H. W. TILMAN

THE EIGHT SAILING/MOUNTAIN–EXPLORATION BOOKS

H.W. Tilman

The Eight Sailing/Mountain-Exploration Books

Introduction by Colin Putt

Mischief in Patagonia
Mischief Among the Penguins
Mischief in Greenland
Mostly Mischief   Mischief Goes South
In Mischief's Wake
Ice With Everything
Triumph and Tribulation

DIADEM BOOKS LTD · LONDON
THE MOUNTAINEERS · SEATTLE

Published simultaneously in Great Britain and the United States by Diadem (Baton Wicks Publications) and The Mountaineers, Seattle.

Copyright © 1987 by Joan A. Mullins and Pamela H. Davis

First published 1987
Reprinted 1989, 1993, 1995, 2000

All trade enquiries in the U.K., Europe and Commonwealth (except Canada) to Baton Wicks Publications, c/o Cordee, 3a De Montfort Street, Leicester LE1 7HD.

All trade enquiries in the U.S.A. and Canada to The Mountaineers, 1001 SW Klickitat Way, Suite 201, Seattle, WA 98134, U.S.A.

British Library Cataloguing in Publication Data:
Tilman, H. W.
    The eight sailing/mountain-exploration books.
    I. Tilman, H.W. 2. Mountaineering –
    Great Britain – Biography 3. Seamen –
    Great Britain – Biography 4. Explorers
    – Great Britain – Biography
    I. Title
    910'92'4   GV199.92.T54
ISBN 0-906371-22-8

U.S. Library of Congress Catalog Card No:
  87-195688
ISBN 0-89886-143-8

Printed in Great Britain by
St Edmundsbury Press Limited, Bury St Edmunds, Suffolk

Contents

Photographs in the Text

Jacket illustrations

Front: Mischief at the Bylot anchorage
Back: Tilman in *Mischief* in a foreign port – probably in the southern hemisphere

Illustrations used at the beginning of each book

Illustrations between pages 284 and 285

Patagonia 1956;   Crozet Islands trip 1959/60;   West Greenland;
East Greenland 1964;   Bylot Island 1963;   Mt Raleigh 1962

Illustrations between pages 700 and 701

The Heard Island expedition 1964/65;   Surtsey eruption;   Upernivik Island;
Angmagssalik Island 1964;   *Mischief* beached at Jan Mayen 1968;
Torssukatak Fjord, South Greenland 1970;   Magdalena Fjord, Spitzbergen 1974

ACKNOWLEDGEMENTS The copyright holders and the publishers wish to thank the following for help in producing this volume: Colin Putt for his Introduction and permission to use his Alpine Journal Obituary notice as a basis for the jacket notes; W. G. Lee for sundry advice and support; Peter Horsfall, Douglas Hughes, Brigadier Derek Davis and Janis Tetlow for work on the typescript; Warwick Deacock, Dr Grahame Budd, Philip Temple and Dr Malcolm Hay for photographs of the Heard Island expedition; Rob Collister and Mike Heller for the introductory photographs for two of the books; Dr Philip Gribbon for caption advice; Ann Rhydderch of the Gwynedd Archive Service, Area Record Office, Dolgellau, for help in locating old photographs; John Morey and Lynne Jackman of The Readers' Union for their support for the project.

INTRODUCTION

by Colin Putt

ON H.W. TILMAN'S Greenland voyage in 1970 someone remarked that 'the Skipper must have been away from home and living on hard tack for nearly all his life.'

This was indeed so. He had gone to boarding school in 1909, aged eleven, and left at seventeen to join the Army and fight through the First World War in France, where he was awarded the MC and bar, and survived where so many did not. Then he went pioneering in Kenya, where he met Eric Shipton with whom he began a famous mountaineering partnership. Through the 1930s he was climbing and exploring in the Himalaya, and on the outbreak of war in 1939 he was back in the Army in time to play a part in Dunkirk. Later he fought in the Western Desert and behind the enemy's lines in Albania and Italy, for which he was awarded the DSO. After the war he was quickly back in the Himalaya, exploring, climbing and making a remarkable series of long journeys in the central Asian hinterland. He then spent a year as British Consul in Burma and returned to England to embark upon the sea-borne mountaineering expeditions described in this series of his books.

Not only was he well used to living on hard tack, he had become an authority on how to do so, for his achievements in mountain exploration had made him famous. These exploits, and many others, are recounted in Tilman's and Shipton's earlier books', and in Anderson's biography of Tilman.⁴ In this present series of Tilman's eight books about sailing to climb, he tells how he applied, on long sea voyages to remote places, the same principles of modest simplicity which had characterized his mountaineering.

In the 1930s, and again in the first few years after the war, the Himalaya and the vast expanse of central Asia beyond offered Tilman ample scope of unvisited mountain country for his explorations, but by the 1950s climbing expeditions were arriving in the Himalaya in rapidly increasing and sometimes obtrusive numbers. At the same time the expansion of Communist control and influence had closed the unexplored parts of central Asia to him. He had suddenly become an explorer with nowhere to explore. When, at the age of fifty-four, he started his Burma posting, perhaps even Tilman thought, as others surely did, that his climbing career had come to an end.

Yet, competent climber that he was, climbing was to Tilman always a means to an end; first, last and all the time he was an explorer. His travels and climbs had been undertaken so that he could become familiar with new places, preferably mountainous places nobody had been to before; for him the first ascent of a great peak simply rounded off an expedition and gave a

3

good view of the country round about. He knew and accepted that mountain exploration usually requires a great deal of difficult travel for a very few summits gained. It therefore seemed perfectly reasonable to replace the long land approaches and steamer voyages that had been the inevitable preliminaries to his Himalayan and Asian travels, with a new and in many ways more flexible form of transport in the form of a tough sailing boat. Thus he was prepared, even eager to endure 'an intolerable deal of sea, as it were, for a halfpennyworth of mountain.' Far from retiring from exploration, in 1952 he decided that his next objective would be the first crossing from the west of the Patagonian ice-cap, still marked 'inesplorado' on the maps, little visited because of its inaccessibility and its atrocious climate, with its ice literally touching tidewater in many places on its western side.

In *Mischief in Patagonia* he describes this first exploratory expedition in which a maritime approach was vital to the success of the enterprise. Both as a seasoned explorer and as a professional soldier, Tilman was well aware that if you want to get to a place at the right time and in good order, you must have full command of your own transport. He wasted no time or effort on attempts to hitch a ride to the Patagonian channels; he set about learning to be a sailor and bought a suitable boat. The expedition was a complete success and became the model for the series of voyages, spanning a quarter of a century, to mountains in the remote regions of both the northern and southern hemispheres. This remarkable catalogue of activity is described in eight highly readable books and comprises a saga of adventure and endeavour of absorbing interest, all the more remarkable in that it was conducted by a man in the latter half of his life.

In transferring the bulk of his activity to sailing Tilman was not making so large a change as might appear. Though there are few links between gymnastic rock-climbing and small-yacht racing round buoys, at the other end of the scale there are close similarities between mountaineering and long distance sailing. On a big remote mountain or on a long voyage under sail you are pitting your skill, courage, endurance and teamwork against the greatest forces of nature, subject to no artificial rules and without any reasonable hope of external aid; your life may be the stake for which you play. Tilman, having become a leading exponent of the one art, was to become a leader in the other, or rather in a new combination of the two.

On his Patagonian adventure Tilman was introduced to the typical problems of this new field of sailing to mountains. He learned valuable lessons about the time taken, the costs and the setbacks. After many vicissitudes Tilman and his five companions arrived, in good order, in the fjords below the ice-cap, and with his usual flair for route-finding he soon had his climbing party ashore at the foot of a large icefall. Tilman's description of his party worrying out a practicable route through this obstacle is typically laconic, but nevertheless can be used almost as a text-book on dealing with such problems. There follows the long slog in foul weather across the ice-cap, where on the very limit of the little party's supplies and endurance, good route-finding was the key to the success of the whole expedition.

The winter of 1956–57 saw Tilman with one successful sea-borne mountain expedition under his belt,* a full year's deep sea experience on top of his many years of mountain exploration, and a small ship in sound condition, ready and able to go almost anywhere in the world where there is salt water.

Mischief and Tilman's two later boats were all Bristol Channel pilot cutters, built about the turn of the century. They were small, around thirty tons displacement, and could carry a crew of five or six men with supplies for a long voyage. They were not yachts, they were strong, seaworthy, practical little working vessels, not very fast but weatherly, safe and easily handled. There are very few of them left now (Tilman used up two of those that remained), but they are described in faithful detail in Stuckey's book.² These vessels were particularly suited to Tilman's requirements because, as working craft, they were able to carry a useful load, and although they had all by then acquired auxiliary engines, they had originally been built as pure, unassisted sailing vessels. Lack of space for fuel made long passages under power impossible, and to make the ocean voyages for which Tilman used them they had to perform reliably under sail alone.

For his second sea-borne expedition Tilman looked even further afield than Patagonia, to the Crozet islands and Kerguelen in the sub-Antarctic South Indian Ocean. The pilot book for the region described a big, permanently snow-covered mountain on the Crozets, and the large island of Kerguelen, like Patagonia, had an unexplored ice-cap. The account of his first attempt to reach the Crozets is given, not in *Mischief Among the Penguins* but as a sort of appendix to the later book, *Mischief Goes South*. On her way to the Crozets from the Cape, *Mischief* broached in a big sea, was damaged and lost her dinghy, so that there was no way to get ashore without the aid of a jetty. She had to return to Durban, and thence to England via the Suez canal. The circumnavigation of Africa had taken a whole year, and the only mountaineering achieved had been a day's rock climbing on Table Mountain. Tilman set out again the next year with a new dinghy and a new crew, and duly arrived at the Crozets, but as the climbing party found their way about the main island in poor visibility the awful realisation dawned on them that the big glaciated mountain was not there! The highest mountain in the place was a thing of about the same size and nature of Snowdon. They went on to Kerguelen and got up onto the ice-cap without too much trouble, but were unable to complete a full crossing from sea to sea. In the book Tilman puts this failure down to the prevalence of fog, but the fact was that there were only two climbers, and a party of two in heavily crevassed country, thousands of miles from the nearest competent rescue party, is not really strong enough. Tilman was starting to discover how hard it is to get together a small but competent party with the necessary climbing and sailing skills, for an expedition of a year's duration.

Nevertheless, this was a very happy voyage, thoroughly enjoyed by all the participants, and the French, who own the Crozets and Kerguelen were impressed by the little expedition's achievements in sorting out previously unknown geographical features of their islands, and named a number of places after *Mischief*, Tilman having declined to have his own name used.

---

* For his Patagonian venture Tilman was awarded the 'Blue Water Medal' of the Cruising Club of America.

By 1961, after these three trips to the southern hemisphere, Tilman was sure that he wanted to continue his expeditions in *Mischief*, but he now made a variation on his theme with some shorter voyages to nearer places in the Arctic. Greenland and the Canadian Eastern Arctic islands are within a few weeks' sailing time from England, and abound in interesting coastal mountains. The coasts themselves are well known and well charted; many of the mountains were mapped and named, and some had been climbed; but the climbing possibilities in the various mountain districts were ill-defined. For shorter voyages, of only four or five months' duration, he might more easily recruit enough competent mountaineers to make an effective reconnaissance of some of these climbing areas. *Mischief in Greenland* gives an account of Tilman's first two summer voyages to Greenland and the Canadian islands, the first of many made over the next fifteen years. Around Umanak Fjord near Disko Island on the west coast of Greenland (and right under the Polar route from Heathrow to Los Angeles) he found many worthy mountains so close to good anchorages that the ship could be used as a sort of climbing hut. Although he came back to his area several times in later years, Tilman and his parties never climbed more than a representative fraction of the mountains; here and in other places he sampled and then moved elsewhere, leaving plenty of virgin peaks and a good written record for those who came after.

On his second Arctic voyage in 1962 Tilman again visited the Umanak Fjord region, and also crossed Davis Strait to Baffin Island, where he made the first ascent of Mt. Raleigh, which proved a relatively easy climb. This was to be a recurrent problem for Tilman: the great peak, planned as the culmination of the expedition, turning out to be too easy and thus an anticlimax.

The next book in the series *Mostly Mischief* is so titled because, sandwiched among the records of three Arctic expeditions in *Mischief*, it gives an account of a voyage to Heard Island in the Antarctic, in the Australian fishing schooner *Patanela*, commanded by Tilman. On the first Arctic excursion in this book, he made the first crossing of Bylot Island, at the eastern entrance to the North-West Passage. While Tilman and his climbing partner were crossing the island, *Mischief*, under the command of Tilman's very able mate, Ed Mikeska, distinguished herself by arriving at Pond Inlet in the entrance to the Passage about a week before the first supply ship of the year. She was small, old and unstrengthened, but in her time *Mischief* got through, or round, a lot of pack-ice.

After this resounding success in the pack-ice Tilman took her next to the East Greenland coast at Angmagssalik, where ice is usually more prevalent and more difficult than on the west coast. On his arrival Tilman found his way to the land blocked by extensive, close pack-ice, and was persuaded to follow a small icebreaker into it. Like others who have tried this in small slow vessels he was unable to keep up, could not steer in the powerful ship's propeller stream, and suffered damage to the hull. Most of the time ashore was spent in making repairs but enough climbing was done to show that here was another promising area. In the following year, 1965, he returned to this district to investigate Skjoldungen Island and fjords some 180 miles down the coast from Angmagssalik and found many worthy mountains of all standards of difficulty.

Meanwhile between Arctic summer voyages, Tilman had taken the big schooner *Patanela* to Heard Island, a round trip of 11,000 miles from Sydney, and landed the climbing party which made the first ascent of Big Ben, a 9,000ft volcano and the highest mountain in the Australian territories. This marked a turning point in his career, for the first time he had transported a climbing party to its destination without himself taking part in the climbing. It is a turning point we must all come to if we want to continue with expeditions after we are too old to go to the top, but it came to Tilman sooner than it should: he was still fit to go to the summit but nobody else on board was fit to take command of the ship while he was ashore.

It was on this expedition that I first met Tilman. He was of short to medium height and strongly but not heavily built. Throughout his long life he had taken a great deal of regular exercise and lived frugally, his basic constitution was exceptionally robust, and in his seventies he could still endure cold, fatigue and lack of sleep such as would have killed many men of half his age. He well understood that 'the art of roughing it consists of smoothing it', but where he could not make himself comfortable he scarcely seemed to notice the hardships.

He was highly intelligent – after the First World War he had considered going to university and if he had done so he would probably have remained there as a don. He was a great reader of very well-chosen books and was a natural scholar. His rapid grasp of the principles of navigation was an example of this, and it was practised not only with speed and accuracy, but with remarkable understanding of what he was doing and of what his results really meant. Sailing as he did in high latitudes, with the compass unreliable or misleading, infrequent and fleeting sightings, weird refractive effects, horizons obscured by mist or by ice, and using only the most basic and old-fashioned equipment, he always seemed to know his position and to understand all the possibilities for error.*

He was one of those rare individuals whose decisions and actions usually arise from logical thought rather than from emotion or instinct; he possessed very good thinking equipment and he habitually used it. His careful, rational way of addressing a problem did not falter under fire; sometimes in an emergency he would seem to be doing nothing at all while he carefully assessed the situation and worked out what should be done; then he would give clear and complete orders. The initial delay might sorely test your faith in him, but his solution to the problem would restore it. He could see the fault at once in any argument or conclusion based on incomplete thinking or an inadequate grasp of facts, and demolish the whole thing with one well-placed shot of logic.

The idea is common among those who know of Tilman but did not know him personally, that he was a crusty recluse, a martinet, and a misogynist. This is a completely false picture, but it is possible to see how it arose. In his

---

* Tilman was elected a Fellow of the Royal Institute of Navigation.

own writings he tended to draw a self-caricature of this kind, and other writers, including Shipton, commenting humorously on his indifference to hardships have given the same impression. With his calm endurance of discomfort and danger, his rigid avoidance of any display of emotion, his laconic conversational style and his concise, ironic humour, he was something of a Spartan, on the surface at least, but there were other reasons for his unmerited reputation as a martinet. At sea in general, and on a Tilman voyage in particular, you cannot afford to have a careless, slovenly, thoughtless, unseamanlike crew; they will wreck the ship. Yet, the great majority of people are impossibly careless, slovenly, thoughtless or unseamanlike until they have been trained in seamanship. Tilman set out regularly on his expeditions with people like this, and he had to train and discipline them to preserve their lives, and his own. He was in the same position as the sailing ship officers who set sail with shanghaied or pressed crews of landlubbers and had to teach them their new trade, quickly, before they sank the ship. He faced the problem squarely, explained what had to be done and how, reminded people quietly at first when they got it wrong, reprimanded them gently when this became necessary, sometimes even moved them on to other duties where they could do less harm. Most of us managed to come up to scratch and soon began to enjoy doing a job properly, but from time to time a man would take to heart the suggestion that he was something short of perfect, and would go away to tell tales about a cantankerous bucko skipper and his unreasonable behaviour. Tilman was not the only skipper who has been given such a reputation in this way: I know of several who have taken crews of landsmen and inshore yachtsmen on long hard voyages and have been made the subject of the same calumnies or worse.

It was not easy to get to know Tilman. He was shy and taciturn with strangers, but with people he had come to know and like he could be the best of good company. I remember so many enjoyable times at sea when he fairly sparkled with quiet humour, erudite comment on any subject you liked to raise, anecdotes and quotations in prose and verse: a feast of good clean fun with everybody joining in. His smile alone could give the lie to stories you might have heard about a grumpy hermit; he was generous, fond of animals, got on famously with children, and enjoyed female company greatly – intelligent, sensible female company that is, for he did not suffer fools, of either sex, gladly. Although unmarried, he was a family man who took a great interest in his two nieces and their children. He was devoted to his sister, whom he described as his 'sheet anchor'. She maintained a home for him in Wales, to which he could retire for rest and comfort in between voyages.

Simplicity had been the keynote of Tilman's and Shipton's mountain explorations together, and Tilman brought the same philosophy to sea with him. His old ships were of a highly developed but very simple design, he navigated with compass, log, lead, sextant and chronometer just as Captain Cook had done, he carried no radio transmitter, his food was cooked on three Primus burners, and in his ships there was a singular lack of stainless steel, plastics and electronics. He always had a perfectly clear view of his ends in going to sea, and of the ship as a means to those ends; he did not allow elaborations or non-essentials about the ship to divert any of his limited resources from their correct application.

In 1966 Tilman set out on his most ambitious sailing and climbing expedition yet (described in *Mischief Goes South*), to Smith Island in the South Shetlands, off the Antarctic mainland below Cape Horn, where there were two large, unvisited and unknown mountains. He gathered together a strong party of able and experienced mountaineers and for his mate he had a professional ship's master on a busman's holiday. Tilman would be able to leave *Mischief* in his hands to go ashore and climb. Everything seemed to be set fair for a truly memorable expedition, until David Shaw, the mate, was lost overboard on the run down the Atlantic to Montevideo. The morale of the remaining crew broke down badly and the voyage turned into a sort of never-ending purgatory. Nothing was accomplished, and it was only by tremendous persistence and the wavering loyalty of one member of the original crew that Tilman got *Mischief* back to England at all. The story is worth reading, to learn how quickly and how badly a seemingly good enterprise can go wrong.

Tilman had never had real crew trouble before, there had been one odd man out on one or two earlier expeditions and that was all. On this voyage however, and on two later ones as well, the majority of the crew had realised too late, that the enterprise on which they were embarked contained an element of risk greater than they had bargained for. Conditions on board the old pilot cutters were often or even usually a little uncomfortable and from time to time some peril or other would become obvious to all. The whole thing went on for months and if you started to worry and to wish things were different, there was plenty of time in which to get very unhappy. If on the other hand you could accept that this was the experience you had come for, that Tilman's methods, judgement and decisions were sound and that he knew a lot more about this particular game than anybody else on board, if in other words you could put yourself unreservedly under his leadership, you could relax and enjoy yourself. This was admittedly a difficult self-discipline to expect from men who had just lost one of their number in tragic circumstances. 'Each one man's death diminisheth me.'

Tilman was a quiet and thoughtful man. He did not attempt total confrontation with his malcontents on this Smith Island failure or on the subsequent occasions of near-mutiny. Nevertheless it is worth noting that most of his voyages, including the two in which I took part, were very happy ones and greatly enjoyed by all, and as with Machiavelli's *Hannibal*, 'There was no slightest whisper of mutiny among his troops.' A number of those who sailed with Tilman were willing and able to come back for more, and sailed on two, three or even more of his expeditions, a kind of action which surely speaks louder than words.

After the dreadful year-long southern voyage, Tilman decided to return to his investigations of the East Greenland coast, this time with an ambitious plan to get into Scoresby Sound. This is the world's longest fjord and gives access to many mountains, but the entrance to it is usually defended by extensive fields of very thick, heavy ice. In the event he could not get into the Sound on this or on any of a number of later attempts, and on this first try he lost *Mischief* off the island of Jan Mayen. His account of this, in the first part of *In Mischief's Wake*, is a good example of the way in which losses of small vessels usually happen, not in one sudden overwhelming disaster but beginning with some small mishap which starts a chain of events leading up to the final wreck. 'The kingdom was lost for the want of a nail.'

To Tilman the loss of *Mischief* was like a bereavement. Of his three pilot cutters she was the first, the best and the most long-lived; his relationship with her was rather like a happy marriage, for he loved her, warts and all, with an enduring, steadfast faithfulness. The work of maintaining an old wooden sailing boat is immense, everlastingly laborious and desperately expensive, but Tilman had maintained *Mischief* faithfully and well, right to the end she was a good little ship, ready for anything. Now she was gone, and he blamed himself for it. He was not one to give up easily however, and by summer 1969 he had another pilot cutter, *Sea Breeze*, fitted out, stored, watered, manned and on her way to Scoresby Sound, only to have the crew (led by the mate) refuse to enter the pack-ice, and insist on sailing straight home again.

After three truly disastrous voyages in a row it was time for some better luck and in the following year, 1970, *Sea Breeze* made a happy and successful voyage to two mountainous areas of south Greenland, at Tasermiut Fjord and at Torssukatak Fjord, the fjord which runs right through Greenland from sea to sea, above Cape Farewell. Interesting mountains were found and climbed in both districts.

Tilman then continued his attempts to get into Scoresby Sound (*Ice With Everything*); he realised that ice would usually keep him out and that he would have to turn up at the right place in the right season a number of times before he struck lucky. In 1971 the entrance was closed as usual and *Sea Breeze* was diverted to Sedhesteds Fjord, 100 miles south of Angmagssalik, where mountains were found to be plentiful and of good quality, although by the time she got there it was too late in the season for much climbing. In 1972 *Sea Breeze* was again repulsed by ice off Scoresby Sound, diverted to the consolation prize areas below Angmagssalik, and was wrecked. As with *Mischief*, a trifling mishap, to the engine this time, set off a train of events ending in shipwreck, which was at least well managed, with no injuries or loss of life.

Old pilot cutters were getting scarce by now and Tilman's next and last one, *Baroque*, was not really as good as the other two. She was old and shaky, had been built with a rather peculiar hull form and construction, and had since suffered a number of major, ill-considered improvements. On her first long voyage to the Disko Island area where Tilman had started his Greenland climbing, her persistent attempts to fall apart were frustrated by Simon Richardson,[3] then only twenty years old but already a man to reckon with, at sea or on a mountain.

The rest of *Baroque*'s voyages are described in Tilman's last book, *Triumph and Tribulation*, which starts with an account of a major feat of small-craft sailing, the remarkable voyage round the island of Vestspitzbergen, going within ten degrees latitude of the Pole itself. The difficulties and dangers were severe and plentiful, and they were overcome by a great skill and a very determined crew (whose concentration on the task in hand was not diverted by any climbing ashore). On each of the remaining two voyages, poor, feeble old *Baroque* was so damaged that she was unable to reach any mountains, and no climbing was done. After the 1976 voyage to East Greenland she was all but a wreck and had to be left behind in Iceland for the winter of 1976–77.

It is clear that Tilman had now decided that he must give up his voyaging, and when he got *Baroque* back to England in June 1977 he sold her, to a good home. He was seventy-nine years old, and before he gave up the ship he had hoped to spend his eightieth birthday, in February 1978, in the Antarctic. The last unhappy voyage in *Baroque* and her subsequent disposal seemed to have put paid to all such plans, but now another chance appeared. Simon Richardson, inspired by his experiences with Tilman, had acquired and re-built a big, ice-strengthened vessel, *En Avant*, and was preparing to have a crack at Tilman's old objective in the South Atlantic, Smith Island, in the South Shetland Islands. No doubt with some trepidation, he invited Tilman to join him; Tilman accepted and as soon as he had completed the sale of *Baroque* he joined the ship at Southampton to help with fitting out.

They sailed in August 1977 for Las Palmas, Rio de Janiero, Port Stanley and Smith Island with a complement of seven men; two more mountaineers from New Zealand were to join at the Falklands. They had an excellent run to Rio: *En Avant* proved to be a good sea boat and the crew turned up trumps, 'A better lot than any I have sailed with,' Tilman wrote from Rio.[4] They left Rio on the first of November, 1977, for Port Stanley.

En Avant never arrived there or anywhere else. No signals were received. Searches were made but no trace of the ship was ever found, she had simply disappeared. Whatever happened to her must have been a rare piece of bad luck: the ship was so strong and well found, and her master and crew were very capable. Some of his friends thought Tilman would have preferred to die with his seaboots on, rather than become old and dependant on others. In his seventies he did not show many signs of old age, but his ships did so increasingly, and in those days his crews must have realised that they stood some slight chance of taking the minor roles in a Viking funeral. I think that most of us sailed with our eyes open to this risk; the experience of a voyage with Tilman made it worth taking.

If such was his wish, it was granted, but he perished together with the man who could have become his successor in sailing to explore and climb, and with the best crew that had ever come together for that purpose. We will never know just when they died, or where they lie. 'They sleep upon the pathways of the sea.'

1 Available in omnibus form: *H.W.Tilman, The Seven Mountain-Travel Books* Diadem Books/The Mountaineers, 1983.
   Eric Shipton, The Six Mountain-Travel Books Diadem Books/The Mountaineers, 1985.
2 *Sailing Pilots of the Bristol Channel* by Peter J. Stuckey, David and Charles, 1977.
3 *The Quest of Simon Richardson* by Dorothy Richardson, Gollancz, 1986.
4 *High Mountains and Cold Seas* by J.R.L. Anderson, Gollancz/The Mountaineers, 1980.

MISCHIEF IN PATAGONIA

Mischief in Patagonia

First Published by Cambridge University Press, 1957

Contents

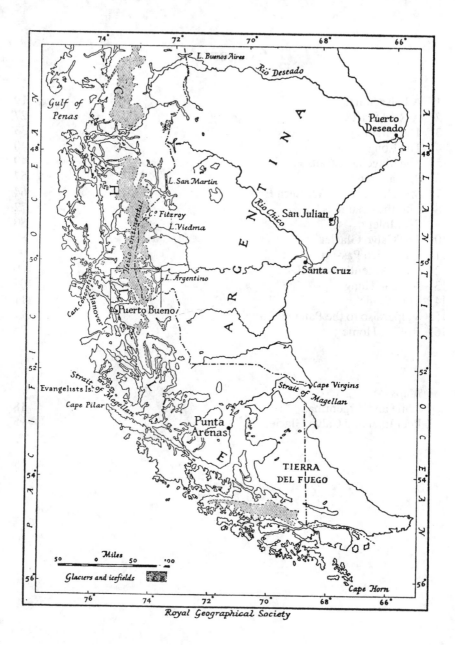

General map of Chile and Argentine Patagonia

CHAPTER ONE

A False Start

We were a ghastly crew The Ancient Mariner

PROVERBIALLY it is not easy to blow and swallow at the same time. So also it is not easy to combine mountaineering and sailing. There are, however, one or two places where such a thing can be done, In the Lofoten Islands a man can sail to the foot of his chosen rock face. On the southernmost coast of Chile, where the high Andes begin to dwindle, there are glaciers reaching down to the sea where a mountaineer can step from his boat and begin his climb at sea-level. A region such as this has an irresistible attraction for a mountaineer who, late in life, catches sea fever and aspires to making an ocean voyage in his own boat.

These Chilean glaciers have their origin in the Patagonian ice-cap (Hielo Continental as it is known there). This covers some 400 or 500 miles between 44° and 51°S., and varies in width from 20 to 50 miles and in height from 6,000 to 10,000ft. I first heard of its attractions in 1945, just after the war, from a friend who had learnt of it while a prisoner in Germany. For the most part the ice-cap was unexplored. No one yet had crossed it, and its glaciers, besides coming so conveniently down to the sea, had other strangely attractive features. Trees grew upon them – one felt this must be an exaggeration. Humming birds and parrots nestled in their branches and penguins paced the ice beneath. On the Argentine side of the range – the accepted way of approach – there were great lakes and forests, and beyond those to the east there were the rolling pampas where millions of sheep roamed, attended by gaucho shepherds, wild characters who lived on meat and *maté* tea, and rode down ostriches with whirling bolas. The more prosaic details of this glowing account were confirmed by the best map then available, the 1 to 1,000,000 sheets of the American Geographical Society. This showed two white, blank spaces bearing the magic word *in-esplorado*. On these two blank spaces, the northern and southern parts of the ice-cap divided by the Rio Baker, were shown numerous glaciers descending to the Patagonia channels on the west, and to the great lakes of Argentino, Viedma, San Martin, and Buenos Aires on the east.

This dazzling picture of a new field for mountain exploration had its blemishes and the chief of these was the weather. Indeed, without some such factor, there seemed little reason why such a large and comparatively accessible region should remain not only unmapped but also unvisited. A little had been done from the Argentine side, for the most part by those interested in its geology and glaciology, and since the lakes offered the readiest access most of the glaciers descending to them had been named. As the prevailing wind and weather are from the west, the Argentine side is more sheltered and therefore drier and less windy than the Pacific side. Even so, of the numerous attempts to reach the summit of the ice-cap or to cross it (the first was in 1914) all except the most recent (1954) had been repulsed by bad weather. The Pacific side, where the weather is worse and where there is nothing but rock, ice, and tangled rain-forest, is for nearly a thousand miles uninhabited and inaccessible except by boat. This had scarcely been touched.

Neither my friend nor the fellow prisoners with whom he had discussed this exciting region were able to follow their ideas up, so that I had to act alone. I must lose no time in getting to Buenos Aires whence I could travel south and west by rail and bus; for there are roads or dirt tracks across the Patagonian pampas serving the numerous estancias some of which lie within 50 miles of the glaciers. At that time I had no notion of crossing to South America in anything but the orthodox way, but a round of the shipping companies soon showed me that there was no getting there at all; or at any rate within the next two or three years, by which time, perhaps, the claims of a multitude of would-be travellers, all with prior or more urgent reasons, might have been met. I forgot Patagonia and went back to the Himalaya.

In the decade after the war, thanks to the opening up of the Nepal Himalaya, to the successful use of oxygen, and to the consequent scramble to be the first upon one of the giants, the tempo of Himalayan climbing became fast and furious. In this decade the year 1949 was almost as noteworthy as 1953, the year in which Everest was climbed, for 1949 marked the throwing open of the Nepal Himalaya. That year one small and not particularly successful party went to the Langtang Himal. The next year saw a similar party in the field as well as the first big post-war expedition, the French party which climbed Annapurna I, the first twenty-six thousander to be climbed. In the autumn of the same year a party of four Americans* and the writer were the first outsiders to visit Namche Bazaar, the home of the Sherpas, and to traverse the Khumbu glacier at the foot of Everest. As if this was the ringing of the bell for the last lap the pace then quickened. With little or no encouragement from our account of what we had seen of Everest, European climbers, or rather nations, began to file their applications to attempt the ascent from the Nepal side; and at the same time numerous private parties set out for this wonderful new field. By 1953 the second applicant on the list (fortunately the British party) had climbed Everest. By 1956 not only had it been climbed again but the six next highest peaks had been, in the classic phrase, 'knocked off', and there were some forty expeditions afoot, eleven of them, employing 5,000 porters, in Nepal.

The Himalaya are extensive, no less than 1,500 miles in length, but a quiet man might well shrink from going, say, to Katmandu, the starting place for the Nepal Himalaya, if he thought he was likely to meet there eleven other parties with their 5,000 porters. Moreover, if he had the misfortune to find

---

* Dr Charles Houston of K2 fame, his father Mr Oscar Houston, Anderson Bakewell and Mrs E. S. Cowles.

himself travelling in the wake of one of these parties he would find food hard to come by, and local transport either unobtainable or at a premium. Such inhabitants as did remain would all be wearing climbing boots and wrist-watches and would drive uncommonly hard bargains. Added to these considerations is the undoubted fact that the Himalaya are high, too high for those who are not 'in the vaward of youth', and though the ageing mountaineer will assuredly find rich solace in its valleys and upon its glaciers he is not likely to resort to them when he knows there are peaks in other parts of the world still within his feeble grasp. So I began thinking again of those two white blanks on the map, of penguins and humming birds, of the pampas and of gauchos, in short, of Patagonia, a place where, one was told, the natives' heads steam when they eat marmalade.

Before this line of thought had led me anywhere I had acquired a stout 14ft. dinghy as a first step to venturing upon the sea. There are a number of mountaineers whose devotion to mountains is not entire, who own and sail boats; but there are few sailors who also climb. Of these, the best known was the late Conor O'Brien. He was a celebrated yachtsman who had designed his own yacht *Saoirse*. Having been invited to join a climbing party in the New Zealand alps for Christmas in 1923 he thought a voyage there an excellent opportunity for trying her out. Going by the Cape and running his easting down in the Roaring Forties he reached New Zealand. He arrived too late for any climbing so he sailed home by way of the Pacific and Cape Horn. One feels that his devotion to the sea came first and that in his eyes the loss of a climbing season was nothing to the accomplishment of such a tremendous voyage.

There is something in common between the arts of sailing and of climbing. Each is intimately concerned with elemental things, which from time to time demand from men who practise those arts whatever self-reliance, prudence, and endurance they may have. The sea and the hills offer challenges to those who venture upon them and in the acceptance of these and in the meeting of them as best he can lies the sailor's or mountaineer's reward. An essential difference is, perhaps, that the mountaineer usually accepts the challenge on his own terms, whereas once at sea the sailor has no say in the matter and in consequence may suffer more often the salutary and humbling emotion of fear.

The sea's most powerful spell is romance; that romance which, in the course of time, has gathered round the ships and men who from the beginning have sailed upon it – the strange coasts and their discoveries, the storms and the hardships, the fighting and trading, and all the strange things which have happened and still do happen to those who venture upon it. For the professional sailor this romantic veil has no doubt become threadbare, but for the amateur there is endless fascination. As Belloc says of the amateur sailor 'In venturing in sail upon strange coasts we are seeking those first experiences and trying to feel as felt the earlier man in a happier time, to see the world as they saw it'. With the mountains there is no romance. Man's association with them is relatively recent and perhaps artificial. With the sea it is as old as himself, natural and inescapable.

From the dinghy I graduated to a friend's four-tonner. In this we twice crossed the Irish Sea and these crossings had given us nearly as much satisfaction as if we had crossed an ocean. Even on those short passages we learnt a lot. We made unexpected landfalls; we lost a dinghy, we were sucked into and finally flung out of the Devil's Tail race near Bardsey Island – a chastening experience – and once in a thick mist we discovered in Cardigan bay a buoy which no one else had ever seen before or has seen since. My apprenticeship was interrupted for eighteen months while I was in Burma but on my return I was lucky enough to be able to sail from Portsmouth to the Mediterranean in the 17-ton cutter *Iolaire* which then belonged to one whom, in seafaring matters, I have always thought of as the *maestro**. Upper Burma is 500 miles from the sea and except near the Tibet border has no real mountains, so that on quitting it my unsatisfied longing was equally poised between mountains and sea. Naturally, therefore, it occurred to me to marry the two by sailing a boat to South America and landing on one of those remarkable glaciers to astonish the penguins and humming birds. Of course, I should miss the long and no doubt enjoyable approach over the pampas in the company of gauchos, ostriches, and whirling bolas, but one can't have everything.

This far-reaching decision was easier to make than even to begin to carry out. I had no boat and not much idea of what sort of a boat I would need. On that, no doubt, advice could be had, but had I a boat I had not the essential experience to handle it. The more I read, the more discouraging was the prospect. There were the gales in the South Atlantic and fierce tides in the Magellan Straits. The channels of Patagonia were beset with strong currents and stronger winds accompanied by incessant rain, sleet, or snow. The shores were uninhabited, inhospitable, iron-bound, and with more or less bottomless anchorages. It seemed wiser to buy a steamer ticket than a yacht. The first and essential step was to find an amateur skipper who not only knew all about boats but who also would regard such a voyage, with its manifold difficulties and discomforts with eager enthusiasm. There were no doubt many such but would any of them have the necessary time? And how was I to find one?

However, in January 1954, I was put in touch with a man who was not only a competent and experienced sailor but also owned a boat of the right type. *Mischief*, built at Cardiff in 1906, was originally a Bristol Channel pilot cutter, 45ft. overall in length, 13ft. beam, and drawing 7ft. 6in. aft. Her register tonnage was 13.78 (by Thames measurement about 29 tons) and her displacement was about 55 tons, which meant that she was heavily built. Her only history known to me was what can be learnt from the entries in her certificate of registry. The first entry was in 1927 when presumably her life as a working boat came to an end and she was bought for conversion into a yacht. Since then she had had nine owners and her latest had bought her in Malta in 1953.

March had come by the time we had arranged for her to be hauled out for survey and, provided she proved sound, for subsequent fitting out. She was lying at Palma, Mallorca, where there was a good yard well used to building and repairing wooden ships. Another month passed before a slip was vacant.

*Robert Somerset Esq., DSO

Time was short for if we were to reach the Patagonian channels by mid-summer (southern summer), enjoy two months on the ice-cap, and be clear of those boisterous regions before the southern autumn, we had to be ready by the end of July. Everything turned on what the survey showed, for unless the hull was sound it was no use going on with the venture. To examine the outside planking the copper sheathing had to be stripped off. When this was done it was not worth putting back, but copper was so scarce in Palma that the yards and scrap-metal merchants fought for it and we got a very good price. The outside planking was mostly sound. Inside she had a foot of concrete ballast which filled the bays to the top of the floor. No doubt it had been put in when the boat was built and it seemed probable that if water had seeped beneath it the planking would be rotten. On the question of cement in yachts it is instructive to note the contradictory opinions of two experts. Claud Worth: 'The bays of *Tern* were filled with Portland cement which made her enormously strong and precluded decay in this region.' The Lonsdale Library *Cruising*: 'Cementing ought to be strictly avoided in a boat built of wood. The evils resulting from cement in the bilge of wood boats have been too often experienced. Moisture gets behind it and may result in dry rot.' *Mischief*'s cement had been well and truly laid. Amongst it were lumps of iron pyrites and the whole was almost adamantine. It took two men two days to chip out a hole a foot square in order to expose that small area of the bottom planks and keelson. Sure enough there was water. Overnight quite a pool collected and our hopes fell accordingly; but the yard foreman, who had spent a lifetime with wooden ships, having done some probing, declared the wood sound. In fact it was almost as hard as the concrete.

I bought the boat and we told the yard to go ahead with the refit. The several pages of our requirements had already been made out by my friend the late owner, to whose knowledge, thoroughness, and hard work I should like to pay tribute. As well as the work on hull and deck – new planks, recaulking, the doubling of all fastenings and keel bolts, new rail cap, stanchions for life-lines, and a hundred and one lesser jobs – all the standing and running rigging had to be renewed. In addition there was a mass of work to be done below – alterations to berths and lockers, the fitting of extra tanks for water and petrol, not to mention galley fittings, lockers for vegetables, sails, and bos'n's stores, rewiring, and so on. The mast had already been taken out for scraping and overhaul, as well as the inside ballast for chipping and painting. This consisted of about a hundred and twenty iron pigs of about 100 lb. each, vile things to have to handle and stow without the help of a professional weight-lifter. Inside ballast conjures up for most owners the dreadful vision of a ship on her beam ends with iron pigs cascading about the cabin. Happily *Mischief*'s ballast never shifted.

In May, after another cruise with the 'Master' in *Iolaire* to North African ports and Malta, I returned to Palma to live on board until we sailed. It was hard lying, for *Mischief* was still on the slip and as the ballast was still out there was no floor to the cabin. Work went on steadily but slowly. There were frequent interruptions for *fiestas*, but on the whole the Spanish shipwrights and carpenters worked well and the cost was half what it would have been in a home yard. At last the time came for her to go back into the water. We slapped on the blue anti-fouling paint with a will and when she was afloat she was moored alongside a floating crane where the mast was stepped and the rigging set up. There were still hundreds of small things to be done before she was ready for sea, but now she was looking like a ship, and a deep sea ship at that, with the after shrouds and the topping lifts swathed in baggywrinkle. The shrouds were the admiration of all. Later they raised many a laugh in yachting harbours, for they were of unyachtlike dimensions, two and half inches wire with bottle screws to match. The forestay was two and three-quarter inches wire and the rest of the standing and running rigging was proportionately sturdy. It paid handsomely. We never need have anxiety about the mast, nothing ever carried away, and we returned to England in 1956 using the same main sheet and jib sheets we had fitted at Palma. Altogether one felt that she was 'fit to shunt ice' as the old whaling captain remarked to Slocum of his famous *Spray*. Though we did not encounter any storm such as drove *Spray* back willy-nilly into the Magellan Straits, we did in fact shunt a great deal of ice, something which *Spray* never had to do.

The new suit of sails having arrived from England, the main-sail was bent on, and at the end of July, late but not too late, we left Mallorca bound for Gibraltar where we had to pick up sea stores sent there from England. These consisted of food for six months. A like amount had been sent to Montevideo to await our arrival. In contrast to my subsequent experience a crew had been found without much effort on my part. As they dispersed with equal facility there is no need to name them. When agreeing with the previous owner that he would skipper *Mischief* for me, an ineluctable condition (on his part) was that his wife should be one of the crew. She was a modern Grace Darling who could hand, reef, and steer, as the phrase goes, and she shipped as bos'n. I had had misgivings about this, not that I questioned her ability but I had at the back of my mind the remark of some sage from China, a country prolific in sages, to the effect that discord is not sent down from Heaven but is brought about by women. But it was both or nothing; no song, no supper.

We made a slow passage of ten days to Gibraltar where we had no sooner tied up than I learnt that the skipper and his wife were going no farther. On passage, relations between Grace Darling and myself had been strained although I had been self-effacing, as an owner should be, and as silent as usual. Perhaps one of the few remarks I ventured had not been well chosen. We took it in turns to cook and the day after Grace Darling's turn, when one of the crew who knew how to cook was officiating, I thanked God aloud for having on board one whose presence ensured our having good meals on at least one day in five. Besides a clash of temperaments there may have been other factors; we were late in starting, were bound for a rude climate, and in spite of all that had been done we were not in every respect ready for sea. With a mind fully occupied with all the implications of this miserable, unlooked-for, and abrupt ending to a promising venture, I could yet feel for the skipper whose hard work in fitting out now went for nothing. But he had no option – a wife's counsel is bad, but he who will not take it is mad.

The other two crew members adjourned immediately to the Yacht Club to celebrate our safe arrival, and it soon became clear that they had no intention of continuing. Neither would they help take the ship back to England although one of them was well able to take charge of a yacht. I could not leave her at Gibraltar where there are land rats and water rats who prey upon laid-up ships, so the only thing to do was to sail her back with a scratch crew. To add to these embarrassments I had to explain to the admiral who had honoured the venture by asking the crew and myself to lunch that we were no longer on speaking terms. On the other hand it was pleasant to be joined the same day by David Drummond, lately an instructor at the Outward Bound Mountain School, Eskdale, who had hoped to be one of the ice-cap party. He knew nothing about the sea but being a mountaineer he would stand by me and not desert like the yachtsmen.

September was well advanced before we cleared from Gibraltar with a scratch crew – the exotic fruits of an advertisement in the local newspaper. The only two who counted were a sergeant and a corporal from a RASC Water Transport unit who had obtained a month's leave in order to come – a month, I thought in my innocence, being ample allowance for a voyage of 1,200 odd miles. They had been to sea but knew nothing about sail. They soon picked it up, were a likeable pair, and failed only in staying power. A private from the Duke of Wellington's, and a Scottish youth from the dock-yard who had come out three weeks before and now wanted to go home, completed the motley crew and irritated beyond measure the novice who was now skipper. In summer strong northerly winds prevail along the Portuguese coast. By late September these should have weakened and have become less steady. I counted on having at least a small proportion of fair winds, but having rounded Cape St Vincent in good style we met with constant, strong head winds with which we battled for the next eighteen days. By going out a hundred miles from the coast we fared no better and succeeded only in demoralising the crew, who would have much preferred noting our progress, however slow, against some land. Having no sextant I was navigating by dead reckoning but thanks mainly to a very friendly Union Castle boat, the *Roxburgh Castle,* I had a pretty good idea where we were. The incessant beating into wind and sea, with one or two nights spent hove to, told on the crew who began to murmur loudly. Unwisely, perhaps, I had told them we were about the latitude of Oporto, whereupon the two NCO's declared that unless I put in and landed them they would no longer stand their watches. In fact, mutiny on the high seas. The situation called for a bucko mate and a belaying pin. I had plenty of belaying pins (there were half a dozen each side in the fiferail) but no bucko mate. I was too old for the role and David was too good-natured. Having little confidence in myself and none in the crew Oporto was the last place I should have picked upon. At the entrance is a bar, the tidal streams attain a rate of 7 knots, and during freshets the ebb in the river has been reported to run at 16 knots.

There was nothing else for it so I headed her for Oporto where we made a good landfall. By sundown we were off the bar. A swell was running and we had no information as to the state of the tide. On board were Tide Tables for all the ports of the South Atlantic, the Pacific, and the Mediterranean, but

none for the coast of Portugal. As we motored slowly in we were startled by
the report of a cannon. Were the natives hostile or was it an old Portuguese
custom thus to salute the setting sun? A moment later a man appeared on the
jetty beyond the bar excitedly waving a newspaper. The sergeant assured me
he was beckoning us in whereas I was quite sure he was waving us out. Even
as I put her round she bumped twice on the bottom. We anchored for the
night well outside the bar.

In the morning a pilot came off, took us up the river and moored us below the
city with warps, springs, and our heaviest anchor. He said they had fired the gun
to warn us and that had we attempted to cross the bar we would surely have lost
the ship. The RASC men departed, leaving me with three weak hands, two of
them unwilling. I had to choose between the cheap but doubtful step of recruiting two unknown Portuguese sailors, with whom I should not be able to exchange a word, or the expensive step of calling for professional help from home.
Lying in a nearby yard with a professional skipper on board was the English
yacht *Iyruna* which had left Gibraltar just before us. She had met heavy weather,
been damaged, and had put back to lay up for the winter. Her skipper was not
able to come but he gave me the name of a likely amateur, W.A. Procter (of
whom more later) who at that time, however, could not leave England. At length
Humphrey Barton and a friend flew out and we sailed the same afternoon.

By now, late October, our old enemy the north wind had given place to
south-westerly winds with drizzling rain. Although the wind was not strong
we managed to break the gaff. This decided us to put into Vigo. We were off
what we thought was the entrance to the bay. It was dusk, the weather thick,
and we attributed to low cloud the fact that we could not see the light, which,
as in many Spanish lighthouses, is sited too high. *Mischief* had now a skipper
of very different calibre, so we stood boldly in and once inside the narrow
entrance picked up the buoys marking the channel. For two hours we motored
on towards the bright lights of a large town and having closed the lights and
duly noted the wharves where, I was assured, Atlantic liners tie up, we began
searching for the Yacht Club. Although we went in close enough to take the
ground, we failed to find it. We drew off a little and anchored in disgust.

The Yacht Club proved to be as elusive by daylight and the reason became
clear when, having hailed a man in a dinghy, we learnt that we were not in
Vigo bay but in the next bay to the north. Still, in this delightful cruising
ground we had a very pleasant sail round to Villagarcia where, although it was
a Sunday, we had the gaff repaired. Off Finisterre it broke again, but under
trysail and headsails with a brave southerly wind we made good time across
the bay until we ran into fog. Out of this a huge French battleship appeared
and vanished like a wraith. While we were remarking this apparition the
Scottish youth – his one active contribution to the voyage, for which I forgive
him all – drew our attention to a pillar buoy on the port bow and breakers
ahead. Having put *Mischief* about and brought the buoy on to the starboard hand we passed close enough to discover that it was the Ar Men
buoy marking the reef of that suggestive name for which we had been
confidently heading. This was the last of our misadventures. Two days later,
on 5 November, we tied up at Lymington town quay where I was left alone to
clear up the mess below and to lick my wounds.

CHAPTER TWO

A Real Start

A man in a jail has more room, better food, and commonly better company. Samuel Johnson

IN SPITE of all that had been done at Palma, *Mischief* still had some defects. No less than three new spars were needed—a gaff, topmast, and bowsprit. The last two, which had always been a bit shaky, were now condemned. But she was full of food and in all other respects ready and, like her owner, raring to go. So much time and money had already been spent that it seemed infinitely more painful to cut one's losses at once than to spend more in the hope of ultimately accomplishing so refreshing an adventure. Yet in the gloom of winter, when the making of these spars had been put in hand and when I myself went frequently to Lymington to work on her, I constantly wondered whether by the summer there would be a skipper to sail her or a crew to man her. The supply of 'rash, inconsiderate, fiery voluntaries' who knew anything of either sailing or climbing had apparently dried up. Perhaps it was that too many of them agreed with the well known description of life at sea quoted above. As for a skipper, although I had more confidence I had no wish to take the job on myself if I could find someone better qualified, someone whose sea experience was such that all qualms and arguments on the part of the crew would have to be kept to themselves; and apart from the voyage out and back I had to have an experienced man to take charge when the shore party had landed.

When I got in touch with W. A. Procter, the man whom I had so luckily heard of at Oporto, I found him eager to make a long voyage and not a whit perturbed either by the proposed cruising ground or the prospect of a year's absence. Nor did he waver, as several others did, from his first decision. Having for several years owned a Falmouth quay punt he knew more about boats than I would ever hope to, though that is not extravagant praise. He was a retired civil servant and when I visited him and found to my alarm that he had a wife and three children I felt like a wrecker of homes. But Mrs Procter took a sensible view of what must have seemed a fairly wild scheme and, putting her husband's interests before her own, decided that a sea voyage would do him good and promised to wish us both God-speed when the time came. The only stipulation was that I should bring him back.

Having now at least the nucleus of a crew I began canvassing the services and the universities for young sailors and/or climbers, inserting advertisements in the yachting press, and generally making my wants known as widely as I could. All came to nothing. Of two naval officers who would have liked to have come, one could not get leave, while the other could have leave but no pay. Some half-dozen undergraduates at different times volunteered and were accepted, only to withdraw later, deterred either by the advice of illiberal tutors or nervous parents. Of the twenty or so who answered the advertisement only two seemed worth interviewing. In the event one wanted to be paid and the other was looking for a passage to Canada. For the rest there were several girls and one married couple (an application which made me wince) while the others faded away after being told what was in store.

In the meantime, hoping much, as always, from time and chance, I went down to Lymington to work on the boat. Scrubbing out lockers and painting the inside; new ratlines had to be fitted to the shrouds ('rattling down' as an old shellback would say); a new net was needed under the bowsprit, while all the blocks had to be stripped down and greased and new strops fitted. The old barrel winch, which must have been born with the ship and which one felt should be turned by capstan bars, was replaced with a very good winch which I bought cheap in a scrap yard. To complete the luxury below, pumps were fitted so that the galley sink and wash-hand basin could be emptied without the necessity of anyone going on deck. The manager of the yard, a man built on generous lines and accustomed to jumping on board from the jetty a few feet above, noted with misgiving that the deck yielded under this treatment like a too-well-sprung dance floor. Shaking his head ominously he alarmed me by suggesting that a new deck might be a good thing, rightly pointing out that his weight was nothing to that of a South Atlantic comber. But Humphrey Barton who knew the ship by now reassured me and we compromised by putting supporting posts under the deck beams. Two of these also served the useful purpose of securing the main water tank (100 gal.) which previously had only been screwed to the cabin deck!

At this stage the means occupied so much of my time and attention that I was in danger of losing sight of the end. What should have been the simple, straightforward job of fitting out and manning a boat to go to South America had become so beset with unknown factors that it was difficult to make any firm plans for the more exacting part and object of the whole exercise, the work on the ice-cap. Ideally one would have wished, having crossed the ice-cap, to wander overland to Punta Arenas to rejoin the ship there; or better still to cross back by another route and be picked up at a fresh rendezvous. But how strong would the shore party be, would it include a scientist, and would there be anyone left in the ship upon whom one could rely to take her safely back to Punta Arenas? When discussing plans with the skipper in 1954 we had decided that the picking up of the shore party at any other place than that at which they had landed would be too hazardous, and that the best place to land would be at some spot in Peel Inlet, a long fjord running inland from the main channel some 300 miles distant from Punta Arenas.

Westward of Tierra del Fuego and stretching along the western coast of Patagonia for eleven degrees northwards from the Magellan Straits is a chain of islands known as the Patagonian Archipelago. In the *South America Pilot* this region is described 'as about as inhospitable a land as is to be found in the globe. The land is mountainous presenting an alternation of matted forest, bare rock, and deep bogs, and is intersected by many deep channels into peninsulas and islands as yet very imperfectly known. The scenery is magnificently stern; cloud and mist usually screen the higher peaks and snow fields.' Between these islands and the mainland are good navigable channels which afford a smooth water route of over 300 miles. By using these channels ships can avoid the heavy seas and tempestuous weather usually encountered when passing into the Pacific from the Magellan Straits. Nowadays it is the usual route for traffic between Argentine and Chilean ports. These channels are lit at difficult or dangerous points by buoys or unmanned lights; at the southern and northern entrances there are two manned lighthouses. The channels and their numerous anchorages are well charted but from the main channel a number of fjords or inlets run eastwards for 30 to 40 miles. These are not charted. They are named and that is all; for no one uses them except a few Canoe Indians and the occasional hunter of sea otters.

These inlets provide the only access to the glaciers and the glaciers are the only access to the ice-cap. We had to decide which of the many was the best. The inlets are not shown at all on the Admiralty charts, which are concerned only with the main channels, but by then I had got hold of a very useful series of maps. After the war, at the request of the Chilean government, the American Air Force had surveyed the whole of that difficult region from the outer islands fronting the Pacific eastwards to the Argentine lakes. It must have been a long, difficult, and hazardous task because the number of days on which a camera could be used are few, the weather is normally bad, and there are no emergency landing strips. The resulting maps had been printed on a 1:250,000 scale and as well as giving a good picture of the ice, showing which glaciers actually reached the sea, they give an accurate outline of the coasts of these inlets. They do not, of course, show any soundings. From these maps we had picked upon Peel Inlet as the most likely for our purpose. It penetrated furthest east so that the ice-cap crossing would be the shorter, and it contained no less than ten glaciers which reached the water as well as several others which came within a mile of the shore. Above all, close to the entrance to Peel Inlet from the main channel, there was a safe anchorage at a place called Puerto Bueno. Thus it seemed best to base ourselves on Puerto Bueno and to effect our landing in Peel Inlet. This inlet had been first visited in 1908 by the Chilean navy store ship *Meteoro* which spent a night there while the Swedish scientific party which it was carrying landed to geologise. Later in 1930 Michael Mason, the well-known writer, traveller, and yachtsman, visited it in *Violeta* a 15-ton steam launch which he had chartered at Punta Arenas. Thus we were not working altogether in the dark. The two books describing these two visits had an honoured place on *Mischief*'s bookshelf.

The adventure of crossing an ocean, the seeing of new lands and little known coasts, and the setting foot on hitherto unvisited glaciers were for me sufficient reasons for travelling so far afield. But in these unromantic days the excuse of mere adventure is not enough. The path of the traveller is made smoother and the official wheels, which sooner or later have to be turned, turn more freely if he or one of his party purpose suffering in the cause of science. Indeed, one is hardly expected to travel – I use the word in the strict sense – for any other reason, and I found that almost the first questions asked by foreign journalists were about our scientific aims. One cannot provide for a yacht and a crew of five in South American ports on a travel allowance of £100 and so when applying for more money to the Bank of England – on the whole a serious-minded body – it would not do to offer a frivolous reason. Apart from the collecting of plants which I proposed to undertake I hoped to include in the shore party a geologist or glaciologist. It was unlikely he would be willing or able to waste four months at sea but I hoped that he could join us at Punta Arenas and then leave as soon as we got back. I have found by experience that the field geologist, the man who plies his hammer in the secret places of the earth, is not a common bird, while the glaciologist is rare indeed. For many years past young geologists who wished to get experience in the field have confined their activities to Spitsbergen and North East Land, a region which surely by now must be in fragments. For the 1954 attempt I had found a young Oxford geologist who was able to come and eager to do some glaciological work as well. He was to join us at Punta Arenas and the Everest Foundation were to contribute towards his passage. Even after the fiasco of that year he agreed to hold himself in readiness for the winter of 1955-56, but within a month of our departure he had the offer of a Fellowship and naturally took it.

In May 1955 affairs looked far from promising. There was a crew of one, no scientist, not even a mountaineer for the shore party. Suddenly things took a turn for the better. Through the Royal Artillery Yacht Club I got in touch with Lieut. M. R. Grove (he got his captaincy while we were in the Pacific) who, with the enterprise expected of gunner subalterns, volunteered to come. We met at Bala, half-way between Barmouth and Oswestry where he was stationed, with the result that he applied for a year's leave. Early in June this was granted – without pay, of course, but with the threat, too, that the lost year would not count for promotion. Over this hard condition the Treasury, with the help of the President of the Royal Geographical Society (himself a gunner), was later persuaded to relent. Michael Grove had had some slight experience of sailing and ahead of him lay ample time to gain more. He would gladly have made one of the shore party, which at this time consisted of only myself, but he had had no experience of climbing and once we had landed in Peel Inlet we would not have the time to train him. At Punta Arenas, when we were still short of the essential third man, I prepared for the worst by getting him a pair of climbing boots. However, he was never called upon to use them.

On the constantly changing list of possible or probable candidates, which for the last few months had kept me on tenterhooks, the name of Major E. H. Marriott, also a gunner, a member of the Alpine Club and an experienced climber, had frequently bobbed up. Having recently joined a party who were to sail a boat to New Zealand, and paying for the privilege, he had been finally struck off. It now seemed that after a difference of opinion with the skipper and owner he was again at a loose end. Charles Marriott, so called because his initials are E. H., had before the war sailed as far as the Canaries on a similar voyage before leaving the ship in much the same circumstances.

But differences of opinion and jarring temperaments, leading often to the dispersal of crews and the abrupt ending of promising ventures, are common form in small boats, an occupational risk which cannot be insured against and which one must accept. The only long voyages free from crew trouble are usually made by man and wife – of which there are several recent examples – or by single-handers. So Charles Marriott was invited to join. As neither he nor Michael Grove was available before the first week of July I arranged to pick them up at Falmouth whence we would make our final departure.

Procter joined me at Lymington in mid-June, sailing day being tentatively fixed for the 24th. We had intended putting the boat on the hard at Falmouth in order to apply between tides a final coat of anti-fouling; but now we decided to have her slipped at Lymington, where she had been lying in a mud berth, so that we could have a look at the hull as well as give it proper time to dry before applying the paint. Meantime there were only the two of us to sail her to Falmouth. In the days when *Mischief* was a working boat and sailors were real sailors, the Pilot cutters were normally manned by two hands – occasionally, I believe, by one. In that delightful book *Messing about in Boats* there is a description of how the dinghy was got on board by the lone hand, by the bold but simple expedient of making the painter fast to the boom at the right place, letting the main sheet out, and then gybing the boom over, whereupon the dinghy sprang on board through an opening cut in the bulwarks while the hand leapt from the tiller to catch it by the stern and secure it. I did not see either Procter or myself attempting such a feat or even taking her quietly round to Falmouth by ourselves. We needed help and help was forthcoming.

An acquaintance of Procter's, near Petersfield, having heard of our project became eager to join in. This was John Van Tromp and I hoped he would have some of the qualities of his great namesake. He ran a small dairy farm. One hears of sailors swallowing the anchor and buying a farm but less often does one hear of anyone selling a farm in order to go to sea. Van Tromp, when he came down to Lymington to press his claim, startled me a little by his deerstalker hat. His claim, however, was one which appealed strongly to me for he volunteered to do all the cooking. On my list there were still the names of one or two waverers who had yet to make their decision and here was a man who had no doubts and who was ready to tackle the least pleasant job. As I was soon to learn, I am not alone in liking good food and plenty of it supplied at regular and not too infrequent intervals. But when a crew takes it in turn to cook this desirable end is seldom attained. On dry land or on calm days at sea cooking can be an agreeable pursuit, taxing and stimulating the imagination and occasioning many surprises; but *Mischief*'s galley is not ideally placed. It is in the fore part of the ship, between cabin and forepeak, where the motion is most lively. And when she is sailing on the wind the fore hatch, the main source of ventilation for the galley, must be kept closed. 'When they bring you a heifer be ready with the rope.' I therefore closed promptly with this welcome offer and John agreed to be with us on sailing day, bringing with him a friend called Tony who wanted to come as far as Falmouth. Tony, who had never been to sea, had a bent for machinery and I unashamedly meant to use it to get out of Lymington river.

On 27 June, the last coat of anti-fouling having been put on, *Mischief* took the water. The engine did not start immediately, but it did as soon as we had turned on the petrol. Unobtrusively we stole away down the river, remarked only by some vigilant friends at the Yacht Club who gave us a one-gun salute which we acknowledged by dipping our colours. The three days down Channel proved uneventful except for the deathly sickness of John's friend, the anxious passage by night through a fleet of drifters, and the mistaking of Gribbin Head for Dodman Point by Procter who, as a Cornishman, should have known better.

At Falmouth we still had much to do. The bolster which supports the starboard shrouds had broken and had to be replaced, a job which the local yard did quickly and efficiently. Half a ton of stores sent down from Liverpool had to be put on board and stowed, formalities for taking on a small quantity of bonded stores observed, and water, petrol, and paraffin tanks refilled. In addition, a large air bubble in the compass indicated a leaking seal; we wanted a day's sailing to try the twin staysails; and another day to go to Newlyn to buy some composite rope. This is a six-strand rope of forty-two wires, each strand consisting of seven wires contained in a manila sheath. It is very strong, neither stretches nor swells, is impervious to chafe, and is the devil to coil. On a long voyage, especially in a gaff-rigged ship like *Mischief*, chafe is the great bugbear, the throat and peak halyards being most susceptible. When the original halyards showed signs of wear we reeved this composite rope and forgot about it.

To those who have to do with them, ships seem to lend a sense of purpose and of service. The compass adjuster might have been a high priest of a religion called terrestrial magnetism who regarded compasses as sentient beings, of more account than the ships and men they guided, and fully responsible for their behaviour. He looked at our compass disapprovingly, shook it, turned it round once or twice, and advised me to drop it overboard. If I insisted he would gladly remove the air bubble without charge, but the compass was old and its period of recovery after deflection so prolonged that it was no longer trustworthy. In defence of an old friend I pointed out that this despised instrument had brought us safely home from the Mediterranean (omitting the story of that horrible apparition the Ar Men buoy), whereupon he merely remarked on the wonderful ways of Providence. In the end I took his advice.

The day allotted for trying out the twin staysails turned out wet, windy, and rough. Tony came with us and enjoyed it but a girl friend of Van Tromp's who came for the sail did not. The mainsail had to come down, never an easy job in a strong wind, before the staysail booms were fitted to the mast, one with a jaw and the other with a gooseneck which dropped into the spider band on the mast. When they were up the twins pulled like mad and we were confident that with some adjustments, particularly to the mast fitting, they would be powerful aids to trade wind sailing. Once more under the mainsail we turned and scuttled back to Falmouth.

The time had come for Michael Grove and Charles Marriott to show up. Every time we rowed ashore we scanned the pier until at last I descried a bearded figure in a white yachting cap who, viewed from far enough off to conceal the slightly motheaten blazer and flannel trousers, had something of the air of King Edward waiting to join the royal cutter *Britannia*. It was Charles Marriott whom we gladly took off, for his appearance did *Mischief* credit. Michael Grove soon followed and on the morning of 6 July we went ashore for the last time to lay in fresh food. At 10 am we got our anchor and sailed out, and very few of those who watched us go knew whither we were bound. 'It is not the beginning but the continuing of the same until it be thoroughly finished that yieldeth the true glory.'

CHAPTER THREE

The First Leg

Where lies the land to which the ship would go?
Far, far ahead, is all her seamen know. Clough

ALTHOUGH it smacks of seamanlike efficiency, to say that we got our anchor and sailed out is not strictly accurate. It leaves much unsaid. In fact we had two anchors down and their cables were so lovingly entwined that for some time the foredeck was the scene of a fearful struggle and resounded with unseamanlike oaths. We passed Black Rock, and the sentiments appropriate to watching from the deck of a small ship, outward bound on a long voyage, the receding shores of one's native land, had barely found expression when the shores ceased to recede. The wind which had hitherto been light now failed altogether and for two hours we drifted off the headland of St Anthony viewing its not remarkable features from many different angles.

After lunching on deck, for it was a warm day for England, we got a breeze from the south-west, hoisted the Genoa and streamed the log in the hope that the voyage had really begun. By evening we had caught many mackerel. To add to our pleasure the wind went round to north-west so that we were able to lay the course for Ushant; or rather 15 miles west of Ushant, for after our experience the previous year I intended giving that noted sea-mark a wide berth. Our next port of call was Las Palmas in the Canaries. Except for the purpose of checking our untried navigation the sighting of any land on the way would have been unnecessary. It is 1,500 odd miles to Las Palmas which we reckoned upon reaching inside three weeks.

With four of us available for watch-keeping – the cook very properly being exempt – we had an easy time. The day from 8 am to 8 pm was divided into three watches of four hours each and the night into four watches of three hours each. Thus, without recourse to dog watches, one's watch changed automatically, and on every fourth day a man had practically the whole day off or the whole night in. In order to make life still easier, when sails had to be shifted we did it if possible at the change of watch. At nightfall we tried by shortening sail to ensure that the watch below was not disturbed. Naturally this did not always happen. A peaceful sky and a steady barometer might belie their promise, wind and weather might change without warning, so that that which might have been done in daylight and at leisure, had to be done in darkness, in a hurry, by men half asleep. More often a disturbed night was our own fault. Because of a natural dislike of slowing the ship when she was reeling off the miles it was too easy to leave our light sails up or the mainsail unreefed, to trust to careless hope and to use reason to thrust aside what we did not fancy.

According to the late Conor O'Brien, a complicated rig on an ocean-going yacht justifies itself in giving the crew something to do. Other than watch-keeping and sail-changing there is not much for the crew of a well-found ship on a long voyage under normal conditions to do, for the sail changing has neither the frequency nor the urgency that obtains in ocean racing. Naturally one tries to get the best one can out of the boat, but the comfort of the crew, the safety of the gear and the wear and tear upon it, are vastly more important than speed. The crew has to carry on for weeks or months and there is a limit to the amount of spare gear that can be carried or to the repairs that can be affected in mid-ocean.

Even so life was too hard for some of the crew, who during their trick at the helm needed cushions to support their body, an awning to cover their head, and a book to distract their mind. But at least one of us, John Van Tromp, had no sinecure. Those who invoke hunters, sharks, wolves, hyenas, or cormorants as examples of voracity have much to learn. Procter, and Michael Grove, too, when he had found his sea legs, could eat their way past any of these with hardly a pause for breath. And since neither Charles Marriott nor I would be described as delicate feeders the cook had his hands full in pre-paring meals and clearing up. In addition, by inclination and because he had more knowledge of it than the rest of us, John attended to the engine when needed and looked after the little charging engine. He also did any electrical repairs. They were often needed as the wiring throughout the ship was amateurish and the fittings not so waterproof as they should have been. He spent his spare time fishing and perhaps once in a thousand miles or so throughout the voyage his efforts were rewarded by a big fish. Those were red-letter days.

Procter was a good carpenter and handyman so that any such work fell to him, while I looked after the rigging. As I have said the amount of wear and tear that goes on at sea sailing night and day, particularly at night when sheets are eased or shortened and the necessary shifting of the anti-chafe material ('scotsmen') is overlooked, is a never-ending source of worry. There are few days when there is not any stitching of sails or splicing of rope and wire to be done. There can be no one who goes to sea for fun who takes no interest in the behaviour of the ship, the set of the sails, the ever-changing pattern of sea and sky, the sea birds which are seldom absent and the fish which, we found, were so seldom present. As long as the ship is moving, preferably in the right direction, one is seldom bored even in the most lifeless ocean and interest is quickly restored by the mere sight of another ship or other sign of life. Only in very light airs or flat calms, when there is no progress and there is nothing to be done or to be seen, is boredom felt, and the effect of such times upon the temper and morale of the crew is very obvious.

Our first night at sea passed peacefully for all except Mike Grove who mistook the rising moon for a sail approaching at speed, shone the torch on our sails, and was on the point of rousing me out. Next day when the wind had freshened from east-north-east we gybed over to the port tack and logged what proved to be our best run for many a long day, 140 miles. How thankful we were for a wind which gave us such a flying start and for a sea which as yet exacted no tribute. The subsequent shortening of sail by taking two rolls in the mainsail and handing the big Genoa served to mark our apprehensions rather than worsening weather; for in the early days we seldom failed to expect the worst, seeing menace in every cloud and a gale in every gust. But by the time we were well into the Bay of Biscay three of us who had not yet found our sea legs were in poor shape. The fair wind took us with a lessening speed right across the Bay and early on the fourth morning, with the wind falling light, we sighted land. During this run three of us had been busily taking sights, more by way of practice than in the expectation of getting trustworthy results. Before setting a course for the Canaries we had intended taking our departure from Cape Finisterre and to make sure of not missing it we had steered a little to the east. The land ahead was undoubtedly the north coast of Spain, somewhere, we thought, in the neighbourhood of Coruña. With the aid of binoculars, the hand-bearing compass, and the appropriate 'Pilot', we speedily identified the Tower of Hercules, a square dark tower at the western entrance of Coruña bay. Procter, who two months before had been there in my old acquaintance *Iyruna* on her way home from Oporto, recognised it, and the adjacent features seemed to fit. After one wrong assumption it is remarkable how easily the neighbouring marks on a coast line can be made to conform and how long it is before discrepancies become so glaring that the original assumption has to be abandoned. Prominent buildings noted in the 'Pilot' are cheerfully allowed to have been knocked down or put up since that invaluable guide was written; woods to have been planted or felled; and awkward hills which refuse to fit into the picture are either ignored or assumed to have been swallowed by an earthquake. Until at last common sense prevails and one is obliged sadly to admit that nothing fits and that one is looking at an entirely different piece of coast. We were all adrift. We were off Cape Ortegal, and in the evening, after we had sailed in desultory fashion some 20 miles along the coast, the Tower of Hercules was unmistakably identified by its light.

That we were out in our reckoning and had made a bad landfall was attributed to our being set in by the tide. The navigator can always attribute his errors – unless, of course, they are fatal – to abnormal tidal sets or the perverse behaviour of currents, whereas the man who leads his party into the wrong valley or on to the wrong ridge has no such scapegoat and is written down an ass. We should have to do better after taking our departure for the

Canaries, for it would not do to miss *them*. We had two sextants, both, judging by their venerable appearance, immediate successors of the astrolabe. Both had Vernier scales, which are less easy to read than micrometers, and unless one had a fearful squint Procter's sextant was very difficult to read. Moreover, it was useless for taking star sights unless one discarded the telescope. But for £5, which was all it cost, one can't expect refinements, and it gave reliable results.

For working sights Procter used the popular Air Navigation Tables. One objection to them is that for a long voyage a great many massive volumes must be carried; for instance, for a voyage like that which Conor O'Brien made, twenty volumes would be needed. The objection I had to them was that until the answer had been plotted on the chart it did not mean anything. Following the example of the 'Master' I used the tables published by the US Hydrographic Office, HO 211, a slim volume of 50 pages. With this and a Nautical Almanac one could circumnavigate the globe. Using these, in less than five minutes one knew without plotting the distance and direction of the ship's line of position from the dead reckoning position. Charles, who in pre-war days had studied celestial navigation at what he called the Military College of Nonsense, was our acknowledged expert, at any rate, in the theory of the subject. But he had refused to move with the times. He preferred time-honoured methods employing logarithms, haversines, cosecants, and God knows what, and these seemed not only to take longer than ours but gave more scope for human fallibility. The scope in fact, was so wide that an error of a degree or so in working became known to us as a 'Charles'. On the other hand a good intercept or, if we were working several star sights, a small 'cocked hat', was called a 'Henry' in honour of the great Navigator. Sometimes when three or even four or five were taking sights it became a little difficult to reconcile the results or even to pick one's way through the spider's web which soon adorned the chart. But I had the last word, and by a combination of the theory of probabilities, a knowledge of the instruments used, and of those who used them, I decided which to accept and which to reject and plotted our position accordingly. It sounds haphazard. A court of inquiry, had we ever had to face one, might have taxed us with awkward questions, but such problems kept everyone's interest alive and before we were through we were at least competent.

The wind falling light obliged us to motor until we were far enough round the corner of Spain to lay the course for Las Palmas. We did not see Finisterre but on 12 July took our departure from Cape Torinana about 10 miles north of it. A day later we picked up the Portuguese Trades, the northerly winds which had so plagued us the previous autumn and which now gave us runs of over a hundred miles a day. As we were running before the wind it did not seem so fresh as I remembered, but the crew of a 14-ton sloop, the *Maid of Pligh*, which was beating to windward homeward bound, probably thought it quite fresh enough. We waved heartily and that was all. In the old days when sailing ships met at sea they would often heave to for a yarn, a pleasant custom that we might well have followed; but we suffered from the universal complaint of being in a hurry, with no time to stand and stare, let alone exchange news with a fellow voyager.

The same night, for a different reason, we not only failed to exchange news but even to exchange names. Shortly after midnight in my watch we sailed close to a large, brilliantly lit passenger liner lying stationary, with two red lights hoisted to show she was not under command. After opening communication with the Aldis lamp and giving our name we found ourselves unable to read morse well enough to learn her name or why she lay there, a failure the more disgraceful since we had on board one serving gunner officer and two veterans. That a yacht should carry a signalling lamp and only be able to use it for the highly improper purpose of scaring steamers ('steamer-scarer' is the yachtsman's name for his lamp) is, to say the least, unseamanlike.

A similar thing had happened the previous year in the same waters in daylight when we encountered the *Roxburgh Castle*. The RASC corporal knew morse, or thought he did, and when asking for our position got on swimmingly until they began sending the latitude and longitude. The figures baffled him. In spite of repetitions he could make nothing of them, so that finally she circled slowly round us – they could almost have shouted to us – making hoists of flags until they were sure we had understood. Just because we could not read morse she had been delayed half an hour. Though one may send morse with great satisfaction to oneself it does not follow that it is always read if one is sending from a yacht. If there is anything of a sea running half the letters spelt out may be obscured by waves. We therefore painted our name in large letters on the dinghy cover. If we thought a ship was going to pass close to us, and sometimes they did alter course in order to do so, we lashed this to the rail, hoisted our ensign, and thus satisfied their curiosity and concealed our signalling inability.

It is astonishing how quickly a southward bound yacht, even though it is not a flyer, reaches the warmer weather for which the crew long. Sweaters and shirts are shed, shorts and bathing bags appear, and the sun-starved northerner's passion for getting his body well tanned by the sun is given full rein. But perfect comfort must not be expected by folks who go a-pleasuring. After a few more degrees of southing the sun-worshippers are wearing dark glasses, rigging awnings over the cockpit, and taking refuge in the shade of the cabin where they do nothing but complain of the heat.

When we had outrun the Portuguese trades a westerly wind carried us along until in about lat. 35° we were caught up in the strong embrace of the true north-east trades. With a wind which never fell below force 4 (about 16 knots) and more often reached force 5 or 6 sailing was exhilarating. We lowered the mainsail and stowed the boom, hoisted the twin staysails and let her go. The sky overhead with little fleecy clouds sailing across was a pale reflection of the sparkling blue sea flecked with foam and dancing spray. Rolling became continuous and sometimes heavy as the pursuing waves surged by, lifting the counter with a friendly shove forwards and slightly sideways before hissing past the rail and depositing a dollop of water on deck by way of salute. Steering was easy, for there was no fear of a gybe. Sheets had scarcely to be touched, and perhaps best of all with this rig the gear subject to chafe was reduced to a minimum. *Mischief* seemed to enjoy sailing before a wind that blew true and steady as the wind of a bellows, as much as did her crew. She frequently showed her pleasure by some very lively rolling. This rhythmic rolling, inseparable from down-wind sailing, becomes a nuisance, particularly at meal times, when a man needs two pair of hands, or when any work has to be done on deck. Every few minutes the ship would glide gently into what would become a crescendo of rolling, each sucessive roll becoming livelier and longer until the dislodging of the helmsman from his seat or a loud crash from the galley, announced that she had had her bit of fun. Then she would sail demurely along until tempted by the laughing waves to do it again. One could amost hear her humming to herself:

> Roll me over, in the clover,
> Roll me over, lay me down, and do it again.

With the coming of the trades we began to see flying fish in abundance and sometimes we got a few on board. For this effortless form of fishing neither patience nor implements are needed, only rough weather. After a night of heavy rolling a search of the scuppers and under the dinghy at times provided enough fish for breakfast. Another welcome visitor was a little brown and white striped pilot fish which perhaps mistook us for the shark he usually attends. He took station a foot or two ahead of *Mischief*'s rushing forefoot and swam there tirelessly for something like 300 miles. Perhaps fish sleep while swimming, as do horses when standing up, but this little chap seemed neither to sleep nor eat food. We watched him carefully, noting in the log at every change of watch whether Fidelio, as we called him, was present and correct. We missed him sorely when he left us as he did the night before we sighted the Islands.

We are never satisfied with the present. Change is what we really like and if there is too much of that we begin to long for stability. Content though *Mischief*'s crew were with life at sea, we eagerly awaited the approach of land, although I for one knew that making port would inevitably give me work and worry. After only 16 days at sea we looked forward with mounting excitement to our first port of call. What sort of a landfall would we make? Or again, would there be any land to see? Grand Canary, on which is Las Palmas, lies between the islands of Teneriffe and Fuertaventura and is separated from them by channels 30 and 45 miles wide respectively. By making a bad shot either way, and attended by the mischance of thick weather, the unskilful mariner could easily whistle through either channel in a matter of hours and not see land at all. In clear weather the veriest duffer should be able to make his landfall, since the Peak of Teneriffe (12,140ft.) can be seen from 70 miles and the other islands have their own mountains.

By the morning of 22 July we had run our distance and in spite of a smoky haze we fully expected to see the Peak towering above it. No such welcome sight appeared. Only the passing of three or four steamers showed we were on course and probably nearing a port. Visibility became worse. We were sailing fast in rough water and we had to decide whether to run off westwards where we thought Grand Canary should be or carry on and hope to see land later when the sun burnt up the haze. In the skipper's opinion, though it would not have been helpful to express it:

> Beyond the clouds, beyond the waves that roar,
> There may indeed, or may not be, a shore.

We raced on until about 10.30 am. The weather was as thick as ever and as the fear of having overshot our mark had become unbearable we handed the twins and hove to under reefed main and reefed staysail, for it was now blowing hard. Thus we lay until about noon when Charles, who is gifted with remarkably keen eyesight, cheered us with a cry of 'Land'. Sure enough to the north-west a blurred shape showed darkly through the haze. We let draw and sailed towards it when it presently resolved itself into Punta Gando, the easternmost point of Grand Canary some 10 miles south of Las Palmas.

Our landfall had been good enough. Had we but had faith in our reckoning and turned west at 8 am we should have sighted the town. As we were now near the south end of the island I suggested sailing round and up the west coast in the lee of the land. This was vetoed on the grounds that we should have a hard job weathering the north end, so we put about and began the long beat back. Weary work it was. It took us the best part of twenty-four hours to make good the ground lost in two hours, but early on the afternoon of the 23rd we dropped anchor off the Las Palmas Yacht Club. Domingo, a man who speaks English and is well known to visting yachts, came off. He startled me by insisting that if we thought of going ashore all together we must employ a watchman, otherwise water-thieves, bold as brass and cunning as monkeys, would strip the ship to the last nut and bolt. One yacht, we were told, had had her entire lead keel removed. Having thus prepared his listeners for bad tidings Domingo added that the watchman's fee would be 15s. a night. I agreed to this blackmail, if blackmail it was, rather than abide the consequences of refusal. So Johnnie the watchman was installed that night and proved a good investment. He rowed us back to the ship at all hours of the night as well as rendering us many other services. Domingo acted his self-assumed part of ship's agent well, saw that we were not cheated too much, and was very grateful for what we gave him.

CHAPTER FOUR

The Long Haul

And where the land she travels from? Away,
Far, far behind, is all that they can say. Clough

UNLIKE our visits to South American ports, in Las Palmas we did not make any friends. But it was from the points of view of climate and amenities the most pleasant. When I say Las Palmas, I mean in fact Puerto de la Luz, the port four miles distant from the city. Here food is as cheap again as in its smarter neighbour, while on the wide esplanade fronting the harbour are places shaded by trees and sheltered by trellises where one can sit and drink and watch the world go by. In the few South American ports we entered, neither the climate nor the streets make any provision for such alfresco idling – in my opinion the best attraction a town can offer.

Visiting yachts are common at Las Palmas, for most yachts bound for the West Indies or America call there; nevertheless, we attracted some attention and were perhaps not altogether unworthy of it. By now Michael had a beard the colour of Yorkshire parkin, shaped like a horse collar, which put me in mind of Facey Romford as portrayed by Leech. While it was worth anybody's money to see Charles, bearded like a minor prophet and still crowned with his yachting cap, strolling along with Van Tromp in his deerstalker hat. Nor were we the only strange types loose in Las Palmas. There was the ex-5th engineer who had saved money while working in some desert on oil installations and was spending it in the Canaries living in a cave with a milkmaid. And there was the ex-Indian Army officer who was extremely correct, but who ate with us at our restaurant in shirt sleeves and braces – on the same principle, one supposes, that if you find yourself among swine it is best to dispense with a plate. On shore, except for the occasional rendezvous at this restaurant, the crew having seen enough of each other at sea, parted company. Michael, while showing a remarkable facility for penetrating almost upon arrival the more select social circles, made a business of collecting all sorts of information dealing with local political and economic affairs. Procter, a classical scholar who spoke Spanish more grammatically, I was told, than a Spaniard, usually seemed to find his way into the family of some earnest student who wished to practise his English. 'When you enter a byre, low; when you enter a pen, bleat,' is a sound maxim, but Procter sometimes carried his affability so far – that is, when on shore – as to lead to embarrassment. Visitors having been warmly invited would arrive on board at the most inconvenient times; or I would return to find the cabin full to overflowing, a painstakingly strident

40

lesson in English in progress over the table, and I would have to take refuge on shore. Both he and Michael were ardent sightseers and made a tour of the island. As we discovered later, however, it was Charles who was the real dyed-in-the-wool tourist. But Las Palmas was to him familiar ground as he had been dumped here on his first deep-sea voyage after a quarrel with the owner of the yacht. Having no money to speak of, he had lived for a fortnight on bananas and had not yet got over it. This time it was John Van Tromp who had no money, there being some hitch over the sale of his farm, so that he was compelled to live like a recluse – though not on a banana diet. While I, besides having much to do, never have difficulty in suppressing any momentary hankering after social gaiety.

As we arrived on a Saturday and were hoping to leave the following Friday, we had only four working days available to us. At Falmouth we had had made a collar fitting to the mast about 5ft. above the deck to take the inboard end of the staysail booms. At least that was the height I liked it to be, but Procter, who is tall, always tried to fix it a couple of feet higher, ostensibly on the grounds that there was more wind up there but in fact to avoid cracking his head on the boom. We had been advised by experts to mount these booms forward of the mast, so now we employed a blacksmith to make an iron fitting which could be bolted to the bitts. At the same time we got him to make a harpoon, so that when fishing we could if we wished transfer the initiative from the fish to ourselves. In a strong wind this new iron fitting proved to be too flimsy. Within five minutes of the twins being hoisted the strain bent it and the bitts themselves shook visibly.

Taking petrol aboard occupied most of a day and involved a cart and horse to fetch the 40 gal. drum, and Domingo's dinghy, a much stouter one than ours, to bring it off. Even so we came within an ace of sinking the dinghy and losing the drum, although when we were discussing the threatened calamity, Charles, after doing in his head a complicated sum, assured us that at least the drum would float. On the last day we took in fresh stores: bread of a particular size, specially baked, and guaranteed to keep the three weeks; potatoes, the best we ever had (they were in perfect condition nine weeks later at Montevideo); carrots, sweet peppers, bags of onions which we ate both raw and cooked, and a hand of bananas; tomato paste, invaluable for *pasta sciutta* and *risotto*; and *chilli* paste, a species of bottled lightning for striking fire from dull dishes.

On Friday 29 July we motored round to the water-boat to fill our tanks. When her crew heard whither we were bound they showed their concern by urging us to fill every container we had, however small. This we did, and then like camels, took a last, long drink ourselves before water became precious. We reckoned that at worst the 4,600 miles ahead of us would take 80 days, so that with 200 gal. we could use two and a half gallons a day. The responsibility for this was put firmly on John. Under his control we were not allowed to drink water except as tea or coffee at meal times and could use only an occasional half-mugful for shaving or tooth cleaning. Later, as it happened, we were able to refill one of our tanks with rain water, but we could have gone to Montevideo on our 200 gal. without inconvenience.

After settling accounts with Domingo and Johnnie we hoisted sail, cast off from the water-boat and began the long haul southwards. Leaving Las Palmas in a sailing ship bound south is as carefree as stepping on to a train. As soon as we were outside we hoisted the twins and metaphorically sat back. By 5 pm our old acquaintance Punta Gando was abeam. We streamed the log and managed to snarl it with the fishing line. It took us two hours to sort out the tangle. As fishermen we were always rich in hope if poor in possession. We usually had a line out, sometimes two, and if these were forgotten when going about or in moments of crisis, as they sometimes were, the consequent lashup was deplorable.

Our next landfall, we hoped, would be St Vincent in the Cape Verde Islands some 900 miles to the south-west. Thence we would stand on to the southward without trying to make much westing, aiming at crossing the equator in about long. 29°W. This was the track used in other days by sailing ships bound round Cape Horn. Where possible we followed the track for sailing ships laid down on the *Ocean Pilot Charts* published by the U.S. Hydrographic Office. There is a chart for each ocean for each month of the year showing not only the recommended track for steam or sail, but also the prevalent winds and currents, the seasonal limits of the trades, percentages of gales and calms, sea temperatures, normal barometric pressures, and much else. These charts are based on observations and information collected by Lieutenant Maury (1806-73), an American naval officer who as a midshipman had spent four years on a cruise round the world. Having been put in charge of what later became the Hydrographic Office he devoted much of his time to establishing which were the best routes for sailing ships on all the standard voyages at any particular time of the year. He did this mainly by distributing specially prepared log books to masters of vessels and thus accumulating a mass of data. Without the information to be found on these charts or in the British Admiralty publication *Ocean Passages of the World,* which comprise the carefully sifted data of thousands of voyages, a sailing ship man would spend many more days at sea.

For the next seven days we ran in the full swing of the trades. These were days of glorious sailing. The sun blazed down till the pitch in the seams bubbled, the dazzling white twins swayed and curtsied until their booms kissed the water, while the ship rolled lazily along on her run of more than a hundred miles every day. All this happened with little or no exertion on our part. We even had flying fish for breakfast every morning with no exertion at all. But the Cape Verde Islands which we were rapidly approaching seem to upset the steadiness of the trades. The wind became fitful and one wondered whether or not the wind would be truer away to the west of the islands. But the idea of taking such a course would be rejected when one remembered what a fillip the interest and morale of the crew received from the sight of land. For me there is something about islands that rouses a more lively interest than a mere line of coast, an aura of romance such as is expressed in Flecker's

A ship, an isle, and a sickle moon.

To sight one, even the smallest barren ash-heap, excites curiosity – whether or not there be a landing place, water, or even any life at all; and to be on one is to enjoy the delights of the sea without the disgusts.

Most of the Cape Verde Islands are ash-heaps, ash-heaps which with their warm colouring appear to be still smouldering. Early on 6 August we sighted the bold headland of Lombo de Boi, Bull Point, at the north-east end of Santo Antao. With light airs we sailed and drifted through the channel between it and St Vincent to the east, past the main harbour Porto Grande, remarking as we passed, the barracks, the prison, the hospital, all the tokens, in short, of civilisation. We crept past the signal station on Ilheu dos Passeros dutifully making our number (the signal flags MKCP) and as usual evoking no response; for a yacht's signal flags are too small to be read at any distance. It is doubtful whether a set of flags is worth carrying. It was very hot and we had barely steerage way; so we ignored the warning given in the *Pilot* that sharks frequent the bay, dived overboard and swam about the ship.

The sun sank and the ruddy glow of the barren hills changed to violet and then to deep purple as we drifted along the rock coast towards Ponta Machado, the western extremity of the island. On this cape there is a light-house called Donna Amelia, a name which occasioned some chaff, mostly at Mike's expense, concerning the lighthouse keeper's daughter. About two in the morning I came on deck, perhaps by chance, perhaps because of that instinct which is supposed to rouse the sleeping mariner when his ship is in danger, but probably because Mike had called me to report the Amelia light abeam. Abeam with a vengeance. The thing was virtually above us. We were so close that I could have sworn I heard the light revolving and had the lighthouse keeper's daughter been on watch she could certainly have blown Mike kisses. Though the ship still had way she appeared to my shocked eyes to be getting sucked into a small bight beyond the headland where evidently – though the *Pilot* forbears to mention it – there lurked what that exemplary work sometimes refers to as a *bastardo*. With the help of the engine we won clear and I was thankful to see Amelia's baleful eye gradually recede and eventually disappear.

Having cleared the islands we had only one more good day of trade wind sailing before the wind failed, leaving us still two degrees north of its normal summer limit. The Doldrums, the belt of calms and rain squalls that lies between the north-east and south-east trade wind systems, is furthest north and at its widest in August when it covers about five degrees of latitude. These limits are, of course, only rough and may vary even from week to week. With luck a ship might be only three or four days in the Doldrums before picking up the trades on the other side, or she might remain more or less becalmed for a fortnight or more, fraying the tempers of her crew as well as the sheets, halyards, and sails. We had a weary time. Instead of handing the sails we left them up, the sheets hard in and the boom amidships, watching every catspaw that ruffled the oily sea in the hope that presently we might be able to let draw. On some days rain squalls burst frequently and with great violence, but if they brought any wind with them it might be from any direction. It was fun turning out naked in this heavy rain for a fresh water wash. We filled one of our 30 gal. tanks with great ease and had lots of water for washing clothes. On our shore-going clothes green mould sprouted freely. When it was not raining a clammy heat enveloped us. Buckets of sea water or a bathe overside brought some relief, but this resource was of little avail when the temperature of air and sea became the same, 80°F.

In the old days patience, a virtue very liable to be fatigued by exercise, was the only real remedy for this state of affairs. Other remedies were usually tried, such as whistling, throwing a pack of cards into the sea, or sticking a knife in the mast. But in order to be really effective the knife should be stuck in by a clergyman and seafaring clerics were not common. We ourselves were not free from these beliefs. When whistling failed we threw coins – Spanish pesetas of very nominal value – overboard on the quarter from which we wished the wind to come. But on the whole it is more effective to make use of an engine and petrol. By using these freely and by taking advantage of every puff of wind we worked our way steadily south, making good about 40 miles a day. The longest continuous running of the engine was nine hours, and how grateful we were when we could shut it off. How we reviled the noise and the fumes in the cabin, and how we rejoiced in the succeeding stillness, with the musical ripple of water along the sides and the slat of the sails as they began to fill. Even with the help of the engine we endured eight days of these trying conditions until our boredom ended suddenly with a day of heavy rain, high wind, and steep seas. This violent but welcome change cost us the light Genoa. We had left it up too long and the clew blew out. When the following day dawned bright and clear we thought we had at last escaped from the Doldrums but in fact four more days were to pass before we felt the first welcome breath of the south-east trades in about lat. 3°N.

But this baffling region is not without its interest. Marine life which hitherto had consisted mainly of flying fish and Portuguese men o'war (the nautilus with its delicate coloured sail which abounds in tropical and sub-tropical waters) became more varied. We thought it was about time. Accounts of voyages, all no doubt written by honourable men, in which bonito, albicore, dorado, and barracouta are seen or even caught on every other page, where the grim triangular fins of sharks ceaselessly circle the ship, and where whales rub their barnacles off on her bottom, had whetted our appetites and roused expectation to a height that was never to be realised. But on a day of oily calm, after a vast school of porpoises had played round for hours and finally taken themselves off, the helmsman did at last raise the cry of 'Shark'. So indiscriminating were we then that any large, unpleasing looking fish was labelled shark, and this may well have been one, for there are many kinds. He never surfaced but remained a few feet below and never far from our stern, a vague, green, disquieting shape. Horace, as we called him, was interested in food but in a languid sort of way. He followed us with some persistence for several days. Bathing stopped immediately, although I entered him in the log as merely a giant South Atlantic sea frog. Then Procter, the mildest of men, went berserk and harpooned an inoffensive dolphin gambolling round the forefoot. By the time we had it on board the harpoon was bent like a hoop. Some of us had an uneasy feeling that the consequences of such violence might rival those that befell the Ancient Mariner. Nevertheless, we ate him and for the first meal or two felt grateful. After that it palled, for the meat is like venison, dark and very rich. Soon after this we caught our first dorado (also called a dolphin). This was literally a very different kettle of fish, glorious to see and glorious to eat. He is anything up to five feet long, with a long fin running down his back, a Roman nose, and brilliant greeny-gold metallic hues which in the dying fish undergo quick changes. It is a fine thing to see him leaping ferociously after smaller fish, finer to see him on deck, and finest of all to have him on one's plate.

Quite apart from this choice of dark or white meat we lived well at this time. As an experiment I had brought a quantity of dehydrated food from the Ministry of Agriculture Experimental Factory, Aberdeen – minced beef, spinach, carrot, cabbage, and meat and vegetable blocks. All were so easily and quickly cooked and so excellent (the cabbage and carrot might have been straight from the garden) that I regretted having made the vulgar mistake of not taking enough. Even on hot mornings we fortified ourselves with porridge as belly-timber, and in the evening we turned hungrily upon large helpings of potatoes, rice or macaroni in various guises, followed often by steamed puddings with which John had a happy knack. A little too much carbohydrate, perhaps, especially considering the heat, but we had no dietician on board to point out that we were probably digging our graves with our teeth, and we thrived well enough. The puddings traced their origin back to an idle day off the Spanish coast when I made a cake. The recipe was no secret, so I handed it verbally to John who speedily discovered that 'Skipper's Mixture', as it was called, was equally adapted to baked cakes or steamed puddings. On Saturday evenings we had a drink, for not one of us was a rigid abstainer. Sunday was curry night. We felt obliged to limit this to one night a week on account of Michael whose appetite for curry was a little immoderate.

For some time now we had enjoyed the full glory of the southern sky at night – the Cross with its two pointers, Canopus, Fomalhaut, Achernar, Antares, and the two Magellanic Clouds glowing faintly and mysteriously like straying portions of the Milky Way. (These cloud-like clusters, though named after him, were known before Magellan's time.) Charles, whom we knew as the 'Astronomer Royal' and to whom we referred, as it were, for heavenly guidance, pointed out these and many lesser stars with curious names like Nunki, Shaula, and Kaus Australis. For sights we used the major stars and planets and left that temptingly easy target the moon for better men; for the working of her sights, with the numerous necessary corrections and the consequent increased opportunities for errors, generally gave startling results. In low latitudes there were few early mornings or late evenings when three or four suitable stars or planets could not be seen, but in higher latitudes we rarely got good star sights. In the North Atlantic there was usually cloud, poor horizons, or rough weather. If one quarter of the sky was clear, the horizon under it would be hazy, or clouds permitted such a fleeting glimpse of a star that even with the approximately correct angle on the sextant before-hand it could not be picked up, much less brought down to the horizon. Considering which exasperating circumstances, the navigator would exclaim against the Creator's arrangements in somewhat the same style as that credited to Lord Jeffrey: 'Damn the solar system. Bad light; planets too distant; pestered with comets; feeble contrivance; could make a better myself.'

On 29 August we crossed the equator in long. 28°W. and celebrated the event with a plum pudding. This was about the right place for a sailing ship bound for South America to cross the line. The south equatorial current sets west at the rate of about 30 miles a day and if a vessel bound south gets too far west there is some danger that she may not be able to weather Cape San Roque. A sailing vessel unlucky enough to be set to leeward of this cape would have to fetch a huge circuit of the North Atlantic before she could regain her proper course towards the equator for a second attempt. Although we were well placed we were being set west more than we liked and we could not steer south owing to the wind blowing persistently from that quarter rather than from the south-east as it should have done. The current, too, seemed to be working overtime. To go about on the other tack and sail away from the American coast demanded more strength of mind than we possessed, so we kept the ship close-hauled and our fingers crossed, praying for a wind that would let us sail a point free so that we should not be set down towards St Paul's Rocks or Fernando Noronha and eventually fail to weather San Roque.

In spite of the disturbing westerly set we could never be in danger of this, provided our sights were correct. We had long since ceased to get any time signals, but we knew the rate of the deck watch, we had not yet forgotten to wind it, and we felt that our reckoning could not be far out. On 2 September a noon sight showed us that we were on the same latitude as Fernando Noronha and still some 90 miles to the east of it. But as yet the south-east trades, which we had expected would blow bold and true like the north-east trades, were weak and variable. Still we were getting southwards all the time and were encouraged by the sight of a steamer, the first we had seen for three weeks. We were about 50 miles off the Brazilian coast and we aimed to keep off until the time came for us to close the land north of the River Plate. We were pretty confident the coast *was* there because when we were in the latitude of Recife we had seen in the sky the loom of the lights of a large city.

Off Cape Frio, when the weather became appropriately cool, we found that one of our two big paraffin containers had leaked, so that we had only one gallon left to last us to Montevideo, still a fortnight away. We had therefore to reduce our hot meals to one a day and to forgo steamed puddings. Perhaps it was the denial of these sustaining rib-stickers that made us complain of the increasing cold. If we were feeling cold off the Brazilian coast, what would we feel like twenty degrees further south? The sea temperature had already fallen to 70°F. – no water for weaklings – and only the hardiest of the crew could any longer face the daily rite of three buckets over their heads before breakfast, hail, rain, or shine. Between John and me there lay an unspoken challenge as to which of us would bathe farthest south, and already each was watching the other hopefully for signs of weakening. We began to see more ships. A tanker, the *Ancap Tercero*, passed close and gave us three blasts on her horn. Not to be outdone in civility we replied with three on our hand fog-horn, hiccuping, as it were, in response to a thunder-clap.

On the morning of 28 September, after a fine run of 130 miles before a biting north-east wind, the wind fell light when we were some 50 miles off Cabo Polonio, where we expected to make our landfall. That we were not far from land was evident from the presence of seals. Having sighted what we thought was some wreckage or floating branches and altered course to avoid them, we found a party of seals asleep on their backs with their flippers in the air. Presently we were becalmed, handed the sails, and amused ourselves by watching the antics of a seal and two big gulls. While they sat side by side patiently expectant of scraps from the galley, the seal would suddenly shoot up between them. Squawking indignantly they would flutter off and settle down anew, whereupon the seal would play the same trick. So calm and so inviting was the sea that I rashly dived in before taking its temperature. This proved to be only 56°F.

Meantime the glass had been falling steadily and by morning we were bowling along in thickening weather with a strong south-east wind. Rice pudding for breakfast seemed to me an indication of worse to come. At 11 am we sighted land and a little later identified a lighthouse as that on Cabo Polonio. The thrill and satisfaction of making our appointed landfall, of sighting a new continent after two months at sea, now gave way to concern that we might hit it. With the wind and rain both increasing we spent a most anxious afternoon sailing fast along a lee shore, glimpsing it just often enough to raise doubts as to whether or not we were being set towards it. In the evening a brief clearing showed Cabo Santa Maria abeam, and that we were now well inside the estuary was evident from the nasty, yellow appearance of the water.

The River Plate estuary is 138 miles wide at its mouth, narrowing to 57 miles at Montevideo which is 60 miles from the sea. At its head the estuary is 25 miles wide. It receives the waters of six rivers, thus comprising the second largest system in the world. The discoloration caused by the silt can be seen 70 or 80 miles out to sea, while this mingling of tropical river water and the colder water from the southern ocean is marked by the presence of large numbers of petrels, albatrosses, seals, and sometimes penguins. The estuary is noted for its sudden and violent weather changes, for its thunderstorms and dust storms, for *sudestadas, zondas,* and *pamperos,* each of which has its own particular unpleasantness. The *pampero* is often preceded by the phenomenon known as *Baba del Diablo,* or Devil's Dribble, which fills the air with the gossamer webs of the aeronaut spider. The *zonda* is a norther; the *pampero,* as its name implies, arises over the pampas and is a line squall which strikes with suddenness and ferocity. The *sudestada,* coming off the sea, brings with it rain and thick weather. Since the estuary is shallow these storms quickly raise a short and nasty sea.

We were about to experience a *sudestada.* Early in the morning after a quiet night the wind rose steadily and heavy rain began driving over the livid water. For us the wind was fair – a wind the sailor is advised not to waste – so we shortened sail as far as we could and taking care to allow two points for leeway we laid a course for the light vessel marking the northern end of the English Bank. This great sandbank lies plumb in the middle of the estuary and in time past has taken its toll of many a ship.* This liberal allowance for leeway could be regarded as a sort of insurance policy, for if the allowance proved to be too much and so caused us to miss the lightship we might perhaps sight instead a buoy lying some eight miles to the south. But since the *sudestada* is accompanied by heavy rain and bad visibility the chances of our sighting a small object like a buoy, which in a rough sea is for half the time obscured, were not good.

In the early afternoon when we had run our distance and had sighted nothing, a change of course became imperative if we were to clear the bank. I had just decided to carry on for another five minutes when to our joy lynx-eyed Charles sighted the buoy about half a mile away on our port bow. With renewed confidence we altered course for the lightship, and at the same time the wind began to moderate and the rain squalls to become less frequent. For the very good reason that it was not there the lightship was never found, for as we learnt later it had been taken off station for repair. However, we soon made out the Isla de Flores some ten miles to the north, and as we passed the island a great box-like thing appeared above the distant horizon. At first we took it for a large ship distorted by mirage – mirage effects are common in the estuary – but when other rectangular shapes began to show on either side of it we realised that we were looking at the skyline of Montevideo still some 12 miles away.

As wind and sea subsided we shook out our reefs. Night fell and we enjoyed a lovely moonlight sail with the lights of the coast road and the eastern suburbs twinkling close on our starboard hand. At length we cut into the dredged and buoyed channel where we began to experience one of the problems of entering a strange harbour at night, the picking out of the aids to navigation from among the even brighter aids to dissipation, the neon signs and coloured lights of bars, night clubs, and such like. After an exchange of marine pleasantries with a steamer and its attendant tug in the harbour entrance, we motored in and dropped anchor at 1 am on 1 October, 64 days out from Las Palmas and all well. Rum and cocoa were served in the cabin.

---

*Mr J. A. Drever, who has made enquiries for me in Montevideo, cannot discover the origin of the name. The oldest document on the subject (he writes) is a chart dated 1685, compiled by a pilot of the Royal Spanish Navy called Andred Emaili. On this chart the English Bank already figures.

CHAPTER FIVE

The Magellan Straits

We found by a miracle, a strait which we called the Strait of the Eleven Thousand Virgins. I think there is not a more beautiful country, or a better strait than this one. Pigafetta

HAVING ENTERED a strange port by night one goes on deck the next morning hopeful as a playgoer watching the curtain rise on another scene. This state of happy expectancy may perhaps be regarded as some slight recompense for the anxieties of the night before. But if it is a busy commercial port one's hopes should not be pitched too high, for in such places few concessions are made to aesthetic taste. The décor is strictly functional. But after nine weeks at sea, even a crane is a refreshing sight, while the majestic view of a grain elevator may move a susceptible seaman to tears.

The first and obvious thing we noted was our ill-chosen anchorage. Evidently it had been determined upon more by the wish to have done than by any seamanlike regard for safety. We found ourselves close to some seaplane mooring buoys. The inevitable visit from some indignant port official was forestalled by Mr J. A. Drever of Messrs Maclean and Stapledon (the agents who were handling our twenty-four cases of provisions which had been lying in the customs since the previous year). He brought with him the port doctor to give us pratique and showed us a better anchorage. He also told us that he was arranging that we should lie at Puerto Buceo, the head-quarters of the Uruguayan Yacht Club. We were congratulated upon our ocean crossing. This had proved easier than we had expected, but any complacency we might have felt was tempered by the thoughts of the next leg of the journey where the Roaring Forties and the Furious Fifties promised a stiffer test. On the whole the weather had been kind to us, and a gale of wind in the tropics is not so searching a trial as a gale under the lowering skies and in the colder waters of higher latitudes.

Next day we motored round to Puerto Buceo, a small, snug harbour lying a few miles to the east and occupied solely by yachts and a few fishing boats. The Argentine coast, 70 miles away, appeared as a mirage with its trees floating in the air. Having first taken the ground as we tried to moor to the jetty and later having parted two warps when tied to a trawler, *Mischief* was finally anchored off the Yacht Club where she lay for the next fortnight. Apart from numerous small jobs, the topmast had to be sent down, the clew of the Genoa had to be repaired, and the seams of the mainsail hand-stitched. Since leaving Las Palmas we had constantly to lower the sail for resewing

49

seams which just as constantly opened at some fresh point. It seemed so worthwhile having the whole sail hand sewn that we struck a bargain with an old coloured sailor. Sitting on a back verandah of the Club, he stitched away happily for ten days until the job was done, and a very good job he made of it. Subsequently we had little trouble with seams opening and still wore the same sail when recrossing the Atlantic the following June. Sewing done by hand is stronger than that done by machine. The stitches are tighter, they sit closer and are therefore less likely to chafe, and if one stitch goes the others are not so liable to pull out as when machine sewn. The high initial cost is the only disadvantage.

In the South Atlantic we should not want to hoist either the topsail or the big Genoa and we should be better off without the weight of the useless topmast aloft. Striking it did not prove so troublesome as we expected. Quite unnecessarily, I thought we ought to lessen the weight by sending down the four wire topmast-stays before starting the spar itself, and consequently I spent a long time at the masthead in a bos'n's chair wrestling with stiff shackles. Had any of us closely examined the topsail halyard from which my chair was suspended before hoisting, I should not have been aloft nearly so long, for one of its strands was found to be chafed through. Having got the topmast down we lashed it on deck. It took up so much room, from abaft the cockpit nearly to the foot of the mast, that we seriously considered leaving it at the Yacht Club until our return. Our plan had always been to return the same way, but, as the great Moltke said, no plan survives contact with the enemy, so we took it with us.

Fourteen days slipped by quickly, each of the crew labouring in his own vocation. Mike became so immersed in the pursuit of local colour and social engagements that we saw little of him. Procter devoted himself to searching for places where one got the most food for the least money, a search for which his fluent Spanish well qualified him and in which his voracity well rewarded him. At times I enjoyed the benefits of this painstaking piece of research. Charles, whose clothes needed constant attention if they were to hold together, fancied himself as a tailor and had begun to make a windproof jacket against the rigours of the ice-cap. To have more light and to give his needle free play he occupied a bedroom on the fourth floor of the Yacht Club's eight-storey building. John divided his time between the ground floor of the club, among the refreshments, and the ship.

We had been given the freedom of the club, a privilege we much appreciated and one which brought us many friends. Among them was the owner of *Blue Disa* which he had sailed out the previous year from England under the Uruguayan flag. She is a sister-ship of the well known ocean-racer *Samuel Pepys*. And there was a Frenchman who lived aboard his modern ketch, sailing round South America, painting scenes of Indian life, and exhibiting his pictures at the larger cities. Another friend, who on our departure made us a present of sugar and butter, was the night watchman, a Pole who had fought in the British Army as a paratrooper. It was remarkable, by the way, the number of Uruguayans with British connections who had come over to fight in the last war. A striking figure always around the club was the bosun, very large, fat, rubicund, and the possessor of a glass eye which at moments of crisis, such as when lifting a yacht out of the water by crane, he popped in his mouth for safety. Many of the club members seemed to have two jobs, neither of which occupied much of their time and one of which was usually connected with the press. We were invited to the offices of *El Pais* where at four in the afternoon we were regaled with whisky and nuts, and interviewed amid manifold interruptions from telephone calls and other business. The printing machinery would have been more impressive had it been working or had our guide had any inkling of what the machines did or how they worked.

My visits to the city were always on business and I always slept on board. (In the course of our year's wanderings I spent only one night ashore under a roof.) In Montevideo I noted a refreshing absence of uniforms, for Uruguay is a free country in every sense – free trade, free currency, free speech. Everyone abuses the government or lack of government, but the principle of giving the other side a turn is well understood. It is the only Welfare State, I understand, in South America. More remarkable is the fact that it has nine Presidents. To me this provision seemed unnecessary in Uruguay, but in more effervescent countries it would be wise enough, for there is safety in numbers. I was impressed by the vast grandeur of the cemetery, the whole surrounded by a high wall with massive iron gates built with a view to baffling body-snatchers. And mention of the cemetery reminds me of another curious building looking exactly like a mosque, from whose history there is a moral to be drawn if philosophy could but find it out. It began life soberly enough as a crematorium, blazed garishly for a short time as a night club until its flames were extinguished, presumably by the police, when it reverted to the housing of dust and ashes and became a museum. But strangest of all was the sight of workmen lighting fires on the pavement on which they broiled great slabs of inch-thick steaks for their 'elevenses'. Montevideo is celebrated for its bathing beaches which, in spite of the coolness of the water and its queer colour, attract many visitors from Buenos Aires.

A few days before we were due to sail Charles complained of a stiff shoulder. He decided that he was not fit enough to make the voyage and that he would travel overland to rejoin us at Punta Arenas. Although four of us could manage *Mischief* it meant harder work and should we meet heavy weather in the South Atlantic we should be inconveniently short-handed. A young German, Gird Breuer, who had often been on board had expressed a wish to come with us to Punta Arenas. He had come out to America as a deckhand with a view to learning English and Spanish before joining his father in business. At 1 pm on the Saturday when we were to sail I got a message through to him to say that we had a vacant berth. By 4 pm he had sacked himself, gathered his few belongings together, and joined *Mischief*.

The trouble about sea voyaging is that you have to start from some port. Throughout the voyage sailing time became more and more a nightmare. There was the last minute round-up on shore, the paying of duty calls, the settling of bills and making forgotten purchases. On board presents arrive and must be acknowledged, hilarious visitors must be persuaded to leave, and finally a hilarious crew must be persuaded to come. We got away before dusk,

motoring through the narrow entrance and then sailing close-hauled for the
'Practicos-Recalada' light vessel, 12 miles to the south-west. This is the light
vessel at the entrance of the dredged channel to Buenos Aires where ships
bound for that place take on or drop their pilot. At midnight we passed close
by it, altered course for Cabo San Antonio at the mouth of the estuary on the
south side, and streamed the log.

The wind being light from the south-east we did not bring the cape abeam
until midnight on the Monday, thus our calm, dignified progress out of the
estuary was in marked contrast to the angry fury of our entrance. We had
time to complain of the cold, for young Gird to be sea-sick, and for some
successful fishing. In the shallow water of the estuary we caught no less than
sixteen fish of about one pound each of a species known locally as *palometa*.
And outside the estuary, while becalmed off Punta Medanos in shoal water,
we were able to catch as many as we wanted of a variety called *pescadilla* – a
fish bigger than the *palometa* and round like a whiting. They were bottom
feeders which took anything from a bare hook to rags, feathers, or a bit of
fish. Shallow water is undoubtedly the place for fish; we never had fishing like
that again. In the course of the whole voyage we caught only about a dozen
dorado and it always seemed to me that in mid-ocean the chances of catching
fish at any particular moment were little better than the chance of catching a
mermaid.

The 1,200-odd miles from Montevideo to Punta Arenas proved to be our
slowest passage, giving an average of only 56 miles a day. For the first six days
we scarcely made 30 miles a day and that only by dint of using the motor in
flat calms. They were pleasant, cool sunny days with plenty to see. On a day
of glassy calm the S.S. *Fitzroy* bound for Port Stanley in the Falkland Islands
ranged close enough alongside for us to speak by megaphone and offered to
report our progress to the British Consul, Punta Arenas. Bird and fish life
became more plentiful, if seals, porpoises, and whales may be called fish. The
last named, great ugly brutes of from 20 to 30ft. in length, with high dorsal
fins, were identified as killer whales. For the first time we saw penguins and
the black and white speckled cape pigeon which followed us right down to the
Straits in small flocks of anything up to twenty. The so-called cape pigeon,
one of the forty different kinds of petrel, was the only ocean bird we met with
which fed readily on scraps. Albatross would follow the ship in their effortless
flight or sometimes sit close by on the water watching us pass and showing not
the least interest when the gash bucket was emptied or biscuits thrown overside. Perhaps they would have taken a lump of pork or fish had we had it to
offer, for the catching of albatross with line and hook was once a common
sport on sailing ships in spite of the superstition of old sailors. Apparently in
those days the price of albatross skins in a place like Melbourne was high
enough to overcome any superstitious fears they may have had.

The albatross did not come up to our expectations. Before reluctantly
concluding that these birds were indeed albatross we must have seen hundreds which, though large, failed to measure up to our ideas. A bird with a
wing span of 10 to 15ft. should, we thought, appear unmistakably huge, and
we were constantly calling one another up from below to pass judgment

upon some newcomer – whether or not he qualified as a genuine wandering albatross. Our imaginations had so bodied forth the form of things unknown that we refused to believe what we saw and still looked for bigger and better birds farther south. At the other end of the scale were the tiny storm petrels. These are the size of a swallow and are the most widespread, companionable, and reassuring of ocean birds. To see such a small bird hundreds of miles from land in stormy weather pursuing his busy, erratic flight, literally dancing on the waves, is most comforting. These are the Mother Carey's chickens of the sailor, Mother Carey being, I believe, a corruption of Mater Cara, an appellation of the Blessed Virgin. Both in the North and South Atlantic and in the Pacific oceans there were few days when Mother Carey's chickens were not seen, so that had one believed that their presence foreboded stormy weather one would have led a most unquiet life.

This tranquil bird-watching life was rudely interrupted when out of a profound calm a sharp gale sprang at us from the south-east. Heralded by a swiftly advancing bank of mist the first puffs increased in a matter of minutes to gale force, compelling us to reef right down and finally to change to trysail, double reefed staysail and storm jib, a rig under which we passed a cold and stormy night. By the following afternoon the wind had dropped enough for us to reset the working sails but with two rolls in the mainsail. The sea was still running very high and young Gird was sick. For that matter so was I, perhaps because of having had soup for lunch or because of the mental exertion of working out sights which is apt to make a weak head spin. After this shaking up we watched the slow downward curve of the barograph with apprehension. However, it was still above normal for those waters and in the event we enjoyed a succession of clear, fine days with fair winds. It was becoming markedly and steadily colder, the sea and air temperatures having dropped to 48°F. and 49°F. respectively.

After passing the great gulfs of San Matias and San George we closed the land in the vicinity of Cabo Blanco (there must be a dozen capes bearing this unimaginative name) and on the morning of 31 October we raised the low, barren coast to the south of the cape. An Argentine frigate came out of Puerto Deseado, Port Desire, and soon we were able to identify Penguin Island some 10 miles to the south. It was at Puerto Deseado that 'penguins' were first given their name by a Welshman sailing with Sir Thomas Cavendish. He called them 'pen gwyn' which is, of course, the Welsh for white head. Penguin Isle is the place where the great seaman and navigator John Davis, having been parted from Cavendish on their second voyage to the Straits, revictualled his ship *Desire* for the voyage back to England. They took on board 14,000 dried penguins. For an estimated voyage of six months this gave a daily ration of five penguins for four men, but long before they reached England (which they did in six months) this vast stock of imperfectly dried meat had gone rotten. The stores, the ship, the men themselves became infested with maggots – 'there was nothing', wrote John Jane who was one of the crew, 'they did not devour, only iron excepted'. When the noisome, worm-ridden *Desire* struggled into Bearhaven in June 1593 only sixteen of her crew remained alive and of these only five were able to stand.

Between Puerto Deseado and Cape Virgins there lies a long stretch of desolate, wind-swept coast, upon which there are only two small ports used mainly for the seasonal shipments of frozen mutton and wool. Besides being remarkable for strong tides with a great range – at Port San Julian the range is as much as 45ft. – these two places are of historic interest. San Julian, 100 miles south of Deseado, is the place where after a violent mutiny Magellan executed two of its leaders and marooned two others, one a priest. Here Drake, sixty years later, had John Doughty beheaded, and before continuing the voyage made a harangue to his crew in which he offered the faint-hearted a ship to return home in and uttered the oft quoted words: 'For I must have the gentlemen to haul and draw with the mariners, and the mariners with the gentlemen; and let us show ourselves to be all of a company, and let us not give occasion to the enemy to rejoice at our decay and overthrow. I would know him that would refuse to set his hand to a rope; but I trust there is not any such here.'

Sixty miles further down the coast from San Julian is Santa Cruz lying at the mouth of the Santa Cruz river which rises in Lake Argentino. When the *Beagle* on her famous voyage round the world anchored there in 1834 Captain Fitzroy with a party of twenty-five, including the young Darwin, set out in three whale boats to explore the river. For eighteen days these indomitable seamen hauled their heavy boats against a five knot current; and then having reached a point about 140 miles from the sea they turned back and regained the ship in only three days, so powerful was the current. Had they persevered for another day, or at most two, they would have been the first Europeans to discover Lake Argentino. But for several days they had been on half rations and as Darwin wrote in his account: 'A light stomach and easy digestion are good to talk about but very unpleasant in practice.' J. H. Gardiner was the first to reach Lake Argentino thirty-three years later, in 1867. Darwin's own ability as a traveller, his toughness and endurance in accomplishing long journeys on foot or on horseback, and his venturesome spirit, are sometimes overlooked.

Now that we were well down in the forties the South Atlantic began to roar to some purpose. No sooner had we left Penguin Isle astern than the coast vanished in a murky haze, while to the south, clouds (which, by the way, I noted in my diary as 'not very threatening') began to gather. The gale struck with stunning force. By evening we were running before it to the north-east under bare poles. But its first fury did not last, for in the course of the night, a glorious night of full moon and cloudless sky, we were able to set the trysail and get the ship once more heading south. By daylight the wind had veered to the north and we got up all plain sail. But again the wind freshened, and again the mainsail had to give way to trysail and storm jib, and later, as she was running too fast, to the jib alone. But at least we were running in the right direction, and *Mischief* had shown herself to be such an able sea-boat that we had no anxiety on her account. After two days of better weather, when we were 20 miles off the entrance to the Straits, the glass fell to 29in. and the wind rose. We made our landfall under the conditions which we had now come to regard as specially reserved for such occasions. At 2 am on the morning of 5 November, with a strong westerly gale blowing, we sighted the Cape Virgins light, a little to the north of the entrance to the Straits. Daylight revealed a long, flat line of white cliffs, except for the lighthouse on the eastern extremity bare as the sea itself. The wind was blowing straight out of the Straits and a high, confused sea was running. We could make no westing so we hove to on the starboard tack and drifted slowly southward. In the evening, with no land in sight, we went about to recover our ground and at midnight we once more raised the light. And so it went on. We stood off until the evening of the 6th, when the wind moderating, we shook out all reefs and stood in to the south-west.

Off the entrance to the Straits the tidal streams are strong and confusing; for the flood stream makes north up the coast from round the Horn and also sets east through the Straits, and in the same way the ebb running south divides, part of it setting west through the Straits. So when the wind fell light we started the engine, fully determined that no false pride should stop us entering the Straits and attaching ourselves firmly to the bottom to save our being blown out or set out by the tide. Bernicot, who in 1936 in the cutter *Anahita* had repeated Slocum's single-handed circumnavigation by way of the Magellan Straits, had had a rough handling just inside the entrance and was twice swept out to sea in spite of all that sail and engine could do. Slocum, too, had no sooner rounded Cape Virgins than a south-westerly gale struck him and for 30 hours his sloop *Spray* managed to hold her ground with no more than a three-reefed mainsail and forestaysail. *She* had no engine and she was *not* driven out to sea; but then *Spray* was *Spray* and there have been few seamen like Slocum.

Inside the Straits the tidal streams are stronger and reach their maximum strength in the First and Second Narrows. In the First Narrows spring tides run at from five to eight knots and are not much less in the Second Narrows. Between the eastern entrance and Punta Arenas a sailing vessel or a low-powered steamer must therefore work the tides, anchoring when the stream is against her. By 10 o'clock that night, when the Dungeness light bore north, we knew we were fairly inside the Straits, and with a nice breeze coming in from north-west and with the flood under us we sailed happily westwards gaining assurance with every mile made good. Early in the morning, when the ebb began to run, we dropped anchor at the tail of the Orange Bank.

Coming on deck that morning with the vague, mysterious coast of Tierra del Fuego on one side and the bold headland of Cape Possession on the other, we felt our adventure had really begun. Until the tide turned we fished unsuccessfully and watched with interest some Commerson's dolphins. These were the first we had seen; they are smaller than most dolphins with black and white colouring sharply delimited, the white part including the flippers and the lower half of the head. When the flood began to make we weighed and stood towards Punta Delgada at the entrance to the First Narrows. As we neared it the wind dropped so we started the engine and with the tide running full bore we swept through the Narrows with a speed of something like eight knots over the ground. The channel has a least width of two miles, the fairway is deep, and the shores steep but not high. An hour later we shot out of the western end and at the same time the engine failed. There was no wind but the tide still ran strongly enough to carry us to a safe anchorage in Santiago bay.

Instead of pressing on that night with the next tide we took a long night in. At noon next day we weighed again hoping to pass the Second Narrows while it was still light, for at this time of year it is light until after 10 o'clock. No sooner had we started, however, than the wind came in so strongly from dead ahead that we had to push the engine hard to get as far as Gregory bay, the next anchorage some 10 miles to the west. In Gregory bay there is a *frigorifico*, a mere collection of buildings with a tall, iron chimney and a wood jetty from which the frozen mutton is shipped. We anchored close off the end of the jetty where only a few children gathered to look at the strange ship, for at this time of year the place was not being used. As if a *frigorifico* was not a strong enough hint that times had changed we could see, as we looked across the Straits that night, the great flames of natural gas from the oil wells on Tierra del Fuego. Thus the voyager in these historic waters, aglow with such romantic names as Famine Reach, Royal Road, Pelican Passage, or Elizabeth Island (so named by Drake), whose imagination has been stirred and who yet cherishes the hopeful illusion that the low coast on either hand is still wild and strange, must here abandon such imaginings, now utterly extinguished by the horrid reality of a *frigorifico* on the one hand and of oil derricks on the other.

Expecting to reach Punta Arenas that day we got under way soon after midnight. Since the Second Narrows are much wider than the First the stream is weaker. In our eagerness to be off we rounded Gregory Point and were at the entrance of the channel before the east-going stream had stopped running. Until the tide turned progress was slow, but by five in the morning, when it was full day, we had cleared the western end. As we altered course for Punta Arenas, for the Straits here bend sharply southwards, we met a rare sailing breeze from the north-west. The day was wonderfully clear. To starboard lay Drake's well-wooded Elizabeth Island, with Queen Channel to the east of it and Royal Road and Pelican Passage to the west. Ahead Broad Reach opened out, its light blue waters ruffled by the freshening wind. Beyond it to the south lay high ground, the slopes green with forest and crowned with patches of winter snow. Far away in the distance, from west round to south, rose a jagged skyline of high mountains, the highest of them glistening with the convincing whiteness of perpetual ice and snow. So unexpected a vision was heartening. There at any rate was country still wild and strange.

As the wind gradually freshened and Broad Reach became covered with white-capped waves, *Mischief* sped along with a bone in her teeth as if eager to finish in style what had been a rather slow passage. The brown huddle at the foot of a bleak, reddish coloured hillside which we had long decided was Punta Arenas began to take shape. In the roads a big four-master hulk lay forlorn and uncared for, and soon we could make out the jetty and we had to decide where to go. We were still sailing fast, a little too fast for accurate navigation, and presently a jar and a shudder warned us that *Mischief* had indeed reached Patagonia. But in a matter of minutes she had bumped over the shoal and we lost no time in handing the sail and dropping anchor a cable's length from the jetty. A pilot launch was soon alongside and towed us to the jetty where we tied up. We had at any rate astonished the natives. The slight contretemps had gone unnoticed by the ancient mariners and long-shoremen who had gathered to see us come in, and who, as we heard later, had much admired our dashing approach, swift rounding-to and stowing of sails. To have made such an impression was gratifying, for it is not every day that an English yacht, or indeed any yacht, comes to Punta Arenas. It was perhaps a pity that our departure was destined to be the reverse of dashing.

CHAPTER SIX

Punta Arenas

Bright and fierce and fickle is the South. Tennyson

IN THESE REGIONS Punta Arenas is the last outpost of civilization. As Sir Fopling Flutter remarked of Hyde Park, 'beyond that all is desert'. Along the coast for 500 or 600 miles west and north there are no settlements, and although the *South America Pilot* states that 'the greater part is inhabited by savages of the lowest civilization', this is, unhappily, no longer true. In the three months we spent in the channels we did not have the good fortune to sight one of their canoes or to hear their poignant cry of 'yammerschooner' (the Canoe Indian's word for 'bakhshish'), the cry which sixty years before had so disgusted Captain Slocum. Had we come across any of these despised savages they could have done nothing for us except possibly to pose for their photographs. They could neither have carried loads for us nor provided any food, so that the problems of mountain travel in this region are less easily solved than in the Himalaya where even in the remotest valley it is usually possible to find food and transport.

Punta Arenas, or Magallanes as it is known, had therefore to be the base where we must make our final arrangements. Once we had left it behind, although we should always be in sight of land, we might as well be in mid-ocean; nor had we any means of communication – an advantage, perhaps, in enterprises of this kind. A Commander F. J. Porta of the Chilean Naval Mission at that time in England, had recommended me to the care of the naval authorities at Punta Arenas and they now gave us all the help they could. As a first instalment we made use of the hot shower baths of a naval tug lying at the jetty. Our brass tiller was badly bent so we handed it to a Lieutenant Hudson of this same tug that it might be sent to the arsenal to be straightened and to have a sleeve brased on. As there is a rule that all foreign vessels navigating the channels must take a Chilean pilot, the naval authorities had contemplated sending Lieutenant Hudson with us. We should have been delighted to have him, both for his own sake and for his knowledge of the channels. But had he come the authorities would have had to arrange for him to be taken off by another ship after we had reached Peel Inlet, and in addition *Mischief* turned out to be not quite the type of vessel they were expecting. After consulting naval headquarters in Valparaiso they waived the rule and we were allowed to sail without a pilot. The navy also helped us with petrol. For navigating the channels we had always intended making full use of our engine. In places they are narrow, the prevailing wind is from the north, and we should have to enter and anchor in many small, rock-strewn coves. Neither had we much time in hand; so that on all counts it seemed desirable to take all the petrol we could. I decided to take two 40-gal. drums on deck – a fairly safe cargo because except for one short reach off Tamar Island the channels are so sheltered that there are no big seas to fear. These drums and our tanks gave us a range of about 500 miles. As this was not enough for the journey to Peel Inlet and back again, the navy promised that if a ship were going that way it would leave a drum of petrol for us at Puerto Bueno. As will appear, they were better than their word.

The Honorary British Consul (T. P. Jones, Esq., MBE) and members of the British community were most helpful and kind. Unluckily not all of us could accept the hospitality offered, especially the invitations to estancias on the mainland or on Tierra del Fuego, because there had always to be enough crew on board to tend the warps and if necessary to move the ship from the jetty. As an old sea captain remarked, Punta Arenas has a strong climate. On most days in summer it blows hard, sometimes very hard; and in winter, although there is less wind, it is very cold. The prevailing wind is off the land, but the roadstead feels its full force and there is not much shelter in the lee of the jetty. Big sailing ships naturally avoided the Straits, going always by Cape Horn, but among the port regulations still quoted in the *South America Pilot* is one that shows what might be expected: 'Whenever the weather is bad, vessels anchored in the port must let go their second anchor, hoist their boats, haul in their guess-warp booms, send down top-gallant masts, and point their yards to the wind.'

On the afternoon after our arrival the wind, normally a pretty vigorous blast, showed signs of becoming something more. Our tiller, it will be remembered, was ashore for repair so that there was no casting off and anchoring in the roads. By dark it was blowing a whole gale and several warps had already parted. Constructed of open timber work the jetty gave little shelter. We were on the lee side but in effect there was no lee for the wind whistled straight through underneath the decking. We had an ample reserve of warps but thinking to fix things once and for all we shackled a length of wire rope to the jetty, led it in over the bow and round the bitts, out over the stern, and shackled that end as well to the jetty. By the time this had been done *Mischief*, lying broadside to the jetty, had been blown far enough from it to prevent anyone getting ashore. Thus, for better or for worse, we were wedded to the jetty by this infernal piece of wire – a wire most unlikely to part for it had been used in raising the Comet aircraft which had crashed off Sicily. We soon found it was to be for worse. The wire began to saw its way into the stemhead and anything it touched. The bitts began to move and life-line stanchions to bend. There was no casting it off – the strain on it saw to that. Shackled as we were to an inaccessible jetty there was no way of freeing ourselves short of cutting the wire. But by midnight something had to be done. Procter offered to haul himself ashore along one of our remaining warps but I thought this a too risky manoeuvre and refused.

Only a few yards ahead of us lay the brightly lit naval tug, snuggly secure in a cocoon of warps. Its two men on watch at first were not aware of the dramatic entertainment going on close under their stern, but presently it occurred to them that all was not well with us. Through the howling of the gale by means of signs and shrieks, we made them understand what was wanted. Since they had no marline spike for undoing the shackles we passed one over on a line, and then sent them the end of our anchor chain to make fast to the jetty. When the strain was on the chain they were able to unshackle the wire, and we then paid out the chain and rode comfortably, well clear of the jetty, for what little remained of the night. Dawn disclosed a haggard trio.

After this all-night performance we moored ourselves on the lee side of a big LCT, an ex-wartime tank landing craft, one of several which were used by the oil company on Tierra del Fuego for landing stores. There we lay quietly enough until the wind decided to blow from another quarter – on to the land from the south-east instead of from the north-west. This sent in such a swell that one after another our fenders began to go, either by being ground to bits against the plates of the LCT or by getting caught under her rubbing strake and breaking their lines. One of these I was particularly sorry to lose because recently I had devoted several days and much loving care to covering its canvas with coir 'needle-stitching'. But now we had our tiller back and after some delay in starting the engine, for the battery was down, we cast off and motored out to anchor west of the jetty. Had it not been for the necessity of going ashore it would have been well to stay there, but on most days it would have been difficult to row ashore, with only an even chance of rowing back. A good friend then gave us three rubber tyres for fenders and we were allotted a better berth at the shore end of the jetty where a steamer lying on the other side made an excellent wind-break.

This desirable berth became vacant through the departure of the spider crab fishing boats, their season having just begun. The spider crab, known locally as *centolla,* is a speciality of these waters. It is large, deep red in colour, and has spidery legs covered with spiny protuberances. We thought its meat far more delicious than that of any other crab and enjoyed them both fresh and tinned. There are canning factories at Punta Arenas and across the Straits at Porvenir and considerable quantities are exported. This crab, I believe, is akin to that species of king crab fished for in the North Pacific and off the Alaskan coast. In the Magellan Straits they catch it in nets in deep water – as deep as 30 fathoms, we were told.

In spite of telegrams to Santiago and Buenos Aires I had as yet heard nothing of Charles' whereabouts, nor had any Chilean climbers volunteered. It was beginning to look as if the effective shore party would consist only of myself, but as a precautionary measure I bought a pair of climbing boots for

Michael. In the long night watches at sea, as I pondered upon this and that, whether physical evil is a cause of moral good or why Procter could not relieve the wheel on time, a constantly recurring question was, when the shore party finally did land after so many months at sea, whether or no its members would have the use of their legs and if not how many days would it take them to recover that use. Now that I had the opportunity I thought it would be wise to try out my own legs and to start fettling up a little.

Inland from the town the ground rises gradually to a flat ridge about a thousand feet high. The forest of oak and Antarctic beech which at one time covered the slopes has since been felled and now there are a few poor farms with wire-fenced fields where cows and a few horses graze. Beyond the farms and below the ridge is a club hut and ski run which is much used in winter. Having visited the ski hut by car on our first day in port I made that my early morning walk. These cross-country walks, climbing over wire fences and seeing nothing but a few haggard hares, were more of a duty than a pleasure, but it was an agreeable surprise to find that I could do the five miles up to the hut and return to the ship without falling or fainting by the way. Leaving the jetty, passing by a saloon of severe aspect appropriately named the 'Bar Antarctica', and under the statue of General O'Higgins (like most South American towns Punta Arenas is liberally sprinkled with statues), one soon reached the deplorable suburbs, wooden shanties, and shacks made of flattened petrol tins, reminiscent of the native quarter of Nairobi forty years ago. As with most developing towns the money is dropped in the centre with a big splash and only faint ripples ever reach the outskirts. The centre of Punta Arenas is well laid out in squares, is clean, and has an air of spacious freshness, largely attributable, one supposes, to the incessant wind.

My only other excursion outside the town was to Rio Seco, the oldest *frigorifico* in Magallanes. As the season had not yet begun there were no sheep to be slaughtered and one could view the silent, immaculate works without the unnerving clamour of a season in full swing. Sheep are, of course, the mainstay of Patagonia and of Tierra del Fuego. That part of Patagonia which belongs to Chile is known as the province of Magallanes, but only the southern part near the Straits is inhabited. The province also includes the western end of Tierra del Fuego, the eastern end of the island belonging to the Argentine. Punta Arenas is the capital and the centre from which the great quantities of wool, frozen meat, and skins are shipped.

While waiting one afternoon for the museum to open, Michael and I spent the time in the next best thing, the cemetery. This presented some novel features. In spite of the bracing climate the graves were well supplied with flowers. Indeed, provided they are screened from the shrivelling wind, European flowers and vegetables thrive out of doors. But in some cases the owner of the grave, as distinct from its occupant, had taken the precaution of building a conservatory or hot-house over it. Some of the vaults were most impressive. In addition to the wealthy families (and some of the families of the early settlers are very wealthy indeed), the police, the army, the navy, and several mutual or co-operative burial societies, had its own vault wherein the neatly labelled drawers or niches round the walls reminded one of a filing cabinet.

The inhabitants, of whom there are now some 35,000, have a weather-beaten air, as well they might. Apart from the business community they are essentially the descendants of gauchos, sailors, convicts, ship-wrecked mariners, gold seekers, sea otter and seal hunters, Alacaluf Indians, Onas, Yaghans, and such like tough *hombres*. The very few indigenes or semi-indigenes seen in the streets were thick-set and short, of high colour, and with thick black hair. Evidently they were no kin to those original inhabitants of gigantic stature whom Magellan met and to whom he gave the name Patagones or 'big feet'.

In its palmiest days Punta Arenas was a more cosmopolitan town or city, for nowadays the majority of its population are of Chilean extraction. It was the British who first introduced sheep and who started the sheep farms both on the mainland and on Tierra del Fuego. When the shipping business of the port was at its height in the years before the opening of the Panama Canal, the British community practically ran the place. More English than Spanish was spoken; wages were paid in sterling and many of the stores marked their prices in sterling. An amusing reminder of this bygone influence are the signs still to be seen over some of the smaller workshops, the 'Gasfiteria' or 'Tinplateria'. The chief engineer of a ship is still known as a 'chiffinger'. One of the old inhabitants who had experienced these halcyon days told me that then there was neither Army, Navy, nor Custom House; that the poorest workman smoked Abdullas, and that whisky and French Champagne cost five shillings a bottle. Can one imagine conditions more conducive to the peace, prosperity, and tranquillity of mankind?

A less amusing relic of those days is the British Club which, like many clubs nearer home, now faces a dwindling membership. On the other hand the Golf Club, the most southerly in the world, where a player might well think himself on the ringing plains of windy Troy, is by no means moribund. There all nations are welcome; Germans, Italians, Frenchmen, Yugo Slavs, and Turks, not to mention Chileans, may drive balls into the sea as freely as any Englishman, Scot, or Welshman. Now, of all the foreigners, the Yugo Slavs are the most numerous. The early comers, then known as Austriacos, were of peasant stock from the Dalmatian coast. Their immigration had been accelerated by the annexation of Bosnia and Hercegovina in 1908. Many of them took to washing gold on the beaches (where a good day's pay can still be made), while others took up land. Some of these early settlers became very rich and today their descendants are prosperous doctors, lawyers, and business men.

In the British Club there is an interesting relic in the form of Admiral Cradock's visiting card which he left when on his way to the disastrous battle of Coronel. And there is also a living relic of those stirring times, an old German sea captain, Albert Pagels. In the Falkland Islands battle of 8 October 1914, the sequel to Coronel, all the German ships in South American waters were sunk except the cruiser *Dresden* which escaped to Punta Arenas. After twenty-four hours (in which, I believe, she managed to coal) she had to clear out. She took refuge in Cockburn channel where for many months she lay hid, playing a successful game of hide-and-seek in these intricate channels, being victualled and in other ways aided by our friend Pagels who owned a small cutter. Eventually, in March 1915, she was found at Juan Fernandez where she blew herself up. Before this interesting episode Pagels had accompanied the Skottsberg expedition as guide and handyman and finished by travelling on horseback right down the eastern side of the Cordillera from Aysen to Punta Arenas. No doubt in the intervening years he had other notable adventures, but he next appears as a public hero (thanks to the Dresden exploit) in Hitler's Germany just before the war. Indestructibly tough, he took part in this war, too, and having been captured by, and escaped from, the Russians (whom he does not like) he returned to Punta Arenas where he was one of the first to welcome *Mischief*.

In Punta Arenas we found plenty of good shops but all suffering from the effects of rigorous import restrictions. With few exceptions everything sold had to be made or grown in Chile. The most welcome presents one could make were things like tea, mustard, golden syrup, fruit salts; and English tobacco or cigarettes were unobtainable. I was always trying to cadge tobacco (British ships being the chief sufferers) while John was reduced to cigarettes of local tobacco rolled in *The Times* airmail edition. Compared with the same edition of the *Daily Telegraph* it was in this respect alone well worth the extra money. These import restrictions, applicable to the whole of Chile, appeared not to be uniformly enforced. Punta Arenas, small, uninfluential, and furthest from Santiago, suffered them in full measure. The current rumour that it was about to be declared a free port was bred, perhaps, by wishful thinking. Our twenty-three cases of provisions from Montevideo 'in transit' had been clutched by the customs and much time, trouble and money had to be spent before we were allowed to take half on board and consign the remainder to Valparaiso. By now we had revised our plan of returning by the same route, a thing always to be avoided if possible. This change became possible mainly because we were ahead of schedule. The governing factor was that we must be clear of the West Indies before the beginning of the hurricane season in July, and provided no undue delays occurred we should be able to go up the west coast, through the canal, and be out of the Caribbean before then.

By now we had been in port nearly a week. We had filled up with water and taken on board the two drums of petrol; but still there was no news from Charles. At last on the 16th I had a letter to say he proposed coming from Valdivia by a steamer and was due to arrive on 26 November. As we had planned to sail on the 20th I cabled him to fly from Puerto Montt just south of Valdivia, and in order to clinch the matter and forestall argument (for I recollected that Charles mistrusted air travel) booked and paid for his seat. Over the week-end the office staff of the air line (who behaved very well) had a trying time. I pestered them daily for news of our wandering boy and for passenger lists of incoming planes. Puerto Montt reported that a bearded figure in a yachting cap had put in a brief appearance, the rest was silence. Finally, to our disgust, we learnt from the shipping company that he had in fact embarked on the S.S. *Arica* as he originally intended. Accordingly sailing day had to be deferred to the 26th. It seems that on the way to the air-field something told him that he would not reach Punta Arenas that day – a premonition that proved perfectly correct as he had no intention of embarking and allowed the aircraft to depart without him.

Meantime from Santiago there came news of a volunteer for the shore party. A young Chilean climber, Jorge Quinteros, recommended by the 'Federation Andinismo de Chile', offered to come. He had climbed in the Central Andes and was a student of ballet and a bee-keeper. He spoke little or no English. He was prepared to fly to Punta Arenas for an interview without any commitment on my part, but I felt that if he came as far as that I could hardly send him back. So I decided to take him. After all a ballet dancer should have impeccable balance and Everest had been climbed by a bee-keeper. But in asking him I made it clear that there would be a great deal more load carrying than climbing and that he would be away at least three months. When Jorge arrived on the 24th he did not seem much disconcerted by the rum-looking characters with whom he had thrown in his lot, by what to his eyes must have been the inadequate size of *Mischief*, or by the rather cramped bunk in which he was invited to spread himself and his gear. I think that thus to commit himself inescapably for a period of three months in the company of strangers and foreigners, in the totally unfamiliar circumstances of a small yacht bound on a voyage of some hazard, required more than common spirit. I am glad to say this gamble came off. I don't think Jorge ever regretted having joined us and our only regret was when he left. On the ship, of course, he was able to converse with Procter who put him in the way of things and told him what had to be done. On the ice-cap journey talking was not so easy, but there are occasions when it is an advantage not to be able to exchange ideas – 'the camel driver has his thoughts, and the camel he has his'.

On the morning of the 26th the S.S. *Arica* came alongside the jetty bringing with her our missing tourist. Sailing time was fixed for 2 o'clock. At 2.30 pm the crew began to assemble and by 3 pm we were complete, a search party having retrieved John from the Hotel de France where he was playing the piano. By then a large crowd of friends, admirers, and no doubt some critics, had assembled to see us start. After some hasty last-minute photography we hoisted the jib so that her head would sheer away from the jetty, and cast off the remaining warps. For some as yet unexplained reason the jib promptly fell into the sea and the next minute saw us stuck hard and fast by the stern less than a ship's length from the waving crowd. The wise man sits on the hole in his carpet, but there was no covering our shame; the critics would need neither telescopes nor binoculars to discern our embarrassment. Having recovered the jib and unavailingly tried the engine which we had hitherto been too proud to use, we sent a warp ashore to the accompaniment of much friendly advice from the experts with the idea of pulling her off the mud. *Mischief*, who had so eagerly taken the ground on her arrival, seemed to have a liking for the place and would not budge. In the roads two Chilean cruisers lay at anchor and at this moment of crisis one of their picket boats was approaching the jetty at the good round pace common to picket boats, a sailor with a boathook standing rigidly to attention in the bow. Either by seaman-like intuition or at the instance of the loud instructions from the crowd, her helmsman grasped the idea that we wanted pulling off. Perhaps he thought we

wanted shoving off, for putting his helm hard over, with little diminution
of speed, he rammed us fair and square, projecting the still rigid, well-
disciplined bowman half-way up our shrouds. It was a Saturday afternoon and
one could almost hear the happy sigh of the crowd as they realised how wise
they had been to spend it on the jetty. However, the aquatic sports were
nearly over. With admirable fortitude *Mischief* uncomplainingly sustained
this assault and rather surprisingly remained unmoved. But by now we had a
line to the still quivering picket boat which, forging ahead, plucked us quickly
into deeper water. With all speed we hoisted sail. Rounding the jetty and
dipping our ensign to the cruisers, we headed south.

CHAPTER SEVEN

Magellan Straits, Western End

*This streight is extreme cold; the trees seeme to stoope with the burden of the weather and yet are greene
continually. Towards the South sea monstrous high hills and craggy rocks do exalt themselves, whose tops be all
hoary with snow.* Hakluyt's 'Voyages'

STILL SOUTHWARDS! We had yet 50 miles to go before we could round Cape
Froward, the southernmost point of the American continent in lat. 53° 56′ S.
We were sailing down Broad Reach which continues south of Punta Arenas
and is some 20 miles wide. Gradually it narrows and leads into Famine Reach
where the Straits are only five miles wide. As if to atone for the shambles of
her departure *Mischief*, with two rolls in the mainsail, went down Broad
Reach at a great clip. The flat, barren coasts of the eastern end gave way to
bold, densely wooded shores, while to the south rose the wild, snow-covered
peaks of Dawson Island. We looked in vain for the twin summits of Mount
Sarmiento (7,215ft.) the highest peak of Tierra del Fuego and a worthy
memorial to one of the bravest, most unfortunate, and most indefatigable of
seamen. I like to think I once saw this peak from Punta Arenas. At that time
it had not been climbed and few attempts have been made since 1898, when
Lord Conway with two Swiss guides, who first set foot on it, attained a height
of 4,000ft. Had we returned by Punta Arenas I would have had a closer look
at it, but in the following February, when we were in the Pacific, the peak was
climbed by an Italian party organised by the veteran Alberto de Agostini SDB,
a man who has done more exploration in Tierra del Fuego and the Patagonian
Andes than anyone. In the evening, as the wind had freshened to force 7, we
took another roll in the mainsail, reefed the staysail, and set the storm jib. It
was a short-lived flurry; by midnight we were drifting past the Santa Ana
lighthouse with barely steerage way. Santa Ana is one of the headlands
enclosing a small bay and anchorage known as Port Famine, the last good
anchorage for vessels bound west before rounding Cape Froward. It is not a

port and no one lives there, but it must be haunted by many ghosts. In 1581, alarmed by Drake's passage in 1578, Spain launched an expedition with the object of fortifying the Straits and so preventing or discouraging any similar exploit. More than two years after the start of what was to be a most ill-fated venture, the Spanish fleet entered the Straits. But before they had even reached the First Narrows, one of the ships was cast ashore. A party of four hundred men and thirty women were landed to salvage the stores. Leaving this party in charge of a Lieutenant Viedma, Sarmiento with a hundred men marched westward along the coast to this Santa Ana point, while a pinnace with stores followed by sea. A fort and a settlement were built and the place named Ciudad del Rey Felipe. On the approach of winter Sarmiento tried to unite his two garrisons, but bad weather drove his ship out of the Straits. Undaunted, he made two unsuccessful attempts in two different ships to succour his starving countrymen. Viedma, having come to the end of his resources, marched overland to Rey Felipe, a move which probably only hastened the doom of both settlements. By the end of the second winter only fifteen men and three women remained alive.

In 1587 Cavendish, on the third circumnavigation of the globe, anchored at Rey Felipe, changing its name to Port Famine. He found there a fort with four cannon and 'several churches'. Of the people who once worshipped there, we are told: 'At last they died like so many dogs, in their houses, in great numbers; and the stench of these putrifying carcasses infecting those that survived they were forced to quit the town with one consent, and go rambling upon the sea coasts living upon roots and leaves and sea herbs, or what animals they at any time happily caught.' It was this tragic story of Rey Felipe which probably gave rise to the legend that there was a lost city somewhere in the mountains far to the north of the Straits, a city founded by the remnants of Sarmiento's hapless garrison.

In the morning, there being no wind, we started motoring in order to round Cape Froward. The glass was falling, the western sky looked dirty, and we had no wish to be caught in a gale from ahead off this notoriously stormy cape. We had with us no Belloc whose love for the sea and sail was equalled only by his hatred of machinery. 'I would rather die of thirst', he writes, 'ten miles off the headland in a brazen calm, than have on board what is monstrously called an auxiliary . . . For it is with headlands as with harbours, if you have machinery aboard your craft is gone.' Whether it is done under sail or power, the rounding of a great cape, more especially a cape that divides two oceans, has about it something both solemn and elating. Although it is a normal and long foreseen step, the moment the cape looms in sight the pent-up hopes and fears of a long voyage focus themselves upon its successful rounding.

Cape Froward is not like Cape Horn. The rounding of it, unlike that of its more famous and tempestuous neighbour, confers none of the traditional privileges such as spitting to windward or drinking the loyal toast with one foot on the table. Nevertheless, it is a noble and impressive headland, in shape and size not unlike the Horn. Both capes are of much the same height, the one 1,200ft. and the other 1,300ft., and in pictures their profiles are alike.

Each springs boldly from the sea to a sort of step before it rises steeply to a summit which is frequently snow-covered. To the west of Cape Froward the climate suddenly changes and becomes both wetter and windier. That a change for the worse is at hand is often foretold by a violent storm off the cape itself. As the *South America Pilot* says: 'The change in the vicinity of the cape is often very striking. The squalls are exceptionally heavy, the weather frequently changes to heavy rain or snow, and the shores will often be invisible.' A sailing vessel bound west round the Horn, upon reaching the pitch of the Cape would not notice any such sudden change; for the weather would no doubt be just as vile throughout Drake Sea or Strait, that 500 mile stretch of stormy, open water between Cape Horn and the South Shetlands.

Equally remarkable, too, is the change of scene as one moves from the east to the western part of the Straits. Just as on land the traveller from the east ascends from the flat pampas through foothills to the Cordillera, so by sea he makes a 'voyage through the Andes'. In his book *South America* Lord Bryce describes the change thus:

Magellan's Straits are unlike any other straits in this respect, that the physical aspect of the two ends is entirely different. The character of the shores on each side is the same in each part, but both shores of the eastern half, from the Atlantic to Cape Froward, are unlike those of the western half from Cape Froward to the Pacific. The former has low banks with smooth outlines, slopes of earth or sand dipping into shallow water, and a climate extremely dry. The latter half is enclosed between high, steep mountains which are drenched by incessant rains. The eastern half is a channel leading through the southernmost part of the Argentine plain, which has apparently been raised from the sea bottom in comparatively recent times. The western half is a deep narrow cut through the extremity of a great mountain system that stretches north for thousands of miles, forming the western edge of S. America, and the rocks on each side of it are ancient. The western half is grand and solemn, with its deep waters mirroring white crags and blue glaciers. The low eastern half has no beauty save that which belongs to vast open spaces of level land and smooth water over which broods the silence of a clear and lucent air. A more singular contrast, all within a few hours steaming, it would be hard to find.

Having got fairly up to this defiant looking headland we stopped the engine and sailed slowly past with a light north-westerly breeze, passing near enough to see clearly the big white cross on the summit. The wind then freshening from dead ahead we sought shelter in the attractively named Snug bay, about five miles north-west of the cape. The bay belied its name, for it is wide open to the west and it was to that quarter that the wind was backing. While lunching below we paid frequent visits on deck to see if the anchor was dragging. It is the kind of place of which the *Pilot* elsewhere advises the mariner that 'anchoring in this bight must be prompted by necessity and not by any hope of tranquillity'.

So far from tranquil were we that at two o'clock, in a rising wind and sea, we got up our anchor and sailed out. As Froward Reach is amply wide enough for manoeuvre we began to beat against wind, sea, and driving rain, for using the engine in such conditions was merely a waste of petrol. We sailed in this way all through the night, for although the reach is unlit there are no dangers and the iron-bound shores are steep-to. By daybreak we were off Pond Sound on the southern side and more than ready to seek shelter after such a wet, cold and anxious night. The necessity of putting the ship about at irregular and frequent intervals had meant that two of us had continually to be on deck, one steering and the other standing by. It was becoming clear that if the conditions met with on this first day and night west of Cape Froward were usual (as they were) a tough time lay ahead of us. The entrance to Pond Sound looked intricate and as we had not yet accustomed our weak nerves to threading tortuous passages beset with rocks, mostly within the proverbial biscuit's toss, we plumped for Port Gallant. This was reputedly one of the best anchorages in the Straits, spacious, sheltered, easy of access, and of moderate depth. Most often the depth is immoderate – a factor which rules out many otherwise safe and charming little holes where the mariner could hope to enjoy a care-free night. 'No bottom at ten fathoms' was too frequently the leadsman's cry, and if one despaired of finding a better hole and went in close, by the time the anchor was dropped in eight fathoms one found oneself within spitting distance of the shore, the ship having no room to swing.

Throughout the day the weather worsened and we were thankful when we reached the shelter of Fortescue bay and anchored in Port Gallant at its head. Since leaving Snug bay, more than twenty-four hours earlier, we had made good about 20 miles. When Slocum passed this way in 1896 he was pursued by savages from Fortescue bay. In 1908 Skottsberg, too, met Indians, one of whom, Mrs Ahichakwarrakwilties (Mission name, Emilia) came on board his steamer. Accordingly our hopes of seeing some of these uncouth people ran high, but, alas, we found there only a naval tanker, the *Maipu*, at anchor with a boat's crew ashore gathering mussels.

In one way we were not sorry to see her, for I had just discovered that as a result of some bad mathematics we had not enough paraffin for cooking to last three months. As our anchor went down the *Maipu* recalled her boat and started to weigh. Hastily we launched our dinghy and got alongside just as she began to move. She carried no paraffin. Barely had the dinghy got back with this bad news when the two cruisers which we had seen at Punta Arenas steamed into the bay and anchored half a mile away. Surely a cruiser would carry a Primus stove as a sort of secondary armament, as it were, a spare *batterie de cuisine* should the electric stove fail? Hunger, or the threatened paraffin shortage with all its implications, made us bold. After consulting the International Code, we hoisted the signal, 'I am in need of paraffin'. At Punta Arenas the good will of the navy toward us had made so deep and lasting an impression that I think we half expected the admiral – if there was one on board – to come over in his barge towing a 40 gal. drum of paraffin. Nothing happened. One of the cruisers made a signal which we could not read and which was probably meant for her consort or the disappearing tanker, so we determined to visit them early next morning.

On a falsely bright morning, after a night of wind and rain, Michael and Jorge rowed to the cruisers which lay well down wind of *Mischief*. After a long pull they got alongside first one and then the other, their stay in each case being so short that we could only conclude that their mission had failed.

As they began the long plug back against the wind it began to blow harder, and through our glasses we watched their desperately slow progress with growing concern. Finally, we weighed anchor and motored down to them. Having picked them up we anchored again while we stowed the dinghy and made ready for sea. We beat out of the bay in a driving snow storm – the weather changes quickly in those parts – dipping our ensign to the cruisers. They, having more sense, remained at anchor.

Although it was late spring both the scene and the weather were wintry. The rain of the preceding night, falling as snow upon the grey hills around the bay, had clothed them with white to within five hundred feet of the sea; and as *Mischief* left the shelter of the bay to begin beating westward along English Reach she was assailed by furious squalls of rain, sleet, and snow. The squalls were prolonged, the intervals between them brief. But in these well-nigh land-locked channels there is never any sea to throw a boat about and *Mischief* was stiff and stout enough to sail happily in all but the strongest blasts under storm jib, reefed staysail, and reefed mainsail. In these waters this became our normal rig and we seldom had occasion to alter it. We had hoped to make Tilly bay, but after one of our hardest day's sailing, wind and tide defeated us. English Reach, the continuation of Froward Reach, is divided into two narrow channels by the Charles Islands which lie in mid-stream, so that the tides run strongly. Late in the afternoon, when the tide turned against us, we started the engine to help the sails. It was no good. Although at the start of a fresh tack we might be pointing at a mark on the far shore a good mile further west, inexorably the tide set us back. We barely held our ground, so after wasting much precious petrol on this treadmill we turned and ran back to Mussel bay where we anchored in five fathoms some 50 yards from the mouth of a small stream. We had made good only 10 miles. For a long day's beating against wind and rain, a discipline to which we had now become resigned, it was a small reward. Yet it was fascinating sailing; rounding miniature capes, peeping into hidden coves, tacking between rocky wooded shores backed by sombre fells of yellow heath and grey slabs, and over all the low, driving clouds. Desolate and forsaken as the scene was, it had the powerful appeal of an untrodden land and the bracing challenge of unsparing harshness.

Early next morning everyone went ashore to collect firewood, mussels, and flowers. As it was our first landing on this wild coast we experienced a most satisfying thrill. As we ranged along the shore and a little way inland through bush and swamp, remarking the trees, the plants, the birds, a lake, and finally the mournful framework of a rude hut, we did indeed recapture something of 'those first experiences, and felt as earlier men felt in a happier time'. Firewood was needed for the cabin stove, now most necessary; the mussels of these coasts are famous for their size and succulence; while by collecting flowers I hoped to pay my modest tribute to science. From its rectangular shape we judged the hut to have been once the temporary home of some seal or sea otter hunter and not that of Canoe Indians whose wigwams were merely poles and withies bent together. The land birds were few and small, like wrens, but on a rock by the shore was a solitary kelp goose. The gander is snow white and in these parts may often be seen, a solitary white figure on some rocky point. The browny black plumage of the female so matches the colour of the surroundings that only a closer inspection will show her standing alongside her mate. A starving man might eat a kelp goose readily, but Brillat-Savarin himself would despair of making from it a dish fit for a gastronome. Placed somewhere between these extremes, we ate this one without enthusiasm, but out of consideration for the marksman we held our comment. Long use and wont might reconcile one to their fishy taste, but these birds are too wary to figure frequently on one's menu.

We sailed out as soon as the flood tide began to make. There was the usual head wind but the strong tide took us up to Crosstide Cape in three hours. Hereabouts three tidal streams meet – by English Reach from the Atlantic, by Crooked Reach from the Pacific, and by Canal Jerome from the miniature inland sea of Otway Water. Off the cape the wind died down and we had to start the engine to reach our chosen anchorage in Butler bay. According to the *Pilot* 'for small vessels with local knowledge Butler bay affords anchorage on its western side over a bottom of rock more or less covered with mud'. Even without local knowledge the information was enough. We were always amazed by the thoroughness of the sailing directions, for they were based largely on surveys by sailing vessels over a hundred years ago. The names of men like Fitzroy, Stokes, Lecky, Wharton, and their ships, *Beagle, Adventure, Sylvia, Nassau,* recur constantly on the charts. We were humbled by the thoughts of those men who had spent so many years in these tempestuous waters, hemmed in among islets and hidden rocks, riding out gales, drenched by constant rain, and who in open boats sought out and sounded all the various channels and anchorages.

In the evening after a day of rain and sleet, we dropped anchor in four fathoms only about 20 yards from shore. Butler bay is not on the mainland but on Santa Ines island on the south-west side of the Straits. It is a large island with a range of snow peaks and many glaciers, all unexplored. As an example of the troubles that may beset climbing parties in these regions it is worth mentioning briefly a recent attempt to traverse Santa Ines from east to west as described by Saint Loup in *Monts Pacifique.* As an introduction the party and its equipment were flooded out of their first camp on the beach by an exceptionally high tide. Having climbed about 2,500ft. over rock and wet snow they reached the foot of a glacier where they established a camp. Ahead they could see a sort of ice basin surrounded by formidable peaks. A blizzard in the night, with wind up to 80 mph wrecked their sodden tents and so discouraged them that after drinking half a litre of brandy each they came down. This last domestic detail calls to mind one of the early attempts on Mont Blanc, but in that case the party suffered from lassitude which they found 'could not be conquered without the aid of liquor'. But no doubt the weather on these outer islands, which receive the first unbroken fury of the Pacific gales, is worse than any we experienced on the ice-cap itself.

For supper that night we had the mussels gathered at Mussel bay. This bay is by no means remarkable for mussels, which abound everywhere. It was so named by Cavendish: 'We put into a cove on the south side which we called

Muskle Cove because there were great store of them.' Mussels were the main food of the Canoe Indians. In most bays and coves are still to be found middens or heaps of discarded shells which mark the sites of their most favoured encampments. Dr Junius Bird of the American Natural History Museum, who had made a study of the culture of the original inhabitants of these coasts, has excavated middens in the Beagle Channel region which were 13ft. deep. He points out three things that did a little to mitigate the harshness of life in the channels – things, rather, which made life possible for people who had no clothes other than a patch of seal-skin and no shelter other than the rudest wigwam of branches and leaves. First there was the 'tepu' tree *(tepualis stipularis)*. This can be cut and burnt when green, and even in heavy rain a fire can be coaxed from its fine twigs. Then the antarctic beech which provided bark with which to make canoes, and thirdly mussels. These provided not only a freely available food but also an essential tool, for from the shell of the giant 'chorro' they made an effective knife.

Darwin, who met numbers of these Indians in the Beagle Channel, thought them less than admirable:

These Fuegians were the most abject and miserable creatures I anywhere beheld. They were quite naked and one full grown woman was absolutely so. It was raining heavily, and the fresh water, together with the spray, trickled down her body. These poor wretches were stunted in their growth, their hideous faces bedaubed, their skins filthy and greasy, their hair entangled, their voices discordant, and their gestures violent. Viewing such men one could hardly make oneself believe that they are fellow creatures and inhabitants of the same world. It is a common subject of conjecture what pleasures in life some of the lower animals can enjoy; how much more reasonably the same question may be asked with respect to these barbarians.

Brutish though they were – a picture in Skottsberg's book shows two who look as if they had that moment come down from their tree – any man who has in more favoured regions tried 'living on the country' cannot but feel respect for a race so intrinsically tough that they could hold their own in so inhospitable a country. Darwin goes on:

Their skill, like the instinct of animals, is not improved by experience; their canoe, their most ingenious work poor as it may be, has remained the same for the last three hundred years. Although essentially the same creature how little must the mind of one of these beings resemble that of an educated man. What a scale of improvement is comprehended between the faculties of a Fuegian savage and a Sir Isaac Newton! Whence have these people come? What could have tempted a tribe of men leaving the fine regions of the north to travel down the Cordillera, to invent and build canoes, and then to enter one of the most inhospitable countries of the world?

Without canoes, of course, these people could not have reached these coasts, for there is no way by land. One can only presume that they were driven there by fear. In the Patagonian channels they were at any rate unmolested. Provided they could survive unclad in the constant rain and cold, and had the skill and the material to build canoes so that they could move from one mussel bed to another – for all movement overland was impossible – they had nothing to fear. Nothing to fear that is, until the coming of their so-called betters; the sailors, sealers, and traders who traded drink for skins; and the missionaries who killed by misguided zeal and ill-directed kindness. As Mark Twain said: 'Soap and education are not so sudden as a massacre, but they are more deadly in the long run.'

'Mussels for supper and snow after' is the last enigmatic entry in my note of Butler bay. The following day, 1 December, we suffered a serious mishap. On a dry, dull morning we motored out and as there was no wind outside we kept the engine running. Two hours later a valve spring broke. The box of spare parts made up for us by the agents for our type of engine had no replacement. The engine could not be used except for short spells in moments of crisis or when making or leaving harbour. Peel Inlet looked an uncommonly long way off.

Meantime a fair wind sprang up. With some help from the tide it took us quickly to Field anchorage. While we were considering what we should now do, for the wind had dropped, we saw our first glacier at close quarters. This was a lovely stream of ice tumbling down from a 4,000ft. peak and ending in a sheer drop to the water's edge. But our course was decided for us, for the wind began to blow strongly from north-west and now that we had no engine we could not afford to waste any wind. We had to push on another five miles to Playa Prada. In the increasing wind accompanied by torrential rain and sleet we gained the shelter of the outer anchorage and turned on the engine to negotiate the extremely narrow pass to the inner one. We passed within a few yards of a wall of rock as straight and smooth as a dockside.

The inner anchorage is a most beautiful cirque of rock and these enclosing walls are thickly covered with trees and ferns. The hanging valley just discernible above the cirque evidently contains a glacier, for two cataracts of water spilt over the wall while yet a third stream had cut back into the rock to form a deep cleft. Save for the roar of the falls the place was profoundly still. Overhead and outside in the reach a gale raged. Curtains of rain swept ceaselessly across the cirque but not a ripple disturbed the steel grey water of the anchorage. Many of these apparently sheltered anchorages are blasted at times by 'williwaws'; in fact, at Playa Prada, according to the *Pilot*, williwaws occasionally blow from all directions with great force. These squalls blow down almost vertically from high ground with appalling fury and are particularly met with near the foot of a valley or below a break in the hills. They are not confined to enclosed anchorages – indeed in such places we were never disturbed – and when sailing close to a steep shore or even in the middle of a narrow channel a ship may be struck and perhaps thrown on its beam ends.

While the rain fell in great gouts we sat below in moderate comfort with a smart fire burning. As is a habit of cabin sky-lights ours leaked a little so that throughout our stay in the channels we had to keep the cover on. The canvas having been waterproofed with a preparation of my own making had a yellowish glaze, and the subdued light reminded us of sitting in an aquarium. It was not only the light that gave us this idea for most things about us were wet. The twilight of the cabin reflected our drooping spirits. We had expected bad weather but not quite so bad as that which we were now experiencing. Rain, bitter squalls of hail and snow, strong winds funnelling their way down

the channels from dead ahead, were our daily and nightly portion. Perhaps
we deserved it, for it resembled the Punishment of Gluttons in the *Inferno*:

> Ceaseless, accursed, heavy and cold, unchanged
> For ever both in kind and in degree:
> Large hail, discoloured water, sleety flaw,
> Through the dim midnight air streamed down amain.

We had scarcely seen the sun since leaving Punta Arenas and the glass now
stood at 28.75, well below the normal for that region. The breakdown of the
engine also weighed heavily on us, and since it could not be repaired our
80 gal. of petrol on deck and the prospect of more at Puerto Bueno merely
added to our exasperation. Equally worrying was the paraffin shortage. We
had already begun to economise and those left on board at Peel Inlet would
have to make do with wood. An almost painless method of economising had
been devised by John in the form of what he called dual purpose pie. One
must imagine a beef steak and kidney pudding (bully beef doing duty for both
steak and kidney) crowned with a six inch thick roof of pastry. One ate half
the roof with the meat and put the remainder aside to eat later with jam or
treacle as the sweet. Since all ills are good when attended by food, we ate one
that night.

CHAPTER EIGHT

Into the Channels

*The general features of these channels are high, abrupt shores, with innumerable peaks; their bold rugged heads
giving an appearance of gloomy grandeur rarely seen elsewhere. In proceeding through them the general rule
should be to keep in mid-channel and avoid all kelp.*   South America Pilot

IT HAD RAINED all night and now it only ceased for a short time as we
weighed anchor and motored out into Long Reach. Fifteen minutes was the
maximum time we were allowed to use the engine, and John, who had charge of
it, was becoming increasingly reluctant to use it at all for fear of making bad
worse. In heavy rain and squalls we tacked back and forth across the reach.
At four o'clock, when we had made good some seven miles, we seemed to be
losing ground. We therefore had to decide whether to make for a cove on the
south side with the discouraging name of Rocky Inlet, or Marion Cove on the
north. The *Pilot* had merely told us that the entrance to Rocky Inlet was
fringed with kelp, but that the depths in Marion cove were so great that even
a small vessel anchored in 25 fathoms would be unable to veer enough cable
to swing. To Rocky Inlet therefore we went, sounding our way cautiously. It
too was deep, but we found bottom among kelp some 30 yards from the shore.

Charles, having in his time learnt the nautical patter for sounding, usually undertook the cold, wet task of swinging the lead. His sonorous cries, 'by the deep six', 'and a half six', 'by the mark seven', or more often, 'no bottom at fifteen', enthralled us and mystified Jorge who, until we enlightened him, apparently mistook 'no bottom' for the equally depressing cry of 'no bottle'. The kelp which surrounded us is a characteristic feature of these waters. 'Keep clear of kelp' had been the reiterated advice of the old salts at Punta Arenas. Certainly, when under way one should not ignore it, for kelp implies rocks. On almost every rock, from low water mark down to very great depths, the weed grows in long streamers. Captain Fitzroy found it growing up from a rock at a depth of 45 fathoms. Since it does not grow directly upwards but lies at an acute angle, it can attain a very great length. Captain Cook, who met it at the Kerguelens – for it is very widespread – affirmed that 360ft. was no uncommon length. Kelp, therefore, may often be seen on the surface in deep water, while the rock from which it streams may be close to the surface and a hundred yards away. If the tide is strong the kelp that is seen is often far from its parent rock, or the current may be strong enough to run it under so that it is not seen at all. The *Pilot* quotes an instance of the danger which may lurk in kelp beds: one of the *Beagle's* boats having sounded a large bed of kelp and considering it might be safely crossed, found a rock not more than four feet in diameter and only six feet below the surface. Besides thus buoying hidden dangers, kelp makes an excellent breakwater behind which a small boat can find smooth water. Sealers, Canoe Indians, and such like, used to moor their boats with a piece of growing kelp and lie to it as securely as at anchor. Slocum himself, in Crooked Reach, when the wind had died, moored *Spray* by kelp in 20 fathoms and held her there for several hours against a three-knot current.

We spent another idle evening in Rocky Inlet, for the rain was such that we could neither go ashore nor carry out the much needed repairs to sheets and sails. The everlasting going-about had caused more wear and tear than a long ocean passage, and the sodden state of sheets and sails had made them more susceptible to chafe and had delayed the necessary repair. It is little use stitching wet canvas or trying to splice a sodden rope. That night for the first time we set an anchor watch; it was very squally and *Mischief* when swinging seemed to us too anxious to nuzzle some nearby rocks.

With the glass rising we expected better times. It was now very cold. The snow which fell during the night did not confine itself to the high ground but covered *Mischief's* deck as well. In the morning the wind was fair and in spite of frequent squalls of snow or hail gave us a grand day's sailing. Instead of beating to and fro across the channel we could now lay a course nearly parallel to the shores which slid past as they had never done before. Further west the scene becomes even more desolate, a succession of low rounded hills, and hummocks of white granite, bald as granite setts. This absence of vegetation was owing mainly to the slate giving place to granite, but the greater exposure to Pacific gales no doubt played a part. By now Long Reach had merged into Sea Reach and we were on the threshold of the great ocean whose throb and heave we soon began to feel. We sped past Cripples

Channel. Ahead of us Cape Tamar, round which we had to pass to reach the Patagonian channels, reared its great bulk. On our port hand lay Desolation island, thus named by Sir John Narborough 'because it is so desolate a land to behold'.

Cape Tamar is a critical point for small vessels bound for the Patagonian channels, for the 12 miles of water which must be traversed before the sheltered water of Smyth channel is reached are exposed to the full sweep of the Pacific. Fortunately the conditions under which we were to approach it could scarce be bettered. Since leaving Rocky Inlet we had tacked only once, and rounding Cape Tamar we should bring the wind on our quarter. Soon the two peaks on Tamar Island showed above the cape and Rhoda Pass opened to starboard. This pass is a narrow channel between the island and Tamar peninsular on which the cape lies. It is used by small vessels to avoid the heavy seas usually met with off the island. Since this pass has at one point a width of less than a cable, and as we were under sail, we thought it best to go outside, heavy seas notwithstanding. At seven o'clock we had the island abeam and having made a good offing squared away for the entrance to Smyth channel. The sea was rough but by no means heavy. Westwards towards the open ocean lay a magnificently stern and wild seascape. To the south stretched the black and fiercely serrated skyline of Desolation Island, terminating far to the west in the unmistakable profile of Cape Pillar, one of the two western guardians of the Straits. Dark storm clouds passed in procession over the savage peaks of Desolation, while from the direction of Pillar a drifting white curtain – a white squall – marched with gathering speed towards us. Even were there no squall in the offing the Evangelistas, the notorious rocks which form the other guardian of the Straits, lying 15 miles north-west of Cape Pillar, would have been hardly visible. The relief of the men who man the Evangelistas lighthouse is a difficult and dangerous task. Winds of force eight or above are reached on about eighty days of the year at the western entrance to the Straits.* An anchorage on one of the nearby islands is called Cuarenta Dias, reputedly because a relief ship once waited there for forty days before being able to effect a landing. At Punta Arenas, Lieutenant Hudson told us that recently his ship had had to wait thirty days before the relief could be carried out.

In these waters the rule never to waste a fair wind applies with singular force. In the ten hours since leaving Rocky Inlet we had covered nearly 50 miles. As this was the equivalent of three of four days of beating against head winds we decided to carry on throughout the night. Smyth channel is by no means plain sailing. It has a sharp bend, small capes project from the shores and small islets lie off them; but there is a lighthouse on Fairway Islets at the entrance and three unmanned lights mark the principal dangers beyond. Fairway is the only manned light in the channels before reaching Tarn bay at the northern exit from the channels into the Gulf of Penas. It was necessary to go carefully, and as a warning and a reminder we had on our starboard hand a group of reefs known as the 'Stragglers' where we could distinguish the gaunt,

*The comparative figure for the western entrance to the English Channel is thirty-two days. Further east off the Needles it is only twenty-five.

twisted ironwork of several wrecks. There was no response when we reported our name by lamp to the Fairway lighthouse, and soon after the light, as well as the shores of Smyth channel, vanished from our sight in a heavy squall of rain. With a promontory thrusting out into the channel ahead of us and some islets beyond, we were profoundly relieved when the rain began to thin. Soon it was clear enough for us to make out the light on the promontory, but when the next light came in sight, that on Shoal Island, a new peril arose. The wind died, and to avoid being set on the island, for the tide was running strongly, we had recourse to our lame engine. This calm stayed with us until dawn when a strongish wind from ahead obliged us to begin beating again. By midday we reached our chosen anchorage in Otter bay where a wood and mussel party immediately went off. I stayed aboard to repair the staysail which for the first time for many days was dry, and having done that I joined the foraging party on shore. When Charles met me there I took him for Robinson Crusoe, a little down-at-heels.

Though the Otter islands are well wooded they are, like many other parts of the channels remarkably bare of life. Cormorants are the commonest birds but small numbers of ducks, penguins and kelp geese frequent the shore. In the nearby woods small creeper wrens, finches, kingfishers, and thrushes may be met with, but nowhere in any number. Although it was early summer neither the song nor the twittering of birds was much heard, and one could well believe that the merriest songster might be subdued by the gloomy solemnity of its surroundings. Indeed, under a thick canopy of both living and decaying trees, dripping with moisture and draped in moss, where the rare shafts of sunlight scarce can penetrate, man himself is oppressed into silence.

The sea-birds, too, went about their affairs quietly. We seldom heard the braying or mooing of penguins, and the steamer ducks only became really noisy when beating the water in frantic flight. This species of duck which cannot fly was given the name 'Racehorse duck' by the men of the ship-wrecked *Wager*, one of Lord Anson's squadron, because of the speed at which it travelled. Captain Stokes, who commanded the *Beagle* on her first commission in these waters in 1826–8, preferred to call them steamer duck after the paddle steamers then coming more and more into use. The local name *patos vapor* is merely a literal translation of the English. Their wings are too small and weak for flight but they scuttle over the water at an astonishing pace half swimming and half running, flapping the water with their wings and making so much splash and fuss about it all that the whole business is extremely comical. We never tired of watching them. On the approach of the strange sea monster *Mischief* they would begin swimming in uncertain circles. Then, becoming a little more agitated, the whole party would gather together and increase speed on what was thought to be a safe course. Faster and faster they went until at last the retreat became a rout when with one accord the whole flock broke into frenzied flight, wings and legs going like pistons, each bird half lost in a cloud of spray. When really worked up their estimated speed is from 15 to 20 knots. Darwin's opinion that their wings move alternately like the legs is disputed. But because of the amount of spray they throw up and the speed at which they move, this weighty problem is not so easily solved.

Amusement is all these creatures provide. For although with cunning, perseverance, and a high velocity rifle they can be killed they can hardly be eaten, for the meat is tough, oily, and fishy. Small shot, even buckshot, rattles off them harmlessly, and Darwin records his failure to break a steamer duck's skull with a geological hammer! After cormorants they were the birds most commonly seen and, since they weigh as much as twenty to thirty pounds, it annoyed us to find them such impossible table birds. It is generally true that where any particular herb grows there lives the ass who is to eat it, and no doubt an all-wise Providence provided steamer ducks for the strong stomachs of Canoe Indians and shipwrecked mariners. The fact that we could not stomach, much less relish them (Procter's disapproval was not very severe), seemed to me to betray our inadequacy as travellers; for proverbially a traveller must have the back of an ass to bear all and the mouth of a hog to eat what is set before him.

The entries in the log were becoming a little monotonous. 'Fresh wind from ahead, increasing later, rain most of the day', was again recorded for the next day. But we made good some 15 miles, coming to rest in the evening in Isthmus bay, a good anchorage on the east side of the channel where we found two broken huts. Mount Burney, 5,800ft. high, always snow covered and only a few miles from the coast, had remained hidden all day.

Michael and I went plant-hunting, and thanks to the forest having at one time been cleared we were able to penetrate half a mile inland, discovering on the way berberis, fuchsia, a fine scarlet-flowered shrub, and strangely enough the remains of a fence. What had induced anyone, we wondered, to settle here to farm, and how long had it been before this courageous or crazy settler retired discomfited? Where the forest had been cleared nothing now grew but moss and a few scattered tussocks of coarse grass. The absence of feed explained the fence, for no sheep would consent to remain there tethered only by his teeth; and, unless the settler himself was as self-sufficient as a Canoe Indian, he would not be able to maintain life and would depend upon supplies from Punta Arenas. It is most unlikely that this long stretch of coast and its innumerable islands will ever be settled. To describe it in the Whitehall farmer's phrase as 'marginal land' would be a euphemism as extravagant as Lord Salisbury's well known description of the Sahara as 'very light soil'. This labyrinth of channels and islands seems to be useless to man. Where the shores are not of bare rock they are covered with scrubby evergreen forest which, a thousand feet above, peters out into boggy moor, rock, and ice. And this whole bleak landscape is swept, summer and winter alike, by high winds and persistent rain.

With more zeal than prudence, the barometer falling steadily, we sailed out next morning hoping to get through Victory Pass into Canal Sarmiento. By noon our hopes had vanished. Squall followed squall until our lee rail, three feet above the deck, was awash. In the afternoon these williwaws, for such they were, continued striking us from all directions with great violence; and while we were reefing the mainsail still more closely we were twice taken aback. On all sides the water was being whipped up into the air, giving the channel the appearance of a rough plain swept by dust-devils. Any port in a storm. Our nearest refuge was Inlet bay, referred to briefly in the *Pilot* as 'for small vessels with local knowledge'; and having fought our way well to windward we turned and ran in. The noises emitted by our suffering engine had become so strange that we dared not use it. So that when entering this small, kelp-strewn cove under sail alone the faces of the crew grew more and more troubled. Until the anchor was down and the sails off we looked, in the words of Uncle Remus, 'like every minit wuz gwineter be de nex'.

Next day as we beat up to the entrance to Victory Pass the sun came out, the wind backed, and with a fair wind we sailed merrily through. Gloomy grandeur is a just description of the scenery of the channels, but how swiftly does a touch of sunlight dispel the gloom. How fair then can be the scene when in bright sun and pearly clear air the lichen covered rocks glow with the rich warmth of an old stone wall, the granite outcrops sparkle, and the flat grey of the fells breaks into light and shade, a patchwork of green and yellow with purple cloud shadows drifting across.

Victory Pass leading into Collingwood Strait at the south end of Canal Sarmiento runs at right angles to the general north and south trends of the channels. With a following wind here one might fairly expect a beam wind in Collingwood Strait. In the channels, however, one hardly ever enjoys a beam wind; for no matter from what direction, the wind is funnelled up or down the reach, so that a vessel always finds it either from ahead or astern. When, therefore, we found ourselves once more beating after having turned the corner into Collingwood Strait, we felt more hurt than surprised. Attracted by the name we had intended to make the Bay of Islands, but when the wind increased we turned into Columbine Cove on the western shore, having done only 13 miles. In more ways than one it was a lucky decision. Rowing ashore I spotted several duck (or geese?) behind a little spit. Putting back hastily I brought John off armed with our .22 rifle. After a short stalk he killed two. These handsome birds had bronze necks and backs, with white wings shading to green at the tips; and after due hanging they provided a memorable meal.

In the channels a day seldom passed without our sighting a steamer. Generally these were small tankers or coasters, Chilean, Norwegian, Danish and German. We learnt later that a German boat in which our friend Gird Breuer was travelling to Valparaiso, dropped a tin container of mail for us to pick up. As we had no inkling of her intention, and as she was steaming at 12 knots half a mile away, it was a singularly careless and unsuccessful way of delivering mail. None of these ships showed any interest in us and we had not thought it worth making an effort to stop one to ask about valve springs. At sundown, however, another ship passed which we recognised as our former acquaintance the *Maipu*. When she slowed down and began to turn towards the cove we became excited. A quarter mile out she stopped, her cable ran out, and before the roar had died away Jorge and I were half-way to her in the dinghy.

As we came alongside and climbed the Jacob's ladder the steel sides of this small ship appeared to us quite vast. With friendly grins we were ushered to the captain's cabin. A bell was pressed and a steward brought beer. Another bell summoned the chief engineer who having learnt our need went through his stores and ultimately found a spring of approximately the right size. With this treasure, a sack of bread, potatoes, and some tinned food we returned to *Mischief* while the *Maipu* began to shorten her cable. Nor was the matter of paraffin forgotten. While we were there the captain had a signal sent off asking that some should be sent with the petrol to Puerto Buno. His only request had been for a picture of *Mischief*. So back went the dinghy with the best photograph we had. Whereupon the *Maipu*, with a farewell blast, steamed out of the cove.

From Columbine Cove our way lay through the narrow Farquar Pass at the north end of Newton island into Canal Sarmiento. Conditions were better that day, the head wind was less violent and by noon the rain had stopped. Anxious to begin work on the engine we put into Wodehouse bay on Piazzi island on the west side of the channel, where a wreck to the north of the entrance provides easy identification. Many of these bays and coves are not so readily identified. Sometimes they are not even seen as the entrance may not open up until one has sailed past it, or it may appear so insignificant that it is just disregarded. It is always important in coastal sailing, and particularly so here, to identify everything in sight and to know at all times where one is.

We had made good some 15 miles. Leaving John and Charles to begin work on the engine the rest of us went ashore to gather mussels and cook them on a wood fire. Wodehouse bay is another lovely anchorage. Indeed all these lonely little bays are endowed with a wild beauty. The wildness and loneliness is intensified by storm and the beauty only reaches its full bloom under a benign sky. The bay seemed devoid of life. The channel being out of sight, *Mischief* lay as if in a landlocked pool nodding very gently to her reflection in the water. In the far distance stretched the long, jagged line of the Sarmiento Cordillera, the higher snow-covered peaks glowing faintly pink in the setting sun, while further to the north two bold spires of rock and ice marked the extreme southern end of the ice-cap.

For six solid hours our two engineers John and Charles (the one supplying the practice and the other the theory) battled to extract the broken spring. Armed as they were with little better than their bare hands – for we had no valve-lifter – it was an unequal contest. Lying in my bunk watching the struggle through the cabin doorway, while our black gang became rapidly blacker, I had leisure to reflect upon how pleasant it is to see a battle from a distant hill. At intervals they would withdraw into the cabin to cool off and to draw diagrams on the once-white table explanatory of the various conceivable ways in which a valve spring could be fitted. Having eliminated by trial and error the two most likely ways, our theorist now voiced his considered opinion, based on what he had heard of the American way of life and their readiness to scrap the outmoded or outworn, that the valves of this American engine were not removable, and that if a spring did break the engine should be incontinently scrapped. This led to a heated exchange, more personal than mechanical, until at last they decided to sleep on it.

Morning brought enlightenment for in a short time they found what had before escaped them, two small, hardly visible collars holding down the valve. Soon it was out. Then, with much ingenuity, a hand vice, pieces of cord, and some strong language they compressed the new spring, fitted it, and by midday the engine was running. In heavy rain we motored out, but on meeting a very strong wind we put back, having at last concluded that the wear and tear on the gear when beating against these winds was not worth the few miles gained. When the weather cleared in the evening we were not tempted out. Instead we bathed and washed clothes in a fresh-water pool, leaving John to cook the Columbine cove duck over a wood fire. Very good it proved, too, with no fishy taint whatever.

By morning (Saturday, 10 December, a fortnight out from Punta Arenas) the weather had again deteriorated; but after lunch, when the barometer rose a little, we ventured out. We should have done better to stay where we were. After seven hours of beating, with everything reefed down, we made good six miles. The tide turned against us, and we were thankful to reach Occasion Cove late in the evening. It had been a beast of a day. Occasion Cove (Caleta Occasion) is at the back of a bigger bay called Lecky Retreat. Captain S. T. S. Lecky is better known as the author of *Lecky's Wrinkles in Practical Navigation*, usually referred to as *Lecky's Wrinkles*. In 1872–4, as Lieutenant Lecky in command of the *Penguin* he was actively engaged in surveying these coasts, giving his name to a harbour, an inlet, a lookout, a monument, a retreat, and a shelf. To compile a history of the exploration and survey of the channels, with full biographical notes on the seamen of various nations who have lent their names to the all too numerous features, would be an absorbing task. A task only suitable, perhaps, for a man with a long vista of years ahead of him, one who was a linguist, and one who believed that labour is its own reward.

The weather still being foul we delayed starting until the following afternoon. While waiting a party went out in the dinghy and after a stern chase shot a steamer duck. Outside in the channel we found a fair wind. Setting all plain sail, and with the engine running, we did not have to touch the sheets until we had cleared Tarleton Pass at the opening of Nelson Strait. Although this strait opens directly on to the Pacific no swell reaches the eastern end owing to the number of islands. In the narrow channel between Vancouver and Evans Islands we again encountered head winds and had to beat up to Mayne harbour on the coast of Evans Island. In six hours sailing we had made good 25 miles – much better than our average run which since leaving Punta Arenas had been only 18 miles a day.

Before the channels were lit, when all vessels had to anchor at night, Mayne harbour was in constant use. On the plan of the harbour the narrow entrance is marked with buoys, but the buoys are no longer there. Next day, in a flat calm, we motored the remaining 20 miles to Puerto Bueno.

CHAPTER NINE

Peel Inlet

The ice was here, the ice was there,
The ice was all around:
It cracked and growled, and roared and howled,
Like noises in a swound.

The Ancient Mariner

A PLACE that has long figured as the penultimate goal, the advance base or springboard into the unknown, is often given in one's mind unwarranted attributes. I can think of places in the Himalaya which from the map appear to be important road junctions or a natural jumping-off place for the crossing of some high pass; a place on which for many days the thoughts of the party have fondly dwelt – the sheep, eggs, butter, beer, or transport likely to be available – only to find on arrival a smoky hovel tenanted, if at all, by some ascetic bent on a solitary fast, who has chosen it as a spot where he will not be tempted to break it.

So, on the voyage out, had Puerto Bueno loomed large in our thoughts, but by now we had experience of the channels and had learnt to expect nothing anywhere, irrespective of whether a place was called a cove, a harbour, or a port. Only in this way were we not disappointed. In the old days, no doubt, a visitor to Puerto Bueno would at least have had company. It was a regular stopping place where, by begging or barter, one could probably make good any deficiencies. But ships do not go there now. There is a good safe anchorage, where wood and water can be had for the labour, and that is all. It is supposed to have been discovered and named by Sarmiento who had been dispatched south from Peru to intercept Drake then thought to be on his way back through the Magellan Straits. But Drake went on westwards round the world and Sarmiento, after a thorough examination of the Straits, went on to Spain. Certainly the amount of wood which has been cut in the vicinity by ships' parties points to its having been a favourite harbour for a long time. Apart from this clearing, and an oil drum planted on a rock either as an ornament, a letter-box, or a leading mark, the place must be the same now as it was nearly four hundred years ago. In such surroundings it was easy to picture a three-masted carrack, not much more than twice *Mischief*'s size, with high carved poop and yellow painted sides, lying at anchor, while a boatload of fierce, swarthy sailors rowed ashore.

In the belief that there would not be any safe harbour in Peel Inlet I had intended that *Mischief* should await the return of the shore party at Puerto Bueno. Now that we had seen the place the idea was less attractive. There seemed to be no life and little of interest in the neighbourhood to keep a party amused for two months. They could not even see passing ships, for the main channel is out of sight from the inner harbour. I was not surprised then when we left, to find that those who were to keep the ship were not looking forward to their stay at Puerto Bueno.

We left next morning, having first made sure that the navy had not already been here. The calm weather of the previous day continued. There was no wind, no rain, no sun. Peel Inlet opens off Canal Sarmiento about eight miles north of Puerto Bueno round Cape Antonio. The northern side of the entrance is formed by the shore of Chatham Island and between cape and island, across the six mile wide entrance, are a few small islets. Off the shore of one of these a large object in the water arrested our attention, and when we realised it was not a boat but an ice floe we examined it with increased interest but with no great concern. A few miles up we passed the very narrow entrance to Pitt channel, a short cut leading to Canal San Andres and thence to the main channel. Several more floes, some of fantastic shape and delicate blue colouring, now drifted by close to the ship and were greeted with pleased cries, much as some ignorant clown might greet the first few ranging shots of a hostile battery. It is ridiculous to think that we went out of our way to photograph these feeble harbingers of the coming hordes.

When ahead of us a long line of what appeared to be white water was seen stretching almost from shore to shore, we at length awoke to the fact that trouble might be at hand. The mood of care-free happiness, encouraged by the near accomplishment of the long outward passage and the closeness of our objective, changed rapidly to one of extreme anxiety, and made me wonder where we could go should Peel Inlet be blocked. These weak fears, engendered possibly by a diet of mussels, proved groundless. That which from afar had looked like almost solid ice, dissolved on approach to a mass of small floes (technically known as 'bergy bits') through which we had no difficulty in steering, though at a very slow pace. There were frequent leads of more open water and with a lookout posted in the bows to signal to the helmsman it was possible to avoid any serious collisions. If one appeared to be unavoidable a man with the boathook and another standing on the bobstay did what they could to deflect the floe. We were surprised, even alarmed, at the weight of impact of a floe no bigger than a small table. From the cross-trees it was possible to see well ahead and to plan one's course according to the shifting ice.

This accumulation of ice was encountered some fifteen miles up the inlet where it divides, a short arm running south-east and a much longer arm stretching north. The glacier which I had chosen from the map lies at the head of the south-east arm which is about four miles long. This comparatively short arm had another attraction for not far from the glacier at its head there is a cove called Caleta Amelia where the *Meteoro* (a 650-ton twin screw steamer) with Skottsberg's party on board had spent two nights while Skottsberg and a geologist examined the shore at the foot of the glacier. As we opened up the south-east arm the glacier came in sight, a huge sheet of ice nearly two miles broad, cleft in its middle by a bald rocky hill, with its upper reaches shrouded in mist. It must have made a thrilling sight to those of the party to whom glaciers were unfamiliar. Even Charles and I were profoundly impressed by its size and by the way in which it flowed out into the deep waters of the fjord, suggesting to an observer the idea of inexhaustible, overflowing abundance, an unmistakable hint of the vastness of the snowfield from which it came. From the practical point of view we were pleased to note the easy angle of its descent, the relative smoothness of its tongue, and the presence of a convenient shelf of rock on which we could land.

We were still a long way off and in between lay a great deal of loose ice as well as half a mile or more of the chaotic water-borne part of the glacier itself, and as we closed the western shore to creep along to Caleta Amelia the thickening ice threatened to make even that unattainable. After poking about looking for a lead we gave it up. We could see where Amelia cove lay but as there was no getting there we had to anchor in another small cove a mile short of it. Three of us then embarked in the dinghy to see how near we could get to the glacier. By our later standards the ice cannot have been thick for we rowed for nearly an hour without having to pole away floes or to haul the dinghy between them with an ice-axe. But soon bigger floes barred our way and we drew alongside one on which we could land to survey the prospect. It was not encouraging. We were still a mile away from solid ice and owing to the dense forest on both shores it seemed as impossible to reach the glacier by land. In 1933 Michael Mason came here in a steam launch and from a photograph in his book *Where Tempests Blow* it seems that at that time the glacier was not split in two by the rock hill but flowed round it and united again at its foot, thrusting out into the sea an unbroken front of twice the present width. Now only the ice stream to the north of the rock hill enters the water; the southern ice stream stops short a hundred yards from the shore. All along the seaward face of the rock hill, many feet above its present level, a distinct line of polished rock shows the height to which the ice once reached.

This setback was severe but was not necessarily fatal to our plans. Since the glacier on which we had set our hopes proved unattainable we had to find another. It seemed reasonable to think that of the many which flowed into the northern arm of Peel Inlet there would surely be one on which we could land. The amount of floating ice and the unexpected difficulty in landing had subdued us a little. All sorrows, we are told, are alleviated by eating bread. By this, no doubt, is meant food in general, but whether steamer duck should be called food is 'a point verging perilously on the moot'. Our duck had been hung for three days, boiled twice, cooked in a pressure cooker, and served curried, yet still it had about it a pungent flavour of steamer duck – that is, of fish oil. Many years have passed since the Rev Dr Folliot justly observed that 'the science of fish sauce is by no means brought to perfection – a fine field of discovery still lies open in that line'; yet in Patagonia the field has been neglected, as yet no sauce has been discovered that will disguise the fishiness of steamer duck.

To sail through these ice-strewn waters in a small boat not built with a view to shunting ice, where a boat needs to be able to twist and turn quickly, would be difficult and dangerous. Without an engine our difficulties would have been insurmountable. On motoring out next morning we steered for the eastern shore where the ice was less thick. Opposite the point where we had turned south-east on the previous day, a small cape projects, and 300 or 400 yards off this cape were several large floes. I was steering, and elected to pass between two of the biggest which were some 50 yards apart. Although we were watching them pretty intently, for they seemed to be unusually still, it was not until we were up to them that I realised they were aground. A moment later we joined them. There was no kelp to warn us and we were a long way off shore. Of course there was no need to have gone between the floes and any fool should have guessed that they were hard and fast from their appearance, for they were sticking high out of the water. We lowered the dinghy, ran out a kedge anchor, and pulled her off with less trouble than such carelessness deserved.

The northern arm which we were now entering is narrow and enclosed by high walls on both sides. Its western wall is formed by the large Wilcock peninsula with mountains running up to 5,000ft., and many small glaciers, none of which reaches the sea; while, of course, the eastern shore forms the foothills of the Cordillera 8,000 or 9,000ft. above. It must be remembered that the latitude here is about that of London, and presumably it is the combined effects of the extent and height of this range together with the weather which accounts for the accumulation of snow and the consequent size of the glaciers. The permanent snow line in this latitude is about 3,000ft. It is said that the coolness of the summers rather than the severity of the winters is the most important factor in maintaining so low a snow line, the glaciers, and the snow field from which they descend. If we include the Darwin range in Tierra del Fuego (where the snow line is about 2,000ft.) this ice mantle covers a length of over 700 miles and is broken only at the Straits of Magellan and the Rio Baker, which separates the two great fields of inland ice at latitude 48°. The two together form the largest glaciated region of the temperate zone. Its northernmost glacier, the San Rafael, reaches the sea in lat. 46° 40′ S., further from the pole than any Alaskan glacier by 10 degrees, and 20 degrees further than the Jökelfjord, the most southern of the Norwegian glaciers which reach the sea. Darwin puts it even more strikingly. He says of this San Rafael glacier, 15 miles long and in one place seven miles broad, that it pushes its ice into the sea at a point on the coast where, within less than 500 miles, palms grow.

After some six miles of threading our way through patches of ice and occasional stretches of clear water we at last turned into a small bay to reconnoitre the approach to the next 'sea-level' glacier. Waterfall bay, as we called it, was magnificent if nothing else. Quite near and high on our left a great white stream of ice swept round the foot of a black ridge to break into myriads of cracks, seracs, and crevasses, many of them scintillating with a vivid blue, as they plunged steeply to the ice-strewn water. On one side was bare rock; on the other, almost as steep, evergreen forest. On the other side of the bay, the waterfall itself, which in any other bay would have been impressive, faded into insignificance before its stupendous, frozen counterpart. Here we could approach near to the glacier but we could see no likely landing place; and even suppose we did land, an ascent of the ice-fall was obviously impracticable, while the rock on the left looked steep. The thought of having to make our first carry on untried legs up such steep rock daunted me. Charles was in two minds about it, but the longer I looked the more certain I became that it might do – but only as a last resort. Perhaps it was that as the time for abandoning the snug shelter of the ship drew inevitably nearer, the more ready I was to postpone it. Anyway it seemed wiser to enlarge the circle of our acquaintance before we finally committed ourselves, so, without dropping anchor we left the bay.

Several miles further north the fjord opens out into a wide reach, the eastern shore receding to form the entrance to what is called on the map Calvo inlet. Inside the inlet we could see three glaciers. There were several more in a very narrow extension of Calvo which penetrated inland for several miles, and yet another which terminated a mile from the sea on the north side of the entrance. Here were infinite riches in a little space. As the wide reach was free of ice we made sail and stood over to an island in the middle of the entrance hoping to find an anchorage. Here the water was deep, so we carried on and closed the northern shore where there was ice. Soon we were creeping through a narrow lead, with the shore close on our port hand and thick ice on the other. We began sounding, determined to anchor as soon as we found a reasonable depth, for evening was drawing on. At last we got 11 fathoms and let go the anchor; we were 50 yards from the shore and about a mile from the nearest glacier. On the whole the day had been fine with a few wintry gleams of sunshine. Thirty miles inland from the main channel in the lee of the imposing range on Wilcock peninsula, the absence of violent winds was most noticeable. Indeed the comparatively fair weather we enjoyed throughout our long stay in Calvo could only be attributed to the shielding effect of this high land.

Our plan now was to take *Mischief* as near as possible to the glacier immediately ahead of us. After a peaceful night in the ice we motored very slowly for an hour-and-a-half through thick floes before we anchored again close in to the bank in six fathoms. As our cable rattled out steamer ducks scuttled away, a penguin bobbed up, and from a nearby cave a sea lion roared in astonishment. After lunch the shore party went off in the dinghy to reconnoitre. The floes were too close together for rowing so we either paddled or hauled ourselves along with the help of an ice-axe with which the bowman reached out, striking the point into the floe ahead. Having passed close under the cave where the sea lion lived with his harem we found an easy landing place, but upon climbing a rock ridge we discovered that an arm of the fjord lay between us and our objective. At the head of this little arm was another branch of the same glacier, but the little arm was chock-a-block with ice and the way along the shore looked long and difficult. But on the other side, where the main glacier ended abruptly in a hundred foot high ice-wall, a little sandy beach beckoned us invitingly. The beach was within 50 yards of the left bank of the glacier, and dare we but force *Mischief* through the ice to anchor there, one problem at least – that of ferrying our stores ashore – would be solved. Whether a way up the glacier could be found was another thing.

That part of it overlooking the sea was impassable, but we had already noticed what looked like a small moraine on the flank of the glacier nearest to the beach. It appeared that the beach with its sand and boulders was in fact the termination of the moraine.

Because of the tide and wind the ice conditions in the bay were seldom static. Our first sight of the cove off the sandy beach showed it to be free of ice and the water between reasonably open. After tea, when we began moving, more ice, including some very large floes, had drifted in. This was added to by the continual discharge of ice from the glacier snout, from which, with a thunderous roar, hundreds of tons of ice crashed frequently into the water, setting up a young tidal wave. Hardening our hearts we drove the long-suffering *Mischief* slowly through a mile of thickly clustering floes, mindful only of her propeller. The shape of a floe above water is no indication of what goes on below and there was always the danger of a floe capsizing under our counter on to the propeller as we brushed past. At last this frightening and heartrending shunting of ice came to an end and by 8 o'clock we had *Mischief* anchored in seven fathoms only 50 yards from the beach.

As anchorages go this one was more spectacular than safe. Within a stone's throw of us there was on the one hand a fantastically furrowed cliff of sapphire blue ice; on the other, and equally close, a heavily forested cliff; while around us lay a slowly circling mass of floes of alarming size, some of them as big as a cottage with the garden thrown in. Although we had reached the haven of our choice I was far from tranquil. It was obvious that more reconnoitring must be done before the shore party could disembark. It was more than possible that if more ice drifted in the ship might not be able to leave or might even be pushed on to the beach. Already the knocking about sustained by poor *Mischief* and her tender was reacting upon her owner as if he had suffered in person; indeed, what with chilblains, back-ache, and a stiff knee his sufferings were at that time not merely vicarious. Even Charles, as our short excursion of the morning showed, was not as spry as he might have been, for he moved with more dignity and deliberation than the occasion demanded.

Next day, Friday, 16 December, we went ashore to try our luck on the moraine. Compared with Himalayan moraines it was despicably small and failed miserably in offering the easy going that they generally provide. (The absence of well developed moraines was a characteristic of all the glaciers we saw.) About half a mile up from the shore, toiling mainly in the trough between ice and moraine or moraine and jungle, we met the first obstacle, a 20ft. high wet slab up which obviously the loads would have to be hauled. About a like distance beyond this we met the type of obstacle we had half expected – a place where the ice so impinged against a rock wall that it left us no way through, round, or over. Thus we were forced to seek a way on the glacier itself which at this point proved more accommodating. We found it to be made up of a series of transverse crevasses, the ridges between them being sometimes very narrow and sometimes a yard or two wide. Where two crevasses merged together, as they often did, there was a void, and where two ridges met there was a pinnacle. On the whole it was a labyrinth which

Charles tackled with more optimism than I felt justified, but after about an hour's hard work, finding a way mainly by trial and error, we emerged in mid-glacier on more or less unbroken ice. So far so good. Heading up the glacier in a crevasse-free trough we gained another 500ft. of height before becoming entangled in a frightful jumble of seracs and yawning chasms. Above and beyond this devastated region we saw what appeared to be a flat shelf promising better going, but there was no reaching it that day.

The weather had been kind. True, it drizzled incessantly but it had been quite calm. When we got back to the shore at six o'clock we found that more ice had drifted in. Between ship and shore it lay so thickly that we had to haul overselves back to the ship by means of a rope. We learnt that down here there had been a lot of wind which had brought into the cove some gigantic bergs. The ship's party had had an anxious time, watching helplessly as these monsters closed in, scraping the ship's side and threatening to crush her, for the ice to seaward was by then too thick to permit escape. The pressure of the ice lifted the dinghy out of the water till it perched forlornly on a big floe. All they could do was to try to stop the bigger bergs from touching the rudder or fouling the bobstay, the bowsprit shrouds, or the bowsprit itself. As soon as the wind dropped, which it did as suddenly as it had begun, the ice began to drift out so that when we returned we saw only the aftermath of this heavy onslaught.

On the whole, despite the inconclusive nature of our reconnaissance, it seemed best for us to gamble on finding a route to the ice-cap by way of what we now called the Calvo glacier; for there are few ice-falls which time and perseverance will not overcome. The essential thing was to get the ship away as early as possible. The morning's inrush of ice had forced her perceptibly nearer the shore and the night's happenings emphasised strongly that this was no place to linger. About midnight an appalling crash close alongside brought us all on deck with a run. We were in time to see the water still boiling and surging and blocks of ice shooting up from below. One of our bigger neighbours had capsized and had broken up with all the turmoil and upheaval of water that would accompany the death throes of a stricken whale.

In the morning, except for two monsters which lay menacingly close, the cove was free of ice. Having made our decision we set about sorting stores and getting them ashore while the water remained open. In the cabin Chaos and old Night reigned. John and I checked food against food lists and filled paraffin containers, while the others weeded out their climbing kit from among sea clothes. Charles' impedimenta for journeying by land and sea for the first time lay remorselessly revealed. From time to time brief glimpses of his treasures had aroused our curiosity and now Michael was able to complete the inventory he had thought it worth while surreptitiously making, either in furtherance of his sociological studies or with a view to equipping himself for some future journey on the lines of his illustrious model. A copy of this inventory which he kindly gave me, perhaps merits insertion here rather than in the obscurity of an appendix:

One tin of anchovies and two of sardines.

Palm and sail needle.

An old piece of canvas.

Yachting cap.

Tattered Balaclava helmet (looks like a crown of thorns)

Assorted empty tins of all shapes and sizes, mostly rusty.

Old pieces of string and cloth

Assorted buttons.

Salt and pepper in empty first-aid tins.

A pair of pliers.

Rusty knife on an enormous khaki lanyard.

Dipping pen and ink bottle with huge cork in silver container.

Compass and binoculars.

Thick tailor's tape measure.

Assorted spices in small tins.

Dilapidated billy-can, half rusted through.

Old sweater and wind jacket, torn to shreds.

Patches with bits of trouser attached, once grey flannels.

A pack of cards, incomplete.

A sextant, too venerable to be cleaned.

Some maps and charts of S. America in general.

Selection of *Reader's Digests.*

A tin of pea-nuts.

Ancient camera, operated by guess-work.

Bottle of quinine.

Home-made solid fuel burner with bits of 'Meta'.

A pair of mittens of very original design.

Badminton Library *Yachting* – very heavy.

Some whisky.

Hooded climbing jacket, home-made.

Although the glass was rising rain fell all day. We ferried the stores ashore, pitched the two tents, and left the stores inside. In the afternoon we made another reconnaissance but it did nothing towards clearing away our doubts. On the next day, with the willing help of the ship's party in carrying loads, we hoped we should be able to make a flying start.

CHAPTER TEN

The Calvo Glacier

Still and blanched and cold and lone,
The icy hills far from me
With frosty ulys overgrown
Stand in their sculptured secrecy.
                              De La Mare

IT IS A CURIOUS FACT that although knowing full well that one will soon be wet through, one always shrinks from starting out wet. After a wet night, rain was still falling and, far from being in a state of raring to go, the shore party sat in the cabin that morning looking like men meditating a cold plunge or even suicide. By 10 o'clock, when there was merely drizzle, and the crew in their oilskins were wondering why we still dithered, any more convincing excuses for delay were hard to find. With the air of dedicated men we began to pack our rucksacks, the last loads to go ashore. Having finished, I in my turn became impatient, and stood, pawing the deck, so to speak, holding the dinghy painter in one hand and an ice-axe in the other; while Jorge, always a slow packer, persistently called out in Spanish enquiring if such or such a thing were necessary: to which I, neither understanding what he said nor able to see through the deck, invariably and confidently answered 'No', which is Spanish, I believe, for 'No'.

Having landed we then had to make up five loads for the first carry, leaving John behind to mind the ship. The large number of tins of 'Lifeboat' biscuits to be carried – flour is no use with Primus stove cooking – gave us some troublesome loads, but we had with us three Yukon pack-boards on which with patience and a little ingenuity one can securely fasten the queerest loads. Jorge, as befitted his youth, shouldered the biggest load, with Mike not far behind. Having hoisted these to the top of the slab, where we had already put a fixed rope, and dumped them there, we all returned to the shore to say goodbye, for I was anxious for the ship to leave. The instructions I had given were that they must return to Puerto Bueno and remain there until 1 January, by which time the navy might have delivered the petrol and paraffin. Then they were to come back, cruise in the bay a few miles off the glacier, and look out for any signs of us. There was plenty of wood for us to make a fire and our bright yellow tents would be readily spotted. This manoeuvre was to be repeated every Sunday until 12 February, the ship meantime lying at a safe anchorage in Calvo fjord – if they found one – or back at Puerto Bueno. The shore party had fifty days food so that we could survive until the middle of February; in fact, I intended, if it was at all possible, to make our ice-cap crossing and return here by the end of January; if we had not shown up by 12 February they were to allow us one week's grace before making their way back to Punta Arenas. The early return on 1 January and the subsequent weekly sighting of our base-camp seemed advisable. It was always possible that if we met with some mischance or had failed in our project that we might wish to be picked up at an early date. It was not an ideal arrangement but in the circumstances I could think of nothing better. I did not want *Mischief* to move about more than was necessary and at the same time I wanted to be sure that the shore party would not have to wait weeks on the beach should they return unexpectedly soon.

In the afternoon the weather cleared up. We carried more loads to the beginning of the ice route, and on the steep moraine between ice and forest we carved out two tent platforms for Camp II. As we trudged back down the moraine with the blue waters of the bay spread out below us, the setting sun shone on the myriad ice floes and upon our small ship beyond. As our tents were pitched we had nothing more to do but collect firewood and start a fire. Considering that rain is an almost daily occurrence it was surprising how easily this was done. Perhaps we inadvertently hit on the 'tepu' tree, for even when we left the channels for good we were still a little hazy about the precise identity of this tree. Charles and Jorge shared a high-altitude Meade tent with sleeve entrance, while I had a one-man tent, so shaped that it resembled nothing so much as a coffin with its lid propped up invitingly. Although sharing a tent these two probably had more elbow room than I who shared mine with the Primus stove, the 'ready-use' stores, saucepans of water or snow, and such like. As I knew what food and paraffin we had and was responsible for them lasting, it was only right that I should attend to the rations and such cooking as there was.

With nothing whatever in the way of food to look for beyond what we could carry and having to carry enough for seven weeks, every ounce had to be of value. In other words the kinds of food we needed had to be chosen on the lines of an Antarctic sledging ration, in which calories are solemnly calculated, rather than a Himalayan ration; for in high climbing the cry is usually 'give us the luxuries and we will dispense with the necessities'. Besides such basic belly-timber as pemmican, biscuit, sugar, and butter (at the rate of eight, seven, six, and three ounces, respectively per man-day) we did have some luxuries such as tea, cheese, chocolate, dried skim-milk, raisins, egg-powder, and oatmeal. The cheese, egg-powder and oatmeal were only for use on alternate days but in the event they did not work out even as well as that. The full allowance for each man was about 29 oz. a day.

This diet must have been totally lacking in vitamins unless perhaps some lurked in the tinned butter. I cannot think that there are any more in pemmican than in a slab of gun-cotton, and since the biscuit was in sealed tins there was no chance of its becoming vitalised by weevils and maggots as was the case in the days of the old sailing ships. Six weeks – the time we were ashore – is no doubt too short a time for the ill effects of such a diet to make themselves felt; but in the three months between Punta Arenas and Valparaiso we did not eat any fresh vegetables other than some rather poor potatoes which were soon finished. Apparently one can do very well without vegetables. In some countries only the rich can afford them and in others they are the only food the poor have to live on. Beau Brummel, who no doubt could afford vegetables and who lived to what was in his day the ripe old age of sixty-two, when asked if he never ate vegetables confessed that he 'once ate a pea'. The more a man travels in remote regions the more will he think how right Thoreau was 'that most of the luxuries and nearly all the so-called comforts of life are not only not indispensable but positive hindrances to the elevation of mankind'.

We devoted the next day to moving everything to Camp II about 700ft. higher up the moraine. This involved two journeys up and down and a third to carry forward what we had left at the half-way dump by the slabs. At this early stage, before we had made any inroads on our loads by eating or by throwing away what had been misguidedly thought indispensable, the total weight to be moved was about 475 lb. – that is to say three carries of over 50 lb. a man. The food accounted for over 300 lb., a figure which, of course, included much inedible packing material. In this respect the biscuit, packed as it was in at least twelve pounds of tin, was the worst offender. 'Satu', the toasted flour which is used in the Himalaya and which can be carried in a sack is, of course, the answer, and had I been a little more alert we could have had it. Not until we reached Valparaiso did we discover that the same thing ('harina tostada') is in common use and easily procurable. Later we took such a supply on board, and although the others did not take it in their tea – as one should – they all liked it.

The pemmican, a very palatable, full-bodied Danish brand, with a grip o' the gob such as Jorrocks liked in his favourite port, was merely wrapped in silver paper in one pound slabs. Greaseproof paper, from which at a pinch the starving explorer might extract some nourishment, would have been lighter and better. Nowadays, such is the march of science, some weight can be saved by using polythene containers for paraffin instead of clumsy tins. Although it was at the expense of the ship's party we had not stinted ourselves of paraffin, for when living on a glacier paraffin is not a thing one wants to be short of. We had about thirty pounds of it to carry and it proved to be too much, for the quantity used depends on whether water is available or snow has to be melted. Having found by trial how many meals a full stove could cook, we dumped a gallon on the glacier intending to retrieve it on our return. Our three personal loads must have weighed nearly 100 lb. altogether. Jorge had too much, my load erred on the same side, while Charles had too little. Either because of inexperience or excessive zeal for travelling light he had not brought anything to put under his sleeping bag. This was such a serious omission that we cut up our big ground sheet and gave him half.

After tea we improved the first part of the ice route by cutting steps, for while one can balance along so-called knife-edge ridges, make giant strides, or jump when unencumbered, one's movements are much more restricted when shouldering a heavy load. A mountaineer normally moves with care, but cut off as we were from any outside help we needed to be doubly careful. On one occasion, as will appear, I did not exercise care enough. After a night of heavy rain I was discouraged to find pools of water at the foot of my 'coffin'. I removed this nuisance by stabbing holes in the floor at strategic points thereby making a sort of self-draining cockpit like *Mischief*'s.

Feeling that we might have overlooked some loophole at the point where the glacier met the rock wall, we examined it more thoroughly but with no more success. The search led us through a narrow tunnel between dripping ice and dripping rock until the rock wall receded. Here, on a bed of gravel, we found growing in close profusion a bank of bright scarlet trumpet-shaped flowers with large dark green leaves – a sight the more beautiful and cheering in the dank gloom of their surroundings. These were later identified as *Ourisia alpina*. After lunching in mid-glacier we ascended as far as the 'devastated area' where we zigzagged about until brought up short by a chasm that could not be turned. Unable to go further up the glacier we began to make for its far side. By a long, intricate, and slightly dangerous route we eventually arrived. To our relief this bank (the true right side) of the glacier consisted of unbroken ice and it seemed likely that the flank of the 'devastated area' could thereby be turned and the shelf gained. This was something, but we returned to camp only a little less dejected for none of us thought the route feasible for a laden party. I took comfort from my companions. Jorge proved active, nimble, and safe, having perfect balance; while Charles, though a little slow, had a wonderful memory for a route, an invaluable faculty in an ice maze where it is so easy to lose the line and hard to recover it – especially when a party has been moving fast and has cut only a minimum of steps.

Even after having a pint of pemmican which should have produced in me more robust thoughts, I was still haunted by a fear that the Calvo glacier might be too much for us. The alternative line, involving a climb of nearly 2,000ft. through the forest above the moraine, had been unanimously rejected. This forest clung to precipitous slopes, slabby in parts and seamed with gullies, and was such a matted tangle of living and rotten, fallen trees, that the carrying of loads up that distance was out of the question. Out of curiosity on one occasion I had penetrated a few yards into it near Camp II where it was not even steep, and had recoiled in horror.

The morning broke wet. It was important, I felt, to maintain the impetus of the attack, so we made a carry to a dump on the glacier and then poked about half-heartedly in the rain looking for a better route to the right bank. Making no progress on my chosen line I stood surveying the troubled sea of ice looking for a smooth patch. Deceived by what from that distance looked like a promising lead through the 'devastated area' to the shelf above, Jorge and I set off hot-foot. By an incredibly bad route which promised to become worse, we did get nearly to the shelf. The higher we climbed the wider and deeper became the chasms and the more profuse and haphazardly heaped the great blocks of ice which half-filled them. Nor were these blocks resting on solid bottom. Jorge, while balancing on one and gazing downwards, withdrew hastily, reporting 'No bottle'. As well as the perils below there were perils from above, and one had to keep an eye lifting to the towering and tottering seracs from which this debris came. We returned to camp very wet. Things were not looking at all rosy: it seemed that we could hardly have selected a worse glacier for our experiment. Had Jorge asked my opinion and had I known Spanish I could only have told him that our situation was hopeless but not desperate.

Our fifth day ashore was another sunless day of showers. Since landing we had scarcely seen the sun, but at least there had been no wind to bother us. Although our hope of ultimately finding a route was not good we carried more loads to the dump in mid-glacier before continuing the search. When we reached the half-mile-wide belt of crevasses and seracs between us and the far side we separated in order to probe it in several places. It was not sound mountaineering practice but it was the quickest way of 'exploring every avenue'. My chosen line promised so well that having got half-way I whistled up Charles who had retired from his, momentarily baffled. With mounting excitement, expecting every moment to be stopped by some impassable gap, we pressed on towards the promised land – for so we had come to regard our very modest objective, the opposite side of the glacier. Once we could see the smooth ice beyond we were not long in reaching it. At last facing up the glacier instead of across it, we moved rapidly over comparatively unbroken ice until we reached the outer edge of the devastated area. Here it was neither so wide nor so broken and very soon we had gained the shelf. So far as we could see this ran diagonally right across to the left bank (on which Camp II lay) and it would bring us out well above the rock wall where with any luck there would be more moraine. Meanwhile there was a pleasant site for Camp III on a rock promontory on the right bank.

On returning to Camp II at seven that evening my eyes were smarting. In such dull weather on dry glacier it had seemed unnecessary to wear snow glasses, but evidently the greater height had increased the glare enough to cause snow blindness. By morning the pain was acute. As the day happened to be fine, with a watery sun struggling to pierce the cloud, we took a rest and spread our wet sleeping bags to dry.

On the 24th we spent five and a half hours in moving to Camp III, the height by barometer being 1,500ft. Though not at all easy to find, the route went well and we did what we could to mark and improve it by cutting large steps; for except in the middle trough there was a complete absence of stones to build cairns. As is often the way after an off-day the party moved with less vigour than before and I had time to cut a staircase off the ice and to level a tent site before the other two arrived. Even with rain falling it was an admirable spot. The rocky promontory formed a sort of island which rose to about 500ft. above the glacier. Round it wound the two arms of the Calvo glacier; one we had just crossed; the other, flowing round its north side, was the one whose tongue we had seen at the head of the little fjord on our first reconnaissance. There was firewood at hand and just below our tents were several little tarns. We felt better in every way. We were in a better camp site and a better frame of mind. Had it not been for the accursed rain, a pressing shortage of tobacco, and for the fact that we were so wet, I could have burst into song. It was Christmas Eve and appropriately enough I had ten socks hanging from my tent roof to dry.

Christmas Day dawned gloriously fine. A six-hour journey down to the dump in the middle of the glacier left us feeling disinclined for more. We brewed up twice – a very exceptional indulgence – and although it was midsummer gathered our winter fuel. While we were so employed a pair of duck settled on the tarn below; their bronze breasts, dove grey necks, and white wings showed that they were of the same species as those John had shot at Columbine cove. Climbing to the top of the 500ft. hill behind our camp we looked down upon the undivided Calvo glacier, a width of some two miles. Our shelf running across the glacier appeared to break into chaos and ruin well short of the dry land of the left bank. Far in the distance, beyond a daunting sea of pinnacles, smooth unbroken *névé* led without interruption to the skyline ridge. Pondering on these observations we returned to our Christmas pemmican with mixed feelings.

Boxing Day might well have seen the end of our immediate hopes. Not because of any major tragedy but because we had lost a pair of snow glasses. Having gone down to fetch the remaining loads we were moving independently and unroped up the unbroken part of the glacier not far from camp. Hereabouts were several open crevasses which could be either turned or crossed with a long stride. My load was unwieldy; a two gallon tin of paraffin had been tied to the top. It was so badly balanced that when I reached out to make a long stride over a crevasse the load swung round and dragged me down. Though fully wide enough at the surface to engulf a man and his load, further down this crevasse narrowed, so that at about 15ft. below I became firmly wedged, unable to move hand, foot, or even my head. What might have easily made matters worse was the fact that I was stupidly carrying both ropes, the one we had recently been using and our spare. Jorge, recovering quickly from his dismay at seeing me thus swallowed up, was soon on the spot and began cutting steps down. Having released my load and passed the rope to Charles, they pulled that up, and eventually I was pulled out, too, like a cork out of a bottle. I still had my axe, but the snow glasses which had been pushed up on my forehead were far down in the Calvo. Had Jorge not had a spare pair (one of the things, possibly, he had not consulted me about when packing) we might have been Rubiconed. In the Karakoram the hardy, rough-hewn men of Askole when crossing new fields either wear home-made goggles, cardboard with a narrow slit, or merely daub soot around their eyes. But they do not do this for more than a day's march and even then their consequent sufferings seem to be almost as great as if they had worn nothing. Apart from a scratched face and a slightly wrenched shoulder no damage had been done. All the loads being at Camp III we now could start unravelling the next knot in this intricate tangle. For this Calvo glacier presented a problem only a little less interesting than the finding of a route up a mountain. Owing to the rise of the glacier we could not see more than a mile ahead and as yet we had no hint of where the *névé* began. We thought probably a thousand feet higher. Although above the promontory the undivided glacier is as wide again as the branch we had crossed, in this wider field of possibilities only the shelf leading towards the left bank seemed to offer any chance. Except for this smooth shelf, the huge sweep of ice resembled a piece of corrugated iron. Had the ridges been intact they might have offered a highway in either direction, but they were broken in so many places by longitudinal crevasses that the nett result was a series of disconnected ice islands. No doubt in the course of movement and melting these islands ultimately formed the seracs and craters of the lower reaches of the glacier. Anyhow no upward progress on the glacier itself could yet be made. We had to escape to the left bank and trust to reaching the *névé* that way.

As we had feared the smooth shelf ended a good quarter mile short of the left bank. Between shelf and bank lay the roughest sea of ice we had yet to cross. By a precarious route, involving the crossing of several frail snow bridges, we reached the ablation valley lying between glacier and rock well above the rock wall. Could we only find a better approach the ablation valley would lead us gently eastwards and upwards. A lower route was worse; we even explored a traverse which took us back above the rock wall through the forest. This fortunately would not go, for it would have meant our starting again from Camp II.

As nothing else offered we returned to it next day, carrying loads to a half-way dump, and set about improving the route. After much trial and error, having made the route much longer but less hazardous, we reached the trough again and went up it, crossing a number of avalanche cones which had fallen from the slopes above. These slopes, sparsely covered with grass, were too steep for a camp site and we had to make do with one on the moraine half a mile up where there was a stream. From a rock bluff 500ft. higher we gazed upon a most satisfying scene. A little way ahead the trough opened out into a shallow snow-filled valley, merging on one side into the *névé*-covered glacier and on the other into the snow slopes of the mountain which flanked it. Several miles away the glacier disappeared from view as it swept round a high rock buttress thrown out by a ridge of the same mountain. Across the glacier on the far side was a magnificent wall of rock and ice which dipped gradually to the place where we thought our col must lie, and the white carpet spread so glisteningly between these mountain walls would assuredly lead us there. Though the carpet might be horribly soft and deeply crevassed we had but to follow where it led.

The soaking we got from a hailstorm on the way back hardly damped the satisfaction we now felt. Provided the pass would go there was nothing to stop us. We were not yet drunk with hope but Charles was elated enough by our brightening prospects to suggest a day off. Mindful of the effects of our last rest I compromised for a half day for him only, so while Jorge and I carried a load to the new camp site Charles left his at the half-way dump. The next day we moved camp and on the following day brought forward all that remained at the dump. It was 31 December. Thus a fortnight had been spent in establishing ourselves at 2,600ft. at a place where we were at last clear of the difficult part of the glacier and whence our further progress would be faster and straighter. By leaving a small food dump here for the return journey and by getting rid of some unwanted tins we could reduce our lifts from three to two. I had already made up my mind that the return journey would not be by way of the glacier. Melting was increasing fast and the snow bridges on the last section would by then be down. Another route would obviously have to be found. It seemed possible that by climbing from this Camp IV for about 2,000ft. over rock and snow until we were above Camp II we could then drop down to it. Though we could not climb up through the forest we could certainly force a way down.

CHAPTER ELEVEN

The Calvo Pass

The vagrant merchant under a heavy load
Bent as he moves and needing frequent rest.
Wordsworth

1 JANUARY 1956, cloudless, windless, hot, was a better day even than Christmas Day. After plodding up the shallow snow-filled valley for about a mile we finally emerged at a col on the ridge dividing Calvo glacier from the valley to the south. Steep snow slopes dropped to a hanging valley containing a large lake while far below was a narrow ice-filled fjord with three big glaciers which crept down to its farther shore. This was the easterly extension

of Calvo inlet which runs inland for another eight miles. It appeared so narrow and so choked with ice that we were glad we had ignored it.

We descended to our glacier by an easy snow slope, carefully picking our way through the maze of crevasses which were now just beginning to open. But the higher we went the less obvious did they become. Sometimes, only a barely perceptible crease in the unruffled surface betrayed a crevasse below. Sometimes there was no sign at all. We moved circumspectly at the full length of the rope, the leader prodding diligently the while. Sometimes a foot would go through and, then, after a brief but sufficing glimpse of frosty blue walls leading down to horrid depths, he would flounder over on his stomach or be hauled out on his back to the accompaniment of superfluous advice to use

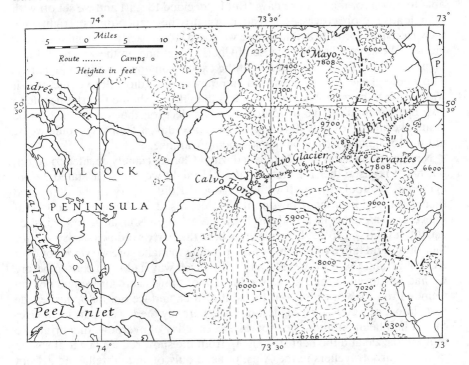

more care. Five hours of this in soft snow and sunshine was enough. At 3,600ft. by aneroid we dumped our loads and plodded homewards in the same steps. This precaution together with a cold night consolidated the trail. Next day we carried more loads to half a mile beyond the dump and then brought that forward as well. It was another gloriously sunny day. The snow softened and we soon got wet. The best part of the day was when we stepped from deep, wet snow on to warm, dry rocks, feeling like tired swimmers wading ashore. These, however, were the last rocks we should tread. This was the last water, too, that we should find. In future we should have to melt snow. We therefore brewed tea twice and laced our pemmican with chilli paste for the last time, for two days of sun on snow had played havoc with our lips.

When rain set in early next morning we regretted not having moved camp when it was fine. For it is most discouraging to pack up in the rain and to strike wet tents knowing that they will be so much the heavier to carry. Nevertheless, having reached the new camp we went back to the dump for more loads before calling it a day. Snow which fell throughout the night disclosed more faults in the design of my tent. Without the protecting eave and a short vertical piece at the side such as in a Meade, it allowed the accumulating snow to press the sides inwards until the cursing inmate found it impossible to move or turn without touching the fabric and starting copious leaks. This, however, was not the sum of my troubles. Charles, who was complaining of sore feet, now expressed a doubt as to whether he would be able to go on for many more days. But he decided to start and we set off with light loads. Soon crevasses forced us on to the slopes on our right. We traversed here for fully a mile before we could strike back to the middle of the glacier. We stopped early because of Charles' feet and on the way back I had plenty to think about. The success of the expedition now seemed in jeopardy. The whole glacier was so crevassed and they were so difficult to detect that it was unsafe to be on it with a party of less than three. Should Charles decide to give up, we should have to return. It was a decision that would have to be made overnight, for only if we started back next day, a Thursday, could we be in time to signal *Mischief* on her second appearance.

Next morning I was greatly relieved when Charles gamely decided to go on, but had I realised the true state of affairs I might well have hesitated before agreeing. He took a day off while Jorge and I did a carry to the dump and then went on for an hour beyond it to select a site for Camp VI. To talk of selecting camp sites in a uniform snow desert sounds absurd. Indeed, they usually turned out to be those placed where the party sat down, as it were for the count, and failed to get up. A little probing to make sure we were not over a crevasse and there we were. Camp VI in such way had been chosen before we had advanced far enough to see the end of the glacier, for we had not yet rounded the rock buttress. But the wall of rock and ice on the opposite side had almost ceased to dip, suggesting that there lay the lowest part of the ice-cap. It had been another fine, hot day. Such a day of overpowering brilliance that the dazzle and the heat striking up from the snow reduced us to the state of some early travellers in the Alps, in need only of an umbrella and a scent bottle.

Such brazenly fine days seemed unnatural after what we had expected. Next day, however, made amends with a terrible storm which began at four in the morning and continued until the afternoon. The wind battered at my tent as though bent on its destruction. The fabric, which was inadequately stayed, flapped wildly and incessantly, and when bursts of hail accompanied the gusts of wind the noise was frightening. Lying thus stormbound, pressing with hands or feet against the fabric in order to tauten and quieten it, I had leisure to reflect upon the folly of voluntarily taking rest days when in all certainty too many idle days would sooner or later be forced upon us by bad weather. On a journey such as this in which the time available for crossing the ice-cap and returning depended on the amount of food carried, an idle day means so much wasted food, and is something to be regarded with the gravest misgiving. On the other hand when the weather allows no choice in the matter idleness can be endured, perhaps even enjoyed, with no pricking of one's conscience. As Lord Curzon used to say: 'It is inevitable, therefore it can be approved.' Although the tents were close together the incessant din prevented my passing on to the others for their consideration the fruits of my profound reflections. Indeed, all talk between us was impossible. As by now I had no tobacco and my only book had been already read twice my resignation was sorely tried. I had already experimented with the smoking of our used tea leaves and had found that whether they were sun dried or toasted over the Primus the smoke was a little acrid. Now, carrying the experiment further, I found that fresh, unused tea smoked very well, and henceforth, regarding it as the quarter-master's perquisite, I allowed myself one pipeful a day.

A cold, clear night succeeded the storm and in the morning as we moved up to Camp VI we found the snow delightfully crisp. A stormy night was the prelude to another blizzard and another idle morning. When the wind abated at two o'clock, thinking anything better than inertia, I turned out the others. We climbed up unladen for two hours with the idea of preparing the track for the next day. The wind, which was at our backs, seemed to be rising again, and when we turned for home we found ourselves facing half a gale and clouds of driven snow. The landmarks disappeared one by one and soon it became questionable whether or no our outgoing tracks would remain visible or be blotted out before we sighted the tents. Very cold and wet we were, and mightily relieved, when at length they loomed ahead. Charles' Spanish and Jorge's English enabled them to converse deliberately, tortuously, but not quite incomprehensibly, and as they lay in their sleeping bags, restoring their half frozen feet and discussing their pemmican, they no doubt said things about this brief sortie which the noise of the storm happily prevented my hearing.

When we started next morning in a brief lull the futility of the sortie of the evening before became even more apparent for not a vestige of a track remained. Half-an-hour later, when snow began to fall, we dumped the loads and fled. We tried once more in the afternoon only to be driven back when the mounting gloom of clouds rolling up the glacier threatened a repetition of yesterday's storm.

But for the time being the weather had done its worst. Our next carry took us beyond the rock buttress and brought into view the full width of the pass – a shallow flattening in the skyline ridge. On a day of stern plodding in bad snow and muggy weather, the leader's half-hour spell of stamping a track seemed never ending. If one glanced at one's watch, time stood still. I found the only way to keep going was to count one's steps.

In these regions a fine day is a thing to be remembered, not so much by its rareness – we were blessed with a good many – but for its perfection. Here are no grudging half measures. The sun blazes benignly from a cloudless sky upon mountains outlined starkly against a brilliant blue. Not a stone sullies the dazzling whiteness of the snow, the only rock in sight is the living rock of the mountains, for no stone ever seems to fall. On these lovely days there is not a breath of air to disturb the serenity of a frozen world suffused with light and warmth. Our spirits and strength restored by the invigorating influence of such a day we reached the dump and went on for another hour before making camp. The height of this Camp VII was 5,750ft. and we judged it to be about 500ft. below the pass. After tea we brought the loads up from the dump, cooked supper and turned in, for it had become very cold.

We went to bed rather pleased with ourselves, the weather, and life in general; but within an hour a blizzard raged. Fearing that the incessant flapping would start a seam in the fabric of the tent I spent most of the night supporting the panels with alternate hands (for this exercise one had to wear gloves) until the snow banking up outside made the task unnecessary. Most of the snow had, I think, drifted, but quite obviously whether it had fallen or drifted it would not do for us to be caught away from camp in one of these sudden storms. By noon the storm had passed leaving in its wake a white mist which seemed to increase tenfold the heat of the unseen sun. In the afternoon we took some loads up to what appeared to be the highest part of the pass. Eastwards everything was hidden in a sea of mist, but to the south-west a deep notch between two mountains showed where yet another glacier rolled down to the eastern end of Calvo fjord.

The extremely violent changes of weather baffled prediction. Reputedly, the fairer the hostess the fouler the reckoning, and in the same way we suspected that the more brilliant the day the worse would be the next. The suspicion proved unfounded, for we now experienced two such successive days. They could not have been more timely. Friday, 13 January, was the first of these marvellous blue days. By nine o'clock of a fresh, cool morning, filled with the exuberance which climbing swiftly on crisp snow affords, we had reached the dump. Having already resolved to do no more relaying we looked at the dump and what we had just added to it with some concern and our exuberance diminished. When we shouldered the newly made-up loads it disappeared for good. As we started contouring round the foot of the ridge on the north side of the pass the crisp snow began to give way under our feet.

We were now traversing a slightly undulating snow field, bounded on the east by a high ridge carrying a peak named on the map Cerro Cervantes (7,808ft.). Although the snow field fell away gradually towards a gap in the ridge which roused our interest and caused some discussion, we ignored it and shaped our course to a little north of east to where the great Bismarck glacier, which flows into Lake Argentino, originates. Still gaining height we plodded on slowly in increasing heat and softening snow. Wordsworth would have recognised us instantly as vagrant merchants, very bent and needing very frequent rest. By three o'clock we had drawn nearly level with the north end of the Cervantes ridge. Ahead of us lay a crest and, slight though it was, it effectually hid everything beyond. But we had had enough. So we camped and brewed tea before walking on to this insignificant crest.

The approach to an unknown pass to look over into unknown country is as exciting as the last pitch of a first ascent; and when the pass lies on a frontier and also forms the watershed between two oceans the thrill is intensified. Ideally, of course, the pass should be steep on both sides, so that one moment the climber sees nothing but the rock or snow in front of him and the next, as though a curtain had been drawn aside, a vast and unexpected landscape. But one can't have everything. Our crest was so broad and the rise so imperceptible that the scene on the other side unfolded itself very gradually. Nevertheless, it was exciting enough and we involuntarily quickened our feeble pace as the first distant blue hills of the Argentine rose above the snow. Then a tiny corner of the lake itself showed almost green against the darker hills, with the long white tongue of the Bismarck glacier projecting far into the water; and at last little by little, far below us, the main glacier unfolded its grey wrinkled mass.

Behind us to the south the ice-cap stretched to the distant rock spires of the Paine region. To the west easy snow slopes led to the summits on the long ridge on which we had gazed for so many days from the other side. To the north rose peak upon peak increasing in height as they became more distant. Most curious, too, was a deep rift in the ice-cap which we could distinguish some 10 miles to the north. There, there is only a distance of five miles separating the northern extremity of Peel Inlet from a little lake which was originally an arm of Lake Argentino but is now cut off from it by a glacier. Should this ice barrier melt or break and the little lake become one with its parent, then a mere five miles separates the waters of Lake Argentino from the Pacific Ocean. So far as distance goes this would appear to be the easiest place to cross the ice-cap, but this northern extremity of Peel is long, narrow, choked with ice, and (as the ship's party were to discover) across its entrance is a reef.

Having savoured to the full this wonderful mountain vision we had to decide what to do. From where we were (7,500ft. above sea-level) what little we could see of the lower Bismarck glacier looked even more tangled and broken than the lower Calvo. On our right the north ridge of Cervantes dropped slowly down to it, to terminate in a high buttress of shaly, yellow rock. At the foot of the buttress the main Bismarck glacier was joined by one almost equally big lying under the east side of Cerro Cervantes. This was fed not only by this mountain but by others further east, and by the ice-cap spilling through the gap in the Cervantes ridge. As we could overlook both glaciers from the buttress we decided to put a camp (Camp IX) on the ridge just short of it.

Owing to either fatigue, excitement, or the tantalising vision of the lake which seemed so near and might yet be so far, I was long in going to sleep and woke only when the sun flooded the tent with a yellow light. It was another flawless day as we moved on over the crest and followed the ridge down about 500ft. to camp on a thin layer of snow overlying a bed of shale. Any idea that we could walk down the main arm of the Bismarck could be dismissed out of hand. Though we might have been able to cross it high up on the névé, its northern or true left bank was cut by two formidably frag-mented subsidiary glaciers. The other branch, which could be called the East Bismarck, warranted closer inspection. It offered the shortest way to the lake and on its farther side, immediately opposite to our camp, the snow slopes above it gave way to warm, red rock. Could we but reach those rocks there seemed good hopes of our reaching the lake.

That night it began blowing and the morning broke overcast, cold, and windy. A few yards from the tents the ridge fell in precipices to the East Bismarck, but lower down where the buttress sprang up for a col there was a snow ramp leading towards the glacier. What lay between the foot of the snow ramp and the glacier could not be seen, but when we got down we found ourselves groping about in a badly broken ice-fall. To escape from this we traversed over to some rocks below the buttress and huddled behind them to take stock and to eat our lunch. The weather was deteriorating and a closer view of the glacier, now only about 500ft. below, was extremely discouraging. Only a short mile separated us from the red rocks, but the sea of ice between broke in tumultuous waves. The only way of reaching the rocks seemed to be to make a long circuit round the head of the glacier on the *névé* and then return along the snow slopes on the far side. As a way of reaching the head of the glacier, the notch in the Cervantes ridge which we had noticed when we first reached the ice-cap at once occurred to us. From where we were the east side of the Cervantes ridge looked impossibly steep. The glacier, however, rose steeply towards its head and might well be accessible from the notch. We would go back and see.

CHAPTER TWELVE

Lake Argentino and Back

Then Alpheus bold
On his glacier cold
With his trident the mountains shook.
                    Shelley

WE WERE ALREADY disheartened as we toiled back up the 2,000ft. of rock and snow, and then that night we had:

> A trifling sum of misery
> New added to the foot of our account

when a short but fierce blizzard raged. Although time spent in reconnaissance is never wasted, we felt that this reconnaissance might have been done with advantage from a camp somewhere near the Calvo pass. If instead of blundering on we had stopped and then made a reconnaissance east as well as north some time and strength would have been saved.

Another brilliant morning went far to comfort us as we began the long trudge back over the wide crest. This crest which we had hoped would be the Bismarck Pass we had now christened the Bismarck Saddle, a name which promised nothing and raised no false hopes. Strictly speaking the name Calvo Pass can only be given to the vague shallow depression on the ice-cap which we had reached from the Calvo glacier. If this depression led downwards to the notch, as it did, and if there was a way through the notch down to the East Bismarck glacier, then the name might well be transferred to the notch itself. In that it proved to be narrow and confined between high walls this notch was more like a pass; but it lay several hundred feet below the true pass showing that the Cervantes ridge where the notch lies is not the watershed.

Having traversed back along the ice-cap under the slopes of Cervantes we shed our loads and began to climb. We hoped to be able to reach a point from which we could look down on the notch to see what lay beyond. When we reached the ridge above it we could see that it marked the entrance to a narrow defile leading easily to the glacier below. A short way down the defile was a convenient shelf lying between an ice-fall above and the seracs below. By traversing along this we could reach and cross the glacier where it was reasonably free from crevasses. This route would pass under a black rock spur where we could camp if necessary. Here was the solution of our troubles, the answer to our prayers.

Having retrieved our loads we brewed up. The air was so still that the Primus would burn in the open. Even though the way led downhill we did not reach the notch that evening. Intending to leave two day's food, spare film, and other things on the ice-cap I had picked on a fold in the snow, half cave, half crevasse, still some way ahead of us, as a useful mark. We had neither wands nor flags and as this was the only identifiable feature in an otherwise unbroken expanse of snow it was only wise to take advantage of it. But the snow was soft and deep and we were feeling uncommonly weary so that we made camp 400 or 500 yards short of it. This slackness was to have consequences. Camp X was 6,550ft. above sea-level.

Six days food seemed ample to take with us – two days to the lake, two days back, and two days in reserve. The rest, enough for two days, together with anything we could leave out of our loads was left behind. This included a great quantity of my exposed film, both colour and black-and-white. As food had also been left at Camp VII on the Calvo side of the pass, and at Camps V and IV, our line of retreat seemed to be secure. We built the dump as high as we could – at least two feet above the ground – and took some bearings.

When we set out for the notch and the red rocks (where we hoped to camp) it was windy and cold. Moving fast over hard snow we were lucky to hit off without hesitation a strait and narrow gate between the ice-fall and the seracs. Skirting under the black rock spur we dropped down to the *névé-covered* glacier and started to cross it, hell-bent on reaching the red rocks which beckoned so invitingly, for we were tired of sleeping on snow. The edge of the glacier close to the snow slopes provided an almost crevasse-free route, but by the time we stepped from soft snow on to dry land in the Argentine, as it were, we were very weary. After some search we found a snug shelf of gravel at the foot of a miniature cliff. Perched a few hundred feet above the glacier this desirable residence boasted a fine view and had water laid on, for a stream trickled down the cliff from a snow bed above. After a fortnight of camping on snow we relished highly the more luxurious warmth of gravel and the abundant water supply. The height of Camp XI was about 4,500ft., the height of Lake Argentino being about 600ft.

We had now pitched our most distant camp. From here we intended to reach the lake and return to camp in the day. Charles, who had not been able to do much in the way of trail-breaking but had kept going with great determination, decided to take a rest, lake or no lake. For Jorge and me it was Pike's Peak or bust, so we started soon after 5 am on 18 January, carrying only lunch and a camera. At this stage in its journey to the lake the glacier assumed the tortured and riven form we had recognised with some despondency from our view-point on the ridge. The *névé* had disappeared and the rough, bare ice close to the rocks was as broken as that of the Calvo. A mile below camp the ice crawled round the foot of a sheer cliff where it seemed more than likely that we might be stopped. We made good progress until we drew near the cliffs which we approached along a wet, black gangway of moraine. With enough time one might have made a laborious but more certain route above the cliff, but it would be at a very high level and we were short of time. When ice and cliff met we had to take to the ice which at this point was as black as the moraine it had deposited. We got past the cliff but it was touch and go. A little later in the season, a little more melting, the disappearance of any one of several slender links, and we would have been stopped.

This was the crux. Once the corner had been turned there was nothing to stop us. Round the corner the cliff dwindled to a boulder-strewn slope where a few hardy shrubs struggled for existence and lower down the slopes became more and more forested. While even better for us, far down the glacier the seracs melted away before a grand expanse of flat, dry ice littered with stones and boulders. On we went at a round pace over ice, moraine, or tree-covered bank – whichever was the easiest. At first the forest was of gnarled, stubby, close-growing trees, scarcely penetrable except by following the bed of a fast flowing stream. Lower down it opened out and provided us with good going; but even that was abandoned when we reached the expanse of flat ice over which we sped rejoicing, remarking as we went several fine examples of 'glacier tables' – boulders perched on an ice pedestal. Near the lake this broad highway suddenly broke up into pinnacles and crevasses forcing us back into the shady forest.

The strangest feature of the Bismarck glacier was the proximity of ice and forest, their line of contact being marked by broken branches and fallen trees. The moraine, where it existed, was a ridge a few feet high littered with stripped tree trunks and apparently as fresh as if deposited only recently. At times the ice almost brushed the living trees. We could walk through open forest of tall Antarctic beech on a carpet of yellow violets, while through the trees, only a few yards off, loomed a monstrous wall of ice. Game tracks were plentiful but we saw neither life nor any fresh spoor. In addition to the violets there were purple vetch, berberis, fuchsia, a yellow flower like a foxglove, very common in the Central Andes, and a holly-like shrub with a pleasing orange flower which we had often seen on the west side.

The shore of the lake is here so heavily forested that we were denied the blessed sight of its milky blue water until the last moment. It was about noon when in the moment of victory we sank down on the bank for our first halt.

The lake itself failed to come up to my high expectation. For one thing we were on a narrow arm so that the opposite shore was barely a mile away. I had hoped to step from the forest on to a grassy sward, graced perhaps by a few flamingos. Instead we sat among nettles and creepers on a steep earth bank, with the water, full of dead branches, about six feet below. In front and on either hand for some way from the shore tops of dead and dying trees rose above the water. Apart from their hindrance to either boating or bathing, to me there is always something peculiarly depressing about black, leafless branches of drowned trees stretched out, as it were, in mute appeal. Still, water is water; and besides my being hot and sweaty enough to make any bathe memorable, here was an occasion – the end of a long pilgrimage over sea and mountain – when not to bathe ceremonially, if need be in boiling spring or ice-bound pool, would have been base indeed. Jorge, with no proud record behind him of ceremonial bathes in far corners of the earth, had no such compelling impulse. Accordingly I rose alone from my bed of briars and nettles, stripped as best I could without getting scratched or stung (there were clouds of virulent horse flies) and bathed. Bathed is, perhaps, an extravagant term for an act which took less than a few seconds to complete; for hard by an ice floe nestled close against the bank.

There were dozens of ice floes and their numbers were being added to at frequent intervals by a thunderous discharge from the glacier tongue which thrusts out into the lake almost as far as the opposing shore. Each ice avalanche was followed by a wave which set the floes rocking on its way towards the shore. This 100ft. high wall of ice with the sun sparkling on its white pinnacles, with ice caverns a more lovely blue even than the water, looked like a section of the Ross Barrier transported from the Antarctic to the more genial surroundings of hills and forest. Indeed, to anyone ignorant of its parent ice-cap nothing could appear more incongruous than this mass of ice, issuing apparently from the depths of a forest, lapped by the placid waters of a lake, and the whole bathed in brilliant sunshine.

Two hours later we started back. Our slow progress soon made it clear that we should not get back that night. Accordingly before quitting the pleasant open forest we chose a flat spot under the trees with a stream hard by and settled down for the night. Having supped on cold water all we had to do was to collect enough wood for our fire. Dead trees lay in profusion and everything was so dry that we had to be careful not to start a forest fire. In contrast to the forest of the western side this looked as though no rain had visited it for months. Higher up, the mountains of this eastern side must surely receive a great quantity of snow, for the snow line is, perhaps, only a thousand feet higher than on the west.

In the night no strange animals prowled round our camp, no ghastly yell from a Patagonian 'yeti' froze our blood, so that apart from rising frequently to replenish the fire we slept well. Hope, reputedly a bad supper but a good breakfast, was all we had had when, having shaken the leaves from our hair and stamped out the fire, we resumed the march. Although we now knew more of the country and could cut off some of yesterday's corners we found it a weary grind; Jorge, whose breakfast evidently had not agreed with him, lagged behind. But feeling that Charles' anxiety at our absence should not be unduly prolonged I went ahead. Traversing high up on the rocks a mile from camp I saw Charles, with a rucksack bulging with sleeping bags and food, moving slowly down the glacier in search of us. Fortunately I was able to stop him and in the course of the morning the three wanderers foregathered to lie at earth for the rest of the day.

In the night it blew hard, so hard that my tent, inadequately stayed with stones, was uprooted. The wonderful weather of the last few days had broken. When we started in the morning the wind which was already blowing strongly increased as we neared the black rock spur where we meant to camp. It was now a blizzard and we might just as well have camped on the snow where we stood, for the twenty minutes climb to the rocks chilled us to the bone. With numbed hands we struggled to erect the tents in the wholly imaginary lee of the rocks across which the snow drove with stinging force. For the next forty-eight hours the gale beat about us with relentless fury. We were in no condition to sit it out and wait for better times. Our limited food, the uncertainty of reaching and finding our dump, and the now visibly weakening seams of my tent, combined to lower our morale and make us anxious. The Primus, too, either because of lack of air in the tightly sealed tent or because of too much outside, now began to give trouble.

On the morning of Sunday, 22 January, the gale was still blowing and outside it was very thick. We had now only food for that day. We had no choice, therefore, but to get on and find the dump. In addition to the initial difficulty of finding the route and hitting off the extremely tenuous line between the ice-fall and the seracs it seemed possible that beyond the notch the storm might well be worse. At last at midday a glimpse of the sun trying to pierce the flying scud encouraged us to try. The slow cold job of packing the frozen tents over, we got under way and accomplished the tricky part of the route without a mistake. This was encouraging but beyond the notch driving snow still hid everything. Having little idea beyond a rough compass course where we were going we camped just in time to avoid another blizzard. We thought we were now not more than a mile from the dump and that night we finished our food.

Although in the morning it was still blowing the sun shone through the driving mist and snow. Visibility was from 200 to 300 yards. My plan was to leave the camp standing and search for the dump. This might take a long time to find, for it would probably be covered by the snow of three days of storm. The others were loth to move far away from camp as it was always possible we might not be able to find it again. There was something in that, but there was nothing at all in Jorge's next suggestion, that having no food and little hope of finding any we should retreat to the Argentine. Charles, who was now feeling the cold, agreed with him. This suggestion implied a two days journey to the lake and then the crossing of some 50 miles rough country before the nearest estancia could be reached. And all this would have to be done on one tin of biscuits which we had foolishly left at the red rocks. Also, such a decision would impose a severe strain on the ship's party who would have great difficulty in returning through the channels short-handed. I therefore exercised my right of veto and at noon we packed up and started for home. If we found the dump on the way so much the better; if we didn't we could go on to the next, or even the next after that. If we had to go hungry it was better that we should move over country we knew and in the direction of our friends.

Visibility was now less than 200 yards but after an hour's plodding I spotted through the mist the hole where we thought to put the dump but didn't. As compass bearings were of no use in such conditions we had to rely on guesswork for its position. Charles and I, taking different lines, moved off to search, Jorge showing an invincible reluctance to being separated from the loads. As we had only a vague idea where to look we could not waste time prodding the snow; our only chance was that a bit of the dump might still be above the surface. After quartering the ground for some time I reluctantly called the search off. This abandoning of all my exposed film was for me, I think, the bitterest pill, for although the morale of the party was shaken I had confidence that once we were over the pass we should be able to keep going until we found one of the lower dumps.

Nothing was said as we shouldered our loads to move on very slowly. Some way past the hole Charles suggested we should try once more before going too far and I gladly agreed for the mist seemed to be thinning a little. Off we went, Jorge again staying by the loads. Once before Charles' keen eyes had served us in good stead and now he was the first to spot at a distance of 200 yards something very small and black. As I did not wish to rouse Jorge's hopes to no purpose I stifled a whoop of joy and joined Charles as he hobbled towards it. It was the dump all right. We were, indeed, lucky, for only about three inches of the corner of the topmost tin showed above the snow.

Seldom can the finding of pemmican and biscuit have given so much genuine pleasure. For this deliverance from black care we declared a holiday and pitched camp on the spot. Replete with food and tolerably secure in the knowledge that there was more to come, we listened with indifference to the persistent wind. Since the 20th it had been blowing and this extraordinary spell of bad weather proved to be by no means over. Late next morning, the wind having dropped a little, but with visibility of only a hundred yards, we started for the pass steering by compass. As we crossed it in deep powder snow, the mist rolled away revealing the familiar mountains to the west, and we went on down rejoicing to be safely over. Near Camp VII we found ourselves at a loss, for we were unable to recognise the landmarks and could not therefore locate the dump with its two days' food. Had we had to cross the pass without food as was so nearly the case, we should have been in a poor way.

As it was we were not yet out of the wood. Our start was delayed by a blizzard which had blown up in the night, but at 11 am we set off steering by compass, with visibility worse than ever. Much depended on our finding the dump at Camp V but even when the mist did clear we had difficulty in recognising such vaguely remembered landmarks as crevasses or queer shaped seracs. It was more by luck than anything else that, late in the day, we stumbled on a box sticking out of the snow. For the time being at least we should not go hungry. Camp IV was on unmistakable rocks and at Camp I there was a three days' supply of food, and provided *Mischief* had not miscarried we should be picked up the day after our arrival there.

We looked forward to the short, easy journey between Camps V and IV, and I pictured myself strolling placidly down the glacier, up on to the little col from which we had once looked down into the next valley, and then on to the rocks where we should knock the snow off our boots for the last time. In the event we had a trying day. Starting in mist we continued in mist. All went well until we halted for a snack near the col, but on starting again we missed the route and became deeply involved in a terrible maze. After following a promising line between two crevasses for a quarter mile or so, we would be brought up short by one running transversely. We would then have to retrace our steps and try another only to finish in the same way. Becoming more and more frustrated I at length decided to follow the complicated pattern of our tracks all the way back to the halting place. There we pitched a tent, brewed up, and waited for the mist to clear. When it did we saw our mistake and within an hour had reached camp. It rained all night but that was the last of a seven day spell of very foul weather. Had we met such conditions on the way up I doubt if we ever should have crossed the ice-cap.

We were now faced with a stiff climb over rock and patches of snow for about 2,000ft. before we could begin the downward traverse towards the tree line. Had the weather not taken a turn for the better it would have been a puzzling journey. Instead we had a lovely clear day and enjoyed looking down on our old enemy, the lower glacier, and to Calvo bay and the Wilcock peninsula beyond. Poor Charles, whose feet for the last few days had been very painful, had a bad time, but he stuck to it nobly. By midday we sat down on a grassy mound just above the tree line to eat our lunch and to select the likeliest point for our attack. We had to drop about 2,000ft. and once the battle with the bush had been joined it would be a case of every man for himself. An hour later, with scratched face and tattered windproofs, I emerged on to the moraine close to Camp II. Jorge followed close behind, and then, *longo intervallo*, the bushes parted and a sort of forest satyr or dryad appeared, leaves in his hair and twigs in his beard. As we forgathered there on the moraine each of us must have looked something like Bunyan's Pilgrim, 'clothed in rags, his face from his own house, and a great burden upon his back'. This final descent through the forest had been a searing experience, creeping under branches, standing on rotten trunks which broke, stepping on to moss hags which had no bottom, slithering down slimy cliffs, dropping like apes from branch to branch, seeing nothing, and able only to go downwards. At one time I had become so firmly lodged in a thicket that I despaired of freeing myself without help. All of us were a little weak.

Down by the shore we pitched our yellow tents on the highest point of the moraine, as a signal, and settled down to wait for the next day but one, Sunday, 29 January. We found two notes which contained bad news. *Mischief* had been aground, had damaged her propeller, and was once again without power. She was anchored in a bay out of our sight some four miles off and we should have to be taken off in the dinghy. On the other hand the promised supply of petrol and paraffin had been delivered. The *Lautaro* (Cmdr. Chubretovich), having failed to find *Mischief* at Puerto Bueno, continued the search in Peel Inlet and finally delivered mail, petrol, and paraffin. Thus, in every sense, the Chilean Navy went out of its way to help us.

CHAPTER THIRTEEN

A Near Thing

Curiosity, like all other desires, produces pain as well as pleasure.
Samuel Johnson

WHILE Jorge went down to the beach to gather mussels, Charles and I collected firewood. If all went well we could expect to be taken off next day; for from the notes left in the pillar-box we learnt that it was their custom for someone to row in on the Saturday, sleep on shore, and then row back on Sunday evening. All the next morning from our look-out on the moraine we played Sister Anne until at last among the distant floes we descried a black speck. Michael with the dinghy arrived in the afternoon, having been rowing and pushing for four solid hours, for the ice was thick. As the dinghy would not hold four men and their kit we left Charles to be picked up the following day. I took the oars, Jorge acted as bowman with his ice-axe, while Michael conned us from the stern. It was hard work for the dinghy was loaded down to the gunwale, and I was relieved when three hours later we turned the corner and saw *Mischief's* stumpy mast. In spite of her recent rough handling she looked imperturbably solid and homelike even among such wild surroundings. She lay off a shingle beach where she had been untroubled by wind or ice although the bay lay wide open to the west. It was a happy reunion – a little marred, perhaps, by the occurrences now to be related.

During the row out I learnt why, how, and where *Mischief* had been nearly wrecked. I blamed myself for not having given more explicit instructions that the ship should not be moved unnecessarily, but I never imagined they would want to go swanning about on their own. Enough has been said of the extreme north end of Peel Inlet to show that it must be a fascinating place, and apparently Procter's curiosity to see it proved irresistible. In 1931 Michael Mason had gone nearly as far as the narrow entrance and we knew from his account in *Where Tempests Blow* that it was full of ice and that a strong current flowed; but it was left for *Mischief* to discover that there was also a bar across it in the shape of a rock reef. Upon this *Mischief* struck, with the result that in this case curiosity produced more pain than pleasure. Once the disaster had happened the small crew, led by Proctor, acted with the utmost energy, resolution, and skill, urged on not only by their fear for the ship but also by the knowledge of the consequences that loss or damage to her might have for the party on the ice-cap. Their experience and the anxiety they naturally felt are well described in Michael's own words:

We headed up the north arm of Peel Inlet. It was wide enough to tack against the familiar head wind which later swung right round until we were running at 4 or 5 knots with the boom wide out. Ahead the channel bent eastwards with a broad, flat forested swamp on the west bank and steep rock on the other. We kept close in to the rock to avoid possible shallows off the west side, but suddenly we touched. In a moment we were off again having been carried over by our own momentum. There was no ice about and the channel was still three quarters of a mile wide, and no sign of kelp. Judging it wiser to go no further without investigating, particularly as we could now see round the bend where there were large ice floes apparently aground in the narrowing waterway, we anchored in 6 fathoms in mid-stream. Bill Procter and I rowed about in the dinghy sounding to find a better anchorage for the night.

The sound of barks and grunts drew us to a small bay some half mile to the south where we saw some sea lions sunning themselves on a rocky cape. There were 20 to 30, mostly of a light brown colour, the sun having dried their shiny black skins. The females became uneasy at our presence behind some bushes and presently the huge old bull roused himself. A grunted order and his large family flopped into the sea one after the other in a frenzy of splashing. The bull remained on the rock as a rearguard, his whiskers bristling and his huge body weaving about as he searched the bushes with indignant eyes. Then he, too, took the water, but he was too curious to leave, and swam around, surrounded by his harem, lifting head and shoulders out of the water to get a better look at us.

On returning to the ship we noted that there was now a strong current and that the icefloes were being carried down towards us. We weighed at once and headed for 'Sea Lion bay' which had seemed an excellent anchorage, taking care to keep in mid-stream to avoid the rock we had touched on the way up. All at once, with a lurch and a shudder the boat ground to a standstill – we were hard and fast. I took the kedge anchor off in the dinghy but could make little headway owing to the current. We had not noticed until now how fast the water was flowing, having been deceived by the slack water at high tide. We heaved on the warp but the boat would not budge, and her stern was already high out of the water. It was about 9 p.m. and in the failing light we could make out a boulder-strewn bottom beneath the swirling water.

The topmast was rigged as a leg made fast to the starboard shrouds and took some of the weight as the yacht began to list. Small icefloes drifted on to us, carried at a rate of 5 or 6 knots over the reef, and we fended them off as best we could with boat-hook, harpoon, or staysail boom. At two in the morning the water was about 2ft. deep, rocks were showing above it, and *Mischief* was leaning heavily on the leg. During slack water we spent two hours sounding the length of the reef which extended nearly a thousand yards from shore to shore. The shallowest part was in mid channel where we had struck, and as it extended 50 yards ahead she would have to come off stern first. Near the west bank there was a gap with a depth of 1½ to 2 fathoms at low water. For one thing we had reason to be grateful – the reef kept off the bigger bergs which had been careering down stream, spinning and breaking up with thunderous roars just before reaching us as they grounded on the edge of the reef. The smaller bergs could be fended off until such time as the stern became too high out of the water for them to be reached. As the tide turned the same bergs came back to us. The bows presented a smaller and less vulnerable target than the stern, but the topmast leg stood out unprotected.

Next morning, 5 January, high water being about 8.30, we laid out the kedge astern but succeeded only in stranding the rope. There was nothing for it but to lighten the ship. Bill rowed ashore with the spare anchor chain and 2 cwt. of ballast and landed on a sand spit between two wooded islands 600 yards down stream. I pumped water out of the tanks while John fended off floes. Bill returned towing a stout trunk of Winter's bark which we erected as another leg, and we brought ballast up from the side lockers and put it on the starboard side of the deck to keep her canted as the tide went out. Rowing ashore with 5 cwt. of pig iron I nearly sank, as the current was so strong that I could not manoeuvre the dinghy and I got caught up in a whirlpool. Even with the empty dinghy I could not row against the current so that we had to wait for slack water for the next load.

Meanwhile Bill and John, when not fending off ice, took up the cabin tank and floor boards and began levering out ballast and carrying it on deck. This was a back-breaking job and the pigs were hard to grip. At slack water between 2 p.m. and 4 p.m. we got three loads ashore. Each 1 cwt. pig had to be lowered 6ft. over the side and a slip would have meant either a holed dinghy or perhaps a broken leg. The boat was now the lighter by a ton of ballast, the spare chain, and about 15 cwt. of water. We continued working on the ballast, getting it up first from the port side and putting it on deck in readiness for slack water, one of us keeping ice-berg watch and the other two handling the pigs. High water was at 9.30 p.m. We had forgotten about eating but we now lit the fire and put some coffee on. A large berg knocked away both legs, but there was enough water to keep the ship from falling over. The difficulty was to get them back in place with the current sweeping them astern.

We rowed ashore two more loads of ballast. By this time Bill was completely exhausted. He had been a tower of strength, but he had had no sleep for over 36 hours and felt the responsibility of the situation. We gave him a sleeping draught and he slept all through the frightful noises of the night, the floes hitting the stern and scraping along the hull. There was a light wind blowing and we were fearful of it increasing and blowing us over. We fixed up the staysail booms on the port side but the ice soon dislodged them. The wind brought the ice down thick and fast. The boathook snapped in my hands as one crashed against the quarter rocking the ship. Others hit the stern and the rudder, and I thought that any moment either this would be smashed or the ship would topple over. Miraculously she withstood the onslaught. By 3 a.m. on the Friday morning the worst was over and we were able to get a little sleep during slack water.

The morning tide brought the ice back and we were now beginning to recognise by their individual shape and size floes as they went back and forth. By daylight, from the dinghy, I looked at the damage. The hull was scraped bare, some of the planking scarred and splintered, the rudder chipped, and the propeller had had one blade chewed to pieces. During slack water we ferried over four more loads of ballast and another three in the afternoon, making a total of 67 cwt. on shore. 'Ballast bay' was now littered with pig iron. Mischief looked a strange sight stuck out in mid channel almost high and dry at low water. It was a beautiful day and we were surrounded by magnificent scenery, but we could not appreciate it.

We cut some more Winter's bark logs and hung them over the stern weighted with ballast in an effort to protect the rudder from ice. On the ebb the topmast was again knocked away by ice, but the Winter's bark trunk took the weight on its own, the boat settling down with a more pronounced list on this remaining leg. The topmast could not get back into its hole among the boulders until low water. In the evening as Bill was taking ashore the first load of ballast just before high water, without the slightest warning the bows swung clear and we were off. I took the tiller while John dashed to the engine, Bill gesticulating madly from the dinghy. We were being carried fast up stream towards the larger ice floes. John threw the anchor over, forgetting to pass the chain through the fairlead. However, we were anchored in about 6 fathoms close to where we had originally anchored on the Wednesday evening.

Bill returned and we surveyed the situation. We decided to wait until low water next morning at about 4 a.m. and then feel our way with the lead through the gap we had sounded, using the engine at its slowest speed. If we grounded again we should have a rising tide to float us off. We put the kedge anchor over and brought up the main anchor and chain with the handy-billy, for the winch could not be used while the chain was not in its fairlead. At last all its 25 fathoms were got in and then let out again through the fairlead.

But our troubles were by no means over. On the ebb the ice came down as before and now we no longer had the protection of the reef against the really big bergs. For the next five hours Bill stood by the winch letting out chain to 'ride' the blows of the bergs and taking it up again, while I steered against the force of the current, veering one way or the other to try to dodge the oncoming ice. From the cockpit I shone the Aldis lamp in accordance with directions from the bow, and put the tiller over at the last moment to see the huge white shape glide grudgingly past, scraping the planking and rocking the hull. But for the biggest this did not work. As the ship swung the mass of ice below water would catch the anchor chain, tauten it, and drag the ship forward to collide with a terrifying crash and spray the deck with chips of ice. At times two bergs would converge on the bows or the bowsprit shrouds, whipping the spar about almost to breaking point, or an eddy would sweep one round to hit unexpectedly on the quarter.

When dawn came the tide slackened and *Mischief* was still afloat. We started the engine, weighed anchor, and crept slowly towards the estimated position of the gap, weaving a way through the grounded floes. As I stood in the bows sounding every few yards the suspense was agonising – 6 fathoms, 5, 4, 3 – John standing by the engine ready to go full astern – $2\frac{1}{2}$, 2, 2, $2\frac{1}{2}$, 4, and we were over. We headed for Sea Lion bay, anchored, and slept for 14 hours.

On Sunday morning we returned to Ballast bay during slack tide at high water, and having anchored some 70 yards off shore began rowing off the ballast. We took off the skylight, rigged a derrick with one of the staysail booms, and with the jib halyard and the handy-billy were able to lift the pigs from the dinghy and lower them into the cabin in one operation. We had to get the job done before the next flood tide which would jam the bay full of ice, whereas during the ebb there was none.

The flood tide began running as we weighed, with all the ballast aboard and looking rather lop-sided, preparatory to returning to Sea Lion bay. Then the worst happened. Just as we came round into midstream the engine stopped. John, cursing wildly, got a few more spluttering revolutions out of it before it failed again. We were being carried back towards the reef. We hoisted sail, but there was not enough wind to stem the tide. Then the engine came to life again making a frightful knocking sound, but we made ground slowly heading in towards the bank where the current was not so strong. The knocking continued and water began pouring in round the propeller shaft. As soon as the engine was switched off the inrush of water subsided to a trickle but we then drifted towards the reef again.

Then the wind freshened. A head wind, but still a wind, and the ship began to gather way heeling over as we hauled in the sheets. Nervously we tacked back and forth, gaining ground each time, and keeping well in midstream until we could fetch Sea Lion bay. The next morning, with a fresh following wind, we sailed back to the anchorage in Mischief cove on the north side of Calvo bay.

CHAPTER FOURTEEN

The Pacific

Seamen are cautioned not to make free with these shores as they are very imperfectly known and from their wild desolate character they cannot be approached with safety. Caution (*Chart No. 24, Channels between the Gulf of Trinidad and Gulf of Peñas*)

THE leak at the inner end of the stern tube was only serious if the shaft was revolving. In the opinion of those on board this had been bent. Later at Valparaiso we found that the bracket supporting the outer end of the stern tube had been sheered through. From Michael's account it seems that the ice had almost sheered through it and then the short time for which the engine had been running had finished the job, so that the movement of the unsupported stern tube as the propeller revolved allowed water to pour in. The noise had no doubt been made by the bent propeller hitting the deadwood. Anyhow we could not run the engine. Neither *Maipo* nor any other ship could now help us. Only on a slip where she could be hauled out, or in a dry dock, could this trouble be cured.

To the north the nearest place with any facilities at all was Puerto Montt but we doubted whether its resources would be equal to the straightening of a bent propeller shaft. It was 700 miles away and Valparaiso, where we had to call for stores and mail and where there would be no lack of facilities, was only 400 miles further. Another plan, and probably the best, was to return to Punta Arenas, only 300 miles away, where we could count on the help of the navy. Bound south, as we should be, we should have better winds and moreover we knew the anchorages. I inclined to this plan but it would have involved great disappointment for the others who had set their hearts on seeing the west coast and making the round of South America.

Without an engine I had strong misgivings about the navigation of the nearly 200 miles of the remaining channels before we reached the open water of the Gulf of Peñas. Among these was the English Narrows, a narrow, tortuous reach about 11 miles long with a five knot current. In its middle section there is a critical point where steamers have to give a blast on their whistle and may only proceed if there is not an answering blast from an oncoming ship. However, we could avoid this and more than a hundred miles of channel navigation by going out into the Pacific by way of Canal Trinidad which opens off the main channels about 60 miles north of Puerto Bueno. So far to the south we might well meet with rough weather in the Pacific but as long as we could make a good offing we should be all right.

The day after our return, which was wet and windless, Procter went off to collect Charles but did not get back until 6 pm. Charles went at once to his bunk and remained there until we got to Valparaiso. His foot was in a worse state than I had imagined. One of the toes was in a bad way, the whole foot red and swollen with the poison threatening to spread up the leg. John took him in charge and finally cleared up the trouble by giving his reluctant patient a course of what we called 'bombs' – large tablets of terramycin, sinister yellow in colour, powerful enough to revive the dying and if used to excess to do the living very little good.

When a breeze sprang up after supper we weighed anchor. At midnight the wind died and morning found us over towards the western shore drifting among ice floes. All morning we kept the ice company. Three times we drifted round one enormous floe close enough to have to fend it off, and three times the monster (for which we had by then found a suitable but unprintable name) drifted round us. In the afternoon a fair wind gave us a fast and pleasant sail into and half-way up the main branch of Peel Inlet where we were at last clear of ice. Night was closing in when we turned from Peel into Pitt channel, the short cut to the north. That we intended sailing on all night through this narrow, scarcely used channel showed how hardened we had become to channel navigation. But we were also in a burning hurry to get on, and the fact that there was nowhere to anchor was an even more compelling reason. When morning came, bringing with it the typical channel weather of rain and head wind, Pitt Channel looked bleak, gloomy, and lifeless. The shores of Chatham Island on the one hand and the Wilcock peninsula on the other, are steep, rocky, and without much vegetation. A few cormorants were the only sign of life. I had been asked to inspect this coast of Chatham Island for signs of former Indian habitation, the middens of mussel shells which are often betrayed by the brighter green of the surrounding vegetation; but from the nature of the coast, the absence of coves and the scanty vegetation, it had been of little interest to such people.

The night set in wet and windy when we were still tacking between these two grim walls of rock and making good only about one mile in the hour. At midnight in heavy rain we cleared the dimly seen northern entrance by rounding a high, beetling crag, and turned westwards in Andrew Sound (Seno San Andres). Like Peel, this fjord extends eastwards into the mountains for more than 20 miles. As the weather was becoming very thick, we hove-to somewhere between the Kentish Isles and Chatham Island to see what the dawn would bring. The current appeared to run strongly and an unpleasant lop such as would be met in a tide race began breaking around us. Through the mist we could catch fleeting glimpses of high, rocky islands, and while waiting for it to clear, which it did about eight o'clock, the breeze of anxiety played very strong upon the brow of expectation.

We then had a good run down Seno San Andres to the main channel, which we entered some fifteen miles south of Canal Trinidad. In strong and increasing wind we began beating up to Portland bay at the south-western end of George Island 'a good and convenient anchorage for small vessels'. Just before sundown we could see that we were not going to fetch Portland bay until long after dark. We could have hove-to for the night, for there was room enough, but we had been on the go three nights, Michael and I, Procter and Jorge doing watch about, and we needed rest before beating out to sea by way of Canal Trinidad. On the west side of Canal Concepcion in which we now were, there were on Madre de Dios Island two possible anchorages, Molyneux bay and Tom bay, both marked by untended lights. Molyneux bay lay over on our port quarter so that it would be a broad reach and we might make it while there was still light enough to find our way in.

By this time, with the wind blowing very hard from the north-west, we were sailing with the main reefed, the whole jib, and no staysail. Running off before the wind we soon romped across to Molyneux Sound. In addition to the light on the northern entrance there is also a buoy marking the sunk 'Fawn' rock on which HMS *Fawn* struck in 1870. Leaving the buoy to starboard we had to stand on to the southern shore before going about and heading for the entrance to the bay. From the bay a wide valley runs inland and down it gusts of wind were being funnelled with terrible force. Perhaps it was with the hope of avoiding another tack that I had delayed so long when I put the helm down only about a cable's length from the rocky shore. *Mischief* came up into the wind sluggishly, missed stays, and hung there with everything flapping madly. Hoping to wear her round I put the helm up but with no more success. By the time she was head to wind again we were drifting backwards. The shore was now only about 30 yards away and if we went on drifting we seemed unlikely to clear it. The shore was steep-to, the water deep, and the bottom rocky. In this moment of crisis Procter ran forward and let go the anchor. More and more chain ran out – we found the depth was 20 fathoms – but at last to everyone's surprise the anchor took hold and the drift was stopped. Hastily we hoisted the staysail and shortened the cable. She was yawing about head to wind, and the moment she paid off on the port tack we let out the main sheet, wound frantically on the winch, and sailed off with the anchor and about 20 fathoms of cable dangling below. It had been a close call, with no one to blame but myself.

Such was the startling prelude to a very dirty night spent hove to in mid-channel. By morning the wind had dropped but the rain had increased. It took us four hours to beat back to Portland bay where we found good anchorage between two islands.

Canal Trinidad is the recommended way for north-bound vessels leaving the channels to avoid the English Narrows. As the *Pilot* says:

The frequent tempestuous weather and heavy seas experienced off the western entrance to the Straits of Magellan render the entrance into the Pacific by the route at times difficult even for full powered vessels. The weather and the sea in Canal Trinidad and its offing, about 150 miles northward of the Straits, are generally more moderate ... It is an excellent channel by which to pass out to the Pacific from the Patagonian channels, when the delay occasioned by Angostura Inglesa will be avoided. The depths in the entrance are not great, hence there is often a short rough sea even in fine weather.

After our recent alarming experience of beating into an anchorage under sail alone I was more determined than ever to get into the open sea; but the forty miles length of Canal Trinidad is open to the Pacific and since it trends north of west the prevailing wind would raise a big enough sea to make beating out against it a wearing business. But Canal Concepcion (we were now lying at its northern end) also leads to the Pacific, and since it runs west of south we should be sheltered from the Pacific swell by the islands of Madre de Dios and the Duke of York. We might even have a fair wind. The distance to the open sea was shorter this way, but we should enter it a degree further south in lat. 52° S.

After considering both routes we decided in favour of Canal Concepcion. We spent a wet morning renewing the rope tails of the wire topping lifts, repairing jib sheets, and clearing the deck of the useless oil drums. There is a peculiar satisfaction to be had in throwing things overboard and the bigger they are the better. The jettisoning of two 40 gal. drums of petrol was, I felt, a magnificently large gesture which gave me great pleasure at a time when pleasures were rare. As it was unlikely that we should be putting into any more Patagonian anchorages we collected a lot of mussels and began a futile hunt for duck. At two o'clock in light wind and rain we got our anchor and headed south-west. Off Moraine Island we streamed the log, as though we were already in the ocean.

By evening the wind had headed us (we thought this spiteful, for we were sailing south) and the night was spent beating into sharp hail squalls. As we forgot to take in the log it had fouled the propeller as we had gone about and was never recovered. The day continued in like fashion and by evening we were wondering whether to take shelter for the night – though none of the available coves looked inviting – when the sky cleared and the wind veered so that we could lay the course. Hardening our hearts we pressed on to the south-west. Early in the morning we were about five miles south of Cape Ladrillero, the southernmost point of the Duke of York Island. Now there was no land to the west of us nearer than New Zealand, and even that was further north. The wind was fresh, the sky cloudy, and a big swell was running, but since on the other tack we could steer no better than north we held south-west. At all costs we must get away from the coast. The weather thickened and soon we had seen the last of Cape Ladrillero. As the day advanced the wind increased to gale force bringing heavy rain and high seas.

This was the sort of rude welcome we had expected from the Pacific in this latitude. Jorge, who was now having his first experience of rough weather took to his bunk and stayed there; and that night I took his watch though feeling far from happy. Charles was already *hors de combat* and now John retired from the scene, too ill to cook. His illness was puzzling since he had never suffered before in bad weather, and it was not until Charles, turning over in his mind the theory of medicine, had recommended quinine, that he began to recover. Apparently it was a recurrence of malaria which he had contracted in Malaya when a prisoner of war. It could not have happened at a worse time than in these few days of storm and stress when only three of the crew were available both for work on deck and for the necessary cooking below.

Having already reefed right down, at midnight we hove to on the starboard tack; but early on the morning of 6 February the wind began to moderate and by midday we were under all plain sail. We were still on a WSW course and the log – for we had streamed our spare – showed 50 miles run since our last sighting of Ladrillero. During the night the wind backed and for the first time allowed us to make some northing. But the weather was by no means settled. Another gale blew up, compelling us to reef closely and also to put about, for we were being driven towards the land. If *Mischief* has a fault, it is a reluctance to go about in heavy weather. At the third attempt we got her round, but once more the log line wrapped itself round the propeller.

This was our worst night. Because we were tired and shorthanded we fought shy of getting the mainsail off and therefore hove to with it reefed right down instead of setting the storm trysail. But the task thus shirked had to be done in the end and then under worse conditions. In the early hours of the morning the leach of the mainsail split and it had to come down. Having stowed and lashed the sail we handed the storm jib and lay under bare poles in the trough of the sea, pointing south-west, thus trying to lessen the drift to the south-east.

Mischief lay there quite happily, taking each wave as it came and shipping very little water. Only occasionally when she was obliged to kick her stern high in the air was her dignity at all ruffled, for she is a wholesome seaboat. The happiness of the crew was less noticeable. Snugged down as she was, with nothing aloft to come adrift, we had no anxiety for the ship; nevertheless the fury and violence of the storm were intimidating. One's eyes became inured to looking out over a wild, angry waste of water; to watching the tumult of seas upon the horizon; and to seeing a wave rear high above the ship to break a few yards away and rush harmlessly by. But it was less easy to withstand the constant uproar – the steady menacing whine of the wind as it tore through the rigging, rising with each gust to a fierce scream; the mournful undertone of protesting creaks and groans from the ship; and the sinister hiss of waves as they broke and creamed by under the lifted counter.

Short-handed as we were and faced by a prospect of repeated north-westerly winds or gales it seemed to me doubtful whether we should be able to beat northward into more genial latitudes. To make any northing at all we had first to bend the spare mainsail, for she would not work to windward under the trysail. I began toying with the idea of hoisting the trysail and running south in order to reach the Atlantic by way of Cape Horn. The stores awaiting us at Valparaiso were of little importance and now that we were in open water the repair of the propeller could wait. In fact, so long as we did not have to go through the Panama Canal it could wait until we got home. But neither Procter nor Michael cared much for this idea and in the event they were right. We agreed to struggle on for at least three or four more days hoping for a favourable slant of wind before finally committing ourselves to the daunting prospect of rounding Cape Horn.

Meanwhile, we had very little idea of how far off or rather how near the coast was. The wind had been mostly from north-west and as the set in this latitude is easterly, I was fearful that we might sight land to the east at any time. In the course of the morning the weather improved and the sun came out. The rough and ready noon sight which I got put us in lat. 51° 30'S. not so far south as I had expected. The deck watch had not been checked for many weeks; indeed, since leaving Punta Arenas we had, more than once, forgotten to wind it, for there was no need to take sights in the channels. The charging engine had broken down and the battery was flat so that we could not get time signals. Sights, therefore, were no help in finding our longitude, but by taking the sun when it was on the meridian (which we could find by trial) we could at least find our latitude. When we had reached the latitude of Valparaiso we would close the land.

In the afternoon we began sailing under trysail and storm jib on a south-westerly course. Our most urgent task was to unbend the torn mainsail. Working on the reeling deck with the wet, heavy canvas was not easy, but by evening we had the sail folded in an unwieldy heap and lashed it on top of the deck water tank between the cabin skylight and the companion way. Next day the wind was still north-west and the sea still ran high, but the sun was shining. The spare mainsail, a brand new sail, had to be got up from its home in the galley. It took three men to lift it. Jorge, who had now got his sea legs, took the helm while the three of us pushed it by main force through the cabin door and out on to the deck. When we stopped for lunch it was bent and ready for hoisting and in the afternoon it went up to the cheers of the crew. A fine sight it was – this great spread of new white canvas. We unreefed the staysail, hoisted the working jib, put the ship about, and steered north.

All night – the stars showing for the first time for many days – we steered north with a moderate breeze and a lumpy sea. In the morning, Procter poking about hopefully under the counter with our home-made gaff retrieved the log-line with the rotator still on it. The quite unexpected recovery of this useful instrument, the weather, and above all the northerly course, had a wonderfully cheering effect, and our satisfaction in watching the steady climb of the barograph needle was checked only by the thought that what goes up must come down. A week had passed since we had reached the open sea and now at last we began to reel off the miles northwards. On the first day 64 miles, rising to 144 on our best day, and averaging 92 for the twelve days between the recovery of the log and our arrival at Valparaiso.

Now that we could look forward to fine and increasingly warm weather, fair winds, and a good kick from the Humboldt current, we could heartily con-gratulate ourselves on not having attempted to go south about. John was up and about, only poor Charles remained prone, barely able to put his bad foot to the ground. Our felicity was only a little marred by the absence of electric light. In the cabin we used an oil lamp but the binnacle had to be lit with a slow-burning carriage candle. As one candle did not quite last the night the man on watch had to change it, a tricky job when we were running before the wind when he could only leave the helm for a matter of seconds.

In these latitudes in the Pacific there seemed to be less life than in the Atlantic. We saw neither fish, porpoises, nor whales. Albatross of various kinds were the commonest birds. Many of them were immature. There is a striking difference between the sight of an albatross in majestic flight and an albatross resting on the water. Family parties of four or five used to sit in a close circle facing each other, and looked comically frumpish and dowdy. They seldom followed in the wake of the ship, but preferred sitting on the water to watch us go by and after a due interval flying ahead of us to settle down for another look.

The Humboldt current, which flows northwards up the coast from about lat. 43°S. nearly to the equator, did not give us the boost we had expected. The air became daily warmer but owing to this cool current the water temperature remained at about 60 degrees. We started bathing again and shed our long Patagonia underpants. Every day we had been expecting to raise the coast but we must have been much further west than we reckoned. However, when a meridian altitude put us in lat. 33° 30′S. we set a course for the Punta Angeles light on the south side of Valparaiso bay, and on the night of 23 February, a fine moonlight night, picked it up dead on the bow. At dawn when the light was close abeam the wind failed and fog came down. We lay becalmed in the midst of a fleet of small, open boats busy fishing off the edge of a reef running north-west from Punta Angeles. Our arrival had evidently been noticed by the lighthouse keeper before the fog closed down, for an imaginative newspaper reported us as 'drifting helpless and exhausted in the last extremity of thirst'. All morning, while the foghorn boomed from the lighthouse, we were a source of free entertainment to the fishermen as we lay waiting for someone to give us a tow. Finally, one of them took Procter ashore and soon after a harbour launch came out, towed us in, and left us in splendid isolation tied to an enormous buoy.

CHAPTER FIFTEEN

Valparaiso to the Panama Canal

Many thousand miles behind us
Many thousand miles before
Sea Chanty

VALPARAISO BAY, edged for half its length by the city and backed in the distance by the Cordillera, is a fine piece of water. Unluckily it is open to the north, a quarter from which in winter some fierce storms blow. There is an inner harbour where big ships may lie protected by an outer wall; but when a norther blows, waves sweep over the wall and the swell makes the quay side untenable. The bay is so deep that the prolongation of the outer wall to gain further protection would be a vast undertaking. Looking at the town from the bay one wonders how it got its name. It lies along the foot of a high ridge, straggling a little way up the slopes. There is not any sign of valley and not the vaguest resemblance to paradise. One wonders, too, where the busy part of the town lies, for there appears to be nothing between the water-front and the half-finished streets which peter out on the arid slopes behind. On landing one finds that the business and shopping centres are strung out for a mile or more along a narrow strip of flat ground at the foot of the slopes, and that this is connected by lifts with the steep residential quarter. At least this used to be the residential quarter, but the most favoured spot now is Viña del Mar, a few miles north along the coast.

For several days we lay alongside the outer wall among the fleet of small trawlers. The harbour is filthy and very soon the ship, the warps, and even our clothes were covered with a film of black oil. Later we anchored off the Yacht Club. Here the water was equally dirty and although we saved our warps we had to use the dinghy to go ashore so that that became smeared with oil. The dinghy caused some amusement. It was clinker built and after its bashing in the ice each plank had long whiskers of wood fibre sticking from it, so that when we had it bottom-up on the deck preparatory to painting, an interested onlooker asked if we were going to shave it. The Yacht Club shared its premises with the rowing clubs – British, German, Italian, French, Chilean. The city fire service, by the way, is organised on similar lines. Each of these communities runs a voluntary fire brigade, and the rivalry in smartness of turn-out and efficiency is intense. Of the three activities – rowing, putting out fires, and yachting – the last seemed the least popular. Owing to what seem to be rather grandmotherly restrictions, yachting in Chile does not flourish. Unless the owner or skipper of a yacht has a certificate of competency in navigation and seamanship, for which he must pass an examination, he cannot take his boat more than a few miles from the harbour. The result is that there are very few sea-going yachts.

The British consul (Mr Dobson) put himself to endless trouble on our behalf, and both he and the director of the Instituto Chileno Britanico (Mr Grant Robertson) extended great hospitality. Through the consul I got in touch with Lloyd's surveyor (Mr James Dobbie, DSC) who arranged for *Mischief* to go into the floating dock. This dock has a remarkable history. In our edition of the *South America Pilot* (1941) it figures as 'reported sunk and will probably become a total loss'. During a norther the dock did capsize and sink with a ship inside (the dock is 350ft. long); the ship remained on the bottom, but the dock was raised by her present owner (Señor Corsson), the head of a large ship repair yard. As there are no slipways capable of taking small fishing boats or large yachts, these are often hoisted out of the water by crane. There was a crane capable of lifting *Mischief*, but even if the inside ballast was first removed the hoisting of her on a couple of slings might well have strained her.

Mischief in company with three large trawlers was not due to go into dock until mid-March, so we had time on our hands. Apart from the sending up of the top mast, painting the deck, and having the charging engine put right, there were no major jobs to be done. This enabled the crew, in turns, to spend a few days in Santiago. Here we were able to visit Jorge in his home, and also from the comfort of a car belonging to the Hon. H. A. Hankey of the British Embassy to see something of the peaks and glaciers of the Central Andes at fairly close quarters. Charles betook himself to a hotel, for according to the doctor's report it did not seem likely that he would be able to finish the voyage in *Mischief*. Michael spent a lot of time at the Seamen's Institute, not so much because of the seamen who frequented it as the several kindly disposed girls who on certain evenings offered their services as dancing partners in the hope of keeping seamen away from the less reputable places. The Institute was presided over by a Mr Henry Boys, a Yorkshireman who had spent most of his life in Chile and who did us many kindnesses.

In due time we entered the dock in the wake of the three German trawlers. The dock rose, and *Mischief* was high and dry. Her propeller shaft was taken to the workshop and found to be undamaged; only the propeller blades needed welding and aligning. The hull was in surprisingly good order, almost free from weed and barnacles, but we used the opportunity to have it scraped and repainted with anti-fouling paint kindly given to us by a shipowner (Señor Alfredo Gubbins). The dock superintendent contributed paint for her topsides, so that *Mischief* emerged from the dock looking most raffish with a bright yellow topsides and a dark green underbody. The dockmaster, Mr Blatt, a Rumanian refugee who had once been master of a vessel, was a genial soul and well disposed towards us. He liked the British. This was all the more strange because we had not been able to do much for him in return for his war-time services to us in the Mediterranean. It was, I fear, a consequence of this preference that the bill for painting *Mischief* must unwittingly have been paid by the owners of the German trawlers which were having their hulls scraped and painted at the same time. Mr Dobbie superintended the refitting of the shaft and the propeller, and thanks to his good offices and the generosity of the owner of the dock we paid nothing whatever for its use or for the repairs which in all fairness should have cost us a very large sum. Such are the extraordinary kindnesses which visiting yachtsmen receive in foreign parts.

On Friday, 23 March, after five days in the dock we motored out and tied up to a buoy. We were now ready for sea and only waited for a young Chilean, George de Giorgio, who was to come with us to England in place of Charles. He had been in his father's yacht as far as the South Seas and the Florida coast and was therefore an experienced sailor. He lived at the small fishing port of Quinteros on the other side of the bay from us, and as at one time I had thought of going there to pick him up I had put Quinteros on our clearance papers as our immediate destination. After his name had been put on our crew list he found his passport needed renewing. Chilean officialdom refused to be hurried. In spite of threats by George's father of speaking to the President himself by telephone, the port authorities struck his name off our crew list. I was determined to sail that day. Postponement meant making out a fresh lot of papers and I was heartily sick of Valparaiso and the attendant troubles of a long stay in port.

I gave George until five o'clock to see what he could do. When the hour came we started hoisting sail but, luckily for George, we were unable to cast off as Mr Dobbie was still on board. He had come to say good-bye and his launch had broken down half-way between ship and shore. The launch finally came alongside at the same time as did another carrying the excited

George. He had got his passport, but as the port office had closed he had not been able to have his name restored to the crew list. All this bother had aroused some interest. A port official came with him in the launch to see that there was no funny business, so I dared not take him with us from Valparaiso. I, therefore, made a hasty arrangement to pick him up at Quinteros and told him to expect us at midnight.

On the south side of Quinteros bay there is a high promontory with a lighthouse. Approaching this just before midnight we saw the headlights of a car climbing the steep road to the lighthouse. George's father was evidently on the look-out, so we gave him a signal with our Aldis lamp for we had no lights showing. Having rounded the cape and entered the small harbour we heard the chug of an engine. A launch appeared out of the night, a kit bag was flung on board, and George followed. Still under way, we turned and headed out to sea.

The run to Callao, a distance of some 1,200 miles, was done in eleven days. The first day was remarkable in that we sighted a solitary sperm whale and also the snows of Aconcagua about 110 miles away. After our long stay in port both Michael and I were sea-sick. We started promisingly with a fresh southerly wind and in a few days we picked up the south-east trades. We hoisted the twins and bowled along at six knots, while *Mischief's* tiller gave little shivers of delight, like a favourite dog waiting for a walk. But owing to the cool Humboldt current we had not the sparkling seas and the radiant days such as we had delighted in, in the north-east trades. The sky remained obstinately overcast. Neither was it 'flying-fish weather'. Apart from one solitary monster weighing a good ¾lb. which came over the stern on the second night, we caught none and saw few. A less welcome visitor was a rat which had evidently joined the ship when we were in dock. We heard him moving about at night and later we found a large hole eaten in the Genoa and the beginnings of a nest. A night or so later we trapped him.

We were well out to sea now and the few sea birds we saw were essentially albatross and the little black storm petrels, but soon an increasing number of cormorants told us that we were approaching the Peruvian coast. This is rich in bird life, particularly so around the Chincha Islands where there are great guano deposits. When we saw the first cormorants we must have been still a hundred miles from land. I took particular note of the distance because of a reference to cormorants in the *South America Pilot*. Referring to the approach to the Falkland Islands it says: 'Penguins may be seen and heard as much as 300 miles from land; they need not, therefore, cause any alarm; the presence of cormorants, however, is well worth noting, as these birds are rarely seen more than ten miles offshore.'

We began to see birds in undreamt-of-numbers. There were many types of gulls but in particular cormorants and pelicans. In the air they looked like trails of smoke or swarms of locusts and when they settled their multitudes covered many acres of sea. More than one cormorant landed on our deck to stay for half an hour or more preening his feathers and allowing himself to be fondled as well as photographed. The pelicans were quite as ludicrous as were the steamer ducks. Long strings of them zoomed past us in single file, their heads and beaks drawn back and chests thrown out, suggesting a file of slightly pompous city aldermen. To settle on the water they merely folded their wings and did a sort of belly-flop sending up a cloud of spray. Their take-off was equally clumsy. In addition there were penguins and vast numbers of boobies or gannets. The latter are always worth watching, particularly when making their spectacular dives. In his book *Autobiography of a Bird-lover* Dr F. M. Chapman gives a graphic description of the bird life in these waters, and of a remarkable 'barrage of boobies' which he witnessed.

As for the birds, who can describe them in their incalculable myriads? Visible link in the chain of life that begins with diatoms nourished by the cool, highly oxygenated waters of the Humboldt current, they animate both the sea and the air. No other coastline of similar extent can show an avian population equalling that of Peru.

On 28 November 1918, off the port of Salaverry where my Red Cross mission had taken me, whichever way one looked from our anchorage, birds could be seen in countless numbers fishing in dense excited flocks, passing in endless files from one fishing ground to another, or massed in great rafts on the sea.

Seaward, like aerial serpents, sinuous files crawled through the air in repeated curves, while low over the waters processions passed rapidly, steadily, hour after hour, with rarely a break in their ranks during the entire day. At times the flocks were composed of cormorants; at others they were composed of white-bodied, brown-winged boobies.

When the birds stopped to feed, the scene commanded the attention of every passenger aboard the ship. The cormorants fished from the surface in a sea of small fry. Swimming and diving, they gobbled voraciously until their storage capacity was reached. Then they floated in dense black masses waiting for the process of digestion to give space for further gorging.

The boobies fished from the air, plunging into the water with great force from an average height of 50ft. to disappear in a jet of spurting spray as they hit the surface. In endless cataracts they poured into the sea. It was a curtain of spearheads, a barrage of birds.

In certain years a warm, southerly counter-current flows down the coast of Peru raising the temperature of the water by ten degrees and more. This is enough to upset the generally stable oceanic conditions. The fish and most of the small living organisms associated with cool waters die, and great numbers of birds die or migrate in consequence. Sharks, tropical dolphins, flying fish, and jumping mantas or giant rays, appear in waters where they are never normally seen. Associated with the phenomenon of the warm current is another known as the 'Callao Painter', a sulphuretted emanation from the sea which darkens the white paint of ships and tarnishes the silver in houses close to the shore. It is thought to be caused by the death of vast numbers of organisms which then give off the gases of decomposition.

The infrequent influx of this warm current (known locally as Corriente del Nino, because it usually begins about the time of Christmas) seriously affects not only the fishing but also the guano industry. The story of the exploitation of the guano deposits on the Chincha Islands is told in Murphy's *Ocean Birds of South America* and is of interest. The remarkable effect of guano as a fertiliser was known to the Incas and to their Spanish conquerors. Early in the nineteenth century, as it was not found elsewhere, it became one of the chief exports of Peru. In 1840 only twenty barrels were brought to England, but a few years later, when the earlier prejudice to it had been overcome, it was in general use and the guano trade had become a huge commercial interest. In 1847 an official Peruvian survey put the deposits on the Chincha Islands at some 23 million tons, the depth of the deposit being 55 metres. At the estimated rate of consumption these deposits would last 170 years. Six years later the deposits had been reduced to a mere 8 million tons and the sales of guano accounted for more than half the total revenue of the Peruvian government. In 1860 no less than 433 large sailing ships loaded guano at the Chinchas and before 1870 the deposits were worked out. It was a time when 'guano fever burnt as fiercely as gold fever, when the Chinchas were a focus of greed and corruption; a centre of dust-gagged misery and slavery as well as of important business ventures represented by calculating Yankee and British sea captains, and by costly ships with towering spars'. At that time the guano was dug by coolies who sweated out their lives on these barren, rainless islands under the lashes of black overseers. Guano is now, as then, a government monopoly, but the working of it is carefully controlled, each island being taken in rotation after a two to three years rest. The amount taken out annually is about a quarter million tons.

On the evening of 4 April Isla San Lorenzo on the south-west side of Callao bay appeared on the bow. With a leading wind we had another glorious moonlight sail round the north end of the island and across the wide bay. The usual difficulty of sorting out sea and shore lights and identifying the harbour lights, was not made any easier by the absence of an important red-flashing buoy at the entrance to the channel. Moving slowly up the channel with the sea wall close on our starboard hand, we saw at last the masts of a great fleet of yachts and we anchored outside them in six fathoms at three o'clock in the morning. The noise of our cable running out woke two fishermen in a rowing boat, who now discovered that their net was wrapped round *Mischief*'s bows. This premature hauling of their net proved quite fruitful, and after disentangling ourselves we bought some fish.

Callao is merely the port for Lima, the capital, which lies eight miles inland. We arrived early on the Thursday morning and we left on Saturday evening, the shortest and least troublesome stay of any we had had. Would that they had all been like that! In duty bound we went up to Lima, Pizarro's 'City of the Kings'. There is an electric tramway to it but the better way is to take a taxi. One merely piles in and the taxi leaves as soon as it is full. No one thinks of taking a taxi to himself.

The climate of Lima is not attractive. According to the guidebook rain rarely falls, but it might have added that the sun rarely shines. For more than half the year the weather is dull, and considering the latitude, only 12 degrees south of the equator, uncommonly cool. On many days there is a fog almost as wetting as rain, and on the day of our visit rain fell heavily. All this cloud and fog is attributable to the cool Humboldt current. Possibly on a clear sunny day, when the neighbouring foothills and the high Andes are both visible, the first city of South America might appear worthy of its setting. For some reason I could never accustom myself to thinking of South American towns as old; yet the Lima Cathedral was begun before Henry VIII died. It was founded by Pizarro and in one of the chapels is a glass vase containing what are believed to be the bones of that fierce conqueror. Fires, earthquakes, and wars, civil and foreign, have not left much of the old architecture and what has taken its place is not remarkable.

So far as trade and currency go Peru is free, like Uruguay, but for those bold spirits who think or say that such freedom is not enough, accommodation is found in a prison on Isla San Lorenzo. Near the quay there was a combined tobacco and trinket shop, with a 'cambio' which would change our traveller's cheques for dollars over the counter; whereas to cash a cheque in a South American bank was a lengthy operation which seemed almost to necessitate calling a board meeting.

On Saturday we came alongside the Club landing stage for water, petrol, and the fresh stores we had ordered. In view of the belt of calms north of the equator and the calms which at that time of year before the rainy season prevail in the Gulf of Panama, we expected to use the engine a lot. In addition to the full tanks, therefore, we took a drum on deck, but after we had lashed it down we discovered a leak. It was a Saturday afternoon and there was no finding the supplier in order to get it changed. But a stranger standing on the Club steps came to our rescue; drove me round Callao in his station waggon until we found a sound drum, and then would not let me pay for it. He turned out to be a Dutchman who had left Holland as a youth in the first World War and was now a missionary among the Indians.

Quite a large crowd had gathered on the landing stage to see us start. There seemed to me to be more than an even chance of our giving a repeat performance of what had happened at Punta Arenas on a Saturday afternoon; nevertheless, we were determined to leave behind a favourable impression of our seamanship by sailing out. We were lying alongside the stage head to wind with only a few yards of deep water between our bow and the sea wall, the way out running parallel to the wall and down a narrow lane bounded on the other side by a line of moored yachts. We made the mistake of not hoisting the jib as well as the staysail and mainsail. When we cast off and pushed the bow out she began forging ahead rather quickly instead of paying off, so that when she finally did swing round the stem missed by inches the blocks of concrete sunk at the foot of the wall. The shrill warning cries from the landing stage were superfluous, for what might happen was all too clear. But we held on, outwardly calm, as though such delicate manoeuvres were a matter of course with us. *Mischief* did not fail, and with gathering speed she bore away down the channel.

North of Callao sailing should be pleasantly quiet. Gales are almost unknown, the weather is variable enough to keep interest alive, and the heat is not oppressive. Since gales are not expected one becomes, perhaps, a little careless, so that once again we managed to blow out the clew of the Genoa by carrying it at night. We found more life in the sea here than in the corresponding latitudes in the Atlantic. Whales were often seen and one big sperm whale surfaced so close to the ship that his spout covered us with spray. The sight of seagulls perched on what looked like small rocks was a little disturbing until we found they were standing on the backs of turtles. We caught a dorado and lost two more while trying to get them on board. George harpooned a squid. This was the ugliest creature imaginable, with a horny parrot beak, prominent eyes, and ten long arms with suckers on the under-side. The two longest arms are used for grabbing his prey while the other eight serve the purpose of knife, fork, and spoon. He weighed about 60lb. Off Cape Blanco we went close inshore in the hope of catching a really big fish, for these waters are reputed to be the best in the world for big game fishing. The largest fish ever caught on a rod, a black marlin weighing 1,135lb., was caught here in 1952. Except for a prolific growth of oil derricks and oil tanks the coast hereabouts is barren.

Longer periods of calms, thunderstorms, and heavy rain, heralded our approach to the Gulf of Panama. When we were still 60 miles from land numbers of swallows and dragon-flies came on board. On 24 April we sighted Cape Marzo, a bold rugged headland on the eastern side of the entrance to the gulf. A strong current sets in here, circles the head of the gulf as if in a basin, and then flows out southwards past the western entrance. We drifted 30 miles in the course of the night and spent a jolly day drifting and sailing northwards with the Pearl Islands close on our port hand. As pearl fisheries the islands once rivalled those of Bahrein in the Persian Gulf. They looked like a beach-comber's paradise – waving palms, little beaches of dazzling white sand, and the warm blue water gently lapping a shore 'where slumber is more sweet than toil, than labour in the deep mid-ocean.'

Once they were visited by men of very different ideas. They brought to my mind *Westward Ho!* which opens with John Oxenham and Salvation Yeo busy recruiting men for a wild adventure which so nearly succeeded. Oxenham had been Drake's second in command when they captured the treasure train in Darien, when together they had looked out upon the Pacific and prayed that God would give them leave and life to sail upon it in an English ship. In this great resolve Oxenham anticipated Drake by three years. In 1575, having made the coast near Nombre de Dios in a ship of 140 tons with a crew of seventy, he concealed the ship with branches of trees and marched inland with all the men dragging two small cannons. On reaching a river that ran into the Gulf of Panama they built a 45ft. pinnace, sailed into the gulf, and landed on one of the Pearl islands. They got very few pearls but after lying in wait for ten days they took a small bark from Peru laden with a staggering sum of gold. 'When you strike oil, stop boring' is a sound maxim, but Oxenham was not satisfied. In a week they took another ship laden with silver bars, but by then the hornet's nest had been properly stirred. News of their activities had reached Panama and a strong force was out looking for them. The story goes that the Spaniards discovered the river Oxenham's men had followed by the number of hen's feathers floating down! The Spaniards recovered the bulk of the treasure while Oxenham and his men were away relaying part of it to their ship. An attempt to retake it was beaten off with heavy loss and meanwhile another party of Spanish soldiers from Nombre de Dios found the ship. In the end all the Englishmen were either killed or taken, Oxenham himself being sent to Lima for judgment. There, after frankly admitting that this was a piece of private enterprise and that he had not the Queen's license, he was executed. Whatever their motive, love of fame, greed of gold, lure of discovery, or hatred of Spain and its religion, the Elizabethan seamen possessed boundless hope, courage, self-reliance, and endurance, of which the like has never since been seen.

After rounding the northernmost island we met a strong breeze from the west and beat up against it till nightfall when we raised the lights of Balboa. Motoring on past a number of ships waiting to enter the canal we were presently picked up by the beam of a searchlight and stopped by a launch. We followed this to an anchorage where the port health officer boarded us. Having nothing else to do he sat yarning until two am and we were not sorry when the arrival of another ship called him back to duty. In the morning, after *Mischief* had been measured for canal dues, we tied up at a wooden jetty while I went to the canal offices to pay. Having parted with the modest sum of 13 dollars I got back to the ship just as our canal pilot arrived, whereupon we cast off and followed a German steamer the eight miles to the Miraflores locks.

Steamers are hauled in and out of the locks by electric 'mules' and are held in the middle by six wire warps, but a comparative mite like *Mischief* merely lies alongside the lock wall, the mast barely showing over the top and the crosstrees almost scraping it. As the water enters the lock there is a considerable surging and the pilot had to watch our bow and stern lines carefully while we stood by to ease or tighten them. We also kept the engine running. The two Miraflores locks raise a ship 54ft. to the Miraflores lake. We had to wait here pending the arrival of a south-bound ship which was being towed. (The canal, of course, trends from south to north, or slightly west of north, and not from west to east as one might expect.) While waiting we housed the bowsprit – that is, we ran it in-board – and it was well we did. The Pedro Miguel lock a mile further on raises the water 31ft. to the level of the Culebra Cut, the highest level reached, 85ft. above sea-level. In this lock we surged about so much that the bowsprit would certainly have been damaged had we not housed it. All the lock gates are doubled as a precaution against ramming, and in front of them is a heavy chain which sinks as the gates open and automatically arrests or slows down a ship that is travelling too fast. In addition the locks themselves are duplicated.

The eight miles long Culebra Cut debouches into Gatun lake, an artifical lake covering an area of 164 square miles on whose surface half submerged hillocks and trees can be seen. We crossed it in the dark, the channel being so well lit, with pairs of leading lights at the bends, that it was like motoring up Piccadilly. Our pilot paced up and down our twenty feet of deck space like a caged lion, urging us to give her all we could. We did our best but *Mischief's* speed under power is only four to five knots and it was midnight before we reached Gatun, hours behind the last north bound ship. So we anchored for the night and our pilot went ashore to sleep in an air-conditioned room. Steamers pass through the lake at eight to ten knots, the whole transit taking seven hours from Balboa to Cristobal.

Having taken on an Atlantic side pilot we got under way about noon when the first of the ships from the Pacific entered the lock. There are three locks at Gatun to lower a ship the 85ft. to the Atlantic. As we descended the surge did not seem so strong as when we had been raised, but as we left the lowest lock the powerful currents demanded full use of the helm to prevent *Mischief* being swept to the side. At Cristobal, six miles from the locks, we moored off the Yacht Club among a number of other sea-going yachts, some of them bound on long passages. There was an Austrian in a double-ender bound for the South Seas single handed who, as we heard, had made a spectacular arrival. Disdaining to anchor, he had jumped overboard and swum ashore with his mooring warp. There were also two young Englishmen in a 21ft. sloop called *Skaffie* which had been badly damaged when crossing the Atlantic. They were bound for New Zealand but owing to shortage of funds for repairs they contemplated giving up the voyage and selling her.

CHAPTER SIXTEEN

Rolling Home

The bunks were hard and the watches long,
The winds were foul, the trip was long.
'Leave Her Johnny' Sea Chanty

ALTHOUGH Cristobal is in the canal zone one has merely to cross a road to reach Colon in Panama. I think it is probably worth while to cross this road occasionally just for the sake of exchanging clean, quiet propriety for bustling life and rowdy squalor. In Cristobal one might as well be in a well-planned garden city in Utopia, only without any shops. In Cristobal the tourist can only buy stamps whereas in Colon there is pretty well everything except rotators for patent logs. George bought a very fine green-eyed stuffed alligator which he polished assiduously with brown boot polish all the way home.

Since we did not expect to reach England before 1 July, by which time Michael's leave would have expired, he had to go home by steamer. Although he had taken the trouble to provide himself with a visa for Panama, the American authorities would not let him disembark at Cristobal, cross the road, and stay at a hotel in Colon. They insisted that if he once left *Mischief* he would have to go to a sort of local 'Ellis Island' and remain there until he embarked. To avoid this semi-imprisonment we transferred him to *Skaffie's* crew list where he nominally lived until his ship arrived. However, authority made some amends for this piece of far-flung bumbledom by allowing me to buy provisions from the canal commissary, the canal employees' emporium for everything from food and clothing to children's toys.

On 1 May, having got our clearance papers, we sailed for Bermuda by way of the Yucatan channel and Florida straits. This route had been suggested by 'the Master', for unless one is going to call at the West Indies it is the best way for sailing ships to leave the Caribbean. Over this sea the north-east trades blow strongly, so that a yacht making for either the Windward Passage east of Cuba or the Mona Passage east of San Domingo must face a beat to windward of more than 700 miles.

For the first three or four days, sailing close-hauled with a wind of force 4 or 5 in a rough sea, none of us felt at our best. We had been wafted smoothly along by breezes from astern, or from abaft the beam, for too long to take kindly to windward sailing. We felt hardly used; our sympathies were entirely with the unknown fair one:

> Oh, for a fair and gentle wind:
> I heard a fair one cry:
> But give to me the snoring breeze
> And white waves leaping high.

The rotator of our patent log had been taken by a shark in the Gulf of Panama, and as we had been unable to get another in Colon we could only estimate the day's run; and each man as he came off watch entered in the log what he thought the ship had done in his watch. A sudden and unaccountable set of 25 miles to the east shook my own confidence as well as that of the crew in my calculations, and let loose a sustained outburst of star, planet, and moon shooting. I had wished to get well to windward of the Mosquito Bank and had perhaps allowed too much for leeway; this new position, however, enabled us to lay a better course direct for Cape San Antonio at the western end of Cuba.This brought the wind free and hereafter sailing became very pleasant.

On the 10th in a flat calm, and shortly before a tropical deluge opened on us, we sighted the Cape Antonio lighthouse. Before the current running north out of the Caribbean sets westwards as the Gulf Stream it enters and circles the Gulf of Mexico, so that if there is no wind a ship can only drift northwards. The next four days, until we got into the Gulf Stream proper, were exasperating and unrewarding. We drifted and sailed north almost into the Gulf of Mexico close to the Dry Tortugas, and then worked our way back again to the coast of Cuba not far from Habana. Going about, we once more headed north and presently we began to feel the effect of the stream. As we neared Florida the lights on its well-lit coast slid past us as though we were in a train. It had taken us a fortnight to get into the Gulf Stream, but it was worth it. Here, in the Florida Straits in the axis of the stream we got a lift of some seventy miles a day. Even well to the north of this we were enough under its influence to benefit to the extent of some forty miles a day.

Off the Florida coast we nearly always had several ships in sight, mostly tankers – even more traffic, I thought, than one would meet in the English Channel. Gulf Stream weather is notoriously unsettled. We experienced calms, light north-easterlies and some terrifying electrical storms with forked lightening stabbing the sky in all directions. A strong norther in the Gulf Stream, blowing as it would against the current, raises a short and irregular sea dangerous to small craft. Even in calm weather we saw some very queer tide tips and over-falls with stretches of smooth water between.

It might have paid us to have stayed in the Gulf Stream almost as far as Cape Hatteras before turning east for Bermuda; for when we quitted it in lat. 29° we met mainly contrary winds. On three successive days, although the glass rose steadily the whole time, we had winds of nearly gale force blowing straight at us from the direction of Bermuda,

At last, thirty days out from Cristobal, we sighted the islands. By evening we were close under Gibb's Hill lighthouse at the south-east end of Hamilton island. In the morning we were still there, for the wind had failed. Starting the engine we chugged quietly along, with the island close to port, admiring the scenery and criticising the ugly and abominably expensive hotels. Steering light-heartedly for the buoys marking the entrance to the channel through the reef, we neglected to check our position by cross bearing. Someone had just remarked upon the increasing paleness of the water when *Mischief* groaned twice and came protestingly to a standstill. Where was now our care-free mood? Crestfallen and with gnawing anxiety we began to unlash the dinghy preparatory to running out a kedge anchor. But before we could launch it two grinning Bermudians came up in a motor boat to tell us they had been bawling themselves hoarse to warn us we were standing in to danger. More to the purpose they added that the tide was making. We got off soon after and followed them back to the channel a quarter of a mile away. After that humiliating experience we diligently picked up, identified, and ticked off in the *Pilot* every buoy – and there must be more than fifty – marking the long, tortuous channel to Hamilton Harbour, a distance of nearly 20 miles.

There are 360 islands or islets in the Bermudas but of these only twenty are inhabited or, one supposes, inhabitable. It is a pity that the people of Hamilton cannot be dispersed over some of the other 240. Although the houses are widely scattered – and very gay they are with their white-washed roofs, pink-washed walls, and windows picked out in blue or yellow – there is hardly a spot in the island which is not overlooked by a house or houses. Perhaps the blight which since the war has killed nearly all the trees (the so-called Bermuda cedar) partly accounts for this feeling of nakedness. The white-washed roofs are a singular feature. It is done, we were told, on account of the water. Rain water is the sole source of supply, and each house has an underground storage tank in which the water off the roof is collected. Whitewash is a panacea for a good many things, but does it purify water? Perhaps, as Tallulah Bankhead remarked, there is less in this than meets the eye.

The ban on motor traffic which had been operating up to the last war did not withstand for long the impact of war and the consequent opening of the American base. The ban might with advantage have been extended to include the harbour traffic where the peace of the many is destroyed by the few who tear round on water skis behind fast motor boats. The sight most worth seeing in Bermuda is the racing of the Bermuda 'fitted' dinghies. This is a class peculiar to Bermuda. The dinghies are 14ft. long. They have a 14ft. bowsprit and a boom which projects over the counter almost as far. They carry 500 square feet of sail and are manned by a crew of six or seven, every man of whom is needed, I imagine, to keep the boat upright and to help with the baling. In light winds it is permissible to jettison some of this human ballast.

In a few days we were ready to begin the last leg. The only major repair had been the welding and rebolting of the gammon iron which supports the bowsprit. Now that Michael had left, only Proctor, George, and myself were available for watch-keeping, though John made it easier for us by taking a watch in the afternoon. We sailed on 7 June.

By great circle course the distance from Bermuda to the Scillies is 3,353 miles. We did it in thirty-two days and for most of the way we had generous gales of wind and usually from a favourable direction. The passage was marked by a number of minor mishaps, attributable sometimes to our own folly or laziness and sometimes to the wearing out of the running rigging on the last few thousand miles of a twenty thousand mile voyage. The first, which might have been more serious, occurred a few days out early one morning in my watch. We had been running all night with whole mainsail and a twin boomed out. When I took over she was rolling and yawing wildly, but probably no more than she had been doing during the night. At length the gybe which I was beginning to fear happened. For a moment the wire boom guy held the boom high in the air; then it broke, and the boom crashed over wrapping the main sheet round the horse and breaking the back-stay tackle. The staysail was flat aback as well, so that when the crew tumbled up in response to my yell they were not a little startled by my new arrangements. With the mainsheet round the horse it was impossible for us to haul the boom in-board so that the sail could then be lowered. Taking a horribly rash decision I told them to stand by for another gybe. Back the boom came with a sickening crash, the main sheet unwound itself in a flash, and all was well. We then handed the mainsail, hoisted the twins, and felt much safer.

Next morning in a wild squall and at the inconvenient time of just before breakfast the sheet of one of the twins parted, and a few seconds later the cranse iron at the outer end of the other boom came adrift. We now had both sails streaming out ahead of the ship like washing on a line. We tamed them after a fierce struggle and fortunately before anything had been torn. The wind then moderated and a period of wet, misty weather succeeded these alarms. We accounted for the mist by our proximity to the tail of the Newfoundland Banks. From time to time we heard ship's foghorns and on one occasion, when a ship appeared suddenly out of the mist, George, who was apt to get excited, started waving his shirt. She was the *Lessel*, a Lamport and Holt boat in ballast. Possibly the look-out had mistaken George's shirt-waving for a distress signal, for she came in close enough to hail us by megaphone to ask if all was well. On our wireless set we could hear St John's giving out the weather forecast for the Grand Banks. A few days later a valve broke and we heard nothing more of weather reports or the much more important time signals. Since leaving Panama we had become accustomed to going without a log, and since Bermuda we had had no stop-watch. It had been dropped in the bilge and had understandably given up. Throwing it overboard was fun. After this we dared not move the deck watch from its little brass bed in the cabin, so when taking sights I had to bawl out to someone below who noted the time.

Another depression soon caught up with us and for two days we sped – everything reefed down – before a southerly gale. I judged we were doing 'twelve knots and a Chinaman', as the saying goes.* Anyhow we ran 350 miles (by sights) in two days while the great following seas took *Mischief* in their arms and hurled her forwards. In our enthusiasm we began shortening the passage by days or even weeks, but I deprecated too much optimism by enumerating all the accidents which might happen to us, including even the breaking of the boom. Sure enough the next day it did break.

That night the barometer dropped very steeply and at three in the morning it was blowing very hard and raining. As usual we had left the mainsail up for too long and no one fancied taking it down in such wild conditions in the dark. As she was going too fast for safety we streamed over the counter the bights of two of our heaviest warps to slow her down and then prayed for dawn. By morning – it was Midsummer Day – the wind moderated and shifted to north-west. A big sea was running and the boom, which should have been hauled in and pinned amidships – for now there was scarcely enough wind to fill it – was slamming about. It had already broken the rope tail of its wire guy when I took over after breakfast. I at once noticed that it had a slight curve. Suspecting that it was sprung I was about to call all hands when it broke, fairly in the middle. We had not yet taken out the reefs, that is there were four or five rolls of canvas round the boom. Having got it inboard we managed to straighten the boom by means of the throat halyards, but unrolling the sail with the boom lying on the deck was quite a job. We cut off a couple of feet at each end of the boom where the fittings were attached and threw the rest overboard. It was a surprise to find that it was a hollow spar; those of us who had had to lift it by the topping lifts had always imagined it as being made of solid iron. Henceforth we used the mainsail without any boom. This arrangement increased our peace of mind and did not much diminish our speed.

Before the next depression overtook us (when racing across the Atlantic the object, I understand, is not to be left behind by a depression) we had three days of light easterly winds and enough sun to encourage bathing. As we were in the traffic lane we expected to see large numbers of ships; a less expected sight in mid-Atlantic was a turtle. When on watch at night I always liked to see the lights of ships. They gave me a feeling of companionship and an interest in making out their course, and whether we should have to advertise our presence with the Aldis lamp. On one occasion I cut it rather too fine. Having assumed that a steamer would pass us about a quarter of a mile off I saw no point in showing a light, but when it eventually became obvious that he was going to come very close indeed I felt it wiser to lie doggo rather than to startle him by showing the light suddenly at such close range. It was always possible that the helmsman might panic and spin the wheel the

*In the old days when the log was hove the reel from which the log line ran out (the time being taken with a sand-glass) was held by a man. Most log lines were only marked to record a maximum speed of 12 knots. The story is that in the 'sixties one of the famous clippers was travelling so fast that the man holding the reel – a Chinaman – was jerked overboard and lost.

wrong way. When their bridge was passing our bowsprit someone saw us and a spotlight was directed *down* on to our deck together with a volley of abuse in some foreign tongue.

Towards the end of June there began a spell of dirty weather which was to last almost to the Scillies. Rain, high winds, and rough seas combined to make life wet and wearing. The companion way was boarded up, the hatch cover closed, the skylight battened down – but nevertheless water managed to find its way below. Although the helmsman was partly protected by the dodger rigged round the cockpit he still had the benefit of enough spray and solid water to keep him awake; and even the briefest of visits to the cockpit to survey the weather compelled one to be fully clothed. As one stood at the foot of the companion struggling into wet oilskins before going on watch, one would call hopefully to the helmsman for some words of comfort, for the least hint of a change for the better. But seldom were they forthcoming. Instead, more briefly and rudely worded, one heard:

> I tell you naught for your comfort,
> Yea, naught for your desire,
> Save that the sky grows darker yet
> And the seas rise higher.

The night of 29 June was particularly bad. The glass having fallen had apparently steadied. We had the trysail up and a twin boomed out. During the night the glass slumped to 29.2in. and at four in the morning, when we must have been doing seven knots, we had to hand the sails and run under storm jib alone. When daylight broke on a grey wilderness of white-capped waves we successfully experimented with a couple of oil bags trailing from either quarter. We found that even the finest film of oil had a remarkably soothing effect when angry waves tried to break close to our counter. Towards the close of a dark and dismal day a German ship altered course to see how we were faring. She came very close to us but signalling was impossible as we were more often out of sight in the trough of a wave than in view.

Discomfort can more easily be borne when one is being driven homewards with such vigour. Every day we ran our hundred miles or more, whether under storm jib alone or with the trysail and a twin. Opportunities for taking sights had to be promptly seized. They were not common and on two consecutive days we could not take any at all. However, on 5 July, in improving weather, we found ourselves only 60 miles from the Bishop rock. That night we picked up the light and by breakfast time on a lovely summer morning we were off St Mary's. A year and a day after leaving we passed Falmouth, but by now we were enveloped in dense fog. For three days as we groped our way up Channel the fog persisted. Because of the tide we anchored in home waters for the first time in Swanage bay, but at last on 9 July we entered Lymington river and tied up at the yard where we had fitted out.

Next day the crew went their several ways and I was left once more to commune with *Mischief*. I will not pretend that at all times throughout this 20,000 mile voyage we were a band of brothers. Patient Griselda herself and a company of angels would sometimes find their tempers strained to breaking point when cooped up in a small ship for months together. 'Ships are all right – it's the men in them', was, I suspect, the thought of each one of us on many occasions; and I know for certain of a few occasions when the same idea was openly and more pointedly expressed. But we were old enough or sensible enough to bear and forbear, and to put the ship and the enterprise in hand before our own feelings. It was this loyalty to the ship, and not my management, that held the crew together and enabled us to bring a worth-while undertaking to a successful end.

MISCHIEF AMONG THE PENGUINS

Mischief Among the Penguins

First published by Rupert Hart-Davis, 1961

Contents

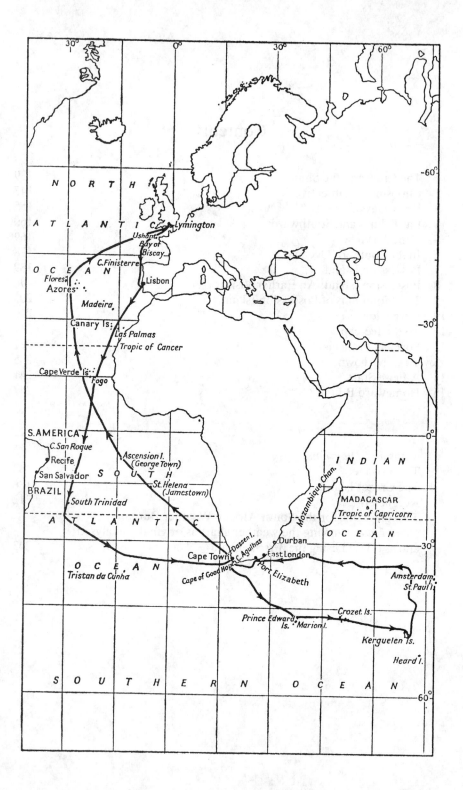

CHAPTER ONE

The Crew and the Ship

'HAND (man) wanted for long voyage in small boat. No pay, no prospects, not much pleasure.' Thus ran the advertisement I inserted in the Personal Column of *The Times* about a month before the day I hoped to sail. In planning a second and, fortunately, more successful voyage to the Crozet Islands in the Southern Ocean, I had run into the usual difficulty of finding a crew. A minimum of four were needed, five would be better, of whom one at least must be a mountaineer or at any rate capable of moving freely and looking after himself on easy rock, ice or snow. Ideally, of course, all should have had some sailing experience. One of them, I hoped, would have an invincible stomach and a turn for cooking on paraffin stoves in cramped quarters in a stuffy, unstable galley; and another should have some knowledge of small marine engines and the numbing effect upon them of sea air and salt water. All must be of cheerful, equable temper, long-suffering, patient in adversity, tolerant of the whims and uncouth manners or habits of others, neat and cleanly, adaptable, unselfish, loyal – in fact, possessed of most of the qualities in which the majority of men, including myself, are notably deficient.

Six months before sailing day such ideas and ideals are all very well but they cannot be long maintained. As the months pass and the men one had in mind fail to come forward, while others change their minds and drop out, such ideals are one by one relinquished until at last the modest aim of filling up the muster alone remains. Indeed, the final stage is reached when one is happy to take almost anyone who offers, regardless of his experience, ignorant of his temperament. After all, we should be away a year, time enough one might hope to demonstrate the truth of what Browning proclaimed:

> The only fault's with time;
> All men become good creatures: but so slow.

For a really long voyage has the advantage that however inexperienced both skipper and crew may be, they begin learning at once and go on learning until the last day of the voyage. One expert, who has written a book about ocean cruising, starts with the premise that either the crew must be found to suit the voyage, or the voyage arranged to suit the crew. If circumstances are such that neither of these is feasible, why then, the crew must in time make themselves fit for the voyage.

Nevertheless, a voyage of long duration rules out many who would be fit to come and would like to come. And experience had already shown me that it was idle to expect any mountaineering friends to join in such ventures as 'sailing to climb'. The keenest mountaineer is not likely to relish the prospect of enduring several months at sea for the sake of a month or two spent in climbing some obscure, unknown mountains. Nor were volunteers from among the yachting fraternity really to be expected, most of whom would have their own boats and their own plans. Very long ocean voyages are not enjoyed by all yachtsmen, and the few who do like them prefer to choose their own cruising grounds. Sun, warmth, exotic faces and places are generally more attractive than uninhabited, barren islands, set in stormy seas under drab skies. For a voyage to the West Indies or the South Seas there might be more than enough volunteers.

But the time factor is the biggest snag. Most men have to take life seriously, and although a knowledge of the art of sailing is pleasant and possibly useful, there is no future in it. A year's absence from bread-winning or getting on in life can be contemplated only by a man who has not yet settled down, or perhaps has no intention of doing anything so humdrum; or by a man of such carefree spirit that he is ready to throw aside everything at the rare prospect of making a long voyage under sail to remote places. I like to think there are still many such in this country – the difficulty is to make contact with them. Thus, rather late in the day, all other means having failed, I had resorted to the above advertisement.

At that time the only certain starter I had was W. A. Procter, who, having refused an early invitation, later changed his mind. As he is a married man with three children, his wife's consent to his going showed admirable complaisance on the part of a wife towards her husband's whims, as well as confidence in old *Mischief*'s ability to look after herself and her crew. Procter had been with me as mate in *Mischief* in Patagonian waters in 1955–56. A Civil Servant, who had been retired prematurely on account of ill-health, he was not really robust then and was not any stronger now; but a long sea voyage, he thought, might set him up, in spite of Mr Wodehouse's conviction 'that the sea is very rarely of use to anybody.' He was keen on boats and sailing, something of a ship's carpenter, and a curious and enquiring traveller of an adventurous spirit. True, this enquiring nature and adventurous spirit of his had all but brought about the wreck of *Mischief* in the Patagonia fjords, but I was now forewarned against it. Above all, he could be relied upon to put the interests of the expedition above everything else and to see it through to the end, however rude the weather or unreasonable the skipper. Both of us knew pretty well the worst of what each was capable, knew each other's bad and good points, and on the whole were seldom surprised by the one or disappointed in the other.

Besides Procter, there were two probable starters whom for good reasons I had not met, for at the time they were in the Antarctic. In July 1958, when on the way home after the failure of our first attempt to reach the Crozet Islands, when I was unwell, more than a little discouraged, and in half a mind to sell *Mischief*, and swallow the anchor, I received in a letter a welcome, bracing tonic from the Antarctic. One Lee Rice, a surveyor on one of the FIDS bases in Grahamland, who had heard of our attempt and the difficulty I had had in finding a crew for it, wrote to offer his services in any such future venture I might have in mind. Besides being a mountaineer and a surveyor, he had made a long ocean passage in a small boat – ideal qualifications for my purposes. Moreover, he had a friend in the Antarctic who would be glad to come too. Roger Tufft had had no sea experience but, having spent three years in Grahamland, was well practised in travelling on ice and snow in rough, mountainous country. They were due home in the spring of 1959. Such an offer from out of the blue was most refreshing and too good to ignore. With two such men I should have the nucleus of a strong crew for a second attempt starting in the summer of 1959.

In the end things went wrong. Owing to its being a bad season for ice, the relief ship *John Biscoe* in which Lee Rice was returning did not reach Southampton until mid-June. Such a late arrival, allowing him a bare six weeks to sort things out before sailing at the end of July with me, seemed likely to prevent his doing so. But when I met the ship at Southampton, Rice told me he would not in any case be able to come, having injured a knee on the way home. He did not think there was time for this to be put right and did not care to run the risk of becoming a passenger in *Mischief*. With him I lost my most likely man and at the same time had to drop the idea of doing any survey work on the islands.

The *Shackleton*, in which Roger Tufft was returning, arrived even later, for she docked at Southampton at the end of June. It was, therefore, with small expectation of success that I went to Southampton for the second time. Amidst the confusion of welcome by relatives, friends, and the Press, the turmoil of disembarkation, and what seemed to me the ungrateful and unnecessary scrutiny by Customs Officials of men arriving from the Antarctic, I began searching for Tufft. Having at last found his cabin, where, by the way, the bookshelf, slightly to my concern, held nothing but poetry, I learnt that *his* knees were all right and that, in spite of his friend's decision and of his own very late arrival, he was still game to come: I might add that Tufft's ability to do a quick turn-round and the very slight regard he has for the blessings of civilisation are exceptional. This was one instance, and I have since learnt of another. Within ten days of our return to England in July 1960, Tufft was on his way to join a party in Spitsbergen.

Thus, about a month before sailing day, fixed provisionally for the end of July, I had only Procter and Tufft. For the remaining two or three I relied upon whatever strange fish might be hooked by the advertisement. I had worded it in a slightly discouraging way in order, as I thought, to save me from being overwhelmed by too many replies. And the carefully inserted stipulation, 'man', would disappoint the surprisingly large number of married couples, women, and girls who lurk in the background waiting to pounce upon just such an offer. Although girls are often more enterprising and some of them more capable than men, I did not care to run the risk of being talked or ogled into an act of folly. For I had already had experience of the truth of the Chinese sage's remark that discord is not sent down from heaven but is brought about by women.

A member of the crew, a man, who turned out to be, in my opinion, a misfit or a bad bargain, would probably be regarded with equal disfavour by the rest of the crew; whereas, in the case of a woman, where one man's meat is another man's poison, there might be some difference of opinion, and I might well find myself in a minority of one. Sanguine though I was, I did not flatter myself that any of the top people who read *The Times* would apply, but when the replies began to arrive I was surprised to learn how far apart, geographically and socially, are some of its readers. As well as the idle rich and the idle poor, there are the romantics and opportunists, who, while scorning solid fare in the news columns of that venerable journal, make a habit of scanning the Personal Column of the front page in the hope of finding something to suit or something bizarre enough to attract them. That class of people, in fact, upon whom I, and perhaps others with more dubious ventures in view, rely for company – the cankers of a calm world and a long peace, ready, as they themselves sometimes advertise, 'to go anywhere and do anything (legal).'

I had over twenty replies, some of them serious, and owing to the limited time available, even that small number had to be dealt with arbitrarily and hastily. It may well be that good men were unwittingly turned down, for it was out of the question for me to make long journeys to interview all the prospective candidates. Inevitably those replies that came from within easy reach received most attention, while those that came from places like Saigon, Madrid, the Channel Islands, or even Scotland and Ireland, had to be dismissed out of hand. The first letter I opened, written apparently by a man of great self-assurance, with a sense of humour, and light-hearted to the point of insanity, seemed to me to be rich in promise.

Dear Sailor, [it began],
Been looking for something like this for years. No worry job – only life at stake – capital. No anxiety as regards shore pay. My qualifying credits: no sailing experience – not my worry but yours, no cook – you'll find this out. We are, therefore, mated for twelve months by virtue, your 'No' items being counter-balanced by mine. Everything equal – when do we meet for discourse?

> Yours affectionately,
> B ... F ...

P.S. Twelve months hence will tell you to go to hell.

If he had nothing else, he had unlimited cheek, which is often an asset, so I gave this brisk character some further details and appointed a meeting place. The rest was silence.

Of the replies from distant places I made an exception in favour of one from The Hague. Jan Garnier wrote at length to say that though he knew little about sailing, he was familiar with petrol engines, that he could cook, and that, being a Dutchman, his habits were, therefore, cleanly to the point of fastidiousness. He had knocked around a lot. He had spent seven years in the French Foreign Legion; had deserted in order to join the Free French, been caught and imprisoned in Morocco; and had eventually succeeded in joining the British Army, where he had collected a Military Medal as well as a Dutch decoration. Since neither Procter, Tufft, myself, nor any of the other applicants professed to know much about engines, Garnier, in spite of the difficulty of meeting him, deserved consideration. Finally, after a further exchange of letters, I decided to take him unseen. A man with his background would certainly be useful, would mix well, and would not expect much in the way of food or comfort. For presumably the Foreign Legion, in its normal habitat, the desert, lives largely on dates; and in a Moroccan prison one lives, I imagine, on even less.

Our number was now four and two others remained to be interviewed, John Lyons and J. G. Osborne. Judging from their letters, neither had any qualifications whatsoever, apart from great eagerness to go. Osborne had sailed a canoe and Lyons had crossed the Atlantic fifty-one times in the *Queen Mary*, playing the double bass in the ship's orchestra. When he produced a Sailor's Discharge Book, one realised how numerous are the various callings with little or no flavour of the sea comprehended by the significant word 'Sailor'. John Lyons' keenest ambition was to make an ocean voyage in a small boat. He had a cheerful and likeable disposition. Moreover, he stout-heartedly volunteered to try his hand in the galley, a thankless and often unpleasant job. The cook is the only man on board with much work to do and his sole compensation is that of having all night in. John Lyons was a retired schoolmaster of fairly advanced age. But I am no chicken, and I did not discover until we arrived at Cape Town, where we had to produce our passports, that he was the older of the two.

Osborne, on the other hand, was youngish, big and strong. He was at the time employed in an office, from which job he was quite willing to give himself a day's notice. Having failed to get a degree, he had not been able to find the work he wanted as a geologist, but he was an ardent amateur of that arid profession, accustomed to tramping many miles over moor and fell, mountain and valley, under a constantly growing burden of rock specimens. Provided it is promptly applied in the right place, brute force is valuable in a seaman, especially so in a boat with such heavy gear as *Mischief*'s is. Another of Jim Osborne's qualifications was taciturnity. Silence, the Chinese say, is worth buying. That it is particularly valuable at sea is shown by the words addressed to his new mate by the skipper of a coasting schooner: 'What I want from you, Mr Mate, is silence, and not too much of that.'

Thus, if I were to take only five, it was a toss-up between Lyons and Osborne. The latter, though no mountaineer, could fill a place in the shore party in the event of Tufft or myself having for some reason to drop out, for he was used to hill-walking and would no doubt carry a gigantic load. On the other hand his strength would be wasted in the galley, for which he was anyway too large and insufficiently nimble. I solved the problem by taking both, making up in numbers what we lacked in skill. For we needed more hauling power on deck, and by having five men available for watch-keeping the long passage out would be less arduous. True, I should have one more mouth to feed, but I was not then aware of how large a mouth Jim Osborne had.

So much for the crew. When it comes to the ship and her fitting-out, where everything depends upon one's own exertions and upon being able to pay for the exertions of professionals, there are not the doubts and uncertainties that surround the finding of the crew. From this brief account of how I got together five men it might be thought that a little patience and common sense is all that is involved. Much is left to be imagined – the alternating hopes and fears as the months go by, the feeling that all the fitting-out and buying of stores may ultimately be in vain, and finally, the last despairing efforts when one feels compelled to make up the required number with no more discrimination than that of a press-gang.

After our return in July 1958 from the abortive attempt to reach the Crozet, *Mischief* spent the winter in her usual mud berth at Lymington. It was not until about November that I had gathered sufficient confidence to decide upon fitting-out for a second attempt, and as a preliminary had her hauled out for survey. Though the hull of an old boat like *Mischief* (built in 1906) may be generally sound, one needs to be always on watch for any slight symptoms of decay. Faults and weaknesses that might be safely overlooked for a season's sailing in home waters must be put right before undertaking a deep-sea voyage. A few days after she had been hauled out I heard the bad news that part of the hull had been damaged by teredo worm. I went at once to Lymington, where with Humphrey Barton, the surveyor, together with a shipwright armed with chisel and mallet, we spent a gloomy morning ascertaining the extent of the damage.

It was mostly confined to the planks forward of midships to about three feet below the water line. The planks had to be examined one by one for small holes no bigger than those made by a one-inch nail, the only visible signs of the worm's ravages. At all these suspicious holes a blow with a chisel would open up a small groove running along the plank, increasing gradually to the size of a man's finger. Each groove had to be followed up to the end until the full extent of the damage was exposed. Sometimes a whole plank had to be condemned, sometimes only part. Some planks were so riddled as to resemble a honeycomb, leaving a bare half-inch of sound wood in planks that were one and a half inches thick. Ignorance is bliss. Whether the attack had started back at Durban or at intermediate places such as Beira, the Comoro Islands, Aldabra or Aden, we must have sailed most of the way home in an unusually fragile hull.

In the days of wooden ships, the teredo worm was rightly dreaded as a deadly menace in tropical waters. No unprotected wood can resist it. In its home-made burrow it grows to a length of a foot, and some species are reputed to grow to six feet. No worms remained in any of the burrows we opened up, the only trace left being a coating of a hard, shelly substance. They rasp away the wood with minute teeth, visible only under a microscope, and the wood dust, after being acted upon by digestive ferments, is their food. As the hole of entry is so small it seems that the teredo gains its first footing when in the embryo stage, and consequently its existence and subsequent growth depend upon its finding a piece of wood as host. Why then are there such multitudes in being in the sea when suitable hosts are comparatively rare? I have had occasion to ponder over a similar question when being sucked dry by leeches in the Himalayan foothills. How do these revolting creatures survive when there are no men or animals to prey upon? For really bad leech-infested country is normally deserted for that reason, and no one travels through it if it can be avoided.

It was odd that we found no worms still in the burrows, for no full-grown worm could get out through the tiny entry hole. They must have died on reaching colder waters and their bodies dissolved away. The only teredo worm I have seen was one solitary specimen which we found lodged in *Mischief*'s keel when I first took her over at Palma, Majorca. At that time her hull was coppered but we had to remove the copper in order to examine the hull, and it was so badly torn in the process as not to be worth putting back. This worm, five inches long and a half-inch thick, had got in where the copper had been torn by touching on a piece of coral rock. Copper sheathing is the complete answer to teredo worm danger so long as it remains in good condition. But it is not a thing you can fit and forget, for if there is a hole the teredo worm will find it.

Anti-fouling paint is an effective defensive measure if the paint is good of its kind and frequently renewed. But it is expensive, the best quality costing as much as £12 a gallon, while the amount needed to cover *Mischiefs*'s hull is nearly three gallons. When we had last painted the hull at Cape Town on the previous voyage in November 1957, I had on board a five-gallon drum of anti-fouling paint of unknown origin which had been given me by a friendly shipowner a year earlier in Valparaiso. Naturally we made use of it and as things turned out we might as well have used face-powder. Two months later bare wood began to show along and just below the water-line. We ought to have done something about it but at none of the places we touched at on our way up the Indian Ocean to Aden were there any facilities for hauling out. So we pressed on regardless and ultimately had to pay for this penny-wise pound-foolish policy, and our subsequent neglect, to the tune of two hundred feet of new planking at a pound a foot.

This wormy digression, painful to write and painful to read, must be forgiven. Most people, especially the elderly, are too ready to discuss their ailments. I feel that *Mischief*, with the garrulity of age, would have much to say about her manifold complaints, the expensive operations she had under-gone, the face-lifts and other attempts at rejuvenation. For it is with ships as with men:

> There is no fortress of man's flesh so made
> But subtle, treacherous Time comes creeping in.
> Oh, long before his last assaults begin
> The enemy's on; the stronghold is betrayed.

After taking advice I had already decided that *Mischief* should have a new deck fitted; and the cost of this so overshadowed everything else that the bill for teredo damage might be considered as merely 'a trifling sum of misery new added to the foot of the account.' But both Humphrey Barton and myself were fearful of what the removal of the old deck might reveal, of how extensive had been the ravages of time, rot and general decay in places that are normally hidden from view. They proved to be less than expected, but while the deck was off the opportunity to stiffen and strengthen the old boat was taken. Extra beams were put in; the half-beams in the way of the mast replaced by through beams; the half-beams each side of the cockpit were tied to the carlines with steel plates; and steel brackets were fitted to the ends of the main beams to tie them to the shelf. When suggesting these improvements Barton wrote: 'The general condition is better than I expected but there is not much holding the two sides of the boat together as the ends of the beams are in poor condition. The brackets should hold her together for many years to come.' To which I could only say, 'Amen, and so be it.'

As all this work had to be done in the open air, the dry spring and summer of 1959 were the greatest of blessings. Work went on uninterrupted by rain, the interior of the boat remained dry, and by the end of May she was back in the water with a new coat of anti-fouling paint and newly enamelled topsides. Throughout the winter I had been able to work on her at odd times, scrubbing out lockers, painting the cabin and galley, rubbing down and varnishing mast and spars. The mast had been taken out and examined, and a soft spot at the heel had had a piece of wood graved in. For the size of the boat the mast looks thin. It is only seven and a half-inches in diameter, and normally it carries a long topmast. When the gaff is slamming about, the upper part of the mast twists in a way that is terrifying to look at. In strong winds the whole mast assumes a graceful curve. But in the course of time one comes to believe wholeheartedly in the theory that what bends won't break.

Besides fairly frequent forays to Lymington, I did a lot of homework such as oiling and wire-brushing all the wire standing and running rigging, renewing block strops and reeving a new net to go under the bowsprit. One could not take the main shrouds home for treatment, for they are not the sort of wire to be coiled up and put in the back of a car. They are of two and three-quarter inch circumference wire, and being fitted in so small a boat are rightly wondered at for their rugged, uncompromising strength. The theory that so long as these stand, the mast, too, will stand, may well be wrong, but it is none the less reassuring. Thus, when the crew joined there should have been nothing left for them to do but to put on board the stores and gear. As is usually the way there remained a multitude of small jobs to be done before *Mischief* could be regarded as in all respects ready for sea. Luckily I had arranged for Procter and Jan Garnier to join me on board ten days before sailing. A few days later John Lyons and Jim Osborne arrived and finally, two days before sailing, Roger Tufft joined.

CHAPTER TWO

Choosing an Objective

THE appetite grows by what it feeds on. After making the voyage to the Patagonian channels and landing a climbing party with six weeks' stores at the foot of a glacier, I felt satisfied that the apparently conflicting aims of sailing and climbing could be happily married. This being so, I was eager for a fresh venture, and the sooner the better, for boats rot from lack of use even as men do. Old though *Mischief* might be, she was still good for a lot of work and seemed eminently suited to the kind of work I had in mind; being capacious enough to carry a crew that included a climbing party and its stores; able to keep the sea for more than two months at a time; and fast enough to reach and return from distant places inside a year provided no time was lost in making unnecessary calls.

Although coastwise cruising, pottering from port to port, or making short sea passages is capital fun, calling for as much seamanship and prudence as the making of long ocean crossings, or perhaps more, I do not think it fully satisfying. In the same way that rock climbing, though very arduous and exacting, is not so satisfying as mountaineering, of which rock climbing is but one aspect, so short passages fail to yield the sense of fulfilment and achievement won from an ocean crossing and a successful landfall on a new continent. And in my opinion even that is not quite enough. There must be an objective to give point to the voyage, and what better objective can a man have than exploring little-known regions or climbing mountains that are in reach only of the seafarer.

Not long after our return from the Patagonia venture in the late summer of 1956, I read of Heard Island in the Southern Ocean in lat. S.53°, some 2,500 miles south-east of Cape Town. The whole island is really a mountain, a semi-active volcano called Big Ben which rises to 9,000ft. and is draped in ice and snow from sea to summit. Here was a challenge to a climber and an objective as remote and inaccessible as the amateur sailor in a small boat could hope to find. After the last war the Australian Weather Bureau had for five years maintained a weather station there. Although it had been abandoned the huts were intact and their diesel power plant, carefully laid up, merely wanted cranking in order to provide visitors with electric light and hot baths. It sounded ideal. Several unsuccessful attempts had been made by the Australians to climb Big Ben. I gathered that the main difficulty was the weather, which at that height in those latitudes can be indeed terrible. One might have to wait a month or two for a favourable spell.

Having examined the chart and read about the island in the *Antarctic Pilot*,

I felt doubt creeping in. There seemed to be no safe anchorage. Accordingly I got in touch with Mr P. G. Law, Director of the Australian Antarctic Division, who knew Heard Island from personal experience.

As regards your getting to Heard Is. [he wrote] I cannot over-stress the dangers which will face you if you proceed in a small boat. As you know, Heard Is. is right in the track of the great westerly cyclones which sweep across the Southern Ocean with almost no intervening good weather of any duration. The seas are mountainous and altogether I can think of no worse place to sail small craft. The obvious thing to do would be to go first to Kerguelen and wait there for reasonable weather before attempting to push on to Heard Is. There is a French station at Kerguelen and I am sure they would be pleased to offer you hospitality.

Although he said nothing about the anchorage, Law's letter served to cool my ardour quite a lot. I passed it on to Dr Brian Roberts of the Scott Polar Research Institute, who agreed with me that the poor anchorage was the chief snag.

The big difficulty [he wrote] is that there is no safe anchorage anywhere round the island where you could leave your boat. I have no doubt you could reach the island in *Mischief*, but she would have to wait for you in an exceedingly unpleasant anchorage where there is small chance that she could remain long enough. Atlas Cove is really very exposed indeed. I think all the accumulated experience shows that the ascent of Big Ben can only be done by a party which is able to await suitable conditions and this would probably mean rather a long wait. Your best chance seems to be to take your boat to Kerguelen where you can find dozens of safe anchorages. You might be able to arrange with the French for one of their vessels to take your party across to Heard Island.

Upon this I wrote to the Chef du Bureau Administratif des Terres Australes et Antarctiques Françaises and had a most sympathetic reply from a M. Heurgon whom I met later in Paris, and later still in surroundings more congenial to us both, at Kerguelen itself. He told me that they had no boat at Kerguelen capable of making the passage to Heard Island but suggested several places at Kerguelen where *Mischief* could safely lie. Heard Island is 300 miles to leeward of Kerguelen and nearly four degrees of latitude farther south. Since the French could not help, and since the only anchorage at Atlas Cove was quite unsuitable for any lengthy stay, there remained only the possibility of *Mischief*'s dropping the climbing party, sailing to Kerguelen to wait, and returning to Heard Island after a couple of months to pick them up again. Rather reluctantly I abandoned this idea as being altogether too dubious. Sailing down wind from Kerguelen to Heard Island might be easy enough but to beat back 300 miles against strong winds was another thing. With her big mainsail *Mischief* goes well to windward in normal weather. With the mainsail reefed right down, or worse still with the storm trysail set (as might well be the rule in the stormy stretch between Kerguelen and Heard Island), she makes little headway and a lot of leeway. Against wind and sea, in the best conditions, she might make good over the ground thirty to forty miles a day; in the worst conditions she would make no progress at all. For example, when coming home in the summer of 1958 through the Mediterranean, where there is generally an east-going current, we met with strong westerly winds off the Spanish coast and anchored in a cove for shelter. Having become tired of waiting, we put to sea again and after beating hard for twenty-four hours fetched up a little farther *east* of the cove we had started from.

Beating for days on end is hard on both boat and crew, and although 300 miles is a short distance, it might take a very long time. After the climbing party had been landed, the crew would be weakened, one or more gales would almost certainly be met, and on the whole I should have felt obliged to stay in the ship and forgo the pleasure of coming to grips with Big Ben. Lying on its snow slopes with the wind shrieking and howling round the tent would be quite enough without the additional torment of anxiety on behalf of *Mischief* and her crew. But no one ever lacks reasons, and often good solid reasons, for not attempting a thing. With a tough, active experienced crew it might have been done. 'Prudence,' as Dr Johnson says, 'quenches that ardour of enterprise, by which everything is done that can claim praise or admiration, and represses that generous temerity which often fails and often succeeds.'

So leaving Heard Island and Big Ben for more favourable times or better men, I turned my attention to Kerguelen. Anyone who has read a book called *Fifteen Thousand Miles in a Ketch* must have had his imagination fired by that distant, desolate island and by a tale of the most resolute courage. Here was a small boat voyage with an objective, with a vengeance. In 1908 two young Breton brothers, Henri Rallier du Baty and Raymond Rallier du Baty, bought an old forty-five ton ketch, little bigger than *Mischief*, fitted her out, recruited four fishermen, and set sail for Kerguelen. As the crew were professionals they had to be paid wages, and the only way to pay them was by filling the ketch with a cargo of seal oil. They took with them the material for making barrels and, before leaving, Raymond took some lessons in coopering. They spent a hazardous and adventurous year on the island moving from anchorage to anchorage, killing seals and trying out the blubber in some old try-pots they came upon, until they had filled all their barrels. Then, in the depths of a southern winter, they sailed on to New Zealand, sold their oil and the ship, and paid off the crew. As one can well believe from this remarkable exploit, Raymond was at heart an explorer. He was a friend and disciple of the French Antarctic explorer J. B. Charcot, and in 1913–14 he returned to Kerguelen to carry out a hydrographic survey.

The island was first discovered in 1772 by the French navigator, Kerguélen-Trémarec, a Breton nobleman. In the belief that he had found the great southern continent upon which the explorers and geographers of those days were so intent, he hurried home and reported his discovery in too glowing terms. The theory generally held at that time was that there must be a large land mass in the southern hemisphere in order to balance the preponderance of land in the northern hemisphere. In the following year he was dispatched with three vessels to explore this great territory, which he had named South France. On this occasion he himself never landed but the truth soon became painfully evident and the unhappy navigator sailed home to confess his mistake. The story that in his disappointment he changed the name to Desolation Island is doubtfully authentic. The latter name was given to it by

Captain Cook when he landed at Christmas Harbour in 1776, in the course of his third and last great voyage. Cook's second voyage, 1773–75, when he traversed almost the whole Southern Ocean between the parallels of 50° and 70°, had finally shown that there was no such thing as a great southern continent in more or less temperate latitudes.

From 1776 until the 1870s the island was frequented by British and American whalers and sealers. It is said that in 1843 there were no less than 500 such ships at work on the coasts of Kerguelen and its vicinity. From then onwards the inevitable decline set in. Thus, the coasts of the island were well known to numbers of seamen who in their small ships visited them year after year sailing, whaling and sealing for months at a time among all the hazards attendant upon navigating sailing ships in a region of violent storms off an iron-bound, unlit, uncharted coast. What superb seamen they must have been, and how great must have been the reward to entice them upon so dangerous a quest. Many were lost. One of the sealers, John Nunn, who was wrecked and spent three years on Kerguelen, has left a record of his sufferings.

It is amusing to contrast their almost yearly visits, their long sojourns, and the taciturnity of these rapacious whaling and sealing men, with the rare, fleeting and slightly portentous visits of scientific expeditions. Nevertheless, it is mostly the latter whom we have to thank for the charting of the innumerable bays, inlets and islets, and the somewhat scant knowledge of the interior. Whaling and sealing being a highly competitive business, those who conducted it were (and are to this day) reticent about their voyages and by no means willing to make their discoveries generally known. A welcome exception to this rule were the ships of the whaling firm of Enderby Brothers, which undertook a series of voyages primarily of discovery. It was interesting to be told, as we were at Cape Town, that few of the whalers which leave there annually for the Antarctic are willing to keep and transmit daily by wireless a meteorological log, for this involves disclosing the ship's position. Such is their ingrained dislike of allowing rivals an inkling of their intentions or their whereabouts.

On the chief scientific expeditions which have put in at Kerguelen for a brief visit, usually on their way to or from the Antarctic, the first was that of James Clark Ross with the well-known ships, *Erebus* and *Terror*. Two months were spent surveying the coast while Dr M'Cormick investigated the geology, and Sir Joseph Hooker the botany. In 1874 another famous ship, the *Challenger*, visited the island to select sites for observing the transit of Venus and to carry out further hydrographic survey. In 1893 a French expedition hoisted the French flag to re-assert possession and extended the survey. In the same year the island was leased for a term of fifty years to two French merchants. Nothing was done until 1909, when, in conjunction with a Norwegian whaling company, they established a large settlement for whale fishing and for hunting elephant seals. In four years the seals were almost exterminated, the whales driven away, and in 1929 the settlement was abandoned. Sheep-breeding had also been tried without success.

The island relapsed into its normally deserted state until 1941, when three

German ships made it their base for raids upon shipping in the Indian Ocean. They sank or captured 200,000 tons of shipping before they were located and destroyed. This incident, together with the realisation of the importance of the island as a weather station and possibly a future air base, stirred the French into activity. In 1949 an expedition of fourteen men reconnoitred a site and in the following year a weather station was installed and is still there. We shall see something of it later.

For me Kerguelen had many attractions as an objective. Though there were no discoveries to be made, the interior of the higher and more rugged western end has rarely been visited, and, so far as I knew, the ice-cap which runs parallel to the west coast, named Glacier Cook on the chart, had never been trodden. Mt Ross, 6,430ft. high, and a number of lesser peaks up to 4,000ft. were all unclimbed. The wide choice of secure anchorages makes it a comparatively safe cruising ground in the summer months, and the presence of the French base lent an added attraction in so far as some help and local knowledge would readily be put at our disposal. But there was no denying that the presence of other human beings detracted something from the glamour. The word 'uninhabited' on a map casts almost the same magic spell as the word 'unexplored', and the attraction of an uninhabited island, small and barren though it be, is scarcely to be withstood.

For this reason, and because they were less known and far less frequently visited than Kerguelen, I began to think that Îles Crozet (these, too, are French possessions) should be our main objective. They were on the way to Kerguelen anyway, being about two-thirds of the distance there from Cape Town. The group consists of five widely scattered islands of which only three, Île aux Cochons, Île de la Possession and Île de l'Est, are large enough to offer any scope. Possession, which is the biggest, is about ten miles long and four miles wide. Of the remaining two, Îles des Apôtres is merely a group of rocky pinnacles, and the Îles des Pingouins consist of a 500ft. high rock with one small outlier. They were discovered in the same year as Kerguelen, 1772, by the French navigator Marion-Dufresne, who also discovered what are now called Marion and Prince Edward Islands. After the murder of Marion-Dufresne in New Zealand, his second-in-command, Crozet, took command of the expedition and his name was subsequently applied to the whole group by Captain Cook. Cook himself did not visit the Crozet Islands.

As with Kerguelen, these islands were the haunt of British and American sealers from about 1805 until 1870, when the seals had been pretty well exterminated. In 1820 the *Prince of Wales* cutter, an English sealer, was wrecked there and an entertaining account of their experiences was written by one of the survivors, C. M. Goodridge. The visits of scientific expeditions to the islands have been rare and usually extremely brief; landing is sometimes difficult and anchorages are scarce and not altogether secure; and the flora, fauna and general structure do not differ much from Kerguelen. All these islands are of volcanic origin. Kerguelen, Prince Edward Island, the Crozet, St Paul and Amsterdam may all be the remains of one extensive land mass.

In 1837 a French corvette spent six days at the Crozet, made a partial survey and rescued the crews of two American sealers. In 1840 James Clark

Ross spent six days there in the *Erebus*, but was unable to land. The *Challenger*, too, was there in 1874, but again no one could land. In the same year an American Transit of Venus expedition landed for one day on Possession Island, and a similar German expedition made observations without landing. From this brief record one might conclude that the only way to spend any time on the Crozet Islands was to be shipwrecked there.

From July 1875 to January 1876 forty-four survivors of the ship *Strathmore* spent seven grim months on the Apostles. In the days of sail, ships bound for Australia or New Zealand ran their easting down somewhere in the Roaring Forties. Hard-driving masters of ships with a reputation for fast passages to maintain, or bent on establishing one, might go as far south as the fiftieth parallel, where the gales are fiercer. Thus, in those days the Crozet might often be sighted by ships.

The *Strathmore*, a new ship from Dundee, was running her easting down along the forty-seventh parallel. Owing to thick weather, no sights had been observed for two or three days and the master intended to check his position and his chronometers by sighting the Crozet. Sail had been reduced so as not to overrun the islands in the dark, but at midnight of 1 July the vessel struck one of the small, rocky islets of the Apostles. A gig and a lifeboat managed to reach the shore and in the next two days the gig ferried ashore those who were still clinging to the rigging and also salvaged some valuable odds and ends—cooking pots, a case of spirits, pickles, blankets, a cleaver and some fire buckets. A whole gale then blew up and smashed to pieces both boats. Huddled in a roughly contrived shelter, the castaways for six months eked out a wretched existence eating albatross, mollyhawks and their eggs. Driftwood from the wreck enabled them to maintain a fire. To add to their misery they sighted two ships and failed to attract their attention. Finally, in January 1876, forty-three men and one woman were taken off by an American whaler. Four had died on the island of cold and exhaustion, and forty, including the master and mate, had been lost with the ship.

It is a striking illustration of the difference modern means of communication make to the perils of the sea and the chances of rescue, that ten months after the *Strathmore* survivors had been picked up, HMS *Wolverine* called at the Crozet in search of them. In 1880, possibly as a result of this disaster, HMS *Comus* established provision depots on the three main islands. In 1887 the depots were restocked by a French man-of-war, the supplies left by the *Comus* having been used up by the shipwrecked crew of a French schooner, none of whom survived. Since then there have been brief visits, usually of only twenty-four hours, by various ships on their way to the Antarctic or Kerguelen. As sailing ships disappeared, so did the need for provision depots on these Southern Ocean islands. Except for whaling ships, those waters are now deserted. No steamer passes within a thousand miles of the Crozet.

It seemed to me that to make a landing on Possession Island would be easiest and most worth while. As well as being the largest, it had, according to the *Antarctic Pilot*, two snow-covered peaks of about 5,000ft. The lee side of the island offered two possible anchorages protected from all winds except easterly. About Île aux Cochons there seemed to hang a faint aroma of roast pork. It was, therefore, all the more fortunate that it had no mountains. East Island, though rich in mountains, had but one doubtfully secure anchorage. I had hoped we might do some mapping, but in the absence of Lee Rice our ambitions would have to be confined to climbing the mountains and making a botanical collection. Roger Tufft had also undertaken to ring as many birds as he could on behalf of the California Wild Life Society. But these were secondary matters, mere by-products, 'In the joy of the actors lies the sense of any action. That is the explanation, that the excuse.'

Possession Island was, therefore, to be the objective, the same objective as that of the previous unsuccessful voyage of 1957–58, which had been made with a crew gathered together in much the same haphazard way. And before going further I may as well describe briefly how we were thwarted on that voyage, and how it was we spent Christmas Day refitting at Durban instead of among the penguins and sea-elephants on Possession Island.

We sailed from Cape Town on 21 November, and on the 26th, when we were only about 350 miles to the south, the glass began falling with every sign of approaching bad weather. By evening we were under trysail and storm jib, and double watches, two men at a time on duty in the cockpit, were arranged. The next day we were running under bare poles before a north-westerly gale, streaming the bights of two big warps to reduce our speed. The glass was only moderately low, 29.15, and went no lower. Later it was interesting to see the weather map for that day published at Cape Town, which showed three depressions in a row, one to the south of us with a barometer reading of 28.6 in its centre. During my watch that night, a lump of solid water came over the counter, breaking several of the iron stanchions of the weather dodger rigged round the cockpit. Wind speeds are difficult to judge and in a small boat tend to be exaggerated. We logged it at Force 9 with long periods of stronger squalls with heavy rain. Meantime the seas had been building up to a mean estimated height of 25 to 30ft. and the crests were breaking. What with rain and sea water, we had to pump out the well every half-hour.

The sea was manageable provided it got no worse and provided she was kept dead before it. But whether *Mischief* was sluggish or whether, as seems probable, the helmsman allowed her to broach to, at six in the morning of the 28th a big sea broke over the portside. At the time I was below, where the immediate results were chaotic. She leant right over, a cataract of water came down the companion-way and through the skylight, and nearly everything moveable alighted on the floor to swim about in the water. The effect of this blow, though not really serious, proved fatal to our hopes. The quarter boards on both sides were stove in, the port coaming of the cockpit was started inboard carryng with it a bit of deck planking. All the gear on deck broke loose and, worst of all, the dinghy, which was lashed down forward disappeared over the side bending the life-rail stanchions flat as it went. With it we lost a bag of anthracite, the working jib, and a couple of spare sheets.

While the other man on watch got her back on course, for she lay wallowing in the trough with the helmsman half-drowned and more than half-astonished, the rest began clearing up the mess below, securing what was left on deck, and pumping out the water which was over the cabin floorboards. Two of us then got the storm jib set to help keep her before the wind. The damage on deck was superficial, but the loss of the dinghy seemed insuperable. All that day we ran on in much the same conditions of wind and sea until early the following morning, when the wind began to take off.

By then, my responsibility weighing heavily, I had made up my mind that we ought to give up and put back to Durban. Although without a dinghy we could not land on the Crozet, we might have gone to Kerguelen, where we could land at the French base. But that was 2,000 miles away. What worried me was that only two of the crew besides myself could be relied upon to steer safely when running in bad weather. We could not afford to broach to again and we had not yet reached the Forties (we were in the south lat. 39°), where worse weather might well be met. The prospect of 2,000 more miles in those stormy waters with only two reliable helmsmen so daunted me that I gave up the attempt.

I may have been excessively prudent. An American climbing friend seemed to think so when he wrote: 'The one thing that troubles me about your last trip is that the Tilman whom I knew would have swum ashore pulling his vessel behind him rather than admit defeat because of the loss of a mere dinghy.' On the other hand there were one or two in Cape Town who had condemned us for temerity in embarking upon so hazardous a voyage. Dr Johnson has a word for that too. 'It can raise no wonder,' he says, 'that temerity has been generally censured; for it is one of the vices with which few can be charged, and which, therefore, great numbers are ready to condemn.' As a footnote to this episode, I might add that in 1959 we carried a rubber dinghy as a spare, stowed in safety below.

One more footnote. We decided to save something from the wreck of this unlucky voyage by circumnavigating Africa. So from Durban we sailed north to Beira, where we lay in a river, the Pungwe, which might well have been the 'grey, green, greasy Limpopo.' Thence out into the Indian Ocean to the Comoro Islands, where they grow vanilla and ylang-ylang, a shrub of grotesque shape with flowers of pleasing smell from which an essential oil is extracted. And on to Aldabra, a small coral atoll where the giant land tortoise abounds and turtle haul out on the beaches to lay their eggs. And having sailed up the Red Sea we passed through the Canal out into the Mediterranean, where, traversing it, we spent two solid months of light, fickle, and contrary winds. So that ships which passed us homeward bound passed us again two or three weeks later when they were once more outward bound, saluting us as they went as an old but rather slow-moving acquaintance. We understood why in the old days galley-slaves were an essential form of propulsion in the Mediterranean. From Gibraltar the passage was comparatively fast, taking only twenty days. The usual summer gale blew us up Channel and we tied up at Lymington thirteen months after leaving it, thus ending a fruitless voyage of 22,000 miles.

CHAPTER THREE

Early Days

THE long-drawn-out preparations for a voyage have about them something unreal. Sailing day is distant and nebulous. The fear begins to creep in that one is preparing for an event that never will take place, and in face of the frustrations and disappointments that arise in finding a crew, this feeling of futility is almost justified. There were times when futility seemed the most welcome as well as the most likely upshot, when the idea of failing to start did not altogether displease. In fact, 'Belial, clothed in Reason's garb, counselled ignoble ease.' Is your journey really necessary? became the question. Why attempt to drag five other misguided men half-way across the world when it is obvious that most of our present-day troubles come from men not staying quietly in their room at home? But upon visiting *Mischief* to see how things are going, such weak thoughts are speedily banished. She and her kind were never built so that men should stay quietly at home. She breathes sturdy, eager confidence, a living embodiment of the truth that the sea is for sailing, that strenuousness is the immortal path and sloth the way of death.

A few words about *Mischief*, the chief figure in this account. She was originally a Bristol Channel Pilot cutter built at Cardiff in 1906; in length 45ft., beam 13ft., drawing 7ft. 6ins. aft, and of 29 tons Thames Measurement. Her gaff rig is still the same but she now has an auxiliary petrol engine. With full tanks the range is less than 300 miles, so that her motive power is essentially sail. The first Cardiff pilot to own her was a Mr William Morgan, known throughout the Bristol Channel as 'Billy the Mischief.' When the individual competitive pilot service came to an end in 1912, she was taken over along with sixty-seven other cutters by the Cardiff Steam Pilot Service, an event which marked the end of those stirring days in the Bristol Channel, when each pilot in his own boat strove to be the first to board an incoming ship. What she did during the 1914–18 War I have not discovered, but in 1919 she was bought by a Mr Unna, who took her out to Takoradi on the Gold Coast, where he was working on the new harbour project. He sold her in 1927, when she was first registered as a yacht. Since then she had changed hands ten times before I bought her in 1954 at Palma, Majorca, when she was in a rather neglected state. As the pilot service required, for they might have to keep the sea in all weathers waiting for an incoming ship, the cutters were fine seaboats with extremely easy motion in a sea-way. All the ballast is inside, the bottom being filled with concrete and on top of that four tons of pig-iron. Moreover, they had to be built cheaply and simply, the average price being about £300. When *Mischief* was taken over by the Steam Pilot Service in 1912 she was valued at £420.

When I had sold my car in order to pay for *Mischief*'s new deck, sent home most of my shore-going clothes, and seen Procter and Jan Garnier come on board with the firm intention of making a voyage, I was finally convinced that the unreal had become real, that the wheels which I had set in motion so many months before were turning, and would go on turning until we reached the Crozet or perhaps a more distant shore. However, *Mischief*'s first move was no farther than the Town Quay, where she had to be propped up against the wall. While overhauling the WC, the plumber had found that the skin fittings outside the hull were corroded. So we took her to the quay, where she could be leant against the wall while two shipwrights worked against time between tides to replace the fittings.

After that we began transferring all the gear from the store to the ship, and bending the mainsail. We carry two mainsails, one spare. As they had been made in 1954 and had sailed more than 40,000 miles, they were beginning to wear thin, but such is the inherent strength of flax canvas that it can become very thin indeed before showing any tendency to tear. On the outward voyage we were incessantly restitching seams until at length we did away with the chief source of chafe by casting off altogether the lee topping-lift instead of merely slacking away. As the sails are old, they have stretched a lot and have too much belly to set well when going to windward; but that is a point of sailing which the deep-sea sailor does his best to avoid. Thin though the canvas is, it does not seem to get any lighter. Three men are needed to carry the mainsail, and to stow the spare sail below we have to remove the cabin skylight. We had a brand new jib and staysail. The remaining sails – twin staysails, Genoa jib, topsail, storm jib and trysail – which are less used, were still serviceable.

Mischief's boom is such a formidable spar that the crew cannot but regard it with dislike and fear however noble it may be in appearance. When coming home across the Atlantic in 1956 we broke the old boom. The new boom is a half-inch thicker and solid, whereas the old one was slightly hollow, and it is, therefore, the very devil to raise from its resting place on the gallows. To make it easier we fitted a tackle, and Procter and I went to Southampton in search of suitable blocks. Modern yacht blocks, in order to save windage, are diminutive affairs, beautifully finished, and made of anything but wood – some, one might think are made of gold. We wanted rough, unvarnished wood blocks big enough to take a hefty piece of rope, the kind of blocks that you can pick up cheap in any fishing port in Spain. While in Southampton we had the compass tested. Except that the card was dim with age, it proved to be in good order, so we had a new luminous card fitted. This luminous card was a good investment. Once or twice the binnacle light gave trouble, and on the way home from Cape Town we had to do without a light altogether.

Stores for six months, which had been ordered some time before, together with fresh vegetables and a small quantity of bonded stores, were delivered from Southampton the day before sailing. Unless the boat is over forty tons, one has to make a special application before being allowed to ship stores out of bond. Of the six of us, only three smoked. Procter smoked cigarettes abstemiously while Jan Garnier practically lived on them. I took twenty pounds of tobacco, which lasted the round voyage. Naturally it did me no good, but I would not have been without it. As the sage – not my Chinese friend – whom I quote too often, remarks: 'Smoking requires little exertion and yet preserves the mind from vacuity', and my mind is in constant need of such preservation. The crew were allowed, or rather given, one drink a week on Saturday night, an amount that was not excessive whether regarded as a promoter of conviviality or as an anti-scorbutic measure. Upon surveying the mountain of boxes and tea-chests on deck, it was difficult to believe that the contents could ever be stowed below. Tins of all sizes and shapes are easily fitted into lockers and crannies, but awkward items like ice-axes, carrying-frames, a tent, and the rubber dinghy, were less readily accommodated.

Fortunately our impending departure roused little interest, so that we were able to get the work done without interruption. On the eve of departure we received kind gifts of eggs and coffee from a Lymington quay-side coffee house. These presented no stowage problem, unlike at Cape Town, where one is liable to be overwhelmed with cases of apples, peaches and apricots, bottles of wine, brandy and home-made cakes, for all of which room has to be made in overflowing lockers. On the morning of departure, 30 July, one of the Yard hands arrived early with half a dozen nice sea trout. Having said good-bye to the few who came to see us off, we made ready to go. When we came up Lymington river the year before, *Mischief*, as if to show how delighted she was to be back, had twice buried her nose in the mud. So this time Ted Mapes, the Yard foreman, anxious that nothing so disgraceful should happen again, led the way in a launch and only left us when we were safely outside.

In the brave days of sail most voyages seem to have been begun either with a crew of able-bodied seamen who were incapably drunk, or a crew of landsmen who were perfectly sober and perfectly incapable. Either way it was awkward for the mates who, with the help of a few apprentices, had to set thousands of feet of canvas. On a smaller scale our predicament was the same, for no one knew what had to be done except Procter, and he was a bit rusty. However, the wind was light and the tide with us and long before we reached the Needles we had everything under control. Having taken our departure and streamed the log, it was time to think of lunch – a memorable lunch of sea trout, of which few partook.

Slight though the sea was, the crew, except for Procter and me, were far from well. The first two or three days at sea can be harassing enough with a raw crew even if they are not seasick, as most likely they will be. Seized of this probability, as they like to say in Parliament, Procter and I dosed ourselves with Dramamine the night before in order to make sure that two at least of the crew should be on their feet. But in spite of all this extra work and worry, what a joy it was to be at sea again with the next port of call more than a fortnight away! Quite apart from the pleasures of sailing a boat, the sight and sound of the sea, the adventure of achieving some distant port aided only by the wind and one's own energy and skill, there are the unspiritual attractions of a life of comfort and security in a pleasant open-air prison, with a minimum of shaving and washing, and without the trouble of undressing at night.

We were allowed ample time to get our sea-legs. There was little enough wind until the following evening, when it freshened, enabling us to reach across the Channel on a course that would take us wide of Ushant. Meanwhile the great *Berlin* passed close by, the *American Guide* saluted us with three blasts and we began catching mackerel in large numbers. These were welcome in the galley, where John Lyons battled manfully in spite of bouts of sickness. As we crossed the Channel that night it was wonderfully clear, so clear that at midnight we could see the loom of both Ushant and the Lizard, the latter forty miles away. The wind held fair and steady until at noon of 2 August we had Ushant abeam twenty miles distant. In sailing vessels it is wise to give this great seamark a wide berth, both on account of the dense steamer traffic inshore and the strong tidal streams which swirl round it.

That evening the mainsail had to come down while we resewed about five feet of seam, a job which took nearly two hours. The same thing happened next day, but by then the wind had hauled round to north-east. We, therefore, stowed the main and hoisted the twin staysails. The persistent rolling which usually accompanies down-wind sailing soon began. The crew, however, had now found their sea-legs. They were also becoming so much more familiar with the gear that they often pulled the right rope without holding a debate. Nevertheless, after three days at sea I found it a little dismaying to be asked what the peak halyards were. Roger Tufft soon adapted himself, and had all the makings of a useful hand both on deck and aloft. He had a keen eye, too, when on watch for any signs of chafe, a most important thing on long passages, when carelessness in this respect may result in a rope becoming stranded in a matter of hours. Try as one may, it is not always possible so to arrange matters that a sheet or halyard leads clear without touching either another rope, the shrouds, or the life-rail. Where a rope touches anything it must be protected with a bit of old canvas, a 'scotsman' as it is called. One cannot carry an unlimited supply of spare rope, and the splicing of a damaged part may not be possible if the rope passes through a block as it usually does. Even 'long splices' as they are called, when made by an amateur, are liable to jam in a block or come adrift. Consequently, vigilance is needed from all concerned, especially at night when the helmsman is in sole charge of the deck. It was sometimes infuriating to come on deck to find that the helmsman, having quite rightly altered the trim of the sheets, had quite wrongly failed to change the position of the 'scotsman' accordingly.

We carried this fresh, favourable wind right across the Bay. *Mischief* has been lucky in the Bay of Biscay, having crossed it six times without ever receiving anything but the fairest of treatment. When the barometer started to fall and the wind to rise, we reefed the twins, and yet managed to make a run of 135 miles by sights. Rolling heartily though we were, John carried on unperturbed in the galley. Thoroughly inured as he now was to the fumes and the motion, even the upsetting of the breakfast porridge and milk twice in one morning failed to damp his spirits. His soaring ambition began to reach out for higher things than stewed apples for supper. The texture of his first steamed pudding may have been so close-grained that a harsh critic might have likened it to soft marble – if that is not a contradiction in terms – but each of its successors became more and more ethereal.

By now it was possible to assess with some accuracy the appetites of the crew, a subject of peculiar interest to me who had to feed them for twelve months, and for John who daily had to satisfy them. With mingled feelings of relief and misgiving I noted that Procter's former voracity had markedly abated, for the abatement was accompanied by some decline in his energy. In his place, as the human equivalent of wolves, sharks, cormorants, vultures and suchlike symbols of ravenous insatiability, we had Jim Osborne. We were not doing any hard work – far from it – and having made all allowances for youth, a big body and sea air, I have yet to see his equal in putting away food. We used him as a sort of sink. Nothing went back to the galley or was thrown away without our first asking Jim if he could make use of it, and the occasions when he could not were rare. Jan Garnier, on the other hand, ate hardly at all. A cigarette and a cup of tea were his idea of breakfast. He lost about two stone in the course of the voyage, but he could well afford it. Unlike the majority of sea cooks, who find that a spell in the galley destroys their appetite, John was a good trencherman, and neither Roger nor myself were delicate feeders.

As this was *Mischief*'s third voyage to Las Palmas the way was familiar. We had no occasion to sight any land on the way, thus sparing the navigator the embarrassment of having to explain away any unexpected landfalls. After an exceptionally good run of 600 miles in the first week, we ran out of wind. For two windless, foggy days we saw nothing and heard nothing; evidently we were well clear of the steamer track. The crew spent the time in bed, getting up for meals like so many invalids. How welcome after a calm is the first ripple of water along the side when the ship begins to speak. The clammy, windless gloom was succeeded by a sparkling day on which, with Genoa pulling like mad, we enjoyed a magnificent sail. At midday, far to the east, the lonely rocks with the lovely-sounding name, the Farilhoes, showed up faintly as we sped on southward in real yachting weather.

By nightfall, when we were some fifteen miles off the coast with the loom of Lisbon in sight, the wind died away. At night, when the wind is light, unless one has the strength of mind to have all the sails down, sleep is difficult for those below. On deck, where a glance over the side assures one the ship is moving, all seems comparatively quiet, but below it is like being inside a drum. Every groan and creak is magnified, blocks slam, canvas slats and occasionally one of the sheets falls slack and gives the deck a rousing thump, whereupon one rushes violently on deck to implore the astonished helmsman in the strongest terms to keep her quiet. That night in the middle watch, when I was thus tormented below, I heard amid the general racket a series of violent thumps along the hull. Everything on deck seemed normal, no derelicts or icebergs were in sight, but on peering over the side, I found a large dan buoy with a pole, such as marks the end of a net, hard and fast against our quarter. As we were unlashing the boathook it cleared itself and drifted way. When Roger went overboard next morning to see if there was any damage, he found a number of bare patches where the anti-fouling paint had been rubbed off. Naturally, after our previous experience, this alarmed me. The whole sea, I felt, must be alive with teredo worms converging on

Mischief's unprotected hull; and at Las Palmas, as I knew, there were no facilities for hauling out.

The weather had now become warm enough for shorts and sun-bathing, and presently the Portuguese Trades, as they are called, began pushing us along. Off the Portuguese coast in summer these fresh northerly winds can usually be relied upon to carry one south of Cape St Vincent, where the Trade winds proper take over. Our speed rose accordingly and daily runs of 120 and 130 miles became the rule. Thus we were soon approaching the Canaries and at midnight of 15 August we sighted the Isleta light outside Las Palmas, whereupon we hove to until it was time to enter the harbour.

CHAPTER FOUR

Las Palmas and Southwards

WE lay in the same berth and employed the same boatman and night-watchman as on the previous occasion two years before – a man of great age and considerable stupidity. He had a free flow of American-English which might have been valuable had it comprised anything besides obscene oaths. His infinite capacity for sleep he indulged while lying in his large and heavy dinghy alongside *Mischief*, with one oar hanging from a rope grommet scraping away idly at the paint on our hull. As this was a sensitive point with me by now, I used to get angry. But Fernando merely spat (he chewed tabacco), swore an oath or two and went to sleep. His duties as night-watchman did not weigh heavily upon him. In the evening we often happened upon him in the town, or while we were having supper in some dockside dive he might drop in, accept a drink, favour us with some choice oaths and take himself off. But he was always at hand with his boat when we wanted to go on board; he was an old though not valued friend, and his younger and more active fellow-boatmen, who would have liked his job, looked too like Spanish spivs to inspire confidence. The fact that we lost nothing while lying at Las Palmas is perhaps more a tribute to the honesty of the natives than to Fernando's vigilance.

Lying near us was the usual small number of ocean-going yachts that are always to be found at a pleasant, easy-going and comparatively cheap port like Las Palmas. One or two bound for the West Indies awaited the passing hurricane season; others waited, with or without hope, for funds which would enable them to leave; and a few merely found it impossible to get away. There was the magnificent and venerable 100-ton schooner *Amphitrite*, built at Gosport in 1887, which had just been bought by an American – rather rashly, one thought, in view of her size, age and the legal complications attending her. She had been sold by the Spanish authorities, who had seized her from the previous owner, an Englishman, who was still languishing in a Spanish gaol. This man, whom I had met two years before at the Consul's office when he was less strictly confined, had a complicated story to tell: how he had agreed to sell *Amphitrite* to a Spaniard at Tangier, but had not been paid: how on arriving at Las Palmas, the Spanish authorities had seized the boat as the property of the Spaniard: and how when the police boarded her, he had struck one for insulting his wife. Since, after two years, nothing had been done to right this apparent injustice, one could not but think that a part of the story had not been told. Next door to us lay a small, neglected, German-owned sloop, whose owner had evidently known better times. He used to depart for the day's shopping with a string bag, while his wife or partner, a strikingly handsome Creole, sat on deck sewing, occasionally blinding *Mischief*'s crew with a dazzling smile. There were also American and Australian ketches whose crews held aloof, and a Canadian with a Dutch-built boat and a Danish wife, or maybe the wife was Dutch-built. Judging from their lack of interest in us, it occurred to me that some of these ocean-voyagers are really sea-going beachcombers, so to speak, and that to them the idea of going anywhere in a boat with a purpose in view is not quite the thing.

My crew, I was pleased to find, were models of decorum, unlike the crew of the previous voyage, who, on arrival at Las Palmas, had disappeared to a man, returning before breakfast next morning much the worse for wear. Or the convivial soul we had with us on an earlier voyage who at every port we visited, whether or not he had any money, was seldom sober and contrived to bring about all kinds of embarrassing situations for me either with the Consul, the local yacht club, or the police.

We had enough work to do if we were to get away inside a week as I hoped. As we might well meet gales in the South Atlantic, we sent down the topmast. Without the topmast we lost only the use of the topsail, for by reeving a wire stay from the end of the bowsprit to the top of the mainmast we were still able to set a big Genoa. In the last few days at sea the Primus stoves had been giving trouble and the reason for it seemed to be water in the paraffin. We carried this in a 30 gal. tank on the port side of the engine formerly used for petrol, and since the outlet was a couple of inches above the bottom, this tank had a permanent residue of rust, petrol, paraffin and water, the mixture being thoroughly stirred when rolling about at sea. Procter and Tufft had a theory that this tank could be got out without dismantling half the ship, and in the course of a long afternoon of shoving and hauling they actually proved it; though not without first removing a few lockers and parts of the main engine. They then took it to the gas works, where Procter had made friends with the manager, and where it was cleaned by steam and the inside sprayed with cement. Putting the tank back took as long as getting it out, but at least we had not the nagging fear that we were attempting the impossible. It now became a water-tank, giving us a total of 230 gal. for the long haul to Cape Town, while the paraffin was carried in a 10 gal. drum on deck. In order not to waste time by putting in anywhere, I wanted to sail direct to Cape Town, a distance of over 6,000 miles. One can either call for water at the Cape Verde Islands, or at a Brazilian port, as we did on the previous voyage, for the sailing ship track passes fairly close to both. But by keeping well out from the coast of Brazil we should save three or four hundred miles, as well as the delay due to entering port.

At Las Palmas, where there are no facilities for hauling out small boats, the local fishing boats are careened in time-honoured fashion. As *Mischief* would not care for this sort of treatment, unless of course we took out all the ballast, I began making enquiries about alternative methods, for I was obsessed by the danger of the bare places on the hull. Luckily it was full moon and spring tides. We discovered that at high tide we could take *Mischief* alongside a wharf belonging to a coal company, where at low tide she would be high and dry on hard ground, the rise and fall being about eight feet at spring tides. At midday we went alongside and by evening we could walk round the hull slapping anti-fouling paint on the bare places where the dan buoy had left its mark.

We soon found that for getting any work done in port only three of us were generally available. Invariably John Lyons, after breakfast, washed his hands of us and the galley in order to spend the day ashore like a gentleman, sipping beer *al fresco* and having his shoes forcibly cleaned by the army of itinerant boot-black urchins that haunt the waterside cafés. Jim Osborne's propensity for absenting himself for the whole day on rock-collecting expeditions had not yet reached full fruition, as it did later at Cape Town, but whenever he could he disappeared with his hammer. Jan Garnier, with his cosmopolitan background – he had spent some years in America as well as in the Foreign Legion – picked up friends easily and in consequence was not much on board. Yet in five days we had completed the major jobs, besides brushing and oiling the wire rigging, painting the deck and turning the jib halyards, which have an awkward trick of twisting themselves into knots.

On the morning of Friday the 25th we made a final shopping round-up with the intention of watering and sailing that afternoon. Bread, wine, fruit, vegetables and 'twice-baked' bread were the main items. The latter, sliced bread or rolls baked a second time, is of the greatest value. There seems to be no limit to the time this 'twice-baked' bread keeps, whereas ordinary bread starts to go mouldy within ten days. To water we had to motor over to the quay where the trawlers lie and Jan presently discovered that the water pump of the charging engine was not working. A passing launch gave us a tow to the water point but by the time we got hold of a mechanic it was clear we should not sail that day. Besides a valve in the pump, two piston rings were broken and these could not be put right till next day.

With a fair wind next afternoon we sailed down the harbour, gybed round the breakwater, and stood out to sea. After gaining an offing of ten miles or so we were in a position to hoist the twins and steer south. Certainly the Trades were blowing pretty fresh but except in very strong winds we can usually get the mainsail off while running, that is, without having to bring the boat up into the wind. On this occasion, owing to faulty sail drill, the peak was dropped before the throat halyards had been started, with the result that the topping lift wound itself lovingly round the gaff. For a few minutes, until we could unshackle the topping lift, raise the peak again and drop the throat, the situation was fraught with anxiety, not to say peril, for until the boom is secured on its gallows anything may happen, from the tearing of the sail to someone being knocked out or knocked overboard by the boom. Lowering the mainsail in boisterous conditions always requires care. But in bad weather, when it will have been close-reefed long before there is any need to get it down, there is never much difficulty in handling the reduced sail however hard the wind.

We have never suffered from lack of wind in the vicinity of the Canaries. By breakfast next day we had reeled off ninety miles and in the three succeeding days we ran 360 miles. We had no complaints on that score but we had good reason to complain of the lack of life in the sea. In these waters we had been accustomed to catching an occasional fish, a dorado or a bonito, both delicious to eat. This time we caught none and were not destined to catch any, so that towards the end of the voyage we were too disgusted even to troll a line. Nor were the flying fish as numerous or accommodating as usually they are. It used to be an everyday occurrence, but now we rarely collected enough fish from the scuppers to give all hands a fish or two for breakfast. Dolphins, too, seemed less common than formerly. And the welcome break in the monotonous days of a long ocean passage which is made by a visit from a school of dolphin cannot come too often.

Those few species of fish which are neither frightened nor fierce are sad and solemn, whereas the dolphin, as befits its warm blood, seems to be always gay and frolicsome. It makes one laugh out loud to see them come scurrying after a ship they have just spotted, leaping into the air and turning somersaults as they come, as if overjoyed at the larks they're about to have. Scorning the dull wake, they make a bee-line for the stem, where a dozen of them begin to cross and re-cross in swift streaks of foam, missing by inches the plunging stem, the bobstay, and their jostling playmates. Everyone crowds in the bows, fascinated to watch these torpedo-like, olive-green shapes with white bellies, the embodiment of lithe speed and grace. Or to see another half-dozen, apparently waiting their turn for a dance round the stem, take station just off the bows in line abreast where together they rise, snort, and plunge while maintaining their dressing like a file of soldiers. I should like to see them having fun with a ship going at thirty knots. *Mischief* provided poor sport for creatures that with a scarcely perceptible flick of the tail shoot through the water like a bullet. Soon they would disappear as suddenly as they had come. Having had our amusement for the day, we would go below and the helmsman back to the tiller:

> Though pleased to see the dolphins play,
> I mind my compass and my way.

We were in the full swing of the Trades, which could be counted upon to carry us at least as far as the Cape Verde Islands some 900 miles to the south. With the twin staysails set we need hardly touch a rope and for the next ten days there would be little to do but steer. In the big sailing ships there was always plenty of work for crews that were proportionately scanty. In fact one wonders how that maze of rigging, literally miles of wire and rope, most of it out of sight from the deck, ever got looked after. In our case there was nothing to be done except the navigation and small repair jobs, both of which I was glad to do for the sake of occupation and a liking for 'sailorising'. Roger, too, soon picked up navigation and his results were a useful check on mine. With five men available, watch-keeping duties were extremely light, one spell of three hours at the helm by day and two hours at night. There was an ample collection of books on board – I will not call it a library – from the *Odyssey* in the original Greek (Procter) to geological tomes, Space Travel, Westerns, and the *Scragged in her Silk Stockings* type. They catered for all tastes, and they might have come off the sixpenny barrow.

Besides reading, most of the crew had an infinite capacity for sleep which, in such circumstances, is of great value. Chess was played too, and Jim was quite insatiable. Sometimes we had to postpone changing sails until a game was finished, but when he and Procter started playing chess on watch I had to draw the line. Chess is usually a silent game but Procter maintained a running commentary for the benefit of his small public, who were anyway reading. It went like this:

'Let's see now. If I go there he'll take me with the bishop. No, that's not a good move. I'll just push this pawn up and wait for my plan to fructify. The situation seems not unpromising.... Hell! There goes my queen! I never saw that knight, Jim. Are you quite sure it was on the right square?'

Thus, day and night, with no help from us but a touch of the tiller, the ship rolled southwards, the long booms of the twins slowly describing wide arcs between sea and sky, the pursuing seas creaming along the hull and spurting through the scuppers at every roll. On the last day of August we had the Cape Verde Islands abeam sixty miles to the east and out of sight. The *Sailing Directions* advise keeping well west of the islands in order to hold a better wind, and on this occasion we got well to the south of them before the Trades began to weaken. On previous voyages, mainly for the sake of seeing the islands, when we had sailed through them, we found the wind fitful. Islands have a powerful attraction for the seafarer, even though they are barren slag-heaps like most of the Cape Verde Islands. But the island of Fogo, the most southern and possibly the most barren of the group, which rises to over 9,000ft. had been a thrilling and inspiring sight when we passed that way in 1958. At dawn we had it close aboard, draped in cloud almost from sea to summit, and as we drifted slowly by, the clouds little by little lifted until the full 9,000ft. of violet-hued slopes towered above us. As the name implies, the peak is volcanic and not yet extinct.

When we were twelve days out from Las Palmas, the Trades at last began to falter, twelve days of indolence and tranquil sun-drenched hours until:

> Languor suffering on the rack of bliss
> Confess that man was never made for this.

As the wind veered and finally settled in south-west, while the sky clouded over and a steady drizzle began, we took in the twins and hoisted all plain sail. Between the North-east and South-east Trades are the doldrums, the two hundred or three-hundred-mile-wide region where calms, light variable winds and rain squalls are to be expected. It shifts north or south according to the time of year and may be narrower or wider. On this occasion we were lucky, for we had fairly steady winds from south to south-west and by standing on the starboard tack we made good progress south or a little east of south. As the Equatorial current sets strongly towards Brazil, it is unwise to go on the other tack until one is sure of having picked up the SE Trades. On account of this current, southward-bound ships have sometimes been unable to weather Cape San Roque, in which case they have to make the circuit of the North Atlantic and try again. On the previous voyage we had stood on the port tack when we met these south-west winds and had fetched up between Cape San Roque and Recife. As we were bound for San Salvador, 300 miles to the south, we had to sail close-hauled or even tack in order to make it.

Thanks to some very heavy squalls of rain we were able to refill the 40 gal. deck-tank. The mainsail makes an excellent catchment area, and if it is reefed with one roll round the boom, the rain runs along the boom and trickles out by the mast. The man on water duty, usually stripped naked, slings saucepans on the boom and empties them into the tank. This is warm, wet fun, while at the same time he can wash clothes and have a fresh-water bath. For Roger and me such baths were superfluous, for we made a solemn rite of pouring three buckets of sea-water over ourselves before breakfast, wet or fine. Having then combed our hair we sat down to breakfast with a warranted feeling of superiority over our frowsy companions, except for John, who had been called at 7 am, had probably already shaved, looked wide awake and was comparatively cheerful, sometimes too cheerful. When John banged a plate by way of a bell, Procter, like a lean, dishevelled fakir, would crawl sideways out of his blankets and slide into his seat, the blankets being left in *statu quo*, so that he could crawl back into them after breakfast. The only time, I think, he folded them was the day we got back to Lymington when he was about to leave the ship. We now had the table covered with some plastic material of a tasteful red, having advanced a long way since the days when we used newspapers. But this meant that there was nothing handy on the table for Procter to read, so he had to rummage among his blankets for his Greek Homer or, failing that, some Space Fiction.

Jim, whose bunk was above Procter's, and, therefore, rather close to the deckhead, had on this account very little freeboard for his face. Since there was no possibility of his first sitting up, he too rolled out sideways, but he did it circumspectly for fear of treading on Procter. By now he had a beard, and since his sparse hair hardly warranted combing, his appearance was less shocking. Jan, who never ate breakfast, put in a sort of token appearance, for it was a rule – enforced against some murmuring – that everyone should be up for breakfast whether or not he wanted any. Under the circumstances it was usually a sombre meal. There was no need to discourage hilarity, for it was never contemplated. Speech, if anyone was foolhardy enough to attempt it, usually concerned the prevailing weather or the ship's progress during the night. All this, of course, is standard practice at breakfast tables and there was no reason why we should depart from it even if we were on the high seas.

Since porridge uses a lot of water, on alternate days we had dried eggs. I confess that dried egg is best eaten in cakes, when one is not aware of it, but if well laced with pepper, or better still chillies, it can be eaten with modified ecstasy. I was shocked to find that Procter, who used to be omnivorous in the full sense of the word, could not face it. When both the bread and the 'hard-bake' were finished we used Lifeboat biscuits for conveying the largest possible amount of butter and marmalade to the mouth. It was mainly out of consideration for these trimmings that we had to ration the biscuit.

For lunch we rang the changes on cheese, sardines, herrings, bully beef or Spam, with dates, Marmite or peanut butter as 'afters'. The cheeses were whole ten-pound Cheddars. Although packed in salt they did not keep well, becoming in time a little dry and more than a little strong. However, with a raw onion to qualify the tang they went down very well, at least John and I thought so. Onions always keep well and it is a time-honoured principle that one should never go to sea without one. Hard, white cabbages also keep, and for the first month or six weeks of a passage we used cabbage for salads. For tea we had biscuits and jam, sweet biscuits and occasionally cake, pancakes or soda bread, depending on the cook's benevolence towards us.

But the evening meal we regarded as our main hope and stay, like so many gross rustics 'whose principal enjoyment is their dinner, and who see the sun rise with no other hope than that they shall fill their belly before it sets.' It consisted of whatever dish the skill and ingenuity of the cook might concoct from ingredients limited to bully beef, sausages, Spam, rice, beans, lentils, peas, macaroni, spaghetti, potatoes and onions, helped out with dried vegetables and soups for flavouring. This would be followed by stewed prunes, raisins or apples, or a massive steamed pudding. The crew took it in turns to help the cook by drawing sea water, emptying the gash bucket and filling the stoves. He washed the pans too, while John did the plates and utensils. Sea water can be used for cooking potatoes, likewise for porridge and rice if sufficiently diluted, and all the washing-up is done with it. I had not been able to get any dehydrated meat such as we had on previous voyages. For cooking it is far better than bully beef, which is best eaten when cold.

The mainsail still had to come down frequently to have seams restitched. In the doldrums, when it was sodden with rain, this was no fun. Sewing wet flax canvas is a tedious job because the needle sticks and has to be dragged through with pliers, a method which sooner or later breaks the needle. Provided we could keep the sail full we had no trouble, but with a gaff mainsail a light wind is constantly spilled from the sail by the gaff swinging about. By means of a boom guy and a kicking strap the boom can be held steady but the gaff is impossible to control. The vang (pronounced 'wang' by Thames bargemen), a rope leading down from the peak of the gaff, is used when lowering the sail but it does not stop the gaff swinging. Thus while the boom remains steady the gaff swings and gives the loose canvas a flick like the crack of a whip which puts a fierce strain on the seams. If the wind dropped in the night, the helmsman had to make up his mind whether to call the sleeping crew to get the sail down or to whistle for a wind and wait hopefully. If he waited too long he might find, when he next flashed his torch over the sail, that several feet of seam had opened. In this respect a Bermuda sail is preferable as there is no gaff to torment the sail. On the other hand, the gaff rig is more efficient down-wind, the commonest point of sailing on an ocean voyage, and is much more pleasing to look at.

Owing to constant cloud and rain we got no noon sight for latitude until 10 September, when we were four degrees north of the Equator. The weather continued uncertain and squally as we worked our way south, first on one tack then on the other, until on the 16th we crossed the line in Longitude 24 west. John celebrated the event with a particularly fine cake iced with Equatorial emblems. By crossing the Equator so far east, we were well placed, being 500 miles to windward of Cape San Roque, in spite of having been set 30 miles a day westward by the Equatorial current. For a vessel bound south, the South-east Trades are not very favourable until she is about five degrees south of the Line, when they begin to draw more to the east, thus allowing her to steer south without being close-hauled all the time. When the wind freed us a little, we set one of the twins in place of the working jib to give us more speed. We got little benefit from it, for the same night, in a squall, the clew split and the remnants we gathered in were not worth putting together. Strong, squally weather with a rough sea continued for several days and gave us a fine shove to the south. Knocking off two degrees of latitude a day, by 27 September, when five weeks out, we had logged 3,000 miles and were half-way to the Cape.

On the long passage, with hundreds or thousands of miles of sea-room on all sides, the course will vary from day to day according to the wind. There is an ideal track to be followed if the wind permits, but it pays to sail free, go faster and to forget the ideal track rather than to follow it by sailing close-hauled. But since the track for sailing vessels bound for Cape Town passes close to the island of South Trinidad, we made every effort to stick to it. Rather than pass the island out of sight, we were ready to forgo comfortable sailing, and, if necessary, to put in some hard beating. As luck would have it we found we could easily lay the course for the island. Sure enough at dawn of 30 September, under a massive ink-blue cloud, an unmistakably harder outline appeared right on the bow some fifteen miles away.

To the modern professional sailor a landfall is just part of the day's work. Short, fast passages, precise navigation, time signals, radio beacons and radar should leave little room for error, so that sighting the land he is aiming for should be as inevitable as sunrise. This, coupled with long use and wont, must banish all the romance with which the amateur sailor surrounds his landfalls. For him the element of uncertainty is still there and in it lies part of the charm. The charm of uncertainty, of course, loses some of its flavour when it becomes apparent that a gross mistake has been made, but unless the mistake has dire consequences, one learns a lesson and hopes to do better next time. Besides the mere satisfaction of proving one's navigation correct, or the anticipated pleasure of stepping on shore, there is a wonderful thrill to be got from sighting a long-looked-for island or headland rising from the sea in the appointed place. The thrill increases enormously with the number of days spent at sea. After a passage of weeks surrounded by an unbroken horizon of water, the voyager feels that the first land he sights is a discovery of his own and it has for him personally a reassuring, friendly quality. An island landfall, especially when made at dawn, has a sharp ecstatic flavour, quite distinct from any other. All these conditions were now fulfilled. After five weeks at sea an island appeared at dawn, more or less in the place expected.

From afar off we could see a fine, jagged skyline, and as we drew near the savage grandeur of the rock scenery grew ever more striking; black ravines, yellow pinnacles, the red scars of landslides and, strangest of all, a circular column of basalt rock rising from the beach to over 800ft., quite detached from the cliffs behind it. This pillar is called on the chart 'Il Monumento'. Some patches of green had the appearance of grass and the 3,000ft. high summit was covered with some kind of scrub. Trees there are now none, though early visitors to the island described it as well forested. The wind fell light and headed us so that we could pass no nearer than three miles off its western shore. The island is steep-to and there are no off-lying dangers, but landing is usually difficult and often impossible owing to the surf. Apart from this deterrent we never had it in mind to attempt a landing, for on an expedition such as ours it is best to keep the end firmly in mind, resolutely putting aside such a fatally fascinating lure as a mountainous, uninhabited treasure island.

For buried treasure is the lure which has attracted quite a few visitors to South Trinidad. The last and most determined effort to find the treasure is well described in *The Cruise of the Alerte* by E. F. Knight, war correspondent and yachtsman, who made the attempt in 1890. The story of the treasure has all the rich, romantic, Stevensonian ingredients. It begins in 1848 on board an East Indiaman engaged in the opium trade. One of her quartermasters was a Russian Finn who, on account of the sinister appearance lent him by a deep scar on the face, was known as the Pirate. On passage to Bombay the Pirate fell ill with dysentery and was nursed by the captain himself. Ultimately the disease killed him, but before he died in a Bombay hospital he sent for the captain and confided to him the story of the treasure; how an immense hoard of gold and silver lay buried on South Trinidad, much of it looted from churches in Lima during the war of independence, including gold candlesticks from the cathedral; and how he himself was the sole survivor of those who had made the cache, his fellow pirates having been caught by the Spaniards and executed in Cuba. Finally he gave the captain a piece of tarpaulin on which was a map of the island with the necessary clues for locating the cache.

Attempts had already been made to find the treasure, for the island is only 600 miles off the Brazil coast and easy to reach. But as Knight says: 'Patience is a necessary quality for those who wish to land on South Trinidad. One must not expect to sail there and disembark forthwith as if it were on Southsea Pier.' Besides the landing problem there are other drawbacks such as a lack of water and ravenous land-crabs. Moreover, a landslide has blotted out the clues. Knight and his party made a really serious bid. They dug steadily for three solid months, shifting thousands of tons of earth and rock, until convinced that further labour would be in vain. All this provides a well-told tale of danger and hardship – the danger always attendant upon landing and the hardship involved in navvy work on a hot, thirsty island. The party took their disappointment gaily. It is amusing to read that after much debate they had decided that if the treasure were found, they would return home in the largest mail steamer; the lives of millionaires being too valuable to trust to a small boat, even to so seaworthy a craft as *Alerte* proved herself to be.

CHAPTER FIVE

Cape Town

SOUTH Trinidad lies in S. lat. 20° 30′. A few more degrees and we would be able to start steering east of south until on the latitude of Cape Town, when we would run down our easting. We had almost finished with the South-east Trades and were about to enter a region of variables, the Horse Latitudes, which extend to beyond thirty degrees south, where the westerlies begin to blow. And since we were now out of the tropics we had to keep a weather eye lifting. In the tropics, or even up to thirty degrees either side of the Line, unless in a region where tropical storms occur, gales are so rare that one is apt to forget there are such things. In the South Atlantic tropical storms are unknown, so that we had nothing to worry about in that respect. Day after day the barograph needle traced a straight line across its chart, perfectly straight except for the slight diurnal variation which occurs regularly around ten o'clock and four o'clock by day and by night. There is a similar diurnal variation in higher latitudes but it is masked by the much greater pressure changes which take place, so that it is only perceptible in very settled weather.

In S. lat. 22° we saw our first albatross and Cape pigeons, a low latitude for such birds, whose normal habitat is in much colder waters. There was no doubt about our being in a region of variables. For a whole day we would just creep along, our one aim being to keep the sails quiet, and the next we would be close-reefed for a moderate gale. For two days we ran before a powerful westerly wind accompanied by driving rain, logging six knots with both main and stays'l close-reefed. Twice the helmsman contrived to scare the life out of me with accidental gybes, my hair standing on end while the boom hung high overhead tugging at the wire guy, the guy quivering like a bowstring under the terrific strain. As the sail was close-reefed, the boom guy held its own, bending one of the life-rail stanchions in the effort. With the whole mainsail set, an accidental gybe might well break the boom guy so that the boom would crash over unchecked and carry away the backstay or worse. In mountaineering jargon an accidental gybe on the part of the helmsman would be classed as a subjective danger. Such dangers are less foreseeable and more disconcerting than the objective dangers threatened by wind and waves.

While it is true that what goes up must come down, it is a pity that once the sea has got up it takes a mighty long time to go down. For a whole day and night or more after the wind has dropped the sea goes on slopping about as if glad to be free of the tyranny of the wind. Such times are hard both on the ship's gear and on the tempers of the crew. There is probably enough wind for sailing if only the sea would stop rocking the boat and spilling the wind from the sails as soon as they begin to draw. The mainsail being useless under such conditions, we boomed out our remaining twin and the stays'l. It was a lopsided, ungraceful rig and while we were under it we met our only ship. Not many ships ply the South Atlantic, so it was with some excitement that we first spotted her and began to calculate how close she would pass. Soon she altered course with the obvious intention of speaking to us and when she was some hundreds of yards off she stopped her engines and let her way carry her slowly by. She was the *Tregarne* of the Haines Line bound north. Her crew were greatly interested in us and lined the rail to ask questions and bandy remarks. Her master having assured himself that we were all right gave three farewell blasts on the whistle and proceeded on his way. Apart from one occasion in the North Atlantic when a steamer nearly ran us down in the dark, this was the closest I have ever seen one come. The meeting and the brief conversation with these fellow-voyagers gave us great pleasure. In a modified way it was like the 'gam' that sailing ships, and especially whaling ships, used to have when they met at sea. The vessels would heave to, and from one or the other a boat with the master in it would row across, and while the respective masters swopped news in the saloon, the boat's crew compared notes in the forecastle.

I expect the *Tregarne*'s people gave us a thought that night when the glass began to fall steeply. We ran all night under a reefed mainsail until by morning, when it was blowing a gale, the mainsail had to come down. As it already had several rolls round the boom there were only about eight feet of the luff hoisted, so that we had no difficulty in getting it in even though the lee side topping-lift was not shackled on. The point being that with no topping-lift on the lee side, the sail is free to belly out to leeward and is less easy to gather in. By this time we were shipping a lot of water. While I was kneeling to relash the spare spars on the weather side a solid lump of it caught me bending, as it were, soaking me to the skin in spite of oilskins. For the first time this voyage we had to fit weather-boards in the companion-way leading down from the cockpit, for in rough weather spray and solid water leap over the cockpit coaming. The cockpit is self-draining; that is it has two drainpipes which drain the water back into the sea. The lockers under the cockpit seats act as drains too, and much more quickly than the proper drains; but their water merely goes into the bilge, whence we have to pump it out.

A few minutes' work with an old-fashioned barrel pump fitted on deck usually suffices to empty the bilge, and we have also a rotary pump below in the 'heads,' and another small pump which works off the charging engine provided that is not out of order. Such a multiplicity of pumps does not imply that *Mischief* is particularly wet. In normal conditions a few strokes of the pump every other day are enough to clear the well, but at this time we were making water through some loose caulking in way of the shroud plates, a fault which we attended to at Cape Town. We had on board a canvas weather dodger which when fitted to stanchions on the cockpit coaming will keep out a lot of the spray. I was reluctant to fit it, and we never did fit it, because it not only interferes with the handling of the sheets but it also cramps the style of the helmsman. Snuggling behind the weather dodger he is apt to become weather-bound, less able to see what is going on around him and, above all, less ready to sense a shift of wind.

By the time this blow had subsided we were in lat. 31 S., about 300 miles north of Tristan da Cunha. Considering the latitude and the season – early spring in the southern hemisphere – we thought it unseasonably cold. Some of the crew took to wearing gloves when on watch. Meantime we had the wind dead astern, an awkward point of sailing with fore-and-aft rig if the wind is at all strong and the following seas big enough to make steering difficult. Except in the Trades one is reluctant or too lazy to hoist the twins, a gesture which is almost certain to make the wind back or veer. A better device is to tack down wind, sailing a couple of points off course and thus keeping the headsails full, sailing faster, and avoiding any risks of an accidental gybe. For a time this method seems highly satisfactory until one begins thinking how absurd it is to be sailing two points off the desired course when the wind is free. So on this occasion, by way of experiment, we squared the mainsail and boomed out a twin on the opposite side. She steered very nicely, dead before the wind, right on course, but with no margin for error. The gybe that I had expected soon occurred. Although the guy did not break, it tore out the fairlead through which it passed, thus giving the boom enough scope to slam over and break the backstay. Hauling in the mainsheet, we gybed back, got the sail down and reverted to the slower but safer rig of boomed out headsails.

On 22 October we crossed the Greenwich meridian. We were already a little south of the latitude of Cape Town and had less than 20 degrees of easting to make. In that latitude a degree of longitude represents only about 44 miles, so we had broken into the last thousand miles. But in a sailing ship distance expressed in terms of miles has little meaning. It all depends where you are. In the Trades or the Westerlies, for example, a thousand miles seems of little account, while in a region where calms or head winds may be expected a hundred miles seems almost unattainable. Between ports, therefore, the distance by the sailing ship route is usually expressed in the number of days an average passage will take.

Stowed in the forepeak we had a new coil of two and a half-inch tarred, Italian hemp which I had acquired in a job lot. It was tough stuff, the sort of rope you can fit and forget, and although when new it was about as kindly and amenable as wire, I intended using it for the main sheet and the main halyards. Accordingly we got a length of it for the main sheet on deck and stretched it for two days before reeving it. It still kinked like the devil and when wet was as hard as a board, but I reckoned that by the time the serious business began south of Cape Town it would handle easily. Of all the minor accidents that might befall a small boat, the parting of the main-sheet, for choice in the middle of the night, seems to me one of the worst. In the opening chapters of *Moby Dick* such an accident happens on board a Nantucket schooner. While the great boom is sweeping the deck, knocking an unfortunate passenger into the sea, the paralysed crew look on from a position of safety. But Queequeg, the redoubtable harpooner, lassoos the murderous spar and brings it up with a round turn. What's more, he then dives overboard – it is mid-winter – and rescues the half-drowned passenger. What sea adventures one might accomplish if skipper and crew were so many Queequegs!

Two more strong blows gave us runs of 130 and 135 miles. They were perfect examples of South Atlantic depressions, the wind and rain setting in from the north-west, later backing and blowing harder from south-west while the sky begins to clear and the sun comes out. On the night of 29 October when we were about 300 miles from land we heard penguins mooing. At least some of us thought they mooed like a cow, while others compared the noise to that made by the old-fashioned motor horn which you squeezed. They were jackass penguins, which breed on various islands off the west coast of South Africa. They are of some commercial importance as producers of guano and their eggs are collected and sold in Cape Town, where they are in such demand that they have to be ordered in advance. The birds are protected and no visitors are allowed on the islands where they breed.

The morning of our last day but one at sea began inauspiciously. While having my morning bathe I lost a canvas bucket over the side, and a little later dropped a shackle pin into the sea in the same lubberly fashion. As the sea temperature was now down to sixty degrees, I took the loss of the bucket as a hint to stop bathing, but Roger carried on until we reached the Crozet Islands. Misfortune did not end there. In the evening as we were swigging up the stays'l, having just boomed it out, the halyard parted and sail and boom fell into the sea. We were going quite fast at the time, and before we could get it back on board, the boom, a new one, broke.

As night fell we saw the lights of two ships to the north, a sign that we were getting near, and a little later the loom of the Slangkop and Cape Point lights. At two in the morning we had an adventure with a trawler. Trawlers should always be given plenty of room, for when they have their trawls down they are unable, or at least very unwilling, to alter course. We were horribly close to one when Roger called me up. By sailing very close to the wind we might or might not pass astern of her, and if we put the helm up we might just shave her bows. Finally, by trying to sail too close to the wind, we got the ship in irons, which was probably the best thing we could have done. She passed less than 50 yards away. I expected to receive a volley of abuse, but no one seemed to notice us.

It can easily be imagined with what satisfaction we watched the sun rise over Cape Point on Sunday, 1 November, after 71 days at sea, during which we had sighted only South Trinidad and one solitary ship. As a shake-down cruise it was perhaps on the long side, but not too long in view of the inexperience of the crew and the slowness of one or two to learn. We had experienced all kinds of weather and although there had been no violent gales, the crew had seen enough of *Mischief*'s ability as a sea-boat to give them confidence.

We ended this long haul with a most enjoyable sail. The day was fine, the wind fair from SSW, and close on our starboard hand stretched the high, bold outline of the Cape Peninsula, with the Twelve Apostles and the vast bulk of Table Mountain dominating the scene. As is very often the way on that coast, by the time we had closed the land and brought Green Point abeam a fresh South-easter was blowing out of Table Bay right in our teeth. Hardening the sheets we began to beat up to the Duncan Dock entrance, and having got inside we handed the sails preparatory to motoring to the Yacht Basin. As our arrival could hardly have been expected, I was surprised to see the Club launch approaching, in it the Club Secretary, Commander F. Windsor, and several other men, some with cameras, who were obviously the Press. Fame at last, I thought. The mysterious grape-vine or jungle drums by which the arrival or passage of important people is foretold had evidently been busy. Still it was smart work. As the launch drew near and Freddie Windsor's face lit up with recognition – for he knew us from our previous visit – I noticed that the Pressmen looked a little crest-fallen. We were soon enlightened. *Mischief* had been mistaken for an American yacht on her maiden voyage from Japan, where she had been built, which was now due at Cape Town from East London. This yacht *Tenba* arrived next day looking extremely smart and yacht-like. No one would make the same mistake twice. However, our welcome was warm enough. The launch wasted no time in towing us to the Club jetty and presently, in the Clubhouse, we were sitting down to the traditional South African dish of steak and fried eggs.

There can be no more congenial place or one with more facilities for the cruising yachtsman to refresh and refit than Cape Town, more particularly the Royal Cape Yacht Club. Help and hospitality are offered so unstintingly that they become embarrassing in so far as one can never hope to repay them. The members are always ready with advice and generous practical help, and since among them they represent many different trades, businesses and professions, there are few problems which one or other of them is not able to tackle. Many of them are keen and experienced sailors and quite a few are capable of building or have actually built their boats. Unlike in England, there are in South Africa no yards solely devoted to building and repairing yachts, so that this practical knowledge and ability is probably more widespread among Cape yachtsmen than it is with us. But there is also a professional shipwright who works on the Club boats and of his services we had to make use.

In spite of the slightly discouraging conditions for local cruising there are a good number of large yachts afloat in the Basin. Table Bay itself is a magnificent stretch of water, but on the coast generally, small harbours or anchorages are scarce. And to make a passage eastwards, a yacht must pass both the Cape of Good Hope and Cape Agulhas, notoriously stormy capes, besides having to contend with the strong Agulhas current. The maintenance, too, of a boat lying in the Yacht Basin has some discouraging aspects. In summer South-easters are frequent and violent, sweeping unhindered across the Basin, filling the air with particles of sand and gravel and thus sand-blasting, with horrible efficiency, a boat's varnish and paint-work. When the wind is in its other most favoured quarter, the north-west, it carries smoke from the docks to blacken all one's rigging. To add insult to injury, large numbers of sea-birds like roosting at night on the yachts, so that those that are not festooned with nets, strings or scarecrows are liable to become miniature guano islands. More serious than all this is the effect that the hot sun of the long, rainless summer has on wooden decks and hulls. But all these disheartening conditions are ignored or overcome and yachting flourishes in South Africa as it does at home.

We planned to leave about the end of November. We had quite a lot of work to do; and as well as the pleasure we should have from a longer stay, if we delayed our departure we should have, for what it was worth, the benefit of a full moon when we were near the Crozet. In those latitudes the December nights would be short and if the moon was full the short nights would hold few terrors. Sighting the islands might well be difficult, so that the help we might have from a full moon was not to be neglected. We had no fear that our time at Cape Town would hang heavily. Thanks to the kindness of various people we had numerous social engagements, I myself becoming doubly involved owing to my interest in climbing as well as sailing.

The Mountain Club of South Africa is naturally centred on Cape Town, where it has its own recently built premises in the city and its principal playground a few miles outside. I thought it a tribute either to the keenness, the loquacity, or the long-suffering nature of Cape Town climbers that their large lecture hall is more or less filled every Friday night through the year, in contrast to our clubs based, for example, on London, Liverpool or Manchester, where a meeting once a month in the winter is deemed more than enough. In the eyes of a mountaineer Table Mountain would be more satisfying if it culminated in a peak instead of being crowned by a great flat plateau. The cragsman, on the other hand, need want nothing more. To him, as he watches its great wall towering aloof from the noisy city, the dark ravines, the gaunt precipices and springing buttresses must be a constant source of solace, inspiration and challenge. And like all mountains worthy of the name, its aspect is seldom the same, one day smiling in sun-bathed serenity, the next frowning gloomily while streamers of cloud from the white blanket enveloping the summit rush fiercely down the gullies.

On the miles of more or less continuous wall encircling the mountain there are up to 300 climbing routes, from easy to very severe, on ridge, buttress, face or gully, some of them of great length and great exposure. On several occasions a few friends in the Mountain Club were kind enough to forgo their own fun for the sake of taking me up some of the easy climbs. The week-end climbing has a far from solemn ritual of its own. On Sunday morning, not too early, numerous cars disgorge parties of men and women, all in shorts with bare legs and arms, at the foot of the pipe-line track. Though the air was balmy the shorts made me shudder. Although it is in a few situations permissible or even essential, I admit that the use of the knees when rock-climbing is the mark of the tyro, though I myself use them whenever convenient. But it was not that which made me marvel at the amount of skin left bare, but the fact that on all the paths to the climb, and more so on the summit plateau, there is a great quantity of assorted vegetation, some of it of a very virulent kind. As well as thorns and cacti with cutting leaves, there is the 'blister bush', which has only to touch the skin to raise a crop of painful blisters. In East

Africa when we had any bush-crawling to do – cissies that we must have been – we used to wear slacks and roll down our sleeves. But the Table Mountain flora is by no means all noxious and is extremely rich and varied. There are many varieties of beautiful flowering heaths, brooms, a profusion of proteas, lilies, gladioli and ground orchids of every colour, including the justly famed Red Disa, the so-called Pride of Table Mountain. These flowers, which make a walk on the mountain so pleasurable, are wisely protected, all collecting being forbidden.

From the climber's point of view this profuse vegetation might be thought superfluous but it is not really so. The steep faces, where most of the serious climbing is done, are clean rock. For climbers on the ridges and in the gullies, though the vegetable covering might offend the purist, it comes in handy for belays, supplementary handholds, and, above all, fuel. For these semi-nude parties we saw assembling on the pipe-track are expedition-minded, fully aware that climbers, as well as armies, march on their stomachs. After an hour's stroll along the well-graded track with the hot, stony slopes of the mountain on one side and on the other, far below, the foam-flecked sea, we come to a convenient spring and abundant firewood. Out of capacious rucksacks come smoke-grimed billycans, veterans of countless bivouacs and *al fresco* meals, to be perched cunningly on stones or on the traditional forked sticks over each party's little fire. After our 'elevenses,' tea, chops and an egg or two, the fires are carefully quenched, and the various parties peel off by lesser tracks leading to the foot of the chosen climb. By now it is getting really warm and one begins to see sense in shorts. If it looks like being very hot, our climb may have been chosen with a view to remaining in the shade, in a gully for example, but this is, of course, a refinement that the traditionally hardy mountaineer would wish to achieve more by accident than design.

In any case, our climb is a leisurely affair as befits a warm day, a party of five or more, including both novices and an elderly seaman, besides all the hauling up of sacks with their precious loads on the steeper pitches. The climb will certainly have been chosen with due regard to luncheon sites, that is to say the presence of wood and water at or near the top of the climb. In high summer when some of the springs and water pockets are dry, a knowledge of where water is certain to be found is essential. The baggage of a well-found party, such as ours, is almost certain to include a length of plastic tubing for sucking or siphoning water out of inaccessible crannies. Water having been found, the party scatters to collect firewood and in no time the billies are boiling and the steaks broiling on long wooden skewers. This is the highlight of the day: perched on our mountain eyrie, replete with food and drink, we gaze down to the deep indigo sea where fishing boats crawl like beetles and the rollers break on dazzling white beaches. The descent is usually by one of the numerous gullies, preferably one on the shady side of the mountain and having a convenient spring at its foot where we can brew up for the third and last time.

The young climbers and Tigers, of whom there are many in the Mountain club, might scorn such a picnic. But in all such clubs there are many who love the mountains for their own sake, for whom it is enough to be on a mountain either in good company or alone; and for those like myself, whose years have calmed their climbing passions without dulling their faculty for enjoyment, such a day is admirably suited. And I have a suspicion that for me the wind was tempered, that out of regard for one who was just home from the sea, the arrangements for the party's welfare were more elaborate than usual. Besides Table Mountain there are in the Cape Province alone many mountains and mountain ranges from 5,000ft. to 9,000ft., little known and little climbed, which offer strenuous climbing and the pioneering of new routes. But Table Mountain by its proximity is naturally the main scene of activity, and the Club is its recognised guardian against encroachment by those who wish to push the suburbs of Cape Town ever higher up its slopes or to make motor roads to the summit. The members also expect to be called out in the frequently occurring cases of mountain accidents to tourists and non-climbers. As is well known, there is a cable-way to the summit plateau. It is, of course, something of an eye-sore, especially the terminus building perched on the edge of a fine precipice. Occasionally, when owing to a sudden change of weather a cable-car load of tourists is stranded on the summit, all available climbers are called upon to shepherd them down.

The Yacht Club has its own slipway capable of hauling out boats as big as *Mischief* with a displacement of 35 tons or more. It is generally in use but we were kindly allotted two days on which we could remain on the slip. Meantime we lay to a mooring with our stern about ten yards from a concrete jetty separating the Yacht Basin from Duncan Dock. Thus we had easy access to the shore, for instead of rowing to the Club jetty we could haul the dinghy along one of our shore warps and scramble up the concrete wall. But with a South-easter blowing this method was out of the question. Waves broke furiously against the wall so that passengers were certain to be soaked and the dinghy likely to be holed. In fact, when this notorious Cape Town scourge, the South-easter, was blowing, any going ashore or getting off again became impossible. One such which blew for three days shortly after our arrival obliged us to spend two nights unwillingly ashore. We would assemble hope-fully in the Clubhouse in the expectation of a lull occurring towards midnight as it sometimes did. But when no lull came we had to bed down for the night in armchairs or on the floor.

Upon *Mischief*'s being hauled out on the slip, we scrubbed the bottom and left it at that, as the anti-fouling paint was in good condition. We painted the topsides again, and Ted Misplon, the shipwright, caulked the leak in the way of the shroud-plates. While preparing the topsides for painting, we found a soft spot in the stern block, the massive piece of timber in the counter to which the after ends of the hull planking and deck planking are fixed. It seemed to be a minor job, which Ted said he would see to before we sailed. Meantime he scarfed and glued the boom for the twins that we broke.

We sent the mainsail ashore for machine stitching. I had all the seams resewn and a new line of stitching run down the middle of each seam making three lines of stitching to each seam. That, together with our technique of always casting off the lee side topping-lift whenever we went about, proved effective. In future we seldom had the mainsail down for repair. At the same time I ordered a new twin to be made ready against our return four months later. It did not seem likely that boomed out twin stay-sails would be in much demand south of Cape Town. Some of our stores needed replenishing. No one would have foreseen that in Cape Town tinned butter is not to be had. But the friendly firm of ship-chandlers got over this by persuading the research department of the Metal Box Company to do some experimental work on packing butter in tins. We refilled our big demi-john with red wine. I was told it was the same as that supplied to the crews of Italian ships, who are apparently choosy about their wine, at six shillings a gallon. Cursed bad wine is better than holy water but this wine was by no means bad in spite of its absurd cheapness. I toyed with the idea of having our 30gal. tank filled with it, the tank we had been at such pains to have cleaned at Las Palmas. As they say in Spain, a day without wine is a day without sun and we might expect many sunless days on the way to the islands.

27 November was the day appointed for sailing. On the day before, Ted Misplon started work on that small job in the counter. As he chiselled away in search of sound wood for the scarf to rest on, the hole got bigger and bigger until at last it became apparent that the whole block was rotten. The only thing to do was to fit a new stern block, a piece of wood about seven feet long and one foot each way, which besides having to be curved in three directions, needed a great number of rabbets cutting so that it would fit into place. If he had been slow in starting the job, Ted wasted no time now. For the next five days he worked from morning till night. *Mischief* lay alongside a floating jetty, so that all measurements had to be made from a dinghy moored under the stern and then transferred to the ponderous block of wood lying on the jetty. The first few days seemed to result in nothing but a constantly changing template and a maze of chalk marks on that massive chunk of South African oak, until at last under the skilful blows of Ted's adze it began to take shape.

Having been keyed up for the start, we all felt this setback. Jan Garnier and John Lyons resumed their former occupation of sitting in the Clubhouse window, an occupation usually reserved for the oldest members, where they spent the day drinking coffee. Jim, armed with a geological hammer like a seven-pound sledge and a vast rucksack, resumed his former walks, extending their range and returning every evening with larger loads of Table Mountain. The rest of us hung around the boat encouraging or assisting Ted, cheerful when the chips were flying from adze and chisel, and gloomy when the endless business of measuring with bits of string and chalk and templates began again. Our worst moment, a moment in which our emotions were too poignant for tears, occurred when the block, which we had come to loathe, was pronounced ready to go in. Ted's sparse tool kit comprised little beyond adze and chisel. He needed clamps and he managed to borrow a couple, things about five feet long, from a neighbouring shipyard. There was quite a crowd of interested spectators – for we had many sympathisers – when Ted, who had just triumphantly brought the clamps, unluckily allowed the moving part of one to slide from its long steel arm and bury itself in the mud under *Mischief*'s keel.

Perhaps it was the fact that the wretched thing belonged to the shipyard that made its loss seem so disastrous. In most novels there occur one or perhaps more moments of pregnant silence, but I'm sure no novelist has ever experienced or imagined a moment so pregnantly silent as this, while we looked at Ted and he looked at the now useless clamp. The perversity of inanimate objects is well known and in reviling them there is no need to prepare a preliminary draft. When the pent up storm burst, Ted's fluency was admirable, some of his Afrikaans words sounding horribly rude. After this comprehensive Ernulphus curse embracing the sea, ships, tools, toolmakers and their ancestors on both sides, the job was resumed with makeshift appliances. With a gang of willing helpers Ted wrestled all day with that stubborn block, belting it in with sledge-hammers and prising it out again with crowbars until at length after five or six trials and much re-shaping, it slid into place. Next morning, 3 December, while Ted nailed up the planks and caulked them, a coloured boy, skilful with a paint brush, put our name on the new stern block. It was time to be off.

CHAPTER SIX

In the Southern Ocean

MAKING ready for sea and finally getting away when watched and sometimes aided by a crowd of friends or mere spectators has often embarrassing moments. One so wants things to go right and all too often everything goes wrong. It is a time for cool, curt commands, but one is not feeling cool and there is probably no one to receive any curt commands, the crew being busy with their own last-minute affairs. The deck has been cleared for action partly by adding to the confused medley in the cabin, where belated presents of fruit, cakes and bottles of brandy lie mixed up with hastily cast-off shore-going clothes, sacks of potatoes, onions and stray cabbages for which stowage has not yet been found. Over all lie the pieces of wood which normally make up the engine housing, and Jim's rucksack with its last load of Table Mountain, his bunk being too full to hold any more. Meantime, one of the crew slips ashore to buy soap or make a telephone call and another is too busy with his camera to attend to anything else. Then while you step ashore to say goodbye, someone begins to cast off and you hurry on board, leaving all the important farewells unsaid, while the chap with a passion for soap makes a pier-head jump. Although we had overstayed our welcome owing to the business of the stern block, our friends were sorry to see us go. Some, I think, felt genuine concern, for one or two pessimists had voiced the opinion that we were not likely to be seen again in Cape Town; that if *Mischief* still floated we should be lucky to fetch up in Australia or New Zealand. And in view of what had happened two years before when we had to put back to Durban for repairs, their misgivings might be justified.

Before we could make a start we had to warp out to some dolphins used by boats when hauling out, and then get *Mischief*'s head pointing the right way if we were to avoid fouling a clutter of boats and mooring buoys. With a smart off-shore breeze blowing and the mulishness which *Mischief*, in common with her owner, sometimes shows, we had difficulty in making her point the right way. She has a playful trick, too, when the engine is ticking over and the clutch in neutral, of forging ahead insidiously but relentlessly, the men in the bows imploring you with loud cries to put the gear in neutral while you bellow back heatedly that it has never been anywhere else. On this occasion, while playing this game, she nearly sank a mooring buoy together with the Club member who was hanging to it trying to let go our warp. Finally we got clear and forged ahead, narrowly missing a yacht on her moorings, until out in the Duncan Dock, where we could draw breath, forget the recent shambles and get the sails hoisted in comfort. The wind was south-east and gusty as we sailed out of the entrance, where a number of friends had motored round from the Club to give us a final wave and take photographs of *Mischief* under sail.

Heading south-west to clear Duiker Point, we had for part of the afternoon a fast, jolly sail, the wind freshening all the time. By five o'clock, however, we were close-reefed and by six we hove to under reefed stays'l and main. As there is no mizzen mast on which to hoist a riding sail, a cutter like *Mischief* will not lie ahead to sea in strong winds unless held there forcibly by an enormous sea anchor. She lies three or four points off the wind and an occasional big sea will knock her broadside-on until she comes up again into the wind. When the wind still increased, I thought we should be safer and more comfortable running under the trysail, even though it meant running to the south-west. As we had delayed reeving the new Italian hemp rope for the main halyards until just before leaving Cape Town, we expected to have trouble in getting down the mainsail. These expectations were fulfilled. We had a fearful struggle, for the stiff rope refused to render through the triple block at the throat. To make matters worse, when preparing for sea we had forgotten to bend on the vang at the peak, so that we were without this invaluable aid for hauling down the gaff. We got it down in the end and sent up the storm trysail, but not before Procter had damaged his hand.

To lose ground to the west in this fashion right at the start of the passage was so unwelcome that before nightfall we hove to once more. We had plenty of sea room and, if we could ride out the night hove to, we should not lose much by drifting. By this time all except Procter and myself were seasick and we were not feeling very strong. All things considered our start could hardly have been more discouraging – a striking contrast, too, to our departure from Cape Town two years before, when for 48 windless hours we drifted in sight of the shore while some friends living at Green Point flashed a mirror at us.

During the night the wind decreased and went round to north-west enabling us to start sailing and to lay the course for Marion Island, 1,100 miles south-east by east of Cape Town. Our plan was to try to sight Marion and thence run down our easting to the Crozet Islands, which are roughly in the same latitude six hundred miles farther east. Since the last war, the Union

Government has established a weather station on Marion, the largest of the two Prince Edward islands. Mr A. B. Crawford, of the South Africa weather bureau, had kindly arranged that the Marion Island station should show a light during the time we were likely to be in the vicinity. Normally a light is shown only when a relief ship is expected. Mr Crawford asked us to undertake the keeping of a meteorological log throughout the voyage, which Roger Tufft did, and did very well, having had experience of this work in the Antarctic. It involved recording air and sea temperatures, barometer readings and wind, rain and cloud conditions at 06.00, 12.00 and 18.00 GMT daily. Since merchant shipping routes lie well to the north of the fortieth parallel and the whalers during the summer operate in the far south, the data available for compiling South African weather charts is scanty. In the same way that the weather of the British Isles is largely governed by depressions passing to the north, so the weather at the Cape depends on the depressions which form well to the south. Our reports could not, of course, be transmitted but they were of considerable interest to the analyst who compiled the daily weather chart, who found that on two or three occasions the lack of data had led him badly astray.

Mr Crawford was also interested personally in what may be briefly described as 'Polar Post.' The envelopes containing mail from remote places such as the Antarctic and the islands of the Southern Ocean, stamped in the ordinary way with, for example, South African stamps, surcharged with a rubber stamp indicating the place of origin, are of interest to certain collectors who specialise in them. His assurance that envelopes posted in this way at the Crozet would soon be worth £5 or £10 quickly roused the avidity of the crew. Rubber stamps with 'Iles Crozet' and '*Mischief*' on them were procured together with an official mail bag and a supply of twopenny South African stamps, while Crawford and his friends gave us numbers of letters, or at least envelopes, to be franked by us at the Crozet and brought back in the mail bag for posting. In view of the modest capital required, only twopence a letter, I invested in this promising racket to the extent of half a dozen letters. But since only two of mine were ever delivered, I imagine that some of the post office officials at Cape Town are themselves collectors.

By next day the weather had mended and the crew were on their feet again. The trysail proved more difficult to lower than the mainsail had. It is the weight of the gaff which brings the mainsail down with a run as soon as the halyards are let go, always providing the halyards run freely. The trysail, which is a triangular sail, is hoisted without the gaff and to get it down we had to put its downhaul on the winch. Jan, whose post was usually at the main halyards, had his work cut out coiling this stiff, new rope. We assured him that by the time we got home it would be as supple as silk. We were still only about 50 miles south-west of the Cape. At nightfall, out of respect for this stormy headland and because our morale was low, we again hoisted the trysail. My spirits had not been raised by a deluge of water through the skylight as I sat playing Patience, ruining the cards and soaking me and my blankets. We had had the canvas sky-light cover improved by letting in larger windows so that we could have it on all the time and yet have plenty of light in the cabin. But when a wave came on board, water still forced its way under the cover and through the skylight, until after suffering for many days we cured this by screwing down the canvas with wood battens. It seemed unlikely that for the next few months we should want to open the skylight, for we would rather be stuffy than wet.

On the way to Cape Town we had occasionaly seen whales spouting but now we saw one at really close quarters. A large sperm whale swam round the boat not twenty yards away. His enormous square head half out of the water and the length of his submerged but easily discernible body contributed an awful impression of might and majesty. Seen at close range from the deck of a small boat, he looked so vast and invulnerable that one marvelled at the hardihood of the old-time whalers, who would have thought little of rowing up to within a few feet, darting a harpoon into him, and so setting in motion all that latent power and energy. No wonder that the rowers in those boats were not allowed to look round; for the turmoil and danger that would follow the strike of the harpoon must have daunted the mind of anyone who dwelt upon it. Modern methods have reduced the whaling business to mere butchery. Indeed, one does not have to be a Colonel Blimp to say that pretty well everything has been spoilt, from whaling to warfare, by the irresistible urge for easier and quicker methods, more certainty and more profit. That in the case of whaling such methods will probably put the participants out of business is no consolation to the whales.

At the other end of the scale of sea-life were two small flying-fish which were washed on board. It meant that we were still in the warm water of the Agulhas current, which sweeps along the African coast from the Mozambique Channel and round the tail of the Agulhas Bank, before it fans out and disappears in the South Atlantic. Even where we were, where the current is weakest, it set us 50 miles to the south-west; farther north it is one of the strongest and steadiest currents of all, running at three or four knots throughout the year. After the first south-easterly blow we had little wind until 8 December, when the falling barometer heralded the first of a series of depressions. It gave us two runs of 120 miles and we might have done better had I not been so prudent or timid, fearful that every depression would develop into a hard gale, reefing down in good time and setting the trysail at night.

We were about 500 miles on our way and had reached the edge of the Forties. For two days running I had been worried by the odd results our sights gave us – a degree or a degree and a half of difference between the observed position and the position we thought we were in by dead reckoning. Even though Roger got much the same results I mistrusted them, for it seemed more likely that we were making some stupid error than that we could be a hundred miles wrong in our dead reckoning. When it could no longer be denied that the sights were correct and that, unless the solar system had gone hay-wire, the dead reckoning must be wrong, I worked out a sight with an assumed position a hundred miles from where we thought we were, and the answer agreed within two or three miles. Thus we had experienced a set of a hundred miles to the north-west in three days.

Hitherto I had looked upon currents which set in unexpected directions, or currents which suddenly began flowing where no current has yet been recorded, as the trump cards which the prudent navigator keeps up his sleeve in case he makes an unsatisfactory landfall or if anything untoward happens to his ship. But whether such a card would be strong enough to play before a Court of Inquiry is more than doubtful. Nevertheless such unexpected sets do occur, as we had just seen, and when the compilers of the invaluable Admiralty *Pilots* state that a certain current always flows in a certain direction, they cover themselves by adding that sets in any other direction may also occur. The general circulation of water in the oceans, caused by the prevailing winds, the rotation of the earth and other factors, is well known. Thus in the Southern Ocean, where westerly winds prevail, the general drift sets east or slightly north of east. For example, a bottle thrown into the sea at Marion Island in 1958 was found on the coast of Victoria in 1960. But as well as this steady, unvarying drift, there are often day to day local variations – except in the case of fast-flowing ocean rivers such as the Gulf Stream or the Agulhas current. Thus in any region at any time currents setting in any direction may be experienced, caused probably by strong winds blowing for a short time from a direction different from that of the prevailing wind. These unpredictable variations are of more concern to the mariner than the general drift, and particularly to us in the Southern Ocean intent upon hitting off a small island. Even a castaway on a raft in the vicinity of Marion Island would be only faintly interested in the certain knowledge that in two years his raft might reach Australia.

Fortunately such strong local sets as we had experienced are not frequent. Navigation would be difficult indeed if every change of wind set in motion a fresh current, and I was already well aware of the difficulty there might be in finding the Crozet. Of all the unpleasant things that might happen to us in those lonely seas, this of missing the islands altogether, or, worse still, of hitting one in the dark, was what scared me most. They are small and scattered, their vicinity is sprinkled with sunken rocks, visibility is very often poor, so that, if owing to bad weather we got no sun sights, we might easily be blown to leeward of them before we knew where we were,

It is questionable whether the advice to ocean cruisers that they should frequently consider all the possible accidents that might happen to them or their boat and the appropriate action for dealing with any such accidents, is really the best. The time to consider them is before one starts so that all possible steps to prevent them happening can be taken. Subsequently an attitude of careless hope is, perhaps, permissible, for at least it allows the adventurer to sleep, eat, and enjoy the passing moment. Though, like most fears, it proved illusory, this fear of missing the islands was often present. Had I added to it the fear of losing mast or rudder, of developing a fatal leak, the fear that the next gale or the one after it would prove too much for old *Mischief*, or the fear that the bowl of my best pipe was about to crack – as it did – I had indeed supped full with horrors. And when a gale or trouble does start, though few of us are lofty-minded enough to do so, one might adopt the attitude of the skipper who, after giving the curt order 'Call me when it moderates', used promptly to go below.

After an interlude of two passably fine days, the barometer fell again, cloud spread rapidly from the north-west, and rain set in. The mainsail was already reefed, so that we were able to collect water to replace that already used. There would be no lack of water at the islands, but it seemed a wise precaution in view of some of the possibilities mentioned above and the long time it might take a disabled boat to reach either Australia or some frequented part of the ocean. After its accustomed shift to south-west, the wind blew hard all night, during which we remained hove to in order to avoid losing ground to the north. An almost windless day followed this dirty night but by evening another depression was on the way. At three in the morning we had to gybe on to the starboard tack, the wind having gone south of west. An hour later, when I took over, the barometer had dropped to 29ins; cold, rain, driving spume and a livid sky were the ugly ingredients of what I regarded as a hopeless dawn. We got no sights that day. As the glass rose, the wind backed in its usual way and again we hove to in order to avoid running away to the north-east before the sea.

But by nightfall we were lurching about with flapping sails, for when the guiding hand of the wind is lifted, the sea begins to run in all directions. What a place, we thought, either a gale of wind or none at all! The pattern of the weather is well shown by our runs for the last four days, which had been 113, 20, 105 and 14 miles. We were too small and too slow to take full advantage of the passing depressions; and since our course for Marion Island was more south than east we could not let her run as we might have done if bound eastwards. For the big clipper ships bound for Australia it mattered little whether the wind was north-west or south-west, and with speeds of twelve to fifteen knots they could probably keep pace with a depression and so carry a favourable gale most of the way.

The temperature remained at about 40°F, which, combined with the all-pervading dampness, we thought extremely cold. The sliding hatch remained closed, the weather-boards up in the companion-way, and all ventilators firmly plugged. Sparta, emphatically, began outside. Even if one merely wanted to poke one's head out to look at the weather, it was not wise to do so without wearing oilskins. Whenever it was calm, albatross used to gather on the sea around us, grounded, so to speak, by lack of wind. They can fly in light winds but in a gale they glide and soar with effortless perfection. In our small world Roger was the greatest living authority on the albatross. He was always being called upon to distinguish for us the Wandering Albatross, the Black-browed (so called apparently because its head is completely white), the Yellow-nosed, the Grey-headed, the Sooty Albatross and the Light-mantled Sooty. To the uninstructed, these are merely albatross which differ, as men do, in size or in the colour of their nose or hair. Just as some rock climbers like to make a small variation on an old route for the sake of giving it a new name, so ornithologists seem to have an itch to create new species or sub-species and to attach new labels. As well as the perplexity caused by minor differences and by the changes of plumage in immature and adult birds, the bird-watcher at sea is bothered by the fact that his quarry is nearly always in flight and that he himself is never stationary. To watch a fast-flying bird through a pair of field-glasses from a heaving deck is a hopeless task. I have been told that there is now a gadget, worked on some gyroscopic principle, that when attached to a sextant, camera, or field-glasses will hold them perfectly steady when the man handling the instrument is shaking with excitement or being thrown about in a small boat. It sounds improbable but no more improbable than those achievements of science before which we bow low while hastily averting our thoughts from their implications. But in the matter of the albatross family, I think that the inexpert might follow the example of the old-time sailor who reserved the name Albatross for the big Wanderer and lumped the rest, together with Giant Petrels, under the name Mollyhawk.

The calm lasted long enough for me to get an accurate noon sight which put us in S. lat. 40° 24'. But by afternoon there was plenty of wind for the albatross to take off and for *Mischief* to be doing five knots well reefed down with a gale from north-east. During the night it backed to north-west and blew harder while the glass fell to 28.80 and by dawn we hove to. It was a wild morning, the sea streaked with foam and the air full of spray, but the sun rose in a clear sky. No weather seems quite so bad when the sun is shining. We needed cheering too, for we had not yet carried out the long deferred battening down of the skylight cover; I had a plastic bivouac sheet rigged over my bunk and in order to dodge the spurts from the skylight those on my side of the table took their breakfast standing up. On that bright but windy day, we might have had a fine sail in a boat a little larger than *Mischief*, and with a little more freeboard than our two feet six inches. We did not venture to let draw until afternoon, when the wind took off a little. Owing to the amount of spray flying and the obscurity of the horizon due to scud, I could make no use of the sun that day.

For the next three days we had all the wind we wanted, usually about Force 7 and accompanied by squalls of rain and hail. The glass remained steady but a little below normal for the time of year in that region. We were becoming inured to these harsh conditions and increasingly confident of *Mischief*'s ability to stand up to them and on the whole to take advantage of them. She seldom took much solid water on board. True, the cockpit coaming got pushed in by a sea, but that had never been quite the same since the bash it received two years before. Personally, I had expected the weather to be worse. So far none of the gales had lasted long enough or been violent enough to build up dangerously high seas with breaking crests, such a sea as had put paid to our hopes two years before and for which I had been keeping a rather fearful watch ever since leaving Cape Town. When the wind had been in the right quarter we had run before it steering without any trouble, and as yet we had had no occasion to slow her down by streaming warps. Nor had we been driven to that last resource of using storm oil, of which we carried a five-gallon drum. However, there was still plenty of time. We had not yet reached Marion.

Altogether there had not been many days when sights were unobtainable, rough and ready though some of them had to be. One needed to be always on the alert for a fleeting chance when the sun made a momentary appearance, quick to snap the sight when *Mischief* was on top of a wave, and able to discriminate between the true horizon and the great hills of water constantly obscuring it. Star sights were seldom obtainable; though the night might be clear it had a trick of clouding over just before dawn. Evening star sights I never much cared for; their working out took a lot out of the battery and the light kept the watch below awake.

On Sunday, 20 December, in spite of an overcast sky, I got a sight which put us thirty miles ahead of our dead reckoning position, and at five that evening, fine on the bow, we sighted an island. We were in some doubt whether it was Marion Island, for which we were aiming, or Prince Edward Island twelve miles to the north-east. Long and anxiously we peered at it until at last we could make out Boot rock, a detached rock 200ft. high shaped like a jackboot which lies off the north coast of Marion, and soon all doubts were set at rest when out of the cloud wrack to the north the hard outline of the other island took shape. When sailing down there in a waste of water which encircles the globe, any land seems unnatural. When it does appear it has an unreal quality, even though one has gazed at it daily on the chart. It has an air of defying the sea, as if it knew that in that vast ocean land had no place.

I don't know what we expected to see, but from the disparaging remarks that passed I gathered that the crew were not pleased with the view of our first sub-antarctic island. Certainly Marion looked grim and sombre enough in the fading light, its 4,200ft. high summit shrouded in cloud, the bleak lower slopes sprinkled with fresh snow sweeping down to the rock-bound shore. By dark we could see some lights in the huts of the weather station at the north-east end of the island, then about three miles on the beam. Having been unable to find at Cape Town a bulb for our Aldis signal lamp we were reduced to some ineffective flashing with a hand torch. It was no night for anyone to be sitting outside gazing seawards and I'm sure we were not seen. We hove to with the intention of closing the land at daylight to make our number.

But by morning we had drifted farther away, the wind was right off the land, and by the time the engine had been coaxed into starting (there was water in the cylinder), I thought we might as well push on. The more so because the wind was fresh from south-west, just what we wanted, so we let draw and soon sank Marion below the horizon. We had now only 600 miles to go, we were roughly on the right latitude, and the fact that we had picked up Marion Island in conditions far from ideal gave us more confidence. Until within a hundred miles of the western-most of the Crozet Islands, we enjoyed a wonderful spell of fine, settled weather; four days of calm seas, long runs under all plain sail and a little sunshine. One day we even brought our bedding on deck to dry. It became colder with the temperature down to 37°F. It would have been churlish not to feel grateful, but every day that passed seemed to lessen the chance of our having good weather when near the islands.

On Christmas Eve the weather still looked settled. In those regions, however, changes are sudden, and I begin to despair of drawing any useful conclusions from the appearance of the sky. One sees the most lurid sunsets and predicts, quite wrongly, the direst consequences, and contrarily, after a

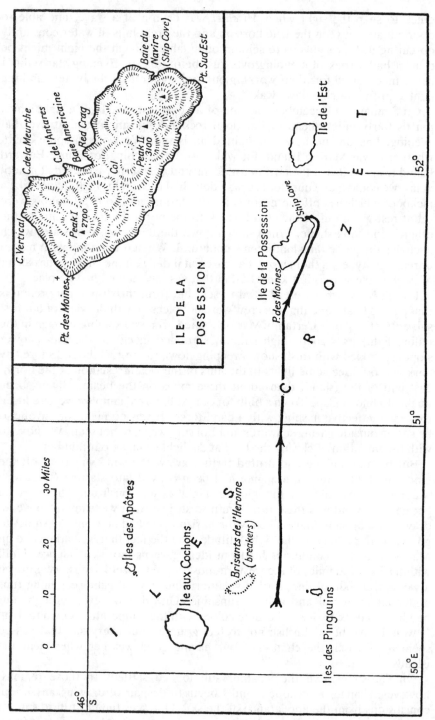

ILE DE LA POSSESSION

C. Vertical
C. de la Meurthe
C. de l'Antares
Baie Americaine
Red Crag
Pt. des Moines
Peak I ▲2700
Col
Peak II ▲3100
Baie du Navire (Ship Cove)
Pt. Sud Est

Ile de la Possession
P. des Moines
Ship Cove

Ile de l'Est

Iles des Apôtres
Ile aux Cochons
Brisants de l'Heroine (breakers)
Iles des Pingouins

30 Miles

0   10   20

S   46°

C   R   O   Z   E   T

50° E   51°   52°

lovely quiet evening sky, the dawn ushers in wind and rain. So it was now. By morning the wind had freshened, the sky became overcast and the barometer was slowly falling. In the course of the day the wind swung to south-east, and the barometer dived to 28.7, the lowest we had yet recorded. Not only could we not lay the course but the behaviour of the barometer indicated that all kinds of devilment were in store. We hove to and nothing much happened. During the night the wind was recorded as Force 6 gusting to Force 7, but it might equally have been of hurricane force, for we had had a lot of mulled wine with our Christmas dinner and were not in an over-serious mood.

Next day I reckoned we were within 50 miles of Île aux Cochons, the westernmost island of the Crozet. It was rough and windy, but the glass was rising after its ominous fall of the previous day. On approaching the islands from the west, one needs to have either good visibility or to know within a mile or two the ship's position. Ten miles north-east of Hog Island are Îles des Apôtres, the group of pinnacled rocky islets where the *Strathmore* came to grief; to the south-east, six and ten miles respectively, are two groups of sunken rocks where the sea always breaks, known collectively by the French as 'Brisants de l'Héroïne' or Heroine Breakers; and seventeen miles to the south is Penguin Island, a small barren rock 500ft. high no bigger than an overgrown fortress. And having got all hot and bothered about avoiding these dangers one learns that the charted position of Heroine Breakers and Penguin Island cannot be relied upon, for they are 'believed' to lie about five miles farther to the south. Sixty miles to the east of this outer fringe, which to my heated imagination began to look like a *chevaux de frise* of rocks, lies Possession Island. My plan was to sight either Hog Island or Penguin so that we could verify our position and lay a course clear of all dangers, in particular the Heroine Breakers.

As we had been sailing briskly all afternoon, I hoped that before nightfall we might raise one or other of those islands. Hog Island is supposed to be about 2,000ft. high and on a clear day would be visible from a long way off. After supper, having seen nothing, I got a star sight for latitude which put us nine miles south of our dead reckoning. Through the delay at Cape Town and through taking longer to get here than we expected, we had overrun the full moon period. The night was moderately clear but, in view of the uncertainties regarding our own position and the position of the Heroine Breakers and Penguin Island, prudence required that we should heave to. At first light it happened to be clear, so I took star sights and went below to work them out. A few minutes later Jan, who was at the helm, gave a hail. Never was it more welcome. He had sighted Penguin Island about four miles to the south. So our luck was in. Whatever the weather might do now, we knew where we were and had a good chance of reaching Possession Island before nightfall. The weather seemed to have decided to take a hand. The glass began to fall and, as the day advanced, the wind rose and a succession of heavy rain squalls began driving across from the north-west.

At eleven o'clock I took over the tiller and remained there for the rest of the day. We were sailing fast under trysail and stays'l before a big quartering sea, and for me it was Pike's Peak or bust. And I was bent on having my fill of pleasure in sailing *Mischief* round an island that for the last two years had seldom been far from my thoughts. Ahead of us in the distance a great black squall seemed to squat as if intent on hiding something, and on this I fixed my gaze. The squall seemed to move very slowly. For some time I thought I could see something more solid than cloud and by noon I was sure of it. Perhaps the earlier sighting of Penguin Island had taken a little of the edge off this landfall, but not much. For here was the long-looked-for prize at the end of a 10,000-mile voyage, a prize with a true romantic flavour – a lonely island set in a stormy sea, and *Mischief* borne towards it on the crests of great following seas, with albatross wheeling in her wake.

It was mostly covered with cloud, but between squalls, when the sun touched it, we thought the island slightly less forbidding in appearance than Marion. We closed the land near Pointe des Moines at the north-west corner and then ran down the coast to round the southernmost point. Pointe des Moines takes its name from a detached rock resembling a monk's cowl which lies off it through which the sea has carved out a large hole. It was exciting sailing along this wild coast, with one eye on the seas chasing us and one on the look-out for breakers ahead. We were far too close, for once when I glanced astern I could see over the port quarter white water surging over a sunk rock which we had passed without noticing. Upon rounding the south corner of the island, we smoothed our water, for we now had land to windward. The wind, however, seemed to gather fresh fury from this obstruction and swept over the low cliffs to scoop water from the surface like the willy-waws of the Patagonia channels. A waterfall dropping over the cliffs hurled water in every direction except downwards.

There are two possible anchorages at Possession Island, Baie du Navire, known to the sealers as Ship Cove, lies on the east coast about two miles round the corner we had just passed. It is sheltered from all winds except easterly. Baie Américaine, the other anchorage, is on the north-east side of the island about seven miles' sailing from Baie du Navire. We intended anchoring in the last-named and when we first saw it about five o'clock that evening we had some doubt about it being the place, or how it came by the name of bay. The English word 'cove' gives a much truer picture. On the chart it looks quite a snug hole, from the sea it looks anything but snug. We regarded with misgiving that slight indentation on an iron-bound coast which seemed to offer so little hope of tranquillity.

There was nothing else in view, the other anchorage might be worse, so we decided to try it. The wind was blowing straight out of the cove and seemed to gain force by being funnelled down the valley which stretches inland. There was no question of beating in, we must either heave to until the wind moderated or motor in. The temptation to have done was so great that we dowsed the staysail and turned on the heat. The engine had to be kept going all out to make headway against the wind. If her head got blown off, as it did twice, I had to let her fall off and go right round to gather speed before she would head into it again.

We first let go in eight fathoms of water, only to find when we had veered enough cable that our stern was far too close to a ledge of kelp-covered rock.

From shore to shore this U-shaped inlet is about 30 yards wide and indents the land for about the same distance. It looked a lot less in both directions and for practical purposes it was a lot less as it shallows fairly quickly and we needed room to swing. With the wind ahead and the rock ledge close under our stern, getting the anchor was a tricky business. In fact it was touch and go and we only cleared the ledge by going hard astern. Our next attempt was more successful and by about six o'clock we were anchored a hundred yards from a beach of black sand, white with penguins.

CHAPTER SEVEN

Possession Island

MISCHIEF being now firmly attached to the bottom, and there being no signs of dragging, we had a moment to look at our surroundings. *Mischief* has been in some rum places but never in any place like this. We seemed to be in a sort of zoo. King penguins not only covered the beach but extended up the valley behind in serried ranks; here and there among them lay huge slug-like creatures which we recognised as sea-elephants; and small colonies of gentoo penguins occupied the rock ledges, where a few fur-seals also lurked. The sand beach covered with the clamorous multitude of penguins extended only along the bottom of the 'U'. Seaward from there on either side the shores of the cove were formed by a rock shelf backed by low cliffs, and above the cliffs were slopes of what looked like lush grass. Numerous white dots sprinkled over the slopes were, as Roger assured us, nesting albatross. Behind the beach a valley with a stream running down led gently upwards and inland till it disappeared in the cloud. Out to sea, about ten miles away, lay East Island, which was likewise cloud-covered. To land on the beach looked deceptively easy. As we found later, it was most often a troublesome business and landing on a rock ledge proved the easiest.

The holding ground seemed to be good. We had down our 'Fisherman' anchor of about 120 lbs. backed by ⅝-inch cable; and to make sure we laid out the sixty-pound 'CQR' anchor on a stout warp as a kedge. Just as Procter got back with the dinghy from laying out the kedge, several long black fins, sticking three feet or more the water, were seen approaching the ship in menacing fashion. They were killer whales, and anyone who has read Bowers' account of how these fierce creatures tried to get at his sledge ponies adrift on an ice floe would not choose to be out in a dinghy in their company. They may be up to 20ft. long, hunt in packs from three to thirty in number, and are extremely voracious, preying upon penguins, seals, porpoises, the smaller dolphins and even whales. In the Antarctic they have been observed making combined efforts to break the ice or upset floes in order to get at seals. The pack of some half-dozen which we saw, having first circled the ship, went close inshore in quite shallow water, no doubt hoping to snap up a penguin or two.

'Sleep after toil, Port after stormy seas, ... does greatly please.' To be safely at anchor with the pleasant prospect before us of all night in was a great joy. As the wind had dropped we set no anchor watch, relying upon the grumbling of the chain and the noise the wind would make to wake us if it came on to blow. Only a gale from south-east or east would oblige us to clear out and gales from those quarters are rare. In fact we lay here undisturbed throughout our stay.

After a peaceful night and a leisurely breakfast, Roger and I had to be put ashore to make a reconnaissance. As was most often the case, cloud covered everything down to 2,000ft. but we could find out what the going would be like and we had to choose a base from which to start. The waves breaking idly on the beach were so small that we landed without difficulty. But launching off the dinghy and pushing her clear of the breaking waves proved a wet job for us who had only knee-high gumboots. Later we gave it up and used a convenient rock ledge. Naturally Roger and I had to stop some time on the beach to inspect the zoo, hobnobbing with the penguins, sheathbills, skua gulls and sea-elephants, all of which, except the last, were just as eager to inspect us – the penguins out of curiosity and the skua gulls out of greed. A sea-elephant must have a limited range of emotions and curiosity is not one of them. If he has any others he is seldom awake long enough to exercise them.

Living on one's fat seems to be the chief requisite for life on a sub-antarctic island. Day and night, day in day out, the penguins did nothing but squawk at each other and nurse their eggs. Sometimes small parties might be seen emerging from the sea as though they had been fishing, but they were a tiny minority, probably only the lunatic fringe. The sea-elephants we never saw enter or leave the water except for a few who played about in the mouth of the freshwater stream. Young and old lay supine in luxurious attitudes of repose, dead to the world apparently, for days, weeks, or possibly months at a time. They were not thick on the ground but they were to be found everywhere, dozing away on this beach and many others, in mud wallows, or in the grass a mile or more from the sea, old bulls up to 20ft. long weighing a couple of tons, and sleek youngsters the size of prize sows. Perhaps those near the beach launched themselves off surreptitiously at night to pick up a few snacks, but those who lay inland, like cows in meadows, had, so to speak, swallowed the anchor, seemingly unwilling to be reminded of the sea and fish. Indeed, to shuffle inland for a mile or so, more or less on one's belly, and carrying two tons of blubber, is not an expedition to be undertaken lightly or frequently. The pups, born probably in September, had all been weaned, yet sleep seemed to be all the food they needed as it was of their parents. Both young and old go to sea in the southern winter in June or July and feed steadily and strenuously before returning to the beaches in the spring for the breeding season and the long fast which follows.

There is no fur on elephant-seals or sea-elephants, as they are equally well called. They were hunted and nearly exterminated solely for the oil their blubber yields. The long snout or short trunk which accounts for their name is only prominent in the old bulls. When angry or excited they inflate it. They have to be angry or excited before they make a good subject for photography and one has to approach very close indeed to rouse them. Then they rear up on their fore-flippers, open their mouths very wide, and snarl ferociously while they shuffle away backwards. Should an aggressive old fellow decide to shuffle forwards one has to step back pretty smartly. The youngsters have better manners. They just lie with one eye open and the other half shut as one approaches, and if one begins stroking them they shut both and go to sleep again.

As is well known, penguins are sociable birds. The more they are together, and the closer the better, seems to be their guiding principle. Consequently we found it harder to make our way inland from the beach than to land on it. The sandy beach near the water was used mainly by the idlers as a sort of promenade where they assembled in small huddles to gossip, show off and generally keep an eye on things. But as soon as we left the sand and stepped on to the muddy gravel by the banks of the stream, we had to barge a way through several thousand close-packed penguins, their serried ranks covering perhaps two acres of ground and extending inland for a couple of hundred yards on both sides of the stream. Except that the stupid people who got in the way were little more than knee-high, it was like the rush-hour in a Tube station. Some birds were so astonished to see a man towering over them that they fell over backwards knocking down several others like ninepins; and if any tried to get out of one's way, they inevitably set in motion a wave which travelled to the outskirts of the rookery accompanied by a crescendo of clamour. But most of them stood firm and showed their dislike of being shoved by reaching up with their long, slender beaks to jab ineffectively at one's trousers. The smell and the state of the wet, muddy ground were both disgusting, but the birds themselves were clean, sleek, handsome. The king penguin is only a little smaller than the emperor, standing nearly three feet high. He has beautiful orange patches on the side of the head, extending down the neck and across the throat, where the orange shades off into the snow-white breast. Like the emperor, he has a dignified carriage and walks upright.

The majority of these birds were incubating eggs, the parents taking the duty in turns. The egg rests on the inturned feet and is covered by a broad transverse fold of skin. They manage it cleverly and can shuffle about, stumble, or even be knocked over without dropping the egg. Like the emperors, they lay only one egg, the incubation period being seven weeks. We saw no chicks and only one young one still in the down stage, who had probably been born the previous year and was evidently a backward child. Poor little Benjamin, as I called him, in his russet coat, who had no play-fellows of his own age and who, I felt, had been orphaned soon after birth. Easily distinguishable by his small stature and comic coat, he was usually to be seen hanging round the idlers on the beach, among them but not of them. Later when I returned from the mountains, I looked in vain for little Benjamin. Alas! he had been knocked on the head, and perhaps it was better so. The sealers had a good name for these youngsters, calling them 'oakum boys,' as the colour of their coats is not unlike that of oakum.

Our passage through the king penguin rookery was gentle and courteous compared with that described by two naturalists off the *Challenger* when she visited Inaccessible Island, near Tristan da Cunha, in 1873. On the beaches, or elsewhere in the open, the naturalists found the rockhopper penguins mild enough, but when they tried to traverse a rookery they describe the experience in the following graphic but unscientific language:

It is impossible to conceive the discomfort of making one's way 'across country' through a big rookery. The grass grows six feet high, matted and tangled, while thousands and thousands of penguins swarm between the tufted stems. You plunge into one of the lanes in the grass, which at once shuts the surroundings from your view. You tread on slimy, black, damp soil composed of the birds' dung. The stench is over-powering; the yelling perfectly terrifying – I can call it nothing else.

On the path only a few droves of penguins, on their way to and from the water, are encountered, and these stampede into the side alleys. You lose your road and in a twinkling you are on the actual breeding ground. The nests are placed so thickly that you cannot help treading on eggs and young at almost every step. If you stop to see where to place your feet, you are instantly attacked by a host of infuriated harpies.

A parent bird sits on each nest, with its sharp beak erect and open ready to bite, screaming savagely 'caa, caa, urr, urr,' its red eye gleaming, its plumes at half-cock, and quivering with rage. No sooner are your legs within reach than they are furiously bitten, often by two or three birds at once. Even if you are wearing strong leather gaiters, they may still be an exposed inch above where you will get horribly tweaked.

At first you try to avoid the nests, but you soon find them so thick that it is useless; so you have just to tramp on as fast as possible, striking out forwards and sideways vigorously, every step knocking down, kicking and treading on an india-rubbery substance, which, if you dare to look down, you will find is a penguin; or smash, smash, as you stamp on eggs by the dozen; or – more dreadful still – squash, squash, as you crush small black creatures – horrible! horrible! Add to this the slippery, dirty ground, the furies biting hard incessantly, the deafening brayings, the insufferable smell, the clouds of small black flies, the hard work fighting through the snarled grass without being able to see where you are going or when it will end.

Then maddened by the pain, stench and noise, you have recourse to more deliberate brutality. Thump, thump goes your stick, and at each blow goes a penguin. Thud, thud, you hear from the man behind as he kicks them right and left off the nests; and so you go on for a bit, thump and smash, whack, thud 'caa, caa, urr, urr', and your wake is strewn with the dead and dying and bleeding. But you make miserably slow progress, and, worried to death, you at last resort to the expedient of stampeding as far as your breath will carry you ... You put down your head and sprint through the grass, treading on old and young haphazard, and rushing on before they all have time to bite.

The air is close in the rookery, and the sun hot. Out of breath and running with perspiration, you come across a mass of rock fallen from the cliff above; this you hail as a city of refuge. You hammer off it hurriedly half a dozen penguins who are sunning themselves there and, mounting on the top, you rest a while, and try to see in what direction you have been going, how far you have got, and whither you are to make the next plunge. Then when you are refreshed, you make another rush, and so on.

After cleaving our way through the thickest of the rookery – without bloodshed – we reached the outskirts, where there were merely a few hundred of the unemployed, the birds with no parental duties. At first we stuck to the valley following a track made by sea-elephants, skirting round many of their sleeping forms and the deep, treacherous mud-holes where they had wallowed. As the going in the valley was bad, the ground soft and wet, and thickly covered with a plant called 'acaena' which grows a foot high, we left it to strike up to the ridge 500ft. above. Even at that low height all vegetation ceased and we found comparatively pleasant and easy walking over reddish lava and stones. Inland this broad ridge merged into another which was evidently the backbone of the island. On it were some high features where a few patches of old snow lay, but these we dismissed out of hand as being nowhere near 5,000ft. high. Farther north where a bank of cloud hung persistently over the ridge it looked more promising. We thought that under that cloud lurked the snow-covered peak we had come so far to climb.

It was a strange, bleak landscape of smooth, easy contours, its uniform drabness relieved only by the fresh green of the valley bottoms and in places by whole hillsides of a warm red colour. From the ridge we had a good view of the coast to the north-east and a bay, obviously American Bay, to which we decided to walk. It was about four miles away but there were four intervening ridges and their valleys to be crossed. At the mouth of each valley were small penguin rookeries and we passed numbers of nesting albatross and giant petrels.

Ridges or slopes from which the bird can easily take flight are preferred to the valleys, and the nests are substantial affairs of earth, moss and grasses raised well above the ground and about two feet across. Most of the birds were sitting on the single egg they lay and they remained undisturbed but watchful at our approach. I wish we had devoted more time on our walks to standing and staring. Had we hung about we might have enjoyed the sight of an albatross making its landing. When they alight on water they look comical enough with their huge webbed feet splayed out and the heels dug in to check their speed, like a man glissading down a snow slope. As one observer writes: 'They appear to dread the act of alighting, flying round and round their nests close to the ground before they make up their minds, and when they finally do, often toppling forward on their beaks. At least half of them make a faulty landing, striking the ground violently with their breasts and turning turtle . . .'

American Bay looked wider than our bay and the protection it afforded no better. The beach of the same black volcanic sand is longer and is bounded at both ends by bold cliffs several hundred feet high, that at the southern end, the Red Craig, being strikingly red in colour. There was a large penguin rookery and great numbers of elephant-seal near the beach and far inland, for the valley which drains into the bay is wide and perfectly flat. The sealers, I should think, frequented it more than Baie du Navire. We found the remains of huts – two floors and a few upright posts – and a couple of big iron try-pots. A little way off was a post which may well have been a cross marking a grave. Of this bay James Clark Ross, who anchored there in the *Erebus* in 1840, wrote: 'The remarkable "Red Craig" came in sight and guided us to American Bay. In this bay and Ship Bay vessels at anchor are well protected from the prevailing winds, but must leave the latter immediately on the springing up of an easterly breeze, as American Bay is the only one where there is room for a ship to beat out. These winds are said to be of rare occurrence, so much so that the French frigate *Heroine*, which was sent in 1834 to survey the group of islands, remained five weeks moored in Ship Bay; since then, however, two English whalers were wrecked in the same bay by trying to ride out an easterly gale.'

For want of a better plan, Roger and I decided to make our first camp at American Bay. Bounding the next valley to the north we could see a long, high ridge leading up into the cloud which lay as if permanently moored over our suspected mountain. In the course of the day the cloud had lifted slightly, perhaps to the 2,000ft. level. Clearly something lay hidden there, yet from the general appearance of things we found it increasingly hard to believe in the presence of a 5,000ft. snow-covered mountain. Still it would be fun to camp on this beach in the company of elephant-seals and penguins, with a fire from the wood of the old sealers' huts, the Southern Ocean lapping at our feet.

Even without a load I found it hard work recrossing the ridges on the way back to the ship. For men straight off the sea it been a long enough walk. We might have saved ourselves some walk and load-carrying by sailing *Mischief* round to American Bay, but I decided against that, reflecting that Jim would no doubt carry an immense load for us and that he would be able to make a second carry while Roger and I extended our reconnaissance. As we sat on the beach waiting for the dinghy we were, as usual, objects of interest to the penguins and the cheeky little sheathbills, the latter pecking at our boots and thoroughly investigating our discarded rucksacks. These small, white, pigeon-like birds, with a horny sheath over the bill, are mainly scavengers. Penguin rookeries are a favourite place and in the Antarctic they gather round any expedition bases. In spite of their feeding habits, which after all are no worse than those of barnyard fowls, they make good eating. The fact that the Norwegian whalers call them ptarmigan indicates that they regard the sheathbill favourably. They are land birds which can swim in spite of their unwebbed feet. From seeing them always running about on the ground one might think they could not fly. Nevertheless, they have been seen several hundreds of miles from land and are known to cross Drake's Strait, the 500-mile stretch of water between Cape Horn and the South Shetlands.

During the night the glass fell to 29in. We woke to find it raining and a south-east wind blowing straight into the anchorage. With the wind in that quarter we must stay on board in case it piped up, and I myself was heartily in favour of taking the day off. For breakfast we tried the penguin eggs collected the previous day. Provided one can stomach their resemblance to jellyfish, the fried eggs are not bad eating – certainly an improvement on dried eggs, though that is not extravagant praise. On the whole I concluded that the eggs of the jackass penguin, which in Cape Town are regarded as a delicacy, must be something different. Of the two I much preferred albatross eggs.

On behalf of a Californian Wild Life Society, Roger had undertaken to ring birds. The south-east wind did not blow hard, so in the evening he went ashore and began by ringing fifteen albatross. He was expert enough to do it single-handed, simply picking the great bird off its nest and holding it with its head and neck under his arm behind him. They squawked a bit but made no resistance. In the evening we had a second and more comfortable Christmas dinner of curry and Christmas pudding, this incongruous and possibly explosive mixture being mollified, assuaged and quenched by a bottle of Van der Hum. Our oil stove, which could not be used at sea, was now brought into action and made the cabin moderately snug. As there were no trees and no driftwood to be found we had done well to discard the three foot high iron stove we had used in the Patagonian fjords, where wood was plentiful. But one missed the fine fug its smoke and heat produced, just as one misses a coal fire when reduced to the miserable make-believe of an electric stove.

On the morning of 30 December, a day of low cloud and drizzle, we assembled our loads and took them ashore by backing the dinghy close to a rock ledge. With a slight swell running one had to watch for the right moment and move smartly. The small colony of gentoo penguins which made these rock ledges their home kept strictly aloof from their larger neighbours. Generally known as Johnnies, they are distinguishable by a white band on top of the head. Formerly they seem to have been as numerous as the king penguins on these islands.

Because, I suppose, the island is so small that we should never be more than a day's walk away from the ship, the adventure of leaving her seemed nothing like so exciting as when we had left for the crossing of the Patagonia ice-cap, when we had cut ourselves off completely on the far side of a 7,000ft. high glaciated range of mountains. Nor, fortunately, had we anything like so much to carry. All told we had about 150 lb. of gear including tent, stove, paraffin, personal kit, rope, and fourteen days food, but we left 30 lb. of this for Jim to make a second carry the next day. Roger and Jim shouldered the main burden, matters being arranged by me so that the weight was in inverse proportion to age. We had now a better knowledge of the route, so that by 1 pm we had reached American Bay, where we pitched our tent on the sand under a low cliff. In spite of the wind, and the sand, which soon covered our belongings, it was a pleasant spot. A family of sea-elephants were our closest neighbours – good neighbours, too, for they never intruded – while penguins from the rookery were constant and welcome visitors.

In the afternoon the weather cleared a little, so we climbed to the top of the rather steep 500ft. high ridge on the north side of the valley. The slope was soft, mossy, and carried a thick growth of acaena, a plant of the genus pimpernel, which together made it a laborious climb. From the top we looked across another wide and flat valley to the high ridge which on the previous visit we had marked down as our most likely line of attack. Cloud still shrouded the far end of this ridge where our supposed high mountain lay, but it began to look more and more merely a high rock peak without a vestige of snow on it. Under it, immediately to the south, a col, lying on the backbone ridge that we had already noted, beckoned invitingly. A long way south of the col and on the same ridge were two peaks which seemed to have some snow on them, but for all that they looked lower than the rock peak. For tactical reasons, and because it looked the devil of a long wind-swept way, we decided to abandon our proposed ridge route in favour of placing a camp under the col. From that more sheltered base we could strike either north or south.

After a night of hard rain and with the glass very low we made ready for a first carry in the direction of the col. Our sleeping-bags were already getting wet, for the light, high-altitude Meade tent we had, the same that we had used in Patagonia, is by no means the best for wet conditions. Now that we were carrying loads the climb to the ridge seemed to me one of several thousand feet. But having gained the ridge we had the pleasure of a long gentle traverse towards the valley bottom, which for the first three or four miles from the sea is wide and flat. It looked as if it might once have been filled by a glacier, and where the valley began rising steeply to the col there seemed to be signs of an old moraine.

In the bottom along the foot of the slope, with the wind strong in our faces, we found very heavy going. But at last when the valley began rising we reached a detritus fan seamed with dry stream beds which offered firm going. By these we entered the narrowing valley below the col, and at a height of about 400ft. nearly all of which we had gained in the last half-mile, we found a camp site in the lee of a great boulder with a brawling stream close by. We estimated the col to be about 1,000ft. above us. Rain set in as we crouched under the boulder eating our lunch, and heavy rain and sleet accompanied us all the way back. But without loads and with the wind behind us we made good time over a better route. Instead of floundering in the soft ground along the foot of the ridge we followed the stream which meanders down the middle of the valley bottom, where we found we could walk on gravel most of the way. But as most wayfarers know, 'whichever way you go there is a league of bad road.' When the time came for us to quit the river for the ridge we had half a mile of flat bog to cross, where if one was not wary enough it was quite possible to be sunk without trace. Having gained the ridge we dropped down to camp, where we found Jim waiting for a last word before he returned to the ship.

CHAPTER EIGHT

Possession Island: an Earlier Visitor

In the evening while Roger went off to ring birds I messed about the camp and its vicinity. As the beaches we visited are on the lee side of the island it is not surprising that we found no driftwood, but some way from the beach I came across a 40ft. wooden spar with its iron fittings, evidently the yard of a small sailing ship. And while prising up a piece of wood from the floor of the old huts, I found a big copper dump or fastening used in ship construction. How peaceful and deserted the island seemed now, with no trace of man but these few bits of wood, and the two iron try-pots close to which a family of sea-elephants dozed, happily oblivious of the fact that their progenitors had been cooked in them. But these few relics led one to reflect upon the hardy men who, a hundred years before, had lived in those huts for months at a time, and upon the scenes of slaughter that must have been enacted on the beach when sea-elephants, fur seals, and even the penguins were ruthlessly butchered.

All the islands of the Southern Ocean as far south as the South Shetlands, most of them teeming with the same kind of life, were ruthlessly exploited. We ourselves killed the odd penguin to eat, but one's gorge rises at the thought of a mass slaughter of these friendly, inquisitive, confiding birds. A great many penguins would need to be killed to obtain oil equivalent to that of one sea-elephant, but there were millions of penguins, and their disregard of man and their sedentary habits made them all too easy prey. In 1834, on Macquarie Island south of New Zealand there were single rookeries of king penguins covering thirty acres each; recently on the whole island there were about 6,000 birds. In his book *Oceanic Birds* Chapman remarks:

The Rockhopper penguins were extensively destroyed for their oil. It was the custom of visiting schooners to hold round-ups when the penguins first came ashore in Spring, and were fattest, and to drive the birds by thousands into corrals. Each penguin yielded about a pint of oil which was worth 2/6. In 1857 at the Falkland Islands four small schooners tried out 50,000 gallons of penguin oil, implying the slaughter of nearly half a million birds during a single season. Much more recently a captain reports killing 70,000 penguins annually. These are revolting figures, but I am inclined to think that it is only the absence of penguins in payable numbers that safeguards them at the present time.

No doubt the owners and possibly the captains of these early sealing and penguin-slaughtering ships made a lot of money, and no doubt, as Chapman says, we should be doing the same thing nowadays if the opportunity were there; except that the slaughter would be to a certain extent controlled, and it would be done by easier, speedier, more efficient means. And owing to these easier means we should not be able to plead in mitigation of the offence of greed and brutality, as they could, that the men engaged in the business risked their lives, suffered great hardships, and were of necessity courageous and resourceful to a degree; and that such employment would encourage the breeding of a race of skilful and hardy seamen.

As an example of the risks run and the hardships endured, an account of life at American Bay in 1821, which I have recently read, is worth relating in some detail. Few can have read it, and besides the intrinsic interest of the story, it illustrates some of the changes which have taken place in the natural history of Possession Island. Above all, it illustrates the immense courage and resourcefulness of sailing ship crews. Charles Medyett Goodridge, who tells the story, was a native of Devon and twenty-five years old when he was wrecked on Possession Island. Since a boy he had been a sailor in the coasting trade and had made voyages as far as Newfoundland; but being of an adventurous nature and Newfoundland, as he says, 'hardly out of the smoke of his father's chimney', he went to London and shipped in the *Princess of Wales* cutter of seventy-five tons burthen, bound for the South Seas 'after Oil, Fins, Skins, and Ambergris.' As well as their pay, which, I suppose, by our standards was derisory, each man was entitled to one out of every ninety skins procured.

They began operations at Prince Edward Island, where they landed a sealing party provisioned for a week or two with salt pork, bread, coffee and molasses, while the remainder looked after the ship and took off and salted-in what skins were procured. Including the master and mate, the crew numbered fifteen all told. The shore party lived under their boat hauled up, turned upside down, and 'tussicked-up'; this means raising one edge of the boat three or four feet on a stone or turf wall leaving an opening for a door. A fire is made with sea-elephant blubber outside the opening and each man sleeps between the thwarts where he usually rows. Besides the discomfort borne by the shore party, there is always the lively apprehension, when a gale forces the parent ship to put to sea, that she may never return.

Finding few fur-seals, they sailed on to the Crozet Islands and landed first on Ile aux Cochons having mistaken what proved to be hogs for seals. It should be noted, by the way, that though Goodridge clearly describes the relative positions of the five islands, he gives none of them a name; nor does he offer any explanation of how the hogs first came to Hog Island. They landed on Christmas Day 1820 and found the hogs numerous, large and ferocious, so formidable in fact that they could not be attacked single-handed. The one big boar and few small pigs they succeeded in killing proved poor eating, for apparently their diet consisted mainly of dead penguins.

The mystery of the pigs is still unsolved, for the following account of their origin is irreconcilable with Goodridge's. In 1840, as we have seen, Ross called at American Bay to land provisions for a party of sealers who had been on the island three years. He says:

> Their leader came on board, and he and his boat's crew looked more like Esquimaux than civilized beings, but filthier far in their dress and persons than any I had ever seen. Their clothes were literally soaked in oil and smelt most offensively; they wore boots of penguin skins with the feathers turned inwards. They were disappointed to find they were not to be removed to Hog Island for the winter which they describe as being so overrun with these animals that 'you can hardly land for them.' The breed was left there by Captain Distance in 1834 and in less than six years have increased in an almost incredible degree, although great numbers are killed by the sealers.

Since the hogs were already there in 1820, the increase which Ross remarks upon is by no means incredible. But to return to Goodridge. Having collected 400 sealskins from Marion and Hog Island they went in February 1821 to East Island, where they landed a party of eight men, the remaining seven going with the vessel to Possession Island, where they anchored in Baie du Navire. The vessel visited the sealing party weekly to restock them and to collect skins for salting. On 17 March, a day before they were due to visit East Island, a south-easterly gale blew up (Baie du Navire is wide open to the south-east). The *Princess of Wales* slipped her cable and stood out to sea to gain an offing, whereupon it fell calm and the ship was left drifting in a heavy swell being set inexorably towards the land. About midnight the vessel struck. Having launched their boat they had a fearful struggle to get clear of the kelp which surrounded them, but by dawn they had landed on a less rocky part of the coast somewhere near American Bay. Their possessions consisted of a kettle, a frying-pan, the knife and steels in their belts and a fire-bag, a tinder box and cotton matches secured from damp in a tarpaulin bag. Having located the wreck they moved camp near her, and before she finally broke up they salvaged only the chests of the captain and mate, some planks, a trysail, the topmast and a Bible which they found floating on the water, which, Goodridge says 'soon became our greatest consolation.'

The hut they built was roofed with the skins of elephant-seals, tussock grass served for beds, and sealskins for blankets. While ranging in search of food they found the remains of a hut built by American sealers in 1805, the year being ascertained by the finding of some tallies of skins with the date cut upon them. Upon digging here they found a pitch pot, which they converted into a frying pan, their own being worn out. Even more useful were an axe, a stone, a piece of shovel, an auger and a number of iron hoops. From the handle of their old frying-pan, with the aid of the sharpening stone, they made a head for a lance with which to kill the elephant-seals upon which they depended for nearly all their wants.

They served us for meat, lodging, firing, light, shoe-leather, sewing thread, grates, washing tubs and tobacco pipes. The parts we used for food were the heart, tongue, sweetbread, the skins of the old ones, the snotters [proboscis], and the flippers. These after boiling a considerable time formed a kind of jelly and with the addition of some eggs, a few pigeons or a couple of sea hens, made a very good soup. The blood served to wash with, as it quickly removed dirt and grease. When we had killed an elephant we used to turn the carcase on its back, and the intestines being taken out, a quantity of blood would flow into the cavity. In this we washed the articles, and then rinsing them in the stream, they were cleansed as well as if we had been provided with soap. The skins also we used for shoes or moccasins, when we were out of King Penguins' skins or wished to make a more durable article; and these we used to sew together with thongs formed from their sinews. Their teeth we used to form into the bowls of pipes, and to this we would attach the leg or wing bone of some fowl, which together formed a very good apparatus. Having no tobacco, we smoked the dry grass, and although it was but a poor substitute we were obliged to be satisfied with it.

Of sea elephants' blubber we made our fires, and their bones we used to lay across on some stones to form grates to lay the blubber on. Of a piece of blubber also, with a piece of rope yarn stuck in it, we formed our lamps, and it produced a very good light. Our cookery consisted principally of soup comprised of the different parts of the sea elephant enumerated, with the addition of eggs instead of vegetables or bread. To this we frequently added the brain of the animal, which was almost as sweet as sugar, and was frequently eaten by us in its raw state. The largest elephants are about 25ft. long and 18ft. round, and their blubber was frequently seven inches thick and would yield a ton of oil. The females come up to have young early in September and continue to suckle them for about five weeks. When first brought forth the young are quite black and their skin beautifully glossy; this formed our most approved material for caps. The old females returned to the sea about the middle of October, by which time they would have lost nearly all their fat in suckling their young. The old male elephants and the young ones would now proceed inland, some as far as two miles, and live together most amicably till about the beginning of December when both old and young would return to the sea, the old ones nearly reduced to skeletons. In February the males were generally up again in great numbers and in very good condition, and are then termed by Southseamen March Bulls. They lie huddled together in heaps (termed pods) like pigs. From December till the following August, however, the yearling and bull elephants make these islands so general a resort that they are always to be found and pretty plentifully.

Great numbers of birds visit these islands. Of the King Penguins I have before spoken but their flesh was not good for food. There were three other species of penguins, named by Southseamen Macaroonys, Johnnys and Rock Hoppers. The Macaroonys congregate in rookeries in great numbers, frequently three or four thousand. The Johnnys build their nests among the long grass, sometimes high up the hills, sometimes on the plains, but seldom more than three or four hundred together. These birds lay both in winter and summer, and by robbing their nests we kept them laying all the year round. When we took the eggs of these birds, they would look at us most piteously, making a low moaning noise as if in great distress at the deprivation, but would exhibit no other kind of resistance; the King Penguins, however, would frequently strike at us with their flippers, and their blows were rather severe.

One kind of bird which proved very valuable to us are called Nellys [Giant Petrel or 'Stinker']. They are larger than a goose and resort to those islands in great numbers. They make burrows in the ground and were easily caught. These birds are so ravenous that after we had killed a sea elephant they would in a few hours carry off every particle of flesh; and unless we kept a good look out, they would unroof our dwelling for the sake of the skins with which we covered it. Their young became very good eating in March and were much esteemed by us. The most useful of all the birds, however, was the albatross. The bird is larger than a swan. They built their nests on the plains, and if the ground is at all marshy they raise their nests about two feet high by digging a trench round and throwing up the soil in the middle. They lay about Christmas, only one egg each, but the eggs are very large, the shell holding about a pint. About May the young were excellent for the table, and provided us with a good dish for a long time as they did not fly off until December.

The smaller birds we used to catch by lighting a blazing fire after dark at the foot of some high cliff; this would attract them in quantities, and they would fly with such force against the rocks as to stun themselves. These consisted of petrels, blue petrels, black eaglets, night hawks and several others. Besides these we caught teal; the latter used to swim about the small ponds when moulting, and then, by wading after them, we caught a good supply. Besides the sea birds, there was a land bird on these islands, which Southseamen call pigeons [sheathbills]. They are quite white and were so tame at our first landing that we could easily catch them with our hands, but after a time they became shy and we were obliged to snare them.

With the help of the sharpening stone, we made fish hooks, and with the remains of cordage from the wreck made some lines. The fish we used to catch were much like gurnet and they made a pleasant change in our diet. At first we used to kill fish with our clubs. Long strips of blubber were laid close to the water's edge, and the fish were so tame that they would creep up the shelving rocks after the blubber while we stood by and knocked them on the head. In course of time they became shy and were not to be taken this way. Thus, fish, flesh and fowl, frequently smoked on our board at the same time.

When we caught a young seal it made us a rare and delicious repast, but they were extremely scarce. Seal skins were in constant request for articles of clothing. I was fortunate enough to save a greatcoat; and when my other clothes were worn out I set to work to manufacture this single garment into a suit. I took out the lining and cut this with some contrivance into a shirt; I then cut off the skirts, and with these I manufactured a pair of trousers, and the upper part served me for a jacket. I could not keep it in wearing trim any length of time, so was obliged at last to resort, with the rest, entirely to sealskin costume. The addition of long beards to our seal skin dresses and fur caps, with knife and steel stuck in our belts, gave us anything but a pleasing exterior.

I have before said that there was neither tree nor shrub on the island; but in the course of our foraging excursions, when above a mile from the reach of tides, we found several trunks of trees about 14ft. long and from 14in. to 18in. diameter – after our most sage consideration we could not solve the difficulty as to how they came there. To remove such of the trees as we wanted we were obliged to split them in several pieces; and this we effected by making a small incision with pieces of iron hoop formed into knives and then with stone wedges rending them asunder. This was a work of some magnitude and labour, but what will not necessity and industry accomplish.

Meanwhile the eight men on East Island were living the same sort of existence with little hope of rescue. They assumed that the *Prince of Wales* had been lost with all hands, the assumption being warranted by finding pieces of wreck washed up on the west coast. In December 1821, after ten months there, the means of existence becoming scarce, they decided to remove to Possession Island. They reached it in the course of a morning, landing in the very cove where their shipmates were living. This wonderfully lucky reunion gave them all renewed hope and energy. They stopped discussing how best to provide each other with a decent funeral when one by one in the course of time they died of old age – a site for the cemetery had already been chosen – and began considering how to build a boat. Plans for a vessel 29ft. feet long of about 12 tons burthen, lugger rigged, were agreed upon, and they began scraping together all the available material. The East Island party had brought with them a bag of nails and a hammer, which was part of the usual equipment of a sealing party for repairing the damage their boat is likely to sustain on rocky beaches. Incidentally they brought with them the knowledge of how to make the Kerguelen cabbage (a plant also found on Crozet) edible by boiling it for three or four hours. Goodridge and his companions had tried it, but through not boiling it enough had found it too bitter. 'This addition to our bill of fare, was indeed a rich delicacy and made to our soup a considerable improvement.'

Since the wood of their house was needed for the boat it was pulled down and another of turf and stones erected. Where the house had stood they laid down the keel of their new boat, formed from the *Princess of Wales*' topmast. Saws were fashioned out of the iron hoops they had found and the carpenter contrived several other tools from the iron bolts from the wreck, beaten out with the solitary hammer on a stone anvil. Sealskins were collected to make the sail, and for rigging they had the rope used by the sealing party for rafting off skins when surf made landing impossible. For pitch they had no substitute, but for oakum they used a mixture of seal fur and albatross down.

Provisions and water for the proposed voyage were a big problem. To carry their water they made bags from the skins of pup sea-elephants, and for provisions they collected large numbers of penguin eggs and salted-down bull elephant's tongues. The East Island party had found an old try-pot, which they now used for evaporating sea water to obtain salt. Meantime, the finding of their daily food for the whole party of fifteen men having become difficult, five of them returned to East Island to pick up a living there. They had to be left there without a boat because, of the two boats they had, one was needed for lining the boat they were building. These boats must have been a good size, for Goodridge remarks that when they went to East Island they were accompanied by six others who remained with them a few days to help build a house and collect wreckage.

In January 1823, one year and ten months after the wreck, the new vessel was ready for launching. A party of seven crossed over to East Island to bring back the five men there, so that all hands could assist in the launching, and take part in the casting of lots for the five who were to embark on what even those men must have regarded as a desperate voyage. By the time the five on East Island had been rounded up it was too late to make the return passage that day. Next day a gale sprang up and their remaining boat was carried seventy yards up the beach and her stern battered in. Since all available wood had already been used, the twelve were marooned on East Island with no means of crossing, and the three on Possession were too few to launch the new vessel. At this moment, the nadir of their fortunes, Providence stepped in. After working for many days to render the smashed boat seaworthy, they were on the point of embarking on what would have been a very risky crossing. Before leaving they went to a king penguin rookery to collect eggs to augment the sea-stock for the projected voyage in the new-built boat, for according to Goodridge there was no king penguin rookery on Possession Island. They were so engaged when round a point came an American sealing schooner. 'Down went the eggs, some capered, some ran, some shouted, and all in one way or other expressed an extravagance of joy, and three loud cheers from us were quickly answered.'

The three on Possession Island were soon picked up. Goodridge never landed to see the completed vessel they had built. Those who had done the work told him 'she was a very tidy craft; and that it was with some regret they left her on the stocks.' How one would have liked to have seen that 'tidy craft' or even some trace of her! But after the ravages of the weather and the visits of numerous sealing parties throughout the next fifty years that would be too much to expect.

Of Goodridge's subsequent adventures, of his three months' sojourn on St Paul Island, of his seven years in Tasmania and final arrival home in 1831, this is no place to tell. After failing with an inn at Dartmouth and a shop at Brixham, he was at length in 1841 reduced to the expedient – more common now than then – of cashing in on his adventures. In those days, however, that was not so easy. The art of advertising was in its infancy, there was no broadcasting, and no national newspapers such as we know them, to which such a story would have been a godsend. So the poor chap started under a severe handicap. Nevertheless, the indomitable Goodridge wrote his book and peddled it personally, price three shillings, round the greater part of western and southern England. And the public of those days seems to have been more discriminating, for he is moved to complain that: 'From a great prejudice against travelling authors, I have found much difficulty in introducing my book to many families in London and other places, in consequence of the many frauds that are practised; any kind friend therefore who after reading my narrative may be induced to patronize it, would confer a great obligation by favouring me with a letter of introduction to any friend or friends.' To such humiliating shifts was our author reduced. But he seems to have succeeded in a modest way, and he well deserved to succeed. In the sixth edition he prints the names of all the places he visited and the names of all who bought the book. They come to about 4,600.

Of the changes in the wild life that seem to have taken place since then, the most remarkable is the absence of king penguin rookeries on Possession Island, which Goodridge reports, and the large rookeries of gentoos. When we were there we saw no gentoo rookeries, only a handful of birds on the rocks by the sea, the whole island being occupied by king penguins. Nor did we see any Macaroni penguins. The giant petrels which Goodridge valued so highly are now comparatively scarce, and there were not many of their old burrows to be seen. His black eaglets and night hawks I cannot identify, though the latter may have been the prion or whale-bird, which is nocturnal. I am sorry we were not aware of Goodridge's success as an angler. Though we could never catch fish we might well have been able to club them. The boat journey they planned seems to me one of the boldest voyages ever contemplated, bolder even than Shackleton's famous journey in an open boat from Elephant Island to South Georgia. For at least the latter had his boat ready to hand, together with preserved provisions, a compass, and a sextant; and they had only 800 miles to go to reach South Georgia, where they knew they would find relief. The *Princess of Wales* men had to build a boat from scratch with the scantiest materials and home-made tools. The sail was of skins, and in the absence of proper caulking material she would probably leak fearfully. Half their provisions were so fragile that they would inevitably break, and the other half would probably go bad. They may have hoped to reach Kerguelen, which was only 700 miles away and where they might have found whaling ships. But without compass or sextant they were more likely to miss it and would then have another 2,000 miles of stormy water to traverse to reach Australia. However, to the brave all things are possible, and these fine seamen seemed to feel as much at home in the Southern Ocean as they did in the English Channel.

CHAPTER NINE

The Mountains of Possession Island

COMFORT must not be expected by folk that go a-pleasuring. The New Year was ushered in by a night of violent wind and rain. The tent collapsed, as those who build their houses on sand must expect them to collapse. So long as one did not move, lying there still moderately warm, but slowly getting wetter, seemed preferable to the rather desperate step of turning out in the driving rain to sort out and refix the tent guys. As men supposedly versed in the ways of tents and the art of pitching them, I wished, for the sake of our self-esteem, that one of the sea-elephants from round the corner had brought about the collapse. But when we surveyed the dismal scene by daylight it was clearly through our own fault of trusting to the pegs instead of tying the guys to boulders.

As the day advanced the storm died away. We got a fire going to dry out our things and to cook some food; and the tent being by this time dry, we packed up and started for what was to be Camp II. After a heavy slog we topped the ridge, where we were met by a terrific wind against which we had to fight all the way up the valley. However, contrary to all expectation we reached our boulder without being rained upon and were soon snugged down in the tent. On our way up the valley the cloud cap over the 'hidden' peak had at last completely lifted, disclosing two rock peaks. Their height, we thought, was certainly less than 3,000ft. The high ridge which we had contemplated using as a route led directly to the summit of the one overlooking our camp. It was too late to get on to it now, for it was steep and a series of rock walls ran across it, but we hoped there would be a way up from the col. At any rate there could be at the most only 2,500ft. to climb, so that we should not have to carry the camp any higher.

During the night some frightful gusts made the tent canvas shake and drum like an unsheeted sail. We were thankful not to be camping on the ridge and grateful for the slight shelter of the boulder, a great block of basalt as big as a small cottage. Except for mosses and a few Kerguelen cabbage there was no vegetation even at this modest height of 400ft. The cabbage is extremely hardy, we found it growing at 2,000ft. It is not at all common on Possession Island and this may account for the disappearance of the rabbits which formerly were said to swarm. On the other hand there is still plenty of other kinds of green stuff; and even on Kerguelen, where rabbits abound, there are certainly not enough cabbage for the rabbit population if that is all they eat. At Camp II the only life was a solitary skua gull which hung about the camp and often followed us on our walks.

As it was raining in the morning we waited until afternoon before going up to the col, intending merely to spy out the land. We therefore carried nothing, not even cameras. In 40 minutes we were on the col, the height according to Roger's aneroid being 1,750ft. We looked over the top down a short valley to the west coast and the ocean beyond. But much more striking than the view was the fact there was no wind. The weather was likely to be our strongest opponent and now it seemed to be off its guard, so without more ado we turned north intent upon bagging the peak. After traversing a wide scree slope we began climbing the western buttress of the peak. Half-way up we entered a steep gully with patches of snow in it and soon came out on the summit ridge, where the snow lay deep. From there we could see the main peak to the north, and by walking along a bank of hard snow which had collected under a steep wall on the east side we found an easy way up. The summit was 2,700ft. and the second peak, which we also visited, was a little lower. Having built a cairn, we went down the same way and were back at the tent after an absence of only three and a half hours.

'Peak I' as we called it, for it seemed a little presumptuous to give names to peaks on a French island, had scarcely justified the trouble we had had in finding and approaching it, to say nothing of a voyage of 10,000 miles. There were no more peaks to the north, and although those to the south might be a little higher it was now quite clear that there was nothing of the order of 5,000ft. as we had been led to expect, no permanent snow, and of course no glaciers. Nor was there any climbing in the technical sense. We had used our hands occasionally to steady ourselves and had scraped a bit of snow away to make a step, and that was all. True, we had been at pains to avoid any steep rock, and very wisely, for the cliffs were a sort of conglomerate of lava and basalt rocks, rounded and smooth, and not too securely cemented together.

Sunday 3 January turned out to be a quite exceptional day and once more we achieved a quite unpremeditated climb. We went up to the col again with the idea of examining more closely the peaks to the south. This col, which later Roger crossed and so made into a pass, is the nub of the island, lying on the backbone ridge with the high peaks either side of it and affording the easiest pass across the island. Apart from a cold wind it was a lovely sunny day and very clear. Three or four miles along the ridge we saw a nice-looking peak with snow on the upper 500ft. It looked far enough off to warrant our moving camp nearer to it, and as the snow-covered part looked steep we walked along the ridge to a minor bump for a closer look. Having got there and seen that there were no real difficulties, and finding it so enjoyable on this bright morning promenading along a high ridge, we decided to make a day of it. For this fine, clear weather was an opportunity not to be missed.

The ridge was broad and afforded excellent going on red, cindery lava, flat stones, or snow, the snow lying in deep banks on the lee side of the ridge. We avoided most of the intervening bumps by traversing these snow banks and by midday arrived at the foot of the last 500ft. of snow-covered rock. As is so often the way its quite formidable appearance belied it, for once we had gained a footing beyond a little rock wall, where we had to cut a step or two, we went up very easily and had no occasion for the use of a rope. On the summit the rocks looked as if covered with a thick layer of white ostrich plumes, the snow having that beautiful feathery formation which wind and warmth combine to give it. On Ruwenzori in East Africa it is a very common snow formation.

The wind had dropped, the sun still shone, and we sat on top of our island for an hour, eating, smoking, and watching the purple cloud shadows drift across a placid sea or hang lazily about the peaks and ridges of East Island. The air was so still that an unguarded match burnt steadily. The aneroid made the height to be 3,100ft. The only remaining question was whether this Peak II, as we called it, was the highest point of the island or yet another half a mile away to the south across a deep dip. The last, although it had cliffs on three sides, was not really a mountain at all but merely the culminating point of a very long ridge which began somewhere south of Baie du Navire. It was a toss-up which was the higher and we could decide only by climbing both. Neither the snow of the peak we were on, nor that we could see on the peaks of East Island, can be called permanent. Before we left the island most of it had disappeared.

We started down as clouds began to gather and the wind to rise; the prelude, as it turned out, to two shocking bad days. The rain that set in that night confined us to our tent for the next 48 hours. Sometimes when the rain stopped pattering on the roof we poked our heads out hopefully, only to find the air full of driving mist through which we could scarcely see across the stream a few yards from the tent. The barometer descended to 28.92 and stayed there, but fortunately there was not much wind. Such off-days are common in all mountains, and those that never have bad weather, and consequently no streams or no snow, are very inferior mountains. On such days the usual recourse is to brew up as frequently as one's resources allow and to eat what luxuries one has. By now it had become clear that we had not much more to do and that we should not need the full fourteen days to do it, so that we could afford to let ourselves go a little. So we drank more tea and ate more chocolate, which was our sole luxury.

Our daily diet was ample if dull. For breakfast we had porridge, biscuits, butter, and jam. For lunch biscuits and cheese, or peanut butter. More biscuits and jam for tea, and at night a stiff dose of pemmican: that is to say, a one-pound slab boiled up in two pints of water. A pint mug of pemmican may not be considered a rich and gigantic vision of the higher gluttony but it is eminently satisfying. The bare pint did my business, but Roger, who was young and hungry, used to scrape the rich sludge from the bottom of the pot, much like the Sherpas, who used to go the length of licking it with their tongues. If calories mean anything, pemmican is about the most potent stuff you can swallow but its relish to some extent depends upon the height at which it is eaten. From sea level up to, say, 20,000ft. it goes down very well, but at greater heights eating it becomes more of a duty than a pleasure; and in order to allay the after effects one may have to lie very still or take a handful of sugar both by way of reward and as a suppressor. Two of us once got outside a mugful at over 27,000ft. an effort rather to be wondered at than repeated. But in normal conditions, since it is so easy to carry, to prepare, and to eat, it has everything in its favour.

On 6 January we could at last leave the tent. From the col Roger had noticed down in the valley to the west a colony of nesting albatross which he was keen to visit. So in order to save time we split up. He crossed the col, while I carried a dump of food forward in the direction of the peak we had yet to climb. Having climbed over the ridge between our valley and the upper end of the American Bay valley, I had another and higher ridge to cross before I felt I could justifiably dump the load. Since cloud covered everything down to about 1,500ft. I could only hope I had guessed right, and that where I had dumped the load would prove a suitable camp site from which to reach the peak. A skua gull, probably the same one, followed me there and back and I saw several families of small, hungry-looking teal. Goodridge says that in the cold season teal were numerous and that they used to catch them by wading after them in the small ponds – a way of bagging duck which is almost as original as clubbing fish. It was great fun moving about in country where no one had been before, for even the crew of the *Princess of Wales* had no reason to go far inland where there was neither life nor vegetation. And whether the hope that one indulges of seeing something new or strange is fulfilled or not, one has the minor explorer's satisfaction of treading new ground.

Roger had had a successful day, having ringed eighty-one birds, both albatross and giant petrels. In spite of his caution, for he was familiar with 'stinkers', as the giant petrels are known, some of the evil-smelling oily fluid which they disgorge when disturbed had got on to his clothes. Albatross have a similar trick. If caught at sea and put down on deck they often throw up, and it is still a matter of conjecture among scientists whether this indicates disgust or sea sickness, which to my mind is much the same thing – a disgust for the sea. The smell of this oily fluid is very strong in the vicinity of petrel breeding grounds, and the smell clings for years to the feathers of museum specimens. According to one authority, the name Fulmar, or 'foul mew,' was given to the large petrel of St Kilda on this account.

Of the oil, Chapman says:

The function of this oil is not known, beyond the fact that it is discharged as a defensive reaction when the birds are approached. Many guesses have been hazarded, one being that the oil serves as food for the offspring, and another that it enables the petrel to calm the troubled waters of the sea about them, during severe storms. The latter idea is not more probable than the first, and yet it is by no means ridiculous, as anyone who has seen the almost miraculous effect of a few drops of fish or sea oil upon raging waters will know.

He thinks it is most likely that the oil is used as feather dressing:

The resemblance of this fluid wax was to that produced by the preen glands of the rail make it appear reasonable that the stomach oil fulfils a similar function. Owing to their environment the petrels and their allies require a larger supply of feather-dressing than any terrestrial birds. The idea of such use is strengthened by the fact that they commonly discharge the oil through the nostrils, as well as through the mouth, and the grooves of the beak may facilitate the distribution of the oil during preening operations while the birds are resting on the water.

On the following day, which was fine, we carried the remaining gear and food to Camp III; and I was pleased to find that the site I had perforce to choose blind was close under Peak III and about 1,300ft. up. As the afternoon was still fine we set out for the peak and reached the top in an hour. On the little rock nob at the end of the ridge, probably the highest point of the island, there was no room for a cairn. On the south side the cliffs dropped almost vertically to a small crater lake. We made the height to be 3,150ft., a little higher than Peak II, but measurement of height by aneroid alone is too rough for us to be absolute about which of the two was higher. There was no snow, and when we looked across to Peak II we saw that most of the comparatively heavy covering of three days before had vanished, washed away no doubt by the forty-eight hours of rainfall. The East Island peaks, too, were free of snow. The main peaks of Possession Island lie much nearer to the south-west coast than the north-east. The sea appeared to be very close below us and we could see the water breaking over the sunk rock which we had skirted so narrowly when approaching the island. On the way up we found more Kerguelen cabbage growing at 2,000ft., as well as a few tufts of coarse grass and a reddish moss which we had not seen before. As most of the vegetation grew within easy reach of our beach, Procter had undertaken to make a collection and he secured pretty well all there was.

When we got back to camp we found that our friend the skua gull had made off with an albatross skull which Roger had left out to dry. Skuas are vultures and hawks in one. Nothing comes amiss to them, whether dead or alive. They will attack even a cormorant and steel the fish out of its mouth if the fish is too big to be gulped down immediately; but the eggs and chicks of the various penguins are their most readily obtainable food. They fear nothing, are enemies of any creature they can master, and live by filching and killing. Chapman gives an amusing illustration of their tenacity of life. A ship's captain who was interested in birds went out in a boat and captured a skua in order to dissect it.

The skua was drawn into the boat and given a sharp rap on the head that we thought was sufficient to kill it, but this only annoyed it, so it was given a regular knock-down blow as we had no desire to see it suffer. It fell into the bottom of the boat apparently dead, but soon revived. Then the second mate, who was pulling stroke oar, grabbed it and gave it a blow sufficient to kill an ox, and wrung its neck. Now it did seem finished. A few moments later the second mate gave a yelp – the skua had given him a nasty jab in the leg and was scrambling over the gunwale. We did not try to detain it, for surely it had earned its freedom.

This excursion concluded our mountaineering, or rather mountain explor-ation, on Possession Island. There was no denying that we were disappointed, but it was not the fault of the mountains that their height had been so grossly over-estimated. A five-thousand-foot mountain in that region would certainly have been glaciated and well worth climbing. I was tempted to say with the Red Queen: 'I have seen hills,' said the Red Queen, 'compared with which these are valleys,' But any ground that is not quite flat is of some interest to a mountaineer and the humblest hill is not to be despised, least of all by a mountaineer long past his youth. However, it seemed to me that there was no more to be done. Even in the absence of a surveyor, I had expected to be fully occupied for a month or more, instead of which we had cleaned up all there was in less than a fortnight. Thus, with time in hand, we must decide where to go. The mountains of East Island looked too like those we had just climbed to be worth a visit; moreover, since there was no safe anchorage there, *Mischief* would have to be sailed back to Baie du Navire to wait. The islands of Amsterdam and St Paul in the South Indian Ocean, more or less on our way back to Cape Town, attracted me, though both, of course, are well known. Our friend Goodridge, along with some of the *Princess of Wales'* crew, at their own request, spent two months on St Paul; living on hogs which they caught and then fattened up on the mice with which the island was plagued; on turnips which they found growing there; and on the crayfish with which the waters abound. On St Paul they found enough wood for fuel, and on Amsterdam fuel is superfluous as there are several springs of boiling water. The third possibility was Kerguelen. True it was 700 miles farther east, rather nearer Australia than Cape Town, and two degrees farther south, but it had both mountains and glaciers. It was a difficult choice. I must say islands with boiling springs, crayfish, and hogs fattened on mice sounded to me like the land of the Lotus-eaters in which it is always afternoon, a place where I could justifiably say to the crew: 'Oh rest ye, brother mariners, we will not wander more.' Once again Belial, with words clothed in reason's garb, counselled ignoble ease; and it was not without a severe struggle that I put behind me the temptation of hot baths, broiled crayfish, and roast sucking pigs.

Next day, 8 January, we started back, keeping as high as possible in order to avoid the squelching green carpet of the valleys. When we were about to quit the ridge to drop down to the penguin rookery I heard the clink of hammer on stone. Jim was hard at work with his sledge-hammer a short distance away. I had not yet caught sight of our familiar mast, so his presence was some assurance that *Mischief* was all right; though the thought did occur to me that Jim with his passion for breaking stones might well be thus engaged even if *Mischief* was a total wreck. He told me all was well and presently we saw her lying in the bay looking very much at home. After fighting our way through the rookery Roger and I had to cool our heels on the beach for an hour before anyone heard our shouts. We amused ourselves with the sea-elephants, provoking them into striking ferocious attitudes in front of the camera.

A stranger stepping on board might have thought from the frightful hurrah's nest of warps and rope ends that she had just arrived after a tempestuous voyage. In fact she had lain there quietly all the time, the only trouble being that, in swinging, the two anchor cables got badly crossed. For lunch we had a large omelette of penguins' eggs which went down well after our ten days on iron rations. We were promised penguin stew for supper. Jim knocked off the few penguins we ate, presumably with his geological hammer, including, I regret to say, poor little Benjamin. I had missed him on the beach and learnt now with sorrow of his early demise. Before leaving we killed one more to take as sea-store, a gentoo for a change. They need to be hung for two days and soaked a long time in water before cooking, the result being a rich, dark stew without any suspicion of fishiness.

During our absence Procter had been busy with plants, and Jim with stones. Jan made a few fruitless sallies after rabbits with the .22 rifle and then took to his bunk, while John firmly refused to set foot on shore. Perhaps he mistrusted the dinghy, which leaked badly, or his agility in landing safely on the rock ledge; but Procter, whose bump of curiosity is fully developed, viewed with disgust the total lack of it in John. Stronger still was his disgust at John's refusal to have any truck with fresh food, either eggs or birds, whereas Procter, besides taking intense interest in food generally, is particularly keen on experimenting with strange, exotic foods, especially when they can be had for nothing. John would neither cook nor eat any of the island products, not even when handed to him on a plate clean and dressed; whether on humanitarian or sanitation grounds we never discovered. In all this lay seeds of discord. If we were to have any fresh food the cooking had to be done by someone else, a task willingly undertaken by Procter, who felt that he had a gift for it; and when at work in the galley contrived to convey the impression that if instead of studying the Classics he had studied cookery, the world would have gained by what the Civil Service would have lost. Few cooks, even if they have abdicated temporarily, like to have their domain invaded and their arrangements upset by alien hands. Long before this the pleasantly donnish manner of the one and the fourth-form humour of the other had sometimes clashed; but now one noticed in the cabin an entire absence of harmony, a sort of cold war of varying tension, sometimes concealed under a forced bonhomie, and sometimes flaring into open warfare, ending usually with one of the combatants quitting the field, in this case the cabin, to finish his meal on deck. In fact the cabin had become barely big enough to hold the two of them. Happily we had no Irishmen among us, so that it remained a private war which the rest regarded with slightly embarrassed detachment. Unless one aspires to his job, the last man to quarrel with on board ship is the cook. But on a previous voyage Procter had quarrelled with the cook – which I confess was not a difficult thing to do – his attitude towards any short-comings in the food or service being perhaps a little too like that of a passenger who has paid his fare. We all like to think our own arrangements are perfect, and neither he, who provided the food, nor John, who cooked it, were good-natured enough to listen with patience to criticisms or suggestions. As the Bengali says: 'The eater of pancakes counts not the holes in them.'

By now we had made up our minds to go to Kerguelen. All that remained was to water ship, which the crew did next day while I squared up on board and repaired the mainsail. Using four jerry-cans, and filling them at a small stream spilling over the cliff by the landing place, they did it quickly in spite of the swell that was running in. Next day, Sunday, 10 January, we got our two anchors up and sailed away eastwards.

CHAPTER TEN

Kerguelen

WITH a good northerly breeze we soon crossed the ten-mile-wide strait between Possession and East Island. In order to have a look at it we sailed close along the south coast of the island, where the rocky shore, the black cliffs springing from it, and the high pinnacled ridges behind made up a forbidding scene. The cliffs continued unbroken except for one small beach and upon that the sea broke heavily. Close under high land the wind is often uncertain and may be dangerous, and we were a little too close. Some powerful blasts of wind from over the cliffs struck at us, and I spent a bad half-hour wondering whether we should clear an off-lying rock without having to gybe to the other tack, or how soon we should experience an accidental gybe. No sooner had we opened the east side of the island than the wind dropped, but a current carried us away from the land.

In spite of mixed weather we made short work of the 700 miles to

Kerguelen, most of the time running under shortened sail. Our best run was 138 and our worst 103 miles, and we covered the whole distance in six and a half days at an average speed of 114 miles. Except that all were cold no two days were the same, rain alternated with sun, and clear weather with thick. One night we spent slamming and banging, making no progress at all, while on the next we ran steadily at six knots under all plain sail with a clear sky and a full moon. As we neared the island the weather worsened as it had done when we neared the Crozet. On the evening of 15 January, when we were some 50 miles off, it was raining hard and the glass falling steeply as we bowled towards it at five knots under trysail and storm jib.

In the time we had available there were two things we might attempt at Kerguelen. We could either explore the ice-cap, a large field of ice marked on the chart as Glacier Cook which extends along the west coast, or we might attempt the hitherto unclimbed Mount Ross, the highest mountain on the island, which lies near the south coast. Besides anything else, we must, of course, pay our respects to the French at their base at the south-east corner of the island. I had no reason to think they expected to see us. Before leaving I had written to M. Heurgon, supposedly in Paris, to tell him we intended trying to reach the Crozet Islands and had been told that my letter would be forwarded to Kerguelen, where M. Heurgon had gone to take charge of the base. It seemed to me that if we visited them first, as politeness required, we ought to make Mount Ross our objective; the point being that it is not a great distance from the French base. On the other hand, if we were to have a go at the ice-cap, after visiting the French we should have to sail back the whole length of the island against the prevailing wind. Except for its height of 6,420ft. we knew nothing of Mount Ross, whether it was easy, hard, or beyond the limits of human possibility; and in view of the weakness of our climbing party, a combination of old age and inexperience, I felt we should be more certain to achieve something by exploring the ice-cap. It would be more interesting, too, for the higher and glaciated western end of the island is less known than the lower eastern end. If we did that, the French base would have to wait. They might think it a little cool of us to make free with their island without first warning them of our presence, but in the circumstances, the island being what it was and we merely far-flung British tourists, I felt they would understand.

In accordance with these ideas we decided to make our landfall at the north-west corner of the island with a view to proceeding to an anchorage in one of the many fjords on the western side of Baie des Baleiniers in what are practically land-locked waters. However hard the west winds might blow, there we should enjoy perfect tranquillity. No anchorage on the west coast itself would be anything like so safe, and since it is a lee shore, leaving an anchorage there might prove difficult and there would always be some swell coming in. A few sample descriptions of west coast anchorages from the *Antarctic Pilot* shows what they are like. Baie du Tonnerre, for example, 'is partly protected by a reef, but the prevailing wind, and ice calving from the glacier, render it insecure.' Or Porte Curieuse, where 'small vessels can obtain anchorage but the channel is often encumbered with ice which has

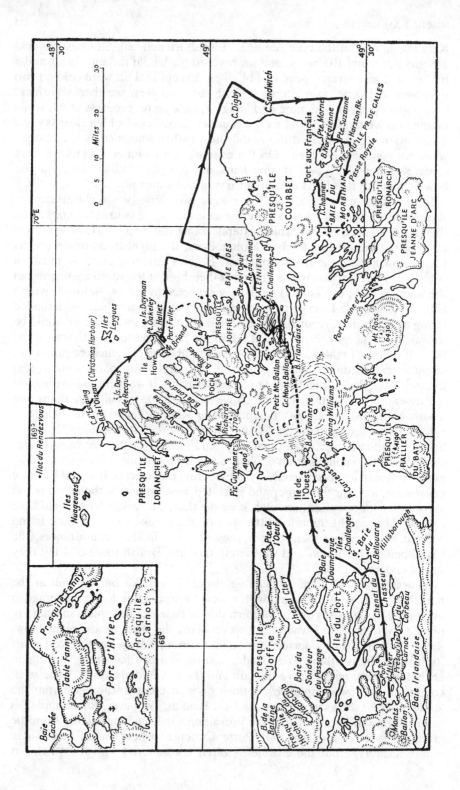

48°
30'

49°

49°
30'

30

Miles

20

10

5

0

70°E

C. Digby

C. Sandwich

Port aux Français

Pte. Mornier

B. Norvégienne

Pte. Suzanne

PRESQU'ILE HarstonRk.

PRESQU'ILE
COURBET

T. Channer

BAIE DU
MORBIHAN

PRESQU'ILE
RONARCH

Passe Royale

PRESQU'ILE
JEANNE D'ARC

PR. DE GALLES

Is. Dayman

Pte. Oakeley

Is. Hallet

Mt. Briand

Pte. de l'Oeuf

BAIE DES
BALEINIERS

Red Chenal

Is. Challenger

Port-Jeanne d'Arc

Port Fuller

Ile Howe

PRESQU'ILE
JOFFRE

Petit Mt. Ballon

B. de Loudres

B. Irlandaise

Mt. Ross
6430

Iles
Leygues

Is. Davis

B. de l'Oiseau

B. des Recques

C. d'Estaing (Christmas Harbour)

ILE
FOCH

Gr. Mont Ballon

Glacier

B. du Tonnerre

B. Young Williams

Ilot du Rendezvous

169°

Mt. Richards
3770

Pic Guynemer
4100

Is. Curieuse

Ile de
l'Ouest

PRESQU'ILE
RALLIER
DU BATY

4100

PRESQU'ILE
LORANCHET

Iles
Nuageuses

Baie
Cachée

Presqu'ile Fanny

Table Fanny

Presqu'ile
Carnot

Port d'Hive

68°

Presqu'ile
Joffre

Chenal Cléry

Baie
Doumergue

Iles
Challenger

Baie du
l. Bellouard

Pte. de
l'Oeuf

Baie
du
Hillsborough

B. de la
Baleine

Presqu'ile
Hoche

B. Club

Baie du
Sondeur

Is. du Passage

Ile du Port

Chenal du
Chasseur

Presqu'ile
Carnot

Is. Hillier

Monts
Ballon

Presqu'ile du
Corbeau

Baie Irlandaise

calved from the numerous glaciers which descend to the coast.' While the bay
with the attractive name of Baie Young Williams is 'obstructed by a bar on
which the sea breaks heavily.' So on the whole I preferred having *Mischief*
anchored in the lee of the ice-cap where nothing could happen to her in our
absence. Some of the place-names of Kerguelen, when the English name has
been left and given a French prefix, sound very odd. The above mentioned
Baie Young Williams, for example, and Baie Supply, Port du Ketch, and best
of all, Baie du Yacht Club.

The landfall we hoped to make was that recommended in the *Antarctic
Pilot* for vessels approaching from the west. It is a round, inaccessible rock
230ft. high, now called Ilot du Rendezvous and formerly Bligh's Cap, lying
twelve miles north-west of Cap d'Estaing, which is the north-west extremity
of the main island. The rock was so named by Cook after William Bligh –
'Breadfruit' Bligh of the *Bounty* – who was sailing master in the *Resolution* on
Cook's third and last voyage. It was a small enough mark to aim at, but
having found Marion and Penguin Islands I had perhaps inflated ideas of my
skill as a navigator and had little doubt about succeeding. At ten o'clock on 16
January we had run our distance without seeing anything of this small rock,
although the visibility was moderately good and although we had checked our
position by getting star sights that morning. After sailing for another hour,
the wind being fresh from north, we went about and steered south-west.
Presently we made out some land where an unmistakable flat-topped
mountain, known as the Bird Table, showed that we were near Cap d'Estaing.
We had overshot Bligh's Cap by about ten miles but the only harm done was
the lessening of my self-esteem.

Just under the Bird Table lies Cook's Christmas Harbour, where he landed
on Christmas Day 1776, unaware that two years before it had been named
Baie de l'Oiseau after the frigate sailing in company with Kerguélen-
Trémarec. In 1840 Ross with *Erebus* and *Terror* remained there from May to
July carrying out magnetic observations. The anchorage suffers from the
fierce squalls that blow down a valley at the head of the bay. Ross called it a
most dreary and disagreeable harbour. He was there in the southern winter
and the fact that he recorded gales on forty-five days out of the sixty-eight he
was there, and that only three were without rain or snow, is some measure of
the violence of the weather at the season. Yet owing to the influence of the
surrounding ocean the winter and summer temperature varies very little.
Ross's most interesting find was fossil trees one which exceeded seven feet in
circumference was dug out and sent to England. Numerous seams of coal
from a few inches to four feet thick were also found.

Apart from its squally reputation, Christmas Harbour was no good to us as
it lay off our track for Baie des Baleiniers. Instead, I decided to spend
the night at Port Fuller, an open anchorage in the safe lee of Île Howe.
Accordingly we went about again and headed south-east for Île Howe, which
we could now see, and as we drew under the shelter of the long Loranchet
peninsula the sea became smooth. Kerguelen, or more properly Îles des
Kerguelen, comprising as it does an archipelago of more than 300 islands and
islets, is remarkable for the number and length of its peninsulas, and the wide

bays and narrow fjords lying between them. In many places the isthmuses at
the roots of the peninsulas between the inlets are so narrow as to form haul-
overs from one sound or harbour to another, and were so used by whalers and
sealers. In relation to its size Kerguelen must have the longest and most
broken coast of any land. At no place on this seventy-five-mile-long island is
one more than twelve miles from the sea.

Every side of Île Howe bristles with off-lying dangers in the shape of islets,
reefs, and sunk rocks. Like most parts of the coast of Kerguelen it is no place
to be sailing at night, and in daytime the mariner must bear in mind the
watchword of the Patagonia channels, 'Keep clear of Kelp.' Having rounded
Point Oakeley at the south-eastern extremity of Île Howe we sailed rather
gingerly along the south coast of the island and finally anchored in eight
fathoms between some islets and a hundred yards off the beach. Although
there is no bay or cove, Port Fuller is well sheltered from the north-west by
the broad bulk of Île Howe. We enjoyed a delightfully peaceful night. The
lifeless beach seemed dull after Baie du Navire, but we were pleased to be
there, pleased with our surroundings and the quiet of the anchorage, and
above all pleased with a fine stew abounding with dumplings, and with the
rice pudding and cocoa, which followed as a way of screwing down the lid on
the stew. After a supper like that, and the strains and stresses of our recent
fast passage, we all slept like the dead.

After poring long over the chart and the *Pilot* I had decided to make for
Baie Cachée as the likeliest jumping-off place for reaching one of the several
glaciers which descend on the east side of the ice-cap. Hidden Bay deserved
its name, for we never found it. To get there we had the best part of fifty miles
to go, first having to sail fifteen miles due east in order to clear the foul ground
strewn with kelp which extends eastwards from the Joffre Peninsula; then we
had to go a like distance south to Baie des Baleiniers before we could turn
west into Baie du Sondeur and the complex channels leading from it. Sailing,
in fact, round three sides of a square.

Luckily I had taken the precaution of plotting the bearing and distance of
each leg, for it was misty when we left the anchorage at 8.30 next morning.
Although we left the main body of the kelp well to starboard we still met with
small rafts of it which might or might not be attached to rocks. At first one
regards all such with alarm and suspicion. If familiarity does not breed
contempt of kelp it certainly breeds carelessness, but in time one can judge
fairly well from the colour of the water whether or not it is deep enough. Kelp
can grow and reach the surface from depths of thirty fathoms and in places
there are thick beds of it in water six fathoms deep. But however deep the
water thick beds of kelp should be avoided because they will almost stop the
way of a boat under sail and will certainly foul the propeller. Rowing a dinghy
through kelp is worse than rowing through thick, broken ice.

The mist cleared as the wind began to pipe up. The glass was falling and the
freshening wind gave us a fast sail on the sixteen-mile leg south to the turning
point at Pointe de l'Oeuf. By then the weather had become unpleasant with
the glass down to 28.8 and heavy rain falling. As we rounded the point to
head west we brought the wind dead ahead. To beat up the narrow Chenal

Clery and the narrower fjords beyond was out of the question if we were to reach Baie Cachée that day, and with the wind blowing straight down the channel there was no good anchorage to be found except at the head of a fjord. Like the Patagonian channels, most of the fjords are steep-to, so that one cannot just close the shore and expect to find water shallow enough to anchor in. So we handed the sails and began motoring, and we had to run the engine full bore to keep her going forward in the teeth of the wind. Although there was no spray to bother one, since in these land-locked waters the sea always remains pretty smooth, the wind and rain made steering cold, wet work.

We kept the northern shore of Île du Port close on our port hand and it was all straightforward going until we reached the western extremity of the island ten miles beyond the turning point at Pointe de l'Oeuf. Here we were faced with an intricate problem in navigation.

Once clear of the island we found channels leading in all directions and a whole cluster of islands and islets hemmed us in on three sides. To the west, where we wanted to go, they were strung like a row of beads. Only one pass to the west was available where all the others were cluttered with obstacles, so that one had to identify the two correct islands between which to pass. It had looked fairly simple on the chart, but the chart was on a scale of four miles to the inch and now it occurred to me that some of the islets might have been omitted for lack of room. Little green jewels as they were, there were far too many of them.

The rain had stopped and I had the chart spread in the cockpit, scanning it feverishly as we motored past the numerous openings. It was no use. Dithering at each and taking none, we finally found ourselves steering south down the broadest opening which offered, hoping that a way to the west by which we could escape would soon present itself. We went on and on, peering round each corner expecting it to open out and always finding a mere cul-de-sac. To go back for another try would waste petrol, nor would the puzzle be any easier to solve at the second attempt. After an unpleasantly long time – for we were steering in the wrong direction – we turned the last corner of what we had now identified as the appropriately named Presqu'ile Fanny. Baie Cachée was on the north side of it and we were now on the south. Fetching up in the wrong fjord in the late evening is no more easy to laugh off than leading one's party to the foot of the wrong mountain after a laborious march. My self-esteem had suffered another jolt. But not to worry. At the head of the three-mile-long fjord enclosed between Fanny's peninsula and that of Carnot there was a good anchorage called Port d'Hiver, so for that we made. I felt that with Fanny on one side of us the opposing Carnot peninsula might well have been named after Fred Karno, a music-hall character about whom we used to sing in the First War to the tune of the hymn 'Greenland's Icy Mountains':

> We are Fred Karno's army,
> No bloody good are we, *etc., etc.*

The rain had stopped, the air was washed clear, and far to the east over the sparkling water of the bay the setting sun lit up the high land of Presqu'ile

Courbet. To the west, beyond the head of the fjord, stretched the level, white band of the ice-cap. On such a calm sunlit evening the scene was far from desolate. Even the stony, barren hills shed their accustomed, dismal inky-blue and glowed warmly brown. Nor was the scene quite lifeless, for on the low green banks of the fjord rabbits scuttled about as if in a field at home. The head of this Port d'Hiver fjord is dominated by the twin peaks, Grand Mont Ballon and Petit Mont Ballon, 2,630ft. and 2,111ft. high respectively. The higher had a light mantling of snow. The sight of these two bulky obstacles blocking the way inland from the head of the fjord impressed upon me very strongly that we were not where we should have been and that we might have to pay for our mistake. Obviously in order to get inland we should have either to climb over them or make a wide detour. Having failed to find Baie Cachée we should have done better by going still farther south into the next fjord, Baie Irlandaise, on the other side of the Carnot peninsula. When examining the chart I had purposely discarded Port d'Hiver solely on account of the presence of the two Ballon peaks, which now appeared to me to be two uncommonly ugly mountains. We had got into the one fjord where there could be no glacier or glacier valley leading inland.

Such were my peevish thoughts as I steered towards the end of the fjord, with one eye on the rabbits – for we were not a hundred yards from the bank – and the other on those absurdly named Ballon peaks in front of us. Soon it was time to start taking soundings. At the first cast of the lead came the unwelcome cry 'No bottom at ten fathoms.' At the next cast the lead landed on the deck forward of the bitts, confounding the leadsman and confusing the skipper. At the third cast – *'longo intervallo'*, for the line had fouled everything – came the startling news of only three fathoms; and as I yelled 'Let go', I noticed some kelp and *Mischief* took the ground. Fortunately we had little way on. By going hard astern and winching in the cable fast, we got clear, and finally anchored in five fathoms some 200 yards from the head of the bay. An unsatisfactory day had ended in an appropriate muddle.

Before going below I got Jan to sound the petrol tank, when we found that we had only two gallons left. We had started the day with about twenty gallons, so, what with the head wind and the extra distance my stupidity had entailed, it had been an expensive day.

No doubt the French would spare us some petrol when we sailed round there, meantime we might as well stay where we were and make the best of it, either by going round the Ballons or over them. The presence of hordes of rabbits and a few gentoo penguins lent Port d'Hiver a more encouraging aspect and we turned in in a more cheerful mood.

CHAPTER ELEVEN

To the Ice-Cap

BEFORE Roger and I could get ashore next morning to make a reconnaissance the dinghy had to be patched up. It had been put in the water the previous evening to 'take-up' and instead had filled with water and was by morning barely afloat. It had given trouble at Baie du Navire, requiring frequent baling, so much so that John, I think, always expected it to sink with us in it. I had bought it second-hand in a hurry the day before we sailed to replace one bought at Durban. Both Procter and I liked its lines and found it a pleasure to row after the Durban dinghy, which was built of teak, as heavy as lead, and as awkward to row as a raft. '*Caveat emptor*' applies to buyers of dinghies as well as of horses. Upon a more leisurely examination, after scraping off a thick layer of weed and barnacles, we found one of the planks sprung; and she was so lightly ribbed that if the thwarts had been removed the two sides could have been squeezed together. Procter stiffened her a bit by putting an extra plank over the gunwale strake, and also put a tingle over the sprung part. However, she had still leaked and the rough usage she had suffered at Cape Town and at Baie du Navire had made it worse.

Some extensive caulking improved matters sufficiently for us to get ashore without recourse to baling, so in the late morning Roger and I set off for a long walk. It was a rough, blustery day but in between squalls it was reasonably clear. Had we thought about it we might have saved ourselves trouble by merely climbing one of the Ballon peaks, sitting there and waiting for the landscape to reveal itself. Strange as it may seem, mountaineers strenuously avoid going uphill unless their objective is a mountain top. They regard highly the principle of the conservation of energy. So rather than climb either Ballon we rushed, like bulls at a gate, up a gently inclined valley on the north side of Petit Ballon. The stream in the valley was small and clear; obviously it could not be flowing from any glacier, much as we wished it might be. In a short time we came to its source in a big lake perhaps a mile long with steep mountain walls on either side. As we had risen hardly at all since leaving the beach we thought for a moment that the lake was an arm of the fjord to the north, Baie Cachée, and we actually tasted the water to make sure it was not.

Proceeding on our way we began by traversing a little above the shore of the lake along the rough, steep flank of Petit Ballon. It generally happens that if a valley is at all steep-sided and narrow, and has water in the bottom, to attempt to traverse the slope is a waste of time. Sooner or later such valleys show their perversity by becoming gorges; the sides get steeper, and the man or men, having an equally perverse tendency to avoid climbing, bent on keeping low, eventually finds the way barred by an impassable cliff. Having out-flanked this obstacle with a minimum of climbing, he begins traversing again and soon runs into another cliff. And so it goes on until he finds himself, as we did, pushed higher and higher and at last he is pushed clean out of the valley. We were not far short of the top of Petit Ballon before the slope eased off and allowed us to move in the direction we wanted.

All things, we are told, work together for good. We had now reached the viewpoint which we might have reached earlier, in a calmer frame of mind, had we set out with the right plan. In the distance the ice-cap showed up dimly and away to our left front a big glacier flowed slowly down to a valley with a meandering river in its wide, flat, gravelly bed. Ahead there was a smaller glacier from which the stream drained into the same valley. The valley and the big glacier were clearly the best way to reach the ice-cap, and if we followed the valley down we should find out whether it drained into our bay round the south side of the Ballon peaks or into Baie Irlandaise, the next fjord to the south.

So having had some food we dropped down to the stream from the smaller glacier and followed it until it disappeared in a deep and narrow gorge just before it joined the main valley. The lips of the gorge overhung so far as almost to form a natural bridge. We got down to the main valley well below the gorge and found it to be half a mile wide, perfectly flat, and with a bottom of firm gravel. We could see the terminal moraine of the glacier about two miles up, and beyond it an ice-fall lying at an easy angle. As ice-falls go it did not appear to be very broken, so we assumed it would be our likeliest route. Looking down the valley we could see the sea about three miles away. Having noted all this we shot off down the valley, delighted to think we should not have to carry loads the way we had come over the shoulder of Petit Ballon.

The slope of the valley was extremely gradual, a fact which we should no doubt appreciate more when we were going the other way. A French guide-book would have described such a gentle slope as 'une pente insensible' and since we were on a French inland I described it as such to Roger. Looking a little startled, he smiled soothingly, for he was unaccustomed to hear from me either flights of fancy or French. The slope, I say, was very gradual, so gradual that when we were still a mile from the water we came upon tide marks, just as one might at Morecambe or Southend when the sea is even more remote. Following the north shore, the true left bank, we came presently to the water and had to take to the rocks. Some small colonies of rockhopper penguin were nesting on the rocks almost under the splash of a small waterfall; but the most common bird of these parts was the Dominican gull, a big, black-backed gull known also as the kelp gull. Later we saw some of these on the rocks by the glacier.

Throughout the day we had come upon rabbits and a great many of them were black. It seemed strange to us that they were so shy, perhaps even more timid than rabbits on a farm which are constantly shot at. When we were motoring up the fjord a hundred yards or so from the shore we had noticed the rabbits scuttling for their burrows long before *Mischief* drew near them. Their behaviour seemed all the more strange when compared with that of the penguins and other birds, because the rabbits knew no more of man than they did. Evidently this fear was instinctive. Just as well for them, I thought, with Jan on the prowl with the .22 rifle.

Any lingering hope we may have had that the water below us was an arm of the Port d'Hiver fjord had by now been dispelled. So instead of postponing the inevitable by slinking along the rocky coast to an indefinite end, we took the more manly course of climbing the steep slopes on our left. We had to slog up nearly a thousand feet to gain the ridge and this was followed by a lot of up and down work before we came in sight of our bay and *Mischief*'s stumpy mast. Beyond her we looked over the Fanny peninsula to the confusing medley of islets where we had gone astray. Compared with the Patagonia fjords, with their dark evergreen forests and steep glaciers, these fjords have a milder beauty: long reaches of still, blue waters dotted with green islets looking as lonely and detached as clouds, nearly all of them untrodden by man.

A calm morning succeeded a very windy night. But our anchors showed no signs of dragging and we were satisfied that we were securely moored. The high Ballon peaks were rather too distant to afford us much of a lee, but we were so close to the shore than even a whole gale from the west would not have scope to raise a sea sufficient to start *Mischief* snubbing at her cable, the action most likely to make an anchor drag. Roger and I made up our loads, together with a load for Jim to carry. We took enough food for a fortnight. At ten o'clock we rowed ashore and started off accompanied by Procter, who wanted to have a look at our glacier. Taking the same line that we had returned by the previous day, in three hours we reached the top of the steep descent to our valley, from where we had a good view of the glacier as well as a long stretch of the ice-cap beyond.

Leaving Procter to return, the three of us dropped down to the valley and began moving up it. As Jim had to get back to the boat we had an excuse for stopping early, so we put our camp on the bank a little above the valley floor. In the event of the river rising it had plenty of channels in which to spread itself, and in the prevailing dull weather the snow-melt did not seem to make much difference to the level of the water. A few days later a spell of fine weather caused a considerable rise in the river. When travelling in the Himalaya this factor has always to be taken into account, for a stream that is easily forded in the early morning may by evening become an impassable torrent.

Next morning, after going for about a mile we came to the stream emerging from the gorge we had noted the previous day. It looked quite shallow, but fording glacier streams, however placid they appear, is never enjoyable. The current is usually swift, the water damnably cold, the bottom uneven and strewn with boulders. There is the unwelcome business of stripping, the question of whether to take one's trousers off or to hope that they will be clear of the water when rolled up; or whether to save one's feet at the expense of having one's boots soaked, or to cross barefoot and thereby suffer a good deal of pain and grief. With these considerations in mind we examined the narrow mouth of the gorge hoping to find an alternative crossing. A great chock-stone jammed in half-way up did in fact make a bridge but it was out of reach either from below or above. So we had to wade. Naturally the water was ice-cold, but only knee-deep and flowing at a moderate rate. As it was a good 30yds. wide our feet were quite numb by the time we got across. We had not been able to carry all our gear in one lift, so we should have two more crossings to make.

We reached the terminal moraine about eleven o'clock and pitched our tent under it on fine black gravel which promised comfortable lying. The ice began about 50yds. beyond the moraine, showing that the glacier was receding in common with the majority of glaciers throughout the world, in the Himalaya, the Andes, the Alps, and in Norway. After some lunch we trudged back for the remaining loads and by five o'clock had settled in for the night. It had been a day of wind and sleet showers with a few fitful gleams of sunshine. Our camp at the snout of the glacier was only about 100ft. above sea level at some six miles from the head of Baie Irlandaise, so that although the glacier is a long way from the sea it is not much above sea level. But as there were no signs of any old moraines farther down the valley it looks as if the glacier never extended beyond its present limits.

The only signs of life were the rabbits, a few pintail duck, and a skua gull which followed us hopefully. The vegetation was very similar to that on Possession, and near the sea the acaena grass grew so plentifully that some hillsides assumed a dark red colour. The roots of this plant can be used as fuel. In the course of the year he spent on Kerguelen in 1908 Raymond du Baty made several journeys inland, when he and his companions were glad to make use of the roots.

One of these journeys brought him to the vicinity of this glacier but from his description it is not easy to follow their route. Two of them landed at the head of Baie Irlandaise – which he names – and 'marched for seven miles across a flat moraine [evidently the gravel bed of the valley] until we arrived at the floor of a great, uncharted glacier and a high mountain range. There was no pass by which we could find a way, but we decided not to be baulked by the mountain but to take it by a frontal attack'. What this range was or even where they were hoping to go is impossible to say; one can only guess that the range was one of the two high ridges enclosing the valley, and that, having been stopped by the glacier to their front, they hoped to cross into another valley. After spending a day among 'endless fortresses of black basalt, jagged peaks, and sharp ridges', and a night in their tent at the bottom of a snow-filled ravine, they forded a glacier stream and got back to their boat. Not content with this they then rowed round into Port d'Hiverfjord, where they had an alarming encounter with whales. 'The sea was crowded with them. Their black snouts and fins made the water black. In every direction we saw them spouting, and wherever we looked there was the gleam of light upon a long, smooth body.' To escape the whales they rowed until their arms ached, and finally beached the boat on Île du Port. This cauldron of whales in the lifeless empty waters where *Mischief* now lay is a striking illustration of the havoc wrought among whales since those days. No wonder a Norwegian whaling company had begun operations at Kerguelen the year du Baty was there.

Our snug site in the lee of the moraine proved to be uncommonly draughty, for the wind seemed to rebound with fresh vigour off the high basalt cliffs on the north side of the glacier. All night the wind beat a devil's tattoo upon the flapping tent. In the morning we started out with loads, intending to make a double carry to Camp III, which we hoped would be located somewhere above the ice-fall. Ice-falls often look deceptively easy when viewed from below and we expected to have little trouble in getting up this one. Only a view from above will show how broken an ice-fall really is or whether there is any through lead. At one time I held the opinion that there were few ice-falls which would not yield to climbers with enough time, patience, and perseverence; but having seen some desperately broken ice-falls in Patagonia, not to mention the one we were about to tackle, I am not so sure.

The cliffs to the north, the source of so many fierce gusts, precluded our finding any route on that side where the ice leant against the cliffs. On the other side of the glacier, the true right bank, the cliffs were low, their top could easily be reached and they appeared to offer a good way of outflanking the glacier. But between us and this promising route lay the river which emerged from the glacier snout, or rather from a dammed-up lake which stretched from the foot of the ice-fall to the snout, a matter of about half a mile. The river was wider than the tributary we had crossed lower down but was not particularly intimidating. However, since the ice-fall looked easy why go to the trouble and discomfort of crossing the river? So without giving it much thought we went bald-headed for the ice.

On most respectable glaciers there is a medial moraine which extends, though in a broken fashion, down the ice-fall, offering a route with some hint of continuity across the transverse crevasses. In this case the medial moraine was so insignificant that it could be traced only by a line of slightly blackened ice; and when this soon petered out we found ourselves stranded in a maze of crevasses running in both directions. In comparison with the notorious ice-fall of the West Cwm of Everest, which I have only looked at from below, it was no doubt a piece of cake. The slope was gradual, the crevasses only some 30ft. deep, no towering seracs threatened to crush us, and we were about 500ft. above sea level instead of 20,000ft. On the other hand there were only two of us, we were not equipped with ladders, nor were we spurred on by feeling that the eyes of England were upon us. We soon had to abandon any ideas of advancing up the ice-fall; it was merely a question of whether to retreat or whether we could escape to the low cliffs on our left. While ranging about looking for a way, Roger went too fast for me, cutting steps and balancing along knife-edge ridges as though he had dealt with ice-falls all his life. I insisted on roping, for my balance was not what it had been, and I did not relish falling into a crevasse even if it was only 30ft. deep. While working our passage over towards the rocks Roger, edging his way along the bottom of a water-filled crevasse, fell in up to his waist. After this cold bath we wasted no time in gaining a footing on the comparatively warm rocks where he could strip and wring out his clothes.

Having wasted four hours on the glacier, most of it in the effort of disentangling ourselves, and reached a height of only 500ft. we decided to call it a day. So, having found a camp site on the rock near a patch of snow where we could get water, we dumped the loads and returned to camp by way of the rocks and the river. The brown basalt rock lay in smooth ice-worn terraces which afforded a delightful promenade. The rocks dropped sheer to the dammed-up lake two or three hundred feet below and some smooth, round boulders lay scattered conveniently to hand. They were not too large to move and there lay the water below, so we fell to work rolling them over the edge. The splash they raised was most satisfactory. The rolling of boulders down steep places is a time-honoured practice, though originally it was done more for business reasons than aesthetic pleasure, when the hardy mountaineers above wished to discourage their enemies below. Nowadays, the mountains being so crowded, it has to be done discreetly.

We crossed the river without much trouble but did not face crossing it yet again in order to move camp to the new site. We postponed that bracing exercise until early next morning, when the coldness of the water, straight off the ice, fully equalled our expectations. After pitching the tent at Camp III we had some food before going on with light loads of food and paraffin. For a mile we climbed easily by the rocks until at about 1,200ft., when we were well above the ice-fall, we embarked on the névé. Our course lay almost west in the direction of a prominent rock gendarme standing at the foot of what we took to be a biggish mountain, for the summit was hidden in cloud. While roping up we scanned the névé anxiously for signs of crevasses. The traversing of an unknown glacier by a party of two, far from any help, is not really sound mountaineering practice. A party of two is extremely vulnerable, for if one falls into a crevasse of any depth his chances of getting out are not good; and if he is injured in the fall he has no chance at all. With this consideration in mind we moved cautiously, treating every crack or the slightest depression of the surfaces with the utmost suspicion, taking nothing for granted and sounding continuously with our axes. There were no open crevasses and those we found, either by sounding or by putting a foot through, were not well covered and were consequently dangerous. The snow itself was pretty firm to walk upon and remarkably free from stones. The only break in the white expanse was a small group of scattered boulders. We steered for these, not only because they would be convenient to sit upon, but because men on a glacier seem irresistibly drawn by anything which offers a break in the white monotony.

The ascent was gradual and as we slowly gained height the wind rose too, so that it became very cold in spite of the sun being out. But in defiance of wind and sun a thick cloud clung persistently to the ice-cap, a fact which we noted with misgiving since in such conditions the crossing of it would be both perplexing and unrewarding.

That we were ill provided for such a contingency I later discovered when taking some bearings. The compass I had with me was an old friend which should have been overhauled or scrapped. In its old age it seemed to have forgotten where north lay, or took such a time to make up its mind that it often got tired of swinging and came to a random stop. Early in the afternoon we called a halt on a shelf among some open crevasses where the wind had swept the ice bare of snow. Obviously it was a windy spot but we thought we might find shelter from the wind as well as soft lying in the bottom of one of the shallower crevasses where snow had accumulated. A little desultory prodding in the proposed site proved so discouraging that we deferred the decision till next day, had some more food, and started back in our tracks.

Even if one has been trudging for only a few hours in snow the relief obtained by stepping on to rock is very comforting, in particular if it has been a day of sunshine and glare. We unroped, kicked the snow off our boots, and sped off down the rocks intent with thoughts of tea. Camp III was at a snug spot, the best site we had yet had. After a day of sunshine the rocks were warm and the evening sun poured through the little back window of the tent. As we basked in the sun sipping our tea, our next proposed camp on that bare wind-swept ice, where the temperature had been thirty-seven degrees, seemed pleasantly remote. A visit from a Dominican gull reminded us of the sea, and from our tent door we had it clearly in view.

The glass remained reassuringly steady, the night was calm, and we woke to find the sun pouring in at the tent door. Yet when we reached the *névé* the same west wind came whistling down from the ice-cap and the cloud layer was only a little above the level of our new camp site. When we arrived there for the second time it seemed even less prepossessing; the bare blue ice, the open crevasses, and the shrivelling wind made one shudder. So we added the dump left the previous day to the top of our loads and pushed on in search of something better. Half a mile on there was a low, flat ridge where the glacier began to descend from the ice-cap proper, a ridge that promised to afford some slight protection from the wind. After some time spent testing for crevasses and searching for a site, we came to the conclusion that the ridge had promised what it could not perform, the wind blowing as freely as ever. Finally we went on to where we should have gone first if it had not been so far, a snug snow hollow at the foot of the mountain not far from the high gendarme.

Again we tested the snow and sniffed about like a dog spinning round on its tail before bedding itself down; and then having pitched the tent across the slope on account of the wind, we up-rooted it and pitched it the other way on account of the slope. However, we seemed at last to have cheated the wind, or perhaps the wind had stopped. But cloud had now come so low that we could scarcely see the rock gendarme a hundred yards away. The height of this Camp IV was about 2,100ft. The absence of wind and the proximity of the rock face of the mountain made the hollow warm and the snow soft. We had to stamp on the tent pegs as hard as we could to drive them in far enough to get a grip. Late in the evening the cloud began to thin away, so we turned out in a hurry to make a quick reconnaissance. We began climbing the snow slope with the rocks of the mountain close on our left, and after ascending some 700ft. it became clear that this supposed mountain was only a great spur of level rock thrusting out from under the ice-cap. Having followed up the rocks until they levelled off on top of the spur we struck off to the west, where the ice stretched away rising very gradually to a far horizon.

By now no trace of cloud remained. Thinking that this perhaps might be our only chance of seeing anything, we set off eagerly towards that distant and ever receding horizon. The great ice plateau seemed to be entirely free from crevasses, but at that late hour the snow was soft, our feet sank a few inches at every step, and for all our efforts the level horizon of snow seemed as distant as ever. Where we had left the rocks the height had been 2,800ft. and after walking for two hours and covering perhaps three miles, we had reached a height of 3,200ft. without seeing anything but snow in all directions. The sun sank lower and lower, while our shadows on the snow reached fantastic lengths. It was time to turn for home, and as we turned our eyes rested on two sharp peaks afloat on a bank of opalescent cloud, their snow summits warmed by the dying sunlight. From their direction and height there was no mistaking the double peaks of Mount Ross nearly 25 miles away in the south-east.

The rock spur might not have existed. We trudged on interminably until it suddenly showed up on the gathering gloom, and by the time we had dropped down to the camp it was almost dark. We had no candles but that was no excuse for a supreme act of clumsiness, when I was giving a final stir to the bubbling pemmican, by which I upset the lot on to the floor and Roger's sleeping bag. The magnitude of this domestic disaster struck us dumb as we fell to work cleaning up the mess and salvaging our supper. We had now to decide what to do. We had had two days of tolerably good weather, and steady though the barometer stood the chances were against a longer spell. There was little to be gained by carrying the camp forward, when, with a whole day at our disposal, and the morning snow in hard condition, we ought to be able to cross the ice-cap and look out over the sea to the west from our present camp. Accordingly we decided to make a push for it next day. A clear starlit night, with the temperature below freezing point, promised well.

Certainly we were in luck. The day proved to be exceptionally fine and windless, the sun shining from a clear sky. There was no cloud on the ice-cap, but below us there was a dense bank which looked like fog rolling in from the sea. It extended up to nearly 1,500ft. and it was to mar to some extent an otherwise satisfying day. The snow was as hard and crisp as we could wish, so that we moved a great deal quicker than on the previous evening. The ice-cap rises so gradually that we found it hard to tell when we were at the highest point, but in less than two hours after leaving camp we felt it was beginning to fall away to the west. The height by aneroid was only 3,300ft. The only way we could tell we were still gaining height was the gradual appearance of peaks to the north as well as Mount Ross to the south, the whole of which was now visible. Undoubtedly it is the only true peak in the full sense of the word that we saw either on Kerguelen or the Crozet. It is a true Alpine peak, well covered in snow where it is not too steep for snow to cling, and from where we saw it, 25 miles away, it had a formidable appearance.

The two peaks to the north had a much milder air. We took them to be Pic Guynemer 4,100ft. and Mount Richards 3,770ft., 10 miles away on the northern edge of the ice-cap. To the west was a thick bank of cloud or fog similar to that we had seen on the eastern side, its top so firm and level that at first we took it for the sea. To the south-west we could make out the much smaller and separate ice-field which covers most of Presqu'île Rallier du Baty, whose highest point is 4,190ft. Mount Ross, too, has no connection with the main ice-cap, which covers some 25 miles from north to south and about 10 miles from east to west, exclusive of the numerous glaciers which extend another three or four miles on both sides. Thus there are no higher mountains feeding this large field of ice, which makes the existence of it at so low an altitude in so low a latitude all the more remarkable. Presumably its presence is accounted for by the fact that rain falls on the island throughout the year, that it is generally cloud-covered and that the temperature is kept down by the surrounding expanse of ocean cooled by cold water from the Antarctic. The mean annual temperature at sea level is about 39°F.

How pleasant it was up there in the cool of the morning, the crisp snow crunching underfoot, on top of our small world where, we hoped, no one had set foot before. But soon we bid content farewell. For about three miles we walked westwards slowly losing height as we went, around us the unbroken snow plain and ahead the level bank of cloud, through which some rounded summits now thrust their heads to appear like islands floating on the sea. Very soon we were suffering all the discomforts attendant upon walking over snow under a bright sun – heat, glare, toil, burnt faces and cracked lips. Short halts became more frequent until at last we sat down on our sacks to eat, scanning the cloud bank below us vainly for any signs of its lifting. We in turn were watched hopefully by a skua gull which had followed us across. A glimpse of the sea, some identifiable bit of coast, or even the crevasses of a glacier below would have satisfied us, but although we sat there for an hour or more nothing happened. By going on down we should merely enter the cloud, fog, or whatever it was that concealed everything below 2,000ft. And I'm afraid the fact that we had already dropped six or seven hundred feet and would have to regain it in steadily softening snow had some effect upon me. Glacier-lethargy and age combined to sap my resolution. I felt like some of the early conquerors of Mount Blanc 'in need only of an umbrella and a scent bottle'. And like them, only with none of the numerous bottles carried by their guides to relieve it, I suffered from a 'lassitude which could not be overcome without the aid of liquor'.

So we started back, and wearisome work we found it retracing our steps over that featureless waste while the snow got softer and softer. Nor were our downhill tracks of any assistance, for they were just too long for us to fit our upgoing steps into them. As we only had six hundred feet or so to rise in a matter of three miles the gradient was almost imperceptible, yet we looked for the first signs of the slope levelling off with the eagerness of men approaching some legendary and almost inaccessible summit. Even when we began going downhill again I was shuffling rather than walking, and once or twice was almost brought to a halt by an attack of mountaineers' foot – the inability to put one in front of the other. Like a man in the throes of sea sickness who hopes the boat will sink, I began to regret there were no crevasses into which one might fall and lie still.

We celebrated our eventual arrival at the tent by brewing up twice, and while waiting for the first brew Roger produced a tin of deliciously cold pineapple slices. He had a welcome habit of fishing up from his capacious rucksack little luxuries like this that we were not supposed to have. Even at late evening the tent was abominably hot and while we were away most of the tent pegs had drawn out. It seemed to us that a heat wave had settled upon Kerguelen. We made up our minds to make an early start in order to get off the glacier while the going was good.

Next day was equally fine, the fourth in succession. Our early start was of little avail, for we encountered soft snow a few hundred feet lower down where it had had no chance to freeze during the night. We went on down to the river, where the warm weather and the increased melting had wrought a change. It was wider and faster-flowing and at times one could hear the nasty, sullen rumbling noise that boulders make when being rolled along the bottom. Roger, who had taken a line of his own, had not yet arrived when I started to cross. When a river crossing looks like being troublesome it is better if two men cross together hand-in-hand, their four feet and the two ice-axes giving so many more points of contact with the bottom. The water was deeper and faster than I bargained for. Instead of waiting for Roger, or looking for a better place, I blundered on, capsized, and crawled out on the far side soaked through, load and all. The load is the danger on these occasions, for once it gets wet it becomes so heavy that one may not be able to stand up again. It is advisable not to have it fastened at the waist, so that it can easily be jettisoned if necessary.

Roger, who had arrived in time to witness my gambols, chose a better place and got over safely. We had lunch at the old camp site while I dried out. It had been one of our windiest camps but now the air was so still that we brewed up on the Primus in the open without pitching the tent. Pushing on down the valley we camped for the night short of the river at the entrance to the gorge, for we hoped there would be less water in it in the early morning. Channels that formerly had been dry were now full of water and it was still rising. Even high up the glacier the temperature at night did not fall below freezing point, so that by morning the level of the water was much the same.

It was not flowing so fiercely as the other and by crossing hand-in-hand we got over without difficulty. By midday we were back on the beach where we sat for most of the afternoon, Procter having taken the dinghy to spend the day on a near-by islet. John, with whom we had a distant and mostly unintelligible conversation, was on board intent upon maintaining his unbroken record by staying there.

CHAPTER TWELVE

Port aux Français

DURING our absence, I'm afraid the crew had had a dull time, for here there was little of the fascinating wild life which had made Baie du Navire so entertaining. Procter had made a fresh collection of plants, and even the breaking of Jim's No. 1 hammer (for he had brought two) did not save the rocks of Kerguelen from his industrious assaults. Jan had kept the table supplied with rabbits. But the flow of fresh food – rabbits, cormorants, mussels, eggs – which should have fired our cook's ambitions had merely disgusted him to the point of practically quitting the galley. Jan and Procter cooked these delicacies and cooked them well, at the cost of some hard feelings. I could understand why Procter had sought a day's solitude on his islet. It was high time to put to sea again.

Our destination now was Baie du Morbihan, about 70 miles away, which we expected to reach in a day and a night. We could stock up with water at the French base but I thought we might as well take some fresh food. I particularly wanted to try cormorant, which the *Antarctic Pilot* describes as being 'rich in fat and meat and good eating.' The opinion of my other authority, Chapman, is cooler: 'I was once served with boiled cormorants,' he writes, 'but the dish left me with no taste for more.' Boiling, of course, is no way to treat game birds, so Jim was sent ashore to murder a cormorant and returned in due course with two penguins. Waiving the small matter of a mistake in species, a mistake excusable in a geologist, we asked him, 'Why two?' 'Well, you see,' said Jim apologetically, 'one got in the way.'

These unlucky victims were gentoo penguins. The absence of king penguins and the fewness of any of the other kinds was common to all the fjords we visited. Perhaps the small squid which is their principal food is found only in the open sea.

But this absence of wild life was only local. Kerguelen is extremely rich in life, only we happened to be at the wrong end of the island for the penguins, albatross, giant petrels, and sea-elephants which made Baie du Navire such an entrancing spot. The long, sandy beaches of the Courbet Peninsula, lying between Baie des Baleiniers and Baie du Morbihan, teem with life. Dr André Migot, who spent a year at the French base in 1953 and wrote a book* about it, describes a rookery of king penguins at Cape Ratmanoff on the east coast of the peninsula with a population of 50,000 birds. And on the north coast, not far from Cape Digby, he saw a rookery of macaroni penguins which covered 12 miles of coastline, probably the largest concentration of penguins

* *The Lonely South.*

anywhere in the world. Four adjacent rookeries of the same species gave a total estimated population on that bit of coast of nearly a million birds. On the east coast, too, besides these and numerous colonies of gentoo and rock-hopper penguins, there were sea-elephants up to a possible total of a quarter of a million; Dr Migot thought that there were about 5,000 of these beasts in a square mile. Alongside these figures Possession Island seems almost deserted.

The calm warm weather we had experienced on the ice-cap still prevailed. On Wednesday, 27 January, we waited until ten o'clock before a gentle breeze ruffled the water and encouraged us to get our anchor up. This wind from the east freshened later, so that we made good progress, beating all the time, down Chenal du Chasseur. Through a gap in the hills to the south we had a last, magnificent glimpse of Mount Ross and far astern the ice-cap glistened like a band of silver. It was the last fair day we were to have. How lovely, we thought, the forlorn landscape looked under the bright sun, and how notably does the presence of ice or snow quicken and augment a mountain scene.

Towards evening, when the wind grew light and wreaths of fog began stealing towards us, we had to find a harbour for the night, for we had not yet reached the wide expanse of Baie des Baleiniers, where we should have had room to drift. We were close under Île Bellouard, which was presently swallowed in the fog, and between it and another small island a pass led into Baie Doumergue and to an anchorage in the lee of our old acquaintance, Île du Port. The pass was full of kelp and although the *Pilot* assured us there was enough water I did not feel happy. The anchorage had evidently been popular with the sealers for there were remains of old leading marks. As we approached the beach a large object lying on it caused much speculation and a wide difference of opinions. Some affirmed it was an elephant seal, others a large boulder, but when a party landed to shoot rabbits they identified it as an enormous 'stinker'. For supper we had rabbit stew and mussels, the latter swimming in a piquant sauce of Jan's making.

We spent the whole of next morning beating up Baie Doumergue inside the Challenger Islands before we could break out into Baie des Baleiniers, here the wind at once left us. Evidently there was a change of weather in the offing, for it was dull and cold. With the night came some wind and all night we steered a safe course to the north. By morning we were far enough out to sea to lay the course for Cape Digby at the north-east extremity of the main island. By then rain had reduced visibility to less than a mile, but we could not afford to waste a fair wind even though it meant navigating by dead reckoning in thick weather past several off-lying islands. We held our course until evening, when we turned south, for I reckoned we had passed Cape Digby. Before darkness fell I thought I heard breakers to starboard, so we headed in a little and soon saw them breaking on a low, dismal-looking shore about a mile off. In the circumstances it was a satisfactory sight as we knew then that we were south of the cape. Even if there had been safe anchorages on the east coast it would have been of little avail to go looking for them in such thick weather. So after gaining a safe offing, we hove to for the night.

This passage of seventy miles to Port aux Français on which we had already been three days gave ample scope for the exercise of patience and prudence. We had some wind in the morning but visibility remained bad, and when the weather cleared at noon the wind died away. However, in the clearing we had identified Pointe Suzanne at the northern entrance to Baie du Morbihan and about 12 miles off. When a breeze sprang up at nightfall, we began to close the land. Coming on watch at midnight I was a little startled to see land on both bows and right ahead a distant light. The French base at Port aux Français could be the only source of light in those parts, and that was what we were looking at over the low spit of land between Baie du Morbihan and Norwegian Bay. Again we hove to and waited for daylight. Jan, who relieved me, was so exuberant at having this light in view that a quarter of an hour later, after I had turned in, he called me up to look at another. But this one was the planet Jupiter rising in the east.

A most miserable dawn broke in wind and rain with nothing anywhere in sight. During the night we must have been set north because when we let draw and began sailing we soon found ourselves surrounded by kelp. Norwegian Bay is full of kelp and a timely clearing of the horizon showed that we were well inside it with Pointe Suzanne broad on the port bow. Altering course, we rounded the point in a strong southerly wind with two rolls of mainsail, and as we opened up Baie du Morbihan, the buildings of the French base came into sight.

Baie du Morbihan is a magnificent sheet of water which with its numerous arms and inlets cover an area of nearly 200 square miles. From entrance to head the distance is 20 miles. The southern and western sides are fringed with many islands and the long fjords, which extend inland, provide many excellent harbours. Two expeditions for observing the Transit of Venus made their headquarters in the bay, and from 1909 to 1929 a French-Norwegian whaling company maintained a settlement at Port Jeanne d'Arc on the western side, where they built houses, workshops, tanks, stores, a factory and a 200ft. wood jetty. All has long been abandoned and is now in ruins. The French base is on the north side of the bay and is wide open to winds from the west. It was probably chosen with an eye to the future in a place where there is enough reasonably flat land to build an airfield.

Meantime the wind had dropped again and we gazed despondently at the cluster of huts and radio masts still some eight miles away. While we were discussing whether we had been seen and what chances there were of a launch coming out to give us a tow, the wind came again from the west with some fury. The reefs we had just taken out were rolled in as *Mischief* went tearing along, the water boiling in the lee scuppers. A motor launch shot out from behind one of the islands to the west and came in pursuit of us without making the least impression. With spray flying all over her, and a crowd of figures in oilskins pointing and gesticulating, she altered course and made straight for the base. We might have followed her but with unnecessary caution we stuck to the dog-leg channel used by the steamers which annually relieve the base. Having rounded Île Channer we pointed for the huts and a little later rounded to and dropped anchor inside a belt of kelp. This is the only protection there is and it is surprising how efficient kelp can be in the place of a breakwater.

We no longer doubted that we had been noticed. The small concrete wharf was thronged with men and as our anchor went down a boat put off. In it was M. Heurgon (Chef del'Etablissement) whom I had last met in his Paris office in 1957; he speaks English, as he had served as a Flying Officer with the Free French air force during the war. After helping us to moor securely to a large buoy, his Breton boatman ferried us ashore. Our arrival could not have been better timed. It was a Sunday and happily the lunch hour. The large crowd on the wharf raised a cheer as we climbed up the ladder. Cameras clicked and ciné-cameras whirred, their principal targets being Jan crowned with a yachting-cap with a white cover and wearing a Newgate fringe, and Roger with his luxurious dark brown mane. With so much hand-shaking to do it was unfortunately impossible for us to return the fire, for our hosts were the more picturesque, with beards of all sizes and shapes and faces of all colours; for many of the staff, such as mechanics, gardeners and kitchen-hands, are recruited in Madagascar. One of the scientists, a short, stout man, had a real hard-weather, dreadnought beard, his face being completely concealed under a thick carpet or rug of hair surmounted by a pair of spectacles.

Dazed and feeling a little sheepish with the warmth of our welcome, we were bundled into a jeep and carried half a mile to the mess where M. Heurgon, his chief assistants, and the 15 scientists lived: a big, light room, with double glass windows, central heating, settees and armchairs, and a large brick fireplace above which was a mural painting of Mount Ross. Fortified by brandy and soda, we then walked round to the main mess-hall, where on Sundays all 67 souls assembled for their *déjeuner*, sitting at one long table and a cross table for the seniors and guests. There, amidst a prodigious convivial clatter, we embarked upon a meal such as only Frenchmen could conjure up on a desolate island.

Judge of our astonishment upon seeing scattered up and down the table whole bowls of tomatoes, lettuce and radishes, and to be assured that they were grown on the island. The long, crusty loaves of French bread were to be expected and were delicious, but the butter that we slapped on pretty freely was fresh, and that also, we were told, was made at the base. Likewise the potatoes, the mutton, the pork and the *pâté de la maison*, which we scooped out by the spoonful, were all home products. To men accustomed to thinking mainly in terms of rabbits and cormorants all these good things were as delightful as they were surprising. Wine, of course, circulated freely, and we concluded this memorable meal with a masterpiece of a cake, a variety of cheeses, coffee and brandy. Speeches were made, John had to be restrained from singing, and Jan, whose fluent French had made him popular, had to be carried out and put to bed.

Presiding over this magnificent affair and supervising everything was the chef in white apron and professional cap, dignified but vivacious, who sat just below the salt, where he kept a watchful eye on the dishing-up and the wants of the guests. He seemed to relish the responsibility of feeding this enormous family of hungry men and evidently enjoyed the life, for he had returned to the island four times. With his love of banter and quick jests I pictured him as a sort of modern Alexis Soyer, born to grapple with gastronomic problems from braising boars' heads to spitting larks or boiling tripe, equally at home cooking for an army in the Crimea or for the crowned heads of Europe.

Sternly overcoming the desire for sleep, those of us who were still on our feet took a walk round the establishment with M. Heurgon to see how all this fresh food was produced; for we were told that tinned and preserved foods played very little part in the diet. We went first to the garden, where a skilful and enthusiastic Malagasy showed us how he grows either in the open, in cold frames, or in a greenhouse, and for most of the year round, radishes, chervil, dandelions, parsley, cabbages, spinach, cress, potatoes and tomatoes. Additional soil has been put down, and manure from the cowsheds and piggery, as well as blood and offal, are liberally applied. Besides the milking cows and the piggery, there is a large poultry yard – wired overhead to protect it from skua gulls – and flocks of geese and ducks roam at large. For fodder they make hay and silage from the acaena grass which grows so abundantly, and they also feed to the livestock an oily meal, a waste product of the sea-elephant factory which we later visited. M. Heurgon, who is a fisherman, showed us a trout hatchery he has started with a view to stocking the streams, and an attempt to breed reindeer is also on foot.

The sheep are run on one of the many islands in the bay. We regretted having no time to visit them, for I felt that homage was due to the providers of the most succulent mutton, I have ever tasted, mutton which combined the sweetness of the mountain, the fat of the valley and the tang of the saltings. Rabbits have long been a curse on Kerguelen as they have been elsewhere, and an attempt to kill them off by introducing myxomatosis failed owing to the absence of fleas to spread the disease. Partly owing to the rabbits there is not enough herbage on the main island – at any rate near Port aux Français – to support even sheep. The flock now numbers several hundred, of which more than a hundred are exported annually as surplus. When one island is eaten out the sheep are moved to another, a system of rotation of islands, so to speak, instead of a rotation of crops. We saw no sheepdogs about and I imagine the job of getting a few hundred sheep on board a tank-landing craft is no mean one, calling for unlimited patience and cunning. We noticed two of these craft at the base, their main use being that of ferrying stores ashore from the relief ship.

Apparently these sheep have begun to thrive only comparatively recently and against all expectation. Xavier Reppe, a journalist, has written in *Aurore sur l'Antarctique* a popular description of all the lands comprised under the name 'Terres Australes et Antartiques Françaises,' including St Paul and New Amsterdam, Adélie Land, Kerguelen and the Crozet. In it he has some amusing stories about the livestock of Kerguelen which I hope are true. He is a man who, like myself, is not displeased to see the scientists and savants confounded by the unlearned, as very rarely they are. Up till 1955 experience, tradition, biologists, botanists and oecologists all agreed and decreed that sheep would not do on Kerguelen. The woe-begone, emaciated appearance of three experimental sheep sent out and borne on the establishment at Port aux Français seemed to endorse this conclusively. A visiting expert who examined them declared that their teeth had rotted away and that owing to the lack of calcium in the soil this was inevitably to be expected. One of the menials, however, a man who knew something about sheep as he had been a shepherd in the Pyrenees, declared that the only trouble with the sheep was their extreme old age. And enquiries showed this to be the case, for the bureaucrat who had the task of balancing the island's stringent budget had ordered the sheep to be bought in the cheapest market. The same ex-shepherd then visited an islet where in 1952 four other sheep had been dumped and written off. When with difficulty they had been rounded up, for they were completely wild, they were found to have multiplied themselves three times and the largest weighed 200lbs.

Another problem which baffled the combined brains of the savants at the time of our journalist's visit to Kerguelen in 1955 was the infertility of the duck eggs. The birds themselves did well enough but they obstinately refused to breed. Lack of minerals in the soil, lack of vitamins, insufficient sun, insufficient moon and all kinds of obscure biological anomalies were canvassed and analysed as possible explanations. The true explanation was imparted discreetly to M. Reppe by a humble labourer who told him in confidence that '*les imbéciles*', as he called them, had not perceived that they had eaten all the drakes, for from the very first these had been sent to the table as the finest birds. Nevertheless, even in those days some of these sub-antarctic farmers knew their business, and M. Reppe seems to have appreci-ated their efforts as much as we did. At their Christmas dinner in 1955 they ate a pig weighing nearly half a ton. Or to put it less grossly and more gracefully, as he does: '*Nous avons sacrifié un sujet qui pesait 320kgs. Mais la specialité la plus prisée des gourmets est le cochon de lait farci, que le chef Perrimond réussit à merveille.*'

Our tour included the meteorological station, whence observations are transmitted daily to various places in the southern hemisphere; the workshops, where the maintenance of the vehicles used about the base seemed to keep them fully occupied; the power station, the men's hutments and the kitchens. No doubt owing to difficulties of transport and labour, and its poor quality, the coal which exists in parts of the island is not utilised. Oil is the only source of light and heat, and it is an expensive one; moreover, the rapidly accumulat-ing dumps of empty oil drums are at once an eyesore and a waste. When we were there, two experts were investigating the possibility of a hydro-electric scheme, for there are several fine waterfalls at no great distance. In the kitchens they use both electric stoves and oil-fired ranges; and all the hutments are fitted with central heating and hot and cold water.

As my scientific knowledge never got much beyond Archimedes' Principles, which I have since forgotten, and as I speak no French worth listening to, I did not accept the warm invitations to see the places where the scientists were busy with research into magnetism, seismology, the ionosphere, cosmic rays and suchlike abstruse matters. For although this research, as well as weather-recording, is the *raison d'être* for the base at Port aux Français, it was of greater interest to me to see how this small band of enthusiastic exiles was fed and housed.

M. Heurgon insisted on our taking all our meals with him, so next morning we went ashore for breakfast. Before leaving the boat we bent another chain on the mooring buoy, for it was blowing very hard from the south-west. Only three of us slept on board. John, who had no qualms about going ashore here, remained there until we sailed, and likewise Jan. The yolk of my breakfast egg was of such a violent red colour that I suspected my sight had been affected by the lunch of the previous day; but M. Heurgon explained that the colour was due to feeding the hens on sea-elephant's liver, and suggested that we should visit the factory where the carcases are processed. A small private company is licensed to kill up to 2,000 seals a year, but the number actually killed is generally less than a thousand. They are shot on beaches several miles away from the factory, the carcases being hauled overland by Weasels. After the inside had been removed the remainder is chopped up by hand and fed into a hopper, whence it passes into large cylinders like pressure cookers. At the end of the process all that remains of a sea-elephant is oil and a brown mealy substance. This meal, rich in oil, makes a valuable feeding stuff for the livestock.

By afternoon the wind had increased so much that when I tried to row off alone to do some small job I had to give up the attempt, and finally regained the shore several hundred yards to leeward of the jetty. At night the wind had abated sufficiently for three of us to get back on board. There had been a cinema show after supper, so it was late when M. Heurgon drove us down to the wharf in the jeep. Jeeps, like yacht-dinghies and maids-of-all-work generally, are apt to suffer from neglect. This one had no lights, so our friend the Breton boatman sat on the forward end of the bonnet to act as navigator and look-out. Our driver seemed to place implicit confidence in the penetrating powers of a seaman's eyes as we shot off with true French *élan* in pitch blackness down the road, or where the road was thought to be. Navigating at that speed, the look-out in the bows never had a chance. As we hit the reef – a dump of empty oil drums – he was projected violently from the bonnet to the top of an oil drum without time to utter a Breton oath, let alone a warning. The jeep, of course, sustained no damage that mattered, but the boatman sprained his wrist.

I had appointed next day, 2 February, as sailing day. Besides feeling that we were imposing too much on French hospitality we wanted to get home in good time. Roger, insatiable in the pursuit of hard experience, had plans for joining a friend in Spitsbergen for the latter half of the summer; and Procter, besides having his bees constantly on his mind, wanted to be home in time for his children's holidays. In the morning our friendly Breton, in spite of his damaged wrist, made several trips in his boat ferrying off water to fill our tanks. As a Breton, and therefore a seaman, he took great interest in *Mischief*. His motor launch gave him plenty to do. Besides making trips to various islands, particularly the island where the sheep lived, she was employed in fishing – another way in which M. Heurgon fully exploited the local resources.

At our farewell lunch we were again impressed with how well and sensibly these Frenchmen lived. But then no men with a M. Perrimond to cater for their bodily needs and to educate their palates would be in danger of becoming what a gifted gastronome has described as 'Gobble-and-gulp-people, who in their melancholy ignorance swallow a *Potage à la Comte de Paris*, or a *Risolette à la Pompadour*, with the same frightful nonchalance as a sailor will devour his pea-soup, or a rustic bolt his bacon.' For *hors d'oeuvres* we had salami and *pâté a la maison*, both home-produced. Our hosts (God forgive them) then offered us snails; but some superb mutton chops with fried potatoes and salad made full amends for this lapse. With the cheese we were persuaded to try honey – pure, unadulterated honey – and needed no second persuasion. We should have preferred to linger over the coffee and brandy but we had to get not only ourselves on board but a whole cargo of good things given us by M. Heurgon, the chef, the doctor, the priest and many other well-wishers. These comprised eggs, fresh butter, bread, potatoes, radishes, lettuce, tomatoes; enough chocolate to last each of us all the way home, and for Jan a like amount of cigarettes; jars of the famous *pâté* and tins of sauerkraut and fruit. Besides that we took on board all the petrol and paraffin we needed, a six-gallon carboy of red wine and a one-gallon jar of Martinique rum. All we could do in return was to take all the letters they could write in two days to Cape Town for posting. The whole party were due for relief in November; but meantime communication with their families was confined to a telegram of so many words which each man was allowed to send fortnightly.

With a hearty cheer from the crowd the last boatload of men and stores at last left the quay. With a fair wind we hoisted sail, let go our moorings and sailed out, accompanied for a time by M. Heurgon in the launch. It had been a most enjoyable and impressive interlude. We left full of admiration for M. Heurgon and his men, the efficient way in which this far-flung French outpost was run, and the keenness and high morale of its occupants.

I must say this state of things, the friendly, cheerful atmosphere, came as a surprise. On landing at Port aux Français I had half expected to find *cafard* oozing out of the windows of the men's huts, for among a party of nearly 70 men of varying rank – officials, scientists, tradesmen, labourers – confined for 12 months on a barren island and living at fairly close quarters, there is bound to be friction. Especially in the case of Frenchmen, who are perhaps more effervescent and therefore likely to go flat more quickly than are Englishmen.

This happy harmony did not always prevail. A striking contrast to it is shown in the description of life at the base given by the Dr André Migot who has already been mentioned. Speaking of the men whom his party relieved in January 1953 he says: 'These men had reached the point where they hated one another with all their hearts and were divided into factions that were more rigid and bitterly opposed than any savage tribes in Central Africa. Many of them were no longer on speaking terms, and among this group of men there were some who would communicate with one another only by letter. Our ears were stuffed with improbable stories of documents being stolen, people being searched and summoned, official reports and so on, the drift of these contradictory tales naturally depending on which clique was telling the story. All this seemed incredibly childish to us. We thought, quite wrongly, that we were different; our mission seemed to be a model of its kind and its members proof against the errors into which the others had fallen. ....'

A few months later Dr Migot writes: 'The perpetual wind and fickle weather have tried the nerves of many. Our daily work is tedious and the diet monotonous; the time-table is inflexible, the camp ugly and the landscape unvarying. Six month's of this life has changed men's characters, embittered their spirits. When this state of mind is aggravated by the tactlessness, unbridled criticism and thoughtless gossip of some, and the bad temper and lack of understanding of others, some members of the mission reach a state of strain that is apt to end in violence.'

Admittedly our visit was short, and I like to think that *Mischief*'s unex-pected arrival and the excitement of seeing fresh faces encouraged at least a temporary uplifting of hearts. So if the minds of the men we met were hag-ridden like those of Dr Migot's companions we did not notice it. For all that I feel sure that M. Heurgon and his men were by no means afflicted with low spirits, rancour, and wretchedness of mind; the convivial uproar which broke out immediately we sat down to our Sunday dinner convinced me of that. No doubt since 1953 the base is better organised and there are more amenities. But the life is still monotonous, the climate harsh, the scenery severe, and it is the job of the base leader and his assistants to see that morale remains unaffected by these conditions. Of M. Heurgon's assistants in this difficult task I should give a high place to M. le Chef. No doubt it will have been noticed that Dr Migot mentions the monotonous diet and I expect that M. Heurgon, too, had long since made a note of it, hence his insistence on fresh food and his keenness on all the farming and gardening activities. On an expedition, where there is generally a sense of struggle and achievement, men will accept a scanty and monotonous diet. A man working at the base on Kerguelen has no such sense to sustain him. When a man is tired of food – not to mention brandy and baccy – he is tired of life, but no one, not even a Frenchman, could tire of the fare provided by a man of Perrimond's genius. Here, I think, lies the big difference between conditions at the base in 1953 and 1960. 'Feed the brute' was M. Heurgon's simple remedy for 'belly-aching.' Or to put it more elegantly, aided by M. Perrimond's practical genius he applied the fundamental Epicurean doctrine that the 'beginning and root of all good is the stomach; even wisdom and culture must be referred to this.'

CHAPTER THIRTEEN

To Cape Town

As we sailed that evening towards the entrance to the bay, the island looked in its worst mood, desolate and grim under a hard, lowering sky. During our short stay we had been lucky to find it generally wearing a more benign face. Having rounded Harston Rock outside Pointe Suzanne, we streamed the log and steered north, homeward bound at last with 10,000 miles to go. To Cape

Town in a direct line was only some 2,100 miles but we could not steer for it until we were far enough north to be clear of the westerlies. We had to go round two sides of a triangle. The proper course for a sailing ship bound for Cape Town from eastwards is to pick up the South-east Trades in about S. lat. 30°, making the African coast about Durban, from where she would have the benefit of the Agulhas current. As it happened, we did not have quite so far north to go; for we found favourable winds in the region of variables in S. lat. 34° when we were about 1,000 miles north of Kerguelen. But before we won clear of the westerlies we expected to be pushed farther east. Cape Leeuwin in Australia was only 1,800 miles away and we feared it might be much nearer before we were able to steer west. The light-hearted suggestion that we might let the westerlies have their way and blow us home round the world did not bear examination. Even going by Panama the distance would have been 15,000 miles and it would not be much fun going round the world with no time to loiter on the way.

Early that night we witnessed a fine display of Aurora Australis; at least it appeared fine to me who had seen nothing of the kind before. In fact, it was probably a weak display, for there were none of the bright green, red and violet colours which one associates with auroras, but merely a broad curtain of whitish-green rays flickering across the southern sky. Since it is the northern lights, Aurora Borealis, which are nearly always mentioned, there is an impression that they are the most common; but this is probably because there are far fewer ships navigating in high latitudes in the south than in the north. Apparently these displays are most frequent in the equinoctial months of March and September, and they have a well defined eleven-year period of greater activity, corresponding with the cycle of solar activity, when the displays are most vivid though not necessarily more frequent. Magnetic storms of any intensity are always accompanied by a display of aurora.

The homeward-bound feeling, coupled with the fact that there were no rabbits, cormorants, or albatross eggs to cook, restored harmony for a time while John resumed his former sway over the galley. *Mischief*'s liveliness as she staggered northwards, together with his recent unbroken bout of eating, drinking and sleeping, had their effect on John's health, but in a few days he was his old, cheerful self. What with the huge amount of stores given us by the French and the trophies gathered by the insatiable collectors among us, the cabin seemed less spacious. The great carboy of wine occupied the place of honour and a lot of space on the floor, cheek by jowl with the box of plant specimens. And in all sorts of unlikely places one came upon pieces of rock, sea-elephants' teeth and albatross heads. Among the rock specimens were some fine examples of volcanic 'bombs', smooth, round or elliptical pieces of lava which, Jim assured us, had acquired their shape on their long fall to earth after being hurled to a great height.

Two days out we passed to the north of what is called the Antarctic Convergence, a zone of some 20 to 30 miles wide where a marked rise in the sea temperature takes place. In the course of 24 hours sailing we recorded a rise of 12 degrees, which Roger and I accepted as a hint to begin bathing again. The line of convergence lies generally near the fiftieth parallel, slightly north of it in the Indian and Atlantic oceans and south of it in the Pacific. The zone is often a region of fog. While navigating south of the Cape we had expected to see some icebergs, and their total absence was at the same time a disappointment and a relief. Even in the best conditions, icebergs are difficult to detect at night and there are no infallible signs to indicate the proximity of bergs. No reliance can be placed upon changes in sea or air temperatures or upon receiving echoes from a foghorn. Even radar would fail to detect growlers or bergy bits, as they are called, which are quite large enough to sink a ship.

On the Pilot Chart the line of the extreme northern limit of icebergs is drawn near the fortieth parallel, or a degree or two north of it in the vicinity of the Cape. Scattered about on the Admiralty chart are numerous notices of localities where icebergs have been seen, but they are all of pretty ancient date. For example, in April 1835, numerous bergs were reported only 70 miles south of Cape Agulhas, and four icebergs from 100ft. to 200ft. high were reported 250 miles south of the same Cape in September 1854. It may be that, as in the case of the Aurora Australis, few icebergs are nowadays reported because there are so few ships in those waters to see them. Or it may be that, owing to the warmer conditions that seem to prevail in both the northern and southern hemisphere, icebergs do not now penetrate so far north.

During the first week we reeled off 500 miles and it was comforting to find that in that distance we had lost only about 50 miles to the east. Without treating us to any extremes, the weather varied widely from wet to fine and from windy to calm. For several days, despairing of catching fish, Procter had been fishing for albatross as they used to do in the big sailing ships. To his own and everyone else's surprise he caught one. The method is to trail on a fishing line a piece of light metal strip shaped like a diamond, with a piece of meat secured in the space in the middle. When the albatross seizes the meat in his beak he finds he is unable to withdraw his opened beak from the metal frame. Though I have not seen it done, the same principle is said to be used to catch monkeys, only in this case it is the monkey's paw, clutching a nut which he has not the sense or is too greedy to drop, which gets caught. It sounds all right in theory but in practice several snags developed. If we were going fast enough to drag the bait along the surface, the albatross had no chance of seizing it, whereas if we were moving slowly the bait sank. One had to be going very slowly indeed, for the bird seemed unable to take the bait when in flight; and having made his usual clumsy landing, he had to swim after it. Procter got over the sinking difficulty by attaching a piece of cork, which no doubt lessened its efficiency as a lure. We were barely moving when his one and only victim managed to grab the bit of salami we were using and got his beak firmly caught inside the metal. In spite of the prevailing excitement he was hauled in and successfully lifted on board, a job almost as tricky as landing a large fish without either gaff or landing net. When Roger had ringed him we let him go. I am glad to say he was not sea sick, as we had been led to expect, and after taking a staggering turn round the deck, he launched himself clumsily over the side and on to the water. There were many subsequent occasions, far too many, when we were moving slowly enough for Procter to let out his line. But surely in vain the net is spread in the sight of any bird. I don't think albatross are such fools as they look, at least not such fools as to think a piece of rather tough salami worth bothering about. The few whose greed overcame their prudence, after a few half-hearted pecks, gave up in disgust.

The extraordinary powers of the albatross in flight and the clumsiness he shows when alighting, especially in calm weather, are well known. This contrasting grace and clumsiness is described by Chapman as follows:

> The flight of the albatross is truly majestic as with motionless wings he sails over the sea; now rising high in the air, now descending until the tip of the lower wing all but touches the crests of the waves as he skims over them. Suddenly he sees something on the water and prepares to alight; but how changed he now is from the noble bird but a moment before all grace and symmetry. He raises his wings, his head goes back, and his back goes in; down drop two enormous webbed feet straddled out to their full extent, and with a hoarse croak, between the cry of a raven and that of a sheep, he falls souse into the water. Here he is at home again, breasting the waves like a cork. Presently he stretches out his neck and with great exertion runs along the top of the water for 70 or 80 yards, until having got sufficient impetus, he tucks up his legs, and is once more fairly launched in the air.

An albatross certainly looks undignified enough when coming in to land on the water but not quite so ludicrous as the pelicans we used to watch off the Peruvian coast; which used to zoom past in single file, their heads drawn back and chests thrown out, like a procession of pompous city aldermen, until the leader, merely folding his wings, belly-flopped into the water amidst a cloud of spray.

That any of the birds ringed by Roger would be found seemed to us a slim chance, but several birds ringed in even more remote places, such as South Georgia, have been recovered. The Wandering Albatross was not so named without reason. Some of the instances quoted by Chapman of how these birds get about are revealing. A bird shot off the coast of Chile on 20 December, 1847, had a vial tied to its neck in which there was the following note:

> December 8th, 1847. Ship, 'Euphrates', Edwards, 16 months out, 2,300 barrels of oil, 150 of it sperm. I have not seen a whale for 4 months. Lat. 43° South, Long. 140.40° west. Thick fog with rain.

According to the figures the albatross had travelled about 3,150 miles in a direct line in the twelve days between the writing of the note and the shooting of the bird. One cannot but wonder at the strange whim of Captain Edwards to confide this concise account of his success, his disappointment, and the state of the weather, to so dubious a messenger as an albatross, as if it might have been a carrier pigeon. Another example is that of a bird ringed in Kerguelen in December 1913 which, almost exactly three years later, was captured by a French four-master near Cape Horn. In this case the distance is over 6,000 miles, and it suggests that some birds in the course of their lives do actually circumnavigate the globe in the region of the westerlies. And since albatross are unknown in the northern hemisphere, even more extraordinary is the case of a black-browed albatross which was shot north-west of

Spitsbergen; and of yet another which for 34 years lived with a colony of gannets on one of the Faeroes. It was known to the islanders as the King of the Gannets, was eventually shot, and is now in the Copenhagen Museum.

Until 14 February, which was the skipper's birthday, the wind hung persistently in the north-west, so that we had to sail close hauled all the time in order not to lose ground to the east. It was a most welcome birthday present when on that day we got our first fair wind. John provided a cake and Jan produced a jar of marinaded mussels which he had preserved when on Kerguelen. We were now in Lat. 35° S., nearly 900 miles north of Kerguelen and still in the same longitude, and we seemed to be already clear of the westerlies. Steering a little north of west we could lay the course for Cape Town, still 2,500 miles away, and for the next eight days made runs of over 100 miles, our best being on the nineteenth, when we ran 148 miles. In fact the wind became a little too fresh. The wire luff of the Genoa parted and soon we had to reef down. Whereupon the wind flew into the west and headed us. Having left the 'Forties' behind, we had been quick to remove the battened-down skylight-cover, but as soon as we began beating in a rough sea we regretted it; and below one needed to be on the *qui vive* when a wave climbed on board and threatened to squirt water through the skylight. But this mattered little, for we were back in a region of warmth and sunshine where we could quickly dry out on deck. We began to get sunburnt again and sometimes conditions allowed of some work on deck, scraping the bright-work and the spare spars.

On the whole we enjoyed a preponderance of easterly winds, so that we made steadily westwards between the latitudes of 35° and 33° S. The Genoa was out of action, its wire luff being too rusty to splice, so for the sake of speed we often ran with the mainsail and staysail boomed out on opposite sides. If the boat was rolling or yawing about it was not at all safe; a gybe seemed always to be imminent and one of the crew even managed to gybe and get the staysail aback as well. To sleep soundly at night, without having one ear cocked for sounds of trouble, I preferred having the twins up when running dead before the wind. Nevertheless, we got along at a famous pace until we sighted land. Then the wind began to falter and with it our hopes of making a fast passage.

On Sunday, 6 March, we saw a steamer, the first to be sighted since leaving Cape Town three months before. A little later we made out some distant land which I took to be Port Elizabeth or thereabouts. As on the previous day we had experienced a westerly set of forty miles from the Agulhas current, I had made an equally generous allowance when working out the dead reckoning. But the only certain way of identifying a distant bit of land when lack of wind prevents one from going nearer is to sight a lighthouse at night. After sunset, therefore, we waited confidently for the Cape St Francis light, 50 miles *west* of Port Elizabeth, to appear, its period being a five-second flash. When the light came up it seemed to flash every ten seconds, the period of the light on Great Fish point 50 miles *east* of Port Elizabeth. It was too bad to believe. But though we timed the flash until we were dizzy, from the deck and from the shrouds, we could not convince ourselves that it was flashing every five seconds as it should have been. We were not lost but a little uncertain of our position. What we had rashly assumed to be Port Elizabeth had, in fact, been East London.

However, next day we really were off Port Elizabeth. By evening, when we had closed the land, we were two miles off Cape Recife at the western end of Algoa Bay or Port Elizabeth. The remaining four hundred odd miles to Cape Town took us eight tedious days. Had the Agulhas current played its part we could have done the distance in the same time in a flat calm, for this two-and-a-half-knot current should give one 40 to 50 miles a day of westing. But, although we kept as far as possible in the axis of the current about 50 miles off shore, we gained from it nothing at all. The passage from East London to Cape Town, or vice versa, has a bad reputation among both Cape yachtsmen and small-boat voyagers on account of the frequency of gales and the high confused seas they raise on the Agulhas Bank, and more particularly along its edge. According to one's point of view, whether beset with impatience or desirous only of quiet, we suffered or enjoyed a week of the utmost tranquillity. On two consecutive days we logged only 20 miles, most of it no doubt due to the current.

On the evening of 13 March, a week after first sighting land, we had Cape Agulhas abeam. As we lay drifting, the *Edinburgh Castle*, bound for Cape Town, steamed close by, and John, who had confided to me that he wished to be home quicker than we should, wondered if he could get a passage in her. We should have to hurry. Next day we made a sudden spurt. After passing Cape Point in the evening, we sailed on slowly throughout the night, and were near the entrance to Table Bay before the wind once more deserted us. As we drifted becalmed, admiring the wide prospect of the bay, watching the smoke from the tall power-house chimneys ascending vertically, and wondering if any of the small fishing boats scattered about would give us a tow, a violent puff of wind hit us and passed on. At the same moment I noticed a familiar cloud gathering on the top of Table Mountain. Fortunately, when the south-easter struck, we were pointing in the right direction, and we tore off close-hauled across the bay, dodging the stream of fishing-boats which were now making with all speed for shelter.

When the dock entrance bore well away on the quarter we went about and headed for it. But owing to the weight of wind and the short, choppy sea, we made too much leeway; although we hung on to the last in hope, we failed to fetch the entrance. As there was more room to leeward, we gybed over and went roaring back across the bay in order to have a second shot. Again we went about too soon and as we sagged away to leeward I was almost sweating with anxiety. To miss the entrance a second time would disgrace us for ever in the eyes of the Yacht Club; and one could be sure that the oldest member or one of his cronies would have his glasses on us, watching our capers. By luffing up, in the harder puffs, we just made it. Shooting between the piers we began to beat up the half-mile length of dock, watched by the steamers moored on either hand.

As the battery was flat and the engine consequently unable to start, we should have to anchor outside the Yacht Basin. But when we saw the Club launch coming to meet us, we dropped anchor and got the sails down while

Commander Windsor came alongside to see what could be done. The wind being too strong for his launch to tow us, he went off to enlist the aid of a powerful Police launch lying at the dock wall. Meanwhile, we had started to drag our anchor and a lot more chain had to be veered before we brought up rather close to the dock wall. Very decently, the Police agreed to giving us a tow, but even their launch had its work cutout towing in the teeth of the blast. Helped by the Club launch we at last got a line to an emergency buoy at the Yacht Basin entrance, where we lay for the next two days while the south-easter blew itself out. It was a rough welcome.

CHAPTER FOURTEEN

A False Start

THOUGH we were all glad enough to be back among our friends and the flesh-pots, we hoped that a fortnight would be enough in which to refresh and to refit for the long haul to Lymington. We intended to stop at only St Helena for water. The important jobs were to slip the boat in order to renew the anti-fouling, to send up the topmast, and to have the charging engine overhauled. Three days after our arrival, John left for England in the *Edinburgh Castle* as he had hoped. I was very sorry to see him go. He had fed us well by making the best use of what we had, and had looked after my interests by being economical. We had seldom, if ever, missed a meal, for even when sick he had refused to give up; and, above all, he was always cheerful and sometimes amusing.

I imagined that among the adventurous youth of Cape Town there would be no lack of volunteers to fill his place for the sake of a free trip to England. Anyone who offered I would be happy to take, for while we could manage well enough with five, we were all lazy enough to prefer having six. But no offers came. Lying in Duncan Dock was an old yacht called *Cariad*, a magnifi-cent 100-foot ketch built in 1896 which, after her racing days were over, had been twice round the world. She had been lying there two years before on our previous visit, looking forlorn and sadly neglected as laid-up ships do. With a new owner she was now undergoing a lengthy fitting-out, and the young crew, who were living on board helping, were becoming a little impatient at the various delays. It occurred to me that some of them might want a change, so I carefully refrained from giving them any encouragement; particularly since *Cariad*'s skipper, a formidable red-bearded figure almost as broad as long, had let it be known that the same ugly thought had occurred to him, and that anyone who tried to entice away his crew would be thrown into the dock.

One morning a slightly undersized black youth came along. He wanted a passage to England, where he hoped to find a steamer going to the Cape Verde Islands, for he claimed to be a native of those islands and a Portuguese subject. He said that the emigration office held his papers together with 40 pounds which he had been obliged to deposit. He added as an afterthought that he was cook in *Cariad*. His absence on this private business must have upset their domestic economy, for when Aluzio Verissimo, or Johnny, as he was known, and I boarded *Cariad* at half-past two, the skipper and crew were just finishing lunch. That this development came as no surprise did not lessen the skipper's rage, particularly with me, whom he regarded as an amateur crimp.

Verissimo, however, braved the lion and in an understandably nervous manner gave his skipper the sack, and having collected his scanty gear, a spare shirt and a key bugle, we started for the emigration office to collect his papers and the cash. The taxi fare was expensive. As a title to Portuguese citizenship Johnny's papers were about as relevant and valid as an unsigned love-letter, consisting merely of a barely legible discharge paper made out by the skipper of a Greek tramp steamer. No wonder the authorities had wanted a deposit of £40 before allowing Johnny to land, and I felt that the immigration people at Southampton might want even more. They could hardly fail to notice the name of Aluzio Verissimo on my crew list and they would not be pleased with me if I tried to laugh him off as an itinerant Portuguese musician bugling his way round the world.

So for the moment we left his £40 in safe hands. If he took it he would have to leave South Africa in some ship or other and I began to think it might not be in *Mischief*. But I was loath to give up. If I was an amateur crimp I wanted to make a success of it. The taxi to the Portuguese Consul's office, our next port of call, was another expensive ride. There Johnny unfolded his life story in what was undoubtedly Portuguese. The Consul listened with boundless patience, a patience exceeded only by that of the crimp, who had to listen without comprehending a word. It was no good. The Consul explained that, much as he would like to, he could not give him a Portuguese passport simply because he spoke the language, and poor Johnny was hazy about the name of his parents and totally ignorant of their address. At the end of a trying day we presented ourselves again on *Cariad*. Johnny, I hoped, felt smaller than I, who had been merely a not unwilling tool in his hand, a sort of spare key to his bugle. His request to be reinstated was, of course, rejected with contumely; but I rejoiced to hear, a few days later, that *Cariad*'s skipper had been obliged to come to terms with the Portuguese virtuoso, who went back to the galley to take it out of the crew.

At Cape Town a visiting yacht is compelled to appoint Agents. The firm to whom I allotted this unremunerative role, without consulting them, took it on willingly and accomplished the tiresome business of ship's papers, involving visits to a string of various offices, for a purely nominal sum. But I had besides a sort of personal agent in the climbing friend who, as well as taking me up Table Mountain, was always ready to put himself and his car at our disposal. So long as *Mischief* remained in Cape Town, the firm for whom Bob Hinings worked, or at least his department of it, might as well have closed; he was either out with me drinking coffee or down at the Yacht Basin to see if we wanted anything done. Knowing Cape Town and speaking Afrikaans, he was useful in all kinds of ways, from knowing where to have climbing boots nailed to bullying a laundry into paying for a pair of trousers they had lost. We met frequently at his flat to dine off the inevitable steak and eggs, and to drink the fine, mellow brandy which he kept in a large medicine bottle marked 'Poison'. Devoted wholeheartedly to mountains and music, he was a man ill-suited to the irksome confinement of an office, and as he had been caught up in the machinery of business, a little of the iron of it had entered into his soul. He was of a strongly independent mind, and though he did not look for trouble he was not unhappy to see it coming, especially if he had been the cause of it.

After the Johnny episode I gave up looking for a new cook and Jan agreed to take over the galley, leaving four of us for watch-keeping. A new twin staysail had been made, a new wire luff fitted to the Genoa, and a fresh lot of stores ordered, including a large amount of twice-baked bread. Before the time came for us to leave, it was gratifying to learn that the meteorological log kept by Roger had been of interest, as the following extract from the *Weather Bureau News Letter*, written by Dr W. Schmitt, shows:

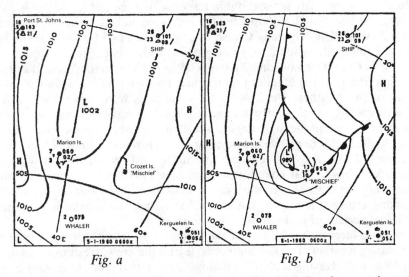

Fig. a   Fig. b

Mischief had no radio on board and the observations were, therefore, not immediately available for current map analysis in South Africa. Merchant shipping in the Indian Ocean normally uses routes north of the 40th parallel while whaling fleets operate in the far south. The observations from *Mischief* therefore provided a crucial test for the skill of the analysts in an oceanic area with sparse and infrequent data. The pressures as reported by the vessel were compared with those interpolated from the current weather charts for the positions of the ship.

It would seem that the forecasters concerned stood the test fairly well although they had some misgivings when the log-book first arrived in Pretoria. To avoid any bias in favour of the analyst, all observations within 100 miles of permanent weather stations, e.g. Marion Island and the Kerguelen base, were excluded from the comparison. The vast majority of the differences between the 145 observations of actual pressure and the 'Map' pressure are between plus 5 and minus 5 millibars, and in 58 cases within 1 millibar. Only nine differences of 10mbs. or more were found, all clustered round three distinct dates, viz. 17/12/59, 28/12/59, and 5/1/60. Here the forecasters erred considerably for one or two days in the particular area.

Figures a and b show the synoptic situation at 0600 GMT on 5 January, 1960, for the regions between Marion Island and the Kerguelen Archipelago. Fig. a shows the map as actually analysed by the shipping forecaster on duty (the writer of the present note). Fig. b shows the revised map, using the *Mischief* data. What seemed to be a weak depression was actually quite an active, deepening, fully-fledged system. A weak low was located north of Marion Island on the previous day and it was interpreted as a cyclonic disturbance within cold air. Owing to lack of data it was not possible to reach a satisfactory conclusion and it was decided to retain it in the form analysed in Fig. a. On the 6th a mature depression with central pressure below 980mbs. appeared at Kerguelen. The maps were not re-analysed immediately to link the low which had been north of Marion Island on the 4th with the depression at Kerguelen on the 6th. This case clearly illustrates the kind of errors which can be expected in current weather map analysis in regions with isolated observations. *Mischief* proved here to have been a real mischief maker for the forecasters.

Cases of fruit sent by many kind friends began to arrive and by the end of March we were ready for sea; but in response to a request to sail out with the Yacht Club fleet on their 'Opening Cruise', we readily delayed our departure until 2 April. The 'Opening Cruise' is ceremonial. Led by the Commodore, dressed over-all, loaded to sinking-point with passengers, including the Mayor of Cape Town or some high official, every boat in the Yacht Basin sails out into the bay, the length of their cruise there depending mainly upon the state of the weather. On 2 April the conditions were miserable – a fresh and freshening north-west wind accompanied by a cold drizzle. At the last moment Jan found the main engine unwilling to start, so, having seen the last over-loaded straggler leave the basin, we got a tow into Duncan Dock, where we hoisted sail. As we began beating out against the north-west wind, the main fleet, having just poked its nose outside the entrance, began streaming in, racing, as it were, for the Bar. It must have been one of the shortest opening cruises on record, but at least they had the satisfaction of seeing *Mischief* under sail in the conditions she liked.

Waving farewell to the last of the incoming fleet, we stood out to sea in worsening weather. It was rough outside and the crew, fresh from land, felt far from well. Having reefed the mainsail, we settled down to gaining a good offing. As darkness fell, the wind began to fail, leaving us lurching about violently in a high, confused swell. When I came on watch at midnight Jim told me that the topmast forestay had come adrift; but since we were under working rig and there was no strain on the topmast, I did not worry much about it. We seemed to be drifting towards Dassen Island, a small island with a lighthouse on it about 30 miles north of Cape Town. So I got Jan up to see if the engine would start, with no effect except to run the battery flat.

At daylight we began clearing up the mess. The thread of the topmast stay rigging-screw had stripped, and the suddenly released stay, while wrapping itself round the shrouds, had torn both jib and staysail and snarled up the jib-sheet pendants. But that was not all. While working on the foredeck we noticed that the bowsprit was badly sprung, cracked across transversely and along one side close to the gammon iron, the iron ring on the stem through which it passes. Probably the sudden release of tension when the topmast stay went, and the consequent fierce whip of the bowsprit downwards, had cracked it. We could fix the stay but we did not think that with splints and wire lashings we could make a satisfactory job of the bowsprit; and if it broke again in mid-ocean, without it we should be a mighty long time getting anywhere. We decided to return to Cape Town despite the loss of the several days it would entail.

The sea had gone down, the day was fine, but the lack of any wind to waft us swiftly back a short 30 miles made this setback more keenly felt. Having repaired the stay temporarily to hold up the drooping bowsprit we had nothing to do but whistle for a wind, tantalised by the fact that we were drifting slowly northwards away from Cape Town, and by the thought of 30 gal. of petrol lying useless in the tank. Conveniences are never missed where they were never enjoyed, as the sage so rightly says. It is probably best to have on board no machinery at all unless one regards it as one does the wind, fickle and liable to stop. For anyone not thoroughly conversant with its workings the only attitude to adopt is one of scornful superiority; like that of an Indian driver I once had who, whenever anything went wrong with a car, used to remark with pitying contempt: 'It is but machinery, Sahib.'

The calm lasted all day, till at nightfall, when a breath of wind came from the north-west, we hoisted the twins and hoped. After a night of scarcely perceptible progress, we were surprised when we sighted Robben Island only a few miles outside Table Bay. All day we crept forward at a very sober pace, until by evening we were once again inside Duncan Dock in tow of the Club launch. No doubt among all the small crowd assembled on the jetty to watch us come in, conjecture must have been rife. The forestay may have looked a bit slack and the bowsprit not steeved up so much as usual, but it would have needed an experienced eye (there was one such) to detect anything wrong. *Mischief* was not down by the head or listing. She had not sprung a leak or been on fire. Perhaps we had lost a man overboard, or someone had acute appendicitis, or perhaps the skipper had merely dropped his sextant overboard or mislaid a pipe. Conjecture was soon set at rest, and while we were still getting our warps ashore, one among the crowd offered to make us a new bowsprit. This was Mike Cattell, a Club member and a shipwright on holiday, so as soon as we had tied up we set to work getting the broken spar out so that he could make a start next morning.

Next day proved to be quite the vilest we had yet experienced in Cape Town. The worst months for south-easters had passed, north-westers were now in season. The south-easters fill the air with sand, but this north-wester, though perhaps less furious, was accompanied by torrential rain. In his car, Mike Cattell and I made the round of all the shipyards and timber yards in search of a suitable piece of wood from which to make a spar 24ft. long and seven inches in diameter. Finding nothing big enough we drove out into the country to the Forest Department, where we found a stick of creosoted 'insignis' pine – no untreated timber can be sold – of the right length and nine inches at the butt. As the whittling down of it might be a long job, and as we should have to hire a lorry to fetch it, we decided that it would be quicker and cheaper to scarf and glue the old one together. It would need to have a piece let in to bring it up to the original length, and Mike recollected that one of the Club members had a short length of broken mast of the right diameter. Having measured the bit of mast and found it would do, we went in search of the owner. The five foot length of broken mast must have been of immense sentimental value, but we bought it and by evening one scarf was finished and glued together. We rigged a little sailcloth tent over it and left our side-lights burning under it to ensure the glue hardened quickly.

Meantime we had the engine-starting motor rewound, Jan having conceived that this was the source of the trouble. Next day, 6 April, was Van Riebeek's day, a public holiday in commemoration of the landing in 1652 of Jan Van Riebeek, the first Governor to be sent out by the Dutch East India Company. Nevertheless, by evening the two pieces of bowsprit were glued together and Mike thought that by the eighth the glue would have set hard enough for us to put to sea again, after a delay of only six days. On the morning of the eighth we put the bowsprit back, omitting the jib outhaul in our haste, so that the bowsprit shrouds and stay had all to come off again. As the engine still refused to start we called in a mechanic, who went off with the carburettor and petrol pump with the promise that he would be back by 2 pm.

As usual when we were about to leave – this was our third departure from Cape Town – Bob Hinings was at hand with his car ready for any last-minute emergencies. No doubt his chief thought that no business Bob could accomplish would be more profitable to the firm than that of speeding *Mischief*'s departure. When a passage is likely to take at least three months, a few hours' delay in starting is really neither here nor there. Such a philosophic reflection never entered my head. The wind was fair and I was dancing with impatience to be off. At three o'clock, when I could stand it no longer, Bob drove me to the garage, where we found the job on the point of completion. Seizing the carburettor, the pump and odd screws and washers, we drove off, leaving the mechanic to follow in his own car with the bill. I had no intention of sailing without paying, or 'paying with the main-sheet' as the saying goes, but after a due pause we began casting off. When he arrived and saw us beginning to move, the mechanic's face registered rage and astonishment; but he cheered up at receiving the cash proffered to him on the end of a boathook by a man standing on the end of the bowsprit, amidst the applause of the onlookers.

Once more I experienced the relief and joy of being at sea again, free from the fetters of the land, with nothing ahead but an almost endless vista of carefree days, no bills to pay, no engagements to keep, no newspapers or telephones; the ship, a snug, secure little world, day by day bravely pushing her way over the trackless ocean. Sitting at the tiller while we headed out past the breakwater, enjoying these trite but pleasing reflections, I suddenly saw flames issuing from the fore-hatch of our snug, secure little world. Jan, I thought, must be making tea. On reaching the galley I found the double-burner Primus the centre of a small inferno and flames were licking up the wood-work surrounding it. Jan brought the galley fire extinguisher into action while I threw a blanket over the stove for good measure. The effect was slight. A fleeting and horrifying vision of yet another return to Cape Town crossed my mind, or even of *Mischief* abandoned, on fire off the breakwater. But our second fire extinguisher hastily brought into play did the trick. Beyond the melting of the lead sheet on which the stove stood, some burnt paint and my severe fright, no harm was done.

CHAPTER FIFTEEN

Homeward Bound

LESSER men might have been upset by this initial holocaust as a prelude to working in the galley, but Jan soon settled down. Since we had taken on board stores for the full complement of six, and now had one less mouth to feed, no restrictions were needed. At first we missed the steamed puddings for which John had developed such a flair, often producing puddings that were fit for a glass case. Nor was he ever dismayed by seeing a gigantic pudding that should have served for two meals vanish in one. By dogged perseverance Jan eventually mastered the art, but some weeks passed before he mustered courage to make a first attempt, and that he had been wise to refrain so long was amply demonstrated by his first attempt. Homeward-bounders seldom grumble, but according to the doggerel rhyme crews had mutinied for less reason:

We haven't been but two days out, when the duff it don't seem to please;
It hadn't the richness of raisins and sichness, so we ups and we mutinies.

Off Robben Island we streamed the log, by midnight we had Dassen Island abeam, the loom of Cape Town faded, and by next day it was 100 miles away. From this flying start we never looked back and in the first week we logged nearly 1,000 miles. But we had one black day, Sunday, 10 April, which I entered in the log as Black Sunday. We were on the fringe of the South-east Trades, which prevail farther south on the African side of the South Atlantic than they do on the other side. The wind backed slowly during the night from south-west, through south, to east of south, which brought it right aft; so that an hour before breakfast, when it was getting light, the helmsman gybed her. The boom guy prevented the boom crashing over and we escaped without damage. Worse, much worse, soon followed. I was at the tiller after breakfast when suddenly an overpowering but delightful aroma of rum billowed up the companion-way. Our precious rum jar, still nearly three-quarters full, had broken adrift and smashed. The smell of rum that pervaded the ship for the rest of the day was a constant turning of the knife in the wound. Smells, I think, recall past scenes more surely than sights or sounds. The smell of certain kinds of petrol fumes, for instance, always bring to my mind the Western Desert. Now, throughout the day, we were reminded of the sundown hour, the glasses, the lemons, the sugar bowl and the rum jar (still nearly three-quarters full) – until at sundown came the moment of truth. But even now our cup of sorrow was not full. With the wind aft, we changed the rig, and while hoisting the old twin, some bungling resulted in it giving one mighty flog and splitting from head to foot. It looked beyond repair but later we buckled to and sewed a foot-wide strip of old cloth the whole length of the sail.

Although the wind was south-east, the weather did not resemble that of the Trades, where usually the days are bright and sparkling, days of continuous sunshine broken only by the drifting, fleecy clouds. Instead we had overcast skies and long hours of drizzle. We were passed presently by an old acquaintance, the *Rochester Castle*, which came very close and greeted us with blasts of the horn. Crews change, but I think someone on her bridge remembered meeting *Mischief* in 1954, 60 miles off the Portuguese coast, when we had asked the *Rochester Castle* by lamp signal for our position. It was the first of those several occasions when, though not lost, I was a little uncertain of where we were. And not without reason, because we had been hove to and drifting for some time and we had no sextant; nor would one have been any use to me, who could not then use one. The figures for the latitude and longitude which the *Rochester Castle* signalled in reply quite baffled our signaller, who, like Lord Melbourne with decimal points, could not understand all the damned dots. So, seeing that we had not understood, the *Rochester Castle* steamed slowly round three times making hoists of flags which we interpreted from the code book. And having made sure that we had the answer, she went on her way, musing no doubt on the inscrutable ways of Providence.

The charging engine, which had had an expensive overhaul, showed its gratitude by packing up for good after doing one short stint. Jan thought the plug might be at fault and had omitted to get a spare. He doubled the role of cook with that of engineer, but, since neither engine would start, this was not so arduous as it sounds. By adjusting ship's time to suit the setting or rising of the sun we could do without lights in the cabin, and for the binnacle we had the luminous compass card. Except in bright moonlight which entirely nullified the luminous effect, the points could easily be read. Half-points were not easy to read but we seldom bothered with those.

After the burst of the first week the Trades became light. With all available sail – mainsail, boomed out twin and topsail – we could do nothing like 100 miles a day. The weather grew steadily warmer, flying fish more plentiful and albatross more rare. We saw the last of them in about S. lat. 20°. As there is a northerly drift of cold water up the African coast albatross are seen farther north than they are on the South American side. And since they follow ships, a northbound ship is likely to have albatross with it farther north and in warmer regions than would be the case with a ship bound south. They have been known to follow ships to within sight of St Helena in S. lat. 16°; but normally they are seldom seen beyond the tropic of Capricorn. Perhaps they follow ships for fun or just for something to look at. The rich scraps thrown from a liner might well be attractive, but the meagre contents of *Mischief*'s gash bucket would scarcely interest a hyena; yet day after day we saw what looked like the same bird or same group of birds. Often one would fly ahead and settle on the water to watch us pass, and much later he would come gliding up from astern to repeat the performance.

At dawn of Sunday, 24 April, we had St Helena in sight about 30 miles away. Here was yet another island landfall at dawn and on that account supremely satisfying. But we were only 16 days out, and for several reasons we could not hope to view St Helena with the same eagerness and apprehension with which we had first viewed those islands in the Southern Ocean. As the last home of Napoleon, St Helena is better known and has had more written about it than, for example, the Isle of Man; and in waters where the Trade wind blows steadily from one quarter, where gales and thick weather are virtually unknown, little apprehension can be felt in finding or approaching it. Should one have the misfortune to miss it, there is still Ascension 700 miles to leeward at which to have a second shot. To impress the visitors and allay the fears of the port medical officer it was our custom when nearing port to wash down the cabin paint-work. Asked to exert himself in this way, the mate, who had a manly disregard for appearances, remarked that he had 'done it on the two previous occasions.' Since we had then been at sea nine months, anyone hearing him must have been strongly impressed both with our slovenly ways and the infrequency of our calls at civilised ports.

St Helena's only harbour, Jamestown, is on the north or lee side of the island. We made the stupid mistake of going round the west end of the island, so that having rounded it, as we did at midday, we spent the whole of a long afternoon beating up to the harbour. To sail round the eastern end would have been equally easy and we should then have had the wind free for running down to the harbour. It was five o'clock before we came to and dropped anchor in eight fathoms about a hundred yards from the small wharf which, with its three diminutive cranes, and a couple of lighters, comprise the harbour facilities. Although it is on the sheltered side of the island the bay is not deeply enough indented to be safe from the slight swell which is usually running. The swell sometimes provides free entertainment when the monthly mail steamer calls and boatloads of sight-seeing passengers are being ferried to and fro. Quite a large crowd gathers to watch the fun at the landing steps, where those waiting impatiently to be taken off suddenly find the sea swirling round their knees, to the ruin of their smart shore-going clothes.

In the morning, after a couple of water-side urchins had helped us to fill our water tanks, we took the battery ashore for charging and did some shopping. Rather surprisingly there was no fruit to be had except bananas, which, by the way, were an extremely good variety – fat, firm, sweet and as good at the ends as in the middle. I am a little fastidious in the matter of bananas; an amateur of bananas, so to speak, having eaten them in many parts of the world and even lived on them for two months in the course of a long cycle ride in a warm climate. These were the more welcome and delicious after the bananas one has to put up with in Cape Town. The Cape Province is not banana country; it is not warm enough. Indeed, I was only persuaded to try one there after watching the extraordinary relish with which a monkey at the Kirstenbosch Zoo ate one. But he must have been hungry and in any case his experience would naturally be limited. The people who eat bananas in England are happy in knowing no better. Fruit picked green and ripened *en route* is about as nourishing, and as interesting to a connoisseur, as processed cheese.

Whatever the residents may think, to the visitor Jamestown is a haven of peace, a quiet, old-fashioned, relic of the past. Looking out from the main square over the old wall and moat one expects to see a square-rigger lying in the bay; and, indeed, on the postcards one still buys such a ship is shown lying in the bay. The town is jammed between the sides of a deep, narrow valley, from which the only exit for wheeled vehicles is a narrow tarmac road which follows the valley up into the interior. Visitors from the country who have no car, or commuters in a hurry, have the option of approaching or leaving the capital by a stone staircase of a thousand steps.

Needing a hair-cut, I consulted a policeman, who advised me to enquire for Mr Clark, probably to be found at that moment – it was 10 am – in 'The White Horse.' But Mr Clark had had his morning snifter or pipe-opener and adjourned to the market, where, when I had had mine, we met. He took me to his house and outside his backdoor, in the shade of an ill-nourished paw-paw tree, he went to work with scissors. He was obviously of mixed descent – British, Portuguese, Dutch, Indians and Africans have all taken a hand in populating the island – but he may have been connected in an irregular way with that Mr Clark, an American, who presented Captain Slocum with a goat. That Mr Clark was a bit of a wag. His ostensible reason for putting the goat on board was, as he said, 'to butt the sack and hustle the coffee beans out of the pod,' for Slocum had received another present in the form of a sack of coffee in parchment. 'Confound all presents wot eat,' said Jorrocks. This 'dog with horns', as Slocum called him, ate a chart of the West Indies, most of the rope on board, and finally Slocum's straw hat, all before the *Spray* had arrived at Ascension, where the goat was marooned.

In the afternoon we took the usual drive round the island including, of course, 'Longwood', where we viewed with great interest the rooms where its illustrious resident lived. House and grounds are maintained in perfect order by a French Consul whose principal task it is to cherish this little piece of French territory. On the central plateau nearly 2,000ft. up, where 'Longwood' is situated, and where the wealthy merchants and slave-owning planters used to live in the days of the island's prosperity, the air is cool and damp; gorse, brambles, broom, bracken, pines and oak trees flourish, in strange contrast to the peepul trees, date palms and banana plants which grow at Jamestown and along the bottom of the little valley behind it. To my mind an otherwise pleasing landscape is spoilt by the ugly New Zealand flax which covers most of the slopes, a plant with dull green, blade-like leaves like an over-grown iris. Flax is the island's main industry and all the larger estates have mills for extracting the fibre. This and a small lace-making industry, together with fishing and the raising of cattle, sheep and vegetables for local consumption, are the only employments for the islanders. Although trials have been made, such as in growing coffee and tea, nothing has yet been found that will provide both employment and revenue. The wide gap between the island's imports and exports is the main problem which the Administration faces. The coming of steamships and finally the opening of the Suez Canal deprived the island once and for all of a modest but seemingly well-founded prosperity as a port of call.

We were woken next morning by a sonorous blast from the siren of the *Durban Castle* as she steamed slowly to her anchorage. As there were now two ships in the harbour, the Governor had kindly invited their respective masters and mates to lunch at Government House. There being no time to take the charging engine ashore for another overhaul, Jan took it off its bed and had it up on deck with a view to taking it apart. When the nut at the fly-wheel end of the crank shaft refused to budge, Jan, who is a hard-hitting mechanic, set to work with a cold chisel. Although almost cut in two the nut stood firm and it was then found that the crank shaft was not as straight as it might have been, a discovery at which one could not with honesty express surprise. The charging engine, as well as the main engine, could now be written off for the rest of the voyage. We should have to reserve the newly-charged battery solely for the wireless set and the reception of time signals, and hope that it would last the course.

After meeting our two fellow-guests at the landing place, we all drove out to Government House, a big Georgian mansion standing in lovely grounds several miles from Jamestown. Like the abbots in England or their opposite numbers in Tibet, our early colonial Governors knew how to choose a site for gracious living, in a place of natural beauty far from the madding crowd; where they might erect a dignified building, surround it with a high wall, and proceed to plant and garden diligently. If exile it must be, then let exile be tempered by living in the same style and surroundings as they were accustomed to at home.

One of the ornaments and curiosities in the grounds of Government House was a giant land tortoise. It was an old resident even in Napoleon's time and its origin is lost in the mists of time. On the voyage of two years before, we had seen some of these extraordinary creatures on Aldabra, a small coral atoll in the South Indian Ocean, the only place other than the Galapagos Islands where they are still found. Frank Bullen, who wrote *The Cruise of the Cachalot*, took a run ashore at Aldabra, where, he says, a sailor reported having come across a giant tortoise which had inscribed on its shell: 'The Ark, Captain Noah, Ararat for orders.'

Back at the landing steps in the late afternoon we had a boat-load of stores to embark before sailing. There was a good swell running, so that while standing on the steps waiting for the dinghy to rise on a wave before dumping in her sacks of potatoes, bread and what not, we got pretty wet. Procter and I in shore-going rig took off our shoes and rolled up our trousers. We had no wish to provide the spectators with more fun than they were already having from the constant flow of passengers to and from the mail steamer. After tea we hoisted sail and got our anchor. Close inshore as we were, the wind came from all directions, funnelled down the valley and bouncing off the cliff behind the wharf. Getting under way was a little tricky. No sooner did

Mischief start paying off than a puff of wind from another direction would take her aback. At one moment we were heading to pass between a lighter and a motor launch, which would have been all right had they not been connected by a tow-rope. At last the sails filled and soon we were passing by the towering side of the *Durban Castle*. As we were now personal friends of her master, all ceremony was observed. We dipped our ensign while she made a hoist wishing us *'Bon Voyage'* and gave us three farewell blasts. To which we replied with three tremulous squeaks on our foghorn.

Seven days later, in the afternoon, we sighted Ascension Island some 40 miles away, and at ten o'clock that night we passed close to it. We were surprised by the number of lights dotted about; besides the cable station at George Town some units of the American Air Force are now in occupation. Ascension Island is remarkable for its 'rollers', a phenomenon which occurs also at St Helena and for which no good explanation has yet been found. At certain times of the year big rollers break with great violence on the *lee* side of the island, that is, in the opposite direction to the waves caused by the South-east Trade winds which blow throughout the year. They continue for perhaps two or three days at a time and when they occur ships have to anchor well outside and no communication with the shore is possible. In the days when Slocum marooned his goat there, Ascension was primarily a Naval Station, known as the 'Stone Frigate' and rated as tender to the South African Squadron. Like St Helena, it is more or less barren up to about the 2,000ft. level, where it is high enough to pierce the Trade wind clouds and draw moisture from them.

Except for flying fish, the tropic sea of the Atlantic is almost devoid of life – no fish, no birds, no ships. We surprised ourselves by catching a small shark and at the same time losing the rotator of our log, the line being cut by the wire trace on which the shark threshed about. Trailing a log line is by no means an essential aid to navigation but it does give a more accurate account of the day's run than is got by estimation. Each man as he comes off watch enters the number of miles he thinks he has done. If one man is apt to over-estimate, another may under-estimate, so that the day's total may well be a pretty fair average. So that while we would willingly have exchanged the log line for a 'dorado' or a 'bonito,' we disliked losing it in exchange for a useless shark. Having eaten shark before and found it nauseating, I was for throwing this one overboard. But allowing hope to triumph over experience, we cooked it, and found it not at all bad. There must be almost as many varieties of sharks as there are of bananas, and I suspect that a fine field of discovery still lies open in that line for the curious gourmet.

Apart from flying fish, which of course deliver themselves on board without waiting to be caught, this small shark was our only victim in the whole 21,000-mile voyage, in my experience an unexampled lack of success. In all likely waters, and in many unlikely, we vainly trolled a line baited with spoons, patent lures, bits of red or white rag, or flying fish. Even off the Cape peninsula, where the waters are thick with tunny and other fish, we had no luck. On previous voyages we used to catch a 'dorado' or some kind of fish at least every 1,000 miles. Like so many other things the ocean seems not to be what it was, but whether we should attribute this to oil pollution, atomic explosions or a Tory Government, it is difficult to say.

What an eventful voyage we were having. That night, in a totally unfrequented part of the ocean three degrees south of the Equator, I observed on the north-east horizon at short intervals five strange, unaccountable flashes, the sort of sudden glow that is made by the loom of a powerful light below the horizon or the flash of a big gun. On Friday, 13 May, an inauspicious date, when we were four degrees north of the Line, I came on watch at 10 pm and saw in the sky a yet more unaccountable phenomenon. To the north-west, about twenty degrees above the horizon, was a luminous glow, bigger than a full moon but nothing like so bright. It moved slowly upwards and in a westerly direction and faded out at an altitude of about sixty degrees having been in view for several minutes. We could make nothing of this. Neither comet, missile nor satellite seemed a satisfactory explanation.

The Equator had been crossed for the second time on 10 May in longitude 20° west, the weather being prematurely like that of the doldrums with heavy rain squalls and light winds. At that season we should have held the Trade wind as far as lat. 2° north, and sure enough, a day later, the south-east wind came back to give us a run of 90 miles. This dying kick of the Trades was succeeded by more rain and thunderstorms, until in lat. 4° north, when a gentle breeze from north-east freshened during the night, we hoped the doldrums were behind us.

For two more days, however, the wind remained light and was frequently upset by heavy rain squalls which were usually preceded by a flat calm. These could be seen forming on the distant horizon in the shape of towering white cumulus clouds which grew black as they advanced towards us, usually across the wind. One of these, with the help of the helmsman, cost us the Genoa, the best pulling sail we had, worth an extra 20 miles a day when the wind suited. We were just finishing supper in the gathering gloom, a gloom intensified by an approaching squall, and Procter was at the helm with oilskins on, ready for the coming rain. He usually took his duty there a little light-heartedly, seldom being able to endure steering for long without the solace of a book; and now, when the rain began falling in buckets, there being at the moment barely enough wind for steerage way, he came down the companion for shelter. He was hardly down before *Mischief* heeled over smartly. 'Plenty of wind now,' I remarked, making a dive for the companion-way. But we were too late in reaching the tiller. She was moving fast and coming up on to the wind. Amidst a frightful racket the Genoa blew to ribbons.

After crossing the Equator in long. 20° west, the track for sailing ships bound for the Channel curves out to long. 40° west before turning north slightly east for the Azores, which are left on the starboard hand. The turning point where the ship begins to head towards the Azores is in lat. 25° north, which is about the northern limit of the Trades. There is then a zone of weak, variable winds to cross before picking up the brave west winds which waft a ship speedily from the Azores to the Channel. Thus although the north-east Trade wind is used to the full, it is not down-wind sailing. The ship is close-hauled all the time, for every mile lost to the west is a mile farther from home.

We hoped to be able to keep well inside this track, cutting across the curve as it were, and so having less distance to sail; but, in spite of our being able to keep closer to the wind than a square-rigged ship, or thinking we could, we had to go out as far west as longitude 38° before we could shape a course for the Azores. Heeled over sharply, and pitching, it was not the easy Trade wind sailing we were accustomed to. Nevertheless, we knocked off our hundred miles a day.

Bowling along in the heart of the Trades, some 300 miles south-west of the Cape Verde islands, we sighted two ships, the first we had seen since leaving St Helena. About this time a strange domestic phenomenon made its appearance. We used to pump the bilge out by means of a barrel pump which drew the water from the well and delivered it on deck. According to the weather, we pumped dry every two or three days, or in the worse conditions every two or three hours. As bilge water goes, *Mischief*'s was usually pure and wholesome, but one day a bright green flood poured out on deck before our astonished eyes. We searched for the cause, especially in the well, where except for a pipe of mine, a stop-watch, a pencil or two and some odd spanners, we found nothing; no dead rats, sheep dip or corroding lumps of copper such as might be expected to turn water green. For the rest of the voyage we pumped out bright green water from the well and have yet to find out why. One suggestion was that it might be due to the contents of the fire extinguishers so lavishly applied in the galley six weeks before, that were now finding their way into the well.*

By the end of May, in lat. 28° north, we had about run through the Trades. For some days the sea had been thick with Gulf weed and innumerable jellyfish brought south by the Azores current, a southerly branch of the Gulf Stream. Our daily runs fell away rapidly. On 4 June we did only 12 miles, a record low which was broken only by a run of five miles on 20 June. During calms most of us went over the side for a swim, and when the speed was moderate we had fun being towed along in the wake at the end of a rope, regaining the ship by coming up the rope hand over hand. As a result of the slow progress we were making, I became so nervous about our water that we gave up porridge and milk for breakfast. But the panic subsided when the wind drew westerly, when for the first time for a month we went on to the port tack, and we began heading for the Azores. Here we did manage to cut a corner off the sailing ship track, for we passed so far inside Flores, the westernmost island, as not to see it. On 13 June we had Pico in sight, 50 miles to the east.

We felt we were already in home waters, As we had logged 5,600 miles since leaving Cape Town, the last thousand miles seemed a mere flea-bite. After leaving the Azores behind we did famously and it was not until we were off Ushant that our hopes of finishing in style were dashed. We were out of sight of Ushant, well outside the shipping lane, when we fell in with calms, light winds from the east, and a lot of fog. Coming up Channel on our way home from Bermuda we had had fog all the way, but on that occasion we were over on the English side and close enough in to be out of the way of

---

* It was due to the marking dye fitted to an inflatable dinghy carried in the pack.

steamers. Now, being out in mid-Channel we had to make the best of it, for the shipping lanes are so many that there is no avoiding them except by keeping close inshore. It took us five days to work our way up from Ushant, taking sights on the rare occasions when the sun appeared, for we had not yet seen any land. At last on the night of 28 June we picked up the loom of Portland light and on the following night we sighted the Needles light some 13 miles away. We missed the tide that night, but next day, with the flood under us and the lightest of westerly breezes behind, we sailed up Lymington river, 65 days out from St Helena.

When *Mischief* had been stripped of her sails, stores and gear, the crew were free to go their several ways, no doubt glad to have seen the last of each other. Eleven months is a long time for six men to be cooped up in a small cabin with frequent, unavoidable spells of leisure and boredom to be endured. As well as being thankful, I am always amazed that *Mischief*'s several crews, picked up at random, strangers to me and to each other, thrown abruptly together with an invitation to like it or lump it, yet contrive to live and work together on tolerably good terms. One firm bond is no doubt the sea and ships, and especially the ship in which they serve. As Conrad says: 'The ship we serve is the moral symbol of our life,' and there could be no better symbol of service than old *Mischief*; symbol of work faithfully performed, first as a working boat, then as a pleasure yacht, and finally, in a very minor way, as an expedition ship.

Only once has one of the crew left me on the outward passage, before completing what he had undertaken to do. Anyone, with or without a sense of loyalty and responsibility, will see an ocean passage through to the end, even if only for the reason that there is no getting off. But to make a series of long ocean passages, such as *Mischief*'s recent voyages have entailed, some other bond is needed to hold men together. Such a bond may be found in the goal the party has in mind, and I like to think that the more distant and seemingly unattainable the goal, the stronger is the bond.

MISCHIEF IN GREENLAND

Mischief in Greenland

First published by Hollis & Carter Ltd., 1964

Contents

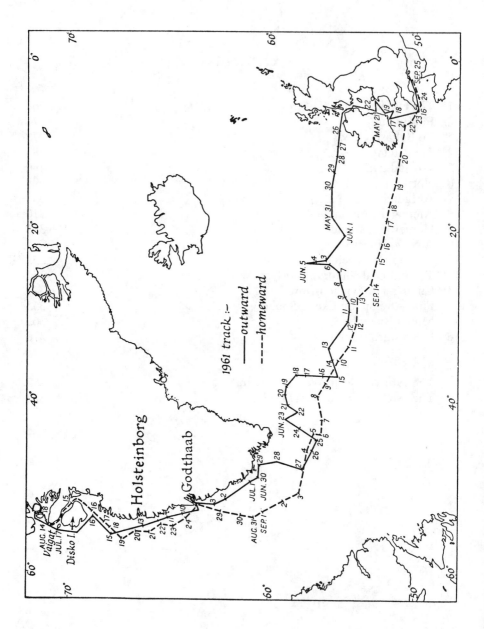

CHAPTER ONE

The Objective and the Crew

THIS THIRD book about my old pilot-cutter *Mischief* is a description of two successive voyages to Greenland and Baffin Island in search of mountains. All that is needed by way of introduction is to state the reasons for choosing those particular objectives. To give reasons for wishing to sail or climb, though often attempted, is difficult and in my opinion is best left alone. If pressed to give reasons for doing such things, perhaps the best answer is found in Stevenson's words: 'In the joy of the actors lies the sense of any action. That is the explanation, that the excuse.'

In the long night watches at sea, or when lying tediously becalmed, even a man whose mind is generally a blank is more or less obliged to think of something. In such circumstances, when homeward bound from Cape Town, with the Crozet Isles and Kerguelen behind us and over 6,000 miles of ocean ahead, it occurred to me that there might be cruising grounds equally exciting but far less distant than the southern ocean. In northern waters, for example. So far *Mischief*'s three voyages, each of about a year's duration and each covering some 20,000 miles, had all been to the Southern Hemisphere. A cruise in that direction has several points in its favour. One enjoys, for instance, three summers in a row, leaving England in August, arriving in the south at the beginning of the southern spring, and reaching home in time for the fag-end of yet another northern summer. Then the course followed by a sailing ship bound south by way of the Atlantic ensures having for the most part favourable winds, reducing to a minimum the unprofitable and uncomfortable business of beating against head winds. Furthermore, until the vessel reaches the latitudes of the Forties, the crew can count on soaking themselves in sunshine. Starved of sun as we are in England this is no small thing and no doubt accounts for the fact that almost every yachtsman contemplating a long cruise confines his choice to the Mediterranean, the West Indies, or the South Sea Islands, places of sun and warmth, blue seas and skies, palm trees and hula-hula girls. And since these voyages are supposed to be pleasure cruises, the fact that one can drink wine almost throughout the voyage is not to be overlooked. One may stock up in the first place at the Canaries or the Azores, and replenish in Brazil or Chile if bound west, or at Cape Town if bound eastwards. True, the wine will be cheap and will not much benefit by keeping or by being well shaken up every day. But, as they say in Spain, cursed bad wine is better than holy water.

Still, even when accompanied by fair winds, sunshine, wine, flying fish, and all the other blessings of tropical seas, 20,000 miles is a long way to go for the sake of a month or so spent climbing some obscure mountains, the more so, if, as had happened on that last voyage, mountains reputed to be 5,000ft. high proved to be only 3,000ft. high. To misquote Prince Hal, this had seemed to me an intolerable deal of sea to one half-pennyworth of mountains. But, it may be asked, what have mountains to do with long sea voyages? Well, in my opinion, a voyage is the better for having some other objective beyond that of crossing an ocean or making a landfall on another continent, and what better objective could a man have than a mountain? This is not to underrate the satisfaction they yield or to belittle the difficulties or even dangers of voyages in small boats. In these respects a cruise in home waters may chance to provide challenge enough. But when crossing oceans or sailing in remote, lonely seas, or on unlit coasts, a man accepts the fact that no help will be at hand. The hazards of being overwhelmed by a storm or of stranding must be faced by himself and his crew alone. If overwhelmed by a storm that is the end of the matter. The consequences of running aground might be worse in some respects, for in such case one would have leisure to reflect upon the loss of one's ship and the carelessness or negligence which had brought about the loss. The amateur sailor, or haphazard navigator, should ponder a remark of the editor of the new edition of Lecky's *Wrinkles*, 'There is nothing more distressing than running ashore, unless it be a doubt as to which continent that shore belongs.'

Provided, however, that the voyage is planned with due regard to seasons, carried through with seamanlike prudence, and attended by a reasonable amount of luck, the risks are small and the voyage comes to be regarded as merely a step towards the final objective. The latter, I feel sure, is an added incentive to the crew, takes their minds off the voyage, and finally gives them a sense of achievement. Moreover, it helps the amateur sailor to adopt a more professional attitude towards the sea and his ship, regarding them as means to an end rather than ends in themselves. There are, indeed, many amateurs who have such an affection for ships and the sea that for them it is enough to be afloat, even if they never go out of sight of land. Whether they are amateur or professional, I suppose all sailors begin their sea careers because of a love for the sea and ships, and the romance of a sea-life. No doubt the professional's first love may soon dwindle into respect, as a sweetheart may dwindle into a wife, while the amateur is rarely at sea often enough or long enough for his ardour to cool.

But to hark back to mountains. The sole object of the three long voyages I had made in *Mischief* had been to combine sailing with climbing, the obvious solution for a man who liked both and was reluctant to give up either. To wish to follow two such enjoyable pursuits at the same time may lay one open to the charge of being too greedy of pleasure, almost gluttonous. Sydney Smith's notion of bliss, his acme of pleasure, was the eating of *pâté de foie gras* to the sound of trumpets. Sailing and climbing are not, of course, comparable with that, but pleasures they must be called, if of a robust kind. To combine the two pursuits might appear to be impossible, just as it is proverbially difficult to blow and swallow at the same time. True, the great mountain ranges, the Alps, the Himalayas, the Andes, are remote enough from the sea, but there are lesser mountains that are almost washed by the sea or closely linked to it and readily accessible by the glaciers they send down into the sea. For example, some of the New Zealand Alps, the Patagonian Andes, mountains in Tierra del Fuego, and several mountainous islands in the Antarctic or sub-Antarctic such as South Georgia, the South Shetlands, Heard Island, or the Crozet and Kerguelen that we had already visited. Some of these places can be reached only by sea. They are all in the Southern Hemisphere, possessed of rude, cold climates, and are remote and not easily accessible.

Though remoteness and inaccessibility are to my mind desirable features they are scarcely compatible with short voyages. One can't have everything. Voyages in the Northern Hemisphere are obviously going to be shorter, for the mountains that can be reached by sea in a small boat lie in Spitsbergen, on both coasts of Greenland, and on the Canadian side of Davis Strait. One might add the coast range of Alaska were it not almost as distant by sea as the Southern Hemisphere; for owing to adverse winds and currents a vessel might have to sail far out into the Pacific before turning north. The hurricane season, too, would have to be considered; in avoiding it one might be bogged down in the Lotus Land of the West Indies and lose one's crew.

Nowadays Greenland can easily be reached by air, but only a man in the devil of a hurry would wish to fly to his mountains, forgoing the lingering pleasure and mounting excitement of a slow, arduous approach under his own exertions. In fact the approach to these sort of places by sea in a small boat will take up most of the time available, will probably be more exacting than the mountaineering itself, and may be the more rewarding part of the enterprise. But a voyage to northern waters, unlike one southwards, has little to offer in the way of pleasure to a yachtsman beyond a bracing climate and spectacular scenery – icebergs, ice floes, ice mountains. There is no care-free Trade Wind sailing to be enjoyed. On the outward voyage at any rate head winds are likely to be the rule rather than the exception. Sunshine, too, may well be less than that of an average English summer, for the North Atlantic on the whole is a region of cloud. Instead of the crew delighting in the freedom of shorts and a shirt, or complete nudity, they may be pent up in winter woollies. As for basking on deck, only the helmsman will spend any time there and he will be wrapped up in sweaters and oilskins.

But a man need not be an ascetic, devoted to hair shirts, to relish a voyage under the moderately adverse conditions that prevail in the North Atlantic, or even in the Arctic, in *summer*. We amateur sailors are of necessity summer sailors, taking our punishment in mild doses, seldom or never likely to experience what professional seafarers, particularly trawlermen, have to contend against when the sea is in its savage winter moods. Men who go to sea or climb mountains for fun derive some of their satisfaction – a lot of it retrospective – in facing and overcoming rough weather and rough terrain, cold, fatigue, and occasionally fright. When undergoing these self-inflicted minor hardships, feeling cold and frightened, eating biscuit and pemmican, they may comfort themselves with the thought that while many non-participants will write them down as asses, there are others to whom their modest sufferings will afford a little vicarious pleasure. A favourite moral reflection of Mr Pecksniff was that if everyone were warm and well fed we should lose the satisfaction of admiring the fortitude with which others bear cold and hunger.

Of the several possible cruising grounds in the north I felt inclined first towards Spitsbergen or its near neighbour Northeastland. I was soon put off by a letter from Roger Tufft, one of the crew who had sailed with me to the Crozet, and who within ten days of our return had joined a party in Spitsbergen. He told me that there were no less than eleven other expeditions in the field. Owing to its being so far north (N. lat. 80°) and at the same time easily accessible from Norway, over the past thirty years Spitsbergen has been overrun with expeditions, mainly from the universities. Northeastland and Edge Island, lying close to Spitsbergen, are less easily approachable on account of ice, but from a mountaineering point of view they are of no interest. Although there may be little left for a climber to do in Spitsbergen, an ambitious sailor might undertake to sail round it. This difficult feat was accomplished by Commander Worsley, one of those who made the famous boat journey with Shackleton from Elephant Island to South Georgia. In 1925, in the auxiliary bark *Island* of about 100 tons, strengthened against ice, with an amateur crew of twelve, he succeeded in sailing anti-clockwise round Spitsbergen in spite of damage to both rudder and propeller from the pack-ice.

Instead of Spitsbergen I began thinking of Greenland. I may be wrong, but I suspect that an average man's knowledge of it begins and ends with the well-known hymn, 'From Greenland's icy mountains'. Supposing him to be a man who has forgotten, like Falstaff, what the inside of a church looks like or who in youth was not addicted to 'hollaing and singing of anthems', he may not know that much. A brief outline of it may therefore be welcome. If we except the continent of Australia, Greenland is the largest island in the world. Geologists, by the way, darkening counsel as they sometimes do, now say it may be two islands. They think that at one point beneath the ice-cap there is a trough which is below sea-level. Assuming, however, that it is one island it is so large that if plunked down over Europe it would extend from the north of Scotland to the Sahara and from the Bay of Biscay to the Po valley. The whole is covered with an ice-cap thousands of feet thick except along the coasts where there is a strip of ice-free country varying in width from one mile to one hundred miles. The ice-cap covers more than nine-tenths of the land and at one point rises to a height of 10,000ft. In 1950 the population of Greenlanders was about 22,000, confined to small towns and settlements along the coastal strip, mainly on the west coast. They are of mixed European and Eskimo descent. The country belongs to Denmark, and there are neither roads nor railways.

For mountaineers the east coast of Greenland, where the mountains are higher and less known, is the more attractive. In recent years an increasing number of climbing expeditions have gone there. But in a small boat, un-strengthened for working among ice, this coast is virtually unapproachable. According to the American Pilot Chart:

'East Greenland has much more pack-ice than West Greenland, and no ship should attempt to navigate in its waters unless it is specially designed. The East Greenland ice is usually broken and rafted into heavy floes of various sizes often with a thickness of 20 to 30ft. It is too great to cut with the prow of a ship. The ice belt is traversed by seeking out the leads of open water, thus the course is tortuous, the ship twisting and turning, worming its way between the floes and fields. A high premium is placed on short turning circles and the manoeuvrability of vessels such as the Norwegian seal-hunter type. Experienced navigators on meeting the ice edge off north-east Greenland are said to insist on clear weather and a steady barometer before attempting passage to the coast.'

On the other hand, West Greenland, according to the same authority, is not regarded as requiring a vessel built especially strong to withstand ice, except possibly so far north as Melville Bay and the approaches to Thule. In West Greenland there are three principal mountain regions. In the south in the vicinity of Cape Farewell (N. lat. 60°); half-way up the coast round about N. lat. 66°; and in the Umanak fjord region in N. lat. 71°. Although it is 800 miles north of Cape Farewell and inside the Arctic Circle I was strongly advised to go to the Umanak region by a friend, Dr H. I. Drever of St Andrew's University. He had himself been there twice and had been completely captivated by it. In his opinion half-measures were a waste of time. I must go the whole hog and sail really far north where the scenery was grander, the icebergs bigger and better, and where the sparse inhabitants still followed to some extent the Eskimo way of life.

Dr Drever, I may as well admit, is a geologist. Many geologists are mountaineers, either of necessity because their studies have obliged them to visit mountainous regions, or because as budding mountaineers they have chosen a profession that seemed likely to furnish excuses for visiting mountains. In one or two earlier books about climbing I may have made some disparaging remarks about geologists and no doubt these were heartily reciprocated. Before the war, and indeed today, parties of climbers intent on visiting far distant ranges such as the Himalayas liked to clothe their more or less frivolous aims with a thin mantle of science. The small party of friends then became an expedition, acquired some standing, and with luck might acquire some cash assistance – a slight token of approval sometimes accorded by various learned societies to those who appear eager to enter what Goethe called the 'charnel-house of science'. For such a party the obvious scientific cloak to assume was the study of geology because it was generally easy to include in the party a man well qualified to geologize as well as climb.

On rare occasions, as might have been foreseen, this dual role led to a conflict of interests or involved the leader in a difficulty such as the following. It happened on the way back from Everest through Tibet where in those days (the 'twenties and 'thirties) one of the conditions of travel, clearly stated in the official pass, was that no stones should be turned over or bits chipped off living rock lest thereby some evil spirit might be released. It was futile to think of our geologist, a single-minded chap like N.E.O.*, complying with that sort of rule, so I had to shut my eyes and ultimately to pay out of expedition funds for a yak or a mule to carry homewards the fruits of two or three

* Prof. Noel E. Odell

months' diligent chipping. One night the box of specimens (which N.E.O. used as an anchor for the guy of his tent) disappeared, the thieves no doubt judging from its weight that it could hardly contain anything but rupees. That put me in a fix. If I complained to the local headman that a box of rock specimens had been stolen we should be confessedly guilty of having broken the rules; while if I said that rupees had been stolen the search might be pressed with such vigour that the box would be found and no doubt opened, proving us to be liars as well as breakers of rules. So I did nothing, thereby convincing N.E.O. that I was both conniving at theft and an enemy to science.

Dr Drever (whose name has provoked these geological reminiscences) put me in touch with a Commander Stamphøj of the Danish navy who gave me charts as well as welcome advice. The next thing was to find a crew. I needed five men and simple though this may sound the finding of a crew is the stumbling block upon which such ventures are likely to come to grief. And even though the crew problem is finally solved the solution often remains doubtful to within a few days before sailing. The long time involved is one great hindrance and for that reason it is easier to find a crew for a voyage of only five months than for one of twelve. There are probably hundreds of men knocking about who would welcome such a chance and who might be suitable; the difficulty lies in making the project known to them. There are also hundreds of sailing clubs and associations a few of whose members might be interested, but an individual like myself can make his wants known only to two or three. So far I have not had any volunteers from the yachting fraternity as represented by clubs. This in no way indicates a lack of enterprise. Such men have their own boats or crew regularly in friends' boats; most are probably interested in racing rather than cruising; long voyages do not appeal to all yachtsmen, and, as I have said, a voyage is more likely to appeal if it is in search of sun and warmth, of exotic faces and places, instead of to cold, barren, uninhabited regions. So in the end one may have to advertise, and those who reply, though they will certainly be keen on the sea and sailing, may know little about it. They may be too young to have settled down; or men who have settled down and found it a mistake; or possibly those who will never settle down – the cankers, as it were, of a calm world and a long peace.

A crew of six all told may seem large for a boat like *Mischief*. As a working boat, a pilot-cutter, the pilot who owned her would have had with him two men, or a man and an apprentice, and after the pilot had boarded the ship that needed his services the two of them would have sailed her home. This was in the years before the First World War when there were still numbers of real sailors about. In 1956 when returning from South America four of us sailed her home from Colon via Bermuda without feeling overworked; and with only four aboard there is plenty of room and more comfort below. The point of having six is that when the climbing party of two goes ashore enough are left on board to handle the boat. She might, for example, have to clear out of an anchorage in a hurry on account of wind or drifting icebergs. With six the work is easy, but ease has to be paid for by having less elbow-room below, stricter rationing of water, and the cost of extra food.

When preparing for this voyage in the autumn of 1960 I had a stroke of luck in hearing from two eager volunteers almost before I had decided where to go. Most people would think that the BBC programme 'Down Your Way', which at that time was going strong, would be heard by only local listeners. They would be wrong. Barmouth, where I live, had a visit from Mr Franklin Engelmann, the maker of that programme. Although merely an English settler and no representative of the Principality, I had to utter a few vocables. I said something about the Crozet Islands voyage and the trouble I had had in finding a crew and as a result had letters from two men, one living in Birmingham and the other in Norwich, offering their services. If this method of making one's wants known were normally available the crew problem would soon be solved.

One of these letters came from David Hodge, a tanker officer on shore temporarily on sick leave. It is not often that among a yacht's crew there is a man with a First Mate's Ticket. David Hodge was about to sit for his and passed the examination before we sailed. He knew nothing of sailing boats but with his sea training he was soon at home on board *Mischief*. I appreciated having with me an adept at navigation, someone who would check my results, keep me up to the mark, and repress any leanings towards carelessness. At the end of the voyage David confessed that on the whole he preferred a 20,000-ton tanker, but I have no doubt that he enjoyed the voyage as much as we enjoyed his company.

David was a Norfolk man and so was the second volunteer letter-writer. Terence Ward was an electrician by trade, keen on sailing, unmarried, and therefore ready to take time off for the sake of making a long voyage. His Broads sailing included experience in the last of the Norfolk wherries so that he was accustomed to handling heavy gear and heavy boats. He knew something about photography and undertook the making of a film with a ciné-camera I had on loan from the Royal Geographical Society. As the Bulgarian proverb says: 'A man can go nowhere without money, not even to church.' It had occurred to me that part of the outlay on this voyage might be recovered if we made a successful film. Like many other apparently bright ideas this one proved to be laughably false. There are films and films, and between those made by the amateur and the professional there is a gulf. An amateur film may be judged by friends, or by fellow climbers and yachtsmen, who see it for nothing, to be highly pleasing, and the same film seen by professionals, who are expected to buy it, will be damned as worthless. It will be either technically a mess or lacking in general interest. On the whole I think that to make a successful film of an expedition one must regard the making of it as the main end and not as a by-product.

The third victim I hooked was Major E. H. Marriott, who had sailed in *Mischief* to Patagonia in 1955-6. Knowing him better than the others I can give him fuller notice. Despite a liking for leaving the ship at intervals to become a tourist, Charles Marriott, as he is generally known, had done well on that venture, especially on our crossing of the Patagonia ice-cap. On the crossing his feet had suffered so much damage that he had had to leave us at Valparaiso to come home by steamer. He is one of the 'make-do-and-mend' or 'do-it-yourself' school, both from preference and because, like John Gilpin, he has a frugal mind. On this occasion he had made out of old sailcloth his own wind-proof jacket. He had not made his own boots, though from the state they were in I thought he might well have done and therein, I suspect, lay partly the cause of his foot troubles.

When he joined us on that voyage he had had more sailing experience than I had. He even went to the length of wearing a yachting cap. In a yacht bound for New Zealand he had got as far as the Canaries where he had been marooned and had had to live on bananas until he could raise the wind for a passage home. In another yacht bound for Vancouver he had got as far as Vigo before the owner decided not to proceed and sailed home. On yet another occasion, when in some Spanish port in a yacht, he had sustained a concussion of the head (not in the bull-ring) and had spent several weeks there in hospital. As a result of this he can focus only one eye at a time, a severe handicap (as will later appear) when on a mountain.

He was a regular soldier who before the last war made the grave mistake of taking the two-year course at the Military College of Science, with the effect that when war broke out he was a marked man and was given the unsoldierly job of inspecting fuses and generally seeing that munitions contractors fulfilled their contracts. However, there is crust and crumb in every loaf. At the Military College of Nonsense, as Charles called it, they had taught him the theory of navigation and the Astronomer Royal himself would be astonished at some of the things Charles could tell him about the solar, stellar, and planetary systems. As a result of this theoretical teaching he became so addicted to logarithms and haversines that a computing machine would have had difficulty in digesting the data Charles assembled when working a sight. But on that occasion he had come in the capacity of climber rather than navigator and I was glad to have him for he is an experienced mountaineer – so experienced that his movements on a mountain are now, like my own, deliberate. For the present voyage, I had hinted he might have to cook as well as climb. He could not join us before we sailed from Lymington, so, making what turned out to be an unlucky choice of rendezvous, I agreed to pick him up at Belfast.

A fourth volunteer was Dr J. B. Joyce, who in the event, at the last moment, decided reluctantly that he was not fit enough to make the voyage. He came with us only to Belfast. He was a climber, too, but was to have doubled the role of cook and doctor – a suitable arrangement because in the old sailing ships the cook was known as the 'doctor'. I hoped that though none of the crew would offer any scope for Joyce's particular line in medicine – he was an obstetrician – his general medical knowledge would cover the more likely emergencies. In none of my crews had we had a doctor and I suppose we had been lucky in never needing one. On this occasion, when we just missed having one, we did at one time feel the need.

When, some three days before sailing, we finally decided that Joyce could not come, it looked as if we must sail short-handed. But in that time I had the luck to find a substitute in young Michael Taylor-Jones who, after a brief telephone conversation, boldly took a chance and came down from

Cumberland to join us. He had just left Oundle and was due to go up to Cambridge to study physics in October. We soon learnt that Charles, too, had been at Oundle. So from the start, although separated by a generation or two, he and Michael were on the old-boy network. Charles displayed such a recent knowledge of the school, acquired apparently from frequent visits, that I suspected he regretted having ever left.

Lastly there was John Wayman whom I got in touch with through a friend. He was a Rugby stalwart and looked the part, a useful man, I thought, to have around in time of need. He captained, we learnt, one of the lowlier teams fielded by the Wasps. In my eyes he seemed young enough but since he had dropped to that Club's eighth or ninth team he was evidently old for Rugby. He was a cotton salesman and a keen yachtsman in his spare time, sailing every summer holiday in chartered yachts with a crew of fellow Rugby hearties. In the nature of things chartered yachts are not likely to be as well found or as well looked after as privately owned boats. In due time we heard something of these holiday adventures across the Channel, adventures that made my hair stand on end. *Mischief*'s voyages may be long but for the most part they are sedately safe.

CHAPTER TWO

Fitting-out

BY WAY of introducing a dull chapter I might take the liberty of transposing the lines of an old couplet:

> To furnish a wife will cost you much trouble,
> But to fit-out a ship the expenses are double.

On the way home from Cape Town on the previous voyage the charging engine had behaved badly and had finally succumbed to the treatment it received at the hands of our hard-hitting mechanic. The battery therefore could not be charged and in order to preserve what life there was left in it we gave up using it to start the main engine. As a result of this long spell of idleness and neglect the main engine, when we reached home, had been condemned as beyond repair. Its interior looked like something dredged up from one of the wrecks of the Armada. So that one big job that had to be done before this Greenland voyage was to install a new Perkins 4/99 diesel engine. The removal alone of the old engine was something of a feat. To the casual eye it appeared that it must either have been installed piece by piece or the boat must have been built round it. Then months elapsed before the new engine was delivered and the installing of it took a lot of time and money. Diesel engines are reputedly more reliable than petrol engines and in a small boat they have the immense advantage of lessening the fire risk. The presence on board of anything up to seventy gallons of petrol had always been to me a source of anxiety, an anxiety that none of the amateur engineers who had sailed with me on earlier voyages had done anything to diminish. They had all been cigarette addicts and generally liked to work over the engine with a cigarette dangling from their lips, their hands being too oily to remove it. Watching them at work, turning over in one's mind the stories of disastrous fires at sea, one felt that at any moment one might become an actor in another such story.

During the winter I visited Lymington several times to work on board and to take back more homework. The cabin and galley needed painting, a job that cannot well be left for the crew to do when they are living on board a week or so before sailing. The daily use of paraffin stoves for months on end has a remarkable effect on white paintwork. The whole of the galley assumes a rich umber tone like the inside of a Tibetan house, while the deckhead immediately above the stoves becomes black as soot. The cabin paint is less affected but it too assumes a faint yellow tinge. Since washing is not very effective the only thing to do – short of stripping the paint and starting afresh – is to cover the dingy surface with more white paint.

Homework implied taking home for cleaning, overhaul, and possibly renewal, most of the wire standing rigging, the guard-rails, and all the blocks and purchases of the running rigging. This is time well spent because when it starts to blow at sea a boat-owner can have no peace of mind unless he is satisfied that so far as he can tell the rigging will stand. At the cost of making *Mischief* look a little 'bald-headed' I saved myself having to work on the topmast rigging by deciding not to send up the topmast on this voyage.

Some critics have remarked that in their opinion *Mischief*'s mast, in the words of Mr Chucks the bos'un, is 'precarious and not at all permanent'; and although it is staunchly stayed with shrouds of two and a half inch wire there have been times when I agreed with them. The extra strain of a heavy topmast aloft – 20ft. of it above the cap – as well as the windage of it and its five supporting wire stays, is hardly offset by the small advantage of being able to set a topsail. The more so on a North Atlantic voyage where we might expect some rough weather and where a topsail could not often be set. The big reaching jib which normally hanks on to the topmast forestay can equally be hanked to a stay running from the top of the mainmast. On voyages southwards we carried the topmast as far as a South American port or Cape Town before housing it and later sent it up again for the homeward passage. Real sailors, I suppose, would think nothing of reefing or sending up the topmast when at sea, a feat we have not yet dared to attempt. To lower or raise the spar is easy enough but before it can be passed through the cap of the mast the five wire stays have to be shackled or unshackled. After a long spell at sea shackles become hard to undo, however well greased they may have been, much too hard for a man working aloft in a seaway who will need one of his hands, if not both, with which to hang on.

'Damn description', said Byron, 'it is always disgusting.' However that may be many novelists devote more space to description than to action and the writers of crime stories usually invite us to study in detail the lay-out of the house or the library where the murder took place. On these grounds, though no one on board was murdered, I think a description of *Mischief*'s lay-out is permissible. Starting from forward below deck there is the forepeak with the chain-locker holding 45 fathoms of five eighths inch chain on the port side and a rack for sails on the other. Stowed there also are a 60 lb. CQR anchor, a small kedge anchor, grapnel, navigation lamps, and lead-lines.

Aft of the forepeak bulkhead is the galley. It is unfortunate that the place upon which the well-being of the crew so largely depends is in the fore part of the boat where the motion is most felt and where the amount of ventilation that can be obtained depends upon the prevailing weather. The fore-hatch is the only source of ventilation and if the boat is on the wind this has to be kept closed. Air in moderation is all to the good but the man working in the galley naturally prefers it unmixed with salt water. Three gimballed Primus stoves and the sink are on the port side with a number of lockers underneath, and on the other side are more lockers and a large open bin in which the spare mainsail is generally stowed. Over this bin is a canvas pipe-cot. No one ever sleeps there and it is used for stowing sails which are passed down from the foredeck through the hatch. The movable ladder leading up to the hatch comes in handy as a chock for the cook's back when he is attending to the stoves. On the bulkhead between the galley and the cabin is a hand wash-basin with a mirror above so that in the rare event of anyone wanting to shave or wash while at sea the facilities are there. Water for the galley is drawn from the main tank under the cabin table by means of a pump and there is also a pump for pumping dirty water out of the sink and the wash-basin. Thus, except that there is no way for the cook to draw the sea-water he requires but by a bucket over the side, the galley arrangements are almost on a par with the most modern kitchen. Sea-water is used whenever possible for cooking and always for washing-up. A pump for drawing it would mean yet another hole in the ship's side and such holes should be kept to a minimum.

There used to be a door in the bulkhead between galley and cabin but this has long since been abolished as an unnecessary nuisance. It might have served a purpose in shutting out smells but personally I think a good sniff of what is brewing in the galley is no bad thing, even if it is only a warning of things to come. And with no barrier between them the crew can partake of the feelings of the cook, hear him cursing vehemently if he and his pots are being thrown about or singing cheerfully if things are going well. In the fore part of the cabin there are three bunks. Of the two on the port side, one above the other, the upper has the advantage of a deck-light which allows enough light for reading. Against that it is farther to fall if one is thrown out. The proprietors of the port-side bunks have around them ample stowage space for their gear, while the man in the starboard bunk has a part share in a narrow though elegant chest of drawers standing against the bulkhead. All three occupants of these bunks are really in clover because this is the warm part of the cabin. Just abaft the foot of the mast is a small stove which burns diesel oil. It is convenient not to have to carry coal, coke or such like fuel for heating and even in a sea-way the stove burns reasonably well. It is safe enough if care is used, though on one occasion when I was on board alone at

Lymington the stove touched off a holocaust in the cabin. It was my fault for not noticing the thing was leaking and that the drip-tray beneath was half full of oil. A fire extinguisher from the galley when brought into play merely fed the flames and filled the cabin with noxious fumes. I got out in time, grabbing another extinguisher from the engine-room as I fled, and this one when brought into action through the cabin skylight saved the day. Still, he who would have eggs must bear with cackling; a man can't expect to enjoy warmth without experiencing the occasional rubs that its generation may entail.

As I have said, the occupants of the three forward berths are pretty snug when the stove is lit, whereas those in the three berths in the after part of the cabin, of which mine is one, derive far less benefit from it. I see no way of remedying this. Here also there are two bunks on the port side and one, the skipper's, to starboard. This is the beamiest part of the boat. The centre space is occupied by the main water tank holding 100 gal. and between the tank and the bunks on each side there is room for a wide settee. No cushions are provided for these but some sybarites bring their own. The table fitted with fiddles sits on top of the water tank. Thus, when the crew are gathered round the table three aside, their knees and feet are more or less in contact with the water tank which in cold weather is the equivalent of a block of ice. Possibly the sort of jacket one fits round hot-water tanks to keep the heat in would in this case be equally effective in preventing the cold from getting out. The table is immediately under the raised skylight which admits to the cabin plenty of light and sometimes plenty of water. There is headroom immediately under the skylight, elsewhere in the cabin the head must be carried bent. On the bulkhead at the after end of the cabin are lockers and shelves, one of the latter holding the small wireless receiving set and the other a barograph where it can be seen by the skipper reclining in his bunk. Beneath bunks and settees there is more stowage space for stores. There is no space for stores under the cabin sole where the inside ballast, four tons or more of iron pigs, lies tightly wedged. Even so we can carry enough stores for three or four months. About the middle of the cabin there is on each side a locker containing a 30 gal. water tank; these are filled from on deck. The total water capacity of 200 gal. is made up by a 40 gal. tank on deck above the after part of the cabin; a pipe from it leads from the deck into the cabin.

A sliding door at the after end of the cabin opens to a narrow passage which gives access to the companion-way up to the cockpit and the deck. The main engine and charging engine are on the port side of the passage and on the other is the 'heads'. Here, besides the lavatory, there is the 70 gal. fuel tank, hanging space for oilskins, a rack for boots, and a big locker where the Aldis lamp, hand-bearing compass, safety belts, and several other things live. The engine is boxed in and since it is seldom in use at sea the top of the box serves as a chart table. As well as the engines there is room on the port side for yet another 30 gal. tank and shelves for tools, bos'n's stores, blocks, shackles, cordage and small stuff. This tank was used originally for water but we now use it for paraffin. I still cherish the hope that on some future voyage, perhaps to the Islands of the Blest, it will be filled with wine. Lurking under the companion-way ladder are the two twelve-volt batteries, one for the wireless and an electric lighting system which is not much used, and the other for starting the main engine. This cannot be started by hand; if the battery is flat the engine has, so to speak, had it. Aft of the batteries is a dark cavern, the space beneath the cockpit floor and the counter, which is used for stowing warps, spare rope, and odd bits of wood.

The well of the bilge lies at the forward end of the engine-room passage-way where it is conveniently sited for catching pencils, dividers, india-rubbers, pipes, and even stop-watches, when they fall off the chart table. Having dropped two stop-watches into this well, thereby stopping them for good, I have long since given up using them. For counting the minutes or seconds that elapse between the taking of a sight and going below to read Greenwich time on the chronometer watch one can either count in one's head or use a wrist-watch. No less than three pumps can suck at this well. The main stand-by is an old-fashioned barrel-pump on deck by the cockpit which does the job handsomely with a minimum of effort. There is a rotary pump inside the 'heads' which is hard to turn, often out of order, and has a nasty trick of siphoning back. More than once, having emptied the bilge with this pump, we have been startled to find it full to overflowing a few minutes later. The third is a pump worked off the charging engine, fitted by me in a misguided moment. It can deliver only a piddle at best, and the futility of fitting such a pump is evident when one considers that at sea charging engines are fickle things, and in conditions when an extra pump might be badly needed, with a lot of water coming below, the charging engine would almost certainly have been put out of action. What a lot of money owners of small boats waste on mechanical devices that cannot always be depended upon and which anyway save only a few minutes' labour!

So much for *Mischief* below deck. From the stemhead on deck the bowsprit sticks out about 12ft. and there are some eight feet of it inboard reaching back to the bitts. Slung between the bowsprit shrouds which support it laterally is a rope net, useful for arresting sails or crew on their way into the sea. In calm weather it has been used as a hammock. The jib goes out along the bowsprit on a traveller and is set flying. The only time a man, or sometimes two men, have to go out on the bowsprit is for hanking the big reaching jib to the stay. It is therefore wise to get this sail in early if the wind freshens. The anchor chain leads out on the port side of the stem, passing first through a chain-stopper, the anchor winch being set back level with the bitts. These are two massive pieces of oak standing three feet above the deck. The fisherman-type anchor weighing about 100 lbs. is lashed on deck near the winch, and on the other side of the foredeck, near the bitts, is carried a nine foot dinghy. This is launched by hoisting it over the rail by means of the jib halyards. There used to be three ventilators let into the foredeck, but their copper cowls have been demolished so frequently either by the sea or rough usage that we have now plugged up the holes. Ventilators on the deck of a small boat are bound to let in as much water as air unless they are high, cumbersome affairs with water-traps, or can be mounted above the deck on the coach-house roof.

The mast is stepped well forward, about one-third of the overall length of the boat (45ft.) from the stem. Mounted on it are two winches for setting up the last bit of the throat and peak halyards. As I have said earlier, the mast has been thought hardly man enough for the job. It is a solid spar only seven and a half inches in diameter and may well be the original mast. All the other spars that were in the boat when I took her over in 1954 have at one time or another been renewed. The only time I have misgivings about the mast, when the possibility that it may be precarious and not very permanent looks menacing, is in a rough sea with insufficient wind to keep the gaff from swinging about. In those circumstances the upper part of the mast looks as if it were being wrung or twisted like a dishcloth. But one should speak well of the bridge that carries one over; what bends will not break; and judging by the number of modern masts that are broken every summer round our coasts I believe it is not as frail as it looks.

By the bulwarks at the foot of the shrouds are two wood kevels each holding half a dozen iron belaying pins. The pins are fitted with a home-made device consisting of a wooden roller round which ropes render easily when swigged on. The wooden rollers are kinder to rope than are iron pins and cause less wear. About five feet up the shrouds the screens for the navigation lights are wired on; and just below the screens a sheer-pole, too, is fixed to the shrouds having attached to it a couple of long pegs for holding the coiled halyards. Between the mast and the cabin skylight there is space for a small deck locker used for stowing the numerous short lengths of rope required frequently for lashings, as well as the handles for both the reefing gear and the mast winches. The reefing gear is the Appledore type and is probably the original fitting. The cabin stove-pipe emerges inside this locker so the lid has to be trimmed to the wind as if it were a ventilator cowl.

The cabin skylight, mounted on a foot-high coaming, is offset from centre so that the port-side deck is at this point wider by a couple of feet than the starboard. The reason for this is that when she was a pilot-cutter, the punt, as the pilots called the dinghy, used to be carried on the port side. By means of a tackle on the mast with its fall led to the cockpit, the man at the helm could raise the punt clear of the bulwarks for his mate to launch her off. The six panes of the skylight, by the way, are of half inch plate glass; even so we once had one of these broken by a wave in the Red Sea of all places.

The twin staysail booms, dinghy oars, boathooks, and harpoon are lashed on one side of the skylight, and on the other, when it is not set up, the topmast. This would come in useful as a spare spar in case of accidents, and it has been used as a sheer-leg when through mischance or mismanagement we have gone aground on a falling tide – as may happen at times to the most prudent mariners.

Aft of the skylight is the 40 gal. water tank covered by a wood grating and on this is lashed an oak water-breaker holding about six gallons and a box for holding chafing gear. This consists of rags, bits of canvas, and ropeyarn to make up the 'scotsmen' to wrap round ropes where they are liable to chafe. Rags may be scarce at the start of a voyage but as it progresses discarded shirts and trousers become increasingly available. Aft of the water tank is the sliding hatch covering the companion-way and between the two is space to lash jerry-cans of petrol for the charging engine and a five gallon drum of fish-oil for calming troubled waters. The staysail sheet winches are on deck alongside the cockpit coaming.

Inside the nine inch high coaming the cockpit is roomy enough, measuring about five feet by six feet by two feet deep. It has seats on both sides, their main use being to provide a stepping-stone to the deck. If the weather is fine enough the crew prefer to spend their leisure hours lying about the deck rather than sitting in the cockpit. The helmsman, too, manages best by standing up as he can thus see farther and has more control of the long brass tiller. Usually there is one among the crew who insists on sitting down throughout his watch, or even lying stretched out on one of the benches, a position from which he can see nothing but the sky and can barely watch the compass. This is mounted on a small binnacle in the middle of the cockpit floor and can be illuminated at night by a wandering lead from the chart-room. Often in the course of a voyage, owing to trouble with the charging engine or shortage of petrol, we have to forgo this lighting and rely upon the self-luminous compass card.

All round the inside of the cockpit are capacious lockers, one reserved for paint and the others for spare sheets, bos'n's chair, handy-billy, and the weather-boards for closing the entrance to the companion-way. The cockpit is self-draining in so far as it has two outlet pipes. They are of small bore, full of bends, easily blocked and difficult to clear; and the amount of débris that collects under the cockpit grating and finds its way into the pipes is really astonishing – matches, blanket fluff, broken biscuit, sweet and chocolate wrappings, and so on. But no hairpins! The pipes drain slowly even when clear, but should the cockpit happen to be half-full of water this rapidly drains into the lockers, thence into the engine-room, and so to the bilge where it can be easily cleared.

Abaft the cockpit stands the gallows for the boom to rest on when the mainsail is down; it is a piece of six inch by six inch oak resting on substantial iron stanchions. The boom is a massive spar some 26ft. long and nearly as thick as the mast so that it is heavy enough by itself; when resting on the gallows it has on top of it the gaff and the mainsail, the canvas probably soaking wet and double its normal weight. Altogether, therefore, when the boom is lashed down to the gallows and the boat is rolling, the stanchions are under a heavy strain. On one voyage we began to fear that they would be torn out of the deck, so that now I have had two iron cross-stays fitted as braces to keep the whole thing rigid.

Finally, between the gallows and the taffrail is the iron horse and buffer for the big main-sheet block, the single-ended main-sheet being made fast to one of two massive samson posts, one on each side of the cockpit. Bulwarks about a foot high enclose the whole of the deck and two feet above the bulwarks a wire guard-rail is supported by iron stanchions. I am told that when she was a working boat there was no guardrail as this would have hindered the launch-ing of the punt and the hoisting of it on board. Wide though the decks are, I should say that without a guard-rail it would be easy enough to lose a man overboard. Without it the crew would feel naked and unprotected, and for my part, if there were any sort of sea running, I should be inclined to go about the deck on all fours. The rail comes in handy, too, for leaning against when taking sights at times when, perhaps, owing to the sails being in the way, one cannot see the sun from the safest and steadiest position – braced against the gallows with one leg curled lovingly round a stanchion.

Mischief's dimensions, by the way, are 45ft. long over-all, 13ft. beam, and she draws about seven feet six inches aft. Her TM tonnage is 29 tons, and deadweight about 35 tons. She was built at Cardiff in 1906.

CHAPTER THREE

To Belfast

THIS FIRST voyage to Greenland seemed to me a less momentous undertaking than the three voyages southwards. The time involved did not amount to more than a long summer cruise, nor did so many ominous question-marks hang over the enterprise as they had, for example, over the voyage to the Crozet Islands – how we should fare in the Roaring Forties, whether we should find our islands, or whether the crew would see through to the end so long a voyage. On the other hand I was not happy about the Atlantic crossing and the expected head winds to which I was unaccustomed. By taking thought the ocean voyager can usually plot a course that ensures avoiding long periods of head winds. If bound for America, for instance, most yachts, unless they are racing, sail south to the Azores or Canaries whence the North-east Trades will quickly blow them westwards. That would be too roundabout for sailing to Greenland. We should have to go direct and make the best we could of the prevailing westerlies. In Davis Strait, too, we might expect trouble with fog and icebergs. Unknown perils loom the larger. I had never seen an iceberg; my experience of ice was limited to the small floes we had encountered in the Patagonian fjords.

Having agreed to call at Belfast for Charles – a matter of five or six days as I fondly imagined – I wanted to leave Lymington about the middle of May. The earlier the better, because in spring there is more chance of having some easterly or northerly winds on this side of the Atlantic. David Hodge and Terry Ward therefore joined the boat early in May. We had enough to do. All the running rigging and some of the standing rigging had to be rove, the deck and deck-fittings to be painted, the anchor chain turned and marked, sails bent, and all the gear and stores to be stowed. For shipping the bowsprit we pulled the boat's head into the quay so that having got the spar in place we could shackle on the bobstay and the shrouds from a firm base instead of from the dinghy. For some obscure reason we did not shackle on the masthead stay, the bowsprit's main support, but left it until the boat was back in her usual position alongside the quay with the bowsprit overhanging the water. I then climbed out on it to shackle the stay. Off the Berthon boatyard at fitting-out time there is much coming and going of yachts, some to marvel at, some to admire. In this busy, narrow river one's own experience leads one to expect that one of these craft may by chance hit something or stick on the mud. A day-boat that I watched did not seem in the least likely to fulfil my expectations; she looked so smart and was so smartly handled that I shouted to David to draw his attention to it. Misunderstanding me, and thinking that I wanted a hand at the end of the bowsprit, he started to climb out to join me. Whereupon, with a resounding crack, the bowsprit, the shrouds, the net, and David and I all found ourselves tangled up in the water together. Luckily it was high water. At low water we should have landed in bottomless mud.

Even if unstayed the bowsprit is stout enough to bear two men. The trouble was that it had broken before off Cape Town where we had put back to have it scarfed, and the scarf had now come unstuck, having been made too short in the first place. When it had been repaired we put it back, this time taking care to make all fast before venturing out on it. On the whole the gremlin that lurked in this unlucky spar behaved considerately. It had broken in the first place when we were close enough to Cape Town to put back, and now it had broken while we were still in harbour.

We were to have one other small misadventure before sailing day. The new Perkins engine had yet to be tried out, so one afternoon with the Yard engineer on board we cast off. In a few minutes, in the narrowest part of the fairway, with expensive yachts moored to piles on either hand and the Yarmouth ferry about to sail, we found that the cooling system was not working. Before the Yard launch arrived to tow us home we had some panic-stricken moments, wondering which yacht we should hit and how much it would cost, or whether the ferry boat would hit us first. After a fresh start the engine behaved perfectly and out in the Solent we even went backwards. I never much care for going backwards in *Mischief*. The propeller is on the port side and whichever way one puts the tiller she seems to go in an unexpected direction. I think on this occasion we may have been covered against third-party risks, for I like to insure against that while in home waters. Outside this, for the sort of voyage that *Mischief* undertakes, the premium is excessive, running into hundreds of pounds. So, like the flies on the mouthful of meat about to be devoured by the old-timer, 'I guess, she just has to take her chance.'

John Wayman joined a few days before sailing, followed by Joyce who then broke the news that he could not make the whole voyage. He was to come only as far as Belfast. I then got in touch with Michael Taylor-Jones who joined us with only a day to spare. Food and stores were to be brought over from Southampton the day before sailing in order that the confusion normally prevailing on sailing day should be to some extent reduced. Bonded stores – drink, tobacco, cigarettes – are brought with the food stores and are accompanied by a Customs officer to see fair play. The Southampton officials must by now be almost reconciled to *Mischief*'s departures and arrivals, each of which they are obliged to witness, clearing the ship in and out with a minimum of formality. Yachts under forty tons have to apply in the first place to HM Customs, London, for permission to carry bonded stores. Whether in fact or in fiction, brandy, rum, tobacco, have come to be associated with life at sea. And the Finns, who are a nation of seafarers, go so far as to say: 'If tobacco and brandy cannot help a man, death is at hand.' Consumption of these things in *Mischief* is usually small. We take enough spirits for us to have a drink on Saturday nights, on rare occasions of stress, or to celebrate landfalls and birthdays. One needs a few bottles in hand, too, for presents or to return hospitality. This time Charles had asked me to bring six bottles for his own private behoof, and since it now seemed almost certain that he would have to cook, I felt this to be a wise provision. As for tobacco, while at home I smoke a pipe moderately, and at sea immoderately, on the principle of making hay while the sun shines. It seems a mistake not to smoke all one can while one can at so moderate a cost. Joyce smoked fairly furiously but he would not be with us long enough to count. David Hodge got through a lot of cigarettes, supporting with equanimity the superior attitude of the rest of the crew who were all non-smokers.

Some slight confusion arose when it came to stowing the bonded stores. On other occasions less rigidly-minded Customs officers had not insisted on sealing the stores but had left them in the cabin where the local Customs man could see that they were still intact just before we sailed. But this time the stores must be put in a locker and sealed up, all the lockers being already full to bursting. There was nothing for it but to take out some forty tins of biscuit and dump them on the cabin floor where there was still some room.

Meeting as they do with all sorts and conditions of men, Customs officers must be in the habit of sizing up people quickly. I wondered what they made of their brief meeting with the odd collection gathered in the cabin. The Master of *Mischief*, as he signed himself on the numerous documents thrust before him, at which he peered through spectacles earnestly but unintelligently, sucking at a pipe in the endeavour to look like a hard-bitten sailor, silent as becomes both an eminent mountaineer and a man who has really nothing to say. David Hodge, officially the mate, but not a bit like the bucko mate all sailing ships should have; slightly built and thin, as well he might be after the complication of diseases that had put him ashore. Dr Joyce, plethoric if you thought of him as a possible climber, but as a ship's doctor merely becomingly stout; perspiring perceptibly in the crowded cabin, and drawing nervously at a cigarette as he hungrily eyed the several thousand that were about to be sealed up. Terry Ward, small, fair, cherubic, like a schoolboy on holiday, though past the thirty mark. John Wayman, also fair and inclining to fat, too fat for a Wasp, I thought, though in mid-May even the Wasps must begin to relax. And Michael, our young physicist, tall and frail, too young to have started shaving seriously and with a long lock of hair which every minute he had to throw back with a disgustingly girlish toss of his head. A gentlemanly-looking lot, the Customs officer might think, with the exception of one or two; but not men to go into the jungle with, if that was his criterion, and certainly not to sea.

On 14 May, watched by a modest crowd of well-wishers, we cast off and motored down the river, preceded by the Yard launch with Ted the bos'n who likes to see us safely off the premises. The slightest deviation on *Mischief*'s part from the winding, narrow fairway, a mere nervous shrinking from collid-ing with an oncoming Yarmouth ferryboat, will infallibly put her on the mud. At the mouth of the river, after a warm handshake from Ted, we hoisted sail and headed for the Needles Channel. It was a pleasure to have for once a crew who knew the ropes. With the exception of Dr Joyce and David, all were familiar with sailing boats, and David with his sea background very quickly got the hang of things. I think what most impressed our steamboat officer was that a sailing boat could not always be pointed in the direction you wanted to go. Outside the Needles the wind freshened and headed us. We had not been butting into it long before we noticed that a seam near the throat of the mainsail was beginning to go. Both the mainsails we carried had seen long service and seam trouble might be expected, though not quite so early as this. As the tide was on the point of turning against us, we headed for Swanage Bay where we anchored off the town to spend a quiet evening repairing the sail. After supper when we got the anchor and were under way we were hailed by the owner of a motor launch drifting down on us who wanted us to tow him in, his engine having failed. As the evening was fine and no danger threatened his appeal fell on deaf ears. I felt a bit of a cad but the pangs of remorse were stilled when presently we heard his engine start. If I were the owner of a motor boat with a broken-down engine, I think I would pretend to be fishing or enjoying a few moments of engine-less peace rather than ask a sailing boat for a tow. As the Persians say: 'The wise man sits on the hole in his carpet.'

At the end of a pleasant day sailing close-hauled all along West Bay we went about to clear Start Point. That night the south-east wind freshened so much that we reefed and by morning, the sea having got up, the crew, except for David and myself, were far from well. To make things easy for us we handed the main and ran under stays'l alone till at tea-time we passed the Wolf Rock. There are no off-lying dangers here so we sailed close to watch the seas breaking furiously at the foot of the lighthouse. At the same time the nuclear submarine *Nautilus* passed, her square conning tower standing up like a house. Meantime the galley to which we looked for aid and comfort had become merely a source of distress. Michael had long since had to give up, Joyce battled with breakfast and lunch, while David came to the rescue for supper. This was no sort of way to run the galley and I hoped for a fast run to Belfast where Charles might take over and put things on a proper footing. But Belfast lay many days away. This wind was the last fair wind we were to have, almost the last wind of any kind.

Instead of laying the course for the Smalls we got pushed steadily west as the wind backed to north. Late on the evening of the 17th we sighted land. Undoubtedly Ireland, but why no glimmer of light from the Tuskar Rock lighthouse near its south-east corner? We were not lost but uncertain of our position. Finally the near presence of a small rockly islet obliged us to go about and at the same time we sighted the Coningsbeg light-vessel twenty miles west of Tuskar! This part of the Irish coast, sprinkled with wonderfully vivid names such as the Brandies, the Barrels, the Bore, the Saltees, held yet another surprise in store. Sailing eastwards towards the Tuskar we presently spotted a red flashing light where according to both the chart and the Pilot book there should have been only the white flashing light of the Barrels buoy. A feverish search through the list of lights in the current *Brown's Nautical Almanac* revealed that a light-vessel with a red flashing light had replaced the Barrels buoy. That my chart and Pilot book had not been kept up to date shocked our professional sailor. He disliked such slipshod methods, though he admitted that while poking around at four knots in a 30-tonner one had more time to correct these little mistakes than when proceeding at 18 knots in a 20,000-ton ship; always provided, of course, that the elementary rule of keeping a good look-out was observed. The professional sailor regularly receives his *Notices to Mariners* and sees to it that his charts are corrected up to date before every voyage. Few amateurs, I suspect, are as careful as that. They buy or borrow their Pilot books and charts, regardless of the edition, leave them uncorrected, assuming them to be as the law of the Medes and Persians which altereth not. The stoutly bound Pilot books will last his lifetime, while the charts need be replaced only when most of their important detail has been obscured by pencil marks, cocoa stains, oil, sea-water, and perhaps pigeon droppings. I mention the last because we were frequently boarded by lost homing pigeons which took up their quarters in the chart-room and turned it into a guano island.

We duly sighted the Tuskar, a light for which I have kindly feelings. When I had last seen it, sailing over from Barmouth in a friend's four-tonner, they had made the signal 'U', meaning 'you are standing into danger', as indeed we were. This time after sighting it we sailed all night on the port tack and fetched up off the South Bishop off the Pembrokeshire coast, having lost ground to the south. The tides in St George's Channel run strongly. The characteristic of this light had also been changed from flashing every twenty seconds to flashing every five seconds. On the next tack between Wales and Ireland we did better but not as well as we expected. The next light which ought to have been Arklow turned out to be the Blackwater fifteen miles to the south. The weather was lovely and the sea calm. We took the opportunity to go aloft to unreeve the jib halyard in order to stretch it and take out the turns.

Having motored up to the Arklow light-vessel in a flat calm we picked up a northerly breeze and set off to have another look at Wales. Early on the morning of the 20th Anglesey showed up more or less where expected. Our navigation seemed to be improving with practice. Back we went again towards Ireland where we fetched up at the Codling light-vessel having made no northing whatsoever. We were suffering on the rack of bliss. As one flawless spring day of sun and warmth succeeded another, the water ruffled fitfully by light northerly winds, life became more and more tedious. I wondered why Charles and I had been such fools as to pick on Belfast as a rendezvous. But at least we avoided crossing the Irish sea again. Four times was enough. It would be tiresome to relate how we drifted, motored, and sometimes sailed up the Irish coast until at last on Monday, 22 May, we rounded Mew Island and entered Belfast Lough. At last we had some wind, enabling us to sail in style into Ballyholm Bay, west of Bangor, where we anchored. A passing yacht, taking part in a race, hailed us to say that there was a better anchorage round the corner in Bangor Bay. I could not see much difference myself as both bays are wide open in every direction except south. Bowing to local knowledge we moved, and as we anchored for the second time I noticed a familiar figure, with yachting cap and beard, gesticulating from the beach.

Charles with his dunnage soon came on board; the crew, I think, being notably impressed with his maritime appearance. He had for the moment discarded his gum-boots, likewise the black patch he used to wear over one eye, but otherwise he fully lived up to the picture I had drawn. It relieved me to learn he had no qualms about taking over the galley, indeed he had come prepared by bringing a private store of spices and a recipe book. As I told him, we had not had a square meal since leaving Lymington nine days before. The crew in turns had done their best but none showed much talent for cooking except perhaps Michael who had a deft hand with pancakes. It is best if possible to have one man in the galley, for if everyone takes a hand things are left dirty, nothing is put back in its place, and the stores and cooking gear become hopelessly jumbled. In fact it is a case of what's everybody's business is nobody's business – the reason offered by an Irishman at the time of the 'Troubles' when asked why a local magnate, much disliked by both sides, had not been shot.

The Royal Ulster Yacht Club, housed in a Victorian mansion overlooking the Lough, is noted for hospitality. We lost no time in making our number there and that evening, having first prepared our stomachs with libations of draught stout, we made good the deficiencies of the voyage. We spent two days at Bangor, replenishing fresh stores and doing odd jobs on board. One of the jib halyard sheaves had worn so much as to fray the halyard, so we hung a block on the mast instead of using the sheaves. This worked in so far as the rope rendered without getting frayed or twisted but the luff of the jib could not be hauled really tight. We sailed at six on the morning of the 25th to catch the north-going tide. The voyage to Greenland had begun.

CHAPTER FOUR

The Atlantic

THE NORTHERLY winds that might have sent us far on our way had we passed south of Ireland still persisted. But at sea as on land, the truth of the Spanish proverb, that whichever way you go there is a league of bad road, is generally borne out. At sea one must accept whatever winds blow, for it is not often possible to cheat the wind like a 'vile politician seeking to circumvent God'. Readers of *Typhoon* may recollect that a similar view was held by that sturdy seaman Captain MacWhirr, a man who 'as if unable to grasp what is due to the difference of latitudes, always wore, at home or in the Tropics, a brown bowler hat and black boots'. He had a contempt even for the laws of storms and thus expressed it to his mate at a moment when his ship was about to be all but overwhelmed by a typhoon: 'All these rules for dodging breezes and circumventing the winds of heaven, Mr Jukes, seem to me the maddest thing.'

When the tide turned against us as well as the wind we could make no progress so we ran into Red Bay where we anchored. There is little shelter from northerly winds in this deserted bay but at any rate we were out of the tide. In the evening the wind veered so that we could steer north and with the tide now under us we went like a scalded cat. The tides in the North Channel run at three knots. At midnight, north-west of Rathlin Island, I came on deck to find her moving backwards, the sails all aback and the tiller lifeless, the sea around seething as if about to boil. We were in the tail of a race, probably in the vicinity of Shamrock Pinnacle. In order to get steerage way we had to start the engine.

Having at last rounded the corner of Ireland we had the wind free and could steer west. By eight o'clock next morning, a big sea then running, we had Inishtrahull Island abeam three miles away. We did not lose sight of the Irish mountains for another two days, but we were now in the open ocean with nothing between us and America two thousand miles away. When presently the wind again headed us we had trouble persuading *Mischief* to go about, the sea being so rough. At the second attempt we got her round but not before the flogging jib had shaken one of the sheet blocks out of its strop. When the wind dropped at midnight we rolled about with the boom slamming wildly. In such circumstances the question is whether to call all hands to get the sails off or to leave things as they are in the hope that the wind will soon come again. Experience teaches that leaving the sails up seldom pays but hope generally triumphs over experience, as Dr Johnson remarked of a man marrying for the second time. Although we steadied the boom to some extent by bowsing it down with the handy-billy, by 2 am a large rent had appeared in the sail so down it had to come. I had hoped that this sail, the weaker of the two we carried, would have taken us across. It had already given so much trouble that we decided to change it, a decision easier to make than to carry out on the deck of a small boat in a rough sea with no sail to steady her. Having first prised the second sail out of its bin in the galley we pushed it by main force into the cabin and on to the deck through the skylight. There are about 700 square feet of canvas in the sail, a lot of canvas to unroll while trying to sort out the head and the foot, the tack and the clew. Having bent it on and hoisted, we bundled up the old sail as best we could and stuffed it below, wet as it was.

On 30 May we had our first good day's run when we logged 120 miles, and on the following day we did 94 miles. We felt we were getting somewhere, for Cape Farewell, the southern tip of Greenland, was less than 1,500 miles away. We began making absurd calculations, little thinking that another 30 days would elapse before we rounded that noted cape. Cape Farewell is 59° 46' north and 43° 53' west, but the mariner is advised not to go north of 58° 30' when passing it on account of the ice which accumulates off the cape. This

1 On the Patagonian Icecap, 1956, looking north from Camp 9 close to the Chile/Argentina watershed at a height of nearly 7000ft.

2 3 4 5   The Crozet Islands trip 1959/60: (above) *Mischief* in the South Atlantic; (far left) Tilman in leisurely mood during the passage; (left) a fine day off the Spanish coast; (below) busy penguins and a querulous elephant seal at Baie du Navire, Possession Island.

West Greenland: 6 (above left) The fjord on the east side of Upernivik Island. 7 (upper right) Mischief at anchor in Holsteinborg harbour. 8 (lower right) The summit ridge of the 6500ft peak Tilman climbed on Upernivik Island.

9 (opposite page) In Inuknaavsait between Qioqe and Upernivik Island looking in the opposite direction to photo 6.

10 (overleaf) An evocative anchorage in an East Greenland fjord – probably on the Angmagssalik visit of 1964.

11   A camp on the crossing of Bylot Island July/August 1963. The Bylot anchorage
is depicted on the cover illustration.

12   Baffin Island 1962: 'False' Mt. Raleigh (Mt. Mischief) from high on Mt. Raleigh.

meant for us roughly a course of west-north-west, a course that we could seldom lay, the wind blowing most often from somewhere between north-west and south-west. We sailed on the tack that allowed us to point nearest to west-north-west and changed to the other tack when that looked the most profitable. If both tacks were equally bad we chose the port tack whereby we got farther north where degrees of longitude measure fewer miles. In the Northern Hemisphere the Great Circle course, which is the shortest possible, lies to the north of the rhumb line course – the course that looks the shortest on a Mercator chart but in fact is not. Sailing thus, generally well off our course, we might log a hundred miles and yet make good less than half that in the direction of Cape Farewell, or even nothing at all.

Meantime the jib halyard continued to be troublesome. The sea being reasonably smooth, I went aloft and changed the block. Later we reverted to using the sheaves on the mast, and finally to the block again. It was unsatis-factory but by using the winch on the mast we could set the halyard up taut, twists and all. I must have been feeling energetic because after that I showed Charles how to make a cake, a task well within the capacity of a man who had spent two years at the Military College of Science. In fact he was already doing well and even beginning to reach out for the higher branches of his present profession. He is blessed with a cast-iron stomach. If the boat is knocking about a lot, as it was the next day, one does not expect anything but the simplest fare for supper. Defying the weather, Charles produced a rich stew with dumplings the size of cricket balls floating in it. I was about to add 'like half-tide rocks', a phrase that might have cast doubts on the wholesome-ness of Charles's dumplings. We still had some fresh bread left. Ordinary bread keeps for about ten days at sea before sprouting a green mould. I suppose sliced bread wrapped in cellophane might keep longer but such bread, even without a green mould, is hardly worth eating. Having finished the fresh bread we go on to what I call 'twice-baked', thick slices of bread or rolls that have been in the oven a second time. This seems to keep indefinitely, only its bulk prevents one from carrying enough for the whole voyage. Baking bread at sea for a crew of six on paraffin stoves is not feasible on account of the time, labour, and paraffin oil needed.

Nothing could be more different from Trade Wind sailing than sailing in the Atlantic in the latitudes of the fifties. No two days are alike, and for that matter the night that follows the day will generally see a change of some sort in the weather. However peaceful the sky may appear as the sun sets, it is a rash gamble to leave the Genoa up if one wants to pass an undisturbed night. Sunshine and rain, winds and calms, reefing and unreefing, followed each other incessantly and at brief intervals. Happily in summer the worst con-ditions seldom last long. What moderate gales we had were generally over in twenty-four hours, and it was rare for a calm to last more than a few hours. Such is the impression I had of our weather and when writing this I expected to have it confirmed by referring to the log we kept. Log-books are normally couched in terse, seamanlike language, but I find that our log-book is terse to the point of dumbness. When the helmsman is relieved he enters in the appropriate columns the course steered, the wind direction, and the reading of the patent log. The space left for general remarks or for noting – as should be done – anything of the slightest interest seen, is too often a blank. If a ship or a whale has been seen there is usually a remark, but on the whole it is difficult to tell from our log-book whether the sun shone or the rain fell, or whether the wind was of gale force or a light breeze.

A log-book entry which causes difficulty is that of the wind direction. When a ship is sailing it is not always easy to say within a point where the wind is from; the truest indication is probably the direction of the waves. But confusion chiefly arises from the magnetic variation, for the wind direction entered in the log should be the true direction after the variation has been added or deducted. In the Atlantic variation increases rapidly westwards, rising to 36° west, or more than three points, off Cape Farewell. Half-way up Davis Strait it is as much as 55° west and increases as the Magnetic Pole is approached. Some find the converting of magnetic bearings into true, and vice versa, puzzling in spite of all the supposedly fool-proof rule-of-thumb rhymes. Any doubts there may be are best resolved by drawing a little diagram. One or two of the crew failed to master the problem and when estimating the wind direction before entering it in the log-book either ignored the variation or applied it the wrong way. In consequence, when looking over the log-book, one is startled by the erratic way in which the wind appears to have behaved. Sometimes, on the change of watch, an entry suggests that the wind shifted four points without apparently affecting the course steered or the set of the sails. When deciding on which tack to sail the large magnetic variation had, of course, to be allowed for. We might, for instance, be steering north-by-east by compass and yet making good two or three points of westing, whereas, on the other tack, perhaps steering west of south, we should have been heading for the Bay of Biscay.

Even in the Atlantic, in the month of June one feels entitled to some warm, sunny days. We experienced on the whole grey, lowering weather with more rain and drizzle than sunshine. On one such dirty, drizzling day, when we were close-reefed and close-hauled in a strong westerly wind the *Empress of Britain* passed close. A little later the *Southern Prince* of the Prince Line overtook us. In spite of the sea running David called her up with the Aldis lamp and asked her to report us at Lloyds. As her freeboard is less than three feet communication by lamp from *Mischief*'s deck when a sea is running is intermittent, the lamp often being obscured in the middle of a letter. Nevertheless the message was read and in due course reached my home.

Sailing to windward in a rough sea is generally wasted effort. For two days we steered NW by N making little or no westing, so we hove-to and had a quiet night. When we let draw we tried her on the starboard tack and in the course of another two days lost about forty miles to the east. I found this discouraging. Besides the lack of progress I was worried by the wear and tear caused by prolonged beating in rough weather. On previous voyages we had generally managed to make ground in the required direction however hard the wind blew. The crew did not seem to mind. Having had no experience of long spells of down-wind sailing they took our slow, arduous progress as a matter of course. But they felt cold, cold accentuated by the general wetness, for there was usually spray flying or rain falling, or both. For the two-hour spell at the helm they adopted the unseamanlike practice of wearing gloves. Woollen gloves were so soon saturated that they devised ingenious waterproof mitts from plastic bags or pieces of canvas. Under these conditions none of us looked forward to a spell in the cockpit holding the brass tiller or the equally cold, wet tiller line. How fast the time passes on watch depends much on how the boat is sailing. When close-hauled in a lumpy sea – which means in effect that she is going up and down in the same hole – the hours seem interminable, whereas if she is going fast in the right direction with the log spinning merrily they pass like a flash. Perhaps the watch passes most quickly when one has to really concentrate on steering her, when running with the wind dead aft and the imminent threat of a Chinese gybe hanging over one.

On this passage we seldom had any inducement to sit about on deck and in the North Atlantic there is seldom much to see except a waste of grey water devoid of life or ships. We were now north of the northernmost steamer track used by ships bound for Scandinavian ports round the north of Scotland. The last ship sighted, an ore carrier called the *Afghanistan*, had altered course to have a look at us and gave us three friendly blasts on her siren by way of encouragement. We returned the compliment with three dismal squeals from our hand fog-horn. The few birds seen, we wrote off as gulls, for we knew no better and had on board no keen bird-watchers such as we had on the later voyage. Most of the way across Terry Ward trolled a line – not, perhaps, such a hopeless gesture as it may sound, for on the way home, in fine, warm weather, I saw some tunny leaping. When there was no work on deck most of the time had to be spent below, usually flat on one's back reading or sleeping. I am told that in a steamer, where there are rivets in the deckhead, an alternative occupation is to count them.

No doubt we had our meals to look forward to and discuss. In that respect we might have been likened to Carlyle's pot-bellied Jutes and Angles, men who 'watched the sun rise with no other hope than that they should fill their bellies before it set'. It is a commonplace that men are more interested in their food than are women (who has ever heard of a female gourmet?), presumably because men are seldom put to the trouble of buying or cooking their food. Yet while women are (or used to be) *ipso facto* cooks, they never become chefs. No woman, I suppose, would be seen dead in a chef's cap, but apart from that objection they lack the inventive genius and poetic fire of a chef. The fact that there are no women poets of great note is perhaps significant. I suspect, too, that the naturally frugal mind of a woman would boggle at the scale upon which a chef conducts operations. For example, Alexis Soyer, that Napoleon of the kitchen, to celebrate the ending of the Crimea war, served up a dish which he called a Culinary Emblem of Peace, containing among many other ingredients twelve boxes of lobsters and 200 eggs.

Charles would be the first to admit that he is no poet and sometimes we had to stimulate his imagination. I was surprised to hear David of all people urging the claims of currant duff as a wholesome, seamanlike sweet. At Lymington, where we used to have supper ashore, he had consistently turned down delicious steamed puddings in favour of cheese on the grounds that when at sea he had eaten enough duff to last his lifetime. Between making a cake, which Charles soon perfected, and making a duff, the difference is barely perceptible. Thus duffs, varying in hue and texture, and sometimes in taste, were included in our homely repertoire of sweets – stewed apple rings, stewed prunes, rice, and (all too rarely) pancakes. Potatoes, and rice, too, figure daily in the main course, yet in spite of all this carbohydrate, much sleeping, little exercise, and lack of worry, no one put on weight. Stews, curries, rissoles, sausages, spaghetti and macaroni dishes, were about the extent of our resources, the meat for these dishes having to be always bully beef or spam. In the matter of carbohydrates, we had now at last had to start eating biscuits. We hoped that the particular kind we started on would soon be finished. I had bought two large tins of them in Cape Town, had thought little of them then, and less now, but could not bear to throw them away. 'Remainder biscuit' has an ominous ring. 'Dry as the remainder biscuit after a voyage' suggest weevils as well as dryness. These were at least free from weevils and they served well enough as a means of conveying to the mouth large quantities of butter and jam. It is on this account, in order to moderate the consumption of butter and jam, that the 'Lifeboat' biscuits we normally use have to be rationed. These biscuits might have been specially packed for a crew of six. There are ninety-six to a tin and at sixteen a man we get through a tin a day.

The fight that we had to get westwards and to round Cape Farewell can best be understood from the brief entries I made in a diary for the latter half of the passage. All bearings, by the way, are true. My hopes and fears are not set down, for I have generally found that in the event these are made to look damn silly.

Tuesday, 13 June. Steering north yesterday till wind backed in the evening. Early this morning wind backed farther to south-west and glass fell to 28.9. Reefed before breakfast when we were doing 6½ knots. A sight at 9 am put us in Long. 33° 14′ west. A new canvas bucket washed overboard. Glass down to 28.7 and a flat calm since 5 pm Handed sails and hoisted again at 8 pm when wind came in hard from north. Reefed. Had to run off to south-west owing to wind. Reefed again and handed jib. Blew hard all night.

14 June. Sea rough and fresh head wind. Steering south-west. Gybed later and steered north.

15 June. Wind fell light in night. Lowered main for repair at 4 am and at 6 am hoisted with all reefs out. Wind south, steering west-north-west, steady rain and glass down to 28.7. No sun, no sights for last twenty-four hours. Very cold on watch. My feet always cold. 4 pm glass down to 28.4. Wind backed to south-east, rain stopped, and sun came out. Wind fell light, violent rolling, handed sails. Hoisted in the night with wind from west. Barometer flattened out.

16 June. Very fresh wind. Took reef out of main but soon had to reef again. Strong wind all afternoon and evening with barometer rising. Overcast. Steering north.

17 June. Same dull windy weather. Went about in the evening and then about again to steer north-west. 10 pm wind freshening, reefed. Midnight reefed again and hove-to.

18 June. Sunny morning but wind about Force 8. Weather sheet of backed fores'l parted. Got sail down with difficulty and hoisted storm jib in lieu. Nut came off starboard shroud shackle bolt. Now about N. lat. 58°.

19 June. Blew hard all day but some sun. Wind moderated by evening when barometer rose and rain set in.

20 June. Reached N. lat. 59° 05′ Went about in the afternoon but by night on port tack again steering north-west. Wind from west-south-west has hardly varied a point since Saturday. Now about 150 miles west of Farewell. All complain of cold.

22 June. Still beating against WSW wind. Sunny until afternoon when some fog came up with a harder wind. Mains'l down for stitching. West about steering south. Small Danish ship *Nancie S.* bound east stopped while we hove-to to speak them. Asked them to report us but don't think they heard as we had no megaphone. The wind has been at WSW for five days. We sail north-west up to Lat. 59° and then go about again. No sign of any ice but still 100 miles west of Cape.

22 June. Still beating but did better steering west by north until heavy rain started and wind headed us. Now about 70 miles south-east of Cape. Glass falling at night so reefed and dropped jib to slow down. We may be farther north than we think.

23 June. All plain sail steering north-west. Noon sight disappointing, not so near Cape as we thought. Lat. 58° 58′ Long. 42° 10′ Went about steering south-west. Strong wind and rough sea, twice failed to stay and had to gybe her round. Strop of jib halyard block on mast parted. Too rough to do anything so now are without jib. 6 pm sighted first iceberg half a mile on port bow. About 30ft. high. My seaboots filled with water when getting jib in.

24 June. Wind freshened yesterday evening. Reefed. About 11 pm a tear in leach of mainsail opened so had to get sail down. Quite a job. Under stays'l only, so can only steer south. Same hard, cold wind all day. Mains'l sodden but repaired with herring-bone stitching a long rub caused by the topping lift. Tear in leach still to do. Had trysail up and steered south-west, but a snap sight this evening showed we had lost 13 miles to east. Poor outlook.

25 June. Same wind all night. Very cold on watch. Some sun today. Got sail patched and hoisted by midday. Renewed stays'l hanks which were all worn through. Now down to Lat. 57° again and evening sight put us 43° 10′ west. Wear and tear continues. Jib outhaul stranded, ditto halyard, also stays'l sheet and wire of port topping lift. Not happy about the mainsail.

This was about the nadir of our fortunes. From a position not far from Cape Farewell, in three days we had been blown a hundred miles or so to the south. Whatever the crew may have thought about it, certainly at this time the breeze of anxiety began to ruffle my brow. We had about three weeks' water left, and Godthaab, the port for which we were aiming, was still nearly 500 miles away. At this comparatively early season the more southern ports of Greenland are difficult to approach on account of ice – the ice that is drifted round Cape Farewell and up the west coast by the Greenland current. We might surely expect more favourable weather in Davis Strait but we were not there yet; in my gloomier moments I even saw us having to run for Iceland to refresh – almost as far away as Ireland. I was worried by the wear and tear occasioned by constant beating and the wet conditions. Wet, sodden rope, with never a chance to dry, seems to fray much more readily, and wet, sodden canvas is hell to repair. The last job on the mainsail had cost David and me several hours work. Such troubles were not serious except that cumulatively they tended to slow us down still more. Happily the crew remained unperturbed, though I warned them that with only three weeks' water left there was a limit to the time we could spend beating about off Cape Farewell. But better things were now in store for us. Cape Farewell had exacted its tribute. We had paid our footing.

CHAPTER FIVE

To Godthaab

ON THAT same Sunday evening the wind moderated and went round to south. We hoisted the jib on the Genoa halyard. On this halyard there is no purchase, so that the luff of the sail sagged disgracefully. But it was better than having no jib. All that night we ran west by north until in the morning the wind failed. Much to our surprise and pleasure the sea fell calm, too, as it had not been for a long time. After motoring for an hour we had to stop. Having lost a pipe and begun looking for it in the bilge as the most likely place, I discovered a lot of oil. The overflow pipe, passing under the floor-boards between the engine and the 'heads', had broken, and Terry Ward had to solder in two new pieces. Rain fell throughout the day and we got no sights, but by dead reckoning we put ourselves in Long. 46°, well to the west of Cape Farewell. To be west of this cape had for a long time been the summit of our hopes so that night we celebrated the event by lacing our cocoa liberally with rum.

For yet another night we continued to sail west and a morning sight put us in Long. 47°, several miles west of where we expected to be. Evidently we had been feeling the benefit of the East Greenland current which sweeps round Cape Farewell. For a hundred miles beyond the cape the coast trends only a little north of west, so that after rounding the cape the current is west-going. A noon sight gave us a latitude of 58° N., a long way south of Farewell, but we were now rapidly closing the land, steering north with a fine breeze from west-north-west. Two days before, when we were fighting to make westing, such a wind would hardly have been designated a 'fine breeze'. We began meeting large icebergs and found them more of an encouragement than a menace. Their presence meant that we were in the East Greenland current and they were no menace because in that latitude at that time of year there is practically no darkness. In the middle of the night, of course, it is not exactly as bright as day, and when fog comes down, as it did that evening, the visibility is poor. I had just come to the conclusion that it would be prudent to have a look-out posted in the bows when the fog cleared away and disclosed a large iceberg close ahead.

On 29 June – a red-letter day for us – fog prevailed almost throughout the day. Although the sun shone brightly overhead we could get no sights, our horizon extending to no more than 200 yards. The clammy fog made it perishing cold despite the sun and despite the cabin stove which we had long since been lighting daily. As we sailed on through the mist it became obvious that we were in a situation that the prudent mariner does his best to avoid.

We had little idea how near we were to some unknown part of a rock-bound and probably ice-bound coast towards which we were sailing in fog, surrounded by scattered icebergs. If we went about, as caution advised, we could steer only south. So we carried on and at four o'clock that afternoon our boldness or rashness had its unmerited reward. A vast berg looming up ahead obliged us to alter course to clear it and at that moment the fog rolled away. After a month at sea the dullest coast looks exciting, but a more dramatic landfall than the one we now made, both as to its suddenness and its striking appearance, could scarcely be imagined. Two or three miles ahead, stretching away on either hand, lay a rocky coast thickly fringed with stranded icebergs and backed by high, barren mountains. Beyond the mountains and over-topping them was the faintly glistening band of the Greenland ice-cap. To identify any particular part of this strange, wild coast was hardly possible, but we guessed that a bold cape a few miles westwards might be Cape Desolation at the western end of Juliannehaab Bight. An evening sight for longitude confirmed this. But on our making towards the cape the fog closed in again and we stood out to sea. Fog or no fog, the novelty of sailing in smooth water, the luck of our landfall, its magnificent aspect, all combined to give us a feeling of elation. From a hidden source Charles dug out a Christmas pudding and took elaborate pains over concocting a rum sauce to help it down – pains that are wasted on this kind of sauce for they merely serve to adulterate the main ingredient.

By a happy chance we had first sighted Greenland at almost the same spot as John Davis had in 1585 and in similar foggy conditions. This great Elizabethan seaman and explorer, whom we remember by the name of his Strait, was the discoverer of Greenland. It is more correct to say that he rediscovered it because Greenland had been settled by Norsemen from as early as the tenth century and it was not until the fifteenth century that their communication with Norway ceased.* On 20 July, 1585, John Davis's two ships *Sunneshine* of fifty tons and *Mooneshine* of thirty-five tons were a month out from the Scillies: 'The 20th as we sayled along the coast the fogge brake up and we discovered the land which was the most deformed, rockie, and mountainous that ever we saw. The first sight whereof did shew as if it had bene in the form of a sugar-loafe, standing to our sight above the cloudes, for that it did shew over the fogge like a white liste in the skie, the tops altogether covered with snow, and the shoare beset with yce a league off into the sea making such yrksome noise so that it seemed to be the true pattern of desolation, and after the same our Captaine named it, the land of Desolation.' Scattered about the world are many capes, islands, bays, and harbours of refuge whose names betray the disgust, despair, relief, or hope of the daring seaman who first saw and named them. In these parts alone there are for example, the Bay of God's Mercy in Hudson Strait, Cape Mercy off Baffin Island, Refuge Harbour, Cape Providence, and Sanderson's Hope. Desolation, too, was the name given to the island discovered in 1772 by

*The last vessel from Greenland returned to Norway in 1410. The evidence found in excavations of Norse burial grounds suggests that they died out either by excessive intermarriage or adverse conditions. There is no indication of absorption by the Eskimo race or of destruction at the hands of Eskimos.

Kerguelen-Trémarac and subsequently named after him. As patterns of desolation there was not much to choose between Kerguelen and the coast of Greenland. Desolate though it might be, we viewed the coast with emotions very different to those of John Davis and his men. As well we might. Ice mountains were probably the last thing they had wished to see whereas we had come in search of them. And we were secure in the knowledge that there were ports at hand where we could refit and replenish our stores as easily as if at home.

In Davis Strait the weather is less boisterous than in the Atlantic. Winds are mainly from southerly or northerly quarters and in summer rarely attain much strength. Force 6, or possibly on one occasion Force 7, was the most we experienced and on the whole we suffered more from lack of wind than too much. In the summer months fog is a great nuisance. If it were coupled with dark nights the icebergs would be a serious menace. Moving slowly, as we were, we could see bergs in time to avoid them even when visibility was down to 200 yards or less. All the icebergs sighted on this part of the coast break off from the glaciers of East Greenland and are brought here by the current. After rounding Farewell the current fans out and presently divides, part of it going west across the Strait to join the Labrador current and part continuing north up the coast. The flow of bergs is mainly from April to August though some are found in any month of the year. None of these bergs reach Newfoundland waters. They end by melting south of Farewell or in the middle of Davis Strait where in summer the water is relatively warm.

Unlike pack-ice, which moves generally with the wind, the movement of bergs is affected almost entirely by currents because of the far greater proportion of ice below water than above. The amount submerged varies with the type of berg. A solid block-like berg with sheer sides floats with only about one fifth above the surface, while a so-called 'picturesque' berg, pinnacled and ridged like a miniature mountain, might have one third or even as much as a half above water. We saw some great blocks of bergs 100ft. high and covering an acre or more of sea in the waters west of Cape Farewell. They became fewer as we went north and disappeared entirely before Godthaab was reached. On this voyage, unlike that of the following year, we saw no pack-ice. The bergs which appear off the Newfoundland banks in spring derive mainly from some twenty huge West Greenland glaciers northwards of Disko Island. It is estimated that 7,500 break off these twenty glaciers each year. An average of 396 drift south of Newfoundland and approximately 35 as far south as Lat. 43° N., that is south of the Grand Banks where the *Titanic* was sunk. After circling the head of Baffin Bay they are carried by the Labrador current down the Canadian coast. A berg calved in summer may reach the Hudson Strait region by autumn where it becomes fixed in the pack-ice, to be released and appear off Newfoundland in the spring.

We never tired of looking at bergs. At first we counted and logged all those in sight but north of Disko Island they became too numerous to count. If some particularly vast or grotesquely-shaped monster hove in sight we sometimes went out of our way to have a closer look at him. According to the light their colour varied from an opaque dazzling white to the loveliest blues and greens. Some had caves or even a hole clean through them in which the blue colour was intense and translucent. When passing a berg it is best to keep on the windward side on account of the number of bergy bits or growlers which break away and litter the sea to leeward. In fog or at night, in waters where there is no reason to expect ice floes, the presence of these bits of ice would indicate a berg in the vicinity. If it is rough waves may be sometimes heard breaking against the berg, but no reliance can be placed upon detecting changes of air or sea temperature in its vicinity or of receiving echoes from it from a fog-horn. Radar would pick up a large berg but would probably fail to show a 'growler' quite big enough to sink a ship. The only certain method is to see it. That a good look-out all round even in daylight is essential was impressed on me the day after we made our landfall. The wind had dropped and there was nothing in sight, no land, no ice. We handed the sails and motored for some eight hours, for most of the time in fog. When the boom and mainsail are resting on the gallows the helmsman's vision is obscured on one side unless he stands up on the cockpit seat and steers with his foot, or has a line round the tiller. For one reason or another I was standing in the cockpit, peering intently ahead into the fog. Happening to bend down and glance under the boom to the port side I was startled by the sight of the large, luminous mass of an iceberg less than fifty yards away.

We had more to look at than icebergs. In clear weather we could see the bold, mountainous coast and there were several ships about. A small coaster passed inside us and we saw for the first time some of the three- and four-masted schooners of the Portuguese fishing fleet. Off this coast there are a number of banks rich in cod and halibut, the resort of Norwegian, German, and British trawlers as well as these Portuguese schooners which, after fishing the Grand Banks in May and June, come north to the Davis Strait banks to complete their catch. They fish from dories with hand lines and later we sailed by some of their dories in action. The schooners we now saw were fishing on the Danas bank, north of the big Frederikshaab glacier. Other important banks are Fiskernaes, the Fyllas of Godthaab, and the Great and Little Hellefiske banks farther north.

When we arrived off Godthaab fjord on the morning of 4 July the weather was fortunately clear, for it is not an easy place to find or to enter. A submerged reef reaches out from the north shore of the entrance and the fairway lies between the tail end of this reef and a dense cluster of islets, possibly some fifty in number. On one of the outer islets there is a small beacon and on the islet directly opposite the tail of the reef there is a concrete pillar, with a light. The pillar which is only about ten feet high, is not readily seen from the offing, and in summer when it is never really dark the light is not much help. On this our first approach we acted with the utmost caution. Having closed the outer beacon we met a small fishing boat whom we consulted as to our next move. To ask, as they say in Spain, is no disgrace. We could not talk to them but they pointed out the way and soon we were passing the lit beacon, noting with interest some white water on the port hand marking the reef. It is safe to pass within a stone's throw of the islet for the water is deep.

The town and harbour lie about fifteen miles up the fjord from the outer islet, though the fjord, with many branches, runs inland for a good fifty miles. The tides run strongly but the navigation as far as the harbour entrance is straightforward. On this lovely summer day we had a magnificent sail up the calm, blue fjord, the black, barren shores close on either hand and in the distance some startling rock peaks over 3,000ft. high, their gullies still streaked with snow. Off the town we handed the sails, started the engine, and began nosing round looking for the harbour entrance. It was extremely puzzling. The entrance is narrow with two right-angle bends in it, so that from seaward one appears to be steering straight for the unbroken shore of the inlet. Presently we spotted the leading marks, small beacons with flashing lights, and gradually the way unfolded. Some of us had a strong impression that out of regard for the natives Greenland was 'dry'. However, on rounding the last bend, bringing in view the quay and the warehouse, we saw a beautiful sight, a twenty-foot-high stack of cases of Carlsberg lager. So we were reassured on one point. Our enthusiasm equalled that of the Rev Dr Folliot, a man with an interminable swallow, who summed up the well-stocked cellars of Crotchet Castle with the remark: 'A thousand dozen of old wine – a beautiful spectacle, I assure you, and a model of arrangement.'

Entering a strange harbour, especially if it is small and full of ships, is to me as much of a nervous strain as entering a room full of strangers. One has no clear idea what to do or where to go. There is more than a likelihood of making a fool of oneself by anchoring in some prohibited area or, goaded to desperation, smack in the fairway. On this occasion we managed remarkably well. Giving the quay a wide berth we headed for a high rock wall on the far side of the harbour. Sounding our way along by the wall we anchored in five fathoms between it and a small Danish naval vessel. This rock wall, by the way, has painted on it in enormous letters the names of various visiting ships. Had we had enough paint we would have added another. The *Mallemuken*, as this naval vessel was called, had a dual role of fishery protection and coastal survey. She was steel-built, whereas all the other survey vessels we met were wood. In Belfast we had met an elderly couple whose daughter was married to a Danish naval officer. Oddly enough the commander of the *Mallemuken*, who presently came on board, proved to be the man. Speaking excellent English he invited us on board *Mallemuken* for beer and shower-baths, both of which we needed. I thought it my duty to wait on board until the harbour authorities and the police had interviewed us and given us permission to land. At five o'clock, when we were still apparently of no interest to anyone, I rowed ashore to find the harbour-master. As befits a harbour-master he was a big, cheerful man, and spoke fairly fluent American. He said he had seen us arrive and since where we were lying was in nobody's way we might stay there as long as we liked. What about coming ashore, I asked. Why not? Having come so far it would be a pity not to land, and provided none of the crew had venereal disease there could be no possible objection. And there the formalities ended. No bother, no police, no Customs, no Immigration, and no health officials to harry us. Would it were everywhere thus!

The harbour has a deep-water quay where ships of several thousand tons can lie and a fish-quay and fish-curing factory were in course of construction. At the shallow end of this land-locked harbour is a slipway and mooring buoys for the Catalina seaplanes which daily arrive and depart for places up and down the coast. The only links between the harbours and settlements along the coast are by sea and air. There are no roads in Greenland. Godthaab (or Good Hope) is the capital of West Greenland, and although founded as long ago as 1721 by Hans Egede, the Lutheran missionary, it has all the appearance of a raw, thriving pioneer town, so extensive is the work in progress. A rough, unsurfaced road about a mile long leads from the harbour to the town itself which is scattered about over a small peninsula of solid rock interspersed with boggy hollows. As a result of this unpromising site all foundations have to be blasted out, all telephone lines and power cables are carried overhead on forests of poles, there is no underground drainage system, and water is laid on to standpipes by the roadside. Except for the stone-built house that had belonged to Hans Egede himself, the buildings and houses are of wood or prefabricated material; the houses are painted in lively colours – green, red, yellow, blue – but the public buildings have a more sober aspect. When we returned in 1962 large blocks of three-storey flats were either finished or nearly ready for occupation. Besides the stores for the necessities, such as provisions, hardware, clothing, and a bakery, there are photographic shops, a bookshop, and another for radio sets and electrical appliances. In fact one can buy there pretty well everything one is likely to need at much the same price as in Europe. One peculiarity is that for successful shopping a local guide is needed. The shops are scattered about, often without any window displays, and are not easily found or identified. Some of them might be mistaken for a private house or a public building. There are many independent traders but the bigger shops are controlled by the Royal Greenland Trading Company which in former days had a monopoly of all Greenland trade. As the result of a Commission appointed soon after the last war the whole set-up has been transformed and the Danish Government and the Trading Company between them are now actively engaged in the development of Greenland, so far as this is possible; and in all aspects of the Greenlanders' life, educational, medical, administrative, and economic, in the hope that in time the country will be run by the Greenlanders themselves and stand upon its own feet. All this will cost and is costing vast sums of money with no prospect of any quick return. The main hope rests upon a rapid development of inshore fishing by helping the Greenlanders to equip themselves with boats and by building and improving harbours, wharves, and fish-curing factories. The trade in sealskins, formerly of the first importance, is now secondary to fishing. A copper mine on the east coast and a cryolite mine at Ivigtut in the south-west are also sources of revenue, cryolite being a rare mineral of importance to the aluminium industry.* No doubt behind all this expenditure there is the hope that other valuable and workable mineral deposits will be found as they have been in the Canadian Arctic. Meantime

---

*A complete list of Greenland exports would have to include shark liver, cod liver, their oils, train oil, sperm oil, eiderdown, blue-fox furs, bearskins, sealskins, walrus hides, various salt fish, canned shrimps, smoked salmon, mutton and wool – these last from the Juliannehaab region where sheep-farming is carried on.

the Greenlanders have their education, technical training, medical care, law, order, and government provided for them by the Danish tax-payer.

In 1944 the total population was about 20,000 and has probably since increased. The population of Godthaab was about 3,000 of whom 500 were Danes. Having been in contact with Europeans for so long nearly all the so-called Eskimos are of mixed descent; and partly as a result of the way they are being cared for they have moved far away from the primitive Eskimo stage and are now a sophisticated people fully aware of the blessings of civilization. They have long had the use of firearms and marine engines and they are now familiar with the cinema, wireless sets, tape-recorders, juke boxes, and jive. There are two houses of entertainment in Godthaab, one patronized almost entirely by Greenlanders – the lower orders, as it were – and the other by both Danes and Greenlanders of substance. The Danish customers were all technicians or workmen resident only for the short summer working season; the more permanent residents, officials and such like, seemed to hold themselves aloof. We usually went to the last, the Kristinemut, where, provided one ordered in advance, an evening meal could be had – eggs, chips, salmon steaks, whale steaks, beef steaks, or smörgenbrod. In both establishments the juke boxes were worked overtime by youthful Greenlanders, so that in that respect there was little to choose. But at the Kristinemut beer was the main attraction and bottled lager was consumed in large quantities. Godthaab's main export at the present must surely be empty bottles, for as yet little fishing is done there.

Most of the crew of the *Mallemuken* resorted in the evening to the Kristinemut where we became friendly with them. There were about a dozen in the crew, nearly all young National Service men, who seemed happy enough to be doing their two years' service in Greenland. As might be expected in a small vessel, well beyond the reach of any Danish naval 'top-brass', duties were light and the discipline far from severe. Their commander, too, had a pleasant life, living mostly ashore with his wife in a convenient house overlooking the harbour. He and his wife were the only contact we made with the upper strata of Godthaab society. A representative from the only newspaper in the world that is published in the Eskimo language, the *Altuagagdliutit*, paid us a visit and subsequently an article about us and some photographs appeared. It may have been as a result of this that we had no other visitors. I was surprised at the lack of interest; many Danes are boat-minded, as it were; no other yachts that I have heard of have visited Greenland waters; and in other foreign ports *Mischief* has usually attracted a lot of attention. One explanation we heard was that the Dane is shy and dislikes intruding upon strangers. Those Danes in Godthaab employed on constructional work were probably far too busy – they worked a twelve-hour day – while the rest were mostly officials who, as a class, stick to their own kind and shrink from compromising themselves with outsiders, particularly with foreign outsiders. Elsewhere in Greenland it was different. We had the kindest reception from the Danes we met, official or unofficial.

We did not want to spend more than a few days in Godthaab. We had still 400 miles to go and were in a hurry to get on, the outward passage of forty days having taken longer than we expected. The day after our arrival was a blank day for it rained incessantly, but the day after that we went alongside the quay for water and fuel oil. The *Umanak*, a large passenger-cargo ship, which runs monthly from Copenhagen, had just arrived and was unloading. She takes eight or nine days from Copenhagen and until recently the monthly sailing was maintained throughout the year. Three years ago, a new ship on her maiden voyage disappeared one stormy January night off Cape Farewell leaving no survivors. The voyages in January and February have since been discontinued, the darkness of those months, and the ice, making it altogether too hazardous. Having warped our way round the stern of *Umanak*, fouling her ensign staff with our mast in the process, we got alongside, filled up with water from a water-cart, and had a forty-gallon oil drum put on deck. In siphoning the oil into our tank we spilt some on deck. Next morning, when we should have sailed, I slipped on this oil and in falling heavily against one of the sheet winches cracked a rib. We had to postpone our departure for two days till 9 July while I lay prone feeling very sore.

Before leaving we filled up with fresh food such as potatoes, onions, and bread. In a country like Greenland everything that a European needs, except fish, coal, and perhaps mutton, has to be imported. Coal of a poor quality is mined on Disko Island and sheep-farming, as I have said, is carried on in the south. Whether things like potatoes, onions, fruit, are available in the shops depends upon the recent arrival of a ship from Denmark. One of two of the residents, I noticed, had attempted the growing of vegetables like cabbage and radishes, while several houses had small built-in conservatories in which flowers were successfully grown. Our bread, by the way, had some remark-able features. It was rye bread – dark, heavy loaves about a foot and a half long and six inches square. This, of course, is baked in Godthaab but it would have been neither fresher nor staler had it been imported, for it has an immutable quality, as unchanging as the leopard's spots or the Ethiopian's skin. Perhaps in the course of weeks it becomes a shade harder, otherwise it remains as good as ever for an indefinite period. We took a lot on board and before it was finished some of us were looking forward to the day when biscuits would once more have to be eaten. Unless one had the jaws and teeth of a shark the slices had to be cut very thin, a feat which demanded a bread knife of exceptional strength that would neither buckle nor break. But perhaps the most impressive feature of this bread was that until one got used to it – and that took an awful long time – it had the effect of a strong aperient.

CHAPTER SIX

Northwards to Igdlorssuit

FOUR DAYS in Godthaab, or for that matter in most ports, is long enough, and if the appointed sailing day is deferred the moral of the crew suffers. I should have liked to have put it off a little longer on my own account and because, too, the day was foggy. But we got our anchor and motored out and after chugging away for six hours against wind and tide passed Agtorssuit, the last of the islands. Outside we hoisted sail and squared away, the stays'l boomed out one side and the mainsail the other, with the wind dead aft.

On clear days it is tempting to sail close to the Greenland coast so that the mountains and glaciers that comprise a great part of it can be fully admired. However, the stranger upon that coast does well not to be too free with it, fringed as it is with islets, skerries, and submerged rocks, some of them extending several miles from the shore. In addition, the absence of sea-marks or anything on shore that is readily indentifiable makes it difficult to tell what part of the shore one is looking at. It is therefore wise to refrain from hugging the coast and to secure a good offing, but having done that the problem of defining one's precise whereabouts has still to be solved, and all too often solved without the help of sights. Ships navigating this coast rely very much on radar. As might have been guessed, these remarks are preparatory to explaining, if not excusing, how we found ourselves astray the very next day.

After making good progress in the night and part of next day we were later obliged to go about and stand in towards the land. The sea was smooth, absolutely flat, and we obtained sights both at noon and in the evening, for the fog lay only in patches. The sights agreed pretty well with our dead reckoning and at 6 pm when we were motoring, there being no wind, we thought we were about 15 miles off the land. An hour later some islets loomed out of the mist only about half a mile away. Moreover, on looking over the side we could see through the dark, still water to the bottom. In the words of George Robey's song, we stopped, and we looked, and we listened. Terry Ward seized the opportunity to drop a bright, spoon-shaped spinner over the side and to our surprise and delight caught a 5 lb. cod. Two more were caught in quick succession. As we found later a spinner is superfluous; anything, a bit of rag, or even a bare hook will do the business. Cod are bottom feeders, so one just keeps the sinker on the bottom and jigs it up and down with the wrist – jigging for cod, as it is called. In that sea classic *Sailing Alone Round the World,* Slocum recalls an old Banks fisherman who from force of habit would, 'while listening to a sermon in the little church on the hill, reach out his hand over the pew and 'jig' for imaginary cod in the aisle.'

When the mist lifted we saw before us a wide landscape – high mountains, glaciers, and on the shore what looked like a small settlement. To identify it was another matter. By our reckoning we should have been off Sukkertoppen, a region of many high mountains. But now the Arctic Pilot came to our aid. Describing the entrance to Sondre Stromfjord, about 25 miles farther north, it mentioned an easily identified mountain with a horned summit and a black strip of basalt running down its face. With the aid of glasses we could make out such a mountain so that it looked as if we were a long way out of our reckoning. Sondre Stromfjord, by the way, is one of the longest of West Greenland fjords, about 100 miles long, and at its head is a big airfield built during the war by the Americans and then known as 'Bluie West 8'. It is now used by Scandinavian Airways, among others, as a stopping place *en route* to the Pacific coast of America. Passengers and mail for Greenland are landed here and distributed thence by Catalina seaplanes.

That we were badly out in our reckoning was confirmed by a sight at noon next day which put us 15 miles farther north than we should have been according to the sights of the previous day. Errors are to be expected if sights are taken with fog about, even though it appears to be only slight fog. If anxious to get a sight one too readily believes the horizon is good enough, but such sights are unreliable. The fog played some maddening tricks. Often the horizon would be perfectly clear in every direction except the one required, immediately below the sun. Lecky, the redoubtable author of *Lecky's Wrinkles*, had a way of overcoming the difficulty of taking sights in fog:

'By sitting in the bottom of a small boat in smooth water, or on the lowest step of the accommodation ladder, the eye will be about two feet above the sea-level, at which height the horizon is little more than a mile and a quarter distant, so that unless the fog is very dense, serviceable observations are quite possible. The writer, on three different occasions, when at anchor off the River Plate during fog, has been able to ascertain the ship's position in the way described, and after verifying it by the lead, has proceeded up to Montevideo without seeing land.'

But Lecky, both as a navigator and as a teacher of navigation, was in a class by himself. He was a hydrographer, as well as a master mariner, who has left his name on various charts, particularly those of the Patagonia channels where there are many reminders of his indefatigable zeal – 'Lecky's Retreat', 'Lecky's Monument', 'Lecky's Look-out'.

Another source of error and trouble for the navigator in Davis Strait is mirage. This is common and when it is present some abnormal refraction of the horizon must also be present. Rocks, islands, icebergs, ships, none of which can be identified for what they really are, appear floating in the air, sometimes upside down. According to the text-book this is occasioned thus:

'When the sea surface is relatively cold (and the wind very light) so that the density of the air decreases for a short distance above the surface, light rays from objects low down near the horizon are bent down, the same way, in fact as are usually the rays of the sun when entering the earth's atmosphere at a low altitude. The effect is to render visible objects which are normally below the horizon. A further occasional effect is produced when the air is appreciably warmer than the sea when an inverted image is seen over the object. This "superior image" is most often seen in high latitudes and wherever the sea surface temperature is abnormally low.'

Having mentioned Lecky I am tempted to repeat here a story which he tells with evident relish and which shows him as a man eager to instruct, but always in a practical and genial way:

'As an instance of ignorance of some of the commonest truths of nature, the writer cannot refrain from introducing the following anecdote. One evening he was pacing the deck with his chief officer and, seeing the sun's lower limb touching the horizon, told his companion that at that moment the whole of the sun's disc was really below it, although from the effects of refraction it was still visible. This the officer could not and *would* not believe. He aptly quoted the saying "seeing is believing, and feeling is the naked truth". However he was convinced some few minutes later by a very familiar experiment. Being firmly seated in front of an empty wash-hand basin, so that the brass plug at the bottom was quite invisible, the basin was about half-filled with water, when, without moving his head, he at once, to his great astonishment, saw the plug.'

After this long and not unlearned digression concerning mirage and refraction, it is time to return to *Mischief*, now stealing very gently away from the coast. We moved that night but only just. The air no more than breathed. It was so still that not a block creaked and even when sailing we made no ripple in the water. Early next morning, smooth though the sea was, I noticed a patch of white water over a submerged rock not a cable's length away. Evidently we were still too close inshore, for this probably was the Pandora reef which the Pilot mentions and locates not over precisely as 'consisting of a ridge of scattered rocks, on which the sea breaks, reported to lie from three to six miles westward of the western extremity of Simiutak' – Simiutak is an island at the mouth of Sondre Stromfjord. The wind now came in strong from SSE so we stood out to the north-west and later gybed to north, the wind being too nearly dead aft to be comfortable. Sure enough before evening we had the father and mother of a crashing gybe which brought me on deck at the run to see if the mast had gone overboard. The hook on the boom guy, a wire rigged to prevent such mishaps, stretching from the end of the boom to the anchor winch, had straightened out leaving the boom free to crash over the moment the wind got behind the sail. Hooks are things which one buys without much thought provided they look man enough for their job, but it would be prudent to buy only those tested or guaranteed as when buying anchor chain. None of the rigging had suffered damage. *Mischief*'s gear is strong, as well it needs to be in view of the strains to which it is at times subjected by some of her crews. My cracked rib, I think, sustained more damage from this gybe than did anything else. In leaping for the deck, galvanized into violent motion by the crash of the boom, I felt it grate. So David cocooned me in yards of sticking plaster, and on account of the pain its removal would inflict I left it on long after the need for it had passed.

The fair wind bustling us northwards did not last long. According to the fickle and variable habit of the wind in those regions it soon died away before coming in light from the north. However, we had crossed the Arctic Circle (N.66° 30′) and had we been so minded might have awarded ourselves a Polar Diploma such as are given to passengers in ships cruising to the North Cape. On 14 July we were off the coast opposite Holsteinborg and among a great many trawlers and a few Portuguese schooners fishing the Hellefiske Bank.

Hellefiske, by the way, which at first sight I translated mentally as 'Hellish good fishing', is in fact the Danish name for a fish not unlike halibut. We sailed close to several dories, either scudding back to the parent schooner under jib and lugsail with a full load of cod, or moored to their long line with the doryman busily starting to haul it in. One man triumphantly waved a big cod which he had just taken off the hook. The dories are flat-bottomed and about fourteen feet long, without buoyancy tanks, without even a fitted thwart, centre-board, or rudder. The absence of inside fittings makes it possible to stow them on the deck of the schooner in nests of six, some sixty dories to a schooner. The mast is stepped for sailing from or back to the schooner and is unstepped while fishing. Those we saw had bright green and yellow sails. The bait used is frozen herring cut up small, or frozen squid, sardines, or caplin. The 3,000-foot-long line has about 500 hooks suspended from it by short lengths of line called snoods. As we sailed by these men we ourselves were suffering no hardships and we could have but a faint idea of what they faced every day, handling such a line with half-frozen hands, tossing up and down in a dinghy in Davis Strait, apart from the task of baiting the 500 hooks, and worse still, removing the hooks from the mouths of heavy, cold, slimy, flapping fish. The doryman stays out until his dory is so full of fish as to leave only a few inches freeboard, before sailing back to the schooner. There, standing up in the heaving dory, he has to gaff his catch one by one on to the schooner's deck. What thorough boatmen and seamen these dorymen must be, and how strong and valuable the tradition that ensures a supply of men eager and proud to follow so hard a calling! None but a doryman could picture with truth the long intervening period spent plying his lone hand far from the parent ship. Alan Villiers, who made a voyage in one of these schooners, thus describes the launching of the dories and their return:

And now here was a vessel which cheerfully put out an anchor upon banks in the open sea, miles from the sight of any land (an anchorage to me had always been at the least a partly-sheltered roadstead) and then proceeded to send away her crew in fragile little boats, without as much as a life-jacket between them or an air-tight tank in any of the boats.

It was wretchedly cold, and raining. The cold sea swept across the schooner's low decks. The one-man dories were neither particularly strong nor especially seaworthy for the work they had to do. They were already laden wih tubs of baited line, buckets of bait, light masts and oiled sails, oars, bailers, anchors and sisal lines, and each held its occupant's personal container, made of wood, brightly painted, and holding his tobacco, a flask of water and a small loaf of bread, a few olives and perhaps a piece of Portuguese ham sausage, and a watch, if he were rich enough to own one. This was generally tied up in old newspaper, where it kept company with a whistle, or a conch to blow in fog. Knives, boat compass, sinkers, jiggers, a honing stone, and grapnels for the long line, completed the dory's cargo. When the doryman himself jumped in, in his heavy woollen clothing and oilskins, and giant leather boots with wooden soles an inch or more thick, the dory had quite a load before it began to look for fish. "Out dories" was the order, and out they went with a will and a rush. There was a tot of brandy for each man who wanted it, and the brandy was dispensed with more generosity than the bait. The cabin-boy poured out the brandy from a kettle. It was traditional for the ship to offer a tot to each doryman before he set out on the day's fishing, just as it was traditional that life-saving gear should never be used. If a man's dory could not save him, nothing could.

The ship was rolling so much, her four yellow masts swinging like pendulums against the grey, wet sky, that I feared some of the dories must be smashed. But these men were experts at getting boats away and a perfect drill had been worked out, probably centuries earlier. The schooner's low sides and low freeboard were a help. The dories were plucked from the nests by overhead hooks which fitted into the protruding grommets spliced into bow and stern. These hooks were manipulated by simple tackles led aloft, with the hauling part by the rail, so that a man or two on each tackle could swing a dory easily from the nest to the rail. Here its doryman hurriedly adjusted its thwarts, saw that the plug was in, climbed the rail and jumped in himself. As the ship rolled towards that side, the tackles were let go at just the right moment and down went the dory with a rush and a thwack upon the sea. Immediately the iron hooks disengaged themselves, alert mariners hauled them back inboard, the doryman shoved off from the side for his life, and dropped astern. Once clear of the ship's side, his little dory seemed smaller than ever, and dancing and leaping in the sea, he rigged his mast and little oiled sail, and away he skimmed towards the horizon, to choose a place to lay out his lines. In a few moments the grey sea all around was covered with the little dories, skimming away like dinghies jockeying for the start at some stormy regatta. But this was no regatta. The shelterless dories looked like an invitation to frostbite, and the black sea was restless and heaving, contorting itself without rhythm as it frequently does on shallow banks. Within a few minutes less than a dozen of our fifty could be seen. Not an accident, not a shout, not a swamped dory, nor a lost piece of gear.

. . . The recall went up at five. Within fifteen minutes the first dory was back loaded to the gunwales. Every few minutes the doryman had to bale furiously to keep himself afloat. For the next two hours we were picking up our dories. Captain Adolfo entered his estimate of each man's catch in the little black book kept for the purpose. The fish were not weighed or measured in any way, but no doryman gaffed up any cod until he had seen the dark countenance of the captain peering down over the rail at his dory. A cold wind came up from the north with a sting of ice in it; nobody worried about it, though the water was lapping at the counters and along the low sides of half the dories. As each came alongside and its catch was recorded, the doryman was handed down a gaff by the deck-boy, and he began at once to heave his fish up and over the rail into the pounds. This in itself was a labour of difficulty, for the cod were big and the schooner's sides high to a dory. The roll of the ship sent the dories jerking in all directions, though they were supposed to be held in position by the deck-boys. There were often four dories discharging along each side, and a dozen others waiting off to take their places. As each dory was discharged it was moved quickly along the ship's side aft, where it was at once hoisted inboard and nested. As each doryman came aboard he joined the hoisting teams, without any time off for a hot drink or a bite to eat, though there was coffee waiting in the galley. No one ate until all the dorymen were back, the fish all in the pounds, and the dories nested and lashed down.

The next time we closed the land we found ourselves at the mouth of Disko Bay. Disko is a large island separated from the mainland by a strait called the Vaigat which extends about sixty miles north-westwards and has a least width of six miles. To go north by way of the Vaigat was longer than by the open sea but we preferred the longer way on account of the scenery, both sides of the strait being mountainous. Moreover Disko Bay and the strait are famous for huge icebergs, some of them up to 300ft. high, calved from the great glaciers of Christianshaab, Jakobshaven, and Ritenbank. These glaciers descend from the ice-cap itself which from here northwards reaches right down to the coast. All along the coast south of Disko there is a strip of ice-free country varying in width from one mile to one hundred miles. The widest part lies inland from Holsteinborg and is of some value as a breeding ground for reindeer.

The mouth of Disko Bay was as far as we got on our passage to the Vaigat. For the best part of a fine, sunny morning we beat up and down across the wide mouth without making any progress. The blue, iceberg-strewn waters of the bay were flecked with white horses by a fierce wind whistling out of the Vaigat. Bowing to superior force we eased the sheets, pointed her head north-west, and went out to sea like a train. The more northing we made the better the weather became. Clammy fog and cold rain were forgotten as one clear, sparkling day followed another, the sun shining perpetually from a cloudless sky. At this time of year, north of Lat. 69°, the sun never set. After sinking towards the west, he hesitated as if in thought, before beginning once more to climb – very strangely to our unaccustomed eyes. We found this phenomenon extremely agreeable. It made the night watches as pleasant as those by day, caused no alteration in our daily life, and abated not a jot our ability to sleep. The brilliant weather we now enjoyed, and continued to enjoy more or less unbroken throughout our stay in these northern parts, seemed to have set in when the sun first remained above the horizon all night, as if before his unceasing vigil the malign spirits of fog and rain dare not show themselves.

The one drawback to these halcyon days was the absence of wind. That north-easterly blow in Disko Bay was the last we were to have. For the rest of the way to Igdlorssuit, a small Eskimo settlement sixty miles north of Disko, we drifted and motored. In these circumstances we had no qualms about using the engine for hours at a time. We were under no critical eyes and we had on board no disciple of Hilaire Belloc who, as a yachtsman, had such a loathing for engines in small boats that, as he averred, he would rather die of thirst laying becalmed than have one in his boat. So we worked our iron tops'l hard, but with discretion. On deck its subdued rumble can easily be tolerated, but in the cabin the noise is barely endurable for the space of a meal. So we often stopped it at meal-times and never dreamt of running it at night, or what our clocks told us was night. Off Hare Island, near the northern entrance of the Vaigat, we began really to see icebergs, spewed out by the tide from this narrow strait in their hundreds to begin their slow journey northwards across the head of Baffin Bay until halted by the winter's sea-ice. Icebergs of all shapes and sizes, some like fortresses with sheer sides, others with pinnacled towers like glistening cathedrals, all floating serenely on the stillest of blue seas.

Now that we were approaching our journey's end, where Charles and I would have to gird up our loins for action, instead of being filled with joyful anticipation, flexing our muscles, doing a little quiet limbering-up on deck, both of us went about our work like a couple of cripples. I had a gathering on one hand and could still feel my rib when breathing – an unavoidable act at

most times and more than ever necessary when climbing. Charles disclosed
for my inspection a toe which looked as if it had been frost-bitten and
required immediate amputation. Naturally he took a more serious view of this
than I did and wanted me to make for Umanak, a small town where, according to the Sailing Directions, there was a hospital. I demurred strongly to this.
As the Arabs say, the camel-driver has his thoughts and the camel he has his.
We were already later than we should have been, and by the time we had
been to Umanak (sixty miles away) and back, and Charles had had his foot
looked at and probably been told not to put it to the ground for a month, we
should have wasted a good many days.

So to Charles's chagrin and with some slight misgiving on my part we held
our course for Ubekjendt Island and the settlement of Igdlorssuit in Lat. 71°
30' Ubekjendt is a name given by the Dutch whalers and means 'unknown';
Igdlorssuit is Eskimo and for that language is a comparatively short name. A
brief glance at the map of these parts had served to disgust me with Eskimo
names. Their length and their doubled consonants combine to make up words
that no ordinary man's tongue is able to pronounce. For their repellent
appearance we must, I suppose, thank Hans Egede who coined the ortho-
graphy for his translation of the Bible into Eskimo. Igdlorssuit lies on the east
side of Ubekjendt Island, an island that rises to over 2,000ft. In my eyes it
looked rounded, featureless, dull; but Rockwell Kent, an artist and a writer,
who in 1933 built a house at Igdlorssuit and lived there for a year, had viewed
it with far different eyes, the eyes of an artist, a man with a soul, as opposed
to a man personifying, as a French writer has put it, *'le mépris de vulgarisation,
du clubalpinisme et des yahous.'* He, Rockwell Kent, thus describes Ubekjendt:

Both by the suggestion of its name and by its position and character – its seagirt
isolation, the simple grandeur of its stark snow-covered table-land and higher peaks,
the dark cliff barrier that forms its eastern shore – there is the glamour of imponderable mystery about the island which dignifies it even at the gateway of a region of
stupendous grandeur. Its cliffs, proclaiming inaccessibility, preclude the thought of
human settlements. When, therefore, on approaching its more mountainous north-
eastern end, where, just ahead, steep mountain walls rise sheer from the water's edge,
the barrier ends, the shore sweeps inward in a mile-wide crescent of smooth strand
and, cupped by mountains, there appears a low and gently sloping verdant foreland,
jewelled with painted buildings, one's spirit, in sudden awakening to a need, exults in
grateful consciousness of its fulfilment.

When we rounded the northern end of the island and started down its east
coast in search of the settlement, we wondered much as to what we should
see. At the time I had not read Rockwell Kent's book and, as I have said, the
island appeared to me an uncommonly dull and barren lump. But it was in the
nature of the settlement we were mainly interested, not the island. Obviously
we could not hope for igloos, for there was no snow below the 2,000ft. level.
Perhaps we expected to see semi-troglodyte dwellings of stones and earth,
their blear-eyed and smoke-grimed inhabitants, clad in furs and reeking of
blubber, crawling out to greet us with cries of 'Pilletay, Pilletay' ('Give,
give'), as we read of their doing in accounts by McClintock and other early
explorers in search of the North-west Passage. It was therefore with mixed

feelings that we finally brought in view a row of some twenty gaily-painted wooden houses (Rockwell's 'jewels') straggling along the beach and in the background what was obviously a church. However, we were cheered when with the aid of binoculars we made out numbers of husky dogs, kayaks, sledges, and racks of drying shark-meat. We felt that the last item should have been blubber, but shark-meat it proved to be.

The settlement lay in no proper bay, there was merely a slight indentation of the coast-line. In such windless waters a sheltered anchorage seems hardly needed; anyway the island protected us from seaward and we were surrounded by land, the nearest being the island of Upernivik some eight miles to the east. Compared with Ubekjendt, or indeed with any island in the world, this really was a magnificently mountainous island. It fairly bristled with peaks, their rock spires and snow domes at that moment aglow in the westering sun, while three glaciers, like broad, white highways, led from the waters of the fjord up into the mountains. These same waters, we noticed, were thickly strewn with icebergs, several smaller specimens lying grounded in our vicinity. We let go the anchor in five fathoms about a hundred yards from the beach. For our first night there we deemed it prudent to set an anchor watch. Drifting icebergs are dangerous and (who knew?) the natives might be hostile.

CHAPTER SEVEN

At Igdlorssuit

BEFORE LONG a boat-load of natives came aboard. Among them, by putting two and two together and judging from what I had been told, I recognized one Bertheson, schoolmaster, pastor, and leading seal-hunter. As well as lesser fry the boat contained a tough-looking character who, I was delighted to see, wore a pair of sealskin trousers. I had understood from my friend Dr Drever that Bertheson the schoolmaster spoke some known language, implying, so far as I was concerned, that he spoke either English or American. Nothing of the kind. Eskimo or Danish – I could take my pick – were all he had to offer, so that our conversation, limited to grins and handshakes, was about as useful and intelligent as that between two apes. Most men visiting Greenland for the first time would at least take the trouble to glance at an Eskimo dictionary, and having had their interest in that language quickly quenched by the length of the words and the superfluity of consonants, would turn to Danish as the next best thing and swot up a few phrases or words. For my part, the true-born Englishman, I set out on my travels with the firm intention of speaking (if speech is necessary) in English, whether to an Eskimo, a Chinaman, or a Canoe Indian. Out of regard for their weak minds one might speak it slowly and clearly so that any fool, one might think, would

understand, but that was as far as I was prepared to go. With some acumen
the schoolmaster had brought with him an English-Danish dictionary, fearing
possibly that his own Danish was a little rusty and that we might fire at him
with words too high for his understanding. With the aid of this we learnt some
striking facts such as his age and the age of his wife, facts which were more
trouble to elicit than they were really worth. When a sufficient number of our
cigarettes had been consumed the party broke up.

I don't pretend that it is not a good thing to be able to talk to the natives in
their own tongue, to glean a few facts about them and their country at first
hand even though the facts may later prove to be nonsense or lies. Indeed, in
my more sombre moments I often think it a waste of time to travel unless one
can talk to the natives – which, of course, is one good reason I have for
preferring to travel if possible where there are none. But I would not have
taken much to heart our inability on this occasion to hold a *conversazione*,
were it not that Dr Drever had suggested that when we went up the fjord in
search of mountains we should take with us two Igdlorssuit men to supply us
with local knowledge, fish, and possibly seal-meat. Obviously we had now no
hope of putting to them this interesting proposition, not to mention the
important details of food and pay which would have to be settled. We must do
without them. Such an arrangement would no doubt have provided amusement for both parties but apart from that I don't think we missed their
services. Fish we could catch ourselves and in the fjords where we went there
were no seals to be shot.

To show what we could do we caught some fish for breakfast before we
turned in that night. They were what are called fjord cod, smaller and less
firm-fleshed than their fellows of the open sea, despised by the natives but
welcome to us. Although we expected to be here several days, and although
one could see from the boat pretty well all that Igdlorssuit had to offer in the
way of sight-seeing, we lost no time in going ashore fully armed with cameras.
In fact we spent five days here, mainly on account of Charles who was now
lying up nursing his foot, still convinced that only a visit to Umanak would
save it. Like the rest of the Greenlanders the people of Igdlorssuit are far
from being pure Eskimos, yet they and their way of life appeared to us more
like the real thing. The huskies, of which each family had some twenty, the
sledges lying about, the kayaks carefully stored high up out of the dogs' reach,
the racks of shark-meat drying in the sun, the women sewing skins on a new-
built kayak, all these led us to believe we were seeing life in the Arctic, even
while we trudged along the sandy beach sweating in the sun and cursing the
heat and the mosquitoes. A walk of about half a mile, the sea on one hand
and on the other a gravel fan sparsely covered with grass and a few flowers
(Rockwell's 'verdant foreland'), brought us to the heart of Igdlorssuit life –
the store and the post-office, and the shed where barrels of sharks' liver
were stored. At least the revolting stuff we watched being weighed was, I am
told, shark liver, and several times up the fjord we saw the fins of these
creatures sticking out of the water. The store, owned by the Greenland
Trading Company, buys all the sealskins and shark liver brought in and sells
all that the community needs in the way of food, clothing, household goods,

beer, tobacco, tools, implements, fishing gear, rifles, shotguns, ammunition, and fuel for their motor boats. Thus although their occupations have not changed and they still live, though indirectly, by their skill in sealing and fishing, yet their way of life has greatly changed from the self-sufficiency of the old days when the seal provided their clothing, boots, tents, and boats, food for men and dogs, fuel for cooking and heating, and oil for lighting.

The three or four motor boats anchored off the settlement were used for going to various islands where at this time of year seals might be found. Generally a kayak was carried on board for use in the final stages of the hunt. Hunting so wary a creature as the seal calls for no little skill and patience even with modern firearms. The only evidence of seals we saw were mere fleeting glimpses of a head poked above water and immediately submerged. The best chance of a shot is when they are hauled out on a berg or floe, or ashore on an islet. They must be shot through the head or they will roll into the water and sink or escape. In winter they are netted or harpooned at breathing holes, or stalked on the ice, the hunter behaving as much like a seal as he can and taking hours over the stalk. A few seals were still being got in July when we were there. I remember seeing a dory with two seals tied behind being towed along by a team of huskies. The beach is steep-to and the water so calm that there was no difficulty in keeping the dory afloat while the dogs walked along the beach. The seals are not the fur-seal, but the skins of these ringed and hooded seals are valuable to the fur trade. As privileged visitors and prospective buyers we penetrated to the back premises of the store where the skins were kept. We were not allowed to buy the quality skins – lovely, silvery fawn skins in prime condition which were reserved for export to Denmark – but we all invested in a few of the lower quality at prices in the region of £1, depending upon the condition. From his purchase Terry Ward knocked up a useful pair of bedroom-slippers. My thoughts were running on sealskin trousers and the figure I should cut in them at home. This novel idea never came to fruition though it seemed to me to be a more proper use for sealskins than the elegant coat for my sister that, as I should have anticipated, they eventually made.

Husky dogs and children, alike, swarmed in Igdlorssuit. Both seemed to be well cared for, the dogs being fed daily on shark meat. In late winter, when the fjord is finally frozen over, when hunting parties go out and when visits are paid to neighbouring settlements, the dogs earn their summer keep by pulling sledges. For the children our visit was a godsend. They played on and around *Mischief*, showed off for our benefit in a kayak, and followed us diligently on our walks. Apparently the sensible arrangement prevailed of closing the school entirely for the summer months. The children were well clad in European clothes – brightly-coloured anoraks were a favourite – as were their elders, apart from one or two old-timers and the young he-men who affected sealskin trousers. Nearly everyone wore sealskin boots. One woman on seeing me approach with a camera darted into her house and reappeared in full-dress costume, with beaded vest and beautifully embroidered white sealskin boots reaching well up the thigh. This dress, we were told, was worn on Sundays for church, but in summer, by a less sensible arrangement, the church, too, seemed to be closed. Both in manner and appearance the people struck me as being very like Sherpas, the same short, sturdy figures and Mongolian features, their brown cheeks suffused with red; cheerful, happy-go-lucky, and always ready to laugh either at us or themselves. The oldest inhabitant was a delightful character; a man like a barrel, as broad as he was long, who walked about (sealskin trousers, of course) aided by a stick, a benign smile on his leathery, wrinkled face and a short cutty pipe stuck firmly in his toothless mouth. They shopped freely at the store buying sugar, flour, jam, sweets, tinned meats and fruits, so that their normal diet seemed to be as humdrum as our own. It must be a sad change from their former régime of blubber, seal meat, and sea birds. In time one can get used to anything and no doubt they still eat enough of these natural, wholesome foods to prevent them from getting scurvy. They certainly looked healthy enough and in little need of the services of a sort of district nurse who visited them about once a fortnight in a small motor vessel from Umanak which brought also mail, stores, and passengers.

Having undertaken to collect plants for the Natural History Museum I spent most of my time botanizing around the settlement where flowers might be found growing up to the 500ft. level. I now had lumbago – 'a trifling sum of misery new added to the foot of my account' – so that I had to be careful when bending to dig out a plant for fear of not being able to straighten up. Really, I thought, I should be far better employed exploring the Brighton front or Cheltenham from a bath-chair rather than Greenland; to be joined there no doubt, in the very near future, by Charles, provided that vehicles of that kind were procurable on easy terms. But Charles was now on the mend. Our second-hand accounts of life's busy scene in Igdlorssuit would no longer serve. He must see for himself. So rising from his bed of pain he announced his intention of going ashore, and in order to save him a long walk we rowed the dinghy to a landing place just below the store. The populace, scenting something unusual afoot, had gathered in strength and they were well rewarded for their pains. In yachting cap and gumboots, his beard a sable silver, monocle in eye and supported by an ice-axe, Charles stepped ashore like a slimmer edition of King Edward VII landing at Cowes from the Royal Yacht. The crowd were speechless with delight. At last, they thought, the captain of *Mischief* had condescended to visit them.

Evidently it was time for us to move. We could loiter on the way and I hoped that by the time I had done a little mountain reconnaissance Charles would be fit to climb. When Dr Drever had first mentioned the possibilities of this Umanak fjord region and had showed me a map, I had plumped for the Qioqe peninsula as the most promising place to begin. This peninsula, some twenty-five miles long and a bare eight miles wide, juts out from the mainland behind the island of Upernivik. We could not therefore see the mountains from Igdlorssuit but according to the map there were plenty of them from 5,000ft. to 7,000ft. high. Maps for a good portion of the west coast have been published on a scale of quarter inch to the mile. These are fairly accurate but in a complicated mountain region such as the Qioqe peninsula we found that some of the peaks marked were not easily reconciled with those on the ground. My choice, as will be seen, turned out to have been a poor one. It was no doubt influenced by the fact that there lay the highest mountain of that region, probably the highest in West Greenland, a peak of 2,310 metres, or about 7,500ft. It is generally true in mountaineering, if not always in life, that 'we needs must love the highest when we see it'. Just before sailing, however, I learnt that the peak had been climbed by an Italian party in the previous summer, but by then the Qioqe peninsula had become for me a fixed idea and we went to it with no very clear idea of what we intended doing there. Plans should certainly be flexible but this was flexible to the point of vacuity.

This Italian expedition of 1960 had been remarkable in more than one way. Most remarkable of all is the fact that the leader, Piero Ghiglioni (who was killed in a car accident later that same year), was aged 77. (A friend who sent me an account of the expedition remarked when he sent it: 'There is hope for you yet.') But Piero Ghiglioni was quite exceptional, a man who had spent a life-time climbing in all parts of the world and who seemed to have the secret of eternal youth. He and his two companions, a doctor and an Italian guide, in the course of three weeks, with the use of a motor boat chartered at Umanak, climbed this highest peak which they named Punta Italia, the highest peak on Disko Island, 6,188ft., and the highest peak on the Nagssuak peninsula, 6,981ft. Moreover all these peaks were climbed in a day from sea-level – no camps, no bivouacs – the climbing of Punta Italia taking eighteen hours. The party enjoyed the same settled weather as we did, and they had before them a clear-cut plan with three definite objectives. They did not mess about looking for a mountain to climb, as we were to do.

Before we left Igdlorssuit we heard of another curious piece of climbing news. Terry Ward, no more gifted as a linguist than the rest of us, soon acquired a knack of conversing more or less intelligibly with these Eskimo, partly by speech and partly by intuition or guess-work. I have often noticed when in foreign parts with the army that the so-called other ranks, men with no pretension to knowing any language but their own, often got on better with the local people, and learnt more of what was going on, than those who had had a supposedly better education and even some smattering of the language. Terry came back on board one day with the story that a week or two before four members of a climbing party of unknown nationality had been killed when climbing on the peninsula just north of Qioqe. We had no knowledge of any other party being in the area and to me it seemed an extraordinary story. Perhaps for once Terry's intuition had been at fault and this heavy death roll pertained to seals, sharks, or polar bears rather than men. However, when we got back to Godthaab the story was confirmed by the Commissioner of Police who was extremely upset about it. A party of nine Belgians had been climbing, four of whom, three men and a woman, had been killed, and the Commissioner had had to organize some attempt at recovering the bodies. Moreover some hard things had been said by the Belgian Minister in Copenhagen about the lack of help that had been forth-coming – as if any help could be expected for mountaineers in such a region, or as if a party of nine were not sufficient to help themselves. At present there are no restrictions on those who wish to climb in Greenland, except for scientific parties or for expeditions venturing on to the ice-cap when, I believe, a deposit has to be made against the possibility of a rescue party having to be mounted. And it is to be hoped that in so fine a field as West Greenland no restrictions upon small climbing parties will have to be made. Mountaineers are aware of the risks they run and in a place where no aid can be expected, where in case of trouble they must rely upon themselves, it behoves them to act accordingly.

CHAPTER EIGHT

Among the Mountains

ON THE same afternoon, having extracted Charles from the thick of an admiring crowd, we got our anchor and sailed out. The wind soon died. After drifting on to a large iceberg and fending off with the boat-hook we started the engine. We had about forty miles to go to the anchorage I had in mind, a bay at the root of the Qioqe peninsula with the remarkable name of Kangerdlugssuakavaak. 'Kangerd' means fjord – the fjords between which our peninsula lay were called Kangerdlugssuaq and Kangerdluarssuk. Since most of the forty miles would have to be done under the engine we anchored for the night on the south side of Upernivik Island off the snout of a dying glacier. In the fjords it is difficult to find water shallow enough to anchor in without being perilously near the rocky shore. Usually the most likely place is off a glacier, or a stream that emerges from a glacier, where silt and débris have accumulated.

Early next morning a small floe got under our bowsprit and we had to move to another anchorage. I spent an hour ashore looking for plants. In West Greenland there are several hundred species of flowering plants, grasses, and ferns. In our short visit we collected only some sixty species but many of the flowers were no doubt over by the time we arrived. There are many familiar forms such as buttercups, dandelions, saxifrage, campions, poppies, harebells, willow herb; and of the larger kinds, creeping willow, dwarf birch, crowberry, and bilberry. As we motored up Kangerdluarssuk, with the Qioqe peninsula on our port hand, we met with a bitter wind blowing straight from the ice-cap. The day was unusually cloudy with cloud down to about 500ft. so that we saw nothing of the mountains but their lower cliffs, broken occasionally by steep and narrow valleys filled with ice. At its upper end the fjord widens. In the middle lies the small island of Qeqertak; in the south-east corner a massive glacier descends from the inland ice, filling that part of the fjord with big icebergs; and in the north-east corner was the bay with the long, unpronounceable name where we proposed to stay, a bay well protected from drifting ice. We dropped anchor in seven fathoms off a wide gravel fan left by a retreating glacier. Even so we found the stern touched the bottom about twenty yards from the shore. We had to lay out a kedge anchor astern to keep her lying parallel to the beach.

David was eager to set foot on a glacier, so next day he and I took a walk up the valley which runs right across the root of the peninsula to Kangerdlugssuaq fjord on the north side. In winter this valley is used as a sledge route. Rockwell Kent describes a journey made in January from Igdlorssuit to Umanak when, owing to open water, they could not sledge direct to Umanak and had to sledge up the northern fjord, haul the sledge over the peninsula by this valley, and continue down the southern fjord and along the coast to Umanak. A short walk up the gravel fan brought us on to the glacier itself which, fortunately for David, for he had on only shoes, was smooth, unbroken ice covered with gravel and flat stones. After about three miles of easy going, passing on our left the mouth of the valley whence the glacier descended, we reached the moraine on the far side of the glacier and were soon on the low divide looking down to the northern fjord. Thick mist covered the fjord while we basked in sunshine. On the evidence alone of this short excursion I began to fear that we had come to the wrong place for a climbing centre. Certainly the glacier led into the heart of the peninsula in the direction of the bigger peaks, including Punta Italia, but its ice-fall, filling the valley that we had passed, seemed to me an effective barrier. The peaks were too far to be climbed from the boat so that we should have to carry loads up the ice-fall, and besides that they looked inaccessible from the glacier head. I did, however, notice a peak of about 6,500ft. which was within reach and which could be got at by way of a steep but ice-free valley less than a mile from the anchorage.

Charles, too, had been out for the day exercising his foot. When we compared notes I gathered that in his view this ice-fall was a minor obstacle. In the course of many years of climbing, mostly in the Himalaya, the times I have failed to come to grips with some peak on which I had set my heart, having been balked and forced to retreat by some ice-fall, are sad memories. Most ice-falls, I admit, can be overcome with time, patience, or possibly ladders, as, for example the ice-fall leading to the West Cwm on the south side of Everest. But unless the goal beyond is all-important they are best left alone by small parties like ours, especially if loads have to be carried up them. Charles, as I have said, did not agree. He judged this ice-fall to be, so to speak, a piece of cake, and persuaded me to try it in spite of my conviction that we were wasting our time. He concluded by saying there was nothing he liked better than worrying his way through an intricate ice-fall. My reply, couched in phrases that might have shocked anyone but Charles, was that I thoroughly disliked messing about in them. However, since I had had my way over the little matter of not going to Umanak I thought that this harmless whim of his should be humoured.

Accordingly next day we started up the ice-fall. I must say Charles did his best while I studiously refrained from any discouraging remarks and even tried to show the enthusiasm I did not feel. As we got higher even a one-eyed man might have seen that there was no likelihood of finding a route up any of the big peaks beyond had we surmounted the difficulties of the ice-fall, but

Charles was so engrossed in mastering it and showing that it could be mastered, that the uselessness of doing so hardly occurred to him. Nothing daunted, Charles pressed on, only a little astonished to find that after one terrace had been laboriously gained there was always another above. We lunched precariously, surrounded by crevasses and seracs in hideous confusion. Shortly afterwards, when we were still some 200ft. below what really was the top we were stopped by a series of gaping crevasses, around, through, or over which, Charles had to admit there was no way. He had had his fun, so on the way back to the boat I pointed out the 6,500ft. peak I proposed we should tackle next day. The steep valley leading to it narrowed higher up to a gully packed with snow. By way of the gully we could reach a high snow shoulder and possibly the rock peak beyond. We could not see what lay between shoulder and summit but the mountain was well worth trying. In spite of the encouraging example of a so much older man, I had some misgivings about my own ability to emulate Piero Ghiglioni's feats. I asked Charles how he felt about climbing 6,500ft. in the day. Many years ago, at a much higher altitude, I had climbed 6,000ft. and back in a day; and Charles searching his memory, thought he had done as much before and could no doubt do it again.

The condemned men ate a hearty breakfast – cod steaks, if I remember right – and at 8.30 we had ourselves rowed ashore. Not the least blessing of climbing in Greenland is that one can start at a reasonable hour; no turning out in the small hours, as one must in the Alps, to cook and swallow some food, that were it food for the gods would be revolting at such a time, and then to stumble out into the cold darkness guided by the feeble light of a candle lantern. All this to avoid being be-nighted, of which in Greenland there is happily no fear. Some loose scree in the valley took a little of the shine out of us but when we reached the gully we found almost continuous beds of hard snow up which we could kick our way. We lunched just below the shoulder, having climbed about 3,000ft. We continued kicking steps until when about 500ft. below a flat snow ridge at the foot of the final rock peak we were obliged to cut steps. Charles, who was in front at the time, thought we might avoid this by making use of some old avalanche snow off to our right. When this proved delusive we came back and I took over the step-cutting, for Charles, even at this early stage, was beginning to suffer from mountaineer's foot – the inability to put one in front of the other.

At four o'clock we came out on the level ridge whence we looked straight down to the waters of the fjord and across it to the great glacier rolling down from the inland ice. A mountain prospect from a high place is enthralling but to look out over sea and mountains is, I think, even more moving – to feel at once the immensity of the one and the steadfast, unchanging nature of the other, both indifferent to man's presence and yet to many men an inspiration and a solace. However that may be, that which concerned us more than the majestic view was the formidable aspect of the rock and ice ridge which sprang upwards towards the summit almost from where we stood. There was nearly a thousand feet of it. It might improve on acquaintance, but to two tired men it looked sufficiently daunting. Charles now admitted that he had shot his bolt and while I might have gone farther I did not feel capable of looking after him as well as myself on what would evidently be the hardest part of the climb. Reluctantly, and keenly disappointed, we accepted defeat. For all that it had been a day of rare enjoyment, of strenuous endeavour in glorious surroundings and in flawless weather with only our own feebleness to blame for our failure. At 8.30 that evening, dejected and humbled, we rowed back to the boat.

Before trying this fairly long climb we had had only the one short day on the ice-fall. We preferred to attribute our failure to lack of exercise rather than to excess of years. But I did not want to sweat up that long gully again and risk another breakdown. I felt we should move to a base where we should have more scope. Before quitting the fjord, however, we wanted to take some pictures of *Mischief* under sail, mainly for the sake of the film which Terry Ward was engaged upon. The wide head of the fjord, tolerably free from icebergs, afforded a good opportunity provided we had some wind. With the first breeze we sailed to the little island of Qeqertak preparatory to sending off the dinghy with the camera party. We had, of course, first to walk round the island, for islands have the power of suggesting to those that visit them that they are treading unexplored territory. Having hoisted sail and got under way we promptly went aground. But she soon came off and we made several runs across the fjord, taking care to have the big glacier as a background when the pictures were taken.

While Charles and I had been amusing ourselves on the mountains the crew had set about giving *Mischief* a new look. At Godthaab we had not been able to find any cream-coloured paint like that on her topsides. At David's suggestion we bought instead some bright yellow paint; he thought that with black bulwarks and yellow topsides she would look pretty rakish so this new colour scheme was now adopted. All Danish ships plying to Greenland, and all the local fishing boats, are painted a standard red-lead colour, presumably to make them conspicuous when among ice. Personally I liked the new colour scheme, but when we returned to Lymington, where yachts are either glossy white or nothing, I failed to detect any gasps of admiration from frequenters of the Yard. To finish this as well as other work we stayed yet another day at this anchorage. Among other jobs the starboard topping lift needed renewal and besides working on board we spent time ashore washing both our clothes and ourselves in a fresh-water pool. Although the water came from a snow-bed not far away, thanks to the continuous sunshine it was not really cold. The weather continued unbrokenly fine and even if the barometer fell the weather sensibly ignored it and remained serenely cloudless and calm.

On 29 July we had a long day's motoring back down the fjord and through the narrow winding channel called Inukavsait between the tip of the peninsula and Upernivik Island. Each glacier we passed we scanned closely as a possible way up into the mountains, but most of them were mere ice torrents. The scenery in Inukavsait is spectacular. Gaunt cliffs tower over it on both sides and at the half-way point, where the fjord narrows and makes a sharp bend, we appeared to be heading for an unbroken face of rock. Beyond this, on the peninsula side the cliffs receded and we made for a beach where a glacier stream debouched. At 8 pm we anchored close inshore opposite the widest part of a detritus fan. After supper, alarmed at the sight of a big berg drifting past within spitting distance at the rate of about two knots, we decided to move to a little cove on the north side of the fan. With no winch to help we had a tussle getting the stern anchor and having reached our new anchorage we found a berg had grounded there leaving us no room to swing. Back at the first anchorage we set an anchor watch, for there were many bergs about drifting up and down with the tide. Some we recognized as old friends that we had passed earlier in the day.

Owing to a couple of days of bad weather and a relapse in Charles's condition – knee trouble this time – we spent nine days in this uneasy anchorage for the sake of climbing one peak. Near the landing place we found traces of recent visits by Eskimos and the reason for these visits became clear when on walking upstream as far as the entrance to a gorge we saw the cliffs were occupied by a colony of glaucus gulls. This was the only bird colony we saw and Terry spent a lot of time on top of the cliff and below it trying to take pictures. Apart from the gulls, a few snow buntings and sandpipers, and rare families of ptarmigan, were the only living things we saw on land, excepting always mosquitoes and midges. They were particularly bad along the banks of the stream which was also the richest collecting ground for flowers. I was nearly driven mad and remembered with shame how at Godthaab, where some of the Danish workmen wore head veils, I had thought them 'cissy'.

The only peak that could be reached from the boat appeared not to be intended for climbing, at least not by Charles and me. Evidently we should have to try up the glacier, the stream from which had cut the gorge where the gulls lived. There was too much water in the gorge for us to walk up it and we had to make a long, high detour crossing a series of old moraines and boulder-strewn slopes. On this sort of ground Charles is greatly handicapped because, as a result of his adventure in Spain, he can focus only one eye at a time. Boulder-hopping is trying for a fit man with two good eyes and it is easy enough to take a bad toss. Charles had to move with caution and deliberation and he had not the turn of speed to make up time when on easy ground. Having sat down on a boulder to wait for Charles I had frequently felt the force of the Nepali saying that 'he who rests on a stone is twice glad'. Heavens knows, I myself move slowly enough nowadays but when climbing with Charles I felt how apt were the poignant lines of one Joseph Cottle, a very minor poet:

> 'How steep, how painful the ascent:
> It needs the evidence of close deduction
> To know that we shall ever gain the top.'

When at 1 pm we finally reached the glacier we were thankful to find that this glacier really was a broad highway, rising very gradually – *une pente insensible,* as the French guide-books say – tolerably free from crevasses, and for the most part clean, dry ice. After going for three hours we had at last got on to *névé* and found the snow soft and deep, and since the col we were making for was still distant we decided to call it a day. But the excursion had not been altogether fruitless. Up a side valley I had noticed a nice-looking peak up which there seemed to be a way.

By the time we got back to the boat we had been walking for twelve hours, so the next day we remained on board. We started to paint the deck with oil and red ochre, a mixture that takes so long to dry that only half the deck can be done at a time. Charles's knee then swelled up again and another three days passed before he pronounced himself fit for action. Upon this we made up four loads and set off for the glacier accompanied by John Wayman and Michael as assistant porters. Unpractised though they were in the aggravating game of boulder-hopping they moved a lot faster than we did. We put the camp by a lake in the ablation valley alongside the glacier. It was only 1,200ft. up and a long way from the peak but we reckoned that a bed on warm gravel instead of on cold ice would compensate us for the extra toil. Having supped richly on pemmican and breakfasted on porridge – for we did ourselves well – we set off about eight o'clock of a dull morning. Two hours later when we turned off the main glacier into the side valley we found it to be a glacier-filled cirque, its head overhung by threatening seracs and its floor strewn with their débris. Charles viewed the scene with disfavour. His mountaineering principles are quite rightly orthodox and they teach that objective dangers such as this are to be shunned. In reality the risk was slight because our route lay up a rock buttress at the head of the cirque and once on the buttress we should be out of the line of fire. The weak point of the buttress lay up a yellow rock gully which proved steeper than it looked and very loose, so loose that we deemed it safer to climb unroped, lest the rope should dislodge something on to the man below – in this case Charles. By lunch-time we had reached easier ground on top of the buttress.

The cloud had thickened and a penetrating wind began to blow as we sat on a wet rock ledge to eat and to view the prospect ahead. It was very discouraging. The buttress that from below had appeared to lead direct to a snow slope, we now found to be cut off from it by a wide, shallow scoop of bare ice, an ice scoop that had been polished by débris falling from some ice cliffs a few hundred feet above. Below us the scoop heeled over steeply to disappear from view. For the moment the cliffs looked stable enough; the difficulty lay in the fact that we had about 150ft. of ice to cross, so that, with only our 100ft. rope, at one stage both of us would be on the ice at once and neither able to check a slip. Having canvassed all possible alternatives, and having decided that the snow beyond the scoop looked suspiciously thin, we were in two minds about going on or giving up. Manlier thoughts prevailed. While Charles belayed himself to the rocks I started cutting steps across the ice; good, large steps, too, for we should have to return the same way. Having run out all the rope I cut a stance and Charles embarked on the ice. Passing below me he cut on till he had reached the snow which, as we had feared, proved to be lying thinly on ice. However, after another rope's length we were in deeper, safer snow and moved freely across it to gain a rock ridge. This steep ridge was also very loose so we unroped again and climbed steadily up into the mist. An ice slope lying at an easy angle, up which I quickly nicked steps, led finally to the snow summit where – *longo intervallo* –I was joined by

Charles. We had got our peak and by bad luck on quite the worst day we had had. Visibility extended to only a few yards and merely the fact that on all sides the slope fell away showed that we were on the top. The height by aneroid was 5,800ft. It had taken us nine hours from camp. All went well on the descent, our steps were still good, and at the top of the buttress we once more unroped. Charles has a flair for remembering a route. Without him, in spite of the odd stones we had placed to mark various pitches, I should have had difficulty in sticking to our line of ascent. At 9 pm we were off the rocks. I reached the tent by 11.30 pm, but by the time I had brewed pemmican and Charles had arrived to eat it, it was one o'clock in the morning.

It was raining when we packed up and started down next day. On arriving at the beach, expecting to be wafted swiftly on board for a pint or two of tea, I was peeved to see that *Mischief* was on the move. Threatened by an iceberg the crew had had to get the anchor with all speed and move to yet another anchorage. At this place, where we had had to stay so long, we enjoyed little peace. It put me in mind of a remark in the Admiralty Pilot about an anchorage on the North African coast: 'Anchoring in this bight must be prompted by necessity and not by any hope of tranquillity.' We maintained an anchor watch all the time and that night at 2 am in my watch a strong puff of wind caused the anchor to drag. Having started the engine and moved to a fresh spot we let go the heavy fisherman-type anchor. Partly to save ourselves labour we had trusted to the CQR pattern anchor, one which holds well in mud or sand but is not much use on a rocky bottom. A CQR anchor is relatively half the weight of a conventional pattern anchor. It is stockless, shaped like a ploughshare, and depends for its holding power upon digging itself in. CQR, I believe, stands for an abbreviated, or perhaps an American version, of the word 'secure'. In the fjords where one has to anchor, as it were, on a mountain side, where the bottom may shelve from six fathoms to twenty fathoms in as many yards, an anchor is easily dislodged.

Mountaineering is happily not yet a competitive sport. There are no medals to be won, no records to be broken. The mountains, whether or not we overcome them, are the prize, and there are as well the rewards which each individual climber finds for himself – health, peace of mind, high endeavour, adventure, a sense of achievement, staunch companionship, and at the end of it all a store of mountain memories. It is not a competitive sport, as I have said, but at times the old Adam will out. A prime example of this, of course, was the struggle for Everest which ended in almost becoming an international affair. Similarly, on a minor scale, I could not help feeling that our activities, if such they could be called, compared ill with the achievements of that swift-moving successful Italian party of the previous year. It was now 8 August, the season was advancing, but we had still time for another foray provided Charles's legs held out. As I pointed out to him, 'strenuousness is the immortal path and sloth is the way of death' – a truth that elicited merely a non-committal grunt. Conditions were certainly less favourable now than earlier in the summer; on the lower slopes the snow had turned to ice while higher up it was soft and wet. Upernivik Island, where we should have gone in the first place, seemed now our best bet.

Accordingly we got under way and after entering Kangerdlugssuaq fjord we turned westwards and coasted along the north side of the island. On the way we had a look at the glacier leading up to a mountain called Sneepyramiden (7,217ft.) on the peninsula north of Qioqe. It was, I think, while attempting this mountain that the Belgian party had met with disaster. There was evidently no way inland by that glacier which lay in a narrow gorge and was guarded by a wall of black ice only few hundred yards from the shore. We felt no qualms about writing that off. Near the north-west corner of the island there is a group of islets and around them a vast congregation of icebergs had gathered, many of them probably aground. Going dead slow we forced a spectacular passage between two sheer-sided monsters each about 100ft. high. While Terry kept the ciné-camera whirring, I kept an anxious eye on the narrow gap of water where any suspicion of a light green colour would betray the presence of a projecting tongue of ice. Threading our way through these and other concentrated dangers we anchored early in the afternoon off the first of the three big glaciers on the west side of Upernivik. Having lost our 7-lb. lead we had to do our sounding now with a home-made lead consisting of a three-foot length of iron piping filled with sand and plugged with a bit of wood. It was a cold, wet day with low clouds. In the evening, when the clouds lifted to reveal a very broken ice-fall, we decided to move on to the glacier three miles farther south directly opposite Igdlorssuit. Here, after nosing round taking soundings, we found a good berth in six fathoms only about fifty yards from the snout of the glacier.

Wasting no time in reconnaissance four of us started next morning carrying loads for a two-night camp. We made good progress, first on moraine and then on dry ice, and at 2 pm at a height of about 2,000ft. began to look for a camp site. At first we feared that Charles and I would have to sleep on ice or, as a refinement of cruelty, on stones on top of ice. But presently we found a little hollow on the mountain side above the glacier which provided all we needed; a few minutes' work with ice-axes levelled a tent site, and at hand a snow-bed supplied us with water. A short walk up the glacier in the evening revealed a peak well within our grasp.

On that climb the finding of some yellow poppies at 3,000ft. and the view from the summit were the only happy memories, for to tell the truth we had a fearful trudge. Near the summit the wide, gently sloping, uncommonly dull snowface up which we had slogged all morning narrowed to a ridge of red rock crowned with a series of rock gendarmes. One side of the ridge, as if it had been sliced off with a knife, fell sheer to the glacier 3,000ft. below. The height was 6,370ft., high enough for us to see over the surrounding peaks and islands to the open sea dotted with icebergs and to the distant mountains of Disko Island. We realized now what we had missed by not coming here first and staying here, where there were glaciers on which one could move freely and many unclimbed peaks of great character. Instead of buzzing, as we had done, like elderly bees from flower to flower gathering very little honey, had we but established our camp high on Upernivik we might have drunk our fill. With these sad thoughts we turned our backs to the mountains. Next morning we carried the loads down and having stowed for good our boots and ice-axes we motored over to Igdlorssuit.

CHAPTER NINE

Homeward Bound

WE HAD only to make our farewells and perhaps buy a few more skins, so we stayed but the night. We had had no dealings with the people of Igdlorssuit other than over the store counter for cash, but they were such a friendly, likeable lot that we were sorry to leave. Our thoughts turned often to them and we wondered what life was like there when the sun no longer rose over Upernivik, when the blue waters of the fjords turned to ice. I suppose really to grasp what life in the Arctic means one must winter there. Perhaps instead of spending the winter months in the mud of Lymington river it would be more in keeping with *Michief's* character, as well as a rewarding experience, if she wintered for once in Greenland ice.

We were now homeward bound, or on the first leg of our homeward journey, for we had still to call at Godthaab. Wind or no wind we made a point of hoisting sail when leaving Igdlorssuit, a gesture that no doubt was largely wasted on the natives who would only conclude from it that we were in no hurry to get anywhere. That evening we got no farther than the south end of Ubekjendt where we anchored for the night. On the next day, too, we did more motoring than sailing, finally coming to anchor at the mouth of the Vaigat in a place where we caught more cod than we could eat. On the way north we had been driven out of the Vaigat by a northerly wind and now a southerly wind did its best to stop us going south. We beat against it all day, made good about thirty miles, and anchored for the night in thick fog close to the Disko shore.

The wind died in the night. We were motoring as we passed by Qutdligssat where the coal-mine is situated. It is the strangest coal-mine – a high yellow cliff and at its foot at sea-level a wide black seam where the coal is dug. A couple of small coasters anchored close in were loading coal from lighters and hard by them lay some large icebergs aground. On this grey, sunless day, the ships, the ice, and the cliff streaked with coal-dust looked forlorn and grim. The yearly output of some 8,000 tons is barely enough to cover the consumption in Greenland. Soon after passing the mine we ran into dense fog. So far north as this the compass is too sluggish to steer by and we adopted the method of keeping the land close aboard. Though instinct may prompt one to keep well away from dangers it is generally a sound rule when navigating in narrow waters or in fog to keep the danger always in sight. But as visibility was less than fifty yards it was not easy to keep the shore in sight and the boat afloat at the same time, for, as we presently discovered, the coast here is not steep-to. When we finally took the ground and came to a more or less

318

grinding halt the skipper was at the helm – a circumstance that allowed no blame to be apportioned to anyone, not even to the compass. We were merely victims of fate. Having for the moment lost touch with the shore and thinking it was time we knew where we were, I had begun closing with it and soon found it. Had we been using the lead, as we should have been, this could not have happened. The tide was ebbing and our efforts to winch her off with a kedge anchor failed. Luckily the bottom was sand but when she took on a heavy list we had to shore her up with the topmast as a leg. When she still listed we swung the boom out and very nearly made her fall over the other way. So we stopped meddling and contented ourselves with guessing how much farther the water would fall. In the space of three uneasy hours the tide began to make and by 8 pm we were able to haul her off. The fog having cleared we put in a couple of hours motoring before anchoring in six fathoms at the unusual distance of half a mile from the beach. Unlike the greater part of the Greenland coast, at this place, appropriately named Mudder Bay, it is a sort of Arctic Southend of shallow mud flats.

Passing out of the Vaigat we motored across Disko Bay in a flat calm. The bay is rich in magnificent and monumental icebergs. We passed some of the largest we had yet seen, their towering sides mirrored in the still water. These more than fulfilled our expectation, but the scenery of the Vaigat, what little we had seen of it, hardly began to compare in grandeur with that of the regions we had left behind. Five days out of Igdlorssuit, and still attended by fog, we reached the open sea where at last we got some wind – wind from ahead. The brief but glorious Arctic summer seemed now to be over as we beat slowly south in rain and bitter cold weather. On 21 August, another day of southerly wind and rain, when we were still 150 miles north of Godthaab, we met a great many trawlers on the Store Hellefiske bank. At one time we had twenty-five in sight. Besides the annoyance of an exasperatingly slow passage we were worried on Terry's account. He had long given up eating and complained of violent stomach pains. He attributed it to stomach ulcers which he had had before. We could do nothing for him but press on to Godthaab. So on the next day, which was calm, we put in twelve hours of motoring. However, that night we had wind enough. When I turned in at midnight, the wind being fresh from south-east, I was in two minds about reefing. Having gone below I was soon up again roused by the noise of a flogging sail. The jib outhaul had parted so I took the helm while David got the sail in. At one o'clock, the wind apparently increasing, I put my head out of the hatch to ask David how things were. According to him we were doing well. We were indeed. To my startled senses, when after struggling into oilskins I went on deck, the rain pelting down, it seemed to be blowing a gale, the boat heeling over and solid water foaming half-way up the lee rail. Without waiting to call the crew – getting into oilskins takes time – I told David to lash the tiller down while we put some rolls in the mains'l. Busy as we were with this I was not too busy to notice that the stays'l had stopped drawing. Rushing back to the tiller I found it had been lashed up instead of down. The boat had paid off, brought the wind aft, and in another moment we should have had an unholy gybe. Moreover we had not yet secured the boom so that all the rolls in it would have come adrift. Nor was that all. In our haste we had forgotten to cast off the vang, a 2½-inch rope knotted round the boom, which when wound up with the reefed sail was enough to split it. All that day the wind blew hard, but we were on course and made good more than sixty miles before the wind packed up. In the evening we got the sail down and David and I held a sewing party in the rain.

On the following night, when we were approaching Godthaab, we came within an ace of putting the ship ashore for good. It was mainly owing to my stupidity. Even now the recollection of it makes me sweat. By this time the nights were dark but on this occasion it was a clear, moonlit night, a swell running but the sea smooth. As we were unable to lay the course for the Godthaab beacon we were pointing for the coast about ten miles north of it and sailing fast. I had not closely examined on the chart the nature of the coast thereabouts, nor appreciated the fact that we had less far to go to reach it than if we had been on course for Godthaab beacon. Anyway, I thought, on a clear moonlit night the mountainous coast should be seen from several miles off. Normally when closing the land, even if it is thirty miles away, I am all anxiety, and I could not have been wholly at ease that night for I was lying down with one eye open and the other only half shut. David had been relieved at midnight but half-an-hour later, rather to my annoyance, he was still clumping about the deck in his heavy seaboots, either enjoying this fast midnight sail or perhaps not entirely happy about our course. Suddenly he let out a startled yell. I reached the deck with a jump to see a string of low islets half a cable's length to starboard and breakers ahead and to port. With no room to gybe I put the helm hard down. She missed stays. Next time, the breakers meanwhile appearing horribly close, with the stays'l backed she came round. Taking care to follow closely the course on which we had sailed into this perilous place, we sailed out again. It had been a near thing and might have been nearer still had not David delayed his going below. Having made a good offing we put about and at 3 am picked up the Godthaab beacon.

Before closing the beacon and sailing up the fjord we hove-to to wait for daylight. When nearing the town, motoring against wind and tide, with the engine going at 1,800 revolutions, we almost stood still and had to increase the revolutions to 2,500 to make headway. We occupied our old berth but at the invitation of the harbour-master, who assured us there would be no ships coming in that week-end, we went alongside the quay. I had mentioned to the harbour-master that Terry Ward was unwell but we were astonished and a little embarrassed when an ambulance drove on to the quay, for Terry was not yet a stretcher case. Off he went, however, in the ambulance and we soon learnt that appendicitis was his trouble. Whether or not he would be able to sail with us was doubtful. He had to go to hospital again for further tests and await the result.

Meantime we had two interesting visitors. The Commissioner of Police, hearing we had been climbing in the Umanak region, came to tell us about the accident to the Belgian party and the uncalled-for complaint made by the Belgian minister in Copenhagen. We then had a visit from the 'steersman', as he was called, of a Norwegian fishing vessel lying alongside. She was a 'long-liner' as opposed to a trawler, fishing with lines up to three miles long. By fishing deeper than the trawlers they can catch bigger fish and on this account 'long-lining' is considered as profitable as trawling. The catch was salted down on board and between April and November they made two voyages to these waters. This salt cod, known as 'stockfish', is exported mainly to Mediterranean and South American countries. Something went badly wrong with what might be called the harbour-master's shipping forecast. At two in the morning the Norwegian had to move to make room for a modern German stern-trawler which then moored so that we lay between her and the quay. No sooner was she fast than pandemonium broke out. Men began to jump from her deck down to ours on their way ashore, and an hour or so later, in much livelier spirits, were jumping from the quay on to our deck. Some insisted on climbing up our shrouds in order to land with a more resounding thud. By breakfast time the party was still in full swing, though the trawler, as we heard, should have sailed again at 4 am. A stream of men and women flowed across our deck, accordions wheezed, and drunken men danced on the quay. Charles himself is no mean beer drinker and on the previous evening had brought on board a small private stock of two dozen bottles which he had carelessly left on deck. The German trawlermen had not ignored this generous gesture, as Charles discovered immediately he came on deck. Had they realized that he was their unwitting benefactor they could hardly have given him a louder cheer when he appeared, and when he tried to discuss the question of the missing beer they merely stroked his beard. By this time, although it was a Sunday and the harbour-master's day of rest, he was down on the quay trying to shepherd the drunks on board. We had had enough too. Casting off one of the trawler's warps we backed out and returned to our anchorage.

After a final visit to the hospital Terry's fate was sealed. The doctor would not risk his going with us; he was to remain and return later in the *Umanak* where there would be a doctor to look after him. I was sorry to lose Terry and disliked having to leave one of the crew in strange hands in a foreign land. We should miss him on the way home both on account of the extra watch we should have to keep and because he alone was familiar with the main engine and the charging engine. The former would not be likely to give trouble but the charging engine was up to tricks of all kinds. I was wrong in saying Terry was the only man among us with mechanical knowledge. As we now discovered, Charles, thanks to his two years at the Military College of Science, had a wide theoretical knowledge of combustion engines as well as some practical knowledge picked up in his palmier days when he ran a vintage Rolls-Royce. He had used it less as a vehicle than as a movable residence – a rudimentary caravan, in fact – the back of it, the bedroom, as it were, being well stuffed with hay.

We sailed for home on the afternoon of 28 August with a fair wind which gave us a flying start of over 100 miles on the first day. In wet weather, with plenty of wind, we worked our way south and were in the latitude of Cape Farewell and a hundred miles west of it by 2 September. By now the nights were long and if they were clear we witnessed every night a display of

'Northern Lights'. The wide zone where this phenomenon occurs runs in the form of an oval from North-west Greenland across Hudson Bay, back towards Cape Farewell and across the Atlantic towards Ireland. Inside the zone activity of some kind may be seen almost every night in a clear sky. At a distance of 500 miles from the centre of the zone the frequency diminishes to some seventy nights in the year. In the zone itself, according to one's position, the lights may be seen in the south, overhead, or in the northern sky. Those we observed took the form of a pale, greenish glow varying in brightness and in form, sometimes like broad shafts, sometimes as a vast arch, or more often a shifting, shimmering curtain of light against the dark background of the sky.

At noon of 5 September, having done six knots most of the night, we had logged 135 miles in the twenty-four hours, our best day's run either outwards or homewards. Five days elapsed before we again reached the hundreds, five days of rain, fog, variable winds, marked by a few minor troubles. The mainsail had to have another big patch added to those already there, a staysail boom broke when we were running with the wind aft, and the charging engine packed up for good. Charles wrestled with it for several days, spent long hours in silent communion with it, but for all that it never went again. As usually seems to happen towards the end of each voyage, we were without light. We adjusted our time so as to have supper before dark and in the galley Charles made do with a tiny oil lamp not much better than a night-light. When homeward bound such small hardships and shortcomings may easily be tolerated; hence the phrase 'homeward-bound stitches' for sails repaired with stitches an inch long.

On the 11th the glass started falling and remained low throughout a five-day spell of wet, windy weather. We reefed down and finally changed the mainsail for the trysail, for I expected worse was to follow. But though the sea was rough – a full teapot landed in Mike's lap – the wind did not exceed Force 6. This long spell of moderately dirty weather coincided with the passage of hurricane 'Debbie' which struck the coast of Ireland and Scotland on 16 September. Between the 15th and the 16th it appears to have travelled 600 miles on a NNE course and must have passed about 200 miles east of us on the 15th. We were out of reach of any shipping forecasts and happily ignorant of any hurricane being at large in the western Atlantic. A friend in the meteorological office has kindly supplied me with a trace of Debbie's track and her brief history:

Debbie was first suspected during the period 5th–7th September in reports from the Cape Verde Islands and from a Danish steamer. On the 7th indications were that tropical storm intensity had been reached with winds up to 50 knots. During the next three days very little information was received, the storm moving into an area of little ocean traffic and out of range of reconnaissance aircraft. Observations were received from a KLM air liner on 10 September indicating that the forward speed had slowed down and that the storm was moving north-west. On the 11th reports from ships and the U.S. weather satellite Tiros III re-located the hurricane near 25° N., 45° W. with maximum winds of 75 knots. The storm moved northwards and during the 12th maximum sustained winds were estimated at 100 knots. On the 13th the storm curved north-east near 35° N., 45° W. It passed across the Azores on the night 14th–15th.

Curving northward on the 15th it passed just off the west coast of Ireland early on the 16th. Gusts reached 92 knots at Ballykelly and 93 knots at Tiree and Snaefell. At least 11 deaths and many injuries were attributed to Debbie in Ireland and extensive damage occurred in Wales and Scotland.

On the 15th we sighted the first ship of the homeward run and a few days later we spoke to the *Iron Age* asking to be reported at Lloyds. On the 20th we picked up the loom of the Fastnet light but it was four days later before we made our proper landfall at the Scillies. The Channel has a reputation for being unkind to yachts returning from long voyages; at least one circum-navigator has recorded that he had met there his worst weather. We had a fast, pleasant sail. Having missed the tide off Portland we anchored in Chesil Cove. Sailing inside between the Bill and the Race we carried a fair wind all the way to the Needles, cheated the ebb by going through the North channel, and anchored off Lymington river on the night of 26 September with 7,000 miles on the log.

Two days later, *Mischief* having been cleaned out and stripped bare alow and aloft, the crew went their several ways. It was sad to see them go, for we were unlikely to sail again together, or even to meet again, and I owed them much. Few sign on for the second time. This, I think, is not because 'once is enough' but because so few have the time or the opportunity to make one voyage, let alone two. Though *Mischief* is hardly a luxury yacht, neither is she a 'hell-ship'. I hope that this brief account has shown that although life on board may not be ecstasy it is at least comfort. Michael had to embark on a University life, while John Wayman returned to City life tempered, one hopes, by days with the Wasps. David had to go to sea again at once to earn money against the day of his impending marriage; there was thus little hope of his being foot-loose again. Charles and I move in orbits that occasionally cross, and no doubt we shall meet again. But the cook in a small boat deserves special thanks and I should like to record both that and my gratitude to him for his long-suffering companionship upon the mountains.

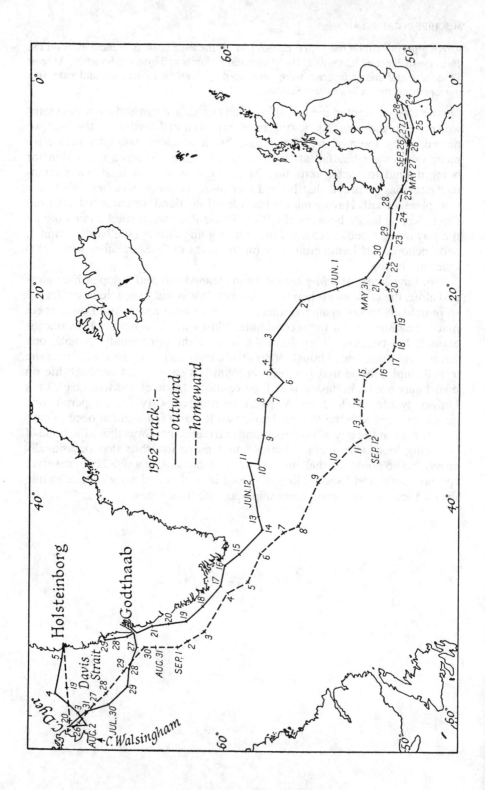

CHAPTER TEN

A New Objective

EPICURUS WAS of the opinion that for most men rest is stagnation and activity madness. It is, I suppose, a question of degree, but if a choice had to be made between the unqualified alternatives most men would no doubt prefer the madness of activity. In my case the activity took the form of another voyage to northern waters. Keeping a boat is like keeping a dog in that both must be exercised, though in fact no spur was needed to persuade me to repeat what had been a successful experiment. The advantages that I had expected such a voyage would have over a voyage southwards had been demonstrated – the time spent at sea and that among the mountains had been less unequal, a crew had been less trouble to find, and, of course, the cost had been less. For a mountaineer Greenland has two great attractions – he will have the mountains to himself instead of sharing them with a horde, and he will find a large number of unclimbed peaks. For the yachtsman, although the east-to-west crossing of the Atlantic may be a cold, rough passage, the Davis Strait and the west Greenland coast, despite the fog, make a wonderful cruising ground; a place where he may see at close range some of the largest icebergs afloat, enjoy the finest of fjord scenery, catch unlimited fish, and possibly have better weather than if he had stayed at home. A summer's day off the Greenland coast has unrivalled charm – freshness and clarity, soft colours, and the serenity of sea, ice, and mountains under the pale, northern sky.

With a second voyage to those regions in view and having a liking for remote, desolate places I turned my attention to the Canadian coast on the west side of Davis Strait. Taken by and large the west coast of Greenland can hardly be called remote and desolate, and it is far from being uninhabited. Letters from Europe reach Godthaab in three days; few of the fjords are without either a small town or a settlement, or that at any rate are not frequently visited by Greenlanders for fishing or hunting; and off the coast the sea is thick with vessels of some kind – trawlers, schooners, coasters, or local fishing boats. On the other hand on the Canadian side of the straits the Cumberland Peninsula is as desolate as a man could wish, more or less uninhabited, and besides that mountainous. In fact at the start of the first Greenland voyage I had had at the back of my mind the hope that we might have time to have a quick look at the Cumberland Peninsula. Before sailing I had been in touch with the leader of a Cambridge party who were about to go there to climb. Lieut R. E. Langford, RE, was then in residence at King's

College – an unusual place to find a Sapper – and I met him there later when both parties had returned. The Cumberland Peninsula on Baffin Island in Lat. 67° N., just inside the Arctic Circle, is about the size of Switzerland and equally mountainous, though its highest mountain is only some 7,000ft. There are two passes across the peninsula formerly used by Eskimos as sledge routes. Few expeditions have been there because access by sea or by land is difficult and only recently has it become possible to reach it by air.

The Cambridge party flew there and spent six weeks in the interior, climbing seven peaks, doing some geological work, and also crossing the peninsula from north to south. It was from Langford that I first heard of Mt Raleigh, a mountain on the coast of the peninsula, seen and named by John Davis in 1585 and still unclimbed. John Davis made his first voyage in search of the North-west Passage in 1585. On 7 August anchored in Exeter Sound on the east coast of Baffin Island, 'altogether free from the pester of ice', as the narrative says, 'we lay under a brave mount the cliffs whereof were orient as gold. This mount we named Mt Raleigh.' Nowadays when pretty well every nook and corner of the earth has been explored, only large-scale Antarctic expeditions, helped by aircraft and Snowcats, and hindered, perhaps, by the pressing needs of science, may still hope to make fresh discoveries. The individual with a taste for discovery has for the most part to content himself with following the tracks of early explorers, obtaining a vicarious thrill from making the landfalls they had made. On our last voyage we had by chance made the same landfall at Cape Desolation as Davis had when he rediscovered Greenland. This Elizabethan seaman and explorer therefore roused my interest, and since he has perhaps been overshadowed by his more famous contemporaries such as Drake, Hawkins, Raleigh, I have subjoined a short account of his life, a life spent for the most part on hazardous voyages in the service of exploration and of his country. Here it is necessary only to mention briefly his three voyages in search of the North-west Passage.

Davis's search for the North-west Passage was no doubt instigated by Sir Humphrey Gilbert's famous *Discourse* published in 1576. The loss of the little *Squirrel* in 1583 with Sir Humphrey and his companions must also have made a deep impression, coming so soon after he had penned the famous words with which his *Discourse* closed, words which in those brave days rang like a trumpet call: 'That he is not worthy to live at all, that for fear or danger of death, shunneth his country's service or his own honour; seeing death is inevitable and the fame of virtue immortal.' On his first voyage Davis, as we have seen, after making his landfall at Cape Desolation anchored in what he called Gilbert Sound, the present Godthaab, where he had friendly intercourse with the Eskimos. Crossing the Strait he discovered and named Capes Dyer and Walsingham, and anchored in Exeter Sound; and finally explored Cumberland Sound in the belief that it was a strait and possibly the desired passage.

In 1586 with the same ships *Sunneshine* and *Mooneshine*, and *Mermaid*, a larger vessel of 120 tons, he landed first at what is now called Old Sukkertoppen. Having again entered Cumberland Sound he sailed down the coast, explored the Labrador coast, and returned home bringing with him some salt cod and 500 sealskins. For his third and last northern voyage in 1587 he had the old

Sunneshine, another vessel *Elizabeth*, and the clinker-built pinnace *Ellen* of twenty tons. In Gilbert Sound he made a heroic decision. To satisfy his backers by making the voyage pay, he dispatched the two bigger ships to the Labrador coast to fish while he continued his exploration in the barely sea-worthy *Ellen* He went north as far as the great cliff now called Sanderson's Hope in Lat. 72° 12', or as he wrote, 'Sanderson has hope of a North-west Passage, no ice towards the north, but a great sea, free, large, very salt and blue, and of an unsearchable depth.' A northerly wind drove them westwards where they encountered the 'middle pack' and were forced once more into Cumberland Sound. Sailing south down the coast off Hudson Strait they met with 'a mighty race, where an island of ice was carried by the force of the current as fast as our bark could sail'. On these three voyages Davis charted long stretches of coast on both sides of the Strait and much of the Labrador coast and took regular observations for the variation of the compass. As Clements Markham wrote:

Davis converted the Arctic regions from a confused myth into a defined area. He not only described and mapped the extensive tract explored by himself, but he clearly pointed out the way for his successors. He lighted Hudson into his strait. He lighted Baffin into his Bay. He lighted Hans Egede to the scene of his Greenland labours. His true-hearted devotion to the cause of Arctic discovery, his patient scientific research, his loyalty to his employers, his dauntless gallantry and enthusiasm, form an example which will be a beacon-light to maritime explorers for all time to come.

Of many remarks made by Chinese sages of the past one of the less pithy (but one that I like) is that of Chang Cha'o: 'If there are no famous hills then nothing need be said, but since there are they must be visited.' Mt Raleigh by its association with John Davis merits fame and as an objective it had for me other desirable features. True it was not very lofty, but lofty enough for a man of whom it might be said that years have tamed his mountain passion without clouding his reason. Besides its romantic name and romantic association it was a mountain lying upon a wild and desolate coast, a coast that would be hard to reach. Indeed when I had read all that I could about the ice conditions in summer on that coast I did not rate our chance of success highly and was prepared to be disappointed. *Mischief's* hull has not been strengthened in any way to make her fit to shunt ice, as she would have to do if we tried to force a way through loose pack-ice. We should therefore have to wait until the ice had cleared away from the coast, and much depended upon our experiencing a favourable season. In any case our time on shore would be short. It would probably be late before we were able to get in, and although we were not likely to be prevented by ice from getting out, we wanted to be home by the end of September.

The conditions governing the movement of ice on that coast and what may therefore be expected are shown in the following extract from the Pilot of Arctic Canada:

The general movement of the ice in Davis Strait and Baffin Bay is controlled mainly by the north and south-flowing currents, and its distribution at any time is largely depend-ent upon the strength and direction of the prevailing winds. It has been estimated that, with the exception of icebergs, not more than two-thirds of the ice in those sea areas is of local origin, and its concentration thoughout the summer season is, therefore, greatly affected by the quantities which enter from the sounds at the head of Baffin Bay, Smith, Jones, and Lancaster Sounds.

Along the Greenland coast the warm north-flowing waters of the West Greenland current keep the more southerly stretches free of ice during most of the winter, and a narrowing belt of open water usually continues up the coast to north of Upernivik until about Christmas. Some time in January, as a rule, the ice becomes consolidated around Disko Island and the heavy west coast pack spreads out to meet it. From here the pack arcs south-westwards and extends as a broad belt off the entrance to Hudson Strait and along the Labrador coast. The south-west coast of Greenland remains practically ice-free until January when it is invaded by the heavy polar ice carried by the East Greenland current. This "storis", as it is called, drifts up the coast as far as Frederikshaab or in some years even to Godthaab, blocking the approaches to the harbours of South and South-west Greenland.

On the western side of Davis Strait the cold waters of the south-flowing Canadian or Labrador current permit the formation of ice along the entire shore-line. All the fjords become covered with an ice-sheet and along Baffin Island the land-fast ice borders the coast as far south as Cape Dyer (near Exeter Sound), extending seaward about ten miles. South of Cape Dyer the belt of fast-ice is usually narrower and over long stretches may be entirely absent. Beyond the fast-ice the heavy pack moves with the great eddy circulation of Baffin Bay along the Greenland coast beyond Disko, around Melville Bay, and from there southwards along the Canadian coast. Although in winter Baffin Bay has generally a 10/10 ice cover, it is not a solid sheet but rather a cemented drifting pack in which the floes may at any time be subjected to violent rearrangement by the gales. In the western part of the bay it appears to drift south at the rate of about four miles a day even in winter.

At the head of Baffin Bay lies the famous polynia, the "North Water", which whalers aimed to reach as early in June as possible, threading their dangerous way through the heavy floes along the edge of the vast sheet of fast-ice in Melville Bay. The ice round this polynia breaks up early and usually by the beginning of June open water extends southwards along the western shore of Baffin Bay to the vicinity of Lancaster Sound.

Because of the atmospheric circulation in the area and of the higher temperatures and salinities introduced by the West Greenland current, the ice in this part of the Canadian Arctic is the first to disintegrate – usually in late May or early June. During June and July heavy fields of close-packed ice move down the Baffin Island coast in a solid belt which has been known to extend 125 miles eastwards from Cape Dyer.

The heaviest concentration of pack – the "middle pack" of unhappy memory to whalers – appears to lie as a tapering north-south belt just west of the central axis of Baffin Bay. As summer progresses this zone gradually shrinks but in its southern limits, extending along the coast to beyond Cape Dyer, heavy ice may persist in some years until late August. Ice may also remain heavily packed until the end of July or even August along the entire coast of Cumberland Peninsula southwards beyond Cape Mercy, blocking the entrance to Cumberland Sound and sometimes completely filling it.

August and September are usually the most ice-free months, in fact in some years the only ice to be seen in these months may be the stream of icebergs moving south to the Labrador Sea. On occasion the early part of October may also be favourable for navigation along the Baffin Island coast but ice usually forms during the last weeks of that month. Failure to realize the relative lateness of the navigation season in those areas led the early navigators to impose a heavy handicap on themselves by their arrival off the entrance to Davis Strait in May or June in hopes of being able to complete their explorations and return home by early September at the latest.

The above source, and many others I consulted, all seemed to show that at the best we could not hope to reach the coast of Baffin Island before early August, and at the worst, or nearly the worst, not before early September. In an exceptionally bad ice year we might not be able to reach it at all. If we sailed, therefore, at the usual time in May we should have practically the whole of July available for climbing in West Greenland. There was a strong temptation to return to the Umanak fjord region where I knew where to go for mountains and where the people were the nearest approach to real Eskimos that we were ever likely to see. But it was rather too far north, both of Godthaab and of Exeter Sound, and we might waste a lot of time in getting there and back. I remembered that the passage south to Godthaab that last voyage had cost us twelve days. For the mountains of Southern Greenland, in the Cape Farewell region, we might well be too early if we arrived as expected by the end of June, for in that month the whole of the Julianehaab Bight may be full of ice (as it proved to be). So there remained for us the mountains of the central part of West Greenland which lie about 100 miles north of Godthaab and are in almost the same latitude as Exeter Sound and at the narrowest part of the Davis Strait.

Mischief, I knew, would be able and willing, so with a rough plan already formed there remained only the finding of a crew. Plans for such a venture as this are best left rough, for as the great Von Moltke said, few plans withstand contact with the enemy. In finding a crew for this voyage I had to start from scratch, no volunteers having presented themselves. There are one or two sailing clubs or associations based on London which notify their members of boat-owners in need of crew and it was by this means that I got my first victim. He did not belong to the Association concerned but happening to see their list of crews needed he introduced himself to me at a lecture I gave there. Hans Hoff was from East Germany. Too young to serve in the war, he had been working as an apprentice to a watch-making firm when the Russian army arrived at his home. (He had some curious tales to tell of those days.) Having got out of East Germany in good time and having spent the last seven years in England he spoke excellent English. He knew something about boats and his keenness on voyaging had led him to attend both navigational and signalling classes when living in London. I had no hesitation about taking him on. The Germans are people with a strong sense of discipline. I could see Hans setting an example to the rest of the crew by springing to execute my slightest command, though to be just no such example was needed. As I was then on the way to Lymington I suggested that before he committed himself he should come down at the week-end to have a look at *Mischief.* Hans duly arrived and I showed him over the boat. There is nothing more depressing, nothing more likely to deter a man bent on making a voyage, than looking over a boat out of commission on a wet, winter's day. Below it is as cold and dank as a tomb, moisture drips from the beams, cupboards gape open, and half the floor-boards are up to encourage whatever air there may be to circulate. A man would scarcely think of housing his dog there, let alone going to sea in it himself. Hans, however, was no stranger to the forlorn appearance of boats when laid up for the winter and the sturdy appearance of *Mischief* from outside impressed him more than the dismal state of things below. So Hans agreed to come and since he was a German I did not expect to be let down.

I then had given me the names of three possible candidates by Charles Evans, a climbing friend who is also himself a boat-owner. Two were unable to come but the third, Michael Rhodes, a research student at the University College of North Wales, Bangor, thought he could. The fact that Dr Charles Evans is the Principal at Bangor probably justified this optimism. When riding over from Bangor on a motor-cycle to see me he got lost on the way and arrived an hour or so late. As I was not looking for a navigator that did not really matter. He was a keen dinghy sailor with the physique of a Rugby player, evidently a man who could put a lot of weight on a rope. His particular line of research at the moment concerned blow-flies, and he astonished me by asserting that he expected to make a rich haul of blow-flies and bugs of all kinds in Greenland and Baffin Island. His presence, therefore, would lend the expedition a faint, if slightly unwholesome, aroma of science. He thought he might be able to borrow a 16-mm ciné-camera, so I took him on in the role of seaman, scientist, and cameraman.

So far, with only about two months to go to the time I hoped to sail, I had two hands. I wanted three more and particularly someone who would be willing to cook. As had happened before when hard pressed, I had recourse to an advertisement in the Personal Column of *The Times*. In the past such an advertisement had always brought a large number of offers, some of them serious, and even one or two acceptances. Unlike when one is hoping to sell something through that medium, when the wording cannot be too bland, it does not do to clothe projected voyages or ventures in words of much promise. It is safer to err on the other side, for there are many who answer such advertisements from force of habit or out of curiosity, as well as many who are ready to fly at anything they see. Thus the advertisement I had used for an earlier voyage merely said: 'Hands wanted for long voyage in small boat; no pay, no prospects, not much pleasure.' The advertising manager who, more than anyone, I should have thought, must have daily dealings with the lunatic fringe, was rude enough to query both the advertisement and my good faith. Even so, when it finally appeared, the response was far too hearty to be dealt with in conscientious fashion.

For the present cruise the advertisement ran: 'Cook wanted for cold voyage in small boat; five mouths to feed for five months.' This, too, was well received but it did not get me anyone. One promising candidate whom I interviewed, having agreed to come, wrote a letter and posted it the same evening to say he had changed his mind; and another, a young flautist, badly wanted to come but would not dream of cooking. But I had let myself in for a lot of trouble by omitting the words 'men only', a mistake that obliged me to write at least a dozen letters of regret to all the women who applied. My regrets were sincere, too, since some of these applicants would have filled the bill admirably had I been able to overcome my fear of having a woman on board for so long in such inescapable circumstances. 'Discord,' as yet another

Chinese sage has remarked, 'is not sent down from heaven, it is brought about by women.' One of these women had crossed the Atlantic cooking for a crew of five men and from the way the letter was worded I gathered that these poor fish might consider themselves lucky to have had her with them. Shrinking hastily away from this seafaring Amazon, I hesitated long before refusing another who wrote less stridently to say she had cruised in several yachts in the Mediterranean, cooking the meals and arranging the flowers, and that she was a *cordon bleu*. Flowers we should have to forgo, but my mouth watered at the thought of the meals we might have. So much for the advertisement – guineas thrown away. Roger Tufft, who had sailed in *Mischief* on the Crozet venture and who still corresponded with me in desultory fashion, knew what was afoot but kept me for a long time in suspense. He is a man who sits loosely in any sedentary job, his usual occupation during his brief stays in England being that of teaching. At length, however, the temptation proved too strong and he wrote to say that he would come. Moreover, failing anyone else, he offered to try his hand in the galley. He was a great acquisition. We knew each other and he was a mountaineer as well as an experienced hand; added to that he was as strong as a horse, able to carry a load or kick steps until further orders. Instead of having time to sit about on stones, as on the last Greenland trip, I should find myself always toiling in the rear. The fact that he knew the boat and the way things were done would be valuable when starting with a strange crew, and there are few men, not excluding some of the rummer birds who have sailed in *Mischief*, with whom Roger would not be able to cope.

I had still two to find and I found them, rather late in the day, and quite by chance. At a lecture in Portsmouth I met the owner – another German – of an old Baltic trading ketch then lying at Gosport. Having a morning free I went on board to have a look at her. The owner and his wife were living on board, so she was not out of commission, nor was this a wet, winter's day; but on going below I felt that even Hans might have thought twice about making a long voyage in her. In the vast, gloomy cavern, formerly the cargo hold and now the main cabin, the only place where the crew could sit or sleep was on top of what I took to be winged-out ballast – two narrow, concrete platforms about three feet high running the length of the hold. But that is by the way. The point is that this tough German concrete-lover subsequently got talking in a train about boats and the sea to another young man from whom I presently had a letter enquiring about the proposed voyage.

Shaun White had a small boat of his own, knew more than a bit about engines and all things mechanical, and was above all a dedicated bird-watcher. I suppose the earnest watching of birds is a full-time occupation – all round the clock in fact if one feels strongly enough about it. Admittedly a lot of birds sleep, but owls hoot all night and there are many others which spend the night dashing themselves against lighthouses. However, young Shaun had another occupation which I discovered later from incidents and from remarks he let fall. It seemed he happily combined – mainly on the shores of the Solent – the pursuits of bird-watching and beachcombing, pursuits which have much in common for both need the use of binoculars and a trained eye. When he joined *Mischief* he brought with him as a goodwill offering a number of useful articles – safety belts, inflatable jackets, a searchlight, rockets, distress signals – all articles concerned with the preservation of life at sea, for Shaun was perhaps a little apprehensive and came prepared for the worst. We learnt that all these things – and these were merely a selection – had either been found on the beach or salvaged from the sea. Indeed in the course of time we began to suspect that some of the things picked up had not been lost until Shaun found them, and could not be regarded legitimately as flotsam, jetsam, or lagan. This weakness of his reminded me of those Texan soldiers of whom Stonewall Jackson, the great Confederate general, remarked that 'the hens have to roost mighty high when the Texans are about'.

By arrangement Shaun, on his way home from a bird-watching week-end on the Isle of Wight, came to have a look at *Mischief* and thereupon decided that he would go with us. On another week-end less than a month before sailing day he visited me again, this time at the head of a small flock of fellow bird-watchers. Till then I had no idea that the disease was widespread among the young, by no means the affliction mainly of retired men, in particular Field-Marshals or eminent Bankers. Luckily none of the yacht-owners, the patrons of the yard, were about or they might have wondered what yachting was coming to. The flock or horde, suitably clad for bird-watching of the roughest kind, bowed down under rucksacks big enough for a Himalayan expedition, having boarded *Mischief* and dumped their loads on the deck, began at once to devour huge chunks of bread which they dug out from the pockets of the rucksacks. One among them, a very tall youth, who seemed to me at least seven foot long, confided that he would like to sail in *Mischief*. Roger Brown was a friend of Shaun's and about due to finish his engineering apprenticeship in Portsmouth Dockyard. Here, I thought, is the man to look after our engine. The difference in design between engines of 40,000 horse-power such as one might find at Portsmouth Dockyard and those, like *Mischief*'s, of 40 horse-power may be considerable; but since the greater comprehends the less I imagined that Roger Brown's knowledge would be invaluable. He had had no sailing experience and his height would be a handicap for working in the galley, but on the understanding that he would look after the machinery and cook I took him on. On the outward passage at least, he did neither. But we had now a full complement and we should soon learn what each could do.

CHAPTER ELEVEN

To Cape Farewell

IN THEORY, when three of the crew joined *Mischief* about ten days before sailing, there should not have been much to do beyond rigging her, bending the sails, and stowing the gear. In the course of the winter I had as usual overhauled the blocks, tackles, running rigging, life-lines, and all movable gear. Having had no time to do the job alone I had had the inside of the boat painted by the yard. The cabin looked so white and clean one hardly dared to sit down. But invariably it takes a great deal longer than one expects before a boat is in all respects ready for sea. In fact we had a lot to do. I went on board on 11 May and three of the crew joined on the 14th. Yet, hindered to some extent by wet weather, we had to work hard to be ready by 23 May.

This time no one fell into the river, but on my first morning on board, when some letters were being handed from the quayside, the whole lot dropped in the brink. Having quickly grabbed all within reach I noticed another drifting past the stern. I was in two minds about rescuing a buff-coloured envelope marked OHMS, suggesting something to do with Income Tax, the loss of which would not be grievous. But having fished it out with the aid of a boat-hook I found I had won a Premium Bond prize of £25. Various sententious sayings appropriate to this happy incident suggested themselves – appearances are deceptive, all cats are grey in the dark, inaction is a crime, or perhaps, cast your bread upon the waters and it will return to you after many days.

Still moderately elated by this windfall I went next day to Southampton to check the stores list with Messrs Burnyeat, the ship-chandlers who have for many years been accustomed to finding for me things like dried skim milk, egg powder, concentrated lime juice, alleged (wrongly, I feel sure) to be fortified with 40 per cent rum; and to packing the dry stores like sugar, flour, rice, milk, oatmeal, macaroni, in 14 lb. and 7 lb. tins with press lids, and the whole 10 lb. cheeses in soldered tins. The application for permission to take bonded stores – cigarettes, tobacco, and drink – had gone through, but I heard the less reassuring news that our calling at Belfast on the previous voyage had not gone unnoticed. Having cleared the ship for Godthaab and then called at Belfast, which is in the United Kingdom, we should have notified the Customs authorities there so that the bonded stores could have been sealed while we were in port.

Before the crew joined I had an interesting and interested visitor, a Mr Rayer, who had served for two years as an apprentice in *Mischief* when she was a pilot-cutter. I felt he was a little critical of amateurs because as soon as

333

he arrived he asked me when I had last had the service over the eye-splices in the shrouds removed in order to examine the state of the wire. His pilot and owner had been one William Morgan, known in the Bristol Channel in those days as Billy the Mischief, a tough character who remained at sea whatever the weather until they had picked up a ship or, failing that, had run out of bread and water. I have read somewhere that Frobisher and Hawkins when cruising in search of Spanish ships used to declare that they would continue to cruise 'as long as the beer lasted'. According to Mr Rayer, who should know, a story concerning Bristol Channel pilot-cutters that has gained wide currency is a myth. He had never seen it done or heard of it being done. It relates to their alleged method of getting the punt on board by making the painter fast to the boom and then gybing, so that in theory the punt leapt from the sea on to the deck where it could be grabbed and secured. As Mr Rayer said, there were then neither stanchions nor life-rail, so that had any bold man attempted this labour-saving method there was nothing to stop the punt from flying inboard. In his day the chain-locker used to be in what is now the galley and they did their cooking on a Dover stove at the fore end of the cabin. This stove burnt day and night and the apprentice had the job of keeping it bright. 'Always a pleasure to look at,' added Mr Rayer reflectively, looking hard at me as we stood in the galley by a rather dirty Primus stove. They used to carry two mainsails, one light and one heavy, a spinnaker, three jibs, topsail, and storm canvas. Instead of hauling out on a slipway they had legs fitted, and for scrubbing and painting, the boats were put on the hard at Ilfracombe. He said that *Mischief* was sold out of the Pilot Service for £80, but this seems an absurdly low figure even for pre-1914 days.

All the ratlines on the shrouds needed renewing, a process which is known as 'rattling down' because, I suppose, one naturally starts at the lowest ratline and works up. Each ratline is clove-hitched round the middle shroud and the eye-splice at each end is seized to the outer shrouds. A real sailor, I imagine, a man whose every finger is a marline spike and every hair a ropeyarn, would have no trouble in turning in splices in 14-inch rope while standing in mid-air half-way up the shrouds. If on the other hand, after guessing the right length (for each ratline is shorter than the one below), you make them up on deck, you invariably find that after the clove hitch has been put on the ratline is either too short or too long. If the job is well done it looks smart and symmetrical, if ill done it looks like the ladder Jacob might have dreamt about. While I was thus busied Shaun White rode on to the quayside on his motor-bike looking like Shock-headed Peter. He was soon followed by Hans Hoff and Roger Tufft so that next day we got down to work shipping the bowsprit, boom, and gaff, and reeving the halyards. The sheaves on the mast for the jib halyard which had given us so much trouble had been renewed. And, not before it was needed, I had had made a new mainsail which next day we bent on. Much to my relief it fitted nicely, for there had been some discrepancy between the measurements I made and those of the original sail (after allowing for stretch) as recorded by Gowen, the makers. On the last voyage we had constantly been stitching, whereas on this new sail we never once used a needle. The lee-side topping lift is the main cause of chafe, but unless we were making short tacks we took care to cast it off altogether.

Michael Rhodes then joined bringing with him the promised ciné-camera and a miniature trunk of entomological gear – poison bottles, test-tubes, specimen cases, a butterfly net, and a young furnace used for extracting mites from earth samples. Shaun then left to spend the week-end at home, offering to bring back a lifebuoy, life-jackets, and a drum of paint, all the harvest of the sea. Unluckily the lifebuoy, the one thing we needed, had been eaten by his dog. In spite of the rain that fell too frequently we managed to paint the deck, bulwarks, stanchions, cockpit, and to cover the bare patches on the hull. The hull was to have been painted by the yard but in view of the weather it would have been time wasted. I was glad we had not had it done because after we had painted the deck with oil and red ochre, a heavy shower distributed much of this over the yellow hull, so that she looked like a pirate ship with blood running out of the scuppers.

When Roger Brown at length joined we were about ready to go. I had reserved for him the longest bunk and had had no difficulty in doing so because it is also the most inconvenient, situated so close to the deckhead that the occupant has to roll in sideways and has not the least chance of sitting up. The stores were then brought over from Southampton accompanied by a Customs officer to seal up the drink and tobacco, and by an Immigration officer to record Hans's departure. On 23 May we cast off and motored down the river, receiving a salute of one gun from the Royal Lymington Yacht Club as we passed. I doubt if *Mischief* has ever before got away to a starting gun. Anyway this mark of recognition was much appreciated by the crew, none of whom were members of the Club. When we hoisted sail outside a fresh westerly wind obliged us to tack several times before passing the Needles and these manoeuvres were carried out without any of the hitches one might have expected on the first day at sea with a strange crew. All except Roger Brown had sailed before in some kind of craft. Soon after clearing the Needles we were overhauled by a blue-hulled pilot-cutter, very like *Mischief*. She passed close and no sooner had this excitement subsided than the crew one by one began to feel unwell. Roger and Hans decided to take their meals on deck, Shaun looked pretty wan, while poor Michael and Roger Brown were prostrate. All recovered quickly except Michael, who was sick off and on most of the way across and who even on the return voyage succumbed in rough weather. Such a state of affairs is more than discouraging, but Michael never allowed it to get him down or to prevent him from doing his work.

The wind freed us during the night. Instead of steering south we could steer west and by the following evening we had Guernsey abeam. After this little shake-up we ran at once into real yachting weather with a light north-east wind and a calm sea. The invalids had recovered but as Roger Brown showed no enthusiasm for taking over the galley, Roger Tufft came to the rescue as he had promised. He had armed himself with a Penguin cookery book and very soon began baking cakes and boiling duffs. We had no oven to fit on the Primus stove and he got over that by putting the cake tin or basin inside a saucepan with an asbestos mat to prevent the bottom burning. Except in port or at anchor, when the crew relieved him in turns, Roger went on cooking until we were homeward bound, and whatever the weather never failed to feed us well. When at length we turned towards home Roger Brown woke up and undertook to show what he could do in the galley. In that he was remarkably successful, the more so because by then all our luxuries and many of our necessities had been finished. But so long as there is enough rice or macaroni on board there is no difficulty about following the Chinese precept: 'A well filled stomach is indeed the great thing – all else is luxury.' Few men in any of the crews I have had could be described as delicate feeders. On this voyage we had some good trenchermen. Michael, or Mick as he was called, between his bouts of sea-sickness naturally ate prodigiously to make up for lost time. Hans, in a methodical German manner, ate his way through whatever quantity might be piled on his plate, while young Shaun's swallow-ing capacity seemed interminable. Both bird-watchers had a peculiar aversion to tea or coffee and insisted on drinking cocoa, a beverage that one associates with Temperance and Little Englanders and on that account holds suspect.

Our bird-watchers lost no time in following their vocation. We had on board one too many, for it seemed impossible for one of them to spot anything without his feeling obliged to draw the other's attention to it, to compare notes, or to have an identification confirmed. At first it startled me out of my wits and by the end of the voyage I had still to get used to it. A profound peace would be reigning above deck and below when suddenly a piercing yell, quivering with urgency, would ring out. Whereupon, according to which of the two was below, there would be an upheaval from the direction of Shaun's or Brown's bunk and a stampede for the door which would be wrenched back and hurled to again with equal violence. No need for alarm; we were neither on fire nor sinking; a bird had been seen. Provided both were safely below it was possible to relax; but Mick and Roger, who were also interested in birds, though less fervently, soon caught the infection, and if they were incautious enough to seek expert opinion on some bird they had seen, a double stampede would take place. In the Southern Ocean birds such as albatross and giant petrels are plentiful and well worth looking at. In the Atlantic and home waters an uninstructed man might imagine birds were few and those few represented merely gulls. Nothing of the kind. Plenty of birds of various species can be seen if they are looked for, and provided one has powerful binoculars, years of practice, and an assertive manner, they can be confidently assigned to their various species.

For a whole sunny afternoon we lay becalmed, the peace broken only by the bird-watchers or by the splash of someone diving overboard for a swim. Those who bathe in May, we are told, will soon lie in clay. I remember on the last voyage having given this piece of news to Dr Joyce as he clambered back on board after a swim in the Irish Sea, and having been quite startled by its unexpected effect. Either my solemn manner must have been convincing, or advice on the care of his health from a layman shook him. He wilted visibly and, much to David's amusement, retired below in a very thoughtful mood. Whatever the weather Roger and I poured three buckets of sea-water over ourselves before breakfast and continued doing so until the sea temperature fell to 40° F. I gave up then but Roger carried on until it fell to 34° F. when he, too, had had enough. Mick joined us only occasionally, flinching less at cold water than at having to get up a moment before it was necessary.

After the calm we had a fast sail throughout the night with a fresh northeast wind and a morning sight put us only ten miles from the Wolf Rock. Fog then came down but we ran on confidently and when the lighthouse duly loomed up about a mile away the crew began comparing me with Henry the Navigator. The wind then headed us so that we had a job to clear the Scillies, sailing past the northernmost island rather nearer than prudence demanded. The amateur navigator cannot bring it off every time. Having achieved one coup I should not so soon have attempted another. We had the broad Atlantic before us, we had made our departure from the Scillies, and we were under no obligation to sight Ireland. However, the wind being fair, I laid off a course that should have taken us within a few miles of the Fastnet rock. Had we been moving a lot faster I might have gone below with the impressive words 'Call me when you see it'. We never did see the Fastnet rock or indeed any part whatsoever of Ireland, and Henry the Navigator had to fall back on the accustomed excuses – bad steering, unusual leeway, currents, poor visibility.

We were undoubtedly a little out of our reckoning but we were going strong and had logged 400 miles in the first five days at sea; and when a racing pigeon alighted on board the crew had something else to talk about than the niceties of navigation. This pigeon must have been out of his reckoning as well, for Ireland was within easy reach if he knew where it lay. Or perhaps he was not trying. As the Bengali proverb says: 'The sight of a horse makes the traveller lame,' and in my experience the sight of a ship has much the same effect on homing pigeons. Their resolution is sapped, they begin to feel weak, hungry, and thirsty, and down they come, forgetting all about their prescribed journey. On one voyage we had picked up no less than five and carried them from the Eddystone to Cadiz. This one took an even longer ride, remaining with us until we were off the Greenland coast, in spite of the fact that we passed one or two homeward-bound ships to which he could easily have transferred himself and found better accommodation. At first he looked peaky and refused to take any food. Then I remembered our lentils. Whereupon he began eating voraciously, grew fat and sleek, and had to be forcibly launched in the air before he would take any flying exercise. He took up his quarters in the engine-cum-chart-room where he showed alike his gratitude and his contempt for my navigation by defecating on the charts. The bird gave us a lot of amusement and the longer he stayed the more he became one of the family and the more we cherished him. So that although he made a proper mess we were sorry when he went.

The glass remained high and steady, the sky overcast, the wind fair. For a week we had been on the same tack on the required course of west-north-west. We had passed outside the limits of the BBC shipping forecasts and had to make our own guesses about the weather. A weather forecast for the North Atlantic as far west as Long. 40° is broadcast from Portishead on W-T. Our small set out of a car could not pick that up nor could we have read it. Hans had attended a signalling class and read morse at slow speeds. He had an opportunity that evening at 10 pm when we spoke to the *Rembrandt* and asked her to report us. Having acknowledged our message she then signalled 'P' which meant 'Your lights are out or burning badly'. In fact this was an understatement because our lights were hung up in the forepeak where they usually remain once we are out of home waters.

At sea, in a world comprising only six people, their personal appearance and what they wear is commonly a subject for comment. At Lymington Mick had had his reddish hair cropped very close; now, when his beard of more or less the same colour had made some growth, it became difficult to tell whether one was looking at his face or the back of his head. Hans also had a reddish beard which developed in course of time into a coir mat through which little could be seen but his eyes. Roger Brown had come on board wearing a beard; now, in a life that for him seemed to hold few other pleasures, he spent a lot of time combing it. Roger Tufft, as one might expect, had a virile mane like a horse-collar, while Shaun had so much hair on his head that none could be spared for his face.

The glass began falling for the first time on 1 June. The wind went aft and in consequence we soon had our first Chinese gybe. In the evening we changed to twin staysails to avoid the risk of any more gybes, and ran all night at five knots. It had been a day of incident. Our passenger pigeon took off and disappeared from sight eastwards, and returned after an absence of five hours. How, we wondered, did he find us again? Then the sighting of a long-tailed skua and an unidentified species of black petrel well-nigh drove the bird-watchers into a frenzy. Bangers and mash, followed by a rib-binding rice pudding, brought an eventful day to a firm finish. The wind freshened in the night and in one two-hour watch we logged fourteen miles. By noon we had done 131 miles and on each of the next two days we ran 120 miles. We spoke to another ship, the *Jessie Stove*, a small ore-carrier, but on account of the sea running she could not read our lamp. At one moment we would be in view on top of a wave and the next we would drop out of sight with the lamp obscured in the middle of a letter. I told Hans to stop sending but to my dismay the *Jessie Stove*, now about a mile astern, swung round and steamed after us. They evidently thought we were in trouble or wanted something. Included in the short list of urgent and important signals to be used by vessels in sight of one another, there is no group of letters or letter signifying 'Buzz off'. The simplest thing to send and the most likely to be understood was 'OK'. This had the desired effect and she soon resumed her course, no doubt cursing us for a lot of incompetent asses.

Our pigeon seemed unsettled, possibly homesick, or remorseful on account of neglected duty. Taking off once more it fell straight into the sea. Having managed to get back on board it was sick, spewing up lentils and sea-water. Again it took off and fell in and this time it drifted helplessly astern while skua gulls gathered round to attack it. This really looked like 'curtains', but the game bird managed to get off the water and flew back to us to be received with a cheer. The pigeon was not the only one sick, for we were enjoying a rough spell. The wind rose to gale force and since by running before it we should lose a lot of ground we hove-to with the mainsail rolled right down and a double-reefed stays'l. Defying the weather Roger produced for supper, sausages, fried onions, and a noble duff. The wind began to take off in the night but in the twenty-four hours we logged only sixteen miles. This was the first wind we had had from any westerly quarter and we were already half-way across in Long. 27° W. June is supposed to be the quietest month in the North Atlantic; gales are infrequent and usually short-lived. This brief blow was follwed by three quiet, sunny days. We had the Genoa up and during the calms some of us bathed overside, the sea temperature being 47° F. Unquestionably we were enjoying far more favourable conditions than those of the first voyage, warmer weather and better winds. We began counting the days to Cape Farewell.

From June 9th to the 11th we had another spell of wet, dirty weather during which we shipped a lot of water through the skylight. In spite of the windows let into it, the fitting of this cover makes the cabin a little gloomy, so that its fitting is usually put off until everything below is pretty well soaked. By now we had worked up to N. lat. 59°, only a little south of Cape Farewell, and we were about 250 miles east of it. There is no fishing bank in that area, where we now had a curious encounter with a Russian trawler from Petsamo, a White Sea port. In the police court phrase she seemed to be loitering with intent, steaming slowly and aimlessly in no particular direction. Having nothing to do she came over to have a look at us. We signalled with the lamp but got no reply. After dropping back she came up again in the afternoon and for some time we cruised in company, each having a good look at the other. I should say almost a third of her company were women and by their appearance active members of the crew rather than floozies. On 14 June a fine, sunny day, we were some forty miles south of Cape Farewell with not an iceberg in sight. We altered course to north-west and before breakfast next morning we sighted high snow mountains. We were only twenty-three days out from Lymington. On the previous voyage it had taken us thirty-five days. The difference in time is actually greater because the figures are from Lymington and Belfast respectively and the distance from Belfast is some 300 miles less. As has been seen we met no contrary winds at all until we were half-way across the Atlantic, no one had complained of the cold, and on the whole it had been an enjoyable trouble-free passage.

CHAPTER TWELVE

To Godthaab and Evighedsfjord

CAPE FAREWELL, so named by John Davis, is the southern extremity of an island 2,700ft. high. Surrounded as it is by high mountains it does not stand out prominently, but like most capes that mark the culminating point of large masses of land it is noted for stormy weather. In addition much ice accumulates round it, sometimes extending as far as 150 miles seaward. But the average distance is seventy miles in April, decreasing in August to thirty miles. For our part we could not have rounded it in fairer conditions. Sailing west-north-west parallel to the coast, mountains glistening all along our starboard hand, we romped along at five knots over a sparkling blue sea on a day of brilliant sunshine. And what fascination there is in the sight of this Greenland coast; how bracing the austere beauty of sea, snow mountains, and ice! In the morning we sighted only one big solitary berg and in the afternoon passed another close enough for us to take photographs. In order to have the best light we passed it on the wrong side, that is to leeward, where we had to dodge a number of bergy bits or growlers which had broken off. A German stern-trawler from Kiel altered course to have a closer look at us and greeted us with three blasts of his siren. The air temperature that day was 36°F. and the sea 42°F.

Next day we lay becalmed. It was an equally brilliant day and the few icebergs scattered about were curiously distorted by mirage. On this account too, we could not make out whether a white bank all along the horizon to starboard was fog or ice. At the same time we were much puzzled by a low rumbling noise. Some thought there must be a fishing boat about, others an aeroplane. True we had a bottle-nosed whale close aboard at the time but we could not hold him responsible for a noise like that. When a breeze sprang up we closed with this white bank and found it to be heavily congested pack-ice so distorted by mirage as to appear twice its height. It was this pack-ice that in spite of the perfectly smooth sea maintained the low menacing growl which we had heard from miles away. In similar circumstances John Davis and his company had been confounded by the noise of the pack; 'Here we heard a mighty great roaring of the sea, as if it had been the breach of some shoare, the ayr being so foggie that we could not see one ship from the other. Then coming near to the breach, we met many islands of yce floating, and did perceive that all the roaring that we heard was caused only by the rowling of this yce together.' We sailed to within a hundred yards of the pack to take photographs before standing out to sea. From so low a viewpoint as our deck photographs of pack-ice proved singularly unimpressive. In the vicinity of the pack the sea temperature was down to 34°F.

All next day as we drifted and sailed up the coast we had the pack in sight, for apparently it filled the whole of the Julianehaab Bight as far north as Cape Desolation. Ghosting along all night we tacked once to avoid a raft of small floes covering a mile of sea. The morning broke clear and sunny and again we found ourselves surrounded by floes with just enough steerage way to avoid them. A seal lay basking on a floe but when we tried to edge close the whisper of wind failed altogether and when we started the engine he dived into the sea. In the afternoon we ran into fog. The air temperature fell to 36°F. and the moisture on the ropes froze. By evening, the fog still persisting, we found our way barred by a narrow belt of pack-ice. Although the water beyond appeared to be clear of ice we hesitated to break through and coasted westwards alongside the ice searching for an opening. For four hours we motored at four knots, dodging loose floes, and still having the more solid ice about fifty yards away on our starboard hand. At length at ten o'clock, tired of dodging stray floes and thinking I saw an opening, I turned her head towards the ice. We were nearly through when in making a tight turn to avoid a floe on the port side we suffered a frightening blow below the water-line from a tongue of ice projecting from a floe on the starboard side. Those who were below were more than a little startled. As one man they rushed on deck to see what had hit us such a sickening thud. Assuming a calm which I was far from feeling I told them we had just grazed a bit of ice, that the ship appeared not to be sinking, and that at least we were through the ice and able to resume our proper course.

So far as Greenland waters were concerned this was our last encounter with pack-ice and had I exercised a little more patience or caution it need not have been so rude an encounter. Such a blow, I felt, could hardly have done *Mischief* any good. For the next few days I watched closely the well of the bilge, but the number of strokes needed to clear it showed no increase. (In calm water she makes very little water.) Of course, inside a boat such a noise is exaggerated. This tap on *Mischief*'s hull had sounded sufficiently like the crack of doom momentarily to scare the crew, and to leave one or two of them with a sense of insecurity that was not finally dispelled until two months later when we had had her slipped and examined the hull. What gave me most concern was our meeting here with so much ice where in the previous year there had been only icebergs. I felt that it did not augur well for our chances of reaching Baffin Island. Before sailing I had had a talk at the Meteorological Office at Bracknell and had been told that the Arctic winter had been more severe than usual, implying that in summer more ice would find its way down from the North. As against that, the sea in the south-western part of Davis Strait was reported to be unusually warm. We had undertaken to keep a weather log for the Meteorological Office, as well as ice reports and notes on the aurora we observed. Roger Tufft took this in hand, as he had on a previous voyage on behalf of the South African Meteorological Service. He had, by the way, spent three years on one of the Antarctic bases as a meteorologist. We could not, of course, transmit reports but the log we kept would ultimately be valuable for analytical purposes, especially as few British ships visit the Davis Strait and West Greenland.

We began sighting numbers of trawlers fishing on the Frederikshaab Bank, including a very smart-looking vessel from Klaksvig in the Faeroe Islands. We were out of sight of land and managed to get sights to fix our position. All the way over Hans had been assiduous in taking sights and plotting our dead reckoning position by means of Traverse Tables. Whenever I got my sextant out he followed me on deck with his, and old and battered though it was, with the horizon mirror only half silvered, our sights generally agreed within a minute or two. Like Charles Marriott he stuck to old-fashioned, time-honoured methods, wrestling with cosines and haversines as he had been taught at his navigation classes. I have a feeling that those who teach navigation are averse to short cuts. With some justification, perhaps, they may think that without a thorough understanding of spherical trigonometry no man can hope to understand the theory of navigation, and that to practise it without understanding the theory is to be no better than a quack. Or, with more reason, they may think that if all would-be navigators took to using trouble-saving tables – for example, the American H.O. 211 that I myself prefer – the use of which any fool can master in half an hour, there would be no more need for instructors.

I was thankful to get sights that day because on the following day, 21 June, we got no sights at all and had to rely upon dead reckoning for finding the entrance to Godthaab fjord in thick weather. In navigating by dead reckoning, estimating the course and distance made good, there is as much luck as skill. Lord Kelvin, whose remarks are quoted in Lecky's *Wrinkles*, held strong views about trusting too much to dead reckoning when nearing land:

We often hear stories of marvellous exactness with which the dead reckoning has been verified by the result. A man has steamed or sailed across the Atlantic without having got a glimpse of sun or stars the whole way, and has made land within five miles of the point aimed at. This may be done once, and may be done again, but must not be trusted to on any one occasion as probably to be done again this time. Undue trust in dead reckoning has produced more disastrous shipwrecks, I believe, than all other causes put together.

I believe it would be unsafe to say that, even if the speed through the water and the steerage were reckoned with absolute accuracy in "the account", the ship's place could in general be reasonably trusted to within fifteen or twenty miles per twenty-four hours of dead-reckoning. And, besides, neither the speed through the water nor the steerage can be safely reckoned without allowing a considerable margin of error.

All things considered, a thoroughly skilled and careful navigator may reckon that, in the most favourable circumstances, he has a fair chance of being within five miles of his estimated position after a two hundred miles run on dead reckoning; but with all his skill and with all his care, he may be twenty miles off it.'

All day we ran with a good following wind until evening when we had expected to sight land somewhere south of Godthaab. In thickening weather we could see nothing so we stood out to the north-west and that night we ran another fifty miles. At four in the morning, visibility being then about half a mile, we went about and pointed at where I hoped Godthaab fjord might be. After we had run about fifteen miles without seeing a thing, a brief glimpse of a cargo ship appearing and disappearing like a wraith in the mist gave us some comfort. She, too, might be in search of the Godthaab beacon. Presently the fog began to thin, and lo, right ahead lay the islands. Had we gone about a bit sooner we should have done even better, for now we were hard on the wind and had to make another board before we could enter the narrow channel between beacon and reef. A small, familiar-looking vessel outward bound proved to be our old friend *Mallemuken*. We exchanged salutes.

As we covered the twelve miles or so up the fjord the wind steadily increased and by the time we neared the leading marks off the narrow harbour entrance we had quite a tussle before we could dowse the mainsail. After threading the channel and opening up the harbour we met this fierce blast right in our teeth. Worse still, the harbour seemed to be occupied by too many ships. A corvette *Thetis* (ex-British corvette *Geranium*) took up a lot of room; a small survey vessel lay alongside her, and in our old berth, between *Thetis* and the rock wall, lay yet another. 'He who knows not whither to go is in no haste to move.' The wind had brought us to a stop anyway, so I signalled to let go the anchor; and as soon as it was down realized that we were in the way of vessels approaching or leaving the wharf. Without waiting for the harbour-master to come out to tell us to move we began winching in. Getting the anchor in a strong wind with a heavy boat like *Mischief* is no easy task. And there is a joining shackle on the cable which does not properly fit the gipsy of the winch, so that if there is much strain on the cable this link persistently slips back. After a severe struggle we got the anchor up and left it hanging ready to drop again. Approaching as near as we could to our old berth I again signalled for it to be let go. Nothing happened. The cable refused to run out and we began drifting rapidly astern before the wind. By this time our activities had aroused the interest of the officer commanding the survey vessel who shouted to us to make fast alongside him. But at that moment the anchor took charge and went down with a run. Seeing our plight the officer quickly sent over a launch with a warp. Slacking away on the anchor cable almost to its full scope we warped alongside the survey vessel and were able to draw breath. We were below discussing the few points about this appalling shambles that would bear discussing when a sailor appeared at the door and handed me a bottle of whisky. Next day when I sought out this officer to thank him both for his help and the whisky, his only comment was: 'You looked as if you needed it.' Our passage to Godthaab this time had taken only thirty days and the log registered 2,200 miles. The previous year from Belfast we had logged 2,650 miles and had taken forty days.

When we went ashore that evening we found that though the old harbour-master had gone the new one was of much the same type – genial (convivial, as we discovered later), and speaking the same seamanlike American. We supped well at the Kristinemut which was full to capacity, and where I was greeted with embarrassing heartiness by the few old acquaintances who were not too drunk to recognize me. The crowding was due to the presence of the corvette and the even greater number of Danes employed on construction work. Much had been done since our last visit. The road from the harbour to the town had been surfaced, some three-storey blocks of flats had gone up, the fish wharf had been finished and a start had been made on the fish-curing factory. The noise of blasting and of pneumatic drills continued from 7 am to 7 pm, for the workmen, brought out only for the summer, work a twelve-hour day. The local Greenlander will have nothing to do with navvy work which is all done by Danish workmen.

The day after our arrival was Midsummer Day, a day marked by celebrations. Several huge bonfires were built, effigies burned, and a gala dance held in the cinema hall. On a brilliantly fine night – it might well have been called a sunny night – the bonfires seemed out of place. Except for Hans, who is very much a ladies' man and therefore given to dancing, the crew attended the dance as spectators. They got better value for their money than they expected when a drunken brawl started. The corvette, dressed over-all for the occasion, held a private dance to which some of our crew subsequently found their way. By the time they got there, however, the guests were beyond dancing, the earlier emphasis having been exclusively on drinking. I had occasion to visit the *Thetis* early next morning, for she was about to sail and I wanted to borrow a large-scale chart of the Sukkertoppen region. Even at that hour there were no traces of the night's disaster in the Captain's morning face as he very kindly went through his charts and made me a present of what I needed.

Evighedsfjord where we had decided to go for our climbing, is in N. lat. 65.50° a little south of Sondre Stromfjord. The chart showed only the first twenty miles of the fjord but we had also a map which included the whole fjord and the surrounding mountains. 'Evigheds' means, I believe, 'never ending', but the fjord is not that long. On sailing day, 26 June, rain fell heavily all day and there was little or no wind. We spent the morning alongside the quay watering and waiting with what patience we could muster for twelve gallons of paraffin that we needed. While waiting I went on board the *Ellen S.*, a small coaster. Her master struck me as being a man fully satisfied with his lot as well he might be. He spent the summer on the Greenland coast and in the winter returned to Denmark, where he had a wife and family, and whence he had to make only one or two short winter voyages. He was interested in birds and wild life generally, had a library of books on the subject, and a battery of guns which he made use of both ashore and afloat.

We had an uneventful passage up the coast, passing the usual numbers of trawlers fishing the banks, experiencing one rough day, and on another a fall of snow. But 30 June, when we tried to enter Evighedsfjord, was a day of incident, thanks to the mistakes we made. I had made a bad blunder the previous evening. Having taken a sight for longitude I decided that we were six miles west of our dead reckoning when in fact we were six miles east of it – a mistake on a par with reading right for left. It is a matter of comparing the angle read on the sextant with the calculated angle that would have been obtained had the ship been in the assumed position. If the angle is taken when the sun is roughly west and is found to be larger by six minutes than the calculated angle, then you are nearer the sun than you thought you were by that number of miles; in other words you are six miles west of your estimated position. Visibility was poor and we were closing the land at a fairly brisk speed on a north-easterly course. With more confidence than I usually feel under such circumstances I turned in, leaving orders to be called when we had run thirty miles. We had run little more than twenty when at 3 am Hans roused me with news of an island about a quarter of a mile away. Having got the ship about on a course away from the land I re-worked the sight of the previous evening and discovered the mistake, a small matter of twelve miles.

The fog looked like staying. As there was no wind, we started the engine and motored towards the coast. An ice-breaker, the *West Wind*, no doubt from the American base at Thule, passed us going south. We had no clear idea where we were until in a momentary lifting of the fog we spotted a glacier which came right down to the water. On the chart the only glacier that answered to this lay in a fjord called Angmarqoq. Turning north we presently passed a group of islands which we could identify and which confirmed our position. The entrance to Evighedsfjord lay about eighteen miles farther north and the entrance could be identified by a small group of islands called Ikermiut on one of which there was a beacon. By the time we had run our distance the fog had come down thicker than ever. We had almost given up hope of sighting anything when an island crowned with a beacon loomed up close on the starboard hand. Cheered by this bit of luck, and thinking perhaps that the difficulty of navigating in fog had been overrated, I put her on course for another island six miles inside the fjord where we hoped to anchor for the night. We were attracted to it by a small settlement marked on the chart. We had not gone three miles when the vague outline of islands began to appear on either hand where no islands should have been. Either we were in the wrong fjord or in a small southern arm of Evighedsfjord. Clearly it was time to stop, so we motored over to the nearest islands and anchored between two of them in fifteen fathoms. We were very close to one island and to prevent her swinging we dropped a stern anchor with fifteen fathoms of chain attached to a warp. Hans let it go while I took a turn with the warp, which promptly broke. We lost the lot. For an hour and more we rowed about in the dinghy dragging a grapnel, but the water was too deep and we caught nothing. We had better luck fishing, and having caught three big cod we set an anchor watch and turned in, the fog being as thick as ever. Fresh-caught cod, by the way, are very different from the shop-soiled variety we get at home.

During the night the fog cleared. How simple everything then appeared. We were, as we suspected, in the southern arm of the fjord; either the tide had set us off course or the compass had played us a trick. With a brisk wind blowing into the fjord we set off for the settlement of Timerdlit six miles up the fjord. We did not expect to go any farther north this year and had strong hopes that Timerdlit would prove to be something like Igdlorssuit, a place with huskies and kayaks, with a stronger flavour of Greenland than Godthaab. Having rounded the island we began to beat up to the settlement lying on the mainland inside the island. As the channel between was barely a cable wide it would have been easier and quicker to motor, but we were being closely followed and watched by a small local fishing boat. By our skilful handling of *Mischief* under sail in confined waters we hoped to astonish the natives, just as earlier explorers accomplished the same end, though with less trouble, by removing their false teeth or their glass eyes if they were fortunate enough to be so equipped. More than once we had to warn our escort to get out of the way as we prepared to go about. We must have gone about at least ten times in that narrow channel. At last, the patience of both parties nearly exhausted, the Greenlanders pointed out the anchorage and we came to rest off Timerdlit, a place comprising one deserted frame hut and the concrete base of what may have once been a store.

The Greenlanders' boat, full of fine fish, came alongside and we at once bought a big halibut for a packet of cigarettes. No words were needed for this transaction and beyond learning that they came from Kangamiut, an island at the northern entrance to the fjord, we got no further information. They wore store clothes – not a pair of sealskin trousers or boots among them – and we realized sadly that so far south as this we should look in vain for huskies, sledges, kayaks, or anything associated with the old Eskimo way of life. We spent the afternoon roaming the hills behind the deserted settlement. The collection of bones, offal, and bits of skin in and around the frame house not only showed that it had been recently lived in but afforded a fruitful field for Mick to begin collecting blow-flies. I began my usual collection of plants. We came upon several graves, remains of old stone huts, and a stone erection about the size and shape of an old straw skep whose use we could not fathom. In the evening a survey vessel, a strongly-built wooden vessel of lovely lines, anchored near by. Her skipper and the chief surveyor paid us a visit.

She sailed early in the morning and later we passed her anchored close in while the survey party toiled up a 4,000ft. mountain to occupy a station. For the first fifteen miles the fjord is wide and the mountains lie well back. (The Eskimo name for Evighedsfjord is Kangerdlugssuatsiaq.) It then makes a right-angle bend at a point where two great glaciers descend from what is known as the Sukkertoppen ice-cap, a field of ice covering some 900 square miles beteen Evighedsfjord and Sondre Stromfjord and quite separate from the main inland ice. Beyond the bend the fjord narrows to a canyon, its abrupt black walls broken only by some desperately steep and narrow clefts filled with ice, looking like mere ice torrents. After another fifteen miles it bends sharply north and continues for another twenty miles, but at the bend there is a wide bay and there we decided to stay. This bay called Kangiussaq lies immediately below the highest peak in the area, a peak of 6,995ft. called Agssaussat. It had been swathed in cloud as we motored up the fjord but as we neared the anchorage the clouds rolled away. As the sun illumined its summit snows and the black crags and pinnacles of its western face, it looked a formidable mountain. But mountains have more than one face and when it came to climbing Agssaussat (which means, by the way, 'Big with child') we found a simple way up. Late that evening we anchored in fifteen fathoms about a hundred yards from the beach. Even in that depth, when the boat dropped back on her anchor, there were only five fathoms under her.

CHAPTER THIRTEEN

Climbing in Evighedsfjord

THE LESSON I had learnt the previous year on our first attempt to climb a peak had sunk in. It never occurred to me to try to climb Agssaussat from the boat. Roger and I started at the very reasonable hour of 11 am to find a way up the glacier. The ice stopped short of the beach by a hundred yards and about a mile beyond this point it rose in a steep ice-fall. Once above that we imagined we should find it all plain sailing and from a camp up there we could strike at Agssaussat and possibly another peak. After some preliminary boulder-hopping we took to the ice where the going was good. At the foot of the ice-fall a snow-filled gully between the glacier and the confining rock wall offered an easy way of gaining height to within a couple of hundred feet of the top of the ice-fall where the gully petered out. Both the ice above and the rock on our left were unclimbable but to our right a shelf traversed the ice-fall to the far side. We followed this and without having to cut more than a few steps we gained the rocks on the far side whence we soon reached the flat glacier above the ice-fall. It was a good route but liable to change. Melting was going on rapidly and the gap between ice and rock which we had easily stepped over would soon widen. At 2,200ft. we found a camp site on a bit of rough moraine and by four o'clock we were back on board. Mick had shot a long-tailed duck. Having no means of roasting it and no apple sauce, we curried it, brutal though that may seem. We curried it, I might add, with full honours, for we had some of the essential trimmings – coconut, dates, raisins, and lemon. Mick, too, has mastered the difficult art of cooking dry rice without which the spiciest curry is but a mockery, so that altogether it was a memorable meal.

As he was ferrying the loads ashore next morning Roger Brown, who was to be one of the carrying party, dropped his camera in the sea and retired on board to spend the day drying it. His load had to be divided among us, and Mick, who was to have come merely as camera-man, had to carry a load as well. In the snow gully we roped up and had lunch at the top of it before shepherding the novices across the ice traverse. All went well and by 3 pm we had the tent up. Roger went down with Mick and Shaun to see them safely off the ice. With Mick busy, as it were 'on location', they took so long that I went down to satisfy myself they were all right.

All next day we were confined to the tent by rain and sleet. We read and played chess. The tent began leaking along the seams, pools gathered on the floor, and as I was unable to keep well afloat owing to a punctured air-mattress, we resorted to stabbing holes in the floor to drain off the water. At last towards evening the rain stopped, the clouds began to thin, and little by little between the cloud rifts we pieced together the south-east ridge of Agssaussat clear to the summit. There appeared to be no difficulties. Next day after a lot of snow plodding and a little rock scrambling we reached the summit in just over four hours. It was a hot, cloudless day. Against the dazzling brilliance of the surrounding snow-fields the fjord looked like a strip of dark green jade and the sky a wan blue. Nearly 7,000ft. below we could make out *Mischief*, a mere speck, like 'a tall anchoring bark diminished to her cock'. As we neared our camp at 3 pm the firm *névé* over which we had sped in the morning had turned to watery slush in which we waded to our knees. The sun temperature was 92°F. and in the shade 76°F.

The weather was equally fine and hot next day when we climbed a peak of 6,125ft. close to camp. Some intricate route-finding at the start up rock and snow made it an interesting climb, and the snow slope by which we gained the summit ridge was so steep that we had to dig our hands in to keep in balance. On the way down, when this slope would be wet and unsafe, we avoided it by traversing the mountain and rejoining the glacier well above camp. There were no other peaks within reach of this camp so that afternoon we packed up and went down. Carrying heavy loads, we cautiously crossed the ice traverse using crampons, and having reached the top of the snow gully we uncautiously unroped. For here Roger slipped and began rolling down, missing the gaping maw of a crevasse by inches. A fall in the gully would have been harmless for it flattened out at the bottom, but the crevasse demanded respect and we had already three times skirted and peered into this obvious receptacle for falling bodies.

The crew had already fitted a new cranse iron, oiled the wire rigging, and rove a new lacing for the mainsail, but we spent another day here to continue work on the boat and to collect plants and bugs. The tropical weather continued and in the course of a botanical excursion to a near-by glacier valley I suffered severely in the cause of science. Instead of following the beach I embarked on a bush-crawl through thickets of alder and dwarf birch, attended by a private cloud of mosquitoes and streaming with sweat. In order to obtain some respite while I had lunch I lit a fire and sat in the smoke, and having stamped the fire out began the return journey by the easier way of the beach. When half-way home I noticed that my fire, far from being stamped out, had taken hold. By evening the whole hillside up to about 500ft. was burning and a great pillar of smoke hung over the fjord. The fire would certainly discourage a great number of mosquitoes and could harm no one, nevertheless I felt slightly guilty as anyone must who is responsible for starting a holocaust. The crew advised that next time before going ashore I should be searched for matches. Three days later, from the top of another mountain many miles away, we could still see the smoke of this infernal fire.

Our next anchorage was down the fjord beyond the big bend in a land-locked bay called Tasiussaq. We discovered a reef across the entrance where we had only five fathoms of water as we sounded our way in before anchoring in six fathoms about 100 yards from the shore. We dined off cod kedgeree and we had the hope that by coming to this bay we might be able to vary our cod diet with salmon. These hopes grew when we came to explore the wide valley at the head of the bay through which meandered a clear, blue stream some twenty yards wide. At one or two of its pools we noticed stakes and a day later a party of Greenlanders arrived to camp on the beach and to net salmon. In a short time they had caught two sacks full. We bought some of these and later, when Roger and I were climbing, the crew caught six. They used a fine nylon net which Shaun had bought in Godthaab for netting birds. It was an expensive net and only his greed for salmon overcame his scruples about allowing it to be used for fishing. Boiled salmon with mussel sauce made another memorable meal to be recorded with gratitude. The stomach has a long memory.

Viewed from afar this verdant valley appeared to offer pleasant walking. In fact the going was deplorably bad. In the flat bottom where the vegetation was rich, one had to leap from moss hag to moss hag, while the slopes above, though bare, were seamed with little gullies. The alder bushes attained a height of ten feet, dwarf willow and juniper abounded, and willow herb grew profusely in great patches of pink. Birds were more numerous here. Besides snow buntings and red polls we saw a sea eagle, several magensa duck, and coveys of ptarmigan. Roger and I had our eyes on a snow-peak about six miles away for which we should have to take a camp up the valley. Before doing that we had a day on a near-by rock peak, 'Amaussuaq', of 4,620ft. The name means 'Like a hand' and four pointed towers standing on the summit ridge make the name apt enough. Leaving the boat at nine o'clock we had an hour of boulder-hopping before reaching the foot of a snow-gully. From the col at the top of the gully, easy rock climbing brought us to the summit by one o'clock. For the descent we found a gully on the other side of the mountain which gave us a thousand feet of glissading down to the main valley.

With Hans and Shaun assisting to carry we started the long slog up the valley. The going, I repeat, was bad – all bog and bother, as Jorrocks would have called it – the day blazing hot, and each of us had our personal swarm of mosquitoes and black flies. I had brought some tubes of a repellent called 'Dusk' which was fairly effective if applied at frequent intervals to face and hands. We made little height till we had crossed the river – where Shaun fell in – and began climbing up a side valley leading to a col. Halts became longer and more frequent. All of us had had enough when we camped just below the col near a patch of snow. Having dumped our loads Roger and I walked up to the col. We were profoundly shocked by the sight of two very deep gorges lying between us and our mountain. The height of the col was 1,300ft. and the bottoms of the gorges were at almost sea-level where they drained into a neighbouring fjord. After taking some food Hans and Shaun had to face the long, hot walk home; but Roger and I, lying in the tent, were on no bed of roses. The sun beat fiercely upon the tent from which all ventilation had been excluded for fear of mosquitoes. The few mosquitoes that were inside , and that had survived our first onslaught, took their siesta on the roof of the tent finding it too hot to start worrying us. We lay there stifling, sweating, unsleeping, not far from the point of having heat stroke.

With the probability of a long day in front of us we left the tent by 7 am and sat for some time on the col examining our mountain. That was our mistake. The longer we sat and looked the weaker became our resolve. We had some doubts about whether or not an ice wall which guarded the whole length of the main ridge could be breached; and then the ridge itself impressed us unfavourably, a good mile or more of snow which long before midday would be like wet cotton wool. Besides that were the two gorges, looking deeper than ever in the clear morning light. We were ready to welcome any change of plan provided it meant less effort. We decided to go for a peak which was actually slightly higher but more accessible. We should have to drop into the far gorge but only in order to follow up it to the glacier whence its stream originated. This glacier happily proved to be dry ice and remarkably un-broken considering the steep angle at which it rose. With the aid of crampons we gained height quickly. So far we had seen only the top of the peak; there might or might not be a route up. But had we brought with us our map we should have noted that near the summit there was a sign indicating a trigonometrical beacon, a fact that would have reassured us about there being a route and might well have stopped us from bothering to climb the mountain.

When the whole face of the mountain at length came in sight we saw on one side of it an inviting gully. The finding of a bit of a rusty tin showed us we were not the first comers and at the top of the gully on a shoulder of the mountain we found a cairn with a plate cemented into the rock engraved 'Trig. No. 1'. The summit lay 700ft. above. We felt the survey party deserved full marks for having found the only easy route, a route which lay hidden from sight until one was right under the face of the mountain. The height proved to be 6,250ft. and even there, on the snow, we were followed by mosquitoes. Thanks to a sequence of snow-beds we shot down the gully at a great rate and soon we were trudging down the glacier with the melt streams pouring off in increasing volume every minute.

In a lake between the moraine and the glacier these combined melt streams caused a most curious effect. At a point in the middle of the lake the water was spouting up with a whoosh like an oil gusher, and surrounding the turbulent spot was a growing mound of gravel deposited by the spouting water.

We reached the tent by five o'clock, much too soon for comfort, for once more we had to lie sealed up in the tent half-naked and sweating. Roger, bless him, produced a tin of deliciously cold Mandarin orange slices – we had nothing of the kind on board – and then we brewed a lot of tea, thus raising the temperature even higher. Some of our bodily needs being met we fell to reviewing the events of the day. At first we felt we had shown a commendable lack of spirit. Roger had surprisingly lagged behind and had been off colour and had we stuck to our first objective we should, I believe, have had only the satisfaction of having tried. But that, of course, is what matters, and matters far more than climbing a peak. In fact by slinking off to bag an easy peak we had lowered rather than raised our self-respect. Was our moral fibre slacken-ing? If so it needed stiffening. So when the evening became cooler I set about preparing the stiffest brew of pemmican we had yet had. Pemmican as thick as this, I noticed, my scientific interest fully aroused, does not bubble when it boils. This hell-broth of mine merely heaved slightly, shivering like a quick-sand, while at long intervals a globule of imprisoned air expired on the surface with a melancholy sigh.

We packed up and started down next morning expecting any moment to meet Mick and Roger Brown who were coming up to help with the loads. Mick we shortly saw but no Roger Brown. Once again he and his camera had fallen into a stream. Shaun, too, we heard, had soaked his camera in the same way, and I remembered that at various times he had thrown overboard a mop and the gash-bucket. Are bird-watchers prone to this sort of thing? Are they unsteady on their feet or it is that their eyes are always in the air looking for birds instead of on the ground? To most of us Shaun's camera appeared to be ruined beyond hope and we told him so. But he took it all to pieces, dried it, and successfully re-assembled it. In fact with him and Hans, the apprentice watch-maker, there were few jobs on board, however finicking, which could not be tackled. One small job, however, that defeated them all were my teeth which I broke by sitting on them. Mick as a practical scientist took this job in hand. He tried first with Aerolite glue and when that failed reinforced the glue with a cunningly made steel pin. This lasted only twenty-four hours and I was lucky to find later in Holsteinborg a dentist's mechanic. A mouth without molars is like a mill without stones.

On 15 July we intended sailing for Godthaab, calling at Kangamiut on the way. It was full early to be thinking of Baffin Island, but for all we knew the season might be an open one and the earlier we got there the better. At Godthaab we hoped we might obtain a report on ice conditions in that area. As we were about to sail that evening a Kangamiut boat came into the bay and presently they came alongside to ask for some oil. We gave them diesel oil but apparently they wanted paraffin which we could not spare. Instead we gave them a tow. For two hours we beat down the fjord, until the Greenlanders, tired of our slow progress and getting uncommonly wet, cast off the line and made for the beach. The wind then died and we enjoyed a wonderfully clear, still evening as we took our last look at the mountains, their familiar outlines reflected in the quiet water. Kangamiut itself lies on an island surrounded by many others. The intricate approach terminates in a long, narrow strip of water almost like a dock. Although it was midnight when we arrived two local men boarded us and helped us to moor with an anchor from the bow and a warp to the shore.

The steep rocky hillside overlooking the harbour is lined with rows of gaily painted little wooden houses where live the 300-odd Greenlanders of Kangamiut. They depend mainly upon fishing and there is a curing factory for salting down the cod and halibut. The salmon in the streams up the fjords are now being exploited. We were told that fifty tons had been caught the previous autumn; these were sent to Sukkertoppen for freezing. We spent the morning at the house of the manager appointed by the Greenland Trading Company, a man responsible not only for trade but for the general welfare of Kangamiut and its inhabitants. He had spent fourteen years in Greenland both on the east coast and the west and had enjoyed it. One of his tasks had been the moving of the entire Eskimo community of Thule, where the

American base is, to a place seventy miles farther north where they could pursue their normal life hunting seals, walrus, and polar bear, free from the distractions of jet planes and coca-cola. The manager showed us his collection of Eskimo curios collected over the years, soapstone and ivory carvings and implements of all kinds. Naturally we were on the look-out for such things, particularly carvings, but nowadays they are virtually unobtainable by the casual visitor. Few are made and those few are bespoke by the residents. While we were there an old man came into the house to offer us a beautifully made model kayak complete in every detail. He asked £5, might have accepted less, but found among us no takers. In the afternoon the manager paid us a visit bringing with him his clerk who very kindly cut my hair. We were sitting down to tea when we felt *Mischief* bump on the bottom, a hint perhaps that she was impatient to be off. We found she had dragged inshore. We were sorting this out when a big naval picket boat arrived from nowhere, dropped anchor too close to us, and then drifted across our warp. So, taking the hint, we bade the manager a hasty farewell, got our lines in, and sailed out.

Going down the coast we experienced the usual calms, light breezes, and, of course, fog. Whenever the fog came down the temperature dropped to 36° or 37°F. On the morning of the 19 July, after being becalmed all night, we were sailing close inshore in foggy weather. The sun shone pleasantly overhead but visibility was less than 200 yards. We were steering south-east for the beacon at the entrance to Godthaab fjord which we reckoned to be about five miles away when suddenly an island loomed up close ahead. After clearing it by gybing we went back on course and soon sighted more islets on the port hand. What they were we had little idea for the whole coast hereabouts is thick with islands, islets, and skerries. An hour later yet more islands appeared ahead but this time when we altered course to clear them we found ourselves hemmed in. Whichever way we turned islets appeared to cluster like peas on a plate. For the next hour we were dodging them as if they were ice floes, following a likely looking lead until it closed and then gybing or going about to try another. Fortunately the sun shone strongly overhead enabling us to judge pretty well by the colour of the water where shoal patches lay; but this did not altogether spare us some frightening moments when on looking over the side we saw the bottom very close beneath us. At length we reached open water – open so far as the fog permitted us to see – and we hove-to to await a clearing. From the number and density of this group of islands we judged we had crossed the mouth of the fjord and sailed right in among the fifty or more on the south side. With a little more luck, we thought, we might have sighted the beacon, for in the course of the morning we must have sailed past nearly every one of the fifty. For some time we had been hearing the noise of an engine and presently a small fishing boat loomed up out of the mist. When hailed he came alongside and proved to be a Faeroe Island fishing boat. Asked where the beacon was, they told us east-south-east and barely a mile, whereupon we let draw and soon found it. As was generally the way, as we drew inland up the fjord we ran into clear weather while the fog lay in a heavy bank out to sea.

This final visit of ours to Godthaab extended to seven days, partly owing to delay in the matter of obtaining an ice report. A Canadian who looked after the maintenance of the Catalina seaplanes run by East Canada Airways proved most helpful. When a signal to the big air base at Sondre Stromfjord produced no results he got in touch direct with the air-strip on Cape Dyer. Cape Dyer is one of the two big easternmost capes of Baffin Island, the other being Cape Walsingham forty miles to the south. Exeter Sound and Exeter Bay lie a few miles south of Cape Dyer. In 1955 Cape Dyer had been chosen for the siting of a link in the Distant Early Warning chain stretching across the Canadian Arctic and an air-strip had been built there. Besides this matter of an ice report the Canadian helped us to find in Godthaab a new solenoid starter for our engine and presented us, rather prodigally, with five gallons of oil. We carried on board, a relic of Cape Town days, a five-gallon drum of fish oil for use as storm oil. This had become almost solid so I asked the Canadian if he could let us have some used engine oil. He told us they dumped used oil and sent our drum back filled with new engine oil.

The *Mallemuken* (what a lot of time she spent in Godthaab!) had a new commander and a new crew neither of whom had paid us any attention. The day after our arrival two of us had a bucket bath on deck. Later, on the quay, I met a petty officer from her crew who asked me if we had enjoyed our bath; I told him we preferred hot showers when we could get them and that afternoon we made free with the shower bath in *Mallemuken*. As the Faeroe Islanders had done us a good turn in giving us the bearing of the beacon I thought to give them a bottle of gin. Rowing over to the fish wharf where they were lying I had a look over their boat which was little bigger than *Mischief*. They come out early in the summer doing the 1,200 miles in eighteen days relying entirely upon their engine. The three of them berthed in a tiny cabin forward where there were actually five bunks, the two spare bunks being occupied by a couple of Greenlanders whom they took on for the summer's fishing. They had five big reels of nylon line ranged along the bulwarks and used as a lure artificial sand-eels. One of them said he once had fourteen cod on at a time. The catch is put in ice and sold at Faeringhaven, a fishing port about twenty miles south of Godthaab. Their galley had the beauty of simplicity. It was merely a cupboard, like a small wardrobe without any drawers, standing on deck aft, and inside it a small gas-ring supplied from a gas cylinder standing outside. There was no going inside this galley. To see how things were going the cook had merely to open the doors; nor could he stir and sniff at his pots as most of us like to do unless he lay down on the deck. In September these hardy souls return to the Faeroe Islands. They pressed on me some cod and a Kingfish, a big red job which made prime eating.

We did some work on the boat. Painted half the deck – which was duly rained on – turned all the halyards end for end, and mulled over the idea of hauling her out to look at the bottom. At Godthaab there is no convenient wall for a boat to be leant against. The harbour-master recommended a little creek near the anchorage where a big trading schooner was at that time hauled out and lying on her side – careened in fact. We had a look at the place but what with the boulders lying about and the difficulty of keeping *Mischief* upright, we thought that more harm than good might result. Finally we went alongside the quay to fill up with water, fuel, and paraffin, for we had no clear idea of what we should do if unable to reach Exeter Sound, or where our next port of call, if any, might be. Against this contingency, and through the influence of our Canadian friend, I changed some Danish money into dollars at the Kristinemut. Our standing there should have been high enough as it was, for we ate there every night, ringing the changes on whale steaks, salmon steaks, beef steaks, and smörgenbrod and shrimps.

At last on 25 July we got a report from Cape Dyer. The main item of it, 'heavily congested pack-ice two to five miles from the coast', was not very encouraging, but we thought we might as well go and see for ourselves. On the following morning we had a final shopping round-up, taking on board among other things no less than twenty-six massive loaves of rye bread. Later that day we entertained two guests, very fortunately for us at different times. Mick had been paying daily visits to the dentist. She – most of the dentists in Greenland appear to be women – having expressed a wish to see over *Mischief*, we invited her to lunch. Having seen this visitor ashore I went along to say good-bye to the harbour-master. It must have been a holiday because I found him in the go-down along with a few choice friends and on the floor in front of them two open cases of Carlsberg lager. The cases were nearly empty but this evidence was hardly needed to tell one that the party had been in progress for some time. Having helped them to finish the beer I began making my farewells. But that would not do. The harbour-master himself must come and see us off. So they staggered across the quay and lowered him down the ladder rung by rung into a waiting boat. It was a much bigger boat than our dinghy, and a good thing too, for throughout the short passage the harbour-master insisted on standing up to sing while he surveyed his watery domain with uncomprehending eyes. Having got him safely over the rail and down into the cabin we gave him a stiff go of rum to calm him, whereupon he signified that his boat's crew must have the same treatment. Getting him off proved to be a more difficult task than that of getting him on board. After a few groping, tentative efforts at cocking his leg over the rail he gave up and collapsed on the deck. So we pushed him under the rail and into the welcoming arms of his boat's crew amid loud cries of 'Bon voyage'. By then it was five o'clock so we got our anchor and sailed out.

CHAPTER FOURTEEN

First Attempt on Exeter Sound

A FAIR WIND took us quickly down the fjord. Approaching the islands we ran into fog and took care to keep them in sight one after another as we sailed by so that we made sure of passing the beacon. That done we pointed her head due west, the nearest we could get to north-west which was the course for Cape Dyer. After three days' sailing hard on the wind, and sometimes having to tack, we were disappointed when a noon sight put us in Lat. 64° 20′, or only some twenty miles north of the latitude of Godthaab. We attributed this poor result to leeway, because out in the middle of Davis Strait there should not have been any south-going current. We were surprised, too, to find that the sea temperature had risen from 40° F. to 44° F., but that could be accounted for by our being north of that branch of the Greenland current which turns westwards just south of what is called the Davis Strait Ridge between N. lat. 63° and 64°. Our first sunny, fogless day was more than welcome, for the weather for the first three days had been thick, raw, and wet, making the ropes and sails perpetually sodden. The next day, too, was so fine and sunny that some of us bathed on deck, the air and the sea temperature being the same at 44° F. There were several big icebergs about and also some bottle-nosed whales.

That night we ran fifty miles north-west, passing at midnight in fog within a hundred yards of a big berg. We reckoned we had Cape Walsingham abeam about forty miles away but on account of fog we could get no sights to verify this. By now it was clear we were in the Labrador current amidst the south-going stream of icebergs. Bergy bits and scattered floes became more numerous and that morning we passed a berg which we estimated to be a quarter-mile long. Not many minutes after this monster had disappeared in the fog we heard a thunderous roar like an avalanche which went on for an appreciable time. Evidently a part of it had broken off and capsized. I fully expected a miniature tidal wave would follow us but nothing happened. Until early afternoon we worked our way north through loose floes and belts of scattered pack-ice when we emerged into what appeared to be open water – open, that is to say, for about a half-mile which was the limit of visibility. A seal rolling about and playing on one of these floes seemed quite unalarmed and watched us with interest as we sailed by only fifty yards away. The wind continued fair so we held on northwards with the intention of reaching the latitude of Cape Dyer before turning in towards Exeter Sound. By now the sea temperature had dropped to 34° F. and the air to 40° F. These are not low temperatures for that region and we had nothing to complain about, but the all-pervading fog and damp made us feel extremely cold. Winter woollies and extra sweaters were now the wear and on deck oilskins had to be worn over-all. All that day we had not the least hint of sun, the sky having an unbroken leaden hue almost as dark as the sea. We began to find the constantly thick weather a little discouraging. But, as Sancho Panza used to say, all ills are good when attended by food. and that night we ate a rich risotto and screwed it down with a monumental plum duff – Michael Rhodes *fecit*.

At ten o'clock that night we had to heave-to, the sea being so cluttered with bergy bits. With a wind we could have steered round them but when the wind dropped, rather than start motoring, we just let her lie while the ice drifted by. Generally the floes drifted clear and only once did we have to poke an intruder out from under the bobstay. Of course if the sea had been rough we should not have viewed our small but dangerous neighbours with such com-placency. Next day, 1 August, we continued motoring towards the land. At last, later in the morning, the fog cleared and we got sights which put us in Lat. 66° 26′ N. and Long. 60° 15′ West, about forty miles from the coast and a little south of Cape Dyer. Early in the afternoon we sighted high land and after examining it through binoculars we could make out a radio mast and some buildings. Although we were aware of the air-strip on Cape Dyer, the reality was a nasty sight for men like ourselves who liked to think that they were closing a wild, desolate coast, unspoilt by man or traces of man. Even nastier, however, was the sight of a vague unbroken line of white close inshore. It might be fog but we feared almost certainly it was ice. Early that evening we reached the edge of this pack-ice, for so it proved to be. We were then ten to fifteen miles from the coast and from the masthead we could not see how far the ice reached for behind it lay a bank of fog. We motored slowly into the loose pack at the ice edge, more for the sake of taking photographs than with any intention of trying to force our way through.

This ice, of course, was no more than what we had expected to find. We had no call to be either surprised or disappointed, the question was what we should now do. Under the circumstances, with no promising leads in sight and ignorant of how thick the belt might be, we should have been foolish to enter the ice in the hope of barging a way through. We were not in a fjord but in the open sea where any wind or rough weather would start all this ice moving and heaving up and down. And merely 'getting through' might not be enough. For all we knew Exeter Sound itself might be jammed with ice. In the seasons of 1955 and 1956 when steamers were unloading stores in Exeter Bay for the building of the Cape Dyer establishment operations were much hampered by ice. On 7 August, 1956, the ice was so heavy that ice-breaker assistance was needed to break the ice in the anchorage so that unloading could continue. In summer the pack-ice moves freely, the ice groups and regroups, leads open and shut, according to strength and direction of the wind. We might, there-fore, hang about, Micawber-like, hoping something favourable would happen. Alternatively we could go back to Greenland and wait there in much more comfortable circumstances. We had still a month in hand and to our inexperi-enced eyes the solid belt of ice in front of us seemed hardly likely to disperse in much less than that. We decided to compromise by going down the coast

as far south as Angijak Island south of Cape Walsingham. If the ice proved
to be continuous and no openings presented themselves we would retire to
Holsteinborg. Southwards seemed our best bet, for north of Cape Dyer the
coast trends to the west, so that ice drifting down from the north would tend
to bank up against the land.

All that night we sailed south. The helmsman, Roger Brown, reported
killer whales but whether they were seen is another matter. Roger Brown had
such a propensity for seeing this voracious kind of whale that he himself
earned the name of 'Killer'. Hans, by the way, had long answered to the name
of 'Uncle'; not that he was rich but that his manner was a little avuncular,
fussy, and prone to giving advice to the younger members of the crew, who,
indeed, sometimes, stood in want of it. At midnight fog came down again and
remained with us throughout the whole of as vile, wet, and foggy a day as we
had yet experienced. The sea temperature was 34° F. and the air 36° F. In the
evening we had to turn west to avoid ice and after resuming our southerly
course we met more pack-ice at midnight. We hove-to for the night in a
position estimated to be thirty miles east of Cape Walsingham.

On a drizzly morning with a fresh easterly wind and no ice in sight we let
draw and continued southwards. What, we wondered, had happened to all
the ice we had seen at midnight? The glass remained steady, but off the coast,
whether it went up or down, the weather remained consistently thick and wet.
Later we again sighted the familiar line of white stretching away both ahead
of us and to starboard. Again we made a board of five miles out to the east
before turning south and once more saw ice ahead of us. Hereabouts, forty
miles off the coast, there seemed to be more ice than around Cape Dyer. So
at noon we gave up and set a course for Holsteinborg 180 miles away across
the narrowest part of Davis Strait. In the evening, when we saw another great
raft of pack-ice covering several miles of sea, we rashly concluded that we had
seen the last of it. About two in the morning Roger Brown called me to say
we were among floes. I went up and took the helm for we were sailing fast in
smooth water under all plain sail. That it was foggy goes without saying. At
first I thought these floes were merely a few stragglers and that we should
soon be clear, though the smoothness of the sea might have warned me that
there was pack-ice in the vicinity. In fact if the sea suddenly becomes smooth
it is a pretty sure hint that there is pack-ice to windward. If loose floes are
scattered over a wide area any wind tends to regroup them and as the wind
rises they collect in belts running in a direction at right angles to the wind. As
we were sailing with the wind just forward of the beam we were likely to
become more involved, as we very soon did.

At first it was fun dodging the floes but, sailing as fast as we were, this
presently became too hazardous. All hands were called to get the mainsail off
and we jogged along under stays'l alone. We had erred in not turning back on
first meeting ice, for by now it was all round us and we were forced to follow
the most open lead in whatever direction it might take us. Although the sea
was smooth a perceptible swell added to the difficulty. At one moment we
would appear to be following an open lead and suddenly floes would heave in
sight on top of the swell. After two hours of it we had got nowhere and were

still unable to see in what direction to steer to find open water. Then the lead we were following narrowed and began to close ahead of us. We downed the stays'l to lessen the impending impact and at the same time noticed with alarm a big tabular floe, much bigger than *Mischief*, making straight at us. It was undercut all along the water-line where even in that murky light the ice shone balefully blue, and as it came towards us, travelling faster than we were, it brushed aside the smaller floes in its path. This big, blue bastard, as we immediately christened it, seemed bent on our destruction. For one or two confused minutes we were hemmed in and to my heated imagination seemed to be lifted up and riding on ice. Then, having started the engine, we began slowly making headway. The floes thinned, the sea became rough, and at last we were in open water. Hard by lay a big iceberg, as white and fresh-looking as if it had just broken off a glacier. Under its lee we hoisted sail and resumed our course. By the time we had brewed coffee and turned in, leaving the helmsman to carry on, it was five o'clock. I suppose an experienced ice navigator, instead of taking fright at the approach of this threatening monster, would have moored his ship to it and allowed it to clear a path for him through the raft of floes.

This ice, we thought, must have been the tail-end of what is known as the 'middle-pack', the great tongue of loosely packed ice that stretches down west of the centre axis of Davis Strait from Baffin Bay to beyond Cape Dyer. We reckoned we were about eighty miles from the Canadian coast when we encountered it. The old whalers trying to reach the 'north water' in June or early July often got into serious trouble in this 'middle pack'. In the year 1830, out of the fleet of ninety-one British whalers, nineteen were lost and at one time there were 1,000 men on the ice, men whose ships had already been nipped and sunk or whose ships were beset. It was known in whaling history as 'Baffin Fair'. On such occasions, thanks to the presence of so many ships, few lives were lost, but some terrible scenes took place. Once a ship was nipped and making water fast so that she looked like sinking, the men would remove themselves and their gear to the ice, the rum casks were broached, and all discipline came to an end. And apparently it became a custom or tradition that a ship so nipped should be set on fire.

By the evening of 5 August, a lovely, calm evening, we were once more off the Greenland coast about twenty miles north of Holsteinborg. It was a Sunday. Two Portuguese schooners lay idle side by side, enjoying like us the sunny, peaceful calm. What a contrast, we thought to the Canadian coast – no ice, no fog (for the moment), and a benign sun. The sea temperature having risen to 44° F. we felt we were in tropical waters. Like most Greenland ports the approach to Holsteinborg is guarded or obstructed, according to the point of view, by islands and rocks. If one is confident enough to use them one has usually a choice of two or three channels. We were cautious and generally followed the course prescribed as suitable for large vessels. The sea-mark to pick up when approaching Holsteinborg from the north or west is Qagssit, one of a small group of low-lying islands with a beacon on it. Having given that a wide berth one steers for Anatsusok, one of a cluster of islands off the harbour entrance on which is a beacon and a light, taking care at the same time to avoid Jacob's Skaer, a rock only two feet high. It is also worth noting that three miles south-east of Qagssit is a rock with less than six feet of water over it on which the sea rarely breaks. On this HMS *Valorous* struck in 1875 – a long time ago, but no doubt the rock is still there. Early next morning, keeping a wary eye on the diminutive Jacob's Skaer and other dangers, we downed sail and motored through the harbour entrance. The main harbour looked so small and so full of shipping of various kinds that we went on to have a look at the inner harbour. This was large enough and completely empty, for it is cut off from the town, so back we went to the busy main harbour. A friendly police boat (one of three similar boats that were newly arrived at Godthaab from Denmark when we were last there) warned us that in a vacant hole we were making for there lurked a submerged rock. We had to go right in close to a floating jetty where the smaller fishing boats lay, where we dropped anchor and laid out a warp to the shore. We were barely clear of the fairway; I felt that sooner or later one of the many fishing boats which were constantly coming and going would fail to notice *Mischief*'s long bowsprit. Luckily it was a period of neap tides. Had it been springs we should have been on the bottom at low water.

Holsteinborg is an important fishing port, with a curing factory and a cannery for shrimps. Having a small shipyard and slipway it is one of the few places on the coast where ships can be repaired and even built. That evening the assistant manager of the yard paid us a visit. He told us that except for the manager and himself the men in the yard were Greenlanders and mostly competent workmen. Apparently we were not quite the first yacht to visit Holsteinborg. An Italian – a rich man, I imagine – had for several seasons kept his motor-yacht there, laying her up in the yard for the winter, and in summer, after flying out with his crew, cruising on the coast. That summer he had taken a climbing party to the Devil's Thumb, a 1,800ft. rock pillar, a well-known landmark, up in Lat. 74° 30′. The yacht had two 300-horse-power engines and a skipper, lent by the Greenland Trading Company, who knew the coast. It is worth recalling that a few of our Victorian yachtsmen, generally wealthy men, preferred the Arctic to the Mediterranean for summer cruises. Of course, in those days yachts were something more than what we now understand by the term and they were generally crewed by professionals. There was Lord Dufferin, for example, who sailed to Jan Mayen and Spitsbergen, and Leigh Smith, who made five Arctic voyages, two as far as Franz Joseph Land. On the last of these in 1873 the *Eira*, a 360-ton steam-yacht, strengthened for ice, was nipped in the ice and sunk. The crew wintered there successfully and next summer, in four of the yacht's boats, sailed 450 miles to Nova Zembla where they were picked up.

Besides the number of small boats engaged in fishing we were impressed by several well-kept, well-equipped fishing boats of about thirty tons, with wireless, echo-sounders, life-saving rafts, and some with a harpoon gun mounted in the bows. These were apparently built in Denmark at a cost of about £15,000 and shipped out to Greenland to be taken over on easy terms by local fishermen. There are some fifteen hundred people in Holsteinborg and we reckoned that every man, woman, and child must have owned a team of huskies. (In Godthaab dogs are absolutely forbidden.) The place fairly crawled with dogs, especially around the harbour, the wharves, and the fish factory where there were fish offal, scraps of whale or reindeer meat to be picked up, and oil barrels to lick. Some swam about the harbour in search of food. Around many of the houses there were dogs which were obviously fed, but the majority, we were told, were not fed in summer and had to fend for themselves. We had noticed on the way in a pack of huskies confined on a small island where it seemed impossible that they could eke out an existence, but we were assured that these, too, were not fed and were parked there to be out of the way. There were almost as many children running loose as there were dogs, clambering over *Mischief* and rowing about the harbour in our dinghy. When they were being unusually trying I sometimes regretted that the harsher methods of dog management had not been applied to the children.

There was no place here corresponding to the Kristinemut, nowhere for the sea-weary mariner to go to wash the salt out of his mouth except a rather dreary coffee bar. Beer could be bought only over the counter at the general store and, as we soon learnt, could not be bought at all until a fresh consignment arrived. When in harbour we liked to have our evening meal ashore and Mick heard from a friendly Dane that we might be able to muscle in, as it were, at a hostel where some seventy Danish technicians and workmen had their meals. Just as at Godthaab a lot of constructional work was in hand, new houses being built, roads made, and drains laid. Accordingly, on our first evening we repaired to the hostel. As George Robey used to sing: 'My word, it was fine; they were just going to dine; my reception gave me quite a shock.' They were all so delighted to see us, or so we imagined as we slid modestly into some vacant seats at the foot of a long table. A very good meal we had, too, conversing brightly with our neighbours, behaving with decorum, and finally paying our bill. Next morning I went up to the hostel to warn them that we should be dining with them again that evening. I was confronted, however, by the manageress, a large, square-rigged Danish woman, strikingly masculine in face and figure, who at once gave me a curt 'no' and with whom I felt no inclination to argue.

Some further slight embarrassment awaited me later that morning when I set out to find the dentist. At the quay a drunken Greenlander attached himself to me and refused to be shaken off. Every passer-by had to be stopped and told who his distinguished friend was, and presently they were being told, too, where I was bound for, the drunk having discovered my destination when I asked a Dane where the dentist lived. At the door of the dentist's waiting-room I tried to shut him out but he followed me in and introduced me loudly to each member of the small suffering assembly. The noise he made brought the dentist herself into the room. Hastily explaining the matter and thrusting my broken teeth into her hand I withdrew before she had time to ask who my drunken companion was. But I had not yet done with him. I had to go to his house where, in a neat room with a polished wood floor, he made me sit while he cranked up an ancient gramophone and turned his wireless on at full bore. This brought in his wife who after viewing with distaste her polished floor, followed him with a floor-cloth as he walked about wiping away the marks left by his muddy gumboots. Finally, seeing no end to it, she made him sit down while she hauled his boots off and threw them out. He had not brought me to his house purely out of affection. Presently he went out of the room and returned with his wife's full regalia – high, embroidered boots, shirt, collar, the lot – which he offered to me for £30. Upon my declining this bargain he asked for a 2/– tip for having shown me the dentist's house!

The drunk's house was perched perilously on a rock above the road and the floating jetty, a wooden staircase giving access to the road. It must have been one of the first houses built, for now they extend inland as much as a mile from the harbour. The floating jetty always presented a busy scene, particularly if a boat came in with a load of whale meat or reindeer meat. This would be cut up into large hunks, weighed, and sold on the spot to a crowd of eager buyers. Behind Holsteinborg and its adjacent coast there is a stretch of broken, hilly country of nearly a hundred miles between the coast and the inland ice, a piece of country well stocked with reindeer. Hunting, we were told, is permitted for two months in the year, August and February. When we tired of watching the activity on the jetty we used to walk round to the other side of the harbour where cargo was landed from lighters and where the larger fishing boats landed their catch for the curing factory. The shore gang handling cargoes consisted of women. At the curing factory the cod were hauled up in baskets to be gutted by one gang of men and filleted at adjacent tables by another. Inside the factory were high stacks of alternate layers of salt and fish which in the curing process have to be moved and restacked with, I suppose, as much expert knowledge as would be required for curing tobacco or maturing Stilton cheese.

With a slipway at hand it seemed a mistake not to have *Mischief* slipped, to satisfy ourselves that our two slight accidents in the ice had not started a plank. The assistant manager said they were too busy. Three ships in turn had been on the slip since our arrival, one of them a survey ship which had hit a rock – an occupational hazard of survey ships on that coast. He suggested we might save time and money by putting her against the wall near the floating jetty where, he said, there were nine feet of water at high tide. We agreed to try and at midday, high tide being soon after, the yard launch came to tow us in. We had already taken some soundings and I was doubtful that there would be enough water for us. Sure enough, when a few yards out from the wall we took the ground. The yard men waited a bit for the tide to rise though to us it seemed already at a stand. They then gave us another violent pluck and succeeded in putting us yet more firmly aground. At my earnest request they then tried to pull her off. She would not budge and there we were, out of reach of the wall, with no visible means of support when the tide ebbed. Happily our friend at the yard, a man of action, saw what had happened. Hailing the launch over, he sent them back with the big wire hawser attached to the slipway winch. It did occur to us that when the electric winch took the strain our samson post together with half our deck might be torn out. But this alarming thought had hardly time to sink in before the wire tightened and we slid off into deep water.

The assistant manager would not be beaten. Night tides, he said, are always higher than day tides, so we must try again at midnight when he would send the launch and his gang to help. That night tides are always higher is a fallacy; it depends on the declination of the moon. It may so happen that for weeks together the night tides are higher; but if this is so, at another period of the year the reverse will be the case. Anyhow before midnight I rowed the head boatman across to where there was a slightly dilapidated tide gauge on which I had marked the height reached by the morning tide. Having pointed out the present level and asked him whether he thought the tide could make two feet in the next half-hour, I found he agreed with me that it was no go. So we gave the boatmen a glass of rum apiece for their trouble and sent them home. The head boatman, a man with a most villainous countenance, downed his at one gulp. As Michael Finsbury said: 'I have never seen a man drink faster; it restored one's confidence in the human race.'

At the shipyard next morning they agreed that we should have to wait for spring tides; they added that in four or five days' time they would be able to take us on the slip. Holsteinborg, amusing and interesting though it was, had no beer and too many dogs, urchins, and mosquitoes. Moreover it was very hot: 80° F. in the sun and 65° F. in the shade. We decided to retire to the country for a few days, to Nordre Isortok, the next fjord to the north only fifteen miles away.

CHAPTER FIFTEEN

Mount Raleigh

THE PASSAGE to Isortok, a matter of a few hours, took us the best part of three days. In the evening when we were rounding the Qagssit group of islands the wind piped up from south and began to blow with some vigour. At midnight, when we thought we were still south of Nordre Isortok by a few miles, we reefed and hove-to on the starboard tack, the wind then blowing about Force 6. We must have been fore-reaching fast because at three in the morning some islands showed up. They may well have been the islands at the mouth of our fjord and had we been bolder we might have run in for shelter. Instead we took fright, let draw, gybed to the other tack and stood away from the land. At the same time the outhaul and lacing at the peak of the gaff began to go. The mainsail, therefore, had to come down and a fine job we had. The new peak halyard of 2½-inch rope that had recently been fitted stubbornly refused to render through the blocks. Once the mainsail was down we could not heave-to. The boat ran off rapidly to the north until the staysail, too, had been taken in when we lay-a-try under bare poles.

We soon renewed the gaff lacing and outhaul but there was now no hope of beating back to Isortok for the wind had increased; nor could we have found it because it was raining hard as well. Throughout a long day, sea and sky one grey wetness, we lay, rolling heavily and drifting to the north-west. Poor Mick was sea-sick all the time. Early next day, the third since we had left Holsteinborg, the wind began to take off. When the rain cleared we found we had two trawlers in company. Close aboard a whale swam around the ship, sometimes turning over on its back. From its white flukes and white belly we identified it as a Piked whale or Lesser Rorqual, not more than thirty feet in length. In the course of the day we recovered the thirty or more miles we had been blown northwards and by evening were off the entrance of our fjord. On our small-scale chart the entrance looked fearfully intricate, as though islets had been scattered over it from a giant pepper-pot. In reality, in daylight and good visibility, the passage proved simple enough. Nordre Isortok is thirty-five miles long. We contented ourselves with a mere twelve miles, anchoring late that night at the head of a short arm called Isortuarssuk. We noticed two Greenlander boats anchored and the light of a camp fire on shore. It was an unusual fjord in that the water shoaled gradually. When we let go in four fathoms we were a good half-mile from the shore and between us and the shore some huge boulders showed above water. By mere chance we had entered at low water. At high water all the boulders were covered so that we might easily have anchored among them and found ourselves sitting on top of one when the tide ebbed. There are no tide tables for these parts – or at least we had none – and one can only tell what the tide is doing by watching closely the water-level along the rocks of the fjord.

I cannot say I enjoyed our visit to Isortok. It had begun badly and continued as it had begun. In retrospect it seems to have been a case of one damned thing after another. The mountains in the neighbourhood are less than 3,000ft. Roger rushed up one alone the first day while I made a botanical excursion up the valley. There were few flowers and few mosquitoes but myriads of little black flies like midges. Having set out without any 'Dusk' ointment I soon found myself being driven demented. A gentle wind blew up the valley; I found that by facing about and walking into it the midges hovering round one were blown away; but those tactics could not be persisted in if I meant to walk up the valley. To stop to collect flowers, taking off the rucksack and getting out the press, was out of the question; even the sight of something as rare as a black tulip could hardly have induced me to stop. I was determined to get as far as a big lake three miles up the valley, a lake shut in by high rock walls with red screes running down to it, not unlike the Wastwater screes. By then I had had enough. The slight wind had now dropped so that no relief could be expected on the homeward journey. Instead I fled violently uphill on to a ridge on the south side of the valley, hoping to escape from my tormentors. Quite useless. At a height of a thousand feet the midges were equally at home. In Kipling's story 'The Vortex' a man takes refuge from a swam of angry bees by hurling himself into the village pond. Nearing home, when a deep pool presented itself, I undressed hastily and jumped in. It was too cold to stay there long and to dress meant standing still. So, snatching up my clothes and boots, I sped naked along the beach towards the dinghy. The next day my face had swelled so much I could hardly see.

After supper that night it began to rain and a wind blew down the fjord raising quite a sea. At first, as we felt an occasional shudder, we thought the anchor was snubbing and let out more chain. Whereupon she began to bump on the bottom in no uncertain way. On taking a sounding over the stern we got only six feet of water. With the tide beginning to ebb we worked hard to get her off but the anchor merely came home and the engine failed to move her. For the next hour she continued to bump and at every bump we winced involuntarily. As she finally settled she heeled at an alarming angle and remained like that until three in the morning. At five we floated again and when we got the anchor in we saw why she had dragged, the cable having taken a turn round the fluke of the anchor.

It continued stormy throughout the day. Nevertheless we went out in the dinghy trying vainly to catch some cod, watching enviously the Greenlanders on shore as they plucked salmon from the nets they had laid off the mouth of a stream. When the weather improved next day I finished painting the half of the deck we had left undone. While kneeling on the deck painting, difficult though it may seem, I managed to lose overside a favourite pipe. On top of that the mainspring of our chronometer watch chose this time to break. Watchmaker Hans could do nothing about that, but we could get on without it so long as we could obtain time signals. Where, when, and upon whom, I wondered, would misfortune strike next? So far no day at this anchorage had been without its minor accident.

Meantime the question of catching salmon was under urgent consideration. We searched the ship for empty bottles and jars to act as floats for Shaun's net and a large party went ashore at low tide to set it – as close to the Greenlanders' nets as we could manage without being accused of poaching. Having laid it out, moored it to two boulders, and fastened weights to the bottom, we watched the floats ride jauntily on the water as the tide began to make. For a few hours we had no more to do but lament the absence of green peas and new potatoes. Nevertheless, when the Greenlanders came to cadge flour we thought it only prudent to take some salmon in exchange. How wise we were. In our net there was not even a piece of seaweed while on the same tide the Greenlanders gathered their usual harvest of fish. Some of the salmon they salted down in barrels and some they smoked in a flue made of stones and sods. For fuel there was abundant dwarf willow and heath. They presented us with a smoked salmon, the most delicious thing we had eaten in Greenland. As well as fishing, the party were out after reindeer, or caribou. We saw fresh tracks and Shaun said he had actually seen one.

Having been away quite long enough we set out for Holsteinborg. In the afternoon when we were approaching Qagssit, the wind fair, the sea smooth, and visibility excellent, I decided to try the inner passage instead of taking the longer and safer way round. The tide setting strongly to the north took us near the shore, but in the fjords one becomes so accustomed to sailing within a stone's throw of the rocks that I thought we had room enough to weather a small projecting point. We weathered it all right though not in a very seaman-like fashion. We bumped once on a rock and slid off again before the panic party called up from below had had time to lower the mainsail. Now that spring tides were running our old berth was useless so we tied up by the shipyard quay with four boats inside us and our bowsprit almost tickling the rail of our old acquaintance *Mallemuken*. She was also waiting to go on the slip. She had discovered the whereabouts of a sunken rock by the infallible method of hitting it and had sustained considerable damage to her bottom plates. In fact the damage was beyond the ability of the yard to repair; she had to be patched up for returning to Denmark. Lying outside the harbour was the survey vessel we had met at Timerdlit. For her the working season was over and she was about to sail for Denmark to be laid up for the winter. That evening we went on board her where a large party had gathered. Her skipper showed me some extraordinary traces recorded by his echo-sounding machine; they resembled the greatly magnified teeth of a cross-cut saw. At one point the trace showed that the bottom rose from a depth of 300 metres to a depth of five metres in what was virtually a vertical line. He thought that with experience, by watching the configuration of the land, one could tell whether the water would be deep or shallow; and that while it was generally safe to go between the coast and a string of islets, it was seldom safe to go between the islets themselves.

A British trawler came in that night to land two injured men and left early before we had time to visit her. A Portuguese trawler, too, lay outside with engine trouble; we were impressed by the smartness of the uniform her officers wore and by the behaviour of her men. An even more interesting visitor was the good ship *Umanak* with 40,000 bottles, or possibly cases, of beer. The news spread like wildfire and there were some ugly scenes at the General Store where we took care to be in good time to buy beer and also some fruit that she had brought. Except for lemons this was the only bit of fruit we had during the voyage.

Yet another arrival was the Portuguese hospital ship *Gil Eanes*. She carries six doctors, has the equipment to deal with any injury or illness, and is responsible for the health and well-being of the 6,000-odd men in the Portuguese schooner and trawler fleets fishing on the Grand Banks and in Davis Strait. As well as taking off sick men from schooners in the open sea, she supplies them with fresh water, diesel oil, and galley coal. Having met one of her doctors, who said he had a Hull trawler man in his care, we went on board to see him and were shown all over her. The Hull man expected to be landed and flown home; he spoke highly of the skill and kindness of the Portuguese. She had several large wards, X-ray room, operating theatre with a lift down to it, and a large, competent staff. The *Gil Eanes* extends a helping hand to any sick or injured fisherman irrespective of nationality.

The *Mallemuken* was at length hauled out and behind her another small survey vessel which was to be laid up for the winter in the yard. On the first attempt, the stern of the *Mallemuken* being in the way, the survey vessel could not be hauled high enough to move her sideways off the slip. So they let her down and put her on the cradle askew so that the next time her bow came up clear of *Mallemuken*'s stern. It was now our turn. The fact that *Mischief* had reclined on her side for a few hours in Isortok and had bumped on a rock on the way back, made us the more set on examining her hull. When she was hauled out that evening we were relieved to find that except for loss of paint her hull showed no sign of damage. This fact surprised both me and the crew, whose apprehensions, if they had had any, were thus set at rest. Quite a crowd gathered to see *Mischief* out of the water, the local boat-fanciers expressing admiration for her shapely, workmanlike lines.

By 9 am we were back in the water and devoted the rest of the morning to shopping and to taking our last photographs before starting for Exeter Sound. There is one small building in Holsteinborg worthy of a photograph,, a small, simple church with blue walls and red roof, with a golden weather-vane on its miniature steeple. It is reputed to be the original Moravian Mission church and has the date 1732 on the weather-vane. It has been superseded by a much bigger church and appeared now to be used as a sort of crèche. Outside it, in the form of an arch, are two enormous jawbones from a whale.

Until we were off Qagssit we had no wind, then with a nice breeze from south freshening all the time we went fast and bang on course. During the night, when I was on watch, I found we were encompassed by about a dozen trawlers. Trawlers at night, I always think, are as dangerous to meet as trams are to a motorist, for they follow an unswerving course. If any avoiding action is called for it is seldom taken by the trawler. At four o'clock I was roused by *Mischief*'s unusual motion, trembling all over like a weight-lifter making a prodigious effort. I found she was doing about 'twelve knots and a Chinaman' under whole mainsail and Genoa with a Force 6 wind. We usually take the Genoa in at night, for we do not like our sleep disturbed. Should one decide to leave it up, however tranquil the appearance of the sky and sea, one can be fairly certain of having to turn out to take it down, such is the perversity of the weather at sea. We took it down and put two rolls in the mainsail. In the morning it was overcast, wet, and still blowing hard, and by midday we had reeled off 100 miles. That evening when we were only about sixty miles off Cape Dyer the weather thickened and we met several icebergs. The sea temperature went down to 36°F., twelve degrees lower than at Holsteinborg. At night the wind died, leaving us rolling heavily and surrounded by fog.

In the morning a fresh breeze dispersed the fog and we sailed fast all day in a rough sea until at 5 pm we once more sighted Cape Dyer. As we drew in towards the land south of the cape we smoothed our water and as yet there was no sign of any ice apart from a few scattered bergs. Our delight at finding the coast clear was no less than our astonishment that so much ice could vanish in so short a time. It was now 20 August so that in a short three weeks the solid belt of ice along the coast had completely dispersed and disintegrated. Even with Cape Dyer as a point of reference we found the coast south of it puzzling, nor could we see any likely anchorage. When it became dark, as it did now by ten o'clock, we let her drift, the wind having died away.

The morning broke fine and sunny. It almost seemed that so close to the land or in the absence of ice the fog had no encouragement to form. Having identified Cape Walsingham to the south and the wide mouth of Exeter Sound before us, we sailed in. When the wind failed we motored for fifteen miles to Davis's Totnes Roads and to an anchorage off the mouth of a small valley. Three tall icebergs lay grounded half a mile from the shore. About three miles up the valley we could see a glacier and overlooking it the cliffs of what I had already assumed to be Mount Raleigh. Strong sunlight playing on the cliffs, as well as a little imagination, were needed to make them appear 'orient as gold'; but these were the only striking cliffs in view and from farther out in the fjord this mountain alone had filled the observer's eye.

After spreading the sails to dry we lost no time in setting foot on a shore that for so long had occupied most of our thoughts, a shore that so recently had seemed utterly unapproachable. We walked along to the mouth of the valley where the river fed by the glacier tumbled over a waterfall into the sea. A more barren, lifeless place it would be difficult to find. Yet in Davis's day there had been life enough, as witness the adventure his party had immediately they landed here:

So soon as we were come to an anker in Totnes rode under Mount Raleigh we espied four white beares at the foot of the mount: we supposing them to be goats or wolves, manned our boats and went towards them; but when we came near the shore we found them to be white beares of a monstrous bignesse. We being desirous of fresh victuall and the sport began to assault them, and I being on land, one of them came downe the hill right against me: my piece was charged with hailshot and a bullet: I discharged my piece and shot him in the necke; he roared a little and tooke the water straight making small account of his hurt. Then we followed him with our boat and killed him with boare speares, and two more that night.

The 7th we went on shore to another beare which lay all night upon an island under Mount Raleigh (this island was about a mile from our anchorage) and when we came up to him he lay fast asleep. Then I shot being charged with two bullets and strooke him in the head. Whereupon we all ran upon him with boare speares. The breadth of his forefoot from one side to the other was 14 inches. They were very fat, so as we were constrained to cast the fat away. We saw a raven upon Mt Raleigh. The coast is very mountainous, altogether without wood, grass, or earth, and is onely huge mountaines of stone; but the bravest stone that ever we saw. The aire was very moderate in this country.

The 8th we departed from Mount Raleigh, coasting along the shoare which lieth south-south-west and east-north-east.

We had with us a Canadian map of the area on a scale of 1:500,000. There have been cases of 'explorers' of the present day penetrating into 'unknown' country and complaining that the maps were misleading. For obvious reasons the surveying of mountainous regions is not regarded as a matter of urgency and when it is at last done the survey need not be rigorous. For a region such as the Cumberland Peninsula, difficult to approach either by land or sea, uninhabited and apparently of no economic value, it is a wonder that there is any map at all. The map in question is therefore, as might be expected, not in a very advanced state: glaciers are shown, cliffs are marked, a few heights are given in round figures, and lakes, rivers, and the coast line are delineated with some degree of accuracy. The only named mountain is Mt Raleigh. No height is given and its position is marked with a very small dot. One felt that whoever put it there might have had doubts and half-hoped that it might be overlooked. However, there was no mistake about it for Roger, too, had a map on which the same dot appeared. What troubled us was to see that the Mt Raleigh of the map lay on the opposite side of the glacier to what we assumed to be Mt Raleigh. It looked as if we should have to climb both.

Roger and I overhauled our climbing gear with unexpected pleasure. When we had at last stowed away boots, axes, rope, crampons, tent, and cooking-pots neither of us had confidently believed that we should need them again that summer. Accompanied by three of the crew we set out next morning to put a camp somewhere near the glacier. In spite of its cliffs Mt Raleigh did not appear to be formidable. From a point short of the glacier snout the cliffs could be avoided and the long summit ridge looked flat and featureless. We moved up the left bank of the stream over rough boulder-strewn slopes and presently came to a large lake. Skirting the shore of the lake we gained little height until we reached a steep rock dyke through which the stream had cut a gorge; above the dyke lay a smaller lake reaching almost to the glacier snout. We camped by the shore of the lake at a height of 400ft. Surprisingly enough – for in most accounts of travel in the Canadian Arctic they are noticed with fervour – there were hardly any mosquitoes or black flies. The vegetation was sparse and the little there was seemed similar to that of West Greenland.

Leaving camp next morning at 8.45 we climbed the moderately steep slopes above it and gained the summit ridge at a height of 3,000ft. By then we were enveloped in cloud and snow fell gently but persistently. As we plodded along the broad ridge, sometimes on rock and sometimes on snow, with the cliffs falling steeply on our left, Roger, deceived by the bad visibility, surprised me by announcing that we had reached the summit. To me such news was very welcome but after years of climbing experience, with failures more numerous than successes, I regarded it with suspicion. We had still some way to go. We ate a remarkably joyless lunch sitting on a wet rock with our feet in the snow. At long length the ridge rose abruptly and we toiled up a wide stony glacis to what was undoubtedly the summit. The height by aneroid was 5,700ft. From here we should have looked out to the 'false' Mt Raleigh on the other side of the glacier but the cloud was now thicker than ever. Having built a massive cairn we started down.

Success must have gone to our heads. From the stony slope we got on to snow and after rattling along for half an hour we began to suspect that things were not as they ought to have been. When the ridge we were following narrowed and ended in a snow dome we realized we were all adrift. In spite of the falling snow our steps, which we now retraced, were fortunately still visible, and towards three o'clock we were relieved when our cairn loomed up out of the mist. This time, by keeping close to the edge of the cliffs on our right, we made no mistake. No mistake, at least, until we forsook the long certainty of the ridge to plunge down a steep gully which we thought would take us more swiftly home. The rock was steep and loose and the snow down which we had expected to glissade turned out to be hard ice. Twice I took a toss – for I was getting tired – cutting my hands and losing my axe which we found again only after a long search. We reached the tent at six o'clock. It had been raining in the valley so the inside of it was a bit wet; but we had climbed one Mt Raleigh and I went to sleep wondering whether I should have the strength to climb another one next day.

Our luck was in. The day broke fine, sunny, and windless. We went up the glacier. We wanted to explore it and we thought it likely that from the col at its head there would be a ridge leading on to the 'false' Mt Raleigh. A snow-ridge led down to the col from the mountain we had already climbed – in fact we had talked of descending by it – and we had expected to find a similar ridge on the opposite side of the col though we could not see it from the camp. We found excellent going on the glacier and gained height quickly, the cliffs of the 'false' Mt Raleigh now in full view on our left and bearing a remarkable resemblance to the opposing cliffs. When we were at a height of about 1,700ft., still short of the col, we could see that the cliffs continued unbroken beyond the col and that the ridge we had expected to find did not exist. We were now almost directly below the summit of 'false' Mt Raleigh, so quitting the glacier we tackled the cliffs. These proved to be not nearly so steep as they appeared. Helped by some snow-gullies we climbed quickly and by lunch-time were only a thousand feet below the top. Lunch was far more enjoyable on that day as we sat on a sun-warmed rock, the glacier far below our feet, and confronted by the massive bulk of Mt Raleigh with cloud shadows drifting across its snow-sprinkled cliffs.

The snow of the previous day lay thick on the rocks but we were soon just under the summit which was guarded by a steep wall of ice. We outflanked this and walked over hard snow to the top. The height by aneroid was 5,200ft. The respective heights of the two mountains do not really matter, neverthe-less we were pleased to find that what we took to be Davis's Mt Raleigh had the advantage by 500ft. From the top, where we built another cairn, we could see over the whole tip of the Cumberland Peninsula, from Cape Walsingham to the south and to a fjord to the west of Cape Dyer. From a mountaineer's point of view this eastern extremity of the peninsula is uninviting, the moun-tains uniformly rounded and uninteresting. Mt Raleigh itself, apart from its southern face of cliffs, has not much character, and might be thought hardly worthy of its illustrious name or of the great seaman-explorer who named it. Nevertheless, it is a mountain that I for one shall always hold dear. We got off our mountain by way of a long and easy glacier which terminated at the lake on the opposite side to our camp. Walking round the muddy shore we were back at the tent by 5 pm, our mission accomplished. From his sack Roger produced another tin of 'Mandarin' oranges.

On the way down next morning Shaun met us below the gorge and gave us the news. They had shot a duck but caught no fish. A fox and an Arctic hare had been seen and a great number of caribou heads. Shaun himself had a particularly fine specimen which had to be sawn in half before we could find a home for it behind the engine. They had found the remains of old Eskimo settlements and a couple of fairly modern traps. At present the nearest Eskimo settlement is on Padloping Island forty miles north of Cape Dyer where in 1955 the population was thirty-one. For supper that night we had stewed duck and a chocolate pudding fit for a glass case.

CHAPTER SIXTEEN

Homeward Bound

WE HAD done what we set out to do, our stores were getting low, and it was time to turn for home. Cape Farewell was nearly 800 miles away, a distance that we expected might take a couple of weeks in view of the variable winds and calms of the Davis Strait. Once to the east of the cape we looked forward confidently to being blown swiftly across the Atlantic by strong westerly winds. As well as being without the use of the chronometer watch, we no longer had the benefit of our wireless set, a valve having broken. Apart from being unable to get time signals, the lack of it hardly mattered. In some ways, I think, we were better without it. If one is going to be at sea for a few weeks in a sailing vessel one might as well do it properly and realize to the full the self-sufficiency of one's own small world by abstaining from communication with the shore or from news of whatever may be happening there. As Belloc well said: 'In venturing in sail upon strange coasts we are seeking first experiences. Trying to feel as felt the earlier man in a happier time. To see the world as they saw it.'

As for having the correct time to the nearest second I think we tended to make too much fuss. In mid-ocean it is nice to know where you are within some miles but I would not put it stronger than that. Ten, twenty, or thirty miles makes no difference out there; and to a watchful eye there are often signs indicative of the presence of land when yet a day's sail or more away, in time enough to begin taking appropriate precautions. Mick's watch was reputedly reliable. Before leaving the coast we checked it by taking a sight, working it out by the time of this watch, comparing the longitude so found with the known longitude, and thus finding the error of the watch. The rough rating of the watch was known and a few days later, in an attempt to check it, we took equal altitude sights either side of noon. That is to say one takes a sight about a quarter hour before noon and, without altering the sextant, takes the time when the sun is at the same altitude on its downward path after noon. The mean of these times should be apparent noon at the ship. It is rough and ready but provided the ship is nearly stationary there need not be a very large error. Lecky damns it as a method 'very alluring to people who either suffer from want of energy, or have been insufficiently grounded in first principles'. We need not have bothered. On board there was a small transistor set of Shaun's which as soon as we got within 500 miles of home waters would give us time signals, the news, or any other unpleasantness we might want to hear. Slocum, by the way, sailed round the world, making very exact landfalls, with no more elaborate timepiece than an alarm clock which he got cheap for a dollar because it had only one hand. He had to boil it, too, before it went to his satisfaction. But Slocum was reputedly highly skilled in the working of what were called 'Lunars', a method of finding the longitude without benefit of a chronometer by taking altitudes of sun and moon and the angle between the two bodies.

We sailed out of Exeter Sound on 26 August, a wonderfully fine, clear day and very cold. The sea temperature was 39° F. and the air 40° F. From a long way out to sea Mt Raleigh stood out boldly from among its neighbours like a true mountain. We had little if any doubt left that this is Davis's mountain and that the map is in error. That night and for the next fortnight, whenever the sky was clear, we observed magnificent auroral displays. The last faint occurrence we noted was when we were in as low a latitude as 52°N. On account of the name Northern Lights one imagines them always to be looked for in the northern sky; now, when we first saw them, owing to our own northern latitude, they appeared in the southern sky. On several occasions when for half-an-hour or so, generally before midnight, the display was at its maximum intensity, the sight was so extraordinary that the man on watch took the undoubted risk of waking up the crew to look at it. Usually a faint curtain or glow would be visible throughout the hours of darkness, but very often round about midnight the smouldering glow would flare up, brilliant bands of pale green light stabbing the zenith or forming a bright, shimmering arch across the sky. The displays were certainly brighter, more prolonged, and more frequent than any we had seen the previous voyage.

We made a mistake in being too intent upon getting to the east rather than the south, for on the fifth day out we found ourselves once more approaching the Greenland coast north of Cape Farewell. It was a day of fog and the wind was such that when we were at last forced to put about we could do no better than steer a little south of west. Just before dark we sighted an iceberg, a peril that had to be taken more seriously now that the nights were really dark. The nights were long too; three times on the way home we advanced the ship's time by an hour in order to finish our supper in daylight or at the worst by dusk. There were limits to this useful expedient or we should have found ourselves having breakfast in the dark. We had stupidly run out of petrol for the charging engine, the battery was flat, and we had only six slow-burning carriage candles for lighting both the cabin and the galley for the rest of the voyage. Roger Brown had by now taken over the galley. He brought to it some fresh ideas and managed very well in spite of having to cook in semi-darkness and with the scantier ingredients of a depleted larder.

We fully realized we had made a mistake by allowing ourselves to be pushed so far eastwards when we met with the adverse Greenland current and re-entered waters where there were still enough icebergs about to give us some anxious nights. We got our first fair wind when we were in the latitude of the cape but still 100 miles west of it. We were doing six knots, we had sighted an iceberg at dusk, and in my watch from two to four, when visibility was remarkably bad, I was at times on the point of shortening sail or even heaving-to. The thought that icebergs were few and the sea very wide was reinforced by the urge of not wasting a fair wind. In the twenty-four hours we ran 123 miles, the best day we were to have until coming up Channel. A lurid red dawn ushered in a day of drizzling rain. We were still too near the land for comfort and had to gybe and steer south in order to give Cape Farewell a wide enough berth. We were twelve days out when we finally passed the longitude of the cape, and were 140 miles south of it when we saw our last iceberg. Hereabouts we fell in with a large school of pilot whales, ponderous creatures about twenty feet long which played round the ship as nimbly as porpoises for several hours. Those of us who had any film left wasted it prodigally on this unusual sight. Among the school were a great many babies. While the elders surfaced with a slow and dignified whoosh, the little chap following hard behind came out of the water like a cork out of a bottle.

The brave westerlies we had so confidently hoped for failed us almost entirely. A rousing blow from north-east, when for twenty-four hours we were close reefed, was merely the prelude to a long spell of light easterly winds, a spell that with one brief break continued until we were off the Irish coast. A vast anti-cyclonic system seemed to have spread over the North Atlantic. Had we been in the tropics the barograph could hardly have traced a straighter line, or the weather remained so damnably settled. As one warm sunny day of light contrary winds succeeded another we grew first ungrateful and then cross. It was strange to have the crew eagerly watching the barometer in the hope that it would fall. Some entries in my diary show what it was like:

11 September. Fine morning, wind still NE. Quite maddening having to sail SE or south instead of east.

12 September. Bad windless night with boom slamming. Very fine and warm. Bathed. Sea temperature 52°F. Barometer 30.2. Strange that we should be longing for a fall. Portuguese trawler with two headsails up going east very slowly. Faster than us, however.

13 September. Very light wind at night, only 9 miles done. Weak aurora: Barometer high and steady. Cut out porridge to conserve water not knowing how long this weather may last. Another Portuguse trawler with stacks of dories on deck. Masts had a cluster of short yards (for launching dories?).

14 September. No wind in night. Glassy calm at 2 am Motored for 5 hours. Wind from WNW later but veering.

15 September. Wind east again. Wonderful fine weather. Last night full moon, cloudless sky, flat sea. About 850 miles to Bishop Rock. Shaun began to get time signals on his transistor set. Mick's watch 1 minute 30 seconds slow. Quite a big error for 20 days. More wind at night but doing no better than south.

16 September. Wind very fresh from east and sea rough. Steering west of south so hove-to on port tack. Remained hove-to all night rather than lose easting.

17 September. Sky overcast. Wind force 5 to 6, reached 7 at times during the night. Sea very rough and an occasional douche through skylight. Glass falling. Maddening not being able to sail, and drifting to west. Drizzle with wind veering south-east and falling. Fried rice and sausage.

I suppose that when homeward bound any delay is particularly irksome to the crew, although we ourselves, with no wives and families waiting expectantly, had no good reason for haste. Perhaps a week of easterly winds in September in the North Atlantic outraged our sense of the rule of right and the eternal fitness of things. In a sailing vessel patience is very necessary but patience, as Dr Johnson observed, is a virtue easily fatigued by exercise. Our five months at sea had not been long enough to rid us of the urge to save time, an urge that seems to be the inevitable curse of a mechanical age whether men are on the road or at sea. In the old days of sail they spent days or weeks at anchor waiting for a fair wind or lying helplessly becalmed and accepted it as part of the game. It was a case of 'It is inevitable, therefore it can be approved,' as Lord Curzon used to say. For all that, I find it hard to believe that such delays were submitted to cheerfully with neither grumbling nor complaint. John Davis, for example, with no least hint of the annoyance he must have felt, merely states that on his first voyage he had to shelter in Falmouth for five days and wait twelve days in the Scillies for a fair wind; and that on a later voyage to the Magellan Straits they lay becalmed on the line for twenty-seven days. It is, I think, fair comment that in accounts of early voyages – in *Hakluyt's Voyages*, for example – too little is said about the long haul across the ocean. The bare facts are stated and no more. For the early voyagers the ocean crossing, whether of the North or South Atlantic, or of the Pacific, was merely a means to an end, an unavoidable necessity hardly worth recording; the detailed description of how the ships fared and what the voyagers felt, and thought, and saw, begins only when they reach another continent or fall upon some strange coast. Whereas nowadays, partly because accounts of voyages are mostly written by amateur sailors and because there are no longer unknown continents or strange coasts, the voyage itself is the end, the ocean crossing is the only romantic part of the enterprise, and the behaviour of the ship and the reactions of the crew make up the whole of the story.

After we had made a little more westing Shaun's transistor set was able to pick up the shipping forecasts. We were still a few hundred miles west of the westernmost areas of Sole and Shannon which the forecasts embrace, but on the fragile basis of the weather prevailing hundreds of miles away to the east our two meteorologists, Roger Tufft and Roger Brown, began compiling synoptic charts. By this means they endeavoured to explain to us our predicament. The data, of course, was slender, but from the little there was we got no comfort. However, on the 19th and 20th the anti-cyclone weakened its grip. We enjoyed two days of north-westerly winds accompanied by rain in which we knocked off 200 miles and an additional bonus of fourteen miles from a current. The sea temperature suddenly rose to 59°F. The wind then flew round to south-east, the barometer climbed to 30.4, and we learnt that another anti-cyclone lay centred over the Irish Sea. Meanwhile everything but the voyage seemed to be coming to an end – no jam, marmalade, coffee, dates, raisins, egg powder, or chocolate. In another momentary panic, for fear of a water shortage, we again knocked off porridge.

Before leaving Exeter Sound we had made a book on the number of days the passage would take. Whoever had taken the shortest number of twenty-eight days was already out of the running, and we began to fear that even the longest guess of thirty-six days would be badly out. But at last, on 24 September, when we were fifty miles south-west of the Fastnet Rock, a spell of thick, westerly weather set in and blew us home in five days at the rate of 100 miles a day. Passing Round Island, our first landfall, on the evening of the 26th, we had a fast run up-Channel to the Start, scattering in our wake quantities of old clothes, tins, and junk as we hastily began clearing up below. On the way over we had sighted no ships but the two Portuguese trawlers and had not been able to report our whereabouts. Better late than never; so when passing Prawle Point, where there is a signal station, we called them up with our lamp but got no response.

Our last night at sea was stormy. The wind backed to south-east and freshened to Force 7. It was raining hard and no shore lights were visible. Sailing as we were, reefed down and close-hauled in a rough sea, I feared that what with leeway and current we might in the course of the night find ourselves caught up in the Portland Race. We held on, sailing as close as we could to the wind, and at midnight were reassured when a small coaster passed close inside us. Between rain squalls at dawn we were lucky enough to get a brief glimpse of Anvil Point light while it was still lit. Taking a bearing and roughly guessing our distance off we set a course for the Needles. Although the wind had taken off, the weather was thicker than before. By nine o'clock we had seen nothing. An ocean-going tug came suddenly out of the murk astern and passed us close on a more southerly course. If *he* was bound for the Needles Channel, I thought, *we* must be wrong. Just before we lost sight of him however he altered course and a minute later we, too, saw dead ahead of us a pillar buoy – the Fairway buoy for the Needles Channel. Soon after, the Needles themselves loomed up through the rain. With a strong tide under us we entered Lymington river and by ten-thirty of a miserably wet morning the voyage was over.

It had taken us thirty-four days, only a day better than Davis's ships *Sunneshine* of fifty tons and *Mooneshine* of thirty-five tons, which returned to Dartmouth from Exeter Sound in thirty-five days. In his day almost every voyage undertaken had been a romantic adventure. As we read the accounts of them they distil for us the essence of romance – the gay pursuit of a perilous quest. In more humdrum times, by following in the track of John Davis, we had sought and at times slightly savoured this elusive essence.

MOSTLY MISCHIEF

Mostly Mischief

First published by Hollis & Carter Ltd., 1966

Contents

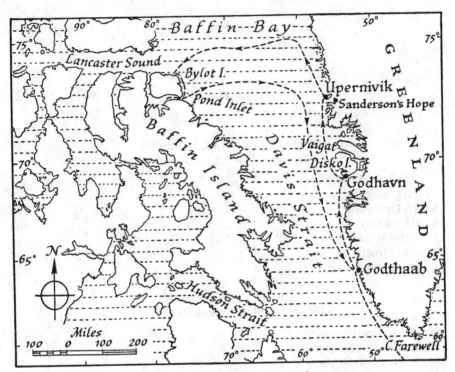

Bylot Island, Baffin Bay, 1963

Part 1

Bylot Island, Baffin Bay
Mischief
May–September, 1963

CHAPTER ONE

Plans and Preparations

AS THE Texan oil-man put it: 'When you strike oil, stop boring.' After two voyages to Davis Strait and the adjacent coasts of west Greenland and Baffin Island I felt that I had also, as it were, struck oil, having found a cruising ground that fulfilled all expectations. In a region to which the voyage is not too long, Arctic waters beat upon coasts that are wild and little frequented and that are studded with unclimbed mountains. Here in summer one enjoys more or less continuous daylight, the pale skies and soft colours of the north, and above all the romance and excitement of icebergs and pack-ice seen at close quarters from the deck of a small boat. When sailing, perhaps, in fog, a little uncertain of one's position, listening to the menacing growl of pack-ice, it is easy to imagine oneself in company with John Davis aboard his 50-ton ship *Mooneshine*, or with any of those hardy spirits, the Elizabethan sailor-explorers in search of a north-west passage. As Belloc wrote of the amateur sailor: 'In venturing in sail upon strange coasts we are seeking those first experiences, and trying to feel as felt the earlier man in a happier time, to see the world as they saw it.'

The west coast of Greenland from Cape Farewell to Cape York (which can be regarded as almost beyond the northernmost limit for a small boat) is 900 miles long, for the most part fronted with uninhabited islands, islets, and skerries, and indented with long, fascinating fjords generously blessed with mountains and glaciers. On the opposite side of Davis Strait the east coast of Baffin Island is not much shorter and has likewise its islands, fjords, and mountains, though these are rather too rounded and lacking in true Alpine character to attract the mountaineer. But from the amateur explorer's point of view this coast has the advantage over Greenland of having no ports or towns, very few Eskimo settlements, and maps that are pleasingly vague.

Compared with the Greenland coast it is frighteningly barren and the climate is cooler and cloudier. The cause of these conditions is the cold, south-going Canadian, or Labrador, current bringing bergs and pack-ice down from Baffin Bay and the great ice-filled sounds leading to it – Smith, Jones, and Lancaster Sounds. On this account, too, except for a brief period in August and September, the Canadian coast is heavily beset with ice. The west Greenland coast, on the other hand, is washed by a north-going current bringing comparatively warm water from the Atlantic, and although the immense Greenland glaciers are the source of nearly all the icebergs met with on either coast, this west coast is in summer more or less free from pack-ice.

In so vast a field, with so many attractive fjords and their attendant mountains asking to be visited, the choice of an objective is difficult; and a voyage in my opinion should have some objective beyond that of crossing an ocean or making a passage. Naturally the amateur sailor derives much satisfaction from hitting off the continent or country at which he is aiming, but nowadays this modest ambition is achieved more often than not and the successful voyager, having bought a few souvenirs to support his claim, has nothing to do but come back:

> Nothing to sing but songs,
> Ah well, alas, and alack,
> Nowhere to go but out
> Nowhere to come but back.

After studying the *Arctic Pilot* I picked upon Bylot Island as a likely objective for 1963. It lies off the north-east corner of Baffin Island separated from it by the ten-mile wide Pond Inlet. It is in Lat. 73°N., further north than *Mischief* had been before and as far north as she is likely to get in those regions. To find ice-free water further north than this one would have to go to Spitsbergen where in favourable seasons one might reach Lat. 78°N. without even seeing ice. Thus even the reaching of Bylot Island was a challenge. There was no certainty that it could be reached, that the ice would have cleared away or be sufficiently open for a small, unstrengthened vessel like *Mischief* to navigate. According to the ice-charts there seemed little doubt that by the end of August and throughout September the sea up there would be navigable. So if the worst came to the worst we could wait. But that would mean a late homeward voyage across the Atlantic in October which the prudent yachtsman would wish to avoid. In the Atlantic in October the percentage of gales shows a marked increase.

The island is named after Robert Bylot who acted as mate to Hudson on his fourth voyage in *Discovery* in 1610. This was the ill-fated voyage when, as the result of a mutiny, Hudson himself, his son John, and seven seamen were turned adrift in an open boat 'without food, drink, fire, clothing, or other necessaries' in the great unexplored Bay to fend for themselves, or in other words to die. Bylot himself took no leading part in the mutiny but the fact that he escaped being put over the side seems to show that he was no very ardent supporter of his captain, Henry Hudson. Perhaps the mutineers had need of his skill, for he was then put in charge of the ship. Before they had won clear of Hudson's Strait four of the leading mutineers had been killed by Eskimos and *Discovery* finally struggled into Bantry Bay on 6 September 1611, with only nine survivors, all in a state of starvation. The survivors were in a position to give their account of events without fear of contradiction, and although an enquiry was held nothing came of it and no one was brought to book. Bylot's services were evidently of value for he went on to make two more voyages both in the same ship, *Discovery*, of only fifty-five tons. The first was with Baffin in 1615 when they again explored Hudson Bay, when Baffin gave it as his considered opinion that no north-west passage would be found in that direction and that Davis Strait offered the only hope. Consequently in 1616 they sailed again, with Bylot as master and Baffin as pilot, when *Discovery* reached Lat. 77°45'N. On this outstanding voyage Baffin Bay, and Smith, Jones, and Lancaster Sounds were discovered and named. No advance of importance towards the discovery of a north-west passage was to be made for the next two hundred years.

In my view, distorted though it may be, Bylot Island had much in its favour, being difficult to reach, little known, uninhabited, and mountainous. In 1939 P. D. Baird, a well known Arctic traveller, had made a single-handed sledge journey with dogs inland from the Pond Inlet coast. Owing to soft snow on the north-flowing glaciers he did not get through to the north coast. In May 1954 a party of American scientists landed by air on the ice in Pond Inlet and spent a month on the island at a base on the south coast. They had climbed two mountains close inland from there, the 5,800ft. Mt Thule, and another of about 6,000ft. A general account of this appears in a book called *Spring on an Arctic Island* by Katharine Scherman, the wife of one of the scientists.

With so little background knowledge I had doubts as to whether the mountains would be of much interest. It seemed probable that they would be like those at the tip of the Cumberland Peninsula which we had climbed the previous year and their description in the *Arctic Pilot* – a 1947 edition – confirmed this: 'Bylot Island is formed of crystalline rocks and in physical character closely resembles the adjacent north-east part of Baffin Island. The general elevation of the interior ranges from 2,000ft. to 3,000ft. and the coastal highlands are covered with an ice-cap which extends 10 to 15 miles inland, the interior, according to the Eskimos, being free of snow during summer. The ice-rim feeds numerous glaciers, some of which discharge bergs.'

This 1947 account is evidently largely guess-work and wrong in several respects; the general elevation is from 3,000ft. to 6,000ft. and the ice-cap covers most of the elevated interior which in summer is by no means free from snow. The 1960 edition of the Canadian publication *Pilot of Arctic Canada*, up to date and more accurate, made the mountains, too, sound quite impressive: 'The second largest ice-field (second to the Penny ice-cap on Baffin Island) occupies the greater part of Bylot Island and is only slightly lower than the Penny ice-cap, mountain peaks rising through it to attain altitudes of over 6,000ft. .... On the south coast the Castle Gables, an Alpine-like mountain rising to 4,850ft. with serrated ridges and three major, jagged crests, is a prominent summit between Kaparoqtalik and Sermilik glaciers. Mt Thule, about 5,800ft. high, stands about five miles north-westward of Sermilik glacier.' This sounded like the real thing but on some air photographs, which I received from a friend in the Canadian Survey, Castle Gables appeared as a ridge of rotten rock devoid of ice or snow, and Mt Thule a rounded summit little higher than the surrounding snow-field.

No mountains are to be despised. At my time of life, especially, one's attitude towards any mountain can hardly be too humble. I had, however, to consider the young, ardent climber whom, I hoped, might be persuaded to accompany me. I could hardly ask him to suffer a four month's voyage for the sake of climbing mountains like Castle Gables or Thule. A more worth-while challenge would be a crossing of the island. It is about sixty miles from north to south, for the most part glaciers and snow-fields. The whole island, by the way, covers some 4,000 square miles – small enough compared with the 200,000 square miles of Baffin Island which is roughly two-and-one-half times the size of the British Isles. If we succeeded it would be the first complete crossing. Much virtue in being the first. To a mountaineer a first ascent is the great prize. In the nature of things there are nowadays, in the more accessible mountainous regions, few first ascents left to be made. Aspirants for mountaineering fame are thus driven to making first ascents by all the remaining possible and impossible routes on an ascending scale of difficulty and danger, first ascents in winter, first ascents by moonlight or by no light at all, and so on, some spurred by dedication to the craft, some perhaps seeking the bubble reputation even in the cannon's mouth.

Mischief has been fully described before. She is a Bristol Channel pilot cutter built at Cardiff in 1906 of 29 tons T.M., 45ft. long, 13ft. beam, drawing 7ft. 6ins. aft. Apart from a 40-hp Perkins diesel auxiliary engine, winches for the staysail sheets and the main halyard, and a wire guard-rail, she is not much changed from when she was a working boat – the same heavy gear and rigging, heavy canvas sails, and accommodation below that might be described as simple. The winches and the guard-rail make her easier and safer to handle, the engine allows for some indifferent seamanship on the part of the skipper and is in any case essential among ice floes and in the windless Greenfield fjords if one wants to cover any ground. Moreover, instead of the two men or man and boy who used to work her in and out of the Bristol Channel, the crew now generally comprises five or six so that they are, comparatively speaking, in clover. On the other hand in her working days she did not cross oceans or spend weeks or months at sea.

The crew began to assemble at Lymington about 13 May, allowing a full week to get the spars and running rigging set up, the sails bent, and stores stowed. This was as well because the weather proved wet and unfavourable for work and at the last moment we found signs of rot in the knightheads, the vertical stem timbers either side of the bowsprit. These had to be replaced together with a new breast-hook, the timber which holds together the bows. In an old boat rot or soft spots in the timbers is endemic and generally to be found if persistently sought. It is a case of the more you stir the more it stinks.

One cannot afford to be too fussy. A boat must be ripe indeed if without any cautionary hints and warnings she opens up like a basket. Apart from when she is occasionally called on to shunt ice *Mischief* is handled with the tender care due to one of her age. We avoid, if possible, prolonged bashing into head seas. If she begins to tremble with excitement, as she sometimes does when doing over six knots, I take it as a hint to reduce sail. In the open sea one can steer a point or even two points off the required course if it will make the motion easier, and since the average helmsman is likely to be that much off course anyway it makes no difference in the long run. Or one can heave to for the sake of peace and quiet, especially if the cook is having trouble in the galley and the evening meal is in jeopardy.

The crews for *Mischief*'s nine voyages have all been more or less inexperienced. Most sailing men either have their own boats to sail or are engaged to crew for friends, while the few who have the opportunity to make a long cruise prefer to go in search of sun and warmth. In 1963 I had what was probably the least experienced crew of any. With one exception I doubt if any of them had been to sea before in a small boat. However the exception had enough experience to make up the deficiency of the rest. Ed Mikeska was a professional seaman who had sailed in all kinds of ships from large yachts to ice-breakers. In fact his last spell at sea had been in a Canadian ice-breaker in the Canadian Arctic. He was a Pole, in his 'teens when the Germans invaded Poland, who had got away to England and served in the war at sea with the Free Poles. I had corresponded with him off and on for some time and he had been on the point of coming with me on an earlier voyage to the Southern Ocean but had thought better of it. This time, since his mind seemed fully made up, I took him on and felt I was lucky to have on board such a thorough seaman. By the time one has got clear of the English Channel and its perilous shipping lanes even a green crew should have shaken down, got over their seasickness, and be on the way to becoming useful, but those first two or three days in the Channel can be very wearing for the skipper unless backed by an experienced hand like Ed Mikeska. Though it may have been for the good of their souls his hazing of the crew was perhaps too much like that of a bucko mate.

Ed took the keenest interest in boats and in all aspects of the sea and was knowledgeable about most of them. On joining he had some disparaging remarks to make about *Mischief*, in fact in his view she seemed scarcely seaworthy – the cockpit was big enough to constitute a death-trap, the companionway facing aft would merely conduct half the ocean into the cabin, and the skylight was another vulnerable point that endangered the ship. The rigging of her, too, could in several ways be improved. A man's most cherished possession be it a woman or a ship, a horse or a favourite dog, is seldom without blemishes, and though the man himself may be aware of them he does not really enjoy having them brought to his notice. I had to remind Ed of the remark of the skipper of a coasting brig to his newly-joined mate: 'What I want from you Mr Mate is silence, and not too much of that.'

Then there was Mike Taylor, young and strong, so reluctant to settle down in the Channel Islands as an estate agent in his father's office that he had been working as a labourer in the Berthon Boatyard. I'm afraid the voyage unsettled him still more; I had a brief meeting with him recently in Sydney where he had just arrived.

Bruce Reid, also young, had left St Andrews University (with which I have a sort of back-door relationship), unfortunately without a degree, his climbing activities having precluded his devoting much time to the study of history. He had since settled for the RAF but would not be needed until October. Stephen Pitt, the youngest of all, after leaving school at Malvern had worked in a London office in the timber business without acquiring any great love for it. His parents were a little concerned at his wanting to go to sea in *Mischief* and since they lived within easy reach of Lymington I soon learnt how they thought about it. Unable to be like the deaf adder that stoppeth her ears I soon began to feel all the guilt and none of the pleasure of a successful seducer of youth.

All these had been enlisted voluntarily and almost painlessly without any advertising or having to scratch around and solicit. None of them, however, had shown any willingness to take on the job of cook, the most important in the ship. My last victim, Bob Sargent, who lived in Edinburgh, I got hold of in a more devious way. My friend Dr David Lewis, in search of crew for a maiden voyage to northern waters in his catamaran *Rehu Moana*, had by no means eschewed publicity and had, in consequence, received a host of applicants. Among those rejects whom he passed on to me was young Bob Sargent. Luckily I had occasion to go north to St Andrews and we arranged to meet for breakfast at Princes Street station in Edinburgh. He was then studying in a business college of the House of Fraser, found it singularly unrefreshing, and was hell-bent on going on some expedition, no matter where. He had never been to sea and had no other useful experience or skills to offer but he said he could cook. Cooking for oneself on a gas or electric stove in a house that seldom rocks is quite different to cooking for six men on a Primus stove at sea in *Mischief*'s galley, a galley, by the way, which is sited forward of the mast in the most lively part of the ship. After I had explained and even stressed all these differences to Bob his confidence remained unshaken. So I agreed to take him as cook, a gamble that happened to come off.

CHAPTER TWO

To Godthaab

HOWEVER MANY times it has been done, the act of casting off the warps and letting go one's last hold of the shore at the start of a voyage has about it something solemn and irrevocable, like marriage, for better or for worse. True, one is not afloat for a lifetime, but when mewed up with five fellow humans for four months, should one or two of them prove to be misfits, it might well seem like a lifetime. One feels uneasy, too, that something vital may have been forgotten, like the proverbial Dutchman who left behind his anchor. To put back would make one feel too much of a fool, while to put in at any other home port after the ship had been cleared for a foreign port would lead HM Customs to suspect some hanky-panky. And there is the fear that things may go wrong in front of the crowd of friends, or even admirers, who have gathered on the quay to wave farewell; such as on a memorable occasion at Punta Arenas when we went aground hard and fast within spitting distance of the crowd of admirers on the quay we had just left; or more recently at Albany in Australia when, upon hoisting the stay-sail to blow the ship's head clear of the jetty, the block strop broke and the sail collapsed on the heads of the chaps hoisting it.

No untimely mishaps occurred when we cast off on the morning of 23 May. In consideration of *Mischief*'s draft and the crowded river, the Harbour Master's launch was in attendance to see us away. In the Solent we hoisted sail. The wind being foul, we had to tack four times before reaching the Needles, thus giving the crew a little sail drill. Outside, the wind obliged by veering more northerly just as if to spite the meteorological boys who had forecast it backing to south-west. We could not have been treated more kindly, the glass remained high and the sea calm. No one was seasick and during the night no steamers menaced us. My personal bliss was only slightly marred by some very queer results from sun sights which put us ashore in West Bay. One's navigation, like everything else about a ship, must be kept in good repair and free from rust.

Our progress down Channel was stately and slow. On the 24th we were still off Start Point and did not sight the Lizard until late that evening, the weather hazy with light easterly winds. Meantime, in these cosmopolitan waters, a Russian sail-training ship passed us under engine, a Dutch submarine was sighted, and a French trawler shot by so close under our stern that we had to haul in the log-line. I thought this friendly of them but unnecessary. Early on the 26th we found ourselves becalmed near the Seven Stones light-vessel with the tide setting us briskly towards the rocks and the white breaking water two miles to the south-west. We had to start the engine to get clear. Formerly the engine used not to start with the promptitude that one would wish, so now we carried ether and whenever the engine was required administered a whiff with gratifying effect. In the march of science I'm afraid I lag far behind and would never myself have suspected that ether would have such a galvanizing effect upon diesel engines.

That evening we had some wind and for my part a restless night. In spite of their gentle initiation the crew were still pretty inept, hazy about which rope to pull or even how to manage the pumps and stop-cocks on the lavatory. A reported alarming leak was the result of someone having failed to turn off the lavatory inflow, and no sooner had this been put right when Stephen reported 'water pouring in at the bow'. This proved to be some damp round the new breast-hook. But Ed remained uneasy and while searching the ship for leaks promised us a gale by morning. We did in fact, put in a reef at 3 am but the morning broke fine and sunny with a moderately rough sea. This pleased the crew who were beginning to think sailing a dull, slow business. Bob proved his worth by producing breakfast as usual and for supper bangers and mash with fried onions. By noon we had logged over 100 miles for the twenty-four hours. We at last felt we were getting somewhere for we were then eighty miles south-west of the Fastnet.

The last four days of May gave us all that could be wished for in the way of weather. With a steady beam wind at north-east we had hardly to touch a sheet. Leaving the genoa up all night, we recorded runs of 90, 95, 131, and 121 miles. Ever since leaving we had had trouble with the charging engine on which the battery and hence the cabin lights, the binnacle light, and the use of the wireless receiver depended. For the time we had to forego weather reports and, more important, time signals. Besides keeping a Supplementary Ship's log for the Meteorological Office, Ed doubled the rôle of mate and engineer. As a matter of routine he spent an hour each day wrestling with the charging engine, the session ending invariably in failure and abuse both in English and Polish. Having found an old sparking plug that looked as if it should have long since been thrown overboard I gave it Ed to try. Whereupon the engine started without a murmur. This much relieved Ed who, for the next few days, until we were out of range, could listen to the weather forecasts to which he was so much addicted. Though we may all like to have our fortunes told few of us are weak-minded enough to believe what we are told. Similarly I think it a mistake to rely for one's peace of mind upon forecasts of fair weather or to become unduly worried by forecasts of foul weather. As Dr Johnson remarks: 'Let us cease to consider what may never happen, and what, when it shall happen, will laugh at human speculation.' When far from land the weather must be taken as it comes and fortunately bad weather seldom springs upon one without warning, leaving no time to shorten sail. If it behaved like that one would want not forecasts but a running commentary.

Perhaps it was presumptuous of me at this early stage to bake a cake. It got away to a bad start, rising very slowly, accompanied, as I noticed, by a rising wind. Before the cake was done we had reefed both main and staysail and a little later we hove to, the wind being from ahead. Sailing hard into it made us leak a bit round the stemhead. The *Clarkenden*, bound west, closed and spoke to us by loud-hailer, offering to report us at Lloyd's. On the following day we let draw and made some westing but the wind soon increased to Force 7 and again we hove to. In rough weather, do what one may, *Mischief*'s skylight is never watertight. We can ship a canvas cover and sit below in the gloom of an aquarium and only a little less wet. Even with the cover shipped, when a sea comes on deck those on the lee side of the cabin get a shower-bath. Matters below were not mended when the teapot upset, scalding Mike's hand and arm. Bob took his watch that night.

In summer in the Atlantic a blow rarely lasts for more than twenty-four hours. By next day, having straightened things up below and on deck, we were under all plain sail with a good quartering wind. But the sky remained obstinately overcast and three days went by before I got a sight, a sight which put us thirty miles south of our dead reckoning position. When hove to, *Mischief* makes about one knot crabwise, which is fair enough provided one has plenty of sea-room. I have since had a brief experience with a parachute anchor and think it might hold a boat even as heavy as *Mischief*. To save that amount of drift would be a useful achievement.

By 4 June we had done our first thousand miles. On the 7th, when about 500 miles from Cape Farewell, we suffered a flat calm from 6 am until midnight. We launched our nine-foot dinghy in order to take pictures of *Mischief* with her sails hanging limp and of the Atlantic in a most benign mood. We ran the engine for an hour to exercise it and in order to appreciate more fully the profound silence when it stopped. As we waited patiently for a wind Ed, our meteorological expert, began to speak of calms that had lasted for six weeks. In view of their recent history the Poles, as a nation, have a right to suspect the worst from their fellow men or at any rate from those who are their immediate neighbours, but Ed Mikeska's suspicions embraced also the weather. Few of the well-known signs that are supposed to promise fair weather found any favour in his eyes while any signs of ill-omen were given full value and filled him with apprehensive gloom. We had some wind that night and when the dawn broke luridly red the prospect of six weeks' calm had to yield place to that of an imminent gale.

In the end we had a fine easterly breeze which gave us a lift of sixty-five miles in twelve hours. This proved to be the last log reading we were to take for some time, the rotator on the log having been bitten off by some marine monster. It is of course satisfactory to be able to read off from hour to hour the distance covered and what speed one is doing, but a sufficiently accurate estimate can be made by the helmsman who at the end of his watch logs his idea of the distance run. One man will underestimate and another will overestimate and at the end of the day the total will not be far out. This, together with the course steered, enables the navigator to plot the assumed position which sooner or later he will be able to check by sights. The easterly wind brought with it a thick, drizzly weather, the air temperature dropping to 45° and the sea to 43°. On this I abandoned my early-morning ritual of pouring over my head three buckets of sea water, and I gave it up more readily because there was no one with whom to compete in this endurance test. On former voyages, as the sea temperature gradually dropped, some of us have vied with each other as to who would or could longest maintain this shocking habit.

In the prevailing thick weather Ed hastened to hoist an umbrella-like radar reflector which, with seamanlike prudence, he had brought with him. The theory is that a wooden vessel does not show up on a radar screen and most yachtsmen carry various kinds of metal devices in the hope that their presence will thus be made obvious to an oncoming steamer. An expert has recently told me that *Mischief*'s massive wire shrouds should act as well or better than any reflector. Pehaps hoisting radar reflectors is merely an act of faith, just as not many years ago Europeans in the tropics used to wear sun helmets. Sitting under the protection of Ed's umbrella I can't say that I felt any more secure, nor would it do to relax one's vigilance on this account. In any case the waters we were then sailing are so unfrequented by ships that only if I had shipped an entire crew of Jonahs were we likely to be hit by one. We ourselves stood far more chance of hitting an iceberg for we were only some 200 miles east of Cape Farewell. Homeward bound round Cape Farewell in 1962 we had sighted an iceberg 140 miles south-east of it.

These icebergs off Cape Farewell and the vicinity originate in the glaciers of the east coast of Greenland. Owing to the inaccessibility of the northern parts of this coast, information about the iceberg-discharging glaciers and their productivity is less complete than for the west coast where the average annual discharge of bergs from all the bigger glaciers is pretty well known. The annual discharge is thought to be about equal for both coasts, but the east coast bergs do not reach the sea so quickly and in many cases are held up by the pack-ice near their sources. Moreover a large number never leave the fjords into which they are calved owing to the shallowness of the water at the fjord entrance. In Scoresby Sund, for example, in Lat. 70°N. the majority of icebergs never leave the fjord. The most productive glaciers are all south of Lat. 68°. The main flow of bergs round Cape Farewell takes place from April to August; off there several hundred have been reported in sight from a ship at one time. In autumn the number decreases rapidly and in winter Cape Farewell is more or less free from bergs.

The only safeguard against icebergs is vigilance and it was partly on their account that on 12 June we spent an uneasy night. With the glass falling steeply, accompanied by heavy rain, the wind increased until it was gusting to about Force 8. We were running fast under twin staysails and in order to reduce speed we dropped one of them. With no visibility at all to speak of we were still going too fast. I was in two minds about having the starboard sail down when the matter was settled for me by its sheet parting. In spite of its violent flogging we got the sail in undamaged. At dawn the wind eased and the sun came out, the prelude to a lovely day, but it had been no fun sailing thus unsighted, and uncertain whether or no there were any icebergs about. The fact that so far none had been sighted did not, of course, carry complete assurance.

On 14 June, a cold, grey day, when we were about fifty miles south of Cape

Farewell we began steering north to close with the land in order to benefit by the current which sweeps round the cape and up the west coast. Sights showed that we had already had a lift of twenty miles from the current. Early next day we sighted pack-ice ahead and to starboard but still no bergs. The wind obliged us to make long boards and each time we came inshore we met loose floes on the edge of the pack. I had expected to find better weather west of the cape but for the next three days we had dull, lowering skies and bitter head winds, the air temperature falling to 39° and then to 34°. The sea temperature remained at 37°. At last we began meeting icebergs though they were remarkably few compared with the previous summer. In the prevailing dull weather the nights were not as light as they should have been and for two hours either side of midnight, when visibility became pretty poor, we usually hove to.

So far we had had a good passage. We had rounded Cape Farewell in twenty-three days, the same time as in 1962, whereas in 1961 it had cost us thirty-five days. Easterly winds at the start had given us a good push and by keeping well north we had perhaps avoided some of the westerly winds. On the 17th we were in Lat. 61°16' and that afternoon when the weather cleared we closed the land north of Arsuk Fjord where there is a cryolite mine. We watched a small cargo vessel work her way in there through scattered floes. Cryolite is used in the manufacture of aluminium and in the enamelling of iron; according to the *Arctic Pilot* 20,000 tons are exported from there annually. By now icebergs had become a normal feature of the seascape; trawlers too, for we were now on the first of the fishing banks, rich in cod and halibut, which extend well up the west Greenland coast. That summer an international body was engaged in fishery research in these waters and on behalf of this Ed Mikeska had undertaken the making of plankton hauls close inshore. We made our first haul that evening. The sample in its glass jar resembled in colour and consistency a weak brew of tomato soup. Hauling in the fine mesh net at the end of some twenty fathoms of rope required two men.

My expectation of pleasant June weather in Davis Strait, based on previous experience, at last began to be realized. On a warm, sunny afternoon the magic of a northern summer day had us in thrall as we sailed silently over a placid, pale blue sea dotted with bergs, while inland the dark outline of the coastal mountains was split by the broad, glistening ice-stream of the ten-mile wide Frederikshaab Glacier. The day before, the 'blink' from this great mass of ice had been visible in the sky. We sailed close past the Portuguese three-masted schooner *Antonio Donnino* at anchor, with her fleet of fifty or sixty dories scattered over the surrounding area. A dog barked at us and the voices of two men talking on deck were carried to us over the quiet water long after we had passed.

Early on 21 June we sighted the cluster of islets at the entrance to the Godthaab Fjord and in the distance the two peaks known as the Beacons of Godthaab – Sermilsiak, nearly 4,000ft. high which is shaped like a saddle with a high pommel, and Hjortataken to the south like a high pillar. Though the entrance between the islets and a reef to the north of them is narrow, on a clear day there is no difficulty, and thereafter the fjord is wide and free from dangers for twelve miles up to the narrow harbour entrance. John Davis anchored here in 1585 – he called it Gilbert Sound – and had friendly exchanges with the Eskimos. I was immediately struck by the amount of snow still lying low on the surrounding hills and even on islands right down to the water's edge. From this, infected perhaps by Ed's pessimism, I began drawing gloomy conclusions about the lateness of the season and the small chance of finding ice-free water in Baffin Bay.

Arrived in the small land-locked harbour with its dog-leg entrance we anchored in our usual berth with the quay half a cable away on one side and on the other, only some twenty yards away, a thirty-foot wall of rock. This wall is decorated, or desecrated, with the names of various visiting ships painted in large white letters. Before we left, Stephen, not to be outdone in vandalism, added *Mischief*'s name to the record. *Mallemuken*, a small Danish naval vessel used mainly for fishery protection, was moored in her usual berth close to us. Almost every time we had visited Godthaab she had been there and we had usually managed to make use of her hot shower bath. We had not to wait before going ashore. At Godthaab there are no formalities for visiting yachts, possibly because, other than *Mischief*, there are not any. Ashore we made a useful friend in Bond Elliot, a Canadian, agent for the Canadian firm that ran the Catalina seaplanes which carry mail and passengers between the various ports on the west Greenland coast. He found for us a solenoid starter for our Perkins engine which had burnt out and had made for us in their workshop a new petrol tank for the Stuart Turner charging engine. He also did his best to obtain an ice report for Baffin Bay but without success. Owing to the amount of snow still about it was undoubtedly much colder ashore than it had been in previous summers. Thanks to the cold there were no clouds of mosquitoes to plague us. In former summers it had been common to see men working in the open with nets over their heads.

The weather was also wetter and windier than usual; in fact we might as well have been in England. On the night of our arrival a heavy southerly gale set in with torrential rain. Three trawlers and the survey vessel *Dana* came in for shelter. Next day, the gale continuing, we stayed on board and set an anchor watch, for we were horribly close to the rock wall. The dinghy, inadequately secured, went adrift and no one saw it go. We expected to find it broken up, as we deserved, on the rocks at the shallow end of the harbour, and by great luck an RC padre returning in his motor boat from a parochial visit up the fjord spotted it there. Taking two of the crew he returned and retrieved it for us undamaged. After having had a dinghy lost overboard on the first abortive voyage to the Crozet Islands I have always carried a collapsible rubber dinghy as a spare, poor substitute though this would be for a nine-foot wooden dinghy.

That evening the gale abated, though not the rain. No one, however, flinched from the mile trudge in pouring rain which separated us from the warmth, noise, bright lights, and beer of the *Christinamut*, the only 'local' in Godthaab and for that matter probably in all Greenland. But a gloom had been cast over the town by a disaster to a German trawler, in which twenty-six of the crew were lost, when she struck a rock outside the nearby fishing port of Faeringerhavnen when making for it in the gale that had just subsided.

Since our first visit in 1961 to Godthaab, the capital of west Greenland, the town has grown; and it is still growing. A quay for fishing boats with a fish-processing factory on it have been built at the harbour, more houses and blocks of flats have sprung up, and the long road from the harbour to the town has been surfaced. There are no seals as far south as this so that inshore fishing, the only means of livelihood for the Greenlanders, is being en-couraged by building houses for the fishermen and by providing small fishing boats on easy terms. Except in the far north the Greenlanders are now a much mixed race, the original Eskimo blood mingled with that of the whalers and seamen of all the various European nations who have been in contact with Greenland over the last two or three hundred years. It would be interesting to know what the less sophisticated Eskimos whom we were to meet later at Pond Inlet, who live in tents in summer and sod and stone huts in winter, would make of life in a three-storeyed flat at Godthaab.

CHAPTER THREE

To Upernivik

GODTHAAB, which means Good Hope, is an odd town. On first seeing the place, built on a barren promontory of bog and rock, surrounded by water and bleak hills, with no communications other than by sea, one wonders why it was built there. One wonders, too, how John Davis happened to make it his Greenland landfall, or why Hans Egede, the first missionary, chose it as his base. The harbour is good but small, and so hidden that anyone who did not know of it would hardly find it. Anyhow Godthaab is the capital of west Greenland and its rapid growth, with neither industry nor a surrounding population to support it, can only be accounted for by Parkinson's Law which seems to apply universally from China to Peru.

The shops of the one shopping street are well stocked and if one knows where to go all necessities and a good many luxuries can be bought at prices comparable with those of Europe. Most of the houses and flats are pre-fabricated and gaily painted. There is one large hall where a film is shown once a week and where occasional dances are held, sometimes followed by a mild brawl. One or two coffee bars, the *Christinamut* licensed restaurant, and a small transit hotel represent the night-life. There are a church, schools, two large hospitals, and no doubt a gaol. The only surviving stone building, which is carefully preserved, is reputedly the original home of Hans Egede, the Lutheran missionary who settled there in 1721. Most of the growth is recent, for it still has the appearance of a thriving pioneer town – open drains and a forest of poles supporting a web of telephone and power lines, while bull-dozers, pneumatic drills, and constant blasting, stridently announce progress.

Before leaving we stocked up with rye bread, the same colour, texture and specific gravity as black basalt, though softer, impervious to mould, nourishing, satisfying, and slightly laxative. After filling up with oil and water we sailed on 28 June with a fair wind down the fjord. We had about 500 miles to go to Upernivik which would be our last Greenland port before we headed north-west across Baffin Bay for Bylot Island another 300 miles away. Allowing a fortnight for this we still had time in hand and I had been debating the wisdom of turning aside for a week's climbing either in Godthaab Fjord or further up the coast. Bruce Reid, I noticed, had been eagerly eyeing these Godthaab mountains. On an expedition it is generally a mistake to attempt too much, to try to snatch a bonus as well as the main prize. And for all we knew, unable so far to obtain any ice information, Bylot Island might be accessible earlier than we expected. The sooner we went there to see the better.

Weather in Davis Strait is variable. In summer gales are infrequent though in this respect we had just had a sample of what it could do. Winds mostly alternate between south-east and north-west with rather too many calms in between. For most of the 30th we lay becalmed off Evigheds Fjord, the grandly mountainous fjord where we had spent a happy fortnight the previous summer. The sight of those shapely summits beckoning from afar slightly unsettled my resolve to press on. The next day a head wind of from twenty-five to thirty knots obliged us to heave to for twelve hours. How cold it was, too, while this wind whistled down from the north. By 2 July we were on the Hellefiske Bank, the most northerly of the fishing grounds on this coast, with several trawlers and a number of the stately Portuguese schooners in sight. The Portuguese cod-fishing fleet is said to be the largest in the world comprising 72 vessels, of which 41 are the dory-carrying schooners, fishing with hand-lines, and 31 trawlers. A hospital ship accompanies the fleet. The schooners sail in April for the Newfoundland Banks and later in the season proceed to the Greenland banks to complete their catch. These dory-men inherit a long seafaring tradition of skill and hardihood, and are content and proud, even in these softer times, to follow their hard calling.

That day the noon sight put us in Lat. 66°36', or just north of the Arctic Circle, an event we celebrated that night with Carlsberg lager, gin, minestrone, curry, tinned fruit and chocolate sauce. Bob, the cook, was doing us well. But in my diary, in which food takes second place only to the weather, I find neither kind nor unkind references to duff. I think that in this respect he may have been lacking. We must have been too docile. Crews have mutinied with less reason:

> We haven't been but two days at sea
> When the duff it don't seem to please,
> It hadn't the richness of raisins and sichness,
> So we ups and we mutinies.

Bob, by the way, though he came from Edinburgh, hotly denied being a Scot – a refreshing trait. He had a round, red face, the redness aggravated by toiling in the galley, and the loudest laugh that I have anywhere heard. In *Mischief* on this cruise there was not that much to laugh about but that did not prevent Bob from making the rafters – or, since we are at sea, the deckhead – ring frequently. Nor was his the 'loud laugh that speaks the vacant mind' for throughout the voyage he devoted himself to one book, an uncommonly dreary, psychological treatise. Perhaps we were a solemn lot. I myself seldom utter; Ed was bowed down with meteorological cares; Stephen busy writing a masterpiece that has still to appear; Bruce flexing in vain his climbing muscles (though he had soon become a reliable hand); Mike writing short stories and tearing them up; and Bob reading himself into a psychological stupor.

A run of 104 miles on 3 July brought us into Disko Bugt, the wide entrance to the Vaigat Channel which separates Disko Island from the mainland. As usual the bight was cluttered with icebergs of all shapes and sizes, some tabular, some like square fortresses, and others fashioned into arches and picturesque pinnacles. The Vaigat is the source of most of the icebergs that, after circling Baffin Bay, drift down the Canadian coast and finally, perhaps two years later, appear on the Newfoundland Banks. They originate in the great glaciers descending to the sea from the Greenland ice-cap which, from the Vaigat northwards, extends right to the coast. It is estimated that the twelve most important glaciers in the Vaigat and northwards discharge annually some 5,400 bergs. But of these only a few hundred survive to reach the Grand Banks and become a menace to shipping. South of the Vaigat the ice-cap lies back from the coast leaving a strip of ice-free country varying in width from one to one hundred miles. Except in the extreme south round Julianehaab, where there is some sheep-farming, this strip of ice-free land, rocky, boggy, sparsely vegetated, is of no value.

The principal settlement on Disko Island is Godhavn, a small port lying at its southern end. In the past it was the place most frequently visited by whalers and exploring ships on their voyage north. While we could hardly flatter ourselves that we were explorers, we were on our way north, so I decided to call there. According to the *Pilot* there was an Arctic Research Station at Godhavn where possibly we might get some ice information. In fact the Research Station concerned itself mainly with ecology on the land and had no curiosity whatever about ice at sea. The harbour entrance is only about a cable wide but except when icebergs are grounded in the channel, as frequently they are, presents no difficulty. The anchorage is land-locked and has a depth of seven fathoms. When we arrived on 4 July we anchored ahead of a small steamer unloading coal from Kutdlisat on the east coast of Disko Island, the only working coal-mine in Greenland. This rather poor quality coal is burnt in the settlements throughout Greenland. In 1961 we sailed close by Kutdlisat. One does not look for beauty near a coal-mine but I must say this place seemed to be the acme of desolation – a high, yellow cliff streaked with coal-dust, at its foot at sea level the black coal seam, a couple of dingy ships at anchor with large icebergs almost alongside, the whole shrouded in dismal fog.

We arrived on a warm, cloudless day, a day that almost persuaded the crew to believe me when I told them that the further north one went the better the weather, and how that in 1961 we had enjoyed a month of unbroken, glorious weather. We were presently boarded by the Danish manager of the shrimp processing factory. We had been puzzled by a large vessel moored in a corner of the harbour that looked like a nineteenth-century relic, and we now learnt that this was where the shrimps were treated. She resembled the ships used by Arctic explorers in the latter half of last century, a sailing ship with an engine, clipper bows, two fully rigged masts, and between them a high funnel. She had in fact spent her life plying between Denmark and Greenland and was now ending her days moored in Godhavn boiling shrimps. This shrimping business was another attempt to find the Greenlanders profitable employment. The men caught the shrimps and sold them to the factory, while some forty girls and women were employed cleaning and packing the shrimps. I noticed that the paper bags in which the frozen shrimps were packed were marked 'Export to UK'. Between the spacious decks all seemed to be eminently hygienic but the smell of cooked shrimps in bulk we found a bit overpowering.

Godhavn is a provincial capital and about 500 people live there. There are the usual brightly painted wooden houses, a church built in the Arctic-Byzantine style, and still a few of the old-fashioned Eskimo houses of stones with a roof of turf carrying a rich crop of grass. In the course of an evening stroll along the beach in search of the Arctic Research Station we watched Greenlanders netting fish for dog-food. A few stray huskies were saving master trouble by catching their own fish but of course in this case there was no stock-piling. In winter when the sea freezes dog sledges are much in use for journeys to neighbouring settlements. Methods of dog management vary. At Holsteinborg (further south) the huskies in summer are left to feed themselves which they do in a fashion by licking the outsides of oil barrels or swimming in the harbour in search of offal from the fish factory. Seeing these voracious animals roaming the town we were surprised they did not devour some of the too numerous children who were also allowed to roam at large. At Umanak, at the north end of the Vaigat, the huskies were better off, for they were kept confined and fed once or twice a week on shark meat.

Before returning to the ship that night we found ourselves involved with the Godhavn fire brigade which presently arrived at the beach in a lorry towing a red trailer with hoses and pump to carry out a practice drill. They were led by our shrimping friend in full uniform, helmet, boots, and fireman's axe at belt. Their first target, a pit full of old sump oil, provided more trouble to set alight than to extinguish. Meantime the whole of Godhavn had arrived on the scene and were warming themselves round the second target, a huge pile of waste wood, chaffing their fire-fighting friends, trampling on the hoses, and occasionally getting hosed down as they deserved.

In spite of the absence of tourists there is in Greenland a market for curios and those who sell them are no less astute than any in Port Said, Singapore, or Katmandu. We were on the lookout for soap-stone carvings and were soon boarded by a Greenlander offering some carved whalebone figures. His prices were inflexible and no doubt inflated, but Stephen and I were weak-minded enough to buy some of these 'tupilaks', as they are called. These grotesque, intricately carved figures are quite small representations of mythical beasts with one foot like a man's, the other a bear's paw, a bird's wing for an arm, and the head, perhaps, that of a musk ox.

To my surprise and chagrin the halcyon weather which I firmly believed had come to stay ended next day in a storm of wind and rain. The wind brought a number of small bergs into the harbour entrance where they grounded. That evening the seaplane with mail and passengers from Umanak, after circling several times, gave up and went back. The harbour is small and a seaplane has to touch down well out in the entrance which was now impeded by bergs. We had intended to sail but postponed it on account of the weather. Two young Danes from the wireless station paid us a visit and gave us the welcome news that a ship had reported meeting no ice on the way to Upernivik.

We left next day, 7 July, threading our way among the grounded bergs. Though the sea was lumpy after the previous day's blow we had a fair wind and could lay the desired course NNW. In the night the wind went round to SSE and gave us a good run of ninety miles. With the wind dead aft we soon suffered the accidental gybe which may confidently be expected in those conditions unless the helmsman is reasonably good and extremely alert. The ship, of course, may assist by giving an untimely roll and once the helmsman allows the wind to get on the wrong side of the mainsail over goes the boom with a crash, sometimes breaking something on the way. This is commonly known as a Chinese gybe, though it is safe to assume that Chinese seamen are not more prone than others to gybing in this lubberly fashion. *Mischief* has a massive boom, massive enough to laugh at such trifling affairs as the wire guy or preventer which is rigged to prevent such accidents. Having broken the guy it swept on unimpeded to break the weather backstay as well. No further damage resulted, for the rigging is strong, as indeed it needs to be to withstand the shocks sometimes imposed on it. After this jarring experience I was content to steer two points off course thus bringing the wind well out on the quarter. It goes against the grain to steer wide when one can lay the required course. Yet on the whole nothing is lost, for the ship sails faster with the wind on the quarter and it is much safer.

The south wind brought thick weather which cleared only when the wind dropped. As it cleared we beheld a great fleet of icebergs scattered over the northern exit from the Vaigat and beyond them Ubekjendt Island and the mountains where we had spent a month in 1961. I had happy recollections of the small settlement on Ubekjendt to which we had come direct from Godthaab, and the delight we had felt to find Greenlanders wearing sealskin trousers and boots, and paddling kayaks, instead of wearing winkle-pickers and dancing the Twist. Sailing, drifting, and occasional motoring marked our slow progress. In Davis Strait light airs and fogs are a little too prevalent. They sometimes go together but neither lasts very long. There are many worse places for fog – the Straits of Belle-Isle, for instance, reputedly 'the place where they invented fog'. The calms oblige one to motor more than one likes, since the only pleasure to be had from running an engine in a small boat is the exquisite relief when it stops.

North of Ubekjendt the character of the coast changes. It is fronted by innumerable islands, behind which the ice-cap approaches to the sea, and there are no mountains worthy of the name. On 11 July, a fine, clear morning, when we began to close the land, we soon descried in the distance a prominent cliff, jet black in the morning light and crowned with snow. We recognized it at once for Sanderson's Hope and the sight of this historic Arctic seamark gave me at least a tremendous thrill.

In 1587 John Davis made his third and last voyage to Davis Strait and waters beyond in search of the North-west Passage, his first having been in 1585. In all three his principal backer had been William Sanderson, a rich London merchant and a patron of exploration. Davis had three ships: *Sunshine* which had been on the two earlier voyages, and *Elizabeth*, both of about fifty tons, and *Ellen*, a little clinker-built pinnace of only twenty tons. He felt that this third voyage should at least pay its expenses so his plan was for the three ships to sail in company to Greenland whence *Sunshine* and *Ellen* should proceed to the Newfoundland Banks to fish while he himself would sail northwards in *Elizabeth*. At Gilbert Sound (Godthaab) *Ellen* was found to be leaking badly. Whereupon Davis took the heroically unselfish decision to dispatch the two sound vessels to the fishing grounds while he went north in the barely seaworthy *Ellen*. On 30 June the little *Ellen* lay under the shadow of this 1,000ft. high cliff which Davis called 'Sanderson his hope of a North-west Passage,' recording at the same time, 'No ice towards the north but a great sea, free, large, very salt and blue, and of an unsearchable depth.' The hig hopes implied by these words were not to be realized and Sanderson's Hope proved to be their furthest north. The onset of a northerly gale prevented progress in that direction and on sailing west they soon came upon the ice of the 'middle pack' which forced them to turn south.

It is interesting to note how ice conditions change over the years or the centuries. As early as the end of June Davis had met favourable conditions and but for the northerly wind might have reached the head of Baffin Bay and anticipated the discoveries made by Baffin and Bylot in 1616. On the other hand McClintock in 1857 on his voyage in search of Franklin in the screw-yacht *Fox* (177 tons), strengthened and sheathed for ice, became iced-in on 12 August when only some eighty miles north of Upernivik, and remained in the grip of the ice until April of the next year when they were released near Holsteinborg. It is thought that ice conditions in these regions at present are generally easier than they were fifty years ago.

I noted regretfully that even on our Admiralty charts, let alone the Danish charts, the name for this historic cape is now given as 'Kaersoarssuak' and under it in brackets, in apologetically small type, is 'Sanderson's Hope'. I expect in the next edition of charts published the English name will have disappeared and we shall have only the unpronounceable Kaersoarssuak which means nothing to anyone except Greenlanders who neither need charts nor use them. Like all primitive people who are also travellers the Eskimo have names for all the features along the coast whether large or small. It is right to use these in the absence of a name with superior claims, claims that the name 'Sanderson's Hope' undoubtedly has, a name that has been used by the seamen of many European nations for 400 years, a name given to a cape that is still of importance to navigators, and a name that evokes memories of heroic men and heroic voyages. The changing of geographical names for national or political reasons goes on apace nowadays and it is of small consequence in most instances. It matters little to outsiders how often the Russians, for example, change the names of their streets, towns, or even mountains. No foreigners are allowed to climb these anyway, even if any such could overcome their repugnance sufficiently to wish to climb mountains with names like Peak Stalin or Peak of the Academy of Sciences. Upernivik is on a small island five miles north of Sanderson's Hope. There are several other islands in the vicinity and before finding our way through them we stood in under the cliff to have a good look at it. A couple of Greenlanders in a small motor boat were busy banging away at the birds that haunt the cliff, so busy that they took no notice of us. The *Arctic Pilot* (1947 edition) remarks that 'the cliff is a famous place for looms (guillemots); the birds congregate in myriads along the face ...' No doubt in recent years, with the acquisition of more firearms, the Greenlanders have taken serious toll of them. The myriads have certainly been thinned, we saw only a few birds.

Sir Leopold McClintock, whose name has already been mentioned, who was one of the most successful explorers, took a lively interest in the feeding of his men, as indeed the Arctic explorer of those days had to do if he and his men were to survive. He fully realized the importance of fresh food. 'Our shooting parties', he writes, 'have twice visited a loomery and each time have brought on board 300 looms. We consider our loom soup incomparable; more like hare soup than any other, but richer, darker, and better adapted to our climate, our appetite, and consequently our tastes. So long as we had the necessary ingredients the following receipt of our excellent steward, James Gore, was strictly followed; it suited well for divers ducks, and all sea-birds, especially those with dark flesh.'

Just in case any of my readers should find themselves in reduced circumstances in the neighbourhood of a loomery I append James Gore's instructions for making loom soup:

Take 8 looms, skin and take off the two white lumps near the tail; clean and split into pieces; wash them well, also the livers. Put them into a large saucepan, cover well with water, and boil for 4 or 5 hours. An hour before serving add ½ lb of bacon cut up small, season with pepper and salt, two tablespoons of Harvey Sauce, a little Cayenne pepper, half a wineglass of lemon juice, a teaspoonful of ground allspice, and a few cloves; thicken with 4 tablespoons of flour mixed in cold water stirred gradually into the soup. Add ½ pint of wine, after which let it boil for a few minutes. The result will be 4 quarts of rich soup.

So much for gastronome Gore. The Eskimos eat their looms raw.

CHAPTER FOUR

Baffin Bay

WE WERE becoming accustomed to small harbours. At Upernivik the harbour besides being small was encumbered with rocks and ice floes. While I was taking stock of the limited choice left by these hazards Ed Mikeska, ready on the foredeck with the anchor, suddenly let it go. I thought we must have run aground. Apparently he had acted on a signal, or an imagined signal, from a man on the quay, and when one's anchor is dropped for one at the instigation of a disinterested spectator some confusion is bound to result. Happily at Upernivik there is no Yacht Club overlooking the harbour, with the usual quota of eagle-eyed members, with nothing to do between drinks but wait for some such distressing incident.

After the shouting had died down, and upon trying to move to a proper berth, we found we had a foul anchor. With toil and sweat we freed it by hanging it off, anchored again, and put a line ashore. There was a small quay with a warehouse and from it four Danes presently put off and came on board. They included the local manager for the Royal Greenland Trading Company who by virtue of that office was the Upernivik Pooh Bah, harbour-master, customs, health, immigration, mayor, and governor of the Province. We got out the gin but this did not stop the manager, a stern-path-of-duty man, from asking to see our health certificates. A regulation provides that visitors to Greenland, presumably coming by air, must have a health certificate issued within forty-eight hours of departure. Some of us did have odd bits of paper showing that at some distant period we had been vaccinated, but that was all. With the assistance of more gin and some talk on our part about the refreshing absence of red tape at Godthaab and Godhavn, and the difficulty of contracting typhoid, consumption, or smallpox at sea, this far-flung piece of bumbledom was strangled at birth.

One of the Danes took us ashore to have coffee in his house. Compared with *Mischief*'s cabin it was like an oven. Our cabin, or at any rate the forward part of it, is heated by a small drip-feed stove using the same fuel as the engine. We asked about seals and were told that as many as 14,000 skins might be handled in a season. Upernivik in Lat. 72°47′ is the most northern principal settlement, the centre to which sealskins are brought for disposal and from where trade goods, food, clothing, ammunition, oil etc. are distributed to small outlying settlements up or down the coast. In summer a small coasting vessel calls weekly but from November to May or June there is no communication at all.

During our very short stay we met with a lot of hospitality, having received none at all elsewhere. It is true, and I suppose only natural, that the stranger can expect a welcome only in places that are really remote. We made another friend in Peter Nissen, a Dane married to an Englishwoman, with a family of four small children at whose house we had drinks, with white bread, cheese, and Godhavn shrimps. He was keen on shooting and possessed a whole battery of firearms. When he heard that we had no weapons on board he was distressed and insisted, much against my will, in lending a .306 American service rifle. It was dated 1917 and looked as if it had never been fired. He talked of our shooting seals with it, or even Polar bears, thinking perhaps that we might need some protection when crossing Bylot Island. He worked in the radio station and thanks to him we obtained an ice report from Baffin Bay through the Danish liaison officer at Thule, the American base some 300 miles to the north.

Having arrived on 11 July we sailed on the afternoon of the 13th. A few houses, the hospital, and the Greenland Company's trading store just about exhausted the sights. We spent some hours patiently fishing with a grapnel for the gash bucket which Stephen had thrown overboard. We watched with interest, too, the methods used to supply the place with drinking water. A launch went out – it had not far to go – and having grappled an ice floe or bergy bit of several tons towed it to the beach. There a lorry awaited with a gang of men who attacked the ice with picks and crowbars to break it into small pieces which were then put in sacks for the lorry to distribute to the various houses. We ourselves, in need of some thirty gallons of water, were kindly allowed to draw on the hospital where they had facilities for melting ice in quantity. The island is waterless; considering, too, the poor harbour, one wonders how it came to be chosen as a settlement. I suppose even if there were a lake or a stream the water would not remain unfrozen for many months in the year. For seventy-nine days in the year the sun does not so much as rise. When we were there the air temperature was 65° and the sea 39°.

The ice report which we had received from Thule in slightly garbled form seemed to indicate Lat. 74° as the northern limit of ice. In Davis Strait and Baffin Bay there are two main ice bodies. There is what is known as the East Ice which in winter and spring drifts round Cape Farewell and up the coast, generally disappearing before it reaches as far as Godthaab. And there is the West Ice, the ice carried southwards by the Arctic or Labrador current consisting of ancient floes of great thickness which come from the Polar Sea through Smith, Jones, and Lancaster sounds, mixed up with icebergs and the ice which forms each winter in Baffin Bay and Davis Strait. In winter this ice extends and meets with the ice forming along the Greenland coast north of Disko so that the whole sea is covered.

In April the ice on the Greenland side begins to open and besides this there is nearly always a large area of more or less open water in the northern part of Baffin Bay. This 'polynia', as it is called, is known as the 'North Water' and for two centuries whalers and explorers have been aware of its existence and have taken advantage of it. Its origin is still not definitely known. By July, in an average year, the North Water is no longer isolated and can easily be reached by the widening belt of open water along the Greenland coast. In April and May the ice from Upernivik northwards might well be impenetrable so that the North Water could not be reached. The whalers of the previous century used to make it their aim to reach the North Water as early in the season as possible in May or at latest June – by forcing their way through the ice north of Upernivik. In these attempts it was by no means unusual for ships to be beset, nipped, and sunk; they always sailed in company so that if a ship sank the crew who had taken refuge on the ice would be picked up by another. But even in mid-summer there generally remains a huge, pear-shaped extent of ice floes reaching from the southern edge of the North Water down to the narrowest part of Davis Strait in about Lat. 64°. This is known as the 'Middle Pack'.

In order to avoid the Middle Pack we should have to reach the North Water before shaping a course for Bylot Island. For a whaling ship mid-July would have been fully late but by small-boat standards it might be too early in the season. And supposing Baffin Bay to be successfully crossed, would the ice in Lancaster Sound and Pond Inlet allow us to reach the coast of Bylot Island? The distance was about 360 miles. If we had to dodge about a lot to avoid ice, steering the sort of course that would make an eel dizzy, it might well be half as much again. Steering a course depends upon the compass and I had already noted that the Canadian chart of those waters bore the discouraging warning that 'The magnetic compass is useless in this region.'

At Upernivik the magnetic variation is already 60°W., at Bylot Island it increases to 75°W., and at the western end of Lancaster Sound it is 90°W. The magnetic pole is at present roughly in Lat. 70°N. Long. 97°W., only some 400 miles from Bylot Island in a south-westerly direction. At the magnetic pole a freely suspended compass needle points up and down having no horizontal force to give it direction. Hence the extreme sluggishness of the compass needle in the Canadian Arctic and its complete uselessness near the magnetic pole. And as a matter of interest, should anyone who reads this be contemplating a journey from the magnetic pole to the true north pole, they will find they will have to steer due south by compass to reach it.

We had, of course, already noticed the increasing unwillingness of our little five-inch compass card to move, but having moved it did point in the right direction. Had it not brought us more or less unerringly to Upernivik? Going west to Bylot Island the horizontal force would become less and less and the compass correspondingly less inclined to bestir itself. However, long before the day of the gyro compass and radar aids, many ships with compasses no better than ours had navigated these waters and we hoped we could manage as well.

We sailed slowly away from Upernivik on a lovely, calm, sunny evening, the placid sea dotted with immaculate icebergs, rocky islets glowing warmly in the setting sun, and astern of us the distant line of the ice-cap faintly tinged with yellow. Even on the more southerly part of the Greenland coast one can only identify one's position vaguely by mountains or the openings to fjords. North of Upernivik there are not even these to provide a clue. Between

Sanderson's Hope and an 1,800ft. high pillar known as the Devil's Thumb 100 miles to the north, the coast presents the same front of indistinguishable islands and featureless ice-cap. We steered north-west aiming to reach Lat. 74° where, if the Thule ice report was right, we might be able to turn west. At midnight when ice appeared ahead we turned north and soon lost sight of what must have been a detached raft of floes and not the edge of the Middle Pack. By noon of the 14th we were in Lat. 73°23′N. 58°W. with no ice anywhere in sight.

That we managed to get ourselves into trouble the very next day was my own fault. Having met some loose floes, less than 4/10 ice cover, I assumed that this was merely another detached raft and began to weave a way through it in a general northwesterly direction. The amount of open water soon began to diminish. We headed northwards and that was no good. Finally we were forced to retreat eastwards and it was late evening before we were clear of the ice, back in square one, having wasted the best part of a day. The night was very cold, the air temperature 32° and the sea 33°. By morning, when we had got well away from the ice, the sea temperature had risen to 35°. Though the presence of an iceberg does not affect the sea or air temperature, the near presence of large quantities of pack-ice has a marked effect. On a day of little wind and a lot of fog the halyards became festooned with icicles and frozen rime. The ice had to be shaken off before the halyards would render through the blocks.

The 17th was yet another day of fog and calms, not a ripple on the water, and so still that the creaking of a bird's wings as it flew by invisibly in the fog could easily by heard. In spite of the comparative warmth, sea and air temperature both at 36°, our halyards were thick with ice while the baggy-wrinkle (the anti-chafe gear wrapped round shrouds and topping lifts) looked like elongated snowballs. Having motored for six hours we felt we had done enough. The fog certainly increased the tension. For all we could tell we might have been motoring steadily into an ice cul-de-sac. But on the whole we were content. The cabin felt all the warmer when one came off watch and we did not mind having ice on the rigging provided the sea remained free.

On the 18th, when by dead reckoning we had reached Lat. 74°40′, we met with ice all along our port hand. For two hours we steered north along the edge until I grew impatient and decided to try conclusions with what after all might be merely a narrow line of floes – much to the dismay of Ed who had a wholesome respect for ice having spent some time bashing through it in an ice-breaker. Forewarned by recent experience I did not persevere too long. We turned north-east and soon reached open water again. On a day of little wind, the sea calm, in a region of no strong currents, there is no danger in poking about among loose floes always provided one has room to turn. *Mischief* unfortunately needs a lot of space in which to turn. But it would be unwise to persevere long amongst ice floes without being able to see open water ahead or at any rate quite certain it was there. On a day of wind, the sea rough, and the ice on the move, it would be courting disaster to be amongst it in a small, un-protected vessel. That day we saw a number of seals on the floes and I was glad they had the sense to dive into the water before we got close enough for a shot.

In the night we had some wind and made good eight miles to the west. All morning the light wind held, increasing to a fresh breeze by afternoon. The sun peering vaguely through the overcast enabled me to take a sight which put us in 75°N. 66°W., about half-way across Baffin Bay. Ice then appeared about a mile away on the port hand but so far our progress had been fairly painless. It looked now as if we had reached the North Water and that the ice showing up to the south must be the edge of the Middle Pack. When ice appeared dead ahead late in the evening our hope momentarily died but having come up with it we found it to be merely a long line of scattered floes projecting from the main body of the pack. Beyond lay more open water. In climbing it is notoriously a mistake to write off by mere inspection a seemingly impossible route. One must come to grips with it. In the same way ice floes that in fact are widely scattered, when seen from even half a mile away from the deck of a small boat – or even from the crosstrees – appear just as unbroken and impenetrable as heavily congested pack-ice. All next day in light winds and showers of sleet we sailed west over perfectly open water, only a strong ice-blink to the south denoting the whereabouts of the pack. The sun made a fitful appearance and our noon position I put at 74°40′N. 66°40′W. There happened that day to be a partial eclipse, so that we were delighted when the sky cleared to allow us to watch the progress of the shadow which began at 5 pm and lasted until 7 pm. A huge iceberg afforded us another remarkable spectacle by heaving itself majestically out of the water as if about to capsize. At each ponderous roll one side lifted and the other sank by twenty to thirty feet. By estimating the number of cricket pitches that could be placed on it end to end some of us reckoned it about 300ft. long, others 500ft. This led to arguments about its tonnage and estimates varied even more widely from a million tons to ten million. There is scope enough for error because the proportion of ice above water to that below varies greatly with the type of berg. A blocky, precipitous-sided berg has about five times more of its volume below water, than above, while a much pinnacled, so-called 'pictur-esque' berg, has only twice as much. As I write this, surrounded by slide rules and assisted by a young relative familiar with hypothetical logarithms and hyperbolic functions, I have worked the sum afresh and find that our rolling iceberg, give or take a few tons, weighed 450,000 tons.

In the evening ice-blink could be seen ahead as well as to the south. Ed swore there was ice to the north too – ice all round, in fact. But he took the same lugubrious view of ice as he did of the weather. Having read more than once *Letters from High Latitudes* and being familiar with it, I was reminded of Wilson, Lord Dufferin's personal servant, who moved uneasily about the deck with the air of Cassandra at the conflagration of Troy. Cassandra Wilson used to wake his master something in this fashion:

> 'Seven o'clock, my Lord.'
> 'Very well. How's the wind?'
> 'Blowing a gale, my Lord – dead ahead.'
> 'How many points is she off her course?'
> 'Four points, my Lord – full four points.'
> 'Is it pretty clear, Wilson?'

'Can't see your hand, my Lord – can't see your hand.'
'Much ice in sight?'
'Ice all round, my Lord – ice all round.'

At midnight we came up with the ice that earlier had been betrayed to us by the 'blink', a yellowish-white appearance of the sky produced by the reflection of pack-ice on the clouds. It proved to be another projecting cape which we presently rounded and resumed our westerly course. Throughout that next day we met scattered floes, so widely scattered that for the most part we could maintain our course. From sights I reckoned we had about 120 miles to go. Seals were fairly plentiful, sticking their heads out of the water or basking peacefully on the floes, and since we were under sail the latter took little notice of our passing. The crew seemed anxious to have one shot and equally in favour of casting me in the role of murderer. I must have been talking too much of my misspent youth in East Africa, of elephants and rhino, for they evidently took me for Buffalo Bill, or such a marksman as the famous elephant hunter Neumann who, because he invariably killed all his game with one shot, earned from his Swahili followers the sobriquet *Risasi moja* – one cartridge.

When voyaging single-handed through the Patagonian channels Slocum felt that in the loneliness of those waters life of any kind should be held sacrosanct. I, too, felt reluctant to reduce the seal population by even one. But public opinion was too strong so, consoling myself with thoughts of fresh meat, I took Nissen's rifle, from which no shot had yet been fired, and lay down in the bows. It would not do to bungle it, the eyes of England, so to speak, were upon me. Waiting until the ship had glided quietly to within about a hundred yards of our unsuspecting victim, I fired. The seal hardly moved. It had either been killed outright or very hard hit, but I gave it one more round to make sure it did not slip away into the sea.

We hove to, launched the dinghy, and Bruce and Mike went off with rope and ice-axe to retrieve the body. The ice-axe was needed to cut a landing place on the floe. It proved to be a big harp seal. Stephen made a good job of skinning it and then put together a wooden frame where he stretched the skin to dry. The skinning is comparatively easy but cleaning a sealskin, removing all traces of blubber, is most laborious and troublesome for the amateur. With various implements we whittled away day by day and still there were bits of blubber all over the skin. Finally it was left for the expert hands of an Eskimo at Pond Inlet who quickly made a proper job of it. We enjoyed the liver and we dutifully ate what little edible meat there was. To enjoy seal meat, perhaps one should be sitting in an igloo or smoke-blackened hut after a day's sledging, a blizzard raging outside, devouring it in one's fingers after slightly warming and smoking it over a blubber lamp.

On 22 July we ran all day through patches of fog before a light wind. Both fog and wind increased at night (there was, of course, no darkness) till we were reaching at five knots with a spanking breeze at north. Seeing a few floes about we put an extra man on watch. At 1 am the fog cleared and at 2 am (ship's time) I took a meridian sight of the sun in the north. True the sun was too low for a reliable sight but I liked the notion of taking a meridian sight in the middle of the night. On a fine, clear morning a bank of cloud away to the west hinted at the presence of land.

Before the weather closed down again, as it did before noon of the 23rd, I thought we had about forty miles to go to Cape Liverpool at the north-east corner of Bylot Island. At 4 pm I got a snap sight which was probably useless on account of the fog, but taking everything into account I reckoned we were only about twelve miles from the cape. Whereupon I altered course to WSW hoping to fetch the land near Maud Bight which is twenty miles west of the cape and well inside Lancaster Sound. In view of the probability of ice in the sound, the reputed uselessness of the compass, and the paucity of reliable sights, this was a considerable act of faith. We were certainly near some part of the Canadian Arctic, we might even fetch the coast of Bylot Island. Beyond that it was anybody's guess.

> Beyond the clouds, beyond the waves that roar,
> There may indeed, or may not be, a shore.

About an hour later, the fog still thick and Ed on deck steering, the rest of us below were startled by an agonized yell, a yell like that from a covey of angry screech owls giving tongue together. Whether it heralded triumph or disaster I could not determine but knowing who had uttered it I surmised the latter. Tumbling up on deck we saw, a short 200 yards away, at about the limit of visibility, a low range of sandhills.

CHAPTER FIVE

Bylot Island

IN LECKY'S *Wrinkles*, of which I had a copy on board, there is a remark to the effect that 'there is nothing so distressing as running on shore, unless there is also present some doubt as to which continent the shore belongs.' We were not quite in that predicament. We were comfortably far from the beach – we had lost no time in anchoring – and in my opinion this was undoubtedly Bylot Island, though what part of it was, of course, a question.

Taking a map of the island I rowed the dinghy ashore. Not that I expected to meet any natives, hostile or friendly, of whom I might ask our where-abouts, or even any of the notices found nowadays on most beaches – 'Deck Chairs 2d.', or 'Bathing Prohibited'. But on the map which, with regard to the coastline, is pretty detailed, there might be some identifiable features. Just west of Cape Liverpool, for instance, there was marked a lagoon where a river debouched. The cape itself is not significant enough, it is merely a bend in the coastline, a slight protuberance, as Dr Johnson might have called it. As far as could be seen in the fog the coast ran straight roughly from south-east to north-west, as the coast near Cape Liverpool does run. In a hurried walk along the beach in both directions I met several small streams and finally a backwater which a liberal-minded man might have called a lagoon. Back on board, with more confidence than I really felt, I assured the crew we were off Cape Liverpool. After supper some of us landed again for further exploration. The fog remained thick and apart from some old bear tracks we saw nothing else of interest. We set an anchor watch.

Though we could make Cape Liverpool our starting point for crossing the island, Bruce and I preferred if possible to start from Maud Bight, twenty miles further west, where a large glacier came right down to the coast, thus offering a broad highway to the interior. At this time of year at that low level the glacier, we thought, would almost certainly have a surface of dry ice, free from snow, on which we would be able to move at a good pace. At Cape Liverpool the nearest glacier was eight miles away from the beach.

Early on the 24th – the fog as thick as ever – we got our anchor and started sailing a little north of west with a good breeze at north. Very soon we began meeting icebergs and large flat floes, evidently at the entrance to Lancaster Sound. With one of these we had a terribly close shave. In the absence of any visible land it was difficult to tell whether we were being set up or down by any current. Stephen was at the helm pointing reasonably clear of a 100ft. high ice monster with a ram like a battleship. Only when we drew near did I realize that we were being set down towards it very fast indeed. By then we were too close either to gybe or to go about. We could only hold on and pray that we were going fast enough to miss it. We shot by with about ten feet to spare. My knees still knock when I think of this near miss.

When the sun showed at 10 am, the horizon below it seemingly clear enough for a sight, I took one which showed that we were about ten miles east of our assumed position. My ideas about Cape Liverpool had to be revised. We must have been well to the south-east of it. The clearing, during which we had seen no land, lasted but a short time. Tacking towards the land we met more floes, stood out again, and continued tacking off and on until the wind died. Having started the engine we once more closed the land where we could make out fast ice (winter ice still fast to the shore) and beyond, very dimly, a low coastline. As we followed the edge of the fast ice westwards we were gradually forced away from the shore by its increasing width until finally the fast shore ice merged with heavy floes and blocked the sound. At 6 pm we had to abandon any hope of reaching Maud Bight or of penetrating any further west in Lancaster Sound.

Coasting back along the edge of the fast ice, keeping a sharp look-out for seals, polar bears, and somewhere to anchor, at last at 8.30 pm we found a little ice-free hole where a river debouched. We anchored there, only a few yards from the shore, with fast ice on either side of us. The strong current from the river which had kept the opening clear of ice also prevented us from swinging. We had barely done congratulating ourselves on finding this snug hole when the fog rolled away in dramatic fashion, revealing a wide stretch of brown tundra and beyond it a tangle of snow mountains brilliantly lit by the westering sun. A hasty inspection of our surroundings showed that the river

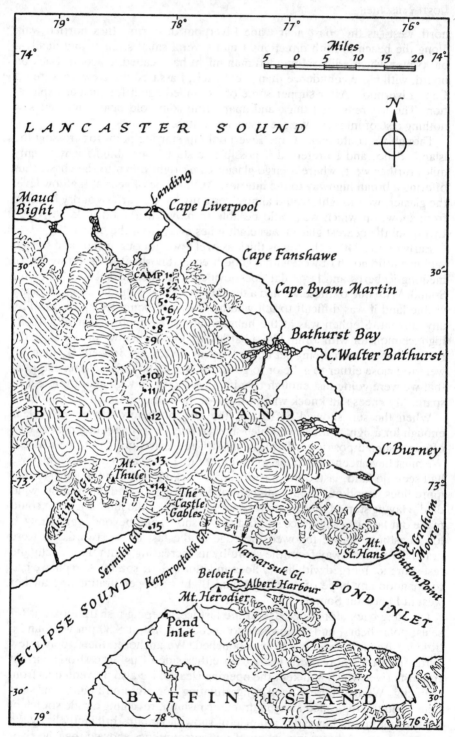

The Crossing of Bylot Island, 25 July - 8 August, 1963

formed an undoubted lagoon and that its course, parallel to the coast, agreed
with that on the map near Cape Liverpool. This was decisive. We had already
had more luck than we deserved and I had no mind to push it any further by
trying to force our way to Maud Bight. As Swift said: 'There is no piece of
knowledge in fewer hands than that of knowing when to have done.' Bruce
and I could very well start our journey from here and we had already marked
down a glacier that would take us inland. Naturally the crew were all agog to
set foot at once upon this barren and almost unknown shore. They proposed a
walk after supper and for once I was quick enough to seize the advantage.
Their energy could be harnessed. 'When they bring you a heifer be ready with
the rope', as Sancho Panza was fond of saying. Accordingly Bruce and I
quickly made up some light loads which we carried inland for a mile and a half
where we dumped them. On returning to the ship I took a sight, hoping to
verify our position. Either I was too tired or there was too much refraction,
for the working of it made no sense at all.

   In contrast to the general run of the weather ever since Upernivik, and
especially of the last few days, we enjoyed on 25 July and for several subsequent days bright, cloudless weather. There were no flowers and hardly any
birds to rejoice and sing but even the bleak tundra assumed a more kindly
aspect. But the thin ice that formed overnight round the ship reminded us of
how far north we were and of the briefness of the arctic summer. I considered
food for eighteen days a sufficiently liberal allowance for Bruce and I to take
for the fifty-mile crossing. One had to assume that nothing untoward would
befall either of us and that the boat would be there to pick us up. Food,
together with our personal loads, tent, cooking gear, paraffin, and rope
would, we reckoned, add up to about 160 lbs. The 15-lb tent was a big item
and I had canvassed the idea of sleeping in snow-holes. But I like my comfort
and in view of the sort of snow we were to encounter I am glad we did not try.
Many years ago I may have been able to stagger *downhill* under an 80-lb load,
and judging by what one reads in climbing journals this seems nowadays to be
a standard load, especially among New Zealand climbers. One sometimes
wonders whether the loads are weighed or whether they merely feel like 80
lbs – as indeed I could swear was the weight of any load that I now attempt to
carry. However, on this journey I had no intention of competing in a weight-
carrying contest. About 40 lb would be more than enough and the idea of
adding to it by taking Peter Nissen's rifle never so much as crossed my mind.
We hoped that for the first march, with the help of two volunteers, we could
carry everything as far as the glacier. After that we should have to relay until
we had consumed enough to be able to carry what was left in one lift.

   Accordingly on the 25th Bruce and I, Stephen and Bob, set out for the foot
of the glacier about eight miles away. Ed had the job of taking *Mischief* round
to the settlement in Pond Inlet and I felt she could not be in safer or more
capable hands. The settlement is on the south or Baffin Island side of Pond
Inlet, more or less opposite and separated by ten miles of water from the
snout of the Sermilik glacier, the glacier by which Bruce and I hoped to
descend to the south coast. The Sermilik is one of four glaciers on the south
coast which have names. These and Mt Thule are about the only names on the

map apart from the capes and bays of the coastline. I told Ed that we expected to reach the south coast about 12 August and that on either side of that date he was to look out for smoke signals at 8 am and noon. If after the lapse of a week nothing had been seen he would have to sail over and look for us up the Sermilik. On shore we had noticed nothing much with which to make smoke. Perhaps on the south side there would be more vegetation, at the worst we could burn the tent.

Bunyan relates in one of his dreams: 'I saw a man clothed in rags and a great burden upon his back.' I thought of this as I watched Bob, all enthusiasm, setting off that morning. He had joined the ship with remarkably little clothing and now that little was fast becoming rags. But he did have a pair of new climbing boots, a pair which he had worn only once before for a very short time the previous evening. At the dump we added that to our loads and set off again. The going was perfectly flat and reasonably smooth, interspersed with patches of bog which had to be avoided. A mouse and a pure white snowy owl were the only signs of life.

Besides his threadbare clothes Bob seemed bent on mortifying the flesh through the stomach. When we called a halt for lunch he produced for his own consumption merely two pieces of very dry black bread. But shortly after he was in real trouble, his new boots having begun to hurt so much that he had to take them off and walk in his socks. True he had on two thick pairs but I realized that very soon he would have to be told to go back, for he was not the kind to give in willingly. We then came to the only obstacle of the day, a fairly fast-flowing river about knee-deep. Stephen and I made the mistake of crossing bare foot. The stones on the bottom were slippery and half-way over both of us took a ducking. Profiting by our example Bruce crossed in his boots. Bob had no choice, his boots being too painful to wear, and when we were all across I sent him back.

The flat tundra now came to an end. We began toiling up a boulder fan, the debris deposited by the glacier above. Our pace became slower and slower, the heat of the day and our weeks of inaction on the boat taking their toll. Stephen had still to return and obviously we were not going to reach the glacier, so at 5 pm, having found a tent site and water, we called it a day. Stephen started back at once while Bruce and I, after pitching the tent and making a brew, went back to fetch Bob's load. The huge, erratic boulder by which it had been left looked a long way off and it was two hours before we were back, intent on our supper. On this and on every succeeding day we had a one-lb tin of pemmican between the two of us, as thick, rich, and satisfying a brew as can be imagined. According to a pocket aneroid the height was 800ft.

The morning dawned fine and clear. We could see right across the ice-filled Lancaster Sound to North Devon Island, low and comparatively free from snow. *Mischief* had gone. We had, so to speak, burnt our boats. Now it was 'Pike's Peak or bust'. How mistaken can one be? We had looked forward eagerly and confidently to setting foot on the glacier where, we assumed, we should tread dry ice or crisp, firm snow. Upon reaching it we sank almost at once into soft snow eighteen inches deep with water underneath. This seemed too bad to be true. We tried the middle of the glacier and found it no better;

the side, and that was worse. The disgust we felt at this belying of our hopes presently turned to misgiving. How were we to carry loads for fifty miles through this sort of stuff in eighteen days? As target for the day we set our eyes on a rock spur round which the glacier bent out of sight. By 2 pm, when still well short of it, we had had enough and made camp in the snow alongside a flat boulder almost as big as a table. It would not quite accommodate the tent which we had to pitch in slushy snow where the deeper one dug the wetter it became. Fortified by strong tea we started back for the remaining loads and were home again by 6 pm.

The rock spur where Camp II should have been put finally served for Camp III. The going continued to be deplorable except for a short half-mile of south-facing slope which the sun had stripped bare of snow where our speed in comparison became that of an express. The leader, by treading cat-like, might remain on top for a few yards, then down he would go thigh-deep with both feet in water to thresh about like a fly in a jam-pot. The man behind fared no better, for a step that had supported the leader generally collapsed when used for the second time. However, we kept moving. As the proverb says, 'be not afraid of going slowly, be only afraid of standing still.' One blessing was the entire absence of crevasses which enabled us to move un-roped. We were already 2,550ft. above sea level and we camped a bit early that day on account of mist and rain. There must have been something very peculiar about atmospheric conditions outside. In the course of many hours spent in small tents at all levels, from sea level to 27,000ft., I have never before encountered such an opaque atmosphere, or fug, inside a tent. Our wet clothes were steaming, the cooking pot was steaming, and I had a pipe going – all, of course, normal conditions – yet I could hardly see Bruce's face lying alongside me, while the far end of the tent seven feet away was completely obscured. When the rain stopped we went back for the loads.

We failed to reach our objective for the fourth day, a distant snow col, by the usual large margin. At midday we took advantage of a bare boulder-strewn slope to make camp. The toil of shifting rocks to build a platform was a small price to pay for a dry lodging. We were here 3,000ft. up. We kept assuring ourselves that the snow was improving, an assurance as often belied when one of us disappeared up to the waist. The constant expectation of suddenly sinking like this was almost as bad as the reality; like at the old Fun Fairs where for threepence one could enter a Haunted House and have one's nerves stretched in a variety of ways, including a dark, narrow corridor where the floor suddenly collapsed. At this camp, while hacking out some ice to melt for water, Bruce broke the shaft of my ice-axe. Bound with a strip of tin and multiple lashings it served well enough for probing snow. There seemed not the remotest chance of our having to use an axe to cut steps.

We reached the snow col (3,600ft.) the next day, 29 July, after a hard yet satisfying day. Each trip, the first, and the second to relay the loads forward, took four hours. At this height the snow proved less consistently bad; we thought seventy-five per cent of it to be relatively good and the rest infernally bad. A few minutes after starting we were always wet to the waist. So far our view had been restricted to the snow ridges either side of the glacier; there were no moraines at the side of the glacier and the snow on it merely merged with the snow of the slope leading up to the ridge. But from the col we enjoyed a long vista down a wide glacier to the sea beyond, probably the glacier descending to Maud Bight. Our route from the col started with a descent to another glacier basin. Thus emboldened we set off with double loads but we soon abandoned them after reaching the treacherous snow in the basin. Again we found a bit of rock to camp on at 1 pm before returning to retrieve the remaining loads. We had lost some height, this Camp VII being only 2,800ft. Although we studied the map avidly and marked on it each day where we thought we were it was of no help in finding a route. The snow-field which we were traversing appears on the map as a mass of vague form lines and none of the glaciers are identifiable except when they approach the coast. Thus we had at least the satisfaction of finding our own way through un-mapped country. We steered south by the sun, selecting some feature that lay roughly in that direction and making for it by the line of least resistance. Had we kept to the ridges we might have avoided losing any height but we should not have found any of those patches of snow-free slopes which afforded such exquisite relief from the snow bog.

We made Camp VIII on 1 August after what we considered a good day. Thanks to some stretches of bare ice we had made good at least three miles. Nevertheless we were obliged to pitch the tent in the middle of a snow-field with not a rock in sight. We met a new and formidable obstacle in the shape of streams that in their meandering course through the wide snow-field had worn a six-foot furrow down to blue ice and had cast up on either side a high bank of snow. I tried walking for a time without snow glasses and suffered for it with a mild touch of snow-blindness.

For the first time we managed to carry all the gear in one lift to the next camp, still at only 2,800ft. Several deep furrows had to be crossed, usually necessitating making a cast up or down stream until we found a place narrow enough to jump. There was no future at all in setting foot on the slippery ice in the fast running water. Once Bruce did incautiously put a foot in and I had to hang on to him to prevent his being swept off his feet. Camp IX was an oasis in a snow desert, a delightful site with a ready-made gravel platform, a few tufts of grass, yellow poppies, a pair of pipits, a butterfly, and at our feet a clear blue tarn. Moreover the day was hot and cloudless, so still that at our lunch halt we brewed tea on an unshielded stove in the open air. In the evening we had tea outside in our garden, admiring what was al-most a mountain prospect, the level snow stretching away to a distant ser-rated ridge.

Once more we began making height, camping on 3 August at 3,600ft. Having only the one trip to make we kept moving until we had covered the record distance of five miles. But we had our troubles. Bruce now began to find his boots hurting him, so much so that he soon became quite crippled. They were Italian climbing boots with a piece of metal inserted to stiffen the heel, and short of pulling the boots to pieces to remove the metal there was nothing we could do. Then when nearing camp – I must have been tired and careless – I came a cropper on a loose boulder and savaged my left arm.

Nothing was broken but for the next two days it was quite useless. Anyway the incident served as a caution.

That night it actually froze. On account of my arm Bruce had most of the packing up to do, but when at length we started we enjoyed for a short time the pleasure of walking on hard, crisp snow. What with Bruce's boots and my arm neither of us felt like a long day so we camped early at a height of 4,350ft. A col that we hoped might be the watershed appeared to be only about two miles away. At this height we were in cloud and mist and for a time saw no guiding sun. Starting on 5 August we steered at first by a rock outcrop looming vaguely through the mist and when this became obscured we had to resort to a prismatic compass. I sent Bruce ahead on a bearing until he had disappeared in the mist where he stopped and waited for me to come up. Climbing steadily all the time we reached the col early in the afternoon at a height of 5,700ft. By then the cloud had dispersed and we estimated the height of a nearby, rounded snow summit to be about 6,500ft. This might well have been the highest or one of the highest points of Bylot Island but neither of us had the inclination or the energy to make the long snow plod to the top.

This col was undoubtedly on the watershed and it behove us to be careful about our next move. A moderately steep slope dropped 500ft. to a snow basin, the main source of a big glacier which disappeared round a shoulder of the mountain. We half suspected this glacier to be the Sermilik. If it were then we were home and dry. But it appeared to run too much east of south, so before committing ourselves and losing precious height by a descent to the basin we began traversing towards another col lying due south. Luckily for us the snow of the traverse proved so vile that we soon gave up in despair and began plunging recklessly downhill. 'No matter where it leads me, the down-hill path for me' was no doubt in both our minds. Whatever this glacier might prove to be it would certainly conduct us to the coast. We camped in the basin at a height of 5,200ft.

We were 'with child', as Pepys would say, to see round the corner so that we should know in what direction the glacier trended. However, making the best speed we could on the morning of 6 August we failed to reach the corner before a great cloud advanced up the glacier to blot out everything. Once more we had to use the compass. Owing to the advance of day and the gradual loss of height, the hard crust on which we had started walking began to soften. Soon we were sinking and floundering every few steps. At last, however, we had turned the corner and far away, through a brief clearing of the cloud, I felt sure I had caught a glimpse of blue, a blue that could not be mistaken for sky. With some difficulty I refrained from crying out, as I should have done, 'The sea! The sea!' I did not want to raise false hopes in Bruce who by now, thanks to his wretched boots, had his work cut out to keep going. The glacier led south so that we were pretty sure it was the Sermilik and we felt pleased at having hit it off so nicely. Lured on by some distant rocks on the left bank we made tremendous efforts to reach them, wading through snow just as bad as that which we had met at the start of our journey. We dumped the loads with the idea of first breaking a trail to the rocks and then returning for the loads. It was no use, we were too tired. After a mile the rocks looked no nearer. We gave in, fetched the loads, and made camp in the snow. The height was 3,700ft.

We were nearly out of the wood. On 7 August after two more hours in really hellish snow we won through to dry ice and our troubles were over. Provided *Mischief* had reached Pond Inlet we did not think there would be any delay in our being taken off. With the sea now in view we pressed on and camped finally on a moraine, the first we had seen. We might as well have stayed on the glacier itself, for on removing some stones and gravel to make a platform we exposed the ice beneath. My air mattress had long been useless so I lay on top of a Yukon pack-board and kept pretty warm. This last camp but one was at 2,200ft. and some seven or eight miles from the coast. We thought that by making an early start we might reach the sea before midday in time to send up the first pre-arranged smoke signal to let the crew know we had arrived.

So on 8 August at 6.30 am off we went with light loads, downhill, and on dry ice. Tired though we both were and with Bruce limping along behind, surely we could make it before noon. At last the time came to quit the glacier which terminated several hundred yards from the sea, and at last the rope which we had carried without having occasion to use came in handy for us to rope down a fifteen ft. cliff of ice at the edge of the glacier. There we first set foot on dry land, so to speak, after a voyage of fourteen days over snow. The last seven miles had taken five hours. We need not have hurried. The whole Baffin Island coast lay covered in cloud.

CHAPTER SIX

Pond Inlet

AT ITS snout the Sermilik glacier is over a mile wide. Only the western corner of it is still washed by the sea, for it is receding and has been receding for a long time as the huge and very old moraine on the left bank showed. It took us a long time to climb this moraine and having reached the top we saw what in our snow-weary eyes looked like a lush meadow. What a contrast, too, was here from the bare, brown, stony waste that borders the north coast. Besides grass and a few flowers we noted with satisfaction an abundant growth of heath that promised to make for us a lot of smoke. Having carefully chosen a site, before erecting the tent we layed down a springy mattress of heath. We promised ourselves soft lying after what I think, taken all in all, had been the hardest fifty miles I had ever done, certainly the slowest. If we were not now in ecstasy it was at least comfort.

We had put the tent about 300ft. above the beach, fully high enough for a fire to be seen from sea level at ten miles distance provided someone looked for it in the right direction at the right time. Tired limbs and a cold east wind kept us inside except for the time spent gathering a supply of heath for the fire. Although the next morning broke fine, a bank of fog still hid the opposite coast. When it cleared later we could make out even with unaided eyes the square outlines of buildings and a steamer at anchor. She was making a lot of smoke, evidently preparatory to sailing, for she presently moved off westwards towards Eclipse Sound. We guessed she must be the annual supply ship visiting the settlements at Pond Inlet, Arctic Bay in Admiralty Inlet, and Resolute on Cornwallis Island. We spent the morning building a big cairn on the beach and gathering driftwood to augment the fire. At noon the great moment had come. It was a substantial blaze comparable, we imagined, to the beacons signalling the arrival of the Armada and, we hoped, with an equally galvanizing effect. For what it was worth we also flashed a mirror and then settled back confidently to wait. An hour elapsed and nothing happened. Except for a few lonely icebergs the ten-mile stretch of water remained obstinately blank.

In the afternoon I took a walk uphill and then gained the beach below Castle Gables by way of a steep gully. As we had guessed from the air photographs this peak is merely a serrated ridge of rotten rock. Walking back by the beach I found evidence of old camp sites – a sheltering wall of stones, tins, bits of box-wood – relics perhaps of the American party of 1954. I collected more driftwood. At noon there had been a lot of wind blowing the smoke away horizontally, so that evening when the air was still we made more smoke.

On the next day we varied our tactics, lighting three fires in widely separated places instead of one big blaze. We had them going just in time, as a belt of fog crept slowly westwards along the Baffin Island coast. Albert Harbour, the best anchorage in Pond Inlet ten miles east of the settlement, had already been blotted out. We were already a little puzzled and as we gazed across the sunlit, smiling sea where nothing moved we debated the absence of response to our signals. If they had chosen to lie at Albert Harbour they would not have seen our smoke that day and might be too far off anyway. But it was unlikely that the crew would stop long at that empty harbour, however good the anchorage, with the hospitality of the settlement and fresh faces so close at hand. We found it hard, too, to believe that our smoke was not visible from the settlement or had not been noticed. Besides the crew who would be looking out, there would be numbers of keen-eyed Eskimos, quick to spot anything unusual, and probably with nothing better to do than ourselves but stare across the sea. There remained only the disturbing possibility that *Mischief* had not arrived, that she had been delayed for some reason, or even caught in the ice. There was no ice in sight now but a fortnight earlier conditions might have been as bad or worse than those we had encountered in Lancaster Sound.

As a result of these reflections we took stock of our food. The few luxuries we had started with – porridge, jam, butter, marmite, peanut butter, and chocolate – had been eaten long since, and on our arrival, thinking that we should be picked up in a day, we had made pretty free with what was left. We found we could now have ten biscuits each for that day and the next and that the pemmican, tea, sugar, and milk would last the same time. We had nothing else bar one slow-burning carriage candle and so far as we knew the resources of the island were nil. We remembered the solitary hare we had seen and the rifle we had not brought with us. And if *Mischief* had failed to arrive no one at the settlement would even know of our existence. Thus we faced the prospect of starving, with the added refinement of starving within sight of plenty. Obviously before that happened we should have to bestir ourselves. Bruce's air mattress was in good condition – a lash-up of that and driftwood might carry one of us safely across if the sea remained calm.

That night it blew hard from the east and continued blowing next morning. But the sun shone cheerfully as we surveyed the same prospect of wind-swept, sunlit, empty waters, and since cloud hung low over the Baffin Island side we need light no fires nor expect any rescue that day. We moved the tent to a more sheltered hollow and I went for a walk along the beach to the west under the front of the glacier. Bruce seemed sunk in lethargy or was perhaps reserving his strength for a voyage by raft. I can well understand the fascination of beachcombing, especially for a man on an island where the only evidence that there is life elsewhere on this planet is to be found on the beach. I found and discarded all kinds of worthless treasures – the runner of a sledge, a broken oar, whalebones, curious pebbles, the skeleton of a seal. The beach, too, was cluttered with bergy bits cast up by the gale. I took home some sea water which in the absence of salt we were using to flavour the pemmican, and that evening, in the last of our pemmican, we used too much.

Next morning, having made a smoke signal at 8 am, we retired to the tent for breakfast. As we were finishing this frugal meal, a mug of tea and three biscuits, thus leaving only seven in the larder, we heard the noise of an engine. In a flash I was outside the tent to see in the distance two small boats. We castaways had no need to wave shirts or light fires to attract their attention. They were obviously heading for our beach and presently two canoes, one large and one small, powered by Johnson outboard engines, landed and out stepped two Eskimos. The man, Kudloo by name, had a smattering of English. A party of Eskimos were apparently camped about five miles west of the Sermilik engaged in hunting seals or perhaps narwhal. They had seen our smoke and had had the sense or the curiosity to come and investigate. They must have been recently at the settlement because they knew of *Mischief* and they did not need to be told what we wanted.

In no time at all we had packed up, carried the loads to the beach, and dumped them in the big canoe, generously bestowing our remaining biscuits on Kudloo's companion, a young lad. In accord with my sense of fitness these chaps should have come in kayaks, though a kayak would not have helped us much. An umiak would have done – the large skin boat light enough to be carried, formerly used by Eskimos for ice-sea travel, propelled by rudely fashioned oars, while Kudloo and his companion should have been wearing sealskin anoraks and bearskin trousers, reeking emphatically of smoke and blubber. The only concessions Kudloo made towards my ideal were a pair of sealskin boots and a short cutty pipe which remained stuck in his mouth, the bowl close under his nose. The canoes were fine jobs of light plywood construction made in Canada, the big one capable of carrying several tons. The lad had to take the smaller canoe back to their camp. He had also to take with him, though Heaven knows why, some of the ice with which our beach was liberally strewn. I noticed he was choosy about what he took, discarding after a brief glance several pieces that to my inexpert eyes looked like perfectly good ice. This done we all embarked and shot off at a good five knots. When about halfway over both wind and sea got up and I began to think Kudloo might be well advised to turn and run for Bylot Island to await a better day. I pondered, too, how an air mattress would have fared in these conditions. But Kudloo drove on, pipe firmly clenched in his teeth, quite regardless of the spray drenching both himself and his passengers. Soon we sighted a mast and a familiar yellow hull and two hours after leaving we were alongside. Having given Kudloo a well-earned five dollars we climbed on board and surprised the crew still at their breakfast. We thought they looked a bit sheepish.

They had arrived about 28 July, the first ship of the season, followed a week later by the supply ship Bruce and I had seen. During the last few days they had, of course, been looking out for signals and apparently had looked in the right place, but they had seen nothing. With no one now at our camp site to make smoke the matter could not be tested, but Bruce and I had to admit that against the dark background of the moraine our smoke might have gone unnoticed. Nevertheless we remained secretly convinced that their combined vision, even assisted by binoculars, must be singularly myopic. At any rate all our anxiety had been needless, though we were not to know it. In the course of the next week, seeing no signals, they would have sailed over to look for us. But whether before this happened, Bruce and I, with nothing to eat, would have decided upon a raft, and which of us would have embarked on this dicey voyage, are questions that I am glad we did not have to answer.

Meantime they were full (in every sense) of the hospitality they had received and of the generosity with which the ship had been crammed with food. Apparently we had on board now more food than when we started the voyage. They also told us of their adventures on the passage round, and since these were sometimes exciting I record them here in Ed's own graphic and sometimes telegraphic style:

After Tilman and his party left for the glacier, Mike and myself kept regular ice watch aboard the cutter until the tidal current became weak enough to prevent the floes from moving along the coast. At low water most of them are grounded, some break under their own weight, and the current from our river is then strong enough to carry them seaward. Satisfied that Mischief was in no immediate danger we went ashore and erected a stone cairn on the south bank of the river. A rum bottle with the names of the crew, date, and other information was inserted at the base and a board put on top. During the afternoon strong refraction showed on the northern horizon, probably the coast of Devon Island. From the masthead open water showed eastwards.

Later I went ashore to look for the returning party. A lonely, staggering figure of a man carrying an empty rucksack appeared in the distance. Sure enough it was Bob, minus his boots which he had left somewhere and which he wanted Mike to fetch as he was unable to walk, his feet being sore and blistered. We took him on board and he soon fell asleep exhausted by the march. Two hours later Stephen returned. We hove up anchor and left at once under power, for there was no wind. East of Cape Liverpool most of the ice floes were left astern. I tried to signal Tilman's camp by Aldis. No answer. Numerous seals were swimming around. We hoisted the genoa and took it down again; some weak catspaws but not enough to move us. First signs of a steadier breeze came off the bold promontory of Cape Fanshawe when we hoisted all plain sail and stopped the engine. Tacking close inshore among grounded bergs. Possession Bay covered with broken ice and bergy bits. Had we known that Ross's cairn is still there unopened we would have gone in to recover it. Slow progress in light catspaws.

Suddenly after midnight wind shifts NW in a sudden strong gust which sent us flying southwards. Masthead look-out reports icefloes ahead extending seawards, and more astern. Refraction always makes them look bigger and closer packed than they really are. Towards morning wind dies down and we motor again for a few hours. Passed the floes which are jammed close inshore. Seals everywhere. Ice-fields in bays and inlets along the shore. Heading for Cape Byam Martin. Hoisted genoa and boomed it out with spinnaker pole with a light wind astern. Closing with Cape Graham Moore with snow-clad peaks of Baffin Island clearly visible. Many ice-floes at the entrance to Pond Inlet.

Wind freshening as we round the cape $1\frac{1}{2}$ cables off shore. Chart does not show any rocks or soundings so are keeping a sharp look-out in the bows. We gybe to starboard tack and discover some people standing on Button Point. This was Father Roselier and his Eskimo party, as we found out later; they were digging up an old Eskimo settlement. Sky clouding over rapidly with drizzle, and a heavy squall hangs over Albert harbour visible twenty-five miles away. Close shave with huge berg on account Stephen's refusal to steer course as ordered. Wind heading us and we have to sail towards Guys Bight on the Baffin Island side. When in the middle of the sound it falls calm. Drizzle, isolated floes. Current running east, sails down, engine on, heading towards Albert harbour. Mike reports long line of floes ahead. Bloody hell! On closer inspection we manage to get through by long detours. These floes stretch in long unbroken lines at right angles to the current. When closing the land I thought of anchoring in Albert harbour but the crew want to go on.

No wind. Measure fuel in tank and decide to carry on outside Belœil Island (Albert harbour). Fine clear weather. Doubled the point of Belœil early in the morning. Mist and fog patches ahead. Saw Eskimo camp close to rocky shore below Mt Herodier. Saw more floes ahead, close pack ice on the water. Motoring more difficult. Dead slow. Can't manoeuvre. No openings towards Black Point near Pond Inlet settlement. Turned back and closed the shore near the Eskimo camp. Motor canoe comes out and Eskimo hunters come aboard. We sound and drop anchor fifty yards offshore on a sandy shelf where a strong current eddy keeps driving the menacing ice away. Crew trying to strike bargains in sealskins but no go. Eskimo want twenty-eight dollars for silver seals. Very fine skins. Old hunter explains by gestures that the best way to reach the settlement is by working close inshore.

We sleep for a few hours and early in the afternoon find that there is a strong movement among the floes. They are driving to the north so with engine on and lookout at the masthead we manage to reach Black Point and can see the buildings of the settlement. A fast motor canoe comes out with two marine biologists, Dr Mansfield and Tony Welch. They show us an anchorage abreast of the RCMP building. Plenty of big floes around moving with east-going current. As soon as the anchor is down these huge chunks of ice start to move down on us, fouling the anchor chain and driving us down the bay despite all our efforts to fend them off. Bob Pilot, the RCMP corporal in charge of the station, comes out in his uniform with questions and papers*, also some mail for us which came in yesterday from Frobisher by Canso amphibian. We are the first ship to reach Pond Inlet this season.

At one moment we are aground. I told Mike to sound. He, not being familiar with the markings of the lead-line, shouts 'eight fathoms'. Full astern! Amongst volleys of swearwords and curses I manage to get her off and decide to go behind Black Point with Mansfield's canoe sounding ahead of us with an echo-sounder. We manage to anchor in a narrow place in 2½ fathoms. Current eddy and rocks off the point keep out most of the floes. Boys went ashore to walk to the settlement and did not come back until midnight. Next day a small float-plane landed nearby and was pulled ashore as the ice situation worsened. [This was a private plane belonging to a young mining magnate who had discovered and was preparing to exploit a 'mountain' of very rich iron ore 200 miles south of Pond Inlet.]

We are now surrounded by closely packed ice. Wind has veered east pushing floes against our anchor chain, and now and again we have to start the engine to take the weight off. Met Dr Mansfield again and agreed to go with them to Ragged Island in Eclipse sound about forty miles west of the settlement as soon as the ice cleared. On every east-going tide there is a great rush of ice through the narrows towards the open sea and more floes come in from Eclipse Sound. Bob Pilot gave us a great quantity of food and we moved to the anchorage off the settlement to load it. The fluke of our main anchor had been broken off by ice so had to use the CQR anchor which holds as well or better than the 'fisherman' type. A strong wind from west helped to clear most of the ice out of Pond Inlet.

We motored out to Ragged Island with Mansfield's whaling gear and stores on deck. [Dr Mansfield, on behalf of the Canadian Government was carrying out research on narwhal which are particularly plentiful in Pond Inlet.] His party in two big canoes caught up with us off Curry Island. Took several transit bearings to make sure of our position as the chart is blank and there are two shoals in this area. Mansfield's transistor echo-sounder was installed in our cockpit as we proceeded towards the north end of Ragged Island, while his canoe party took the short cut to the south end. Sounded off the point, a

* It seems a very inopportune moment. H.W.T.

cable distant, and found a sudden shoaling of the water from no bottom at 200 fathoms to seven fathoms in five minutes. At 1 am anchored in a bight near the southern point, gravel, three fathoms. Mansfield's camp on the beach.

Next morning, after setting narwhal nets, two canoes went back to the eskimo camp on Curry Island to collect provisions. Some of the crew went with them taking soundings in the narrow rock-obstructed passage and finding depths of one fathom. Afterwards when Mansfield decided to move south towards Eskimo Inlet we motored back to Pond Inlet, no wind, calm sea. Took some plankton samples in the area where narwhal blew. Except for a few large bergs Pond Inlet was now free of ice.

Proceeded to do some deck and maintenance work, but the crew mostly ashore visiting friends. One night found myself adrift during strong south-east blow with anchor dragging. Started engine and motored back to anchorage alone, blowing whistle to attract attention of crew ashore. All signals useless, as the boys were having a party in Jack Russell's house. We had a row after they came back. Next two days devoted to painting and rigging work. Tilman and Reid arrived in a canoe from Sermilik.

Thus the honour of being the first ship of the season to reach Pond Inlet, about a week before the regular supply ship arrived, seems to have been won not without difficulty and danger. I think Ed should have been presented with a gold cane, like that given to the master of the first ship to pass up the St Lawrence to Montreal. One judges from Ed's account that the excitement of arriving at the settlement and the welcome they received there proved at times too much for the crew. In rather different circumstances the crews of the old Arctic whalers, when their ship was beset, piled out on the ice, broached the rum, and generally behaved in what is popularly supposed to be a seamanlike fashion. However, both ship and crew looked in good shape, the crew in no hurry at all to leave Pond Inlet where they were thoroughly enjoying themselves. The tiny community had certainly given them a warm welcome.

CHAPTER SEVEN

Homeward Bound

POND INLET was so named by John Ross in 1818 after John Pond (1767–1836) who was Astronomer-Royal at that time. That fame is ephemeral is a trite remark but the truth of it is fully borne out in the one small example of Bylot Island. Only a few of the names sprinkled round its coast have been mentioned in this account – Maud Bight, Cape Fanshawe, Cape Byam Martin, Cape Graham Moore, Guys Bight – and who now knows or cares who these men were. None of the residents at Pond Inlet could tell me who Pond was, and I confess it took some trouble on my part to find out.

When we were there the community comprised Corporal Pilot of the RCMP and his wife; the manager of the Hudson Bay Company's store who, needless to say, was a Scot; the engineer in charge of the power plant; the Roman Catholic padre, the keen ethnologist whom Ed had glimpsed in action at Button Point; and an Anglican padre with his wife and child who had only just arrived in the supply ship. In addition, for the summer only, there were two technicans putting up more buildings, and the two marine biologists enquiring into the narwhal population and its habits. Of the natives of those parts there were some thirty Eskimo families living in tents who, I understood, mostly returned to outlying settlements in the winter. Corporal Pilot exercised control over a large area and in winter spent much of his time touring his domain by dog sledge.

The Hudson Bay Company store was similar to those of the Royal Green and Trading Company along the Greenland coast. Furs, sealskins, and narwhal horns were bought or exchanged for food, clothing, arms, ammunition, oil, tobacco, etc. We were told that some 1,000 sealskins had been bought that season. Thus the Eskimos still live as they have always done by hunting, though nowadays in indirect fashion, merely earning money by hunting instead of having to depend on it for food, clothing, and all their necessities. Like most other things the price of sealskins is on the rise. In 1961 at Igdlorssuit in Greenland we had bought average quality skins for £1. In 1963 at Pond Inlet similar skins were worth £5. In the store there were a few narwhal horns from five to seven feet in length. For what purpose the male narwhal uses this formidable implement, no one seems rightly to know. Of two horns still unsold, which I had my eye on, one was imperfect and the other was earmarked as a present for the Governor of the Bank of England. I imagined this financial mogul nonchalantly throwing his silk hat on to it as he clocked in – or, perhaps it would symbolize the horn of plenty.

On the return voyage, instead of sailing the two sides of a triangle by which we had come, we had some hope of steering straight for Godthaab by sailing south-east parallel to the coast of Baffin Island. A signal to 'Ice Control Halifax' asking about the ice conditions and for advice as to our best route, brought a very detailed ice report and a recommendation to take the northern route as we had done on the way up. The Middle Pack had receded southwards a little but near the Canadian coast the ice remained too thick for us to navigate. It seems easier to get a report on ice conditions in the Canadian Arctic than for the coasts of Greenland.

In return for the kindness we had received, before leaving we had a party on board. Those of our guests for whom there was room had scarcely got themselves below before the party was diminished by two. The slight motion of the boat at anchor proved too much for Mrs Pilot who had to be taken hurriedly ashore by her husband. Later we were joined by the mining magnate and his pilot who touched down almost alongside in their small plane, and by the narwhal research party. The latter told us that they had netted fifteen narwhal in the narrows off Ragged Island, one with an eight-foot horn.

After making our farewells ashore we sailed out on the morning of 15 August with a very light wind. The deck and hull had been painted, we had filled up with oil at a cost of only twenty-eight dollars with a drum of furnace oil thrown in; and we had on board enough food for several months, much of it of a kind that *Mischief*'s crews seldom see. An austere sufficiency is usually their portion. We had eggs in the shell, bacon, huge tins of ham, pickles, fancy biscuits, tins of lime-juice and orange juice, meats and soups in be-wildering variety, fishcakes, olives, salted peanuts, jams, honey, and maple syrup. I have long been of the opinion that all tinned foods taste much the same after the initial impact of surprise or disgust has worn off. At sea in a small boat, where tinned food is for the most part inevitable, there is no remedy for this dull uniformity except to carry enough onions, garlic, and above all Tabasco sauce. All this variety simplified Bob's problems, the crew having so much scope for browsing that the main meals hardly mattered.

On our way out we passed inside Belœil Island in order to examine Albert harbour, before sailing slowly down the inlet on a lovely evening, the snows of Bylot Island bathed in sunshine. For two days the sea remained so void of ice that we began edging south a little too soon. In Lat. 72°44' we saw ice to the south and at midnight of the 17th we found ourselves in fog amongst floes. At 1 am I went below thinking we were clear, leaving Ed and Bruce on deck. The continuous uproar that ensued as they repeatedly went about to avoid more floes was more than I could stand, so we hove to rather precariously with floes on all sides. We should, I suppose, have had the sails down but by leaving them up we could steer clear of any threatening floe merely by letting draw. Finally Mike contrived to lay us smartly alongside a big floe and the wind in the sail defied all our efforts to part company with it. Down the sail had to come and with the engine in reverse we got off with no harm but loss of paint.

This tendency to edge southwards had to be suppressed. We motored due north through scattered floes with solid pack still to the east until by evening we were able to start sailing. Our wire rigging was covered with verglas such as the luckless climber sometimes finds on rock, the air temperature being 34° and the sea 35°. Next morning we were again wrapped in a clammy blanket of fog. When at length the sun shone on an empty sea we began sailing south-east until a distant fog bank and the low growling of pack-ice once more warned us away.

The danger that one can see is much less fearful than the unseen danger. The nights had now begun to get dark so that we were much relieved when by 20 August we had seen the last of ice and icebergs. We passed some ninety miles west of Upernivik and sighted the Greenland coast first in the neighbour-hood of Disko Island. Several Portuguese schooners were still busy filling their holds with salt cod. On the Hellefiske Bank we saw a four-master and later sailed through a fleet of dories. A falling glass and a rising wind heralded a long spell of dirty weather as we closed the land north of Godthaab. Having picked up the beacon on the outer islands we sailed up the fjord and gained the harbour as the wind rose to gale force. Even the prospect of beer at the *Kristinemut* failed to persuade us to venture ashore on that wet and windy night.

Despite continuous rain next day we were all ashore shopping, stocking up with bread, and making arrangements through our Canadian friend for the return by air of Nissen's rifle. When we went alongside for paraffin and water on the 29th the air was damp, muggy, and still. The calm before the storm, as we might have guessed, for no sooner had we cleared the harbour than it began blowing hard from south. With the wind in that quarter we should do no good, but rather than put back into Godthaab we took shelter in the lee of an island on the south side of the fjord. All that night, the next day, and the following night, while the glass fell to 29.2, the rain drummed incessantly on the deck and the waters of the fjord were whipped into foam. The man on anchor watch amused himself by catching cod. When the wind at last veered and moderated we beat out past the islands in a heavy swell. As we took our departure from the last island we were able once more to stream our log, having now collected the new rotator that we had ordered from England upon first arriving at Godthaab.

The sails and ropes that had been sodden for a week had just begun to dry out when late that night another gale hit us from south-east, the glass again falling to 29.2. Unluckily we were still within reach of the Godthaab weather forecasts; or at least Ed could listen to them because he was the only one who had any Danish. Besides experiencing our own bad weather we suffered vicariously as Ed recounted for our benefit all the gales then howling round the coasts of Greenland, including a monstrous one of Force 10 off Cape Farewell. This, he assured us, would inevitably move in our direction. In fact for the next six days we enjoyed reasonably pleasant weather for the time of year, and withal managed to put so many miles between ourselves and the Voice of Godthaab that its croaking could no longer be heard. At this period we enjoyed many very beautiful nights. Even the moon at full failed to dim the splendour of the aurora as it flung vast glowing arches across the sky or draped it with shimmering curtains of pale, green pulsating light.

By 7 September we were already sixty miles south of Cape Farewell, the weather raw and drizzly, and no wind until nightfall when we began a fast run under twin staysails. On the two previous homeward voyages in September the weather had been no worse than in June which is reckoned the quietest month in the Atlantic. According to statistics, however, more gales can be expected. And, of course, everyone assumes he will be blown out of his bed or bunk round about the equinox, 20 September. Lecky, however, who even if old-fashioned can be accepted as an oracle in all sea-faring matters, holds that there are no such things as 'equinoctial gales'. 'Equinoctial gales', he writes, 'constitute one of those prejudices of which it is well-nigh hopeless to disabuse the popular mind. Most careful observations prove conclusively that storms have no special connection with the equinoxes; yet how often does one hear a gale, occurring even three weeks one side or other of this event referred to as an equinoctial gale.'

On 11 September, when we were some 360 miles west of Cape Farewell, after rolling becalmed throughout the morning watch, by afternoon we were hove-to with a forty-knot wind from south-west. We had the storm jib up and gradually increased the number of rolls in the mainsail until only about five feet of the luff remained hoisted. She lay quietly enough, forereaching crab-wise at nearly two knots. By midnight the wind had moderated and veered. We started sailing and by noon next day were doing six and half knots, a speed at which *Mischief* begins to tremble with excitement. In fact we had another gale at our backs and when a great dollop of water fell in the cockpit we took the hint, handed the sails, and let her run. At dusk we ventured to hoist the staysail but soon had it down again, the wind increasing throughout the night.

When I came on watch at 4 am, an hour when a man is very easily impressed, when the size of the seas hissing by begins to be dimly discernible in the murky light of dawn, I rated the stronger gusts at Force 10. Towards the end of my watch another wave flooded the cockpit and its unhappy occupant. Most of this water found its way below thus rousing Ed who thought the time had come to stream a drogue to slow us down. Ed had recently renewed the canvas of the drogue but not the roping. Certainly its launching over the stern appeared to quieten her down. We were all delighted, especially Ed, until half an hour later, when we gave the warp a tug and discovered that the drogue was no longer at the other end. I believe it had parted almost as soon as we streamed it. This violent depression, a secondary following that of the previous day, soon passed. But Ed did his best to diminish the satisfaction that its passing afforded us by predicting that such weather might last from September to March, though, of course, we hoped to be home before then. Things below were becoming a bit damp, particularly my bunk which is the most vulnerable on account of having no other bunk above it.

For the next two days, reefed and in thick weather, we tramped along at the rate of over 100 miles a day. We met a ship, the *Manchester Merchant*, which came close to have a good look at us but did not reply to our lamp signals. When approaching Ireland in poor visibility we were on the wrong tack to clear it, the wind being south-east. We could not have made so free with the desolate coasts we had recently quitted where there are no warnings for the mariner. Soon, out on the starboard bow, we heard the friendly bellowing of the Bull lighthouse. There is quite a farmyard off this south-west corner of Ireland. Bull Island, off Dursey Head, had for its immediate neighbours the Cow, Calf, and Heifer, not to mention the Cat or Crow rocks.

Thanks to Ed's devoted attention our battery had remained fully charged. We did not have to sup by candle-light and perforce observe wireless silence as had usually been the case at the latter end of a voyage. Naturally gale warnings began flowing in. Certainly in the last days of the passage from 20 September to 25 September we had a lot of wind – the equinoctial gales as, no doubt, the uninstructed would think? All day of the 25th and the succeeding night, when we had been told to expect that the violent north-west wind then blowing would back south-west, we carried on for the Scillies on the port tack. When we had overshot the Bishop by some forty miles the wind did at last go round and blew to such purpose that forty hours later we passed the Needles, twenty-six days out from Godthaab and a record passage. In 1961 it had taken us twenty-nine days and in 1962 no less than thirty-four.

Happily after all this wind and rain, both the day of our arrival and the next

day were fine enough for us to dry the sails and to strip *Mischief* bare ready
for laying up. It was time for our small self-contained community to part.
After so many days at sea together between water and sky the crew went their
several ways – Ed to a merchant ship, Bruce to train with the RAF, Stephen
to learn farming, and Mike to Australia. Bob disappeared as mysteriously as
he had come and I have not heard of him since. We had made our voyage, as
the saying goes, had achieved what we had set out to do. I felt we had been
lucky. There is no water anywhere that is fool-proof, and northern waters are
less so than average.

Part 2

East Greenland
Mischief
May–September, 1964

CHAPTER EIGHT

The Objective and the Crew

NOTHING LASTS like the provisional. When I bought *Mischief* in 1954 for a voyage to the Patagonian channels for a specific purpose I did not expect her to last many years, or that I should have the opportunity to go on sailing her year after year until our lives, so to speak, had become intertwined. But as the years went by, the ship showing less sign of wear than her owner, I came to believe that she would last my time. During the winter of 1963–64, however, our partnership very nearly came to an end. When cleaning up below in the cabin on our return in September, we found some rot in the lining of the cabin. So before leaving *Mischief* to enjoy her hard-earned winter's repose in the mud berth that she has occupied since she first came to Lymington in November '54, I asked the yard to take out the plank lining and replace it with peg-board which would allow more ventilation. In old boats it is generally the case that the more you stir the more it stinks, the removal of one bit of wood leading to the discovery of further horrors. On removing the lining it was found that many of the oak frames were in places soft, in other words rotten; there was plenty of sound wood in the frames but it meant that some of the fastenings, on which everything depends, could not be trusted to hold.

According to the Persian proverb, 'the wise man sits on the hole in his carpet.' This plan is not really applicable to faults in boats, at least not in a boat that you wish to sail yourself. So before long I returned to the boatyard and went on board together with a friend who was also a surveyor. The interior of a boat out of commission in winter is never a cheerful scene, and *Mischief*'s cold, dank cabin, condensation dripping from the beams, looked the worse for having apparently suffered at the hands of wreckers. It reeked of desolation, decay, death, and as the surveyor began methodically prodding the frames with a thin spike I sensed his face growing longer at every prod.

In his opinion the old boat – not quite sixty years old – which had carried me and my crews for so many thousands of miles had, so to speak, had it. She had reached the end of her tether so far as deep water voyages were concerned though she might be good for several more years of pottering round the coast. He strongly advised me against allowing myself to be talked into spending more money on her, even the expense of having her hauled out for a proper survey would not be justified. This was bitter medicine.

> The first bringer of unwelcome news
> Hath but a losing office; and his tongue
> Sounds ever after as a sullen bell
> Remembered tolling a departed friend.

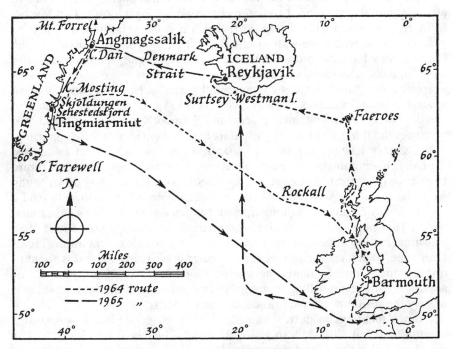

East Greenland, 1964 and 1965

Nothing has an uglier look than reason when it is not of our side. Sentiment is no good guide for action, but the old boat had come to mean a lot to me and when I looked at her lying there, to all appearances as stout as ever, I could not bring myself to write her off then and there as one might an old car. A second opinion is usually asked for in the hope rather than the belief that it will contradict the first. Nevertheless before coming to a decision I had another surveyor to look at her after she had undergone further stripping inside. The verdict was the same: 'She is no longer fit for the sort of use you require – extended cruising – though she could still give several years service for inshore sailing where she is unlikely to be subjected to prolonged heavy weather stresses.'

What to do with her was then the question. Apart from the fact that it was not what I wanted, I did not think that short cruises would repay the expense of fitting out or the trouble of finding fresh crews every season. Nor did I want to sell her, to hear of her later rotting away neglected, or ending her days ignominiously as a houseboat. Perhaps some one could be found who would be interested in preserving her as an example of a Bristol Channel pilot cutter. Apart from models, and with the notable and magnificent exception of *Cutty Sark*, nowhere are there preserved any relics of the days of sail, any examples of the various types of fishing and working boats that even fifty years ago could be found around our coasts. By now it is probably too late. As it happened I had to spend the inside of a week in America that winter to attend a climbing reunion. I took the chance of having a look at Old Mystic, formerly a Connecticut whaling port, which is being refashioned as it once was, complete with rope-walk, sail-loft, smithy, and the rest. Lying in the harbour they have the old whaling ship *William Morgan*, the barque *Joseph Conrad*, a big schooner yacht noted for several Arctic voyages, and a number of lesser craft. Another maritime museum I visited at Newport News also had several original examples of sailing vessels. In America there are plenty of wealthy men to endow such places and I understood that in these two instances the interest shown by the public makes them almost self-supporting.

In January I began the search for another old or oldish boat to replace *Mischief*, having in the meantime received some enquiries about her future from people interested in encouraging boys to sail. On the way down to the west country to look at a boat I stopped at Lymington and naturally paid a visit to *Mischief* looking, I thought, most forlorn and disconsolate in her mud berth. That time and chance play a greater part in arranging our future than we would care to admit has been noted before by even less penetrating minds than mine. When chance intervenes to change one's plans – as it was about to do to mine – one is almost persuaded that history itself is a chapter of accidents, or is even willing to accept the degrading notion that our world is merely the result of a 'fortuitous concourse of atoms'.

Chance meetings in pubs seldom lead to much good. But it was such a meeting that led ultimately to giving *Mischief* a further lease of life. In *The Ship* I got talking to Wing Commander R. H. A. Coombes whom, by the way, except for brief greetings in the boatyard, I had not met before. He listened to my dismal tale with an understanding ear, for he was then engaged in refitting, almost rebuilding *Isoletta*, a seventy-ft. ketch built in 1909, having bought the bare hull cheap. He took a robust view of *Mischief*'s troubles and recommended having her hauled out and properly examined. He was confident that she would be found sound enough below the water-line, in which case the upper frames could very well be made good by doubling up. This was the sort of advice I wanted to hear and it was therefore quickly accepted, thus contradicting Dr Johnson's dictum that 'Few things are so liberally bestowed, or squandered with so little effect, as good advice.' Besides advice I had absorbed a few pints. Doubly fortified I went straight back to the yard and made arrangements to have *Mischief* hauled out for inspection.

The result answered expectations. The timbers below the water-line were sound enough and by doubling the upper parts of the frames she could be made seaworthy. Obviously it was not going to be cheap but it would be less expensive than buying another boat, especially an old boat with which one might also buy trouble. I had, too, some misgivings at flying in the face of professional advice and, perhaps, at allowing myself to be too much influenced by sentiment. In the end I decided to have the work done.

Once this piece of folly, as some would call it, had been committed, I began thinking of committing another that coming summer. Instead of making a fourth voyage to the west coast of Greenland I thought of visiting the east coast, a place that hitherto I had regarded as unsuitable for a small boat. One authority is emphatic on this point: 'East Greenland has much more pack-ice than West Greenland and no ship should attempt to navigate in its waters unless it is specially designed. The east Greenland ice is usually broken and rafted into heavy floes of various sizes often with a thickness of twenty to thirty feet. It is too great to cut with the prow of a ship. The ice-belt is traversed by seeking out the leads of open water, thus the course is tortuous, the ship twisting and turning, worming its way between the floes and fields. A high premium is placed on short turning circles and the manoeuvrability of vessels such as the Norwegian seal-hunter type. Experienced navigators on meeting the ice-edge off north-east Greenland are said to insist on clear weather and a steady barometer before attempting passage to the coast.'

Although the foregoing is certainly true it refers chiefly to the more northern part of that coast. A study of the ice-charts for the months of July and August showed that there was not much ice on the coast south of Lat. 63°. As the *Arctic Pilot* says: 'Throughout the period December to June inclusive the ice along the entire length of the coast from Lat. 80° to Cape Farewell (Lat. 60°) is wholly impenetrable. With the advance of summer the pack becomes lighter and more open along the southern part of the coast, particularly from the region of Scoresby Sund (Lat. 70°) southward. In an average year, the ice in this region is mainly navigable by ordinary vessels in August to October inclusive; along the most southern part of the coast from Lat. 64° to Cape Farewell there are large stretches of open water in September and October. In July from Lat. 61° to Cape Farewell the ice is mainly navigable, but patches of unnavigable ice may be met.'

Thus if one kept south of Lat. 64° there seemed to be a fair chance of reaching the coast. This coast, like the west coast, is fringed with islets and islands and, in the south, by a narrow strip of ice-free land. It is likewise much indented with fjords – an arm of Scoresby Sund forms the longest fjord in the world. Life of any kind is more scarce than on the west coast. Its mountains are higher. Mt Watkins (12,139ft.) is the highest mountain in Greenland and further south is Mt Forrel (11,024ft.). There are only two trading stations on the coast, at Scoresby Sund and at Angmagssalik (Lat. 65°36'). Since the war, an increasing number of mountaineering parties have visited the regions of the higher mountains, usually going by air from Iceland to Scoresby Sund or Angmagssalik.

South of Angmagssalik, the only part of the coast that we could expect to reach in *Mischief*, the mountains are of the order of 4,000 to 6,000ft., quite high enough for me. The place I picked on after reading the *Pilot* and studying the chart was Skjoldungen (Lat. 63°) where two fjords, North and South Skjoldungen, run inland for about twenty-five miles where they are joined together by a deep channel. The mountainous island of Skjoldungen lying between the two fjords seemed a fascinating bit of little-known country. The *Pilot* noted that a valley at the head of South Skjoldungen contains a good salmon river and has a comparatively rich vegetation; but my main reason for choosing this fjord was because in it there is no great glacier descending from the ice-cap to clutter it up with floes and bergs as is the case in many of the east Greenland fjords.

Whether or not we called first at Angmagssalik depended to some extent upon ice conditions. It would be the correct thing to do in order to make ourselves known to the Greenland authorities. In any case it would be little use to arrive off the coast before the latter half of July, so that if we started at the usual time at the end of May we should have time to visit both the Faeroes and Iceland. Making a rough plan is easier than finding a crew to assist in carrying it out. Experience had shown that I need not try to collect a crew of seasoned yachtsmen or even a nucleus of such. There is less in this than meets the eye, as Talulah Bankhead remarked. It was not so much that experienced hands knew better than to embark in *Mischief*, but rather that such men either sail their own boats or crew for their friends. My recruits are found mainly among young chaps with a taste for adventure who have not yet settled down or have settled down prematurely in a job not to their liking. If they have any qualifications so much the better, but if not it is no great matter. It is unfortunate from my point of view that none of these young men ever have any money to contribute towards the expenses. On the other hand, if they did contribute they might feel themselves entitled to make suggestions or even to complain, like passengers who have paid their fare. As the Chinese say, quietness is worth buying.

Having before had some contact with Bangor University I had two recruits from that source. Roger Coward, a history student in his last year, was not entirely inexperienced having sailed racing dinghies. He was keen to make a film and in a position to borrow a 16-mm camera provided I would supply the film. In spite of having done this before and found it not repaying, I agreed. Besides the cost of the film, the shooting of it involves a certain amount of pain. It would be an exaggeration to say that if a man fell overboard the camera man would ask him to do it again slowly, but all the more usual activities on board have to be rehearsed for his benefit or done when there is no occasion to do them. The other Bangor representative was Charles Sewell, a young laboratory assistant and an active rock climber. Bangor University, having at its doorstep the Menai Straits for sailing and Snowdonia for climbing, should have a high proportion of sane undergraduates – and professors, too, for that matter.

M. Wareham was a young engineer apprentice at the Berthon Boatyard, Lymington, thus well acquainted with boats and with *Mischief*. Although barely eighteen he was a useful acquisition. He was generally known as 'Noddy' from his habit of wearing a wool cap with a bob on it perched precariously on a mat of curly, copper hair. This particular cap soon went overboard.

L. D. R. Cook had spent some years in a RAF Mountain Rescue team in Scotland where he had acquired an interest in climbing. His size and weight made up for the lack of brawn in the others who were mostly lightweights. He had enjoyed what one assumes must be only a spasmodically active life in the Mountain Rescue team but was none the less evidently a misfit in the RAF with a strong dislike for authority and 'bull' – a common attitude of present day youth, admirable only up to a point. At this time he was employed in London as store accountant by a firm importing French cosmetics, though what Bob Cook could have in common with French cosmetics is almost beyond conjecture.

Finally I got hold of an old friend Major E. H. Marriott. The initials must be some sort of under-cover address to fox the enemy for I have never heard him referred to as anything else but Charles. He had sailed with me on a voyage to the Patagonia channels as a climber, and on the first Greenland voyage when he both cooked and climbed. Thus he was now to make a third voyage in *Mischief*, a triumph, some might say, of hope over experience. We already had two climbers on board, three including myself, and since Charles Marriott at that time was not over-fit he was prepared to forego any mountaineering. He agreed to come as cook, a rôle that is exacting and always difficult to fill. It requires a strong stomach, the balance and agility of a juggler; indifference to being sprayed with cold sea water from the galley hatch and very hot water from the stove; the ability to work in a confined space breathing rather foul air; and the same energy, patience, and goodwill as that needed by a hen cormorant to sustain her mouth-gaping offspring. All these Charles had to some extent, particularly the first and the last. Besides this he was an experienced hand who in the first few trying days of the voyage could take a watch and help to show the greenhorns how things should be done. He was also good company if you like the company of a chap who will argue any point or no point, and he had a fund of anecdotes and doubtful stories. Some of these would be new to the crew, and even to me who had been with him twelve months on the first occasion and four on the second, for I have a very short memory.

CHAPTER NINE

To the Faeroe Islands

THE EXTENSIVE repairs to *Mischief*'s ribs having been completed the crew began to assemble from 20 May onwards. One or two of them I had met only once before for a few brief moments, so that when they stepped on board, instead of a welcoming smile, my face must have worn a look of shocked surprise. Had I or had I not met this chap before somewhere? Surely I had not asked him to come? The lean, wiry Charles Sewell bore a horrible resemblance to someone I had sailed with many years before and when he upset the varnish tin twice the first day this fear was almost confirmed. Charles Marriott ran true to form by deferring his arrival from day to day and consequently our departure. It did not matter. Rain delayed the fitting out and for two days I myself felt more like going to bed than going to sea.

Our wireless set, a type that is fitted in motor cars, had at last succumbed to sea-air and damp. I invested in a Decca transistor set, supposed to give world-wide coverage, so that we need no longer depend upon the battery and the charging engine. With a good chronometer watch a wireless receiving set is not essential. Watches, however, have been known to stop, especially if one forgets to wind them, and if Test Matches are being played a reliable receiving set is important. Weather forecasts can be obtained only for home waters and need not necessarily be taken too much to heart. West of the areas Shannon and Rockall forecasts for the Atlantic are transmitted in Morse too fast for the average yachtsman, while those for Iceland or Greenland waters will be in some unknown tongue.

Charles Marriott arrived on 30 May at 11.30 and we cast off at 12.30 after a hurried lunch. As we motored down the river the Royal Lymington Yacht Club honoured us with a salute from their starting gun. With the ebb tide and a light wind we soon cleared the Needles, but in the evening a violent squall ushered in a night of torrential rain, thunder, lightning, and squalls from all points of the compass. Not at all the sort of night to be at sea with a green crew. We had several Chinese gybes, were scared by steamers, and enjoyed five minutes pandemonium when the staysail sheet got out of control. The next night was a repetition of the first, worse in fact, for Charles Marriott lost overboard his yachting cap, a veteran of many voyages, at least ten years old to my knowledge, much prized by him and greatly admired by the crew. No longer would a slimmer edition of King Edward VII be seen disembarking from *Mischief* as though from the royal yacht *Britannia*.

By 1 June the weather had faired up and the wind died down to leave us rolling heavily. A corvette steamed slowly past and hailed us by name to know if we were all right. The crew, discomfited by the heavy rolling, might not have agreed with my affirmative reply. We discovered now that the metal collar for the twin staysail booms had been left behind, like the proverbial Dutchman's anchor. It was infuriating to have the sails on board and no means of setting them. Our course down Channel had no doubt been tortuous. On 2 June the visibility being poor, I reckoned we must be somewhere near the Manacles. But life is full of surprises. When the wind fell light we handed the mainsail in order to stitch a seam and while I was busy with this Noddy sighted through the haze a slender tower to the north-east – no doubt, the Eddystone. But when the sun went down and the light came on it proved to be the Wolf Rock light. We were at least twenty miles and two points out in our reckoning. I concluded that *Mischief* knew the way down Channel better than her skipper.

Astonishment is an emotion salutary for the young – and the old, too, for that matter. Presently we were to have even greater cause than this for astonishment, and these two strange occurrences went far to confirm my belief that navigation is far from being an exact science. Bound for east Greenland via the Faeroes and Iceland our best course lay up the Irish Sea and through the Minches. Upon rounding Land's End, therefore, we set a course for the Smalls. Thick weather obliged us to go about before sighting them but on the evening of 4 June we had the Tuskar rock abeam five miles off. Taking our departure from this unmistakable mark we set a course for Holyhead eighty miles away, a course that enabled us to make the most of a fine quartering wind. The wind held steady all night and next day, which was hazy, we were puzzled but not dismayed when we found we had run 100 miles without either hitting or even sighting Holyhead Island. At last about tea-time, when land began to loom vaguely to port, to starboard, and also ahead, we realized that we were near the head of Cardigan Bay, two points off course and some forty miles from Holyhead. Currents, the compass, the helmsmen, even the navigator, may be responsible for these anomalies. It is not, however, for the navigator to accept responsibility for them or to show surprise, or he may sap what confidence the crew have in him. Attack is the best form of defence. A few remarks about the impossibility of navigating the ship if it is not steered straight will restore his own confidence and subdue and mystify the crew.

> Where lies the land to which the ship will go?
> Far, far ahead is all her seamen know.
> And where the land she travels from? Away
> Far, far behind is all that they can say.

The tide being foul we went outside Bardsey Island and headed across to Ireland, the wind by now round at north. In poor visibility we were lucky to sight St Johns lighthouse whence we set a course to clear South Rock, the most easterly point of Ireland. The night closed down dark and foggy and we were sailing fast, so mindful of recent events I prudently decided to heave to. Several ships were about with their foghorns blaring and before dawn we received aid and comfort by hearing away on our beam the bleating of Mew

Island lighthouse south of Belfast Lough. Approaching the North Channel on a clear, sunny evening, the wind light, we had the doubtful pleasure of watching the Stranraer-Larne ferry cross and recross no less than four times. Here the tides run strongly and, perhaps, I had not been explicit enough about the course to steer if the wind freshened. Coming on deck early next morning I found we were up behind the Mull of Kintyre, none of the helmsmen in the night having realized that he was steering blithely into a cul-de-sac. By the time we had regained the North Channel, and once more sighted the ferryboat, the tide had turned against us, leaving us no choice but to steer west for Red Bay and anchor there.

Leaving on the north-going tide, by 1 pm of 9 June we had Inishtrahull abeam, whence we set a course for Skerryvore. Inishtrahull and Skerryvore! What stirring, romantic names for the two lonely, Atlantic-facing outposts of Ireland and Scotland! Skerryvore is one of a shoal of above-water and sunken rocks extending for twelve miles to the south of the Isle of Tiree. It must be a fearsome sight in a gale when the whole of this twelve miles is a mass of breakers. The lighthouse, designed by Alan Stevenson and finished in 1844, must be one of the most exposed of any, wide open as it is to the unbroken sweep of the Atlantic.

After passing Skerryvore we had a grand sail through the Passage of Tiree, the five-miles-wide strait between Mull and the two bleak, barren islands of Tiree and Coll. Johnson and Boswell in their tour of the Hebrides were driven by a storm to take refuge in Coll where they remained weatherbound for nearly a fortnight:

'We were doomed to experience, like others, the dangers of trusting to the wind, which blew against us in a short time with such violence that we, being no seasoned sailors, were willing to call it a tempest. I was sea-sick and lay down. Mr Boswell kept the deck. The master knew not well whither to go; and our difficulties might well have filled a very pathetic page, had not Maclean of Coll, who with every other qualification that insular life requires is a very active and skilful mariner, piloted us safe into his own harbour.'

Boswell devotes several pages to this adventure of which the following is a brief sample:

'. . . a prodigious sea with immense billows coming upon the vessel so that it seemed hardly possible to escape. There was something grandly horrible in the sight . . . As I saw them all busy doing something, I asked Coll what I could do. He, with a happy readiness, put into my hand a rope, which was fixed to the top of one of the masts, and told me to hold it till he bade me pull. If I had considered the matter I might have seen that this could not be of the least service but his object was to keep me out of the way of those who were busy working the vessel, and at the same time divert my fear by employing me, and making me think I was of use. Thus did I stand firm to my post while the wind and rain beat upon me, always expecting a call to pull my rope.'

From what we saw of Coll and its small harbour as we sailed by I think Boswell had good reason to be afraid, running as they were for a small, unlit harbour, in a gale, on a black night. Among the Hebrides with their strong tides, strong winds, and much rain, the perils of navigation when there were no harbour lights or lighthouses are hardly imaginable. Nowadays, in summer at least, there are no difficulties thanks to the numerous lights. Rounding the north end of Coll we stood across to Ushinish lighthouse on South Uist passing on the way the rocks of Oigh Sgeir where there is also a light. From Ushinish we made for the Little Minch at the north end of Skye, faithfully following the pecked line on the chart, the recommended route for north-bound vessels, like a hen following a chalk-line. Once through the pass of the Little Minch we were in the clear, for the North Minch is over thirty miles wide.

It seemed a shame to pass non-stop through this perfect cruising ground with only the vaguest glimpse of the mountains of Skye. These western isles were no more familiar to the crew than Greenland but at this stage of the voyage they were more interested in sleep than in scenery. On the evening of 11 June we passed the Butt of Lewis and sailed out into the Atlantic. The Faeroes lie due north, only 180 miles away, with nothing in between but the small uninhabited islands of Sula Sgeir and Rona. We sighted the former on the 12th; it is visited in summer by people from Lewis to collect the eggs of the gannet or solar goose. A mixture of rain and fog, flat calms and high winds, made this short passage slow and uncertain. I got no sun sights, only a sight of Vega, and one star by itself is not of great value. Sailing north in summer the nights soon become so light that only planets or the very brightest stars are visible – visible, that is to say, to the navigator with a sextant that is a little antique like mine, with a telescope that hinders rather than helps the picking up of stars. Even when the nights are dark the North Atlantic sky, after remaining clear all night, has a mean trick of clouding over before dawn when one is hoping to take star sights. The exasperated navigator then feels like echoing the impious outburst ascribed to Lord Jeffrey, a contemporary of Sydney Smith, though what circumstances occasioned the outburst I have not discovered: 'Damn the solar system; bad light; planets too distant; pestered with comets; feeble contrivance; could make a better with ease.'

After remaining hove to most of the night in a near gale and heavy rain, still uncertain of our position, we let draw on the morning of the 14th, steering east. Two trawlers were in sight and at noon a high island showed up on the starboard bow some 20 miles away. It could be only Syderö the southern-most of the Faeroes. There are altogether eighteen islands, all but one inhabited, spread over about 60 miles of sea. There are many good harbours, a few of them classed as 'winter harbours' safe in all weather conditions, and the rest are 'summer harbours'. My only knowledge of the Faeroes, strictly practical, came from the *Pilot*; we did not know where to find the choicest beauty spots or the cheapest beer; even Charles Marriott, a rich storehouse of general knowledge, was at a loss. I inclined to the capital, Thorshaven, or Vaag Fjord on Syderö, both on the east side of the group and therefore sheltered.

Three miles off the south end of Syderö is a 37ft. high rock called Munken and in the vicinity of the rock there are heavy tide rips even in fine weather. That evening we were sailing eastwards about two miles south of Munken, thinking that was enough. Apparently it was not. The wind dropped and almost at once the sea, as if glad to be free of its control, began to boil like a pot. All around us waves shot up and collapsed in confusion. As we had no steerage way the sails and spars slammed and banged, the mast quivered. Broken water extended as far as the eye could reach. We were being set westwards anyway, so we forgot about Thorshaven and Vaag Fjord, started the engine, and steered north-west, intent only on getting out of this miniature maelstrom.

When we were well west of Syderö conditions improved except for a heavy swell running and an absence of wind. We handed all sails except the genoa which we stupidly left up with the result that it split right across. But we had by no means finished with our Faeroe Island troubles. Our best bet now seemed to be Vestmanhavn in Vestmanha Sund, the narrow channel between the main island Strömö and the westernmost island Vaagö. From there, to continue our voyage to Iceland, we should merely have to complete the passage of the Sund to fetch clear of the islands and be out in the Atlantic. Entering Vestmanhavn we should have to fly a 'Q' flag which we now discovered we had also left behind. So while waiting for a wind I made up a flag with canvas and curry powder.

Towards noon a breeze came in from west enabling us just to lay the desired course. All seemed set fair for a quick passage to Vaagö Fjord followed by a quiet night at anchor in Vestmanhavn. In the afternoon, however, the weather deteriorated, squalls of wind and rain became gradually heavier and more frequent, blotting out all the land except for two 1,500ft. high islands close on our starboard hand. Prudence suggested reefing or even standing out to sea for the night, for the wind had in it a note of malice and we were on a lee shore in thick weather. But without the driving power of the full mainsail we should never clear Kolter, the northernmost of the two islands now fine on the lee bow. With Vaagö Fjord and its promise of shelter only five miles away we drove on under all plain sail, the lee scuppers awash, praying that the gear would stand and that we could weather Kolter. As if to enhance the wild, adventurous aspect of the scene – the hard-driven ship, the angry sea, the dim, menacing outline of the island – a blue whale, close aboard, jumped half clear of the water, fell back with a splash that could be heard above the roar of the wind, and then towered, head and shoulders clear of the water, before sounding.

With Kolter gradually drawing safely aft we could turn our attention to what lay ahead, peering through the gathering gloom of rain and nightfall in search of the fjord entrance. Between the heavier curtains of rain that swept across we made out the black outline of an immense vertical wall of rock fine on the weather bow. For this we steered, certain that it would provide us with a lee and trusting that it marked the entrance to the fjord. In the smooth water in the lee of this precipice we got the sails off, for the wind now whistled straight down the fjord which lay directly ahead. Vestmanhavn is some eight miles up the fjord and we had not gone more than a couple of miles, motoring into the teeth of the blast, when we began to have doubts about reaching it. Either the wind had increased or the tide turned against us, for we almost stood still. There was no anchoring anywhere in this wall-sided fjord so once more we abandoned our immediate objective, turned tail, and shot back down the fjord.

About three miles west of the fjord entrance and the great cliff which we now knew was Stakken there is a small harbour called Midvaag. Although it was on the weather side of Stakken we hoped that by creeping close along the shore we could cheat the wind and find moderately smooth water. As we rounded close under Stakken we regarded with awe its lesser but more extraordinary neighbour, a detached pinnacle like a gigantic Napes Needle, over 1,000ft. high, called Troldkonefinger. Bucking the wind and sea, our speed reduced to a crawl, we watched the rocks close inshore anxiously as we crept slowly by. Soon we were in more sheltered water and at last at midnight we let go in three fathoms between some fishing craft and a small breakwater. There had been no time for supper in the stress and strain of the last few hours. Before turning in Charles dished up soup, bully, and spuds, alleviating this austerity with cocoa and rum. Midvaag is not a 'winter harbour' and since the wind and rain continued unabated we set an anchor watch.

CHAPTER TEN

Surtsey and Reykjavik

IT IS fun to arrive by night at a strange harbour, wondering what daylight will reveal – unless it happens to be one of those busy ports where one may well be knocked up long before daylight to be told that you have anchored in the fairway or a prohibited area. From our short acquaintance with the Faeroes and the seas around, the tide-rips, the cliffs, and the grey clouds covering them, we did not expect much in the way of habitation. But any place that has afforded the seafarer shelter on a stormy night is bound to be regarded with kindly eyes.

No doubt on a wet, windy morning Midvaag was not looking its best, but the line of white cottages nestling below the green hillside where a few sheep grazed had a pleasing appearance. When the rain stopped in the afternoon we rowed ashore. Some fishermen unloading their catch promptly gave us half a dozen haddock and one of them attached himself to us as guide. The post office was officially shut but our guide led us into the living room where the postmaster was dining *en famille* off some uncommonly strong fish soup. In spite of our protests he insisted on interrupting the meal to stamp our letters. Continuing our walk up the main street, ignoring a hardware shop and a clothes shop, we came to what looked like the third and last shop. Among a meagre window display we detected a ray of hope – a writing pad, an ink bottle, a packet of cigarettes, a few Westerns, and a bottle of beer. The stock inside was not much richer but we bought the beer bottle and had a suck all round, not forgetting our guide, for it was terribly expensive. The people of Midvaag, we decided, inclined to the literary life rather than the convivial. In the midst of this drinking bout it occurred to me that I had not yet entered the ship. There were no formalities at the Harbour-master's office beyond a cigar and a chat, and after he had rung up his confrère at the Customs house to tell him of our arrival, that concluded the ship's business. In the evening Charles and I followed the road out beyond the village and came eventually to a big lake, the Sorvaags Wand. The lake is peculiar in that it has no river emptying out but spills abruptly into the sea over a natural weir. The road, which leads to Sorvaag harbour on the west coast of Vaagö, was built by British troops during the war, as was the airfield on Vaagö, the only one in the Faeroes. From it there is a service to Glasgow and also to Iceland. The capital, Thorshavn, only two hours away by sea, is linked by a mailboat. We were told that out of a total population of 36,000, 10,000 live in the capital; but this may be no more precise than another news item fed to the gullible visitors. We learnt that Midvaag's chief import is sheep's heads from Aberdeen, and considering the number of sheep to be seen grazing in the vicinity, all with heads, I found this hard to believe. Vaagö like most of the other islands rises to over 2,000ft. and the grazing is on the lower slopes near the sea. I doubt if anyone lives out of sight of the sea from which comes their food and their livelihood.

The Faeroe islander, therefore, is above all a seaman. In boats not much bigger than *Mischief* and less seaworthy, because they are powered only by an engine, they follow their calling across the Atlantic as well as round their wind-swept islands. The banks off the west coast of Greenland are well known to them. We had met Faeroe island boats at Godthaab. Crossing in May they spent the summer there, selling their catches to the local factories, and went home in the early autumn. Generally they had a crew of five, all housed in the foc'sle which was about the size of our galley. Their own galley was nothing more than a sort of wardrobe lashed on deck aft with a single gas ring inside. There was no question of working inside the galley, the cook merely opened the wardrobe door and stooped or knelt on deck to give the pot a stir.

From the Faeroes we had about 600 miles to go to Reykjavik which would be our port of departure for east Greenland. On the way there I had in mind a visit to the new volcanic island which had appeared off the south-west coast of Iceland on 14 November, 1963. To say the island 'appeared' is a mild description of its tumultuous birth, a birth attended by violent explosions which hurled clouds of smoke, steam, ash, and pumice thousands of feet into the air. By the next day, when wind blew away some of this cloud, it could be seen that an island had emerged from the sea. *Notices to Mariners* of 23 January, 1964, contained the following warning: 'A submarine volcanic eruption has formed an island about half a mile in diameter and 250ft. high, in position 63°18'N. 20°36'W. Eruption is continuing and mariners are warned to keep clear of the area.' By April the island had grown to nearly a mile in length and 500ft. in height. It had been given the name Surtsey and the volcano itself was christened Surtur, after the Fire Giant Surtur of Norse mythology, who comes from the south when the world ends and burns up everything. In view of the overcast skies, the rain, and the fog that are common in those waters, I was not at all confident of being able to find this exciting island, let alone make a landing.

Before leaving Midvaag we stocked up with bread, fresh and warm from the bakery, neither so dark nor so heavy as the bread obtainable in Greenland. While I could stand any amount of it, one or two of the crew conceived for it such a dislike that they preferred to eat biscuit. By now Charles and I had repaired the huge tear in the genoa, a sail that we were able to hoist more often than I had looked for in those windy regions. Making over towards Iceland, generally under overcast skies, our navigation could not be as precise as one would wish when approaching that coast. 'The advisability of keeping at a distance cannot be too emphatically enjoined,' says the *Pilot,* 'and the numerous wrecks of British, German, French, Norwegian, Belgian, and Icelandic fishing vessels demonstrate strongly that the locality must be navigated with the utmost caution. For long stretches the coast is perfectly flat and from seaward it is difficult to make out the low coast against the high land of the interior, and it is frequently not seen until breakers are sighted. The land is bare of vegetation and the sand of which it is composed is, in many lights, indistinguishable from the sea.'

By 24 June we were some fifty miles east of the Westman Islands or Vestmannaeyjar, Surtsey lying to the west of them. Of this group of islands twenty miles off the south coast of Iceland only Heimaey, the largest, is inhabited. The islands are remarkable for the wealth of bird life on their cliffs – puffins, fulmars, gannets – of which large numbers are taken by the islanders for food. Much now depended upon the weather. That afternoon we had a bit of a blow which soon subsided and the sunset looked promising. In northern latitudes, however, when the sun gets towards midnight and dawn follows soon after, a fine-weather sunset might equally be interpreted as the 'red sky in the morning when the sailor takes warning'. But 25 June proved to be our lucky day, bright, calm, and clear. At 6 am we sighted the stacks and skerries of the westernmost islands and hard by them a great plume of cloud drifting away from a hump-backed island, its easy contours contrasting strangely with its wall-sided neighbours.

We spent the whole morning coming up with it and a large part of the afternoon poking about along its eastern shore for somewhere to anchor. To our surprise the shore shelved so steeply that close to the beach we found 4 fathoms of water and when we let go the anchor it merely slid off or through the ash into deeper water. As holding ground it was no better than a heap of flour. Finally we gave up and were content to let her drift while we launched the dinghy for Roger and I to go ashore. A small surf breaking on the beach did not hinder our landing though it did give a little trouble when we came to launch off.

The beach, of reddish-black sand or fine pumice, offered firm walking and even at that early period it had acquired some litter in the way of tins, bottles, and bits of wood. Beyond the narrow beach the ground sloped upwards to the summit at an angle of about 30°. On this ash slope it was like climbing a sandhill, two steps up and one down. I classed the climb, in Baedeker's words, as 'fatiguing and not rewarding', for the crater into which we finally peered belched merely smoke and fumes instead of the cauldron of molten, fiery lava that I had expected and hoped to see. There was a beacon on top, no doubt for survey purposes, so that evidently ours was not a first ascent except, no doubt, the first ascent by a British party. The whole place smelt like a coke oven. One sensed, too, that the thing was alive and growing but I must say I was staggered to see later in *The Times* of 9 October a picture of Surtsey and to learn that it had by then grown to 800ft. high.

The timing of our visit had been unlucky, or perhaps lucky, according to the point of view. I have since learnt that until 4 April, 1964, Surtsey had been merely evidence of a marine eruption but on that date a lava eruption began when fountains of lava shot up to heights of 100 to 200ft. and numerous rivers of lava overflowed the crater to run into the sea. The greatest velocity in the lava flow was observed on 22 April when a white-hot wave of lava covered a distance of 300 yards in fifteen seconds. The lava flow ceased at the end of April and for the next two and a half months no lava flowed over the crater rim, though it was probable that lava continued to flow into the sea from a vent below sea level. On 9 July lava began pouring out of the crater again, the level having by then become higher, and formed a lava lake about 100 yards in diameter. Thus at the time of our visit there was probably lava inside the crater but obscured from our view by smoke and steam. With the advent of lava, Surtsey's life is not likely to be as ephemeral as that of other volcanic islands. Of ten marine eruptions off Iceland in historic time, four built up islands and all four islands have been swallowed by the Atlantic. As long as Surtsey consisted only of volcanic ash and cinders its future was uncertain but since lava started to flow it is likely that the island will withstand the onslaught of the surf for a very long time despite the inroads that the surf has already made. In the winter of 1964, for example, a large chunk of the highest peak together with the survey beacon fell away, having been eroded at sea level.

The following account of Surtsey in action is from an article by Dr D. C. Blanchard, a scientist collecting data on the lightning and other electrical phenomena in the vicinity of the volcano:

'By this time Surtsey was three months old but the eruptions were still frequent. We approached from upwind and when we arrived Surtsey put on a magnificent display of the forces at her command. The eruptions were occurring from a crater near the edge of the island partially open to the sea. The contact of the cold sea water with the hot pumice or lava appeared to be the cause of giant explosions that sent geysers of ash-streaked cloud and water hurtling upwards to over a thousand feet. Cloud masses continued upwards until there was a long cloud column that extended from near the sea to heights of 20,000ft. In the lowest thousand feet of the column there was frequent lightning and thunder; our instruments recorded the electrical activity. In addition we could see huge rocks or fire-bombs thrown out of the main plume to crash back on to the island or into the sea. Numerous mushroom-like clouds and smoke rings could be seen and from the lower parts of the plume a waterspout was visible against the dark curtain of ash that fell in long streamers to the sea.'

With *Mischief* unattached to the bottom we did not want to linger long. When Roger had finished filming we collected some lava as souvenirs for the crew and then ran down in long, plunging strides as one might descend a slope of soft snow. We had been lucky with the weather. A day later there would have been no landing on Surtsey, a day of fierce and frequent squalls when we had to hand the jib and put four rolls in the mainsail. Having rounded Reykjanes, the south-western extremity of Iceland, we sailed briskly all night with a fine beam wind and early on 27 June anchored outside the dock entrance at Reykjavik. Our curry-powder '*Q*' flag attracted no attention so finally Bob Cook and I rowed ashore. Securing the dinghy, we climbed up a sea-wall and over some railings to land in a main thoroughfare where cars had stopped and a small crowd gathered to watch this English invasion. A man who spoke English at once offered to drive me to the harbour offices. There, with little ado, *Mischief* and her crew were entered and cleared at the same time at a cost of ten shillings, and the Harbour-master pointed out a fish wharf where we could lie.

Having motored in and made fast alongside a small fishing boat we were boarded by one of her crew, already more than a little drunk. Our gin was too mild for friend Gunnar who produced from his pocket a bottle of evil-tasting spirit known locally as 'Black Death', a name it richly deserved. It was a Saturday, after one o'clock and the shops closed, and we looked like being without either bread or beer over the week-end. Gunnar, his good nature inflamed and his wits unimpaired by 'Black Death', grasped the implications in a flash. He assured us we could forget the beer because in Reykjavik, or all Iceland for that matter, there was no such thing unless you counted the non-alcoholic beer brewed by permission of a government which knew what was good for you. As for bread, we should have that at once. Gunnar, Charles, and I, linking arms for mutual support, started for the town. Hailing the first available taxi Gunnar took us to a ship's chandlers where he battered piti-lessly upon the door until it opened. As friends of his we received a moder-ately hearty welcome. There was, of course, no bread there but Gunnar, after receiving advice, went off again with Charles in the taxi, leaving the ship's chandler and I to drink each other's health in non-alcoholic beer. So we got our bread and presently managed to get rid of Gunnar. He would not hear of our paying off the taxi but continued in it alone, evidently feeling the need of fresh air and carriage exercise.

On Sunday we had a stream of visitors, some sober, some drunk. Charles and I who were on board alone almost had a fight with one who could not be persuaded to leave. In spite or because of the strict drinking rules the people of Reykjavik seemed of a convivial nature. Many of them are fishermen and sailors, traditionally free spenders, bent on making the most of their short spells on shore. The State bewery responsible for the revolting beer also makes spirits which are strictly rationed and which are in consequence readily obtainable 'under the counter'.

We thought Reykjavik an expensive place, particularly for eating. But we soon found a well-run Sailor's Institute where good, cheap meals were served cafeteria fashion, the helpings liberal, and a second helping to be got for nothing. At the same place there were hot showers. Most of the private houses, shops, and buildings are heated by natural hot water pumped from thermal springs at Reykir, ten miles distant. At Reykir, too, there are extensive greenhouses where things like tomatoes are grown. They even grow bananas there, though speaking as a banana-critic, one who has eaten them in most of their natural habitats and who once lived entirely on them for nine weeks in the course of a long cycle ride. I should regard Iceland bananas more as a curiosity than as edible fruit.

Reykjavik has 70,000 inhabitants out of a total Icelandic population of 170,000. In this respect it seems to be comparatively an even more powerful magnet than our own Great Wen. There are now too many corrugated iron and cement buildings, but the small Parliament House of stone, set in a neat little square, is solid and dignified. The most attractive feature to me is the way the town surrounds and is a part of the harbour and docks, a street having on one side houses and on the other ships. Fish and fishing are its business. Where we lay the small inshore fishing boats were in and out almost every day, lorries awaiting to take the fish to the nearby processing factory, one of several. We had to pass this on our way to town and were frequently given half a dozen fish from the heap that a lorry had just dumped on the floor. Naturally in our neighbourhood the smell of fish was all pervading. 'He who would have eggs must bear with cackling.'

Prince Philip was about to visit Reykjavik in the royal yacht and a number of British journalists were gathering there. Two, representing a popular daily, had arrived prematurely and while kicking their heels waiting tried to make some 'copy' out of *Mischief*. It had been expected that if the royal yacht met a British trawler off Iceland the Duke of Edinburgh would probably board her, and these two journalists, taking a sporting chance, had taken passage on a trawler from Hull. Unluckily, while hanging about south of Iceland in the hope of meeting *Britannia* the trawler had caught no fish. The skipper, soon tiring of this, sailed for north Iceland and landed his two passengers. They came to see us one evening, taking the needless precaution of bringing their own whisky. They were good company, the night wore on, until at around midnight they decided that their paper would like some pictures of *Mischief* and her crew. It seemed to me a little dark for successful photographs. Maybe they had some confused notions of being in the Land of the Midnight Sun. However, we obliged them by draping ourselves round the shrouds in picturesque attitudes and with difficulty dissuaded the photographer from climbing the mast.

On 30 June most of the ships in the harbour dressed over-all in honour of *Britannia*'s expected arrival. As we were the only British representative we took it upon ourselves to sail out into the roads to pay our respects. In the afternoon, with our big Blue Ensign flying from the peak of the gaff we sailed out of the harbour into the buoyed channel. Fortunately we had time in hand because in making a trial salute the halyard parted and we had to lower the mainsail in order to reeve another. Except for an Icelandic gunboat we were the only vessel waiting outside. At 4 pm, exactly on time, *Britannia* and her escort HMS *Malcolm* hove in sight, and, the wind being fair, we sailed past her on a reciprocal course about a cable's length away. Grand she looked with her shining dark blue hull and three slender masts flying the Icelandic flag, the

Royal Standard, and the Duke of Edinburgh's own standard, and at her stern the largest White Ensign I have ever seen. It was a proud moment for *Mischief* and her crew when this huge ensign was dipped to acknowledge our salute and when the Duke stepped out of the chart-room to give us a friendly wave. We were back in time to witness the official reception when he landed at the harbour steps.

Before leaving Iceland a few days later the Duke held a reception for all British residents in Reykjavik at the British Ambassador's residence. I scarcely qualified, but having known the Ambassador some years before in Rangoon, I too, was invited. There must have been at least a hundred people present and it was most impressive to see how the Duke conversed in turn with everyone there and often managed to joke with them. On a less exalted plane we met one or two interesting people. There was the Reykjavik golf professional, a Welshman. Iceland and golf seem somehow incongruous, though no more so, I suppose, than golf in the Magellan Straits where it is played at Punta Arenas on what surely must be the windiest course in the world. Then there was the Iceland Airways pilot who came to have a look at *Mischief* – a native Icelander, and in 1940 barely out of school, he had gone to England to join the RAF as a fighter pilot, a quite remarkable case, I thought, of enterprise and courage. We found a good friend, too, in the captain of a Danish cargo vessel who dispensed Carlsberg lager with the utmost generosity. He had with him a handsome Alsatian dog which he oddly named Henry Morgan. Like beer, dogs are prohibited in Reykjavik, but the police were wise enough to look the other way when Henry Morgan took a walk on the quay.

Charles Marriott, who has a tourist's mind, contemplated an excursion. He could not bear to leave Iceland without seeing a geyser and a waterfall. Enquiries showed that Great Geyser and Gullfoss waterfall could be reached by bus and that there was a hotel nearby. Even when on pleasure bent, Charles, like Mrs Gilpin, has a frugal mind; so he took a rucksack and a one-man tent, determined to sleep outside and eat inside. Geysers have generally to be encouraged before they will perform. One approaches them, as it were, according to the Pathan proverb, 'a lump of gur* in one hand and a stone in the other' though in the case of geysers it is soap or sods. In *Letters from High Latitudes* we read how Lord Dufferin's party spent three days waiting for Great Geyser and were rewarded only after a sharp emetic in the form of a cart-load of sods had been administered. Since his time quantities of soap have been found more effective. Charles spent a wet night in his tent and from his subdued account we gathered that neither he nor the other tourists present at Great Geyser were sufficiently provided with soap or sods. Roger Coward, who wanted film material, persuaded the rest of the crew to club together to charter a motor car for their sight-seeing tour.

The only ice information obtainable concerned Icelandic waters where the pack-ice was reported unusually close to the north coast – within twenty miles in fact. I therefore visited HMS *Malcolm* where they listened to and interpreted for me the ice report broadcast daily from Angmagssalik. It indicated

*gur – a jaggery or unrefined sugar.

the presence of heavy polar ice extending fifteen miles out from Angmagssalik and the adjoining coast. This was certainly discouraging. At Skjoldungen 100 miles further south conditions might be better, and during the week or more that it would take us to cross Denmark Strait things might improve. It was still early in the season and should the ice on inspection prove to be unnavigable we could always go round Cape Farewell to the west coast, either to find some mountains to climb or to wait. On 6 July when we had intended to sail it was blowing hard. On the advice of the fishermen, reinforced by a weather report from HMS *Exmouth* who had just arrived, we postponed our departure for a day.

CHAPTER ELEVEN

Angmagssalik

THE CAUTIOUS delaying of our start did not save us from running into some rough weather. *Mischief* is so good a seaboat that down below amidships the motion is seldom violent, yet on this occasion our teapot – a heavy, squat, six-pint affair – leapt right off the table. After so long a spell ashore poor Noddy was seasick and I lost overboard what I called my Hudson Bay hat, a hideous thing such as is worn by baseball players, given to me gratis at the Hudson Bay Company store at Pond Inlet because none of their Eskimo customers would look at it. We had knocked off 100 miles before this blow subsided and left us becalmed. We did some repairs to the sails and four of us had a very brief swim over the side. Has anyone before bathed voluntarily in Denmark Strait? The sea temperature was still 50°, for the Irminger current, a branch of the comparatively warm Atlantic current, impinges against the south coast of Iceland before flowing west across Denmark Strait to merge finally with the cold East Greenland current.

A halo round the sun and a falling glass heralded another blow which overtook us that night when we had to heave to, the wind being contrary. After this the wind settled in north-east and remained fair and light for the rest of the passage. We sighted a small Danish cargo vessel bound west; she had the characteristic red hull of most of the vessels seen in Greenland waters. We tried to speak her but she went on her way. On 12 July, in spite of some fog, I managed to get sights which put us some twenty miles east of Cape Dan. At this point the coast changes direction from south-west to west, forming a sort of bight at the back of which lies Angmagssalik about fifteen miles west and a little south of the cape. Off the cape the currents are strong and much ice frequently accumulates. It surprised us that so far we had seen neither bergs nor pack-ice for we were well in the East Greenland current. Both sea and air temperatures had dropped to 40°. In these waters, too, the presence of fog, such as we were then meeting, often indicates the presence of ice.

On account of more fog that evening we set a double watch and at 1 am, in very murky conditions, we passed a big berg and some scattered floes. We sailed slowly on under staysail alone steering west until at 6 am of the 13th we became entangled among thick floes. Starting the engine we retreated south-east into open water. In spite of fog we could distinguish the ice edge, so we began sailing south well outside it hoping that in the latitude of Skjoldungen there might be less ice. Obviously the ice off Angmagssalik was too heavy for us to navigate. Whether or not we reached Angmagssalik did not much matter. Politeness required that if possible we should report our presence on the coast and we were naturally curious to see what the only town in east Greenland looked like.

There now occurred another of those chance meetings that so often decide the course of events for good or for ill. In this case the chance meeting, though it resulted in our reaching Angmagssalik, brought about nothing but ill. In the course of the morning we sighted a cargo vessel of about 4,000 tons, stationary. By midday we were within speaking distance of each other and having a good 'gam'. Like the royal yacht she was named *Britannia*. Bound for Angmagssalik from the west Greenland coast she had been waiting there six days for ice conditions to improve. Her captain added that a local vessel was on her way out to lead him through the ice and he appeared to assume that we would take advantage of this opportunity. *Ejnar Mikkelsen* presently arrived. She was small, possibly about 200 tons, a Norwegian sealer-type specially built for manoeuvring in ice, with 240 h.p. engines, enormously thick hull, and rounded bows – a sort of miniature ice-breaker. Without the debate and deliberation that such a dubious step required it was taken for granted that we should follow in the wake of these two vessels. I suppose I ought to have known better, but I confess I did not anticipate our having much difficulty in following behind them. So, in happy ignorance of what was in store, we now devoted ourselves to getting into trouble with complete success.

The convoy got under way and for the first half-hour, the ice cover being 5/10 or less, we managed pretty well. Even so we failed to keep close under *Britannia's* stern as we had been adjured to do. Going at our best speed of five or six knots in order to keep up, with ice all around we were bound to hit some, and this we could not afford to do however small the ice might be. When the floes thickened to 7/10 or more they had to slacken speed while *Ejnar Mikkelsen* opened a way through, thus allowing us to come up close astern of *Britannia*. We were not there long. As soon as she forged ahead the wash from her propeller made *Mischief* unsteerable. Her head was thrown off to one side and sometimes we found ourselves facing the wrong way. Nor could we prevent ourselves from falling further and further behind. The floes that closed in *Britannia's* wake slowed us down or stopped us altogether, so that eventually we would become completely boxed in by ice, unable to move in any direction, and the two ships ahead almost lost to sight in the fog. Twice *Ejnar Mikkelsen* had to come back to open a lead for us or even to throw us a rope in order to haul our bows round. With her small propeller on the port quarter *Mischief* is about as manoeuvrable as a steam-roller and quite impossible to turn round in a confined space.

At 4 pm when we had done about two miles and were again completely stuck we noticed that the two ships ahead had also stopped and were apparently conferring together. We stepped on to the ice to take photographs of *Mischief* in trouble as well as to warm ourselves. It was bitterly cold in the damp fog, the temperature just above freezing point. *Ejnar Mikkelsen* then started back towards us, shouldering aside massive floes as big or bigger than herself or smashing them under her bows. She stopped nearby, her Greenlander crew grinning cheerfully, very much at home in these dismal, frigid surroundings, her two or three passengers huddled up in coats and mufflers regarding us, we thought, with sour looks. Her skipper joined us on the ice. Niels Underborg, who now and later proved a good friend to us, thick-set, ruddy complexioned, bare-headed, looked a proper seaman. He and *Britannia*'s captain had been discussing what was best to do, whether to push on or whether to take us back to open water; they had agreed that *Britannia* should make her own way and that *Ejnar Mikkelsen* should look after us. We expressed regret at making a nuisance of ourselves but he did not seem to mind and fully appreciated our difficulties, especially in keeping close astern. On the other hand, the two or three passengers he had on board seemed to mind quite a lot. A Danish girl, smoking a pipe, had been particularly vociferous and vehement in word and gesture, urging us to go faster. More important than this pipe-smoking Amazon was the Governor of Angmagssalik District who was also on board, and who, impatient at the delay, wanted Niels to abandon us. He, of course, would not hear of this, knowing that we had no chance at all of getting out of the ice without assistance. He said we had still about 12 miles of ice to negotiate and again urged us to keep close, for owing to the strong currents no lead remained open for long.

We started once more, the ice as thick as ever, the fog worse, no hint anywhere of land. There is a radio beacon on Cape Dan so presumably Niels was using that and the Angmagssalik radio station to maintain direction. Again we became hemmed in by ice and had to be extricated and several times we just scraped through between moving floes at a cost of nothing but loss of paint. Many of the floes had long under-water projections, easily discernible by the light green colour above them, though it was difficult to guess what depth of water covered them. One of these projecting tongues now proved both our undoing and our salvation. When trying to squeeze through a gap between two floes our keel grounded on the projecting tongue of one. Unable to move we stuck there while the floe to port, topping our deck by a good six ft. inexorably closed. Poor *Mischief* gave a shudder as she was lifted up, canted over, and the port-side bulwarks crushed in with the frightening noise of rending timber. I had just begun to think of what we most needed to take if we had to pile out on the ice in a hurry, when the floes drifted slowly apart and *Mischief* slid off the ice. Apparently the projecting tongue had hit the opposing floe and had rebounded. Our relief was premature. Noddy, who was below at the engine controls while I steered and shouted orders down to him, reported the well full and water overflowing into the cabin. Manning the barrel pump on deck we soon had the leak under control. But we could not let-up. She was leaking freely and the pump had to be kept going. It was now about midnight, still foggy, and still no sign of land. But the ice showed signs of relenting. We began to find long leads of more or less open water in which we could do our five knots and in these easier conditions I handed over the tiller where I had been for the last 12 hours. At last at 4 am some high land showed close at hand above the fog, and shortly after we sensed rather than saw that we were within a fjord entrance. The floes were thicker in the fjord and the fog worse. We lost sight of *Ejnar Mikkelsen* and stopped, for we had no idea where the harbour lay. She soon came back, we half heard some shouted instructions about avoiding a wire, and then we followed into the harbour where she anchored. We made fast alongside her, thankful to have arrived, albeit in so leaky a condition. It was a bit early for breakfast but not too early for a drink. Niels Underborg, before retiring to his house on shore, joined us. He spoke excellent English having served for three years during the war with the Worcestershire Regiment. He thought that we were lucky to be in and that it might be three weeks before we should be able to get out.

Leaving the pump manned the rest of us turned in for some sleep. When we came on deck again we might have been in a different world. Instead of the cold, Stygian gloom in which we had been enveloped for so long, we beheld the fairest of sunlit scenes. From a cloudless, azure sky the sun shone benignly, flooding with warm light the rock ridges and snow couloirs of the mountains across the fjord. The ice floes dotting the fjord, which yesterday had been dull, grey menacing shapes, now sparkled joyously on the crystal blue water. The 100-yard-wide harbour entrance was bounded on one side by an unoccupied wharf and on the other by a wall of rock. Between, supported on buoys, lay a wire which served more or less effectively to stop floes from drifting into the harbour. The small harbour shallowed quickly to where a fast-running river with a bridge over it flowed in. At this shallow end were landing steps and a wharf for small craft with two big warehouses on it. Behind, clustered on the steep hillside, lay the brightly coloured buildings of the town.

Niels had advised us that at the shallow end there was a bit of beach where we could lay *Mischief* on her side, and that a Danish shipwright carpenter, Martin, would be able to patch her up. Meantime we had to keep the pump going and on that account maintained the usual two-hour watches. A few strokes of the pump every minute or so sufficed to keep the water in check. I went ashore to have a look at the hard where we were to beach *Mischief* and to make arrangements with Martin. He, too, had some English and told us that we could beach the boat that evening at high water and that at midnight the water would be low enough for him to start work. At that time of year it was light all night and Martin was willing to work at any hour.

We were a little uneasy about laying *Mischief* over with all the stores and ballast inside. If the bottom were uneven or if she lay down on a bit of rock, we might do her more harm than good. However, we could see the bottom clearly and at the top of the tide we got her in a good position, put plenty of weight on the starboard side, and as the water fell she lay down quietly enough until she came to rest on the turn of the bilge at an angle of about 50°. On the port side we could see two separate damaged places where several planks had been sprung. At midnight Martin turned up and he had time to cut out some of the damaged planks and insert short lengths of new wood before the water returned. As the water rose and began lapping over the starboard deck *Mischief* lay inert, seemingly content to end a life of toil on the beach at Angmagssalik. We suffered a few minutes of extreme alarm. The trouble was that she had a lot of water inside. When the tide went down and she began to list over the pump had no longer sucked; all this water was now swishing about in the cabin up to the top of my bunk. Moreover, as she began to list to starboard, we had forgotten to haul back the boom which we had swung out to weight her on that side, and once she was on her side it was impossible to shift it. Needless to say she came upright long before the water had risen enough to lap over the cockpit coaming, but not before I had become grey with anxiety.

We remained where we were until at 1 pm next day, when she was again on the beach, Martin completed the repairs on that side. Before putting her down again starboard side upper-most in order to have a look at that side we went back to a buoy to get some sleep, having had only about three hours in the last two days. It was impossible to eat or sleep on board while she was lying over. We ate on the beach surrounded by urchins, huskies, oil, and harbour offal, and slept where we could. Charles took his tent and camped by the river. She still leaked, though nothing like so badly. When we came to look at the starboard side we found the wood badly scarred forward of midships. Martin probed this carefully and apparently satisfied himself that none of the planks had been cracked right through. He did some caulking there and also round the rudder trunk.

By now *Britannia* had come safely in and was unloading at the quay. Her captain proved most friendly, bore us no grudge for the delay we had caused him, and seemed more concerned at our misadventures. In between high and low water, when we were either putting *Mischief* on the hard or floating her off, we explored Angmagssalik. Beer could be bought at the Greenland Trading Company store, but not drunk there, and there was a small coffee bar. Down by the river we found a communal wash-house where for ten ore one could have a hot shower and the use of a washing machine. There were usually a number of Greenlander women gossiping there and since they were more familiar with washing machines they seldom allowed us to wash our own clothes. For the fourth time we careened *Mischief*, as she was still making a lot of water. This time we put her on stern first in order to have the stern well clear of the water for inspection. Martin could find nothing there. We turned her round and went on again bow first. At 4 am Martin came to put a sheet of lead, felt, and finally a sheet of zinc, covering the whole of the damaged area on the port side. This appeared to do the trick.

We had hoped to get away that day. As yet there was no chance of our going out to sea and south to Skjoldungen, but we could at least cross King Oscar's Havn, as the local fjord was named, to climb a mountain there; or we might possibly go up the much larger Angmagssalik Fjord between Cape Dan and the mainland which runs north for nearly thirty miles. By keeping close inshore we could avoid the heavy ice which still blocked our escape to sea. And not only our escape. *Britannia* had already made an attempt to sail and had had to return. But the brilliant weather we had enjoyed now broke; a gale of wind ushered in four days of incessant rain. Nor was this the only 'trifling sum of misery added to the foot of our account'. Too late we discovered that between Friday and Monday no beer was to be had; a local bye-law to that effect ensured that on pay-day the Greenlander would have to take some of his money home. Niels Underborg asked us to his house where he showed us a number of charming pictures of Greenland scenes which he had painted. He told us of the fate of *Ejnar Mikkelsen*'s predecessor which had been capsized by an ice floe off Cape Dan and had sunk in less than five minutes. He and the crew all managed to get on to the ice whence they were soon picked up. Ejnar Mikkelsen, by the way, is the name of a noted Danish explorer and administrator of east Greenland who, although now eighty years old, still visits the country. We were entertained, too, by our pipe-smoking girl friend to coffee and delicious cakes. She proved not to be the Amazon I had feared but a charming, friendly schoolmistress who taught in the local school and who thoroughly enjoyed life at Angmagssalik. Her gestures during our adventures in the ice had evidently been of encouragement rather than of impatience.

Although on the Tuesday, 21 July, rain still fell we made an attempt to reach Angmagssalik Fjord. By ten o'clock we were back at the buoy having found the ice too thick and *Mischief* too unhandy. From our first day here a peak on the far side of King Oscar's Havn had roused our interest, a peak named on the chart Poljemsfjeld, or in Eskimo Qimertajalik, of graceful shape, with two steep ridges enclosing a long snow couloir. So a day later, having collected some white bread kindly baked for us by the wife of the harbour master we motored across to an anchorage within striking distance of our mountain. It is only 3,380ft. high so that even I could expect to get up and down in the day. Bob Cook, Charles Sewell, and I left the boat at 10.30 and an hour later had reached the foot of the peak. Two hours scrambling over easy rocks brought us to the bottom of the snow couloir. In spite of the late hour the snow remained in prime condition for kicking steps. For the next hour we climbed in this glistening couloir, encouraged by the knowledge that it would bring us out close to the summit. By 2.30 pm we were on top, happy in our success and in the magnificent prospect extending over miles of ice-covered sea to the blue water beyond. In a small cairn we found a tin with records of two earlier ascents – the first in 1931 by two Germans, and the second in 1954 by two Danes.

By the time we started down the sun had softened the snow in the couloir. We roped up with Charles in front and Bob, the heavyweight, in rear as anchorman. Care was needed, for our upgoing steps were apt to give way and underneath the snow lay ice. At a point about half-way down Bob was not quite careful enough. The step broke and down he shot knocking me off my steps and finally pulling off Charles. Fortunately the couloir made a sharp bend just below and before we had fallen fifty feet the three of us fetched up on the rocks in a tangle of rope and ice-axes with no hurt except to our self-esteem. On our way back to the boat we took what we hoped would be a shorter route. Whichever way you go, the Spanish proverb tells us, there is a league of bad road. Having made long detours to avoid cliffs and crossed innumerable gullies, we reached the boat at 7 pm in about twice as long a time as that of the outward journey.

CHAPTER TWELVE

Homeward Bound

ON RETURNING to the harbour we saw a very stoutly built, wooden, Norwegian trading vessel. *Ardwark* had just returned from Skjoldungen where there is a small settlement and her captain told us he had met a lot of ice and strongly advised us not to try yet awhile. On the 25th, therefore, we made a short excursion into Angmagssalik Fjord. Dodging among ice floes until evening we finally anchored in a branch fjord called Sangmalik. We noticed that although we were only some fifteen miles from Angmagssalik heavy banks of snow lay all along the beach while a lake, only a few feet above sea level, was covered with ice two to three ft. thick. Nothing whatever grew there, whereas at Angmagssalik grass and flowers abound. I attributed this to the fact that Sangmalik, on the opposite side of the peninsula on which Poljemsfjeld lies, faces north.

Bob and I had a day's climbing on Sofiasfjeld, much the same height as our first peak, treading snow all the way except for a bit of loose rock on the summit ridge. We could look inland to the ice-cap and seaward to Cape Dan where the ice appeared as thick as ever. The glacier by which we descended had its foot in the lake, a fact which would certainly encourage the lake to remain frozen. On the return passage we took advantage of a breeze to launch the dinghy and take pictures of *Mischief* under sail. Beating down the main fjord against the wind we met in turn *Ejnar Mikkelsen* and *Ardwark* bound up the fjord to the settlement of Kungmiut. We were a little dismayed to find that this short spell of beating in sheltered water sufficed to reopen the leak.

Martin came on board and although we pulled up floor boards and emptied lockers we failed to track it down. He had brought with him a bag of sawdust. Securing the boathook to the handle of a bucket filled with sawdust he plunged the bucket down beneath the hull and at the same time contrived to spill out the sawdust. In theory the sawdust is sucked into the leak by the ingoing water and bungs it up. Provided one knows whereabouts on the hull to spill the bucket this trick works; and it worked then although the leak had not been located and was not very pronounced. With that we should have to be content. Having already beached her five times we were not likely to discover anything fresh by doing it once more.

After nearly a fortnight we were becoming impatient to go. As Dr Johnson observed: 'Patience is a virtue very easily fatigued by exercise.' We filled up with oil and water, made our farewells to the harbour-master, Martin, and other wellwishers, and on 31 July sailed out to try conclusions with the ice. By 4 pm we slunk back. Two miles out we had met with heavy ice and from the masthead had seen nothing but ice. For the sake of exercise most of us at various times had walked up the hill behind the town known locally as Seaman's Hill. I preferred to call it Spy-glass Hill. Close on 2,000ft. high, it afforded an excellent view seawards. When I went up there before breakfast next day I saw what I took to be a possible lead through the ice. We motored out at 9 am steering for some icebergs I had noted as leading marks. From deck-level the lead looked a lot less open and owing to a heavy swell the floes were rising and falling in a frightening way. After getting ourselves nearly shut in, and taking ten minutes to turn the boat round, we scuttled back to harbour in a chastened mood.

Early next morning I was again up Spy-glass, this time climbing to the higher southernmost summit, known as Somansfjeldet (2,400ft.) whence one could see south along the coast. What I saw inspired me with fresh hope. We started after breakfast, hugging the coast until we came to an unmistakable berg which I had marked down as the point for us to turn seawards. Motoring up a wide lead with only a few scattered floes we congratulated ourselves on having won clear. But at midday we ran into pretty solid ice and from the masthead no open water could be seen. Back we had to go. I climbed Spy-glass Hill for the third morning running less in the hope of seeing a fresh lead than with the need to convince myself that we had really met ice the previous day and had not imagined it. This useful exercise showed me convincingly how quickly ice conditions could change. Where we had been motoring in open water was now all ice.

In order to leave more room in the cramped harbour we moved outside to a small bay where we were sometimes woken by being nudged by stray floes. On one occasion we found ourselves sitting, as it were, on an ice saddle, our keel over the sunken middle section of a floe with the two above-water parts of it on either side. On yet another pilgrimage up Spy-glass Hill on the evening of 4 August I met a solitary Dane coming down. We had a brief and baffling chat from which I concluded that either his English or mine must be faulty. 'Have you been to the top?' I asked. 'I live there,' came the reply. 'Oh! What do you do there?' 'I cook!'

The ice still looked unpromising but Niels, who came on board that night, spoke encouragingly and told us that on the way back from Cape Dan he had seen from his wheelhouse for the first time that summer the open sea. I spent the next two days in bed with a chill but when our look-out returned from Spy-glass on the evening of the 6th he reported the bay more or less ice-free. We stupidly deferred sailing till next morning when Roger, who had gone up the hill early to confirm this, reported ice all across the fjord entrance. Early on the 8th the report was the same, but that afternoon, which was marvellously fine and clear, several of us climbed Spy-glass for what was to be the last time. Nowhere could we see any ice thick enough to stop us. Our chance had come.

We sailed on 9 August and by midday had reached the open sea. Until we were clear of the ice it was bitterly cold. We hoisted sail and drifted southwards with the current, the sea perfectly calm, the afternoon warm and sunny. Throughout the next day in light airs we progressed slowly, noting with some misgiving the bergs and pack-ice all along between us and the shore. We knew, however, that the appearance of pack-ice from a distance is often deceptive and we felt that when the time came to go in the ice would be navigable. We were to have no chance of testing this.

On the 11th in fog and a fresh south-east wind we began at last to move smartly. The wind presently backed north-west and freshened to Force 5 as the fog cleared. Closing the land we identified Cape Mosting, about thirty miles from Skjoldungen, and were then forced further out to sea by a projecting cape of ice. That was as near as we were to get to our objective. Under the strains of fast sailing the leak had started again and every two hours at the change of watch about 500 strokes of the pump were needed to clear the well. By 7 pm this had increased to 900 strokes and after a brief talk with the crew, who were naturally disappointed, I decided to head for home. I felt that with the menace of this leak hanging over us we should not much enjoy the short time we had left for Skjoldungen. Nor could we mend matters by returning to Angmagssalik to put the boat once again on the beach. We could steer a northerly course towards Iceland and the Faeroes, so that if the leak worsened, as I feared it might, we should have a chance to put in.

So in the gathering gloom of a wild night of wind and rain we turned her head eastwards. We wanted to steer north-east but it was by now blowing hard and we did not want to make the leak worse by sailing close on the wind. As it was the pump had to be kept going more or less continuously. We doubled the watch, one man steering while the other stood by in the cockpit to pump vigorously every few minutes until the pump sucked dry. Rain continued throughout the next day and when we found ourselves unable to steer better than south-west, we hove to. This lessened the leak considerably and we derived much comfort from the knowledge that at the cost of standing still we could at any rate keep afloat.

Two days of wet, gloomy weather, accompanied by northerly winds that prevented us steering a northerly course, did little to cheer us. We found that she leaked most when on the port tack and that in light winds one man could cope with both steering and pumping. During a calm spell we launched the dinghy to see if we could repeat Martin's successful trick with sawdust, having brought a bag of it with us. There was too much of a lop. Apart from covering the surface of the water with sawdust we achieved nothing. We even tried hauling an old sail under the hull, a remedy that obviously could be effective only if there was a large hole with water pouring in. Another search inside the hull led nowhere. The number of damp patches and weeps we discovered did not account for the steady trickle into the well. I suppose we became accustomed to living in a leaking ship just as in time one becomes accustomed to living with noise, pain, and the other ills of life. As the sage observed: 'Human life is everywhere a state where much is to be endured and little enjoyed.' We forgot about Iceland, still as far off as ever, and decided to steer direct for the Western islands and the North Channel.

Homeward bound across the Atlantic one expects and seldom gets a steady stream of westerly winds. A fine northerly breeze lasted for a day and a half giving us a good push to the south-east, and with brighter weather we were able to get sights. At various times two large schools of porpoises chased us for hours leaping clear into the air and turning somersaults. 'When the sea-hog jumps', they say 'stand to your pumps.' On this occasion, as on others, the adage proved false and in any case our pump was already manned. The wind died at night and even a crimson sunrise provoked nothing but light winds for the next two days.

It was not until the 20th that we began really to move as the wind increased slowly to gale force until by the next day we were running at three knots under bare poles. As often happens we neglected to rig the canvas cover over the skylight before those below had suffered some salt water showers. The deck pump which had seen some pretty hard usage in the last few weeks chose this moment to break, the wooden plunger coming adrift from the actuating rod. The spare rotary pump fitted in the heads was awkward to use and called for a lot of effort. Nobody much cared for it. So Charles Marriott and Noddy, representing respectively advanced scientific theory and applied mechanics, got to work, and with screw-hooks and wire contrived a lash-up for the barrel pump. It worked provided it was gently used.

On a warm, windless day after the gale the *Ocean Ranger* of Manchester passed close by. When we called her by lamp asking to be reported she merely responded with three blasts on her siren. At dawn of the 27th I got a fix with star sights and in consequence altered course in order to have a good look at Rockall, the lone rock out in the Atlantic 200 miles west of St Kilda. Having come up with it we sailed round half a cable away from this remarkable rock upon which very few landings have been made. The sea being perfectly calm I had entertained hopes of landing, but as we drew near we could see that even the slight swell then running broke in violence as it hit the rock. Rockall is 70ft. high and about 80ft. on the water-line, steep all round and the east face quite sheer. Nothing like granite. For ages this diminutive rock has faced the fierce Atlantic gales and there it stands defiant and apparently little diminished.

On the evening of 29 August we sighted the Dubh Artach light off Iona and for good measure the loom of Skerryvore, Inishtrahull, and Islay lights. I for one was not sorry to know that at last we had some land within reach. With a favouring tide we whistled through Rathlin Sound and had arrived off our old acquaintance Red Bay just as it turned against us. On three occasions we have had to anchor there to avoid a foul tide but this time with a light northerly wind we could just stem the tide.

At Barmouth, where I live, *Mischief* was known only by name. I had promised to bring her there one day and now was the chance. At least we could have the barrel pump properly repaired; and although I wanted to be back earlier than usual, having engaged to fly to Australia on 20 October to sail a vessel to Heard Island in the Southern Ocean, we still had time in hand. Accordingly, instead of heading for Land's End we altered course to pass south of the Isle of Man and thence to Holyhead, the nearest port to Barmouth at which we could get Customs clearance.

We had run into an anticyclone with fine, hazy weather and easterly winds, blowing, as winds so often do, from precisely the place for which one is bound. The haze became fog which persisted off and on for the next week. We spent an unpleasant night off the Isle of Man with not a glimmer of the Chicken Rock light and ships hooting anxiously all round us. As we beat towards Anglesey on 1 September against a hard south-east wind we were only dimly aware of our position. However, we sighted the Skerries late that evening and at 2 am anchored outside the Holyhead breakwater. At daylight we entered the New Harbour and anchored near the coastguard station attracted there by the sight of a man cleaning the windows. Rowing ashore I explained that we were bound for Barmouth and asked him to rouse out a Customs officer to clear us. He knew the Barmouth coastguard, Mr R. H. Williams, commonly known as Bob Henry, a Barmouth worthy, town councillor and monumental mason, a sociable man who, if need be, could outsing a choir of convivial canaries. He promised to telephone Bob Henry and I was not quick enough to stop him, for I feared the consequences.

At eight o'clock a Customs officer came off and cleared us with a minimum of fuss and an hour later we sailed. We were just in time. Shortly after, as we heard on the wireless, fog prevented any ships entering or leaving Holyhead. It was about sixty miles to Barmouth and had we motored all the way, as we had no intention of doing, we could not have arrived before 9 pm, too late to cross the bar. As it was we took our time. Having drifted past the South Stack we were accosted by a launch and told pretty shortly to clear out five miles to seaward as we were in a guided missile range. The day, though hazy, was altogether too lovely to be marred by motoring. We pointed to our idle sails, asked them to send us a wind, and left it at that. Throughout the afternoon, in happy ignorance of what was then passing at Barmouth, we sailed and drifted slowly on, passed through Bardsey Sound at 10 pm, and at midnight sighted the Causeway buoy.

This buoy marks the western end of Sarn Badrig, or St Patrick's Causeway, which reaches out twelve miles into Cardigan Bay from a few miles north of Barmouth. At low water springs parts of it dry out and in the brief but glorious days of the Welsh schooners trading out of Portmadoc, Barmouth and Aberdovey, several vessels were wrecked there. This natural causeway runs so straight that it is easy to believe it to be man-made, one of the embankments of the legendary kingdom of Cantref-y-Gwaleod, the 'lowland hundred', now sunk beneath the waters of Cardigan Bay. Those who have read Peacock's *Misfortunes of Elphin* will remember the immortal drunkard Seithenyn, watchman of the embankment and answerable to the king for its safety, whose neglect allowed it to decay. During the great storm that finally engulfed the kingdom, breaching the neglected embankment and sweeping away all that were on it, Seithenyn, instead of being drowned like the rest as he deserved, got safely ashore on one of the hundreds of wine barrels to which he had devoted his life industriously emptying.

The entrance to Barmouth harbour is buoyed but not lit. Having run our distance from the Causeway buoy we took soundings and anchored in four fathoms at 5 am. I assumed we were off Barmouth but a wrong course had evidently been given to the helmsman or steered by mistake. When daylight came the familiar landmarks showed me that we were four miles to the south. Off we went motoring at speed in order to cross the bar on the flood tide. Going up the channel towards the harbour we were met by a local lobster boat: on board, the unquenchable Bob Henry with a television camera team. As we made towards the little stone quay, where flags and welcoming banners were still hanging, we realized what we had escaped, and what disappointment we had caused the previous afternoon, by failing to perform the impossible. Owing to miscalculations of distance, time, and *Mischief*'s abilities, a great part of Barmouth, led by the mayor, had awaited our arrival from three o'clock until dusk, telescopes sweeping the horizon and boats ranging the sea in search of us, at the time when we were still the wrong side of Bardsey Island.

Having made sure that *Mischief* would not fall over, for the quay dries out, I went home for breakfast. By the time I got back the flow of visitors had begun and throughout the day we were either showing people round the boat or were ourselves being stared at from the crowded quay. With *Mischief* high and dry no pumping was required and all hands proceeded in relays to Bodowen for baths and food.

Having had the pump repaired and spent a wet night at the Last Inn we sailed early on 4 September. An easterly breeze took us as far as the Sarn-y-Bwch buoy off Aberdovey where we were becalmed in fog. All night and next morning fog persisted until a south-westerly breeze sprang up accompanied by rain. Visibility was not much improved but we identified Cardigan Island and that night picked up the loom of the Strumbles light. Passing well outside the South Bishop and Smalls we crossed the Bristol Channel with a fresh breeze at north-west and a rough sea. Next morning dawned thick and drizzly, the wind having backed south-west. It was no sort of weather in which to be approaching Land's End. We had neither seen or heard anything since passing the Smalls and were pointing, so we thought, for the Scillies. The Bristol Channel and the adjacent coasts of Devon and Cornwall are the scenes of *Mischief*'s youth but I can't understand why she chose at this time to take us into St Ives Bay. Steering a little west of south and seeing through a brief clearing in the murk some pleasantly green scenery on our starboard hand, I naturally took it for the Scillies. How fallible are human assumptions! Charles Marriott, who lives in these wild regions, tentatively suggested it might be St Ives, and when a factory chimney came into view I could no longer doubt.

At any rate we now knew where we were and it was the wrong place from which to round Lands End with a south-west wind. Tacking on and off we made no progress at all until ten o'clock that night when the wind shifted to west. With the change of wind the weather cleared, all the familiar lights came up, and at midnight we passed the Longships and headed up Channel. Two days later, again at midnight, we were closing the Needles in clear weather with wind and tide both in our favour. A large passenger steamer outward bound, after clearing the Needles Channel, turned south and stopped, no doubt to drop the pilot. That done she incontinently turned west and rushed straight at us. Not wishing to gybe all standing I held on and she passed ahead of us within a biscuit's toes, as the saying goes, without even seeing us. At least no one on the bridge used a loud-hailer to blast us and the quiet of the night.

When my heart had stopped thumping we continued up the Needles channel, most of the crew gathered on the foredeck admiring the sights and the lights, while I sat happily steering, the wind dead aft and the boom squared off to starboard. The crew evidently assumed I had seen or heard the Warden buoy hidden behind the mainsail, for when they suddenly and simultaneously uttered a startled yell the tip of the boom was almost caressing the buoy as it slid by. Safely anchored off Lymington river to wait for daylight I had leisure to reflect on the varied perils that beset our coasts, while only the gentle clang of the pump reminded me of those we had escaped in Greenland waters.

Alongside next morning we set to work unloading and unrigging the ship. For yet another night the pump had to be manned but by the next day she had been hauled out. On stripping the lining in the galley it was found that water had been coming in at the damaged planks that Martin had thought were not cracked through. Insomuch as we had not reached Skjoldungen the voyage had been a failure. But it had been full of incident and we had all enjoyed it. Leigh Mallory's reputed answer to the question of why anyone should want to climb Everest – 'Because it is there' – has been quoted *ad nauseam*. I should have thought that a better answer to that question or to why a man undertakes any adventure or enterprise is to be found in Stevenson's words: 'In the joy of the actors lies the sense of any action. That is the explanation, that the excuse.'

Part 3

Heard Island, Southern Ocean
Patanela
November, 1964 – March, 1965

CHAPTER THIRTEEN

Fitting Out

HEARD ISLAND in Lat. 53°10′S. Long. 73°35′E., is an uninhabited sub-antarctic island lying about 300 miles to the south-east of the much larger island of Kerguelen. Measuring only some twenty-three miles by twelve miles it culminates in the peak known as Big Ben which is 9,005ft. high. Thus the island is nearly all mountain, a mountain heavily glaciated on all sides; many of the glaciers terminate in ice cliffs that are washed by the sea.

As far back as 1957 I had had an eye to Big Ben but enquiries had shown that there was no safe anchorage where *Mischief* could be left. A letter, too, from Mr P.G. Law, then (and now) Director of the Australian Antarctic Division, had been discouraging. 'As regards your getting to Heard Island,' he had written, 'I cannot overstress the dangers which will face you if you proceed in a small boat. As you know, Heard Island is right in the track of the great westerly cyclones which sweep across the Southern Ocean with almost no intervening period of good weather of any duration. The seas are mountainous and altogether I can think of no worse place to sail small craft.' More than that, the lack of safe anchorage meant that the boat, after dropping the shore party, would have to be sailed to Kerguelen where there are many good anchorages. With *Mischief*, with a crew of only six, I did not think this was on. It was the usual difficulty of being in two places at once. I myself would certainly want to land on Heard Island, and equally certainly I would not like to leave a reduced crew with the responsibility of navigating to Kerguelen and back again. I should have felt extreme anxiety both on their account and on my own, for if for some reason they had failed to return, the shore party would have been residents of Heard Island for a long time. From 1949 to 1954, when it was abandoned, Australia had maintained there a scientific base – huts, electric light, and hot baths – so perhaps we should not

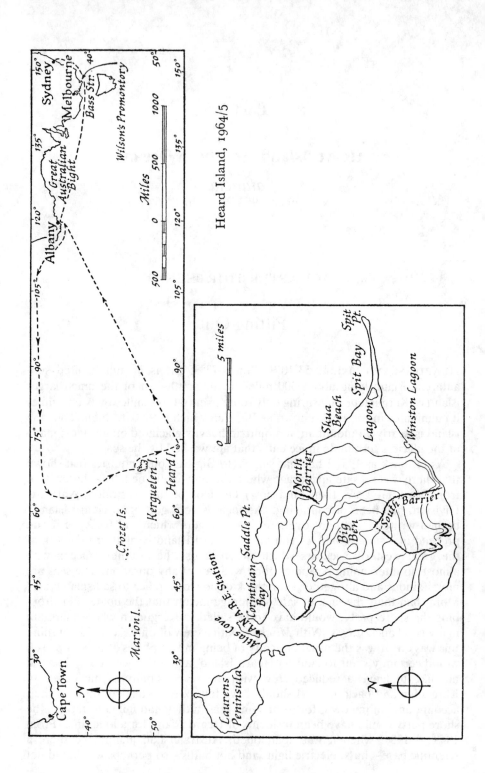

Heard Island, 1964/5

have been badly off. But in the end I decided to leave Big Ben for better men and went instead to Iles Crozet and Kerguelen. At least we went there at the second attempt, the first having ended when we suffered some storm damage, after which we had to be content with circumnavigating Africa.

In the winter of 1963–64 I heard from Warwick Deacock, an ex-Army officer and a climber, then living in Australia, who was organizing a private expedition to sail to Heard Island with the object, among others, of climbing Big Ben. *Patanela*, a 63ft. steel schooner, had been chartered for five months and he asked me to act as navigator, knowing that I had once been interested in Heard Island and had visited Kerguelen. A large amount of money had still to be found including £A8,000 for the charter. For several years *Patanela* had been employed in cray-fishing in Bass Strait and the charter figure was based – over-sanguinely, one thought – on the amount that could be made in a season's fishing. At that time the two owners and active managers of the boat, the Hunt brothers, were to have come with us. In the end they had to drop out and I was then asked to skipper *Patanela* as well as navigate. Since my experience had been limited entirely to sailing a small cutter, to be asked to take charge of a big, unknown schooner and an unknown crew was no light matter. Nevertheless, both the destination and the aims of the expedition were things after my own heart. After learning from an independent source in Australia that *Patanela* was a capable boat and in sound condition I did not long hesitate to accept. Arriving in Sydney on 20 October, more dead than alive after a long flight, I was met by Warwick Deacock and several members of the expedition. From the airport we went straight on board *Patanela*, then lying at the jetty of the Cruising Club of Australia who, besides allowing us to fit-out there, also allowed us to use the clubhouse. As is inevitably the way with a boat undergoing a major refit she was in a chaotic state, the deck almost impassable from the accumulation of junk. Work on her was not nearly so forward as I had expected and the chance of our leaving on the advertised date, 1 November, seemed to me remote. Apart from a mass of work below deck, all the running rigging had yet to be fitted, there were no cleats, nothing on which to hang rope-coils, no fittings on deck for sheet-blocks or tackles, and no binnacle.

Compared with the accommodation in *Mischief*, which is not luxurious, that in *Patanela* seemed to me only a little superior to what would have been found in a better-class slaver. Berths were needed for ten, a number that could not well be reduced. If five men were to be put ashore on Heard Island, we must have five left on board to work the ship. There were four good bunks in the foc's'le, the only snags there being that it was awkward to enter and pitch dark. An escape hatch on deck which would admit daylight, would normally be closed at sea. One entered it through a small steel door, after assuming a kneeling position on deck, and then climbed down a ladder backwards. I wondered where the remaining six were to be interred, and when our tour of inspection finally finished up aft in the small combined galley and saloon I was a little shaken when I learnt that this was the only remaining space. In here there were two spacious fore-and-aft bunks and the plan was that two should sleep side by side in each while the remaining two were somehow to be slung from the deckhead like bats. Where these six unfortunates were to stow their gear was a question that had also been left hanging – bat-like.

Being a bit of a cissy, I thought some other arrangement desirable. Amidships there was a huge hold, the cray-tank, that normally held seventeen tons of sea-water and cray-fish and had now been earmarked to carry 2,000 gallons of fuel oil in drums. But the idea was to *sail* to Heard Island and we had space in the engine room for 1,000 gallons of oil. I therefore suggested that we put only 1,000 gallons in the cray-tank in the form of a single layer of drums on top of which we could build a temporary floor and four bunks. Like those in the foc'sle, the four men in the cray-tank would depend entirely upon electric light but they were better off in that being amidships they were in the steadiest part of the ship. Only the saloon-cum-galley had any daylight and the two bunks there, though uncomfortably wide, were obviously designed for the skipper and for the leader of the expedition. Nor would even they be exactly in clover. The floor space, measuring about nine ft. by nine ft., contained a gas-stove and a sink, a table and two benches at which four could sit in discomfort; and at mealtimes, if not at other times, the whole crew, less the two men on watch, would be sitting or standing there. Washing, which at sea is admittedly an infrequent and possibly superfluous operation, would have to be done on deck with a bucket; there was no lavatory; and nowhere to hang or even dump wet oilskins except on the floor of the wheel-house. 'Conveniences', as Dr Johnson said, 'are never missed where they were never enjoyed.' Our crew of young, eager, resourceful Australians and New Zealanders, whose morale, I feared, might be affected by this too ungracious living, took it all in their stride, making light of deficiencies and of their gloomy quarters. The steel door of the foc'sle soon bore the legend 'Saloon and Bar'. Over the cray-tank door they painted 'All hope abandon etc.', and below, in lighter vein, 'Knock twice and ask for Maisie.' The galley-cum-saloon was labelled 'The Dirty Spoon', and the engine-room 'The Sauna'.

Warwick Deacock had undertaken to cook, the most onerous job on board, and manfully he performed his duties. 'All ills,' Sancho Panza used to say, 'are alleviated by food.' At sea, in ships more comfortable than *Patanela*, the ills can be many and various, and food becomes of supreme importance. Meals must be good, plentiful and punctual. On this store we were to have no complaints, we lived like princes. *Patanela* had a refrigerated hold which before we left had been stuffed full of steaks, chops, sides and shoulders of beef, mutton, pork, besides hundreds of thousands of meat pies, sausages, bacon, and eggs; and in Warwick we had a man born to grapple with these ingredients on a scale of the necessary grandeur. Thrice daily throughout the voyage he satisfied ten voracious appetites, his only relief coming on Sundays when the crew took it in turns to vie with each other and with the master in the splendour of their menus. The meat remained good throughout the voyage except for a side of beef that might have come from the Durham ox itself, a monumental piece of meat that became known to us as 'Mary', and which after we had been hacking at it for a few weeks, and making little impression, had to be thrown overboard. Nor, amidst this superfluity of solids, was drink lacking. We had each a can of beer every day, and spirits for high days and holidays.

But I am anticipating. Having seen the ship I felt it was no good teetering on the brink. Forthwith I unrolled my swag (we are now in Australia) and lived on board for the next five months. Young Douglas Hunt who unfortunately was not coming with us, gave us invaluable help during the fitting out and shared with me the rigours of living on board. The rigours were more severe then than they would be, I hoped, when we got to sea; but 'what does misery matter if we are all miserable together?' The small wheel-house aft through which one entered the saloon, the saloon itself, and the foc's'le, were being given a lining of special material to prevent condensation. In the various stages of this long process Doug Hunt and I lived like nomads, moving our bedding from the saloon to the foc's'le and back again two or three times. Cooking was out of the question. For breakfast we walked up to King's Cross, a sort of Australian Leicester Square, where an eating place remained open all night; we lunched on board off meat pies and beer, and after work went ashore for a meal at night.

Once the running rigging had been set up and the sails bent we could go for a sail in the harbour to see how they set and to mark the leads for the headsail sheets. But before that she needed more weight in her, so we motored up the harbour to the big Mobil oil depot where we received (gratis) 2,000 gallons of oil, putting half in the engine room and half in the cray-tank. Some of our friends who knew we had gone to load oil were concerned when that afternoon a fire broke out in the depot, destroying storage tanks and doing £250,000 worth of damage. Fortunately we had left about an hour earlier. Manoeuvring *Patanela* to and from her berth at the Club jetty through lines of closely moored, expensive yachts was quite hair-raising. Doug Hunt handled her in masterly fashion and on one occasion, when she had to be slipped, he turned her in her own length. With her 160h.p. Rolls Royce engine and big propeller she was in fact easy to handle once one got the hang of it. Unaccustomed as I was to wheel steering and to a boat of her size I was thankful to have Doug Hunt there from whom I could learn.

Patanela had been brought round from Melbourne to Sydney for fitting out by a scratch crew. Happily, at an early stage in the passage they had learnt to ignore the compass located in the steel wheel-house. On some points it was 50° out, more on others. There were two wheels, one mounted inside the wheel-house, the other on its outer side aft. From inside the wheel-house one could see very little, certainly not the sails, so that wheel was useless to us; and though the outside wheel was good for manoeuvring in harbour there was no place to put a binnacle and compass. So we took the wheel from inside and put it on deck abaft the mainmast where one could both see and steer, and connected it to the steering gear with a long shaft bracketed to the starboard side of the wheel-house. The tricky job of rigging this wheel with the necessary shafting and gear wheels was done by an engineering friend of the expedition. Indeed a great many hardworking friends with various skills rallied round to help us.

Having got the wheel in its new position we bought a binnacle for £30, lined it up fore and aft and fixed it to the deck. This left the wheel-house free for use as a chart-room where with a lot of bother we fitted a chart-table, a rack for charts, and a secure home for my sextant and chronometer watch. There is much to be said for steel yachts – strength, freedom from leaks, freedom from attacks by teredo worm – and in Australia, especially ocean racing yachts, more are built of steel than of wood. But in a steel boat small fittings such as these, or shelves for books and clothes, are not to be had by knocking in a few nails or screws. All deck fittings, too, such as ringbolts, have to be welded on or have a hole burnt for them. We carried a welding outfit on the voyage.

Meantime we were being badgered by the Australian Shipping Board who, with the professional distrust of amateurs, rather hoped to save us from our folly by preventing us from sailing at all. At their request we had to slip *Patanela* again in order that they could take measurements to work out her angle of heel. They did not regard our brand new suit of sails of the heaviest Dacron made as enough. We must have a spare suit made. Alternatively, as this might take a few months, we must carry enough cloth to make a suit ourselves. None of our navigation lights complied with the regulations and must be changed. And finally, the unkindest cut of all, we must sign on a certificated navigator as a spare in case I got washed overboard. Enough is enough. Warwick Deacock got himself elected a member of the Australian Cruising Club, had *Patanela* registered as a yacht, and from that secure ground told the Shipping Board, so to speak, to jump into the dock.

Not all the crew were available for work on board. Of those that were Ed Reid, who had spent seven years as radio operator in the Australian navy, was fully occupied installing our own transmitting and receiving set (on loan from the Army) in the engine room and rigging the aerial aloft. An engine room is not ideal for a radio but we had no other place to put it. Phil Temple, a writer and an entomologist, who had been on two New Guinea expeditions, was also busy with his own devices, rigging a string of outsize butterfly nets that could be hoisted to the cross-trees. When these were aloft it was hoped that any wind-borne insects on passage in our vicinity would be caught, thus providing food of a kind for scientific thought.

Later we were joined by John Crick, a young New Zealand student teacher, a climber with no sailing experience, black-browed and given to modern poetry, songs of the out-back, sheep-shearing, Ned Kelly, and such like. Tony Hill was a young law student who might be described as debonair when he was not looking scruffy, though seldom quite so scruffy as Phil Temple or John Crick. He had done some sailing and soon proved active and able both on deck and aloft. He acted as mate and was of great help to me, competent, reliable, and able to jolly the crew along.

Two who were working all the time on the boat were coming with us only as far as Albany. Alec Theakston was busy mainly in the engine room, but he could turn his hand to most things and his ability as an acrobat might have come in useful later in the voyage. Jim McCormick, red-headed and consequently fiery, had a seaman's card and in our first days at sea his presence among a more or less inexperienced crew was more than welcome. He had sailed in the coastal trade and regaled us with stories of a full-blooded character, master of a trading schooner, known as the 'Beast of Bass Strait,' a nautical Jack Dempsey who, if provoked, would knock a man the length of the deck. The Beast had a less violent but equally unpleasant way of dealing with any man he found steering half a point off course by merely telling him not to bother to call his relief.

Members of the expedition who were still occupied with their own affairs used to come along in the evening to do some work. Dr Russell Pardoe (we had three doctors in the crew) had been twice to the Antarctic and had earned an MBE for his work on those expeditions. Russ, as we called him, was quiet, thorough, and painstaking in everything he did, whether rigging lazy-guys or treating boils. His particular pets were two inflatable rafts for the landing party, together with their Johnson outboards. He brought, too, an Aqua-lung which we were to have occasion to use. Colin Putt, our king-pin and sheet-anchor, was another New Zealander employed by Imperial Chemicals in Sydney. He was coming as engineer and climber, but he knew a great deal about boats and could make or improvise anything a boat might need. Any insoluble problems we had we left to him, a man of infinite resource and sagacity. It was mainly upon his advice that *Patanela* had been chartered.

Much hampered by visitors and Press photographers the work gradually got done. The inevitable question of when we were going to sail could only be answered by 'When we were ready'. The junk on deck had now grown to mountainous proportions and had to be got rid of. Much as I, and others, enjoy throwing things overboard one can't indulge in that habit too freely in Sydney Harbour, or for that matter in any other. Finally all hands were turned on to make a grand clearance by carrying it all ashore whence Colin Putt took it away in a five-ton lorry. No one asked what he did with it. *Patanela* now began to look like a ship and we made arrangements to have the compass swung.

With the compass adjuster on board, a retired sea captain who had served in sail, we went up harbour beyond the bridge where we put the boat's head on various known bearings. Finally we spent a long time circling round a buoy. By this time the adjuster was obviously a worried man. He could neither account for nor correct the erratic behaviour of the compass. The magnets that corrected it for one bearing would make it hopelessly out on another. At the end of the long morning, dizzied by our circling of the buoy and the antics of the compass needle, and running short of magnets, our sea captain asked to be put ashore. He needed, he said, leisure to reflect, to think of something that he had not yet tried. On our way back it struck me that if his musings resulted in our having to find a new position for the binnacle, and hence the wheel, as seemed probable, we never would sail. I persuaded him, therefore, to give it another try and back we went under the bridge to repeat the morning's performance. The short interval that we had unwittingly allowed did the trick. To the surprise and delight of all the compass, having had time to settle down in its new surroundings, now behaved like a witch. The deviation on all points was slight.

As soon as we got back to the Club we announced that we would sail next day, 5 November. It meant working up to the last minute, the most essential job being the securing of three 100gal. drums of water and some small drums of petrol which we were obliged to carry on deck. When the Press photographers were at last satisfied, we cast off at 3 pm and as soon as we were clear started getting sail on. As we passed Sydney Heads we shook off the last of the following launches, streamed the log, and headed south with a good breeze at north-east.

CHAPTER FOURTEEN

To Albany

ALTHOUGH WE had still to call at Albany to pick up three members of the expedition and to fill up with water and oil, the voyage had at last begun and we were heartily glad to be at sea. For my part I believed and hoped that the most worrying part of the expedition was behind us; for the next few months our only contentions would be with the elements. It is probably true of all such sea adventures that the stresses and strains are most felt while fitting out and if this has been thoroughly done there should be no need for worry during the voyage.

A thunderstorm soon killed the wind. Outside the Heads there was enough lop to give the boat some motion so that by nightfall the crew's joy at being at sea had begun to diminish. Warwick, who was among those afflicted with seasickness, characteristically refused to give in and dished up a stew for those feeling strong enough to eat. Nor were our invalids given much chance to recover. On the next day we had a head wind gusting up to Force 7 which at length obliged us to heave to, and a rare tussle we had dowsing the big mainsail with our crew of novices. She hove to very comfortably under the foresail alone, a tip I had had from *Patanela*'s original owner who had paid us a visit when fitting out.

We did not expect to enjoy much sailing on the 1,800 mile passage to Albany. In November along the south coast of Australia fresh to strong westerly winds prevail and the current is also adverse. According to the *Sailing Directions* no sailing vessel leaving Sydney at this time of year should attempt to go west along the south coast of Australia. With our 160h.p. engine we could afford to ignore this advice and indeed we had no choice, for the passage north-about would have been longer and more difficult. Moreover having started five days late we had no time in hand, so whenever the wind blew from forward of the beam we handed the sails and made full use of the engine.

By the 8th we had rounded Gabo Island, the south-eastern extremity of Australia and about 240 miles from Sydney. For the first day or two the working of my sights produced some bizarre results. In working sights in the southern hemisphere east of Greenwich, as against in the northern hemisphere west of Greenwich, to which for the last four years I had been habituated, there are some small but important differences to be observed. Any neglect of these is bound to result in a nonsense. Fortunately, although the Australian coast is for the most part barren sandhills and scrub, without towns, villages, or even caravan parks, it is plentifully sprinkled with lighthouses. Thus by closing the land one could always verify one's position even if the lighthouse sighted was not the expected one.

After Gabo Island the next important landmark on the way round Australia is Wilson Promontory, the southernmost point of Australia in Lat. 38°55'. When nearing it on 10 November in the teeth of a strong head-wind and short, steep seas, we went inshore to coast along the great, empty stretch of sand known as Ninety-Mile Beach where we had smoother water and less current. The weather report spoke of twenty-two-knot winds off the Promontory, so when Jim McCormick began hinting at the snappers that might be caught thereabouts, we decided to have a quiet night in Sealer's Cove in the lee of the Promontory. On the way we fell in with a shoal of barracouta. In a mad ten minutes Jim hauled them in as fast as he could free the hook to throw it in again for another to take. When he had caught fifteen, the fish stopped feeding as suddenly as they had begun. Having already caught and eaten a tunny we found the barracouta disappointing. They are all bones and the flavour hardly repays the trouble spent in eating them.

Sealer's Cove is a delightful anchorage surrounded by steep slopes of dense scrub and eucalyptus trees from which some enormous granite boulders stand out. Apart from the men in the lighthouse on Wilson Promontory there were probably no human beings within 50 miles, a pleasing thought for anyone familiar with our own crowded coasts. Possibly at the request of the Shipping Board, our bowsprit had been decorated with a terrible tubular steel pulpit extending its whole length. We were surprised it had stayed there so long. At Sydney I had made a rope net to hang between the bowsprit shrouds so we took the opportunity to cut the steel monster adrift. No tears were shed as it sank beneath the quiet waters of Sealer's Cove and its absence greatly improved *Patanela*'s appearance. Warwick laid on an abundant meal and after lingering over cigars and whisky we set an anchor watch and spent a peaceful night.

The wind had dropped by morning. As we motored past Wilson Promontory in calm water we felt our wait had been justified. There is a deep, five-mile-wide channel between the cape and Rodondo Island, a magnificent, conical mass of granite 1,100ft. high, an unmistakable seamark. Curiously enough, though the island lies so close to the shore of Victoria it is accounted as part of Tasmania. Cape Otway, which we passed next day, was the last land we should see for a week as we embarked on the long 1,200-mile haul across the Great Australian Bight. More than anything, I think, the extent of the Bight made me fully aware of the size of this great southern continent. The Bight is reputedly stormy but we did not encounter anything much in the way of weather. Albert Rogers, our temporary engineer, worked with Imperial Chemicals in Sydney as an engineer and was thus taking a busman's holiday.

Although he appeared to be enjoying it he was in a hurry to get back. Perhaps the heat of the 'Sauna' was too much, for he was a little on the stout side. So we gave him his head, the revolution counter shot up, and we went bumming along at seven knots, knocking off 170 miles a day. The racket was appalling, and the heat which Albert had to endure in the 'Sauna' increased accordingly. In addition, a big swell running made her roll heavily with no steadying sails. There can be no nastier or more wearing a way of getting about the ocean than motoring in a small boat.

On 19 November we began to close the land somewhere near Albany. When land appears at a distance the navigator is tempted to begin at once to identify various features. This is a mistake. The first surmises he makes are as often as not false and once made they are only grudgingly abandoned. On this occasion the nearer we drew the less I could reconcile my first ideas with the chart, and I had worked up quite a stew before we satisfactorily identified the lighthouse on Breaksea Island, when at once everything fell into place. Provided one has confidence – and it is a large proviso – it is easier to close a strange harbour at night when the lights are readily identified. Beyond Breaksea Island we entered King George's Sound – discovered by Vancouver in 1791 – and were soon in the dredged channel leading to Princess Royal Harbour.

No friendly launch came out to meet us as expected. At a loss where to go, we went alongside the vacant steamer wharf where we were soon found by a large body of friends and well-wishers. We had to move to a slightly dilapidated wooden jetty further up the harbour. Quite a crowd had assembled there, too, to watch us, and they did not assemble in vain. Our first attempt to come alongside nearly carried away part of the jetty and we spent what seemed to me like an hour going ahead and astern before we got safely berthed in the rather cramped space. There was a strong wind blowing but even so my handling of the ship must have been far from impressive. At that time of year Albany is a little too subject to strong westerly winds and though the harbour is surrounded by land its spaciousness allows the wind full scope. During our week's stay the wind blew almost daily and we delayed our departure by two days while a gale blew itself out. Lying at an open pile jetty broadside on to wind and sea we had often to let go all warps except the bow lines in order to ease the strain. When lying thus, head on to wind and sea, we had no more to worry about except the difficulty of getting ashore. The young and agile managed it by lying face down on the warp and hauling themselves across with an ankle hooked over the warp to steady them.

Once one had got ashore the rewards that Albany had to offer were meagre. Australian beer is strong and that is about all that can be said for it, while the pubs are bleak and tawdry to a degree, not unlike the dreariest of British Railway's waiting rooms except that there is nowhere to sit and no coal fire. When it is not wind-swept the town of 10,000 inhabitants is pleasant and quiet, with an extremely wide main street, so wide that it has always a slightly deserted air. A kangaroo loped down it early one morning and instead of motor cars I half expected to see some mounted bushrangers. As Sir Fopling Flutter said of Hyde Park, 'Beyond, all is desert,' so beyond Albany township all is scrub. One has to motor many miles in order to see a farm. During our stay there only one ship entered the harbour. But this fine harbour was busy enough during the war and may in the future again be busy. This corner of Australia is now attracting attention and land once considered worthless is being taken up. Whaling, too, is carried on in a small way. There is a whaling station and the three catchers that serve it went to sea daily if the weather was reasonable. They had the assistance of a small seaplane spotter. The whales are on passage and are all taken on the continental shelf.

At Albany we were as free from formalities as if in Greenland. No Shipping Board would have worried us had we started from there. We made friends everywhere, were entertained officially and privately, and got all the help we needed. Colin Putt joined and eagerly took over the engine room from Albert. Dr Malcolm Hay joined, too, having just arrived from England where he had been to pass an examination in surgery. He took over our ciné-camera. And lastly Dr Grahame Budd who had not been able to make the passage from Sydney. Thus with three doctors on board we were heavily over insured against illness and accident and, as if often the way, we suffered none. Grahame was an experienced mountaineer. Having been twice to Heard Island with ANARE expeditions he knew the island well, its peculiar weather, and the best way to tackle Big Ben.

On 23 November we took on oil at the steamer wharf preparatory to leaving next day. As an expected spare sextant had not yet arrived and the wind was still at west we decided to wait. For the next two days we lay to our bow lines while a moderate gale blew, but by the 27th we were ready to go. Wishing to atone for our unseamanlike arrival we proposed to astonish the natives by sailing from the jetty without using the engine – an easy enough feat because we had only to hoist the staysail for the wind to blow her head round. As we let go aft the staysail was run up smartly and to our discomfiture came down no less smartly on the heads of the chaps hoisting, the strop on the block having come adrift.

With everything set we sailed down the narrow buoyed channel, on the point of gybing most of the time, while Malcolm Hay followed in a launch with the ciné-camera. Sailing freely in the open waters of the Sound, *Patanela* no doubt made a fine picture which Malcolm seemed never to tire of taking. The launch buzzed around hither and thither, Malcolm busy with the camera, until a performance that had looked like going on for ever was suddenly cut short when Malcolm dropped the camera and dived, fully clothed, into the sea. Apparently the case of his exposure meter had fallen overboard. Having picked him up and said good-bye to those in the launch we made our last farewell of all to the pilot of the whale-spotting seaplane who came down close by and stood on top of his cabin to shout to us.

Outside the Sound we could steer no better than south by west, and next day, making little headway, we hove to. At Sydney we had been given a parachute anchor to try out, a thing that when folded took up less room than a bucket. After wetting it to prevent the wind taking charge, we shackled it to the anchor cable and dropped it in with about five fathoms of chain. When the 'chute had opened, which took a few minutes, we were surprised at the way this thirty-two ft. diameter piece of silk held a boat of *Patanela*'s size and weight head to wind. Later, off Heard Island in a hard gale, when we hoped it would lessen the drift to leeward, the anchor held us for an hour until the enormous strain proved too much for the bronze fitting between the parachute cords and the cable shackle.

Contrary winds were almost a certainty until we had rounded Cape Leeuwin (Lat. 34°22'S.) and made some northing. We could not steer a direct course from Albany to Heard Island for this rhumb-line course of about 2,500 miles lay entirely through the region of the strong westerlies, the Roaring Forties. We planned to make our westing roughly in Lat. 33°S. where we might expect variable winds, in the so-called Horse Latitudes. On the 29th, with the engine assisting, we were some fifteen miles off the cape, making poor progress in a rough sea against a Force 6 wind. Violent squalls continued throughout the day. We seemed hardly to move, but by evening I was relieved to note that we were out of sight of land. This south-western extremity of Australia was named by the captain of the Dutch vessel *Leeuwin* which rounded the cape as long ago as 1622. As with most capes at the extremities of continents the weather is often stormy, moreover reefs extend far out to sea and the current sets on to the land. It is a place that needs to be given a wide berth. As we drew north the weather improved and on 1 December we were doing five knots under all plain sail with a fresh south-east wind. Grahame, who had undertaken to make deep plankton hauls throughout the voyage, thought it time to make a start. Having rigged a boom and dropped the net and its two-cwt sinker over the side we discovered the electric winch was not powerful enough to haul it up. We had to be content to make surface hauls over the stern. It was not a popular pastime. The hauls had to be made after dark, several hands were needed, and our speed had to be reduced to two knots by shortening sail. The haul itself was the least trouble but the net had then to be taken forward to be hoisted on the staysail halyards, and the pump and hoses rigged for washing it down. However fine the weather, oilskins were the wear. The catch, sometimes as thick as minestrone, was bottled in preservative. In the past my own contributions to science, acting, of course, merely as a collector, have been few and grudging, none perhaps so grudging as this. But Grahame's enthusiasm or sense of duty were not to be withstood. Only if conditions were really bad could I bring myself to disappoint him and gladden the rest by refusing to allow a plankton haul.

Though in our chosen latitude we escaped having westerly winds, sometimes we had no wind at all. One windless spell lasted for three days, days when we had no qualms about using the engine. And we began to enjoy some really warm weather. I had not thought much of the weather at Sydney and at sea off the coast it had been like an English summer, wet, blustery, and not very warm. We began having our lunch on deck and Tony, who had brought a deck chair, could occasionally sit in it. On one of these calm, undeniably pleasant days, we stopped the engine for an hour for all hands to bathe.

Even with their occasional calms the Horse Latitudes, between the Trade Winds and the Westerlies, are pleasant to sail in. In the Trades one reels off the miles but the unvarying wind and weather become monotonous. Our changeable winds were interspersed with calms and our fine days with days of cloud and drizzle. Apart from the work of the ship we kept ourselves occupied. There were endless discussions about plans for Heard Island and for the prior landing we should have to make either at Amsterdam Island or Kerguelen in order to re-organize ourselves. As the voyage drew on these plans became settled and committed to paper, each man being given a particular responsibility. We had a more tedious occupation in the signing of several thousand postcards. A surprising number of people both in Australia and abroad had subscribed five shillings in return for which we undertook to send a postcard we had had printed signed by members of the expedition and stamped with an expedition stamp – an extension of the Polar Post racket.

Warwick thought up other ways of depriving the crew of sleep, the occupation that generally fills the leisure hours of most crews. Every Sunday someone inflicted a lecture upon his fellows, and beside this we had to furnish material for the ship's newspaper that John Crick had been told to edit. In time the first number of 'SOS' appeared, the letters standing for 'Spirit of the Storm' which, I was told, is the meaning of *Patanela*, a Tasmanian aboriginal word. Needless to say there no longer are any of these, Tasmania having made a clean sweep of its aboriginals. The first number, amusingly illustrated by Ed Reid, proved to be the last. Though the material for it had been collected the second number never went to press as we were then too preoccupied.

Another calm day gave us the opportunity to empty and clean out the refrigerator hold which by then looked like an abandoned snow cave. Warwick and his helpers got half frozen as they worked inside sending up the food – and what masses there were! – before scraping off the accumulated ice, hosing down, and then baling out the water. By 15 December, having averaged about 100 miles a day mostly under sail, we were in the longitude of Amsterdam Island (Lat. 37°40′ Long. 77°30′) and about 180 miles north of it. There is a French meteorological station there and an achorage of sorts. We had expected we might have to call there in order to transfer fuel from the cray-tank to the engine room bunkers, a job that could not be done at sea; but having used little fuel since Albany we decided to defer this until we reached Kerguelen. We had wind on most days and once we had turned south into the region of the westerlies we expected to have more than enough wind. Kerguelen is in Long. 70°E and I did not intend turning southwards until we had reached Long. 65°E. a good two hundred miles to the west of it.

CHAPTER FIFTEEN

To Kerguelen

THE RUDE, intemperate Southern Ocean is rich in bird life. Many more birds are seen here than in the Tropics, the Trades, or the Horse Latitudes. As we edged southwards so the bird-life increased. In our small world Russ Pardoe was the greatest living authority on sea birds and he recorded methodically all that were seen. The various kinds of albatross were the most common and the most to be admired for their majestic, effortless flight; when sitting upon the water they look a little gawky and stupid. The big Wandering Albatross, the Sooty, the light-mantled Sooty, the Yellow-nosed, Black-Browed, and Grey-headed, could all be seen, and could be identified if one was enough of a conjurer to follow a bird in flight through field-glasses while standing on a heaving deck. Shearwaters or Mutton birds, petrel of many varieties, Cape Pigeons and Prions, were always about. At night the latter were attracted by our stern light. Sometimes, looking aft at night, the Prions were so numerous that one almost thought that large snowflakes were falling. The little Storm Petrels fluttering over and sometimes dancing upon the storm-tossed sea, no bigger than sparrows, and possibly a thousand miles from the nearest land, seemed to epitomize gay courage and contempt for the worst the elements could do.

Any tendency to edge south too soon had to be resisted. On 19 December when we were in the longitude of Kerguelen and 900 miles north of it in Lat. 35°, a strong westerly breeze led me to fear that we were already in the grip of the Westerlies. It proved a false alarm. After shifting north and then south, the wind stopped altogether. Four days later, having made all the westing we wanted (in fact we reached as far west as Long. 62°30′), we shaped a course for Kerguelen. The weather soon became harder, the skies greyer, and the sea assumed that steely look which one associates with southern latitudes. Reefing and unreefing the mainsail, or lowering it altogether, became a daily and nightly occurrence. The main boom had no roller reefing gear, in fact it had no reef fittings in the way of bee-blocks or sheaves. Moreover the after end was out of reach from the deck, being above the roof of the wheel-house. Colin therefore bolted a block on the boom aft through which we rove a long rope from the clew earing forward to the mast so that several hands could tally on and haul the earing down to the boom by brute force. Since the boom had not to revolve we had fitted lazy guys, light lines from the topping lifts to the boom, which helped to prevent the sail from bellying out when being lowered in strong winds.

The weather was constantly boisterous but on the run down to Kerguelen we did not record any winds stronger than Force 7. 24 December was particularly boisterous, a day of vicious squalls. We reefed before breakfast, handed the mainsail soon after, and ran hard all day under foresail and headsails. At midnight hands were called to make sail, the wind having eased, and before turning in we hung up our Christmas stockings. Sure enough some seafaring Father Christmas boarded us in the early hours. After breakfast we displayed our various gifts and even smoked the cigars found among them. Our Christmas dinner we had decided to defer until lying in some snug anchorage at Kerguelen. A few days later, while Warwick was cooking breakfast, a big wave struck us and the resulting lurch flung him right across the saloon. He was cushioned to some extent by landing on me but he hurt his back and was out of action for that day. Except for the loss overboard of a lifebuoy we suffered no damage on deck. After this we built a strong pen round the stove for we could not afford to have the cook thrown about.

On 31 December, only some 150 miles from Kerguelen, we ran fast all day before a big following sea. At midnight most of us joined the watch on deck to see the New Year in with song and the ringing of bells, and early on 1 January, 1965, we sighted Iles Nuageuses at the north-west corner of Kerguelen. The surprise shown by the crew at this precise landfall was, I thought, a little uncalled for. Later we sighted the isolated rock Bligh's Cap, now called Ilot du Rendezvous, which is twelve miles north-west of Cap d'Estaing on the main island. The rock was named by Cook after William Bligh – 'Breadfruit' Bligh of the *Bounty* – who was sailing master in the *Resolution* on Cook's third and last voyage. The discoverer of Kerguelen was not Cook but a Breton nobleman Kerguelen-Trémarac who sighted the island in 1772. Thinking that he had discovered the great southern continent upon which the explorers and geographers at that time were so intent, Trémarac hurried home to report his discovery in glowing terms. Having merely sighted some land he rashly concluded that he had proved the generally held theory that there must be a large land mass in the southern hemisphere to balance the preponderance of land in the northern hemisphere. The next year, with three vessels, he was sent to explore the new continent which he had named South France. The smallness and the uselessness of his discovery soon became apparent and Trémarac had to sail home to acknowledge his mistake. There is a story that in his disappointment he renamed the island 'Desolation', but this is the name given to it by Cook when he visited it in 1776, unaware that it had been discovered four years before.

The island is about ninety miles long and its coastline is remarkable for the number of great bays and fjords reaching far inland, so much so that nowhere on the island is more than twelve miles from salt water. The eastern side is comparatively flat while the west is mountainous and has an ice-cap of some extent known as Glacier Cook, the ice-cap that two of us crossed when we were at Kerguelen in *Mischief* in 1960. From it several glaciers descend to the sea. The coast of Kerguelen was well known to the hundreds of whalers and sealers who visited it in the course of the last century. In 1843, for instance, there were said to be 500 such ships at work on the coast. But these men generally kept their own counsel. The first extensive hydrographic survey was by the French explorer J. B. Charcot in 1913–14, accompanied by Raymond Rallier du Baty. The latter had already spent a year on Kerguelen in 1908 when he sailed there with his brother and four Breton fishermen in the small ketch *J. B. Charcot*. Raymond du Baty's account of this voyage, *Fifteen Thousand Miles in a Ketch*, is one of the best sea adventure stories ever written. A striking thing about this book is that it was written in English and published in England and is unknown in France. In 1960 at the French base in Kerguelen no one had so much as heard of it. 'A prophet is not without honour, except in his own country.' One of my treasured possessions is an autographed copy of the book which I received very recently from Raymond du Baty himself.

Even as late as 1908 the big bay on the north coast known as Baie des Baleiniers was swarming with whales. In 1909 a French-Norwegian company established a whaling station at Port Jeanne d'Arc which was abandoned only in 1929. The island then relapsed into its normally deserted state until in the Second World War three German raiders used it as a base for raids upon shipping in the Indian Ocean. This incident, together with a realization of the importance of the island as a weather station and possibly a future air base, stirred the French government into activity. In 1949 an expedition of fourteen men reconnoitred a site and in the following year a weather station and scientific base was installed. Port aux Français at the south-east end of the island has since increased both in size and scope. In the last three years complete surveys both of Kerguelen and Iles Crozet have been made and maps published.

Before leaving for Australia I had corresponded with the 'Bureau des Terres Australes et Antarctiques' in Paris to warn them that in the event of our not finding a safe anchorage at Heard Island we should like to bring *Patanela* to Port aux Français; which was, of course, agreed. But we did not want to go there *before* proceeding to Heard Island. What we wanted was a quiet anchorage, free from social distractions, where we could put in a couple of days hard work preparing the stores and equipment for landing on Heard Island. The place I had in mind was Baie du Recques, a few miles south of Christmas Harbour, and the last thing we wanted to see at that moment were Frenchmen, admirable hosts as they are.

Upon rounding Cap d'Estaing we could see the Bird Table, an unmistakable flat-topped mountain near Cook's Christmas Harbour. He had landed there on Christmas Day 1776 unaware that it had already been named Baie de l'Oiseau after the name of one of the frigates in Kerguelen-Trémarac's squadron. The *Antarctic Pilot* does not recommend Christmas Harbour and for that reason we avoided it: 'Good ground tackle is necessary as squalls blow with tremendous violence down the valley at the head of the harbour. In 1939 the *Bougainville* dragged her anchor while lying in this bay.' In 1840 Ross with *Erebus* and *Terror* had remained there from May to July carrying out magnetic observations. He called it a most dreary and disagreeable harbour and recorded gales on forty-five of the sixty-eight days he was there and only three without rain or snow. But that, of course, was in the southern winter.

We therefore carried on past the entrance to Christmas Harbour, admiring, as we went by, Pointe de l'Arche, a remarkable wall of rock originally forming an arch, though the top of the arch, the keystone as it were, has since collapsed. Suddenly, out of the blue, a helicopter appeared and proceeded to 'buzz' us. Were we being warned off or welcomed? And how did the French at Port aux Français, ninety miles away, whence we assumed the helicopter had come, know of our presence? Mulling over this strange happening we sailed on and turned into Baie du Recques where we met a strong head wind. It was late evening before we anchored in Ainsi du Jardin at the head of the fjord a cable's length off the shore. By then Warwick had our delayed Christmas dinner well under way and presently all ten of us squeezed into the saloon, overflowing up the steps leading to the wheel-house, to begin some serious eating and drinking – savoury, soup, roast beef and Yorkshire pudding, the whole screwed down by a monumental duff.

The mystery of the helicopter was resolved next morning when it appeared again high to the south and having spotted us landed nearby on an impossibly small, flat bit of ground. Russ who already had the rubber rafts in the water went to fetch off the five occupants. Only a fortnight before, a small summer base had been established at Christmas Harbour whence with the help of two helicopters a geological survey of the west end of the island was in hand. They had been as much astonished at the sight of *Patanela* sailing by as we had been by the helicopter, and they had expected us to see their two huts there and go in. We explained that we would be fully occupied for the next two days but promised to lunch with them the day we left.

Having watched our lively visitors soar into the air we went back to work. The bunks in the cray-tank had to be partially uprooted so that the oil from the drums underneath could be pumped into the main bunkers. Food and equipment for the shore party had to be broken out and made up into loads, and all the rigging overhauled. Thanks to a fine day we broke the back of the work. Overnight the weather changed. We woke to a day of rain and violent squalls and made the unwelcome discovery that we had dragged our anchor. The cliffs beyond the beach, down which a waterfall cascaded, which should have provided a good lee, merely acted as a wind shute. We anchored again as close to the shore as we dared, seeking to avoid the willy-waws which struck down from the cliffs whipping the water white.

Oiling having been finished and the cray-tank restored to order we wanted to erect the tents on shore and to give the eighteen-foot USR raft a trial run. Except that we were in sheltered water the weather conditions would make the trials realistic. The loaded raft with five on board went off down the fjord in search of rougher water. As I watched them through binoculars, the craft half hidden by spray as it bounced violently over the short waves, I felt relieved when they at last headed back for the ship. In the afternoon the wind still blowing and the rain hissing down, four of us took the raft to visit a wreck lying on the opposite shore. Besides satisfying our curiosity we wanted a few pieces of heavy timber. She had been a schooner, not much bigger than *Patanela*, the main mast in a tabernacle, and probably a Breton schooner judging by the word *St. Malo* which could be read on the single cylinder Bollinder engine. The type of engine indicated that she had been built early in the century. She was for the most part buried in sand but we prised off some lengths of sound timber. Launching off in shallow water and breakers was a tricky business and at the first attempt we sheared off the pin of the propeller. Russ had a spare in the tool kit and when we finally got off we went back to the beach by the anchorage to see how the tent-erecting party were faring. One tent, one of these new-fangled, pole-less affairs, depending for rigidity upon being pumped up, might have been all right on the Lido but was obviously out of place on Heard Island or even Kerguelen. Inside the big pyramid tent, which we entered with difficulty through the sleeve entrance, we found a slightly disconsolate party sitting counting the drips. We had now only to water ship. Standing in the mouth of the stream below the waterfall we filled the USR raft by means of buckets; Russ then drove it back to the ship where they pumped the water out of the raft into the main tank. Finally the tents were struck, both rafts deflated and stowed, and we sat down to a well-earned supper. In two days, in spite of the vile weather on one of them, we had got the work done and were ready for Heard Island.

At Kerguelen fine days are few and perfect days are memorably rare. In 1960 on the ice-cap we had enjoyed four such days in a row, days when the snow at 3,000ft. turned to slush and when the reflected heat and glare almost brought us to a standstill. Now, on 4 January, when we visited the French at Christmas Harbour, we enjoyed another such day, calm, cloudless, warm. After waiting a bit to dry the tents we sailed at 10 am and at noon motored past the rock arch into the harbour. At one or two places the steam rising from the drying ground had all the appearance of a hot spring. As our anchor went down two sportsmen paddled out to welcome us on a crazy raft of oil drums, while rockets, Verey lights, and cheers went up from the party on the beach. Confident that on this bright, windless day *Patanela* could safely be left, all hands went ashore in the rubber raft to make the tour of the base – two huts, two tents, two helicopters, and three wine barrels. A long table had been contrived outside and presently some twenty of us sat down to what the French – and we, too, for that matter – regarded as serious business. After some shots of cassis and hors d'oeuvres we embarked on the main course, rabbit stewed in wine, cooked to such perfection that it might have been mistaken for chicken.

Rabbits are plentiful, too plentiful, on Kerguelen, as are sea elephants and several kinds of penguin. None of the latter shared our meal but a flock of skuas and sheathbills soon gathered round the table. One of the helicopter pilots, with a skill evidently born of long practice, caught a skua and administered what the French call a 'coup de Scotch'. The effect was remarkably sudden. Flying was out of the question, even standing became difficult, while the other skuas hungrily awaited its expected demise. Skuas, looking like ill-favoured scavenger crows, are not likeable birds, otherwise one could have been sorry for it. Towards four o'clock, for it had been a protracted lunch, both the weather and the guests showed signs of change, of impending dissolution. Once more we sang the *Marseillaise*, Grahame playing the accompaniment on his recorder while lying under the table, then arm-in-arm we went down to the beach, a swaying picture of international fellowship. The sails went up with a will, albeit a little raggedly, and as we swung round to face the entrance the oil drum raft launched off, more Verey lights soared up, and both helicopters took off to zoom dangerously round our masts. In gathering cloud we got clear of the coast before the wind died and left us tossing in a cross sea in rain and darkness.

CHAPTER SIXTEEN

Heard Island and Port aux Français

THE STRONG north-west wind that presently got up enabled us next evening to round Cape Digby at the north-east corner of the island. There, on the lee side of the island, we had smooth water and ran fast all night down the east coast. By daylight Kerguelen was out of sight. The cold now became more appreciable, the sea temperature 39°F. and the air 43°, for we had now crossed what is called the antarctic convergence where there is an upwelling of cold water. At 8 am of the 7th, fine, sunny, and windy, we were some ninety miles from Heard Island and early that afternoon, when we were still sixty miles away, we sighted Big Ben. There was no mistaking the characteristic lenticular cloud sitting over the summit and below it the glint of white snow slopes. That evening we sailed close by the McDonald Islands, three barren rocks, steep-to all round. No one has yet landed on them and it was in our minds to make an attempt. For this we needed a calm sea and the sea at this time was far from calm. The islands are some thirty miles west of Heard Island and in a freshening wind we ran towards it at five knots until midnight when we hove to about ten miles short of Winston Lagoon.

In 1962 the ANARE ship on its way to Mawson, the Australian Antarctic base, had landed on Heard Island a party of four which included Warwick Deacock and Grahame Budd. In the course of an attempt on Big Ben, after putting a camp at 4,000ft. they had been driven down by snow and gales. The route they had then taken, starting from Winston Lagoon, had appeared most promising, and on this account Winston Lagoon or its vicinity had been chosen as the place to put the present party ashore. Moreover, we entertained a faint hope that we might take *Patanela* into the lagoon itself where not only could a landing be easily made but where *Patanela* might safely remain while the party were on the mountain. There was no sheltered anchorage elsewhere. Even at Atlas Cove at the north-west end of the island where the Australians had their base, one would need to be in constant readiness to clear out at short notice.

By next morning the wind had died and except that the glass was falling conditions for a landing seemed fair. When we anchored in five fathoms about a quarter-mile off the lagoon the wind showed signs of stirring but fortunately from offshore. We had envisaged sending a raft in to the lagoon to take soundings but we had not to worry long about that. Even with the slight swell then running the water broke white right across the entrance, and seaward of the shingle spit that almost enclosed the lagoon huge boulders showed above the water. Both rafts were inflated and launched, one to be used as a stand-by rescue launch, and the loads got on deck. The breaking water on the bar discouraged any idea of taking even a raft in but west of the lagoon was a small beach where we could see some sea elephants and a penguin rookery. From the beach access could easily be had to the ridge called the South Barrier and so on to the mountain.

At that moment a raft might have got ashore but in order to establish the shore party for a month two trips would have to be made and the unloading and reloading would take some time. Before committing ourselves we waited a bit for the weather to declare its intentions. We did not have to wait long. The wind quickly rose to gale force. The strain on the cable proved too much for the electric winch so we got the anchor by hand and let the boat drift off shore. The wind had settled at north-west and when about a mile out we got the parachute anchor overboard in the hope of stopping or lessening the inevitable easterly drift. All along we had been at great pains to get to windward of the island and to stay there, to avoid at all costs having to beat back to recover it. The anchor held us almost stationary for nearly an hour until under the combined weight of wind and boat it gave way. The fitting between the anchor chain and the nylon parachute cords parted and although we re-rigged it with more shackles we finally had to haul it in and resign ourselves to drifting eastwards.

Hove to on the port tack we drifted to the south-east for the best part of two days until the wind moderated enough for us to begin motoring. A sight at noon of the 11th put us fifteen miles nearer the island than I expected, our total drift having been only about forty miles. Soon we sighted the island and at the same time the wind increased again to nearly gale force. But we had the island in sight and this time we were determined not to let go of it. We plugged on until we had gained the lee of the east side of the island and by evening were anchored off the Compton Glacier. Except that it afforded shelter from any wind between north-west and south-west the anchorage had few charms. True we could see the snow slopes and ridges of the mountain, but shorewards, instead of a beach, we beheld merely black ice cliffs about 100ft. high. The Compton Glacier extends into the sea and owing to the amount of debris it carries the ice is more black than white. To the south of us, where is Spit Bay, we could make out the seas breaking on the low gravel spit which extends sea-wards to the east for five miles.

This spit which protects Spit Bay and the east coast of the island from southerly winds lay between us and Winston Lagoon. To round it and reach the lagoon we had about twenty-five miles to go and in order to be there in good time we started soon after 3 am on the 12th. Owing to the swell left by the recent strong winds the sea breaking on the bar across the lagoon looked worse than it had three days before. We anchored off the small beach while Warwick, who had to make the decision, gazed long and earnestly at the surf.

The decision made, no time was lost in loading the raft and at 11 am it started for the beach with the five men of the shore party, Colin driving. In case of mishap Russ stood by with the Zodiac raft which by now was less seaworthy than one would wish. The rest of us watched their progress with anxiety as the heavily-laden craft vanished in the trough and reappeared on the top of the swell. Soon we saw them stop outside the breakers to await their opportunity. What happened in the few, critical moments among the breakers we were too far off to see but we were heartily glad when we next saw the raft being hauled up the beach.

Nearly an hour then elapsed before we were in contact with the shore party and learnt how they had fared, both ship and shore party being provided with 'Walky-Talky' sets. All had gone well until the raft capsized in shallow water at the edge of the beach with three of the party underneath it and the Johnson outboard still running. The load had been well secured so that nothing was lost but a camera, and since the party were wearing 'wet' suits they remained more or less warm in spite of their ducking. Warwick added that the surf was then too bad to launch off for the second trip. We agreed to wait until evening in the hope that it might go down.

We saw them put the tents up high above the beach and then early in the afternoon we heard that they were about to launch. This they achieved and Warwick with Colin came off for the second load of stores. All went well on the second trip and by 4 pm the shore party were safely established with a month's food and we had squared up on board and were ready to go. 11 February was the day appointed for our return. I wanted to pass round the west side of the island, a part we had not yet seen. But off Cape Lambeth only a mile to the west, the tents of the shore party still in view, we met a strong breeze while ahead of us stretched a long line of white water. No reef or spit lay in that direction, the water was being lashed by sudden and violent wind. We stood to the south to make an offing, handed the sails, and lay to under bare poles.

By next morning we were able to set the foresail and start sailing assisted by the engine. After a night of drifting we were not likely to fetch the west of the island and in due course the east coast showed up wide on our port bow. At noon, in bright sunshine we had Spit Point abeam. For the moment we were in calm water and in spite of being short-handed we hoisted all the sails hoping that the shore party would take note of this defiant gesture. A freshening wind soon made her too hard to hold. When the island disappeared that evening in a bank of fog we were once more under short canvas. Gales, sunshine, rain, and fog – we had had them all in the inside of a week. Happily, the vexed seas round Heard Island are free from ice and icebergs.

With a crew of five we had only one man on watch. Tony Hill, Russ Pardoe, Malcolm Hay, and I did two-hour watches, while Ed Reid who had the wireless to look after did the cooking. We missed Warwick. Ed positively liked food out of tins but he soon learnt to his dismay that his favourite, baked beans, was on the proscribed list. Ed's wireless transmissions, or attempted transmissions, took up a lot of time. We were a long way from anywhere, certainly too far from Australia to make contact. The news that the party had landed on Heard Island went by way of Mawson in the Antarctic. Some of his messages went by way of Cape Town and one by Singapore.

With Kerguelen lying 300 miles to the north-west, that is to windward, I expected a hard passage. In fact, with moderate winds, and those generally from west or south of west, we had no trouble. On the evening of the third day we sighted Presqu'île Monarch at the south-east end of the island and next day we were motoring against a strong head wind up the broad Baie de Morbihan. This bay has many ramifications and Port aux Français, the French base, lies up in its north-eastern corner in what is probably the most exposed part. The bay is big enough to provide a long 'fetch' so that in a hard gale there may be waves two to three feet high outside Port aux Français. Its saving grace is a patch of kelp across the entrance, thus the small piece of water inside remains pretty smooth even in a gale. Since *Mischief*'s visit in 1960 three mooring buoys for three landing craft have been laid. There is therefore not much room left for anchoring and none at all for dragging.

We had timed our arrival to a nicety. When the 'Chef de Mission' came on board to welcome us he announced that lunch was on the table. Jeeps took us the few hundred yards from the little concrete jetty to the common messroom where the odd hundred men and one woman who then comprised the base were already seated. Amidst a great welcoming uproar of cheers and banging on the table we took our seats. We had an undeniably excellent meal, a meal such as only Frenchmen could produce on what is a desert island if you exclude innumerable rabbits and the quarter million sea elephants and a million penguins that inhabit the flat beaches of the east coast. I noticed my companions going at it hammer and tongs, Malcolm having a slight edge on the others, but to me it lacked the relish and refinement of our first meal here in 1960 when M. Perrimond presided over the cuisine. Or perhaps then, after the Spartan fare of *Mischief*, I was in a more appreciative mood than now after weeks of high living in *Patanela*.

As coffee was being served the whole assembly began chanting a refrain 'Cognac, Odot, Cognac Odot, Cognac!' I grasped the significance when after about five minutes of chanting M. Odot rose to his feet and produced his keys and presently the brandy began to circulate. He was the quartermaster, intendant, or steward, a short, stout man with an imperial, far more respectably dressed than anyone else. The chanting then began again: 'Cigar, Odot, cigar Odot, cigar!' and once more M. Odot complied, and cigars were handed round. Perhaps the presence of guests made him more amenable. Once more the chanting broke out: 'Merci beaucoup, merci beaucoup, merci!'

After lunch we made a tour of the base, visiting the various huts where extremely intricate machines were ticking away day and night recording upon reams of paper whatever they were recording – obscure phenomena from the ionosphere or maybe the stratosphere. Their earnest, bearded attendants explained to me what each was doing. After the lunch we had had I was not in a receptive mood. My French being little and my knowledge of science less, I felt that they might as well have addressed their remarks to the moulting King penguin that I had observed standing forlorn and disconsolate by the flag-staff outside the messroom. Aided by the woman scientist who spoke some English

I found the launching site for hydrogen balloons slightly more intelligible. While on our way in we had remarked the huge screen erected for protecting the balloons while being inflated and had mistaken it for a block of flats. In connection with the balloons, a mast seventy metres high was in process of erection, a considerable feat of engineering in view of the rocky ground and the force of the winds it had to withstand.

I was surprised at how few of the French, several of them very learned men, spoke any English, far more surprising than the fact that only one of us far-from-learned men spoke any French. Russ and Malcolm could sometimes be heard uttering what they thought might be French, but Tony who had spent a year studying in Paris spoke it pretty fluently and acted as interpreter. The base had expanded considerably since 1960 when the personnel numbered only seventy against 120, though we were told that in winter only about thirty are left there. And besides the new base at Christmas Harbour, a base had been established on Ile de la Possession in the Crozet group at Baie du Navire, the anchorage where we had spent a fortnight in *Mischief*. I was told that a 'téléferique' now passed directly over the King penguin rookery through which we had so often fought our way – a piece of news that decided me to write off Baie du Navire as a place to be revisited.

Another change that had taken place was the closing down of the plant for extracting oil from sea elephants – they had, of course, first been slaughtered. This had been run by a private company which had permission to kill up to 2,000 annually. The late manager of this, a tall, fair Frenchman speaking excellent English, known as the Viscount (and I believe he was a Viscount) was marooned at Port aux Français with neither instructions, money, nor even a passage home. We had thoughts of taking him to Australia but before we left we heard that a passage for him had been arranged.

We had arrived on a Saturday when they had their weekly film show. Before attending we went back on board to change our anchor. The Breton boatswain in charge of all the craft, a man who answered my ideas of a real Frenchman – black hair and moustache, red-faced, stout, with a very loud, hoarse voice – did not think our anchor man enough and loaned us a much heavier, stockless anchor. On this anchor we lay quietly enough till the Monday when I thought it time to move on. We had more than a fortnight to put in before our Heard Island rendezvous and did not wish to trespass for so long on French hospitality. On the Sunday they had insisted on our having all our meals ashore and for our part we had needed little pressing. As no doubt they would have done at home, they devoted Sunday to 'la chasse', most of the garrison setting out heavily armed and returning at dusk either with nothing or perhaps a scrawny rabbit.

With difficulty we persuaded the Chef de Mission and some of the hier-archy to visit us on board for drinks. In the end we mustered quite a crowd. Having given them all their 'coup de Scotch' I noticed they were not drinking very heartily and when I took a swig myself I understood why. I had given them whisky and sea water. While they were on board I explained to the Chef de Mission that we would like to spend some time at Port Jeanne d'Arc to which he agreed and at once began organizing things to ensure our enjoying our stay there. From my point of view the chief attraction of Port Jeanne d'Arc lay in the fact that there was a vacant mooring buoy which we could use. Anchoring at Port aux Français was too much like anchoring at a place mentioned in an *Admiralty Pilot*, of which it remarks: 'Anchoring in this bight must be prompted by necessity and not by any hope of tranquillity.'

CHAPTER SEVENTEEN

Port Jeanne d'Arc, Heard Island and Sydney

ON THE Monday morning we found awaiting us on the quay a whole barrel of wine. I asked to be allowed to take only a couple of jerry-cans. We all liked our 'coups de rouge', or 'plonk' as the Australians called it, but I felt we would make little impression on a barrel. With us we had the Breton boatswain as pilot, three men whom we were to drop at Ile Longue where the French run a flock of 700 sheep, and two climbers, both good chaps known to us as Jacques and Claude. They were to show us round Port Jeanne d'Arc and its neighbourhood.

We motored all the way, the trip taking about six hours, including an hour's delay at Ile Longue to effect the relief of the shepherds. From this flock came the mutton we had been eating so heartily over the week-end, mutton that combined the sweetness of the mountain, the fat of the valley, and the tang of the saltings. According to our Breton friend the narrow pass at the north end of Ile Longue contained mines. A German raider that had used Port Jeanne d'Arc during the war had laid them and they were reputedly still there. No one professed to believe seriously in these mines but I noticed that as we passed through the suspected area everyone on board gathered in the after part of the ship. We secured to the buoy at 6 pm and settled down to a cheerful evening entertaining our French guests.

The remains of the whaling station at Port Jeanne d'Arc that had been in use from 1909 to 1929 are still substantial – huge wooden flensing platforms, whale-boats, boilers, vats, storage tanks, a wooden jetty with a light railway, blacksmith's shop, carpenter's shop, and two separate barracks. Part of the barracks are still habitable and are used by the French who, during the season of winter gales, launch their hydrogen balloons from Port Jeanne d'Arc instead of from Port aux Français. Thus the balloons have a chance of gaining height before passing over Port aux Français 20 miles to leeward. The helicopter arrived next morning to take back the Breton boatswain and to allow the Chef de Mission to inspect Port Jeanne d'Arc. Meantime Claude and Jacques had established themselves in the barracks and were busy cooking lunch for us. Quite rightly they believed in living on the country. They had shot a rabbit in the doorway and had a big pot of mussels boiling over a fire outside. They had brought bread with them and the barracks kitchen was fully stocked with tinned food and a barrel of wine.

In the afternoon we walked up Dome Rouge (1,150ft.), a bare stony ridge where winter snow still lay in drifts. Returning by the shore of the fjord we put up some duck and a brace of these rather scraggy birds was duly shot for supper. We came upon some sea elephants enjoying their two or three months' repose and a few stray King penguins. This handsome bird, next in size to the Emperor penguin, with blueish grey back and white breast, has a bright orange patch on the side of the head merging with a similar band at the neck. The two Frenchmen and three of us were to make an excursion to the lower slopes of Mt Ross (6,430ft.) the highest peak of Kerguelen. Claude and Jacques talked of starting at 4 am but in the course of the evening, helped by some 'coups de Scotch' they became more reasonable. Russ, Malcolm and Ed went off to the ship to pack their rucksacks before returning ashore where they were to sleep. For ship-to-shore transport we had now only a two-man rubber dinghy so that the ferrying business took some time. It was long after midnight before Tony and I got back on board.

We did not rise very early, nevertheless, as I had suspected, we were in time to see the climbing party shoulder its burdens and slouch off. Two days later they returned, very late in the evening and tired. They slept at the barracks where Tony and I most unwisely joined them for a continental breakfast. Coffee and rolls are very well, but we found them drinking Ovomaltine and eating sweet cake. This was not only revolting but annoying because we now had fresh bread on board. With our gas oven and some dried yeast it had been simple enough to make. I rather fancy myself as a master baker but Malcolm, fired by my example, soon took it out of my hands, and began turning out better bread and in addition spice buns. With only five on board baking need not be quite incessant. Henceforth, until we had re-embarked the shore party, we enjoyed bread every day.

The following Saturday a landing craft brought a large party of visitors including two more climbers. With them, Tony and Malcolm left that after-noon to have a look at Mt Ross. Tempted though I was I did not feel happy about leaving the ship. We had had one hard blow on a day when Tony and I had been ashore separately. Arriving back first I had been horrified to see the staysail, which had not been properly secured, flapping madly half-way up the stay. The rubber dinghy had not blown away, for we always weighted it down with stones, but having paddled a short way out I came back. There seemed to me to be every chance of missing the ship and being blown down the fjord, or of grabbing the ship and losing the dinghy. The line which we had rigged between ship and shore in anticipation of such happenings had been sub-merged in kelp. Even when Tony came back we had to wait for the fiercest squalls to subside before we could go on board to secure the sail.

On a fine, clear day I went a long walk to the head of Baie Swain whence Mt Ross showed up well. There are two summits to this fine snow peak, the smaller appearing fairly simple and the main peak extremely difficult. I met several elephant seals and King penguins. The latter seemed to be moulting and in that state preferred the company of a sea elephant to that of their fellows. A sea elephant lay in a mud wallow, only its eyes and mouth showing, while a King penguin stood a foot from its mouth in deep meditation. On the way back I approached this sea elephant to stir it up, and when it opened its mouth wide and bellowed so ferociously that involuntarily I started back, the penguin never so much as moved.

The climbing party were away four days during which Ross, Ed, and I amused ourselves cooking, collecting mussels, baking bread, and playing chess. Grahame had taken his pocket chess set with him but Ed had carved some pieces with which we had a lot of fun. We were all much in the same class, a pretty low class, and defeats were not taken to heart. On 31 January the landing craft came to retrieve the Frenchmen and on the following day we ourselves set out for Port aux Français. It was already blowing very hard as we approached the anchorage where, we had been told, there was now a vacant buoy, one of the landing craft having been slipped for repairs. Three times we tried and failed to pass a warp through the shackle on the buoy, the wind increasing all the time. Rather than anchor there I thought we should be safer in the lee of Point Molloy a few miles away. There is a hut there and two leading lights to show the anchorage. We set an anchor watch. In the course of the night the gale increased and both the land and the light became obscured in pitch blackness. It was therefore difficult to tell whether or not we were holding. At 4 am a resounding bang on the keep brought all hands on deck with a rush. We were close inshore among kelp. Within a minute we had the engine going and after a few more bumps got into deeper water. We motored back under the Point, dropped anchor, and at once drifted away fast, the wind blowing as hard as ever. Three times we anchored in different places and each time the anchor wrapped itself in kelp on the way down and failed to hold. At the fourth attempt we succeeded.

We remained there while the wind blew itself out and on the next day secured to the buoy at Port aux Français where we learnt that during the gale gusts of Force 10 had been registered. Using his Aqua-lung Russ examined our hull and reported no damage. We dined ashore, watched an amusing film of life at the base, and agreed to have lunch ashore next day before sailing for Heard Island. It was another windy day. The confidence that we had expressed at lunch and had still felt as we went down to the quay, had waned by the time we climbed on board. The Breton boatman took us off, and in spite of the comparative calm behind the sheltering kelp we had a job getting ourselves and our belongings – gifts of food and drink – from the launch on to *Patanela*. To leave in such conditions, when a failure of the engine or a mistake in casting off would at once put us in danger of hitting a landing craft or the rocky beach, seemed unwise and was not necessary. We still had six days in which to reach Heard Island. We waited, and in consequence spent another anxious night. How I wished we had been safely at sea instead of lying to a buoy in cramped surroundings with a gale blowing! It seemed to blow harder than it had two nights before and here we had no sheltering land close to windward. We doubled the chain to the buoy and remained on deck though we could do little except pray that the buoy would not budge. At 3 am, when the wind showed signs of moderating, we turned in.

After a late breakfast we sailed and went so fast that by noon next day we had only 150 miles to go. We hove to that night and remained hove to all next day while it blew hard from north-east, the barometer high and steady at 29.5. On the 8th we were drawing near the island and since we preferred to be at sea rather than at some uneasy anchorage we hove to well west of the McDonald Islands. Early next morning we let draw in a rough sea and high wind at south-west. As we closed the north-west end of the island the weather became more violent, squalls accompanied by sleet and rain lashing us in rapid succession. Under bare poles, chased by huge following seas, we shot past Red Island at three knots. Atlas Cove and Corinthian Bay, two of Heard Island's supposedly better anchorages, were mere sheets of foam where frequent willy-waws swept the water high into the air. It was a boisterous welcome.

Once past Rogers Head we could set the staysail but not until we were off Compton Glacier did we find any sort of a lee. Further round still we went to anchor off Skua Beach in Spit Bay in seven fathoms. Although on the next day, 10 February, we would be a day ahead of schedule we did not think the shore party would take it amiss if we gave them the chance to come off. Accordingly we started at 6 am to motor round the Spit to the landing beach. We were relieved to see the tents there and at length a moving figure, though it seemed to us that they took our arrival very calmly. In fact it created so little stir that we began to wonder if they were all there or even all alive. After a tense hour Warwick came on the air and we listened in awe-struck silence to a remarkable bulletin. He had not forgotten his army training: 'Shore party to *Patanela*, Shore party to *Patanela* [could it be anyone else?]; the ascent of Big Ben has been accomplished; all the aims of the expedition have been achieved.' Whereupon Tony grabbed the set from Ed and asked Warwick to give us his news in Australian.

All the party were well and all five had stood on top of Big Ben. This was what we wanted to hear. Meantime they were more than ready to come off but the surf was bad. We said we would wait until 6 pm. We should have to go back to Spit Bay to anchor and wanted to round the Spit before dark. I doubt if the surf had gone down much when at 5 pm they decided to try. Of course by next day the surf might have been as bad or worse, nevertheless, looking back, I regret that we did arrive a day early. The fact that we were there waiting no doubt persuaded them to try when conditions were not good enough. They got off without mishap but at the cost of leaving behind all personal gear and all the expensive equipment. They had climbed Big Ben but I felt that the island had had the last word.

Late that evening we got under way and headed south to clear the Spit. The ice of Winston glacier, its black moraine, and the little landing beach below, faded in the gathering gloom as we drew rapidly away, leaving Heard Island to relapse into its customary solitude. A solitude that seems unlikely to be broken for some time, for now that the mountain has been climbed there is little left to be done. Great is the incentive of profit but even if the elephant seals again become plentiful there, I doubt if in these days of ease anyone would be found willing to emulate the men who sailed to Heard Island a hundred years ago. In ships not much bigger than *Patanela*, men returned to this forbidding island year after year as a matter of course; when small parties would leave the comparative comfort of their ships to live on the beaches for six months or even a year in rough huts built of stones and bits of driftwood, cold, squalid, subsisting on seal meat and blubber like so many castaways.

The following notes on the sealers of last century have been sent me by my friend Mr Barnes, curator at the Mariners Museum, Newport News.

The *Roman*, 350 tons, sailed from New London on June 24th, 1870, to Heard Island and returned May 3rd, 1871, with 1,500 barrels of sea-elephant oil. She sailed again on June 26th the same year and returned June 9th, 1872, with another 1,518 barrels, as well as 21 barrels of sperm oil. Her third voyage from July 16th, 1872, to March 31st, 1873, resulted in 1,225 barrels of oil, and on a fourth voyage from May, 1873, to April, 1874, she again brought back 1,440 barrels of sea-elephant oil and some whale bone.

A smaller vessel, the schooner *Roswell King*, 97 tons, sailed from New London on June 29th, 1870, for Heard Island and returned with 1,750 barrels of sea-elephant oil on April 26th, 1873. She sailed again on August 5th, 1873, and returned April 29th, 1875, with only 55 barrels.

Sir Joseph Hooker, referring to his landing on Heard Island in 1842 when he was on Sir James Ross's Antarctic expedition as botanist, wrote: 'We saw six sealers; two were Americans and two Portuguese from the Cape Verde Islands. They were left on the island by the whaling vessels we met with at Kerguelen, their duty to hunt sea-elephants. The men engaged to remain three years on the island, and see the whale ships only for a short time in the spring of the year.'

A naturalist on the *Challenger* expedition 1872–76 wrote: 'There are said to be 40 men on Heard Island. Men occasionally get lost upon the glaciers. Sometimes a man gets desperate from being in so miserable a place, and one whaler that we met at Kerguelen said, after he had had some rum, that occasionally men had to be shot: a statement which may be true or false, but which expresses at all events the feeling of the men. But they had good clothing and did not look particularly dirty. They lived in wooden huts, or rather under roofs built over holes in the ground. Around the huts were oil casks and a hand barrow for wheeling blubber about. Their principle food was penguins and they used penguin skins with the fat on for fuel. Captain Nares saw five such skins piled on the fire one after the other.'

Our castaways looked none the worse for their month on the island, though we gathered that it had not been altogether a picnic. Having established a camp at 4,000ft. they waited for several days for a quiet spell, determined to do the remaining 5,000ft. in one jump. When their chance came they started very early and were all on top by midday, but they had hardly had time to look around and to examine the crater (Big Ben is a volcanic mountain) when the weather broke with its customary suddenness. In wind and driving snow they had had some difficulty in finding their way down. Besides climbing the mountain they had spent time surveying, collecting, and making counts of the sea-elephant and penguin colonies – colonies that are recovering but slowly from the ravages inflicted by the sealers of the previous century.

In the first week after leaving the island we ran over 1,000 miles. Homeward bound, with a good ship under us, we did not care how hard the following gale. Even when under only staysail and foresail she reeled off the miles and if the gale moderated we hoisted the reefed mainsail. On 14

February the crew obstinately refused to let me stand my watches (it was the skipper's birthday), and to have all night in at sea is about as nice a present as a man could wish. By the 20th we were already up to Lat. 41°S. and the brave westerlies showed signs of faltering. Indeed, on the next day when still 500 miles out from Albany we were reduced to motoring – but not for long. We stopped the engine for all hands to bathe and we had lunch again on deck.

Two days later, eighteen days out from Heard Island, we picked up the Eclipse Island light and early that morning were fast alongside at our old berth at Albany. After taking on oil and water we sailed next day for Sydney. We were in a hurry. Having never taken part in ocean racing, and having generally preferred comfort to speed when cruising, I found it a salutary experience to be asked to make Sydney in thirteen days. In common with most expeditions nowadays we were under obligations to the Press and it was at the request of *The Australian* newspaper that we aimed to be off Sydney Heads at 9 am on 14 March, a Sunday. By using the engine we could do it easily but there were limits to what we were prepared to endure and we hoped to be able to sail most of the time.

We made good progress across the Bight until on 5 March, during a heavy squall, when we were trying to reef, something let go with a bang. At first I thought the mainsail had split. Having got the sail down we discovered that a lug at the foremast head holding up the starboard shrouds had broken. We had to lower all but the staysail, yet so strong was the wind that we did four knots for the rest of the day and part of the night. Three days later we put into Portland behind Cape Wilson and anchored in the roads. We put a length of chain round the masthead to which we shackled the shrouds, and at the same time transferred seven drums of fuel from the cray-tank to the bunkers. At this point we had logged 10,000 miles and we took time off to celebrate this with a superlative curry before getting under way again at 10 pm.

The next night we passed Wilson's Promontory. Although the night was clear and cloudless the smoke from bush fires then raging in south and south-eastern parts of Australia made the lights difficult to spot at even half their normal range. Having passed Gabo Island and turned north we lost the wind and for the first time in the voyage the engine chose to misbehave. The thermostat stopped working and everything came to the boil. It seemed highly probable that the reception committee off Sydney Heads were going to be disappointed but at that moment a breeze made itself felt and rapidly strengthened. Soon we were fairly romping up the coast.

We arrived off the Heads two hours too soon and jilled about until some launches appeared when we went in and met them. This time a berth had been arranged for us at the Motor Yacht Club, a club with magnificent premises and a slightly decrepit jetty which I nearly knocked for six on coming alongside. Among the welcoming and admiring crowd – their admiration no doubt diminished by this unseamanlike finish to the voyage – were the owners of *Patanela*, the Hunt brothers, delighted to see her back and to have such good accounts of her from us.

In his famous description of a prize fight Hazlitt summed it up as 'a complete thing'. In my opinion, devoted as I am to both sea and mountains, to sailing and climbing, this expedition deserves to be so described. A long voyage, much of it in unfrequented waters, and at the end of it a remote, uninhabited island crowned with an unclimbed mountain. It was an enterprise that needed to be undertaken, one that I myself had shrunk from attempting, and that now, thanks to Warwick Deacock's initiative and drive, had at last been accomplished. From first to last we had been a happy party, each man pulling his full weight. I may have regretted not to have set foot even on Heard Island, much less on Big Ben, but that was implicit in the job I undertook. Besides enjoying every minute of it, I considered it a great privilege to be skipper of so fine a vessel and to sail with so eager, lively, and resolute a crew.

Part 4

East Greenland: Return Engagement
Mischief
June–September, 1965

CHAPTER EIGHTEEN

To Iceland

TEMPTING THOUGH it was to spend a month or two seeing Australia and New Zealand, I had at the back of my mind the thought of a return match with east Greenland. Defeat rankles. Our failure to reach our objective there in 1964 was reason enough for having another go in 1965. Having seen *Patanela* unloaded, cleaned up, and back in her owner's hands, I came home before the end of March in time to begin scratching around for a crew. 'Strenuousness is the immortal path,' as some sage has observed, 'sloth is the way of death.'

While on a quick visit to Lymington to inspect *Mischief* and to take home some of her rigging for overhaul, I had an assurance from 'Noddy' Wareham who had been with us the previous year, that he would like to come again. Then I had a letter from R. Bradley, a stranger, who hinted that he might be rash enough to volunteer. He kept a day-boat on the east coast and had a longing to make a deep-sea voyage. Like me he was well stricken in years and though at one time he had been a long distance cyclist he was no longer in racing trim. In view of this and the weight of *Mischief*'s gear he was not really up to work on deck and offered to come as cook. 'When they bring you the heifer be ready with the rope,' as I have quoted before. I took Bradley to Lymington to look at the boat and when we parted he said he would think about it. I therefore expected a refusal and was agreeably surprised when he wrote to say that he would come.

Brian Hill, a young man from Weymouth, I acquired through a friend of a friend. No stranger to the sea, he had worked as a hand on a small tug on a delivery voyage to S. America; moreover, he left me in no doubt, as some do, that he really meant business. I hoped to start towards the end of June a month later than usual, the idea being that by the time we arrived off east

Greenland ice conditions were likely to be easier. On another visit to Lymington in mid-May, when I still had only these three starters, I had an offer from Brian Thomas, a young shipwright apprentice in the boatyard. He was as strong as an ox and altogether a likely looking chap. These inroads of mine on the labour force of the Berthon Boatyard were not altogether welcome. It was not until the end of May, when I was becoming agitated, that I knew for certain that he and Noddy would both get leave.

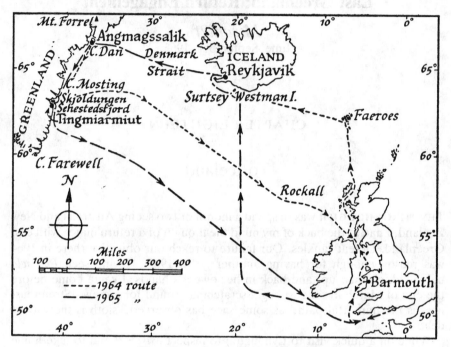

East Greenland, 1964 and 1965

As often happens, in the last week or so I had several offers and finally picked Brian Holloway (the third Brian), a young, footloose New Zealander. Many young people from overseas come to England to see Europe, to make the modern equivalent of the Grand Tour, very much on the cheap. They work at various odd jobs merely to make enough money to travel about. Young Holloway seemed to be living mainly on charm and hope. In a small van, accompanied by two girls and a cat, he called on me at Barmouth on the way back from a tour of Scotland. He had no commitments – except subsequently to one of the girls – and had cruised in a yacht from New Zealand to the South Sea islands, so I took him on, hoping he would prove as good as the New Zealanders we had had in *Patanela*. He was, besides the only one of the five who looked like being of use on a mountain. I had no climber. One whom I had hoped would be coming had been unable to make up his mind. Brian Holloway had done a lot of ski-ing but no mountaineering. The previous year, when we had three climbers on board, we had failed to reach our mountains, so that for a man who wanted to climb the prospects were too uncertain.

We began fitting out about 14 June and had to work hard to be ready by 25 June. The weather hindered us and neither Noddy nor Brian Thomas were immediately available. In the end we missed the morning tide of the 25th, having to wait for a reconditioned cabin heater to be installed, and for the Customs, our authority to draw bonded stores having been delayed. We were not sorry. For some days the shipping forecasts had been uniformly depressing, nothing but strong westerly winds and rain. Towards evening the weather seemed to improve a little and we decided to go. Accordingly at 5.30 pm in drizzle and a fresh south-west wind, we cast off and motored down the river. Having hoisted sail and made one board across the Solent in which we lost a little ground, I decided to anchor for the night in Yarmouth roads. With a strange crew, most of whom would probably be seasick, it would be no fun beating out at night into the Channel. At least we had made a start.

By morning the rain had stopped and the wind moderated. At 8 am we got our anchor and beat out past the Needles in good time to avoid being overrun by the two hundred-odd yachts setting out on the race round the island whose sails we could see far astern. So much for our departure as I saw it. But a friend, Mr W. G. Lee of Lymington, who observed it narrowly from Hurst Point, who shares my romantic notions of the sea and is better able to describe them, saw it thus:

Mischief moved slowly away from her anchorage into the fairway while a figure twice clambered out on to the bow-spit. She headed up into the freshening breeze while the jib was hoisted. Then the gaff could be seen to lift with the mainsail following, and with these sails set *Mischief* moved away on the port tack. After ten minutes or so she went about and beat across towards Yarmouth and then returned on a long tack to the Pennington side of the channel. I feared she was, in fact, putting back into Lymington for some reason, but eventually she went about again and thus confirmed her intention of putting to sea. Now on the starboard tack she sailed right across under the Island shore west of Sconce Point and made quite a bit of ground, but the next tack was across the last of the flood tide through the Narrows and she barely made any progress before finding herself close in under Hurst Point. Here she went about again, close under my position on the beach, to make a long beat through the narrow channel. Major Tilman was clearly visible at the helm and four of the crew on deck. A dark clad figure made his way out on the bow sprit as *Mischief*, meeting her first waves, plunged and reared a few times to remind him of his position.

She carried this tack past the NE Shingles buoy and passed inshore of the Warden buoy. It was now clear that the second headsail was due to go on, but there seemed to be some difficulty because Major Tilman left the helm and went forward to help. Meanwhile *Mischief* was forging ahead towards an inhospitable lee shore between Totland and Alum Bay. Then the bunt of the headsail could be seen and the ship bore off temporarily, as I thought, to free the sail in some way, but in the process heading directly inshore as though a novel ascent of Tennyson Down was intended. After a somewhat agonizing interval (at least for the observer from the other shore whose binoculars foreshortened the distance to give an entirely false impression) the second headsail went up and *Mischief* went about to stand into the regular channel.

All the time the wind was freshening and was such at Hurst Point that I could not keep my eye to my camera viewfinder for more than a few seconds before it watered intolerably and left me to guess what was in view. After one more tack inshore *Mischief* went away on a long tack to clear the Needles. As she beat out into the shipping lane the sea around and ahead was visibly rougher with a lot of white showing over the Shingle shoals. Near the Middle Shingles buoy she came on to the starboard tack which let the sun show off the full curve of her main, and showed up her headsails as taut triangles of light. Sailing thus on the horizon with her gaff rig and headsails emphasized, she reminded me of a nineteenth-century print – a lovely sight but a bit too distant to appreciate with the unaided eye.

On this tack she cleared the Needles but the glasses showed it to be an exciting stage of the passage, for where the seas lifted over the shoal between the Bridge buoy and the Island they were steep and confused. I clearly saw *Mischief*'s forefoot rise high in the air time and time again, and then her stern and counter as she plunged and lifted until she passed behind the lighthouse. In due course I caught sight of her again, hull down, but with her gaff still discernible, making hard progress due south, getting little help from the strong south-wester and none as yet from the west-going tide. And so I watched until it became a strain to see her at all and the time had come to turn for home. As I did so I casually glanced eastwards along the Solent and an amazing sight presented itself. It was as though a barricade had been thrown across the whole width from Bouldnor to the Beaulieu river as the two hundred and fifty yachts participating in the Round-the-Island race beat out towards Hurst and the Needles Channel. I became aware, too, of quite a crowd having collected along the beach. So here I was, at the crossroads, so to speak.

On the one hand I had a fleet in which teak and mahogany, nylon and terylene, glassfibre, tufnol, polyurethene, stainless steel, titanium, radio DF, echo sounders, remote reading anemometers, sophisticated electronics and all that ingenuity has yet devised, being harnessed for a circuit of the Isle of Wight, while hull down on the other hand was a 1906 working cutter with flax canvas, wooden blocks, hot dipped fittings, tarred seizings and scotsmen in her rigging, and thousands of sea miles behind her, bound for the ice floes of east Greenland. I wondered how many, if any, of the now swollen crowd, knew or cared. It may be that in one sense I was still as alone as Hurst Point as I had been nearly five hours ago. Curiosity held me there while the leading yachts came through, but I had made my choice, and with scarcely a glance at the approaching fleet I walked back along the shingle spit well rewarded for my morning vigil.

Outside the Needles the sea was still rough enough to make a camera of mine, kept on a shelf above my bunk, jump off, find its way out of the cabin, to finish up in the bilge near the engine. This bath in a mixture of oil and sea water did it no good, but I had another camera with which I could take black-and-white photographs. Brad, the cook, and Brian Hill quickly succumbed, and Kiwi, as we now called Brian Holloway, cooked our supper. Three Brians on board were too many. Brian Thomas, who came from South Wales, we renamed, with great originality, Taffy.

Early on the afternoon of the 29th we passed the Wolf rock where a Trinity House vessel lay effecting the relief of the lighthouse crew. Three hours later we passed her again lying to by the Seven Stones lightship. The wind had freshened and gone north, where it stayed for a week or more, and although Brad managed to prepare for supper a noble stew and a stiff duff, he could take no further interest in it himself. On occasions when the weather was boisterous this happened throughout the voyage, with the result that poor

Brad lost a stone in weight. It had the effect, too, of making me feel slightly ashamed to be stuffing myself with food, in preparing which the cook had rendered himself unfit to partake. But I never allowed myself to be entirely overcome by these considerate feelings or to suffer my appetite to be impaired by them. Taffy, too, felt no such scruples, besides having an inordinate appetite. As I have said he was powerfully built and had even brought with him a chest expander to increase that power. This miniature Tarzan from the jungles of South Wales needed a lot of nourishment.

Noddy, on the other hand, always passed over breakfast in favour of sleep and spent the rest of the day waiting for supper. At this he did more than his duty before retiring, like a small, sea-going boa-constrictor, to await the passing of another food-less twenty-four hours. Brian Hill was a poor trencherman, too. In fact we saved so much food on this voyage that the necessity of making another to consume what was left over soon became apparent. Brian had another idiosyncrasy. Whatever the weather, sunshine or storm, he never went on deck other than fully equipped in oilskins, seaboots, gloves, and cap of some kind. He put me in mind of a Sherpa we once had with us on Everest who, possibly because he had never before worn anything but homespun wool, wore everything we gave him – windproofs, mittens, Balaclava, boots, snow-glasses – even at base camp in the finest weather, as if a blizzard was imminent.

At about this early stage we first noticed a strange smell in the cabin, all pervasive and difficult to pin down, which I attributed to either a dead rat, fermenting rice, or uncommonly bad cheese. We had on board, stowed in the cabin, six whole ten lb Cheddars, each in a soldered tin. The smell having become intolerable we got to work with a cold chisel to open up all the cheeses. In three of the tins – and it is still a mystery how it got there – we found an inch or two of water. All was not lost. I housed the three sickly invalids in a box on deck where they could enjoy the sun and the wind. They were the last and by no means the worst to be eaten. Good judges, such as Taffy and myself, spoke highly of them, especially when alleviated with a raw onion.

The north wind blowing straight down the Irish Sea resolved any doubts I may have had about which course to take. We steered west or a little north of it and in the next week logged over 600 miles. So persistently did the wind hang in the north that when ten days out we had not even reached the latitude of Barmouth. Still we were well out in the Atlantic, 300 miles west of Ireland, where it is usually harder to make westing than northing. In spite of this it proved to be a slow passage. In the twenty days it took us to reach the Vestmanaeyjar, south of Iceland, the average run was only sixty-three miles a day and on only four days did we log over 100 miles. On the 13th, with the wind dead aft, we resorted to the twin headsails boomed out from the mast, having this time not forgotten to bring their iron collar. Progress was slow, only thirty-four miles in the day, and while we were reverting to fore and aft rig a ship came in sight. The sail changing seemed to worry those on board her. From a position several miles astern she turned and came back towards us. So we hove to while she ranged close alongside, her engines stopped, to ask if we were all right. She was the *Teneriffa* of the Norwegian Wilhelmsen lines whose ship's names all begin with a 'T'. Her captain offered to report us and we much appreciated their having gone out of their way to speak us.

In making the Vestmannaeyjar, a group of islands twenty miles off the Iceland coast, we intended putting in at Heimaey, the largest and the only inhabited island of the group. Close by is the volcanic island of Surtsey which we had visited the previous year, and just before sailing I had heard that a new island had appeared close by. Accordingly we steered for Surtsey. On the 15th at 9 am we saw a huge column of smoke about thirty miles off. As we drew near we could see that the smoke issued from this island and that Surtsey, about a mile west, was practically dormant. In comparison with its diminutive neighbour which was making all the fuss Surtsey looked enormous. It is now about one and a half miles long, a mile wide, and 600ft. high. Its smooth contours contrast strangely with the steep-sided islands and islets of the Vestmannaeyjar. The new island was in full eruption and we hove to about a half-mile off to watch. The vast white column of smoke and steam ascended continuously while every few minutes an explosion flung a jet black cloud of smoke and ash, and lumps of pumice hundreds of feet into the air. Away to leeward, below the white smoke, curtains of ash drifted down to the sea. After about an hour we let draw to resume our passage to Heimaey and as we started a plane arrived from Iceland to watch the volcano. Whereupon the eruptions stopped, the smoke ceased, and the unlucky plane, after circling for some time flew home. Surtsey and the new island have enabled a few enterprising people to earn some money. Besides the chartering of planes for interested spectators, coloured picture postcards of the volcanoes in action are sold in large numbers.

With a very fresh beam wind we made about seven knots for most of the twenty miles to Heimaey. To reach the port at the north-west corner of the island we had to pass close under an 800ft. high cliff whence the baffling down draughts and wind eddies obliged us to down sail and motor. To find the way in we had only to follow the numerous small trawlers and drifters, one of which overhauled us close enough to throw on board half a dozen fine haddock. As we turned to open up the narrow harbour entrance, passing between the cliffs and Faxasker, an islet about a quarter mile off, we met a confused sea and a violent wind blowing straight on to those appalling cliffs. The fishing boats, going faster than we were, plunged their bows under amidst sheets of spray. We were reminded of how dependent we were upon our engine at that moment by the sight of the wrecked British trawler *Goodwood* lying under the cliffs just outside the entrance. Her engines, we were told, had failed.

At the first fish quay we passed a small crowd were watching us, so we stopped to ask where we could lie. Several English voices directed us to a berth. In Heimaey there are a surprising number of young English, Scots, and Irish who go there to work either in the fish factories or the fishing boats for what seemed to us to be princely wages. Some intended to stay only for the summer, others had been there two or three years. It is the second busiest port in Iceland, devoted entirely to fishing, and the boats that use it – trawlers, herring drifters, seine-netters, ring-netters, or long liners – are all local boats, most of them small. Although they are all Icelandic boats they are supposed to have regard to various fishing limits according to the type of boat. Trawling, for instance is not allowed within six miles of the shore. But they told us that the fishery patrol vessel had a hopeless task. Its movements are passed on from fishing boat to fishing boat, and even the time when the air patrol takes off from Reykjavik is immediately known.

We lay astern of a cluster of fishing boats lying three, four, and five abreast at the quay. We were glad to be in, for it was now blowing a gale and raining. There are two fish processing factories that work day and night, one of them turning fish and fish offal into fish-meal and fertiliser. We lay downwind of the latter and suffered accordingly, but we could not complain for they allowed us to use their hot showers.

The owners of the fishing boats reputedly make a great deal of money and in Heimaey there are not many ways of spending it. One way is to buy a motor car and this they do in spite of the fact that there are only nine miles of road. Another way, I imagine, is at the cemetery. Nowhere else have I seen such massive and elaborate marble and granite tombstones, some of them, family vaults, constituting a whole wall about twenty yards long. The most avid cinema-goer could not spend much money because there is only the one, and the shops are few and remarkably unattractive. The cemetery happened to lie in my way on a walk up to the volcano, or rather the grass covered crater of a long defunct volcano, for Heimaey, like the other islands of the group, is of volcanic origin. At the crater there was a pillar with an inscribed copper plate pointing to various prominent landmarks, including Hecla on the mainland. On our second day there I took a solitary walk up the very steep, mostly grass-covered rock called Klif, nearly a thousand feet high. In the prevailing gale and driving rain, coupled with the oilskins and the gumboots I was wearing, I rated the climb as 'very severe!' On the summit ridge I came across a rope, formerly used no doubt by those who took the sea birds – auks, fulmars, kittiwakes, and gannets, that haunt the cliffs.

CHAPTER NINETEEN

Reykjavik and Angmagssalik

THE SEASON being still early we decided to go first to Reykjavik where we might be able to get some news about ice conditions. On the 15th we sailed and the next evening passed through the channel between Reykjanes, the south-western extremity of Iceland, and Eldey, a steep rock 226ft. high which is reputedly one of the largest gannet colonies in the world. Even at this distance away streaks of ash and pumice from the new volcano could be seen on the water. Very early in the morning as we lay becalmed about thirty miles from Reykjavik we were passed by the *Bremen*, a large German cruise ship. Late that evening, as we crept slowly up the buoyed channel into Reykjavik, she passed again outward bound, her tourists having 'done' Iceland.

Reykjavik lies at the back of a fifty-mile-wide bay called Faxafloi. It was a warm, pleasant day, clear, the wind light, and we were in no hurry – all conditions conducive to carelessness. Moreover, having been there before, we thought we knew the place. So instead of laying off the course from the chart, I thought I could recognize various features and went bumming on to what on closer inspection proved to be the small fishing port of Keflavik where there is an American air base. Thus, a long way off course, we still had twenty miles to go and did not reach Reykjavik until late evening. Anxious to have supper we made fast at the first fish quay we came to and were busy eating one of Brad's curries when we were told in strong Icelandic to shove off. At the same moment two Customs officers arrived. They were genial enough, spoke good English, and told us where to move to when we had finished supper. The fishing boat to which we finally made fast at a nearby jetty was undergoing repair so that we lay there undisturbed throughout our short stay.

Next morning I went to the harbour offices to clear the ship and pay light dues. The young clerk made out a bill for 400 kroners, a kroner being worth about 2d. I remembered that the previous year we had paid 50 kroners and I resolved that on this occasion, like the hero in Stanley Holloway's *Runcorn Ferry* episode, I would rather be 'drownded than done'. The battle was prolonged. Fortunately the office kept very complete records and when the clerk turned up those for 1964 there it was in black-and-white: *Mischief*, 50 kroners. I got the impression that unlike the previous year, when we had benefited by the goodwill reflected by the Duke of Edinburgh's visit, we were not popular. None of our former acquaintances, either the drunk or the sober, showed up, and no one gave us any fish. Then it had been, so to speak, British week, now it was very much German week. Besides the *Bremen*, two more German cruise ships arrived to make a long stay, one of them a very modern vessel from Rostock in East Germany.

Thinking that our best bet for obtaining an ice report would be through the American air base at Keflavik I went to the British Embassy to ask for an introduction. The young lady receptionist evidently thought I looked like a Distressed British Seaman waiting for a free passage home, as I suppose I may have done, but even when I had eluded her and reached the Ambassador, whom I knew slightly, I got no change. Keflavik and the American base were seemingly beyond human ken. It occurred to me then that the harbour-master at Angmagssalik who had been helpful the previous year in several ways, including the lowering of our stock of whisky, might still be there. So I invested some capital in a reply-paid cable asking whether by the end of July ice conditions would allow of *Mischief* entering the place. Two days later came the laconic reply: 'Should be possible'.

Upon this we decided to sail on 24 July and got busy buying what stores we needed and taking on water. Before leaving I went out to the meteorological office which is housed in the control tower at the airport. Reykjavik must be one of the few capital cities of the world where the airport is within easy walking distance. The airport is also remarkably free and easy. I merely walked into the control tower and having explained what I wanted was at once made welcome. Two of those on duty in the meteorological office were busy playing chess and the third was free to devote himself to discussing the Greenland ice and weather. What they knew about the ice confirmed the harbour-master's signal – only about 3/10 ice cover in the neighbourhood of Angmagssalik. I was shown all round the control tower and from the roof they pointed out the mast of a twelve-ton ketch, recently bought and sailed over from the Clyde, the first yacht to be based in Icelandic waters. It had been acquired through the combined efforts of forty members of a newly formed yacht club who deemed it shameful that a sea-faring nation such as Iceland should be unrepresented in the yachting world.

From Reykjavik to Angmagssalik across Denmark Strait is about 400 miles and seven days elapsed before we sighted Greenland's mountains. The summer in Iceland had been exceptionally fine and the first two or three of these seven days were quite flawless provided one did not mind standing still. For a whole day, the sea like a mirror and the sun hot, we lay on deck watching the snow-capped Snaefell (4,000ft.) some sixty miles away. I had my last bucket bath, the sea being still comparatively warm at 50°F. We saw several whales, schools of porpoise, and small flocks of fulmars always gathered round the boat when she lay becalmed. When over a hundred miles from Iceland we picked up a 'dan' buoy that had broken adrift. The two stout twelve-foot bamboo poles were floated by means of nine metal floats like small footballs roped together in a net, and were kept upright by a length of heavy chain. When we began hauling in the rope we thought it would never end and finally finished up with a 300ft. coil of good two inch manila. One of the bamboo poles from this useful find came in handy later on.

On the evening of the 29th in Lat. 65°30' Long. 29°50', when we happened to be steering in that direction, I thought I could see ice 'blink' to the north, a characteristic yellowish tinge in the sky which often denotes the presence of ice below. It seemed improbable, for we were nearly 200 miles east of Angmagssalik, but at midnight I was called on deck. Sure enough ice lay ahead. At first I took it to be a stray raft of floes or a mass of bergy bits left by the collapse of an iceberg. On climbing the shrouds, however, I could see ice stretching away interminably to the north-east. The sea temperature near this pack-ice was 39°F. and an hour later, having gone about and steered south, we found it to be 52°. The presence of an iceberg has no effect on the sea temperature; as might be expected, the presence of pack-ice has a very marked effect.

Angmagssalik, in Lat. 65°40', is a little north of Reykjavik, in Lat. 64°10'. Some fifteen miles east of Angmagssalik and slightly north of it is Cape Dan, marking an abrupt bend of the coast to the west and forming a sort of bight at the back of which lies Angmagssalik. The south-going East Greenland current extends to about fifty miles off the coast and, as I had an exaggerated notion of its strength, I made the mistake of aiming for the coast north of Cape Dan, a neighbourhood where ice notoriously accumulates. On the 30th with a bitter north-east wind, overcast, and some patches of fog and sea-smoke, we got no sights. At midnight, when it was still quite light, the fog cleared revealing a magnificent stretch of wild, mountainous coast about forty miles away. No ice anywhere in sight, not even a berg. The day remained wonderfully fine and by evening when we had closed the land, we had many bergs in sight and could hear the ominous growling of the pack-ice. In the absence of any wind we let her drift and enjoyed a quiet night.

Motoring west in the morning we soon met the pack. Encouraged, perhaps, by the harbour-master's signal we thought to try conclusions with it but we had not to penetrate far before prudence advised a retreat. All day we drifted, sailed, and occasionally motored south with the ice edge close to starboard until, by evening, the ice forced us to steer east of south. Rather than waste fuel we stopped and let her drift with the current. We reckoned we were about twenty miles east of Cape Dan with ice all in between. It was another perfect evening, not a breath of wind, no ripple on the water, only a gentle swell. As the sun dipped briefly behind the jagged peaks, now a deep indigo, the open water between us and the ice edge, assumed a coppery sheen, and as each swell passed and the back of the swell lost the evening light, the coppery sea became streaked with bands of steel.

The following day was just as perfect as with a light south-west breeze we stood away from the coast on a long board until, towards evening, we turned once more in the direction of the land. At midnight, sailing slowly, we had a glimpse of ice to the north but we appeared to have rounded the bulge, for by morning we had open water in sight everywhere. According to my dead reckoning Cape Dan now lay about twenty miles to the north-west. It is the one mark on the coast that can be recognized for it has on it a great radar reflector globe, part of the Distant Early Warning System. I took three sights all of which put us twenty miles further west. I refused to believe them, attributing these odd results to mirage of which we had had some notable examples. We had noted with astonishment the previous morning the ice edge, about a mile distant, looking like an ice cliff 100ft. high. So we held on steering north-west and wondering what the devil had happened to Cape Dan, searching with binoculars all along the coast ahead, until at 11 am Noddy suddenly spotted the great globe about ten miles to the *north-east*.

It is embarrassing for the navigator when making his final approach to have to order an alteration of course of nearly eight points. One cannot claim that the target has moved or is moving. How stupid is it possible to be if after so many voyages I could believe even doubtful sun sights to be less trustworthy than dead reckoning? We met no ice at all until near Angmagssalik when we had about five miles of scattered floes to traverse. I appreciated then the mistake we had made in closing the land too far north. Had we approached Angmagssalik from the south-east we should have seen no pack-ice and saved two days.

On the afternoon of 3 August we anchored in our old berth outside the small harbour with a warp to a holdfast on the rock shore twenty yards away. From the harbour-master, who soon paid us a visit, we learnt that the ice had been very heavy up to about 15 July when it began clearing rapidly. The old

Ardvark, a wooden Norwegian vessel, had been caught in the ice and spent a month in it drifting south. She is chartered for the summer and seems to spend most of her time fetching sand for cement work from a neighbouring fjord. The new three-storey warehouse on the quay that had been begun last year was well advanced. Later our old friend the *Ejnar Mikkelsen* came in and her skipper Niels Underborg came on board. The previous autumn he had taken her to Denmark for repairs and to the dismay of the Greenlander crew, who were not used to the open sea, they had had a rough passage.

We collected our mail, had showers, and allowed the Greenlander women to put our clothes through the washing machine. Martin, the Danish shipwright-carpenter, rowed over to see if we were still leaking, and when the harbour-master came for his evening peg he brought two beautiful white loaves baked by his wife. We learnt that a plane was due in with mail on 6 August so we arranged with the harbour-master to go alongside the quay on that day for oil and water. Mail is brought from Sondre Stromfjord in west Greenland and the plane lands at Kulusuk near Cape Dan where there is an air strip. On the afternoon of the 6th, *Ejnar Mikkelsen* duly came in with the mail from Kulusuk and an hour later we were on our way. On the previous voyage we had spent three weeks in Angmagssalik more or less ice-bound; this time we spent only three days.

During our short stay I had gone twice up Spy-glass Hill, partly for old time's sake and partly to look at the ice. What I saw of the ice had led me to suspect that we might have more trouble in getting out than we had had coming in, and so it proved. Once outside King Oscar's Havn we met a strong southerly wind. Even motoring close in to the shore we made little headway and I decided to sail through the belt of ice floes and out to sea where we could make some use of the wind. With the wind abeam we were soon among the floes, with the wind moderating. We continued under sail and since the wind became less and less we started the engine to help the sails. This was a mistake. We ran foul of a floe and the wind in the sails, light though it was, prevented us from getting clear. By this time fog had come down and the floes proved to be much closer packed than those we had come through a few days before.

When manoeuvring in ice it is very easy to run against a floe or to get oneself boxed in. It is a case of he who hesitates is lost. Enough way must be kept on for making quick turns and one must decide quickly which way to turn – especially when visibility is restricted as it was then, when we could not see where open water lay, and where what looked like a promising lead either became too narrow to turn in or ended in a cul-de-sac. Steering by compass as near east as we could, ignorant as to whether that was our best course, and becoming more and more frustrated, at last at ten o'clock we saw the open sea about a hundred yards away. The floes at the ice edge were tossing violently in the swell and we passed them with the utmost caution. We hoisted sail again and headed south-east.

The passage of 180 miles to Skjoldungen proved to be as troublesome as it was short. Fog and light winds persisted all the next day and similarly on the 8th except that the fog was denser and wetter. We heard two ships close by, hooting, presumably, at each other and not at us, and we were relieved when the sounds gradually drew away. There are no fishing banks off that coast and we wondered what these two ships were and whither bound. In the evening, the weather as thick as ever, I was startled by the helmsman's report of 'Land on the port bow', the nearest land in that direction being Iceland. It proved to be a large iceberg about a hundred yards off and since we were making a lot of heavy leeway we missed it by less than I liked.

A brief clearing next morning showed the coast about fifteen miles off and the incessant grumbling of the pack-ice warned us that we were too near. There were over many bergs about, too, for comfort, so that when a fresh north-westerly breeze sprang up, accompanied by drizzle, we took advantage of it to steer south, a course that would take us steadily away from the coast which trends south-west. We had what would have been a day of glorious sailing had it not been so cold and wet. We did five knots most of the time and during my watch I scored an extremely near miss on a whale. He surfaced less than twenty yards ahead and *Mischief*'s stem cut across the smooth slick he left as he dived to avoid us. In the evening when I thought we had run our distance we ran west for about twenty miles until having sighted icebergs we hove to for the night. The bergs drift with the current and the majority of them are generally within twenty miles of the land. At night at this time there were several hours of darkness.

In the morning we let draw and started to close the land in good visibility but a completely overcast sky. I badly needed a sun sight, preferably a noon sight to give us our latitude. We had not much idea where we were and still less about how to recognize Skjoldungen. The mass of jagged peaks ahead meant nothing to us who had nothing by which to identify them. It is hard to identify any part of the Greenland coast. The innumerable islands that fringe it all look much alike while few of the capes are unmistakably prominent. Fjords occur every few miles so that it is easy enough to enter the wrong one. All depended upon our seeing the sun and the sky remained obstinately and heavily overcast. But luck was with us. Just before noon a wan sun showed faintly through the cloud and we found we were about five miles south of the fjord entrance. There was little ice about and it now became a simple matter to recognize and reconcile the islands and capes shown on the chart with those on the ground. That evening we found a good anchorage ten miles up the fjord.

CHAPTER TWENTY

Skjoldungen and Homewards

WE HAD learnt at Angmagssalik that the settlement at Skjoldungen where, besides Greenlanders, there was a Greenland Trading Company store, was about to be removed. One reason given to us was that the natives had taken to brewing some kind of hooch from sugar; another, that owing to the few seals there they could no longer support themselves by hunting. Anyhow they were being moved to the Angmagssalik district and when we passed the settlement that evening there were obviously only a few Greenlanders left. By 15 September we were told, all would have gone, and Skjoldungen Fjord would be deserted. There were the usual painted wood huts, quite a number of them, but I thought it looked a fairly grim spot, stuck under some dark cliffs. As we passed some children waved to us from the slightly dilapidated huts.

We anchored in a well sheltered bay, fronted by an island, called Halvdans Fjord, a much more cheerful spot, with plenty of vegetation on the surrounding shore and a good stream running in. That night only the rumble of a distant avalanche broke the profound stillness. South Skjoldungen where we were is about twenty miles long and generally about a mile wide. At its north end it is connected by a narrow, deep channel with North Skjoldungen, so that the land between the two fjords, Skjoldungen proper, is an island. Both sides of the fjord are mountainous and many small, steep, broken glaciers descend to the water. The peaks vary from 3,000ft. to over 6,000ft. are of all grades of difficulty and all unclimbed.

As we motored up the fjord next morning, and as I scanned the snow-plastered faces, the stark walls of rock, and the steep, aspiring ridges that no climbing party had as yet seen, much less attempted, I began to wonder whether such a weak party as ours had any business there. Perhaps I had never quite believed we would get there, for only now did a fact that I had known from the first begin to bother me. Kiwi had joined with no ice-axe and boots that were not all they might be, and I had done nothing about it. A peak on the north side that I finally decided we might manage seemed about 5,000ft. high, too high, I felt, for me to climb from sea level in the day. Its glacier ended about 1,500ft. above the sea and could be reached by a steep slope of rock and scree. Two miles short of it we found a small bay where the water was shallow enough for us to anchor. Next day, carrying light loads, four of us set out along the beach, intending to put a camp on the glacier. On rounding the last corner we found that another glacier, hitherto hidden, cut us off from the foot of the rock slope. Its snout entered the water and higher up

499

it was broken by a 500ft. wall of rock down which cascades of snow and blocks of ice were constantly falling from its upper section. Frightening though it was we were out of range of this cannonade, but we had some 400yd. of crevassed, rotten, and steep ice to cross and I decided that we had better not cross it. Three of us had never been on a glacier and two would have to recross later alone. So we ate our lunch and walked back to the boat in increasing wind and rain. A prudent decision that saved Kiwi and me thirty-six hours of discomfort in a wet tent. All that night and throughout the next day it rained hard and blew unceasingly.

Having moved the boat two miles up to beyond this unfriendly glacier four of us toiled up the slope of rock and scree and gained the glacier above – a gently flowing glacier of rough ice almost free from crevasses. For a camp site we appeared to have the choice of the glacier which was at least flat or a chaotic mound of boulders where we should be warmer. Having had some experience in these things I climbed up the mound and soon found a place that with some delving and heaving could be made to hold the tent. None of the boulders or embedded rocks could defeat Taffy once he got his back to them. We soon had the tent up and were able to give the carrying party, Taffy and Brian, a cup of tea before they went down.

We passed a surprisingly warm night and set off across the glacier to the foot of our ridge on a perfect Greenland morning, clear, warm, and still. After some easy climbing on rock and snow we gained the crest of the ridge and could see where it rose steeply to the summit about a thousand feet above. The snow slope leading to the rock summit looked much steeper than I had imagined from below. I should not have cared to be on it myself without a steadying axe and we should have to descend after the sun had been on it for some time. We would, of course, be roped and although Kiwi was eager to try I did not think it good enough. There is a disadvantage about my plan of sailing to remote regions in order to climb, especially in the circumstances in which I am often placed, as I was then. At the back of my mind there is always the thought that any mishap on the mountain would also involve *Mischief* and the crew in great difficulty. This, perhaps, made for over-cautiousness. As Dr Johnson said: 'Prudence quenches that ardour of enterprise, by which everything is done that can claim praise or admiration, and represses that generous temerity which often fails and often succeeds.'

That hot, sweltering afternoon we carried the camp down. The glacier stream entered the fjord near where *Mischief* lay in a series of cascades, and while waiting for the dinghy to take us off Kiwi and I sat under one of these to wash off the grime and sweat of a long hot day. The sun had brought out the mosquitoes in force. On board they were less troublesome than on shore where they drove one quite frantic, and at night on watch (which we always kept) they ceased to trouble us. My watch that night passed quickly. The night was dark and the sky clear and I watched the northern lights weave strange patterns of scintillating colour. The putter of a motor boat came from across the fjord and I signalled what I hoped was the Esquimo equivalent for 'What ship?' She came alongside, two men on deck and two asleep below. I shone the torch over her hopefully, expecting to see some salmon – there is a salmon river at the head of Skjoldungen – but all I saw was one huge seal and a small one, the latter half-skinned. I gave them some cigarettes and they chugged off for the settlement.

Re-entering Halvdan anchorage I realized we had a peak on our doorstep, a peak of about 3,000ft. that could be climbed from the boat, that looked both interesting and within our limited abilities. A glacier covered with hard snow took us to a col at about 2,500ft. whence moderately steep rock led to the summit. At only one point, where we had to cut a few steps across a patch of ice, did we have to use the rope. Having lunched and built a cairn we started down by a different route and, after many false casts down gullies that ended in cliffs, contrived to get ourselves lost. Ultimately we reached a valley on the wrong side of the mountain where we enjoyed a brief and icy bathe. It had been a brilliant, hot day, we ourselves were tired, hot, and sweaty, so that this refreshing dip in a Greenland tarn certainly merited inclusion in my list of memorable bathes. Walking back along the shore of Halvdan we came upon a motor boat from the settlement with a party of youngsters gathering bilberries and bathing in the fjord. I had always imagined that Eskimos were averse to water but here they were larking and swimming in the icy water as if it were a South Seas lagoon. On reaching the boat we discovered that our own brave efforts in the tarn, or even those of the Greenlanders, did not rate very highly, for Taffy had just swum from the boat to the island, a distance of about 300 yards. True, he had taken the precaution of being accompanied by Brad in the dinghy and when we returned he was still a little purple.

One of the most shapely of the Skjoldungen peaks lay on the south side opposite to Halvdan Fjord. It had taken my eye immediately upon our entering Skjoldungen but I did not think it was within our grasp. In order to have a closer look we crossed the fjord and anchored off a very large glacier which stopped short of the water by a quarter mile. Although the surroundings were grim the anchorage was excellent, the water shoaling gradually and there was good holding ground. On a grey, misty day, Taffy, Noddy, and I walked over the rough ice of the glacier for about five miles to see if this peak had any easier ridge than those we had seen. In such matters the weather may affect one's judgement. On a sunny day this peak might have appeared to me less daunting than it did then as I sat caressed by an uncommonly cool wind while wisps of mist writhed round its distant summit. For that time anyway its challenge was to remain unanswered.

So much for Skjoldungen where, had we arrived the previous year, when I had with me a comparatively strong party, we might have attempted some worth-while peak. Before leaving for home I wanted to have a look at Sehesteds Fjord, the next fjord to the south. We had first to water the ship, preferably at a stream that did not flow direct from a glacier. We headed for the narrow entrance of a small bay nearby where a likely looking stream entered. The first cast of the lead gave 'no bottom at ten fathoms, and the next 'one fathom'. As *Mischief* draws seven feet we were obviously aground but we had gone on so gently that we hardly noticed it. Nevertheless with the engine 'full astern' she refused to move. We lost no time in running a kedge out astern and bringing the warp forward to the anchor winch. With the combined power of the winch and engine she came off so fast that we had not time to stop the engine before the warp had taken a turn round the propeller shaft. With no sails up, the engine useless, and the rocky shore close at hand, we hastily dropped the big anchor which fortunately took hold.

So there we were in deep water with the sixty-lb CQR anchor dangling from the propeller shaft on a three-inch warp. After about an hour of patient grappling, arms and shoulders under water most of the time, Taffy managed to get hold of the warp below the propeller and we got the anchor on board. The bamboo pole, a product of the 'dan' buoy incident, now came in useful. After securing a knife to it with Jubilee clips we sawed away at the warp where it went round the shaft until the free end eventually dropped off and sank. Finally we went back to Halvdan to water at the stream there. Floating the rubber dinghy right into the mouth of the stream we filled it with buckets and towed it back to the ship. Unable to rig a pump we passed the water up in buckets, through the cabin skylight, and so into the main tank under the table.

By then, 23 August, the coast was free of ice except for bergs but in the entrance and all the way up Sehesteds Fjord big floes and bergs were extremely numerous. They came from a glacier at the head of Sehesteds Fjord which descends direct from the ice-cap. On this account, though Sehesteds is a fine, mountainous fjord, it compares unfavourably with Skjoldungen as a place for climbing. The quantity of ice about made anchoring a problem and at 4 pm I took advantage of the first little ice-free bay we had seen and anchored on the south side. In the course of a brief walk ashore I was attracted by a peak on the opposite side, so later we got our anchor and set out to look for an anchorage on the north side. In mid-fjord, floes and bergs clustering all round, we met two Danes, armed to the teeth, in a small motor boat. They were on holiday from the weather station at Tingmiarmiut thirty miles to the south and were bound for the Skjoldungen settlement. We slowed down while they came alongside for a 'gam' but I did not ask them on board as we had yet to find our night's anchorage. It was, I think, the feeling that we had been inhospitable, that later induced us to call at Tingmiarmiut. The north shore proved to be steep-to and heavily infested with ice. At length we found a place off a glacier that had long since receded from the shore, where the water was shallow enough, and prepared for an uneasy night fending off floes.

Early in the morning in my watch a large floe drifted in and shoved its projecting shelf of ice right under the keel. I had visions of the floe capsizing and of *Mischief* being catapulted into the air by the ice underneath. The above-water part of the floe could just be reached with the bamboo pole and I was able to keep shoving the boat clear. Kiwi and I had another cloudless, windless day for our third and last climb. Having reached the summit ridge on good, hard snow we thought the peak was in the bag. But we came to a series of deep gaps in the ridge, the last forcing us to descend 500ft. before we could traverse across and gain the summit. This peak was at the junction of Sehesteds with a branch fjord in which there was far more ice on the surface than water. In fact so congested were the floes that the fjord looked like a continuation of the glacier we could see at its head from which all the ice came. When we got back to the boat in the evening we learnt that she had had to be moved once on account of ice. Several bergs were still menacingly close so in order to avoid being pestered by them during the night we went back to the anchorage on the south side.

The weather station of Tingmiarmiut is on an island at the entrance to a large fjord of the same name. On the chart it looked as if it should be approached from the fjord side but I had learnt from the Danes we met that the best approach was from seaward by a narrow inlet about three miles long. Instead of going back down Sehesteds and out to sea we saved ourselves a few miles by going up the fjord and then cutting south through a narrow channel behind an island. Once at sea we set a course for Tingmiarmiut twenty-five miles down the coast, having enough wind to sail most of the way. The weather was clear. There was a small group of islands close off the entrance to the inlet which appeared narrower and even more uninviting than I had expected, with some rocks showing on one side. The doubts that I felt about this being the right entrance were dispelled when we spotted on one side of it a small concrete beacon.

It is astonishing to see the sort of places into which large icebergs will find their way. At a sharp bend in this narrow passage, its width varying between a cable and half a cable, we found three icebergs lying across it. We might, perhaps, have squeezed through but decided not to try. Instead we anchored there in a tiny bay with an even bigger iceberg close at hand. This monster was almost certainly aground and would not worry us. From the chart the station must be about a mile beyond the bend. We could hear nothing, and see nothing but the rock walls of the channel, so we uttered a few bleats on our foghorn and then had supper, intending to defer our visit till the morning.

Although by morning the three bergs blocking the way had drifted off I thought it better to walk to the station to see first what the anchorage there was like. Accordingly three of us landed and after a quarter of an hour of rough walking came upon the huts. Twelve husky dogs picketed in a line on a bed of winter snow set up a frightful clamour and presently a man appeared. He offered us coffee but the coffee was accompanied by bacon and eggs, smoked eels, and other delicacies. The fact that we had just had our breakfast made no difference to Taffy and Kiwi. The other six men then began to drift in and in due course they took us back to *Mischief* in their launch so that we could bring her up to the anchorage. Before doing this we could not resist visiting the huskies who were quite besides themselves with delight at being fondled and spoken to. We went solemnly down the line having a word with each.

The anchorage at the head of the inlet where the station lies is wider than the channel with room for a ship of several hundred tons. There are two big huts, a wireless hut, and a large store. In the living hut is the kitchen with an oil-fired range, dining room, and a big, comfortable lounge with a small billiards table. The two Land-rovers they have cannot be overworked, for they are mainly used for bringing up stores from the jetty when a ship arrives which happens only twice a year, in July and October. Mail can be received all the year round by having it dropped, but it cannot be sent. We spent a cheerful day with the Danes, a day devoted largely to eating and drinking – a meal of half a chicken each and ice cream in the afternoon and another at night.

When we came ashore for breakfast we brought them some rum and cigarettes and before we left we were taken to their store and told to help ourselves – which, on our behalf, Brad did in an all-embracing way. With three of the Danes on board we then motored down the inlet, dropping them at the entrance where a very unpleasant, confused sea was running. With no wind to steady us we were thrown about all day by a sea that was running in every direction. Frequent tide rips added to the confusion and not until we were twenty miles off the island did the sea calm down.

The fast passage that one always expects to make homewards across the Atlantic seldom happens. On this occasion we logged over 100 miles on only four days, and for the twenty-two days from Tingmiarmiut to the Needles the average run was only seventy miles. An unusual occurrence in the North Atlantic was our being able to run for three consecutive days with twin staysails set without touching a sheet, the wind never varying a point, while we logged 270 miles. Few ships are sighted to the north of the main shipping lanes and those few that we do sight always seem to be Manchester Liners. In Lat. 56° the *Manchester Renown* came close to have a look at us and on the same evening after dark I signalled another ship to ask to be reported. She got our name and duly reported us but my reading of Morse is not very hot and I did not learn her name until we got home when I found we had been reported by the *Manchester Engineer*. We met a strange ship in the way of an extremely dirty Russian trawler with apparently nothing to do beyond having a look at us. She would not respond to signals in any form, lamp, flags, or foghorn.

At length, on the night of 13 September we picked up the Bull light at the corner of Ireland and before dawn next morning, Mizzen Head and the Fastnet lights. On the 16th we were three miles south of the Longships, the wind light at south, so light that by evening we were still eighteen miles south-west of the Lizard. One of the concessions to modernity on board *Mischief* is our wireless receiving set and since entering home waters we had begun listening to the Shipping Forecasts. Most yachtsmen, I suppose, listen to these forecasts. A few, perhaps listen with the reverence that they would have accorded to the living voice of one of the major prophets, never dreaming of quitting their moorings, if only to cross the Solent, until they have learnt what is in store.

That evening we were a little surprised to hear a gale warning for the Channel and most parts of the coast, a deep depression being about to pass over the British Isles with its centre somewhere about Liverpool. If one picks up a gale warning it is prudent to act on it, especially if, as on this occasion, winds of Force 9 and 10 are mentioned. The wind was still light at south and the glass just beginning to turn down, but while we still had daylight we changed the mainsail and working jib for the trysail and storm jib, leaving the staysail set. Throughout the night we sailed on to the south-east in order to get well away from the land. In the morning, the glass falling steeply and wind about Force 6 or 7 at south, with rain, we continued sailing with the staysail set until the increasing wind obliged us to drop it about noon. That afternoon the sea built up considerably, short, steep, and breaking. In fact the seas seemed to be more vicious at that time than they were later when the gale had fully developed, when the wind blowing at full blast appeared to smooth them out. At 4 pm on account of the wind direction and the breaking seas, we hove to on the starboard tack. Had the wind been west instead of south we could, I think, have safely run before it.

That evening the forecast for 'Plymouth' was laconic: 'Gale Force 10 southerly, veering west later.' The wind certainly went on increasing until towards midnight when the glass began to flatten out. Unluckily we were hove to in a busy shipping lane and since our navigation lamps refused to burn with that amount of wind blowing we had some tense moments. Perhaps nowadays no one can make proper oil lamps, but surely a hundred, or even fifty years ago, when oil lamps were in common use at sea, a gale of wind did not promptly blow them all out.

We had our Aldis lamp for emergency use but I dislike flashing it at an oncoming, unsuspecting ship, especially on a stormy night, partly because it might be taken for a call for assistance, and partly for fear of so upsetting the officer on watch that he might give the wrong helm order. I think it best to refrain, like Brer Fox who 'lay low and said nothin'', unless pretty confident that there is some danger of being hit. But just before dawn of the 18th my judgement was at fault and this policy of masterly inactivity nearly caused a nasty mishap. When at the eleventh hour, so to speak, I switched on the Aldis lamp the chap at the wheel of the oncoming ship certainly reacted with admirable promptness. She passed to windward at short spitting distance while a stream of abuse in English flowed down to us from her bridge.

As the day advanced and the wind eased we began sailing and that night in lovely, clear weather we raised the Portland Bill light. Having anchored off Yarmouth for the Customs to clear us we went up Lymington river on the Sunday afternoon and made fast.

Two days later we had stripped *Mischief* bare and the crew went their several ways.

Gratifying though it would be I cannot hope that anyone who reads of these voyages will partake of the pleasure of those who made them, or even of the pleasure that I have had in thus reliving them. Possibly the book may be dismissed as a picture of an elderly escapist in full flight. I do not think that label applies. Besides the voyages themselves, representing our feeble challenges to Poseidon, each voyage had a purpose, frivolous though to many the purpose might seem. Rather than escaping from anything we were facing up to reality. As Belloc said: 'Everywhere the sea is a teacher of truth. I am not sure that the best thing I find in sailing is not this salt of reality. ... There, sailing the sea, we play every part of life: control, direction, effort, fate; and there can we test ourselves and know our state.'

MISCHIEF GOES SOUTH

Mischief Goes South

First published by Hollis & Carter Ltd., 1968

Contents

Part 1: Islands of the Southern Ocean
(July 1966 – July 1967)

Part 2: Round Africa
(June 1957 – July 1958)

Maps

Scale of Nautical Miles at the Equator

Part 1

Islands of the Southern Ocean

July 1966 – July 1967

CHAPTER ONE

The Objective and the Crew

WHAT ORNITHOLOGISTS, speaking *ex cathedra*, as it were, like to tell us about the habits of birds sometimes takes a lot of swallowing – an elegant phrase, but apt enough in this context. For instance, one Forbush affirms in his whimsical way that the Arctic tern 'nests as far north as the most northern Eskimo live, while in winter its tireless pinions beat along the distant shore of unexplored lands of the Antarctic continent.' I am more willing to concede this because recently *Mischief*'s movements have been equally erratic, though less rapid, sailing off the east coast of Greenland in 1965, and in 1966 beating her tireless pinions far down in the Southern Ocean. With less compelling reasons than the Arctic tern has for its long journey, such behaviour may seem strange, especially after I had decided that from my point of view Greenland waters were the ideal cruising ground and that there was no need to look elsewhere. The point of view is important and since mine is not widely shared the following description of my ideal will be of help:

A region to which the voyage is not too long, where Arctic waters beat upon coasts that are wild and little frequented, and that are studded with unclimbed mountains; where in summer one enjoys almost continuous daylight, the pale skies and soft colours of the north, and above all the romance and excitement of icebergs and pack-ice seen at close quarters from the deck of a small boat. A region where it is easy to imagine oneself in company with John Davis aboard his 50-ton ship *Mooneshine*, or with any of those hardy spirits, the Elizabethan seamen-explorers in search of a North-west passage.

A man must be allowed to change his mind. As Benedick remarked: 'When I said I would die a bachelor, I did not think I should live till I were married.' It is a mistake to get into a rut. Fired by the divine spark of discontent or out of cussedness, after five voyages to Greenland waters I felt in need of change.

No doubt the most striking change would have been a cruise to the West Indies or the South Sea Islands, regarded as the Islands of the Blessed by most right-minded yachtsmen who, if they live in England, pine, not unreasonably, for sunshine, hula-hula girls, and bananas. Something could be said against such places but my main objection is that they have no mountains, or only mountains that are covered with a lush growth of tropical vegetation, suitable for bushwhackers but not for climbers. Instead my thoughts turned to the far South, to Antarctic islands; and since this would be a longer and more arduous undertaking than a Greenland voyage it was a case of now or never, before *Mischief* and her owner grew any older. Many would say, I suppose, that both should long since have been in a museum.

There, as in northern waters, one would enjoy the blessing of continuous daylight and would lack for nothing in the way of icebergs, glaciers, and mountains. Moreover, the Southern Ocean is richer in life – albatross, giant petrels, penguins, whales, seals, and sea elephants. Nor would romance be quite absent, though the sealers of the nineteenth century are not perhaps such heroic characters as the Elizabethan seamen-explorers. In Antarctic waters, lacking the incentive of an imagined North-west passage, exploration began at a more recent date; yet, even in the days of sail, many adventurous spirits found their way there, in search of a living rather than of fame.

Obviously a southern voyage has one or two drawbacks. The weather for one, which is likely to be ruder and colder, with a marked absence of the prolonged sunshine that is a heartening feature of the Greenland scene. Worse still is the great distance involved, a round journey of some 20,000 miles of twelve months duration. *Mischief*'s earlier voyages had been to the south, to the Magellan Straits and Patagonian channels, and to the sub-antarctic islands of Crozet and Kerguelen. And of these I had said, mis-quoting Prince Hal: 'An intolerable deal of sea for one half-pennyworth of mountain.' The voyage I had in mind meant going farther south, to the South Shetland Islands, 500 miles south-east of Cape Horn and only some 60 miles from Graham Land, the northernmost tip of the Antarctic continent. This peninsula, by the way, whose name has long been in dispute between the Americans and ourselves – the Americans calling it Palmer Peninsula – is now known as the Antarctic Peninsula. The South Shetlands comprise eleven islands and in the *Antarctic Pilot* there is the following general description:

These islands were discovered by Mr W. Smith in the brig *Williams* on February 18th, 1819, when on a voyage from Buenos Aires to Valparaiso, and standing far to the southward. Smith again attempted to make the islands in June 1819 but met the pack-ice and had to abandon his project; but he succeeded during a third voyage in October of the same year, landing on King George Island. The commercial exploitation of the islands by numerous British and American sealers followed immediately upon their discovery. The valuable fur seals were taken in such numbers that by 1822 they were almost exterminated, though some sealing continued until 1828. During this period the coasts and harbours became well known and some of the early charts which were produced compare favourably with modern surveys.

The islands, which are largely volcanic, extend about 290 miles in an ENE and

WSW direction between the parallels of 61° 00′ S. and 63° 22′ S. and the meridians of 53° 50′ W. and 62° 50′ W. and are separated by some navigable channels. The northern parts of the coasts of the islands abound with islets, rocks, and breakers, but the southern coasts are almost entirely clear of dangers. In the early part of spring the southern coasts are blocked with ice, which may also extend a considerable distance northwards from the islands during winter, making the islands inaccessible to vessels other than ice-breakers.

The interior of the islands consists generally of high mountains, Smith Island (Lat. 63° 00′ S. Long. 62° 31′ W.) the highest, being 6,900 feet high. The islands are almost entirely ice-covered all the year round, and it is only after midsummer (in January) that a few tracts which are free from snow carry lichens and mosses, in some places supplanted by small patches of grass. The summer may be compared with a mild British winter. Sea birds, principally penguins and petrels, are very plentiful as in the South Orkney Islands. Elephant seals are found on many of the beaches and their number appears to be increasing. Fur seals were abundant until their practical extermination during the nineteenth century. A few Weddell seals breed on the islands and the crab-eater seal is a rare visitor.

The particular island I had in my sights was naturally Smith Island, the most westerly of the group and the most mountainous. Livingstone is the only other island of the group with mountains of interest. Smith Island has on it Mount Foster (6,900 ft.) and Mount Pisgah (6,000 ft.). Neither have been climbed. Indeed, so far as I can learn, no one has even landed on the island since James Weddell in 1820, a year after its discovery by William Smith. Many place-names in the Antarctic serve to remind us that sealers such as Smith, Weddell, Biscoe, Kemp, and Balleny were foremost in exploring those waters, prompted equally by a love of exploration and by the wish to find new, untouched sealing grounds. Weddell, a retired Master of the Royal Navy and a sealing captain, is famous for his penetration of the Weddell Sea in 1822 in the 160-ton brig *Jane* and the 65-ton cutter *Beaufroy*. In his *The White Road: A History of Polar Exploration* L. P. Kirwan writes:

Weddell in his devotion to science was typical of these sealing captains of the first three decades of the nineteenth century. Despite the lack of proper instruments and the disgruntlement of his sailors at so apparently profitless an occupation, he did what he could, testing the direction and strength of currents, taking temperatures of the sea until his thermometers were smashed in a gale, puzzling over differences in magnetic variation, scrupulously observing even in moments of danger the nature, form, and movements of the ice. To persevere with such tasks in vessels cruelly exposed to the violence of Antarctic weather required a singular devotion. The experience of Weddell's ships on this lengthy pioneering voyage were not unusual. A whaleboat overboard, a rudder frozen into immobility; bulwarks, decks, and rigging so heavily encrusted with ice that the ship could scarcely rise to the sea – such experiences were common in the brigs and cutters of the Antarctic sealers in the early years of the nineteenth century.

No doubt Conrad had in mind more distant times, but the earlier years of the nineteenth century, at least in the Antarctic, might equally be included when he speaks of 'Days when the sea was great and mysterious, ready to surrender the prize of fame to audacious men.'

From my point of view, therefore, the South Shetlands were highly attractive – remote, inaccessible, mountainous, The fact that they were inhabited was a slight drawback. At least on one of them, Deception Island, there are British, Chilean, and Argentine bases. Smith Island offered a supreme challenge to the sea-going mountaineer, an even sterner challenge than that accepted recently by Warwick Deacock and his party of Australians and New Zealanders when they sailed to Heard Island in the sub-antarctic and climbed its 9,000ft. peak Big Ben. For at Smith Island a party would be starting from scratch, without fore-knowledge of a possible landing place – there might well not be any – or of any route up the mountain. But apart from the island and its problems, the voyage alone would be an ambitious undertaking for an old 30-ton cutter with a skipper verging on the Psalmist's age limit. An old boat can, of course, be strengthened. But the man whose strength is diminished by age can only strive to emulate Beowulf's well known exhortation:

> Harder should be the spirit, the heart all the bolder,
> Courage the greater, as the strength grows less.

Ambitious or not, the voyage was within *Mischief's* powers. Size is no criterion of a boat's seaworthiness. The sealers used to sail small boats in the Antarctic, but these were either carried there on the deck of the larger vessels or built on the spot. They did not try to sail them across Drake Passage, the stretch of water between Cape Horn and the South Shetlands. Edmund Fanning, an American sealer who was active in these waters, describes how he acquired a fleet of three such tenders, or shallops, as he calls them:

Raising and decking our launch for one; then purchasing another which had in the previous season been built here by the crew of an English sealer; then taking the spare topmast of our vessel *Aspasia* for a keel, and a spare mainyard for a mast, together with some fifty oak knees roughly hewn that we had on board to support our battery deck; with these materials and a number of 3-inch planks which had been used to floor the ballast over, and sundry articles purchased from the wreck of the *Regulator*, we proceeded to lay the keel of the third shallop on an iceberg, in a valley at the starboard side of the harbour. She was a first-rate seaboat, as well as the fastest sailer among the fleet.

The 'iceberg in a valley' is a puzzle. Does he mean an iceberg aground, or a glacier? And one would like to know why they laid the keel on an 'iceberg'. Was this the only flat ground available? Or was it to facilitate the launching? Or just for the hell of it?

Other than those built on the spot or carried there, no boat comparable to *Mischief* had sailed in Antarctic waters, much less crossed Drake Strait – with one memorable exception. Shackleton's famous do-or-die voyage from the South Shetlands to South Georgia in May, one of the worst weather months, is not likely ever to be forgotten. This voyage in the *James Caird*, a ship's lifeboat, was a rescue operation, a life or death matter, not only for the six men on board but for the other twenty-two men of the *Endurance* marooned on Elephant Island, the easternmost of the South Shetlands. Behind *Mischief's* endeavour there would be no such compelling motive. The interest of the voyage itself and its ultimate aim must suffice to make it, as I thought, a worth-while undertaking. Anywhere at sea there are hazards, otherwise small-boat sailing would have less appeal. No waters are foolproof and Antarctic waters perhaps less so than any. As regards ice dangers, icebergs are visible even at night, and in low visibility one can always heave-to. Pack-ice we would avoid, for in summer the South Shetlands are normally ice-free. At Punta Arenas, through the Chilean navy, one could get reliable information about ice conditions, and if necessary wait there until the islands were reported free from ice. In summer a frigate or a naval tug plies frequently between Punta Arenas and the Chilean Antarctic bases.

The weather might have a more threatening aspect than the ice, but *Mischief*, in spite of her age, is staunch and a good seaboat, well able to stand up to the weather of those latitudes, the so-called Roaring Forties, Furious Fifties, and Shrieking Sixties. That is, of course, in summer conditions, between November and March. Ed Mikeska, a professional seaman, who had sailed with me to Baffin Bay and who had always regarded with apprehension *Mischief's* vulnerable skylight and too roomy cockpit, wrote to me encouragingly in his own peculiar, semi-seamanlike, staccato vein: 'I see you are to be a flying-fish sailor again, Cape Horning? Going to spit to windward now! Have a couple of good bilge-pumps fitted. Old *Mischief's* timbers will be a'shivering, and mind yer blooming skylight, not to mention the snug, dry cockpit you have. If you are lucky and hit a gale period in the South you will make the Shetlands under bare poles and baggy-wrinkle.' But much smaller boats than *Mischief* have successfully rounded Cape Horn. One hoped that the weather might not be quite so fearful as has been painted, and one knew that it does not become progressively worse farther south. In winter the weather could no doubt be hell, just as it can be in the North Atlantic.*

To find crews for *Mischief's* three voyages, which were all of twelve month's duration, had involved me in much effort and trouble. On the whole the results had been highly satisfactory so that none of this effort had been wasted. There must be plenty of men of the right stamp who would come forward if they knew what was afoot or if one could make contact with them, but the publicity that could easily be had and that would solve this problem is not all that welcome. One would like to have the benefit without paying the degrading price, like an American firm that proudly proclaims: 'We eschew publicity but we know how to use it.' However, despite this desire to let things speak for themselves, a policy that in these strident days might almost pass for reticence, *Mischief's* voyages have become better known. For each succeeding voyage the need to shop around for crew or to advertise, became less. To find crews for her most recent voyages I had really exerted myself very little,

*Note. Here is a specimen of winter Atlantic weather quoted recently in the Meteorological Office publication, *The Marine Observer*. Trawler St Barr, Hull to Labrador.

15th Feb. 1966 18.00 Wind WNW force 12, gusts to 87 knots, vis. 50 yds.
16th Feb. 00.00 Wind NW force 11, snow, seas 35ft. vis. 50 yds.
16th Feb. 06.00 wind NW force 11, continuous snow
16th Feb. 06.10 Wind NW increased and blew off wind-cups.
17th Feb. 00.00 Wind NW force 11, main aerials down.
17th Feb. 12.00 Wind NW force 7–8, snow showers, vis 2½ miles.

merely lurking in my fastness behind the Welsh hills, vetting the letters of hopeful applicants, and sallying forth at invervals, like a spider from his web, to inspect and secure another victim. One had to take them on the principle of first come first served, for it was not reasonable to defer a decision for long. This often had unfortunate results. Sure enough, when the muster roll had been filled, a man with better claims and in every way preferable, had to be turned down.

In spite of this inevitably haphazard method of collecting a crew – for it could not be called picking one – on all the Greenland voyages we had been a reasonably happy ship. On a comparatively short voyage of four to five months it is easy enough to:

> Be to their faults a little blind.
> And to their virtues ever kind.

And this cut both ways, the crew being prepared to tolerate anything I might do or say seeing that they had not to endure or suffer me for all that long. The crew's ability to get on with each other and to work together is more important than what seamanly qualities they may have. In this respect the enormous crew of ten which had sailed with me in *Patanela* to Heard Island (see *Mostly Mischief*, London, 1966) was remarkable for the absence of friction. But those were picked men, known to each other or to mutual friends, men with like interests and with expedition experience.

My system, if system it could be called, had worked well enough so far. Even if it could be arranged, a short preliminary voyage to try out the crew would have little value. They would be on their best behaviour, zealous and willing to an embarrassing degree, and if one did take a dislike to one of them, a replacement would still have to be found at short notice. Always on past voyages the crews had soon shaped up to their jobs, took whatever was going in the way of food, and made themselves as pleasant as they knew how. I hope I did the same, though no man can be expected to make bright, chatty remarks for five months on end, much less for twelve. It is sometimes difficult to say 'Good-morning' and quite impossible to continue the conversation beyond that. Doubts have been expressed as to whether the Christian virtue of good temper is binding on a man before breakfast. There is a story, quite apocryphal, of a pre-war voyage to India in a P & O liner with a Himalayan climbing party. On reaching the open sea from Tilbury the writer is reputed to have exclaimed, 'H'm, the sea', and on nearing Bombay, after a silence of eighteen days, to have startled his expectant listeners with another profound remark, 'H'm, the land'. But no one goes to sea in a small boat in the hope of leading a social life.

Naturally the finding of a crew for a twelve month's voyage is harder than for one of only five months. Fewer men are able or willing to spare that amount of time. There are therefore fewer from whom to choose. Whether this means that the chances of picking a dud are greater or lesser I am not a mathematician enough to say, but the presence of any such will inevitably be that much more difficult to tolerate. For the sort of voyage now in prospect, where conditions would be tough, at times perhaps even daunting, the quality of the crew, their reliability, their devotion to the ship they served and their sense of obligation to finish what they had undertaken to do, became of prime importance. Again, unlike a Greenland voyage, there would be stops in strange, sunny, exciting lands where the temptation to swallow the anchor is strong. Places where:

> Slumber is more sweet than toil, the shore
> Than labour in the deep mid-ocean, wind, and wave,
>   and oar;
> Oh, rest ye brother mariners, we will not wander
>   more.

Besides the attractions of the shore there may be other yachts which, at any rate in port, seem to offer more ease and comfort than hellship *Mischief*, and whose skippers appear to be less of a bastard.

As I say, no special exertions were made to find a crew for this voyage and there was no lack of applicants. Of these many withdrew when they learnt the time involved and our destination, and in the end, as is usually the case, it was touch and go whether we should have a full complement, with no scope left for manoeuvre. In the case of the first few applicants, one is so glad to have any at all that, like the first swallows of summer, they meet with a less critical eye. What unexpected virtues may not lie hidden under that unprepossessing appearance and manner? If this man is turned down, on possibly flimsy grounds, will any more be forthcoming? These are the questions that arise, and one has nothing to go upon but one's own fallible judgement.

Early in 1966 I roped in the first applicant, young Roger Robinson who approached me in person after a lecture I had given at Lymington. He was then at Southampton Technical College taking a course in Yard management, and in the happy position apparently of being able to break off and resume after a year's absence. He had had considerable sailing experience, had seen *Mischief* and knew what he was in for, and seemed uncommonly keen. I thought this quality would compensate for lack of size and weight, for he was dimunitive. As Falstaff said: 'Will you tell me, Master Shallow, how to choose a man? Care I for the thews, stature, bulk, and big assemblance of a man? Give me the spirit, Master Shallow.'

Next I had a letter from John Ireland, a stranger, who had heard of me and *Mischief* through a friend of mine in New Zealand. He then came to Wales bringing with him a friend of his, David Shaw. John Ireland hailed from Liverpool (my home town) and had the Liverpool sound, talking that language so fast that I had always to ask him to repeat what he had said. He had recently done a long trip in a Land Rover, climbing in New Zealand and the Andes on the way, for he was primarily a climber. He had also done some dinghy sailing. The friend, David Shaw, looked the more likely and proved to be just the man I always hope to have with me and so seldom get. I took to him at once; red-haired, sturdy, quiet, and self-reliant. He had been a Conway boy and was then in the Royal Mail Line and had just got his Master's ticket. He had not done much sailing but with his sea background would very soon learn. He would be invaluable to have, both as a competent mate and an experienced navigator, and should we succeed in landing a climbing party on Smith Island he would be able to take charge of *Mischief*. The question was whether he would be granted a year's leave. It would be a bit of a busman's holiday for him but he hankered after a closer familiarity with the sea in its varying moods than can be obtained from a glass-enclosed bridge. If *Mischief* had to proceed at 20 knots in all weathers one would certainly want to lurk behind glass. On my advice they went down to Lymington to look at *Mischief*, with the result that both wanted to come. It would be some time before David heard about his leave and it was up to me to keep a place open until he had heard.

The first few days down the steamer-infested English Channel with an inexperienced and probably seasick crew can be very wearying, conducive to nightmares and stomach ulcers. On this account alone the presence of a man who has sailed before in *Mischief* and knows the ropes is more than welcome, besides the comfort to be got from having on board from the start a man whom one knows and in whom one has confidence. Nor is this wish to have on board a second-voyager quite so absurd and improbable as may be thought. Not all past crews think that once is enough. Charles Marriott, for instance, has made one long and two short voyages in *Mischief*, thus deserving my gratitude and a medal, too, if I had one to bestow. Roger Tufft was another who had made one long and one short voyage, a man who liked it the hard way, having previously done three years in the Antarctic, subsequently making a crossing of the Greenland ice-cap manhauling a sledge. Bill Proctor, too had taken part in two long voyages when he was of the utmost value to me, having had far more experience. Later he built his own boat, a little 21ft. sloop, in which he had got more than half-way round the world before – alas – coming to grief. In July 1965 he left Guadalcanal for New Guinea, since when no trace of him or his boat has been found.

Setting considerable store, then, on having on board an old hand, I wrote to Bob Cook who had been present on the first, unlucky trip to East Greenland when *Mischief* had been nipped in the ice. I knew he was neither married nor in a job so promising that it could not lightly be thrown up, for he was a long-distance lorry driver. I was glad when he agreed to come. As well as being a climber he was valuable on deck, a big man whose weight on a rope would be worth about three of my more diminutive crew. There remained one place to fill, the hardest to fill in both senses. It is rare to find a man eager to cook at sea, and this is not strange, for dedicated men are rare. *Mischief's* galley is forward of the mast, the liveliest place in any seaway, and the cooking is done on Primus stoves, primitive, smelly, but safe and reasonably efficient. I have described it elsewhere as 'a rôle that is exacting and always difficult to fill. A rôle requiring the balance and agility of a juggler, a strong stomach, and indifference to being alternately sprayed with cold sea water from the galley hatch and boiling water from the stove; the ability to work in a confined space breathing rather foul air, and the energy, patience, and goodwill shown by a hen cormorant in feeding her mouth-gaping offspring.'

A friend of Roger Robinson's, a Swede, volunteered for the job, but owing to the Easter holidays, and his departure for Sweden before he had received my glad acceptance, he managed to escape. A young lad on a motor bike bound for Snowdonia and dressed for the part, a little shaggy withal, then turned up unannounced at Bodowen. Having heard through John Ireland of what was afoot he was on fire to come in the hope of doing some climbing. He had made one or two voyages as a trawler hand and was now learning the trade of welding, two jobs that in my opinion augured well of a prospective cook, the one hinting at a cast-iron stomach and the other familiarity with great heat. Tom O'Shaughnessy hailed from Birmingham and was, of course, Irish, and quick to take offence. His keenness for the adventure overcame his reluctance to cook. We already had two possible climbers but his willingness to cook made me glad to take him.

We were now complete provided David Shaw got leave and I had to put off several possible recruits while this hung in the balance. In mid-July we were due to sail so that it was disturbing for me to learn a month before that Bob Cook had fallen off the top of his loaded lorry on to a concrete floor, chipped the bone in both wrists, and would be unable to come. Those whom I now had to fall back on, having previously refused them, were committed to something else or for some reason unable to come. One had taken an Alpine holiday and spent all his money. Time was running out, but having at last heard that David Shaw could come I became reconciled to sailing with five all told instead of six.

At the end of June, just before I left for Lymington to start fitting out, Bob Cook wrote to say that he might be fit enough to come provided he could take things easy for the first few weeks. This welcome news came a fraction too late. Chance governs all. Before I had replied telling Bob to come I had a telephone call from a Mike Edwards, another of John Ireland's acquaintances. He, too, came from Birmingham. 'I have no great hopes of Birmingham', said Mrs Elton, 'there is something dire about the sound of it.' Be that as it may, I should have plumped for Bob Cook, chipped wrists notwithstanding, had not Mike Edwards told me that he was a professional photographer and suggested the possibility of making a film. On two earlier voyages we had made a 16mm film and I had found the exercise expensive and not repaying. But hope springs eternal in even my breast and I arranged to meet Mike Edwards in Ludlow next morning on my way to Lymington. Besides his photographic background he had sailed racing dinghies and had done his national service in the Navy. True, he had served only as a photographer but he should have learnt something of the sea and the need to keep things shipshape below. As later he showed, he had.

We met in the bar of The Feathers. He was tall, very fair, with a handsome beard of the same hue, a relic presumably of the Navy. Answering a question in the Commons about shark repellants, Churchill began his reply by saying, 'HM Government is totally opposed to sharks'; and, stupid prejudice though it no doubt is, I feel totally opposed to young men with beards. However, beard or no beard, I had to decide quickly between these two possibilities and I decided on trying to make a film. This gave Mike barely a week to settle his affairs, collect his kit, find, buy, and have tested a suitable second-hand camera with the necessary equipment. That he managed to do all this and join

Mischief a couple of days before sailing says much for his energy and ability.

So, for better or for worse, I had my crew, and on paper they looked pretty good. On previous voyages I had sailed with crews of less experience and less promise who had turned out well. How many of this lot were men with whom, according to Monty's well known criterion, one would care to go into the jungle, remained to be seen.

CHAPTER TWO

To the Canaries

AT THE END of a voyage *Mischief* is stripped bare. The crew put in two days hard word carrying ashore the sails, the gear, the accumulated junk of a voyage, unreeving the running rigging, and unshipping and sending ashore all the spars including the bowsprit. The Yard then take out the mast for storage under cover, and the standing rigging, the shrouds and forestays, go into the loft with the rest of the gear. *Mischief* is then taken to her mud berth where she is left to withstand the ravages of winter, no doubt feeling callously neglected. Rot and decay now have the chance to make their insidious attack. To help fight this off a big cowl ventilator is fitted over the hole in the deck normally filled by the mast, and additional ventilators have been let into the foredeck.

Whether the pole mast is the original mast dating back to 1906 is not known. Certainly it is getting on in years and has one or two very long shakes which happily run the right way, up and down the mast instead of across it. These are left open so that no water lodges in them, a plan that is probably better than filling them with stopping material. The mast has practically no taper. An elderly lady, whom I absolve from any rude intentions, once asked me if it had been a telephone pole. Some critics regard the mast, in the words of Mr Chuck the bos'un, as precarious and not at all permanent. It is stoutly stayed with $2\frac{1}{2}$ inch wire, but out of respect for any possible weakness we no longer send aloft the topmast, a heavy spar which extends another 20ft. above the upper cap. The extra weight aloft, as well as the extra windage of its five supporting shrouds and stays, is hardly offset by the ability to set a topsail. Nor in the Atlantic off Iceland and Greenland, where *Mischief* had cruised for the past five summers, would there be many days when a topsail could be carried. Over the years I have become accustomed to her baldheaded look and am not likely to see her fully rigged again until she is reduced to making coastal passages. All the other spars, boom, gaff, and bowsprit, have been renewed since I bought her in the spring of 1954 at Majorca. The gaff had broken off the Spanish coast when bringing her home in the autumn of that year; the boom broke in 1956 between Bermuda and the Scillies, and the bowsprit broke off Cape Town in 1960. The present boom is a massive affair almost as thick as the mast, strong enough in itself to laugh at the most violent 'Chinese' gybes and heavy enough to smash anything that stands in its way. Even when laying in stately repose on the gallows, its dimensions strike a new crew with awe and dismay; for it is obvious that the least tap from this heavy, blunt instrument would stun the strongest elephant. But, like the threat of nuclear war, its formidable powers are a safeguard and a deterrent. One keeps out of harm's way. So far it has neither killed anyone nor swept them overboard.

Throughout the winter I had been taking home bits and pieces of the running rigging – bowsprit shrouds, backstays, topping lifts, tackles – replacing the wire when necessary, renewing block strops, and overhauling the blocks. In stormy weather, the knowledge that this work has been properly done ensures some peace of mind. On this long voyage south of 21,000 miles, except for a broken sheave in the throat halyard block, nothing in the rigging came adrift. It is not easy nowadays to find old-fashioned wood blocks or the sheaves to go with them, modern yacht blocks being made of anything but wood, diminutive in size as they are high in cost. The main shrouds and forestay are too heavy to be taken home, nor would I care to undertake the job of splicing wire of that size. These are examined by the Yard before the mast is stepped, which is done after the boat has been hauled out for its annual coat of anti-fouling. On this occasion, when towards the end of June the mast was about to be stepped, the shrouds, which had been fitted in 1955, had to be condemned. Under the serving and parcelling of the eyes that go over the masthead, it was found that only a strand or two remained serviceable, the rest being rusted through. Why the mast had remained standing on the voyage home from Greenland the previous autumn is another unsolved mystery of the sea; the mast must indeed have been precarious and not at all permanent. This discovery meant a rush job making up new shrouds and forestay, and in order to save time and money – the usual excuse for any unsightliness – I consented to 'talurit' splices for the lower eyes instead of hand splices. This quick method of swageing wire is reckoned to be as strong or stronger than splicing by hand but it looked out of place in *Mischief's* old style rigging.

Before this, young Roger and I had started painting below-peak, galley, cabin, and engine-room – a job that must be done before the crew can start living on board. By the time I got down early in July to start fitting out he had about finished the painting. The new shrouds had already been set up but the forestay had been made a foot too long and had to be done again. Pleased though I was to see the new shrouds already up I felt disgusted with myself over the 'talurit' splices which stuck out blatantly, as inappropriate as a tin roof on a tithe barn. Keen-eyed visitors to the old boat commented on their incongruity. They feared that it might be the thin edge of the wedge, that before long she would have stainless steel rigging, chromium-plated winches, a metal mast, nylon rope and terylene sails. Such things may be good in the right place, though where that is I would not care to say; but in an old gaff cutter they strike a bizarre note, as if some venerable elder statesman had had himself rigged out in Carnaby Street.

When David Shaw joined we did our best to hoodwink people by serving over the 'talurit' splices with marline. These whims and fancies of mine have to be paid for and I suppose this is done through some loss in efficiency. Sails and ropes made from artificial materials, of which new versions are constantly appearing, cost much more but are stronger and more enduring than those made from natural fibres. but the greatest advantage of such sails is their immunity to rot and mildew, so that if need be they can be stowed wet. They have some slight drawbacks. The stitching on such sails stands out proud and is liable to chafe, and bends and hitches taken in ropes of man-made fibres are apt to slip. Personally, I shrink from the noise that some of these new materials make; the flapping of the sails when going about often sounds like small-arms fire. Tom had a windproof smock made from one of these new materials and when he was on deck in a breeze the racket it made was frightening.

By the time the crew began to arrive I had the ratlines made up so that we could get aloft to hang the blocks and reeve the halyards. David and John Ireland limped into the Yard in an ancient and halting car that seemed about to wheeze its last wheeze. John at once advertised its sale. After some hard bargaining it went to a chap in the Yard for £5, the removal of its last seat add to the amenities of *Mischief's* cabin having significantly diminished its value. With the arrival of Tom O'Shaughnessy work went on apace, and with everything well in hand David and I spent a day in Southampton for a last shopping round-up and the collection of log books and thermometers from the Meteorological Office. On the Greenland voyages we had recorded observations for the Meteorological office at Bracknell. Having no transmitter we cannot transmit observations when they are made as is, of course, done by the large fleet of voluntary observing ships.* At the end of the voyage our log books are sent to Bracknell where they are used for analysis. They are of value mainly because the observations, particularly of sea temperatures and ice, are from little-frequented waters. When I wrote to Bracknell about the impending voyage I suggested that the Southern Ocean might lie outside their parish. 'So far from being out of our parish,' was the reply, 'we are very interested indeed in those parts. Since the demise of British whaling we are virtually starved of marine observations from the Southern Ocean. The Royal Research Ships *Shackleton* and *John Biscoe* are our only source of marine data. That is why observations from *Mischief* would be so valuable.'

Mike Edwards having joined two days previously we sailed from Lymington on Friday, 14 July 1966, bound for the Antarctic by way of the Canaries, Montevideo, and Punta Arenas. A few local friends gathered to see us cast off and on our way down the river the Royal Lymington Yacht Club, according to their friendly custom, gave us a starting gun. Wind of our departure, however, had reached as far as Southampton, so that Southern Television sent a camera team to accompany us out into the Solent where we would hoist sail. As our jib halyard has a perverse habit of twisting I had had the jib made

---

*There are some 500 of these selected ships,covering between them the Seven Seas and representative of the best of the Merchant Navy. The P. & O., for instance, have been recording observations since 1855. In addition there are 65 supplementary ships, 108 coasting vessels, 13 lightships, 20 trawlers, and 50 auxiliary ships whose observations are less full than those of the selected ships.

up in stops and when the moment came all the sails went up without any hitch. Only the vang, the rope leading down from the peak of the gaff, got adrift. From my position aft in the cockpit I should have secured the lower end of the vang to the boom, but with my eyes on the crew and conscious that the eyes of England, or at least Southern England, were upon me, I failed to grab it in time. Since then I have not met anyone who watched our departure as it appeared on illustrated wireless; anyone who did must have wondered whether the long rope streaming gaily from the peak was *Mischief's* paying-off pendant. When the television boys arrange to take such pictures they probably think they are doing one a favour, whereas the boot is really on the other foot. The camera team, one hopes, enjoy a nice little outing, and in the course of it, at no cost, obtain the material to fill an otherwise dull programme. The idea of insulting one by offering some payment in return, even to the extent of a coil of rope or a bottle of whisky, never occurs to them.

On a fine, clear morning, the wind at NW force 4–5, we cleared the Needles and headed down Channel. None of the crew except John showed any interest in pilchards for lunch, and unless the sea is unusually calm this is how fresh crews usually react whether or not they have taken anti-seasick pills beforehand. It is a state of affairs that is to be expected and must be allowed for when starting out with an unseasoned crew. It is always a bad thing to have to postpone one's departure but it would be unwise not to do so if really rough weather prevailed. In the Channel, where even in summer fog or thick weather may develop quite quickly, it is a good thing to know one's position. As soon as we had sunk the coast of England below the horizon I took a sun sight, but before obtaining a reasonable result I found I had to work it several times. Rust is the enemy to combat in maintaining a boat, and a man's brains, after some months ashore, are not immune to its ravages.

At midnight we passed the Casquets and had Les Hanois abeam next morning. Standing away from the French coast we had to reef down in the afternoon, and when the forecast predicted winds of force 6–7 we hove to for the night. The crew were far from well and I wanted to ensure our having some supper. Tom being out of action, Mike gave us a scratch meal of onion soup, cold bully, and spuds. That the forecast proved correct deserves mention, for it is only the mistakes that are usually recorded, often in indignant terms. Conditions were less wild when we started sailing again at 4 am steering WSW with Ushant 50 miles away. Both Tom and Roger remained in prone positions and David was not sure of himself, having to abstain from the cigarettes he delighted in. None of the others smoked. I smoke a pipe and smoke far more tobacco at sea than on land in order to extract the utmost benefit from duty-free tobacco – making hay while the sun shines, so to speak. David, who had never before been sick at sea, felt injured, while I took it as a reflection upon *Mischief's* sea kindliness, one of her great virtues.

On the Sunday night, a clear night with moderate wind and sea, we raised the Ushant light and by next morning had it abeam with a stream of shipping well inside us. For the skipper at any rate the rounding of this noted seamark had been fairly painless, except that our meals had been a little too simple. On the Monday night, however, Tom made amends by giving us a curry with really dry rice. In the matter of curry I can be a little swinish; it was probably gluttony at supper, and the consequent drowisiness, that led to my having a close shave with a trawler. I had to put the helm hard down to avoid being rammed.

Women who spend much time with horses are said to acquire faces not unlike a horse; in the same way, having spent much time with Sherpas, Tibetans, Khirgiz, Afghans, and such like, I have acquired a taste for hot dishes. These otherwise happy folk never taste meat as we know it in the form of Welsh mutton or Scotch beef. When in luck they may partake of a scraggy goat, a scrawny rooster, or a yak whose diet has been mainly gravel, the kind of meat that needs to be thoroughly disguised even if it means blistering one's mouth in the process. Nor is their liking for fiery food confined to meat dishes. The Sherpas, for instance like all their food spiced; were they to eat anything so anaemic as porridge they would flavour it with chillies rather than sugar. Once alone with one in the Assam Himalaya, I made a note of how he doctored his ration of half a mug of peasoup:

Taking six large chillies, a dozen cloves of garlic, an ounce of salt, he ground them on a stone to form a thick paste. This was scraped off the stone and dissolved in not more that a quarter cupful of water to which only half the soup was added. Then, with an occasional shake of the head and a blink of the eyes, the only hint that he was taking a powerful blister and not an emollient like bread and milk, the fragrant mess was quickly hoisted in. The Sherpa likes his sauce piquant.

I was fortunate in once taking a short course in how to eat curries, if not how to make them, in the Western Desert where, in quiet periods, the officers of a Punjabi battalion used to lay on a special curry lunch on Sundays, a rich and gigantic vision of the higher gluttony. The Colonel, a Falstaffian figure in shirt sleeves and shorts, always began by putting towel round his neck as a sweat rag. Disgusting, no doubt, but highly practical and a mark of respect to the mess cook. Before concluding this dissertation on curry and returning to the Bay of Biscay, I might add that our having curry for breakfast, harmless though it may sound, played some part in the ultimate defection of the crew. On such small things have depended ere now the fate of dynasties. The War of the Austrian Succession, we are told, was ostensibly caused by the loss of his ear by one Jenkins, master mariner, at the hands of the Spaniards.

We made fast time across the Bay with runs of over 100 miles on four successive days, so that when only six days out we were nearing Cape Villano north of Finisterre. There were the usual tunnymen about, gaily painted craft with tanned steadying sails, their crews hauling in tunny with monotonous ease. This irked us, for we caught nothing on the line that we trolled persistently over the stern; as some wag remarked, we would have no fish on our plate until we got to that river. For a week the crew were kept occupied, if not amused, by scraping the deck. Hitherto the deck had been painted with a mixture of linseed oil and red ochre which looked well and was non-skid. With a painted deck, however, there is a tendency for water to get under the paint and lie there. Our bare deck when wet seemed to me much more slippery and whether with bare feet or in gumboots one had to move with caution. Unlike the single-handed sailor whose time is fully occupied, a large crew in a small boat never has enough to do. Four men could manage *Mischief* comfortably. In her working days, manned by real sailors, two were enough. We had to have six so that if a climbing party were put ashore there would be enough men left to work the boat. We therefore had five watch-keepers, and since in normal weather we keep single watches, a man has a lot more time off duty than on. The few major repair jobs that crop up from day to day are easily handled by one man. On passage, painting and varnishing are not often possible and seldom profitable, while the making of chafing gear such as baggy-wrinkle or fenders, is limited by the amount of old rope on board – usually not a lot. How different from the life of hard labour for the crew of big four-masted sailing ships with their miles of rope and wire and acres of canvas to be maintained, too few men and too much work:

Six days shalt thou labour, and do all that thou art able,
And on the seventh – holystone the decks and scrape the cable.

So that apart from watch-keeping and the occasional call to change sails or reef, the crew of a small boat are thrown much upon their own resources – reading, writing, sleeping, or sun-bathing and day-dreaming on deck. In fact, 'stretched on the rack of a too easy chair'.

Having carried us swiftly across the Bay the wind fell light and finally left us becalmed, in fog and in the shipping lane, 30 miles north of the Farilhoes. *Reina del Mar*, a cruise ship, slid by going dead slow, while other ships, to judge by the noise of their engines, were bashing on regardless, some not even sounding their fog-horns. Compared with the strident, threatening blare from a big steamer, the note from our foghorn, blown by mouth, is politely plaintive and of limited range. On some calm foggy day it would be instructive to row off in the dinghy to learn how far its squeak does carry. I suspect that one would not have far to row.

A breeze thinned the fog a little but it did not clear until next day when we found we were 20 miles south of our dead reckoning position. Nothing had been seen or heard of the lighthouse on the Burlings. Whether we had passed between the Farilhoes and the Burlings, or outside both groups, worried David, a most conscientious navigator. Evening star sights were his forte, taking four or even five stars and producing the answer in a very short time in spite of the indifferent cabin lighting. I preferred morning star sights when there was daylight in which to read the tables; even so the results were sometimes less than perfect, the triangle of error that resulted from the plotting, generally known as a 'cocked hat', too often resembled a nine-gallon Stetson. My sextant, made by Bassnett of Liverpool, a firm long defunct, must be pretty venerable. Old shoes, old coats, old friends, are best, but, perhaps, not old sextants. In picking up a star I find it better to discard the telescope, which leads one to suspect that it may be dim with age. However, since the Polynesians navigated successfully with a coconut, price 1/–, one grudges spending £50 or so on a new sextant. An authority on these matters, though not himself a Polynesian, tells me that celestial navigation by means of coconuts is a myth. But I propose letting it stand. We suffer too much from matter-of-fact people who take pleasure in demolishing our cherished illusions.

The northerly wind off the Portuguese coast soon began to veer east, merging into the north-east Trades which at this time of year are at their farthest north. With 500 miles to go to the Canaries we set the twin staysails and sat back to enjoy an even more leisurely life. Sailing downwind with twin staysails or a square sail brings peace of mind to the skipper and makes for a fast passage. In the latitudes of the Trades the chances of a gale are remote, the gear is free from chafe, and whatever antics the helmsman may be equal to there is no great boom for him to bring crashing over in a 'Chinese' gybe. But like most good things one can get tired of this kind of sailing. The sheets have not to be touched, the helmsman has only to keep the wind on the back of his neck, and the ceaseless rolling becomes a bore. This year the Trade wind seemed less fresh than I remembered on earlier voyages, and since the following seas were not so big the rolling never became so violent as that described on *Mischief's* first voyage South:

She seemed to enjoy sailing before a wind that blew true and steady as a bellows, and frequently showed her pleasure by some lively rolling. This rhythmic rolling, inseparable from downwind sailing, becomes a nuisance, particularly at meal times, when a man needs two pairs of hands, or if any work has to be done on deck. Every few minutes the boat would glide gently into a crescendo of rolling, each successive roll becoming livelier and longer, until the dislodging of the helmsman from his seat or a loud crash from the galley, announced that she had had her bit of fun. Then she would sail demurely along until tempted by the laughing waves to do it again. One could almost hear her humming to herself:

> Roll me over, in the clover,
> Roll me over, lay me down, and do it again.

By now we were in flying fish waters but only rarely did enough come on board to provide a breakfast. Flying at night they hit the sails or some other obstruction (once when steering I was hit in the face by one), or if the boat is rolling heavily they may be scooped up over the bulwarks. I attributed the scarcity of flying fish for breakfast to the fact that we were not rolling enough. Porridge, therefore, or a scramble of dried eggs, was usually our morning fare. Dried eggs are at their most exquisite in a cake or a duff where their flavour passes unnoticed among the more wholesome ingredients. If taken neat they need to be laced liberally with Tabasco sauce, a sauce that is hot by our feeble standards, for I doubt if it would blister the skin. Tom had now found his feet, and – thoroughly mixing the metaphor – began to pull out all the stops, playing every possible variation within our limited range. Based firmly for the most part on bully beef, these consisted of stews, risotto, past'asciuta, dried hash, sausage and mash, and, of course, curry. As yet my gastronome's diary makes no mention of duffs, the mariner's prime belly-timber, but they were to come. I read, however, that we had some difficulty about mashing spuds. 'Have we anything on board for mashing spuds?' someone asked. 'What size are your feet, Mike?'

We were now nearing the Canaries after a pleasant enough passage, but a little worried by the amount of water she was making. The trouble was traced to a broken cockpit drainpipe. Later in harbour, when we could plug the outlet with a cork, John put in a length of polythene tubing. At midnight of 29 July we sighted the Isleta light on Grand Canary and hove to until daylight before entering the harbour. *Mischief* wears well. Unlike her owner she does not get slower and slower each year. On the four occasions that she has visited Las Palmas, from 1955 onwards, she has taken exactly 16 days from Lymington.

CHAPTER THREE

Tragedy at Sea

SINCE *Mischief's* last visit in 1959 alterations and extensions have been made to the harbour of La Luz. Because there were no ocean-going yachts anchored off it, we ignored what was obviously a new yacht club and went on to anchor off where the club had been when we were last here, which was now waste land. We found ourselves among a thick cluster of local small craft and had not been there five minutes before a policeman on the nearby wharf told us to clear out. So we moved to the head of the harbour, an oasis of quiet, as we thought, until a bucket dredger close by started to work. When no one had shown any interest or come to clear us I rowed ashore and got a lift in a truck to the port office on the opposite side of the harbour. It was open, but only for the sake of a bevy of hostile charwomen who soon brushed me aside. At last I found the office of the port police where a chap who sat smoking a cigar, listening to a commentary on a World Cup match, stamped our passports in between goals. On this Saturday afternoon no doubt the port authorities in many other countries were similarly busy. Having made our number at the Yacht Club, where a swimming gala was in progress, we dined in a cheap joint in La Luz. Tom had stayed on board and in spite of the racket from the dredger (which worked all night) heard us when we shouted for the dinghy.

As the dredger seemed unlikely to shift for some time we decided to move to the Club, having first found that the water off it would be deep enough. With a view to astonishing the natives we thought we would sail there and make a running moor. Two natives at least we astonished, gave them in fact the fright of their lives. What with our being near the head of the harbour and the wind offshore, the dredger on one side and a wooden jetty on the other, we had little room in which to tack. Moreover, *Mischief* was in one of her obstinate moods. On the first two attempts prudence decided me to bear away at the critical moment. On the third attempt, without doing the fresh thinking that the situation obviously required, I held on, much to the surprise and dismay of two men in a dinghy fishing close to the wooden jetty. Probably neither could swim, for they stood by their ship like heroes, awaiting our onslaught, without jumping overboard. Our bowsprit cleared the jetty by an inch or so and out of the corner of my eye I could see that the two heroes were still afloat; nevertheless, our manoeuvre, daring though it was, had not been really seamanlike.

Shaken though I was, and indeed the crew as well, no one flinched from the carrying out of the second part of our programme, the running moor. After a couple of dummy runs this went without a hitch. Dashing, in a manner of speaking towards the shore, we turned into the wind, let go the anchor, and had the sails down in a jiffy. Only when a launch full of yachting characters appeared on the scene did we realise that a small buoy close ahead of us marked the finish of a race. Soon the contestants at the end of their eight-mile race hove in sight and our presence close to the finishing mark gave them a last minute chance to display their skill. From the noise made by the excited crews as they were obliged to go about and again about to fetch the mark, one sensed that in their opinion we were in the way. These racing boats were the size of whalers with a big crew and one big lateen sail which demanded smart handling as they went about, loosing the tack, carrying it round the mast, and making fast again at the stem.

Several launches with spectators were in at the finish and presently one of them came alongside. A thin, grey-haired man in a battered black velour asked in excellent English if he could do anything for us. Gravino, as he was called, proved an invaluable ally during the rest of our stay, bargaining with shopkeepers, arranging for stores and water, and dealing with officials. Among us only John had a smattering of Spanish, having spent some months in Montevideo on his world tour. Gravino, a widower, lived alone with a pet dog in an ancient fishing boat moored in the harbour. He had been a fisherman and gave us much unavailing advice on how to catch fish; his English had been learnt while at an American base during the war. He made heavy inroads on our whisky, though protesting his dislike of it, his favourite tipple being bacardi rum and coke. He was seventy odd, and when we remarked on his agility and fitness he told us, much as a man might boast of doing twenty 'press-ups' before breakfast, that he daily drank 65 small glasses of rum and coke. The night before we sailed we joined him at his favourite bar, his home-ground so to speak, where he scored a century not-out.

No one from the Yacht Club paid us a visit; perhaps we looked too much like a working boat. A big French ketch came in for a couple of days and later a Fairmile launch from Durban. The latter must have had a foul time bucking the north-east Trades; an ocean voyage in a small power boat is my idea of hell, it must demand from the crew uncommon endurance. The short stay made by these two and the absence of any other yachts contrasted strongly with the dozen or so that had been present on our earlier visits, yachts that had been manned mostly by what I call seagoing beachcombers who were in no hurry to move. Most of them – American, Canadian, Australian, German – had been bound for the West Indies and were awaiting the passing of the hurricane season. Others might be waiting the arrival of funds, or waiting there to earn funds, or merely waiting, Micawber-like, for something to turn up. I remember vividly a small weather-worn sloop lying next to us, whose owner, a bearded German, old enough to have known better, had with him as partner or crew a sort of Gypsy Queen, all flashing eyes and teeth. While he went shopping with a string bag the Gipsy Queen, or Princess Pocahontas as I called her, sat on deck ogling *Mischief's* crew. There may be fewer cruising yachts at Las Palmas but a vastly increased number of fishing vessels now use the harbour, small trawlers of many nationalities but mainly Japanese. In recent years the waters off the African coast opposite the Canaries have proved to be one of the world's richest fishing grounds.

Except for Tom who was short of cash the crew spent their days ashore and seemed fully occupied. Mike, in particular, as was his way in every port, gave the impression of being rushed off his feet, a man working against time, writing notes, and taking the name and address of everyone he met. But they were all models of decorum, unlike the crew of 1957 who on arrival had disappeared to a man, returning for breakfast the worse for wear, one of them having been robbed of all he possessed. We made a point of meeting about 11pm at the Club jetty in order to avoid someone having to turn out later in the night to fetch off belated arrivals. The descent into the dinghy down a long, iron ladder presented no difficulty but one night David, who was cold sober, missed the dinghy. His anger on being fished out of the water was so evident that our natural impulse to laugh had to be quickly suppressed. His smart, shore-going rig had all to be rinsed out in fresh water.

On 6 August we went alongside the fish wharf to take in water. If we were to fetch Montevideo at one hop as intended we needed all the water we could carry and a bit more. The main tank in the cabin, on top of which is our table, holds 100 gallons; a deck tank holds another 40 gallons; and there is another side tank in the cabin holding 30 gallons. Besides this there is a 5-gallon iron-bound water-beaker lashed on deck, which many people think ought to be full of brandy, and a few smaller containers. Altogether we can carry about 180 gallons which, at 3 gallons a day, would allow us to be at sea for 60 days. This would not be enough and we relied upon collecting 30 to 40 gallons of rain water in the doldrums, an expectation that in my short experience has never failed. The water is in charge of the cook and no one gets any to drink except in the form of tea, coffee, or cocoa. The washing of either body or clothes is, of course out, except with sea water. Shaving water is allowable but only Tom and I availed ourselves of this. While watering I went with Gravino to collect our clearance papers. On the way back a fisherman friend of Gravino's presented me with a fish, a big, red, roman-nosed brute whose coarse looks belied its fine quality.

Having paid Gravino for his services with a bottle of the whisky he despised and drank so heartily, we sailed out. We were well stocked with provisions and one or two of our containers had in them something better than water. As the Spaniards say, a day without wine is a day without sun, and at all our ports of call as far south as Punta Arenas wine is to be had good and cheap. It had been a moot point whether we should take our departure for the South Shetlands from the Falkland Islands or from Punta Arenas, and the fact that we should be able to stock up with wine there may have tipped the scale in favour of Punta Arenas. We took a large quantity of twice-baked bread, 'tostada', which is merely sliced bread or rolls put in the oven and toasted. In less than ten days bread is usually too mouldy to be eaten even by the least fastidious while 'tostada' seems to keep indefinitely. We had no less than three sacks full.

Having obtained a good offing to clear the southern end of Grand Canary we set the twins and let her go. The Trades blow pretty fresh in the vicinity of the Canaries. Leaving Las Palmas bound south is like stepping on to a train; for one can hoist the twins secure in the knowledge that for the next 800 miles one will drive steadily on course logging over 100 miles a day. That afternoon the wind increased to force 6 or 7. In one watch we logged 6 knots and in the next 7 knots, just about as fast as *Mischief* can be expected to go without coming apart at the seams. Chased by the following seas she yawed about a lot, so that until the wind moderated after midnight we had two men on watch. The point was that the helmsman in order to call his relief has to leave the tiller for a minute or two to nip down to the cabin, and under the twins she does not hold her course nearly so steadily as under fore and aft rig, no matter how cunningly the tiller is lashed. With no one at the helm to correct it, a violent yaw might fetch one of the sails aback. On one occasion some genius at the helm brought off the almost impossible feat of getting both the twin stay-sails aback. My metaphorical train on to which we had stepped when leaving Las Palmas proved to be a stopping train. After a run of 520 miles in five days, on the next day we did only 25 miles. Whether he is concerned with the erratic behaviour of a storm or the ordered regularity of the Trade winds, a seaman counts on nothing from the weather except its power to surprise him. As Captain MacWhirr remarked of the Laws of Storms: 'All these rules for dodging breezes and circumventing the winds of Heaven, Mr Jukes, seem to me the maddest thing.' Still, the Trade winds at least ought to conform to the rules; their northern or southern limits shift and may exceed or fall short of the accepted average, but a sudden failure of them at their very heart gives good reason for surprise. On the night before this sudden lull – though it cannot be cited as cause and effect – we had admired a dazzling display of phosphorescence during which a school of dolphins struck streaks of fire as they crossed and recrossed the ship's glowing wake. For two days the wind picked up again enabling us to score runs of 108 and 90 miles. The rougher sea brought on board some flying fish and for the first time we had enough for breakfast. In my opinion they are as good as fresh herrings. I see, too, from my gastronomic notes, that Tom had mastered the technique of duff making. The gannets among us, which was our term for the gluttons, had barely finished breakfast before they were speculating on what the day might bring forth, that is to say, the size, shape, flavour and richness of the evening's duff – like those men of whom Dr Johnson speaks, 'whose principal enjoyment is their dinner and who see the sun rise with no other hope than that they shall fill their belly before it sets.'

On the 14th the wind failed again and as we lay becalmed that evening – though nothing could be seen – we reckoned we were only a few miles north of Boa Vista, the easternmost island of the Cape Verde group in Lat. 16 N. These islands are supposed to lie within the belt of the north-east Trades throughout the year. The sailing ship track passes to the west of the islands, where it is possible we might have had steadier winds. But I wanted to sight the islands, or at least to let the crew see them, in particular the island of Fogo and its 9,000ft. volcanic cone of which on an earlier voyage we had enjoyed a spectacular glimpse. Islands, ships, whales, marine monsters of any kind, birds, even bits of seaweed, all arouse the keenest interest and break the tedium of a long ocean passage. They form subjects for argument and give the crew something to talk about other than the shortcomings of the skipper. Alas! We saw nothing. For us the Cape Verde Islands might not have existed, for the haze that so often prevails in their vicinity in summer had reduced visibility to less than two miles.

On account of this, the indefinite horizon, as well as the unreliability of a meridian sight, the sun being now almost overhead, we were uncertain of our position – an uncertainty that could not but cause anxiety in view of what the *Admiralty Pilot* has to say of this region:

Chart 366 should be used with great caution, especially in the vicinity of Boa Vista, off which many uncharted dangers exist. The haze over the whole group is often so thick that the surf is sighted before the land. The eastern islands more especially feel the force of the south-westerly set and several wrecks have been caused by disregarding it. It is recommended to give the east coast of Boa Vista a berth of at least 7 miles.

Admiralty Pilots necessarily abound with gloomy remarks of this kind, painting the worst possible picture, so that the mariner who comes unstuck cannot say he has not been warned. Therefore, upon hearing what I took to be the noise of breakers, at the first breath of wind we stood away to the south-east.

> Beyond the clouds, beyond the waves that roar,
> There may indeed, or may not be, a shore.

The crew suggested the noise was that of a jet plane warming up, but I could see no possible connection between jet planes and an island like Boa Vista, and this mythical jet continued warming itself up so long as we remained in earshot. By the following evening, when a west wind had cleared away the haze, we were too far south to see any of the islands.

The sights that we did at last obtain put us 20 miles south of our dead reckoning. We were having difficulty in getting time signals and at this juncture David managed to put the chronometer watch back in its case upside down, thus effectively stopping it. This watch had been purchased ten years before, secondhand for £5, and on only one voyage, when the mainspring broke, has it stopped. It has a steady rate, generally gaining two or three seconds a day when the temperature increases, and losing again by a similar amount in colder regions. For news and time signals we carry a Decca transistor receiving set, and normally an aerial inside the cabin suffices for picking up the BBC Overseas service in any ocean. Now, in order to make sure of receiving a time signal, we rigged an outside aerial, and having got one we were able next night to restart the chronometer.

During the next few days the wind varied greatly in strength, one evening a flat calm and in the succeeding night enough wind to split the genoa. During the evening calm, the weather bright and sunny, we piped all hands to bathe and skylark. Skylarking was the word, ducking each other, diving from the rigging, belly flops and bottom flops. And for supper we had what we called a cheese flop followed by a jam sponge. Flop consisted of potatoes, cheese, and onions churned together and baked. At last on 19 August, in Lat. 8°N., we had the rain we expected and needed. With a roll in the mainsail water trickles off briskly to be collected in saucepans and buckets hitched at various points along the boom. Later we rigged the canvas skylight cover under the boom like a canvas bath. A watering party, stripped naked, stands by to empty the saucepans and buckets into the deck tank. The single roll that we had put in the mainsail for collecting water soon had to be increased on account of wind, the prelude to a black, wet, thoroughly unpleasant night. This bout of rain lasted for 24 hours.

The wind now settled down at south or a point or two either side of it, the very direction in which we hoped to steer. Whichever tack we sailed on, owing to leeway, we could make but little to the south, perhaps 10, or at the most 20 miles of southing as a result of 24 hours sailing. Why worry, one might ask, South America lies to the west so why not steer west? The snag is that a ship which fails to cross the Equator far enough to the east is set to the west in the grip of the Equatorial current at the rate of 20 miles a day until it finds itself hard up against the coast of Brazil. In the days of sail a square-rigged ship that found itself unable to weather Cape San Roque at the north-east corner of South America might have to fetch a circuit of the North Atlantic in order to try again. One is well advised not to go on the port tack to start steering west until south of Lat. 4°N.

Notwithstanding, our reluctance to sail in the opposite direction to our destination overcame reason. For the next two or three days we steered stubbornly westwards on the port tack, always hoping that the southerly wind would free us by hauling more to the east. In fresh winds and a moderately rough sea we were going west at the rate of 80 miles a day and very little to the south; and it was in these unsatisfactory conditions that a most unexpected and inexplicable tragedy overtook us. Coming on deck at 7.40 am on 27 August, I found the ship on course, the helm lashed, and no sign of the helmsman. It was hard to believe but it did not take long to satisfy myself that David, who had the watch from 6 am to 8 am was not on board. After a hasty look in the peak, the galley, and the cabin I gave the alarm, turned out all hands, and gave the order to gybe. In a few minutes we were sailing back ENE on a reciprocal course with all hands up the shrouds scanning. The sea flecked with white horses, dark cloud shadows moving slowly across it, the sea that for the last few weeks we had sailed over so care-free and unthinkingly, had suddenly assumed a pitiless aspect.

We soon noticed that the patent log had stopped rotating and on hauling in the line we found that this had broken about two-thirds of its length from the counter. It is by no means unusual to lose a rotator; on the present voyage we lost two. Either it is bitten off by a shark or a porpoise, or the line frays at the point where it is attached to the rotator. But the line is less likely to break or be bitten through at any other point, accordingly we assumed that it had broken when David grabbed at it, or even later on when his weight on it had combined with a sudden lift and snatch of the counter to put too much strain on the line. The entry in the logbook by the man whom David had relieved at 6 am was 1,830 miles and the log had stopped recording at 1,831. In short, we concluded that if the line broke when David grabbed at it, as seemed most probable, this must have happened about 6.15 am, so that he had already been overboard for an hour and three-quarters. My heart sank. In so far as we were not shipping any water on deck the sea could not be called rough, but for a man swimming it was far too rough. I did not see how a man unsupported by a lifebelt could long survive.

Assuming the worst I decided to sail back a full seven miles, which in theory would take us to the ship's position at 6.15 am, the time at which the accident had probably occurred. After that we could start searching back across our track. I say 'in theory' because it could be only the roughest guess-work. How much leeway would she make? Would it be the same that she had made on the opposite tack? Would the speeds be the same? Even an error of a half-point would in the course of 7 miles bring us to a position that differed by nearly one mile. And in the conditions prevailing, the white horses and the increasing glare of the sun on the water, we should be lucky to spot a man's head even three or four hundred yards away. When so much depended, or might depend, upon the course we steered, upon our making a lucky guess, my feelings as I sat watching the compass may be easily imagined.

By 10 am, when we had run our distance and sighted nothing, we handed the sails, started the enginge, and began to motor back across our track, ranging about a half-mile either side of it. A sound enough plan if we were approximately in the right place, otherwise perfectly futile. Nor could one suppress the terrible feeling that we might have already sailed past David, that he had watched *Mischief*'s familiar mast go by and that we had failed to spot him. The crew continued their watch from up the shrouds where they remained throughout that most dismal day, one of them in turn coming down for a bite of food. Standing on the ratlines, hanging on to the shrouds hour after hour, taxed both strength and determination. With no sails to steady her *Mischief* rolled and pitched heartily and the higher a man is above the deck the more violently is he flung about. For the first two or three hours hope buoyed us up but as the weary day dragged on we became increasingly despondent; until at last the lengthening hours since the first news of the disaster finally extinguished hope. A small school of dolphins chose this day of all days to accompany *Mischief*, leaping out of the water and turning somersaults with a gay abandon that contrasted bitterly with our despairing gloom.

At 6.30 pm, the sun about to set, I decided that no more could be done. Setting main and staysail, we hoisted a riding light and hove to for the night, unwilling to leave the scene of the tragedy and uncertain of what course to steer. Were we to continue to South America or turn for home? It seemed best to sleep on it. In the morning I could ask the crew what they wanted to do. Apart from all its other sad aspects, the loss of David Shaw was a wellnigh fatal blow to my hopes and expectations. As mate, as a competent navigator, a reliable, likeable man with whom I could get on, a man whose training imbued him with a sense of loyalty to the ship in which he served, his loss was irreparable. None of the others had the knowledge, the experience, or the force of character needed to take his place. With no one now who could take charge of the ship in my absence, Smith Island at any rate was out of the question. Had I known what might happen, as by then I should have guessed, I need not have waited to consult the crew before turning for home.

Although it has no bearing on the present case, I thought that to end this chapter, a brief account of a 'man overboard' incident that had a miraculously happy ending, might be of interest; an account for which I am indebted to my friend Commander Erroll Bruce.

In 1951 during the trans-Pacific race to Honolulu a man fell overboard from the yacht *L'Apache*, just before breakfast in broad daylight, the weather clear, wind and sea moderate. A white lifebuoy was immediately thrown to him. The yacht was running with every possible sail set and with a spider's web of preventers, downhauls, and stays rigged to keep the sails full. In these circumstances half an hour elapsed before the yacht was under control and able to steer towards the scene of the accident. But in that comparatively short time those on board had lost their position relative to the man and they never found him. Meantime the man, who was not wearing oilskins, had got inside the lifebuoy which was fitted with an automatic light. By daylight, however, the light was useless, and by nightfall its battery had run down.

An American naval fleet that happened to be exercising in the vicinity intercepted distress signals from *L'Apache*. A widespread search with destroyers and aircraft began. Several of these passed close to and were seen by the man sitting in the lifebuoy, but it was not until next day, in a final sweep before the search was abandoned, that he was sighted and safely picked up.

As Erroll Bruce points out, the vital thing in such circumstances, when for some reason a boat cannot immediately be turned, is to keep the man in sight or to know how his position bears relative to the boat. As well as the lifebuoy for the man himself, anything that floats should be thrown overboard at intervals as markers for the track on which to sail back.

CHAPTER FOUR

Arrival at Montevideo

THIS ACCIDENT, so obscure, so unexpected, and unnecessary, hit us hard. For the first day or two one could not realize that it had actually happened, that there was not some mistake, and that David was not merely absent from the cabin on watch and would presently come below. An accident calls for some explanation and it is the more distubing when no reasonable explanation is forthcoming. We discussed it at length that night and on subsequent occasions without any useful result. David had kept the meteorological logbook and 6 am was one of the times when observations were made. When taking the sea temperature he had what I thought the bad habit of leaning out under the guard rail to lower the thermometer into the sea, instead of drawing a bucketful of seawater. As *Mischief*'s freeboard amidships is less than 3 feet this was easy to do. That he might have been doing this and had leant out too far occurred to me at once, but when we found both thermometers on board in their usual place this possibility had to be ruled out.

Again, the vang, its lower end clove-hitched round the outer end of the boom, sometimes comes adrift and has to be recaptured, usually by a man leaning out over the rail with a boathook. I have had occasion to do this and have then stood on the bulwarks at the counter (where, by the way, the guard rail ends) to refasten it round the boom. I have done this when no one else was on deck to see me fall in, or likely to come on deck for some time, which goes to show how careless or over-confident one can be. But, as we could see, the vang was fast nor could we find anything loose in the rigging or adrift on deck to account for David having lashed the tiller and left it. That it had been so securely lashed that *Mischief* had held her course for so long was another puzzle, though I knew that David enjoyed playing with the tiller and so adjusting things that *Mischief* sailed herself. How fatally successful he had been! If the helmsman leaves the tiller to put something right on deck he would normally take a few turns round it with the tiller line and a couple of hitches. This would be good enough for the few minutes before the line worked loose, the tiller shifted, and the boat came up into the wind. Even when on the wind *Mischief* does not sail herself for long and I was astonished that on this occasion she had held her course for nearly two hours. If only David had not been so successful in lashing the tiller! She would have flown up into the wind, when the ensuing racket, the flapping of sails and banging of the boom, would inevitably have woken and brought me on deck to see what was happening. In which case we should have had more chance of saving David.

That night it rained heavily, a sure sign that we were still in the region of the south-west Monsoon and not yet near the south-east Trades. In fact our dodging about on the previous day and heaving to at night had probably lost us more ground to the north. In the morning, much to my surprise, not one of the crew expressed any desire to turn back, a desire to which I would have been ready, even glad, to accede. In fact I felt like turning back and had opinions been divided would have done so. But to insist upon turning back seemed unfair because it would have been easier for me than for them to give up the voyage and arrive home unexpectedly. True, my arrangements for a year's absence had been made, but had I returned I should not have had to start looking for a job, as they would, or in some cases for lodgings. Nor would it be for me, as it might be for them, the only chance of making a long voyage to strange lands.

So we decided to proceed, though I made it clear, or thought I had made it clear, that there could be no attempt to land on Smith Island. On the other hand we were a quite strong enough crew to take the boat to the South Shetlands, even though morale had been a little shaken. And for my part, without David to back me, there would be more work and worry. We agreed to remain on two-hour single watches, and in order to prevent the four watchkeepers having always the same watch Tom volunteered to take the afternoon watch. As a meagre compensation for cooking, the cook had all night in and could afford to miss the afternoon siesta when most of us like to get our heads down. 'Sleep that knits up the ravell'd sleeve of care,' or what the sailor vulgarly calls a good kip, is probably more valued by seamen than by anyone because their sleep is usually brief and often broken. A thorough-going seaman can sleep at any hour in any circumstances. For my part daylight sleeping is hard to come by except in the afternoon, and the more welcome therefore I found Tom's assurance of always having the afternoon siesta, however sordid one usually feels after this indulgence.

A noon sight for latitude (Lat. 05°15′N.) showed that we had been set north as I had feared and that in the three days that we had been on the port tack we had made little or no southing. We therefore went back to the starboard tack steering ESE, determined to remain on it until in Lat. 4°N. Wet and windy conditions continued until September 1st, when the weather brightened and the light, fleecy clouds sailing overhead had all the appearance of a Trade-wind sky. We began to steer towards our destination instead of away from it, and as a bonus we collected no less than eight flying fish from the scuppers. Dorado, too, were seen in numbers, those big, brilliantly-coloured, swift-darting fish, sometimes confusingly called dolphins, a fish that when caught makes a dish fit for Lucullus. When caught! Alas! Our lures were tried in vain, whether bright bits of tin, white rags, or red rags, all were alike ignored or bitten off.

Just as the full moon excites lunatics and makes wolves howl, at sea it gives me the itch to take star sights. The stars are so much easier to see than at dusk or dawn, and since the horizon appears to have a razor-edge sharpness it seems a sin to ignore such perfect conditions. On one such calm, velvety moonlit night I took a sight of Fomalhaut at 1.30 am when it happened to be on the meridian, and on working it out found that we ourselves were exactly on the Equator. The result may well have been a mile or so out but when the sum of latitude came to precisely 0 degrees it gave me peculiar pleasure. Indeed, such pleasure that I thought of rousing out the crew to share it. There is, as the Bible tells us, a time to keep silence, and a time to speak, and on the whole, 1.30 am is the time for silence.

The value of star sights by moonlight is debatable. So great an authority as Lecky, author of *Lecky's Wrinkles*, has no doubts on the matter and willing even to dispense with the moon: 'A man of ordinary vision, using a good star telescope and well silvered sextant glasses, will find little difficulty at any time on a clear night (especially if the moon be up) in obtaining all he may want in the way of reliable sights.' Commander Cobb, on the other hand, the editor of a modern edition of *Lecky*, is not so sure:

We all know that the moon possesses a 'mysterious influence', the moonlight plays many tricks of fancy. One of these tricks may well be to present to the mariner a false horizon, be the latter's appearance ever so sharply defined. Nevertheless, stars have been and will continue to be observed on a moon horizon, but such sights are not recommended and should always be treated as suspect.

To offset this warning the Commander goes on to quote the interesting case of the grounding of a cruiser on Quelpart Island off Korea early in the century:

The navigator, in default of any better means of ascertaining his position, had been able to obtain a hurried latitude by Polaris in moonlight. This latitude placed him some ten miles to the northward of his dead reckoning, a state of affairs which he considered to be highly improbable. His horizon had been uncertain; he therefore ignored the observation, despite the fact that he was approaching the island from southward. Alas! At the court-martial which inevitably followed, it was discovered that his latitude by Polaris was more accurate than that of his dead reckoning. The moral here is an old one – if a choice of positions presents itself, always consider the ship to be in the position of greatest danger.

No question of danger arose in our case, for we were still a good 2,000 miles from Cape Polonio where we hoped to make our landfall. All this moonlight navigation or, as some might say, moonlight madness, was of merely academic interest. Nevertheless the South Equatorial current was setting us west at such an astonishing rate – on one day a difference of 40 miles between the course steered and the course made good – that at times we seemed more likely to make a landfall on Cape Recife, at the north-east corner of Brazil, than on Cape Polonio 1,500 miles to the south. After crossing the Equator we took advantage of a calm sea and a moderate breeze to launch the dinghy and embark a camera party to take pictures of *Mischief* under sail. Mike Edwards had the 16 mm. cine camera and with him went John Ireland festooned with all the cameras on board, while we sailed off down wind preparatory to making several runs close past the dinghy.

The wind began to haul more easterly, as it should further south, but it also blew harder than one expects in the SE Trades. In ten days we logged 1,130 miles, hard on the wind for most of the time, a point of sailing which makes *Mischief* creak and groan. She also leaks more than one cares for when sailing hard, especially in way of the chain plates and around the stemhead. Leaks at least keep the bilges sweet and exercise the pumps. We have an old-fashioned barrel pump worked from on deck near the cockpit with a minimum of effort and with satisfactory results, and another, a most efficient 'Whale' pump, mounted in the heads. In view of the serious nature, as I thought, of the voyage I had it fitted in place of a rotary pump which demanded a lot of effort and had a nasty trick of siphoning back. We even had a third pump but as it had been carried for years without being used this had rusted solid. In Montevideo I passed it on to a mechanically minded boat-owner on condition that he removed it. This had been worked, or should have been worked, off the charging engine, an imperfectly reliable source of power, as engines must be. 'It is but machinery, Sahib,' was the excuse offered to me by an Indian truck driver when his truck broke down. The theory behind the fitting of this expensive, worksaving appliance was that after days of gales, *Mischief* half full of water, the crew would be too exhausted to work the pumps, but in such conditions I think, the charging engine itself would have been the first thing to have its spirit quenched by the quantity of water on board. In order to save a few minutes hard labour there is a tendency nowadays to waste money on mechanical devices that at an inopportune moment may let one down.

Meantime the over-fresh winds obliged Tom and I to put in a lot of palm and needle work maintaining the genoas. We had two of these big sails. One had already done several voyages and was not expected to last long, while the other, a second-hand sail bought for the voyage, had turned out to be a thoroughly bad buy. 'Flapping Fanny', as we called the latter, was not robust enough to start with and soon wore itself out, the leech flapping incessantly even when running. Having wasted much time and sail twine on it we stripped off the hanks, bolt rope, and cringles, and threw it over the side. It had lasted just long enough for Tom and I to patch a tear of twenty feet or more in the older sail.

The dorado that now began to haunt the ship and our inability to catch them drove us well-nigh frantic. They lived under the hull in perfect peace and amity with scores of lesser fry, the whole aquarium menaced only by man, their common and not very deadly enemy. Neither by fair means or foul could we kill one. John Ireland managed to lodge a harpoon in one which wriggled off just before we had got it on board, while Roger lost another which he had foul-hooked when jigging a bare hook over the side. At the same time we lost another rotator but I doubt if a dorado had tried to make a meal of that.

Having run through the Trades we entered the region of variable winds. Variable indeed! After a prolonged run under The Twins before a northerly wind, we had to drop them in the middle of the night for a sudden shift of wind to the south accompanied by a deluge of rain. The rain came in useful. By now, 45 days out, we were well into the main tank and had just lost two gallons by upsetting a container in the galley. The southerly wind and sea increased all day until after being hit an awful crack when a sea leapt on board we decided to heave to. At first I feared that this sea had broken the skylight. In rough weather we rig a canvas cover over the skylight, but even so jets of water force their way through. As my bunk has no upper berth above, it is the more vulnerable and frequently gets soused. All ills are good that are attended by food, says the philosopher, and that night, being Sunday night, we had curry and a treacle duff, a pudding fit for a glass case. Maybe the rough weather had affected the appetites of the crew. So much curry remained uneaten that I told Tom to dish it up for breakfast. Like Mrs Gilpin, though on pleasure bent, I have a frugal mind.

That human life is everywhere a state where much is to be endured and little to be enjoyed was a thought that had not yet penetrated the minds of the crew. John in particular, a great traveller by his own account, had not learnt that a traveller should have the back of an ass to bear all, and the mouth of a hog to eat what is set before him. The curry, appearing at an unusual hour, was still hot enough to inflame him. On this occasion I caught his drift quick enough when he violently voiced his disgust at being expected to eat curry for breakfast. This chap who had eagerly volunteered to come on this voyage, who would have been disappointed had he been refused, who was now enjoying a free holiday, had apparently persuaded himself that he was doing me a favour. It is a question whether those who contribute nothing towards the expenses of a voyage have any right to complain, if they do complain it needs to be done tactfully.

Running parallel with the coast of South America, now about 60 miles away, we began sighting ships. Nowadays the sailing ship route to South America is so lonely that one can safely forget about navigation lights. Until one begins to close the land the sighting of a steamer would be a rare and memorable event. Nor is there much life of any kind in this watery desert, the North and South Atlantic on either side of the Equator, where the sighting of even a bird almost warrants calling those below. Perhaps one might see the odd storm petrel, the smallest and commonest of all ocean birds, ranging from the Southern Ocean to the North Atlantic. More rarely, always aloft and never on the water, one might see the lovely and highly predatory frigate bird with its long forked tail; or perhaps a bos'un bird with an even longer tail, the bos'uns marline spike. As far north as Lat. 20°S. we saw the first albatross, the yellow-nosed albatross which is found much further north than the big wanderers. Cape pigeons, too, sometimes gathered round the boat, and these pintado petrel are one of the commonest birds of colder southern waters and the most attractive. Owing to their chequered black and white plumage, they have the rare merit of being easily identified by the most myopic bird-watcher.

Having been at sea for fifty days, and with less than a thousand miles to go, we all felt the passage had lasted long enough. It had so far been fairly fast for *Mischief*, and had we not unnecessarily covered three or four hundred extra miles through going on the starboard tack when too far north of the Equator, we should have been even quicker. The twice-baked bread, fresh to the very last, had now given out and we went on to biscuit. With Primus stoves, the baking of bread for a crew of six would consume too much time and paraffin to be feasible. The 'Lifeboat' biscuits we use are small, tasty, and not too hard; they serve so well for conveying to the mouth large quantities of butter and jam that they have to be rationed. Our porridge, too, ran out, and this at least had the advantage that we used less water for cooking. The small amount of paraffin we had left gave me more concern. After four consecutive days of light winds when we did less than 50 miles a day, I decided to reduce our consumption by cutting out the mid-morning tea or coffee – our 'elevenses'. The crew took this hard, blaming me, quite rightly, for not buying enough paraffin. However, when we had done three runs of over 120 miles a day everyone cheered up. At sea there is nothing like swift progress for keeping tempers sweet.

Overnight on 2 October the sea temperature dropped from 67° to 60° F., indicating that we had crossed what is called the sub-tropical convergence ... upon which my early morning bucket baths became less frequent. On some voyages these early morning showers had been carried to extreme lengths, or extreme north and south latitudes, an unspoken but well understood challenge between one or two of us leading to a contest of obstinate politeness as to who would be first to quit. A 'sudestada', a moderate southeasterly gale accompanied by heavy rain, sent us scurrying along under close reefed main and jib throughout a murky night. By morning it had cleared and that evening we sighted land fine on the bow and about 15 miles distant. By midnight, drifting with all the sails down, we had Cape Polonio abeam.

Motoring through thick fog on a windless morning we presently came up with a small fishing boat engaged in long-lining. In exchange for cigarettes they gave us dogfish, edible enough in spite of their name. Small rockhopper penguins were bobbing out of the water, and what appeared at first sight to be wreckage or floating branches turned out to be seals sleeping on their backs with their flippers in the air. They breed on the island of Lobos at the entrance to the Plate estuary, which we passed about a mile off at 3 am of a wonderfully bright, moonlit night, the seals and penguins making noises according to their kind, barking and braying. As the day advanced the breeze on our quarter freshened so that we finished this long passage with a flourish, romping through the dirty, yellow water of the River Plate at a good 5 knots. As we passed Flores Island near Montevideo the wind grew fresher raising a short, choppy sea. Puerto Buceo, a small fishing port and the headquarters of the Yacht Club, is about 9 miles east of Montevideo. It was too insignificant to appear on our chart and my memories of the place were faint.

Closing the land in search of it we had trouble in making out any landmarks at all owing to haze and the glare of the westering sun. Despairing of finding it I was about to make for Montevideo harbour when we spotted the breakwater and the nine-storey club building. Off the entrance the water is shallow and each time we dropped into a hollow between the steep waves I felt sure that *Mischief's* keel would hit the sandy bottom. All went well and we anchored in a most undesirable berth in only 1½ fathoms of water, the fishing boats inside the breakwater and the yachts lying off the Club leaving us little choice. Nor was that the worst. When the anchor went down we found that Mike Edwards, intoxicated by the city lights, had omitted to put the chain through the fairlead. Not wishing to have the bulwarks chewed to pieces by winching up the cable, we hauled all 45 fathoms of it up from the locker, passed the bitter end back through the fairlead and restowed. Tom, who is not loquacious, thought this an occasion that called for remark. He had served in trawlers, so he gave Mike, and us, a fairly close idea of what the eloquence of a trawler hand would have been in like circumstances. We were 60 days out from Las Palmas, having sailed 5,300 miles.

CHAPTER FIVE

Trouble at Montevideo

AT A British port a yacht flying a 'Q' flag would probably be boarded by the Customs and Immigration officers in a matter of hours. At Puerto Buceo we lay for weeks unvisited, and only when we showed signs of leaving did the authorities sit up and take notice. On our first visit here in 1955 things had been different, but then we had gone to the main harbour where we unwittingly drew and promptly received attention from a whole posse of officials by anchoring in the fairway for the arrival and departure of seaplanes. Their present unconcern seemed the more surprising because there is a water-guard in permanent session in a room on the ground floor of the Clubhouse where several policemen, in pseudo naval uniform, sleep, eat, smoke, and drink *maté* tea, their job being to keep an eye on visiting yachts. These rare visitors are mainly Argentine yachts on a week-end sail from Buenos Aires a hundred miles away up the river.

Ignoring the police, and ignored by them, we all went ashore the morning after our arrival to take a bus into the city. A member of the Club from whom we enquired about bus routes pressed upon us an ample sum of Uruguayan money to pay our fares. The first essential was to report the presumed death of David Shaw to the British consul who would no doubt find means of informing his parents in England. At all costs I wanted to avoid their first learning of this through the newspapers, and for that reason I intended saying nothing to the Uruguayan authorities. From them the local press would probably have got wind of it and the news would not be confined to Montevideo. Accidents to yachtsmen or climbers are meat and drink to the British press to whom the news would undoubtedly be passed. In the crew list I had made out for the Port authorities, expecting them to show some interest in us, I had omitted David Shaw's name. Subsequently this led to a bit of bother.

It took about half-an-hour to reach the city by bus, the fare then being 2½ pesos or about 6p. When we returned in the spring of 1967 the fare had doubled. In the course of the next three weeks I made this journey so many times that it became wearisome. Its distance from the city is one disadvantage of Puerto Buceo, but on no account should a visiting yacht lie in the main harbour. 'There be land-rats and water-rats, land-thieves and water-thieves', and Montevideo abounds in both. They operate on a wholesale scale. We heard of one steamer that had had fifty 5-gallon drums of paint removed from her deck in the course of a night.

Nowadays journeys by land are more perilous than sea voyages. This bus ride had its hazards. The buses have three doors, front, middle, and rear, operated by the driver. On some you enter by the rear door and leave by the front or middle, on others this order is reversed. A comparatively bucolic customer like myself found it puzzling. On one occasion, having put a hand inside the middle door, the wrong one, preparatory to entering, the door closed and the bus moved off. Had it been the left hand (we drive on the right in Uruguay) I might have sprinted alongside to the next stop, but with the right hand jammed in the door I was facing the wrong way and had to start running backwards. Fortunately a passer-by, who had less contempt for gringos than the bus driver, persuaded the driver to stop before he had gone far. It would be charitable to think the driver had not seen me, but more probable that he wished to teach the gringo to use the right door.

Now that we had arrived events moved quickly and trouble came thick and fast. Only later, when Tom and I were alone together, the sole survivors of the crew of six which had left Lymington with such high hopes, did I learn what had been brewing for some time. Had I known I might have been more circumspect. As the Swahili say: 'Cross the river before you start reviling the crocodile's mother.' John Ireland I expected would leave and his loss was no great matter: even if we got no one else the four of us could have managed. Apart from curry for breakfast he had some complaints about our fitness for the voyage. A bolt securing the gaff saddle to the gaff was worn, the sheet winches slipped, as, too, did the anchor winch. As a matter of personal interest I let the offending bolt remain and it was still there when we returned to Lymington. With a full crew sheet winches are a luxury on a cruising yacht; in any case, if it is blowing hard and the sheets need hardening the boat can be run off or brought to the wind. The links of the chain did not exactly fit the cogs of the anchor winch so that a link or two occasionally slipped back. Short of a new cable or a new winch, patience and a foot pressed hard on the chain are the remedy.

His real grievance was that we had no distress signals and carried no life-raft. In my view every herring should hang by its own tail. Anyone venturing into unfrequented and possibly dangerous waters does so with his eyes open, should be willing to depend on his own exertions, and should neither expect nor ask for help. Nor would equipment of this sort be of much use in Drake Passage where the chances of being picked up are so slim as to be hardly worth considering. A yacht is supposed to carry distress signals but is not over much reliance placed upon them by owners of small craft? A man with a boat that may be in many respects unseaworthy will happily put to sea secure in the knowledge that at least he has his distress flares. Yearly around our coasts so many calls are made upon the various rescue organizations that by now the average man should be ashamed to think of adding to their number. The confidence that is placed, and successfully placed, in being rescued fosters carelessness or even foolishness, and condones ignorance. More care and thought might be taken if there were a penalty for the firing of distress signals, say £25 a flare, the proceeds to be collected by the RNLI, the fine to be remitted only if proof were forthcoming that the boat had started out in all respects seaworthy and had been in real danger. The perils of the sea are less apparent than the perils of climbing and have to be carefully assessed. In climbing the penalty for a mistake is obvious and is sometimes exacted instantaneously, so that on the whole there are fewer foolish climbers than foolish amateur sailors.

But to return to John Ireland with whom I now parted company, feeling that he and I would not get on together however many life-rafts we carried. To my surprise and chagrin Mike Edwards, with whom I thought I had got on tolerably well, then announced that he would go too, and forthwith they both packed their gear and went. If possible this show-down should have been postponed until we had reached the South Shetlands where there would be neither the opportunity nor the temptation to leave the ship. One regretted the unfortunate proximity of the Yacht Club where rooms could be had comparatively cheaply, where there were all the attractions of gracious living and convivial company. The defection of the older men could not but affect young Roger who, though he professed to be still game, was obviously in two minds about it. He seemed to be waiting for an excuse to book a room at the Yacht Club – if he had not already done so – and the opportunity soon came.

As I have said we were in a poor anchorage. The water was so shallow that at times we were sitting on the bottom. The tidal rise and fall is only a few feet and the depth of water at Buceo depends more upon the wind, a strong blow from anywhere between SE and SW having the effect of raising the level considerably. What with the shallowness and the little scope we had to swing, we had very little chain out. Two days later a hard wind from SW soon showed how insecure we were. We began to drag and to drag fast, fortunately in broad daylight.

Close astern of us lay an 8-metre yacht which some months before had sunk at her moorings where her owner seemed quite happy to leave her, and where she had become part of the scene, a natural hazard, as it were. Before our engine could be started we had slid past this wreck and I fully expected that our anchor, which Tom and Roger were struggling to get up, would foul it. By some miracle it came clear and having got it in we steered for the breakwater, now swept continuously by waves, in order to secure alongside a fishing boat. Owing to the strength of the wind, and the difficulty I had in steering and seeing to the engine throttle at the same time – I almost ran our bowsprit through the remaining rigging of the wreck. Imagination boggles – at least mine did – at the thought of a sunk yacht with another securely fastened on top of it. After this shambles, when we were finally made fast alongside the fishing boat, Roger instantly repaired to the Club, to take advice as he put it, and presently returned to announce his departure. He had lost confidence, he said, we were too short-handed, without life-raft or flares, sheet winches slipping, anchor winch slipping etc.

Tom, who remained steadfast and extremely cheerful at this crisis in our affairs, told me that he had fully expected something of the sort. For the last few weeks of the passage the three malcontents had been discussing their course of action on arrival at Montevideo. Our own course of action now needed discussing. There are over a million people in Montevideo and it would be strange, I thought, if we could not find two or even three enterprising enough to sail south-wards with us. By now we had come so far that to turn back hardly bore contemplation, the time for that had been when we were still north of the Equator. So having done what needed doing in the way of maintenance I made almost daily journeys to the city calling at the consulates and shipping offices, particularly the German and Scandinavian. Though sympathetic none of them knew of any likely candidates. The most obvious recruiting ground, the Yacht Club, was also the least likely to provide anyone. Apart from dinghy racing one suspects that their sailing is done in the bar. The club had very kindly given us the run of its facilities, and very useful they were, but none of the members were sufficiently interested to pay *Mischief* a visit. Perhaps they had heard all they wanted to know from our late crew who were now resident members, but the main barrier was probably language. Surprisingly few spoke English.

The British consul required from each of the crew a written statement concerning the loss of David Shaw and did not think that there would be any need for an official enquiry. The news of his death had been sent to his parents through the Foreign Office and soon appeared in the British press whence it rebounded. Soon the news appeared in the Montevideo papers and we had visits from Reuters agent and from the *Daily Express* man at Buenos Aires asking for more details. Meantime the search for crew had drawn blank. Even Punta Arenas looked far away and the South Shetlands right off our map. Tom and I discussed the idea of the two of us sailing to Cape Town, shorter and easier than the voyage homewards. Tom would get some climbing and a crew to take the boat home would have been easily found. By then the season would have been too far advanced for going south, and in any case, owing to contrary winds, it would be impossible to sail to the South Shetlands from Cape Town. For two men in *Mischief* it would have been a hard voyage.

The onward march of progress has inevitably extinguished a few trades and professions – chimney-sweeps for instance, body-snatchers, crimps. At Montevideo I regretted that there were no longer any crimps, men dedicated to making more widely known the benefits of a seafaring life. Two or three bodies delivered on board, drunk or doped, might have cost money but would have saved time; they would have been as useful as those we eventually got and might have been less of a nuisance. In the absence of crimps, or of resorts like Smokey Joe's or Big Nellie's, I had in the end to apply to the Sailor's home run by the Salvation Army.

The home did not cater only for sailors, all were welcome. Most of the inmates were perhaps men who had had losses and deserved them, modern examples of Falstaff's ragged company, 'revolted tapsters and ostlers trade-fallen; the cankers of a calm world and a long peace.' The Home lay near the docks and its cleanliness inside contrasted with the dirtiness of the street outside, for the Major in charge, an Australian, saw to it that his lodgers earned their keep. Montevideo, by the way, struck me as having become a little unkempt. The standard of living had gone down, too. One never saw what had been a common thing on our visit in 1955, workmen sitting round a fire on the pavement broiling 2-inch steaks for their lunch.

In a short time the Major found three men for me to interview. They were anxious to get to Europe, to Germany for preference, were willing to work their passage, and did not shrink from the idea of going there by way of the South Shetlands. One of them who had no trade, no skills, no experience, and not a word of English, I thought better to discard forthwith. The second Uruguayan was quite black, looking like a more refined negro. The majority of Uruguayans are European in appearance and this chap, Carreo Javiel may have had his origin in Brazil. Mixed crews in small boats, like mixed marriages, need thinking about. We are all as God made us, some of us much worse, and no one can help his colour. Racial integration is a subject much to the fore and I felt sure that Tom, who hailed from Birmingham, would assimilate or stomach a black crew as easily as I could. Besides we could not afford to be choosy and this man Carreo had one skill which we needed. He was a marine engineer, having served as such in the Uruguayan navy, from which he had a discharge book alleging him to be of good character. He was intelligent and had a fair smattering of English. As it would take a little time to get used to the idea of living with him at close quarters, I deferred my decision. But Carreo was more than anxious to come and determined not to be put off. For several successive nights after supper we would be hailed by a lanky figure on the breakwater requiring to be brought on board. Having him on board for a cup of tea and a cigarette was good practice for Tom and I in the matter of racial integration. He certainly had a noticeable smell and no doubt he thought the same of Tom and I and *Mischief*'s cabin. His anxiety to please and his persistence wore down my instinctive resistance. I agreed to take him – no pay, find his own gear, and a passage to Europe by way of the South Shetlands and Cape Town. His geography may have been a bit scattered but he must have understood our general direction and we impressed upon him that the climate would not be like that of Montevideo. I could see that Carreo meant business and that he would undoubtedly be with us on sailing day.

The last of the trio was a young German, Herbert Bittner, aged about 30, fair, slim, nimble and active – physically the makings of a sailor but, as we were to learn, totally lacking in any sea-sense or the ability to acquire it. His life history was obscure and his habit of romancing added to the obscurity. Apparently he had been in Montevideo about six months and in that short time had gained some notoriety. Many people had heard of him or of the incident in which he had rather mysteriously figured. According to his account he had been found lying on the steps of a church, having been knocked on the head and robbed, and instead of the aid and comfort which he naturally had expected he had enjoyed a short spell in the 'calaboos'. Some said he was a Jew, in South America on the track of Nazi war criminals, and that this knock on the head had been by way of a hint to lay off. About one period of his life there was less doubt. He had once been a racing cyclist and at the slightest provocation he would produce his most treasured possession, a packet of press cuttings in which the great Bittner hit the headlines – pictures of him and his bike, Bittner and his silver cups, or Bittner being garlanded in Delhi. He was extremely plausible and self-confident – 'no problema' was his favourite expresion – and assured me that he had had some sea experience and could cook, the experience having been gained on a voyage to India in his father's yacht. Well, he may have had a father, but the yacht, I am sure, was as imaginary as his sea experience. He had, however, the great merit of cheerfulness, chattered a lot, and was amusing in small doses. He spoke a little peculiar English and enough Spanish to help us out with Carreo whom, of course, he knew as a fellow lodger. I had a word with the German consul. In his opinion Bittner was mad and that anyone thinking of going to sea with him could not be quite sane. For all that he would be extremely grateful to anyone who took him back to Germany as he, the consul, could then close the Bittner file. Certainly Herbert was what might be called excitable and perhaps that tap on the head had done nothing to calm him. My friend the Major spoke well of both of them, eager to have them taken off his hands. But there is less in this than meets the eye, as Talulah Bankhead used to say. Neither of them had given him trouble, only as a good Salvation Army man he would naturally be delighted to see any of his down-at-heel, out-of-luck lodgers shifting for themselves, or at least eager to do something rather than hang around the Sailor's Home. So I decided to include Herbert Bittner in our growingly assorted company. If he proved equal to taking over the galley, as I hoped, Tom could be more usefully employed on deck.

We had been in Montevideo over a fortnight, and now had a crew of four, when the unexpected happened. Our three deserters had made themselves at home in the Club where they might be seen taking their mid-morning coffee on the terrace whence they could keep an eye on *Mischief*. Like two countries whose hostility towards each other has reached the point of severing diplomatic relations, my only contact with them, if contact were needed, was through a third party. One day Tom, the third party, told me that Mike Edwards would like to come back. He was evidently one who acted on impulse; his having left seemed as unreasonable as his wish to come back. His desertion had no doubt influenced young Roger with the result that I had been obliged to take on two questionable characters. Still, if only for the sake of continuing the film that he had begun I welcomed this news and after a brief talk he decided to rejoin. Bygones were to be bygones. For all that he took care not to do any work or to return on board until the day we sailed. As I am writing of real people and not fictitious characters it will not do to impute motives. Why Mike thought fit to rejoin is nearly as beyond conjecture as what song the Sirens sang. It is even possible that he thought, as most people would think, that the least to be expected from a man who volunteers to crew is that he sees the voyage through even when things turn out to be less agreeable than he anticipated.

No sooner had we thus increased our crew to five when along came a young Argentinian and a friend. The Argentinian had just started life in the merchant service and hankered after more experience, while His Uruguayan friend was studying medicine. They were far better types than my two from the Sailor's Home, but I could not take both and the one would not go without the other. We would therefore have to sail with only five. The plan was to go to Punta Arenas and make a final decision there according to how the crew shaped. Either we could continue southwards, or spend some time in, say, Beagle Channel, where Tom and I could climb something, or at the worst head straight for Cape Town. The latter would be the quickest way home. I had friends to see there, and *Mischief* could be hauled out for a scrub at the hospitable Royal Cape Yacht Club. That was the general idea, but I knew that having arrived at Punta Arenas, with the South Shetlands just the other side of Drake Passage, I would be extremely reluctant to abandon our original aim:

> ... But something ere the end,
> Some work of noble note may yet be done

So we began to get ready. Carreo and Herbert came to live on board and the necessary stores were delivered. Carreo, eager to please, cleaned and repainted the engine and made a thorough job of it. I had to wait for some money from home and we had still to take in water. All the Montevideo Banks were on strike, mere chaos reigned, all correspondence, including my credit note, lay unopened. Buying stores proved far more expensive than I had bargained for and I regretted having spent £10 on yet another rotator for the log, a second-hand one at that. When we first streamed this, by the way, we found it to be an Irishman's rotator, going widdershins, against the sun. Nowhere in Montevideo could we find a *Nautical Almanac* for 1967 and I had little hope of finding one at Punta Arenas. Twice-toasted bread, 'tostada', was another important item that we had to go without.

One of the shallower parts of Puerto Buceo is off the Club quay where we had to go for watering. A steady SW wind piles up the water and one evening, having taken a sounding and consulted the Club bos'un, I thought we had a chance of getting near enough. Since the anchor-dragging debâcle we had been lying to a buoy which had become vacant, so we had therefore no anchor to heave in. This was just as well because Tom had gone ashore and only Carreo and Herbert were there to help. We managed to approach within 30ft. of the quay, which was as near as we dared to, and ran a hose on board, a hose that provided such a meagre trickle that we looked like being there all night. While busy attending to this I was peremptorily ordered on shore by one of the police, evidently alerted by our preparations for departure. They were extremely annoyed at my failure to report to them the loss of David Shaw and there were complications arising out of the changes that had taken place since our arrival. Before anything else I must provide a certified copy in Spanish of the relevant log entry lodged with the British consul.

We finished watering as darkness fell. Much to my surprise we were still afloat, the water holding up well, and by now Tom was back on board, slightly drunk and in uncommonly high spirits, responding to every order with hearty, seamanlike Ay, Ayes. We had not room to turn *Mischief* round – she needs a lot of room – so the passage back had to be made stern first in the dark, a short voyage but one pregnant with disaster. When going backwards one never knows how *Mischief* will react to the rudder, the propeller being offset on the port side; whether it will have the normal reverse effect, the opposite effect, or no effect at all. Strictly speaking we should have hoisted two red lights to show that we were not under control. To assist in this manoeuvre and to pick up the buoy, I had one half-drunk Irishman and two aliens, one of whom did not understand what I said, while the other may have understood but did not know what to do. But *Mischief* behaved like a witch. With the tiller steady amidships she described what mathematicians call a Cartesian oval, a beautiful curve which took us safely round the head of a jetty, past innumerable yachts, and to the vicinity of the buoy. With more hearty Ay, Ayes Tom, armed with a torch, went off in the dinghy and to my relief at once found the buoy.

One day when the bank opened for a few hours, while the senior members of the staff who had no reason to be on strike, dealt with their angrier customers, I collected my travellers cheques. But the police were being awkward and refused to give us a 'salida' or clearance. An old friend, Mr McClew, of Maclean and Stapledon, an old established firm of shipping agents with whom we had dealt in 1955, came to the rescue. His years of experience in dealing with officials had not been wasted and his *suaviter in modo* approach seldom failed. We hurried back to the ship, collecting Mike on the way. Having put Mr McClew ashore we were just hoisting the dinghy in when the police launch came alongside to tell us the port was closed. In gale or near gale conditions Purerto Buceo is closed to yachts and fishing vessels, and its closure is signalled by a red flag. We could have got out safely but in view of our recent relations with the police it was wiser to conform. The police wanted to take away our clearance papers to ensure that we did conform, a request that we quickly refused.

CHAPTER SIX

To Punta Arenas

WE SAILED next day, 28 October. The distance to Punta Arenas is not much more than 1,200 miles; that we had to sail nearly 1,700 miles and took 28 days to do it shows how fickle and contrary were the winds. Calms, light airs, and fogs, broken by an occasional short-lived gale, were our portion. In 1955 on this passage we had managed to average only 56 miles a day. Such conditions are unlooked for since one is traversing the Forties and Fifties, from Lat. 35° S. to Lat. 55° S., where one might expect to be pushed along by strong westerlies for most of the way. As well as fast, this passage should also be smooth because with the Argentine coast lying all along the weather side the sea has no great fetch. It is probably the effect of the land, too, that makes the Westerlies off this coast so comparatively feeble.

At sea with a fresh crew the wind for the first few days can hardly be too light, and a number of quiet nights without any alarms made up for our lack of progress. By dint of drifting, motoring, and a little sailing we crossed the 120-mile-wide estuary and started down the Argentine coast. According to our £10 Irishman's rotator we were going backwards and to remedy this we pasted over the face of the patent log a new clock face that read anti-clockwise, if that is possible. As we had only four watchkeepers we each did a four-hour watch in the morning instead of the usual two-hour watch. Herbert performed in the galley according to his lights but could eat nothing himself in spite of the flat sea. The most that could be said of our meals at this period was that they had the merit of the unexpected. On one unmemorable evening, having finished our prunes and rice, we sat for some time awaiting the arrival of a non-existent main dish, on the false assumption that Herbert had got the courses back to front.

But he surprised and delighted us by catching two fish and an albatross, one of a flock of twenty or so which had swiftly gathered round us, as we lay becalmed, to fight for the fish offal. These were of the species known as the 'Shy albatross' and their behaviour belied their name. Nothing could drive them away. We ate the fish and put the albatross back in the sea. In the days of sail the catching of albatross with line and hook was common practice despite the widespread belief that to kill an albatross is to ask for trouble. It seems that in those days the price obtained for albatross skins, especially in Australian ports, effectively overcame any superstitious feelings the sailors may have had. Birds quickly increased in numbers and kind – Magellan penguins, albatross of several species including the wanderer, giant petrels, prions, Cape pigeons, and the ubiquitous storm petrel.

One evening when we were south of Mar del Plata in Lat. 40° S. we fell in with a fleet of Russian trawlers. We sighted the first of them as we ran fast to the south-west under the twins having already logged 143 miles, by far the best day's run of the passage. Alarmed by a fall in the barometer from 1025 mbs to 1010 mbs, we then put a reef in the twins. But no evil came and need not have been feared for the barometer was merely returning to normal after having been abnormally high. Later, when the wind suddenly backed to west it brought with it a blast off the land that felt like superheated air. Whereupon it fell calm and we lay there for the rest of the night surrounded by the lights of fifteen Russian trawlers. Our nearest neighbour turned a searchlight on us and could only be persuaded to turn it off when I signalled by lamp the letters BYM, or Bon Voyage.

With a morning breeze we continued on our way. Soon the father and mother of the fleet, a big factory ship also fitted with a stern trawl, closed us and steamed along on a parallel course less than fifty yards away. Her skipper spoke a rude sort of English and we had quite a long 'gam'. Then they switched on a loud-speaker and played Beatle records for us, or so Mike interpreted the hideous din. As is the way with Russian ships there were a number of women on board, floosies, or in this case perhaps fishwives, to whom our crew made the appropriate grimaces and gestures. Whether these were interpreted as comradely or lascivious it would be hard to say. Herbert, besides being a bit of a comedian, never wasted an opportunity. When he waved aloft a frying pan the Russians at once took the hint and threw overboard a parcel of fish with a buoy attached. So we drew away and hauled round to pick it up. To my shame the two attempts we made to grab it were unsuccessful. With the genoa up and a freshening wind, manoeuvring became difficult. Twice we came up into the wind over the buoy and each time we drifted back before it could be grabbed with the boathook.

Between them the Russians and the Japanese have led the way in discovering new fishing grounds. For more than 100 miles off the Argentine coast the depth is less than 100 fathoms and further south the continental shelf grows wider until in Lat.51° S. it extends to the Falkland Islands, over 300 miles from the mainland. If there are fish there this constitutes a vast trawling ground.

This pleasant episode had been marred only by my bungling of 'catching' the fish, and it cheered us on a cheerless, grey day. On the blackest of black nights, with a rising wind. Carreo had the watch till midnight. Generally I tried to keep awake when he was on watch, but this time the banging of the boom and the slatting of sails woke me up. He had got her in stays, the whole mainsail proving too much for him and the boat. A man who has never before sailed a boat cannot learn to steer in a matter of days, but Carreo never learnt and owing to our inability to communicate we could not teach him. Nor did he much care for being taught anything. He knew the points of the compass; that is to say, if you told him to steer, say, south by west, and indicated the point with your finger, he would stick to it regardless. If the wind shifted so that the boat stopped sailing, well, so much the worse for the wind.

Perhaps to keep the crew amused and their minds off the sea we were following the coast at no great distance. Usually I like to get well away from the land; as Conrad rightly observed, 'the true peace of God begins at any spot a thousand miles from the nearest land.' The following night I had hoped to pick up the Punta Delgada light, but at dusk the weather thickened so we altered course away from the land. For supper Herbert gave us fried spuds, and cabbage with custard, a meal that together with the fog filled me with gloom and foreboding. We stole along very quietly over a smooth sea, the silence broken only by the ripple of water along the hull or the melancholy mooing of a penguin, seeing nothing but the guard rail three feet away and the light of the stern lamp reflected in the fog. I had the impression that we had somehow got into a landlocked gulf where imaginary currents were sweeping us on shore. Joy cometh with the morning. By 5 am the fog had cleared and I got some star sights.

As the sun rose higher the wind died away to nothing. The hardier among us basked on deck stripped, the air temperature being 65° F. and the sea 55° F. Presently a halo formed round the sun, the glass had been falling, and a low bank of cloud or fog to the south-east put me in mind of what had happened in 1955 when a like bank of cloud had advanced upon us before a wind which in a matter of minutes had risen to gale force. This time the cloud heralded nothing more than a hard breeze which by nightfall began to moderate. Another exasperatingly calm day followed and yet another windy night.

At the witching hour of 2 am Mike treated us to an imperial 'Chinese' gybe, the boom flying over with an almighty crash carrying all before it. Nothing had broken, but rather than lie awake below waiting anxiously for an encore I decided to heave to until daylight.

Having sighted land at its northern end we ran fast across the 120-mile-wide Gulf San Jorge in weather more like what it should be in Lat. 47° S. We were still running fast close-reefed when we sighted the land on the southern side of the gulf and a lighthouse which we took to be that on Penguin Island. In my *South American Pilot* this was described as a circular iron tower painted in red and white bands, and the slight discrepancy between what we saw and what we should have seen we ascribed to bad light, bad paint, or possibly my out-of-date *Pilot*. Penguin Island awoke memories of John Davis, the Elizabethan seaman-explorer whose tracks in Greenland waters I had sometimes tried to follow. In 1591 he, too, had deserted northern waters and had gone south in company with Thomas Cavendish. This side of Magellan Straits they were separated and Davis, after persistent attempts to pass the Straits, was finally driven back. He put into Port Desire near Penguin Island to refit for the voyage home. As the name implies penguins were to be had in some quantity. They killed and dried 14,000 which for an estimated voyage of six months allowed a daily ration of five penguins for four men. The voyage home did take six months but long ere this their stock of imperfectly dried penguins had gone rotten. The stores, the ship, the men themselves, became infested with maggots – 'There was nothing', wrote John Jane, one of the crew, 'they did not devour, only iron excepted'. When the noisome worm-ridden *Desire* at last struggled into Bearhaven in June 1593 only sixteen of her crew remained alive and of those only five were able to stand.

Later that night we raised the Cape Guardian light 30 miles to the south, a light that we were fated to see again. Another of those curious blasts of hot air off the land heralded a south-westerly gale throughout which the glass steadily rose. By dawn we were hove-to close reefed, and before breakfast we rolled down the mainsail even more. Despite the lively conditions Herbert produced porridge for breakfast, his swan song. All complained of his cooking and Mike had some hard things to say about the state of the galley – saucepans containing remnants of food growing a crop of mould, bits of bread and rotting potatoes stuffed away in odd corners, the stoves coated with congealed fat and bits of rice and macaroni. A deplorable mess that would have made a soft-hearted sanitary inspector weep. In my opinion it does not do to be too fussy about the milieu in which food is cooked so long as the final product answers expectations, but in Herbert's case it did not. Anyone accustomed to native cooks, using 'native' as a convenient label for the black, brown, or yellow inhabitants of wherever it might be, knew better than to intrude upon the kitchen which was probably a grass hut with an earth floor and an open fire.

Mike generously offered to take over the galley where he soon had things shipshape. But we had other troubles on our hands. Herbert who had been unwell from the start now had toothache and talked of retiring to hospital at Punta Arenas. Carreo, so zealous and resolute before we sailed, also talked of leaving; one day because he could not have three hot meals a day, and the next because Tom had sworn at him. We were aware that defection on the part of either of these two new recruits would put in jeopardy the continuation of the voyage southwards. Carreo we decided, must be kept sweet, more difficult though this became every day. He was extremely touchy, so that anything said to him that he did not immediately understand, and that applied to most of what we said, he took to be an insult.

The gale took off by the following evening, but this south-westerly blow, together with a north-going current, had set us back about 35 miles to the north-east. A day later, when we were again becalmed, we once more sighted Cape Guardian. For the next week we averaged only some thirty miles a day. In the Roaring Forties, as in other notoriously windy regions, placid conditions may often prevail. It is much like giving a dog a bad name. Off Cape Horn, or the Cape of Good Hope, the so-called Cape of Storms, or in the Roaring Forties, though the yachtsman may expect to be blown out of the water it is a comfort to know that such forebodings are not always fulfilled.

The generally light winds had a mean habit of piping up at night. At midnight on a night of howling wind and driving rain we sighted the San Julian light; by 8 am, when we had it abeam, the wind dropped to a gentle breeze. Herbert, who had been promoted to the deck, had the afternoon watch, and while we were all asleep took the boat within a few hundred yards of the beach. With him, as with Carreo, a given course became a fixed idea, something to be adhered to even if it meant taking the boat overland. San Julian, 100 miles to the south of Port Desire, is where first Magellan, and then Drake sixty years later, both stayed for some time in order to refit and to nip in the bud incipient mutinies; where Magellan hung two of the leading trouble-makers and marooned two others, one of them a priest; and where Drake had John Doughty beheaded. Drake's subsequent exhortation to his followers is well known:

For I must have the gentlemen to haul and draw with the mariners, and the mariners with the gentlemen; and let us show ourselves to be all of a company, and let us not give occasion to the enemy to rejoice at our decay and overthrow. I would know him that would refuse to set his hand to a rope; but I trust there is not any such here.

Once more we closed the land near the sonorously named San Francisco de Paula, remarkable for its three – or four-hundred-feet-high white cliffs. Though having a resemblance to the white cliffs of Dover these are not of chalk but of clay and gravel. By this we had left the Forties for the Fifties and still the winds remained light and inconstant. Our consecutive runs of 25, 25, 84, 17, 48, and 6 miles show the pattern of the weather. At sea in sail patience is very necessary, but as Dr Johnson remarked patience is a virtue easily fatigued by exercise. As crews often do under such slow progress, we were all becoming a little irritable in spite of the vast improvement in our fare that Mike had wrought. Even Carreo condescended to eat and to approve his curries. In the important matter of duffs his use of Quaker oats instead of flour marked, I believe, a revolutionary break-through in the field of marine duff-making, and resulted withal in some masterpieces of angelic lightness.

Pudding is perhaps too coarse a word for the sort of thing that should be eaten on bended knees.

By the evening of 20 November we were by dead reckoning about 8 miles east of Cape Virgins at the entrance to Magellan Straits. We had run our distance so we hove to in thick fog with a force 6 wind at north. Uncertain of our position, and not daring to let draw, we drifted slowly to the south-east all next day in the same dismal fog. A seam in the mainsail opened and part of the leech rope came adrift, so we changed it for the trysail while Tom and I put in a long, cold spell stitching. Next day the fog cleared and in the evening we sighted a great flame of natural gas from an oil well near Cape Nombre on Tierra del Fuego. We had drifted some 30 miles south of Cape Virgins and had to work back north to enter the Straits. The number of oil wells both on the mainland to the north of the Straits and on Tierra del Fuego has increased greatly in recent years. Many of them are marked on the chart and where there is also one of these perpetual flames they are readily identified and make valuable land-marks.

Punta Arenas lies about 120 miles inside the Straits and the navigation of this eastern section involves the passage through the First and Second Narrows where the tidal streams run strongly – 5 to 8 knots at springs in the First Narrows and slightly less in the Second Narrows. A small vessel must therefore work the tides. An important factor is that the west-going stream, the flood, begins to run three hours before high water by the shore and continues running for three hours after, the reason being that the tidal range outside the Narrows is 42ft. while inside it is only half that. Thus the water level outside has to rise 21ft. before it can begin its rush through the Narrows.

On the 23rd, the wind being light, we resorted to the engine. After puzzling my head over this tidal conundrum I reckoned that with the help of the engine we should arrive within striking distance of the First Narrows in time to catch the evening tide. When still some eight miles away we picked up a strong northerly wind, cut the engine, hoisted sail, and went along at a rare bat, the flood tide having begun to run. I made a mess of the approach and the current swept us to the south side of the entrance where we had some anxious moments on the edge of the Orange Bank in a patch of turbulent water. In the Narrows, which are about 2 miles wide and 10 miles long, there are alarming looking eddies and whirlpools hinting at submerged rocks, but the strait is in fact deep and free from dangers. Shooting out of the Narrows, the flood still running, we made for the northern shore where we anchored for the night. We lay wide open to the west, whence all the weather makes, so we set an anchor watch.

When we weighed anchor at 5 am to catch the tide for the Second Narrows and so to Punta Arenas the same day, we were soon baffled by head winds. Giving up the unequal struggle we squared away and came to anchor off the north shore in Gregory Bay a cable's length from the beach. Waiting for the tide to turn we spent the day there, watching trucks passing along the road which now links the numerous oil rigs to the east with Punta Arenas. Alas! A hundred years ago, when these coasts were really wild and strange, we might have spent the day parleying with Patagonian Indians. The *Beagle* on her famous voyage anchored in Gregory Bay and Darwin thus describes their stay:

Came to an anchor in St Gregory Bay. On shore there were the Toldos of a large tribe of Patagonian Indians. Went on shore with the captain and met with a kind of reception. These Indians have such constant communication with the sealers that they are half-civilized; they talk a good deal of Spanish and some English. Their appearance is rather wild. They are clothed in large mantles of the guanaco (a deer) and their long hair streams about their faces. They are much painted, many with their whole faces red, others black. One man was ringed and dotted with white like a Fuegian. The average height appeared to be more than six feet; the horses who carried these large men were small and ill-fitted for their work. When we returned to the boat a great number of Indians got in; it was a tedious and difficult operation to clear the boat. The captain promised to take three on board and everyone seemed determined to be one of them. At last we reached the ship with our three guests who had tea and behaved quite like gentlemen, used a knife and fork and helped themselves with a spoon. Nothing was so much relished as sugar. They felt the motion and were therefore landed. A large party went on shore next day to barter for mantles etc. The whole population of the Toldos were arranged on a bank having with them guanaco skins, ostrich feathers, etc. The first demand was for fire-arms, and of course, not giving them these, tobacco was the next; indeed, axes, knives, etc. were of no esteem in comparison to tobacco. It was an amusing scene and it was impossible not to like these misnamed giants, they were so thoroughly good-humoured and unsuspecting.

Unhappily, and quite naturally, the last of Darwin's good-humoured giants has long since been extinguished. As Mark Twain said: 'Soap and education are not so sudden as a massacre but they are equally deadly in the long run.' The captain with whom Darwin had gone ashore was Robert Fitzroy who in 1854 became the first head of the newly formed Meteorological Office. Fizroy's rules for deducing what weather may be in store from the appearance of clouds and the colour of the sky are familiar to all weather prophets.

We entered the Second Narrows late that evening and at 10pm in teeming rain, anchored in the lee of Elizabeth Island. This island, which the Chileans call Isla Isabel, was named by Drake who had anchored there in August 1578. In Henry's *Collection of Voyages* we read:

On August 20th they entered the Straits of Magellan in which they struggled with contrary winds, and the various dangers which the intricacy of that winding passage exposed them to. When they had passed the narrows and had entered a wider sea, they discovered an island to which they gave the name of Elizabeth, in honour of their sovereign.

Royal Road and Pelican Passage, on the west and south side respectively of Elizabeth Island, were also named by Drake, but his ship, the *Pelican*, had by then been given a new name. Apparently, upon reaching the entrance to the Straits, he had renamed her *Golden Hind*, in remembrance of his friend Christopher Hatton whose crest was a hind. It is very remarkable, and exemplifies Drake's boldness and skill as a navigator, that he not only passed through the Straits in winter when the days are short and the winds strong, but that he took only sixteen days. On this Henry, who published his *Voyages* in 1774, remarks: 'A passage the more extraordinary, as none of our late voyagers made it in less than thirty-six days in the middle of summer.'

By 9 am on a fair morning, with a fair wind, we had Punta Arenas in sight. Some snow-drifts still lay on the hills above. We arrived at noon, a month out from Montevideo. Making for the inshore end of the wooden jetty, just before reaching our chosen berth alongside a small fishing vessel, the only vacant place, we took the ground. It was almost the same spot where on our departure in 1955 we had suffered a like embarrassment. It is natural that such incidents, moments of failure or ignominy, should be more easily and more vividly remembered than our moments of success because the former are so much the more common. On that unlucky occasion a crowd of at least thirty friends and well wishers had assembled to watch us depart, a crowd that by *Mischief*'s standard of publicity amounted to a multitude. We let go our warps, the multitude raised a reedy cheer, we waved our hands airily, when, lo and behold, we were hard and fast aground, where we remained, within a few yards of our embarrassed friends, for the next hour.

On the present occasion a touch of the engine soon got us off and we moved round to the west side of the jetty where several small naval craft lay. A naval tug with the odd name of *Colo Colo* invited us to secure alongside which we did. The Chilean navy were here in force, a cruiser and several frigates lying anchored in the roads. Punta Arenas is a naval base, there is a naval barracks, a small dockyard, and an old fourmaster hulk moored in the roads is used as a prison for naval defaulters. In 1955, armed with an introduction from the Chilean naval attaché in London, we had received a lot of help from the navy at Punta Arenas. Indeed there was talk of putting a naval officer on board to pilot us through the channels, an idea that, upon seeing *Mischief*, they relinquished. We had no introductions this time and they were not needed. *Colo Colo* invited us on board for showers, and the commander of another naval vessel made us a present of two 40-gallon drums of oil. One of these had to be left behind as I did not relish carrying any deck cargo on our next leg. The Chilean navy maintain the Chilean antarctic bases and we learnt from a vessel that had recently returned that the South Shetlands were free of ice.

Had it not been for the development of the oil field I doubt if I should have noticed much change in Punta Arenas since 1955. Although nowadays there is everywhere a general exodus from the countryside to swell the population of the towns, around Punta Arenas there are no villages and no rural inhabitants to be attracted. Beyond Punta Arenas, as Sir Fopling Flutter said of Hyde Park, 'all is desert'. Owing no doubt, to the oil field there has been some building of new houses and new shops. The town never had any pretension to beauty so that no development of this kind can make it any worse. By the jetty new warehouses and a post office had sprung up, and one noted landmark, the *Bar Antartica*, a saloon of appropriately forbidding aspect, had been swept away – as also the old Hotel de France where our cook of those days, Van Tromp, used to play the piano, and where we had made some memorable meals off the succulent spider crab, or 'centolla', a crab peculiar to these waters. The new houses were all of very modern design and happily no towering blocks of flats have yet been built. Punta Arenas has a strong climate, days when it is not blowing half a gale or more are few, so that high buildings might well be too draughty. Supermarkets have, of course, appeared to make shopping more inhuman and shoppers like things on a conveyor-belt; and there is a new, flash hotel where no one, least of all our friend Van Tromp, would dream of playing the piano.

The British Consulate still transacted decreasing business in the same dingy building that also houses the British Club, even more moribund, and sad to see. Ichabod, the glories are departed! In its hey-day, before the opening of the Panama Canal, Punta Arenas was practically a British colony, the *estancias* of Patagonia and Tierra del Fuego were nearly all British-owned, as was most of the shipping that passed through the Straits and the coal that the ships called for. English was more useful than Spanish, wages were paid in sterling. The late Mr T.P. Jones, British consul at the time of our first visit, who had himself experienced those halcyon days, told me that then no Chilean soldiers or sailors were to be seen in the streets, there was no Customs House, the poorest workmen smoked Abdulla cigarettes, and that whisky and champagne cost five shillings a bottle. For the British community, at any rate, the millenium had already arrived.

The hospitable *Colo Colo* left next day and we moved back to the east side of the jetty alongside a crab-fisher. We bought two 'centolla' for about fifteen shillings. As Herbert, the economist, remarked: 'For that money you become a good, fat chicken.' That day a new figure made his appearance. A Norwegian vessel *Hardanger* came in and one of her deckhands, a young Canadian, Louis, visited *Mischief*. He showed the keenest desire to join us; adventure, he said, and a more intimate knowledge of the sea than can be had from a 10,000-ton steamer, were what he wanted. He had left father to look after the Saskatchewan farm while he went globe-trotting on the cheap. Such a strong, young chap, would, I thought, be a useful acquisition and would be an insurance against Carreo's possible departure. Together we went on board *Hardanger* to learn if his captain would pay him off there and then. The captain refused to do this but agreed that it might be managed at Buenos Aires where they would be in four days. We left it at that. If Louis got his discharge he would cable me and fly down to join us. While on board I had a look at his quarters, a spacious cabin to himself, radiator, fan, washbasin, the lot.

During our stay of ten days we were obliged to shift our berth at least seven times. Whichever side of the jetty we lay, sooner or later the wind would start blowing us hard against it. Whenever the bashing looked like becoming severe we moved out and anchored. Except for the difficulty over the dinghy we should have done better to stay there, but the crew came and went when they pleased and sometimes remained on shore all night. In these circumstances I did not like being long away from the boat. We lost all our fenders and had to replace them with tyres picked up on the beach. Edward Allcard, the single-hander, had apparently suffered as much as we did: a note which he had left for me was appropriately headed: 'Sea Wanderer, Pier Basher, Punta Arenas.'

Allcard had wintered, as he described it, in Beagle Channel, and had sailed from Punta Arenas for Valparaiso three weeks before we arrived. He knew that we were due and had assumed that we would be following him north-bound through the Straits and the Channels.

His note to me therefore ran as follows: ' . . . Hope I will have the pleasure of meeting you. I am now leaving for Port Gallant. In January 1967 the master of *Swallow* climbed to the highest summit and deposited a bottle under a cairn, and I might have a look for it. I will paint a white arrow on some prominent rock pointing to a spot below which will be a note for you.' The master of *Swallow* was Carteret who set out from England for a voyage round the world in company with Wallis in the ship *Dolphin*. In Henry's *Voyages* I find this reference:

. . . Came to an anchor in the bay near Cape Gallant, where they catched wild duck in such numbers as to afford them very seasonable relief. Near this spot are very high mountains, one of which was climbed by the master of the *Swalloe*, with the hope of getting a view of the South Sea; but being disappointed in his expectation, he erected a pyramid, and having written the ship's name and the date of the year, he left the same with a shilling within the structure.

Finding arrows painted on rocks and picking up notes in remote places like Port Gallant is right up my street. There is nothing I should have enjoyed more. But unless we went west through the Straits and back round Cape Horn it would be well off our course. However, the story has a sequel. On returning to England I found another letter from Edward Allcard which I again take the liberty of quoting:

Re the mountain in Port Gallant, between two gales I was lucky enough to reach the summit – the bottle left by Wallis' squadron had been pinched by American tourists 117 years ago, and they had left a copper plaque which I pinched in turn, plus what might have been the remains of Wallis' flagpole. The summit was a most satisfactory one, a sharp serrated ridge which I could sit astride, although the rock whizzing away under my left foot lowered my morale a couple of points. I built you a cairn on the shore, axed a tree to mark it and hoisted a rather nice face towel. Your letter I put in an up-turned NIDO milk can telling you I had been lucky.

After receiving that I felt under strong obligations to one day visit Port Gallant. One would love to know whether or not some latter day American tourists have also pinched Allcard's NIDO milk can. I have never heard of tourists in those regions, but unlikelier things have happened. American tourists are now being taken to the Antarctic.

I spent one day away from the ship when a mountaineering friend, Derek Walker, then head of the English school at Punta Arenas, drove three of us out to Fort Bulnes and Port Famine. The country south and west of Punta Arenas is not attractive, lying on the border between the arid flats of Atlantic Patagonia and the uninhabited, densely forested, mountainous regions of Pacific Patagonia, the dividing point being Cape Froward at the southernmost tip of the American continent. On the foothills where forest had grown, the trees have all been felled or burnt and all along the inland side of the unmade road there is mile upon mile of charred stumps. Occasionally one passed a house, or rather a tin shanty, with a grass field enclosed by a broken-down fence. Fort Bulnes is the reconstruction of an old Chilean fort and a popular place with the citizens of Punta Arenas for their Sunday outings. Although it is now merely a historic monument and museum it is still firmly held by the Army who require visitors to first obtain a pass. Port Famine has a longer history but there is nothing there now except the newly built clubhouse of a skin-diving club – almost the last activity that one would expect to see flourishing in Magellan Straits. In 1581, alarmed by Drake's incursion, the Spanish sent an expedition under Sarmiento to fortify the Straits. One would have thought that for this purpose only at the First Narrows would it be any use; nevertheless, a settlement was made at this useless spot, a fort built, and the place named Ciudad del Rey Filipe. Six years later, when Cavendish called there, on the third circumnavigation of the world, nothing remained but 'four cannon and several churches', and the putrefying corpses of the garrison. Four hundred men and thirty women had starved to death. Cavendish called the place Port Famine.

On 3 December, a Saturday, Louis arrived by air from Buenos Aires as arranged. No sooner had he got his gear on board than a strong westerly blow obliged us to haul off and anchor. On the Sunday we were back alongside and on the Monday, when I had planned to sail, a strong easterly wind discouraged that idea and again drove us off to anchor . . . We were all ready to go, water and stores on board, and the ship 'entered out', in the curious phrase of shipping agents. Through the good offices of the vice-consul we had a good supply of 'tostada', but no *Nautical Almanac* for 1967 had been obtainable.

CHAPTER SEVEN

To the South Shetlands

THE FURTHER a man goes, the more reluctant he naturally becomes to turn back. As might have been expected, the thought of tamely giving up at this stage was unbearable, even when weighed against the bleak prospect of sailing south with a disgruntled and discordant crew. Only a mutiny on their part could have persuaded me to think differently and they had not yet reached that stage. Though the prime objective had long since been given up, a voyage to the South Shetlands could be regarded as a reconnaissance, either for myself or for some future party, and I had still some hope that Tom and I might do something on Livingston Island, provided we found a secure anchorage. Moreover only some 800 miles now separated us from our goal, albeit the greater part of those miles lay across the cold and reputedly stormy waters of Drake Passage.

This sea between Cape Horn and the South Shetlands is too wide to be called a Strait, as sometimes it is, and its name reminds us that Drake was the

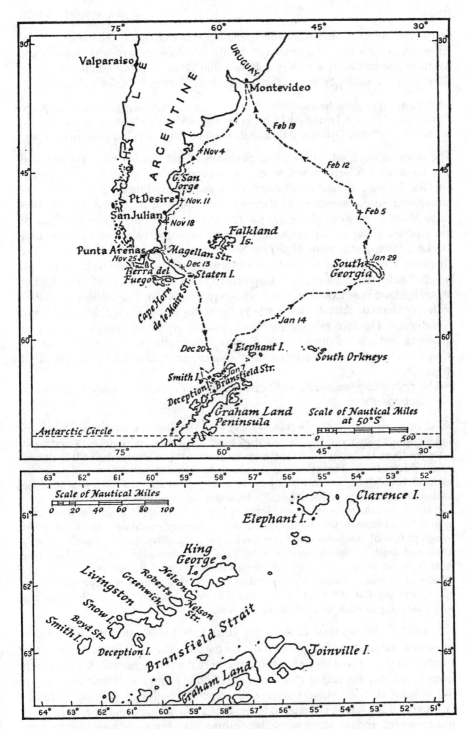

Track chart for Southern Ocean expedition: Montevideo – Southern Ocean
The South Shetland Islands

first to sail upon it, thus discovering the existence of open water south of the American continent – an entirely fortuitous discovery wrought through the wrath of the winds. It is widely believed that Drake sighted and landed upon Cape Horn, a belief based on the narrative of Fletcher, Drake's chaplain:

The uttermost cape or headland of all these islands stands near in 56 degrees [Cape Horn is Lat. 55° 59′ S.] without which there is no main or island to be seen southwards, but that the Atlantic Ocean and the South Seas meet in a most large and free scope.

The devious track and the various positions of the *Golden Hind* for the next fifty days after 8 September, when she passed from the Straits of Magellan into the Pacific, are not at all clear, for a sequence of heavy gales drove her hither and yon somewhere to the west and south of the Horn. In his book *Cape Horn* Felix Reisenberg has plotted the various courses and positions of the *Golden Hind* during those fifty stormy days from the brief log kept by Drake's Portuguese pilot Nuño da Silva, a better guide probably than the chaplain. His conclusion is that the southernmost island that Drake landed on was 200 miles west and south of Cape Horn in Lat. 57° S. It is unfortunate that no such island now exists, but as Reisenberg points out, the position coincides with Burnham or Pactolus bank where the water shoals from 2,000 fathoms to 70 fathoms. He accounts for its disappearance either by volcanic activity or the wear and tear of three hundred years of pounding by heavy seas and, no doubt, icebergs. It is an interesting theory, incapable of either proof of disproof.

The prevailing weather conditions in Drake Passage are thus described in the *Antarctic Pilot:*

North of about Lat. 60° S. winds from some westerly direction strongly predominate, and their mean force is high. The 'Roaring Forties' is a well-known term to navigators in the southern hemisphere for the strong, predominantly westerly winds which prevail south of Lat. 40° S. The name might seem to imply that the winds were less strong south of Lat. 50° S., but this is not so. In most sectors the westerly winds continue unabated as far south as about Lat. 55° S., and in many sectors, in January, nearly to Lat. 60° S. Any decrease in velocity south of Lat. 55° S. is not so much a real decrease in speed as an increase in variability. Considering average conditions, the circum-polar trough [a line of minimum mean pressure] is the limit of the predominantly westerly winds and south of this [normally Lat. 60° to 65° S] easterlies predominate. Gales are most frequent in the zone of the Westerlies to the north of the circum-polar trough. Observations from whaling ships show that gales reach a frequency exceeding 20% in places between Lat. 40° S. and 55°S., and that they generally decrease in frequency with increasing latitude to a minimum in Lat. 63° S.

Lat. 63° S., by the way, is about the latitude of the South Shetlands so that we should be heading for a region of comparative calms. Bearing in mind the wind conditions I had thought preferable to make our departure for the south from Punta Arenas rather than from Port Stanley in the Falkland Islands, on the ground that we should start with some 200 miles of westing in hand. However, if the winds ran true to form, as they so seldom do, the advantage is less apparent, indeed there would be nothing in it. For having first been swept away to the east, when we reached Lat. 60° S., we should conveniently be swept back again by the predominant Easterlies. Happily *Mischief* is not a cork to be swept about at the mercy of winds and waves as such calculations might imply. Except when hove-to we have some control over her direction, and in mid-summer, even in those latitudes, one need not expect to be hove-to for days on end. It might therefore have been as easy and more politic to call at Port Stanley to make our number there, since the islands we were bound for are part of the Falkland Islands Dependencies. We were, I believe, expected there and our failure to turn up may in part have accounted for the coolness of our reception at Deception Island.

We got our anchor at 8 am and sailed away unnoticed. With the ebb tide still under us we carried on to the Second Narrows through which we passed escorted by a large school of Commerson's dolphins,* a species peculiar to these waters, some five feet long and genuine piebalds. The grace and speed of these lithe creatures, clearly visible in the smooth, pale green water, held us fascinated and kept our cameras busy; but I strongly suspect that one of them snatched our left-hand rotator which disappeared about this time. For the rest of the voyage outwards and homewards we dispensed with a patent log, making the man on watch responsible for recording his estimate of what mileage the boat had sailed during his watch. The tide turned against us as we left the Narrows and we did not come to an anchor in Gregory Bay until after midnight. While sounding our way up to the anchorage Tom hove the lead without making it fast with the result that we lost the lead-line and its 7 lb. lead.

Next morning we passed the First Narrows and anchored again a few miles beyond where we remained for the rest of the day and the night waiting for a fair wind. Shortly after starting on the following day we sighted the RRS *Shackleton* which altered course to close us, her deck crowded with bearded figures peering at us from behind cameras. Next day she passed us again bound south having made a quick turn-round at Punta Arenas where she had called to land a sick man from one of the Antarctic bases. On neither occasion did they speak to us. One could not but feel that they regarded us with a faint air of disapproval.

The weather behaved in its usual erratic way, the wind hanging obstinately in the east, bringing with it a lot of rain and some fog. By the third day since leaving the Straits we had got only as far as Rio Grande where there is a large '*frigorifico*' and a wireless station. The Rio Grande marks the dividing line between the pampas country of the northern part of Tierra del Fuego, where the sheep-runs are, from the mountainous regions to the south. At last we got a breeze from the west, hoisted the twins and ran fast to the south-east. At 8 pm wind and sea having increased, we reefed the twins, and when I came on at midnight we were north of the entrance to Straits de la Maire. These straits were first discovered and traversed in 1616 by a small Dutch private expedition that had been launched mainly with the hope of breaking the monopoly

---

*Commerson's Dolphin (*Cephalorhynchus commersonii*) is perhaps the most conspicuously marked small cetacean to be found in the Southern Ocean. It has the alternative common names of Piebald Porpoise and Le Jacobite, the latter Commerson's own name for it; both refer to the striking black and white colour of the body. It has been observed in the Straits of Magellan, near Tierra del Fuego, and at the Falkland Islands.

of the Dutch East India Company by finding a new route to the Far East. Two ships, *Unity* and *Hoorn*, sailed from the port of Hoorn with Schouten in command and the two brothers le Maire on board. Their father, Isaac le Maire, who had quarrelled with the East India Company, had been the moving spirit behind the voyage. While careened at Port Desire having the weed burnt off, the smaller of the two ships, *Hoorn*, caught fire and became a total loss. *Unity* went on through Straits de la Maire and was the first to round the cape to which Schouten gave the name Hoorn.

Dangerous tide rips extend for many miles from both sides of the entrance to the straits, and when southbound it is necessary to enter at high water. I much wanted to pass through the straits but not only had we ill-timed our arrival; we should have to lower the twins, set the main and steer south with a biggish sea on the beam. There are never any lack of reasons or excuses for inaction. I decided to leave well alone and to carry on eastwards along the north shore of Staten Island. In the morning we had glimpses of the lower slopes of this mountainous island, thickly clad in Antarctic beech, glimpses that were soon blotted out by cloud. According to some doubtful sights we were 10 miles east of the island when the wind dropped. The glass had fallen to 29 inches, so we set the trysail fully expecting a dirty night. Nothing came of this but next morning with the island still in sight, we lay tumbling in a horribly confused sea for many hours making no progress at all. The meeting of the current coming round Cape Horn with that through the various channels of Tierra del Fuego causes an unusually agitated sea off the coasts of Staten Island. As the *Pilot* warns: 'There are very dangerous overfalls off the eastern extremity of the island when the wind is against the tidal steam; they have been reported to extend 18 miles from the island.'

Given a knowledge of Spanish and the right frequency one could no doubt receive weather forecasts from the Rio Grande station. As we were not so equipped we were not liable to be frightened by any forecasts. The warnings of the barometer are at least silent but in a small boat, when the sails can be handed and all made snug in a few minutes, one sometimes wonders whether they too could not be dispensed with. Why disturb one's peace of mind by trying to peer into the immediate future? 'Let us cease to consider what may never happen,' said Dr Johnson, 'and what when it shall happen will laugh at human speculation.' It seemed to be the custom in these parts for the wind to fall light as the barometer fell, and only when the barometer rose did things begin to happen. On the 15th it fell to 28.6 inches, and that evening, when it had started to rise, the wind came in so hard that we set the trysail and double-reefed the staysail. Whereupon the wind began to moderate. It had become noticeably colder, the air temperature 36° F. and the sea 39° F., and we shifted into our winter woollens. We had minor worries besides the cold. First the cabin heater, which burns diesel oil, caught fire and had to be extinguished with the help of one of our appliances, and then the lavatory got blocked. I was glad to see that our marine engineer Carreo made no bones about tackling this.

I'm afraid that by now Carreo thoroughly disliked us all, with a special aversion for Mike Edwards whose blond hair and beard he may have found provocative. He seldom opened his mouth except to quarrel. In arranging the watches I took care to precede him so that I was the one to call him. When woken in the middle of the night he might be in a belligerent mood and he would be less likely to start a fight with me than with one of the others. Herbert had developed such a crop of boils that he could not work on deck and had to revert to the galley, but in spite of all remained remarkably cheerful. Since neither of these two had much in the way of warm clothing we all subscribed what we could spare towards their wardrobe. Tom, who so far had been most loyal, now turned sour. He claimed that had he known we were to attempt no landing on Smith Island he would not have left Punta Arenas. Ignorant of what the people at the British base on Deception Island were like, I promised that if we found a climber among them, as seemed likely, he could accompany Tom while I looked after the boat. I felt sure that a man would be allowed time off for such an enterprise.

Books about sailing ships in the waters south of Cape Horn naturally lay stress on the gales encountered, so that one is left with the impression that gales seldom cease and that seas are always mountainous. At first one thinks that 5,000 miles of ocean unbroken by any land must inevitably give birth to gigantic waves, forgetting that the depressions, and the winds that cause the waves, probably extend over less than 500 miles. One imagines, too, that in the seemingly infrequent lulls between gales an endless procession of great combers, the Cape Horn greybeards, marches on relentlessly from the west. This is not so. The sea behaves here as elsewhere, and when the wind is not blowing, as happens frequently in summer, there are no waves. From my own very limited experience of four voyages in the Southern Ocean I should say that in summer the gales of the Roaring Forties, Furious Fifties, and Shrieking Sixties, are no more frequent or fierce than in similar latitudes in the North Atlantic. Gale frequencies may well be higher off the pitch of the Horn, as is generally the way off capes at the extremities of great land masses, like the Cape of Good Hope (the so-called Cape of Storms), Cape Leeuwin, and the Snares. But in the southern hemisphere these latitudes are colder than their northern equivalents and more cloudy.

With a beam wind and a smooth sea we had a fine run of 100 miles on 18 December, a pleasant enough day except for a snow shower which lasted about half an hour. That night we crossed what is known as the Antarctic convergence, marked by a sudden fall in sea temperature, the boundary between the colder, less saline Antarctic water to the south, and the warmer more saline sub-antarctic water. Overnight the sea temperature dropped from 39° to 35° F., and next day to 33° F., where it remained until we had recrossed the convergence on the way homewards. In a paper to the Royal Geographical Society, Dr Dilwyn John, of the *Discovery II* expedition, thus vividly described the meaning of the Antarctic convergence:

One might well ask, what can this boundary be, far away in the open sea? It might be supposed that sea-water throughout the oceans mixed readily, that there would be something like an even and gradual transition from the water of minus temperature, poor in salts because of melting ice and falling snow, at the Antarctic ice-edge, to the warm water rich in salts in the tropic. It is not so: there are successive zones from north to south separated by sharp boundaries. Antarctic surface water is very cold, and although it is poor in salts it is heavier than the warmer more saline water of the neighbouring zone to the north, the temperate zone of the southern hemisphere. This temperate zone is called the sub-antarctic. Now Antarctic water moves for the most part towards the east because of the prevailing westerly winds, but it has a northern movement too. Where it meets sub-antarctic water the very different densities of the two do not allow of ready mixing, and the heavier Antarctic water sinks sharply below the lighter sub-antarctic and continues its flow northwards below it.

This line along which the heavy Antarctic surface water meets the lighter surface water and sinks below it, is the boundary in the surface of the open sea that I spoke of. It is called the Antarctic convergence. It is a physical boundary very easily and precisely detected with a thermometer by the sharp change in temperature as one passes from one zone to another. It can be detected as easily if not so precisely by a zoologist with a tow-net because each of the two waters has a distinctive fauna of floating animal life. But we, whether sailors or zoologists, know and will remember the convergence best in another way; as the line to the north of which we felt one day, after months in the Antarctic, genial air again and soft rain like English rain in the spring. In the southernmost lands in the sub-antarctic, the islands about Cape Horn, the earth smells as earth should smell and as it never does in the Antarctic. It is no doubt the north-easterly course of the convergence between the longitudes of Cape Horn and South Georgia, so that the former is left far to the north and the latter to the south, that accounts for the vast difference in the climate of two islands that are precisely in the same latitude and only 1,000 miles apart. The lower slopes of Staten Island are clothed with beech trees with so rich an undergrowth that it is difficult to push through. South Georgia, the other island, is a true Antarctic land. The snow line of South Georgia is lower than the tree line of Tierra del Fuego.

On 19 December we had a good run of 90 miles under the twin staysails, an unusual rig for these waters, and by next day I reckoned we were about 90 miles north of Livingston Island. The wind increased that night so that at 2 am, when two small icebergs were sighted, we hove-to on account of the wind and the poor visibility. In this latitude, 62° S., it never became properly dark, only the two hours either side of midnight were a bit murky. Deception Island lies to the south-west of Livingston Island and the approach to it from the north is guarded by a chain of islands stretching for nearly two hundred miles from Smith Island in the west to King George Island in the east. The northern side of the chain abounds with islets, rocks, and breakers, and most of the islands are separated by comparatively narrow channels, so that the only safe and sensible approach for strangers like ourselves, is by the 20-mile wide Boyd Strait between Smith Island and Snow Island. It had become increasingly rare for us to get a reliable sight, especially noon sights for the all-important latitude. Either it would be cloudy, raining, snowing, or foggy, and on one occasion, having already had the sextant dowsed with spray, I found that the wind made my eyes water too much to take a sight. Not that one need complain about difficulties that must be expected and allowed for when by choice one visits such regions. As Byron said: 'Comfort must not be expected by folk who go a-pleasuring.'

Having been hove-to for most of the 21st, when by dead reckoning we were 25 miles north of Livingston Island, we let draw in the evening in fog, visibility less than half a mile. But by next morning we were again hove-to in a heavy sea and south-easterly gale, the weather too thick for us to see anything except two moderately large icebergs. By now we were more than a little uncertain of our position. Snow Island should have been only a few miles away and with the wind at south-east we were drifting safely away from it. In order to lessen the drift we tried out a parachute anchor I had brought for just such a contingency. On the voyage to Heard Island, such an anchor, a 29ft. diameter parachute on 5 fathoms of anchor chain, had held *Patanela*, a boat twice as heavy as *Mischief*, more or less stationary for an hour in a severe gale. Finally the fitting between the cable and the parachute had parted, but the parachute itself remained intact. The material of our present parachute must have been inferior or maybe it got foul of the cable. In five minutes we were hauling inboard its tattered remnants. Normally when hove-to one might expect to drift 25 to 30 miles in 24 hours, a distance well worth trying to save.

That it never became completely dark did something to lessen the anxiety that a stormy night naturally inspires. I had a chill and stood no watch and might have enjoyed the luxury of undisturbed sleep had it not been for the whining and howling of the wind. Only by plugging one's ears could the mournful and nerve-racking dirge played by the wind upon the rigging be shut out, and then one would be fearful of missing some more significant noise – a hail from the deck, the breaking of a skylight, or some worse disaster. Long before there is any reasonable hope of the gale abating one begins to time the intervals between the gusts, in the hope that if the lulls lengthen the wind is taking off. The glass remained high and steady throughout and each lull served only to make the next gust sound fiercer. The wind by itself is of less consequence than the sea it raises, except that its noise, like the noise of a bombardment, in time wears a man down. In the open sea waves have to build up to 20ft. or more before their breaking crests become dangerous to a small boat, however seaworthy, and if the wind blows hard enough for long enough this is bound to happen. Whether hove-to or running the chance of being hit by a breaking sea is always there, and though a bad helmsman can increase the chances, a good one cannot do much to lessen them. Not all seas run true, on a dark night a man cannot see, and a heavy boat like *Mischief* is not quick enough on the helm for a man to take avoiding action.

On the afternoon of the following day, when still hove-to, we had to lower the mainsail to repair a seam. When it is reefed right down the sail and the massive boom are not too difficult to control even in a hard blow. Even though the wind had blown steadily for 24 hours the sea had in it no real malice. The wind, even in gusts had not risen above force 9 and since it was blowing from south-east the sea had no long fetch. Our steady drift away from the islands caused us some concern but it would have been far greater had we been drifting towards them. On the early morning of 24 December we let draw again and sailed slowly southwards in cold, wet fog. When the wind died we continued southwards under the engine until a fresh fall in the barometer frightened me into stopping to await clearer weather. For three days we had had no reliable sights and our rate of drift could only be guessed at. We might be in Boyd Strait, for all I knew, between Smith and Snow Islands, not a good

place to be in if another gale started either from east or west. In fact, as the
next day showed, we had enough sea-room.

On Christmas morning at 3 am the fog rolled away, revealing to my
surprised gaze an unbroken horizon, no land anywhere in sight. I put the
visibility at about ten miles so that had we been near Smith or Snow Islands,
as I thought, we should certainly have seen something. This clearing did not
last long. A wind sprang up from north-east, bringing in its train sleet and
rain, and with this fine quartering breeze we sailed southwards at 4 knots. If
we missed the islands, we could hardly miss the Antarctic continent some
sixty miles beyond. Long before breakfast I had to call all hands to change the
main for the trysail, a call that they did not respond to with much alacrity; not
for the first time I sensed how bloody-minded they were becoming. And,
Christmas Day though it was, I felt out of humour, angry with myself more
than with anyone for not knowing where we were. In the brief diary I kept, I
notice that under the heading 'Christmas Day' there is the query, 'My worst?'
It had a faint resemblance to Christmas Day 1955 when we were not exactly
lost but in doubt about our next move. We were in a tent on the Calvo glacier,
dining largely off pemmican, uncertain as to whether we should find any route
ahead or be forced to retreat to the boat. It is not so much where you are that
matters but whom you are with, and on that occasion I had two staunch
companions.

Meantime snow began to fall and the cabin heater created another diversion for us. After Carreo had tried in vain to make it burn, Herbert had a go
and was only too sucessful, setting the whole thing on fire. The extinguishers
finally subdued it, but their fumes made the cabin untenable for some time.
Thus we were all on deck, but it was Tom, I think, who first sighted land.
Vaguely through the murk, not much more than a mile away, we saw a white
blur with a dense black rock to one side of it. This most welcome and
dramatic landfall we took at first to be Snow Island, which has off its western
shore the 500ft.-high Castle Rock. But as we drew nearer our 'Castle Rock'
became a part of the island, a part too steep to hold snow, and we realized
that the broken glacier we looked at, and the steep snow slopes above, must
be descending from high, cloud-hidden peaks. It could only be Smith Island, a
magnificent landfall achieved entirely by accident. We closed the shore, if an
ice-cliff lapped by the sea can be called a shore, and had to stand out again
when the wind showed signs of failing. Before the weather closed in, as it did
when the wind died, we had time to discern what looked like a cape to the
north-east. We confidently hoped that this was Cape Smith at the northern
extremity of the island, for the island is 20 miles long from north to south and
we were on the wrong side, that is the west side of it. From some hidden store
Herbert produced a bottle of beer and we had buns for tea, thus thriftily
celebrating both Christmas Day and a successful landfall. Having started the
engine we soon rounded what proved to be Cape Smith and set a course for
Deception Island some sixty miles to the east. After supper, the fog having
become dense, we stopped.

'There is something personal and compact about an island, no matter how
desolate it may be.' These words of Shackleton, which probably applied to

Elephant Island where his party took refuge, seemed to me equally applicable to Smith Island. It is as compact as could be, no bays, inlets or fjords, as desolate an island as any I have seen, and it had a grim enough personality even though some 5,000ft. of its more daunting aspect remained hidden. In the very short distance that we coasted along it, sheer ice cliffs, glacier tongues, rock cliffs, or boulders, forbade even the thought of a landing. Yet somewhere along that considerable coastline there must be some kind of a cove and a beach. To search for it from a small boat might take days and would involve the risk of being caught in a gale on the wrong side of the island; for it would not be easy, in view of its 20-mile length, to nip quickly round to the lee side. And having found a landing place there is the problem of the 6,900ft. Mount Foster which unfortunately we never saw. It would be too much to expect that the landing place would also be the most convenient spot from which to tackle the mountain. In mountaineering the means are more important than the end, so that one must hope that this rich prize does not fall to some party that has been landed conveniently adjacent to the mountain by helicopter.

It is a great pity that no logbook or account of James Weddell's 1820 voyage has been found or is now likely to be found. Where he made his landing on Smith Island is not known. His later voyage, when he penetrated deep into the Weddell Sea, is described in his own book *A Voyage towards the South Pole* published in 1825, and in this book occurs the brief reference to his having landed on Smith Island: 'Of the South Shetlands, the highest and most forbidding in aspect is the western island which in 1820 I named James Island as I was the first who landed upon it.' Dr Brian Roberts, of the Scott Polar Institute, assures me that James and Smith Island are the same. It had been discovered by William Smith in 1819 and it was his name that the British sealers used during the next few years until it became firmly established. These early sealers either did not know of Weddell's name (which was not published until 1825) or they knowingly used the earlier name.

CHAPTER EIGHT

At Deception Island

NEXT MORNING, in the absence of any wind, we began motoring, intent upon reaching Deception Island that day. Although the fog had thinned we were too far away to see anything of either Smith, Snow Island, or Deception. We had not been motoring for long when a wind from the north-east set in but by then the island had become dimly discernible and we made haste to close it. When we had got up to South Point the wind had developed into a snow blizzard and we were faced with a three-mile plug into the teeth of it north

along the coast. The entrance to Port Foster is narrow and in our anxiety not
to miss it we kept within a quarter mile of the low steep cliffs which even at
that range were frequently blotted out by snow squalls. At times we seemed
to stand still. Driving into the blizzard from dead ahead, and a short, steep
sea, the engine just managed to push us along at about one knot. Thus it was
late afternoon before we were off the entrance to Neptune's Bellows and in
the most welcome lee of the high cliffs to the east of it. The crew emerged
from the unheated cabin to see the sights while I at last felt some life returning
to my half-frozen hands, having been steering since we sighted the island.

Neptune's Bellows is the name given to the entrance to Port Foster by
American sealers in the early years of the nineteenth century. The name is
suggestive enough for sailors, but in point of fact, both on the day we entered
and the day we left, the Bellows were not working. Even with a north-easterly
blizzard blowing outside we met no furious blasts inside the Bellows, and on
the day we sailed out the wind barely filled the sails. Nevertheless, the striking
scenery at the entrance fully merits so imaginative a name, for on both sides
are high cliffs of vividly coloured red and yellow rock. That on the north side
is a true, uncompromising cliff, the rock rising vertically out of the sea for two
or three hundred feet; the south side is less sheer and on a smaller scale. The
width between these cliffs is about 3 cables but the navigable width is only half
this, for in mid-channel there is a sunken rock. On the south shore lies the
forlorn, rusty wreck of a whale chaser, a strong hint to the stranger to stick
close to the north side of the channel.

Deception Island, like most of the neighbouring islands, is of volcanic
origin, and is one of the few volcanoes that have been breached and inun-
dated by the sea. It is for all the world like an atoll, Port Foster representing
the lagoon and Neptune's Bellows the pass; but the surrounding reef, instead
of coral, is a ridge of a mean height of 1,000ft. permanently covered with
snow, the rim of the original volcano. Despite Byron's 'Damn description, it
is always disgusting', the following details from the *Antarctic Pilot* will be of
interest:

The whole island is of volcanic origin, forming one of the largest and most remarkable
crater islands in the world. The principal rock is lava. Brickstone is dispersed upon the
beaches and in large fragments on the hills, giving relief to the dull scenery. Numerous
hot sulphurous springs occur, the temperature of the hottest from 185° to 190° F., hot
enough to boil an egg. In January 1936 the hottest water found in Whalers Bay was
127° F. in a brackish stream flowing down the beach near the whaling station. At low
tide the temperature of the sea along the shore was 95° F. At high tide the temperature
of the sea at this point was 43.5° F., but one cable offshore it was 38.5° F. It is reported
by the whalers that at times the water in this anchorage has been hot enough to blister
the paint on the factory ships. In April 1927, the RRS *Discovery* found much
evidence of volcanic activity. Clouds of steam frequently arose at the water line in
Whalers Bay and at low-water mark. At 8 inches below the scoriae and ashes on the
beach the temperature was found to be 133° F.

Turning sharp right – to starboard, I should say – on emerging from
Neptune's Bellows one enters Whalers Bay at the head of which is the British
base and the derelict whaling station. We brought up first in unexpectedly

shoal water of only 2 fathoms. As this would not do we anchored again in 7 fathoms and immediately began to drag. Unlike the cliffs of Neptune's Bellows, the snow-covered ridge behind the base did not afford much of a barrier to the north-east wind which still blew with great force. The third time we let go, the anchor appeared to be holding so I went below to gather myself together before visiting the base. Meantime Tom and Louis already had the dinghy in the water and were in such haste to get ashore that they were about to push off. Unwilling to be preceded by two such uncouth heralds I hastened to join them. The voyagers who landed on islands inhabited by savages were at first often kindly treated; only later, reasoning perhaps from the uncivil behaviour of their visitors, did the natives turn hostile. So it was with the savages of Deception Island. A reception committee some half-dozen strong gave us a warm welcome, though the base leader himself was not there. As we walked towards the huts a short distance away I remembered to ask if among the dozen or so men at the base there were any climbers, and learnt that there were not. Had there been one he would not have been able to accompany us; no one was even allowed to visit *Mischief*.

We were on the point of entering the hut when, happening to look back, I saw *Mischief* moving rapidly away from the shore with no one on deck. Muttering some hasty apologies to our would-be hosts I turned and ran for the dinghy, to be followed presently by Tom whose seaman's instinct for the moment overcame his ill-will. Louis remained there. We were told later that he had had a bath and used up all their hot water, a fact which conceivably may have contributed to the blighting of our prospects. As Tom and I rowed off in haste to overtake *Mischief* before she fetched up on the opposite shore, our former acquaintance *Shackleton* turned the corner out of Neptune's Bellows. As soon as she had anchored and put a warp ashore her launch came over with an invitation from her captain to lie alongside her for the night, an offer we gladly accepted. They were a cheerful crowd, both the crew and the men bound for the various Antarctic bases, and treated us well. After a hot shower I had a drink with Captain Turnbull who told me that for the last four seasons he had been looking in vain for a possible landing place on Smith Island. He also told me that about three days before Christmas they had visited Port Foster and found it full of pack-ice. At that moment there was not a fragment of ice anywhere.

Port Foster is the Port of Entry for the South Shetlands and the base leader is also the resident magistrate. Accordingly I went ashore next day with the ship's papers and crew's passports. Christmas, or Boxing Day, had apparently exhausted the stock of goodwill at the base. I got no further than the outer office where I had a formal interview with the base leader who expressed surprise at our visit and some disgust for Louis and Herbert, for he, too, had been there the previous night for a bath. I mentioned that I would like to buy a small quantity of stores and learnt that it was unlikely that any could be spared. I was surprised at this and had no complaint to make but one could not help comparing the treatment strangers received at similarly remote foreign bases, where one had not even to ask for anything. At Kerguelen, for example, the French had loaded us with bread, butter, potatoes, enough chocolate to last the voyage home, jars of pâté, tins of fruit, all the petrol and paraffin we needed, and finally a barrel of red wine. At Pond Inlet the Royal Canadian Mounted Police post had so stocked us up that we left with more food on board than when the voyage began. At Tingmiarmiut in East Greenland, where seven Danes maintained a weather station, we were shown into their store and told to help ourselves. Such places are usually overstocked, for they keep a year's supply in hand in case of accidents to the relief ship. This may or may not have been the case at Deception Island, but we heard of, and later saw for ourselves, cases of tinned butter, dried eggs, dried milk, dried potatoes, etc. rotting away in one of the several disused oil tanks, once part of the whaling station. These tanks had been holed by the navy in the last war to prevent their possible use by German raiders.

Meantime we enjoyed brief popularity on board *Shackleton* where we had been invited to take our meals in the mess with the British Antarctic Survey party. We particularly welcomed this invitation because Carreo had dismantled the stove, strewing the cabin with bits of iron and soot. With the help of one of *Shackleton*'s engineers he was busy constructing it on a new principle. Though the effects of any action are plain enough, their causes are sometimes obscure; and there were two reasons currently offered for the sudden eclipse of our popularity – no more meals were to be served to *Mischief*'s crew, and a little later Captain Turnbull asked me to move *Mischief* elsewhere. One version was that the wardroom had been left without enough sausages for breakfast, the other that Tom had somehow fallen foul of the captain. Since our arrival I had seen little of Tom who had transferred himself to the seamen's mess where he had been the life and soul of the party. But he had been seen having a short talk with the captain and judging from Tom's own version of what had passed I was not altogether surprised at being asked to shove off. Before we parted company we filled our water tanks from *Shackleton*'s hose, thus saving a lot of trouble later. She was taking on water from a well on shore. There are several wells and it is said that each whaling ship had its own well. The *Pilot* recommends taking water when the tides are low as occasionally salt water may seep into the well when the tides are high. Captain Turnbull also gave me a chart of South Georgia but could spare none of their 1967 *Nautical Almanacs*. He also assured me, and his position enabled him to give the assurance, that we should be able to buy what stores we needed.

So we anchored once more off the base, this time using our 1 cwt. Fisherman type anchor instead of the 60 lb. CQR anchor which was no use in this bottom of ash and cinders. We also took a line ashore, made fast to a boiler, the debris of the whaling station. Having attended to this I once more sought out the base leader to give him a list of our modest requirements. He was busy with the construction of a small jetty but took time off to give me a lecture on the irresponsibility of sailing a small boat to the Antarctic. He looked like the earnest young head of Dr Whacko's Academy and I felt like a newly joined urchin, too dumbfounded to utter. I can only think that this far-flung Government official, monarch of all he surveyed – provided he ignored the two foreign bases – greatly resented private intruders upon his small domain.

Back on board Mike cleaned up the refuse habitually deposited in the galley by Herbert, and with the stove put together and burning the cabin had become almost inhabitable. Carreo's reconstruction was not a success. It burned dangerously fiercely and gave out volumes of filthy smoke. Rather than perish by fire at sea, or become as black as Eskimos cooking over a blubber fire, we preferred to be cold. Long before reaching South Georgia we gave up using it, and later on had the satisfaction one always finds in throwing things overboard. Louis had now developed boils and since the British base had no doctor, the three of them, Louis, Herbert, and Carreo, walked to the Chilean base three miles away. A dry glacier of black ice, black with cinders, had to be crossed, so mountaineer Tom, who had long dissociated himself from any work on board, showed them the way. They did not go there entirely for their health. As I was told by Louis, whom I had come to regard as a seagoing bum with neither manners nor principles, all three hoped to arrange a passage to Punta Arenas. This hope was not fulfilled, though while we were there a naval tug arrived and departed. Louis attributed his boils to a low diet, the same diet that Mike, Tom, and I had been living on for six months, free from either boils, scurvy, or any other disease. Louis was another example of an adventure-lover who wanted his adventure on a plate without the attendant discomforts or risks. Not only should we have had the latest drugs on board but also a radio transmitter, distress signals,etc.,

Shackleton left next day bound south and if any of us had expected her to leave us a sack of potatoes or a few loaves of bread they were disappointed. Some of the BAS party, however, who were particularly friendly, had given us some luxuries from their private stores. Having seen her off Mike, Tom, and I walked over the ridge behind the base to visit a penguin rookery on the east coast. The route lay mostly over hard snow, lying presumably on top of ice, for the snow line is only a little above the beach. There were a few crevasses but they were open and not deep. The Antarctic terns that were nesting along the beach became very aggressive if their nests were approached and repeatedly, as it were, dive-bombed us. There is no grass anywhere on the island, only mosses and lichens that in places form a carpet over what might be mistaken for soil – very light soil, perhaps, as Lord Salisbury once described the Sahara Desert. The rookery was on rocky, snow-free ground a hundred feet above the sea, very noisy and smelly. They were Macaroni penguins, about 2ft. in height, rather truculent, and smelling like goats. They did not seem to bother with nests but just layed their eggs in any slight depression. None of the eggs were hatched.

We had no further contact with anyone at the base. One or two of them had rowed past in their boat, eyeing us curiously from a safe distance but never coming alongside, much less on board. They must have had their orders. I was therefore surprised when Dr Whacko himself brought off the promised stores – 20 lb. each of flour and sugar, 5 lb. of tea and coffee, 30 gallons of diesel oil, 5 gallons of paraffin, and 1 gallon of methylated spirit. It is to his credit that he did not demand cash down, but in due course the bill came and was paid. This visit must have been prompted by curiosity or, perhaps, as may happen to anyone, he had been suddenly overcome with friendly feelings. It was a beastly morning with a cold north-east wind and snow, so when the boat had been unloaded we naturally asked him and his underling on board for a drink. The alacrity with which he accepted surprised us and gave us the warm, satisfying glow felt by those who turn the other cheek, a warmer glow than can be got by retaliating in kind, tempting though that is. Despite two snorts of whisky the conversation remained stilted, consisting mainly of questions on our part about their life at the base. One felt sorry for them, for it must be a damnably dull life on Deception Island with no prospect of travel as there is at some of the bases. One of their jobs, too, was the breeding of huskies to be used for sledge journeys at those bases. They climbed into their boat and we saw no more of Whacko and his academy.

Since Herbert and Louis were daily walking to the Chilean base to have their boils treated I decided to go there and remain until they were reported fit. On the last day of 1966, a fine day with a good sailing breeze, we sailed round, a better way of going there than by walking over a dry glacier. The Chilean base is on the same side of Port Foster at Pendulum Cove, the place where in 1829 Captain Foster, of HMS *Chanticleer*, established his pendulum station and carried out experiments for determining the force of gravity. The cove has since silted up. Where there was once a considerable inlet there is now only a small cove and beyond the beach a freshwater lake. We anchored in 6 fathoms and put a warp ashore, the wind by now blowing offshore in very violent gusts. Tom and Mike, who heartily despised each other, had a fierce slanging match over the proper way to run out a warp.

The Chilean base is large, modern, and fitted with all conveniences, electric light, hot water, central heating. In summer there are over 100 men there and at the moment they were engaged in building a runway for a seaplane. The Commandant, an Air Force officer, who had already seen something of our quality in the shape of Louis, Carreo, and Herbert, did not welcome me effusively. Still he proved more hospitable than stern, path-of-duty Whacko, inviting us to have our meals in the men's messroom, and to ask for anything we needed.

We had not yet eaten a large, home-made Christmas pudding and New Year's Eve seemed the time to eat it. For twenty minutes I occupied myself in the galley making a rum sauce to help it down, and on returning to the cabin learnt that Mike and Louis had gone ashore to have a fight. This was better, of course, than staging it in the cabin, and their showing so much consideration left me astonished. Nevertheless it boded no good. This crew of mine should have shipped with Fanning, the sealing captain already mentioned. 'It was always with me,' he writes, 'a cardinal duty to state, on shipping of crew, that it must be well understood by them, as a prominent part of our agreement, that all the quarrelling and swearing was to be done by myself and the work by them.' Since they could not devour each other like Kilkenny cats, I rather hoped that Mike would win, but it was not to be. Louis was a bit of a pugilist as well as a bum, he read books on prize-fighting, and presently returned to announce, rather disappointedly, that a couple of punches had been enough for Mike who had refused to return on board with him. I found Mike, now with a fruity black eye, pacing the shore in bewildered fashion, and persuaded him to come back to the boat. Even before this it was clear that the crew hated each other, that we all hated Carreo, and that they were united only by their hatred for me. Except that Dr Johnson himself was by no means hated, our situation reminded me of life in what he had called his seraglio, three elderly, indigent females whom he charitably lodged in his house along with one Levett, an equally indigent, unqualified medical practitioner: 'Mrs Williams hates everybody; Levett hates Mrs Desmoulins and does not love Mrs Williams; Mrs Desmoulins hates them both; Poll loves none of them.'

New Year's eve continued its eventful way. The crew, less Mike and I, were to go ashore for a party with the Chileans. While they were changing into their best rig Carreo, already half drunk, made determined efforts to push off by himself in the dignhy. The only way to checkmate him was to take the oars below. Having got rid of them Mike and I had to divide the night for anchor watches, the wind now blowing offshore with gale force. Towards midnight Tom brought off Herbert with news that could not wait, news confided to him secretly by a Chilean friend, that proved to be stupid enough to have been invented by Herbert – so puzzled was the Chilean doctor by Herbert's various ailments, that if we did not sail next day we would probably be put in quarantine for a month.

Leaving me to think this out they re-embarked, missed the warp by which they could have hauled themselves ashore, and were rapidly blown out of the cove, Tom rowing furiously but in vain. We lost sight of them about a cable's length away trying to round a point where they might find a lee. If they failed they would be blown two miles across the bay to somewhere near the Argentine base, that is if the dinghy did not fill and sink in the rough sea further out. I remembered they had no baler. In the morning, the wind still blowing hard, we could see no life on shore where the effects of the New Year's party had evidently been severe. Mike and I discussed the chance of the dinghy surviving a two-mile voyage across the wind-swept bay. I felt ashamed that we had made no effort to go after them, hard though it might have been with only the two of us on board and a wind that might have been too much for our engine to fight against. The suspense lasted until midday when, happening to go on deck, I caught sight of a figure wearing Herbert's unmistakable red balaclava. Later we saw him and Tom walking out beyond the point, where they had evidently got ashore, in order to retrieve the dinghy. In the afternoon all hands came off bringing some eggs and tomatoes as a peace-offering. No more was said or heard of the quarantine problem, had it ever existed outside Herbert's fertile imagination. 'No problema', by the way, was still his favourite, over-worked idiom, expressing his unbounded and singularly ill-founded optimism.

The following day being fine with only a light breeze, the crew ashore and no hostilities, I took the opportunity to reeve a new peak halyard, making spare sheets out of the old one. I had lunch in the men's mess – mutton, lentils, pineapple, red wine, and coffee. Carreo, I noted, was evidently regarded as a figure of fun by the Chileans who, of course, had not got to live with him. Three Air Force officers accompanied me on board for a drink.

They so much preferred English cigarettes to their own that I gave them a carton of a hundred, part of the 5,000 that had been got for David Shaw, our only cigarette smoker. These were fast melting away, either Carreo or Herbert being busy flogging them to the Chileans. In the evening a naval tug arrived and anchored hard by. When their whaler was rowed ashore with a warp, the ship's dog, an Alsatian, jumped overboard and swam ashore with it. The wind having gone round to south-west we were now stern on to the beach, about five yards off and our rudder touching the bottom, so we ran out a kedge anchor to hold her off. At this cove steam rose from along the water's edge and immediately below the surface the sand felt quite hot. Up to 1936 there were hot springs along the beach and large patches of steaming hot sand.

3 January was clear, calm, and sunny. Such days, I imagine, are far more common on the Antarctic mainland than on the off-lying islands. So fair a day could not be wasted so for the first and last time I put on some boots and climbed the easy snow slope leading to the ridge, the rim of the old volcano. Behind Pendulum Cove this attains to a height of 1,800ft. and is the highest point of the island. Below lay Bransfield Strait, blue enough to have been taken for the Straits of Gibraltar were it not for the numerous icebergs sparkling in the sun. Across the water sixty miles away, though in appearance no more than twenty, were the mountains of Graham Land. Smith Island was in cloud but to the north and close at hand was Livingston Island, dazzling white snow and ice from end to end and from sea to summit. At its eastern end I could see Mount Bowles (3,314ft.), the peak I had had in mind as a poor consolation when Smith Island had to be written off. There is said to be a secure anchorage at Livingston Island, though not very close to Mount Bowles, but by this time I had no heart left for climbing and indeed felt reluctant to leave the ship even for a day.

The others, except Carreo, had gone off for the day to visit another penguin rookery at the north-east corner of the island. When they had not returned by nightfall I felt uneasy about them and annoyed, too, because Carreo and I had again to share an anchor watch, the wind having come in strong from south-west. It seemed more likely that they had spent the night at the Argentine base than that any mischance had befallen, so in the morning I went ashore to find out, the two bases being in contact by radio. Sure enough they had been there and at midday they turned up, very pleased with themselves, and went straight on shore for lunch. A small snow-covered island is not the place for men to jump ship, otherwise I doubt if *Mischief* would ever have left. But when I named the next day, 6 January, as the day of our departure for South Georgia en route to Cape Town, no objections were raised. Herbert, accompanied by Tom, immediately set out for the Argentine base where he said he must have a blood test. In reply to my objections, he said that for him this was a matter of life or death.

Carreo, who had spent the last 24 hours in his bunk, neither eating nor drinking, then took his gear ashore. He was last seen trudging slowly along the shore evidently bound for the Argentine base, and late that evening, on their way back, Tom and Herbert found him floundering in bewildered fashion in a snow drift and brought him back. On sailing day it took the Chileans a long time to convince him that he could not stay with them. Late in the evening they escorted him down to the beach with his kit and a large box of tinned food, his private sea stores. He had also acquired a crimson, peaked, American-style cap with a flap that came down over the back of his neck. In spite of this fine cap, which henceforth never left his head, he looked even more out of place in these arctic surroundings. Peary took his faithful negro, the stalwart Matthew Henson, to the North Pole, but our sub-tropical species did not flourish in high latitudes.

At 7 pm, to my untold relief, we sailed. In Neptune's Bellows the wind failed and we drifted slowly past the great cliff now glowing golden red in the light of the setting sun. From the top two men from the British base watched us go. They did not wave. Perhaps Dr Whacko had told them not to.

In December 1967, as I wrote this chapter, Deception Island began to erupt violently. First reports spoke of a threat to the safety of the British base. My reaction was like that of Churchill's who, on hearing of the illness of a political opponent, remarked cheerfully, 'Nothing trivial, I hope'. The threat proved far from trivial. Both the British and, more regrettably, the Chilean base, had to be abandoned.

CHAPTER NINE

South Georgia

MY ORIGINAL intention had been to sail direct from the South Shetlands to Cape Town, distant about 4,000 miles, but with both wind and current in our favour all the way. But by calling at South Georgia we had the slight possibility of finding there a ship and no chance, however slight, of relieving ourselves of Carreo, our black incubus, should be missed.

In a flat calm we started the engine and coasted the south side of Livingston Island, its higher peaks lit by the sun until nearly midnight. Throughout the night we had an escort of penguins, dashing through the water and surfacing like a school of porpoises. Slow moving and awkward enough on land, in the water they are very much at home, as lively and fast as any fish. In the morning, after passing Greenwich and Roberts Islands, both encased completely in ice, we turned north into Nelson Strait between Roberts Island and Nelson Island further east. After Boyd Strait this is one of the easiest passages between the various islands because all the dangers are above water, but it is no place to be in thick weather on account of strong tides and fierce tide rips, not to speak of icebergs. We had some thirty of them in sight. Meeting a strong adverse tide we did not clear the strait until afternoon. Nelson Island, too, is ice-covered except for a few small rock exposures. On Harmony Point, at its north-west corner, there is a refuge hut and a light, and as we passed it

two helicopters flew low over us and landed there. Just as sail had to give way
to steam, so the dog team and sledge of the heroic days of Antarctic travel are
yielding to aircraft. Had helicopters been in use in Kipling's day his lament for
the passing of Romance might have read:

> Farewell! Romance, the skipper said:
> He vanished with the oil we burn,
> And the helicopters overhead.

For a week the weather remained fair and the winds mainly light, and, what
with icebergs to marvel at and penguins to watch, this sail through the Scotia
Sea would have been enjoyable enough but for the strained atmosphere on
board and the daily scenes with Carreo. The Scotia Sea lies between South
Georgia and the South Orkneys which were now about 150 miles to our
south. It is named after the Norwegian steam whaler *Scotia* in which in 1903
the Scottish Antarctic expedition penetrated deep into the Weddell Sea and
later wintered on Laurie Island in the South Orkneys. In default of home
support, Bruce, the leader of the expedition, handed the Laurie Island base
over to the Argentine Republic, thus providing a starting point for their claim
to the sovereignty of the South Orkneys. In Lat. 59° S., for the first time for
some weeks the air temperature rose above 40° F. and since by now we had
written off the stove this small rise was the more welcome. The genoa, too,
had had to be written off, having split badly. Instead we used one of the twin
staysails, a sail that gave a lot more drive than the working jib but was too
heavy to be of much use in light winds. On the 14th, as a reminder of where
we were, a bitter south-east wind covered the deck with snow, and on the
following night a moderate gale from the same quarter obliged us to heave to.

Although by now the nights were sufficiently dark we were disappointed
not to see any aurora displays. On most nights the sky was anyway too cloudy
and star sights were seldom obtainable. For working sights I had now to use
the 1966 *Nautical Almanac*. I think I am right in saying that neither Brown's
nor Reed's, the two Almanacs generally in use by yachtsmen, offer any help
to the mariner who finds himself at sea with only an Almanac for the previous
year, whereas the Almanac published by HM Nautical Almanac Office of the
Royal Greenwich Observatory, containing nothing but the astronomical
ephemeris, provides for this contingency with a simple rule which enables one
to work out sun and star sights. It cannot be used for the moon or for planets.
I am told that if you keep a *Nautical Almanac* for four years it again becomes
current, so that the thrifty navigator who has plied his trade for four consecutive years and has kept his Almanacs need never buy another.*

By 20 January I reckoned we were about 100 miles off South Georgia. The
penguins that we had heard mooing all night were, I hoped, natives of the
island, and sure enough at 10 next morning we sighted land. By evening we
were off First Rock near the south-west corner in a freshening wind and snow
squalls. When Carreo, in a violent squall, executed a Chinese gybe, I took the

---

*I am also told on high authority, second only to that of the Astronomer Royal, that this four-year rule holds good only for the
sun. Since most amateur navigators rely mainly upon sun sights, the value of this tip to the impecunious or parsimonious remains
undiminished.

hint and hove-to. The night was dark and earlier we had sighted some small bergs. We had taken fifteen days, an average of 70 miles a day, whereas Shackleton in his ship's lifeboat, living in appalling conditions, had taken sixteen days. Elephant Island, whence he had started, is 150 miles nearer; on the other hand his *James Caird*'s sail area compared with *Mischief*'s must have been derisory. The fact that she went so fast is no doubt accounted for by the different weather in January and in May. In May 1915 the indomitable crew of the *James Caird* had suffered and at the same time benefitted from gales or near gales for most of the voyage.

Although it is 500 miles further north, South Georgia, particularly at its southern end, is in appearance almost as arctic as the South Shetlands. As has been noted already, the Antarctic convergence lies well to the north of the island. From a few miles off we could make out nothing but snow peaks, steep glaciers, and precipitous, black headlands. The island was discovered, or rediscovered, by Cook in 1775 on the first of his three great voyages. 'The wild rocks', he wrote, 'raised their lofty summits until they were lost in the clouds, and the valleys lay covered with everlasting snow. Not a tree was to be seen, nor a shrub even big enough to make a toothpick.' The name of Cape Disappointment at the south-western corner of the island perhaps reflects his feelings upon seeing unbounded ocean to the south, convincing proof that he had discovered only an island and not a southern continent. 'The disappointment I now met with,' he says, 'did not affect me much; for to judge of the bulk by the sample it would not be worth the discovery.'

Sailing up the east coast next day we encountered a strong headwind and rather than stand out to sea to tack all night we anchored in Hound Bay, sixteen miles short of Grytviken, the Port of Entry for South Georgia. Except for the grunts and groans of numerous sea elephants the night passed quietly. Proceeding up the coast next day I found the number of small inlets so confusing that we came to Right Whale Rocks at the entrance to Cumberland Bay unexpectedly soon. A small lighthouse stands on these rocks which are covered with tussock grass. The day was sunny and serene, and the broad, calm expanse of the bay with its grass-fringed shores and low surrounding hills might have been likened to a Highland loch but for the great Nordenskjöld glacier that filled the whole of its southern end. The two-mile wide and seventy-foot high ice front of this magnificent glacier is lapped by the sea and is constantly calving.

The bay appeared so empty and devoid of any trace of human activity that we were puzzled as to the whereabouts of King Edward Cove and the settlement. When we had sailed a few miles towards the glacier the wind died, and as we handed the sails the narrow entrance to the cove began to open out. On a rock bluff overlooking the entrance, Hope Point, we could make out the white cross of the Shackleton memorial. Shackleton, of course, did not make his landing here but at King Haakon Bay on the north-west side of the island. Thence the three strongest men of the boat party made their extraordinary forced march of 36 hours over unknown mountainous country, bemused often by fog, and without tent or sleeping bags, till they arrived at the whaling station in Stromness Bay to the north of Cumberland Bay. A whale catcher soon picked up the three men left at King Haakon Bay, and in August after many setbacks, a Chilean vessel with Shackleton on board rescued the 22 men marooned on Elephant Island. The Boss, as his men called him, never let them down. Shackleton (as a schoolboy before the First World War I once heard him lecture) was a man whom nothing daunted, a man equal to any emergency by sea or by land, but of this journey he wrote:

When I look back at those days I do not doubt that Providence guided us, not only across those snowfields, but also across the stormy white sea which separated Elephant Island from our landing place on South Georgia. I know that during that long march of 36 hours over the unnamed mountains and glaciers of South Georgia it often seemed to me that we were four, not three.

Soon the big whaling station at Grytviken and the small British settlement on King Edward Point came into view. Here the works of man do not obtrude too much upon the scene. For a man who likes his scenery stern and wild – provided he turns his back on the red roofs of the settlement – Grytviken is one of the loveliest harbours. The wooden, weather-worn buildings of the whaling station, the white church with its black steeple, nestle below snow-covered hills, while beyond, near enough for the details of their aspiring faces and ridge to be seen, tower two glorious mountains. Sugartop (7,023ft.) and Mount Paget (9,625ft.) are only two of the stronger and more monumental summits of many on the Allardyce Range which, together with the Salvesen Range, forms the island's formidably, rugged backbone. From it many icy, lofty ribs extend towards either coast. Here are the Alps in miniature, their attractions augmented by exotic fauna, sea views, and a total absence of huts and armies of climbers. Much has already been done there by expeditions but now that the shore whaling stations are closed the difficulties of transport are greatly increased. It becomes therefore an ideal objective for a man with a boat who is addicted to climbing, the more so because of the many beautiful fjords and safe anchorages that abound on the coasts of South Georgia.

A small crowd had assembled on the little wooden jetty at the settlement, where willing hands soon helped us to secure alongside. Here we had something like a welcome, the warmest and kindest that *Mischief* has anywhere enjoyed. A customs' officer, delighted to have something to do, soon cleared us, the doctor came on board with kind enquiries, immediately followed by the administrative officer and his wife, Mr and Mrs Coleman. Within minutes an electric heater and electric light had been led into the cabin, and we were accorded the freedom of Shackleton House, a large two-storey building where the bachelors lived, where baths, beds, and meals would be provided. Mr Coleman, himself a retired sea captain, having arranged for a board for *Mischief* to ride against, then took me to his own house for a bath and a meal. Showers are no substitute for the real thing and I was in the mood to appreciate a bath, having been without since we left England. The beautifully fitted house, the warmth, carpets and easy chairs, compared very favourably with *Mischief*'s cabin. Adjoining the living-room was a built-on conservatory where under Mrs Coleman's devoted care, geraniums, roses, fuschias, and other flowers flourished exceedingly. Nor can there be many, if any, other conservatories in the world whence you can look down upon families of sea elephants lying blissfully asleep in their mud wallows among tussock grass. Indeed, if you opened the conservatory windows you could smell them.

There were about a dozen people at the station including four married couples who had their own bungalows. All houses and offices were linked by telephone. The station had been established primarily to keep a check on the whaling operations, to attend to ships' business, and to maintain order among the shore staffs and the crews of the whaling ships. This was no sinecure. In 1958, for example, the population of the three whaling stations at Grytviken, Leith Harbour, and Stromness amounted in the summer to 1,265, including 7 women, and if the whaling fleet was in the number might be swollen to 3,000. All shore-based whaling has now ceased, so that the only ships to call are relief ships on their way to or from the Antarctic. This news practically extinguished any hopes of getting rid of Carreo, but Mr Coleman agreed to send a signal to Port Stanley to ask if he could be put on board a relief ship due in about two months. I had a peaceful night alone on *Mischief*, the crew sleeping at Shackleton House where, I gathered, they had had a fairly riotous time.

The whaling station occupies the far end of the cove and is about half a mile from the station by a jeepable track. In winter when the snow lies deep one would have to go on foot on skis. Snow banks still lay by the track, and we were told that a former administrative officer had been killed by an avalanche when ski-ing along the track. Next day I walked over to the whaling station to meet the manager, an English-speaking Norwegian. In spite of a natural disgust for the slaughter of the harmless, majestic whale, I felt sad at seeing this remote, little town into which much money must have been poured, now almost dead – the huge flensing platforms, power plant, boiler rooms, work-shops, barracks, clubhouse, football ground, church, the two forlorn whale catchers at the jetty, all deserted. On the other hand, had the brutal and bloody business of chopping up whales been in full swing one would no doubt have thought that the sooner it ended the better.

The manager's house, a fine, big building, comfortably furnished and brightly decorated, was still in use, though some of its windows were already being boarded up. In front on what in more genial climates would have been the lawn, stood a massive flagpole and a mounted harpoon gun, flanked by two enormous, old time trypots. A care and maintenance party of five men were busy about the place where a few years ago there would have been three hundred. Four of them were due to leave on the next relief ship, leaving a single caretaker who would live over at the British station. The manager having asked if we were in need of any stores, we made a tour of several well-stocked store-houses, including a refrigerated store, and got together a liberal collection which the manager undertook to ferry over in his boat. While over that side I visited the well-kept cemetery where Shackleton is buried. He died of a heart attack on board his ship *Quest* on 5 January, while off South Georgia.

From the sublime to the sordid and the ridiculous. Upon returning to *Mischief* I found Louis drunk and Carreo incapably drunk, kneeling on deck crooning quietly to himself. The binnacle had been badly bent by someone falling on it – happily the compass was all right – and the locker containing what remained of the ship's liquor bashed open with a hammer. On the table were two empty gin bottles and a half-empty bottle of cherry brandy. The latter must have been given them or stolen, but the two gin bottles were the last of our stock. Henceforth *Mischief* would perforce be a 'dry' ship. Leaving them I walked up to Shackleton House for lunch, pursued by desultory abuse from Louis, imploring me, amongst other things, to jump into the dock.

By evening Carreo was on his feet, roaming about in a maudlin state, and reported to be carrying a knife. Mr Coleman thought he should be locked up for the night, and having had in the recent past three whaling stations to look after he was fully qualified to handle drunks. Together with his henchman who acted as the local police force, he led Carreo unsuspectingly into a room with a bunk and turned the key on him. He did not appear to be carrying any knife. Later in the voyage Herbert, for reasons unknown, presented me with a signed statement concerning this incident. No statement signed by Herbert is of any value but it is worth inserting even if only on account of some curiosities of spelling:

For the Lookbook.

On the 26th January 1967, 20.15 hours at Gritiven, South Georgia, I went on board the yacht *Mischief* with Mr Vera the Chilean cook of the Shackleton House. The engineering officer Carreo Artigas was drunk on board and in possession of a knife. He said to me, 'I will kill the skipper when he returns from his visit to Mr Coleman's house.' I asked him to give me the knife and he repeated his threat to kill the skipper. I asked him again for the knife and he began to fight with me. Mr Vera was witness to all this. At 21.30 Mr Coleman arrested Carreo Artigas and put him in gail overnight. In my opinion Artigas althoogh drunk was responsible for his actions at that time.

By the following day we had a reply from Port Stanley concerning Carreo, firmly declining to help. He had sobered up and looked the worse for wear, slouching around in a blue greatcoat, his brown complexion, slightly mottled after his drinking bout, set off not to advantage by the crimson cap. He presented a new problem for us by firmly refusing to go to Cape Town. Mr Coleman, who had kindlier feelings towards him, talked to him like a father but failed to dissuade him or to convince him that he would get no passage in the next relief ship. Apparently versed in the tradition of resistance movements, albeit his was a private one, he talked of taking to the hills. Meantime the rest of the crew expressed their apprehension and their reluctance to sail with him. True, there was no longer any drink on board but they disliked the thought of Carreo awake on watch and them asleep below. As Macbeth said:

'Tis better thee without, than he within.'

Having brought the man there I had to take him away. Port Stanley in the Falklands, where Chileans and Uruguayans were said to be working on the roads, was only 900 miles away; but that had to be ruled out because it lay dead to windward. Quietness, according to the Chinese proverb, is worth buying. Realizing that it was a devilish high price to pay, and sorely against the grain, I decided to deposit him where I got him. If he knew that we were bound for Montevideo we had some chance of peace on board, whereas if we ignored his violently expressed objections and sailed for Cape Town I felt that anything might happen, including his disappearance overboard. The others, while they saw the sense of this decision, were annoyed and bitterly disappointed at having to alter our plans on account of this wretched man. We had all looked forward to Cape Town and our mail awaited us there. I felt particularly exasperated. Friends were expecting me, I had counted on having the boat hauled out there, and the voyage homewards from Cape Town is quicker and far less troublesome than it is from Montevideo.

The news that we would return to Montevideo almost decided Herbert to start his resistance movement. Hours of brooding in the night watches had given his thoughts a new turn. No one, I believe, at Montevideo cared tuppence about this German ex-cyclist who now interviewed Mr Coleman in his office and solemnly demanded 'political asylum'. Nothing less than his life was at stake, for if he returned to Montevideo it would be in danger! Incidentally Herbert's disease which had baffled the combined wisdom of the Chilean and Argentine medical staff had been swiftly diagnosed and successfully treated by Dr Parker – scabies. On learning this we took care to keep Herbert well clear of the galley.

Throughout our stay none of the crew showed up on board. In spite of orders from Mr Coleman that they were no longer to sleep there they continued to eat and sleep at Shackleton House. With the help of the engineer who ran the power plant I got the boat watered and stocked up with diesel oil and paraffin. He also fixed up a winch and persuaded the galley pump to work, and, the Norwegians having brought the promised stores, we were ready to leave. Except for one day when snow had fallen the weather had been remarkably pleasant, notwithstanding the moans of the oldest inhabitants about the wretched summer. But for the paramount desire I had to get on with the voyage and to see the last of the crew, I should have enjoyed an excursion to the Nordenskjöld glacier, or to Cumberland West Bay where, we were told, reindeer could be seen.

But before we got safely away one more curious incident gave me food for thought. I appointed the morning of Saturday, 28 January for our departure, reserving some doubts as to whether the appointment would be kept. On the Friday night I dined at the Coleman's with the doctor and one or two others. About 11 pm the telephone rang. Mike was at the other end and here was an occasion when he recognized his duty towards me and the ship and practised it. Speaking very guardedly he said that during the evening there had been some 'wild talk' and that I had better get back on board. Walking down to the jetty I could see that though no light was on somebody was on board with a torch. Tom and Herbert were standing in the galley. Herbert's wits were nimble enough to have offered some plausible explanation, but without answering any questions they went up the companionway and walked off into the night. With Mr Coleman I hung about for a bit and then I turned in and read until daylight. Following hard upon Mike's warning this midnight visit looked suspicious. A forced stay or delay at South Georgia might have suited some of the crew. But this is conjecture, as conjectural as the number of battalions there were in a Chinese horde.

Having made all secure on deck preparatory to sailing I watched the kind people of the station assembling to see us go, and then to my relief the crew came on board. Having made our farewells we cast off in drizzling rain and a flat calm.

CHAPTER TEN

Montevideo and Homewards

MONTEVIDEO LIES about 1,700 miles north-west of South Georgia, a distance that we might have run in about three weeks; but until we were clear of the Westerlies and in the region of variable winds we could not expect often to lay the required course. In fact we logged 2,000 miles and took four weeks. With the wind hanging in the north, and light at that, three days had elapsed before we were clear of South Georgia. At least I hoped we were clear, for the radio receiver had packed up and we could get no time signals. Carreo diagnosed a fault in the condenser so I resigned myself to doing without time signals until we reached Montevideo. According to the Taoist doctrine – and it sounds very sensible – if you practise inaction nothing will be left undone. As practised on this occasion it worked like a charm. We did nothing, and in a few days the wireless came on again as suddenly as it had gone off.

On 1 February we suffered a minor calamity for which I was entirely to blame. When the barometer fell to 28.6 we expected something in the way of wind. Nothing happened until the barometer started to rise about midnight when we had to reef down and heave to, the wind blowing with some violence from dead ahead. At 4 am a small tear appeared in the leach of the mainsail just above the reef, but as the wind had backed and moderated we started sailing. This kept the sail quiet. Two hours later, in my watch, the tear had not increased and I reckoned it would hold until the crew turned out for breakfast when we could lower the sail. Then the wind suddenly dropped, the boom started kicking, the leach rope broke, and before one could say 'Jack', let alone 'Jack Robinson', the sail ripped right across from leach to luff, all 24ft. of it. Moreover it was not a seam that had gone, but a tear in the cloth, a jagged tear. When the sea had gone down a bit we got the spare mainsail up and bent on. The spare sail had been very tightly folded, nevertheless we had a mightly struggle to get it through the cabin door. As the torn sail could not be mended properly at sea, and as there was no hope of stowing it below, we had to lash it on deck. At Montevideo we could take it ashore and make a job of it.

The spare sail, an older sail and thin in places, had to be carefully watched. At the least sign of a seam going we had it down for repair and in hard blows we set the trysail. The early hours of the following morning were equally eventful. Carreo had the 4 am to 6 am watch and the wind and incessant rain may have given him an added touch of gall. When Herbert came up to relieve him they at once fell to exchanging blows in the cockpit, the appropriate place for two such birds to fight. But *Mischief* sailed placidly on giving me time to intervene. Half an hour later, when Herbert had brought off a smart Chinese gybe and I went up again to assess the damage, the rain had turned to snow. The weather soon mended, we put in a good day's run, and that night we recrossed the Antarctic convergence. The sea temperature went up from 37° to 45° F.

On 6 February a full gale at north-west set in. By night-fall we set the trysail and jogged along all night heading east of north, a direction which provoked a wild outburst from Carreo. Those who know little suspect the most. In spite of the daily positions marked on the chart for all to see he remained un-convinced that we were not bound for Cape Town. If only we had been bound there these predominant north-westerly winds would have given us a rare lift. Instead we had always a fight to gain any westing.

At last in anti-cyclone conditions we enjoyed a fair wind at south-west and in four days logged 430 miles, all in the right direction. A small school of killer whales swam around for several hours. Even at a distance these tigers of the sea are easily distinguished by the long, narrow dorsal fin standing three or four feet above the water. These were close enough for us to see also the characteristic white mark abaft the eye and their white bellies. In Lat. 45° S the sea temperature had risen to 53° F. and the next day, 17 February, it rose to 62° F, whereupon we shed our woolly garments and I had a bucket bath. This was evidently the sub-tropical convergence, the transition from sub-antarctic water to what is known as the Central Water Mass. The winds pay no heed to convergence; they continued extremely variable, from near gales to flat calms or dirty rain-laden squalls. Reefing and unreefing, nursing the slightly delicate spare mainsail, kept us alert and occupied.

By 15 February the light green colour of the water warned us that we were in soundings and by next day we were crossing the great estuary of the Plate, neither land nor ships anywhere in sight. The water turned yellow and looked so alarmingly shallow that one expected every minute to feel the keel grate on the sandy bottom. A sounding gave us 2 fathoms. We were on the English Bank, an extensive shoal south of Montevideo, where in places there is not enough water to float *Mischief*, and where the buoys that are supposed to define its limits have always eluded us. It was gratifying when the high buildings of Montevideo, shimmering like a mirage, at last came up dead ahead, and I could not refrain from giving Carreo a final jolt by telling him that we had arrived at Cape Town. At one time I had thought of going instead to Buenos Aires, a hundred miles up the river, where there might be less difficulty in finding the two or three hands that would be needed to get us home. There are many more yacht clubs there, for the Argentinians are more boat-minded, or perhaps richer, than the Uruguayans. As events soon showed, Buenos Aires would have been a serious mistake.

There being no mooring buoy available at Puerto Buceo we had to anchor. Carreo and Louis departed that evening, unregretted, followed next day by

Tom and Mike. Tom I had expected would go, for he now looked upon me as a man who had deceived him by issuing a false prospectus, persuading him to invest time – happily no money – in a South Sea Bubble. Mike's departure surprised me for the second and what I imagined would surely be the last time. After so many arduous days at sea he thought it preposterous that I should hope to sail within a week, and that he should be immediately asked to help get the torn mainsail on shore was quite outrageous. Both he and Tom made themselves at home with some Uruguayans living on board their boat moored at the club jetty.

This speedy reduction of the crew to one was not so serious a blow as another that fell upon me the same day. A man can go nowhere without money, as the Bulgarians say, not even to church. I now discovered that an unused book of Travellers' cheques for a large amount had disappeared. Naturally, and probably wrongly, Carreo came under suspicion. Herbert assured me that he had taken and flogged them at Punta Arenas where there was reputedly a market for such things. When Carreo returned to collect his gear he denied any knowledge of the cheques. By rummaging the ship I collected some working capital, 5 pesos, enough for the bus fare into the city, the fare, by the way, having doubled since our last visit. What a good thing it was that we had not gone to Buenos Aires where I should have been right up the creek. At Maclean and Stapledon's, the shipping agents, I could rely upon aid and comfort; upon Mr Maclean for cash and upon his able assistant Mr McClew for comfort. Having cashed a sterling cheque for £100 I returned to the boat with this amount in 1,000-peso notes. Herbert and I were now living alone on board. He had always appeared to me honest in money matters, but I waited until he was out of the cabin before putting this cash away in a place where it was not likely to be found by pickers-up of unconsidered trifles.

After a severe struggle Herbert and I got the torn mainsail on shore and spread out on the Club lawn where I spent the next week pleasantly enough sitting in the sun plying the needle, first herring-boning the whole thing together and then covering the tear with long strips of 9 inch wide canvas. Soon I had an able assistant in a Mr Hills, almost a professional sailmaker, who took on the job of repairing the working jib which was also in a bad way. He had been at sea for many years around the Falkland Islands and had a son who was second engineer in the *Darwin*, a small ship, the only ship, that plies regularly between Montevideo and Port Stanley. Mr Hills and I had met at the Sailor's Home, the fountain source of some of our troubles, where he had been to see his friend the Major. I had no intention of tapping that source again, my visit was merely to retail our experiences to the Major, and to tell him, in sorrow rather than anger, how his swan Carreo had turned out an ill-favoured duck.

This time, for a free trip direct to England instead of via the Antarctic, I anticipated less difficulty in finding a crew; but at the various shipping agents and consulates I had no more success than before. I had struck up an acquaintance with a Swede, an ex-sea captain who lived alone on his small motor boat moored by the sea wall. He was a convivial soul with an interminable swallow so far as whisky was concerned; a man who, like the rest of us, had had his troubles and possibly deserved them. Cigarettes and other dutiable articles thrown overboard from passing steamers and picked up by a motor boat that happened to be around, found a ready sale in Montevideo. But all good things must come to an end. After his boat had been confiscated my Swedish friend had luckily been able to buy it back, but now it was not allowed to leave the harbour. To come to the point, the Swede had in his employ a Uruguayan lad, Roberto, who had an urge to travel. He had been a fisherman, was cheerful, willing, capable, and a good cook. The Swede spoke highly of him and encouraged me to take him on. Roberto had to get a passport, and judging from the dilatory habits of officials the world over, I thought this might take three weeks. To the credit of Uruguay he had it in three days.

So we were now three, for I assumed that Herbert's desire to revisit the Fatherland was unabated. He had learnt no sea sense, and never would, but he remained always cheerful, and I had come to regard him as a part of *Mischief*, a part that should not be leant upon too heavily. One day, while I worked on the sail, Mike came by. We exchanged a few words, words became an argument, and the argument grew heated. In reviling it is not necessary to prepare a preliminary draft. By the time I had said my piece I did not expect that he would want to talk to me again, but about a week later I learnt from Mr McClew, in whom both Tom and Mike confided that he wanted to rejoin. Well inured now to Mike's vagaries, I agreed. He did some work on board, including overhauling the charging engine, but continued to live with his friends in the other boat until the last possible minute.

At about this stage I had a cable from a friend in England asking if I would take on a lad of 18 who had just left Pangbourne, and was desperately keen to make a voyage. Nor was he deterred when I suggested that an air passage to Montevideo would be a high price to pay for what would inevitably be a rather humdrum voyage. No sea voyage can be dull for a man who has an eye for the ever-changing sea and sky, the waves, the wind, and the way of a ship upon the water; but in tropic seas there is not much else to look at and the weather is unlikely to provide a challenge for an ardent young sailor. More cables passed and in the end young Robin arrived on 19 March at the airport where Roberto and I met him. We were due to sail in two days so he had little time in which to see Montevideo. Happily that was not part of his programme; his sole wish was to buy a gaucho's hat. Gauchos are not a monopoly of the Argentine, Uruguay has them, too, and the necessary pampas on which to deploy them. But Robin had no luck, either the shops were shut for a fiesta, or the gauchos, like everyone else, have stopped wearing hats. He had to content himself with an apparatus for drinking *yerba maté* – very much cheaper, I believe, than hats.

But I am anticipating events. Herbert and I continued to live placidly on board until 10 March. In the mornings he did the necessary shopping and in the afternoon went into the city whence he usually got back about 11 pm. He had apparently forgotten that in Montevideo his freedom or even his life might be in danger; or perhaps his political enemies were no longer in power, for there had recently been an election and a new President reigned. Herbert had little or no money so I was naturally curious about how he paid his way on these visits. He told me he spent the time at the Cyclists club where old friends or rivals reminisced about long days in the saddle. I felt tempted to join him and thought I would qualify, having once spent some very long days in the saddle when riding a pushbike from Kenya to the Cameroons.

Anchored in Puerto Buceo one never felt quite at ease. Even in summer hard blows from south-west, the 'pamperos', and from south-east, the 'sudestada', are by no means infrequent. In the mornings there might be no one on board *Mischief*, or perhaps Herbert alone, who by himself could not even have started the engine. On the night of the 10th it began blowing very hard from south-west. By midnight, which was unusual, Herbert had not returned. I passed an anxious night, going on deck at frequent intervals to see if we were dragging. Early in the morning we began to move slowly but surely stern first towards the inner breakwater, a jumble of huge concrete blocks. Alone, there was little I could do except stand by with the engine going, but when we were a short fifty yards from what looked like destruction the anchor somehow took a fresh hold and held us there steadfastly.

When Herbert had not returned I began to think he might have had grounds for his fears, or perhaps he had been roughed up by thugs as had happened to him before. On the third day I bought a newspaper to see if any body had been fished out of the river, as bodies frequently were. A body had been found but it was not Herbert. There were a few of his belongings in his bunk but his cherished package of newspaper cuttings were missing – an ominous sign. On the fourth day after his disappearance I had occasion to open up what I fondly imagined to be the secret cache and found it empty. Herbert had vamoosed with 18,000 pesos, about £90, and no doubt with my Travellers cheques, too, for what they were worth. For him at any rate the voyage had not been unfruitful. As a matter of form, for Herbert had four days start, I informed the police who were not altogether surprised. From the water-guard at Buceo I learnt that prior to his departure he had been enquiring about the bus service to Brazil. This may have been a blind – he was a wily bird – and he might easily have gone to Buenos Aires. The German consul who had been so relieved when I took Herbert away, learnt with sorrow that he was again at large in South America. He would have to reopen the Bittner file. Once more penniless I again had recourse to Mr MacLean. I thought it advisable to lower my sights. The £40 he let me have would have to see us through.

Our number was again reduced to four and I might well have left it at that. We had made long passages before with that number but a three-months voyage with only three watchkeepers is hard work. With some misgivings I put an advertisement in one of the newspapers and the consequent flood of applicants reached alarming proportions. At least sixty came on the first day and not many fewer on the next. With the help of my Swedish friend we soon weeded them out. It was not a matter of asking whether a man had any sea experience, the important point was whether they had a passport and some money. Already having Roberto on my hands I did not want to bring to England another Uruguayan whose fare home, if the worst came to the worst, might be my liability. Few of them had passports, fewer still had any money, and only about two of them had both. The young Italian student, Sergio, whom I finally took on looked a bit of a 'cissy' but spoke excellent English as well as Spanish and Italian. He could interpret to the non-English speaking Roberto and would be company for him. He proved a most regrettable choice but at that stage of the voyage it hardly mattered.

We were about ready to go. The stores that I could afford came on board and I noted with dismay how little cash remained to spend at the Azores, our next stop. We had no need to go alongside for water, enough having been ferried off by Herbert and I in the course of our long stay. Roberto's local knowledge came in useful for he readily found a baker who prepared for us about 70 lb. of 'tostada', a thing that the ship chandlers had never been able to do. With the essential help of Mr McClew we got our clearance; by noon of 21 March all were on board, and having got our anchors (we now had two down) we sailed out.

This passage from Montevideo to the Azores in which we logged 6,260 miles took 86 days, an average of 73 miles a day. This is the longest that *Mischief* has been at sea, her previous record being 74 days between the Canaries and Cape Town. Had we started this homeward run from Cape Town, as originally intended, we should have had the south-east Trades behind us almost from the first day. Starting from Montevideo, before we could hope to pick up the Trades, we had to make about 1,500 miles to the north-east which at this time of year, the southern autumn, is precisely the direction of the prevailing winds. In addition there is a south-going current. At times, when progress seemed pitifully slow, I feared we might have to put into Recife for food, if not for water. Water was no problem. So heavy and frequent were the storms of rain that we crossed the equator, 49 days out, with all tanks and containers full. It cost us 30 days' sailing to reach the region of the Trades, and then, instead of carrying us 2° or 3° north of the equator as they should have done, they petered out in Lat. 3° S. But that is all part of the game. The wind bloweth where it listeth, and those whose pleasure lies in making use of the wind must make the best of it.

Our modest rate of progress may have been the reason why we caught some fish on this long passage. One reads with envy of raft voyages such as *Kon Tiki*, or of Dr Bombard in his rubber dinghy, and the number of fish that daily gathered round asking to be caught. On days when our progress was raft-like we usually had numbers of dorado in attendance. The barnacles and lush vegetation that by now decorated our hull attracted schools of small fish that swam tirelessly just ahead of the stem or lurked under the keel, darting away at intervals to inspect some choice morsel. The Sargasso weed, too, that drifted by, provided these hungry little beggars with plenty of small crabs and shrimps. At first we despised their small size, nor did they appear likely to be caught, but after long perseverance Mike found a way. The record for one day was seventeen. Besides the small fry there were others of 1 lb. to 2 lb. in weight of which we caught several. These had tiny but exceedingly powerful mouths which they used, we were pleased to see, for wrenching barnacles off the hull. One always associates crabs with the foreshore and it seemed strange to find crabs that measured 3 inches across in mid-ocean. The small crabs found on the weed were fierce cannibals; if several of them were together in a bucket of water they tore each other to pieces.

The flying fish needed no catching and often provided our lunch. All was grist that came to our mill including the commonly despised garfish – all snout and tail, green bones, but perfectly edible. The dorado were too smart for us; we got only one which Roberto killed with a superb shot from his home-made harpoon; the handle of our broom tipped with the cunningly filed leg of a Primus stove. This dorado, with lovely iridescent green and gold colouring, was about 3ft. long. Twice Roberto hit a shark with this harpoon. The shark appeared soon after we had all been bathing over the side and although only some 5ft. long caused as much alarm as if he had been 20ft. long. It soon rid itself of the harpoon but reappeared a week later; at least we were convinced that this was the same shark by a white scar on its back just where the harpoon had hit. This second time Roberto lodged the harpoon in his head whence it did not draw until after some wild threshing and the running out of all the line.

Before we reached the Azores we were glad to eke out our food stocks with fish. We were low on bully beef and right out of cheese, jam, and butter. Our twice-baked bread had lasted for 64 days and I reckoned it would have lasted another week had it not been for Sergio. No one but him ate bread at supper, the big meal of the day, and this extravagant habit had always been frowned upon. Frowns were wasted upon Sergio, whose self-esteem rendered him impervious to criticism. Italians are gluttons for carbohydrates, flour in all shapes and forms, but no Italian that I knew – and I have lived with some hungry Italian hordes – could hold a candle to Sergio. And he took his time over it. Compared with Sergio, Gladstone, who chewed each mouthful thirty-two times, merely gobbled. The first man to finish his meal usually relieved the helmsman, a custom that inevitably absolved Sergio from this duty. Having relieved the helmsman, and having in turn been relieved by him when he had finished his meal, one would go below to find Sergio still calmly hoisting it in. Though intelligent enough, he never tried to learn, and when we reached Lymington he no more knew which rope was which than on the day he embarked. So much did he grate on me that I looked forward to the day of our arrival mainly because it would signify, I hoped, Sergio's departure. When, therefore, six weeks later I returned to Lymington and found him, unasked, still living on board I felt as Macbeth felt when he heard that Fleance, whose death he had confidently expected, still lived: 'Then comes my fit again.' Normally I am not much worried by my cabin companions however odd their behaviour, but evidently at this stage of a trying voyage my dislike for this harmless Italian youth had become morbid. So long as he does not go to sea and avoids jobs that involve hurrying over his meals, I imagine, I might even hope, that Sergio will do well.

Few of us are without one redeeming feature. Sergio did his stint in the galley in turn with Mike and Roberto and did it very well. Robin took so long to learn how to light a Primus that we were unwilling to suffer while he learnt how to cook. In him I sustained another disappointment, having looked forward to having on board for a change an eager, willing, cadet-type, the first to reach the deck when called and the last to leave, foremost when any work involving dirt or difficulty needed doing. With Mike, Roberto and Sergio vying with each other, we had some delectable and exotic meals. Roberto had brought with him a round oven to sit on top of a Primus, thus enabling us to have syrup tarts, soda bread, toad-in-the-hole, *canalones*, Cornish pasties, and cottage pies.

We met few ships. A Russian tanker altered course from about five miles away to pass close along our lee side, dipped his ensign, and gave us three blasts on the whistle; and the *Aragon* of the Royal Mail line also closed us to let her passengers take photographs. We suspected that the Russians had heard vaguely of Sir Francis Chichester, who was in the South Atlantic at that time, and had paid us these marks of respect in mistake, though few things could be more difficult, one imagines, than to mistake *Mischief* for *Gypsy Moth*, either in appearance or performance. We met the north-east Trades when we were due south of the Azores in Long. 30° W. and consequently, before we had run through the Trades, sailing close-hauled all the time, we had been pushed as far west as Long. 41°. Being then, in theory, in the region of the Westerlies, we were able to steer more or less towards the Azores. As we were approaching the islands from a little south of west the nearest port of entry for us was Horta on Fayal, the other possible port, San Miguel, lying 100 miles further east. We were in the grip of the Azores 'high' with very light winds, so that 100 miles meant for us a matter of days. At Montevideo, undecided as to which particular island we should fetch, and since England would then be only three weeks away, I had advised the crew not to have mail sent to the Azores. They now told me they were all expecting mail at San Miguel.

At midday of 15 June we sighted the high ground on Fayal distant about 20 miles. We were surprised that the neighbouring island of Pico and its 7,000ft. summit had not shown up long before. In the late afternoon this summit did manage to poke its head above the cloud but the rest of Pico might as well not have existed. Following in the wake of a small tunnyman we were met at the harbour entrance by the Pilot who took us to a convenient buoy. When we were secured, the Pilot entered and cleared us and we were free to land – no Customs, no police, no fuss. Would it were ever thus. Five other yachts lay in the harbour, two of them single-handers. At Horta, the Café Sport, presided over by the ever friendly and helpful Peter, is, in spite of its name, the Mecca for all visiting yachtsmen. Their comings and goings are all faithfully recorded in Peter's log-book. We had missed meeting the Hiscocks by two days and we sailed before the arrival of Dr David Lewis and his family in *Rehu Moana*, whom I had much hoped to see.

Horta is a delightful little town, beautifully kept by people who take pride in its appearance – flowers, shady trees and seats everywhere, speckless, tesselated pavements in black and white, a white-washed sea wall, *brass* ringbolts in the quay, brightly coloured houses, wine good and cheap, friendly people, few motor cars, no bearded weirdies, television aerials, fun fairs, or juke boxes. A paradise, in fact, for squares.

Pleasant though all this was after so long at sea I was impatient to get on and to write *finis* to an unlucky voyage. So that it was with reluctance that I waited for five days until a boat from San Miguel arrived with the crew's mail. Mike ran true to form till the last. Although at this stage it was hardly worth while going through the motions of deserting for the third time, yet in order to make sure that we waited for the mail, he and Sergio left the boat. When the mail arrived on the evening of 20 June these worthies refused to come off until after midnight. The strong temptation to sail without them had to be resisted; the Portuguese would not like it, and we should probably have been pursued next morning by the Pilot's launch, a journey for which I might have had to pay. When Robin finally brought them off in the dinghy all three went below, shut the cabin door, and turned in. From now on, Mike said, they were going to please themselves rather than me, thus proclaiming a sort of seaman's strike, or merely working to rule. So Roberto and I hoisted in the dinghy, let go from the buoy, and motored out. Outside the harbour we hoisted sail and shared the watch on deck until the ineffable Mike appeared to take the 6 am to 8 am watch.

From the Azores to the Channel is about 1,200 miles. Afflicted by light perverse winds, or no wind at all, we logged 1,500 miles in 25 days, making in fact the slowest leg of the whole voyage. When we ran 300 miles in the first three days we thought we were almost home. Thereafter we only once exceeded 100 miles and on one day we logged 15 miles and on another 20 miles. The familiar, brightly painted tunny boats soon made their appearance, the first when we were nearly 500 miles west of Finisterre. They were catching tunny all right and, presently, to our infinite surprise, we had one, too, a fish of about 25 lb. This was the one and only fish to be caught on the line that we had trailed over the stern for the greater part of the voyage. All kinds of lures had been tried, white rags, red rags, shiny bits of tin, even a dead flying fish. When we caught this one we were sailing through frequent patches of discoloured water, so red that they might have been caused by the slaughter of several whales. In fact the discolouration was due to myriads of small shrimps. At Horta, the local boats fishing round the islands daily brought in catches of more than a hundred tunny of 40 to 50 lb. weight.

The Azores 'high' followed us northwards, Fine, hazy weather with light easterly and north-easterly winds prevailed right across the Bay of Biscay. Sailing on the port tack we failed to clear Ushant and made a lubberly sort of landfall to the south of it. Haze concealed the land but the presence of three French warships at exercise showed that we were off Brest. In the haze a radar scanner mounted on top of a funnel looked so like a tower that we mistook it at first for the Armen lighthouse. At night, when the lights came on, we saw this light to the south, Ushant to the north, and St Mathieu to the east. In settled summer weather the yachtsman might guess when he was in the Channel either by running into fog or by the number of racing pigeons that settle on his boat to cadge a lift. We emerged from the fog without being frightened by any steamers, and before we were off the Needles the last of our passengers had flown, though not without leaving their abundant traces behind.

On 15 July, a year and a day since our departure, we motored up Lymington River, having first cleared the Customs at Yarmouth. A nimble friend, who spotted us in the river, reached and warned the Yacht Club in time for them to give us their usual welcome of a one-gun salute. Two days later *Mischief* had been stripped bare and made ready for a long rest in her mud berth. She was none the worse for her experiences. As Conrad's shell-back, old Singleton exclaimed: 'Ships are all right. It's the men in them.' My relief at having arrived was more heartfelt than it normally is. More than once, at Deception Island and South Georgia, I had wondered when, if ever, *Mischief* would return home.

As the reader may have gathered, this 21,000 mile voyage had not furnished the enjoyment that is desirable and is expected on such voyages. Nor had it resulted in any achievement. We had nothing to show for it except the fact that the Antarctic, or the least hostile part of it, can readily be reached in a small boat. A voyage like this naturally entails the endurance of small privations and wearisome duties, and obviously all were not up to it. A man, however, must do his work with the tools provided, and if he himself provides the tools and finds them unsuitable, then so much the worse for him. On the other hand when we sail the seas we expect to be confronted with difficulties – that is one reason for doing it – so perhaps with a crew of thorough seamen and agreeable, staunch companions everything would have been too easy. But to have four misfits in a crew of five is too many.

Track chart for Round Africa expedition

Part 2

Round Africa

June 1957 – July 1958

CHAPTER ELEVEN

The Start

AN ACCOUNT of a voyage that took place ten years ago may seem dangerously like the writer's reminiscences. A man's experiences are said to be the
name he gives to his mistakes, and his reminiscences are often written when
his mistakes have been forgotten. It has been a bad habit of mine generally to
write an account of journeys made by land or by sea. From the start the task
was not easy and practice has made writing no easier, which is one good
reason, coupled with the need for filling the winter evenings, why the habit is
kept up. The reason that no account of this voyage came to be written was
that I did not feel equal to it: not that the voyage was such an epic that no
account could do it justice, but that I did not feel strong enough. As I still
have the brief diary and the log-book of this voyage the following account is
factual and not vaguely reminiscent.

Making a voyage round Africa had never been the intention. It resulted
from trying to save something from the wreck of our hopes, hopes that had
centred upon reaching the Crozet Islands, an enterprise of far more pith and
moment than a circumnavigation of Africa. At this time, the autumn of 1956,
Mischief was back from the voyage to the Patagonian channels and home by
the west coast of South America and the Panama Canal, a voyage made solely
for the purpose of landing a climbing party in the most favourable place from
which to make a crossing of the Patagonian ice-cap.* With this first venture
accomplished I felt satisfied that the apparently conflicting aims of sailing and
climbing could be happily married, and that point being settled I began to
look for a fresh venture.

Three likely objectives suggested themselves. The most ambitious was

*See *Mischief in Patagonia*, London, 1957.

Heard Island, in Lat. 53° S., some 2,500 miles south-east of Cape Town, a small island that is really one big mountain, 9,000ft. high and draped in ice and snow from sea to summit. But there was no secure anchorage; the boat having landed its climbing party would have to be sailed to the much larger island of Kerguelen, 300 miles more or less to windward in stormy latitudes. Moreover the crew faced with this task would be weak, having been depleted by the landing of the climbing party that necessarily included the climbing skipper.

Deciding that this was not on I turned to Kerguelen, a big island abounding in good anchorages, its western end extremely mountainous. Kerguelen belongs to France, and some 700 miles to the west in Lat. 47° S. is another small group of French islands, Iles Crozet, comprising five scattered islands. Ile aux Cochons, Ile de la Possession, Ile de l'Est, Iles des Apôtres, and Iles des Pingouins, the last two being mere clusters of rock pinnacles. They were discovered in the same year as Kerguelen, 1772, by the French navigator Marion-Dufresne, who also discovered what are now Marion and Prince Edward Islands. After the murder of Dufresne in New Zealand, his second-in-command Crozet, took command of the expedition and his name was subsequently applied to the whole group by Captain Cook. Like Kerguelen and Heard Island, the Crozet were the haunt of British and American sealers during the first half of the nineteenth century until all the seals had been pretty well exterminated. A few scientific expeditions on their way to or from the Antarctic had paid brief visits to the islands, but only the crews of ships that had been wrecked there made any prolonged sojourn. The survivors of the wreck of the *Strathmore* had the worst time for she was wrecked on the Apostles, the least hospitable island of all. The story is worth relating.

In the days of sail, ships bound for Australia or New Zealand ran their easting down in the Roaring Forties. Hard driving masters with a reputation for fast passages to maintain, or bent on establishing one, might go as far south as the Fifties in the hope of finding stronger or more prolonged gales. Thus in those days the Crozet were often sighted by ships. The *Strathmore*, a new full-rigged ship from Dundee, was running her easting down along the forty-seventh parallel in the southern winter of 1875. Owing to thick weather no sights had been obtained for several days and the master intended to check his position and his chronometers by sighting the Crozet. Sail had been reduced so as not to overrun the islands in the dark, but at midnight of 1 July the vessel struck one of the rock islets of the Apostles. A gig and a lifeboat reached the shore and in the next two days ferried ashore those still clinging to the rigging and salvaged some valuable odds and ends – cooking pots, a case of spirits, blankets, a cleaver, and some buckets. A whole gale then blew up and smashed to pieces both boats. For six months, huddled in a rudely contrived shelter, the castaways eked out a wretched existence by eating albatross, mollymawks, and their eggs. Driftwood from the wreck enabled them to maintain a fire. To add to their distress they sighted two ships but failed to attract their attention. Finally in January 1876, forty-three men and one woman were taken off by an American whaler. Four had died on the island from their privations and forty, including the master and mate, had perished with the ship. A striking illustration of the difference modern means of communication make to the perils of the sea and the chances of rescue, is that ten months after the *Strathmore*'s survivors had been picked up HMS *Wolverine* called at the Crozet in search of them.

Even in 1957 the Crozet were little known. The *Antarctic Pilot* of that date described Possession Island, the largest of the group, as having snow-covered mountains of about 5,000 feet. This piece of erroneous information and the fact that they were little known weighed in their favour if it came to making a choice between Kerguelen and the Crozet. The high and rugged western half of Kerguelen, too, was little known; the ice-cap named Glacier Cook had never been trodden; Mount Ross (6,430ft.) together with several lesser peaks had never been climbed. The many secure anchorages were an attraction, as was the presence of a French scientific base where help and local knowledge would no doubt be at our disposal. On the other hand there was no denying that the presence of other human beings did to a large extent detract from the glamour. The word 'uninhabited' on a map casts a spell almost as powerful as the word 'unexplored', and the lure of a remote, uninhabited island is hardly to be withstood.

Thus when we sailed in 1957 the Crozet were the main target. I might as well add here that when we succeeded in reaching them at the second attempt we were disappointed only by the mountains. Instead of 5,000ft. they proved to be only 3,000ft. high and their snow cover was not permanent. We were only just in time. A year or so later a French official expedition surveyed Possession Island and established a scientific base near the bay where we had landed. A *téléférique* now runs from the beach to the base above suspended over the large rookery of King penguins. The penguins may not care but any desire of mine to revisit Ile de la Possession has been greatly lessened. I am glad to say that on the French map there is a Mont du Mischief, a tribute to a valiant and much enduring old boat.

In 1957 when *Mischief*'s voyages were little known I had few applicants and consequently some difficulty in finding crew. I have no record and do not remember how I collected the crew for this voyage, but I do not think I resorted to advertising as I did for the later more successful voyage. For that I had to put an advertisement in the Personal Column of *The Times*: 'Hand-(man) wanted for long voyage in small boat. No pay, no prospects, not much pleasure.' I remember, however, that Mike Clay applied for a place when I gave a lecture at Cambridge where he was studying geography. He was a climber not a sailor. Jim Lovegrove, who lived in the same county as I did, must have been listening to the Welsh jungle drums. He was an artist who could turn his hand to many things, including wood carving. He carved a very handsome name-board for *Mischief*'s counter. Having had some experience in Thames sailing barges he knew how to handle heavy gear. I was a bit dubious about taking him, and indeed felt like a wrecker of homes, because he was a married man with a small infant and another on the way. As we were to be away a year I thought it pretty callous both on his part and mine.

How Gerry Levick heard of the enterprise I cannot imagine. He was an engineer working for a firm in Lancashire and I believe our first contact was by telephone when I was already at Lymington fitting out. He quickly gave himself the sack for the sake of making the voyage. No doubt he had sea fever, probably incurable, for since then he has been many years in the Mediterranean as professional skipper in various craft. Finally I got hold of two South Africans – this too must have been sheer accident – Pat Green and Howard Davies, both young, active, likely lads. The former, an experienced hand who had done a lot of sailing, was a valuable acquisition. Howard had no sea experience but bravely volunteered to cook and proved to be the better bargain of the two. I made it clear that in return for a free passage I expected them to complete the voyage to the Crozet and to disembark in South Africa only when we had returned from the islands. To which they agreed.

At that time *Mischief* carried her topmast, giving us the benefit of setting a topsail, and herself a proud, yachtlike appearance. The genoa halyard also went to the topmast head but even without the topmast we can set a genoa of much the same size. Whether or not the topsail gave her any more speed, the first leg to Las Palmas took 16 days, exactly the same as on all the other occasions. Sailing from Lymington on 30 June 1957, by 2 pm we were off the Needles where, with Mike Clay trying his prentice hand at the tiller, *Mischief* bounced smartly off the Bridge buoy, the ebb tide running strongly. It was strange and most appropriate, since Jim Lovegrove was on board, that in the Channel we met a Will Everard sailing barge. We have always been lucky in the Bay, lucky from the point of view of the 'fair one' in the following verse, not the hard-bitten 'snoring breeze' chap:

> Oh, for a fair and gentle breeze:
> I heard a fair one say,
> But give to me the snoring breeze
> And white waves leaping high.

We had calms and light airs all the way across until we picked up a fresh northerly breeze 70 miles north of Finisterre.

When we met the north-east Trades and set the twin staysails, which we did about 9 July *Mischief* took the bit in her teeth and logged an average of 120 miles for the rest of the way. One night when we were doing $6\frac{1}{2}$ knots, *Mischief* trembling with excitement, the log rotator air-borne, the seas building up and water coming on board, I decided rashly to lower one of the twins. Instead of helping to muzzle the flogging sail Jim, for reasons unknown, smartly let go the halyard of the other sail. The boom dropped in the water and not surprisingly, at the pace we were going, snapped like a carrot. The other boom was sprung, too, but we made it last to Las Palmas. On 17 July we rounded the breakwater and anchored off the Yacht Club.

I see an entry in my diary – 'back-ache, cramp, headache, otherwise all right'; an entry which referred to my own infirmities. But it might well have applied to the crew, to Mike certainly, for they went ashore together, spent the night out, and returned with the milk. Mike, by then almost a stretcher case, had had his wallet and other things stolen. Remarkably enough the police recovered them. While staysail booms were being made we painted the deck with red ochre and linseed oil, and the topsides, which at that time were white. Close by lay the 20-ton ketch *Jenny Wren* bound for Cape Town with a South African crew with whom we naturally fraternized.

The sailing ship route to Cape Town is the same up to a point as for South American ports. After crossing the Equator a vessel stands to the south within a 100 or 200 miles of the Brazilian coast. Provided one can carry enough food and water, or replenish with rain water, there is no need to put into a Brazilian port as we did on this voyage. By sailing direct to Cape Town, as we did on the second Crozet voyage, there is a great saving of distance as well as of the time spent in port. Sailing direct we spent 71 days at sea and logged 6,100 miles. In 1957, when we called at Bahia, or Salvador, the total distance increased by 1,500 miles. The fact that we spent only 11 more days at sea was owing to the fast passages we made, averaging 96 miles a day from Las Palmas to Bahia, and 92 miles a day from Bahia to Cape Town. Normally on a long passage I would not expect much more than 70 miles a day. Perhaps the topmast helped.

We sailed on the evening of 23 July escorted out by *Jenny Wren*. Hoisting the twins we put her head south-west and went off like a train, logging 770 miles in the first week. As often happens near the Cape Verde Islands, the wind fell light. There were fish about but we could neither hook nor harpoon them. After some assiduous practice at transfixing a tin with the harpoon Jim took his stand at the end of the bowsprit where he remained for hours without any success. Arriving off the island of Sal in the middle of the night we closed what looked like the loom of a light in order to identify it. It was lucky that there were three of us on deck ready to put about, because quite suddenly the loom resolved itself into the lights of a small town, while land, high and menacing, appeared on either side. The next night I spent hours on deck looking for the light on St Jago, the island itself showing as a vague blur on the port bow. No light ever appeared. As someone remarked the Cape Verde islanders ought to have been told that the war was over. In four visits in the vicinity of these islands only once have I seen a light, a light with the pleasing name of Donna Amelia on St Vincent. On that occasion the helmsman, a young, sociable chap, must have thought that Donna Amelia herself lived in the lighthouse. Before he saw fit to call me we were practically alongside it, near enough for Donna Amelia, had she been there, to blow kisses.

There is usually so much haze round the islands that one sees nothing and would do better to pass well to the west. But this time we were rewarded with a magnificent and dramatic view of Fogo and its peak of 9,281ft. As the sun rose the clouds slowly lifted like the safety curtain in a theatre revealing bit by bit the steep, violet-coloured slopes of the mountain. Fogo soon disappeared in the haze, for we were sailing fairly fast when Mike chose to go for an involuntary swim. Apparently he fell in while skylarking on the bobstay. I was below trying to sleep when a loud shriek brought me on deck. The lifebuoy had already been thrown over, and after trying in vain to hold on to the log-line Mike let go and swam to the buoy. The correct drill of gybing could not be carried out because we were under the twins which had first to be lowered before we could start motoring back. With a man in the shrouds to keep Mike in sight we handed the twins and within about 20 minutes Mike had been hauled out. I have no record of what was said to the chastened Mike but in any case it would not look well in print. To keep the man in sight is the vital thing and even on this occasion when we acted fairly quickly he was a long way astern and not easy to see.

On a hot, windless day we were all in the sea trying to keep cool when a shark joined the party. Our flailing arms and legs as we rushed for the ship should have frightened it out of its life, but it remained quite calm waiting to be fed. It swallowed a cabbage, a rotten one, with apparent gusto, and nosed broodingly at an empty bully beef tin, but nothing would induce him within the harpooneers reach. The south-west rain-bearing winds which we presently met are known as the south-west Monsoon and are a sort of continuation and deflection of the south-east Trades. They enabled us to fill our tanks, gave us all fresh-water baths, and lasted for a wet, depressing week. At this stage of a voyage to South America only a crew of seagoing philosophers, pranked in reason's garb as well as oilskins, would retain their good humour as the ship bears them steadily away from their destination on the starboard tack. When we had reached as far as Long. 15° W., less than 200 miles from the African coast I became alarmed. Then the wind backed slowly to east of south, we went about, and at last pointed towards Brazil. Pointing towards it though we were, Brazil is a large country with two thousand miles of coastline and we hit it in the wrong place. We made a mess of things. Having crossed the Equator several degrees too far west and plagued by winds that were more south than south-east, we took the easy course and sailed too free. Consequently, helped by the Equatorial current setting us west at the rate of some 30 miles a day, we fetched up 3 miles off Recife, dimly recognized through a rain storm. Recife is near the extreme north-east corner of South America and over 300 miles north of Bahia. It was humiliating for me, the navigator, to have to go about and stand out to the east. The wise man sits on the hole in his carpet. Recife would have served me as well as Bahia and I could have boldly proclaimed that this had all along been our target. Spending as little time as possible on this unprofitable tack we went about again to steer south, where-upon, the wind heading us, we were soon enjoying a remarkably close and dangerous view of a charming, rustic village, palms, thatched huts, and boats drawn up on the beach. It is not well to make too free with the shore in these parts. From north of Recife down to Bahia the coast is fringed with a barrier reef of coral which lies from a mile to three miles offshore. This reef is about 16 feet wide at the top, slopes seawards, is abrupt on the land side, and is in general under water.

South of Cape Agostinho the coast trends more west so that we were able to follow it down without having to tack. On 30 August we entered Bahia and anchored off the old port packed tight with local craft. The wide bay that stretches away inland has the lovely, resounding name of Baia de Todos os Santos, the port itself is simply Baia or Bahia, and the city is San Salvador. It is one of the oldest South American cities, founded in 1549. One tends to think that nothing old should exist in the New World, but in San Salvador, or

Lima and Santiago, for example, there are great cathedrals and churches dating back three hundred years or more. San Salvador was once the capital of Brazil and the chief port of entry for African slaves; hence the wonderfully mixed population of all colours including full-blooded negroes.

Besides the many richly decorated churches, some built of marble brought from Europe, there are the gloomy stone-built mansions with massive curved doors that were the homes of great merchant princes, their wealth founded mainly on sugar and slaves. The city is in two parts. The old, so-called, built on a narrow strip of land along the water at the foot of a steep, black, 240ft. high cliff. This is the busy commercial quarter surrounding the old port and containing the main market. The upper city is on top of the cliff, and to reach it, besides steps and steep motor roads, there is direct access by means of passenger lifts. After making one lift trip out of curiosity I preferred using the steps, and that these were preferable may be seen from the account of a lift ride in 1880, when E. F. Knight was at Bahia in his boat *Falcon*. In 1957 the aroma of castor oil was not so pronounced but there were many others:

We take our tickets for the elevator, and enter a half-dark sort of wild-beast cage, where we sit down beside several of the gorgeous fat negresses, for the production of which Bahia is celebrated, and a few dark gentlemen smoking huge Bahia cigars. A strong and not delectable aroma pervades the cage, which seems in some strange way to call up reminiscences of childhood. I have it – it is castor oil. The machinery of the elevator is evidently lubricated with this horror of my youth.

Between us and the shore the old port was choc-a-bloc with strange local craft manned by piratical looking mulattoes and negroes; small fishing boats like spoons, and various big trading craft painted in bold colours, some lateen-rigged with unstayed masts, some fore-and-aft schooners, and some with a loose-footed gaff mainsail and a tall, oblong sail on the foremast. In Knight's book *Cruise of the Falcon* there is a pleasing sketch of one of the latter.

Having taken on provisions, water, and petrol, we sailed for Cape Town on 9 September. *Mischief* then had a petrol engine, the Chrysler 'Crown' engine which had been in her when I bought her in 1954. If given attention it did good service and in Gerry Levick we had the man to give it attention. On the next voyage, partly through neglect and partly through the running down of the starting battery when for two months the engine lay idle, it became a solid mass inside of salt and rust. In addition to supplies we took on two passengers, a pair of budgerigars. They were bought in default of a parrot, for parrots even in their native haunt were outrageously expensive. These two may well have been cock and hen but we called them Peter and Paul; too prophetically, as it turned out, for Peter did fly away. We used to let them fly around in the cabin until one day we forgot to close the skylight and poor Peter vanished. Since we were in mid-ocean there was no hope for him. Paul reached Lymington safely.

CHAPTER TWELVE

Cape Town

UNLESS, LIKE the traditional sailor, one has a wife in every port, most ports of the world may be left without regret. It was good to be at sea, away from the heat, clamour, and smells of Bahia. Even to a man who is willing to take things as he finds them, it did not appear to be a salubrious spot – especially the old town, where the refuse of the market and the quayside provided the luxuries as well as the necessities of life for a vast colony of rats. The sight of them at night scurrying across the road and into the covered market was itself enough to induce symptoms of Bubonic plague. In the words of the old sweat's song: 'There were rats, rats, big as bloody cats, in the Quartermaster's store'. Only in the trenches and dug-outs of the First World War were to be seen such sleek and cheeky rats. Nowadays the sailor has only the peril of the sea to face, whereas not so many years ago, if he stayed long at a place like Bahia he stood every chance of being buried there, a victim to Yellow Jack or typhoid.

From Bahia a sailing vessel has to get further south before it can steer direct for Cape Town, as far south as Lat. 35° S. when there is a good prospect of having mainly westerly winds. As well as southing we made a lot of easting, so that by the time we had run through the south-east Trades and were in the region of variable winds we were on the same meridian as when we had crossed the Equator. The variable winds and variable weather, albatross and whales, were a refreshing change after the tame sameness of Trade-wind regions and lifeless tropical seas. Whales do not seem to mistrust small, silent sailing ships. One evening we had one swimming slowly and majestically around only some 20 yards from the boat. At night he was still there, startling the helmsman whenever he came up for a blow. In common prudence no one dreamt of stirring him up with our small harpoon but in any case a whale is not the sort of creature one would wish to harm:

> We do it wrong, being so majestical,
> To offer it the show of violence.

Seen at close range from the deck of a small boat a whale appears so invulnerably vast that one is amazed afresh at the reckless hardihood of the men who used to kill their whales in hand-to-hand fight, as it were – and as they still do at the Azores where they hunt them in sailing and rowing boats. It is one thing to row up to a whale, but the boldest, one imagines, would pause before launching a harpoon at that latent mass of power and fury. It must be like throwing a match into a powder magazine.

The albatross were just as interested in us as we were in them. Having watched us go by they would take off again in their clumsy way, flapping their great wings and pedalling hard with their feet, fly ahead of us and alight in order to have yet another good look at *Mischief*. If we were becalmed a small flock of them would gather round, more out of curiousity than in expectation of food. We tried floating potatoes out to them on a bit of board but they were not amused. When a shark appeared, we were surprised that it took no notice of these sitting albatross, for it would have had no difficulty in hoisting in one or two to make a juicy and satisfying meal. Perhaps feathers are too indigestible even for a shark. Anyhow this unfortunate shark paid for its indifference as to what was going on. Jim harpooned it and after a brief struggle we got him on board. He was only about 6ft. long and his small teeth did not look very formidable. We ate it, and except that there were no bones it was quite the nastiest fish that I have ever eaten, tasting like warm, slightly greasy, blanc-mange, and eminently sickmaking. Jim, who had a vested interest in it, professed to enjoy it and astonished us by eating the liver for breakfast.

On 11 October we crossed the Greenwich meridian, thus marking another milestone on our long passage. For the next eight months we were to remain in the eastern hemisphere. The weather, like the British economy, continued to be of the 'stop-go' variety. On one of the 'stop' days we recorded an all-time low of 10 miles, followed hard by *Mischief*'s best ever, a run of 151 miles in the 24 hours. At Jim's instigation we had unlaced the mainsail from the boom and ran with it loose-footed. Thus the sail had a lot more belly, and although the risks of a 'Chinese' gybe were not obviated, the consequences would have been less damaging – provided, of course, that the helmsman avoided being strangled or beheaded by the main-sheet. The great drawback was that the sail had to be lowered for reefing.

The sighting of ships, seals basking on the surface, and the mooing of penguins at night, assured us that land was not far off. Some thought these penguin noises were like cows mooing, while others likened the noise to that made by the old-fashioned motor horn that one squeezed. They were Jackass penguins which breed on a few of the islands off the west coast of South Africa. They are valued and protected on account of the guano and eggs they produce; few people are permitted to visit the islands. The eggs are in so great demand at Cape Town and Johannesburg that they have to be ordered in advance. It was a supremely satisfying moment when we sighted land early on the morning of 3 October. To cross an ocean and make a landfall on another continent gives the amateur sailor similar satisfaction to the climbing of a peak. By evening, when Table Mountain and Lion's Head were easily recognizable, we were still 20 miles away. The lights of Robben Island and Green Point came up and at midnight we sailed slowly through the wide entrance to Duncan Dock. We had hoped to anchor there till morning but a police launch drew alongside and brusquely ordered us to anchor outside. In spite of our two South Africans who spoke the same language they regarded us with suspicion. Next morning they made amends by bringing off a pilot who took us into the small, crowded yacht basin, the home of the Royal Cape Yacht Club. We had been 44 days at sea.

We stayed a month at Cape Town, a week longer than I had anticipated owing to the defection of Pat Green and some delay in finding a replacement. For the whole period my diary is a complete blank and for the two interesting facets of Cape Town, the mountain and the sea, I have drawn largely from the account of the second visit. There can be no more congenial a place, or one with more facilities for the cruising yachtsman to refresh and refit, than Cape Town, in particular at the Royal Cape Yacht Club. Help and hospitality are offered in embarrassing profusion. The members are ready with not only advice but with practical help, and since among them there are men of almost every trade, profession, or business there are few problems that one or other of them cannot tackle. Among these keen, experienced sailors, there are many who have built or are capable of building their own boats. Perhaps the absence of yards devoted to building or repairing yachts is even more pronounced in South Africa than in Australia, so that practical knowledge and ability in that line is more common than it is at home.

Although conditions there are not altogether favourable, a goodly number of ocean-going yachts, day sailers, and dinghies are maintained afloat. Table Bay is a fine stretch of water, but along the coast to the east or to the west small harbours and anchorages are scarce. And in order to reach, say, Port Elizabeth, East London, or Durban, one must pass the notoriously stormy Cape and contend with the fast-flowing Agulhas current. Merely maintaining a boat in the yacht basin has some discouraging aspects. In summer south-easters are frequent and violent, sweeping across the unsheltered basin, carrying with them so much sand and gravel that a boat's varnish and paint-work is most efficiently sandblasted. Alternatively, when the wind is north-west it blows smoke from the docks to blacken the rigging. And if that is not enough there are numbers of sea-birds that love to roost on the boats in the yacht basin, in defiance of their being festooned with bird-scarers in the shape of fluttering rags, nets, and such like, so that a boat's deck soon becomes a miniature guano all colours including the justly famed Red Disa. These flowers, which alone make a mountain walk worth while, are wisely protected, all collecting being forbidden.

From the climber's point of view this profuse vegetation might be deemed superfluous but it is not really so. On the steep faces where most of the serious climbing is done the rock is fairly clean. On the buttresses and in the gullies, though the plants and trees might offend the purist, they come in handy for belays, handholds, and above all fuel. For the Sunday parties that we left assembling are expedition-minded, fully aware that climbers as well as armies march on their stomachs. After an hour's stroll along the well graded track, the arid, stony slopes of the mountain on the one hand, and on the other, far below, the boundless ocean, we come to a convenient spring and abundant firewood. Out of capacious rucksacks come the smoke-grimed billies, veterans of countless bivouacs and *al fresco* meals, to be balanced cunningly on stones or on the traditional forked sticks over swiftly kindled fires. Of what use are spirit lamps and similar 'cissy' contrivances when there is meat to be broiled or charred? After our modest 'elevenses' tea, chops, and a couple of eggs, the fires are carefully quenched and the various parties peel off on lesser tracks leading to the foot of their chosen climb. By now it is sizzling hot and shorts seem the only wear despite blister bushes and thorns. If the heat threatens to be excessive, our leader may pick on a climb with a view to remaining in the shade, a refinement that the traditionally hardy mountaineer would seem to adopt by accident rather than design.

In any case our climb is a deliberate affair, fitting in the circumstances; a hot day, a party of five or more, and the presence of an elderly mariner straight from sea, besides all the hauling up of sacks with their precious contents. Shady or sunny, the climb will certainly have been chosen with a proper regard for luncheon sites, that is to say the necessity for finding wood and water at or near the top of the climb. In high summer when some of the springs and water pockets may be dry, someone in the party skilled in bush-craft, a descendant possibly of the 'vortrekkers' will know where water may be found. The equipment of a well-found party such as ours will certainly include a length of plastic tubing for siphoning water out of inaccessible crannies. Water having been found, the party scatters to collect firewood, and in no time the billies are boiling and the steaks broiling on long wooden skewers. This is the highlight of the day. Perched on our mountain eyrie, replete with food and drink, we can gaze out upon the deep indigo sea where fishing boats crawl like water beetles and the rollers break lazily on dazzling white beaches. The descent is usually by one of the many gullies, preferably on the shady side of the mountain, and having at its foot a convenient spring where we can brew up for the third and last time.

The younger climbers and the Tigers, of whom there are plenty in the Club, might scorn such a picnic. There are those, however, who love the mountains for their own sake, for whom it is enough to be on a mountain either alone or with good companions; many like myself whose years may have calmed their climbing passions without dulling their faculty for enjoying the sort of day I have described. I suspect that on this occasion the wind may have been tempered, that out of regard for one who had not yet got his land-legs the arrangements for the party's well-being were slightly more elaborate than usual.

Besides Table Mountain there are in Cape Province alone mountains and mountain ranges from 5,000ft. to 9,000ft. high, not well known and little climbed, which offer plenty of strenuous climbing and the pioneering of new routes. The only drawback to South African mountaineering, and I see no way of remedying it, is that there are no glaciers. By its proximity Table Mountain is the main scene of activity, and the Club is its vigilant guardian against those who would like to push the suburbs of Cape Town ever higher up its slopes or to build a motor road to the summit. The Club, too, is organized to take care of the fairly frequent accidents to pedestrians and visitors. Tourists disgorged on the summit by the cable-way get lost and have to be brought down; or sometimes, owing to a sudden storm, the cable-car is unable to descend, and the whole car-load of tourists stranded on top have to be shepherded down. To a newcomer the cable-way is inevitably something of an eyesore, especially the terminus building perched on the edge of a fine crag.

The Yacht Club has its own slipway with a winch powerful enough to haul up a boat of *Mischief's* displacement, about 35 tons. We had no drawings from which the experts could see the under-water shape of her lines, but they made a good guess, adjusted the cradle accordingly, and hauled her up without mishap. After a good scrub down we put on a fresh coat of anti-fouling paint, using the contents of a 5-gallon drum that had been given me at Valparaiso by a generous shipowner. We might as well have applied face powder. By the time we were on the way home we could see patches of bare wood below the water-line. At Lymington, when the boat had been hauled out, we found that many of the planks, mostly forward of the beam, were riddled with toredo worm. Sections of the planks were like honey-comb, and for part of the homeward run we cannot have had as much as half an inch of sound wood between us and the sea. Some two hundred running feet of planking had to be renewed.

Pat Green, as I have noted, did not keep his word and volunteers to take his place were by no means as plentiful as blackberries. In fact we had but one, young Allen Jolly aged eighteen, who after dithering for some time finally made up his mind to come. It surprised me that the hard-bitten sailing men of the Club did not consider our prospects were very bright. In their opinion, if we were still afloat, we might fetch up in Australia, certainly not at the Crozet, and shook their heads mournfully at so rash an enterprise. It is always gratifying to confound the experts, so that when their dismal fore-bodings were in part fulfilled, the pill was the more bitter.

CHAPTER THIRTEEN

Defeated

WITH STORES and water on board, and *Mischief* having been stripped for the fight by the sending down of her topmast, we made ready to sail. On the afternoon of 21 November we weaved our way out of the yacht basin and hoisted sail in the spacious Duncan Dock. In spite of the size of the dock the wind played some odd tricks. I noticed that as we passed about a hundred yards from a vessel moored alongside, her ensign and ours were streaming out in exactly opposite directions. After twice going about in a reasonably sea-manlike manner we cleared the entrance where a crowd of wellwishers and photographers had assembled. That was almost as far as we went that day, and two days later we were still drifting on a glassy sea a few miles from the Green Point lighthouse. At last, drifting and sailing, we had enough wind to take our departure from Cape Point thirty miles south of Table Bay. Cape Point at the extremity of the Cape of Good Hope is not quite the southern-most tip of the continent. Cape Aghulas, 80 miles farther east, is some 30 miles farther south.

Out of regard for the tales of woe told us by the Club Cassandras we treated the waters south of the Cape with respect. From the start we had two men on watch in four-hour watches. It meant a short sleep, for if one had the first watch from 8 pm to midnight, one came on again at 4 am. Formerly we had been doing single watches of three hours. Young Jolly was at first off colour, unable to enjoy the tunny we caught and which Howard served up poached in white wine and herbs. But it was not long before we had other things to think about than fishing. On the 26th, when we were about 500 miles on our way, in Lat. 39° S., the wind hardened to a moderate gale; a heavy swell from north-west, rain, and a steadily falling glass, promised worse to come. We had already reefed down but by nightfall we changed to storm canvas, trysail and storm jib. Next day as we sped south-east before rising wind and sea we tried to slow her down by handing both sails and streaming a heavy warp. It made little difference, under bare poles she still ran at 4 knots thanks to the windage offered by the heavy shrouds and rigging. Two more warps were streamed in big bights but on the 28th we still logged 100 miles. It was certainly blowing.

Without any sails to help, steering became tricky and if a big sea kicked her stern round, prompt, vigorous action was needed to correct the slew. No storms last for ever and I began to think after two days that this one had lasted quite long enough; for the sea was building up and waves beginning to topple over and break with ominous frequency. That evening the glass steadied at 28.6, the wind backed a couple of points, the sky momentarily cleared, and for a brief moment sunlight glistened upon the streaming, lurching deck of old *Mischief*, the lonely centrepiece of a wild, desolate scene. As night closed in fierce and increasingly heavy squalls of wind and rain, accompanied by thunder and lightning, began sweeping across the sky, the prelude to a foul night. Although the glass showed signs of a rise, when I went below at 8 pm I could not offer the crew much comfort:

> I tell you naught for your comfort,
> Yea, naught for your desire,
> Save that the sky grows darker yet
> And the seas rise higher.

Two days of gale conditions damp the spirits and impair the efficiency of most crews; the incessant whine of the wind, the hiss and surge of great seas breaking alongside, at length begin to daunt even the least apprehensive. The general uproar, the ship's motion, and the strain of waiting for something to happen, make sleep hard to come by. Knowing that it is useless I never even try, but just lie with ears cocked waiting for a new note in the wind or some unwonted noise that might spell calamity. Of the two men on watch one sat lashed in the cockpit steering, the other stood by on the companion-way steps looking out astern over the top of the weather boards that in rough weather are fitted to keep water out of the combined chart and engine-room. As the waves increased in height the helmsman's job became more difficult, trying to keep her stern on to the seas either by steering the given course or by watching the run of the waves. In daylight the latter method is at times frightening and on a dark night impossible. Waves do not all run true and with a heavy boat like *Mischief*, slow on the helm, the smartest helmsman cannot act quickly enough to dodge or square her up before a dangerously breaking sea. When she yawed wildly the helmsman had to sweat to get her back on course before she broached to, a position in which, without sails, she would no longer steer.

At this time we had a canvas weather dodger mounted on heavy iron stanchions practically surrounding the cockpit. It was a nuisance in that it hindered a man from moving quickly from the cockpit to the deck; and I had a feeling that it tempted the helmsman to keep his head down in shelter thus preventing him from keeping a good look-out all round. In this storm the dodger got swept away and I have not yet fitted another, contrary to the present day tendency to shut the crew in behind dodgers, hoods like motor cars, and perspex glass screens. No doubt these keep the helmsman dry but they must impair the efficiency of the look-out. In crews I have had, some are apt to think that the helmsman's job ends with steering, forgetting that he has also to keep a faithful look-out, noting everything in sight, ships, birds, clouds, the wind, the waves, and much else. In fair weather some go on watch with a book under their arm so that as soon as the skipper is away below they can lash the tiller and enjoy a quiet read.

Coming on watch again at midnight I thought the weather had worsened, the wind backing west and blowing harder as the barometer rose. Hardly any two people will agree in their estimate of wind force, and probably no two people when it comes to estimating the height of waves. I thought this wind had been blowing at force 9 for most of the time, more in gusts. I had not been long in the cockpit, too busy with the tiller to ponder much over the vicissitudes of life at sea, when a wave broke over the counter, ripped away most of the dodger, broke off two of its stanchions, and half-filled the capacious cockpit with water. The cockpit drains itself by means of two pipes leading outboard, but the pipes are small, and long before much draining has been done most of the water finds its way below by way of the lockers under the cockpit seats. No harm in that, because it all collects in the well of the bilge whence it can be pumped out. What with rain, spray, and the working of the boat there was always some water below which we cleared by a few minutes pumping every half-hour using the rotary pump mounted in the heads.

Gerry and I rerigged the dodger after a fashion, more as a gesture of defiance than for the protection it gave. How illusory this protection was Mike Clay presently learnt. Soon after six, daylight, and Mike at the helm, a sea struck the port side just forward of the quarter. It seemed that Mike had bent down under the cockpit seat trying to light a cigarette, a difficult feat in the driving spray and a dangerous one, for we had nearly broached to. The sea demolished the remains of the dodger, flattened all its stanchions, and started inboard the cockpit coaming which in turn wrenched up the adjacent deck plank. Water spurted through every seam of the sky-light while the fenders and two heavy blocks lashed abaft the skylight went for six. The square spars lashed on deck came adrift but luckily remained on board. On its way forward the wave swept the dinghy overboard, bending at right angles the life-line stanchions as it went. With the dinghy we lost a bag of anthracite, two small water tanks, the working jib folded and lashed, and several coils of rope. So much for the deck; except, of course, for the unlucky Mike who had been thrown violently to the cockpit floor, half drowned and half dazed.

At the time I was below where the immediate results of the blow were chaotic. She leaned right over, a cataract came down the companion way and through the skylight, and everything moveable alighted on the floor to swim about in the water. In the engine room all the bos'uns stores and tools had leapt off the shelves to finish up in the bilge or less accessible crannies. While the other man on watch struggled to get her back on course, the rest began clearing up the mess below, salvaging sodden books and clothing, and pumping out the water swilling about over the cabin sole. Jim and I then went forward to set the storm jib to help in keeping her before the wind. Meantime the weather had begun to improve in so much as the sun shone brilliantly, though wind and sea showed little sign of abating. A veil of spray blown off the wave tops covered the surface of the sea which now became more confused as the wind backed to south-west. Frequently two monster waves would collide and tower up into a fearsome pyramid of water.

By next day the wind had gone down. We took in the warps, streamed the log and set more sail. As the wind moderated the waves that had long been subjected to its tyranny expressed their new found freedom by leaping higher and running all ways. One such now sprang on board and completed the run on deck by breaking up the deck locker abaft the mast. The time had come for us to take stock of the damage and decide what to do. The damage was superficial and easily repairable but the loss of the dinghy was fatal to our plan of landing on the Crozet Islands. An American climbing friend, when he heard what had happened, disagreed on this: 'What worries me about your last trip,' he wrote, 'is that the Tilman I knew would have swum ashore rather than admit defeat.' Well, may be not. Even twenty years before, the time when he and I had been climbing together, I should have had more sense than to try swimming ashore at the Crozet.

No, the only reasonable alternative was to go to Kerguelen where we should be able to land at the French base. But Kerguelen was still the best part of 2,000 miles away in Lat. 49° S. and we were only on the edge of the Forties. 'If they do these things in the green tree, what shall be done in the dry?' I wondered weakly how many more such batterings we would receive in the course of those 2,000 miles, whereas a man of more robust mind would have argued that the weather had done its worst, that we had come through in tolerably good shape, and that since the summer was advancing we were unlikely to meet with any more such breezes lasting for three days. Another worrying thought was that besides myself only two of the crew could be relied upon to steer safely in bad weather, and the prospect of that long haul under those conditions so daunted me that prudence decided me to give up and sail back to Durban. 'Prudence', as the Sage says, 'quenches that ardour of enterprise by which everything is done that can claim praise or admiration, and represses that generous temerity which often fails and often succeeds.' Had we not succeeded at the second attempt two years later this feeble decision would have been another cause for life-long regret, one more to be added to a fairly long list of might-have-been's. On balance I think we did right to give up since we no longer had any chance of achieving what we had set out to do.

So in fine bright weather, a long uneasy swell still running, we put *Mischief*'s head north-east. Though naturally oppressed by our acknowledged failure, none of the crew demurred and none were in favour of trying to reach Kerguelen. We were much nearer to Durban than Cape Town and by going there we should not be obliged to listen to the inevitable refrain, 'We told you so.' Ten days of light winds brought us to a point 60 miles south of Durban, on the edge of the Agulhas current. From the Mozambique Channel southwards the Agulhas current extends from 30 to 100 miles off the coast and runs at nearly 2 knots, sometimes much more. The greatest strength recorded is 120 miles a day in the month of September. Close inshore there is a counter-current setting up the coast. Steamers bound east from Cape Town hug the coast so closely that when seen from the offing they appear to be navigating with the utmost recklessness. Helped by a fine north-east breeze we made across the current and got well in under the land. Our proximity to the shore, a black night, and an appalling thunderstorm, combined to give us some anxious hours. In the early hours of the morning the peak halyard parted, but we were about to lower the mainsail any way on account of the wind, the opening blast of an approaching gale that sent us scurrying along until by morning we were outside Durban. A pilot boarded us and laid us alongside the fish wharf against which we were unmercifully pounded by the wind, now at gale force. Seeing our plight, the Vice-commodore of the Yacht club directed us to a sheltered spot where at half-ebb we bumped on the bottom. We then sought to make fast at the end of the steamer wharf but were chased away, and finally we found a home in the yacht basin moored at the uttermost end of a long trot. In the princely way they do things in South Africa the Yacht club ran an all-round-the-clock launch service for taking crews ashore. To signal for the launch the yacht hoisted a 'G' flag. That was the theory, but before we had provided ourselves with another dinghy we had some very long waits. I managed to buy a second-hand 8ft. dinghy made of teak.

Howard Davies left us here. He had played his part manfully, and in fair weather or foul stuck cheerfully to his uninviting task. Throughout the recent gale, when cooking in our galley might have baffled a seagoing conjuror, he had served meals bang on time and in between kept the watch on deck happy with frequent mugs of coffee or cocoa. Alan Jolly returned prematurely to his anxious parents in Cape Town, and with him went Mike Clay. To use an out-dated expression, courting rather than climbing had occupied much of Mike's time in Cape Town, and now he was all on fire to clinch matters by getting married. It was not for me to stand in his way; I could only pronounce a seamanlike blessing and express the hope that married life would run smoother than his brief life at sea. We had thus three berths to fill and for a voyage to England through tropic seas there were enough volunteers. David Smith, a tall lad of 18, whose ambition was to be a London 'bobby', took over the galley. Douglas Moor and Ian Sibbald, both inexperienced, came as hands.

In order to salve something from the wreck of our hopes we wanted to return home by way of the Indian Ocean where there were one or two islands of interest that we might visit. Some stores for the homeward voyage, which originally would have been through the Atlantic, had been left at Cape Town, and I now had them sent on to Beira for us to collect. Our friends at the Durban Yacht Club were almost as discouraging as those at Cape Town had been. They were not prophets of doom but they went so far as to say that the passage to Beira in a yacht was not possible. The few yachts that had left Durban for Beira had all had to return, baffled by light winds and the Aghulas current.

Feeling no temptation to spend Christmas in Durban, which at this time of year is exceedingly hot and muggy, I intended sailing on 22 December. As the Arabs say, the camel-driver has his thoughts and the camel, he has his. The crew, who had been ashore all night did not turn up until late afternoon, evidently not in a seagoing mood; and since it was raining and blowing hard we probably did well not to sail. When we left on the 23rd we started to tack up the coast close inshore hoping to gain some northing before launching out across the current. By evening all the new hands were seasick, so rather than spend a sleepless night working the ship short-handed, we stood out to sea. A force 6 wind at north-east sent us along at 6 knots and although we lost a lot of ground to the south, by Christmas Day we were out of the current and able to steer north. The crew, too, had recovered sufficiently to face our Christmas dinner of cold ham, Christmas pudding with rum butter, port and cigars.

We made a fast and trouble-free passage to Beira, utterly confounding the Durban prophets of woe. Keeping 200 miles off the coast until well inside the Mozambique channel, we luckily picked up a fresh north-easterly breeze just when we were ready to make our run in across the current. On that day of the passage we logged 150 miles. The chart for the approaches to Beira is a discouraging document, the absence of water and the presence of shoals makes it look more like a map. For fifteen miles out from the port there are acres and acres of sandbanks, or rather mudbanks, deposited by the Pungwe River, a twin brother of the 'grey-green, greasy Limpopo'. Through the banks runs a tenuous, buoyed channel, a channel that at low water ceases to be continuous. Like politics, navigation is the art of the possible, that is to say that sometimes one must be content with an approximation to the intended aim. At dawn of 3 January 1958, when we were off the mouth of the Pungwe hoping to see one at least of the many buoys, even if not the precise one aimed at, nothing could be seen at all – no buoys, no ships, no land. Staring without inspiration at the monotonous brown sweep of the horizon at last we made out a ship apparently at anchor. On closing it we found the *Tintagel Castle* anchored near 'P' buoy, the pilot station, and nearby the pilot cutter. When the flood started to run, a pilot came on board. We would have liked to impress this Portuguese mariner with our smooth efficiency. But the engine refused to start, under a strong wind and tide the cable was bar taut, and we had a rare struggle getting the anchor. The mainsail went up in a fashion that suggested we were hoisting it for the first time, and the couple of crashing gybes that we presently executed must have made the Portuguee think that some of us would not live long enough to hoist it again. We made No. 3 buoy without having to gybe, and with the wind on the beam and a 3-knot tide under us we rushed from buoy to buoy as if bent on overhauling the *Tintagel Castle*. The pilot anchored us in 2½ fathoms less than a cable from the wharf in what we were assured was excellent holding ground. It needed to be. The flow of the ebb tide at springs with the river behind it made one dizzy to watch.

Beira, the original Sofala, was visited by Vasco da Gama in 1502 and a few years later the Portuguese established a settlement. San Salvador had been settled at much the same time, both places are in roughly the same latitude, well within the tropics, yet no two places could be more unlike. At Beira there are no sixteenth-century churches and no mansions fitting for merchant princes; none of the busy, teeming life of the waterfront no picturesque sailing craft; no vast covered market, not even any fresh vegetables, potatoes, or eggs. It is modern, neat, orderly, fairly clean and remarkably dull. On account of the strong tides and the cluster of boats round the one landing place it was not easy to get ashore; and having got there a walk through the town proved to be, in the words of Baedeker, fatiguing and not repaying.

For watering we had to have three 40-gallon drums brought alongside, and having done that and got our provisions from Cape Town on board we were ready to go. As usual the crew made their last night a late night, only David and I stayed on board for supper. It was the height of springs, two days after the full moon, with the ebb, which runs for seven to eight hours, going like a mill-race. Sitting quietly below after supper in a state of semi-somnolence we were presently aroused by noises off. It seemed a bit early for the crew to have returned. Going on deck I was surprised to find two launches alongside. The town of Beira, the wharf, and the ship that had been lying just ahead of us, seemed in some mysterious way to have receded almost out of sight, and were in fact still fast receding. We were adrift, nearly two miles on the way out to sea. A steamer anchored nearby and several others lying downstream, must have all just missed being run down. Apparently *Mischief*'s departure outward bound, stern first, like a ghost ship with nobody on deck, had been noticed by some alert chap in the port office. While we were being towed back – and against the sluicing tide the launch had its work cut out – David and I got up the anchor. The motor car tyre that now adorned one of its flukes must have been hooked 'en passant', as chess players say.

CHAPTER FOURTEEN

Comoro and Aldabra Islands

AS THE Comoro Islands lie athwart the northern exit from the Mozambique Channel we decided to visit Ile Grande Comore, the biggest of the group of four. This island is the seat of the French Resident and it also has on it a Mont Kartala, 7,874ft. high. Mont Kartala is a volcano, having last erupted in 1918, and it was therefore unlikely to be of much interest. The majority of volcanoes have placid, cindery slopes – Teneriffe is a steep exception – rather to be avoided than climbed.

Sailing early on 8 January we made our way from buoy to buoy down the channel, taking our departure from the outermost. Again we started by hugging the African coast where hot, clammy weather, light winds and little progress, soon frayed our tempers. Taking advantage of a fine northerly breeze we stood over to the Madagascar side of the channel, losing some ground to the south on the way and not finding much better winds. We had already been out a fortnight when we sighted the casuarina trees and buildings on Juan de Nova, a small guano island 60 miles off the Madagascar coast. Another 100 miles to the north-west is Chesterfield Islet and I must have thought myself on a par with Henry the Navigator to expect to sight that, for the islet is a mere 10ft. high rock fringed by a sand-covered reef. According to my reckoning we had already passed it when Gerry, climbing the shrouds to retrieve a pair of shorts hung up to dry, spotted the rock fine on the bow. As we passed it a few cables off we noticed that the reef was covered with frigate birds. We did well to get away from the small islands and islets that lie far out from this part of the Madagascar coast, and not to try to spot any more. During the next four days we experienced some remarkably bad weather, an unbroken pall of low cloud, prolonged squalls of wind and rain, and a rough sea. To account for such an unusual spell I suspected there might be a tropical storm in the vicinity and felt accordingly anxious. January is the worst month of the cyclone season in this part of the Indian Ocean. While it is rare for these storms to cross the high land of Madagascar, a few occasionally pass north of the island and recurve to enter the Mozambique Channel.

When the weather at last cleared we made out Anjouan, one of the Comoro Islands, some 40 miles away, and three days later we fetched Moroni on the west side of Grand Comoro. It is the only harbour and a bad one, encumbered with coral reefs and wide open except to the east. Lying at the small stone pier a boat spends much of the time bumping on the bottom and when afloat it is bashed against the wall by the swell. The anchorage is on the seaward slope of the reef where with offshore winds the anchor may drag into deep water, while with onshore winds the stern hits the reef. The inner harbour, used by dhows, dries out. The six-thousand-odd inhabitants live clustered round the inner harbour and the mosque in a rabbit-warren of flat-roofed houses built of coral rag. Beyond, slightly aloof, are the Residency, a bank, and the Grand Hotel, fighting a losing battle against dilapidation and an absence of guests. The people are a mixture of Arab, Persian, Malagasy, and African negroes, speaking various dialects with Swahili and pigeon-French for common use. There are a few French settlers engaged in growing vanilla and ylang-ylang, a shrub of grotesque growth having pleasantly scented flowers from which an essential oil is extracted. Grand Comoro is the least fertile island of the group, parts of it being mere lava desert, and in spite of a copious rainfall there are neither rivers nor wells. As might be expected the inhabitants are of a conservative nature, either too proud, too poor, or too wise, to delight much in progress. I saw only two jeeps and not a boat in the harbour that boasted an engine. While we were there a Messageries passenger ship arrived with hundreds of deck passengers who, with their baggage, had all to be landed in rowing boats or even in dug-outs propelled by paddles. Admittedly one or two of the rowing boats were more like State barges rowed by twelve pairs of oars.

As we passed through the rabbit-warren in search of the Residency the white-robed Arabs lounging round the mosque either scowled at the infidels or religiously averted their gaze. But the Resident welcomed us kindly and waived all formalities. Having had a drink at the dreary hotel we had about exhausted Moroni's attractions, but Gerry made friends with some of the French with whom he made a successful assault on Kartala. We had long had this great bulge in view during our deliberate approach to the island and it had every appearance of offering another of Baedeker's fatiguing and not repay-ing excursions. Nor was I willing to leave the boat for the couple of days that would be required in view of the hazards of the harbour, the likelihood of theft, and the habit the crew had of absenting themselves when needed. The possession of one's own boat certainly enables one to visit many outlandish places, yet in some cases the need to look after the boat may prevent one seeing much of them.

I was not sorry to get away on the evening of 4 February, the more so because we had just suffered a long spell of pier-bashing awaiting the belated arrival of two of the crew. Our immediate destination was the small coral atoll of Aldabra about 220 miles to the north-east. None of us had seen a coral atoll and my interest had been aroused by reading about Aldabra in *The Cruise of the Cachalot*, the stirring story of an old-time whaling ship by Frank Bullen. Whaling captains of the old school were strongly averse to calling anywhere, both to avoid port dues and desertion on the part of the crew. After cruising round the Comoro Islands and collecting 800 barrels of sperm-whale oil, the skipper of the *Cachalot*, in need of water, put into a cove, rather than any of the ports.

No whaling captain [says Bullen] would be so reckless as to incur port charges; the islands offer great inducements to whaling captains to call, since no one but men hopelessly mad would venture to desert in such places. That qualification is the chief one for any place to possess in the eyes of a whaling captain.

After watering, the *Cachalot* had proceeded to Aldabra, where desertion was even less likely, in order to give the men a run on shore and to collect seabirds eggs and green turtles.

We were a good deal slower than even the lumbering old *Cachalot*. Four days elapsed before we had sunk the great bulk of Kartala and another five before we sighted Aldabra. Across this stretch of the Indian Ocean the Equatorial current sets briskly to the west, the atoll is but a few miles wide and only some 50ft. high, so that here was a case when the navigator experienced the breeze of anxiety playing freshly upon the brow of expectation. An island landfall, preferably at dawn, has a sharp, ecstatic flavour of its own. At first a pale green shimmer in the sky ahead, the reflected light from the shallow water of the lagoon, hinted at what lay beneath, and presently the dark green of its few trees broke the sharp, blue horizon. As we approached the settlement at the north-west corner of the atoll the manager came off in a pirogue rowed by six muscular, cheerful negroes. Visitors are rare, and the schooner from the Seychelles on its bi-annual trip was not due for a month, so they were pleased to see us and to exchange small gifts – cigarettes and bully beef on our side, eggs, coconuts, and limes, on theirs.

There are actually four islands, West, Polymnie, Main, and South, divided by narrow passes, the whole forming an atoll enclosing a lagoon. They are a dependency of the Seychelles and leased to the Seychelles Company. The *Pilot* thus describes Aldabra:

The atoll is either coral or coral rock. The seaward face has abrupt overhanging cliffs from 12 to 15 feet high; the surface of the islands is from 12 to 20 feet high and the sand dunes reach an elevation of from 50 to 60 feet. The islands are clothed in places by a thick almost impenetrable jungle of pemphis, the plants being from 12 to 15 feet high, and mangrove forests flourish, some of the clumps being from 70 to 80 feet in height. The fringing reef is everywhere narrow, never extending more than 3 cables offshore. The chief industries are the preparation and export of dried fish, calipee, dried turtle meat, fish oils, and a little copra. The giant land tortoise is to be found in some numbers on Main Island, and less commonly through the rest of the atoll. Green turtles are to be found, of which there are two distinct groups; one resident, the other migratory and visiting the atoll in vast hordes from December to April to breed. In 1923 wild goats were plentiful. Rats are a great plague and the islands are also infested with jiggers.

The population, or perhaps crew, of the island comprises some 70 souls, men, women, and children, natives of the Seychelles and employees of the company which leases the island to exploit the fishing and the turtle. Every two years the crew is relieved and twice a year a schooner brings stores – mainly rice for the fishermen and their families, and salt for curing – and takes away dried fish, turtle meat, calipee, and turtle shell. A minor source of income is the giant land tortoise, akin to those found on the Galapagos, a few of which are suppled to various zoos. On the beach we saw a pen containing about thirty of these creatures dozing in the sun, awaiting shipment.

The turtle are harpooned in the sea or turned over and subsequently killed when they come up the beach to lay. A turtle lays up to 200 eggs in a hole in the sand dug with its fore-flippers well above tide mark, and goes back to sea on the next tide. After 40 days the eggs hatch out almost simultaneously but only a few of the baby turtles survive. On the short trek down to the beach to the sea for which they instinctively make, many are killed by the rapacious frigate birds, while those that reach the sea are preyed upon by sharks and other fish. Only some ten per cent reach maturity. Down wind of the manager's house were the racks where the turtle meat and calipee were drying. Calipee (beloved of Jos Sedley) is well enough in turtle soup but smells vilely when being dried. It is a product of the green turtle, so called from the colour of the fat, and is the tissue joining the flesh to the shell. Only about 3 lb. of calipee is got from a turtle, their average weight being 300 lb.

Piloted by the manager, we motored round the north-west corner of the atoll to enter Main Channel, the deepest pass into the lagoon, where we anchored. At springs the tide runs through the pass at the rate of 6 knots with scarcely any slack water. Some of the crew went off in the dinghy to explore West Island, but exploring on Aldabra is a formidable, time-consuming task. The surface of metamorphosed coral rock – it rings like metal when walked upon – is jagged and pitted with large and small cavities. Much of it is covered with a stubborn jungle of pemphis wood, the living trees and the dead trunks so hopelessly intertwined that without a cutting party it is well-nigh impenetrable. We only fully realized the strength of the tide when the dinghy party's first attempt to return ended in failure. They had to seize their brief chance at slack water. In the evening I went ashore alone with a sleeping bag and some food to spend the night on Polymnie Island on the east side of the pass. Besides other reasons it was my birthday so I gave myself a present of a romantic but far from comfortable night. It was the only night I had ashore in the course of this 13 months' voyage.

Pirates used not to restrict their activities to the Spanish Main. The Indian Ocean offered a wide and rich field for these enterprising mariners, and its many islands secure places for their refreshment – particularly a place like Aldabra with its turtle and giant tortoise, for the latter's ability to live without food for many days provides a ship's company with an ideally economic supply of meat on the hoof. It is fitting then that this lonely, tropical island should be credited with a pirate's hoard, and the actual presence of a mysterious grave makes it all the more probable; for we know well enough from *Treasure Island* that, having buried one's treasure, one then buried the burial party. On Polymnie Island, according to the manager, there were an ancient anchor and a grave, and the few who visited the grave had been frightened away by a ghost.

I could not find the anchor but I found the grave, marked only by two pieces of bar-iron riveted together in the form of a cross. It lay in an open space under a casuarina tree so I brought my gear from the dinghy, lit a fire, and settled down for the night. As dusk closed in a weird cry shook me not a little, just as the pirates on Treasure Island had been shaken by the cries of Ben Gunn. Then I remembered that the manager had spoken of wild goats on Polymnie Island. Mosquitoes were the next worry. Having changed from shorts to slacks and rolled down my sleeves I lit a pipe to defend my face and fell to musing upon the grave and what lay beneath. Even if no murder had been done, supposing one of one's crew had died what better place to bury him than on top of the hoard as a deterrent to squeamish treasure hunters?

I piled on more logs. By the light of the fire I could just make out the grave. Glancing in its direction I realized I was being watched, watched by two hideous, goggle eyes that regarded me with a cold, fixed, expressionless stare. They were nearly a foot from the ground and in front of the eyes two great pincer claws waved slowly but menacingly as if feeling for the victim that the eyes had already detected. The huge land crab, for such it was, made no move as I stood up, nor any further move after I hit him with the back end of a hatchet. Another appeared, to be dealt with in the same way, and then several more. Apart from what their claws might do, the notion of sleeping there under the baleful stares of these creatures became abhorrent; nor would the bodies of those that I had killed, which were already being devoured, long stay their insatiable hunger. Retreating to the hauled-up dinghy I contrived a rough bed with the oars laid across the thwarts. More horrible eyes began staring up at me from the sand, but in the dinghy I was safe from crabs and slept fitfully in spite of the mosquitoes.

Near my bivouac I had seen numerous, well-worn tracks made by the giant land tortoise – game trails, in fact, if a tortoise can be regarded as game. I watched one of the creatures lumbering along but did not attempt to ride him as Frank Bullen reports having done on his walk ashore on Aldabra. He measured his mount as 4ft. long and 2ft. 6in wide and affirms that it eventually carried him to 'a fine stream of water, sparkling out of the hillside'. These tortoises are reputed to live for hundreds of years. They have one at Government House, St Helena (or had when we called there in 1960) which is believed to have been about the place when Napoleon was in exile there. Bullen also speaks of a patriarch upon whose back a sailor claimed to have seen inscribed: 'The Ark, Captain Noah. Ararat for orders.'

Once more back at the anchorage off the settlement we found the sea too rough for a pirogue to come alongside with water. Early accounts of Aldabra mention a well of fresh water, but the manager had no knowledge of this, nor of Bullen's 'sparkling stream'. We hung on there waiting to water while wind and sea increased alarmingly. A prudent mariner would have spent the night at sea, for the wind was onshore and fifty yards astern of us the seas were breaking on a coral reef. At the settlement they hoisted a white flag, a warning, as we learnt later, for us to clear out.

Before having done with Aldabra I ought to mention a threat that has been hanging over this strange island, an island that in 1958 few had so much as heard of. Briefly there has been a plan for the RAF to use the island as a staging post to the Far East. At an estimated cost of £20 million a 12,000ft. runway would be built at the eastern end and joined to the living quarters, offices, and stores located on West Island by a road having swing bridges across the passes. Apart from the arguments for and against on strategic grounds there is a strong body of scientific opinion against the plan for reasons summed up by Charles Douglas-Home in an article in *The Times*:

Aldabra is unique. It is an elevated atoll, which is rare in the Indian Ocean where most atolls are sea-level atolls. The higher the atoll the wider the range of plants and animals which exist upon it and the more valuable it is for scientific study. Aldabra has never been mined for guano and thus, unlike most other Indian Ocean Atolls, it has not been stripped of its vegetation and the pure ecology of it has been largely uncontaminated. Parts of Aldabra have been contaminated by human contact. On West Island there is a small settlement of Seychellois fishermen. Their presence has already resulted in the near extinction of the Flightless Rail from South Island because of the incursion of rats and cats from the settlement. But most of the atoll remains unaffected, particularly the east end where the giant tortoise live, which also provides the largest breeding ground in the Indian Ocean for the frigate birds and one of the few remaining breeding grounds of the green turtle. The scientist's main argument against the establishment of the base, however, is the fact that except for those areas contaminated by the settlement, the rest of the island in undisturbed. Thus Aldabra provides a unique opportunity for scientists to study the island's ecosystem and the ways in which it has evolved over centuries without being affected by any outside influence.

To get back to the boat. As I have said we stupidly hung on there throughout an anxious night. As I watched apprehensively the white water close astern of us, Jim expounded the novel theory that our position was nothing like so bad as it looked. We would be most likely, he said, to drag at high water, in which case *Mischief* would be washed over the coral reef and would only be wrecked on the comparatively harmless sandy beach beyond! By morning the wind had dropped and we all went ashore for a last meal of turtle's eggs, meat, and fish provided by the manager's hospitable wife. By evening the sea, too, had gone down and the pirogue came off with our water which we manhandled on board with buckets. Amid cheers and waves from the friendly Seychellois we sailed away.

CHAPTER FIFTEEN

The Red Sea and Homewards

OUR COURSE took us west of the main group of the Seychelles. On a day of exceptional clearness the bold silhouette of Mahé, the principal island, showed above the horizon when over 50 miles away. That night, still, warm, moonlit, we stole quietly past Bird Island, only 8ft. high, a white beach, trees, and the light from a solitary hut, endowing it with romance. By dawn we had Denis Island abeam, as low and flat as Bird Island, but having on it a lighthouse; in 1892 it was cultivated, covered with trees, and inhabited. That was the last Indian Ocean island we were to see; the next land sighted was Cape Guardafui on the horn of Africa, after a calm uneventful passage of thirty days. We scraped and varnished the beams inside the cabin, black-leaded the stove, scaled and painted the anchor and its winch, and fitted new light screens. Jim finished carving the new name-baord, and some genius, Gerry I think, made a rotator for the log, the last of several having been taken by a shark. He carved it from wood, giving it the necessary correctly-shaped fins, and filled the inside with lead. After a little adjustment to the length of the line it recorded pretty accurately.

We raised the Guardafui light on the night of 19 March and ran up the Gulf of Aden escorted by two sharks who were in turn accompanied by their pilot fish. The sharks were strangely bright blue in colour but they were not a species new to science, they merely enjoyed rubbing off what was left of our anti-fouling. Arriving at Aden on a Sunday night, bemused by the multitude of lights, ships, oiling buoys, and whatnot, we anchored well clear until the Monday morning when a pilot took us to a berth off the Post Office.

Aden was no longer the drowsy place that I remembered from visits in the thirties when bound to India – a place that came to life only when a mailboat disgorged its passengers for a brief sight-seeing tour, that boasted the one dingy hotel where for sixpence one could see a mermaid, or in other words a dugong. The oil refinery across the bay and extensions to the harbour had changed all that. We were told that 500 ships called every month, mainly for bunkering. Messrs. Luke and Thomas, the shipping-agents, looked after us and we were watered by their water-boat without charge. The port authorities, on the other hand, took their pound of flesh in the way of light dues, etc., the first port in which such charges had been levied against *Mischief*. While walking about in Aden I had a momentary fit of vertigo which later had significance. It lasted only a second and I attributed it to the sun, although at that time of year Aden was still comparatively cool.

We were just too late to expect an easy passage up the Red Sea. By April the southerly winds that prevail during the winter months are failing. We could expect favourable winds for about half the 1,200-odd miles, thereafter we should have to beat against fresh northerly winds. At Durban they had warned us in all seriousness against Red Sea pirates – such is the enchantment that distance lends to a scene. Possibly if the crew of a small boat were imprudent enough to anchor off some small village on the Arabian coast they might find the natives hostile. We had no intention of stopping anywhere on the way if it could be avoided. Even without pirates the Red Sea provides enough problems for the small-boat sailor – the stream of shipping, strong currents, baffling winds, steep seas, scattered reefs, and only partially lit shores. Another navigational hazard is caused by refraction. On one occasion a light with a range of 14 miles was seen when we were 37 miles distant. The Brothers, two islands at the northern end about 200ft. high, have been seen at a distance of 100 miles. Thus, owing to the displacement of the horizon, sights particularly sun sights, are liable to considerable error.

Sailing from Aden on 27 March we went along at a good clip and at dusk next day we passed Perim. That night I woke up feeling fearfully giddy, unable to stand without holding on to something, and vomiting. A few days later I felt strong enough to take my watch, but sights had to be taken sitting down and any quick movement of the head threw one off balance. In the course of the passage matters slowly improved, yet on reaching Lymington three months later I still felt weak and out of balance. Time the great healer, aided by a specialist who had diagnosed a lesion of the labyrinth, affected a cure, but not before I had reached such a low ebb as to put *Mischief* up for sale. Fortunately nobody wanted her except as a gift. Having recovered I felt ashamed of this piece of treachery and thankful that *Mischief*, clever as she was at sea, could not read advertisements.

At that stage of the voyage, enjoying a fair southerly wind, we could lay the desired course and had only to keep the stream of ships in sight. The skipper could very well have stayed in his bunk. The log book, in which we recorded ships in sight, showed a total of between twenty and thirty every day. Having run 400 miles in five days, by 1 April we had the 800ft. high Island of Jabal al Tair abeam, but these easy days of rapid progress were drawing to an end. In about the latitude of Port Sudan the southerly wind died to be replaced almost at once by a stiff northerly blow that soon lashed up a short, steep sea. We now began to make long boards, trying if possible to avoid crossing the shipping lane at night. Standing over to the Arabian side we made out one night the loom of Jedda, and on the next tack towards Africa we had ahead of us the granite peaks of the Berenice Range.

This mountain range lies inland of the justly named Foul Bay, a wide bay thickly studded with rocks and reefs. Here our navigation proved badly askew. We were on the starboard tack steering north-west, confident of weathering Ras Banas, the northern arm of the bay, when over the starboard quarter we saw breaking water. We were already well inside Foul Bay. Going about we steered east with a man aloft who presently saw dead ahead another long line of white water. Thoroughly agitated I stayed on deck until Foul Bay and its horrors were well astern of us. We had now crossed the Red Sea twice and had made good about ten miles to the north. Had it not been for a lucky break in the weather pattern we might still be there. In the next few days a light south-easterly wind brought us to Shadwan Island, the noted seamark at the end of the Red Sea proper and the beginning of the long, narrow Gulf of Suez. It is the crux of the passage, for the prevailing wind is north-westerly, blowing straight through the narrow Strait of Gubal at the entrance to the Gulf. The strait has a navigable width of less than seven miles. Sure enough, out of a clear sky, a moderate gale from north-west descended upon us as soon as Shadwan Island came in sight. We were bashing into it, reefed right down, when one of those short, steep seas curled over and broke on deck, smashing a pane in the skylight as well as one of the twin booms and the deck locker. This glass pane was pretty thick but since then plate glass has been fitted in the skylight. When two seams in the mainsail opened we had to set the trysail and with that sail we had no hope of beating through the Strait of Gubal.

When one door closes, another opens. In this case it was the back-door entrance to the Gulf of Suez by way of the narrow channels west of Shadwan and Gubal Islands. Keeping a look-out aloft for reefs, which are easily seen except when the sun is low, we found sheltered water and anchored for the night off a desolate open beach. The chart names the place Port Endeavour and it is marked by one flat-roofed house in which nobody lives. In this peaceful haven we effected what repairs were needed. Having passed west of

Gubal Island we emerged in the gentler winds and seas of the Gulf of Suez, delighted at having thus cheated those malevolent Straits.

For the most part the Gulf of Suez is little more than ten miles wide and the shipping appeared to be even more heavily concentrated. We had to tack pretty well all the way, so that at night, not wishing to make too free with the shore, we were obliged to cross and recross the shipping lane. The 150 miles to Suez took us six days and in the narrowest part of the Gulf, when for a day and a half it blew hard, we had to reef right down. Arrived in Suez Bay we anchored off Green Island, miles away from the shore, so fearful were we of intruding upon the Canal entrance and the busy shipping. Perhaps in the course of a day or two we might have plucked up enough courage to draw nearer to the centre of things, but that evening a roving bumboat-man with an eye to business drew alongside. When everything and everybody appears or is suspected to be hostile the least show of friendship is accepted with fervour. We welcomed this man as a brother and delivered ourselves into his hands. At the Quarantine station, where he at once took us, we were soon dealt with by the port doctor and the police.

Our doubts about our reception were owing to the ill-fated Suez affair, for we were there in time to reap the aftermath. These doubts were well founded. We found ourselves objects of suspicion, but the worst result of the affair from our point of view was that there were no longer any European shipping agents at Suez to arrange for our transit through the Canal. Difficulties arose about my going ashore and finally, at the suggestion of our friendly bumboat-man, I left it to him to arrange our clearance with the Canal authorities.

No sooner said than done. By next morning we had the necessary papers and attached to them our agent's bill for £27. The correct figure should have been something less than £10. He must have felt, like Clive, astonished at his own moderation, for he had us neatly impaled. Pay or stay; either we paid and went or remained stewing in Suez. The one-sided argument raged till midday when the arrival of the Canal pilot showed that at least we should get what we paid for. So with something less than urbanity I handed over the money. But our cup was not quite full; there was still a trifling sum of misery to be added to the foot of our account. About an hour later, when we were in the Canal, Douglas discovered the loss of eight gold sovereigns, worth, I suppose, about £40. They had been in the pocket of a suit in the cabin and we had little doubt about who had them. Up to the time of his presenting his bill we had been altogether too friendly with the bumboat-man and his myrmidons whom we had allowed to roam all over the boat. One could not but admire the keenness of their scent for what was worth having and the sleight of hand by which they had secured it. There was nothing to be done. No one in Suez would believe our story, much less take any action.

After spending the night at Geneffe at the entrance to the Little Bitter Lake we arrived next day at Ismailia where we anchored again. There we had welcome showers and learnt the unwelcome news that all our mail had been returned to sender. A fresh pilot took us on to Port Said and we implored him to find us a quiet berth where we could lie for a few days to refit. Accordingly we went alongside the Esso oil berth short of Port Said so that the pilot could telephone the Canal office to ask where we could lie. We never saw him again. The Esso watchman, a rough type, told us to shove off, and after some telephoning on our own behalf we were told to moor in Sherif basin. A less quiet berth could hardly have been found. We lay alongside a trading schooner surrounded by lighters full of onions where the police promptly arrived and put a guard on board. For the next two days we were held incommunicado with nothing to do but sleep and nothing to look at but onions. Through the kind intervention of a man called Marco from one of the shipping agents we were at length given shore passes but our policeman still lived on board. Life became more pleasant when we were allowed to move to the Club Nautique at Port Fuad opposite Port Said. The Club, of course, was dead, all its dinghies and speed boats lying around, sunk, but we lay alone in a little basin surrounded by green lawns. We now got some work done, sent up the topmast, and prepared to sail.

From Port Said to Gibraltar is roughly 2,000 miles and the really remarkable feature about our passage was that it took two months. Expecting to do it in one hop in the course of a month, we found ourselves forced to put in at Malta, the halfway mark, to refresh. *Mischief* had been there before, had in fact spent five years there, from 1949 to 1954, in the hands of a Maltese ship chandler who now paid us a visit. They had not been happy years for her. Before Ernle Bradford bought her and took her to Majorca shortly before turning her over to me, she had been grossly neglected.

Unlike the eastern half of the Mediterranean, in the western half we had plenty of wind, but it nearly always came from ahead and sometimes in such strength that we had to seek shelter. Having been pushed over to the African coast we had to lie up behind Cape Farina in the Gulf of Tunis, in company with a number of other small craft, while a westerly gale blew itself out. With the help of a few days of easterly winds we then made a great leap forward until another westerly gale drove us to shelter in a cove near Caba de Gata east of Almeria. Three times we had to anchor in small bays along the Spanish coast. On one occasion, having prematurely left our snug hole to try conclusions with the west wind and east-going current, after beating for 24 hours we were happy to reach the coast again five miles *east* of the anchorage we had quitted. Meantime ships that had passed us in the Eastern Mediterranean homeward bound now began to repass us outward bound. One of these on recognizing us again gave us an encouraging cheer. She happened to be a ship I knew, the *Jan Olden van Barneveldt*, one of a large convoy that had sailed from Liverpool to India in 1941. She was a fine passenger ship that had only recently been requisitioned, with all her peace-time chefs and stewards on board and stuffed full of the sort of food and wine demanded by first class passengers on the Atlantic run. The purser, who abhorred as much as we did, the thought that all these good things might go to the bottom unused, was easily persuaded to let us consume them. It reminded me of a similar precaution that had been taken by the famous climber Mummery and his guide Bergener on the Furggen ridge of the Matterhorn; 'Immediately in front, the long, pitiless slabs, ceaselessly swept by whizzing, shrieking fragments of all sorts and sizes, suggested to Burgener – who had a most proper and prudent objection to every form of waste – that it would be well to drink our Bouvier, and consume our other provisions, before any less fitting fate should overtake them.'

At Gibraltar where we arrived on 3 July we lay in the 'Cormorant' camber, normally reserved for vessels of the Royal Navy. *Mischief* was once more on familiar ground, for in 1954, her maiden voyage as far as I was concerned, she had lain in the same berth for some weeks while I sought to replace the crew that had brought her from Majorca and then left. The Rock, its apes, and its caves, was thus familiar to me and I had time to spare to repaint the deck and the topsides. Jim Lovegrove left us here to attend to his growing family, but for the last leg to Lymington, which we accomplished in twenty days, we needed no substitute.

Warned by my bitter experience in 1954, the result of ignorance, we sailed well out into the Atlantic 200 miles west of Portugal before trying to head north. In 1954, with a scratch crew culled from the Gibraltar garrison, we had attempted to beat north up the coast against the so-called Portuguese Trades. After 18 days, having reached somewhere near Oporto, the crew, who had had enough, forced me to put in and land them. This time our strategy was successful. We dodged the north wind and soon picked up Westerlies. As I say, we thus circumvented the winds of heaven, though one might well ask, like Captain MacWhirr, how did we know that the winds we had dodged were in fact blowing?

The moderate gales and immoderate rain we met in the Channel assured us that we were home again in time to enjoy an English summer. We reached Lymington after a voyage of 22,000 miles and an absence of thirteen months. A voyage in which we had suffered defeat, and from which I brought back only a piece of red coral, some hard-won experience, and many happy memories.

IN MISCHIEF'S WAKE

In Mischief's Wake

First published by Hollis & Carter Ltd., 1971

Contents

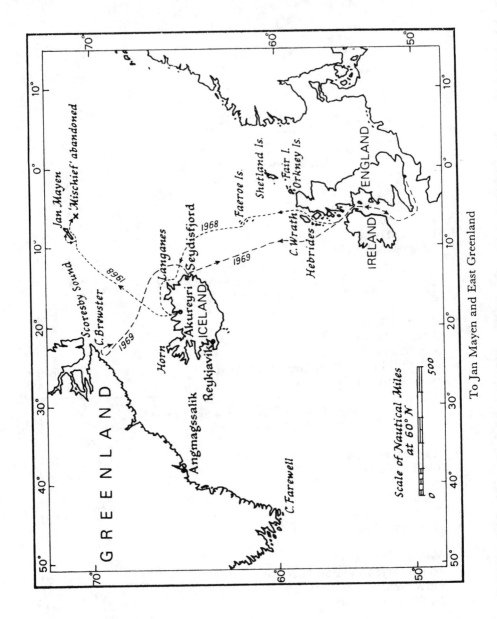

To Jan Mayen and East Greenland

Part 1

Mischief's Last Voyage

Summer 1968

CHAPTER ONE

An Ambitious Plan

IN THE YEARS between 1954 when I bought her, and 1968 when I lost her, the possession of an old pilot cutter called *Mischief* enabled me to visit some remote regions north and south. In those fifteen years she sailed some 110,000 miles. She was not that big, 45ft. long over all, but she was an able sea-boat, kind on her gear and kind on her crew – that is, she did not throw them about. The loss of a man overboard on one unlucky voyage had nothing to do with the boat. All those visits were in search of mountains, and since mountains are the better for being glaciated, the regions visited were either in the Arctic or in moderately high southern latitudes. There is no need to go far south in the southern hemisphere to find glaciers at sea-level. South Georgia, for instance, where the Nordenskjöld Glacier is lapped by the sea, is in the latitude corresponding to that of Whitehaven in Cumberland. In 1966–67 *Mischief* was at the South Shetlands in Lat. 63° S. and in the following year she sank off Jan Mayen in Lat. 71° N. Thus she ranged widely and, had I not lost her, her range by now might have been still wider.

That 1966–67 voyage (described in *Mischief Goes South*) had been far from happy. The loss overboard early on of the one man upon whom I relied, desertions, bickering, more desertions, were a few of our troubles, besides those imposed by the weather in those latitudes. I might have called it a troublesome voyage had I not just been reading about what Hakluyt called 'The troublesome voyage of the right worshipful Sir John Hawkins', a voyage on which four out of six ships were lost together with several hundred men. Even allowing for the fact that in those days most voyages outside home waters were attended by manifold dangers, hardships, and sickness, this appears as a gross understatement. Trouble is evidently an elastic term and fortunately seafarers of today do not meet with anything that Hakluyt would have recognised as such. As Brer Tarrypin said to Brer Fox: 'Lor, Brer Fox, you don't know what trouble is. I'm de man what kin show you trouble.'

Nevertheless the constant unease, if no worse, experienced on that twelve-months' voyage came as something of a sickener; enough almost to make one foreswear long voyages and to take to week-end sailing. But owing to her size and the problem of finding crews, a boat like *Mischief* is really only suitable for long voyages, and I had no intention of exchanging her for a handier, modern yacht whose fittings alone would cost more than *Mischief* would fetch if sold. We had been together too long even to think of it. I could not have endured seeing her in other hands, however well those hands looked after her. Not that week-end sailing, the most that the great majority of yachtsmen can find time for, is to be slighted. It is better than no sailing at all and has the great merit that for so short a time much can be overlooked and much can be endured. What does misery matter if we are all miserable together, is all very well, but the period should be short.

Shortness, then, being desirable, the decision to confine future voyages to northern waters had to be taken. It was taken grudgingly. I should have liked at least one more Antarctic voyage, aimed again at Smith Island, the island where, on that last voyage, we had hoped to land and had instead merely looked at. But it would have been time wasted unless by some happy chance a crew of like minds with hearts that beat as one could have been got together; men, possibly, with an expedition background who would not lightly give up what they had undertaken to do. The Southern Ocean and points beyond have a strong fascination – empty seas, lonely, remote, uninhabited islands, and the romance of the sealers and whalers who sailed those unknown seas long before polar expeditions were thought of, sailing admittedly for gain but not ignobly since they staked their ships and their lives.

In penetrating to Arctic shores there may be less sense of achievement, yet there are strange and little visited coasts to be seen and mountains to be climbed. Even the ice-bound east coast of Greenland, or at least the mountains behind that coast, are now becoming well known to the climbing parties that go there every summer in increasing numbers. Since their time is limited they naturally fly there, thus avoiding the delays, difficulties, and dangers – in short, the fun – of reaching the coast by sea. For there is no doubt that this coast is not easily approached, especially by a small, unstrengthened vessel such as a yacht, since it is guarded for most of the summer by a wide belt of heavy ice. This ice consists of old polar floes, two to three years old, thick and hard as rock, mixed up with immense icebergs. The floes come from the polar basin and the bergs are calved off the great glaciers of North-east Greenland, the whole lot drifting down the coast in a 20-mile-wide belt with the East Greenland current.

Mischief had twice reached the east coast at Angmagssalik in Lat. 66° N., which is not very far north. On the first occasion she got nipped and in consequence some planks were started. In a small, unprotected vessel the prudent mariner obviously keeps clear of ice. I am normally prudent but on this occasion we were following in the wake of two much larger vessels, one a miniature ice-breaker, not exactly at their invitation but at least with their consent. It had seemed a safe bet and like many such bets it came unstuck. This was about the middle of July which is full early for that coast. The next year we were later and on 3 August had little difficulty in reaching Angmagssalik and fjords to the south. Ice conditions vary from year to year but it would be unwise to count on reaching the coast before the beginning of August. That is, of course, a serious drawback for it leaves only a short month for climbing or any other activity before having to start for home. By staying until the end of September there would be little or no risk of being frozen in. The snags are that it is becoming too cold for climbing and that October is not one of the better months for a small boat in the North Atlantic. The real answer is to winter there. Danes who live in Greenland – mostly in houses with central heating – speak with enthusiasm of the winters, the clear atmosphere, cloudless skies, the beauty and purity of the frozen landscape. I have thought of wintering there, *Mischief* frozen-in in some snug anchorage, a foot or two of snow on deck to keep her warm, while the Northern Lights flickered overhead. That would be something like a voyage, always provided the ship's company were of the same opinion.

Two voyages had been made to Angmagssalik and fjords south, and it had been my belief that anywhere north of that there would be too much ice to make an attempt worthwhile. A publication of the US Hydrographic Office supported this belief:

East Greenland has much more pack-ice than West Greenland and no ship should attempt to navigate in the waters of the former unless it is specially designed. The East Greenland ice is usually broken and rafted into innumerable heavy floes of various sizes with a thickness often 20 to 30 feet, it is too great to cut with the prow of a ship. The ice-belt is traversed by seeking out the leads of open water; thus the course is tortuous, the ship twisting, turning, and worming its way between the floes and fields. A high premium is placed in short turning circles and the manoeuvrability of vessels such as the Norwegian sealer type. Experienced navigators, on meeting the ice-edge off North-east Greenland, are said to insist on clear weather and a steady barometer before attempting passage to the coast. The same holds true on departing from the coast, because after September, owing to the liability of gales, tightening of the ice, and nipping, navigation of the pack becomes risky.

The remarks of the *Admiralty Pilot* are more encouraging:

Throughout the period December to June inclusive the ice along the entire length of the coast is wholly impenetrable. With the advance of summer, the pack becomes lighter and more open along the southern part of the coast, particularly from the region of Scoresby Sound southward. In an average year, the ice in this region is mainly navigable by ordinary vessels in August to October inclusive.

When, therefore, a Danish friend wrote to me actually suggesting Scoresby Sound I began to revise my ideas. He wrote in glowing terms, such terms as would fire the most sluggish imagination: 'A most beautiful place, the largest fjord in the world, with two big mountainous unexplored islands, Milneland and Redland.' He also put me in touch with a Captain Toft, a Danish skipper with long experience of Greenland waters gained in small survey vessels, built to withstand heavy ice. He, too, lent encouragement, and thought that in normal ice-years by August a small boat might reach Scoresby Sound. It is in Lat. 70° N. some 300 miles up the coast from Angmagssalik. The Sound, by the way, was named after his father by William Scoresby who in 1822 surveyed and charted 400 miles of the east coast. Besides being one of the most successful whaling captains sailing out of Whitby, he was an explorer and a Fellow of the Royal Society. Having made his first voyage with his father at the age of eleven, after twenty-five years at sea he went to Cambridge, took a degree, and entered the Church. He was with his father in the whaling ship *Resolution* in 1806 when she reached Lat. 81° 30′ N., then the furthest north yet attained. Sailor, explorer, scientist, scholar, parson – this kind of man is not found nowadays.

By leaving at the end of June and going direct one should arrive off the Sound at about the right time early in August. It would be a pity, however, to lose the whole of June, a pleasant month to be at sea, when the crew might enjoy some real yachting weather, the sort of weather that would do little to inure them to the rigours ahead but would at least afford some compensation. Moreover, with time in hand, we could call at the Faeroes, Iceland, and Jan Mayen. This island is in Lat. 71° N. and only 300 miles east of Scoresby Sound, thus making a convenient kicking-off place; and from the Norwegian weather station on the island we might learn something of the ice conditions off the Greenland coast. More than that, there is a big mountain on Jan Mayen – Beerenberg (7,677ft. high). It is an old volcano and therefore not very interesting from a climbing point of view. On the other hand, though lacking in steepness and technical problems, it is all ice from sea to summit and the weather at that height could well be atrocious.

As plans go, this promised to be one of my better ones, a voyage full of interest aimed at two major targets, so that if one were missed we could always say we had been aiming at the other. The boat was ready, there remained only the trifling matter of finding a willing crew. 'Live in hope, if you die in despair,' is the Australian opal-gouger's motto, a motto, that I, too, have adopted after some recent disappointments over crews. *Mischief*, a Bristol Channel pilot cutter built at Cardiff in 1906, seemed to be feeling her years less than her owner. Indeed, provided the man or men who then had her looked after her as well as I had done, I expected her to be still happily sailing the seas while I was twanging my harp. After her last 20,000-mile voyage to the Antarctic she had needed little in the way of repair, but the two mainsails we carried had both seen long service and were worn out. I had been obliged to order a new one and even in 1968, before prices had really begun to get out of hand, this cost an appalling sum, something over £300. When I grumbled about this to the sailmakers they asked me how many miles I had had out of the old sails. It worked out at about 1d a mile, and with the cost of jib, staysail, and genoa thrown in, still came to less than 2d. Wind costs nothing, so the sailmakers, proud of the lasting quality of their work, thought I was getting my transport cheap. I might have reminded them that over the years, to keep them going, the sails had had a lot of amateur stitching and patching.

Charles Marriott, who had made three voyages in *Mischief*, now decided to make a fourth. He would not wish to be introduced to readers again since he has figured so often before in these annals. Enough to say that he was a retired Army officer, younger than I, who lived alone in a cottage in Cornwall adjacent to the sea cliffs where they climb, being himself primarily interested in climbing but equally at home on the sea. It would be a kindness, I thought, to ask him, and his coming could do me great service. Twice before he had successfully taken on the irksome job of cook. He would not claim to be a chef, no modern Soyer, inventor of stoves and sauces, the self-styled gastronomic regenerator of the Reform Club, but Charles had a cast-iron stomach, a prime necessity for sea-cooks, especially in *Mischief*'s galley which is forward of the mast where the motion is most felt. But to my regret, he elected for this voyage to work on deck, having had enough cooking, and I had to agree. He was not really fit and his eyesight, which had been exceptionally good, had suffered as a result of some obscure incident in a Spanish port on one of those several voyages in boats other than *Mischief* that Charles had embarked on and failed to complete.

Simon Beckett and Kenneth Winterschladen (a Yorkshireman, by the way) both aged twenty-four and likeable young men, hunted in couples. They had blown into Bodowen one winter evening on the way home from some rough-shoot in Wales. They had heard of *Mischief* at the Agricultural College, Cirencester, where they had met young Stephen Pitt who had sailed with me on the Bylot Island, Baffin Bay voyage. Kenneth professed to cook and volunteered his services as such. 'When they bring you a heifer be ready with the rope,' as Sancho Panza advised. Men with no sea experience whatsoever will volunteer as deckhands, feeling no doubt that they can learn as they go along, whereas in the galley that process would be neither possible nor acceptable. Simon knew a bit about sailing and I was glad to take them both and so complete the crew. The fourth man, whom I had already secured, was experienced in sailing and worked in a shipyard as a shipwright. I regarded him as my key member and within three weeks of sailing, provisionally fixed for the end of May, he cried off, having been offered a better job in another yard.

A friend came to the rescue by putting me in touch with Ian Duckworth, a young man who had served in the Marines and was then waiting to go to a university. He had achieved some eminence as a rugby player and was also a rock-climber so that he promised to be a welcome addition. Thus the crew, collected in this haphazard way, was complete. Except for Charles, whom I had asked in the mistaken belief that he would be content in the galley, choice hardly came into it. The only times I have had to exercise my fallible judgement were when I had advertised for crew, and provided enough offer themselves of their own accord one is reluctant to resort to advertising. I may be wrong but I like to think that many more would come forward if they knew what was afoot. Of dedicated amateur sailors such as members of yacht clubs, I have had hardly any, presumably because they either have their own boat or a friend with whom they usually crew. On the other hand at various times I have had three professionals, officers from the Merchant Navy sailing for a change in an amateur capacity, who sought a closer knowledge of the sea and its moods than can be got from the bridge of a liner or a great tanker. They enjoyed, too, the contrast of proceeding at a leisurely 5 knots instead of 20 knots with no time schedules to be kept or tides to be caught.

Expecting to sail on 31 May, the crew assembled ten days beforehand. The crew, that is, less Charles who ran true to form by not showing up until two hours before sailing. While busy fitting-out, young Simon managed to strike a jarring note by asking whether I intended carrying a life-raft. The argument that since *Mischief* had been sailing for fourteen years without a life-raft there was no call to carry one on her next voyage, would probably not be accepted as sound. That rigid opponent of change, the Duke of Cambridge, held that there is a time for all things, even for change, and that time comes when change can no longer be resisted. As the Duke himself would have done, I told Simon that I did not propose investing in a life-raft. Besides the cost, somewhere about £120 then, the carrying of one seemed to betray a lack of confidence in *Mischief* or in me, and too much readiness to quit the ship if she got into difficulties. The decision cast a damp over the crew, but not for long. Simon had a brother in the marine store business through whom he could get a life-raft on loan. Would I mind? This removed one objection. I had not suggested it but thought that if the crew felt strongly about it they could attain peace of mind by subscribing among themselves. The life-raft duly arrived and a home was found for it by the cockpit. Strangely enough, at the sight of this white blister installed on *Mischief*'s deck my mind filled with foreboding.

A delay of an hour or so prevented us from getting away on the top of the tide. Since Lymington is blessed by having two high waters this did not matter and the ebb would still be running to carry us through the Needles Channel. We had shipped a new anthracite-burning cabin-heater and had to wait for its chimney to be fitted. We might as well have gone without, the stove never burnt properly and in Iceland anthracite proved to be unobtainable. Hoping to make things easy for the raw crew I put the jib in stops before hoisting, that is to say the sail is rolled up lengthwise along the luff and the roll secured with light ties, so that when hoisted a pull on the sheet breaks the ties and the sail is set. Evidently we overdid the ties most of which refused to break. The sail was not in its first youth and by pulling ever harder to break it out we tore the sail which had then to be got in and another set. So much for making things easy.

With a contrary wind we beat out through the Needles Channel without hitting any of the numerous buoys, a mishap that I have known to happen with a strong ebb running and a novice at the tiller. Outside the wind died so we went over to Swanage bay to anchor, to avoid being swept back when the flood started to make. While there, we repaired the torn jib. The great thing is to have made a start even if our start had been something less than dashing. The cares of the land fall away, all the worries of fitting-out are over, and for the next four months there will be no bills to pay, no newspapers to read. Though we were not yet a thousand miles from the nearest land where, according to Conrad, the true peace of God begins, we were on the way.

CHAPTER TWO

To Iceland

EXCEPT FOR Charles, whom I have never known to be sea-sick, the sea next day took its toll of the crew. Ken battled on manfully in the galley and was first to recover. With a raw crew one must accept the probability that the boat will be shorthanded for most of the way down Channel, that there will be a lot of shipping around, the land not far enough away, and possibly contrary winds. By keeping the boat under easy sail we managed well enough. I even found time to start taking sights, for after eight months ashore one cannot be too quick about beginning again. The tangles that first resulted made me wonder how on earth we should find the Faeroes, or even Iceland which is quite a large island. In the Channel, by closing the land, the lost navigator can generally learn where he is, though in thick weather it would be a mistake to make too free with the shore.

Bound up or down Channel, we have on occasion taken seven days and once only two days. So we were not doing so badly when on the fourth day we rounded Land's End and set a course for the Tuskar Rock. We had our minor worries. The barrel of the bottle screw on one of the starboard shrouds dropped off and with the usual perversity of inanimate objects found its way overboard. Happily we were on the port tack at the time and we had a spare. The mould that at this early stage attacked our stock of hard-baked bread was more serious. This is thickly sliced bread rebaked that, when so treated, usually lasts for the outward passage. This had not been rebaked enough, consequently we had to start on the 'Lifeboat' biscuits normally held in reserve. Baking at sea for five men on a Primus stove is not really on. There is first the difficulty of finding a warm place where the dough can rise; and then the limited oven space that would permit of only one loaf at a time, a loaf that would vanish at one meal. The cook would be at it all day and every day, and the consumption of paraffin would be frightening. If I may be permitted a toot on my own trumpet, I, who consider myself a master-baker, would not undertake it and would not guarantee the results. In one of the present writer's Himalayan books there is a picture of the 'Master-baker' looking ineffably smug, standing by an ice-axe stuck in the ground on which is balanced one of his masterpieces. Making bread in the Himalaya, or at least on the approach to the Himalaya, where there is a hot enough sun to raise the dough and any amount of fuel, is child's play compared with making it on a Primus stove in a boat. I make the bread at home but as I am the only one who eats it the task is not onerous.

With bread and iron one can get to China, as the French Revolutionary

637

commissars (who had no intention of trying) liked to tell their ill-fed and ill-equipped troops. We were merely going to the Faeroes and had plenty of biscuit. Having passed the Tuskar and later the Arklow lightship we soon had in sight the Isle of Man and Scotland. The expensive new mainsail set beautifully and we now had it down to haul out once more the head and the foot. If this stretching is not done with a new sail the leach goes slack and may remain slack, flapping incessantly, wearing out itself and the patience of the crew. They were by now beginning to know their way about, how things should be done and what should not be done, such as, for example, reading a book or even trying to play chess when on watch. Normally we keep single watches so that the man at the helm is in sole charge of the deck and responsible for the ship's welfare. He has not only to watch his steering but keeps an eye on the gear, the sails, any other ships, the sea, the sky, and anything else of interest. If this is done conscientiously there should be no question of boredom or any need for its relief by reading a book. Nevertheless it is not uncommon nowadays for yachts that are not going to be sailed single-handed to be fitted with self-steering gear so that the crew can avoid the tedium of having to steer. One presumes there is still someone on watch even if he is not steering. I should have thought that those who can only get away to sea for brief periods would be only too happy to steer, to feel a boat under their hands, and be jealous of time so spent.

On the evening of 9 June we were off the Maidens north of Belfast when, as had happened before, the wind died and the tide turned against us. To avoid losing ground we anchored in Glenarn Bay, a few miles south of Red Bay, the anchorage we generally used. Without waiting to be piped to 'Bathe and Skylark' the hands bathed and rightly complained of the cold. North of Rathlin Island, which we passed next afternoon, there are numerous overfalls marked on the chart as 'dangerous in unsettled weather'. One could well believe it. With the weather extremely settled, the sea glassy and no wind at all, these overfalls were boiling away, showing like white water breaking on a roof. On a lovely, still summer evening, disturbed only by the fog signal from Rathlin Island, we drifted along the south coast of Islay, until at midnight, the tide in our favour and under a full moon, we shot through the Sound of Islay at 5 knots. This welcome spurt was but brief. Anti-cyclonic weather, haze and light airs, persisted as we slowly worked our way north through the Minches. Had we been able to see anything, the mountains of Skye for choice, it would have been pleasant enough. Too pleasant, really, because the crew were not yet fully seasoned, as they realised when at last we had cleared the Butt of Lewis and met some wind and sea. All were unwell again except, of course, Charles. Sula Sgeir is a rocky, uninhabited island about 35 miles north of the Butt of Lewis. We passed close by it at mid-day of the 15th, going fast under reefed main and small jib. That night, with supper reduced to soup and cold bully, one realised that speed and comfort are seldom compatible.

Approaching the Faeroes from the south on an earlier voyage we had run into trouble when we found ourselves in a fierce adverse current and a confused sea some 5 miles south of Syderø, the southernmost island. On that occasion we had been nominally making for Thorshavn on the east side of the

Faeroes but our plans were sufficiently elastic to allow us to turn sail and make for another harbour on the west side. There are altogether eighteen islands spread over some 60 miles of sea. Harbours abound, most of them 'summer harbours' and a few classed as 'winter harbours' reputedly safe in all weather conditions. On this voyage we had some obligation to make Thorshavn, the capital, as I had promised to meet my Danish correspondent Captain Toft who would be there in his survey vessel *Ole Roemer*. Thorshavn is on the east side of Strømø, the largest and most important island. Owing to cloudy weather we had had no sights for latitude and only a snap sight or two for longitude so we steered to keep well to the east of the islands. When on the morning of the 17th we began closing the land the wind faded away and we soon found ourselves being swept by a swift-running current into the well-named Dimon Fjord between Syderø and Sandø. We identified our position by luckily sighting the two unmistakable islands of Lille Dimon and Store Dimon which one would naturally, and probably wrongly, translate as Small Imp and Big Imp. The Small Imp looks like a haystack and they are both over 1,200ft. high. Such heights are not remarkable in the Faeroes where, especially on the northern and western islands, there are even greater cliffs, the home of innumerable sea-birds. By running the engine flat out we at last got clear of Dimon Fjord and we kept the engine going in order to catch the north-going tide that would take us into Nolsø Fjord, the approach to Thorshavn. Fog then came down in earnest, reducing visibility to less than 500 yards. All was not lost for we soon heard the foghorn from the lighthouse at the south end of Nolsø Fjord, at first ahead, then abeam, and finally drawing aft. A wraith-like steamer passed us, we caught a momentary glimpse of a mysterious ketch towing a dinghy, and then we almost ran down a lone man in a dory shooting guillemot. It is no disgrace to ask, at least not in thick fog, so we hailed him and were told to stand on until we heard the nautophone on Thorshavn pierhead.

Having passed the pierhead, vaguely visible in the fog, we made a tour of the small harbour looking for some resting place other than the wharves used by fishing and commercial vessels. At length we made fast to an untenanted buoy, having first to launch the dinghy, the buoy having no ring. All formalities were waived by both harbour-master and Customs from whom I learnt that *Ole Roemer* was out but would be back in two days. We had a bath and supper at the Sailors' Home – no bar, no beer. Moored close to *Mischief* was a beautiful ketch named *Westward Ho*, built at Hull in 1880, and now maintained in tip-top order by the community as a show-piece. She has no engine and had recently sailed to Copenhagen. The Faeroes, by the way, belong to Denmark but have their own flag and a modified form of home rule. The flag is easily confused with the Icelandic flag and I once committed a *faux-pas* by entering Reykjavik flying the wrong courtesy flag. I gathered that *Westward Ho* made the Denmark voyage every summer to show her off and possibly to raise funds for her upkeep. Like most, though not necessarily all islanders, the Faeroese have the sea in their blood. Fishing is their main standby. In the harbours of West Greenland one meets Faeroe-Island boats of about the size that we would deem suitable for inshore fishing. The crew of three, augmented when hand-lining on the Greenland banks by two Greenlanders, bunk in a fo'c'sle the size of *Mischief*'s peak where the sails are stowed, and their galley resembles a small wardrobe lashed on deck amidships. If you want to see what's cooking you open the wardrobe door and go down on your hands and knees, for the little gas-ring is at deck level.

It is a mistake to think that as one goes north, morals, like the climate, become more severe. The day after our arrival we had two bottles of rum and a bottle of gin stolen in broad daylight by some youths who boarded the boat from a dinghy while Charles watched unsuspectingly from the shore. Since the Faeroes are theoretically 'dry' hard liquor ranks as liquid gold. The police professed interest, even though they knew the lads concerned, and left it at that. Too much should not be expected in Thorshavn. When the shutter of a new camera of mine went haywire I found there was as much chance of having it repaired as there would have been in Barmouth. Rather than having the camera rust and grow fungus at sea, I posted it home.

Ole Roemer having arrived, I had a talk with Captain Toft and we agreed to meet again for a longer yarn and perhaps a convivial evening at Vestmanhavn on 21 June. *Ole Roemer*, which I would translate – certainly wrongly this time – as 'Old Roamer', was a small, powerful double-ender built for working through ice, with some 18-inch thickness of hull sheathed with greenheart and steel plating. She is used by the Royal Geodetic Survey of Denmark. After completing some work at the Faeroes she was proceeding to Scoresby Sound.

When Charles slept ashore at some hotel I was both surprised and relieved to see him back. There was always the chance of his adopting his familiar role of tourist. Once in South America he had been away from the boat for a month 'seeing the country', and at Reykjavik he had embarked on a bus tour along with fifty other like-minded or misguided tourists. He has an insatiable thirst for sight-seeing, merely for his own satisfaction, with no view, such as some of us have, of inflicting his more or less hard-won knowledge on innocent readers.

On the 21st, with a near-gale at north and the glass still falling, we should have stayed where we were had I not engaged to meet Captain Toft at Vestmanhavn. I believed that with a northerly wind we should find a good lee under Strømø once we had turned the corner at its southern end. Not a bit of it. We sped down Nolsø Fjord in thirty minutes with the wind right under our tail but on turning west into Hestø Fjord between Strømø and Hestø Island, met the wind head on. We might have known. No matter what direction the wind outside may be, in a fjord it blows up or down, usually in the opposite direction to which one wants to go. Even in the sheltered waters of the fjord, a strong wind against an equally strong tide raised a nasty sea against which we could make little or no headway. With the engine going we were no better off, for the propeller spent half its time out of the water.

On an earlier occasion, similarly bound for Vestmanhavn, we had been in trouble hereabouts. But then we were west-ward of all the islands on a black, wet night with a gale blowing; and although we had got as far as Vestmanna Sund leading to Vestmanhavn, the strong tide in the Sund proved too much. We had turned tail and sought refuge in the small harbour of Midvaag – precisely what we were now obliged to do for the second time. What puzzles me about the Faeroes is that although the rise and fall of the tide is slight – at Thorshavn about 3ft. – yet the tidal currents round the islands and in the fjords are extremely strong.

We reached Midvaag that afternoon and, whether or not they remembered *Mischief*'s earlier visit, the people were as friendly as before. The crew of a fishing boat lying next to us at the jetty gave us fish and the harbour-master, a Mr Thomson, arranged to take Charles and me for a drive – an irresistible offer to Charles and one from which, out of politeness, I could not escape. Motoring on Vaago Island is simplified by the fact that there is only one road and that on it there are no competing cars. There may have been another car on Vaago but it was not out that day. The road winds below treeless grass hills past a big lake, Sorvaags Wand, a remarkable lake in that instead of a river outlet it spills abruptly into the sea over a natural weir nearly 150ft. high. After a brief stop at the infrequently used airfield built, like the road, by British troops during the last war, we went on to Sorvaag, a small fishing harbour at the end of the road. Over coffee there we learnt once again that the chief import to Vaago consisted of sheep's heads from Aberdeen. We had been told this in 1964 and found it hard to believe, seeing that the sheep on the island, all with heads, far outnumber the population.

Back at Midvaag, we at once cast off to continue the passage to Vestmanhavn where I hoped we might still find *Ole Roemer*. At the entrance to Vestmanna Sund there is a great, gaunt cliff called Stakken and beside it a detached pinnacle over 1,000ft. high looking like a gigantic Napes Needle. It is called the Troll's Finger. While intent on tracing an imaginary route up this challenging rock spire we sailed almost close enough to be within that hypothetical biscuit's toss. The fjord favoured us with the customary head wind so that we had to motor most of the way to Vestmanhavn where there was no sign of *Old Roemer*. We therefore continued through the fjord to the open sea where we found a big swell running and no wind at all. We spent an uneasy night.

As this is the last mention of *Ole Roemer* and Captain Toft, I might insert here part of a letter from him showing how he fared. It confirms the wide extent of the ice that year and shows that even professionals have crew troubles. The 'Storis' he mentions is the Danish name for the East Greenland pack-ice. It means large ice:

We had a lot of trouble with ice during our trip to Scoresby Sound. We met the Storis already a few hours after we had passed Langanes in Iceland, and we only got out of it just before our arrival at Scoresby Sound. We did not get through the Storis without being damaged. The port rail smashed in and the rudder stock twisted about 5 degrees. That was the material damage. The crew could hardly face it, which made the last part of the voyage a bit difficult. The sailing in Scoresby Sound was easy. Fine weather and sunshine nearly every day. The trip home went well without trouble from ice.

After a night's tossing about, only Charles and I could face breakfast, but soon the swell subsided and a fine north-easterly beeze sped us on our way. A sprinkling of snow at the north end of Strømø, where the hills rise to over 2,000ft., reminded us that we were getting north. The sea temperature remained at 50° F. and the air 46° F. I had picked on Akureyri, a port midway along the north coast of Iceland, as the place at which to refresh before going on to Jan Mayen. This involved the rounding of the Langanes Peninsula at the north-eastern extremity of Iceland about which the *Arctic Pilot* has some discouraging remarks:

The neighbourhood has a deservedly bad reputation on account of the frequent fog and strong tidal streams and currents, and the unreliability of the magnetic compass in the vicinity, all of which have contributed to the loss of many vessels. Moreover additional dangers and difficulties may be caused by the presence of polar ice, and finally, Langanesröst, a heavy race, may extend far out to sea even in calm weather.

Of these manifold perils we might, I thought, safely discount the ice. At the end of June, though it might still be off Horn at the north-west corner of Iceland, it would hardly extend so far east as Langanes. In the light of Captain Toft's letter this optimism was ill-founded; he gave no dates in his letter but he was probably there a week or so before we were.

On 25 June we experienced a sudden drop in the sea temperature from 48° F. to 39° F. and on the following day we sighted land some 25 miles to the south-west. Intent as we were on giving Langanes and its dangers a wide berth, a strong westerly set seemed equally intent on pushing us into the land. Langanes, when first sighted, bore north-west but by the afternoon of the same day we were well inside it with no hope of weathering it on that tack. We were reluctantly steering south-east on the other tack when an Icelandic Fishery Protection vessel bore down on us. Our consciences were clear, we had not even a line out over the stern, for I have long abandoned hope of catching fish near the surface in northern waters. On the next tack we must have had everything in our favour. We passed close under the dreaded promontory without let or hindrance, the weather remaining bright, the compass behaving as usual, and even Langanesröst seemingly asleep. It is a drab looking peninsula running out to the north-east for some 6 miles, high and perfectly flat with yellow-red cliffs dropping to the sea. There is a lighthouse at the extremity which we rounded less than a quarter-mile off on 28 June. One of the numerous small boats fishing in the vicinity came near enough for the crew to throw nine large cod on to our deck.

Langanes in Lat. 66° 23′ N. is only 7 miles short of the Arctic Circle. On rounding it we steered north for more than this magical 7 miles in order to clear the next cape. It seemed strange to cross the Arctic Circle under twin staysails, a rig that I always associate with trade winds and tropic seas; but there we were bowling along under the twins on a cold, brilliantly fine day with snow mountains ranging all along our port hand. We were passed first by a cargo vessel and then by three sea-going swans, while high overhead the geese were flying north. That night the sun remained just above the horizon so that even at 1 am, we had no difficulty in making out the entrance to Akureyri Fjord.

CHAPTER THREE

To Jan Mayen

AKUREYRI LIES 30 miles inland at the head of a fjord properly called Eyjaffjordhur. The *Pilot* refers to the fjord as 'the most populous and most frequented inlet on the north coast, and is one of the places where the herring fishery is of considerable and increasing importance.' Written in 1949, this hardly holds good today. Herrings are no more set in their ways than restless mankind and they have now almost completely deserted the north and east coasts of Iceland. The several herring-oil factories dotted along the fjord lie idle.

The fjord is wide and we tacked up it, hoping to astonish the natives by working in under sail. As we drew near the town that evening the wind failed and we turned on the engine. How often does one write those words – always with a slight feeling of guilt, that it is not quite playing the game; and how comparatively easy does the action itself make life at sea – no drifting about in fog off Thorshavn at the mercy of strong currents, wondering which bit of the coast you are going to hit; no drifting helplessly off Akureyri in the rain wondering when the bars close.

At Akureyri, apart from the commercial wharf, there is a so-called main harbour with a narrow entrance that looked small even by our standards. So we finally anchored in 4 fathoms off what looked like the Town Hall to make enquiries. By now rain fell heavily, but it was a Sunday evening and the rain had by no means stopped the rush to the coast which, just as in England, was in full swing. The road ran along the sea-front and the sight of a strange boat from England anchored nearby soon caused a traffic jam as one by one drivers stopped to look. Rowing ashore and climbing up the sea-wall on to the road I accosted the slightly astonished driver of the nearest car. Fittingly enough he happened to be a Customs officer who, in spite of being off duty, took me to his office, gave us clearance, and recommended our moving into the main harbour. We lay there in perfect peace, disturbed only by an occasional lorry and the dust it raised from the untarred dock road.

In the evening we entertained the harbour-master who brought us our mail. After lamenting the disappearance of the herring and its consequences for Akureyri, he told us that only a fortnight before the fjord had been half-filled with ice. We had indeed noticed one or two small floes aground on the shores of the fjord. Despite the wet day, he told us that they were having the finest summer that northern Iceland had enjoyed for many years; in fact the same held good for Norway (as we found later) and the western half of the British Isles. Herring or no herring, Akureyri seemed to be thriving, motor cars thick on the ground and new houses and roads being built. It is in a favoured region for sheep and dairy farming, and the three hotels testified to an increasing tourist industry.

Though the resultant heat had been slight we had already burnt our anthracite and wished to buy more. No one in Akureyri used the stuff but we could have a bag sent up from Reykjavik 150 miles away for £10. Feeling like Stanley Holloway's Yorkshire Noah who declined paying three halfpence a foot for the bird's-eye maple needed to panel the Ark's saloon, saying he would 'rather be drowned than done', I decided to do without. The crew, young and presumably hardy, ought not to mind, while Charles and I, old and frail, would have to buy more sweaters. Meantime Charles, taking advantage of the blazing hot weather that had now returned, almost persuading him to buy dark glasses and a sun helmet, adopted his tourist role and departed by

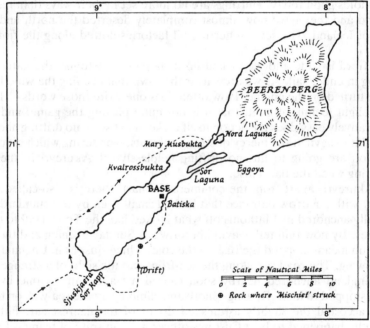

Jan Mayen

bus for Mytvan Lake. This picturesque lake, dotted with volcanic islands and alive with water-fowl, is a great tourist attraction. I learnt later that he had slept out by the lake, either to commune with the water-fowl or, more likely, since he has a frugal mind, to avoid paying for a bed. Anyhow he returned from Mytvan with a painful arm, diagnosed by a doctor as arthritis, and asked me to delay sailing until he was satisfied he would be all right.

The three youngsters decided to go for an all-night walk to climb a peak about 10 miles away. The neighbouring mountains run up to about 5,000ft. and still had on them a lot of winter snow. It is not likely to be permanent snow. Less ambitious, I started alone at the more reasonable hour of 8 am for a peak about 5 miles away. The technical problems were all at the start, finding a way through the surrounding farms without getting into trouble by climbing their wire fences. On the wrong side of the valley there was a good road leading to the Ski Hotel and its ski lifts high up on the opposing slopes. On a hot, flawless day I had the satisfaction of treading the more or less eternal snows, and reaching the top at mid-day, spent an hour there basking in the sun. A fatiguing climb but not altogether unrewarding. It encouraged me to think that with the aid of a half-way camp I might yet reach the top of mighty Beerenberg.

Before I left for my excursion the other three had got back from theirs and naturally retired to bed rather the worse for wear. They were still there when I got back at tea-time, so a little unfeelingly I routed them out and set them to cleaning up below and sorting out a bag of potatoes which was smelling to high heaven. At sea such routine duties are done as a matter of course and it is a bad sign when a crew have to be told to do them. In harbour there is a tendency of some crews to regard the boat as a hotel which they can leave in the morning to go about their affairs and return to at night, trusting that the hotel porter – that is the skipper – will have done whatever needs doing.

The Hull trawler *Portia* came in under tow for engine repairs. Only after she had gone did we learn that the trawler that towed her in had on board a large stock of anthracite. I had a talk with *Portia*'s skipper who invited us to take our meals on board. Reputedly she had the best cook sailing out of Hull, as we could well believe when we had our first meal in the crew's mess. Before the break-down she had been fishing off Horn at the north-west corner of Iceland with a lot of ice in sight. There was evidently more than the normal amount of ice about for the time of year and *Portia*'s skipper did not think much of our chances of reaching Jan Mayen. He felt his own luck was out. They had almost completed their catch just before the engines broke down and the whole had to be sold in Akureyri for what it would fetch as fish-meal. Apparently her engines were something special and the fault in them baffled both her own and the local experts. An electrician familiar with them had to be flown out from England with the necessary part in his pocket or in a suitcase and within an hour of his arrival *Portia* went out for a trial run. On the next day she sailed for the fishing grounds and a fresh start.

Our restaurant having, so to speak, closed, it was time for us to go, and after waiting yet another day on his account, Charles at last agreed to start. We were not really pressed for time and I felt that the delay and the hot weather combined could not fail to improve our chances with the ice. So we sailed on 7 July and this time began tacking *down* the fjord. Rather than spend the night thus occupied, allowing no one any sleep, we stopped at a place called Hjalteyri where we secured to the jetty of a herring-oil factory. It appeared not to have been in use for several years. A crowd of youngsters had watched us come in and without a word the crew went off with them to the nearby village, two arriving back at 3 am and young Simon, our Don Juan, at breakfast time.

We reached the open sea that morning, passing the stern trawler *Pricella* from Fleetwood at the fjord entrance. Twenty miles from the coast is Grimsey, a small, grass-covered, inhabited island which we failed to see, leaving it well to windward. Another island, Kolbeinsey, uninhabited, lies 36 miles north-west of Grimsey beyond which there is nothing until one reaches Jan Mayen some 300 miles north of Iceland.

So light was the wind on the following day that we had the genoa set. Some ominous fog banks lay on the horizon ahead and by nightfall we were in the thick of one listening apprehensively to the beat of an approaching engine. We had a glimpse of the vague outline of a small fishing boat before it vanished in the fog, but then the noise, instead of receding seemed to draw near again. Once more the boat appeared out of the fog and this time came in close while a man shouted across to warn us of ice 5 miles to the north-east. This was a seamanlike act and we thanked them warmly for the unwelcome news. By ten o'clock we could hear the distant growl of pack-ice and shortly after sighted an outlying floe. Sea and air temperatures were both 35°F. So close to the ice, the fact that the sea temperature was no lower seemed to indicate that this was a detached field of no great extent. Soon we had floes on either hand and hastily handed the genoa to reduce speed, having all our work cut out dodging floes and steering a course that would have made an eel dizzy. As the ice persisted I altered our general course to east and finally south-east. We began to draw clear and soon after midnight had passed the last straggling floe.

By morning we were out of the fog-bank and enjoyed a fine sail all the day, reeling off 10 miles every watch. A noon sight put us at 67° 25' N., 17° 50' W. I spent the next two days in bed with a bad go of 'flu and since there was practically no wind we could heave to without any sense of time wasted. I hoped that the 'flu had been picked up at Akureyri and had nothing to do with our living in an unheated cabin. Weakening at the last moment I had invested in a bag of coke, cheap enough but more productive of fumes than heat. Usually at sea, since we are not racing, we try to avoid disturbed nights by making no unessential sail changes. On the night that has stuck in my memory on account of disturbance there was barely enough wind to justify our keeping the sails up. Having come off watch at midnight I looked forward to six unbroken hours sleep. The first two hours passed quickly enough as I listened to the sails slamming, until at the change of watch I went up to help set the genoa, hoping that would get her moving. Half-way through his watch at 3 am Charles came down to whisper some tidings, thinking apparently that by whispering he could impart what he had to say without waking me. I never discovered what the good news was, probably some weather secret. An hour later I got up to open the skylight, feeling that we were being poisoned by the stove. At last at 4.30 am I slept and dreamt, dreamt so vividly that I had cut a finger that I woke at 5.30 to stop the bleeding. By then my six hours unbroken sleep were nearly up and it was time to get into oil-skins to go on deck for a rest.

In these waters, properly known as the Greenland Sea, cloudy weather and fog are a serious hindrance to navigation, that is unless one had these new-fangled aids such as radio direction-finders. Ideas of what is needed to find one's way at sea have changed. Slocum's ideas about this, set down in 1900, show the extent of the change: 'The want of a chronometer for the voyage was all that now worried me. In our new-fangled notions of navigation it is supposed that a mariner cannot find his way without one; and I had myself drifted into this way of thinking.' As we know, Slocum solved this worry by the purchase of a tin clock for a dollar.

July and August are the cloudiest months and the average number of fog days in summer is ten a month, but ships have been held up sometimes for days or even weeks off Jan Mayen. We were therefore lucky to get a sight on the morning of the 15th and another at noon just before the fog closed down. I reckoned we were then about 10 miles to the south-east of South Cape. The chart agents had informed me, wrongly I think that there is no Admiralty chart of Jan Mayen. The only chart I could find on which it figured in any detail was one where the 30-mile long island occupied little more than one inch. The long axis of the island runs from south-west to north-east, the middle of the island being barely 2 miles wide. Almost the whole of the north-eastern half is filled by Beerenberg's massive bulk. The *Arctic Pilot* records how in the seventeenth century the island acquired a confusing variety of names:

In the early part of the seventeenth century the island was always being discovered and renamed. Hudson first saw it in 1607 and named it Hudson's Touches. According to Scoresby the whalers of Hull discovered it about 1611 and named it Trinity Island. The Dutch tradition was that Jan Cornelisz May discovered it in 1611; but this is a mistake, J.Cz. May of 1611 having been confused with J. Jz. May of 1614, and the name Janmayshoek given to one of the capes, having been transferred to the island in the form of Jan Mayen. Jean Vrolicq, the Biscay whaler, claimed to have discovered it in 1612 and named it Isle de Richelieu. Finally in 1615, Fotherby, the English captain, discovered it again and named it Sir Thomas Smith's Island. In the great days of the whale fishery, the Dutch called it Mauritius Island. In the early part of the seventeenth century the island was in undisputed possession of the Dutch, whose occupation extended into the eighteenth century, when it died out. After a long interval, during which the island was almost forgotten, Norwegian sovereignty was proclaimed as from May 8th, 1929.

Normally the island is ice-free from early July until the winter but the variations are considerable and 1968 was a bad year for ice. Yet on our near approach to the island and the first sighting of its adjacent rocks we met no ice at all. We were making for the west coast where, according to my inadequate chart, the Norwegian weather station was to be found, and were on a course that should have taken us some 5 miles south of South Cape. On the evening of the 18th, in fog, at about a cable's distance, we suddenly sighted and counted seven rocky islets, the highest about 100ft. high, with white water breaking close off them to the south-west. These were Sjuskjaera rocks lying about a mile off South-west Cape, which is itself about a mile west of our South Cape. Evidently my sights had not been all that accurate or we had experienced a strong northerly set. Still it was a great satisfaction to have seen something, to know that the island was there, and not to be left in the same doubt as the poet:

> Beyond the clouds, beyond the waves that roar,
> There may indeed, or may not be a shore.

Lord Dufferin describes, or even over-describes in his *Letters from High Latitudes* a far more dramatic landfall when in 1856 his schooner *Foam* was off Jan Mayen in mid-July amid quantities of ice. His main reason for visiting the island was an intense longing to see the great Beerenberg and he tells how the vision was at last vouchsafed him:

Up to this time we had seen nothing of the island, yet I knew we must be within a few miles of it and now, there descended upon us a thicker fog than I should have thought the atmosphere capable of sustaining; it seemed to hang in solid festoons from the masts and spars. To say that you could not see your hand ceased almost to be any longer figurative; even the ice was hid. . . . Thus hour after hour passed and brought no change, while I remained pacing up and down the deck, anxiously questioning each quarter of the grey canopy that enveloped us. At last, about four in the morning, I fancied some change was going to take place; the heavy wreaths of vapour seemed to be imperceptibly separating, and in a few minutes more the solid grey suddenly split asunder, and I beheld through the gap – thousands of feet overhead, as if suspended in the crystal sky – a cone of illuminated snow. You can imagine my delight. It was really that of an anchorite catching a glimpse of the seventh heaven. There at last was the long-sought-for mountain actually tumbling down upon our heads.

Actually, of course, the mountain did not tumble down, and shortly afterwards Lord Dufferin landed on the east coast, leaving a ship's figurehead as a memorial, and departed for Norway. One wonders whether this figurehead has ever been found.

Sheering hastily away from these savage looking rocks we left them at a safe distance before we turned northwards following a coastline that we had yet to see. Next morning in better visibility we closed the coast and sailed slowly along it about a mile off. We were on the look-out for some land-mark that we could identify, Fugleberget for example, described in the *Pilot* as 'an enormous, prominent and perpendicular rock 551ft. high, the jagged outline of which resembles the broken battlements of a ruined castle. . . . Thousands of birds of many species make a deafening uproar with their cries.' Striking features abounded and we were still arguing about two possible headlands, whether or not they were crowned with broken battlements, when Ken drew our attention to some radio masts which in our search for ruined castles we had overlooked. Turning in we anchored in 4 fathoms a cable off the beach of a wide bay. This bay, Mary Musbukta, is sheltered from south and east but wide open to west and north. There are no identations on Jan Mayen deep enough to afford all round shelter; if caught by a gale from the wrong direction one would have to clear out and endeavour to reach the lee side of the island. South-easterly gales are supposedly more frequent than gales from north-west, so that the west side of the island is the better bet, particularly so since, unlike the east side, it is free from outlying dangers.

There was no sign of life; the extensive hutments clustered near the radio masts seemed deserted. On landing we found them in a poor state of repair, snowdrifts half filling some of the rooms; evidently they had not been occupied for several years. A large dump of coal did not seem to be needed so we collected a bagful to see if it would suit the stove. The *Pilot*'s location of the station did not tally with this; it was said to be half a mile inland at the south end of Nordlaguna, a freshwater lake. We could see the lake but no sign of anything at the southern end. We were 200 or 300ft. above the sea and, looking seawards, could see a line of ice some 4 miles to the north extending far out to the west. On the beach and on the shore of the lake, which must once have been open to the sea, were masses of driftwood, big logs. These are said to come from Siberia.

Had we but stayed in Mary Musbukta and set about reconnoitring a way up Beerenberg, ignoring the Norwegians, all might have been well. Sooner or later the Norwegians would have discovered us for themselves. Instead, I thought the first thing to do was to make contact with them. Accordingly that afternoon I set out alone to search for the weather station, leaving the others to look after the boat. Charles had retired to bed, as he had been doing off and on since leaving Iceland, so that I could not afford to be long away. Having drawn blank by the lake I crossed a ridge of black gravel and lava in the direction of the east coast. The ridge was the backbone of the island at its narrowest part. On his island Robinson Crusoe was dumb-founded by a footmark. On top of this ridge on Jan Mayen I was equally puzzled by a mechanical digger, sitting forlorn and deserted by the trench that it had dug.

The trench led upwards into the mist but I followed the tracks of the digger downwards and soon came upon a hut; no one was there but it was apparently used judging by four bunks with sleeping bags, skis, and ski sticks. A well-worn track led westwards to the lake. I followed this and found several more huts, all deserted. Back at the first hut I decided to back-track the mechanical digger, to follow the spoor of the monster to its lair, and although the spoor was not fresh one did not need to be a bushman to puzzle it out. Pursuer rather than pursued, I became engrossed in the chase, wondering where it would lead and what I should find.

The tracks led down a steep, sandy escarpment to a vast expanse of beach extending north, south and seawards. A dense but quite shallow fog lay over the beach; from the escarpment I had looked out over it to the sea beyond. The spoor led south but I had now detected a faint distant rumble like the noise of tracked vehicles – tanks, perhaps – out towards the sea. I walked and walked, and still saw nothing. Was it surf making the noise, or possibly ice? No. Presently over the top of the mist I spotted the cab of some vehicle moving south. The whole scene, the sand, the mist, the noise, and a vague reek of exhausts, took me back to the Western Desert. Putting on a spurt – not easy in climbing boots and soft sand – I still looked like being left behind. The truck stopped and then started again coming my way – a Weasel with a crew of six bearded men.

None of them had a word of English so to cut matters short I climbed on board and no one tried to throw me off. Except that I had no beard they must have thought that I had been forgotten and left behind, possibly under a stone, by some Jan Mayen expedition of many years ago. With the tide coming in we began ploughing through the sea until we reached dry land where a jeep and a truck with more men were waiting. I was transferred to the jeep which set off southwards at what seemed a neck-or-nothing race against time, first along the beach, then by a newly-made road, past a landing strip with landing lights on its seaward side, past a large building (the weather station), to arrive at the main base, a huge place, lounge, mess, dormitories, workshops, stores, radio masts, scanners. It dawned on me at last that there was more to Jan Mayen than a weather station. The shadow of the Cold War had fallen upon it.

We were only just in time for the big meal of the day and I could now see why the jeep had almost burst itself. My presence took a lot of explaining to the Commandant as we sat down, fifty strong, to rissoles and assorted trimmings, followed by great slices of cream cake. Not everyone's idea of a balanced diet but after my long walk I had no complaints. The Commandant expressed concern on our account about ice and wanted us to move round to the small bay by the base where they landed their supplies – or maybe he felt he should keep an eye on us. He had already enquired about passports. He told me that a naval vessel expected in had been turned back by ice, so that there was evidently ice about on the east side.

After supper we had a look at the bay, Batiska, which did not seem to me at all inviting, being half-filled with ice floes. Since we were there uninvited, without even giving notice, I thought it polite and prudent to comply, and undertook to move round in a couple of days by which time the ice might have moved out. It was a fateful decision. Having lent me a very good map of the island, of far more value than our chart, the Commandant drove me by a tarred road back across the island to Kvalrossbukta, a small bay 3 miles south of where *Mischief* lay. We had missed it on our way up the coast, though the two large oil storage tanks should have easily been spotted. A pipeline follows the road from the tanks to the base. There was also a hut with a radio-telephone of which the Commandant gave me the key; he wanted us to spend the night there as he thought it safer than where we were. At the top of the ridge I left the jeep and walked back to the boat. We parted on good terms. Had all gone well we should have spent a most agreeable time at Jan Mayen, possibly climbing Beerenberg into the bargain. A party from the base had made the ascent and the Commandant promised assistance, advice as to the route and help in carrying our gear to the foot of the mountain.

Dense fog forced us to stay where we were that night; indeed, having made a tentative start we had difficulty in groping our way back. Dense though the fog was, it could hardly have been so thick on the foredeck as to prevent the proper reeving of the anchor chain over its roller when we re-anchored. In the morning we had to break the anchor out by sailing her off and winch the cable in when under way. This had happened once before in a small harbour at Montevideo where there was no room to sail the anchor out. We had had to haul the whole 45 fathoms of chain out of the locker, drop it overside, and pass the bitter end back through the fair-lead over its roller.

The wind died and we drifted slowly northwards. But for the ice that we had observed to the north we could have gone north about round the island with the possibility – if fog allowed – of seeing Beerenberg from all sides. In the event we did have a wonderful view when the next morning dawned cloudless and clear. We were not far away and the whole mass of the mountain shone dazzling white from sea to summit. Its great bulk is more impressive than its height, for it measures some 30 miles round at the base, allowing ample space for numerous separate glaciers. It is very like a smaller version of Big Ben on Heard Island which is also a volcano. After being long dormant it erupted again this year (1970) and the following extract is from a report obtained from the Scott Polar Research Institute:

On September 19th–20th the Beerenberg volcano on Jan Mayen Island became re-activated after being dormant for several hundred years, perhaps thousands of years. Reports by whalers at sea of activity on the southern slope of the volcano in 1732 and 1818 have been subject to doubt. But steam and carbon dioxide occur in fractures, and earthquakes are common.

The present eruption was preceded for one or two days by earthquakes with epicentres which were, however, some distance to the north-east. On the morning of September 20th smoke and steam rose to 30,000 feet from the north-east flank of the volcano, apparently coming from a 5–6 km. long fracture with five main parasitic crater centres. Geologists from the Norsk Polar Institutt were rushed to the island and are observing the activity from land, sea, and air. After two days, explosive activity decreased, but a great amount of basaltic lava continues to emerge and cascade down the slope to build up a new coastal platform at least 500 metres wide and 3.5 km. long. Because most of the volcano is covered by glaciers, a great deal of melt water has caused floods that have formed deltas.

The upheaval and melting of glaciers must have been a tremendous sight. On a voyage to Iceland in *Mischief* we once watched the eruption and formation of a volcanic island where the successive explosions under the sea and the uprush of steam, smoke, and ash to a great height were sufficiently awe-inspiring.

CHAPTER FOUR

The Loss of *Mischief*

IN A FLAT calm we started motoring south until a wind sprang up from dead ahead. As we tacked down the coast the brilliance of the morning faded. Beerenberg's shining splendour was dimmed and finally extinguished and soon we were enveloped in the familiar wet fog. Upon making our final board to the east which I judged would lead well clear of Sjuskjaera, we again sighted those seven rocky fangs close aboard. Unable to weather them we went about and on the next tack cleared the rocks but had the breakers off South Cape too close for comfort. The wind failed and left us drifting, the breakers and some ice-floes close on the port hand. So we handed the sails, motored due east for half an hour, and lay to for the night, the fog still thick.

All this was the immediate prelude to a disaster for which I must take the blame: primarily for not getting far enough away from the coast, a coast off which there were outlying rocks and towards which the northerly set we had already experienced would certainly set us. I had the watch from midnight and in view of the fact that we were not moving or so I supposed, did not spend the whole time on deck but came up at frequent intervals. Ian had the next watch and like a fool I told him that he need not be on deck all the time but to come up frequently. Stupid enough orders! How frequent is frequently? Admittedly it was perishing cold and clammy on deck and one tries to make things as easy as possible for the crew, but there is only one place for the man on watch however safe the conditions may seem. Lying to a mile from a rocky shore in fog, visibility some 200 yards, we were by no means safe. Nevertheless what followed need not have done. Ian must have interpreted my imprecise orders liberally. Had he been on deck any time after three o'clock he must surely have heard or seen something to rouse concern. At 3.30 am I woke to a horrible crash and it hardly needed Ian's hurried dash below to tell me we had hit a rock. On reaching the deck the first thing I saw was a rock pinnacle looming above us – I could almost have touched it with a boathook – and *Mischief* was aground on its plinth bumping heavily in the slight swell. I had lost no time in reaching the deck but the panic-stricken Ian had been even quicker to pull the cord of the life-raft without first launching it; and if that were not enough was even then hastily cutting the dinghy lashings. Had there been any rats on board they could not have been smarter about attempting to leave the ship. The great yellow balloon of the inflated life-raft now obstructed the starboard deck. Over the top of this I imparted to Ian a few first thoughts and told him to stop mucking about with the dinghy. The engine started at once and in a matter of minutes the boat slid off but not before the hull had taken some hard knocks.

She was making a lot of water but not more than the whale pump could handle if used briskly. The only plan seemed to be to beach the boat in the hope of being able to get at the damage. The bay we had been making for was not far off if we could find it, and I felt sure the Norwegians would give us all the help they could. The outlying rock on to which we had drifted, the only rock in the vicinity, lay about half a mile out from the shore; we must have drifted north some 3 miles at the rate of nearly half a knot. No land could be seen so we steered north-west to close it and the nearer we got the more infested with floes the water became until, when within a cable's length or less from the low rocky shore, we could scarcely find a way through. After some messing about I spotted the runway lights and knew we had overshot the bay. We turned back keeping as close inshore as possible in order not to miss it. In the clear water the rocky bottom showed close under our keel. The bay seemed to have even more ice in it than before, so we anchored off while I rowed ashore to give word of our plight. The Commandant agreed that ice or no ice it would be best to beach the boat there rather than at Kvalrossbukta where we would be too far away for them to give much help.

Threading our way between the floes we ran *Mischief* up on the little beach of black sand at the head of the bay. To my dismay we found that the rise and fall of the tide was a mere 3ft. meaning that unless she were hauled much further up we would not be able to get at the keel or even the planks above the keel, where most of the damage must be. Only the forefoot would be clear of the water. The beach shelved steeply, too, so that there would always be 2 or 3ft. of water round her stern, the boat drawing 7ft. 6ins. In order to haul her higher we began the heavy task of lightening her, removing the ballast, emptying the water tanks, and dropping the cable over the side.

We started on the ballast that afternoon and made little impression. Each pig, some weighing 100 lb., had to be hauled up the forehatch, carried across the deck, dumped over the side, and then carried up the beach above tide-mark. Had we left them by the boat they would have soon dug themselves into the sand just as *Mischief* herself proceeded to do. Lying on her side at low water, the floorboards out, she had become untenable. About 50 yards inland and high above the beach was a small wooden hut with four bunks which we now occupied, carrying up bedding, food, Primus stove, and cooking gear.

Work began in earnest next day. The Commandant arranged for one of his men, an engineer and an excellent chap who spoke good English, to give a hand. In the bay they had a big float which they used for landing stores and this was now beached alongside *Mischief*. We rigged a tackle for hauling the ballast up the hatch whence it could be swung across the deck, lowered on to the float and stacked there. Except for a few pigs that could not be reached we soon had about 4 tons out. Ian, a strong lad, now in an extremely morose mood, nevertheless did the hardest work down below, starting out the pigs and carrying them to the foot of the hatch. Charles was *hors de combat* but the other two worked with a will, Simon and I manning the tackle while Ken stacked them on the float.

On the next day a bulldozer did its best to haul the boat higher and gained but a few feet. I then rigged a stout line to the masthead by which the bulldozer could haul her down, careening fashion. We got her well over but perhaps I was too concerned about breaking the mast to heave down really hard. For I still had every hope of sailing to Iceland where she could have been hauled out on a slipway and made tight enough for the voyage home. Charles, I knew, would stand by the ship, while Ken and Simon, though apprehensive, were game to try. Ian had other ideas. The day we beached her he had arranged with the base for a passage to Norway in *Brandal*, a small sealing vessel chartered to bring stores and due about 2 August. Had he expressed any regret for what had happened, or sympathy, I might have felt sorry for him. The work on the ballast finished, he sat in the hut, a silent picture of gloom. The only words we exchanged were several days later when I asked him to fetch water and received a convincingly rude reply. Nor did he have much to say to the others, particularly Simon, with whom, as nominal owner of the life-raft, that incident rankled. As there was no CO_2 available for inflating it again the raft was of no use.

Life in the hut, therefore, could hardly have been more depressing. Charles had soon withdrawn to the base where he lay in bed in their sick-room having his meals brought to him. Visitors from the base, to whom we could at least offer a drink, sometimes dropped in in the evening to give us the news or to commiserate. As well as the staff there were four young students out for the summer on an archaeological expedition, searching for traces of the seven

Dutchmen who in 1633 were landed to observe through the winter the facilities for whale-fishing. They all died of scurvy, the last survivor, who died just before the return of the fishing fleet the following spring, having kept a diary recording their observations right up to the end. Having no worries other than the possible loss of a boat, it was with some shame that I found on coming to write this account that my brief diary of daily events had stopped the day after we landed.

When the engineer and I examined the port side we found no serious damage, no sprung or started planks, only a lot of spewed-out caulking, Underwater aft, where it could not be got at, a piece of the keel some 10ft. in length, and its iron shoe, had broken away. This in itself would not be a source of leaking but a keel bolt might have been moved or the garboard strake started. It was now too late to try to turn her round and haul out stern first, and what with the rudder, the shape of the heel, and the soft sand, it would have been hardly possible. Having covered the suspect parts with a huge tingle of tarred felt and copper we moved the bow round and hove her down on the opposite side. With the starboard side treated the same way I felt sure that the leaks had been reduced though by no means cured. When the tide was in she made far less water.

One of our most frequent visitors, a Mr Holvik, whom I called the Viking, was an enormously strong, red-bearded Norwegian, equally at home driving a giant bulldozer or painting a 200ft. high radio mast. He greatly admired *Mischief*, showing as much concern for her as I did. He propounded a plan to haul her right up out of reach of ice and winter gales on to solid ground near the hut, where in their spare time he could work on her. In the following summer I would return and together we would sail her back to Norway. Much as I admired the Viking – I could well imagine him in a longboat with Erik the Red – I doubted whether even he and his bulldozers could haul *Mischief* that far out. Between beach and hut the ground rose steeply and was the sort of sand that overflows into one's boots. With a cradle for the boat and skids or rollers I suppose it might have been done: the builders of Stonehenge, for example, would have thought nothing of it. One main snag was the attitude of the Commandant who discouraged the idea, rightly so from his point of view, for he foresaw, as I did, that the Viking's plan would inevitably mean borrowing from the base plant, material, and probably time.

Shortly after our arrival ice had moved in and completely filled the bay. Had this happened a day sooner there would have been no chance of beaching *Mischief* there. The ice helped in one way by completely damping down any swell; no waves, hardly a wavelet, broke on the beach. Having done what could be done we began preparations for refloating her. We put back the ballast, all but a ton which I decided to leave out thinking she would be that much easier to refloat. By the time that had been done most of the ice in the bay had gone out except for a line of heavy floes right inshore and probably aground, while outside the bay no ice could be seen. The fact that no waves had been breaking on the beach, owing to the presence of the ice, had lulled us into a false sense of security. Only my engineer friend realised that the boat might now be in peril and urged me to get her off quickly. At the moment though, an unbroken line of floes prevented this. As the result of most of the ice having gone waves now began to break on the beach. Either that night or the next – I had lost count of the days – we had some wind and when I went down to the beach in the morning I found about 5ft. of the bowsprit broken off lying in the water in a tangle of wire. The float had been shifted from alongside, but not far enough, and even the web of mooring warps we had laid out had not prevented the boat surging about and hitting the float with the bowsprit. We had reefed the bowsprit by hauling it inboard but not completely so.

Sailing to Iceland without a bowsprit would be slow work. Instead I arranged through the Commandant for *Brandal* to give us a tow to Norway. They agreed to this and also to bring out a small, portable motor pump to ensure our controlling the leak while on passage. By 27 July only the line of massive floes fringing the beach still prevented us from getting afloat and ever since the rest of the ice had gone out *Mischief* had been bumping on the sand. As well as doing her no good it distressed me to watch. Floating her off would mean living on board and keeping the pump going until *Brandal* arrived when, perhaps, the motor pump would give us a spell, but the engineer and I both thought we should try. By means of a wire led from the stern to a block slung from some nearby rocks and thence to a bulldozer we tried hauling her stern back into the water. After we had gained a few feet she stuck immovably, that much nearer to the floes through which, anyway, there seemed little hope of forcing a way.

Next day, a Sunday, the Commandant came down armed with dynamite sticks and detonators to see what could be done. A big floe threateningly close to *Mischief*'s rudder succumbed to this treatment, splitting into two after a few sticks of dynamite had exploded alongside. A bigger floe only a yard or so from the port side proved too tough and massive, and I feared that repeated explosions so close to the boat might harm her more than the ice. Having done what he could the Commandant departed.

Towards mid-day the wind blowing into the bay had increased to nearly a gale. The waves rolling in set the floes to rocking up and down and lurching forward, and *Mischief* began to bump even more heavily on the sand. The crew had for some days since lost interest but I rallied them for a last effort to shift her by means of a warp to the anchor winch and the engine. With the wind behind it the water was now deep enough under the stern for the propeller to bite. Their efforts lacked conviction. Ian in particular showing more concern for what would happen when she floated than for the consequences of letting her remain. I thought that with the water so high, a couple of bulldozers might do the trick, and that she might just squeeze through a gap by the big floe. With that in mind I ran to the base as fast as I could and found hardly a soul there, certainly no one with power to act. By the time I got back the big floe that had been close aboard, urged forward by the rising sea, had battered a hole in the hull just below the engine water intake, and started several of the adjacent planks. That evening, in despair, I wrote her off. She was one third full of water, so we took ashore anything of value below, books, charts, instruments.

The Viking came along next morning, refusing to admit that all was lost, more convinced than ever that his plan was the best, and determined to have a go at hauling her out whatever the Commandant might think. Clutching at straws I agreed and persuaded the crew to start taking out the ballast once more. The gale had pushed her higher up the beach and most of the water had drained out. Late that evening the Viking brought down a big bulldozer with which he succeeded in moving her about 2 yards. The soft sand and the steep ascent, where the real tug-of-war began, were still yards away. Even then at high tide she still lay among the breakers, the wind continued to blow, and the waves rolling in lifted and dropped her heavily on the sand. She was a heartbreaking sight.

The Viking's plan was tacitly abandoned. Either failure had subdued him or the Commandant had put his foot down. Instead, on 30 July, he came down to patch the fresh damage, the Commandant being equally bent on seeing *Mischief* safely away under tow. After a drive round the base stores to collect material, the Viking and I set to work to put on a tingle. But with another gale on 1 August the breakers tore off our rudder. This, I feared, might put paid to towing, but the skipper of *Brandal*, with whom the base was now in touch by radio telephone, reckoned they could still tow. *Brandal* arrived on 2 August according to schedule, having first fetched up well north of the island in spite of radio beacons, radar, and Loran. The same morning the sea tore off the big patch or tingle. Upon which the Viking and I together sought out the Commandant, hoping that after this last blow he might be persuaded to fall in with the Viking's plan. Obviously for success, the use of men, material, and machines would be required. They were very busy, a lot of work having to be done in what remained of the short summer season, as well as the routine work of the base. The Commandant was therefore right to refuse and to limit his assistance – already generous – to getting *Mischief* afloat and ready for towing. This proved to be no easy task.

Accordingly the Viking and I put on another patch. He had built a stage from which to work slung over the side, and with waves continually sweeping the stage it proved a wet job. The base had a big whaler with a powerful engine which they used for ferrying, and that evening I went out in her to *Brandal* anchored well outside the bay. The skipper spoke no English and seemed to me a little fuddled; the mate, young and confident, spoke very good English. At the suggestion of the Commandant they agreed to put on board *Mischief* an electric pump to be supplied with power by a cable from *Brandal*, to reinforce the little petrol-driven pump that they had brought which was already installed in our cockpit. I could not see this running more or less continuously for three of four days, nor were I or any of the crew capable of giving it the necessary nursing. I had to sign a guarantee against the loss of the electric pump, the implication being that *Mischief* was not expected to last the journey and that we might have to leave her in a hurry. The tow was to be on a 'no cure no pay' basis; I urged the mate to take it easy and he assured me that *Brandal* was no flyer. The Commandant did everything he could to ensure success and our safety, bespoke for us one of *Brandal*'s life-rafts and arranged for a walkie-talkie set and a field telephone as well to keep the two ships in touch.

Overnight we rove a 3-in. wire through the big block slung on the nearby rocks, and passed a 6-in. nylon warp twice round *Mischief*'s hull. At 7 am on 4 August, a fortnight to the day since we had first put her ashore in this ill-omened bay, the Norwegians rallied in force to get her off. Since we were not going to sail we had not attempted to restow the ballast – I doubt if the crew would have consented – but abandoned it on the beach. Light as she was, hauling her off took the united powers of two bulldozers, and the whaler pulling from seawards. Either she had dug herself in or the sand had piled her, because at first she refused to budge. So the bigger bulldozer, a real monster in the capable hands of the Viking, dropped its scoop into the sand and using the sand as a cushion advanced on *Mischief* to push her bodily sideways. Having so to speak broken her out they then harnessed the two bulldozers in tandem on to the wire, the whaler took the strain, and *Mischief* slid slowly into deep water. All the ice that had at first hindered us and that had been her undoing, had been swept away by the gales of the last few days. Simon and I were on board with the petrol pump going. It needed to be for she leaked like a basket.

Having secured to a long warp astern of *Brandal* we remained there tossing about in a moderately rough sea until late that afternoon. We found that we could just keep the water at bay by running the pump for five minutes and resting it for five minutes. Meantime the float made several trips out to *Brandal* and finally took off seven men from the base and the rest of our crew. The young archaeologists and my engineer friend were among those going home. Charles, whom I had not seen for the last few days, was to travel in *Brandal*, while Ken and Ian were to help in *Mischief*. Since we were to be in company, Ian had agreed to come. He had in fact reconsidered his earlier decision when we were still hoping to sail away, but only under certain rigid conditions. As with two unfriendly powers when relations have been severed, his ultimatum was handed to me by a third party. I still have the scrap of paper stating his terms:

1. There must be a transmitter on board.
2. Adequate life-saving gear including another life-raft.
3. A forty-eight hour trial run in the vicinity of Jan Mayen.
4. Direct return to England.

On the whole I thought that the chance of *Mischief*'s survival and the morale of the crew would be better without him on board.

After the float had made its last journey to *Brandal* it came alongside bringing Ken and Ian (who was promptly sea-sick), the mate and a sailor to make up the towing line, as well as their electric pump, a life-raft, and the walkie-talkie set and telephone. For the tow they used a nylon warp shackled to 10 fathoms of our anchor chain on which they hung three big tyres to act as a spring. The remaining 35 fathoms of our chain with the 1-cwt. anchor attached we led to the stern to drop over when the tow started. This served in place of a rudder to keep her from yawing about. The heavy electric cable, to supply current from *Brandal* to the pump, they had merely dropped loose in the sea. Its own weight imposed a heavy strain, no current ever passed, and immediately the tow began they told us it had broken. Had it been hitched to the towing line or to another line, as it could have been, *Mischief* might have survived. It meant that the little petrol pump must function for three days without fail and I did not think it would.

At 8 pm that evening the tow started. For the vicinity of Jan Mayen the conditions were good: no fog, no gale, and a moderate sea. An hour later Simon and I, who had been at it all day, went to lie down, leaving Ken and Ian to carry on pumping for the next four hours. With a lot of water sloshing about inside sleep was hardly possible; I brewed some tea and we made do with hard tack. I must have dozed because just before midnight Ken woke me to say the pump had given up; the motor ran but it was not pumping. The crew were ready enough to quit and I confess that the skipper and owner, with so much more at stake, had no longer the will to persevere, a fortnight of toil, trouble, and anxiety having worn me down. Communication with *Brandal* was not easy either with the walkie-talkie or the telephone but she had already got the message. She lay to about a cable away and we were told to bring off only our personal gear. In a final round-up in the dark cabin, already a third full of water, I dropped a note-case and all my remaining money. After scrabbling about vainly in the water for a few minutes I gave up and joined the others on deck where they had already launched the life-raft. Since *Mischief* was not insured this 'trifling sum of misery new added to the foot of the account' hardly counted. The premiums demanded for the sort of voyages *Mischief* undertook were always so high that it had never been worth while to insure her.

Thinking that water might ruin it, before leaving we hoisted the heavy electric pump up through the skylight, having quite a tussle. When the other three had stowed themselves in the life-raft I climbed over *Mischief*'s rail for the last time and joined them. Paddling over to *Brandal* we went on board while three of her crew took the raft back to salvage the two pumps. These met with scant ceremony. The electric pump, that we had so thoughtfully tried to keep dry, was thrown overboard on the end of a line and hauled through the sea to *Brandal*. She was soon under way while I remained on deck in the fading light watching *Mischief*, still floating defiantly, until she was out of sight.

As I have said, ice conditions in 1968 around Jan Mayen were bad. Apart from human failings ice had been the main cause of *Mischief*'s loss or that had certainly prevented her from being saved. For me it was the loss of more than a yacht. I felt like one who had first betrayed and then deserted a stricken friend; a friend with whom for the past fourteen years I had spent more time at sea than on land, and who, when not at sea, had seldom been out of my thoughts. Moreover, I could not but think that by my mistakes and by the failure of one of those who were there to serve her we had broken faith; that the disaster or sequence of disasters need not have happened; and that more might have been done to save her. I shall never forget her.

> The world was all before her, where to choose
> Her place of rest, and Providence her guide.

Part 2

First Voyage in *Sea Breeze*

Summer 1969

CHAPTER FIVE

Buying a Boat

ON THE fiNE sunny day that *Brandal* landed us at Bodo in northern Norway it was hard to believe that we were still well inside the Arctic Circle. Without ship or money, but otherwise in fair shape, I qualified as a semi-distressed British sailor. A journalist, who having already interviewed the crew had no ulterior motive, took me in hand and while conducting me round the sights of Bodo persuaded someone to cash a small sterling cheque. The same day a Norwegian Air Force officer, met casually in the street, did his best to get me a flight to Oslo in an Air Force plane. As there was nothing immediately available he failed to pull this off, but at his instigation I asked for and got from the civil air line a seat at half-price.

At Oslo the British Consul cashed another cheque and introduced me to the people in the Norwegian Ministry of Defence who were concerned with Jan Mayen, whom I had made the journey to Oslo to see. I wanted to tell them how much I appreciated the help given us at Jan Mayen and to find out what we owed them. All that copper we had used, for instance, and, far worse, that brand new 6-in. nylon warp that in the attempts to float *Mischief* had suffered such a mangling that it would, I feared, have to be written off. Another item was the food we had eaten and were still eating in *Brandal* which was then on her way down the coast with the rest of my crew. They were interested in the story and assured me that an account would be rendered. When this eventually came it was for quite a small sum on account of *Brandal*.

On the spectacular train journey from Oslo to Bergen I regretted that Charles was not with me to share this great tourist attraction. I quote:

The Bergen Railway is one of the engineering wonders of Europe; it is also one of the greatest scenic railways of the world. All the features which combine to make the

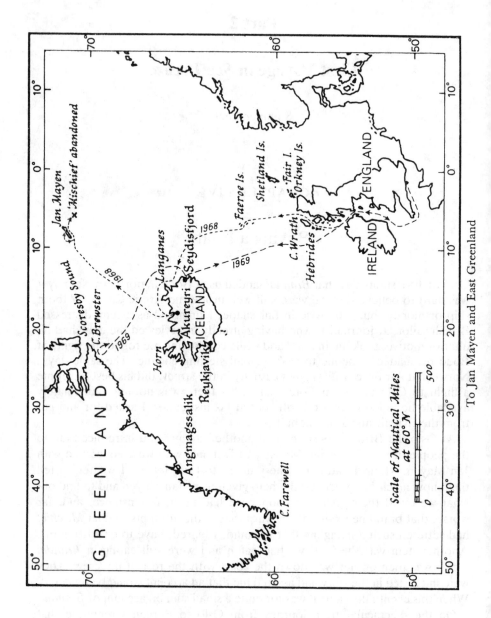

To Jan Mayen and East Greenland

scenery of Norway so alluring to visitors are unfolded along this line in panoramic succession.

How Charles would have enjoyed it. I could see him, for instance, risking his neck by leaning out of the carriage window when inside the Gravehalsen tunnel ('3 miles 514 yards and took 12 years to bore') to take those murky indecipherable photographs in which he specialises. He might even have insisted on leaving the train to visit 'the great Storskvalen glacier to which expeditions can be made.' Nevertheless, I admit the novelty of looking out upon glaciers from inside an over-crowded railway carriage, even if the glaciers were a little scruffy and obviously suffering from an exceptionally hot summer. At Bergen I boarded the Newcastle boat where, besides finding my late crew, I had the luck to meet a friend who had been climbing in Norway. Having his car with him and bound for Wales he thus solved for me the ticklish problem of reaching Barmouth from Newcastle by rail.

Although something of an addicted pipe-smoker I never find any difficulty in abstaining if no tobacco is available. In the absence of a boat there should have been an equal chance of giving up sailing. The craving, however, was still there and within a few days of returning home I found myself scanning the advertisements in the yachting papers and writing to various agencies. A big boat lying on the Clyde, magnificent in a photograph, almost tempted me to go north in spite of some natural apprehension about finding oneself alone and unsupported in a strange environment, surrounded by men reputedly dour and undoubtedly businesslike. Were it not even further from Barmouth than the south coast, much could be said for keeping a boat on the Clyde, thereby cutting out the English Channel and saving at least a week's sailing when setting out for or returning from northern waters. Having started on the downward path by beginning these enquiries, the pace naturally quickened. It became not merely a question of finding a boat, taking, too, the ample time that such a search really demanded, but of finding a boat that was ready or could be got ready for a voyage the following summer. No doubt, time's winged chariot hurrying near makes for haste.

The loss of *Mischief* had been fully reported in the Norwegian press but only one or two English papers had noticed it in a very brief paragraph. Few people could have known of it. I was therefore surprised when at Lymington, within a month of returning home, I got what seemed to be the answer to my hopes in the form of a telegram: 'Regret loss of *Mischief* can I offer you *Sea Breeze*. Oakeley.' On looking her up in *Lloyds Yacht Register* I found that *Sea Breeze* was a Bristol Channel pilot cutter belonging to Sir Atholl Oakeley. Built at Porthleven in 1899 she was certainly a bit long in the tooth, but no more so, in fact a year less, than her prospective owner. For that was how I already began to see myself; the fact that she was of the same breed as *Mischief* investing her immediately with all the qualities I desired. No wonder Barnum believed that a sucker is born every minute.

More to the purpose, she was lying at Hamble where she could be seen at once and, supposing she changed hands, could be brought to Lymington to be thoroughly overhauled during the winter and raring to go by the time summer arrived. Sucker or not, I did not for a moment suppose that a boat of that age would not need a lot of time and money spending on her before she was fit for a deep-sea voyage. Obviously a boat that is used for day sailing or for short hops across the Channel need not be so entirely seaworthy or so well-found as for an ocean voyage. If only for one's own peace of mind there must be no half-doubts about a boat's fitness for a particular purpose.

There and then I went over to Hamble where I found her lying in a mud berth. The boat was in commission but, the owner not being on board, I could not see below. Superficially she looked in good shape, smartly painted and fully rigged, topmast and all. She had deadeyes and lanyards for setting up the shrouds, eminently more in keeping with a boat of that type and vintage than *Mischief*'s rigging screws. The bobstay, too, the forestay and topmast forestay, were all set up with tackles instead of rigging screws. Certainly in keeping, but carrying things too far, I thought, unless one believes in having plenty of 'give' in the standing rigging. This idea of 'give' had apparently been scotched long ago by Dixon Kemp, an expert writing for Victorian yachtsmen:

It has been contended that a yacht's main rigging should be stretchable, because, if she were sailing in squalls, if the rigging did not give to some extent, it would be like attempting to drive a railway train by a succession of blows from a sledgehammer. In stating the case thus ludicrously the fact is entirely overlooked that a vessel's heeling facility affords much greater relief to such shocks than could the yielding property of any rigging, unless indeed the latter were so stretchable as to be perfectly useless as stays. The rigging cannot be set up too rigidly and the less it stretches the better. It was found that in very heavy weather with a ship rolling and pitching heavily, three-fourths of the ultimate strength of the mast and rigging might be tried at any one moment, and that a succession of such trials would inevitably end in disaster.

Compared with *Mischief*'s her cockpit was minute. A mate I had had on one voyage would have heartily approved. He had considered *Mischief*'s cockpit an open invitation to the ocean to come in and fill it, thereby sending the boat to the bottom. Needless to say, on only one occasion had the cockpit been filled to the brim, and then the water readily found its way below whence the pump soon restored it to its rightful place. This diminutive cockpit lay under the shadow almost of a great wooden tiller, the sort of thing John Davis might have had on *Mooneshine*, decorated with spirals running the entire length and culminating in a cunningly carved Turk's Head. I could see myself grasping this massive masterpiece, smiling with content. Striking a more modern note was a large hydraulic winch just forward of the mast that served both as anchor winch and for hoisting the mainsail by means of chain halyards. I believe this had been fitted by a previous owner addicted to single-handed sailing where obviously the main problem in a boat of this size would be that of hoisting the correspondingly large and heavy mainsail.

Other vital statistics for *Sea Breeze* are: overall length 49ft., waterline 43ft., beam 14ft. 3ins., draft 7ft. 5ins., sail area 2,100 square feet. She was fitted with a Kermath two-cylinder diesel engine. Thus she was 3ft. longer than *Mischief* and 1ft. wider, and their respective gross tonnages were 33 and 29 tons. When first built, I am told, she was several feet longer. Concerning this I have a letter from one who served in her when she was a working boat in 1911. Mr Tom England writes:

The *Sea Breeze* was built by Bowden of Porthleven to the order of Mr Morgan

Griffiths, a Newport pilot. Now Mr Griffiths was never a pilot to go too far to the westward and when he saw the *Sea Breeze* he said that she was too long and too big for him. So he gave the order for her to be shortened but of course her beam could not be altered so he had to accept her shorter in length but with the same beam. He was a person never satisfied and being fairly well off was able to satisfy himself in many ways; so he bought a smaller boat and sold the *Sea Breeze* to Mr Goldsworthy and in 1911 I was transferred to him to finish my apprenticeship. From my first trip in her I was happy. She was light on all her gear and never failed to stay in any kind of weather, even when she carried her forestay away and we worked her for a week with just the mainsail and jib. With the foresheet and jib sheets half drawn and four rolls in the mainsail she would sail herself and make good headway, and she was very comfortable when one was down below. When she was hove-to with the sheets to windward and the helm hard down she made very little leeway. She was not so good as some cutters when beating to windward but when reaching and running before the wind she was great. I would never wish to be in any other craft whilst she was about.

A fine tribute to a fine old boat.

A week or so later I went down again to meet Sir Atholl Oakeley and to be shown over his boat. One could not help comparing her with *Mischief*, the only boat of any size that I have ever owned and accordingly my standard model – the only one I have – for judging what a boat ought to be like. Well, perhaps, not quite. She had some faults. The siting of the galley, for instance, forward of the mast where the motion is most felt, whereas in *Sea Breeze* the galley was well placed between the saloon and the cockpit. In *Mischief*, by having the bunks on two tiers, one on top of another, the whole crew were accommodated in the main cabin or saloon, making for mateyness or un-pleasantness as the case might be. *Sea Breeze* had only two bunks in the saloon, two more amidships and forward, while the owner had a cabin to himself with a double bunk, a bunk that, like the proverbial goose, was too big for one and not big enough for two. There were even doors, but these, I reflected, could be easily demolished; for the inside of a boat should be like a church where you can see from one end to the other, the few necessary bulkheads having openings but no doors. The galley had a gas stove and when Lady Oakeley brewed tea for us one realised how painless gas could be compared with the routine of priming and lighting a paraffin stove. On the other hand no one wants to be unexpectedly blown up, and on a long voyage there would be the necessity of carrying a battery of cylinders on deck. True, we had done this without any trouble in *Patanela* on the Heard Island voyage, but she was a bigger boat with high, solid steel bulwarks instead of light wire guard-rails. However, as yet there was no need for me to contemplate throwing the gas stove overboard, for the boat still belonged to Sir Atholl; but since I had not seen anything to put me off completely we discussed terms, the upshot being that I would buy the boat subject to survey. To carry that out the best place would be at Lymington where the Berthon Boatyard had a slip available for hauling her out. Impatient to know the worst or the best, I had imagined that the owner and I would cast off there and then, or at least when the tide served, to motor round to Lymington. I found there were several objections to this, the principal being that the boat would not be afloat until the next spring tide. In the end I had to arrange for the boat to be towed round and met with another snag. For some odd reason the act of towing needed covering by extra insurance. On the face of it a boat under tow with presumably someone steering and an anchor ready to drop would be at no more risk than a boat under its own power.

The tow took place safely, she was slipped on arrival, and a surveyor friend of mine began work on 25 September. I took care to be there. Like *Mischief* and other pilot cutters there was an awful lot of boat below water so that on the slip she looked huge. The men in the yard, who from force of habit kept on alluding to her as *Mischief*, thought I had found a worthy successor. As a surveyor taps and probes his way round a boat there is no call for him, even in the presence of a prospective owner, to conceal his emotions as a doctor must when tapping and probing his patient. On the first day nothing much amiss came to light, but as the survey progressed John Tew's face lengthened until it was as long as the list of defects that he ultimately drew up.

An estimate of what it would cost to have these put right proved to be formidable. Nor would that be the end. Estimates never are the end, especially with a boat, because while the work progresses more faults are inevitably exposed. A survey is bound to be more or less superficial. Short of having the boat pulled to pieces, and in the event of 'no sale' incurring the expense of putting it together again, one cannot expect the surveyor to discover all possible defects. Particularly is this so in old boats like *Sea Breeze* that have had a number of owners altering and re-altering, where there are nooks and crannies that only an agile caterpillar could crawl into, and John Tew was no caterpillar. The massive construction, too, of an old boat may serve to conceal defects, though at the same time it means that a beam or a frame has to be pretty rotten before it becomes dangerously weak. In *Sea Breeze*, for instance, John Tew found a soft spot in the stem that he warned me might prove extensive when gouged out and correspondingly expensive to put right. Altogether he advised strongly against buying the boat.

Once before I had flown in John Tew's face, or at least in the face of his advice. It had cost me a lot and I had not regretted it, for I had thereby given *Mischief* a new lease of life and we had enjoyed many more voyages together despite her having been 'condemned'. On this occasion a repetition of such obstinacy would be going to cost a lot more and I finally decided to take his advice. I had to make up my mind quickly. The boat was now occupying a slipway that the yard wanted to use, it being the end of the season with boats waiting to be hauled out. Either John Tew's bore-holes and other minor havoc must be made good for the boat to be returned to the Hamble, or if the work was to be done, the mast must be taken out and the boat hauled up again under cover. So I telephoned Sir Atholl to tell him that in view of what it would cost to have the boat made really seaworthy I could not buy her. Having expressed surprise that so much needed to be done, and made some observations about both the surveyor and the Berthon Boatyard, he finally suggested a substantial reduction in the purchase price. With some misgivings I agreed and *Sea Breeze* had changed hands.

It would be tedious to list all that had to be done. Apart from refastening the hull throughout, which meant burning her off to the bare wood, the major jobs were the removing and replacing of the covering boards, the sheer strake and the extra thick plank below the sheer strake, as well as 32 bulwark stanchions and the frame heads with them. The ballast had to come out and when out was an astonishing sight, worth anyone's while to come and see. Some of the pieces were so large, weighing 2 or 3 cwt., and so shaped as to fit the hull, that it almost looked as if the boat had been built round the ballast. There would be no taking of that out by the crew. Twice *Mischief*'s ballast had had to be got out by the crew, once in the Patagonian channels and again at Jan Mayen. For the kind of ballast that *Sea Breeze* had, a crew of professional weight-lifters would have hardly sufficed. In the Berthon yard they got it out easily enough by removing the bottom planks and dropping it through the hole. One would like to know how it had first been put in at Porthleven in 1899 – possibly before the deck was lain – and I did not see anyone in Lymington in 1968 capable of putting it back. It did not go back. It was sold as scrap, to the considerable dismay of the chap who was sent to fetch it. In view of what had happened twice in *Mischief* and might happen again, we put in lighter pigs that could be handled.

Just as John Tew had feared, the rot in the stem had gone far. It proved to be a very difficult job and the cement inside and behind the lower part of the stem made it no easier. As the soft wood was gouged out and the hole grew bigger and bigger, a colony of Wharf beetles were discovered. They are a sort of marine hippy squatter and there was some apprehension that having been dislodged from *Sea Breeze* they might take up residence in *Sceptre*, the America's Cup boat, lying in the same shed. Unless she had some rot in her, which seemed improbable, there was nothing to fear as the following authoritative account of Wharf beetles shows:

Wharf beetle (*Nacerde melanure*), as its popular name implies, is associated with timber on the water-front, the reason being that such timber, unless of a resistant species or pressure-treated with preservative, is liable to decay, and forms yet another instance of the close relation between beetle damage and rot. The beetle is soft bodied, a quarter to half an inch long, with a narrow reddish brown body, the tips of the wing-covers darkening to black, the antennae long. The larva is slender, from ½in. to 1½in. long, dirty white, with a yellow head wider than the body, and having behind it on the dorsal surface of the first segment a protruding hump. There are three pronounced pairs of legs. Infestation is not confined to wooden marine works but is found inland in unpreserved soft wood culverts and like places where the wood alternates between wet and drier conditions.

Webster's Dictionary adds to the above description:

Somewhat like Longhorn beetles. The adults are strikingly coloured and frequent flowers. The larvae feed on decaying wood.

CHAPTER SIX

A False Start

WHILE *Sea Breeze* underwent renovation and rejuvenation I had to make a plan for the following summer's voyage and to find a crew. There is no record of the boat's history since the time she ceased to be a working boat. She must have changed owners frequently but I have no reason to believe that she had ever sailed outside home waters. It is never too late to start. All waters come alike to pilot cutters and there would certainly be no need to break her in gently by limiting our first season together to a series of trial runs in the frequented waters of the British Isles. A trial run might as well be a real trial and what better place for that than the North Atlantic and the Greenland Sea?

Obviously a return match with Jan Mayen had its attraction, but apart from thus tempting Providence rather blatantly I doubted whether we should be altogether welcome having so recently made a nuisance of ourselves. No such objection applied to Scoresby Sound which was still no more than a name to me and which could be reached without going anywhere near Jan Mayen. We could call again at the Faeroes and Iceland, preferably at some port other than Akureyri so as to provide a little variety. Thus it would be all new ground, Scoresby Sound excitingly new, and if we failed to reach it on account of ice we could retreat south to Angmagssalik to at least make sure of landing somewhere in Greenland.

Starting all over again with a new boat meant that I was faced with an uphill task, and on top of that was the finding of a crew without any nucleus round which to build. Living, while at home, in a remote part like a hermit, albeit in a pretty comfortable cell and not underfed, I have no large circle of friends and acquaintances through whom to put out feelers; while diffidence, or idleness, makes me unwilling to write and canvass possible sources such as universities, youth organisations, or even yacht clubs. Sitting back and waiting for sea-going enthusiasts to write to me has the dubious merit of sparing me the trouble of having to choose. The number who write are seldom more than the number required; should they happen to be less I have to bestir myself. The critical might well say that the man gets the crews he deserves.

Quite early that winter a letter came from Mike Brocklebank who had heard rumours of *Sea Breeze* and wished to volunteer his services. He showed he was serious by adding that since leave of absence would not be forthcoming he would have to give notice in good time. His job was to teach mechanical engineering at a secondary school: he was interested in boats, sailing, rock climbing, and had spent two years in the Corps of Signals.

Teaching is not necessarily the same thing as doing but I felt that he would be well able to look after a small diesel engine. To me our Kermath diesel engine was a bit of an unknown quantity; so far it had lurked behind the companion-way ladder untroubled and unquestioned by John Tew, by me, or by anyone else. I met Mike at Chester and accepted him as the first recruit. He was thirty-two, single, strong, and enthusiastic.

One thing leads to another, as they say. A colleague of Mike's who taught woodwork at the same school now wanted to come too. I seemed to be off to a flying start – two tradesmen volunteers almost before I could look round. Again I went to Chester, a convenient half-way point, to meet Ralph Furness. Except that we met in the car-park instead of in a pub I felt like that Lieutenant Ayscough recruiting naval seamen in 1770 whose recruiting poster invited 'All true-blue British Hearts of Oak to repair to the Roundabout Tavern, Wapping, where he would be damn'd happy to shake hands with any old shipmates or their jolly Friends in general – Keep it up, my Boys – Twenty may play as well as one.' And in very small print below this warm invitation: 'For the encouragement of Discovering seamen, that they may be impressed, a reward of Two pounds will be given. ...' Ralph, though rather stout for a young man – a fault that a voyage in *Sea Breeze* would correct – seemed otherwise fit and a suitable candidate. My own woodworking talent extends little further than what in Africa we used to call bush-carpentry. In *Sea Breeze* a lot of new fittings would be needed below and Ralph would be the man to do them. He came from the Isle of Man and had messed about in boats.

My next recruit, whom I got through a mutual friend, was as old again as these two and of a very different occupation, being a retired bank manager. As such he inspired confidence at first sight, as all bank managers should, though in the case of Brian Potter it was not so much that he would not rob the till as that in no circumstances would he let a man down. He was big and burly and had kept himself fit by climbing, ski-ing, and canoeing. He had not the slightest experience of sailing or of small boats, yet I felt that my friend Lieutenant Ayscough at the Roundabout Tavern would have given two pounds for him on the nod. He offered to come as cook despite the fact that his cooking experience was little greater, extending no further than camp cooking, the sort that is done on a mountain or on the way to the mountains. Nor would his banking experience stand him in good stead at sea, but he had one valuable asset having been for many years an amateur cabinet-maker.

To meet him I had to make a wide deviation from the rhumb-line course from Barmouth to High Wycombe where Brian lived. It proved to be well worthwhile for I saw there his workshop and the furniture he had made – most of that in the house – and I came away thinking that carpenter Ralph would have little to do beyond handing tools to the maestro. From sales and junk-yards he collected Victorian pieces such as gigantic mahogany wardrobes which he would take to pieces and use in the making of reproductions of antique cabinets, tables, chairs. Brian, a married man with small grandchildren, had always allowed himself freedom to roam. Mrs Potter encouraged these numerous excursions abroad, or at least allowed him to decide whether all or any of these journeys were really necessary. As she told me, in the course of their lives she had on several occasions given Brian advice or directions that, having been reluctantly taken, had invariably turned out wrong. As Sancho Panza said, 'A wife's council is bad, but he who does not take it is mad.'

Finally, from information received, as the police say, I wrote to John Murray, an instructor (more teaching) at an adventure centre; the information coming, by the way, from Mike Brocklebank who did not know John but knew of him. After an exchange of letters John proved keen to come and we met at Lymington. The necessary leave of four months had been readily obtained, as indeed it ought to have been from a place devoted to fostering the spirit of adventure. He appeared neat, almost dapper, an appearance that struck with more stunning force as being in contrast with my own. He looked fit and agile, evidently a useful man aloft, as indeed he proved. We met on board *Sea Breeze* in the early spring when she was not looking her best, looking rather like a building site with the builders on strike. Even so she inspired confidence and John liked the look of her. As well as being a climber he knew a lot about boats and had sailed in most varieties with the exception of gaff-rigged boats. Thus it seemed to me I had a crew of all the talents; like the ministry of that name which, if I remember history rightly, had a short life.

Since we were not going to Jan Mayen and it would be of no avail arriving off Scoresby Sound until the end of July at the earliest, I decided to sail about mid-June. There was still a great deal of work to be done that the crew could do, far more, of course, than would have been called for in *Mischief*. The crew therefore assembled at the beginning of June, John bringing with him to help a lad from the adventure centre who made himself useful. The standing rigging was in order except that the forestay, a piece of wire even thicker than *Mischief*'s notoriously thick forestay, had needed shortening in order to fit to an equally massive rigging screw at the stemhead. Similarly with the topmast forestay, except that that was of wire of a size that an amateur could shorten and splice. The ratlines on the shrouds had to be renewed, a job that had to be done first so that we could get aloft. The old lanyards, stiff with tar and hard as iron, had had to be cut, probably with a hacksaw, when the mast had been taken out. New lanyards of Italian hemp – not easily found in these synthetic times – had to be rove and for this I had the help of Ted Mapes, an old sailor and formerly bos'n of the yard. By means of tackles and plenty of tallow we got them pretty tight. Whether old shellbacks would approve I can't say, but the best way to get lanyards really tight is to set them up under sail. The lee-side shrouds being slack their lanyards are easily set up good and tight, and the other side are similarly done when on the other tack.

During the winter I had taken home all the running rigging for overhauling; it remained merely to discover where it all went, hang and reeve the blocks, and to make sure that the numerous halyards were leading fair and not chafing. The last is the most important and the hardest to achieve. Those peak and throat chain halyards that I had abolished would, of course, have laughed at chafe, but it would have been worse than unseamanlike to hoist the mainsail with the engine while the crew looked on admiringly. After her first three voyages we had sailed *Mischief* without a topmast, detracting a little from her appearance and not much from her performance. The topsail that the topmast enables one to set is always the first sail to come down when the wind freshens and in the North Atlantic, even in mid-summer, it would not often be set. And what with the topsail sheet and halyards, the topmast's shrouds and backstays, and the tackle for lowering the topmast, the gear aloft is almost doubled, involving more care and maintenance and muddling the minds of a strange crew. The slender spar on *Sea Breeze* certainly added to her good looks and I felt so proud of these good looks that I decided to leave the topmast up and await the event. Compared with her mainmast it looked like a toothpick and in the words of Mr Chucks the bos'n 'precarious and not at all permanent'. My correspondent Mr England tells me that in her working day she had a polemast, that is, a mast of the same height but in one piece.

Having spent so much already I could not afford any alterations below. Except for the removal of doors, carpets and curtains, the accommodation remained as before. A sail rack had been built forward in the peak and on one side of the galley a chart table, still leaving the whole of the port side as the cook's domain. The engine, too, is at the after end of the galley behind the steps leading up into the cockpit where it is remarkably inaccessible. An old Lymington friend of mine, Sandy Lee, wanted to improve the companion-way ladder. The steps were awkwardly placed and it was too functional for his aesthetic eye. He made a new one of oak with a pleasing curve, so well-designed that a blind man could climb up without missing a step or hitting his head on the sliding hatch above. Thus in effect I had three craftsmen embellishing *Sea Breeze*, or say two craftsmen and a carpenter.

Many shelves were needed, shelves over the foot of each bunk for personal gear, shelves for books, barograph, and wireless set, racks for charts, bottles, and tumblers, and a removable fiddle for the saloon table. With the abolition of the gas stove the entire re-arrangement of the galley fittings and shelves gave Brian plenty of scope even if the standard of work required and the time available meant rough carpentry instead of cabinet making. Mike did us a good turn by retrieving from a dump a discarded vice, still serviceable and amply big enough. The boat already had a substantial work-bench up forward where we could mount it and where queues began forming up to make use of it.

All the electric wiring had to be renewed, the plumbing re-arranged, and a new whale pump added to supplement a pump driven off the engine.

> To furnish a wife will cost you some trouble
> But to fit out a ship the expenses are double.

The fresh water was carried in four 30-gallon tanks underneath the two bunks in the saloon. They prevented any doubling up of the bunks and they proved devilish awkward to fill. With the original plumbing – and the replacement was not much better – unless you turned various cocks in the right sequence you might find that when all four tanks were supposedly full, three were still empty and the overflow from the fourth had flooded the saloon.

The ship's compass was very small and so far as one could see had been held in the hand while steering. *Mischief*'s compass had been mounted on the floor of her capacious cockpit where in *Sea Breeze* there was no room for it. The only place for it we could find was over the top of the companion-way hatch and the only type of compass that could be read at that height and distance away from the helmsman was a Sestrel. Mr Lee made a little bridge over the sliding hatch to mount it on and a brass cage to protect it from the knocks it might suffer in such an exposed position. Visitors to *Sea Breeze* are often puzzled by this sort of parrot cage so prominently displayed, and in the absence of any bird they take it to be some new-fangled radar device. This compass is marked in degrees instead of points, good enough for a steamer which is not much concerned with the wind but not for a sailing ship where the wind and its direction is all that matters. The wind direction is always named by the points of the compass and it is confusing to switch to degrees when ordering the course to be steered. To add to the confusion this type of compass is read from the back instead of the front, as it must be to be read at all by the helmsman, so that on an alteration of course one has to think twice before deciding which way to push the tiller. Like most things about a boat it is a compromise solution of what is desirable and what is possible, and I shall have to find another solution before throwing it overboard.

Before coming to the action, and to conclude this long-drawn tale of preparation, there is only a little to add. The boat's large and heavy dinghy, so heavy that it had to be launched from a davit, had also to be abolished, or at least I abolished the davit and swapped it for a lighter 9ft. dinghy. Owing to the great hydraulic winch we could find no room on the foredeck, so that even this smaller dinghy had to be carried amidships where it cluttered up the deck and was much in the way of the jib and staysail sheets. Having seen enough of anthracite-burning stoves I reverted to a Kempsafe cabin heater that conveniently burns the same fuel as the engine. We had used one in *Mischief* and except for an occasional holocaust due to carelessness it had given no trouble. The skylight immediately above the stove has to be kept firmly closed, and even so has been known to let in water, and finding a suitable exit for the stove-pipe presented a problem. Engineer Mike's solution involved two right-angle bends and we lived to regret them.

We were not in all respects ready for sea until 17 June. The nearer the day came the more I wondered whether we were in all respects ready, for we were starting from scratch. Putting *Mischief* into commission after being laid-up for the winter was a simple matter; everything required was in the store on shore and had merely to be put in the right place on board. Now one had to think afresh of all that might be needed. Galley equipment, for instance, of which, with the boat, I had not inherited enough to stock a picnic basket. There were no tools of any kind, but happily for this voyage we were exceedingly well off because Brian, Mike, and Ralph all brought their own. Then there were all the bits and pieces that we were wont to carry, things that might never be used but without which one would not feel the boat was really well-found. Spare blocks, wire strops and grommets, short bits of chain, handy-billy, shackles, wire, rope, copper, canvas, bos'n's stores of all kinds, and a hundred other items. But we were not sailing for some unknown shore and most of what a small boat may need can be readily found at the Faeroes or Iceland.

For reasons already given I never insured the boat for the voyage but I usually took the comparatively cheap precaution of insuring her while in home waters, these being the most dangerous. Mere prudence warns one to keep as far as possible from any steamers, especially from trawlers, yet wide as the sea is, ships frequently collide and yachts are occasionally run down. A graver risk for me in a big, heavy boat that is not as handy as a modern yacht, and that has 14ft. of bowsprit sticking out ahead, was that of hitting another yacht. Lymington river is narrow and lined on both sides by expensive yachts lying at their moorings, and in one's anxiety to give the Lymington-Yarmouth ferry room to pass it would be all too easy to foul one of them. Or, perhaps, in the event of some unseamanlike behaviour by both parties, one might impale on the bowsprit some lofty gin-palace.

With all this in mind and a strange boat under me I took care when we cast off on 17 June to have Ted Mapes in a launch to escort us half-way down the river where the bends are narrowest and sharpest. As we passed the club-house of the Royal Lymington Yacht Club they gave us a starting gun, an encouraging gesture that we had long been honoured with in *Mischief*. Strong, blustery, south-westerly weather had prevailed for the last day or two, weather entirely unfavourable for beating down Channel in a strange boat with a strange crew. I had therefore decided to sail about in the Solent to see how she went and to anchor for the night in Yarmouth roads. Clear of the river but before we had begun hoisting any sails I noticed a lot of water coming into the galley high up on the starboard side, and on removing a bit of the lining we enjoyed a view of the Isle of Wight between two of the water-line planks where a foot or two of caulking had spewed out.

Having anchored in the roads I went ashore to see the harbourmaster and to inform the yard at Lymington. We then moved inside the harbour preparatory to leaning the boat against the quayside wall towards midnight when the tide served. By mid-June Yarmouth harbour is bursting at the seams and manoeuvring *Sea Breeze* into her allotted berth shook my weak nerves. How thankful I was for that insurance policy. The ornate gangway of a large Royal Yacht Squadron power boat narrowly escaped destruction at our hands, and the crew of the yacht lying ahead of our mooring must have thought their time had come.

Later on a wet and windy night we were towed alongside the quay and at high tide we turned out to haul the boat forward and heel her over by swinging out the boom. Early in the morning the yard launch came over with two men who recaulked the planks. We had yet to see the sails hoisted and since the weather remained too discouraging to start we went out into the Solent to hoist them. The boat sailed well, went about with no fuss, and after two hours sailing, mostly hard on the wind, we returned to the anchorage well pleased with her performance. But there seemed to be a lot of water in the well, and by the time I had given it 600 strokes I felt something akin to despair. After all the time and money that had been spent the boat was obviously in no condition to take to sea. After more telephone consultation with the yard we repeated the performance of the previous night, laying her once more against the quay wall. In the morning quite a party arrived early enough for a cup of tea – John Tew and the yard manager with their attendants.

After inspecting the hull John Tew's verdict was that the boat must be recaulked throughout. The weather being what it was we had so far lost nothing, but it maddened me to think of the boat lying all that winter in a shed and that no one – neither John Tew, the yard, nor the owner – had had the gumption to examine the caulking. In defence all that could be said was that it looked sound, that the boat had made no water on passage from the Hamble, and had remained dry when put back in the water in the spring. But an hour's sailing in the quiet waters of the Solent had soon found out the rottenness of the caulking. By 20 June she was back at Lymington once more hauled out on the slip. The crew dispersed to foregather again in a week's time.

CHAPTER SEVEN

Second and Third Start

THIS DISCOURAGING, costly setback had at least occurred at the right time, before the voyage had even begun. If any of the crew were given to conjecture they could exercise it by wondering what might have happened had the caulking started coming out in chunks when we were on our way and far from land. In order to lessen the windage aloft while the boat was in the cradle on the slip we had sent down the topmast. By 30 June, the topmast once more set up, we were ready for a fresh start. In far more genial weather we beat out through the Needles Channel, sighting a Thames barge under sail and a Dutch botter, the three of us the only sailing vessels about. In the past week at home Brian must have made some study of an art new to him, surprising us all by serving up curry and a noble duff on our first night at sea.

Fitful winds by day and windless nights made for slow, peaceful progress until 4 July when we made a run of 95 miles that took us somewhere south-east of the Scillies. With both genoa and tops'l set, the topmast bending like a fishing rod, I took fright and had both sails taken down. Five days out and we had not yet rounded Land's End. Next afternoon in thick weather and a near gale we sighted Round Island at the north end of the Scillies and had to go about to weather it. Close reefed and with no jib set, we tacked again at nightfall to weather Cape Cornwall, the small jib having blown out when Mike inadvertently let the sheet fly. We spent a wet night, close-hauled, just maintaining our distance from the Cornish coast and a lee shore. The more or less halcyon days and nights spent drifting down Channel had not prepared the crew for the rough usage of the last two days when they found that yachting had pains as well as pleasures. They were far from well and the boat proved decidedly wet. She needed 500 strokes of the pump every watch though most of this water found its way below from the deck. The beam in the galley dripped generously over Brian and the chart table, as did the beam in way of the mast, wetting my bunk on the one tack and Brian's on the other. Another source of water was the stern gland which later John succeeded in tightening. But in the last windy twenty-four hours the boat had logged 146 miles. We were well pleased with her sailing ability and the way she went about in rough water even when close-reefed, never once missing stays as *Mischief* had sometimes done, obliging us to put her about by gybing.

Brian, the landsman, alone remained unaffected by the weather and seemed to be the only one of the crew enjoying life. He was never idle, which is perhaps half the secret, always having in hand some carpentry job in addition to normal work in the galley. With such a crew to help he preferred to do his own washing-up. The crew usually take turns as galley-slave, washing-up, drawing sea-water for the cook, peeling spuds, and cleaning up below deck. John at least knew what had to be done and was almost too enthusiastic about keeping things below sweet and clean by generous swabbing down. Had we had the means I could see him wanting to smoke the boat out to ward off incipient scurvy.

The crew had a welcome respite in smooth water when we passed close under the lee of Lundy Island. Off Lundy we sighted the royal yacht *Britannia*. I had last seen her at Reykjavik in 1964 when *Mischief*, the only British vessel in harbour, had sailed out to pay her respects as *Britannia* steamed in with the Duke of Edinburgh on board. With the wind still at north-west we held on northwards until midnight of 8 July when we raised the light of the lightship off Worm Head west of Swansea. Upon the new heading of slightly south of west the boat began to pitch heavily in a short, steep sea. It must have been this violent pitching that brought down the topmast. I had barely settled down in the cockpit at 4 am when with a loud crack the topmast went, a bit of it caressing me lightly on the head as it fell on the deck nearby. A minute or two later I realised that the bowsprit, too, had gone. Without the topmast forestay and with no jib set it was no longer supported. All hands were called to clear the wreckage. Using the jib halyards we first got the bowsprit inboard, for it had broken at the gammon iron and was bashing against the hull. A large piece of the topmast hung athwart the main forestay in a tangle of wire and rope, shrouds and halyards. Working from a bos'n's chair shackled to the forestay John at length had it all down.

The topmast could be regarded as expendable but the bowsprit was indispensable. We were well placed for making Appledore, only 25 miles down wind, so with a fine sailing breeze we eased away the main sheet and let her rip. There is a bar across the entrance to Appledore and we had the tide to catch. Having no large-scale chart we had to follow carefully the directions in the *Pilot* and as soon as we had picked up the bar buoy found it all plain sailing. The two Customs officers who presently boarded us did not allow sympathy for our mishap to overcome their duty of sealing up our bonded store locker. The tides were at neaps with not enough water for us to lie alongside the wall. We had to anchor out in the river where even the neap tides run with great strength. Having put the Customs officers ashore in our dinghy, and getting them thoroughly wet, I sought out Messrs Hinks boatyard to put in hand a new bowsprit.

This small yard had recently completed the building of *Nonsuch*, a replica of the seventeenth-century ship whose voyage in 1668 had marked the founding of the Hudson Bay Company. In 1668 two French traders, De Groseilliers and Radisson, supported and financed by Prince Rupert (cousin of Charles II) and his friends, sailed for Hudson Bay in two small ships, *Nonsuch* and *Eaglet*. Storm damage forced *Eaglet* to turn back but the *Nonsuch* under Captain Zacharia Hillam reached the mouth of Rupert River and wintered there. When they returned to England the next year with a fortune in furs on board, the Hudson Bay region, hitherto explored only in the hope of finding a north-west passage, became attractive in its own right. In 1670, under the patronage of Prince Rupert, the Hudson Bay Company was founded, and received a charter giving it almost sovereign rights over all lands whose waters drained into Hudson Bay. It was to celebrate this tricentenary that the *Nonsuch* had been built for the Hudson Bay Company who intended her to sail across the Atlantic to take part in the celebrations. She had proved a bit tender for an Atlantic voyage and in the end was shipped over in a freighter.

The yard had no timber long enough for the bowsprit and had to order it from St Austell. On arrival the timber turned out to be 24ft. long instead of 25ft., but to avoid delay I accepted the shorter length even though it meant our having to make up new bowsprit shrouds. By 10 July the tides had made sufficiently for us to go alongside the wall, a change much to the better. Except at slack water, rowing ashore was difficult. If the dinghy were laden, the perspiring oarsman might finish up half a mile below or above the point aimed at. At low water alongside the wall we had a chance to examine the hull and found it in good shape except for a bit of stopping that had come out near the stem. We had a line from the mast to the wall to prevent her falling over as the tide dropped, and once or twice we would either forget to shorten up the line as the boat took the ground and began to lean over away from the wall, or to slack away as the boat rose at high tide. On these occasions a loud warning cry testified to the professional alertness of the old salts who spent their days on the quay regarding and criticising the passing nautical scene. Were they thinking:

> How pleasant to gaze on the sailors
> To gaze without having to sail.

Among the trippers and retired seafarers who kept an eye on *Sea Breeze* was Captain Jewel, lately owner and master of a beautiful three-masted trading schooner *Kathleen and May*. At least ten years before, on a visit to Appledore by land, I had seen the schooner lying alongside and had admired the yacht-like fashion in which this trading vessel was maintained. *Kathleen and May* was now lying up the river towards Bideford, laid-up but not neglected. I went on board and as I gazed up at her lofty spars I was not surprised when the present owner told me it had taken him two months single-handed to scrape down and varnish those three tall masts. I had a word with Captain Jewel who remarked on the absence of our topmast and considered it a grave mistake to sail, as we intended, without one. For his part, he said, he would sooner sail without a bowsprit.

On the 12th men from the yard wheeled our bowsprit along and lowered it over the wall for us to reeve. It went in with less trouble than I had expected and we could then measure the length for the new bowsprit shrouds and for a new stay from the masthead to the cranse iron at the end of the bowsprit. Turning in a splice in plough-steel wire takes time so that it is important to get the measurements right.

By now I had other things to think about as well. The two schoolmasters had decided to quit. Mike had heard at second hand that his mother was ill, and although we urged him to get some reliable information, say from a doctor, he merely said he ought to go home. Ralph lingered, idle and sulky, while he made up his mind and then he likewise departed. It seemed that their early experiences had fallen short of their expectations. So much had gone wrong since first leaving Lymington that they may have likened *Sea Breeze* to Milton's:

> Fatal and perfidious bark,
> Built in th' eclipse, and rigged with curses dark.

At times I had been tempted to think the same.

Here was a facer. I had no reserves to call up; either we must find two local volunteers or expect a delay of several weeks and the consequent abandonment of most of our plans. John remained staunch and full of hope in spite of this latest and worst setback, while Brian I knew was not the man to stop stirring till the pudding was done. Surely, I thought, in Appledore or Bideford, home of Sir Richard Grenville, not to mention *Westward Ho* and all that that implied, the spirit of adventurous seafaring must still flourish. The first likely covert to draw seemed to be the North Devon Yacht Club at Instow across the river to which I now went by ferry. Keen racing men they were, no doubt, but a little parochial. I could forgive them for never having heard of *Mischief*, but whence we had come, Lymington, and whither we were bound, Greenland, were equally beyond their ken. Even the magic word 'the Solent', the yachtsman's Mecca, roused no flicker of interest in these Devon infidels. One of the youngest members did indeed seem momentarily to catch fire at the mention of Greenland, but unluckily mother was at hand to stamp it out.

Nevertheless this Instow visit bore fruit. The boatman who ferried me over – our needs were now common knowledge – gave me the name of a Welshman, an intruder on the Devon scene, whom he thought might come. Dai Morgan, or Ken as he was rightly called, was living in a caravan pending the renovation of a nearby cottage that he had bought. He was doing everything himself, brickwork, plumbing, heating, lighting, glazing, the lot – evidently a king among handymen. He had been an agricultural engineer in South Wales and had now retired to Appledore having conceived no great love for his own countrymen. Besides a lifetime's experience of engines he had a great liking for the sea, had helped her present owner to bring *Kathleen and May* round from Southampton, and also to bring an old trading ketch to England from the Baltic.

On the debit side he was elderly, far from spry, and did not look robust. He would be no help on deck except for doing his two-hour trick at the helm if well wrapped up. Having had a look at *Sea Breeze* and talked to John and Brian he expressed his readiness to join. Readiness was the word. I could not but admire the carefree way in which he arranged his affairs for a three months' absence by putting together a few necessities, parking the cat with a neighbour, locking the caravan and the half-finished cottage, and repairing on board next day. As might have been expected, he proved of great value as engineer, methodical and painstaking to a degree, and withal a good shipmate, except that throughout the voyage, in spite of many disappointments, he always expected the worst to happen. To me he will always figure as Cassandra Ken.

The ripples from the stone cast at Instow spread. On the 13th a young man came along to see the boat and those in her, and promised to return that evening with a definite answer, which he did. Colin Kavenan had heard about us from a friend in the Yacht Club. He was at a loose end waiting to attend some course and could get himself ready by the next day, parents no obstacle. He had done some boating and was a keen fisherman. Colin wore a beard, but at this crisis in our affairs I would not have minded had he worn beads and had hair down to his waist. Thus in a week after putting into Appledore we had a new bowsprit fitted and had replaced our two deserters with rather more promising material; and unless another spar carried away pretty soon, a change of mind on their part would be of no avail.

It was late on the evening of the 15th before we cast off. We had had to cut some links out of the bobstay chain in order to get it bar taut, and Ken and Colin had some last minute arrangements to make. The following morning in poor visibility the Smalls lighthouse appeared as expected, a feat that I attributed more to luck than to good navigation. With the Bristol Channel to the east and St George's Channel to the north the tidal streams hereabouts are both strong and complex, owing apparently to the difficulty the stream has in deciding into which of the two channels it should be running. The *Pilot* devotes five pages to the subject and to hoist it all in requires a clearer head than mine. *Sea Breeze* seemed bent on making up lost time by reeling off over 90 miles to pass the Codling lightvessel next day. We had Snowdon in sight, nearly 60 miles away, and for supper, mackerel with cheese sauce and a treacle duff. Colin had brought a short spinning rod. If there were mackerel about, and he seemed to know when they were, he would catch them.

A falling glass and a southerly wind presaged some wet, windy weather. In order to get well clear of the Irish coast we ran off to the north-east, and a great dollop of water through the skylight hinted that the sea was becoming rough. In the course of the voyage we tried various dodges with the skylight, making it more water-tight but never quite water-proof; if a sea hit the skylight coaming with any force it always managed to lift the skylight just enough for a jet of water to burst through. The place of honour – the head of the table where the skipper sat – was, as it should be, the place of danger. Later that afternoon in heavy rain and poor visibility we hove to as we were rapidly closing the Isle of Man. Between squalls we sighted the island and started sailing, the plan being to run up the coast to the north until we had a good lee and smoother water in which to gybe the boat round. Off Point of Ayr we were in relatively calm water and should have stayed there. Clear of the land, conditions became so bad that I decided to heave to for the night. In strong winds it is almost impossible to keep oil-burning navigation lamps alight, and ours were probably out when we had an alarmingly close shave with a small tanker. When the tanker stood on in spite of a powerful torch directed at him we hastily let draw and gybed away so that he passed some 50 yards off. Perhaps the trick of making oil lamps wind-proof is no longer known. A hundred or even fifty years ago, when oil lamps were in common use at sea, it is hard to believe that a gale of wind would promptly extinguish them all.

In more moderate weather we made rapid progress, sighting the Maidens north of Belfast the next evening. On the previous windy night even Brian had had to restrict supper to soup and bully beef sandwiches, and to give him a chance to make up for this with a curry, as well as to cheat an adverse tide, we anchored once again in Red Bay. Sailing after lunch next day, wind and tide both in our favour, we were soon off Rathlin Island. As we sailed by close to the shore Colin stood by, rod in hand, and on seeing what he judged to be a fishy-looking eddy made a cast and hauled out four huge mackerel at one go. Originally we had intended calling at the Faeroes where my Danish friend in *Ole Roemer* would be. We were a month late; *Ole Roemer* by now would probably be on her way to Scoresby Sound, so I decided to sail direct to Iceland. Accordingly, when south of Skerryvore, we headed north-west out into the Atlantic where we enjoyed fine weather and fast sailing. The fine weather lasted only two days but for the next six days we ran over 100 miles a day. Even on the 25th, when we were hove to for several hours during a southerly gale, we still made good our 100 miles. When hove to, we found that the boat forged ahead much too fast, mainly because, unlike *Mischief*, there were no sheet winches and it was hard to haul the staysail flat aback. Later, to correct this, we used a tackle. Macaroni cheese and treacle duff for supper.

On this headlong rush towards Iceland we got too far south and fetched up in the vicinity of Hvalbakur, or Whaleback Island, only 16ft. high, 25 miles out from the land, and, of course, unlit. In approaching this east coast one needs to be wary on account, as the *Pilot* stresses, of the off-lying streams, and the unreliability of the magnetic compass when near the land. One reason for our having picked on Seydisfjord for our landfall was its freedom from off-lying dangers and we had no business to be closing the land when still 40 miles to the south. Having steered north we headed in again on what I thought was the right latitude, but a snap meridian sight, the sun having been for the most part hidden, showed that we were still to the southward. Under the lee of Iceland, in a region of prevailing Westerlies, one would expect to find pretty smooth water. Not a bit. The nearer we approached the land the more lumpy and irregular the sea became owing, no doubt, to strong tidal streams.

On 28 July, after another southerly gale and in a horribly confused sea, as we steered gingerly towards the land, visibility grew worse and worse. At midnight, when it was down to about 2 cables, we altered course to the north, roughly parallel to the coast, my frayed nerves unable to stand it any longer. Ken had been on watch but being ill-clad and feeling the cold he had had to be relieved. We had done well to alter course. Shortly after I had taken over something more solid than the fog loomed close on our port, the vague outline of a high island. From the description in the *Pilot* I took it to be Skrudhur, 520ft. high: 'This islet is an excellent landmark, both on account of its shape and of its height, as all the other islets on this part of the coast are low.' It was then too late, but had we known earlier that we were in its vicinity more attention might have been paid to the remarks in the *Pilot* about local magnetic anomalies:

Eastward and southward of Skrudhur the compass is especially affected, the greatest observed anomaly being 22° E. in a position 3 to 4 miles south-eastward of the island; three-quarters of a mile northward of this position the anomaly was 11° W., and it ceased altogether a quarter of a mile southward of the position. About 4¾ miles eastward of Skrudhur an anomaly of 17° E. has been observed, and between Skrudhur and the mainland, one of 11° E.

Such large anomalies could hardly be called niceties of navigation, but in a small sailing boat, where precise navigation is hardly possible, content as one is to steer within half a point or so of a given course, they would generally be disregarded. No wonder that in the days of sail before happenings as strange as these had been observed and recorded for the benefit of sailors, every stress was laid on what they called the four L's – lead, log, latitude, and look-out, the last being the ultimate safeguard on which all depends.

When the wind died away to nothing and the gaff began to jerk wildly as the boat tossed about in the confused sea, I took the extreme step of calling all hands well before breakfast to hand the mainsail. Then she really began to dance about but with no longer the chance of doing herself any harm. Brian, always on a level with circumstances, cooked the usual breakfast porridge, and by the time that was finished we had the land in sight. The sea quietened down and with the dispersal of the fog I could check by sights that the island we had seen was undoubtedly Skrudhur. With no wind and 20 miles to go to Dalatangi lighthouse at the entrance to our fjord we started the engine. It had been a remarkably fast passage. In eleven days from Appledore to Iceland we had covered 1,083 miles. We did nothing like as well on the homeward run, or indeed on the voyage the following year. On long passages I found it wise to count on nothing better than 70 miles a day.

CHAPTER EIGHT

A Polite Mutiny off the Greenland Coast

THE PORT OF Budhareyri at the head of Seydisfjordhur, whither we were bound, is thus described in the *Pilot*: 'The town contains a hotel with 15 beds, and numerous fish-filleting, freezing, and fish-oil factories. There are fifteen piers and jetties.' Naturally we expected to see a busy, thriving port, perhaps with a Seaman's Home like that at Reykjavik where meals can be had, but these expectations had to be modified. Upon reaching the place one could tell at once that it was far from busy, in fact almost moribund. The departure of the herring from Iceland waters has changed things here as on the north coast, but unlike Akureyri there is no farming in this region and no tourists, so that Budhareyri has been hard hit. The hotel was closed, only one fish factory worked part time, and the piers and jetties were largely deserted. A Customs officer who came on board advised us to move to another part of the harbour where we lay in solitary state at a quay long enough, if not deep enough, to accommodate the *Queen Mary*.

Having reached Iceland in spite of so many setbacks I began to think that Scoresby Sound was in the bag, but even as we chugged quietly up the fjord these sanguine hopes received a jolt. John, who for the past week had complained of being ill, having perked up on reaching the calm waters of the fjord, chose that moment to hint that we had come far enough; but considering the weakness of the crew and his own infirmity, we would do well, after perhaps seeing something more of Iceland, to start for home. Naturally I could not agree to that and told him that we would push on as far as we could and that I could judge for myself when the time had come to turn back. He attributed his illness to those unlucky mackerel caught off Rathlin Island, a fish to which, he said, he was allergic. There was talk of seeing a doctor as soon as we arrived at Budhareyri, but having arrived he said no more about his health and consulted no doctor.

For all the depressingly dull, wet weather, so unlike what we had experienced at Akureyri, we enjoyed our stay. The natives regarded us with friendly amusement, a provincial paper having recorded our advent under the unkind headlines 'Old men in an Old Boat'. We made good use of some communal shower baths and began finding our way around. There was no High Street or shopping centre. The shops were of a retiring nature, looking like private houses, and had to be searched for. Local knowledge was indispensable. At a shop like an old-fashioned draper's Ken and Colin found all they lacked in the way of thick sweaters, wool shirts, long pants, and even oilskins. There was a well-stocked liquor store selling every kind of spirit from whisky to Black Death. The Iceland authorities regard beer, rather than gin, as the original Mother's Ruin. The only beer permitted is the non-alcoholic variety brewed by the state brewery with Black Death as a profitable by-product. Brian, who believes in and practises living off the country, treated himself to a bottle. It tastes like surgical spirit laced with aniseed.

The parson of the Lutheran church was a surprising and amusing visitor. He arrived just as we were having our tea, and having laced his tea with whisky from a bottle that emerged unobtrusively from a pocket as if by a conjuring trick, between puffs from a cigar, he devoured with relish biscuits well spread with jam. He had spent three years in London, spoke idiomatic English and appeared exceedingly well-informed. In return we were invited the next evening to the Manse or its Lutheran equivalent where, though a little hampered by the attentions of the parson's seven children, we set about a fine array of cakes, savouries, biscuits, and some notable shrimp mayonnaise. Coffee, of course, with endless doses of Black Death in small glasses accompanied by the usual 'Skolls'. Another guest was the manager of the fish factory from whom we hoped to elicit the solution to the herring mystery. His explanation, confused by indifferent English and too much Black Death, was that the mature herring, having learnt sense, swim low and escape the nets, while the inexperienced young, the breeding stock of the future, are caught. Anyway over-fishing had finished off the Iceland herring.

We returned late from the party in driving rain and a wind so strong that before turning in I put out more warps. Brian and I resolved to climb Strandertinder (3,310ft.), the peak that towers in modest fashion over the town. The rain that had been falling since the previous night let up towards evening allowing us to set off. Starting right from sea-level, scratch as it were, we had every foot of it to climb, a long slog that took two hours and a half. The extensive view from the top suffered from sameness, all the surrounding mountains appearing much the same size and shape. We found a better way down where patches of surviving winter snow gave us some long glissades.

Sea Breeze has two port-holes, one in the saloon and one in my cabin. It was usually under water and I never really became accustomed to watching all that green water surging by, separated from it by only a small piece of glass.

> When the cabin port-holes are dark and green
> Because of the seas outside;
> When the steward falls into the soup tureen
> And the chairs begin to slide.
> Why then you may know if you haven't guessed
> That you're fifty north and forty west.

But the fear that they might be broken by a stray piece of ice was really what decided me to cover them with an iron plate outside, a dead-light. The stove pipe also needed a cowl and when that had been fitted we tried the stove. In port, where there is no down-draught from the mainsail, it burnt well despite the two bends in the pipe.

By Saturday, 2 August, having set up and tarred the lanyards, filled up with water, paraffin, 60 gallons of diesel oil, and black bread, we were ready to go. John had said no more about cutting short the voyage and I assumed, with reservations, that all was well. That I was not over-hopeful is confirmed by an entry in my brief diary – 'wonder how far we shall get?' Much depended on what we met in the way of weather. Outside the fjord we picked up a north-easterly breeze and were able to lay a course that would take us well clear of the Langanes Peninsula. But next day the wind veered south-east bringing with it the fog that was to persist more or less continuously for the next five days. We were still making too much water, 600 strokes of the pump every watch to clear the bilge, until John had another go at the stern gland when the number of strokes required fell to 100. Until then he had been gloomy but after being sick as a result of crawling under the counter he brightened up a lot. That night after a supper of macaroni, hash, peas, and a sad but neverthe-less satisfying duff we crossed the Arctic circle. No ceremonies, no sky-larking, no visit from 'Le Père Arctique' marked the occasion.

In spite of a backing of the wind on the next day to north of east, the thick, wet fog lay heavily over the sea as if part of it. Indeed one found it hard to determine where the one began and the other ended. Fog, as the *Pilot* notes, is more likely with southerly winds, but there can be no cast-iron rules for the insidious comings and goings of this depressing frequenter of northern waters:

During the summer, when gales are rare and the wind is generally light, fog is often widespread and persistent. It sometimes continues for days or even weeks. ... Fogs are most general with winds from some southerly point; with northerly or north-westerly winds they usually disperse, although sometimes persisting for several hours after a shift of wind northward following a long spell of southerly winds.

It began to get cold, the air temperature 41° F. and the sea down to 38° F., high time for long woolly pants and vests. Combined with the fog it had a discouraging effect upon a far from eager crew and the refusal of the stove to burn properly did not mend matters. Ken decided that the right-angle bends must be eliminated, and together with John set to work as though their lives depended on it. They effected a great improvement though the cowl had still to be carefully trimmed according to the wind. Renewed mutterings came from John who until our arrival in Iceland had struck me as entirely reliable, the last man to want to quit, and one of the best mates I had had. How much longer did I propose bumbling about the Arctic in thick fog with a weak crew, no communication with anybody, no variety in the food, and himself unfit? For supper that night, a melancholy feast, we had sausages, cabbage, and a prime treacle duff.

On the morning of the 6th, after some heavy rain, a northerly wind sprang up. Obeying the rules, for once the fog became less dense and our horizon widened. Unfortunately the sun remained obstinately hidden and no sights could be obtained. We sailed fast for most of the day and at 6 pm, when I took the sea temperature for entry in the meteorological log, it had fallen to 32° F. The hint that ice could not be far off was confirmed a little later when we sighted a small berg. More scattered floes appeared, the flotsam and jetsam of the main pack, and at 7 pm we hove to. The sighting of ice caused John concern though, as I pointed out, anyone who embarks on a voyage to the Arctic would expect to see something of the sort sooner or later.

I should have been happier myself had we known where we were. For four days we had had no sights and this meeting with the ice showed that the coast could not be far away. Our respite from fog did not last long. But next day, for a change, the sun shone brightly while the fog returned as thick as ever – a shallow fog with blue sky overhead. To have a sun and no horizon is far more maddening than to have no sun at all. In desperation I brought the sun down on to the back of a fulmar sitting on the water a 100 yards from the ship and directly under the sun. After making due allowance for height of eye, height of fulmar, etc., the sight when worked out put us well up on the Greenland ice-cap.

8 August is a day I always remember. It was our black day in 1970 just as it had been Hindenberg's black day in 1918, on which the unit I was happy to be with played an active part. With a light easterly breeze we had sailed quietly all night until the morning when the wind backed north and began to freshen. As the fog slowly thinned we sighted first pack-ice to the east. Then suddenly, like the raising of a curtain, the fog dissolved and we were gazing with astonishment at a wild, mountainous coastline stretching far into the distance on either hand. After having been more or less blindfold for so long it seemed to me more like a revelation than a landfall. Directly opposite were two big glaciers, evidently descending from the ice-cap, for the mountains in the vicinity carried remarkably little snow. A cluster of jagged pinnacles far to the south stood out black against the morning sky.

What a time one could have, I thought, poking about in those numerous, largely unknown fjords if one could only reach them, forgetting that if it were not for the ever-present ice they would not have remained so long unknown. To the north-east the coast seemed to terminate in a cape 20 to 25 miles away. A hasty sight taken from an assumed position 15 miles from the coast gave me a clue and comparing the lie of the land with the chart I took this cape to be Cape Brewster at the southern entrance to Scoresby Sound. Instead of an unbroken mass the pack-ice seemed to lie in scattered fields and my hopes began to rise. Sailing north in increasing wind we soon came up with one of these fields and turned in towards the coast in the hope of finding a lead.

Rain now accompanied the rising wind. Intent on seizing the chance that our first fog-free day had given us, thinking the barograph had risen whereas in fact it had begun to fall, I did not pay much heed to these warnings. As Lecky says: 'A falling barometer with a northerly wind conveys a warning that cannot be disregarded with impunity.' Upon meeting more ice we followed its edge to the north-west but were always confronted by more ice ahead. By this time, late afternoon, the wind looked like increasing to a gale and the rain fairly pelted down; but the sea remained perfectly smooth thanks to the protecting fields of ice that almost surrounded us. Under the engine, I thought, the ice might well be navigable. The question was whether to try it here or to go out to sea clear of the ice and make the latitude of Scoresby Sound before attempting to reach the coast. The last would probably be the better course, but meantime we could heave to where we were in calm water and wait for the wind to abate. Between the widely scattered fields there would be room to keep well away from any ice.

John would have none of it. Like Brer Rabbit, in the language of Uncle Remus, he seemed to imagine that 'every minnit wuz gwineter be de nex'. In order to pacify him we began sailing east in search of open water. While running along the edge of some ice that seemed to stretch interminably southwards, looking for a break, and getting tired of losing so much ground to the south, I took the boat in close and realised that the ice was no field but a thin line of floes. We sailed through without difficulty and the roughness of the sea beyond showed that there was no ice to the north. Whereupon we hove to on the starboard tack to ride out the night. A dirty night it proved and I soon realised we had hove to on the wrong tack when the boat, by fore-reaching, brought us back within sight of the ice. We went about and lay to on the port tack heading east.

The rain stopped before morning but the wind continued to blow with some fury throughout the day. As I listened vainly for any lulls that might herald a lessening of the wind I felt that this unlucky gale would be the breaking point for a half-demoralised crew. Instead of getting somewhere we were fast losing ground to the south. By evening the wind had eased enough for us to let draw and start making north again towards Scoresby Sound. At least that was my proposal but the crew, the mate their spokesman, thought otherwise – demurred strongly and refused to do anything of the kind. Brian, of course, was as keen as I was to persevere but felt that his inexperience and his position as cook did not allow him an equal say. There we were in a stout ship, plenty of food and water, suffering a few inconveniences but certainly no hardships, and only some 40 miles from our objective at just the right time of year.

Brian, John, and I argued, standing for some odd reason round the foot of the mast below. I knew it would be no use. I am not eloquent and it would have needed the fiery eloquence of a Drake or a Garibaldi to stiffen John's spine. Even the suggestion that if Scoresby Sound were ruled out we could go south to Angmagssalik, thus at least landing in Greenland, met with no favour. John reckoned that he had stretched himself to the limit for my sake, that he had reached the end of his tether, and that any delay might have serious effects upon his health. Cassandra Ken concurred and thought that if we were to go on, the chances of any of us even surviving were no better than fifty-fifty. Colin, with slightly less conviction, agreed. To give up when so near, in an able boat with ample supplies, was hard to stomach, but with an unwilling crew there was nothing to be done. 'Home, and don't spare the horses,' was the cry.

Once before I had had the melancholy experience of sailing homewards with a disillusioned crew. On this occasion the passage would be much shorter, so short that it should not be difficult to maintain harmony, to be polite instead of resentful. It proved not to be so short, and Brian did not feel it incumbent upon him to conceal his disgust at our ignominious flight and the man mainly responsible. For the first ten days we were almost as fogbound as we had been on the way out. For the sake of the record, not by way of complaint, I see from the logbook that between 4 August and 18th we had fog every day except on the critical 8th, when it rained. In the Greenland Sea fog is to be expected and like any other vexations and hazards of the sea must be borne with what cheerfulness one can muster. Like the ice conditions, fog may vary in intensity from year to year. On the Jan Mayen voyage of the previous year we had not nearly so much fog. We had struck a bad year, and the same had apparently held good, contrary to my belief, for the ice conditions. A friend in the Meteorological Office sent me this report:

Our sea-ice charts for August and early September show that ice conditions for most of the time were excessive in the Scoresby Sound area. For the period 1st to 8th August open pack at the entrance and to seaward quickly became close pack within the Sound. Belts of close pack, 20 to 30 miles wide, existed to the north and south of the entrance and during the period 9th to 18th August, these belts merged, filled the entrance and combined with the close pack already within the Sound. The area of close pack extended 40 miles seaward of the entrance but a 10 to 20 miles wide bank of open pack lay along the coast to the south of Cape Brewster. The close pack gradually melted, more slowly within the Sound than outside, and by September 7th open water existed over the whole area, though a belt of close pack lay just to the northward. After September 7th open and close pack continuously threatened and sometimes closed the entrance to the Sound.

Thus the 'season' for Scoresby Sound was a very short one. *Sea Breeze* may well have been unable to make much progress into the Sound until late August and would have had considerable difficulty in clearing the entrance after the first week in September.

So much for the reports, but I have also an eye-witness account of conditions. Captain Toft was there again in *Ole Roemer*, met as much fog as we did, and concludes his letter with an interesting remark about the moral effects of fog and ice.

We left Thorshavn July 30th and arrived at Scoresby Sound August 2nd. For most of the way we had dense fog with SE winds, but about 30 miles from the Greenland coast the fog disappeared and we got clear weather. Very nice, but we then sighted a big area of heavy ice. Fortunately between the ice and Cape Brewster it was possible to force the ship through. It was very difficult and quite impossible for a vessel without ice protection and very strongly built. We tried to go to the roads (anchorage?) of Scoresby Sound but it was impossible owing to heavy ice.

We stayed in the area of Scoresby Sound until August 28th and from the first to the last day we had trouble with ice, sometimes being jammed in and drifting with it. The weather was bad, a rotation of three days of fog and snow, so it was an exceptionally bad season.

When we left we had difficulties with ice for the first eight miles. The weather was good until past Langanes when we had gale Force 9 for 36 hours. We arrived at Thorshavn August 31st after what I call a bad season.

After my experience, the best way to enter the Sound is from south-east close to Cape Brewster, but sailing along the east coast of Greenland will always be a little hazardous but quite interesting. Another problem is the crew. Not every man is fit for that job. I think that fog and ice is depressing for a young man.

At the time, from the little I had seen of the ice, I had thought that our chances were good. It is obvious from these reports that this was not so and that even with a less faint-hearted crew, though we might have got into the Sound we could have done nothing, and might not have got out. Still that is no reason for not having tried.

CHAPTER NINE

Homeward Bound

FOG ALONE was not responsible for our slow progress, but the light winds and calms that generally go with it. It is, however, possible to have the worst of both worlds and to enjoy fog and a gale at the same time, or even fog and a thunderstorm. Almost at the start of his historic voyage Slocum records:

About midnight the fog shut down again denser than ever before. One could almost stand on it. It continued so for a number of days, the *wind increasing to a gale*. The waves rose high but I had a good ship. Still, in the dismal fog I felt myself drifting into loneliness, an insect on a straw in the midst of the elements. I lashed the helm, and my vessel held her course, and while she sailed I slept.

Lecky records a severe electric storm in the North Atlantic, the lightning forming a complete network of flashes, while the prevailing fog was so dense that the funnels could not be seen from the bridge.

Now that we were running away from Greenland we had nothing to fear from ice and therefore no necessity to heave to at night, or at least during the murkiest hours around midnight, as we had been doing. Bergs and floes generally show up whiter than the surrounding fog far enough away, say 200 or at the worst 100 yards, for a slow moving boat such as *Sea Breeze* to steer clear or stop. The ugliest menace is from bergy bits or small floes nearly awash that may not be seen at all, especially if the sea is a little rough; and there are the exceptional big bergs and floes that for some reason are an off-white colour or worse and blend perfectly with the surrounding fog. When such a berg does at last loom up and disclose itself it is likely to be close enough to frighten the helmsman out of his wits.

Ships were an unlikely hazard in fog in these waters. We did hear one ship hooting away as she crossed our bows some way off, near enough, however, to agitate John. With nautical punctilio he blew away on our squeaker fog-horn two blasts every minute, indicating, at any rate to the fulmars sitting on the water nearby, that we were a sailing vessel on the port tack. It would be valuable to know how far one of these lung-driven fog-horns carries, and on some calm, foggy day I must row off in the dinghy (with a compass!) to find out. One might not have far to row. Soon after this fog-horn contest, we observed another mystery of the sea that baffled even conjecture. We passed an open box measuring about 6ft. by 2ft. carrying at one end a short ensign staff flying a small flag with a St Andrew's cross. Had the box had a lid like a coffin one might have taken it for the funeral ship of some latter-day Viking of modest means launched on the ocean on its last voyage to Valhalla.

Head winds pushed us so far to the west that we had trouble in clearing

Iceland and when the fog lifted we saw again the high land west of Langanes Peninsula. At last on the 20th we had all the wind we wanted. In one two-hour watch we did 14 miles and made a day's run of 140 miles, urged on by big, following seas. We were on the wrong tack and I reckoned there was too much wind to gybe safely, so after supper – curry and macaroni cheese – we dropped the jib, brought her up into the wind, and round she went. Next day we went almost as fast, passed a Russian trawler and a factory ship, and sighted St Kilda well away to the north-east. There is little or no darkness in northern waters in June or July, only on the way home in late August or September is there any chance of seeing auroral displays, and since the night must also be cloudless, the opportunities are rare. The night after passing St Kilda we witnessed such a display, beginning with shafts of light like the beams of some colossal searchlight that soon dissolved to form a luminous band whose arch spanned the northern sky.

We made our landfall in the customary thick weather on 23 August. Making a landfall infers some preciseness; it would be more correct to say that we inadvertently found ourselves close to a confusion of islands and islets at the southern end of the Hebrides. The wind being light and southerly I was tempted to make a fair wind of it by running off to the east through one of several unidentifiable sounds – Pabbay, perhaps, or Mingulay. I was not certain about any of them. Prudence, therefore, prevailed and we held on down the coast until we sighted the lighthouse on Berneray and knew exactly where we were. Off Barra Head we met plenty of wind and set a course for Skerryvore. Brian celebrated our arrival in home waters with curry and an apricot duff assuaged by white sauce.

After a windy night the day broke with vicious squalls hurrying down upon us from the north-west across a white-capped sea. What followed was probably my fault for not telling the helmsman, John, to steer wide, keeping the following wind well out on the quarter. Running fast before wind and sea with the whole mainsail set, the boat yawed quite a bit. The sight of a particularly threatening squall coming up astern, whipping the water white, decided me that it was time to reef. While down below getting into oilskins I felt the boat gybe and got back on deck to find the gaff dangling in two halves astride the topping lift, John having executed an imperial Chinese gybe. Taming the flogging mainsail and the flailing pieces of jagged wood took time and caution. That done, we set the topsail as a sort of trysail. Not a word of regret came from John who seemed to think that gaffs should be made of sterner stuff. Rathlin Island was already in sight and even under our diminished rig we went fast enough. The brave west wind carried us through the North Channel in style, enabling us to laugh at the adverse tide, a tide that on every previous passage had obliged us to anchor somewhere in order to escape it. Near Mew Island off Belfast Lough the wind began to take off.

Except in the unlikely event of carrying a fair wind all the way to Lymington, our trysail rig would prove a handicap and possibly a danger. Without a mainsail, for instance, we would not be able to claw off a lee shore, and the very next day we found ourselves in just those circumstances. We therefore decided to make for Holyhead to have the gaff repaired, and having gone there it would be only kind to look in at Barmouth to astonish the natives with a sight of *Sea Breeze*. That night the wind went south so that by morning we were off the Isle of Man coast south of Peel instead of south of the Calf of Man as we had hoped. The difficulty of sailing without a mainsail now became apparent. We were close to the shore, the wind blowing on to it, and whichever tack we tried, to the north-west or to the south-west, we could not get away from it. As we sagged to leeward towards an inhospitable bit of rugged coast I had the anchor got ready and told Ken to start the engine. The next ten anxious minutes passed slowly. Both fuel tanks were blocked and Ken was hastily rigging a jerrycan from which to feed fuel to the engine.

As we made down the coast with one perilous incident safely averted, I voluntarily incurred another. Wishing to cut short the pains of motoring I chose to take the passage through Calf Sound instead of going round outside the Calf of Man and Chicken Rock. If one stuck to mid-channel there were no dangers, though the *Pilot* did warn that the tide ran strongly and that the passage should not be attempted without local knowledge. I must say, when we came up to the pass and, when it was too late to turn back, saw the line of breaking water extending right across the extremely narrow opening, I began to have doubts about the wisdom of taking short cuts. Cassandra Ken had already given us up for lost. But all went well and on the east side of the island we soon picked up a wind. My mentor Lecky severely admonishes the mariner who tries short-cuts, and instances a 'major marine disaster that had recently occurred due to a fine ship being navigated at night through a narrow channel between a group of small islands and the mainland – all for the sake of a saving of five miles in distance steamed, during a round voyage (never completed) of some 12,000 miles.'

More recent experience confirms a suspicion that listening to the Shipping Forecasts is seldom of value. Out in the Atlantic beyond their range one forgets about forecasts and takes the weather as it comes, with no sense of any lost benefit; but in home waters listening becomes a habit that is not easily broken. There is always the chance of hearing something to one's advantage – a probable shift of wind, for instance, that might help to decide a course of action – and if not no harm is done. At six o'clock that evening, when half-way to Holyhead, we were surprised and a little disconcerted – for it might be right – to hear a gale warning for the Irish Sea. We expected to reach Holyhead by midnight but did not relish being caught in a westerly gale while searching for the entrance. On the other hand if we were to heave to to await the worst, we must do so forthwith while we still had ample searoom. The sky at sunset did not look strikingly ill-omened so we decided to stand on. The wind did increase to Force 6 – no more – but thanks to being set down by a strong tide we did not pass the Holyhead breakwater until well after midnight. Entering a strange port at night is not an exercise I enjoy and that night Holyhead seemed more than ordinarily confusing owing to the construction of a new breakwater then in progress and the presence of a floating crane with its web of mooring wires. We got in the way of the mail boat and in the end anchored too near the crane.

The Customs, who came on board early, treated us leniently, as they generally do if the case allows, and then piloted us to the boatyard where we landed the broken gaff. There was not enough water to stay there so we anchored off among a fleet of yachts. The boatyard had evidently suffered from some yachtsmen who 'payed with the mainsheet' as Slocum expresses it. Their first question was how I would pay them and through what bank? Three days elapsed before we could sail owing to the time needed for the proper hardening of the glued scarph. The gaff being ready, we bent on the mainsail and sailed out at mid-day of the 30th. More trouble with the fuel system had left us temporarily without the engine. In a light and fluky wind the tide carried us close to the North Stack which we narrowly avoided hitting thanks to a timely puff of wind and a hasty gybe. On so fine and warm a day, idling off the Anglesey coast was time well spent except that we wanted to catch the tide at Barmouth next day. There is a bar across the entrance that with our draught must be crossed within an hour or so of high water.

By midnight we were off Bardsey Island with a brisker wind and set a course for the Causeway Buoy that marks the seaward end of Sarn Badrig or St Patrick's Causeway, a dangerous rock ledge stretching from the shore for 11 miles out into Cardigan Bay. In the brief but glorious days of the Welsh trading schooners plying into the ports of Aberdovey, Barmouth, and Portmadoc, the Causeway claimed many victims. It is a natural causeway but runs so straight that it is easy to believe it to be the work of man, one of the embankments of the legendary kingdom of Cantref-y-Gwaleod, the 'Lowland Hundred', now sunk beneath the waters of Cardigan Bay. Readers of Peacock may remember the immortal Seithenym, a mighty toper, guardian of the embankment and answerable to the king for its safety, by whose drunken neglect it fell into decay. In the storm that one day breached the embankment, sweeping away all who were on it and engulfing the kingdom, Seithenym, instead of being drowned like the rest as he deserved, got safely ashore on one of the hundreds of wine barrels to which he had devoted his life industriously emptying.

We neither saw nor heard the Causeway Buoy, having evidently given it so safe a berth by keeping well south, that at ten o'clock next morning we fetched up near the Sarn-y-Bwch Buoy just south of Barmouth. From the sea the familiar long, flat ridge of Cader Idris that I have been looking at for the last twenty years appeared like a sharp peak, but Diffwys. a 2,900ft. hill behind Bodowen, was unmistakable. Disregarding John's objections that we were off Portmadoc, we sailed up to the Outer Buoy where we jilled about waiting for high water. On *Mischief*'s one and only visit to Barmouth we had disapointed an official welcoming party by arriving twelve hours late, but on this gloriously fine Bank Holiday week-end people were too busy amusing themselves to bother about *Sea Breeze*. However, we were presently boarded by the harbour-master accompanied by an old friend of mine, Bob Henry, coastguard and Town Councillor, than whom there is no cheerier company. The Holyhead Customs, as I said, had treated us leniently, so we sat on deck watching the dinghy sailors and the bathing belles on the distant beach while the tide slowly rose and the level of the gin bottle swiftly fell. The wind had fallen away to nothing, so, assisted by our now inspired guests, we handed the sails and motored in to lie at the small stone quay, the harbour-master imperiously shooing away a lobster boat to make room for us. After the boat had settled on the bottom and we had made sure she would not fall over we adjourned in relays for baths and food at Bodowen.

Next day we sailed with a gradually freshening north-easterly wind, made our departure from the Sarn-y-Bwch Buoy, and saw nothing more, except the Fishguard-Rosslare ferry, until Land's End loomed dimly out of the haze on the evening of 3 September. Good going for 180 miles, and for me, good navigation. The Fishguard-Rosslare ferry, unlikely to be off course, gave us our latitude, and a combined sun and moon shot on the morning of the 3rd a fairly good fix. The mistakes one makes, when one is all adrift and off target by 20 or 30 miles, are seldom forgotten, so that it is heartening to record a bull's-eye.

Off Land's End the wind left us, apparently for good. Three days later we had struggled as far as the Start, some 80 miles on our way, and a laconic diary entry for that day reads: 'What a passage! Omelette and prunes.' Two days later in the same dull, thick, windless weather we were somewhere south-east of Portland Bill and making little progress. Having decided to motor the rest of the way we began a frantic search for a tin of engine oil that Ken reported the engine could not do without. No joy. (Emptying the ship at Lymington the tin was found lodged behind a frame in the stern locker.) Ken reckoned we could motor safely as far as Weymouth which we had already passed so back we went. Even that was not our last stop. Having missed the tide we anchored for the night in Swanage Bay to reach Lymington on the morning of the 9th.

Although *Sea Breeze* had taken us safely to the coast of East Greenland and back we had landed nowhere and achieved nothing. From that point of view the voyage could hardly be reckoned a success. On the other hand, if regarded as a trial run in a boat new to me, a shake-down cruise, it had won several prizes by the shaking down of no less than three spars. Despite that, and the leaking deck, I was happy with the boat and given time, which in my case is getting short, I shall become as fond of her as of *Mischief*.

The crew had scarcely come up to expectations. When they had assembled in June they had struck me as a most promising lot. Alas. As the hapless Duncan remarked:

> There's no art
> To find the mind's construction in the face:

and were there any such art I had at that time no alternative candidates upon whom it might have been exercised. At Appledore I had been lucky, and being then willing to take anyone at all to make up our numbers I had no reason to be dissatisfied. Three days later, *Sea Breeze* having been stripped to a gantline, the crew went their several ways. Looking at the old boat before I, too, started for home, I reflected that in the course of her long life she must have carried even rummer crews – skippers, too, for that matter; men who, unlike the boat herself, were not built to withstand the stress of sea and weather. Ships are all right, it's the men in them.

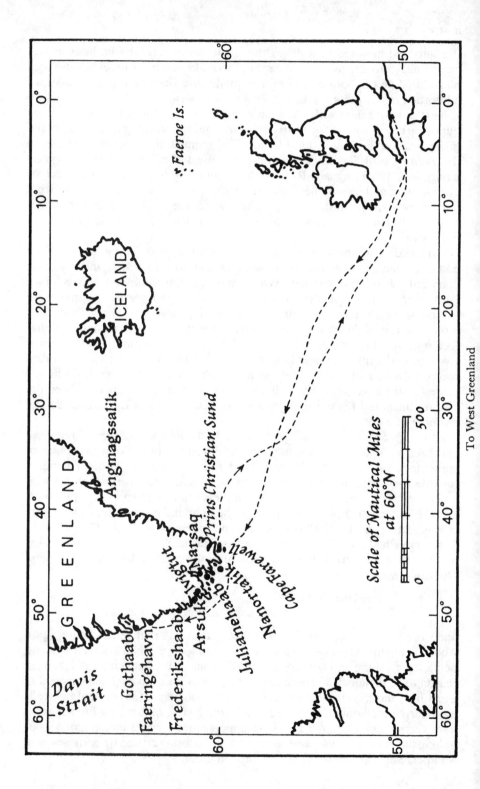

To West Greenland

Part 3

Second Voyage in *Sea Breeze*

Summer 1970

CHAPTER TEN

A Different Crew

THREE MONTHS went by while I pondered over the vicissitudes of life's voyage and voyages in general. In November of 1969 I had not even begun to think of crews or of where to go in 1970, nor had I had any of the usual enquiries. In fact since the loss of *Mischief* the assumption among those who made such enquiries may have been that I, too, had sunk or, at any rate, was fast sinking. After three successive setbacks one needed to be resilient – the troublesome voyage south of 1966–67, the disastrous voyage north of 1968 when through bad seamanship and worse luck I had lost faithful *Mischief*, and then the first futile voyage in *Sea Breeze*. But hope springs eternal even in my breast and to nourish it there came, like a ray of winter sunshine, a letter from Colin Putt whom I had not heard from since we had sailed together in *Patanela* in the winter of 1964–65 from Sydney to Heard Island:

David Lewis tells me that *Sea Breeze* has turned out to be a basically good ship, but that there is some difficulty in getting suitable crews; it struck me that this last point, awkward though it must be, might present me with an opportunity. There is between three and four months leave due to me in the next year; it becomes available in April and I can no doubt scrape up a return fare to England. If you are going on a short voyage in 1970 is there any possibiity of my getting a berth in *Sea Breeze*. I should warn you that in addition to my established vices of eating and talking too much, and compulsive fiddling with rigging and machinery, I would probably be too short of leave to be of much use for fitting out. My friend Iain Dillon has asked me to make a similar plea on his behalf. He is an Australian, mountaineer and student of the classics, and has done a year in the Tasmanian cray-fish schooners. He is definitely no piker and although only 22 is one of the old school and believes in discipline for himself as well as others. PS. What sort of engine has *Sea Breeze*? I might be able to start reading about it.

Colin was then in charge of an ICI chemical works in Sydney and, as I had fully realised in *Patanela*, was a man of infinite resource and ability. Probably, as Monty would say, a good man to go into the jungle with, had we been going there. More to my point, he was a good man to have if one was cast away on a desert island, where he would build you a boat were there enough driftwood about, and an engine, too, given some old iron. He has in hand at the present moment the building of a boat which is to be called *Reconnaissance*; as Colin explains, quoting a trite military maxim, time spent in reconnaissance is never wasted. Besides his technical abilities he has had long experience of expeditions in the mountains of New Zealand and New Guinea, as well as on Heard Island; and while not likely to do anything rash or ill considered he would not easily give up anything he had set himself to do. Nor was that all. He would more than make up for my own taciturnity. As the life and soul of any party, his copious loquacity, embellished with wit, wisdom, and anecdote, would take the weak minds of any crew off the small inconveniences of life at sea, such as cold, wet bunks, or seasickness.

Iain Dillon was an unknown quantity whom I was more than ready to take on Colin's recommendation. The word 'piker' is not in my vocabulary, but it is expressive enough and I thought I knew what Colin meant. Perhaps the majority of the crew on the previous voyage might have been shortly described as pikers. Besides his year spent at sea cray-fishing, he had evidently done a lot of climbing; apparently unable or unwilling to settle down and content to earn enough money to enable him to go on expeditions. If he was anything like the Australians and New Zealanders that comprised *Patanela*'s crew, who regarded the ship they served in and the expedition they were part of as their only responsibility, I should have little to worry about and everything to hope for. Thus with these two as a solid nucleus, sheet anchor and kedge, so to speak, it would not much matter what the rest of the crew – supposing them to be pikers – either thought or did.

I had great hopes of Brian Potter coming again as cook, for the chances of finding any one in that capacity half so good, or so useful on board in every way, were remarkably slight. He had offered to come on the previous voyage mainly in the hope and expectation of climbing a Greenland mountain and had not even set foot in the country. Apart from his usefulness to me I felt I owed him another chance. But owing to some congenital defect his right hand was slowly seizing up – a brother of his suffered in the same way. The surgeon who operated in December assured him that the hand would be right within a month. Spring came and Brian's hand was of less use than Captain Hook's iron claw. He could hold a hammer with difficulty and did not think he was capable of grappling, as it were, with the problems of cooking at sea on an unstable platform, or even of moving about safely, when a sudden lurch of the boat might call for an equally sudden, strong grip of something. In the end I had to reconcile myself to counting him out.

Thus there were still two berths to fill. A friend connected with the Sail Training Association kindly had a notice of the intended voyage inserted in their news bulletin *Sail* – now for reasons of economy defunct. The two training ships *Sir Winston Churchill* and *Malcolm Miller* have between them made some one hundred and fifty cruises, carrying some thirty youngsters each time. I half expected, therefore, to be submerged by a flood of eager applicants for a four months voyage for which they would not pay a thing. Two replied, one of whom, on hearing from me, silently withdrew. I met the sole survivor, Bob Comlay, on board *Sea Breeze* on one of my infrequent winter visits. Inside the boat in winter is like being in a crypt or a cave, one of those dripping caves. Water, a film of condensation, covers and drips from the deckhead and the beams. I am always surprised not to find incipient stalactites and stalagmites growing up to meet each other. Presumably the woodwork lacks carbonate of lime, or perhaps these visits I make, when I sleep on board with the stove going non-stop for forty-eight hours, are enough to nip the budding stalactites. Not only do these visits momentarily dry the boat out but I like to think that *Sea Breeze* feels she is not forgotten.

When Bob Comlay came, Brian Potter was also on board taking measurements for a locker door and a plate rack he was making for me. In those dank surroundings Bob looked a little pale and woe-begone but he made a good first impression. Instead of flicking cigarette ash about he asked for something to put it in, and when I started fiddling with the pump strum-box in the well of the bilge he at once lent a hand and seemed to enjoy having his arms blackened with oily bilge water. He was very young, waiting to go to a university the next October, and was also slightly built – not likely to break a rope by heaving on it. Nevertheless, liking the look of him, I decided to take him and never had the slightest reason to regret it. Besides the high-light of the cruise in *Sir Winston Churchill* he had long been familiar with boats, had a brother who was a naval diver, and a sister who had done far more sailing than he had. A sore point, but a Greenland cruise would put that family quarrel right. He therefore knew something about boats and, as I soon found, was never backward in making suggestions, a few of which, annoyingly enough, turned out to be right. He was extremely keen, put the boat first and foremost, did not forget his obligations to me, always asking for more work, and was generally first on deck and last to leave. In short the type of lad that one has a right to expect from those who offer to go on voyages of this kind.

I had yet to find a cook and since time was getting short played my last card, a card that before now had turned up trumps. I advertised in *The Times*, taking care to say that I wanted an amateur cook of the male species. It was a perfectly straightforward advertisement, no glamour or flat-catching bait, even stating where we were going, and it brought a dozen replies. Things and men are not what they used to be. A similar but much earlier advertisement had brought twice as many replies, though that may have been owing to the tantalising way in which it had been worded, giving nothing away: 'Hands wanted for long voyage in small boat. No pay, no prospects, not much pleasure.' Half the replies to that came from girls or women and I had to pay for my failure to be explicit by writing a great number of explanatory letters giving my reasons for not taking them.

In spite of the precise stipulations in the present case a few of those who did reply obviously expected to be paid for their services, and one confessed to being of the wrong sex. Georgina did not claim to be a *cordon bleu* as one or two of those earlier applicants had, nor did she say anything about her ability to arrange flowers, but she sounded the right sort, 'devoted to slave labour and amateur cooking'. She said not a word about sea experience or even the sea, so perhaps she had never seen it. But neither had Brian Potter for that matter, except from the deck of a steamer. I was sorely tempted to take Georgina at her word until I considered what effect the springing of such an unlikely and possibly unwelcome surprise might have on Colin and Iain. Would Colin's conversational flow have to be muted or even stopped? Was Iain accustomed to mixed bathing?

From the twelve possibles I had little difficulty in choosing. After eliminating the professionals out of hand, Georgina with reluctance, and one or two others who sounded odd, the remaining six, all but one, eliminated themselves. When I met him, though I did not tell him so, Andrew Harwich was the only candidate. He lived in London, as so many people do, and playing for safety I arranged to meet him at the Royal Geographical Society. I remembered that on one or two occasions I had foolishly arranged to meet an unknown candidate at a suitably square club that I occasionally haunt, and the consequent embarrassment caused by my having to borrow a tie from the hall-porter before my man was eligible to enter. Besides their own far-flung Fellows, the Royal Geographical Society give house room to the Everest Foundation and the Institute of Navigation, so that they can ill afford to be stuffy about whom they allow to pass their doors – perhaps, they are not stuffy enough. Their hall-porter must be well accustomed to admitting some queer fish, foreigners and such like.

When a youth with hair down to his shoulders walked in I knew, or rather feared, that this was the chap, for I had noticed him walking up and down in pensive fashion just before the appointed hour. If Andrew was equally taken aback by my appearance he managed to conceal it, as I hope I did my own misgivings. Like Bob he was young and also waiting to go to a university, as it happened St Andrews with which I have a suitably vague and tenuous connection. He could not be expected to have had any experience of the sea or of expeditions but he said he could cook and enjoyed cooking, which is half the battle. At this stage not wishing to discourage him, I did not tell him I had seen Colin eating, and that probably Iain, that much younger, was not likely to be left at the post in the table stakes. Andrew was then passing his time and earning pocket-money by working in a garage as a petrol-pump attendant, an experience that might come in useful to us though at the moment I could not see when. At this interview he may have been over-awed by the picture of some famous explorer leering down at him, Stanley perhaps, or Doughty. He did not say much, I am not fluent, and in a short time he was due back at his petrol pump. For the sound reason that I had no one else in view I agreed to take him and he agreed to come, and I could not have made a wiser decision. His long hair, apart from getting in the way, did not unfit him for life at sea. Without any break Andrew cooked every meal, and cooked them well, from start to finish. Curries and duffs, which in my view more deserve the name of 'sea-food' than lobsters, crabs, and such like, flowed from the galley in agreeable abundance. By the time we were homeward bound, appetites having grown by eating, the duffs had to be cooked in a bucket. Besides this Andrew took an afternoon watch and allowed neither gales, fog, nor ice to perturb him. If Colin, the New Zealander, and Iain, the Australian, set an extremely high standard, my two young Englishmen, were not far behind.

In 1968 we had been in the same latitude and within 300 miles of Scoresby Sound, and in 1969 we had sighted the cape to the south of it. Before the news of Colin's advent I had naturally intended having a third go. But in any one season the chances of success are sketchy and it would not do to court another failure with Colin and Iain on board. They were coming to climb, coming a long way, and I could not afford to disappoint their hopes in that respect as might well happen. Even if we were successful we were hardly likely to be inside the Sound before the middle of August, allowing us a bare fortnight ashore before having to start for home. Reluctantly therefore I abandoned the Scoresby Sound plan, the more reluctantly because I looked like having the sort of crew that would succeed were success at all possible.

I decided instead to try South-west Greenland, Julianehaab and fjords to the south, where there are plenty of mountains of the order of 5,000 to 7,000ft., and where I myself had not been before. Owing to badly underestimating the severity of the ice conditions this proved to be a mistake in that we had too little climbing. On the other hand we had a voyage full of incident and gained a great deal of ice experience. I was aware that we would meet ice off that coast but did not imagine that it would make us nearly a month late in reaching our chosen fjords.

Ice conditions off the west coast of Greenland are peculiar. In early summer north of Upernivik in Lat. 72° N there will be ice near the coast, part of the Baffin Bay ice which is known as the Middle Pack. From there southwards to about Lat. 63° N, around Fiskernaesset, there is unlikely to be any ice other than icebergs; while south of that again, right down to Cape Farewell, there will be heavy pack-ice. This is what the Danes call the 'Storis' or Large Ice, massive floes two or three years old originating in the polar basin and carried down the east coast of Greenland by the East Greenland current. By early spring the 'Storis' will have reached Cape Farewell and begins to extend west and north-west as a belt of ice anything from 20 to 30 miles wide following the trend of the coast. By April it will have filled the Julianehaab Bight and spread further up the coast to as far as Fiskenaesset or even Faeringehavn some 350 miles from Cape Farewell.

On its journey from Cape Farewell it becomes less dense owing to the comparatively warmer water of Davis Strait, and with the advance of summer it begins to disintegrate, more quickly towards its northern limit. By the end of June in a normal year, though the Julianehaab Bight will still be choked with ice, north of that the ice will be widely scattered. Thus a small vessel bound for Julianehaab would hope to be able to reach the coast to the north of the Bight early in July and then by means of fjords and the open water generally found inside the skerries that fringe the coast, work her way back to Julianehaab or any of the fjords to the south.

Obviously then, in order to reach the coast early in the summer and to enjoy a full climbing season the place to go is between Lat. 63° N and Lat. 70° N where one would meet no pack-ice at all. *Mischief's* first and second voyage to Greenland had been to that region and it was on that account less attractive to me for 1970; and if it had been a 'normal' ice season the plan we had chosen would have worked out pretty well.

The fjords at the back of the Julianehaab Bight – the worst place on the west coast for ice – are those where the Vikings had their principal settlement, the Osterbygd or Eastern settlement. Having seen the quantity of ice off this coast, the first question that occurs to one is how the Vikings had managed. They were undoubtedly bold and skilful seamen but surely, one thought, even the boldest and most land-hungry Viking would have thought twice before choosing to settle upon such an ice-strewn coast. The accepted explanation is that the climate was then warmer and that there was in fact no ice. Professor Gwyn Jones in *The Norse Atlantic Saga* has this to say:

There is a wealth of evidence of various kinds which allows modern scientists to conclude that during the climatic optimum of A.D. 1000 to 1200 the mean summer temperatures in southern Greenland were 2° C. to 4° C. higher than now and that sea temperatures in the northernmost Atlantic were of the same order of increase. The area of permanent ice lay north of 80° N., drift-ice must have been rare south of 70°, and very rare indeed south of the Arctic Circle. There is therefore no reason rooted in climate for disbelieving the Norse voyages to Greenland and the mainland of North America.

But in terms of the Greenland settlement the important thing to establish is not that the climatic optimism was warmer than our own warm period but that it was succeeded by a period decidedly, and in the event, fatally colder. Here, too, literary, historical, archaeological, meteorological, and climatic evidence leads to the same conclusion; that after A.D. 1200 the climate of the northern hemisphere fell progressively for two hundred years or more and that by c. 1430 Europe had entered a little Ice Age. Over much of Europe the glaciers were beginning to advance, the tree line fell lower, vegetation and harvests were diminished by the cold; and, worst of all for the Greenlanders, the sea temperature sank, causng an immense increase in the drift-ice which comes south with the East Greenland current.

In an article in the *Geographical Journal* Mr H. H. Lamb of the Meteorological Office, who is in charge of research on climatic variation, wrote as follows:

There is no reasonable doubt that the Arctic was a bit warmer, and that there was less ice on the northern seas, when the old Norse voyages to Iceland and Greenland were made, especially between A.D. 1000 and 1200, than has been the case since. Ice was increasingly encountered on the old sailing route, which crossed to East Greenland near the Arctic Circle, from 1203 onwards; and by 1350–1400 this route had to be abandoned for one further south, rounding Cape Farewell. After 1410 there was no regular communication between Europe and any part of Greenland until the 1720's; the old Norse colony died out, and no European ship ever got in through the ice even on the south-west coast after 1605.

CHAPTER ELEVEN

To Cape Farewell

SAILING DAY had provisionally been fixed for 5 June. Colin could not arrive before the end of May and Iain not until 2 June. I gathered he was earning money for the air fare by working in a West Australian mine. Since there were only three of us available for fitting-out, Bob, Andrew and I lived on board from 20 May onwards. During the winter, if the boat could be got dry enough, I had begun brightening up inside by slapping white paint over the original pastel blue. Slapping is the word, for I was working against time. Bob, who lives at Portsmouth, managed to complete the job in time for us to make ourselves at home on board. Having renewed the ratlines and set up most of the running rigging we faced the problem of the boom, a very heavy spar that the combined strength of two striplings and a man weak with age could barely lift. It had to be got out of a shed, trundled over to the boat, and hoisted to its fitting on the mast. Like the pyramid-builders, but without their advantage of numbers, we had to use our brains, and by dint of a trolly and tackles succeeded admirably. Compared with the boom the weight of the bowsprit is trifling but it cannot be rove from inboard as there is not enough room on the foredeck. The stern of the boat has to be swung out and the bow brought in so that the bowsprit can be launched from the quayside butt-first through the gammon-iron.

With all that done and the boat fully rigged we had time in hand and set to work scraping the deck to the bare wood. At various times the deck had had several coats of paint of different colour and quality and there were numerous worn patches where water could get under the paint and remain so that some of the planks never dried. Some of the old paint could be peeled off with the fingers but there were places where it withstood the attack of the largest scraper we had, a two-handed weapon with a head like a three-sided battle-axe. The bare deck looked well enough when finished though I suspect this treatment made the leaks worse, some of the pitch between the planks having been disturbed by the scrapers.

Colin wasted no time in London. Having arrived at mid-day of the 29th, he joined us that evening, bowed down by a colossal rucksack and clutching a correspondingly heavy ice-axe. The axe, like most of his gear, was of his own making, designed to deal with adamantine New Zealand ice, and modelled, one thought, on the axes with which Swiss guides hewed their way up Mont Blanc early in the last century. His rucksack, and climbing gear such as windproof and gloves, were all home-made, a little outré, perhaps, and lacking in finish, but undeniably effective. If all of us were as proficient, many shops would have to put up the shutters. Vehicles, of course, are well within

Colin's scope. I remember seeing at Sydney – indeed I must have ridden in it – the 'Puttmobile', a hybrid monster, part truck, part motor car, part mobile crane, reminding one of those Eskimo carvings known as 'tubilaks' that portray a mythical creature with the head of a musk-ox, the body of a bird, and the feet of a bear.

Colin had sent by sea two large drums, one containing an armoury of tools – spanners, chisels, saws, a 7 lb hammer, mallets, files, and a full-size adze. All the chisels, by the way, were made from old files, and were looked after, like the rest of the tools, with a craftsman's care, wiped over daily when at sea with a secret mixture to keep rust at bay. In the other drum were six gallons of Australian wine or 'plonk' and a quantity of dried fruit. The wine in big glass jars had stood the journey well and no more deserved the pejorative name of 'plonk' than most of the red wine we drink in England. Within minutes of arriving Colin had changed into working rig, opened up the tool drum, and begun making tentative advances towards the engine.

Iain arrived as planned and instead of the lean-faced, hungry-looking clean-shaven Australian I had expected, he wore a beard, and the removal of this beard some months later revealed an almost chubby face. More surprising still was his voice – quiet and rather more English than the English. So we were able to sail as planned on Friday 5 June. Only a few Lymington friends watched us go – no one from the yard who, perhaps, thought they would soon see us again as had happened before. *Sea Breeze* may be regarded there as an anachronism but she is useful as a sort of chopping-block upon which apprentices can be let loose to try their unpractised hand, for since she is thick little harm can result. On a fine day with an easterly breeze we could not have wished for a better start. Outside the Needles the slight sea affected only Andrew who had so far recovered by the Sunday that we had our usual curry and a masterly duff, washed down with Australian Moselle. Off Anvil Point, of all unlikely places, we were pursued by a patrol boat and brusquely told to steer south as a missile was about to be fired. We ran down Channel at record speed until the Saturday night when, with the Wolf light in sight, the wind headed us. So we bore off to the south and next morning in fine, but hazy weather rounded the Bishop Rock and set off westwards.

Colin apparently disliked carrying birds as passengers. When a racing pigeon settled down to roost on the masthead, out of harm's way and harming no one, he lashed a broom to the burgee halyards and promptly dislodged it. Besides pigeons we had some minor worries. The log, which had recently been overhauled, revolved only by fits and starts. Until the spinning rotator had wound the line into kinks, the register mechanism refused to budge when it would suddenly let go spinning madly and stopping again as soon as the line had unwound. No line could stand that sort of treatment for long and in a few days the line broke and we lost the rotator. It was not much missed. With a little experience the man on watch can estimate within a mile or so how many miles he has done in the watch. Bob made a Dutchman's log which we used occasionally, or we would throw a chip of wood over at the stem and time its passage for the length of the boat. If Andrew was handy he would give you the speed in knots before you had time to write anything down. My sextant had likewise been overhauled with the result that when taking a sight I found I had three suns to choose from, a bright sun in the middle with lesser luminaries above and below. A little confusing at first, but so long as one stuck to the same sun the sights worked out all right.

After sighting the Fastnet light we ran out of wind and into fog, hearing in due course the explosive fog signals from Mizzen Head and later the bellowing of the Bull lighthouse. There is a perfect menagerie of names in that region – Bull island with its neighbouring islets of Cow, Calf, and Heifer, not to mention the Cat and Crow rocks. Winds remained light and progress slow in spite of having everything set including the genoa. Try as we might the wind could not be persuaded to fill both headsails, there was not enough of it. I could sympathise with the good people of Steeple Bumpstead, Bucks., who are said to have refused to allow the building of a second windmill on the grounds that there was barely enough wind for the one they already had. Even after that rush down Channel the whole passage proved slow, so slow that the average daily run for the Atlantic crossing was only 68 miles.

On the 16th, when we had some wind and a lot of rain we did our best run of 130 miles. The rain, and the water that *Sea Breeze* scooped up as she heeled over, soon found a way below. We had to rig a sort of plastic aqueduct along the beams to canalise the drips, leading the water into a tin suspended at one end of the beam. No one seems to have thought of rigging a tin at both ends, so that if the boat were put on the other tack one had to remember to transfer the tin to the leeward side. The hydraulic pump started a leak, too, turning the galley floor into a skating rink. To put this right involved draining the whole system of oil which Colin managed to do without losing too much.

A few hundred miles west of Ireland put us beyond the range of the BBC Home Service and in order to get time signals we listened occasionally to the Overseas Service, and, having got the time signal, usually switched off before the tale of world events began to unfold. At sea only the events within our small world bounded by the visible horizon were of much interest, the sighting of a ship, a school of dolphins, or a whale, having far more impact than wars and rumours of wars. We saw nothing of pronounced interest except on the night Bob called me up to look at a mysterious, luminous object astern which I had no difficulty in pronouncing to be the rising moon.

As I said, we seldom listened to the news, but quite by chance on 19 June, when we were still some 500 miles from Cape Farewell, we heard the result of the General Election. Our two 'colonials' took the news calmly but were happy to join me in what the cheerful Frenchmen that Colin and I had met at Kerguelen called a 'coup de whisky', while Andrew appropriately dished up bully in batter and Cabinet pudding. I see from my gastronomic diary that he had begun reaching out for higher if less filling things than duffs, such as chocolate soufflé and apricot pie. Besides wine we had our full ration of spirits, usually broached only once a week on Saturday night. Except on the homeward run, when with a large surplus on hand, on which duty would have to be paid, we set ourselves seriously to reducing it.

Although we met no full gales we were sometimes obliged to heave to. On one occasion in the early hours of the morning, when the crew were having trouble handing the jib preparatory to heaving to, I lashed the tiller and went forward to offer some unwanted advice. The boat came up into the wind and before I could unlash the tiller she went about with a violent lurch accompanied by a quite appalling crash from below. A big shelf carrying all our wine jars, sextant, binoculars, and spare Primus stoves had come bodily away. Only one jar had broken but obviously the rest would be the better if drunk quickly. Mummery and his guide Burgener, on the Furggen ridge of the Matterhorn, had reasoned similarly: 'Immediately in front, the long, pitiless slabs, ceaselessly swept by whizzing, shrieking fragments of all sorts and sizes, suggested to Burgener – who had a most prudent and proper objection to waste – that it would be well to drink our Bouvier before any less fitting fate should overtake it.'

Head winds rather than lack of wind accounted for our poor average mileage. For us the distance to Cape Farewell was about 1,700 miles, a little less than the distance from north of Bergen in Norway whence the Vikings sailed in their long ships and apparently sailed faster; only seven days to Horn at the north-west corner of Iceland, and four more days to Greenland. Professor Gwyn Jones in a *History of the Vikings* quotes these 'sailing directions' culled from Icelandic sources – most concise directions, no need to be written, capable of being carried in the thickest Viking skull:

Learned men state that from Stad (north of Bergen) in Norway it is seven days sail west to Horn in the east of Iceland; and from Snaefellsness, where the distance is shortest, it is four days sail west to Greenland. And it is said if one sails from Bergen due west to Hvarf (a south-east Greenland landmark) that one's course will lie some seventy miles or more south of Iceland. .... One sails north of Shetland so that one sights land in clear weather only, then south of the Faeroes so that the sea looks halfway up the mountainsides, then south of Iceland so that one gets sight of birds and whales from there.

The Gokstad Viking ship, built about AD 850 and retrieved from a burial mound in 1880 looks a fast ship. In 1893 a replica of the Gokstad ship was sailed across the Atlantic from Bergen to Newfoundland in twenty-eight days. The original ship was 76ft. overall with a beam of 17ft. and she had a keel of 57ft. made from a single oak timber – the similar piece of timber for the replica had to be imported from Canada. On the direct route north of Iceland there would certainly be a good chance of favourable easterly winds since most of the depressions would pass south of Iceland, but towards the end of the Viking period *circa* 1300 the worsening ice conditions had forced the abandonment of this route. It is thought, and it must be almost certain, that the big single squaresail slung on a yard some 37ft. long on a mast some 35ft. high was fitted with a kind of sprit, making it like a lugsail, so that the boat could sail 'on the wind' as well as with a following wind.

Despite head winds, and the drips from which all our bunks suffered in some degree, the crew were in remarkably good spirits. Alone on watch in the cockpit, the rain perhaps pelting down, it did one good to hear the gales of laughter wafted up from below as the crew sat yarning after a meal while the sea-water used for washing up was heating. Iain had one of the heartiest laughs I have ever heard, a laugh easily aroused that far out-bellowed any-

The Heard Island expedition, 1964–65:   13   (above) Russ Pardoe, Warwick Deacock and Ed Reid relaxing in the galley. *Photo: Grahame Budd*

14   Reefing Patanela's main sail during the outward passage. *Photo: Warwick Deacock*

15 (right)
Running under
foresail only
on a fine day.
*Photo: Philip
Temple*

16 (below) The
1963 camp below
the crater rim
on Big Ben. The
pass is on the
right dominated
by a 7600ft peak,
and the main
summit – Mawson
Peak (9005ft) –
is on the left.
This was finally
reached by Putt,
Temple, Crick,
Budd and Deacock
in 1966. *Photo:
Grahame Budd*

17 (top) The south side of Heard Island.
Photo: Malcolm Hay

18 (above) Tilman, with splinted thumb, at the wheel of Patanela. *Photo: Grahame Budd*

19　The Heard Island team on their return to Sydney: (back row) John Crick, Dr Russ Pardoe, Ed Reid, Colin Putt; (middle row) Dr Grahame Budd, Philip Temple, Warwick Deacock; (front row) Tony Hill, H. W. Tilman and Dr Malcolm Hay. *Photo: Grahame Budd*

20　The climbers returning to Patanela after the Big Ben climb. *Photo: Philip Temple*

21   The volcanic eruption at Surtsey near Iceland in 1966.

22   Mischief at anchor off Igdlorssuit. Upernivik Island is in the background, with Tilman's Peak (see photo 8) the prominent summit at the head of the right-hand glacier.

23 Mischief noses through ice floes on the north side of Angmagssalik Island, East Greenland, 1964.

Opposite page:

24 (upper left) Mischief at Jan Mayen, threatened by the ice floes which later gathered to cause critical damage.

25 (lower left) Sea Breeze hemmed in with ice off the coast of East Greenland.

26 (right) Tilman, still a fit man in his seventies, navigating on Sea Breeze.

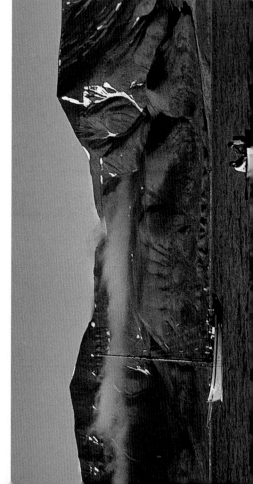

27 (top left) Sea Breeze in Torssukatak Fjord. S. Greenland, 1970.

28 (lower left) Baroque in Magdalena Fjord. Spitzbergen, 1974.

29 (above) Neptune (John Shipton) welcomes Tilman (78) across the Arctic Circle in 1975 during his penultimate arctic voyage.

thing that wind or sea might be doing in that way. Well furnished with argument and exposition, Colin had, too, an endless fund of stories and anecdotes, mainly about the strange characters who still haunt the outback, as the Australians call their hinterland. He had read widely, having at one time, I think, been a teacher, and what is more difficult, remembered what he had read. Bob's studies were to be directed to electronics and computers, Andrew's to mathematics, so that they had something in common to expound – subject to correction by the omniscient Colin – and much to disagree about. Unlike with some of my past crews, no roster for the duty of galley-slave had to be kept. As a matter of course all lent a hand with the washing-up and the sweeping or washing down of the saloon. Colin hardly ever sat still. He was either busy at the work-bench making something – an oven, perhaps, or new chocks for the dinghy – or working on the engine. Among many other things he entirely reorganised the fuel system. During the winter the three tanks that had given us trouble on the previous voyage had been taken out and cleaned. Whoever put them back had omitted to chock them off properly, as we discovered when they began to move in the first rough weather we met.

On 30 June we were by account 60 miles south of Cape Farewell. For the last few days we had had to fight to gain any northing having early on been too intent on getting to the west. On a crossing to Greenland, when head winds are met, it generally pays to stay on the port tack thereby at least saving a little distance. At this stage we began reaping the first fruits of Colin's oven. Iain made currant buns for tea, eaten hot, and we were able to have our potatoes baked in their jackets. Food plays an important part at sea – all ills are good when attended by food – and I hope these frequent references to it may dispel a myth, current since Himalayan days, that to climb or sail with the writer spells slow starvation.

Icebergs are sometimes seen 100 miles from Cape Farewell and the *Pilot* recommends giving the cape a berth of 70 miles. We were surprised, therefore, next morning when I reckoned we were only some 30 miles to the south-west that no icebergs were in sight. When the sky cleared I got a noon sight and found that we were 40 miles west-south-west of the cape and still no ice in sight. The afternoon turned out gloriously fine. Our first iceberg came in sight, the growling of pack-ice could be heard, and presently we made out the long line of ice stretching far to westward. By seven o'clock of a calm, sunny evening, the wind having fallen light, we lay to about a mile off the edge of the ice. The sea temperature had fallen to 33° F. Icebergs, however big, do not seem to affect the sea temperature in their vicinity, but in the proximity of a field of pack-ice the effect is very marked.

Thinking in all innocence that the crew might not have another such favourable chance of observing pack-ice at close quarters we sailed in close enough for them to take photographs. Often at the edge of the pack there is a wide region of scattered floes that tempts or obliges one to penetrate further in order to discover whether the main body of the pack is likely to be navigable. At this stage, of course, we had no such design and, had we had, could at once have laid it aside. On that bright evening, the sun still high in the sky, we lay to within a cable's length of a solid, glistening white wall of anything up to 20ft. in height. Such dense, closely packed ice I had never seen.

CHAPTER TWELVE

In the Ice

WITH JUST enough wind to sail we let draw and followed the ice-edge to the north-west. That night – it was, of course, light all night – an east-bound Norwegian whale-chaser closed us in order to exchange greetings. An Irish monk Dicuil, writing in the year 825, describes with accuracy the light northern nights of Iceland:

The setting sun hides itself at the evening hour as if behind a little hill, so that no darkness occurs during that very brief period of time, but whatever task a man wishes to perform, even to picking the lice out of his shirt, he can manage it precisely as in broad daylight.

Incidentally, in what sort of craft did these Irish monks, who were neither trained seamen nor expert boat-builders like the Norsemen, reach Iceland a hundred or two hundred years before the latter?

For the next week, mostly in fog, drizzle, or heavy rain, we made up the coast, standing out to the west when headed, and then standing in again to keep in touch with the ice, always expecting, as we got further north, to find it becoming more open. We had no intention of trying to reach the coast until in the latitude of Nunarssuit, an island about 120 miles to the north-west of Cape Farewell. The island lies on the north side of Julianehaab Bight, separated from the mainland by Torsukatak Sound, the channel commonly used by trading vessels when coasting inside the skerries and by which Julianehaab can be reached by a sort of back-door entrance, thus avoiding the ice-filled Bight. The success of this plan much depended on our obtaining sights for latitude and whether ice would permit our getting close enough to the Torsukatak entrance to identify it. To make out the small beacon marking the entrance to the Sound we should have to be well within the 3-mile limit.

After twenty-four hours of steady rain, the following day found us hove to in a short, steep sea raised by a stiff north-westerly breeze. For what it was worth, and at the cost of a shower-bath, I managed to take a sight. When we let draw that evening we soon sighted ice a mile ahead, went about, and steered west. When we next closed with the ice we had a fair wind which allowed us to keep the ice in sight as we sailed to the north-west. We had had no sights for latitude but I assumed that we were beyond Nunarssuit. Our hopes now centred on Arsuk, a small port 30 miles further up the coast.

Close north-west of Torsukatak Sound there is a group of no less than 150 skerries, a feature, I had thought, by which the Sound would be far more readily identified than by any beacon. Early on the morning of 5 July the sight of a number of black objects convinced me that my reckoning was out and that we had most opportunely and by accident stumbled on these skerries. Calling Iain, I put the boat about and steered to pass round their western edge. On this drizzly morning, even from quite close, it took us a long time to decide that the black things were in fact icebergs, and the improving light left no room for doubt. Turning back to continue along the ice-edge, an edge that looked as dense and uncompromising as ever, I happened to glance astern and saw a large passenger ship of some 5,000 tons with a tripod mast, slowly emerge from the ice about 2 miles away. Outside the ice she stopped and lay to. I expected her presently to steam north-west in our direction. But she remained stationary and before I could make up my mind to go back, fog came down. Thus we missed a chance of speaking to her and at least finding out where we were. We learnt later that she was the monthly passenger ship on the Copenhagen–Greenland run trying without success to reach Arsuk and Ivigtut.

For most of the day we held on north-west through widely scattered floes, gybed once to escape from a cul-de-sac, and towards evening were again forced out to the west. After losing the little we had gained towards the east, and still surrounded by scattered floes, we hove to for the night. Curry and duff as usual, for it was Sunday night. Since our near encounter with the ship we had seen no heavy ice. I began to hope that the scattered floes we were among marked the northernmost drift of the Storis and that even if we could not fetch Arsuk, then Frederikshaab, the next port up the coast, would be easily attainable. As we learnt later, Frederikshaab was at this time closed to all shipping by ice. Fog held us up next morning until noon when a wan sun and a vague horizon allowed me to take a sight for latitude. It put us in Lat. 61° 30' N., half-way between Arsuk and Frederikshaab, which was probably correct. We gained some more miles towards the land through gradually lessening ice until dense fog obliged us once more to stop. With the air temperature 35° F. and the sea only 31° we needed a lot of clothes.

'A long and trying day' is how my diary describes 7 July. In a small, unstrengthened vessel it is mere prudence not to enter close pack unless one knows that there is open water beyond and how far beyond. If the floes increase and the open water between them becomes less it is folly to persevere and common sense to turn back. These solemn truths were not learnt that day, they were merely heavily underlined. I knew them before, and for that reason the anxious hours that now followed were the more galling. In a flat calm we started motoring north-east through open pack that soon threatened to become worse. Instead of turning back we headed more to the north on the facile assumption that we were near the northern limit of the drift. In a short time there was no longer a question of steering a course, we had to take whatever lead offered, and many of these so-called leads led to nothing but trouble. When we got stuck, which was far too often, it might take a quarter of an hour or more to free ourselves. With her small, offset propeller, *Sea Breeze* needs a lot of room in which to turn. For manoeuvring in ice one wants a boat that will spin round in her own length.

Bob and Iain spent the day in turns high up the shrouds conning the boat, spying out the leads, and looking for signs of open water. They could not see far, visibility being about 300 yards. As the day wore on I had uneasy visions of spending the night and even being crushed in this icy wilderness, cheek by jowl with some of the ugliest ice I had seen, jagged, misshapen, old polar floes 10 to 20ft. high, and, what was worse, always on the move, the leads closing and opening with bewildering speed. Like men in a maze, lost to all sense of time and direction, we sought only to escape. Having probed in various directions, we now ignored all leads except those that trended south, the way by which we had entered our maze, and at last towards evening, to our great joy, the ice began to relent and we reached a large polynia (space of open water surrounded by ice). There we hove to while we supped appropriately off pasta and prunes. The fog then lifted and we sighted land a long way off. Much heartened we pushed on through fairly open water until at 1 am we stopped for cocoa and rum and some much needed rest. When hove to, even in the largest polynias, there were always some floes about; the man on watch had to watch our drift, and on drawing near to a floe had to judge whether we would drift safely by or whether he must let draw and sail clear.

Andrew took my watch and I turned in thankful to have won clear and pretty certain that I knew where we were. During that brief glimpse of the land I was sure I had seen the Frederikshaab glacier away to the north-east. I had seen it before on an earlier voyage from well out to sea, and it is the only glacier on this part of the coast. This 10-mile wide glacier flowing down from the ice-cap some 35 miles beyond Frederikshaab makes an unmistakable landmark. No bergs can calve from this glacier for it ends on a flat which dries. The glacier showed up clearly enough in the morning when we hoisted sail and set off hopefully to the south-east in the direction of Frederikshaab. As the floes increased again we resorted to the engine. For sailing, the floes must be pretty wide apart, five-tenths ice cover at the most. Given room and a fair wind the floes can be dodged easily enough under sail, but if the wind is fresh the boat may be going too fast to stop in time should a mistake have been made and a collision appear imminent. For that reason fore and aft rig is less handy than a squaresail which when backed stops the boat short. A few Victorian yachtsmen who were rich enough to have large paid crews had a liking for northern waters. One of them, Leigh Smith, who has a Spitsbergen cape named after him, eventually lost his yacht *Eira* in the ice off Franz Josef Land in 1881. Another, James Lamont, whose hobby was killing walrus, used to sail his 142-ton schooner to Spitzbergen and then transfer to a much handier 30-ton sloop with a squaresail, having discovered that his fore-and-aft schooner was unsuited to ice navigation.

When the engine had to be stopped for a minor repair we tried the experiment of mooring to a floe in order to stop the boat drifting, the wind being very fresh. Selecting a good big floe with a clean-cut edge and no projecting tongues – nothing like those craggy miniature icebergs of the previous day – ideally with a little indented bay like a small dock, we would put our stem gently against the ice while two of the crew jumped from the bowsprit with ice-axes and mooring ropes. The floe needed to have some hummocks that with ice-axes we could quickly fashion into bollards, for in an otherwise well-found ship we lacked ice-anchors. That our first floe had not been well chosen we realised when a large piece broke off. We moored to another where we decided to stay for a while, the wind having freshened to a good Force 6, and blowing, of course, straight from Frederikshaab. We were low on fuel and could not afford to waste any by punching into a strong head wind. With so much ice still about we realised that we depended largely on our engine.

The floe to which we moored, as well as all the ice in the vicinity, was constantly in motion. Consequently we soon found ourselves hemmed in. At midnight we managed to escape and moored to yet another floe. Twice more we repeated the performance until on the afternoon of the 9th, when we felt we were secure for some time, attached as we were to a really well chosen floe with a mile or more of open water to leeward. Not a bit of it. Within an hour ice began streaming into the polynia and this time we were not smart enough in casting off surrounded by several miles of tight-packed floes of all shapes and sizes intermingled with some vast icebergs. The floe we had picked on was a beauty, nearly 100 yards in length, the one half flat as a lawn, and on the side we were moored amply provided with hummocks that afforded bollards for head-ropes, stern-ropes, breast-ropes, springs, the lot. They came in mighty handy when we had to warp the boat forward or back to avoid some threatening neighbour. Through pressure and rafting these old polar floes are thick, unlike the sea-ice that results from one winter's freeze, which would not be more than 5ft. thick – the sort of ice in which the old whalers and sealers were able with ice-saws to cut themselves a safe dock. In the clear water one could follow the emerald green face of our floe down for 20ft. and there would probably be as much again below that.

During the five days of our imprisonment we kept normal watches except when at night, if the ice was restless, we kept double watches. The two men might well find themselves sweating while they fended off floes with our spiked poles or trudged about on the ice shifting mooring lines. On first realising that we were well and truly beset Colin had suggested having some survival gear ready on deck or on the floe in case the boat got nipped and we had to abandon her. We would, I thought, have good warning when any pressure started, and I doubt if we ever were in danger of being nipped, the few yards of open water that generally surrounded our floe affording that much 'give'. Nor was there ever any tossing about of the ice which would soon have knocked holes in *Sea Breeze*, for the many miles of ice that lay between us and the open sea perfectly damped any swell or motion. We lay as quiet as in a dock. Nevertheless we were by no means free from anxiety, especially at first before we had become inured and reconciled to our strange position. Even with several northern voyages behind me I had no experience of this sort of thing. Perhaps I had had more sense then. In Baffin Bay, in Lancaster Sound, off Baffin Island, or on the east coast of Greenland, we had seldom become entangled with ice and never for long. On the east coast of Greenland we had once been in heavy pack and had suffered for it, but it had been only for some fifteen hours and then we were under safe escort. The crew, for whom all this was novel and who had hardly bargained for being beset, remained quite undismayed and in excellent spirits. What, I wondered, would the crew of the previous year have made of it?

We needed to be always on the alert, fending off or warping out of danger, the situation changing almost from hour to hour. It was surprising how floes, covering perhaps half an acre, could be persuaded to move away a little by steady shoving. We were not vigilant enough. A small floe drifted under the counter and by jamming the rudder hard over broke our beautiful carved, wooden tiller, the pride of the ship. We had a spare iron tiller which we now got ready but for safety's sake did not fit until our escape from the ice. Icebergs were the greatest menace. The pack, and *Sea Breeze* with it, was moving steadily north-west with the current at the rate of about 1 knot. The bergs, drawing several hundred more feet, were unaffected or perhaps felt a counter-current, so that we had the impression that they were moving in the opposite direction at a similar speed, brushing aside everything in their path and causing all the ice within a quarter mile of them to jostle and gyrate. Here, then, was some danger of pressure. Any berg to the north of us we watched apprehensively, striving to determine its course and whether or not this would prove to be a collision course. Happily, none of them passed within a quarter of a mile, and great was our relief when they had drawn abeam and then safely astern. One monster, some 200 yards long and 50 yards wide, resembled an aircraft carrier steaming majestically by, complete with flight-deck, bridge, and funnel.

By 10 July we were well north of the Frederikshaab glacier and abeam of some skerries 2 or 3 miles off to which I took a bearing. In two hours time the bearing had altered 90° which, if our distance off was correct, gave us a speed of 1 knot. Besides this coastal navigation I also tried some celestial navigation, though with a horizon of ice the results had to be used with caution. I took a meridian sight from up the shrouds in order to cancel out the height of the ice on the horizon. It put us in Lat. 62° 53′ N. opposite Fiskenaesset, or 80 miles north-west of Frederikshaab. We were certainly getting on, though not in the right direction. The day being windless I took another sight of the sun reflected in a little pool of perfectly still water alongside, halving the angle so found. It agreed approximately with the first sight. Later, on our way to Arsuk, on a foggy day with a bright sun overhead, we tried the same dodge using a tin of oil on deck, with results so erratic as to be useless.

Some of us used to take a daily walk, pacing our ice lawn back and forth twenty times to accomplish a mile. There was a good pool of melt-water lying on the floe from which we replenished our tanks, the water being perfectly fresh. The *Arctic Pilot* gives the reason:

The enclosed brine in frozen sea water is itself seldom frozen; it tends to sink through the surrounding crystal network on account of its density being greater than that of the ice. With the summer rise of temperature the process is more rapid, and level ice, as the young ice of this age should be called, may lose almost all its salt content. If there is hummocking the progress is again speeded up and a single summer is enough for the ice to become fresh. No taste of salt can be detected by taste and ice of this nature is a source of the purest possible drinking water.

The weather was as usual mixed – fog, rain, drizzle, even one flawless day of unbroken sunshine when an aeroplane and a helicopter flew low over the ice. No doubt they were taking advantage of the weather to fly an ice patrol and we sincerely hoped we had not been spotted, later to be involuntarily rescued. It might be thought that had any of us had the wit to understand a little Danish we might have benefited, or at least kept out of danger, by listening to the ice reports broadcast daily by Godthaab radio and local stations. To make use of such information we would, of course, have to know where we were, but apart from that there is always the time lag and the rapid changes that take place in the ice picture. And, as we have seen, the infrequency of weather clear enough for ice patrols to be flown must affect the accuracy of the reports.

By 13 July, another foggy day, we could detect signs of a loosening of the ice. Later, when the fog thinned, we could see a lot of open water inshore of us. Next morning, to avoid the pressing attentions of a neighbouring floe, we carried out what proved to be our last warping manoeuvre. The fog then cleared, disclosing nothing but scattered floes to the eastward, and after a hasty lunch we cast off from our faithful friend. After motoring to get clear we set all plain sail and sped north-eastwards in more or less open water.

A passing fishing boat ignored us, but presently we sighted a small coaster coming our way. Having about reached the navigator's nadir of having to ask a passing ship where he is, we hove to and hoisted our ensign, whereupon, after circling round, he came alongside and we passed him our lines. The crew were Greenlanders, deaf and dumb so far as we were concerned, but the skipper, a young Dane, spoke good English. He was delighted to see us, delighted, that is, to see so strange a sight as a boat under sail in those waters. In the wheelhouse I had a good look at his large-scale chart. Faeringehavn was our nearest port, 20 miles distant, north by east magnetic, and no ice. Our five-day drift in the pack of just about 100 miles had carried us off my large-scale charts. I had brought no charts for north of Frederikshaab, never thinking we should find ourselves even that far north. Having inspected *Sea Breeze* and passed over a case of Carlsberg – refusing any gift in return – the Dane went on his way to Fiskenaesset. That night, instead of enjoying the bright lights of Faeringehavn, we were once more hove to in fog and a bitter north-west wind dodging stray ice floes. Pasta and stewed apples.

CHAPTER THIRTEEN

To Julianehaab

OFF FAERINGEHAVN next morning, without a chart for the entrance, we relied upon the directions in the *Pilot*. These are usually, perhaps intentionally, full of foreboding, and those for Faeringehavn were no exception. 'The entrance to Faeringehavn, which is encumbered with islets and shoals, etc., etc. . . . No vessel should attempt to enter the harbour without local knowledge.' The key to a safe entrance seemed to be Sorre Sker, described in the *Pilot* as 'a small rock with an orange circular mark painted on it, as the beacon is frequently destroyed during gales.' While looking for this rock we hove to, and a Canadian vessel, *Blue Cloud*, which then appeared from northwards, hove to for the same reason. He, too, was a stranger in these parts. On the principle of always putting the stranger nearest the danger we proposed letting him lead the way and had to keep the engine going flat out to keep him in sight. Just as he made his last turn, which happened to be the wrong one, a bank of fog came down. There are three harbours; a very small basin serving the administrative part of the town, the fishing and commercial harbour a mile up the fjord, and the oiling jetty south of the fjord. *Blue Cloud*'s skipper had mistakenly entered the first and had great trouble turning round to extricate himself. When he was out of the way we went there, too, to make our number with the officials and to post letters, before moving on to the main harbour.

We lay at the end of a long quay where the local fishing boats were busy discharging their catch for sale to the Norwegian-owned fish factory on the quay. The catch was almost exclusively cod. Our thoughts were centred on salmon but there were none to be had. While we were there the first boat of the season left to take part in the controversial deep-sea salmon fishing which is thought likely to lead to a big diminution of the salmon running up European rivers, our own rivers in particular. We were told that the fishing starts on the Baffin-Island side of Davis Strait and follows the salmon as they head for the Greenland rivers later in the season. A Norwegian-owned fish factory is something new, for until 1950 all Greenland activities were the monopoly of the state-owned Royal Greenland Trading Company; now, even in small ports, there are privately owned shops and supermarkets. At a so-called 'Boutique' in Faeringehavn I bought two large-scale charts. At the Sailor's Home, a common feature of Icelandic ports but rare in Greenland, we had showers and substantial meals. Shipping gossip travels fast in Greenland. On the evening of our arrival I had a pleasant surprise in the form of a signal from a Danish friend, Captain Stamphøj, sent from his ship then homeward-bound 40 miles west of Faeringehavn, congratulating us on our safe arrival in Greenland. The owner of a small motor boat lying alongside us had with him two paying passengers, Danish ornithologists. Armed with binoculars and expensive cameras they were working their way down the coast bird-watching.

Having come or been driven so far north I was tempted to take the easy course by going on to Godthaab, the capital of Greenland only 30 miles away, and to the many mountainous fjords further north. We would have met no ice and would have had more climbing, but by now Julianehaab, lurking behind its ice barrier, held something of a challenge. At first we thought of following the coast down, taking advantage of the lead of open water supposedly to be found between the ice and the shore. From our later experience we found that this 'open' water contained large quantities of ice, and a passage with innumerable islets, skerries, and rocks awash on the one hand, and pack-ice on the other, is not at all inviting. We happened to meet on the wharf a Danish naval officer, Captain Jacobsen, whose ship was then taking on oil.

He took Colin and me off to her. There was no question of being piped over the side or of saluting the quarter-deck, if that is what naval etiquette demands, for the only way of getting on board was by climbing monkey-fashion along a mooring warp. The ship, a large frigate or a small cruiser, could not be accommodated alongside the jetty. Over drinks the captain showed us the latest ice reports, by which he did not set great store, and finally advised us to go right out to sea clear of the ice and then to sail south-east as far as the latitude of Arsuk where he was confident that by then the ice would be navigable.

Accordingly on the 17th, having stocked up with black bread and received a present of six large cod from a happily drunken Faeroe islander, we moved to the oil wharf where we took on 60 gallons of diesel oil and 10 gallons of paraffin. A mile or two outside the entrance a line of white seemed to suggest impenetrable ice until one got close to it. Looked at from afar from a small boat all ice looks alike, one has to get really close in order to see whether or not it is navigable. In this instance the ice proved no hindrance and as we left the coast astern it became steadily less. After some 18 miles of motoring we hoisted sail in open water but with the barometer falling from 1,010 mbs. to 994 mbs. in a matter of hours, trouble might be expected. By evening we were hove to for a short-lived gale-force blast. Even when hove to *Sea Breeze* moves crab-wise quite fast and by midnight we had come up with some unexpected ice to the west. Hove to on the other tack heading east, we spent the rest of a dirty, wet night dodging small floes and growlers. So far out in Davis Strait, or in dire straits as Colin called them, we had not bargained for this.

With less than 200 miles to go to reach the latitude of Arsuk, four days in the open sea should have been enough. Thanks to fog, heavy and sometimes prolonged rain, head winds and calms, we took ten days. Five days elapsed before I could even take a sight, and that put us no less than 120 miles out from the coast. A fair wind then gave us a good shove and on the 24th, in the accustomed fog, we heard once more the growl of pack-ice close to the south-east. The next day, remarkable for excellent visibility, we rounded the northern edge of this ice and steered for a point where some far distant ice-blink appeared to end. The ice hereabouts was in the form of large fields or rafts that had broken away from the main body, and given clear weather, they could be avoided. A temptingly deep bay of open water lay all along our starboard hand but beyond it the sky showed the pronounced blink of more ice. This ice-blink is a valuable guide, just as in tropic seas a pale green light in the sky may betray the presence of a lagoon. The *Arctic Pilot* thus describes it:

The ice-blink is quite unmistakable over solid and extensive pack. On clear days, with the sky mostly blue, ice-blink appears as a luminous yellow haze on the horizon in the direction of the ice. On days with overcast skies or low clouds the yellow colour is mostly absent, the blink appearing as a whitish glare on the clouds. In fog, white patches indicate the presence of ice at a short distance. When approaching pack-ice or when wholly or mainly surrounded by it, the band of ice-blink may be sharply broken by one or more dark patches known as water sky. These indicate the direction of leads or open water. If low on the horizon, water-sky may possibly indicate the presence of open water up to as much as 40 miles beyond the visible horizon.

To pick out all these signs infallibly would need a life-time of experience. All is not ice that blinks.

Frequent climbs had to be made to the cross-trees whence one surveyed the sea and the sky to judge as best one could the course to steer. We should have had a crow-nest fitted, and to make life easier – which is the aim of everyone nowadays – such a one as I saw on the *Kista Dan*, an Antarctic relief ship. It was heated, closed all round with glass (fitted with windscreen wipers), and could be reached without exposing oneself to the air by means of a ladder *inside* the mast. Still steering east we were at last brought up short by a barrier of ice that apparently could not be turned. Open water lay beyond, as we could see from aloft, and since the ice was barely a mile in width we chose the weakest spot and gingerly sneaked our way through. On the weather side, where the swell rocked the floes up and down, *Sea Breeze* sustained some hard knocks; in fact by now the water-line planks had bristles like a tooth-brush but as yet the hull had suffered no serious damage.

By evening we came up with what looked like the main body of the pack and since we were still too far north we followed it south during the night for about 40 miles. We saw a whale and a seal, and had our usual Sunday supper of curry and a duff swimming in treacle. Having run our distance by the morning we headed boldly eastwards into the ice, only the windward edge at all thick, and navigable even under sail as we got further in. Between drifting banks of fog I managed to take a reliable noon sight which put us plumb on the desired latitude. All afternoon and evening we chugged on – the wind had died – through scattered floes, fog all round and blue sky overhead, until I began to doubt that Greenland did in fact lie ahead. At last at 11 pm the land loomed up and we came to anchor off what I earnestly hoped was Sermersut Island at the entrance to Arsuk fjord. It is 3,150ft. high and the summit, if one can see it, is serrated. In our haste to have done we had anchored in the first likely looking cove. It had an uneven rocky bottom and was occupied by a large floe, so we got the anchor up and moored to a convenient floe in mid-fjord. As we were having a nightcap of tea and rum the watch on deck reported lights to the north. If we really were off Sermersut no lights, either of a settlement or of a navigational aid, could possibly be seen.

In the morning we made out a cluster of radio masts high up on a headland 5 miles to the north. At first I thought of going there where, in the course of casual conversation, we might learn where we were without the shame of asking. But the more I looked at the lie of the land the more assured I was that we were in the right fjord. The crew remained sceptical until after motoring eastwards a few miles we spotted a beacon, convincing evidence that we were right for Arsuk. The beacons marking the recognised channels through the fjords consist of a small red or yellow triangle mounted on a 10ft. high metal staff. If the triangle points downwards the beacon is left to starboard and vice versa. The radio masts we had seen, ignored on the chart, were evidently a link in some Early Warning or tracking system. Since they are conspicuous enough from seaward they might as well figure on the chart.

We passed the small settlement of Arsuk without stopping and went on another 10 miles to Ivigtut. Our first day in the fjords was enjoyably summer-like. We sat on deck sunning ourselves and tracing imaginary routes up the almost sheer rock walls on either hand, walls that at one point were less than a cable apart. So far the weather had been unkind but in the fjords there was a marked improvement; there is far less fog in the fjords than at sea, and the further inland the fjord penetrates the better the weather. Over the ice-cap the sky seemed to be always blue. I may be wrong, but I believe that to enjoy hot, summer weather in Greenland one needs to be north of the Arctic Circle.

I felt a little nervous about entering Ivigtut. The *Pilot* has this warning:

Vessels are forbidden to enter Arsuk fjord until permission has been obtained immediately before entry from the Cryolite Mine Administration and every vessel must display her national flag while proceeding through the fjord and while approaching and entering Arsuk and Ivigtut roadsteads.

Accordingly on arrival, not wishing to obtrude, we made for a small cove where we would be inconspicuous. The harbour-master, who was then busy berthing a cargo vessel, took time off to rush over in his launch to shoo us away, directing us instead to a small-boat harbour where we lay alongside in the snuggest berth we had had for some time. Some Danes who came on board for a drink took the crew away for beer and smorgbrod at the club. I turned in for a long sleep.

The importance of Ivigtut lies in its cryolite mine, a rare mineral used in the aluminium industry. The only other source, I believe, is in Russia, though the stuff can be made synthetically at a price. The Ivigtut mine, a large hole in the ground now full of water, is worked out, but we were told that the ore stock would take ten years to shift at the rate of 50,000 tons a year. The mine has been worked since the last century and was discovered as long ago as 1794. In spite of intensive search no similar deposit has yet been found in Greenland, but since Greenland has a coastline of over 24,000 miles, equal to the circumference of the earth, there is room for discovery. In its palmy days the low grade ore was used for road or wharf foundations or dumped in the fjord. Some of this is now being recovered by dredging. No Greenlanders are employed at the mine and the present Danish staff is down to about fifty.

Next day I visited the cargo ship *Edith Nielsen* that had come in the previous evening. The captain told me that he had taken three days to come from Frederikshaab going dead slow all the way; he said that among floes radar was of little help. The brother of the King of Denmark, an elderly man and a director of the Royal Greenland Company, was that day to visit the mine having arrived by helicopter at the nearby naval base of Gronnedal. *Sea Breeze* has a full locker of signal flags and here was an occasion, perhaps the only one, when they might be used. So we dressed ship over all and could only hope that her gay appearance was duly noted by the Prince as he drove by in a jeep. *Edith Nielsen*, the only other vessel there, was too busy loading cryolite to pay attention to etiquette, Danish though she was. We could obtain no black bread, more desirable for us on account of its excellent keeping qualities. The Danes at Ivigtut had not come to Greenland to eat black bread, so the twenty loaves that had been ordered for us from their bakery were white. They were so good and vanished so quickly that mould never had a chance to start. We took on more fuel because for the remainder of our time we would be using the engine a lot in the fjords, and since we would be in fjords we could afford to carry a drum on deck. We got this 40 gal. drum in exchange for a bottle of gin. Torsukatak, the fjord we had originally aimed at, was now the objective, and we reached it by way of an inshore passage through the skerries, meeting little ice and using sails for part of the time. Just south of the entrance to Torsukatak is Cape Desolation so named by John Davis in 1585, 'the most deformed, rockie, mountainous land that ever we saw ... and the shore beset with yce a league off into the sea, making such yrksome noyse as that it seemed to be the true pattern of desolation.'

We anchored for the night inside the fjord at a recognised anchorage called Bangshavn where we caught a few cod. Cod of 3 to 4 lb. weight, enough for our needs, could be caught at most of our fjord anchorages by dangling any kind of lure a few feet up from the bottom. For a long time, until we got sick of the sight of them and threw them overboard, we had cod hung from the boom gallows drying in the hope that they would be eaten on the voyage home. From Torsukatak we entered Bredefjord, wide and long, extending some 45 miles inland from Julianehaab Bight to terminate close to the ice-cap. Half-way up the fjord was a mountain we wanted to examine and also a branch fjord by which we could reach Julianehaab. Saturday 1 August was a perfect summer day with just enough wind for us to sail. We lunched linger-ingly on deck in the hot sun. The wind had died and for some time we were content to drift, loath to break the profound calm by turning on the engine. We had our peak in view less than 10 miles away – not very interesting, I thought, but with the days slipping by and no mountain yet climbed Colin and Iain were champing at the bit.

Right from the start the fjord had been moderately strewn with floes and icebergs and their numbers now began to increase. For some time we had been going dead slow, threading a most tortuous course through ever thicken-ing ice, and twice I had predicted that the next opening ahead would prove to be the last and that we were wasting our time. At last even Colin, at whose pressing urge we still persevered, had to admit defeat in the face of a high, unbroken wall of floes and bergs stretching from shore to shore. We were then a short mile from Narsaq, a settlement in the branch fjord, and behind which lay our mountain. Some of this ice may have come from the ice-cap at the head of the fjord but most of it was probably the result of the meeting of the two fjords and the fact that at this point Bredefjord had narrowed to less than a mile wide. So with a wasted day behind us we rethreaded our way through the mass of ice to find an anchorage for the night in a less crowded part of the fjord. There was a lot of weed on the bottom in many of the fjord anchorages and we gave up using the CQR in favour of our heavy Fisherman-type anchor. Baked potatoes, sausage and French beans.

I regretted our not having visited Narsaq, the place the Vikings called Dyrnes, where there are the ruins of several of their homesteads and a church. In the ruins of one of the homesteads was found a runic staff, reputedly the oldest yet found in Greenland and said to date from the time of Erik the Red, *circa* 986. Erik's own homestead was at Brattalid in the next fjord south of Narsaq and about 20 miles away. The so-called Eastern settlement stretched from Torsukatak Fjord in the south up to Ivigtut, and in it the remains of 190 farms, 12 churches, a cathedral, and a monastery have been identified. In the Western settlement, concentrated around Godthaab Fjord, there were 90 farms and 4 churches. It is thought that in its hey-day there were some 3,000 Norse settlers, all from Iceland. As well as making the Vinland voyages from Greenland they seem to have ranged far to the north, probably on hunting expeditions – to Upernivik in Lat. 73° N., for example, where in 1824 an Eskimo found a stone inscribed with runes telling that in 1333 three Norsemen had wintered there; and cairns, thought to have been built by Norsemen, have been found in Jones Sound 76° N., and near Ellesmere Island in 79° N.

While much is known about the Viking settlements, what still remains obscure is how and why they vanished from history. Various theories have been advanced but for none of them is there any real evidence; that they died out through physical degeneration; that they died of the plague, the Black Death that ravaged Norway in 1349; that in the face of pressure from the Eskimos moving southwards they migrated to the adjacent parts of Canada; that they blended with the Eskimo and disappeared as a separate race, or that the Eskimos exterminated them. The Greenland carrier made its last voyage in 1369 and in 1406 the last vessel known to have reached Greenland arrived there by mistake and did not get away for four years. The rest is silence. In his *History of the Vikings* Professor Gwyn Jones sums up:

In the present state of knowledge it seems safest to conclude that the Greenland colony died out for no one reason but through a complex of deadly pressures. Of these its isolation from Europe, the neglect it suffered from its northern kinsmen, the lack of trade and new blood, the worsening conditions of cold, and above all the encroaching Eskimo, were the most important. Even in theory they sound more than enough to bring down the curtain on this farthest medieval outpost of what had been the Viking, and was now the European world, and extinguish it with all the trappings of inexorable and heart-chilling doom.

After a long day, fog all morning and rain all afternoon, we anchored short of Julianehaab in Motzfeldthavn. As I had spent all day on deck, puzzling over the intricate windings of the passage and looking out for beacons, the crew stood by anchor watch. Fishing whiled away the tedium of anchor watches and overnight the crew caught between them a fine lot of cod. Next day, 3 August, some three weeks behind schedule, we reached Julianehaab. We secured first alongside a local boat where we were immediately overrun by a swarm of small Greenlanders who, having pried into everything on board, settled down on deck to jig for cod. For the sake of quiet we removed the children and went to an anchorage among a fleet of small craft.

Compared with Godthaab, the town is modest enough and it is not easy to see why a place that is not easy to reach, especially in summer, should be of importance, except that it is in the centre of the sheep-farming region. In Greenland there are no roads outside the townships, yet in Julianehaab, where one could walk from one end to the other in ten minutes, there are numerous cars and even taxis. There are plenty of shops and in one we all bought anoraks which seemed good and cheap; all, that is, except Colin who of course makes his own. There was even a well-stocked bookshop where Iain and I both invested in an expensive illustrated account of the life of Jakob Danielsen, a famous Greenland hunter and artist who lived at Godhavn up by Disko Island and died in 1938. In it there are many delightful drawings and water-colours portraying hunting scenes and the Eskimo way of life throughout the year.

That evening we were whisked away by speedboat to visit an experimental farm 10 miles away up the fjord. The sheep – of Icelandic stock – were out on the hill but we saw the stables where they are housed in winter, and the few acres of Rye and Timothy grass that provided their winter keep. In a large nursery potatoes, cabbage, and carrots were doing well while radish, a cool-climate product if ever there was one, waxed fat. Rhubarb, which we had noticed growing outside a few houses in Julianehaab, would not win any prizes for giant sticks, but at least it grows. Strawberries were growing under glass and looked well, but the young trees, mostly conifers, were not thriving. In the absence of forests, the forest officer, whom we met, has a discouraging job. He had been there for seventeen years and consoled himself with a Greenlander wife, a large family, and home-brewed beer – lacking a little in head, but clear, amber, and hoppy. I speak as a home-brewer.

CHAPTER FOURTEEN

To the Mountains

TO REACH Tasermiut, the fjord where we hoped to find some good mountains, we skirted the inside of Julianehaab Bight, keeping generally inside the numerous islands and skerries. These serve as only a partial barrier to the ice in the Bight outside; like water, ice-floes seem to penetrate the merest cracks. We set out on an overcoat afternoon having first gone alongside to fill up with water and to collect forty loaves of black bread. Once outside Julianehaab Fjord we were among floes where two hunters in kayaks were prowling about on the look-out for seals. On that grey day the scene reminded me of the drawings in my Jakob Danielsen book. In this part of Greenland seals are not plentiful and kayaks are rare. Yet they are regularly hunted and at the smaller settlements we would be offered skins, usually at a staggering price. Bob and Andrew bought their sealskins at a shop, dressed skins that had been to Copenhagen and back. They were small and comparatively cheap. The skins offered to us at the settlements were mostly prime specimens that may have been in the family for years pending the arrival of suckers and tourists like ourselves.

We anchored that night near the tip of a horseshoe-shaped island, the two arms enclosing a wide reach of water, and from the shore of our little bay the ground ran up to a col 200 or 300ft. high. No re-assuring anchorage symbol appeared on the chart but it looked safe, reasonably snug, and almost free of ice. Throughout the next day fog held us prisoners there and towards evening the barometer dropped quickly from 1,011 to 1,004 mbs. Very violent gusts of wind then began to sweep down from the col, tearing up the water in sheets of spray. The anchor soon dragged. Having shortened up I tried to get the boat further into the cove but in the fierce gusts the boat's head kept falling off. Having narrowly missed hitting the rocks with the bowsprit we abandoned the cove and anchored again further inside the horeshoe, veering 40 fathoms of chain at a mere 30 yards from the rocky shore. The gusts here were perhaps slightly less violent than those sweeping down from the col which seemed to act like a wind tunnel. We kept the engine going to ease the strain on the cable, all hands stood by on deck, with a man at the tiller to meet the wild yaws that were bringing the stern horribly close to the rocks. There was no question of seeking safety outside where the Bight was full of ice. Had the anchor not held we had no other card to play short of motoring up and down in mid-reach where willie-waws danced across the water and more ice kept drifting in. With the glass rising to 10 mbs in two hours the wind began to take off and by midnight all was calm. This short-lived storm bent both palms of the anchor. Happily, we had finished supper just as the trouble started – fillets of cod with a delicate fish sauce of Andrew's invention, and mashed potatoes. As Dr Opimian said: 'Whatever happens in this world never let it spoil your dinner.'

Upon emerging next morning from this ill-starred horseshoe we were stopped by a mass of floes and bergs driven inshore by the brief gale. A few miles back on the way we had come there was an alternative route which we now went back to try. The crux was a 50-yard wide pass between an island and the mainland where, as we now found, two big bergs had drifted in and grounded. In trying to squeeze through between the shore and one of the bergs we went aground, got off with difficulty, and withdrew to a nearby anchorage. From there we went in the dinghy to explore a similar narrow pass which proved far too shallow for *Sea Breeze*. Next day we tried the original route where we were once more foiled by a combination of ice and fog and had to spend another night in the horseshoe. The nights were by now becoming dark and for the first time we saw the Northern Lights.

At our third attempt we were doing well until mid-day when the ice became so thick that I decided to go back. Easier said than done. The oddly-shaped bergs or floes that we had noted on the way were still in sight to guide us back but the pattern of the ice in between was no longer the same, the leads by which we had come having closed. We wasted hours backing and filling in order to turn the boat round after getting stuck in some blind lead, and finally we managed to plant the boat's keel firmly astride a projecting tongue of ice. Nothing would shift her. It looked as if we would be there until the ice melted, until we resorted to the old dodge of rocking the boat by combined rushes of the crew from side to side. Though it was not the course we wanted, when a lead towards the shore offered we took it thankfully and anchored in Zacharia's Havn. We had made a good 12 miles in ten hours. Iain and Andrew bathed under a handy waterfall to the astonishment of some natives who had walked over from the nearby settlement of Sydproven. We were running short of time or we should have visited Sydproven where, according to the *Pilot*, 'the church and houses are built of stone in a style of architecture far superior to the wooden edifices usually seen in this country.'

Even on the next day we did not quite reach Tasermiut Fjord, being stopped by a sudden and furious head wind which made close steering among ice-floes altogether too hazardous. This short-lived blast came with a sharp rise in the barometer. We could only account for all these recent setbacks by the presence on board of a Jonah, and the lot fell on Abdul, the name we had given to the carved head of a coloured gentleman, Moor or Malay, who leered down on us from his place under the saloon skylight. He had a sardonic sneer and shifty eyes and had been inherited by me with the boat. We therefore committed Abdul to life on an ice-floe instead of in *Sea Breeze*'s warm, wet saloon. Zacharia's Havn provided us with seven fine cod, and that night we witnessed another fine auroral display, great shafts of greenish light that for more than an hour waxed, waned, flickered, and finally died.

At the entrance to Tasermiut Fjord is a small township, Nanortalik, where we stopped for an hour to shop, thinking that this was our last chance before starting homewards. At Julianehaab we had been advised to call on a Mr Jensen who owned a sheep-farm in Tasermiut, so 10 miles up the fjord we turned off through a narrow pass to emerge in a wide bay where at its northern end we could make out the Jensen homestead. It was a lovely bay of bright blue water and beyond the olive-green slopes that ran gently down to its shores stood a fierce array of jagged peaks. They were mostly rock and uncommonly steep. We anchored off a sandy beach on a calm, sunny evening, and had not some of the peaks been decorated with small hanging glaciers we might have been in some Highland loch. We felt we had at last got to the heart of the matter. Supper consisted of steamed fish and cabbage cooked in water with a drop of Stockholm tar that gave it a pleasing smoky flavour. Andrew garnished the fish with another sauce of his own invention that would have pleased Dr Folliot. As that worthy observed: 'The science of fish sauce is by no means brought to perfection, a fine field of discovery still lies open in that line.'

Colin and Iain having sorted out their climbing gear set off to reconnoitre a big peak overlooking the anchorage, while I walked up to the Jensen's house to introduce ourselves. Mr Jensen spoke no English and his wife only a little, haltingly. Which was unlucky because we had many questions to ask about sheep-farming in Greenland and about the Viking ruins hard by the house which we were presently shown. Expecting to see at least the remains of obvious stone walls, I was disappointed. These were, so to speak, completely ruined ruins. It needed some creative imagination to transform two holes in the ground like disused sawpits, and three straight lines of stones, into two Viking houses within their protecting walls. Nevertheless the artefacts that Mr Jensen had found on this unpromising site were convincing evidence.

These were mostly weights for looms, small flat stones with holes drilled in them. More, perhaps, may have been found, for we were told that some Danish archaeologists had recently visited the site.

Strictly speaking, therefore, the Jensens were not pioneers, some unknown Viking having farmed the same land a thousand years earlier. For all that the two holes in the ground were not much to build on and the Jensens had in fact started from scratch; housing first themselves, building stables for 400 sheep, and clearing and ploughing the 10 acres from which Mr Jensen was at that moment busy harvesting Rye grass for winter fodder. All this and the running of 1,100 sheep was done with no help but that of two Iceland ponies and three friendly Border collies. The ponies did the ploughing and the mowing, too, if the state of the ground allowed, otherwise Mr Jensen had to use a scythe. The sheep ranged over a vast area, though strictly limited in height by the short distance up the mountain slopes that vegetation could survive. They were rounded up in the autumn and all but 400 sent away for slaughter. They were so scattered that one seldom saw any. Plodding through the dwarf willow, juniper, and heath that made walking an arduous exercise, one might come across two or three at the most, and these would immediately take to their heels like so many wild antelope.

The Jensens visited us the next evening bringing some rhubarb, radishes, and carrots. The talk – helped out by a dictionary – turned to salmon, a fish that had been on our minds for some time. A large lake 2 miles away was apparently full of salmon and although we had no means of catching them, the Greenlanders at a nearby settlement had and visited the lake frequently for that purpose. In asking us to eat salmon next evening Mrs Jensen had therefore every confidence that they would be available, as indeed they were in abundance. For that memorable meal alone we reckoned the voyage had been worth while. Their house was spacious and well furnished; cooking by Calor gas and oil lamps for lighting. The only modern gadget was a radio telephone which kept them in touch with Julianehaab.

The mountaineers' first reconnaissance had been foiled by mist and they now went off in another direction to look for a suitable mountain. Colin, accustomed to New Zealand mountains, liked them with plenty of ice and none of the needle-like peaks in the vicinity seemed to offer him much chance to ply his mighty axe. While taking a stroll towards the salmon lake, a turquoise gem set amid high snow peaks, I thought I could see just what Colin wanted, a mountain about 6,000ft. high abounding with ridges and shoulders, glaciers, ice-falls, snow couloirs, and *névé*. It lay far away at the head of the lake, but distance meant nothing to them and Colin and Iain took fire at my report.

We were enjoying a brief spell of marvellous weather when they set off for this distant peak carrying four days' food and no tent. Evidently, even in the Antipodes, the rumour has got around that armies march on their stomachs. I provided them with a couple of days' food in the form of two old tins of pemmican, a food new to Colin and one that on this trip earned his highest esteem. I gave him the Copenhagen address where it could be obtained, but he rather thought he would be making it himself, meat and fat being so plentiful in Australia. But they wanted more than this snack and as well as necessities took luxuries like flour, potatoes, currants, spaghetti, just as if they were going on a camping holiday. We had a good supply of real farm-house cheese – no soapy, processed stuff – of which they took a liberal share. As Colin said, even if they failed on the mountain they could have a Cheddar gorge.

In their absence the ship-keepers did a lot of walking. I found my first walk to a distant tarn at about 2,000ft. fatiguing and not repaying; mosquitoes and midges were maddening and I had to cross a fast-flowing and frigidly cold glacier stream. Still, the mosquitoes of southern Greenland are nothing like the torment they are further north. We also paid a visit to the lake which discharges into the fjord by way of a wide channel, hardly deserving the name of river, for it is only 200 or 300 yards long. Judging from a few small patches of smooth, rich green grass on the banks of the channel, Vikings may have lived there, too. It seemed to be a favoured spot climatically, where there were groves of birch growing to a height of 20ft., twisted and warped by wind, but real trees.

The climbing party returned on the third day having had the worst of luck with the weather. The fine spell broke on the second day when they were on the summit ridge not far from the top, whence they were forced to retreat in a hurry before the onset of a severe storm. Nevertheless they had had some good climbing, Colin had used his brain-biter with effect, and accustomed as they were to the frustrations of New Zealand weather, defeat did not rankle. The fact remained that we had only a fortnight left and that so far we had nothing to show. We intended leaving Greenland about 1 September by way of Prins Christian Sund, the eastern end of the inland waterway that links the west to the east coast well inside Cape Farewell. The western end of the waterway is Torssukatak (two S's this time), a fjord bristling with mountains where we could profitably spend the remaining time. Having said good-bye to the kind Mr and Mrs Jensen we started back down the fjord leaving Nanortalik well on our starboard hand. As we turned south for the 20-mile run down the coast we had a brisk wind dead astern. Frederiksdal, a small settlement at the fjord entrance, was our goal for the night. With a fair wind the boat romped along through pretty ice-free water, but with the wind aft we had to tack and in moderate visibility were seldom close enough to the shore to distinguish any beacons. At 7 pm, having run our distance, we gybed confidently for the run in to Frederiksdal and Torssukatak Fjord. On reaching the fjord entrance we were surprised at the absence of any beacons or of any glimmer of light from the settlement. It rather looked as if someone had blundered. In the gathering gloom we stood on into the fjord where it took us another two hours to find an anchorage. In these deep fjords it is always a problem. Only at the mouth of rivers or off a valley that once held a glacier, is there much chance of finding shallow enough water. Even so one may find oneself closing the shore, the distance becoming perilously less, while the mournful cry of 'no bottom at ten' still echoes back from the leadsman.

My guess was that we were short of Frederiksdal but nothing that we had seen on the way in could be reconciled with any of the fjords as shown on the chart. As we repassed the fjord entrance on our way out to sea next morning I noticed a little hook-shaped cape which gave me an inkling of where we were and from further out I could identify Cape Christian, only 5 miles from Cape Farewell and the end of Greenland. We had overshot our mark by two fjords. We took a beaconed short cut to Frederiksdal from which an accumulation of ice forced us to retire, and then near the settlement we luckily met a venerable and genial Greenlander returning in his dory with a nice catch of cod. We took him on board, made fast the dory astern, and handed him the tiller. He told us the harbour was chock-full of ice and took us instead to a place we should never have found for ourselves, a small cleft among the rocks, deep water and just room for *Sea Breeze* and not much else. To our alarm a small coasting vessel *Narwhal* now appeared evidently heading for the same hole. Her skipper turned her in her own length, backed into the gap between us and the rock wall, and having made fast to it began discharging his cargo on top of it.

The Royal Greenland Trading Company had a store here where we bought honey, lemons, coffee, and some galvanised nails for tingles. By now there were some deep gashes along the waterline that would need to be covered before leaving Greenland. Our pilot took us to his house – neat, clean, and warm – where we discussed the merits and price of a large sealskin. It was too dark in colour to be really attractive and no sale resulted. Outside most of the houses there were hanging rows of cod's heads that had been cleaned of everything except the teeth. We were told they were good for making soup – tasty, no doubt, but hardly nourishing. I should like to have had Dr Folliot's opinion. There was a dance that night in the local Town Hall, a bleak shed lit by one Aladdin lamp, and only heavy rain prevented Bob and Andrew from attending.

Motoring next day up Torssukatak we met *Narwhal* on her way back from the even smaller settlement of Augpilagtoq, the last in southern Greenland. We stopped short of it at a marked anchorage called Stordalens havn close to a 6,000ft. peak that looked extremely difficult, steep and probably rotten rock as most of it is in those parts. We were roused out early by an intruding floe that obliged us to move twice before it went on its way. I went up to a snow col at about 2,500ft. to spy out the land and I got the impression that some of the formidable rock towers in the vicinity would go if approached from the ice-cap side as opposed to the fjord side. There were difficulties about that, too, for the snow basin to which the col gave access was cut off from the ice-cap by a high rock wall. Coming back, hot and sweaty, I had a far from memorable bathe in a shallow runnel and had a long walk across flats of hard sand to reach the water, the tide being out. Several big floes were sitting high and dry on the sand which was thick with worm-casts. The mixture of ice-floes and worms struck me as incongruous and I wondered what Darwin, who wrote a monograph on worms, would have said of it.

Colin was temporarily 'crook', as they say in New Zealand, so that for once time spent on reconnaissance was wasted. We decided to move on, a large iceberg drifting down on us providing an immediate spur to action. In backing away too hastily from this menace we ran hard aground and had to wait for the tide to refloat us. Clearly it was not our day. On the way to Augpilagtoq, with supper long overdue, we were tempted to anchor short of the place in a bit of a cove. Some small pieces of ice drifting by showed that there was a fast current. No sooner was the anchor down in 11 fathoms than a much weightier bit of ice drifted athwart the anchor chain and hung there, threatening to break both it and the bobstay. By going full astern and winching in cable at the same time we shook it off but not before both the shank and fluke of the anchor had been bent.

The harbour at Augpilagtoq is a long, narrow cleft in the rocks into which it seemed unlikely that any floes would drift, yet even there we were pestered by them. If there were any traffic other than small boats it would be easy and worth while to stretch a wire across the entrance as is done at Angmagssalik to keep out ice. Besides the usual cod hung out on drying racks, we were surprised to see a lot of what looked like seal blubber; 40 miles or more from the sea in either direction seemed a long way inland for seals. At this small place, with a population of a hundred at most, an enterprising Greenlander had opened a café. He entertained us to coffee and biscuits while Bob entertained an audience of two small Greenlanders with the guitar that was part of the café furnishing. I paid in kind with a packet of English matches with which he was delighted.

Near Augpilagtoq three fjords meet in a broad stretch of water called Ilua. Taking advantage of a sunny day and a little wind we sailed about in Ilua while Bob and Andrew in the dinghy took photographs. That done we went on up an arm of the fjord called Kangikitsoq where we at last found an anchorage that was free of ice. Entering this arm we passed an immense piece of ice. What name it deserved, whether floe or berg, was hard to determine, for it was perfectly tabular, measured a good hundred yards either way, and was about 20ft. high. This monster was still drifting quietly to and fro in the same place when we left and promised to survive at least another summer if not two. Whence it could have come was another puzzle. Hard by, a big glacier descending from the ice-cap pushed out well into the fjord, but it looked far too wrinkled and crevassed to be the source of such a perfectly flat and symmetrical piece of ice. We looked at this glacier to see if it might provide a route up on to the ice-cap whence the climbers might have found a way up the highest peak in the fjord. It was far too broken, so we returned to our ice-free anchorage where we remained until sailing day, 30 August.

CHAPTER FIFTEEN

Homeward Bound

AFTER A LONG walk up the main valley Colin and Iain reported having found
a good camp site at the foot of a glacier by which, they thought, an attractive
peak could be reached. Taking five days' food and a tent they left next day for
what sounded like an idyllic spot, juniper wood for a fire, a small tarn for
water, the glacier highway beckoning them onward and upward. The ship-
keeping party settled down to work and short walks. Bob and I spent most of
the time working on the deck, gouging out any soft wood and putting in
graving pieces, hammering in caulking cotton and pouring pitch into the
seams. Colin had already put tingles over the deeper gashes along the water-
line, but below that, where we could see there was some damage, nothing
could be done. In the calm waters of the fjord she made hardly any water and
although in the open sea the story might be different I did not think the case
warranted our trying to beach her in order to get at problematical leaks. Most
of these wounds, I regret to say, were self-inflicted, that is to say by mis-
judging the width of a gap between floes or by moving too fast when we
should have been going dead slow, we had too often given poor *Sea Breeze*
some terrible and avoidable knocks.

Andrew took up archaeology, having found what he thought was an old
house site. With my ice-axe – which I implored him not to break – he delved
away industriously and at length unearthed a piece of wood that looked
suspiciously like part of a soap box, evidently of the post-viking period. I took
a walk up the main valley, crossed the river, and came back on the other side
among some of the largest boulders I have ever seen. Some of them offered
the weary traveller a fine bivouac and they had evidently been used as such
judging by the rough stone walls that some bygone occupant had hoped would
keep out the draught. But what would bring anyone to this valley? Salmon in
the river? There are no reindeer to hunt in this part of Greenland, and we saw
nowhere the least sign of life except the spoor of what was probably a fox. I
reached the fjord again so far from the boat that I had to light a signal fire to
summon the dinghy. On a pleasant grass flat near the shore was a hut,
probably some Greenlander's fishing lodge, and, more interesting, a line of
man-laid stones. I thought them far superior to those at the Jensens' farm, but
instead of being in a straight line the stones were laid in a graceful curve for a
length of some 50 yards. Laid, possibly, by a deformed Viking, one leg
shorter than the other.

The climbing party returned after four days having had plenty of fun but no
great success. So late in the season snow conditions were becoming unsafe.
They had found the *névé* beyond their glacier highway so seamed with

crevasses, and their snow bridges so frail, that they considered it dangerous, especially for a party of only two when if one falls in there is not enough hauling power available to get him out. Accordingly we decided to leave as arranged on 30 August. Our ice-free anchorage lost its good name on the morning we left when a great floe drifted in to settle down almost alongside.

We had nearly 40 miles of motoring to reach the eastern end of Prins Christian Sund where there is a Danish weather station at which we intended to call. This long passage is spectacular and in sunless weather a little grim, the rock walls of the fjord extending for mile upon mile, their continuity broken but rarely by the steep ice-fall of a glacier cascading down from the ice-cap. Not only was the day sunless but a canopy of cloud accentuated the gloom by concealing the heights and leaving nothing to be seen but a few hundred feet of forbidding rock wall lapped by steel-grey water. Some 15 miles from the weather station we met a small speedboat driven by two cheerful, young Danes bound for the bright lights of Augpilagtoq, the café and the guitar. At the rate they were going it would not take long always provided they failed to hit a small piece of ice. They must have a girl friend there, more likely several, because they insisted on giving us two out of a collection of large chocolate boxes stowed under their canopy.

We did not make the weather station that night. We anchored on the south side of the fjord having inspected and discarded a more attractive spot on the north side owing to the amount of ice there. It was strange to be thus still pestered by ice so late in the summer when there was practically no ice coming down with the East Greenland current. Presumably this ice was mostly debris from the local glaciers most of which came right down to the fjord. Next morning we anchored close inshore near the little wharf of the weather station, the vicinity of the wharf itself apparently so encumbered with rocks that we funked going alongside. However, a reception party on the wharf waved us in so we crept nervously into the smallest harbour I have ever seen. But there was deep water alongside and just enough room between the wharf and a rock wall to warp the boat round, as we did later to make our exit easier.

The chief of the station came on board and we had barely finished a second round of drinks before a fork-lift truck, summoned apparently by telepathy, began shovelling crates and cartons of food on to our deck. Potatoes, long-life milk, eggs, cheese, hams, wrapped bread, biscuits, sauces, shrimps, honey, jam, in endless variety until, I think, we had more food on board than on the day we left Lymington. From experience I suspected that something of the sort might happen and had hinted as much to the crew, but I was quite taken aback by the enormity of the happening. With one exception, these far-flung establishments, whether in the Arctic or the sub-Antarctic, especially if they are not British, have always been excessively kind to visitors like myself. This station was manned by sixteen Danes who do a two-year stint and are sustained by the most modern conveniences, showers, sauna baths, and real water closets, the only ones of their kind in Greenland. They are well paid during their exile, as they deserve to be, for they lead a monotonous life with no high days or holidays. One would need to have an indoor hobby or an outdoor activity such as ski-ing in winter and perhaps sailing in summer. Throughout the year they get mail every three weeks from Nanortalik because in winter the fjords do not freeze over. But this year their first supply ship arriving from eastwards had not been able to get in until 14 August. She was, by the way, *Britannia*, the same ship that *Mischief* had followed through the ice to Angmagssalik in 1964.

A flight of wooden steps, several hundred of them I should guess, led from the wharf to the main establishment on the headland. A wire-rope railway hauled up supplies. After sampling the showers we had drinks in a large, well-furnished ante-room before adjourning for supper in an equally large dining hall. The cook had two assistants. One felt that he needed them, especially on that evening when he had to provide for my crew of cormorants, worthy descendants of Carlyle's 'gluttonous race of Jutes and Angles who saw the sun rise with no other hope but that they should fill their bellies before it set.' Most of the Danes whom we met enjoyed their life in Greenland but few regarded the country as anything but an incubus, a financial incubus on the back of Denmark that they would be better without. A great deal of money has been spent in the past, and is still being spent, almost entirely for the benefit of the 30,000 or so Greenlanders who by now would be hard put to it to support themselves if support from Denmark were withdrawn. Inevitably their former self-sufficient life of bare subsistence has vanished, to be replaced by a life in which food, clothing, and other necessities have to be bought with cash.

Instead of porridge, that well-tried belly-timber, Andrew could now provide what might be called a hotel breakfast – fruit-juice, cornflakes, and real milk. After which we cast off and sailed out to sea. In a bitter north-east wind accompanied by flurries of snow we watched the desolate coast recede. By now, even on this coast, all the ice had vanished, all but some bergs that had grounded on a reef 3 miles out. These, the last we were to see, managed to give me a final fright. Until we had drawn near I did not appreciate how fast we were being set down on them, what with leeway and current, and that if we ran the boat off we would pile up on the reef to leeward of them. We should have gone about but by dint of sailing hard on the wind we scraped by with little enough to spare. We were going fast and by evening had got clear of the East Greenland current, as we could tell when the sea temperature rose from 35° F. at mid-day to 47° F. at 6 pm.

As expected, the amount of pumping required increased suddenly from 40 strokes to 200 strokes a watch, and next day in a rising easterly wind to over 300 strokes. By evening the wind had backed north-east and risen to a gale, the glass having fallen from 1,010 mbs. to 986 mbs. Once more I was reminded of Lecky's warning, that a falling barometer with a northerly wind conveys a warning which cannot be disregarded with impunity. Throughout the night vicious squalls of wind and rain drove at us without intermission. Not wanting to lose ground to the west by running, we were hove to with everything close-reefed. The leak naturally increased, so much so that in one hour 500 strokes were needed to clear the well. This alarmed me considerably and we set double watches, one man on deck and the other pumping. By morning the wind began to take off but Andrew and Colin, unused to this rough treatment after so long a spell in calm waters, were not at all themselves. We searched diligently for a leak that, short of stripping the lining, looked like worrying us for the rest of the voyage. Two days later, however, poking about under the floorboards near the 'heads', Colin discovered a small stream coming in where a plank had started away from a frame. By fitting a strongback, and shoving oakum and tallow between plank and frame before tightening up, he practically stopped it. Easy enough to describe but the job took two days of hard work.

Three days later we had another gale, happily from north-west so that with only the staysail set we ran before it at 5 knots; and hardly had that blow subsided before it piped up again from north, the squalls becoming increasingly violent as the barometer rose. We reefed down successively until there were so many rolls on the boom that only about 6ft. of the mainsail's luff remained hoisted, but by afternoon we had to take the sail down altogether and run under bare poles, still doing 3 knots. We did well to hand the sail. As we got it in we saw that the gaff was badly sprung about a third of the way along from the peak. Nothing could be done at the moment, nor did we have any present use for the mainsail, the gale continuing to blow all the next day.

In all this rough weather, despite our having stopped the leak, she still made a lot of water, most of it by way of the deck where there was always water sloshing about. Certainly things were a bit damp below. The chart table, where the chronometer watch in its wooden case was screwed down, and the sextant on a shelf above, suffered from constant drips. The horizon glass of the sextant began to mist over and became progressively worse so that before the end of the voyage the sun needed to be bright to be seen at all in the mirror. Star sights were out of the question. Worse still, the winding spring of the deck watch broke. I took the time by Colin's wristwatch which was pretty steady, backed up by frequent time signals. When the wind moderated we set the topsail as a sort of trysail and with the winds remaining in a westerly quarter we made good progress. As soon as the sea had gone down and the boat steadied, Colin began sawing up a 14ft. length of 9in. by 3in. timber, exulting, I think, in having foreseen some such occasion when this great baulk of wood he had so long treasured would be put to use. In order to select the best of it he began by ripping the whole 14ft. lengthways, a task that took a whole morning. He had already made two iron brackets and, having got his two 7ft. lengths, was able to fish the gaff.

So far we had met only two ships, both Russian, one of which altered course to have a close look at us while the crew waved and took photographs. We were then some 500 miles from the Bishop Rock where we wanted to make our landfall. That night a large bird alighted on Bob's head as he sat in the cockpit steering, Colin, the bird-fancier, was safely asleep so we put the bird in a box in the saloon hoping that when he got up to go on watch the bird would either crow or peck at him. Except that it was not a domestic fowl – though almost as big – none of us knew enough about birds to identify it. It was a queer bird, quite tame and seemingly familiar with the boat, and judging by the sardonic glint in its eye my opinion was that Abdul had adopted this disguise in order to fly from his ice-floe to haunt us. I could imagine him chewing the matter over, pondering ways and means, what disguise would best serve, and perhaps receiving inspiration for his plan from some lines he had heard me quote:

> The feathered race with pinions cleave the air;
> Not so the mackerel, and still less the bear.

When I showed the bird's photograph – he liked being photographed – to a knowledgeable friend he at once identified it as a juvenile, or immature, as the ornithologist would say, Icelandic gull. In spite of its immaturity it knew it was on to a good thing and stayed with us for two days while we fed it on pilchards and Greenland shrimps. Then one dark night he suddenly vanished. I suspect Colin could have told us why.

By the 15th we were once more under full sail, and a near gale on the following day thoroughly tested Colin's handiwork. Personally I never had any doubts, the fished gaff appearing strong enough to withstand a hurricane. This blow, for which the barometer hardly moved, went on for two days while the shipping forecast handed out gale warnings for each of the twenty-three areas it covers except for those in the Channel. Being then well south of Mizzen Head we were quite content to put up with the windless day that followed the gale, since it was so gloriously fine. With so much of our gear hung out to dry the boat looked like a second- or third-hand clothes shop. Happy in our ignorance, we could not know that this fine day marked the beginning of a spell of anti-cyclonic weather that was to prevail over the British Isles for the next fortnight, a fortnight of easterly winds and thick weather.

After breakfast on the morning of the 20th I got a sight that put us 10 miles west of the Bishop Rock and two hours later I sighted the lighthouse fine on the starboard bow, all the islands to the north of it hidden in fog. The crew began comparing me with Henry the Navigator, but even my own modest impression that I was becoming moderately competent in this difficult art had, within the next twenty-four hours, to be revised.

With the wind at east we steered south to clear the islands, and that evening in fog, visibility about 500 yards, when we were back on the other tack steering north-east, we heard the Bishop's explosive fog signal fine on the bow and rather too close. Going about we made another long board to the southward. By next morning we were again steering north-east, still in poor visibility, when we sighted land close on the port hand. All agreed that we were east of Land's End and just about entering Mount's Bay, though to me the presence of some rocky islets close inshore was puzzling. They must have grown up since the printing of the chart. A hastily taken sight put us 20 miles to the west-north-west, somewhere off the north Cornwall coast, the land, if anywhere, on our starboard hand. Most confusing! Was this the right continent? As Lecky's editor says: 'Nothing could be more distressing than running ashore, unless it be a doubt as to which continent that shore belongs,'

I discarded the sight as being too bad to be true, attributing the strange result to the poor horizon, the fogged mirror, and Colin's wrist-watch. I did not even bother to plot the position line that the sight had given, a line that ran nearly parallel to our course; had that been done I would have noticed that the line passed close to St Mary's (which was, of course, the land we had seen) and the Seven Stones lightvessel. However, we carried on into our supposed Mount's Bay. It seemed uncommonly wide and although the visibility was poor it became every moment more difficult to account for the absence of any land ahead. At length, when we had been sailing for two hours, Bob drew my attention to the Seven Stones lightvessel, just becoming visible less than 2 miles away on the port beam. The moral seems to be that the most suspect sight is more trustworthy than dead reckoning and guess-work.

By nightfall we were back on the right side of Land's End and the next morning really were in Mount's Bay with Penzance in sight. Outside the bay we hove to, unable to make any ground against an easterly wind that had increased to Force 6. The wind did nothing whatever to disperse the fog. We had a close shave in the night with a trawler and early in the morning passed close under the stern of a big Norwegian freighter, hooting away on his foghorn and going dead slow. It was unusual and reassuring to see the Regulations for Preventing Collisions at Sea being so strictly obeyed – perhaps her radar had broken down. The fog lifting and the wind moderating, we paid another visit to Mount's Bay, far enough east this time to see St Michael's Mount instead of Penzance; and in order to let *Sea Breeze* see the place where she had been built seventy-one years ago we went in close to Porthleven.

Since for the last three days the barograph needle had drawn a perfectly straight line across its chart we had little hope of any change in the weather, but the wind did at last veer south and we made a great leap forward to Prawl Point where at night we lay becalmed amidst a stream of shipping. Naturally in these conditions we listened hopefully to the shipping forecast which again gave gale warnings for every area except the Channel where the wind was to be south-west Force 5 to 6, and by morning perhaps gale 8. In fact we had a fair wind at south and sailed fast in a perfectly calm sea until with Portland Bill in sight the wind died.

On Sunday the 27th, the last day of the voyage, with a fair wind and the tide under us we went fast past St Alban's Head while Andrew attended to the cooking of a duff to end all duffs to celebrate the event. Like most of our homeward bound duffs it had to be cooked in a bucket to give room and scope enough, and when it appeared on the table, smothered in Golden Syrup, even Colin had to admit that his vision of the higher gluttony had at last materialised. Anchoring for the night off Lymington River we made fast next morning at our old berth, eight days after sighting the Scillies. It had been a frustrating week but at least the sails were dry.

With able and willing hands two days sufficed to strip the rigging and take everything out of the boat and into the store. Colin and Iain lingered in England for a few weeks, returning to the boat at week-ends for Colin to lay-up the engine and Iain to repaint the whole of the inside. If they had not had all the climbing they expected, they felt, I think, that our unforeseen and uncalled for adventures in the ice more than made up for that. For my part it had been a good voyage, if not the most successful then certainly the happiest which is almost as important. Those who took part had more or less chosen themselves, so that I could take no credit for that, but only congratulate myself that for once I had sailed with an able and willing crew who thought only of the ship they served and the success of the voyage. With as good a crowd a few years earlier who knows but that something of note might have been accomplished.

ICE WITH EVERYTHING

Ice With Everything

First published by Nautical Publishing Co. Ltd. in association with George
G. Harrup & Co. Ltd., 1974

Contents

CHAPTER ONE

To the Faeroes

FOR MOST MEN, as Epicurus has remarked, rest is stagnation and activity madness. Mad or not, the activity that I have been pursuing for the last twenty years takes the form of voyages to remote, mountainous regions. In more recent years this has invariably meant a summer voyage to the Arctic, either to the west or east coast of Greenland. By now such voyages have become a habit, and a worse habit is that of writing about them. In these pages are descriptions of the three most recent voyages, those of 1971, 1972 and 1973, the first comparatively humdrum, the second totally disastrous, and the third exceedingly troublesome.

Upon her return from the 1970 voyage to south-west Greenland *Sea Breeze* had been hauled out in order that the hull could be examined. The ice she had encountered, besides inflicting some deep scars, had started one or two planks, yet considering that throughout the two months spent upon the coast she had never been out of sight of ice and had spent five days in the pack moored to a floe, she had got off lightly. The defects having been put right, she received her annual coat of anti-fouling and went back into the water for the winter. *Sea Breeze*, by the way, is a Bristol Channel pilot cutter built in 1899, length 49ft., beam 14ft. 4in., drawing 7ft. 6in., and of about 33 tons TM. A boat built in 1899 may seem on the old side for such voyages, but I have a liking for craft of traditional lines and rig and a foolish liking for doing things the hard way, for apart from her engine *Sea Breeze* is much as she was when a working boat. Nothing, of course, could be more untraditional than an engine, but to be without one on the Greenland coast is a grievous handicap. Apart from ice or skerries upon which a sailing vessel becalmed might drift helplessly, there is the matter of making progress. In the fjords winds are light and fitful so that without an engine one might spend days drifting about unable to reach one's goal or even to reach an anchorage. Pilot cutters are necessarily old, for none were built after 1910, but they are eminently suitable for these voyages – ample stowage space, sturdily built, and able sea-boats – qualities that had been impressed upon me in the years from 1954 to 1968 when I had been the happy owner of *Mischief*, a pilot cutter built in 1906.

Barmouth, where I live, is 230 miles from Lymington where *Sea Breeze* lay. Why not, one might think, move the boat to Wales or oneself to Hampshire? Long use and wont and the inability to get out of a rut together make one reason and besides that there is the absence of hills in Hampshire and the scarcity of boatyards in Wales. In winter a boat out of commission is a forlorn habitation and on my periodical visits I used to put up at a guest-house. When this closed I had perforce to sleep on board, a salutary exercise that brought home to one the dangers that beset a boat laid up for the winter. 'Death and decay in all around I see' would be a mild description. From stem to stern the deckhead dripped moisture, mildew bloomed on the varnish, and one half expected to find toadstools sprouting in the lockers. In the dark and more inaccessible corners that are features of old boats, they probably did. *Sea Breeze*, I believed, would last my time, but not unless steps were taken to combat damp and decay during the winter lay-up. A big canvas cover supported on booms over the whole length of the boat not only kept the rain off the deck but allowed all hatches and skylights to be left wide open. This made a big difference and since on these visits I had a stove going non-stop the cabin soon became less like the family vault.

Northern waters offer a wide choice of places that are accessible to a small boat in summer – Spitsbergen, Jan Mayen, Baffin Island, and both the coasts of Greenland. Including fjords, some of which are a hundred miles long, Greenland has a coast line of some 20,000 miles, hence inexhaustible riches for anyone who has at command his own transport in the form of an able boat. One is often asked what is the attraction of Greenland and the reply would be, where else would a man who desires both hills and the sea want to go. Where, within a month's sail from home, he can see mountains that are Alpine both in character and stature and glaciers vastly in excess of Alpine stature; where there are numerous uninhabited, little-known fjords; a coast fringed with islands, islets, and skerries equally devoid of human life; where a man in his own boat, though hardly to be called an explorer, even at this late date can, in Belloc's words, 'feel as felt the earlier man in a happier time, and see the world as they saw it'. Added to that are the icebergs of all shapes and sizes, their massive grandeur all the more impressive when seen at close quarters from the deck of a small boat; finally, and best of all, the austere beauty of a summer's day off the Greenland coast, sea, snow mountains, and ice, and overhead the pale northern sky.

Wide though the choice of objectives in northern waters may be, I had no doubts about where we ought to make for in 1971. No one likes being defeated and our tame acceptance of defeat when trying to reach Scoresby Sound in 1969 still rankled. On that occasion, when some 20 miles south of C. Brewster, the southern entrance to the Sound, what I called a polite mutiny on the part of the crew had obliged us to give up and return prematurely home. Admittedly, our five days of groping in continuous fog had not been encouraging and when the fog had cleared sufficiently to reveal a lot of ice – a phenomenon not unexpected in the Arctic – the crew decided they had seen enough. Ice reports that I obtained after our return showed that we might have had trouble entering the Sound and certainly more when leaving it, but this is what the voyager likes to discover for himself and this is what a voyage of this kind is all about.

Scoresby Sound is in Lat. 70° N. on the east coast of Greenland. The Sound was named after his father by William Scoresby, who in 1882 surveyed and charted some 400 miles of the east coast. Like his father, he was one of the most successful whaling captains sailing out of Whitby and, not content with this, he went on to become an explorer, a scientist, a Fellow of the Royal Society, and at last a parson. Having made his first voyage with his father at the age of eleven, after twenty-five years at sea he went to Cambridge to take a degree and entered the Church. His two-volume book *An Account of the Arctic Regions*, with a history and description of the northern whale-fishery, should be read if only for the story of how they saved the whaler *Elsie*, nipped and badly holed a hundred miles inside the pack.

The earlier statement that the east coast of Greenland is accessible in summer to a small boat needs qualifying. South of Angmagssalik (Lat. 66° N.) the coast is usually fairly free of ice by the end of July, while north of that it seldom is. Ice conditions vary a lot from year to year but in most years there is little chance of finding Scoresby Sound open before the beginning of August. The *Arctic Pilot* has this to say:

Conditions are very variable. The ice in the Sound generally breaks up about the middle of July. Navigation is usually possible in August and September and frequently also in the latter part of July. Navigation after mid-September may be risky owing to the onset of gales. The approaches to Scoresby Sound are more likely to be free from ice in late September than at any other time but in severe ice years they may not uncover at all.

Navigable in this context means for moderate-sized steamers or small sealers built to withstand ice. Obviously for an unstrengthened boat such as *Sea Breeze* conditions need to be unusually good. It is a matter of luck. Ice conditions cannot be foreseen or predicted and even ice reports received a few days beforehand are of little value since, by the time one gets there, the situation may have entirely altered. The only way is to go there and see, and in the case of Scoresby Sound, by the time this has been done, say in mid-August, supposing one is repulsed, there is no time left for anything but to go home. A target like this, more likely to be missed than hit, is not to be aimed at too frequently. In 1970, for instance, I gave up Scoresby Sound in favour of West Greenland because I had in the crew two Australian climbers who had come all that way in the hope of climbing a Greenland mountain and I could not afford to disappoint them by attempting Scoresby Sound and failing. Moreover, for climbing purposes, reaching the Sound, though meritorious, is not enough. The real objective is two little-known, highly mountainous islands on which no climbing, I believe, has yet been done, and these lie some 70 miles inside the entrance. Seventy miles is no small distance and since the Sound would be by no means entirely ice-free it would probably have to be done under the engine. There are therefore difficulties and hazards enough in the way of winning this particular prize. Scoresby Sound, by the way, is the largest fjord in the world. Some merit would be acquired by getting there in a small boat and at the back of it are these two islands studded with unclimbed peaks.

Provided with an able boat and a highly desirable objective there remained only the matter of crew, a crew that must not include any 'pikers', as my Australian and New Zealand friends call them, those whose hearts are not in it and who are ready to quit at the first sign of trouble. I already had one man who could be relied upon in Bob Comlay; he sailed with us in 1970 and wished to do so again. Once is not always enough, as some might think would be the case with these voyages. Several have made two voyages, while one, Charles Marriott, even more eccentric, has made four. I had equal confidence, too, in another candidate, though I had not yet met him. He had been recommended to me by Phil Temple who had been on the Heard Island voyage, and I had therefore no hesitation about taking Max Smart, a New Zealander living in England. While on a visit to Snowdonia he came over to Bodowen to see me. Hairy as a prophet and strong as a horse, he lent an energetic and powerful hand clearing some of our local jungle. On *Sea Breeze* there are no winches to assist in setting up halyards and sheets, nor are they needed, provided one has a Max Smart or someone as strong on board.

For a cook I had to advertise as I had done for the previous voyage and for several others before that. The market for this commodity, 'cook for a cool voyage' as I put it, seemed to be barely steady, the number of replies received being down on that of the previous year. Of the ten who replied most were for various reasons self-cancelling and all but one of the few left in the running either disliked the tone of my letters or had second and better thoughts. A line I remember from some children's book ran, 'Little Hippo, bound to win, was the only one left in', and on this occasion the only one left in was Marius Dakin, an art student, or rather hoping to qualify as an art student in the coming autumn. He had no sea experience but he could cook and what is more he enjoyed cooking. He was something of an expert photographer and for this trip hoped to borrow father's expensive camera, father being a professional. Wise in his generation, father thought differently. So instead Marius undertook to make a film using the second-hand 16 mm. camera that I had bought for the southern voyage of 1966–67. Like the other films taken on past voyages, and indeed like many that are inflicted on the public, the result hardly justified the expense.

The name of the man whom I had secured for fourth place escapes me, as he himself escaped by dropping out at the last moment. By then we were fitting out and it seemed as if only a miracle could save us from sailing short-handed. Though three watch-keepers could manage well enough, it would be uncommonly hard work on a four-month voyage. In their working days pilot cutters were sailed by two men or even a man and an apprentice, but they would be out for a few days or a week at most and they were real sailors. The unexpected happened. I had a letter from one Peter Marsh who had done a lot of week-end sailing and had built himself a catamaran in which he proposed sailing to Iceland. He wrote mainly to ask for advice but also implied that he would like to gain some first-hand experience in northern waters. 'When they bring you a heifer be ready with the rope', as they say in Spain. I sent him a telegram, he arrived at Lymington on 29 May, and the crew was complete.

Max arrived next day humping a vast load, and then Marius, in pink bell-bottom trousers and green velvet jacket, with a guitar slung behind, looking more like a troubadour than a sea-cook. Bob Comlay, a student at Bangor University, had examinations to take and would not join until sailing day, which was to be 12 June. Marius, the aesthete, shocked by the décor of the galley, got to work on it. Nominally the galley is painted white, until after five months with three Primus stoves in action it assumes a darker hue, pale yellow in the outer parts, becoming dark brown towards the centre, and finally jet black immediately above the stoves. Having stripped off the mixture of paint and carbon – no light task – Marius painted the bulkhead eggshell blue, picked out the beams in black, and the deckhead between in white, and very smart it looked.

With the weather remaining on the whole unfavourable and only three hands available we needed all the time allowed for fitting out. Art is long and time is fleeting, I thought, as I watched Marius so preoccupied with painting the galley that he had no time for anything else. In a ketch lying outside *Sea Breeze* were a Mr and Mrs Habens who were always ready with advice and assistance, urgently needed when it came to the tricky manoeuvre of moving *Sea Breeze* to the outside berth and turning her head in the right direction for off. Sorting out the bow lines, breast lines, stern lines, and springs by which the boats were moored might have baffled a professional dock-master.

With the arrival of Bob Comlay on 12 June we were ready to go. For some days I had been dithering over the question of whether to sail east or west-about, up Channel or down, and had still only reached the infirm decision of waiting to see what the weather might be when we were outside the Needles. We were bound first for the Faeroes, a convenient stopping place on the way to Iceland, and thence to East Greenland. By way of the North Sea it is possibly 100 miles shorter than by the Irish Sea and the Minches, a difference too slight to be of much account to a sailing vessel where the length of a passage is reckoned in the number of days it takes rather than the distance between ports. Calculations as to the length of the rhumb line course are of little use since the distance that will have to be sailed depends upon the winds encountered. If foul winds prevail one might sail many miles and still make no progress. The only real reason I had for going by way of the North Sea was that we had not been there before, while among several other reasons for not going that way was the density of steamer traffic in Dover Straits. Curiosity is said to betoken a generous mind and on this occasion curiosity prevailed. Meeting a westerly wind outside the Needles we turned eastwards and when it had taken us far enough in that direction to preclude any idea of our turning back the wind swung round to the east. So on the next day we found ourselves approaching the most congested shipping lanes in the world with a contrary wind and in thick weather.

The passage of the Straits proved less harrowing than I had anticipated, but it was luck rather than skill that brought us through. The thick weather prevented us from knowing where we were, a piece of knowledge that is particularly essential in a place like Dover Straits. Buoys abound, but the only one we passed we failed to identify, distracted perhaps by the German tanker that appeared out of the murk astern, hooting and going dead slow. Nor did we make rapid progress. On consecutive days, on different tacks, we twice sighted Dungeness to the north-east, until at last on the evening of 15 June a breeze at north-west sprang up to continue all night and all the next day, by which time we were clear of the Narrows and had the Galloper light-vessel abeam. Meantime all was not well with the unlucky Peter who had been seasick from the time we passed the Needles, gamely taking his trick at the helm with the appearance and alacrity of a corpse. He proved to be one of those rare cases of seasickness for whom time and wont is no cure, and the sailing that he had previously done, confined to week-ends, had not lasted long enough for him to discover this. He stuck it out until we reached Iceland when it had become abundantly clear that his sickness was chronic. Rather than face another two or three months' misery, during which time he would be little use on board, he rightly decided to quit.

For the whole of a sunny afternoon, with all sails down, we drifted quietly back to the Newark lightvessel which we had passed earlier in the day. Various jobs that needed doing to the mainsail could now be done, hauling out the peak and clew, tightening up the gaff lacing. On the shrouds *Sea Breeze* had the appropriate lanyards of 1¾in. tarred Italian hemp (not easily found nowadays) instead of rigging screws, and these had to be set up again until they were bar taut. These sort of 'sailorising' jobs which are fun to do are neither needed nor known on modern yachts.

In the North Sea one expects to see oil rigs, just as in the Arctic one expects to see icebergs. Like bergs, these are not marked on the chart, at least not until oil or gas has been struck when the rig is likely to become a semi-permanent feature; so that when we sighted a cluster of lights where according to the chart no lights should have been it was not difficult to guess what they were. No doubt the positions of rigs not yet marked on the chart are notified in *Notices to Mariners*, the weekly publication to which amateur sailors like ourselves should pay more attention. When to the west of the British Isles and listening to the shipping forecast I always have the impression that the North Sea has more than a fair share of gales and have accordingly felt sorry for any yachtsmen there. Perhaps we were lucky. The only gale warning we had proved to be a false alarm. We made good progress and by dawn of 23 June found ourselves off the entrance to Pentland Firth, so confused, I confess, by the profusion of lights in sight that it took me some time to grasp the fact. I had intended going by the way of Fair Isle through the wide strait between the Shetlands and the Orkneys, but the settled weather combined, of course, with curiosity induced me to try the Pentland Firth. With the tide running the wrong way we foolishly tried bucking it, helped by a fresh south-easterly breeze and with the engine going, an impossible feat for *Sea Breeze* even with a favourable gale. Off Duncansby Head we started going rapidly backwards, so we ran off north-east towards the Skerries where we were chased in a frightening way by an advancing tide-rip. When the wind died the tide turned in our favour and by evening we were through the Firth and admiring the Old Man of Hoy all aglow in the setting sun. There were now only some 200 miles to go and two days later, thanks to fair winds we sighted the familiar Lille Dimon, the 1,200ft. high rocky island, shaped like a haystack, an unmistakable mark when approaching the Faeroes from the south-east.

CHAPTER TWO

The Faeroes and Iceland

A FRESHENING northerly wind and the onset of rain that evening seemed to betoken a dirty night. Not liking the prospect of beating north to Nolso fjord and Thorshavn, which was our destination, we ran off west into Skuo fjord where, at its head, there was the sheltered anchorage of Sands Vaag. The fjord did not provide the lee that we had expected. Fierce gusts swept down from the cliffs of Sando Island to the north, tearing the water white as they hit. The whole mainsail when full of wind is hard to tame so we rolled in several reefs in order to have things under control before reaching the anchorage. By 6 pm when we anchored off the village, the wind had risen to gale force, the rain streaming down. The anchorage is sheltered from all but a south-east wind when it would become untenable. We set an anchor watch.

The wind had eased by morning though still at north, and since it was a thick, mizzling day we lay at earth, as Jorrocks would say. There are some 600 people in Sands Vaag, a village remarkable in that not only several of the houses but also the fairly large church have roofs of turf. At this time of year the grass on the roofs was long enough for hay-making; the roofs rippled in the wind and one wondered whether they were ever scythed. The people live by sheep-farming and inshore fishing from open boats of traditional Norse lines.

It is strange that although the rise and fall of the tide at the Faeroes is but a few feet, the tidal stream runs with great force in the fjords and off the headlands. While carefully timing our departure to catch the north-going stream I stupidly overlooked the fact that the north-going stream would also be flooding into Skuo fjord. The engine had to work hard until we reached the sea where we hoisted sail and had the tide under us all the way to Nolso fjord. Failure to keep charts and *Pilot* books bang up-to-date, as well as the neglecting of *Notices to Mariners*, is another fault of the amateur sailor, a fault that caused us some embarrassment off Thorshavn. Look where we might we could see no sign of the entrance marked by a beacon on the end of the breakwater. There seemed to be no end to the breakwater and consequently no entrance. To enquire is neither a disaster nor a disgrace so we hailed a youth cavorting about in a speed-boat. The breakwater was being extended, the beacon had been removed, and the new entrance temporarily marked by an inconspicuous buoy. All of which would no doubt have been noted on an up-to-date chart.

We picked up the same buoy that we had used on previous visits close to *Westward Ho*, a fine big ketch built at Hull in 1880. They were giving her a major refit and in consequence she looked a bit dishevelled. After rowing ashore and walking to the Customs Office I found when I got there that they had already been on board to seal our liquor store. Like Iceland, the Faeroes are nominally 'dry'. I had the impression that they had not been much taken by my hairy crew. Max who had started out hairy now looked like the Wild Man of Borneo himself, his eyes just discernable through a matted under-growth of hair. He and Peter forthwith went ashore to stretch their legs on the hill behind the town where they bivouacked for the night. Though Max enjoyed life at sea his real love was for mountains, to climb them or to camp among them. Peter, half inclined to give up here, decided to wait and see how he fared on the next leg to Iceland.

Having taken on water at the fish-wharf we sailed on 30 June for Reykjavik going north-about round the top of the Faeroes. Next day as soon as we met a bit of wind and sea Peter succumbed, nor was Max quite himself, showing less than his usual interest in the pasta and duff that we had for supper – a little heavy on the carbohydrates, perhaps, but as the Chinese say, a well-filled stomach is the great thing, all else is luxury. One expects plenty of wind south-east of Iceland, the track followed by most of the depressions that cross the Atlantic. The harder blows seldom lasted long, which was just as well because we were short-handed. Owing to his inability to eat anything Peter was not up to doing much beyond his two-hour trick at the helm.

On 6 July, in thick drizzling weather, we were somewhere south of the Vestmannaejar, a group of islands and rocks 20 miles south of the Iceland coast, noted for volcanic activity. Heimaey, the fishing port of the Vestmannaejar, had recently been overwhelmed by a volcanic eruption. Also in this group is Surtsey, the volcanic island which suddenly appeared on 14 November 1963. 'Appeared' is hardly the word for its tumultuous birth, a birth attended by violent explosions hurling clouds of smoke, steam, ash, and pumice thousands of feet into the air. Only when the wind blew away some of this cloud could it be seen that a new island had emerged from the sea. *Notices to Mariners* of 3 January 1964 had this warning note:

A submarine volcanic eruption has formed an island about half a mile in diameter and 250ft. high in position 63° 18′ N. 20° 36′ W. Eruption is continuing and mariners are warned to keep clear of the area.

That mariners had to wait so long for this news to be published may have been owing to the Christmas holidays, or more likely it was in the hope that the island might disappear almost as suddenly as it had appeared; for unless and until lava begins to flow the existence of such islands may be only ephemeral. By April 1964 the island had grown to nearly a mile in length and 500ft. in height. The Icelanders called it Surtsey and the volcano, which was still active, was called Surtur after the Fire Giant of Norse mythology, who comes from the south when the world ends to burn up everything. On passage to Iceland in *Mischief* in June 1964 two of us had landed on Surtsey, complete with cine-camera, and climbed to the rim of the volcano. The crater into which we had peered belched merely smoke and fumes instead of the cauldron of molten, fiery lava that we had hopefully expected to see. The whole place smelt like a coke oven, and one sensed, too, that the thing was still alive and growing. Our visit had been well or ill timed according to the point of view. Lava had only begun flowing on 4 April when rivers overflowed the crater to pour down into the sea. At the end of April the flow ceased and did not begin again until 9 July, a fortnight after our visit.

On 15 July 1965, still in *Mischief*, we again visited the area, guided from 30 miles away by a vast column of smoke. This came from a new island that had just erupted about a mile away from Surtsey which by then lay dormant. We hove-to to watch. The vast white column of smoke ascended continuously, while every few minutes a fresh explosion flung a jet-black cloud of smoke, ash, and lumps of pumice, hundreds of feet into the air. Away to leeward, below the white smoke, curtains of ash drifted down to the sea. For an hour we lay and watched this remarkable sight until at length the activity subsided.

Having thus a proprietary interest in Surtsey I much wished to see it again in 1971. In the thick prevailing weather, however, I doubted our finding it even had there been a column of smoke to guide us; but by luck we spotted a lone rock which from its shape I recognised as one of the Vestmannaejar lying close to Surtsey, and soon after a big island, which was undoubtedly Surtsey, came into view. It had grown considerably in six years and the small island that had been so violent in 1965 had linked up with its parent. Except for some slight smoke or steam from four widely separated fumaroles there was no hint of activity. Scientists of various 'ologies are keeping a close watch on Surtsey to see how nature starts work on virgin territory. In 1964 we had noticed only some beer bottles.

Two days later, helped by light westerly winds, we sailed up the 50-mile wide bight of Faxafloi and between the piers into Reykjavik harbour. While we were handing the sails and wondering where to find a berth we were hailed from the shore and directed to one of the many steamer wharves, at that moment vacant. Usually a yacht is ignored and left to find its own accommodation from whence in short time it will be told to move. This seemed almost too civil and we found it was merely for the benefit of the Custom who wanted to seal our stores and go home, for it was getting late. A looker-on who spoke English then kindly drove me to the Harbour-master's office where the duty-man, who seemed to be slightly tiddly, advised us to berth alongside *Odinn*, the outermost of four fishery protection vessels, the whole Icelandic navy in fact. There, he assured me, we would lie undisturbed throughout our stay (*Odinn* has recently figured conspicuously in the so-called cod war). In fact, there were two smaller vessels outside *Odinn* so we secured to the outermost. The first disturbance came before breakfast to let *Odinn* out, and the second after breakfast to let yet another similar vessel in. Meantime the topsides of *Avahur* to which we were fast were being scaled with pneumatic hammers. So we looked round for a better and quieter hole and finally went alongside a tanker, *Haforninn*, moored at a nearby wharf and apparently out of commission. We were told that ten years previously, before the herring deserted Iceland waters or had been fished to extinction, she had been employed as a sort of fleet herring-carrier and that her tanks had suffered from this misuse. She was now for sale. We found a rope-ladder by which we could gain her deck and thence access to the wharf only a few minutes' walk from the town. We lay there very comfortably with no need to tend any shore-lines, while *Haforninn* acted as a buffer between us and the occasional drunken Icelander, full of Black Death and *joie de vivre* who invites himself on board. Black Death is the appropriate name for a fiery and lethal by-product of the State brewery's non-alcoholic beer, the only beer allowed in Iceland.

This was my third call at Reykjavik and I learnt with regret that the Sailor's Home where we used to be able to get showers and cheap, abundant meals had been closed. A fine, new bath-house had been built at the far end of the docks, but for supper we had to look for cheap eating places in the town. Peter now decided to take passage home and we could not blame him. He had been ill on and off all the time, eating little, and too feeble to do any work. We had to find a replacement. The more difficult part of the voyage lay ahead, not to mention the passage homewards, and I wanted a full crew. From as far back as 1954 I had learnt that even in England suitable crew are not to be picked up like blackberries; in Iceland the chances seemed remote. The size of Reykjavik's population, some 70,000, really has no bearing because the field of choice is restricted to the small band of nomadic youngsters from Europe and America who in summer walk, hitch-hike, or bus themselves all over the island. There is a small sailing club at Reykjavik from which a recruit might be had, in which case one would either have to drop him on return, leaving one shorthanded for the homeward voyage, or take him to England and pay his fare back. The yachting boom that in recent years has seen boats turned out on production lines like motor cars has not hit Iceland. There are not enough people, for the climate is not all that inimical to yachting. Nor are all yachtsmen fair-weather sun-seekers, as the offshore and ocean racing fraternity bear witness by having to take the weather as it comes. Even if in summer the Icelandic climate can be a little harsh; to offset this there are extensive and exciting cruising grounds and well-sheltered fjords.

Our search for crew did not have to be hurried. We had time in hand, for having regard to ice conditions we did not want to be off Scoresby Sound until the first week of August at the earliest. Bob and Marius made the standard tourist trip to Gulfoss and the Great Geyser, and on their return Max and Peter embarked in a bus intent on a five-day walk over the glaciated Mirdals Jokull, 70 miles south-east of Reykjavik. I remained at home. So far as tourist attractions go my feelings are those of Dr Johnson who would have liked seeing the Giant's Causeway but would not like the trouble of going to see it.

The Youth Hostel, where there was a steady trickle of visitors, was the most likely cover to draw and there the crew made known themselves and our need. Indirectly this worked. The news got around among the foreign community and we were soon in touch with a young American, Jim Collins, who had been working on a small, local fishing boat. The boat was now laid up for repairs on account of engine trouble. According to his account Jim had been knocking about the world for three years and even after five weeks in an Icelandic fishing boat, usually a profitable occupation, his accumulated capital amounted to 10 dollars. Wishing to get to Europe he readily cast in his lot with us and we never had cause to regret it. He soon got used to our ways and proved himself a most able hand and a cheery shipmate.

Bob had an introduction to an Icelandic woman, a journalist, who very kindly asked the whole lot of us to her house for what proved to be a memorable meal, memorable at least as regards the solids. The sweet came first, an old Icelandic custom, and since it consisted of yoghourt and straw-berries we had no grounds for complaint. Except, perhaps on the score of size, for having travelled through real yoghourt country in Central Asia where a normal portion is a washbasinful I found the small bowls a little meagre. After this promising opening we had salmon caught in a local river, so good that the accompanying vegetables and other trimmings hardly mattered. Unfortunately, this highly civilised meal had to be washed down with non-alcoholic beer, and there was no escaping this even on a plea of teetotalism.

In our turn we entertained a Dutchman, Dr Hartog, who turned up one morning sailing single-handed in an aluminium-alloy 8 tonner to moor along-side us. He was not a single-hander by choice. He usually sailed with his wife, a combination that can and has resulted in famous and formidable crews, such as the Smeetons, the Hiscocks, and the late Dr and Mrs Pye. On this occasion he had unwisely declared his intention to reach Greenland to which his wife had responded with 'Include me out' or the Dutch equivalent. The doctor had not enjoyed his lone voyage and on meeting contrary winds had put into Reykjavik prior to returning to Scotland where his wife was waiting. He may have been pining for his wife's cooking and I doubt if our curry and duff would abate this longing.

There are not many capital cities where one can walk out to the airport in twenty minutes. I walked out there frequently to talk to the Meteorological boys who were always ready to pass on what news they had of ice conditions off Greenland. This news was invariably bad, whether it came from photo-graphs taken by satellites or from air reconnaissance. They were naturally more interested in conditions off Iceland which were unusual for that time of year, the ice lying within 30 to 40 miles off Horn, the north-western extremity of Iceland. I also had a report at first hand from a pilot whom I knew who had just flown a party to a landing strip north of Scoresby Sound. He happened, too, to be the Commodore of the Odinn Yacht Club from whom in the following year we received valuable help. He had seen heavy ice all the way to Scoresby except for a wide lead well south of it. Since at least three weeks would elapse before we were up there or thereabouts we were not unduly discouraged; nevertheless the indications were that conditions were not going to be favourable.

CHAPTER THREE

To the North

WE SAILED on 21 July, and since it was still full early in the season we intended calling at Isafjord, a fishing port in north-west Iceland. Iceland was enjoying a rare bout of hot weather and as one bright, cloudless day succeeded another we trusted that the ice would soon feel the effect. Glorious weather, indeed, for everything except sailing. For six days of faint northerly breezes, or no wind at all, we tacked and drifted up the coast until on the 26th a stronger breeze gave us a welcome push into the wide entrance of our fjord. There it left us. Isafjord lay 30 miles up so we started the engine. Nothing happened. The kraken, or its Icelandic equivalent, must be gripping *Sea Breeze* by the keel. Bob, who was our engineer, then peered over the stern where the absence of any propeller explained her reluctance to move. We then recalled that on leaving Reykjavik under power the engine had suddenly revved up, probably signalling the shedding of the propeller; by then we were hoisting sail, having finished with the engine, and we had paid no more attention.

A few minutes before this painful discovery a local fishing boat had come alongside to present us with several fine cod, and we watched with regret as he disappeared down the fjord towards Isafjord. For a bottle of whisky they would no doubt have been delighted to give us a tow. The calm that prevailed that evening after supper looked like lasting for days. We tried towing with the dinghy but she barely moved. Then we got our two pairs of oars and a long piece of 6in. plank – more effective than the oars – using the life-line stanchions as thole-pins. We may have had some tide with us but I reckoned that in three hours we moved her two or three miles. At 1 am we gave up, for we were no Vikings. To wait for a wind, however long the wait might be, seemed preferable, a decision that Vikings themselves might have come to in the absence of women, slaves, or prisoners of war to row for them.

The calm did not last that long. By mid-morning of the next day we were in a short arm of the fjord with Isafjord close ahead. Isafjordhur, to give it its full name, is built on what is called an *eyri*, a long spit of sand and gravel. As the *Pilot* says of these parts:

The deep-water fjords running for considerable distances south-eastwards between high steep coasts, all possess good harbours or anchorages behind an *eyri* or moraine which is peculiar to most of the Icelandic fjords. These *eyris* are low spits of shingle or sand which extend transversely across the fjord and are the remains of terminal moraines of the Ice Age.

This particular spit sticks out across the fjord to within half a cable of the other side, leaving a buoyed entrance channel with a navigable fairway of only 50 yards width. The channel is dog-legged and there are three pairs of leading marks indicating the points at which course must be altered. Another curious feature of the channel is a runway on the side opposite to the *eyri*, so that one may have a plane taxi-ing along the runway a few yards from the ship.

We had the tide under us but the wind contrary as we boldly began tacking up this narrow channel, the crew right on their toes, putting her about smartly at extremely short intervals. We were about half-way through and doing well, having hit neither the *eyri* nor the runway, when a launch came up astern and a stentorian voice asked if we needed help. It was the local pilot, also acting British consul, an ex-trawler skipper, familiar with English ports and English, and married to a Yorkshire woman. Having no false pride I gladly accepted this timely offer. With the launch made fast alongside we proceeded to the harbour while I explained to Mr Johanssen our predicament and our immediate needs – a wall against which we could lie where at low water we would be able to get at the propeller shaft. We anchored off the jetty and after lunch, at the top of the tide, the pilot took us alongside where we warped her back until the stern took the ground. Having canted her over with the boom and put a line from the masthead to hold her, we waited for the tide to go down. In the meantime Mr Johanssen had betrayed a liking for rum. I have never seen a man drink faster. Michael Finsbury, whom readers of *The Wrong Box* will remember, remarked admiringly of another equally fast drinker that 'it restored his faith in the human race'.

We found that we had not only lost our propeller but that the shaft had broken off a few inches inside the 'A' bracket. One of the nuts holding this bracket had come off thus causing excessive vibration. Besides finding a suitable propeller, which looked like being difficult, a new shaft would have to be made. Without Mr Johanssen we should not have got much done. He persuaded an engineering firm to start right away drawing the old shaft while he himself scoured the town for a left-handed propeller of the approximate size. By next day he had heard of one that belonged to the local diver who at that moment, as one might expect, was under water. Together we watched from the quayside while he cut away the trawl net that had wrapped itself round the propeller of a German trawler, the trawler having been towed in by a compatriot. That job done we went off to inspect the diver's propeller, a trifle smaller than our own and a good deal worn; we were not likely to find anything better in Isafjord and we soon came to terms over a glass of rum in *Sea Breeze*'s cabin. Meantime, the engineers had had trouble drawing the broken shaft, the bolts of the gear box having seized up. To free them they used an oxy-acetylene torch and succeeded, much to our surprise, before the engine caught fire. We stood by with an extinguisher just in case. Finally the shaft inside had to be cut in order to get the coupling off, and it was the Thursday evening low tide before they had withdrawn the broken shaft, not forgetting to insert a wooden plug. Nevertheless they promised the job would be done by Friday evening, a promise of some consequence because the next three days were public holidays.

At low water on Friday evening, about 7.30 pm they brought along the new shaft. Even the face of the foreman – whom for good reason I had christened Dismal Jimmy – showed that he was trying hard to conceal a smile of satisfaction and he very easily succeeded when they discovered that the new shaft was several inches too short. Tableau! Evidently someone, possibly Dismal himself, had blundered by forgetting that a bit of the shaft had broken off with the propeller. Their reaction to this disaster was both astonishing and admirable. Instead of throwing the job in with a promise to be back after the holidays they rushed back to the workshop to make another shaft. They had not much time, in two hours or less the water would be over the plug. Bob and I watched anxiously as the water slowly rose. When they brought back the new shaft at 10 pm it was an inch or two above the hole. Nothing dismayed, Dismal yanked out the plug, got the shaft in, and began tightening up with his hands under water. Then they had to go back for coupling bolts, having brought the wrong ones; but by 11 pm the job was done and Dismal went off to enjoy or possibly suffer the coming holidays with a well-earned shot of rum under his belt. We had plenty of rum and we needed it – a sort of Daffy's Elixir, a universal solvent and lubricant, especially in Isafjord. When Bob started the engine everything seemed to work, and at low tide next morning he put pins through the nuts of the 'A' bracket to obviate their working loose again.

This north-western peninsula of Iceland known as Vestfird is pretty remote, joined to the rest of Iceland by a narrow neck only 6 miles wide; and although of considerable size the peninsula is so indented with fjords that no place on it is more than 12 miles from the sea. In this remote place visiting yachts are naturally rare and inevitably we had a great number of curious spectators gazing down at us from the jetty. Besides the natives we were inspected by a party of six American climbers bound for Scoresby Sound, needless to say by air. They did not seem to think much of our way of getting there and they may have been right. But to be carried by air to the mountains of one's choice, either in Greenland, Alaska, or even nowadays the Himalaya, as all climbing parties are, is a poor introduction. Unless told, one might not know in which continent one had arrived. Much depends on one's point of view, whether arriving or travelling hopefully is the aim. Another visitor provided me with some amusement. He was an English tourist off one of the Icelandic steamers that do the round of Iceland starting from Reykjavik. The usual questions were put – how many days from England and where were we bound for – and on being told Greenland he remarked brightly: 'Ah! Following in Tilman's footsteps.'

By the Saturday morning (31 July) we were ready to go. Having filled up with water, settled our debts, and paid a grateful farewell to Mr Johanssen we cast off. Under power, with the new propeller working well, the dog-legged channel gave us no worry. Once clear we hoisted sail and beat out to sea down the main fjord. On its northern shore drifts of winter snow still lay almost down to sea level. Before breakfast next morning we had crossed the Arctic Circle which runs a few miles north of Horn and just fails to touch the north coast of Iceland at any point. The island of Grimsey, half-way along the north coast, is the only bit of Iceland inside the Arctic Circle. The reports of ice off Horn that we had heard at Reykjavik were confirmed next afternoon when we sighted a line of ice to port and scattered floes ahead and to starboard. At midnight we met the ice edge and had to go about, steering south through scattered floes with two men on watch; for by now the nights were getting dark. Had it been at all rough, with white horses making the bits of ice difficult to spot we should have hove-to. With ice about the helmsman gets out of the cockpit and stands on deck where he can see more, but even so a look-out in the bows is needed to warn him of ice directly ahead. In spite of steering back towards Iceland we did not get clear of the ice until noon next day and when visibility had improved we could still see a line of ice to the east trending towards the coast. The air temperature was 39° F. and the sea 36° F. so we lit the cabin stove.

This unusual accumulation of ice off the coast in August involved us in beating about for several days before we reached open water. An ice report that I saw subsequently showed that on 3 August Denmark Strait, the 300-mile wide stretch of water between Greenland and Iceland, was completely bridged by pack-ice, obliging a British trawler to return home south of Iceland instead of north-about. On that particular day we were between the coast and the south edge of the ice which still extended eastwards. The question was how far east we should have to go round it, for we were already a long way off the direct course for Scoresby Sound.

That evening, in a deserted sea, no trawlers anywhere in sight, we again made up to the ice-edge to see what the prospects were and found that we were about to be embayed. Standing south with what little wind there was, we reached open water by next morning having made good only some 14 miles to the east. Another attempt to steer north was baffled on the morning of the 5th when once more we met the ice-edge and had to sheer off to the east yet again. But this time an easterly course took us into more ice and for the rest of the morning we devoted ourselves to getting into trouble with complete success. By the time fog closed down, reducing visibility to a hundred yards, we had been motoring for an hour or so, the floes having drawn closer together. With the wind free it is possible to sail through scattered floes, with a head wind one soon finds oneself wildly off course or with the sails aback and the boat jostling a floe. Conning the boat from up the shrouds I soon managed to get her into a cul-de-sac where, with little room for manoeuvre, we spent a long time turning round. Such mistakes are costly in time. Worse still, if the ice is on the move one's retreat from the cul-de-sac may be cut off.

For two more anxious hours I conned the ship as best I could from aloft until at last I detected open water ahead. At the same time, just showing above the shallow bank of fog, I made out the crow's nest of a ship steaming slowly along the edge of the ice that we were about to break out from. We emerged from the ice just ahead of him and the slight swell we met confirmed that we were in open water. As we began hoisting sail the Norwegian whale-chaser, for such he was, closed with us for a gam. After greetings, a heaving line landed on deck and we were invited to haul away. Attached to it was the biggest lump of meat (whale meat) I have ever seen, a great block of it, 2ft. by 2ft. by 1ft. thick, no bone, fat, or gristle, all prime steak.

The fog lifted, the sun came out, and as we sailed northwards we counted no less than eighteen trawlers, mostly British, fishing on the Spordagrun bank. We were thankful to be among this lot in daylight; with their trawls down they are reluctant to alter course so one does well to keep clear of trawlers, especially by night. That evening we were becalmed south of another field of ice which, when we began sailing, forced us still more to the east. In fact before we were free to steer the desired course we were in the longitude of Akureyri half-way along the north coast of Iceland. I was hoping to sight the islet of Kolbeinsey, only 26ft. high, and was rash enough to tell the crew where to expect it, somewhere on the starboard bow. It finally showed up some 5 miles away on the port quarter, which was a pity. According to the *Pilot* Kolbeinsey lies west of its charted position; no distance is given so one is no wiser.

A good south-easterly breeze on the 7th gave us a lift north-wards, the sea temperature up to 45° F., and no ice anywhere in sight. The glass was falling and next morning a strange cloud formation to the south boded mischief. So hard and firm was the outline of this sugar-loaf mountain of cloud astern that we had to look long and closely before deciding that it was merely cloud. The wind freshened and we ran on close-reefed to the north-west where we soon sighted a line of ice all along the port hand. Our position, 68° 40′ N. and 19° 00′ W., put us nearly a hundred miles out from the Greenland coast, and it was disconcerting, to say the least of it, to meet ice so far from the coast. Even had we not seen the pack the drop in the sea temperature to 35° F. would have told us that it was not far away. The air temperature was 36° F. For the next two days it blew fresh from north and at night either fog or ice obliged us to heave-to. We had no reason to complain. In the Greenland sea fog, ice, and northerly winds are to be expected.

By 11 August the weather improved and by steering north true we reached 70° N., the latitude of Scoresby Sound. Accordingly we turned west. Having already seen ice a hundred miles from the coast we did not expect to make much westing and sure enough we soon descried a hard line of white stretching away to the north and to the south. On a calm, sunny evening we closed the ice to make sure, for from a few miles away scattered floes will have the appearance of an impassable wall of ice. Here were no scattered floes, but close, heavy Polar ice, an uncompromising barrier that offered no temptation to start probing, an obstacle from which one could retreat with a clear conscience. A small boat had no business there and even had the floes been fairly open we were so far from coast, a good 60 miles, that to attempt to pass through would have been foolhardy. Provided one knows what lies beyond no harm would come from attempting a passage of a few miles through scattered floes, assuming one has the sense to retreat if they start thickening. A passage of 60 miles, measured in days rather than hours, offers too many hostages to fortune in the shape of changes in the weather and the vagaries of machinery. Sailing among floes is not easy and to find oneself a few miles inside the pack with a broken-down engine might have all kinds of consequences, none of them pleasant. The Greenland whaling fleet worked among ice as a matter of course, ships of 300 to 400 tons massively built with crews of forty to fifty men of a kind that is not bred nowadays. Most important of all, they cruised in company so that if one were beset help or a refuge was at hand.

To satisfy ourselves that there were no open leads or that the ice did not suddenly fall away to the west, we went north for another 20 miles only to see it stretching away into the distance as far as the eye could see. There remained only to follow the ice-edge south on the chance of finding an inshore lead in a lower latitude, an unwelcome decision that meant throwing away our hard-won northing. As we went south the hard edge gave away to loose floes, sometimes in the form of capes projecting from the main pack. Fog on the 13th made for despondency but when it lifted the next day a clear horizon all round gave our spirits a wonderful lift. The only ice in sight was a solitary berg. After a moderate gale had obliged us to heave-to a fine easterly breeze encouraged us to steer west to close the ice. We were about in Lat. 68° 5′ N. or 70 miles south-east of C. Brewster at the southern entrance to the Sound. With no ice in sight ahead we began steering direct for the cape but by noon we were again among scattered floes with the hard edge of the pack showing all too clearly to the north. We spent the night hove-to and next day began motoring due west through fairly open ice. We went on into the ice for some 6 miles before prudence prevailed. Conditions were no easier and there was every possibility that we would be motoring through ice all the way to the coast. Nor was there any certainty of finding ice-free water along the coast had we reached it, a process that would have involved something like twenty-four hours of motoring. My faith in machinery hardly extends that far and we had on board no mechanical genius capable of dealing with any emergency. An Indian driver I once had shared my incompetence with machinery and the consequent lack of faith in it. When the truck broke down, as it frequently did, all he could say was: 'It is but machinery, Sahib.'

Steering south did not get us out of the ice as we had expected. We had to retrace our steps to the east and did not win clear until late that night – a mis-spent day if ever there was one. So far as Scoresby Sound went we had shot our bolt. It was evidently a bad ice year and we had to accept defeat. 'Prudence', as Dr Johnson says, 'quenches that ardour of enterprise by which everything is done that can claim praise or admiration,' but Dr Johnson was no mariner upon whom caution and prudence are enjoined. Instead we decided to sail direct to Angmagssalik to stock up for the homeward passage, before going on to one of the many mountainous fjords further south for the brief time that remained.

CHAPTER FOUR

Angmagssalik and Homewards

FOR THE next two days we were constantly edged away to the east of our desired course by ice of various kinds, big floes, growlers, and bergy bits, evidently the lingering remains of what had recently been close-pack-ice. Such bits of ice generally show up white and are easy to see, but not all of them. On a calm, clear night, as we were sailing along quietly, a piece of ice about 15ft. long, completely awash, nothing showing, only betrayed its presence a few feet from the hull by the waves slapping against it. This happening in my watch gave me a salutary shock and towards the end of the next day I was to have another. During the first watch that morning, blowing fresh and snowing, the boat had a real Arctic appearance with snow lying about the deck and encasing the shrouds. We did 12 miles in that watch. As the day advanced the wind increased and the snow turned to rain with visibility not more than half a mile. Anxious to make up for lost time we let her rip, sailing full and by with all plain sail, running her off to south-east during the frequent heavy squalls. For the last few days, since we were far from land, particularly from Greenland, I had been navigating on a plotting chart, a blank sheet except for the lines of latitude and longitude. So at 4 pm when I was below, enjoying tea and wads, the cry of 'Land' from on deck gave me a rude shock. Sure enough close to windward through the murk loomed a gaunt cliff with a solitary house at its foot.

A glance at the appropriate chart would have shown that on the course we were steering and the rate we were going we should soon be nearing Horn, and that the frequency with which we had been obliged to run her off still more to the east would ensure our fetching up on the wrong side of it, as indeed we had. At this awkward moment the wind increased in violence. Nevertheless we had to gybe, which we did without breaking anything, and were relieved to see that grim headland fade away in the rain. Overnight the barometer rose 10 mbs. and the wind moderated. By morning the wind had swung round to the east and by noon we had rounded Horn and soon left Iceland astern.

Denmark Strait, which on earlier voyages had been placid enough, seemed in a disturbed state. Again the wind increased until by midnight we had reefed down so far that only some six feet of luff remained on the mast. Rain set in, and when an iceberg showed up with its litter of bergy bits stretching for hundreds of yards to leeward, we hove-to. As a general rule one should pass up-wind of icebergs. In a hard blow, even when close-reefed, *Sea Breeze* will not lie still, but makes almost a knot crab-wise, so what with the way she had on and the breaking seas that made ice difficult to see we passed an anxious day and a worse night. For by night, though the wind had dropped, we were enveloped in fog, and more than once that night a fearful thump and the trample of feet overhead would announce that the watch on deck were fending off a chunk of ice. In the persisting fog I became concerned to know where we were until at last on 23 August, through rifts in the fog, I got both a morning and a noon sight. They were not easy to take. After waiting patiently on deck for the horizon under the sun to clear, no sooner had one brought up the sextant than in the cold atmosphere the mirrors misted over. By now, of course, the nights were quite dark, and what with fog and the presence of icebergs we kept double watches.

We were nearing Greenland, and at length the sort of weather that I have come to associate with the east coast set in – flawless, windless, sunny days when the calm blue water reflects the majestic shapes of glistening icebergs. On 25 August we sighted the coast, marvellously mountainous and wonder-fully clear even at 40 miles distance. We were north of Angmagssalik and of C. Dan where the coast recedes abruptly to the west. This marked turning away of the coast makes the cape easy to identify and besides that it has on it the only radio beacon on the coast. Having no RDF equipment we were more concerned to see it than to hear it, and the big, silvery domes are easily seen from a distance. By evening we were south of the cape and heading west in search of Angmagssalik. This is less readily found. One steers for a bold, brown promontory that looks like the end of the land, where the coast makes another sharp turn to the west. The promontory is steep-to and can be approached safely, and one needs to be close to make out the narrow entrance to King Oscar's Havn or the small, dimly lit beacon on its northern side. The harbour lies about a mile inside the entrance and is small, small enough to be congested even by the few diminutive local vessels that are usually there. So we anchored outside near the root of the breakwater within a few yards of the rocky shore and some brightly painted Greenlander huts. It was near midnight when we let go the anchor to a chorus of howls from all the huskies in the town – a bright, clear night with the aurora shimmering overhead like a curtain of pale fire.

We were last here in *Mischief* in 1965 since when the town has grown – a new wharf and warehouse at the harbour, more roads, more houses, and more shops. Then there had been only the one store, that run by the Royal Greenland Trading Co. which used to have the monopoly of all trade in Greenland; now there are several privately-owned shops and even a coffee-bar complete with juke-box and fruit machine. The Greenlanders – the men at any rate – are happy-go-lucky, free spenders, and born gamblers; the fruit machine seemed to suffer accordingly, taking a hard and incessant pounding. The helpful Danish Harbour-master who had been here in 1965 was no more, his place having been taken by a Greenlander, while the shipwright carpenter who had patched up *Mischief* after her passage through the ice, was away on leave. The local boat *Ejnar Mikelsen*, which on that occasion had helped us through the ice, had been replaced by a new version under the same skipper, our good friend Niels Underborg. He and I had a long gam. He told me that another English boat, a converted motor fishing vessel with a crew of twelve, mostly mountaineers, had called and that he had taken them up the coast to Kangerdlugssual. As far as that apparently the coast had been almost ice-free, while north of that, as we had found, the ice spread far to the east.

Max went off on a solitary glacier walk while the rest of us busied ourselves with repairs to the mainsail, turning halyards end for end, and putting a tingle over a suspected leak under the counter. For old time's sake I went up what we used to call Spy-glass hill. This was the hill just behind the town, close on 2,000ft. high, that on our first slightly hazardous visit in 1964 we climbed frequently, sometimes before breakfast, in order to see if the ice in the offing opened sufficiently for us to escape. Having got into Angmagssalik early that year, with the essential help of *Ejnar Mikelsen* and the springing of some planks as well, we were then unable to leave and had been held prisoners by the ice for three weeks. From Spy-glass hill one had been able to see what the ice conditions out to sea were like, but this time, instead of time spent on reconnaissance being never wasted, it almost invariably was wasted. For having rushed down the hill back to the boat, got under way, motored down the fjord, and arrived on the scene, one found that the ice had moved and that the wide lead spotted from Spy-glass hill no longer existed.

Having gone alongside in the harbour for water we sailed on 29 August bound for the Sehesteds fjord about a hundred miles to the south. The *Pilot* thus describes the fjord:

Sehesteds fjord extends about 23 miles north-westwards with several branches. At its head are mountains which reach an elevation of as much as 6,700ft. On the northern side is a narrow inlet named Rans Sund which is reported to afford good anchorage for small craft. In August 1932 the *Veslekari* anchored in Rans Sund and observed that new ice began to form in the harbour on 11th August.

Rans Sund then seemed to be the place to make for, and one could only hope that the formation of new ice in August was the exception rather than the rule. Seldom can so short a passage have taken so long – five aggravating days, the wind light and fitful, pestered by bergs, and rolling horribly for a lot of the time in a quite unaccountable swell. Big sailing ships lying becalmed were said to draw together by some sort of mutual attraction. The same thing happened as we lay becalmed near a big iceberg, only we drew together so fast that we imagined the berg to be self-propelled and bent on running us down. There were at least fifty bergs in sight that morning and the largest of them, a real monster, lay close at hand. Seeing that he was drawing uncomfortably near we started the engine and headed out to sea to get clear. It is hard to believe – and we had not lost our propeller this time – but for a good ten minutes neither the bearing nor our distance from this brute appreciably altered. We felt we were being pursued. However, he was not as quick on the helm as we were and by altering course to south-west we shook him off.

By 2 September we were, I hoped, about off the entrance to our fjord, some 7 miles out from the land. Like the rest of Greenland the coast here abounds in fjords, off-lying islands, islets, and skerries, all unmarked.

Identification is difficult and in our case was essential. Owing to the absence of any features that could be described as 'unmistakable' or even 'remarkable' the *Pilot*'s description of the coast hereabouts did not much help. Of the numerous capes mentioned the added characteristic of 'bold', or 'brown', or 'steep reddish-brown' seemed to fit most of them. Meantime we were being thrown about by a very lively swell that ran in all directions and for which there was no accounting. It would be a relief to gain the quiet waters of the fjord but before closing the land I wanted to be sure of our latitude. It was near noon and though the sky was overcast we waited in hope. The sun duly obliged and now that we knew our latitude for certain the distant scene began to fall into shape like the pieces of a jigsaw puzzle.

So we started the engine and the next few hours of motoring through that infernal lop were my idea of hell. The violent swell, big enough at times to lift our propeller clear of the water, reduced our speed to a crawl, and as it broke against the numerous bergs sheets of spray were flung into the air. A great deal of camera film was wasted on this impressive spectacle, for the breaking waves offered a target as fleeting as that of a surfacing dolphin. Some skerries at the fjord entrance were not shown on the chart and Bob, who pointed this out, was convinced we were in the wrong fjord. I myself had some doubts. Except for the immense number of floes that cluttered the surface it looked remarkably like Skjoldungen, the next fjord to the north which we had visited in 1965. These doubts were soon dispelled, the features agreed with the chart, and some ten miles up we boldly took a short cut into Rans Sund by way of a narrow gut. Like most short cuts it would have been better avoided, encumbered as it was with rocks and ice floes. Great was my relief when we emerged safely into Rans Sund, a lovely anchorage, spacious but sheltered, free from ice, a stream for watering, and two fine peaks within striking distance. A solitary seal and a couple of wheatears were the only signs of life.

The higher of the two peaks, which was also the furthest away, at once attracted Max. To climb it from the boat would be a longish day and since its lower slopes were hidden by intervening ground he decided to make sure of it by taking a camp. I tried to dissuade him and urged him to devote the first day to the nearest peak whence he would almost certainly see enough of the other to decide on the best route. I suspect Max wanted an excuse for carrying a load and camping on snow. Anyhow, the advice of the superannuated mountaineer was not taken with the result that both peaks remained unclimbed.

The climbing party, Max and Jim, left at 9 am next day, 3 September. The rest of us had sails to mend, the main sheet to turn, water to get, and finally to build a large cairn on the beach. The rain that set in at midday continued all night and most of the following morning by which time everything above 500ft. was plastered with snow. This augured ill for the success of the climbers. The glass fell to 985 mbs. Even with a companion, or if the snow had not fallen, or Jim had not borrowed my ice-axe, I think the nearer peak would have been beyond my reach. I got only as far as a col on the long ridge leading to the summit. Below the col some six inches of new snow lay on top of hard ice so without an axe I had to take to the neighbouring rocks. Thick mist obscured everything except when through an occasional rift I had a glimpse of the fjord and *Sea Breeze* far below. Having waited in vain for two hours I started down when, of course, the mist began to disperse, revealing on the far side of the fjord two noble glaciers. The climbers got back at 7 pm. On the previous day they had camped on a glacier at the foot of their mountain and on the following morning a complete white-out had prevented their doing anything but strike camp and stumble back down the glacier as best they could. Max had no regrets. He has the right idea about mountains – happy to be among them, preferably camping, even if he can't be on top of them.

The cat-ice that formed overnight on the still water of our anchorage hinted that summer was over and that it was time for us to go. Early in the morning as we sailed down the fjord the rising sun tinged the high peaks astern of us with warm Alpine glow. Offshore the swell still ran though with reduced violence and as we sped eastwards with a fair wind the almost unknown mountains of this splendid coast faded in the distance. That night, in spite of a brilliant full moon, we watched a vivid display of aurora when for nearly five hours the northern sky was lit by long shafts and flickering curtains of pale green fire. Next day we sighted our last berg, fully a hundred miles out from the coast.

The gremlin that lurked in the spars of *Sea Breeze* was still there. The spars had always been in trouble. On her first voyage with me in 1969 the topmast, bowsprit, and gaff all broke, the first two early in the voyage, the last on the way home. In 1970 the mended gaff broke again and now the same spar, once more scarfed, broke for the third time. In spite of this I had great confidence in the mast, the most important of all, which was a good inch thicker than *Mischief*'s mast, as well as in the boom which was nearly as thick as the mast. The gaff broke on the afternoon of the 12th when a German tanker altered course to have a look at us and passed a cable's length away. With a farewell blast of the horn she sheered off and a minute or so later our bow hit a wave with some violence, a wave that was probably caused by the tanker's wash. The gaff promptly broke, snapping clean in two. Having handed and lashed the mainsail we set the tops'l abaft the mast like a trys'l.

Colin Putt, the make-do and mend maestro of the previous voyage, would have enjoyed himself, but between them the crew seemed well able to cope, Bob providing the brains and Max the brawn. He spent most of one day hammering stubborn pieces of metal tubing flat and bending them to the required shape. These were brackets designed to hold in place the two wooden splints, 6ft. lengths of 3in. by 3in. By the following day all was ready for assembly, a tricky job since the spar was in two separate pieces, not merely sprung; while the rolling of the boat, with no steadying mainsail, made it difficult to line up the two pieces. The gaff had evidently outlived its usefulness – a new one would certainly be needed – so we had no mercy on the old one, driving into it through the splints a great number of 6in. nails. The final nail driven, we unlashed the mainsail and hoisted; what a joy it was to feel the boat respond, her customary liveliness restored. Although I bet Bob a pint or two that his gaff would not last, I had little doubt that it would see us home.

In spite of this delay and yet another when the mainsail had to come down again to splice the broken leach rope, we made a fast passage. By the 16th we were within 600 miles of Mizzen Head, beginning to meet Irish gannets, and practically in home waters. Once more we resumed the bad habit of listening to shipping forecasts and by changing ship's time to British Summer Time found ourselves having breakfast by candle-light. On the 23rd we passed a fine Russian passenger ship without any passengers, and early on the following night we picked up the Bishop light. Even in the Channel we met neither fog nor head winds. By 27 September we were in Lymington river receiving from the Royal Lymington clubhouse the finishing gun, their customary generous salute on our return.

CHAPTER FIVE

1972. A Change of Plan

THAT THE account of this voyage is not as full as it should be is partly owing to the absence of records and partly to that convenient faculty the mind has of forgetting what it does not wish to remember. That this faculty of forgetting is not at all times absolute many of us no doubt regret when some of the unfortunate or unworthy incidents from our past involuntarily come to mind.

Although in 1971 we had had an enjoyable and comparatively trouble-free voyage we had failed to reach our objective and had not achieved anything elsewhere. For us Scoresby Sound remained inviolate, unseen even from afar, and no Greenland mountain had been climbed. I began to feel that in trying to reach Scoresby Sound we were 'standing for some false, impossible shore, still bent to make some port he knows not where'. The odds against a small boat reaching the Sound are long and, as we found in 1971, the attempt has to be made so late in the summer that failure leaves too little time for the carrying out of any alternative plan.

My thoughts reverted to West Greenland, particularly the northern part which is, of course, much further away. There, one was more likely to be defeated by distance than by ice. In 1963 we had followed the west coast up as far as Upernivik (72° 47′ N.) with little trouble and had then crossed Baffin Bay to Bylot Island in Lat. 73° N. The ice we met had been easily avoided nor was there much of it, for that part of Baffin Bay is what the whaling men called the North Water, a large piece of ice-free water or polynia. The reasons why this particular area should be free of ice are not fully understood. Beyond Baffin Bay in Lat. 76° N. is the south coast of Ellesmere Island, highly glaciated, mildly mountainous, and sufficiently remote to be of great interest if one got there. A number of geologists, glaciologists, and the like do go there, and Mr Hattersley Smith, a friend of mine who knew the island well, strongly recommended it to me; he also provided the necessary Canadian charts and maps.

Obviously this was an ambitious project, for it is a long way north, though on the whole the chances of carrying it out compared favourably, I think, with those of reaching Scoresby Sound. Anyway, why start for a place that is almost certain to be reached? The first requisite, an able boat, was at hand, for after three voyages *Sea Breeze* was getting into good shape. The new gaff had been made a half-inch thicker than the old one and she also had a new mainsail of heavy flax canvas, roped all round. One's whims must be paid for. Compared with terylene, from which sails are made nowadays, flax canvas is heavy and therefore harder to hoist, is less immune to mildew and rot and therefore cannot be stowed away wet. It is also less durable, less durable, that is, in temperate climates – terylene will not stand too much hot sun. On the other hand flax canvas is in keeping with a boat built in 1899, is cheaper, and when flapping in the wind does not crackle like a machine gun. Quietness is worth buying.

The deck had been treated with a heavy, viscous paint which went some way to stopping the drips. No doubt, re-caulking, an expensive operation, would have stopped them entirely. Besides this, improvements had been made below, particularly in the galley which Brian Potter had now reorganised to his liking: Brian had been cook on the first eventful and disappointing voyage in *Sea Breeze*, and he was sailing again in what proved to be her last. He is an efficient sea-cook but, as a craftsman in woodwork, is more interested in making things, so that jobs like fitting shelves, cupboards, plate racks, while hardly taxing his skill are done with gusto, *con amore*. During the winter we had put in several week-ends together, sometimes with Colin Putt, another ex-crew, who had undertaken the overhaul of the engine and the making of a new exhaust pipe. In the theory and practice of machinery of any size or degree, from a tractor to a clockwork train, I regard Colin as the maestro. Had he been sailing with us it is highly probable that the voyage would not have ended as it did.

The second recruit for this voyage was a Richard Capstick who was contemplating throwing up his job as Industrial correspondent of the *Daily Mail* in Hull. Besides its own telephone system, I believe Hull has its own *Daily Mail*. He was not without experience having done some ocean racing, and that he had some enterprise he showed by making a trip in a Hull trawler to Iceland in the early spring before joining *Sea Breeze*. I took the precaution of meeting him in London beforehand, but such interviews are not much to the purpose for gauging a man's fitness for life in a small boat along with four other strangers. For me they merely ensure that when the man turns up at Lymington and says he has come to join one can believe him; not invariably because my memory for faces is not that good and in this case, since our first meeting, the man had grown a beard. Expedition experience, which is seldom forthcoming, would be a fairly sure means of finding out whether a man will turn out well or ill, for one can enquire from those who were with him how he shaped.

The third candidate I had not even the slight advantage of seeing before he joined. Like Max Smart of the previous voyage I took him simply on the recommendation of a friend whose judgement could be relied upon, an act of considerable faith since Brian McClanagan, the man in question, had no experience either of sailing or climbing. He was then in Australia and would not be able to join until a few days before sailing. In recent years I have probably had more offers of crew from Australia and New Zealand than from England.

My last recruit, picked up at the last moment in a great hurry, when someone else had dropped out, was another New Zealander. Mike Clare had been recommended to me earlier on so that when this unexpected vacancy occurred I had him to fall back on. He was working at Llanberis and consequently easily met, and only two days before I was due at Lymington to start fitting out we foregathered at Portmadoc. Mike was eager to come, had no ties, and the people he was working for, making mountaineering ironmongery, were entirely sympathetic. Besides climbing he had had some experience of boats in New Zealand.

Enough work remained in spite of what had been done at week-ends during the winter, while the unsettled weather in May did not help. The new mainsail when set looked a picture, the new gaff it hung from looked worthy of it, and the boom, we thought, quite indestructible. Since our objective, Ellesmere Island, was a long way off we proposed starting earlier than usual. 27 May, the Saturday of Whit week-end, had been fixed for sailing day. Even without the help of the shipping forecast anyone could have guessed that the weather for going down Channel with a green, untried crew would be far from favourable. However, ships and crews rot in port so I decided to sail as planned and to anchor in the Solent to await better times. We had a long wait. For three whole days we lay there while with monotonous regularity the shipping forecast issued gale warnings for every sea area around the British Isles. It blew pretty fresh even in the Solent where we lay at anchor near the Lymington Spit buoy watching the Lymington–Yarmouth ferry-boat cross and re-cross. There was little else to watch. We were rolling heavily and in Lymington it was reported that we were lying there so that the crew could get their sea-legs. Bad though the weather might be, on this holiday week-end quite a few yachts were prepared to brave it, scurrying about with only a reefed mainsail set.

On the 31st we got our anchor and sailed, the wind moderate but still at west. While beating up to the Needles we gave ourselves a severe fright by staying too long on the port tack thus getting close to the Shingles bank on the north side. Gripped by an eddy *Sea Breeze* spun completely round to face the way she had come, the sails all aback. The lop left by the recent rough weather coupled with a fresh head wind made for slow progress and we tacked over to Swanage Bay to wait there until the ebb tide early next morning. When another westerly gale brewed up as we were nearing the Start I thought we might cheat it by anchoring in the lee of Start Point. To get there we sailed round the north end of the Skerries Bank which is marked by a buoy. Having rounded this we needed the engine to make up to the anchorage close inshore in the teeth of the rising wind. So frightful was the clattering noise which ensued that we quickly stopped the engine, hoisted the sails, and went back round the buoy to spend the night hove-to in Lyme Bay. In the course of the night we lost some ten miles of hard-earned westing. By then we had found that the alarming clatter originated from the companion-way steps which were backed with sheet metal.

After passing between Land's End and the Scillies we did better and by 5 June were south of Mizzen Head. Then progress became fitful. A series of depressions, none of them severe, kept us always hard on the wind and seldom pointing in the required direction. We made more northing than westing. When the choice between two evils is nicely balanced, when which-ever tack is chosen means pointing 50° off the proper course, the port tack is probably the best. By so doing one is steering approximately a Great Circle course and the further north one goes the shorter the degrees of longitude.

Thus when we had already reached the latitude of C. Farewell (59° 46' N.) on 19 June we were still some 500 miles east of it. While on watch that evening Mike noticed a very slight crack in our indestructible boom. The gremlin had struck again. The slight crack did not seem to threaten immediate disaster so instead of getting the sail off, as we should have done, Brian went to work fashioning some metal bands to be bolted on. The weather then took a hand by obliging us to reef down and to remain reefed for the next thirty-six hours. However many tight rolls of canvas there may be round a cracked boom they are not much good as splints, as one might suppose. The boom assumed an ominous bend and when we began reefing and took out the last roll it broke clean through. The mainsail, when unbent and with difficulty manhandled below, occupied most of the fore part of the boat. Having lashed the remains of the boom on deck we set the tops'l abaft the mast as we had on the previous voyage. With the weather we were having I rather funked setting the mainsail loose-footed as it could not be reefed. It meant the whole sail or nothing. None of us had suspected a weakness in the boom or dreamt that it would break, nor did anyone, I think, who had seen that massive spar. Size is not everything; the bigger they are the harder they fall. Breaking booms, I have heard, was alleged to be a fault of Pilot cutters in their working day; it was attributed to the roller-reefing gear which necessitates the main sheet (where all the strain comes) being attached to the boom at only one point and that at the extreme end of a spar that might be 30ft. in length.

Under jury rig it would take a long time to round C. Farewell and besides that we were not likely to have a new boom made or the old one repaired anywhere in Greenland. Reykjavik, still some 300 miles north, seemed the best bet, although our going there would probably mean changing our plans. As the great Von Moltke used to remind his staff, few plans withstand contact with the enemy. By this time, too, I suspected that Richard intended leaving at the first opportunity and if it came at a Greenland port there would be no hope of finding a replacement.

The winds now were mostly northerly and north-westerly, reasonably favourable for C. Farewell, but no good for Reykjavik in our lame condition. After beating for three days, sailing about 180 miles, we had made good to the north only some 30 miles. I became concerned about our water supply.

Brian used it with strict economy, certainly less than 3 gallons a day, but one or two of the crew had a habit of drawing it off in the night watches. Water needs to be husbanded on a longish voyage, the supply being limited and unforeseen delays always possible. No water is drunk except as tea or coffee, and those who shave may do so only if they don't do it too often. Washing, either of plates, pots, or persons, is done in sea water. At this time we suffered another minor misfortune for which I blamed myself. The rigging screw on the forestay, a vital piece of the standing rigging, came adrift, its barrel falling into the sea. The barrel had been wired to prevent its unscrewing but no one had kept an eye on the wire. At sea there are very few things that one can fit and forget. With a block on the stemhead to lead a rope to the anchor winch we set up the stay reasonably taut.

Then we had a stroke of luck. One fine, calm afternoon we noticed a vessel ahead, bound nowhere apparently with any urgency. She proved to be a French fishery research vessel, *Thessala* of Brest, bound ultimately for Rockall. The skipper, noticing our queer rig, closed us to enquire if we needed anything. When we mentioned water he manoeuvred skilfully alongside, large fenders out, and one man with a fender detailed specially to watch our bowsprit. Warps were passed to make fast, then a small hosepipe, and finally a yard or so of French bread. Having filled five jerry-cans, a good ten days' supply, we cast off and went our respective ways. There were a number of bearded marine biologists on board, or at least we concluded they were something other than sailors.

Emboldened by this lucky encounter we began setting the mainsail without a boom. Since it could not be reefed we had to watch the weather, especially at night, and besides that the heavy triple block on the clew and the direct pull of the mainsheet did the sail no good. Meantime, Richard's unconcealed impatience to reach Reykjavik confirmed our suspicions. Sea-cook Brian had suspected him almost from the start on the rather flimsy grounds that he refused to eat sardine spines and wore a yachting cap. I felt that a man with the unseamanlike habit of wearing gloves at night in summer in the Atlantic would not prosper on a voyage of this kind.

Even with the mainsail, which we were able to set nearly all the time, we were not off Reykjavik until 2 July, thirty-six days out from Lymington. Since the breaking of the boom twelve days before we had made good 300 miles, having sailed many more than that in the process. Not expecting to be anywhere near Iceland on this trip I had bought no Iceland charts, nor for that matter any charts of East Greenland which it now seemed we might need. In spite of our previous visit I made a mess of the approach to Reykjavik by standing towards it from the west instead of from the north. We presently found ourselves in shoaling water, surrounded by the buoys of a regular web of fishing nets, and too close to a reef that was barely awash. Here was a situation where good advice would have been worth much but instead of that the engine stopped. It stopped for the very good reason that the fuel tank had run dry. To right this involved the lengthy and complicated process of 'bleeding', and young Brian, our inexperienced engineer, confessed himself at a loss. Meantime we had got some sails set in a hurry and headed out to sea. The wind had freshened and in order to make sure of fetching the harbour on the next tack we went about four miles. While we were beating back towards the harbour Mike had a go at the 'bleeding' process and succeeded beyond our hopes. Helped by the engine we weathered the point and by evening we were safely secured to the quay. The tanker against which we had lain the previous year had gone. We occupied her vacant berth alongside the quay with the inconvenience of having to tend our warps.

CHAPTER SIX

North from Iceland

IN REYKJAVIK the Customs people are fussy but friendly. After sealing up our liquor they stayed yarning until nearly midnight and on leaving they promised to telephone my air pilot friend, the Commodore of the Odinn Yacht Club. I wanted some advice as to where the boom could be repaired. He himself could not come, but next morning a club member arrived bringing with him the owner of a small boat-building yard. Taking the boom away to his yard to examine properly he returned that evening to report that in his opinion the boom could not be repaired. He proposed making a new one by laminating together eight 1in. planks, the job to be finished by the end of the week. To this I agreed.

With that fixed we had only the delicate question of Richard's future and that settled itself almost as speedily. That afternoon Brian and I were on deck chewing the cud, discussing this and that, and among other things Richard's shortcomings, perhaps in terms less than civil. Richard, who must have already made up his mind, was below packing his voluminous gear. He evidently overheard us. Coming on deck to announce his immediate departure he touched briefly and rudely on some of our shortcomings, particularly Brian's, but for whom, he said, he would have gladly remained. Four months is not an eternity. I always warn prospective crew that however much they may come to hate me or each other, such sentiments will have to be suppressed until the end of the voyage, and that the success of the venture and the welfare of the ship come before any personal feelings. Richard, however, would not have stuck it out anyway.

Once more we were obliged to make known our want in all likely quarters, particularly at the Youth Hostel where in summer there is a steady stream of tourists of the younger and more active kind. It would be expecting too much to pick such another winner as we had the previous year in the shape of Jim Collins, the American. We did, however, hook another American. Late one evening as I sat on deck musing on the vicissitudes of life I was haled by a long, lanky figure gazing down from the quay through outsize spectacles.

Invited on board the boat (then lying a long way below the level of the quay), he groped tentatively with his feet for the ratlines, missed them, hung by his hands for a brief space, before landing on deck with a portentous thud. It occurred to me then that if he were a prospective crew, of the 70,000 odd inhabitants of Reykjavik at that time, the one least likely to make a sailor had come on board. John Lapin said he was a student from California, a student of agriculture. To make sure I had the name right and to air my French I suggested John Rabbit, to which he assented, his French being as good or perhaps better than mine. He was on his way to Ireland to visit friends. He had no sea experience but was game to try and since so far all coverts had been drawn blank I took him on. 'Mortal men', as Falstaff said in reply to disparaging remarks about his recruits, 'Mortal men, they'll fill a pit as well as better.' No sooner had I committed myself to John Lapin than Brian received a cable from a friend suggesting that his son should fly out to join us. According to Brian father was a keen and experienced yachtsman. About the son, whom he had never met, he was a little vague, thought he must be in the early twenties and no doubt as keen as father if less experienced. With this yachting paragon on offer I could only kick myself for having taken on an agriculturalist.

The boatyard were as good as their word. On the Saturday, six days after our arrival, they brought the new boom, shipped it, and gave it a preliminary coat of varnish. They had done a good job at about half of what it would have cost in an English yard. By this time I had become reconciled to giving up the west coast of Greenland, Baffin Bay, and Ellesmere Island. I reckoned we should not get there before the middle of August, a highly optimistic estimate, leaving a brief two weeks before having to start back. Instead, since we were still east of C. Farewell, we might as well stay there and make another attempt, the third, at reaching Scoresby Sound. I had already provided the necessary charts. Meantime, as it was still early in the season and we did not want to be there until early in August, we could visit Jan Mayen. This island is in approximately the same latitude as Scoresby Sound (70° N.) and only some 300 miles to the east. We had lost *Mischief* there in 1968, but forwarned is forearmed.

Accordingly we sailed on 10 July. Sailed, perhaps, is not quite the right word. With a fresh breeze blowing straight on to the quay *Sea Breeze* showed great reluctance to leave it. After a lot of futile manoeuvring and bumping against the quay we slowly moved out crabwise under the eyes of a large and critical audience. Worse was to follow, worse at least for our new hand John Lapin who remained on deck only briefly before retiring groaning to his bunk. There for the next five days he lay as if in a coma, a bandage over his eyes, neither eating nor drinking, not even moving. After the lapse of three or four days, when he still showed no sign of life, it became clear that we should have to land him. Whether or not his seasickness was chronic, like that of Peter Marsh, he obviously had no intention of trying to overcome it. Nothing would rouse him.

> Now my weary eyes I close
> Leave, ah, leave me, to repose.

Fortunately our progress up the coast had been slow. We had not yet passed Isafjord where he could be conveniently put ashore and where Brian could telephone to his friend about the son. The changing and inconsistent moods of sea have not escaped remark. On the previous voyage nothing could have been more tranquil and untroubled than the sea at the entrance to the fjord, while at this time it seemed to boil, white water breaking all round and well inside the fjord. Even when the light wind had died to nothing the sea continued to break. There must have been a strong tide running. With the engine going flat out it took us all our time to make over to the southern shore where we anchored for the night. Iceland fjords are less sheer-sided than those of Greenland. To my surprise we got bottom in 10 fathoms a good fifty yards out from the shore. Even the noise of the cable running out and the unwonted stillness that followed failed to rouse our passenger about whose presence on board we had almost forgotten. He might have been dead. Nevertheless, he was alive enough to realise that his short voyage was not quite over and that until then, like Brer Rabbit his namesake, his cue was to lie low and say nothing. And no sooner had we secured alongside at Isafjord next morning than he was up on deck, his gear packed, and looking remarkably well considering his five days' ordeal.

One of our earliest visitors was our pilot friend, Mr Johanssen. I got out the rum. But he had with him his wife, who refused to come on board and refused to be left on the quay. As Sancho said, 'A wife's counsel is bad but he who will not take it is mad.' After a severe mental struggle Mr Johanssen gave in, resolving not to leave her alone on the quay. Brian lost no time in going ashore to telephone to England and find out if his friend's son was still available. He was our last hope, we would find no volunteers in Isafjord, so that I was greatly relieved when Brian reported that the young man would be with us in three days' time. Brian, I noticed, took the news thoughtfully, his responsibility for introducing this unknown quantity lying heavy upon him.

The sights of Isafjord are soon exhausted. On the third day after our arrival Brian and I went for a walk up the hill which towers high over the town. We hit on a road that led to a ski-lift, the ascent gradual, the surface smooth. Even so I nearly succumbed to an attack of mountaineer's foot, and it was not until we struck up on to the ridge over rough and steep going that I felt better. On top of the ridge we had the satisfaction of setting foot on the more or less eternal snow, the height being not far short of two thousand feet. In the distance across the fjord we could see the Drangajökull, a sort of miniature ice-cap over 3,000ft. high. Descending the other side of the ridge we found our way back to the town and so to the boat where we learnt that our new hand, Dougal Forsyth, had already arrived and had gone shopping. And rather to Brian's dismay we also learnt that he was a schoolboy of sixteen and that his experience extended only as far as Poole Bay. This piece of news shook me, too. While I myself might be too old I certainly thought sixteen to be too young for this kind of voyage and would not willingly set out from England with anyone of that age on board. However, he undoubtedly had father's consent, if not more, and it was too late to demur. When he did show up young Dougal looked uncommonly sturdy for his age and had no qualms on his own part about his suitability. For the short time the voyage lasted he did very well and looked like making a useful hand.

On 18 July, the day after Dougal's arrival, we sailed for Jan Mayen. Besides filling up time, or rather allowing time, as we hoped, for the ice off Scoresby Sound to clear, I expected to meet there a Danish friend, a member of a Danish expedition to the island. In a letter to me before his departure for Jan Mayen, where he was to be in charge of the commissariat, he had asked about the making of chapatties on a Primus stove. Chapatties are merely a dough of flour and water beaten between the palms of the hands until wafer thin and slapped on to a hot plate for a minute or two. Thinness is all important otherwise the outside is burnt black before the inside is cooked. Eaten hot, with butter oozing out, they are food for the gods as any traveller in the Himalaya would agree. On an expedition the beginner might find a bottle available as a rolling pin and even something that might serve as a board if the party is not travelling austerely; but the professional would scorn such aids and so should the aspiring amateur. All the skill and half the fun lies in achieving a paper-thin round of dough – not shaped like a map of Scotland – about the size of a plate, before it falls to pieces or wraps itself round one's wrist. Cooking it on a Primus is not easy as the heat is too fierce; over hot ashes is best. So much for chapatties.

We had no trouble with ice off Horn this year. We sighted the edge of the pack to the north-west, further away from the coast than in 1971, and had an uneventful passage. On 25 July, from a good 40 miles away, we made out the bold, black cliff at the southern extremity of Jan Mayen, the bowsprit happily pointing straight at it. With no lowering, leaden sunless skies, and a minimum of fog, navigation becomes easy. Since that first sighting of the distant pack there had been no hint of ice and in fact this year there was no ice within a couple of hundred miles of Jan Mayen. It is not often thus. Had similar conditions prevailed in 1968 *Mischief* might be still afloat. Wishing to make our number to the Norwegians we headed for the small bay close to their base near the south-east end of the island, the bay of evil memory where *Mischief* had been so battered by the ice. It lies 4 miles up the east coast from Sorkapp and is a poor anchorage wide open to all winds from north-east round to south.

As Mike and I rowed ashore a small party gathered on the beach of black sand ready to give a hand hauling the dinghy clear of the surf. The English-speaking member of the reception committee shook hands with the remark; 'Mr Tilman, I presume.' He had been at the base in 1968 and upon seeing another yellow-hulled cutter in the bay had put two and two together and concluded that it was that man again. Over a glass of brandy and innumerable cups of coffee we learnt with disappointment that the Danish party and my friend Dr Jensen, the would-be chapattiemaker, had already left the island. On the other hand, I was delighted to hear that with or without the aid of chapatties they had succeeded in climbing Beerenberg, the great volcanic peak 7,677ft. high, ice from sea to summit, that dominates the island. At long intervals the peak has been climbed by various parties and it was recently in the news on account of renewed volcanic activity. We found we could post letters, a plane visiting the island once a month in summer, and we also collected a 40 lb. bag of flour which we needed.

Next day we moved round to Kvalrossbukta, an anchorage on the west coast. There are no safe or sheltered anchorages on Jan Mayen but those on the west coast are preferable as that coast is free from any off-lying dangers. On quitting the bay that morning we ran into thick fog. We lay becalmed in this fog not much more than a mile from the coast and the outlying rock pinnacle upon which *Mischief* had struck in similar foggy conditions, I made sure that history did not now repeat itself. Keep the danger in sight is a sound maxim, so on hearing the melancholy sound of breakers from where we thought Sorkapp lay we motored in that direction and presently made out the loom of the cape. West of the cape the fog lifted and we enjoyed a brisk sail up the coast to Kvalrossbukta in bright evening sunshine. The Norwegians have oil tanks there, the oil being piped across the island, which at this point is only 2 miles wide. Besides a hut used by the Norwegians there are a few graves of earlier visitors, the names upon the wooden crosses no longer decipherable. It is highly unlikely that any are the graves of the seven Dutchmen who wintered hereabouts in 1633, the first men ever to winter on the island. The island was first sighted in 1607 by Henry Hudson and in 1633 the Dutch whaling fleet left seven of their men there to observe through the winter the prevailing conditions. They all died of scurvy, the last, who kept a diary right up to the end, dying only a week or so before the return of the whaling fleet in the spring.

The two Brians spent the next day walking over to the base to post letters. We found a meagre spring where Mike and Dougal employed themselves filling jerrycans and ferrying them off to the ship. I rove a new peak halyard and a few days later had the mortification of seeing this brand new length of rope stranded at one of the upper blocks. Close and constant vigilance is needed to see that all ropes are running clear. Short splices will not render through blocks, and long splices, unless really expertly made, are apt to come adrift, so this meant reeving another 60 fathoms of rope. We carry a lot of spare rope and obviously we need to. That evening a Norwegian sealer anchored in the bay having brought out and dropped at the base a French expedition.

CHAPTER SEVEN

Prelude to Disaster

THE TIME had now arrived for us to try our luck. Three hundred miles to the west lay Scoresby Sound and in a matter of a few days we should meet with success or failure. Although up here in summer the winds are generally light they most often have an easterly component and would be in our favour. Having last year's experience vividly in mind, when ice stopped us 60 miles out from the coast, I was prepared for the worst, but as we sailed on in bright, cloudless weather with not a vestige of ice in sight my hopes revived. Would it be a case of third time lucky?

Sailing along quietly one can hardly say we ran on with bated breath but that was how I felt as the hours went by and still no ice appeared ahead. At last on 3 August when only some 10 miles off the entrance to the Sound we began meeting floes. They were well scattered and having found a suitable one – large, flat, straight-sided – we moored to it and passed a peaceful night. We had learnt the mooring technique in 1970 on the west coast where we had spent many days moored to floes. Besides the charm of novelty, if one wants to stay put for the night it saves the trouble of jilling about or heaving-to and drifting. Next morning, and not without strong hopes, we started motoring through scattered floes towards the Sound. For four hours or so, going slowly, we had no serious trouble and we must have been within a few miles of the settlement at C. Tobin on the northern side before the leads gradually became harder to find, narrower, and sometimes ending in a cul-de-sac. The view from the masthead offered little comfort and regretfully I gave the word for retreat. It was high time. The day had clouded over and a freshening wind from the east had set up enough swell to start the floes rocking up and down in a way that made contact with them something to be avoided, while the business of mooring to one became difficult if not hazardous. If we were to spend the night among floes, mooring was preferable to heaving-to, because when hove-to we should be constantly drifting down on floes and having to let draw to get clear.

As we retraced our steps eastwards and the ice became more open none of the floes we passed quite answered our specification – a respectable size, somewhat bigger, say, than a tennis court, a straight sheer side against which to put our stern while the mooring party jumped ashore, and a few ice bollards or embryo humps which could be quickly fashioned into bollards with an ice-axe. While manoeuvring close to one to assess its suitability our stern sustained a sufficiently hard knock to further cool my waning interest in mooring to a floe. Better to get out to sea clear of the ice. In the course of implementing this decision we passed a floe that looked more promising. It had no bollards ready made or even embryo bollards but a crack or miniature crevasse running across it seemed to be designed to hold a grapnel.

By this time the freshening wind and the swell that was running would have persuaded anyone less pig-headed to desist. We approached up wind and while I put her stem against a short stretch of clean-cut, steep-to ice Mike leapt off the bowsprit with the grapnel. By the time Mike had fixed the grapnel the wind had blown the boat's head to one side so that short of running off and making a fresh approach head to wind it was impossible to put her stem back against the steep-to edge. To save time and to make sure of recovering Mike I ran her forefoot up the sloping shelf of ice immediately ahead while Mike, an athletic chap, waded down the shelf, leapt for the bowsprit end, and swung himself up. We backed off the shelf readily enough then lay to the warp and grapnel. We soon realised that we had wasted our time. The floe was not massive enough to lie immovable. More floes drifted down, joggled against it, and started it spinning slowly round until after a couple of uneasy hours the grapnel pulled out of the crack. Recovering both warp and grapnel intact we went out to sea for the night.

For the next few days we jilled about in the offing, greatly encouraged by the rapid disappearance of all the ice outside the Sound. From C. Tobin, off which we lay, for 17 miles south to C. Brewster the sea was clear of ice while the Sound itself remained chock-a-block with ice, mixed with great icebergs. Meantime, away to the south, unknown to us, a small vessel that was, however, a great deal more powerful than *Sea Breeze*, after a battle with the ice, successfully penetrated the Sound. The skipper of this vessel, then engaged in geodetic survey, was a friend of mine from whom I subsequently had the following letter. They had sailed for Scoresby Sound from Angmagssalik on 3 August.

On the way to Scoresby Sound we were forced by ice to go east and at one time were not more than forty miles from Iceland. From there we went direct to Scoresby Sound but at the entrance were stopped by heavy, close packed ice, and were beset for twelve hours near C. Brewster. We got in a bad position and could not move and during this time five big bergs were forced out of the Sound by under-currents. One of them passed our ship only 15ft. away with a huge forefoot underneath us. When the bergs had passed the ice slackened a little and we were able to make our way behind C. Brewster where we found a shore lead two miles wide along the coast to C. Stevenson. From there we found the area nearly free from ice. We stayed for a week and had excellent weather. The ice we forced was heavy and too much for a ship like yours not ice protected.

In this letter Captain Toft makes no mention of having crossed the Sound to the settlement at C. Tobin so what the ice thereabouts may have been like remains unknown. Had we but known beforehand of this visit we might have cruised off C. Brewster instead of C. Tobin and so fallen in with Captain Toft. Meeting him would have been fun. On the other hand we might have been tempted to follow his powerful ship through the ice with unfortunate results. We had tried that several years before in *Mischief* off Angmagssalik and had got ourselves into trouble with complete success.

For want of better our only plan at the moment was to wait and see whether the ice would move out of the Sound. Just as patience is a virtue easily fatigued by exercise, so waiting about at sea in a small boat is a tiring game to play. One thought of the blockading ships in Nelson's day lying off some French or Spanish port for months on end in fair weather or foul. But they were under orders and not on a pleasure cruise, and they were buoyed up, too, by the prospect of imminent action or of prizes to be taken. Some islands a few miles north of C. Tobin offered a chance of finding an anchorage but having gone there we found the ice lying thick jammed between the islands and the coast. Our hopes were similarly dashed when we inspected a bay just outside the Sound close to C. Tobin where there were a few Greenlander houses. There, a belt of shore-fast ice extended out for several hundred yards, and this was the more frustrating because we could now see the wireless masts of the settlement sticking up from behind the cape only a few miles away.

The engine in *Sea Breeze* was a two-cylinder Kermath 'Hercules', an American engine, installed in 1958. Apart from a reluctance to start from cold it had given no trouble since I had had the boat. In these cold waters we made a point of starting it every two or three days, and if it had not been in use would run it for an hour to keep the batteries charged. On 8 August, a black day in the annals of *Sea Breeze*, it made a queer noise when started and on being stopped refused to start again. I remembered 8 August because on that day in 1969, with C. Brewster in sight, the crew had refused to go on. (Incidentally 8 August was what Hindenberg called the German army's 'black day' on account of the successful British attack at Amiens in 1918 when I happened to be serving as a subaltern in 'I' troop RHA.) Various were the suggestions made but no one among the crew could diagnose the fault, much less cure it. Colin Putt, the maestro in these matters, believes the trouble to have been a broken valve spring and had he been with us perhaps the engine could have been run on one cylinder.

Later that day, various remedies having been tried in vain, we reluctantly concluded that the engine had 'had it'. From then on we were a sailing ship in the strict sense of the word and a more prudent man might have taken this as a hint that it was time to quit the coast of Greenland where, without an engine, or even with one, it is easy for a small boat to find itself in trouble. No waters are foolproof and Arctic waters are less so than any. Before the days of engines ships that plied their trade in the Arctic were built for the job and usually cruised in company so that if one was holed or nipped in the ice help was at hand. Anyhow, we would gain nothing now by waiting; ice conditions in the Sound might become easier but they would not become easy enough for us to manoeuvre in without an engine. Before starting for home we needed water and stores, and instead of some Iceland port I thought we might get them at Angmagssalik, thus giving the crew the slight satisfaction of having set foot in Greenland. The entrance to Angmagssalik is narrow but quite wide enough to sail through if unencumbered by ice, and I reckoned that by the time we got there, say about 20 August, there would be little of that left.

The fact that the ice seemed to be confined to the Sound, the offing remaining more or less ice-free, led me to suppose that the coast to the south would be equally free. The prospect of sailing south, helped by the east Greenland current, keeping this magnificently mountainous coast close aboard all the way to Angmagssalik gave me great pleasure. How wrong can one be. A few miles south of C. Brewster we began meeting ice and the further south we went and the further from the coast – for the coast trends south-west – the more we met. When a large field of ice appeared on our port hand to the east we had something to worry about, for by holding on southwards we might find ourselves embayed. We went about and sailed north again until with open water to the east we could safely sail in that direction. It proved a slow passage and not without some alarms.

A long way from Greenland and in fact within 70 miles of Iceland, we were not expecting to meet any ice when in the darkest hours of a foggy night we found ourselves sailing among scattered floes. These were evidently the remnants of the pack that we had seen in the distance on the way to Jan Mayen three weeks before. We hove-to until daylight and then had to sail further east to win clear, and what with this and contrary winds we had Iceland once more in sight before we were able to head west for the passage across Denmark Strait. One might almost think that a watchful Providence was trying to keep us away from Greenland. There were a surprising number of icebergs roaming widely over Denmark Strait, even within sight of Iceland, for it is not usual to meet them so far away from the Greenland coast.

On the night of 19 August, when only some thirty to forty miles east of C. Dan, we encountered a hard north-easterly gale, quite the hardest blow of the voyage and one which went on for twenty-four hours. We had sea-room enough, for at C. Dan the coast falls away to the west, and we needed it as we drifted away to the south-west, hove-to and with only some six feet of the luff hoisted. On the morning of the 21st, the gale being then spent, we had land in sight to the north, but a heavy bank of fog lay over the sea, only the mountains showing above it, and it was impossible to identify anything. In the distance there was a ship evidently making for Angmagssalik and presently a Norwegian whaler appeared out of the fog and closed with us for a gam. He had been sheltering in Angmagssalik during the gale and was now on the way out to sea seeking.

One of the crew spoke a little English but we had difficulty in making ourselves understood. We told them of our engine trouble and finally managed to get from them what we wanted which was the course and distance to Angmagssalik – 15 miles north-west. They then sheered off into the fog but presently we heard his engines again and once more he ranged alongside. They said they had spoken to Angmagssalik radio station and had been told in return that we would be helped in. We had not asked for a tow nor did I think it likely, in spite of what the Norwegians said, that anyone at Angmagssalik would bother their heads about us. On the other hand I felt pretty confident that if we did meet a local vessel near the entrance a tow would be forthcoming if we needed one – especially if the local vessel happened to be *Ejnar Mikelsen*, for example, whose skipper was an old friend. Later on we were to hear what the reaction had been to this friendly effort on our behalf by the Norwegian whaler.

The fog slowly dispersed and by evening we had closed the land a few miles south of Angmagssalik, a narrow belt of ice floes ahead and beyond that open water and a rocky shore. The wind was light and what little there was unfavourable and I had half made up my mind to spend the night at sea. However, when an opening appeared in the thin line of floes ahead I decided to sail through and try to find an anchorage for the night in Sermilik fjord which lay temptingly wide and open to the south-west, a fateful decision that was to have consequences. This was an error of judgement. Sermilik is one of the fjords that has at its head a large glacier descending from the inland ice so that there is a constant supply of ice lurking somewhere in the fjord. Still there was little enough in sight at the moment and even if we failed to find an anchorage we were not likely to come to harm, the weather apparently settled and the glass still rising after the recent gale. Having sailed through the belt of floes without hitting any of them very hard and having reached open water, I felt satisfied. After more than three weeks at sea it would be pleasant to be at anchor in a Greenland fjord even though it was not in Scoresby Sound.

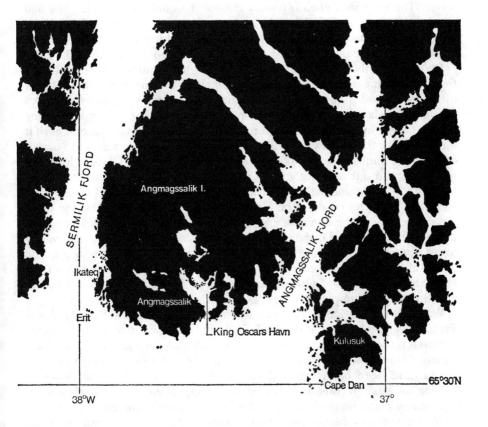

CHAPTER EIGHT

Wreck of *Sea Breeze*

THE WIND became fluky and finally died when we were still a mile or more from the shore. We tried towing with the dinghy without success, nor were we so well equipped with oars and planks as on the previous voyage. A couple of long sweeps would have done the business. The glass had been rising smartly and was now high, the more unexpected therefore was the fierce onset of wind that came in suddenly from the north just as darkness fell, the herald of a dirty night. The first blast laid her over until the lee deck was half under water. The boat shot ahead, rapidly closing the dimly seen shore. She had way enough on, I reckoned, to take her in, and the rate we were going and the fear that we might hit something induced me to get the sails off in a hurry. I had misjudged the distance and we could get no bottom with the lead.

By this time the wind or the tide had brought quantities of ice down the fjord. Increasing numbers of floes were spinning by, so many that the thought of rehoisting and trying to sail among them in the dark with that strength of wind was too daunting. In fact all hands had their work cut out fending off the floes. The dinghy was still lying astern and we had no hands to spare to hoist it on board. For the next two or three hours we drifted slowly across the mouth of the fjord until some rock skerries loomed out of the darkness to leeward. In an effort to sail clear we got the stays'l up and we might have succeeded had not a floe got under the lee bow and stopped her. Her heel caught on a ledge and she spun round to be pinned by wind and waves against the rock, the cranse iron at the bowsprit end striking sparks from the rock face as she plunged in the surge. Dropping the stays'l we shoved desperately and vainly to get her off. She was hard and fast and taking a terrible hammering as she rose and fell on the ledge. Fearing she would soon break up or slip off the ledge into deep water I told the crew to take what gear they could and to abandon ship by jumping for the rock.

Waves swept the ledge on which she lay but from the ledge dry land was within easy reach. A sack of hastily collected food was first thrown ashore followed by Mike who took with him a line which he anchored to a boulder. Young Dougal then tied himself on and got ashore safely, though the line would have been better secured on board to use as a handrail. Without waiting for Mike to coil and throw back the rope Brian, the cook, clambered over the side and jumped for the ledge. A wave caught him and washed him back almost under the boat before the next wave took him shorewards to be grabbed by Mike and hauled to safety wet through from head to foot. The wind, the breaking waves, and the crashing noise made by the boat as she pounded prevented any communication with those on shore who still had both ends of the line. The lead line being the only rope handy young Brian tied himself to that and jumped while I held him. This left me with the weighted end and thinking, rather stupidly, that 7 lb. of lead round the waist might be a hindrance if it came to swimming I had to go below for a knife to cut the lead off. Normally I wear a knife on my belt and to be without one then was unseamanlike, as indeed was much of our behaviour that night.

Total darkness reigned below. Nor could I find a torch. But after first being thrown violently to the floor with a crash that made me think the deck had caved in I found my knife, regained the deck, and presently joined the others, wet only from the waist down. I am ashamed to confess that from our first striking, while all this was happening, it never even occurred to me to collect such essential and easily postable things as diary, log book, films, money, or sextant, all of which could have been stuffed in a rucksack and got ashore. As Dr Johnson well says:

... how often a man that has pleased himself at home with his own resolution, will, in the hour of darkness and fatigue, be content to leave behind everything but himself.

We moved a few yards inland to seek shelter under a low rock wall from the wind and from the rain that had now set in. I found I could not walk without support, the ground seeming to go up and down as it sometimes does on first landing after a rough passage. On taking stock our position seemed to be grimmer than it need have been. We were all wet, some wetter than others. All had sleeping bags but precious little else. Mike had done best by bringing a very light bivouac tent. I had a tin of tobacco, a dry box of matches, but no pipe. Brian, who had not spent the night on deck like the rest of us, had no oilskins and wore carpet slippers instead of gumboots. On the other hand he had a wet and useless camera. No one had brought any food and the sack that had been first thrown ashore had been washed away.

It was then about 1 am and after a couple of hours of fitful dozing, at the first hint of dawn, some of us got up and went down to the wreck. By then I had recovered my balance. Only the top of the mast showed above water. She had evidently filled and slipped off the ledge, but whether this had happened soon after our leaving or/later we could not tell. Even had there been time it would have been difficult and indeed perilous to go back on board to retrieve anything. Jumping down and getting ashore was one thing, but it would have been quite another to maintain a footing on the wave-swept ledge near enough to the boat to grab something and climb up her heaving side.

At full light we moved up to the top of our rock islet which was, I suppose, some seventy or eighty feet high and nearly a hundred yards across. On the chart it is called Erit. There we pitched the bivouac tent and Brian and Dougal, who were wettest and coldest, were put inside. We other three explored every nook and cranny of the rock, finding it rich in nothing but pools of rain-water. At least we should not die of thirst. Returning to the scene of the wreck we searched vainly for flotsam, or even for the jetsam we had thrown overboard – the sack of food. I examined closely a narrow crack full of brash ice. Among the ice was a piece of white board from the after hatch and, Heaven be praised, a pipe, one of several that I had on board. That was all that came ashore.

After this lucky find, there being no interlude for breakfast, Mike, young Brian, and I, spent the morning pacing up and down, scanning the sea (empty except for ice), and speculating on our future. The nearest shore of the fjord was about 2 miles away. Brian's suggestion for paddling across on an ice floe seemed fraught with difficulties, not least the lack of paddles. Out of sight and a few miles up the fjord there was, as I knew, a small settlement, Ikateq, and no doubt there would be communication by boat between this and Angmagssalik. How frequently or infrequently was the question; and supposing a vessel of some kind did pass, would we be seen? We had no flares and no means of making smoke except by burning the tent or somebody's gumboots. Once a week, I thought, might be a reasonable guess, and we ought to be able to keep alive for that long. Perhaps if the sun had been shining and our clothes getting drier instead of wetter, for it was still raining, the prospect of a week or so without food might have been less daunting. Some might consider fasting no hardship, indeed beneficial. As Mr Pecksniff said: 'If everyone were warm and well-fed we should lose the satisfaction of admiring the fortitude with which others bear cold and hunger.'

After lunch – one gets into the habit of so apportioning the day – or say, two o'clock we tried squeezing three into the tent where it was warmer than outside but no drier. Young Brian took the first spell and an hour later I began crawling in for my turn. At that moment Mike let out a yell, 'A boat'. There had already been one false alarm and I expected this too would turn out to be an ice floe. But there was no mistake. Close to the north shore and bound up the fjord was one of the small, local boats with the familiar red hull. At that distance, on a dull, drizzling afternoon, I doubted if they would spot us. All five of us gathered on the highest point of the rock and began waving our sleeping bags. Some even started shouting, futile enough considering the distance and the fact that her Greenlander crew would be sensibly and drily ensconced in their wheelhouse.

To our dismay she held steadily on course and we thought bitterly how stupid they must be to fail to notice five men standing on top of an uninhabited skerry. Or perhaps they mistook the flapping figures for those grotesque and frightening mythological creatures depicted in Eskimo carvings, known as *tubilaks*, and had wisely decided to give Erit a wide berth. We had about given up hope when the boat slowed and turned in our direction. They had seen us all right as one might have known they would. No Greenlander worth his salt could fail to see us. Besides being keen-eyed they have an abiding interest in seals or anything shootable and while on passage, however routine it may be, are always on the alert and keeping a good look-out.

The crew of three set about the rescue in a seamanlike way. While the boat lay-to they launched a capacious dinghy which two of them brought close in to the rock stern-to, taking us all off in turn without mishap. Below in the cuddy they had an oil stove roaring away and relays of hot coffee were soon produced. Meantime the boat continued up the fjord to Ikateq where there were forty drums of oil – the winter fuel supply – to be landed. The crew of

Sea Breeze lent a willing hand, young Brian in the hold slinging the drums, Dougal on the derrick guy, with Mike and Brian on the beach man-handling the landed drums. I was thankful when Brian and the last drum emerged from the hold, for the wire sling was so badly stranded that the most careless stevedore would have condemned it at sight.

Half-way to Angmagssalik we were met and taken on board a far superior vessel, one used by the doctor for visits to outlying settlements. On board were the doctor himself and the head of the Angmagssalik police force. We disappointed the doctor in that we needed no treatment but we were able to reassure the policeman who was a worried man. News travels too fast nowadays. The Danish naval authorities on the west coast had already heard of our rescue and were asking how and why *Sea Breeze* had come to grief. Apparently the message from the Norwegian whaler had been passed to the policeman who in turn had consulted the Harbour-master as to whether anything should be done. His opinion had been that since a tow would cost £200, and that since from the Norwegian's unflattering description we were not likely to have that amount even in pennies, nothing should be done. Since we had neither asked for a tow nor expected one the policeman had no cause for worry.

We spent that night in the hospital where we were given a room to ourselves and most kindly looked after. Next day I had to give a full account of the stranding to our policeman, with my friend, the skipper of *Ejnar Mikelsen*, acting as interpreter. The head of the Administration was in a hurry to get rid of us. A Danish ship about to sail had only two vacant berths and since none of the crew had any money or passports we had to travel together. The quickest and cheapest alternative was to charter a small plane from Reykjavik and we arranged to be picked up next day which was a Friday. Near C. Dan, on the island of Kulusuk, there is an airstrip. Money proved to be no problem, the Administrator, acting for the Danish Government, being delighted to lend me as many thousands of kroner as I needed, on note of hand alone as the money-lenders say. Leaving the hospital we messed and slept that night in the huts used by the Danish technicians and workmen who in summer are employed in Greenland.

Early on the Friday we again embarked in the doctor's boat for passage to Kulusuk, a matter of about an hour and a half. In dense fog and with large numbers of bergs and floes about the skipper made full use of his radar. The harbour at Kulusuk, too, was cluttered with floes and a U.S. naval transport lying there looked uncommonly forlorn in those bleak surroundings. Fog persisted throughout the day and on the last of my several visits to the control tower they told me there would be no flight that day. This was awkward, since it meant our arriving at Reykjavik on the Saturday when the bank to which I had had money for our fares home sent would be shut. Taking my family home was proving expensive enough without having to spend the week-end in a Reykjavik hotel. There is a pretty large staff at Kulusuk (it is part of the Early Warning System) so we ate in their mess and were given rooms in a hostel (all on payment) used by visitors and passengers in transit.

Our plane, a five-seater Apache, arrived next day at noon and after lunch we embarked. Our luggage hardly needed weighing and slight though it was we had a job stuffing it in. Our pilot, long-haired, nonchalant, extremely youthful, a cigarette dangling from his lips, did not inspire confidence. This, together with my reinforced mistrust of engines, made me, if not apprehensive, yet looking forward with some eagerness to a safe landing on the far side of Denmark Strait. I need not have worried. The manager of the charter company, who did a lot for us later at Reykjavik, assured me that he was the best pilot they had ever had.

Late that evening we reached Reykjavik where happily the British Consul had got wind of us. I had met him before in Reykjavik in 1965, and the manager of the charter company now drove me to his office where we were fixed up with a bit of paper that served as a passport for the whole crew and seats on a flight to London next day, for which the Consul paid. The manager of the charter company kindly allowed us to bed down in the top storey of his office in a room that originally had been the airfield control tower. Although we arrived in London a day later than I had indicated we were met and shepherded through the formalities by a relative of mine, Brigadier Davis, accompanied by Bob Comlay. No one having been drowned the loss of *Sea Breeze* happily escaped publicity, but an ITV man lying in wait sought an interview with the persistence of the importunate widow until some rude words from Bob Comlay silenced him. Colin Putt, too, just missed us but came along next morning to drive me to Wales.

At the moment there are few if any amateur sailors likely to profit by it, but for me the lesson of this sad story is not to mess about in Greenland fjords without an engine, especially when they are full of ice. For all that I feel we were victims of an unlucky chain of circumstance – the calm that prevented us from finding an anchorage, followed shortly by a wind of such force that we could not sail safely among the ice brought down by the wind, but for which we would have come to no harm. *Sea Breeze* had made four voyages north and each voyage had seen some small improvement introduced. At the end I felt as proud and confident of her as I had of *Mischief* and thought her to be as able a boat as on the day of her launching in 1899. The fact that she had on her last voyage a new boom and a new mainsail was merely another trifling sum of misery added to the account. Certainly a staggering enough blow for me and only the fact that we had not sailed the seas so long nor had so many adventures together made her loss a little less heart-rending than that of *Mischief*. For fourteen years *Mischief* and I had sailed together and at the end I had to watch helpless while she lay on the beach, so battered by sea and ice that she did not long survive when finally got under tow.

Concerning regrettable incidents, and this ranks as such, Sir Winston Churchill's advice was never to look back, look to the future. Such advice is easier to give than to take, but in a case like mine it would help if I had another boat. Within a short time of getting home I heard of a boat that was to be sold in November, and having had a look at her I felt that, all being well, the future was arranged. When in October I learnt that she was not going to be sold I had to think again and these thoughts led back to *Sea Breeze* and the possibility of raising her. I kicked myself for not having stopped in Reykjavik on the way home to make enquiries, but that had not been possible as I had to take the crew home. There were no facilities at Angmagssalik, if anything were to be done it would be from Reykjavik.

From Lloyds I obtained the name of a firm in Reykjavik to whom I wrote. They thought it a wild idea, a moonbeam from a larger lunacy, but were extremely helpful. Even if it could be done, they said, the cost of salvage and repair would be out of proportion to the value of the ship, and in any case, before approaching a salvage company the wreck would have to be examined by a diver. They reckoned that a diver could be flown to Kulusuk and taken by boat to the wreck for about £550, given favourable conditions. This preliminary stake, which would probably be lost anyway, seemed to me to be worth putting down. I felt I owed it to *Sea Breeze* to make an effort, and the diver, besides reporting on the state of the wreck, might with a little encouragement be persuaded to retrieve a few valuables. I had in mind particularly a couple of sextants and £70 in Danish money.

All this took time and clearance had to be got from Copenhagen. But at length Messrs. Könun, the agents, laid on a diver and a charter flight for him and me for 15 November. On this I booked a flight to Reykjavik and for the second time had money transferred to a bank there. The day before I was due to go the following cable came from Messrs. Könun who, by the way, were not sparing of words either in their letters or their cables:

We have today received following from airfield manager Kulusuk in reply to our queries. Regarding *Sea Breeze* stop undersigned plus helicopter crew ascertained 28th October from helicopter in spite of clear water and visible bottom no sign of *Sea Breeze* stop it is assumed that the wreck has been washed away during heavy storms regards manager Kulusuk. In view of this information which must be relied upon we do not consider it in your interest to send diver stop.

At first I thought there was something fishy about this, even that the airfield manager had an eye to salvaging the boat himself and did not want a visit from me. Accordingly I asked Messrs. Könun why he had bothered to fly a helicopter over the wreck on 28 October and how did he know where to look. To which they replied that the wreck had been observed in about 30 metres of water several times from both speed-boats and helicopter; which implied that she was already in deeper water than when we left her with her mast showing, and that by 28 October she had gone deeper still and out of sight. In their reply they added a suggestion from the airfield manager that if I wanted to look for myself I could hire a helicopter for £250 an hour.

I had to withdraw my suspicions about the airfield manager and after much heart-searching decided to throw in my hand. The approach of winter was a decisive factor. If the wreck were located, if the diver succeeded in reaching it, and if he reported favourably – three big 'ifs' – nothing could be done until the next summer, by which time the wreck might have slipped further down. I consulted my friend Captain Toft who wrote: 'I am sure it is quite impossible to find *Sea Breeze* now because of drifting ice, strong tides, and deep water close to shore. Any money spent on a search has to be lost money.' Another Danish skipper also wrote to me: 'I think there is a deep round Erit and *Sea Breeze* has slid down to the foot of the islet, so I think you are right to forget her and look for another ship. It will be too expensive to raise the yacht and get her repaired. A wooden ship will get very severe damage when hammered on rock broadside on.'

I now had to reproach myself for not having done something early in September when at least the boat might have been found and examined, and to regret that the prospect of acquiring another boat had led to neglecting the slight chance of saving my old one. Thus having muffed both possibilities I had to bestir myself if I were not to be left high and dry with no voyage in view for 1973. I will not say that the idea of giving up, calling it a day had not occurred to me, but I regarded this as the prompting of Belial who 'with words clothed in reason's garb, counselled ignoble ease'. We hear sad stories of men retiring after a life of toil and trouble who instead of enjoying their well-earned ease and freedom from care find it so insupportable that they soon fall into a decline. No doubt a friend, evidently a classical scholar, had this in mind when he sent me the following snippet of ancient wisdom: 'The man who would be fully employed should procure a ship or a woman, for no two things produce more trouble.' (Plautus 254–184 BC). The year ended on a happier note with a promise of full employment and a stock of trouble. *Baroque*, a Pilot cutter of 1902 vintage, was for sale, and needless to say I bought her.

CHAPTER NINE

Baroque

ONE CANNOT buy a biggish boat as if buying a piece of soap. The act is almost as irrevocable as marriage and should be given as much thought. Even if the boat is bought merely to look at, as some are, it has to lie somewhere. Expenses begin at once and if the boat is an old one they will rise in arithmetical progression until either something happens to it or the owner finds himself in Carey Street. When I first heard of *Baroque* she was lying at Mylor near Falmouth and early in January 1973 I went down there. Mylor is in the uttermost parts of the West, as the Psalmist has it, though to me, driving from North Wales in winter, it seemed like the uttermost part of the earth. On this first reconnaissance I broke the journey, but on subsequent visits did the 350-odd miles in the day, straightening one's back with difficulty at the end of it and continuing to vibrate for several hours afterwards.

Baroque measured 50ft. overall, 13ft. 6ins. beam, 7ft. 6ins. draught, and 32 tons TM; thus she was a foot longer than *Sea Breeze* and a foot less in beam. She lay against the harbour wall, drying out at low tide, and at first sight the doghouse that some misguided person had stuck on her, and the tall pole mast, rather put me off. Pilot cutters should have flush decks or at worst low skylights, so the doghouse was incongruous and spoilt her looks. The tall pole mast was in keeping, but it meant extra gear and weight aloft without much gain. The occasions on which one would want to set a tops'l in the North Atlantic are so few that such a sail is hardly worth carrying. Both *Sea Breeze* and *Mischief* had topmasts that could be lowered or dispensed with altogether, as in the end they were. *Baroque*'s upper and lower backstays were lavishly lapped with baggywrinkle, lending her a picturesque appearance and adding weight and windage to the stays. This stuff, easily made up from strands of old rope, preserves the mains'l from chafe. Normally, however, the lee backstays would be cast off and secured by the shrouds so that the wire stay would seldom be against the sail. Probably previous owners had used her mainly for day-sailing and were content to ease away the lee backstays without casting them off altogether as would be done on a long passage. She had been built in 1902 and since her working days had suffered at the hands of various owners all with various ideas, most of them wrong.

It is time to go below and at the risk of being tedious I ought to describe what I found and my reactions, which were those of a man who has already half made up his mind to commit a folly and is already thinking of ways to mitigate it. Starting at the forward end the peak was roomy – a sail rack would have to be built in. Nor was there any chain locker and no chute for the chain to be led down from the winch. In fact she had no substantial ground tackle at all, only a little Fisherman type anchor suitable for a dinghy and a CQR anchor of about 20 lbs. with a few fathoms of $\frac{1}{4}$in chain. On the other hand she had a fine, big winch. A chain locker and chain chute would therefore have to be made, while a Fisherman anchor of about 1 cwt., a 60 lbs. CQR, and some 35 fathoms of $\frac{1}{2}$in. chain would have to be bought. This want of ground tackle, and the absence or flimsiness of various fittings, confirmed that if she had been sailed at all it had been as a dayboat, a day's sail and back to a mooring. Cleats were scarce and small, there were no sheet-leads for either jib or stays'l, and the compass was a small plastic affair mounted on a bakelite bracket screwed to thin plywood.

Abaft the peak came the galley, sink with taps, gas cooker and refrigerator. All would have to be abolished. So far forward the motion is felt most and it would be a long walk carrying food from the galley to the saloon. Instead of the sink I could have a work bench with vice and there would be room, too, for a huge locker with five shelves big enough to hold all our stores. A bunk occupied the port side and a ladder and forehatch gave access to the deck; the presence of the hatch led one to suspect that this bunk might prove to be wet. The art of making watertight hatches has not yet been perfected.

A bulkhead separated this from the next compartment aft which had two bunks to port and one to starboard. Aft of the two bunks a sliding door led into the 'heads'. The mast came down aft of the bulkhead and overhead was a small skylight. The galley would have to go here, the two bunks being sacrificed in favour of a sink with shelves below and above. The proximity of the galley to the lavatory might not please a sanitary inspector but that could not be helped. This sliding door, by the way, soon gave up sliding and had to be abolished like all the other doors, the only door left being that between the chartroom and the cockpit. The throne in the 'heads' had been built for someone with abnormally long legs. We had to put in a foot-rest. At one end of this small compartment a shower had been installed. Pipes writhed everywhere, a Laocoon coil of them, hot water and cold, salt water and fresh. The plumber, not one of the brightest, had a job sorting them out and sealing off the unwanted majority.

Next came the saloon or main cabin, very ornate with mahogany panelling, red baize inside the panels, gimballed brass lamps looking like old-fashioned oil lamps but in fact electric, the whole spacious enough but nowhere to put anything and no table. Brian Potter, cook on the previous voyage, who later came down to lend a hand with *Baroque*, thought that these gimballed lamps (a dozen of them) would be of value to antique dealers. The dealers thought otherwise so Brian converted them back to oil for use in *Baroque*. The two settee berths in the saloon had under them little locker space and only meagre cupboards for the occupants' kit. In fact, in spite of her size there seemed to be little room to stow anything. By putting another bunk over the one on the port side I could have five bunks, the number required, and there remained only the table problem. In *Mischief* we had a 100 gallon water tank in the saloon with a table on top and the same could be done here; owing to the shape of the hull the final result was a tank of only 60 gallons, leaving just enough room for a passageway on one side and barely enough room to sit at the table on the other.

Two steps led from the saloon up into the combined chartroom and engine-room comprising the doghouse, standing a good four feet above deck level, made of plywood, and large perspex windows all round. Apart from its ugliness it was a source of weakness, but nothing much could be done. A wave might abolish it but I could not very well abolish it myself since it housed the engine, and without it there would be nowhere to do any chart-work. The main water tank of 60 gallons lay underneath with a 40 gallon header-tank to one side. Here, too, were the fuel tanks winged out on either side. These were two 40 gallon oil drums, effective enough, one supposed, until they rusted through. The charging motor for the batteries, which were also housed here, was a portable Honda. The engine, a Ford diesel marine conversion, looked huge and lurked below floor level on the port side with a lot of vacant space round it.

Aft of the doghouse was a deep and narrow cockpit, lockers either side and a big locker under the seat. The helmsman had to stand on the seat in order to see over the doghouse roof; in the end we had to add something more to stand on so that he could see enough. Steering was by wheel with a not over-robust looking worm gear and this, too, would need to be abolished in favour of a tiller with less to go wrong and more positive action. Except for the bowsprit the spars looked in good condition, while the sails, which were almost new, were of terylene with not very stout stitching. This certainly has the no mean advantage of being light, easy to hoist and handle, easy to stow, and stowable when wet without fear of rot. On the whole, however, I would still prefer heavy canvas, if only as more in keeping with an old boat. It would be a better bet, too, in tropical waters since terylene does not stand up well to prolonged sunshine. Except for the bowsprit shrouds the wire standing rigging was in good shape. The shrouds were attached to the chain plates with rigging screws, whereas I would have preferred lanyards like we had in *Seabreeze*. These again are more in keeping with a boat built in 1902 and having more give are possibly less cruel to the hull. The chain plates looked short.

> Be to her faults a little blind
> And to her virtues ever kind

is advice equally applicable when proposing to throw in one's lot with either a woman, a horse, or a boat. *Baroque* might have virtues and some of her more obvious faults could be corrected, if not ignored. At that late stage, January, if I were to have a cruise that summer it would have to be in *Baroque*, for there was no other boat in sight. Much needed to be done but nothing like so much as we had had to do with *Sea Breeze*, and she could probably be got ready by the end of May. A cruise to northern waters every summer had become almost as essential as breathing, so strong is habit, and since in the natural course of things there could not be many more I did not want to leave 1973 blank; if a year were missed to start again would be all the harder. Another persuasive factor in *Baroque*'s favour was a specification I saw of work done to her in 1970 for her then owners. She had had then a major overhaul and they had spent a lot of money. As events were to show they had not spent nearly enough.

Or perhaps, as I presently discovered, the work had not been as thorough as it should have been. Even on this first visit I noticed that no new keel-band had been fitted as specified, the old one being still in place with a break in it. On a second visit made a week or so later to discuss terms with the owner, John Smith, who had owned the boat for only a few months, we made a worse discovery. Since my first visit he had on his own behalf taken out the gas cooker and the refrigerator thus exposing three or four frames on the starboard side. Two of these were rotten, without any fastenings, and could be waggled about by hand. I began to think I had been a bit hasty in making an offer. Thanks to a friend who lived in that rather lush region I got in touch with the owner of a nearby boatyard, Bob Pizey, extremely knowledgeable about old boats, who agreed to come over next day to do a quick survey.

The day started badly for Bob Pizey with an accident in his yard when a boat fell over and broke the leg of one of his men. In spite of that he came over to Mylor and devoted several hours to *Baroque*. Outside, the hull appeared to be in good condition, only one soft plank to be renewed and a short graving piece let into another. The propeller, shaft, and 'A' bracket were corroded and needed renewing. The difficulties for a surveyor begin inside where, short of pulling the boat to pieces, he cannot see nearly as much as he would wish. On the other hand, in dealing with old boats, the more you stir the more it stinks. One needs to take a certain amount for granted, adopting the motto of the Australian opal-gouger, 'Live in hope if you die in despair'. We took out what mahogany panelling we could in order to inspect the frames behind and the nett result was two more rotten frames to add to the two already found. It might have been much worse and I made up my mind to go ahead, to buy the boat and to have the necessary work put in hand by the local yard.

On this brief visit to Mylor I acquired not only a boat but also the second of two prospective crew. Brian McClanaghan, not a whit discouraged by the disaster of the previous year, had already offered to come if I succeeded in finding a boat. This time I intended going first to West Greenland and then as far north as we could, a point that I hoped would turn out to be Ellesmere Island, the original objective in 1972. In an untried vessel, making as it were a trial voyage, this might seem ambitious; but to be of any value, to disclose defects and weaknesses, a trial voyage must be long enough to ensure experiencing a few gales. There are exceptions to this. On our first voyage in *Sea Breeze*, for instance, the urgent need for re-caulking became apparent even before we had left the Solent.

My acquaintance with John Harradine, the second volunteer, had begun the previous year soon after the loss of *Sea Breeze*, by his sending me a telegram in Latin, thus astonishing Barmouth Post Office and enhancing my bogus reputation as a man of learning. Latin is undoubtedly the right language for telegrams because one can say an awful lot in very few words. *O passi graviore revocate animos et haec olim meminisse juvabit* the telegram read, and with the help of a dictionary I translated this as 'Ye who have suffered even greater trials gather courage, perhaps one day it will be pleasant to remember them.' The sender gave no address and this had to be got with the aid of the Post Office sleuths. On our corresponding I found him keen on making a northern voyage and promised to let him know if I found a boat. In January he was in England on leave from Norway where he taught adult classes English, not Latin. I had told him of *Baroque* and of my impending second visit to Mylor.

The evening of the day when I had discovered the loose, rotten frames I was in the bar of the inn at Mylor Bridge, about $1\frac{1}{2}$ miles from the harbour, in a very uncertain frame of mind and deriving neither aid nor comfort from the beer provided. A short, young man with reddish hair, wearing a duffel coat, walked in: 'Mr Tilman, I believe.' This feat of detection impressed me. Mylor harbour and its vicinity is a maze of narrow roads leading in all directions., and to find his way from Watford to the boat and then in the dark of a January evening, guided only by his own resourcefulness, to run me to earth at Mylor Bridge showed him to be a man of determined enterprise. Neither the inn nor its beer encouraged conviviality. We had a quiet evening together while I explained the difficulties of my position and expressed the hope that by next afternoon as a result of Bob Pizey's survey I would know what to do. And just before closing time John Harradine supplied the last missing word for *The Times* crossword puzzle, a problem that had been worrying me all evening almost as much as the boat – an erudite man, as I had gathered from his telegram. As I had the only room in the inn John said he would go back and doss down in the boat. After he had left I remembered that the boat was locked up and that I had the key, but I did not think a trifle like that would baffle this resourceful man. In any case, 'I'm all right, Jack,' I thought, as I went up to my room, but on finding it extremely damp and chilly I was not so sure.

I had just finished my bacon and eggs when John, having slept in his van and breakfasted off a packet of biscuits, joined me and we adjourned to the boat to await Bob Pizey. Fortunately the tide was out and the hull accessible. We did a little more wrecking inside to expose more frames and on the whole the survey, as I have said, proved satisfactory. I decided to go ahead and John felt sufficient confidence in the boat to want to come on the projected voyage. He even went so far as to ask me to reserve the bunk forward of the galley for him, an unwise request.

CHAPTER TEN

Fitting Out and Crew

MYLOR YACHT HARBOUR could now start on the work that I had planned, perforce hastily. The galley to be moved amidships and a work bench where the former galley had been; a big, new locker with five shelves to hold three or four months' food, a new bunk in the saloon, and water tank with table on top. (Owing to a strike on the part of galvanisers the tank had eventually to be made of fibre-glass.) A new bowsprit, chain plates for the topmast backstays (there were none), a wood tiller and an iron emergency tiller in lieu of the wheel. A Whale pump to be installed in addition to the semi-rotary; and new propeller, shaft, and 'A' bracket. Later the stern tube was condemned as well and a new one had to be made. The ravages of electrolytic action seemed to be excessive, whether caused by Mylor sea-water or by the web of wiring, ancient and modern, which festooned *Baroque*'s interior. I should have liked to have done something with the doghouse either by removing or lowering it, but this meant an excessively expensive and time-consuming major upheaval. A radio telephone and an echo-sounder were part of her equipment. The latter had a fault which baffled the expert who spent two days trying to put it right. Regretfully I disposed of it. I had felt vaguely that we should fit one in *Mischief* and *Sea Breeze* but had never done so, partly owing to a dislike of making more holes in the hull and partly from a mistrust of mechanical devices. The radio telephone, I learnt, could have been flogged for £200 had I owned the boat before 1 January when the enaction of some new regulations by the Post Office rendered it worthless. As already noted, the electric wiring needed simplifying. Like the water pipes, wires led everywhere, under the deck, along the deck, up the mast, under the cabin sole. We restricted the lighting to a binnacle light, and a light in the doghouse, cabin, galley, and peak. With the water pipes, as I have said, the plumber had a field day and lost. When we tried the pump in the galley sink water came out where the shower bath had been in the 'heads'.

The yard reckoned the work could be done by mid-May. Sailing day had already been provisionally fixed for 29 May, and I had now to complete the crew, a job that proved even more tricky than usual. Even with a poor boat much can be achieved by a good crew and since *Baroque* was an unknown quantity an experienced and reliable crew was more desirable than ever. Brian McClanaghan, his enthusiasm undiminished and his confidence un-shaken by the loss of *Sea Breeze*, knew the ropes and the way things should be done, and was completely reliable. John Harradine owned a small boat of his own so presumably knew quite a bit, and he was also a mountaineer. An American who had been recommended to me by a trusty friend thought he would come and delayed until April to tell me that he would not. Early in May he cabled to say that he had again changed his mind and would join immediately, but this hardly merited the expense of a reply. One or two other prospects faded out and by mid-April the situation might have been described as desperate though not hopeless. My letter to this effect to John Harradine who was back in Norway, and who wanted to know the state of play, led to embarrassing consequences – for him, at least, if not for me.

In the past an advertisement in *The Times* for 'a cook for a cool voyage' had been successful. Just before sending it for insertion I noticed that someone else in reduced circumstances was advertising for 'experienced crew for an Arctic voyage'. My curiosity roused I wrote to the Box Office number to enquire about his voyage, at the same time asking the advertiser to let me have the names and addresses of his rejects. He turned out to be Merton Naydler whom I knew of as having sailed with David Lewis to Iceland in a catamaran, subsequently writing a book called *Cook in a Cool Cat*. He planned to sail to the Murmansk peninsula, an objective that seemed to me to lack not only the prime requisites of an Arctic voyage, namely ice and icebergs, but also to involve the likelihood of having one's boat confiscated and ending up in Lubalanka gaol. His rejected replies, he told me, had already gone into the waste-paper basket but his secretary luckily retrieved them and passed them to me. I wrote to one or two that sounded likely and later found that I had picked a winner in one, Simon Richardson, active, energetic, knowledgeable about boats and engines, and a thorough seaman so far as an amateur sailor can attain to that honourable title.

My own advertisement for cook produced fewer replies than expected, only eight in fact, the number having decreased steadily over the years. Whether this decrease implies a weakening of moral fibre on the part of the young or on the contrary a strengthening of the mind, only the sociologists would be likely to know. All eight very wisely asked for more details about the proposed voyage and on these being supplied all faded out except Ilan Rosengarten, another Australian in England on a working holiday. We exchanged several letters without getting any further and I had the impression that he had by no means made up his mind whether or not he wanted to come. By this time, early May, I was at Mylor living on board and starting to fit out. In fact I spent most of the time in Falmouth, Newlyn, and other places in search of the thousand and one things we needed. For the third time I was starting from scratch to collect what is necessary for a well-found ship and finding it uphill work.

Brian had arranged to join by 7 May, while John Harradine, who had talked of joining by Easter, was still in Norway. For the first week-end Colin Putt and Brian Potter, both highly skilled, came down to lend a hand, and having accomplished a lot in a short time left me in a more robust frame of mind, a little less daunted by the amount of gear still to be got and work to be done. The same week-end Simon Richardson and a friend of his came to see me and the boat, having spent the night, I gathered, in a tent on Bodmin Moor. I agreed to take Simon and thought there might be a berth for his friend as well if Ilan Rosengarten proved to be a non-starter. My last letter to Ilan had suggested his coming to Mylor to take stock of me and the boat if he was really interested; to my surprise he came. He did not tell me much about himself except that he was presently teaching in London and had not the least knowledge of boats, the sea, or expeditions. On the way back to Truro, where I took him to catch his train, I had to make up my mind, and it was with some misgiving that I finally told him to join. These misgivings were mainly owing to his total ignorance of boats and the sea, the difference, for instance, between cooking on a firmly based electric stove and on a most unstable Primus stove. Selfishly, I felt less concern for Ilan's prospects than those of the crew who would be put to some inconvenience or worse if we found our cook unable to cope.

As it happened, Ilan proved to be one of the best cooks I've ever had, either as regards cooking, housekeeping, or as shipmate. I take no credit for this. I had not, merely from his appearance, judged him to be willing, even-tempered, imperturbable, a man eager to overcome difficulties and able to rise to any occasion. I have long since given up trying to assess a man's character by his appearance or his behaviour at a brief interview, and in consequence of numerous errors of judgement have often lamented, like the hapless Duncan, that:

> There's no art
> To find the mind's construction in the face.

The fact is that it is easy to pick a winner when there is only one in the race, as was the case when Ilan came to Mylor to see me. For the first ten days or more my earlier misgivings looked like being justified for Ilan was far from well and took a long time to settle down. Having once recovered he never looked back and readily adapted himself to a strange way of life. He flavoured his cooking with imagination, always trying something new, and always busy in the galley except when beating me at chess. He served all meals on time whatever the weather, kept a close eye on water and stores, took a spell at the tiller when needed, and got on well with the crew. All ills are alleviated when attended by food and since the ills of this voyage were many we had frequent occasion to bless the cook.

With the arrival of Simon and Brian things began to move and I could look forward to more help from Colin Putt and Brian Potter who had promised to come down again before we sailed. The latter, with the experience of two voyages in the galley behind him, would impart some of this know-how to Ilan and start him off on the right foot. I still had to spend time running around looking for various things. Wooden blocks, iron hooks, bull's-eyes for sheet-leads, were all hard to find; which surprised me since one would expect such traditional gear to be more readily obtainable in the West country than elsewhere. Years before in *Mischief*'s time, I remembered having paid a visit to the Great Grimsby Salt and Fish Co. at Newlyn to buy some composite rope such as was then used by trawlers. I went there again only to find it re-named CoSalt and that CoSalt had gone all 'yachty', nothing but plastic and polythene, and fancy clothing for dinghy sailors. The sheet-leads were eventually made for me by a chance-met acquaintance, one-time skipper of the well-known yacht *Tai-Mo-Shan*, who had some lignum vitae on hand. In Cornwall I found a fund of goodwill to be drawn upon, not to me personally but as a man who happened to be fitting out for a serious voyage. So great was the difficulty of finding anchor chain that we looked like being held up for lack of it. Only on the day before sailing John Smith, *Baroque*'s late owner, drove me over to Redruth and we came back with 30 fathoms of ½in. cable in his station-wagon. Happily the links fitted snugly to the winch gypsy or we should have been sunk.

John Harradine still showed no sign of life until ten days before sailing when I received a telegram from Bergen: 'Colorado geophysicist will be a useful addition.' It was obviously not in Latin but to me it was equally obscure. I could make nothing of it. Perhaps it was in code or an acrostic but however hard I tried its meaning remained as elusive as the identity of the dark lady of the Sonnets.

The explanation came in a letter a few days later. He had been delayed looking after a sick friend but hoped to join forthwith; meantime he had solved my crew problem by persuading an American scientist, one Steve, to join us. I reacted smartly to this with a telegram to Watford where he had then arrived, telling him on no account to bring Steve. His honour was at stake, came the reply, his promise to take Steve could not be withdrawn. This left me unmoved. My withers, at any rate, were unwrung. Quite apart from Steve's suitability or otherwise we had no spare bunk and a crew of six gave rise to catering and watering problems. John did not turn up until Whit Sunday three days before we were due to sail, bringing with him the unlucky Steve, a lean, gangling chap about 7ft. long with no sea experience whatsoever. John, as we know, had earmarked the bunk which I had faithfully kept for him. They had brought a mass of gear and Steve, who fancied himself as a carpenter, set about making a shelf over this bunk to accommodate it all. After a day of hammering and sawing up forward I began to wonder what they were doing. The shelf, I found, was to extend over the whole bunk, in effect another bunk on top of the other; possibly it was designed for receiving Steve, either as a stowaway or as a result of presenting me with a *fait accompli*, no longer worth arguing about.

A busy Whit week-end started on the Friday afternoon with the arrival of our stores and their stowage. For the bonded stores the only place left was the 'heads' where they were put and duly sealed up by the Customs. Some 60 lbs. of tinned butter for which the ship's chandler had been scouring England were promised for the Tuesday, together with my tobacco which had been overlooked. At home I smoke a pipe with moderation, at sea with duty-free tobacco I smoke like a factory, making hay, so to speak, while the sun shines. Colin Putt with his wife and one of the boys, young Harry, arrived to camp in their Land-Rover in the car-park. We kept young Harry amused over the week-end by sending him afloat in our 7ft. pram dinghy. *Baroque* had a rubber inflatable, which we never used, and also a life-raft. I viewed this with mixed feelings, since the only voyage on which we had previously carried one had ended in the loss of *Mischief*.

Colin had made a new exhaust pipe which came up through the deck and ended above the coach-roof, whereas the original exhaust had led straight through the ship's side with no 'U' bend, thus allowing the sea free access to the engine. The new one made a hellish noise and with the wind in the right quarter the helmsman had the benefit of breathing diesel fumes to remind him of life ashore. He had also made us two massive 15ft. sweeps out of the old bowsprit. We tried them out later in a Greenland fjord with success, regretting all the more that we had not had them on the previous voyage which might then have ended more happily. Brian Potter came, too, with a fiddle he had made for the table and then busied himself making shelves for our library and for the wireless receiving set. On this we could get weather forecasts until about 500 miles west and thereafter its main use was for time signals obtained on the Overseas Service of the BBC. We had all the sails up in turn and fitted the leads for the headsail sheets – not perfect but the best that could be done with the dinghy taking up so much of the foredeck. On the Sunday morning, in the middle of what was already considerable confusion, John and Steve arrived to add their quota. Their small car was too small to accommodate 7ft. of Stephen who had to doss down on the floor by the work-bench. Surveying the busy scene, and mindful of the voyage ahead, I felt like Milton's Satan on the brink of Chaos:

> Pondering his voyage; for no narrow frith
> He had to cross.

That evening Ilan dished up curry for nine, the whole mollified by a bottle of champagne which visiting friends of his had kindly left.

Meantime we had a serious last-minute problem with the engine which threatened delay. When the new stern tube went in it could not be lined up with the engine. The stern tube had to go back for alteration and the engine had to be moved bodily about a ¼in. We should not know until after the holiday whether this would do the trick and sailing on 29 May as intended looked unlikely. Colin had to leave on the Tuesday morning, much to my regret, because he could talk to the engineer in his own language, deep calling to deep. Greatly to the discomfort of his passengers he took with him all our spare junk, life-belts, light anchors, the wheel and its worm gear, batteries, and a stainless steel stove-pipe. Perhaps, I was too hasty over the stove-pipe. Just after it had gone I had a telephone call from the makers of the diesel-burning cabin heater that I had ordered three months earlier to say that it was ready. We made do with a Valor paraffin burner. Much the same thing happened with a storm trysail that I had ordered long before. In this case the makers finished it ahead of time and then sat on it, no doubt acting on the Taoist principle that if you practise inaction nothing can be left undone. Coming home across the Atlantic in stormy weather we had frequent occasion to bless them.

To my surprise the stern tube came back on the morning of Wednesday the 30th. The engineer got it in and when the tide had risen enough started the engine to try it out. He was a perfectionist in these matters, talking in terms of thousandths of an inch. Rather grudgingly he thought it might do, to which I, knowing nothing about it, hastily agreed. It was not a difficult conclusion to come to because short of taking it out and starting afresh the engine could not be moved any further.

Accordingly after lunch, on the top of the tide, we left, taking the wise precaution of a tow by the yard launch to see us through the clutter of yachts and yacht moorings outside the harbour. That this had been sensible we soon learnt and re-learnt after several startling episodes in the course of the next four months. The propeller is so far offset that with the engine in gear and the rudder hard over in the contrary direction the boat can barely be kept straight. Turning to port is out of the question. Once clear of the moorings we hoisted sail to a light westerly breeze. By 4 pm we were off Pendennis Head and on our own, the two friends who had accompanied us in their boats having turned for home.

CHAPTER ELEVEN

Early Setbacks

WE NOW FELT the benefit of starting from so far down Channel. To spend our first night at sea off the Lizard instead of Anvil Point was a welcome change. Even the light wind that prevailed managed to blow out our navigation lamps twice in my watch. No lamps that I have ever had have remained alight with any wind blowing. I have tried colza oil, which is the proper oil to use, and found it made little difference. One wonders how they managed in sailing ships, or in steamers, too, before the days of electricity. Were the lamps better designed or did the lamp boy spend the night relighting them?

A bit more wind when we were south of the Scillies obliged us to reef for the first time and laid out both John and Ilan who succumbed to seasickness. John, looking the picture of misery, spent the night hunched up on the chartroom floor having already discovered the defects of his chosen berth. While lying there he successfully dispelled the pleasure I felt in being at last on our way by saying that he had a septic wisdom tooth and asking to be landed forthwith for treatment. With unusual foresight, on the chance that at the start we might find something seriously wrong with the boat, I had taken the precaution of bringing charts for the south Irish coast and one of Cork harbour. We therefore set a course for Cork and by the Saturday evening were some 35 miles south-east of the Daunt light-vessel. The wind was fresh and fair and in spite of reefing down we would be off the light-vessel by midnight. Early though it was in the voyage some of the drawbacks to a life on the ocean wave had become manifest. The boat was wet and needed a lot of pumping. Besides copious leaks through the topsides there were drips everywhere. The galley skylight leaked badly, the forehatch worse. John's bunk at its foot, with kit lying everywhere and most of it sodden, was a shambles. Ilan carried on cooking but would eat nothing himself except dried apricots. I recalled Peter Marsh, for whose seasickness use and wont had been no remedy, and began to wonder how long Ilan would stick it out. To find a replacement for John, as we might have to do, would be quite enough without having to find another cook as well. For the crew to cook in turn on a long voyage is not satisfactory. Nothing is put back in its right place, no one knows where to find what he wants, and before long both galley and store are all hugger-mugger.

We hove-to off the Daunt light-vessel at 1 am and waited until after breakfast before going in to anchor in the Quarantine anchorage with our yellow Q flag hoisted. We were in Ireland, moreover it was Sunday, so one did not expect anything would be done with a rush, but by tea-time, John getting restive, I had begun contemplating a long row ashore to make enquiries. Just then the kindly-disposed skipper of a big yacht out for a Sunday afternoon sail hove-to near by to tell us that if we were waiting for the Customs to come off we might wait for ever. He advised our going to the yacht harbour at Crosshaven where he would show us a mooring and enquire about a dentist for us, and since the entrance was tricky we had better follow him. At the moment we were not ready to move as we were having tea, but I did not mention this as it seemed an unseamanlike reason for delay. By the time we had got our anchor he had gone but we negotiated the entrance on our own and began looking for a vacant mooring. Yachts and yacht moorings stretched for the best part of a mile up river where I decided we would not intrude. Mindful of *Baroque*'s behaviour under power the idea of threading our way past so many expensive yachts looked like madness so we anchored well short of them. Though we were insured against such accidents, collisions are bound to cause delay and possibly some ill-will. The insurance that I had inherited with the boat covered us against all marine risks while cruising in coastal waters. As a matter of interest I had asked the company concerned if they would like to extend the cover to Greenland waters, to which they replied tersely, 'On no account.'

We spent six days at Crosshaven. John returned from Cork next day with bad news, the dentist having told him that even after treatment he ought to remain within reach for another ten days in case the trouble recurred. In view of this I thought he should quit. With this he agreed, but his suggestion that it was not too late to get hold of his friend Steve fell on deaf ears. Instead I put in the first of several telephone calls to Mylor. During our stay there two young fellows had made enquiries about the voyage and my hopes rested on capturing one or other of them. Knowing the name of neither made things difficult but through the yard manager I got in touch with the first who promised to be with us by the Thursday. So far so good. The Royal Cork Yacht Club, the oldest yacht club of all, had made us welcome and allowed us to use their delightful clubhouse overlooking the river. The crew spent every evening and a good part of the night there.

On the Wednesday evening a telegram advised me that the first man had changed his mind. My second string, I knew, had worked for Bob Pizey and through him we eventually made contact. John Barrett, or Jonno as he called himself, had left Cornwall and gone back to London. He readily agreed to come and hoped to be with us by the Saturday, so provided he remained firm of purpose or was not got at by anxious parents we were back in business. Meantime there were odd jobs to be done on board and shopping expeditions to Cork. The pressure cooker that Ilan got there was money well spent. At Cork the proximity of ships and docks to the shopping centre put me in mind of Reykjavik.

We neglected one job that might have been done here at the cost of a few days, a job that in the end cost us the best part of a fortnight. The chain plates, which according to the specification of work done in 1970 had been 'strengthened and rebolted', were in any case too short, being fastened to only three of the upper planks. Slight cracks showing in the paint on the port side in way of the shrouds indicated that the planks were already under strain. *Mischief* had had the same trouble but only after several voyages did we have to take drastic steps by lengthening the chain plates enough to take up three more planks. There was a boatyard at Crosshaven where this could have been done – a stitch in time that would have saved several times nine.

After nearly a week of warm, sunny weather that would have been better spent at sea, Saturday, 9 June, came and with it John Barrett. In spite of his youth he had done a good deal of sailing and, as we soon found, seldom hesitated to pass on the benefit of his experience to the rest of us. Garrulity is not, as I thought, confined to the old. Talkers, we are told, are of two kinds, those who talk because they have something to say, and those who talk because they want to say something. Our Jonno was irrepressible either by me or by the crew. One just had to get used to his running commentary as men who work in factories get used to the background of noise. But that is a trifling fault, less irksome most people would say than gloomy reserve, and I was thankful enough for his coming to our aid at short notice, embarking in a strange boat with a strange crew for strange waters. It was a stout effort.

We had already taken on water and fresh bread so at 2 pm we got our anchor and motored out. Off the coast that evening we caught a dozen fat mackerel, enough for supper and breakfast. Boiled mackerel are less alluring than when fried or grilled, but Ilan made amends with a fish sauce and topped up with Canary pudding and custard. His sauces were the product of imagination and invention, such as would have deserved or even earned the approval of Dr Folliott, a reverend gastronome who held that the science of fish sauce was by no means brought to perfection and that a fine field of discovery still lay open in that line. By trolling over the stern one sometimes catches fish, as on this occasion, but more often one merely catches the log-line and produces a devilish tangle. One even catches birds. For some time I had watched a gannet trying to take off from the water close astern. I thought he had a broken wing until at last I realised we had hooked him. We hauled him on board and while, Simon, well gloved, held the savagely snapping beak we extracted the hook from his wing.

In spite of the caulking we had done at Crosshaven she still made a lot of water which the Whale pump failed to clear. It worked better when I had dredged out of the well two bucketfuls of coke and oily sludge – a trifle to what Simon got out a month later. By that time the water that was always sloshing about inside had done a real scouring job, like a river in spate. Clearing the well is a dirty job and the best way of cleaning one's hands was to wash-up. Out of gratitude the cook was never allowed to do this chore for which we used hot sea-water and Tepol. The leaks were mainly in the topsides and by 10 June, when we were already 200 miles west of Ireland, the port side chain plates caused us not only alarm but despondency about our making a voyage at all. Besides nearly an inch of daylight to be seen between the planks the adjacent beam and the deck above were lifting. Crossing the Atlantic in that state was not really on, and besides that there would be no chance of effecting repairs in Greenland. Since we must put back to Ireland the obvious place seemed to be Crosshaven where we knew there was a boatyard; the crew, however, reckoned they had seen enough of Crosshaven so we decided to try our luck in Bantry Bay, which was 50 miles nearer and where there should be a yard either at Castledown or at Bantry at the head of bay. The necessity of this decision made it no less hard to take – the loss of 200 miles of westing and an unknown number of days filled me with gloom, besides the possible loss of some of the crew whose confidence in the boat might be on the wane. As to that I need not have worried. They were as determined as her owner to sail *Baroque* to Greenland.

As if sensing the need for haste *Baroque* got a move on, logging over a hundred miles a day for the next two days. By the 16th we were rapidly closing the land in very poor visibility. It was so thick that after supper we hove-to but later that night the weather cleared and the Bull light showed up where expected a few miles to the north-west. There is quite a farmyard hereabouts, the Bull, Cow and Calf rock, and Crow Head. In the morning we made for Castletown gaining the harbour through an excessively narrow entrance. Fortunately, the leading marks were prominently displayed for I had no large-scale chart. After anchoring off the quay Simon and I rowed ashore to consult the Harbour-master. On this Sunday morning the main street was crowded as we stood there talking to Danny O'Neill, brushing off cars, cows and pedestrians, thirsty souls many of the latter making their way from church to the nearest bar in quest, as it were, of more spiritual refreshment. We, too, adjourned to a bar, not so much to drink but so that Danny could use their telephone. He had suggested our going to Lawrence Cove on Bear Island where a friend of his, Finbar Murphy, had a small boatyard. In the back-room Danny talked to Finbar on a telephone that looked like Graham Bell's original model. If it's obsolete it works. Finbar would be going to Cork next morning but he offered to come to Lawrence Cove that evening to see what needed doing. He lived 7 miles from his boatyard at the west end of Bear Island opposite Castletown. The Harbour-master, a friend indeed, offered to pilot us into the cove.

He came off after lunch accompanied by a young man whom I took to be a friend out for the ride but who proved to be the Customs officer, polite, diffident, almost apologising for intruding. The entrance to Lawrence Cove is dog-legged and at high tide an unwary stranger steering a bee-line for the harbour would find himself on a reef. While we were there an English visiting yacht did nearly impale itself before being frightened off by a tumult of shouting. I was glad we had a pilot. We anchored off the quay where one small fishing boat took up all the room available. Finbar's boatyard, which comprised a slipway and a small shed, also had a quay of sorts. If Mylor had seemed the uttermost part of earth this might have been outer space. I wondered if we had done wisely in coming to a place with one shop, one pub, its only communication with Castletown a ferry run at the whim of the shopkeeper. Meantime, Simon had stripped out all the shelves behind the sink, thus contributing handsomely to Ilan's problems, so that when Finbar came, as he did that evening, he could see what had to be done. Most of the chain plate bolts, we found, were loose, one had sheared, and the wood strongback supporting the plates was far too short. So much for the 'strengthening and rebolting' alleged to have been done.

Finbar undertook the job and his quiet, soft-spoken manner inspired confidence. We no doubt mentioned time but he was not a man in a hurry or one who would like being hurried. No man hurries except when catching flies, is the Arab proverb, and since there are few flies at Lawrence Cove there is no reason for anyone to hurry. Only a handful of people live at the place which consists mainly of empty, substantial houses, relics of the days when Bantry Bay was used by the Navy. The old people, Finbar's father for instance, liked to remember the days when the line of battleships anchored in Bear Haven, the roads between the island and the mainland, stretched almost to Castletown – Kipling's 'Fleet in Being'. Some of the houses have been taken over by a sailing school where young people, many of them French, were taught dinghy sailing. The kedge anchors and their warps which later we had to lay in the small harbour lent an additional hazard to their tuition while they themselves afforded congenial company for my crew when they fore-gathered every evening at the pub. Mindful of crabbed age and youth I remained hermit-like on board.

The few walks I took about the island were, as Baedeker says, fatiguing and not repaying. It is dotted with small white cottages set amid stony fields and unkempt hedges, where a few cows grazed. Pigs and potatoes, supposedly the Irishman's mainstay, were notably absent, so it must be dairy-farming and not subsistence farming that keeps them alive; fishing too, perhaps, though there were few boats about. We met a marine biologist who had ideas for throwing discarded motor cars into the sea to encourage the lobsters to breed. There were several discarded motor cars to be had, the difficulty seemed to lie with the fishermen. He was a rum chap living there on his own, his sole equipment a wet suit and an aqua-lung, carrying out his research as a private enterprise and finding it hard going. He had a small motor car, one, I thought, that would soon be joining those already discarded, in which he drove me to a fort at the east end of the island. Around it was a beautifully cut dry moat about 20ft. deep. The fort had a couple of 6in. guns and though, of course, unoccupied, it was visited periodically by someone from the Irish Army to make sure the guns were still there.

Finbar got back from Cork with the steel for the plates and the necessary bolts on the Wednesday, while Thursday, we learnt, was a public holiday. Meantime Simon had removed the old plates and with two young lads – Finbar's entire work force – was fashioning a massive piece of Iroko wood for a strongback. I had some splicing to do, shortening the wire topping-lifts, and also managed to set up the slack forestay by means of the winch and a length of chain. Ilan went to Castletown with the shopkeeper and brought back some fresh prawns which we had for supper in the form of prawn curry followed by banana sludge, an expressive word, all cooked under difficulties, the galley having been turned upside down and inside out in order to get at the port side. In Ilan we had a cook for all seasons. Local mussels gathered by the crew provided another memorable meal in spite of the time they took to cook.

My hopes that the job could be completed afloat without having to go alongside proved in vain, for the new chain plates extended to below the water-line. We tried first alongside Finbar's little quay where we were still afloat and where our marine biologist friend, acting as frogman, failed to get the bolts in. To finish the job we had to go alongside the wharf where she would dry out, so at midnight of 24 June, when the tide served, we put her alongside where she settled down nicely. By next day the job was done. Taking advantage of the wharf we laid out the chain cable in order to repaint the fathom marks (5 fms., 10 fms., 15 fms., etc.) which had already rubbed off. I went to Castletown via the shopkeeper's ferry to cash a cheque and to thank the Harbour-master for his help. He was busy with a Spanish trawler that had been towed in by a compatriot, its net round the propeller. Remembering the German trawler we had seen at Isafjord in similar circumstances I judged this event, distressing enough to the skipper, to be not uncommon. Having settled with Finbar, who had done the best he could for us, we sailed for the third time on 26 June. The loss of twelve days that this caper had cost merely left us more resolved than ever to sail *Baroque* to Greenland.

CHAPTER TWELVE

To Greenland

BY EVENING we were well past Mizzen Head, catching another fine lot of mackerel on the way. Even at this early stage the amount of pumping needed to keep the water below the level of the cabin sole provided food for thought. When heeled over with the covering board awash – and the tall mast heeled her over fairly readily – it took 300 strokes a watch to empty the well, which at that time we thought a lot. Reefed down and heeling less she made less water, so the leaks were evidently high up. Later, when rough seas had removed some of the rubbing strake, we found gaps in plank butts that needed caulking. Unfortunately these proved to be not the only source and we just had to get used to living with leaks, as one does. Old salts are said to have welcomed a few generous leaks on the ground that they helped to keep the bilges sweet. If the pumping increased to 1,000 strokes a watch we reefed down and at 2,000 we reckoned it time to heave-to.

We did well the first few days and by 30 June, in spite of having to heave-to more than once, we were nearly 300 miles west of Ireland. 30 June was a Saturday, the day we have our weekly drink. We must have just emptied a gin bottle for Simon took advantage of this to post a letter. He sent no message to mankind, as I suppose he should have done, but merely gave the ship's position, 53° 40′ N. 60° 30′ W., and his address. Some time after we had got home he had a letter to say that the bottle had been found on a beach in Galway Bay east of the Aran Islands, 4 miles south of Black Head, 53° 08′ N. 9° 30′ W., late in August. Using the normal channels, postcards or even first-class mail have been known to take longer. Bottles were emptied and cast into the sea frequently and several of them contained messages but so far this is the only one to be found. A more original and far swifter way of posting a letter is recorded in Murphy's monumental work *Oceanic Birds of South America*. On 20 December 1847 a Wandering Albatross was shot off the coast of Chile in 45° 50′ S. 78° 27′ W. and tied to its neck was a vial with a message from a whaling captain: 'Dec. 8th 1847. Ship *Euphrates*, Edwards, 16 months out, 2,300 barrels of oil, 150 of it sperm. I have not seen a whale for 4 months. Lat. 43° S. Long. 148° 40′ W. Thick fog, with rain.' According to these figures, the albatross had travelled 3,150 nautical miles as the crow flies during the twelve-day interval between the writing of the message and the shooting of the bird.

According to Byron comfort must not be expected by folks that go a pleasuring. I suppose that with increasing age the desire for comfort increases and at the risk of being accused, probably rightly, of having become soft I should say that *Baroque*'s accommodation was sub-standard, at any rate well below that of either *Mischief* or *Seabreeze*. In the saloon there were, as I have said, three berths, the two on the port side, one above the other, occupied by Simon and Brian. The only fault of these two was that they were in the line of fire, or rather water, when a wave hit the cabin skylight on the starboard side. This, of course, was the fault of the skylight, not the bunks, and was remedied by rigging a plastic sheet as a weather dodger. Better still would have been to screw down permanently the skylight as we had done in the galley, but there were occasional fine days when we wanted to open the skylight to introduce some much needed fresh air. The settee berth on the starboard side belonged to Ilan. I had dithered a long time over taking this berth myself because it gave ready access to the chartroom and the cockpit. This settee, however, is the only place in the boat where anyone can sit and its use as a bunk in daytime would preclude this. Besides this, anyone going on deck or coming below, usually in wet oilskins, brushed past it; so I relinquished my claim in favour of the cook who since he had all night in did not need any sleep in the daytime. Ilan rigged a roll-up curtain which he let down at bed-time to fend off passers-by and the odd shower from the skylight; for he, of course, was in the line of fire from that when on the port tack.

Forward of the saloon in the galley was a single bunk on the starboard side, opposite the galley sink, with the foot of the mast between in the middle. Into this single bunk the skipper eventually settled. Perched, perhaps, is *le mot juste*, because it was a good 4ft. from the floor and one had to climb in and out. Underneath, where there should have been ample stowage space, were three miserable drawers with the habit of falling out. Only by leaning out over the side could one get enough light to read by in daytime, and owing to its proximity to the mast and shrouds all the groans and complaints of the rigging were transmitted to the occupant as if by a sounding board. When on the wind the jib halyards, too, played a most eerie accompaniment, like the mournful howl of a pack of wolves baying the moon only more intimidating. Compensations were the gratifying smells of cookery and the appreciable rise in temperature when the Primus stoves were going. Moreover, in this bunk no shower baths need be expected, only a persistent drip from the deck beams. Plastic guttering fixed to the beams with drawing pins were the answer to this. Indeed, we all rigged ingenious aqueducts of which Archimedes himself would not have been ashamed.

The bunk forward of the galley on the port side opposite the work bench probably had the highest rainfall, as it were. John Harradine had unwisely chosen this and John Barrett inherited it. The fore hatch just above was the most generous source of water, but there were others. John or Jonno lived under a more or less permanent polythene tent. Besides high humidity he had the benefit of being thrown about more being so far forward; but John, like Shakespeare's 'wet sea-boy upon the giddy mast', had an infinite capacity for sleep, spent more time on his back than anyone, even foregoing meals in favour of sleep, and made no complaints. The mention of meals reminds me of another slight imperfection in our arrangements. The table I had put in on top of the water tank, for which Brian had made a patent adjustable fiddle, came to be used merely as somewhere to put things. No one sat around and ate off it in civilised fashion. Three of us sat on the settee out of reach of the table with our plates in our laps, the fourth in a corner on the opposite side also out of reach of the table. But sailors can hardly expect to eat off tables. On a five months' voyage in 1964 to Heard Island in a 50-ton schooner ten of us ate our meals in a cabin rather smaller than *Baroque*'s, occupied, too, by a large gas stove on which the meals were cooked. There may have been a small table but at meal-times some of the ten sat on it while the rest perched or stood where they could clutching their plates.

Dr Johnson had great contempt for anyone so lacking in ideas, so feeble-minded, such a blockhead in fact, that he needs must fall back on the weather as a topic of conversation. The great Cham of literature himself would have found it hard to describe a voyage without mentioning the weather. Some long-distance voyages mention nothing else and even those who are more restrained – the weather being what it often is – cannot help appearing querulous. This is not really so. Most amateur sailors who go to sea for pleasure want that pleasure to be occasionally spiced with the stresses and strains that usually accompany bad weather, spiced even with some hazards and the bright eye of danger. That this is what appeals to men, though on a more lofty plane, is what Garibaldi knew when he offered 'neither pay, nor quarters, nor provisions; but hunger, thirst, forced marches, battles, and death'. On those carefree, sunny days, the wind free, the sails full, the crew will no doubt express their delight. 'This is what we came for' will be the cry, but if of the right sort their happiness, though unexpressed, will be the same when wet and cold, struggling against adverse conditions.

June and July are reckoned as quiet months in the North Atlantic. Quiet is a relative term and much depends on the kind of vessel concerned, a ship of 30,000 tons, say, or a boat of 30 tons. Quiet or not the weather at least offered variety, from flat calms to gales, fog, drizzle, torrential rain, even some occasional sunshine. We had no trouble in making northing, reaching within a hundred miles of the latitude of C. Farewell (59° 46′ N.) when we were still 300 miles to the east. To be a hundred miles south of the cape is not an excessive margin because on account of the possible presence of icebergs vessels are advised to give it a berth of at least 70 miles.

When far from land it is not of vital importance to know exactly where one is, yet without at least a daily fix the mariner tends to feel frustrated. Even in summer in the North Atlantic sights are not all that readily obtainable owing either to heavy and persistent overcast, rain, fog or high seas. Apart from the roughness caused by a gale the wind may blow so hard that watering eyes make it impossible to take sights. I see from the log that for four successive days south of C. Farewell we were without any noon sight, the sight that provides an accurate latitude, without which the other sights when worked out may indicate a position that is in fact many miles out. Star sights are particularly hard to obtain. It is more often cloudy at dawn and dusk than at midday. If the sky clears it will be at night when, even if it is a bright moonlight, the prudent navigator will put little faith in any star sights he may take, and, of course, north of, say, Lat. 58°, in summer it is not dark enough for stars to be visible. In these circumstances the peevish navigator feels inclined to agree with the remarks attributed to Lord Jeffery: 'Damn the solar system; bad light, planets too distant, pestered with comets, feeble contrivance; could make a better with ease.'

We met only one ship on this passage. On 12 July in Lat. 57° N. the wind taking off after a night at nearly gale force, the *Haralde*, registered in Monrovia, startled us by coming within about twenty yards down wind and passing very slowly across our bows. In my panic-stricken eyes he appeared much closer. I really feared our bowsprit would hit her or rather that he was about to break our bowsprit. A chap on the bridge with no loudhailer shouted unintelligibly into the wind, and not content with that they turned and came back almost as close on the other side. I expect they wanted to know if we were all right, which was friendly of them but frightening. A gam with another ship in mid-ocean is a great event but for such social occasions the weather needs to be good.

After his too prolonged bout of malaise Ilan had long since found his feet; our fears that he might prove to be another Peter Marsh were finally set at rest. A long voyage can be made or marred by the cook and the meals he provides. At sea meals predominate even more than they do on land and in the inevitable monotony of a long passage the crew were apt to become like Carlyle's gluttonous Jutes and Angles, 'men who see the sun rise with no other hope but that they shall fill their bellies before it sets'. For breakfast porridge was the general rule, providing for most of the crew a convenient way of conveying to their mouths large quantities of sugar; though Ilan became a dab hand at turning out omelettes from dried egg of which we had a large amount. These would be generously laced with Tabasco or with melted cheese, or sometimes filled with curry left over from supper. Curry for breakfast used to be the normal thing on ships plying to the East or on any ships that had Goanese or Lascar cooks and stewards. On *Mischief*'s last voyage south, however, left-over curry for breakfast had disgusted one of the crew and the high words that followed this refusal to eat what was given had led ultimately to his deserting at Montevideo and taking most of the crew with him. The traveller, as the proverb says, should have the back of an ass to bear all and the mouth of a hog to eat what is set before him.

For lunch we rang the changes on sardines, pilchards, spam, or cheese, with either coffee or cocoa. Peanut butter and Marmite were popular, while hard white cabbage and raw onions provided a salad of sorts. Tea at 4.30 pm was not to be lightly missed, for besides bread, butter, and jam Ilan frequently baked us a cake or a sort of shortbread made from Quaker Oats. Bread is no great problem on a Greenland voyage. Bread taken at the start will last nearly ten days before going mouldy and after that we go on to twice-baked, sliced bread re-baked, which if properly done and kept in a plastic sack lasts indefinitely. It takes up too much space to carry enough for the whole voyage but on arriving in Greenland one has rye-bread (*rugbrod*) which again lasts for months. This stuff also has the advantage that the crew find it less palatable and eat less of it as time goes on. Our twice-baked bread gave out two days before reaching Greenland and Ilan bridged the gap with chapatties and soda-bread. Proper bread could be baked at sea even on a Primus stove, but in the absence of a hot sun or a warm place in the boat the difficulty is to get the dough to rise. Moreover, freshly baked bread is far too palatable and to satisfy the crew the cook would be at it all day and every day, using far too much paraffin.

For supper, the highlight of the day, Ilan exerted his powers and the rougher it was the more he liked to defy the elements by dishing up something elaborate. His sauces have already received honourable mention. Of some one might say, like the French gastronome, '*Avec cette sauce on mangerait son père.*' Curries, of course, *pasta sciuta*, *rissotto*, lentil soup (a meal in itself), stew with dumplings, fried rice, sausage and mash, potato pie with grated cheese on top (the cheese toasted with a blow-lamp), and one or two Greek dishes, *moussala* for one if I have the name right. Besides the duffs that took pride of place as a second course, open tarts of short pastry filled with dried fruit figured largely. The duffs were all what might be called visions of the higher gluttony, chocolate duffs with chocolate sauce, feathery Canary puddings, or weightier belly-timber like spotted dog, rich in raisins and sultanas. No grounds for mutiny on that score:

> We hadn't been but a week at sea
> When the duff, it don't seem to please,
> It hadn't the riches of raisins and sichness
> So we ups and we mutinies.

All this cookery had to be done on a double-burner gimballed stove and a single-burner with no gimbals. Space had not allowed of gimbals for the latter and happily my fears that on this account it would not be much use at sea proved groundless. The galley being amidships, and Pilot cutters sea-kindly boats, Ilan had no trouble with it even in rough weather. Except on the way home when during a gale it jumped off its stand and sustained a hair-crack which put it out of action.

This domestic digression had led me away from the weather. A gale that lasted longer than we liked set us nearly 60 miles to the south and two almost windless days went by before we got the southerly wind we needed to get round C. Farewell. The warm southerly wind brought with it rain and fog that prevailed for the next three dank and dismal days. On the morning of 19 July the weather brightened and we made a far from precise landfall somewhere to the west of the cape. The southernmost point of Greenland does not stand out boldly and unmistakably like some more famous sea-marks, the Cape itself for instance, or C. Horn. Like them, however, or any cape at the extremity of a land-mass it can at times breed dirty weather. As the *Arctic Pilot* remarks: 'C. Farewell is notorious for foul weather and heavy seas.'

Soon after sighting the land we were overtaken by a violent thunder-storm accompanied by lightning, wind and rain. At the height of this short-lived storm we ran fast past two icebergs, the first we had met. When the sun came out that evening I got a sight confirming our position, or at last confirming that we were at last west of the cape. By then we had twenty-five bergs in sight. Since we were not more than 15 miles from the coast I had expected to

see pack-ice as well, and the fall in the sea temperature from 5.75° C. to
0.25° C. indicated that it could not be far away. As usual on these voyages
in waters seldom covered by British ships we were keeping a meteorological
log for the Meteorological Office; though unlike the other three hundred-
odd voluntary ships that keep meteorological logs we cannot transmit
observations at the time they are made. I regret the sudden transition from
Fahrenheit to Centigrade or Celsius. It is really the fault of the Meteorological
Office who, having gone all metric, supplied us for this voyage with thermometers marked in the latter scale.

The fog that prevailed after supper warned us that later in the night, during
the darker hours either side of midnight, we would be well advised to heave-
to. If the fog is not utterly dense icebergs can generally be seen in time for a
slow-moving ship to avoid them. Not always, or at least not without disquiet.
At 11 pm Brian in a state of agitation rushed down, muttered something
about going about, and rushed back on deck. Not waiting to put any more
clothes on I was on deck in a minute in time to see that we should just clear a
large berg some thirty yards to port. At a safe distance from it we hove-to.
Next morning I put on my winter woollies, had the Valor paraffin stove lit,
and ordered the chart-room door to be kept shut. The stove did raise the
cabin temperature a little and was always good for drying clothes.

Davis Strait may not be as bad as the Strait of Belle Ile, the place where
they invented fog, but it enjoys quite a lot, sometimes merely in shifting
banks, at other times a wide-spreading blanket. Navigation became uncertain.
Steering east of north on a course that would close the land, the wind fresh
and visibility under a thousand yards, I had an uneasy night. Early on the
22nd there was still nothing to be seen until at last around 9 am we sighted a
high island a few hundred yards away. Later the fog cleared sufficiently for us
to identify this island, 700ft. high and a half-mile long, as Qioqe, some 30
miles south of Frederikshaab. That we could close the land like this without
encountering any ice showed a great change from the conditions we had met
in 1970. The fact that we were now a fortnight later makes some difference,
but in that year no ships could enter Frederikshaab and we ourselves were fast
in the pack some 10 miles north of it. This, by the way, is not ice that has
remained over from winter. It is what the Danes call the Storis, or Great Ice,
consisting of old and massive floes from the Polar Sea brought all the way
down the east coast of Greenland by the current, round C. Farewell, and up
the west coast as far as or beyond Frederikshaab where it begins to disperse
and disintegrate.

Closing the land again on the 25th we sighted what I took to be the
Hellfiske Øer, a straggling group of islets and rocks marked at their southern
extremity by a beacon which we failed to see. Like the east coast, the west
coast of Greenland is strewn with islands and islets, barren rocks all very
much alike. Unless one can spot the rare one crowned by a beacon identification is largely guesswork. We guessed right this time. Having stood out for
some 6 miles we went in again expecting to see and identify Faeringehavn, as
we did that evening in the fading light. Light-houses are still rarities on the
Greenland coast and they are not the structures we are accustomed to seeing.

We had gone into Faeringehavn in 1970 after being released by the ice and I do not remember any lights. The latest edition of the *Pilot* now told us that 'a light is exhibited at an elevation of 53ft. from a concrete column *3ft. high* situated on the summit of Den Smukke Ø', and sure enough there it was blinking every five seconds. On a filthy night of wind and rain we stood out once more to heave-to at midnight.

Godthaab lay only about 20 miles to the north and all we had to do was to find the entrance to the fjord, a task that looked fairly hopeless in the fog that enveloped us next morning. As we motored and sailed north the visibility slowly improved and at midday we sighted numerous islands. Several of the islands off the fjord entrance carry beacons, none of these showed any. When the sun broke through briefly I got a snap sight close to the meridian which put us 5 miles north of the entrance, so we started south and presently made out the essential island and its beacon. Although the fjord entrance is wide the navigable channel is restricted to a cable's width between the beaconed island and a reef.

The fjord is long as well as wide. Godthaab itself, the capital of West Greenland, is 15 miles up, while the main fjord and its branches extend as far as the inland ice 70 miles from the coast. Around the inner fjord was the so-called West Settlement of the Norse colonists comprising some ninety farms of which seventy have been located. The Eastern Settlement, or Osterbydd, founded by Eric the Red in AD 986 around Julianehaab in south-west Greenland was much larger, comprising three hundred or more farms. It had its church and a bishop. When all communication with Europe ceased in the fourteenth century, probably because of worsening ice conditions, the colonists died out. Besides the ruins of Viking homesteads dotted about, moving testimonies to perhaps the hardiest colonists of all time, the region is mountainous, so that Godthaab, which on four occasions hitherto I have regarded merely as a place of refreshment before pushing on elsewhere, would amply repay a long visit. As we were already too late, I thought, for Ellesmere Island we might have stayed there this time had I not more or less promised to meet a friend further north. Nor would the crew have been happy had we stopped short of the Arctic Circle.

CHAPTER THIRTEEN

North to Igdlorssuit

WE SECURED that evening alongside a fishing vessel close under the rock wall that bounds the west side of the harbour. On this wall are painted the names of numerous visiting ships, among them the only two British names, HMS *Whitby* and *Mischief*. I had half forgotten our having painted it and the familiar name moved me almost to tears. We had left this record in 1963 and before we left this time we repainted it. In Wales the more fervent Nationalists sometimes express their feelings on suitable rock faces and are duly condemned for vandalism by all right-minded people, but in this case, where I was personally involved, I felt proud as well as sad. We ought to have found the time and a space on the wall on which to paint *Baroque*.

Greenland is not immune from the fashionable disease of 'growth'. The harbour had changed almost out of recognition. Along the foot of the rock wall where formerly two or three vessels might be anchored, was now a long wooden jetty with fishing vessels moored three abreast. The main quay has been lengthened and large warehouses built on it, and room has been made for a fish quay and an adjacent fish factory.

Nevertheless, the same informality prevails and for a visiting yacht at any rate, entry to a port could hardly be simpler – no papers, no passports, no Customs, no harbour dues. I was about to add that such a happy state of affairs in this form-filling age must be unique until I remembered Cork where officialdom had ignored us, and Castletown where the Customs officer had almost apologised for coming on board.

According to the *Pilot* the population of Godthaab is now about 6,000, of whom 5,000 are Eskimos, or Greenlanders as they are now called. In 1960 it was about 3,000. The *Pilot*, by the way, which as regards navigation one assumes to be infallible, credits Godthaab with a narrow-gauge railway connecting the harbour with the town, whereas there is no such thing. The town was founded as long ago as 1721 by Hans Egede, the Lutheran mission-ary, although the great Elizabethan seaman-explorer John Davis is believed to have anchored in Godthaab fjord on his first voyage in search of the North-west Passage in 1585. He named it Gilbert's Sound, presumably in honour of Sir Humphrey Gilbert. On our visits in the early sixties Godthaab had impressed me as a raw, thriving pioneer town with much work to be done and no time to be lost, and that impression did not need much revision in 1973. The town itself, a mile from the harbour, is scattered over a peninsula of solid rock interspersed with boggy hollows where cotton grass used to flourish. On this unpromising site all foundations have to be blasted out, telephones and power lines carried overhead on a forest of poles, the drains on the surface, and the water supplied in boxed conduits to prevent it freezing in winter. Hans Egede's house built of local stone has been preserved, but all other buildings are of imported materials. The private houses painted in lively colours – green, red, yellow, blue – are now almost lost among sober-hued blocks of three-storey flats.

Either in supermarkets or shops one can buy pretty well anything one is likely to need at not much more than European prices. Only in the matter of copper-sheet did we have any bother. Having tried all the likely and unlikely places a helpful taxi-driver took us to a huge Government depot covering acres of ground which seemed to stock everything needed for building a town from scratch. Several lower grade officials were nonplussed and it was not until we reached the man with whom the buck had to stop that we got what we wanted. When confronted with enough sheeting to copper-bottom a battle-ship I felt a bit of a fool asking for two square feet. However, they cut it off and after a lot of paper-work – we might have been signing a treaty – we got our copper. A Seaman's Home down by the harbour was new and most welcome to us as a place where we could get shower-baths and meals. Even at Godthaab one cannot escape television. On our first night at the Seaman's Home we watched Frank Sinatra in colour. Besides the two hotels which we assumed would be beyond our means there are two low-grade cafeterias. We had some food at one around midday but by night apparently one could only drink. Putting my head inside one night I found it crammed with Greenlanders in convivial mood and hastily withdrew. The old Kristinemut where formerly we had gone for beer and whale steak had become a hotel.

Throughout our short stay the weather remained cool and wet. Patches of snow still lay about at sea level and we were told that three weeks earlier there had been a heavy fall. It is not always thus. On previous visits we had suffered from heat and mosquitoes and the Danish workmen by the roadside, sweating as they wielded a pneumatic drill, all wore face veils. Expecting to use a lot of fuel on the way north we wanted a 25 gallon drum of oil. Rather than imperil others as well as ourselves by moving *Baroque* alongside in the congested harbour we went to a pump at the old harbour across the peninsula and brought back the drum in a taxi. The springs just held out. Having rolled the drum into the water at the head of the harbour we left it for John to tow off with the dinghy. Oil drums are not all that towable but a friendly motor launch came to his assistance.

The night before we were due to sail the wind began blowing from north-west with some ferocity. By dawn the bow lines of the fishing vessel to which we were secured had parted with the result that our counter began to take some hard knocks from a vessel lying astern. Starting the engine, we let go our warps, dropped the big Fisherman anchor under-foot, and veered cable until we were riding clear. All that morning it blew hard. Brian, who is not an expert waterman, tried to put Ilan ashore, a matter of twenty yards or so. The wind took charge and off went the pram dinghy down the harbour with every prospect of being bashed against the rocks at the far end. The harbour launch, seeing their plight, steamed after them, picked them up, and landed them.

When Brian started back with the dinghy he once more lost his battle with the wind and once more the harbour launch went to the rescue. This time, taking no chances, they came alongside and handed over first Brian and then the dinghy.

When the wind dropped that afternoon we went over to the main quay for water. The nearest we could get was outside two other vessels across which they passed us a long hose. Having collected Ilan and the stores he had bought we were ready to go. Twenty loaves of black bread, each loaf nearly 2ft. long, took some carrying, as well as sacks of potatoes and onions. Never board a ship without an onion, is sound doctrine.

The Harbour-master, hearing we were bound for Umanak fjord, gave me a letter for my friend Dr Drever whom he knew, and at 6 pm we cast off. On a windless evening we had a long, noisy chug down the fjord. Further north in Davis Strait in summer the winds are generally light and most often northerly. We were three weeks late and I reckoned it would be nearly the end of August before we reached Ellesmere Island, just in time to start the voyage home. Instead we would make for Igdlorssuit, a small settlement in Lat. 71° N. where we had been on the first Greenland voyage in 1961. Mountains are plentiful in that region and Dr Drever would be there until 13 August. It is only some 450 miles from Godthaab, but we were to need all the time allowed.

Off this coast, from Frederikshaab in the south up to Lat. 70° N., there are fishing banks rich in cod and halibut. It surprised me that we met hardly any trawlers and we were particularly disappointed not to see any of the famous Portuguese three-masted schooners, a common enough sight in the sixties. These schooners, after fishing on the Grand Banks in early summer, proceeded to the Greenland banks to complete their catch of cod, all by hand-lining from dories. Having anchored on the bank the schooners launched their dories of which each carried some sixty. These are flat-bottomed, about 14ft. long, without thwarts, centre board, buoyancy tanks, or rudder, the absence of such fittings making for easy stowage in nests on the schooner's deck. For sailing out and back to the parent ship a mast is stepped and jib and lugsail set. The doryman has a 3,000ft. long line with some 500 hooks on 'snoods', which he baits with frozen squid, sardines or caplin. Tossing up and down in a dinghy, handling the line with half-frozen hands, the baiting of 500 hooks, and worse still removing the hook from the mouths of cold, slimy, flapping cod, is a job that only men bred to the life would undertake. Having filled his dory with cod until only a few inches of freeboard remain, the doryman sails back to the parent ship, and standing up in his heaving dory gaffs the catch one by one on to the schooner's deck.

If there were any trawlers or Portuguese schooners about we met none, instead we were pestered by drifters engaged in netting salmon. Particularly on the Little and Great Hellefiske banks north of Godthaab and beyond Holsteinborg we kept sighting the dan buoys marking the nets and their attendant boats – Norwegian, Spanish or Greenlanders – standing by. Though not as lethal as icebergs these nets seemed to me to constitute a worse menace for the unwary in that part of Davis Strait. Twice we fell foul of nets, on both occasions with the skipper at the helm. This was, perhaps, just as well. It gave rise to no harsh words, as otherwise it might have done, and it gave the crew a laugh and a feeling, if only temporary, of superior skill – what a fool the man must be to run into a marked net, not once but twice. The nets are about a mile long, with small plastic floats on top and at each end a dan buoy, a buoy with a 6ft. pole and flag. Having laid its net the boat stands by two or three miles off until it is time to haul. This distance between the net and the boat that layed it, as if trying to disclaim responsibility, caused us some inconvenience. I never understood why they lay off so far unless they thought the boat's presence might scare away the salmon.

Three days out from Godthaab, on the evening of 2 August, having closed the land we had gone about and were standing out to sea. On this placid evening, admiring the sunlit coast astern, I may not have been fully alert, nor as yet had we fully hoisted in the implications of dan buoys with stationary boats in the offing. When a line of yellow plastic floats suddenly appeared ahead almost under our bows I thought we might safely slide over them. I think we might, too, had it not been for the broken keel band which we had not been able to put right at Mylor. Firmly held by the net, as we promptly were, we handed the sails and did all we could to free ourselves by hauling on the net from various directions. No go. The small Greenlander boat to whom the net belonged lay about two miles away and took no notice. The first rocket we fired, a parachute flare, failed to flare so we touched off an orange smoke canister. *Baroque*'s equipment which I had inherited had been sparse enough except in the way of distress signals and fireworks of various kinds – no doubt previous owners had felt they might be needed. Roused by our orange smoke screen the Greenlanders soon came to our assistance. Having launched their dinghy they passed us a rope and while the men in the dinghy held on to the net they towed us off stern first. We came off easily enough, no damage to the net, and no hard feelings on either side.

The very next day, though this time with some excuse, I committed a similar blunder, a blunder which caused far more delay and which had consequences for both parties. Having tacked twice during the night, for the wind was northerly, we were again standing out to sea when I marked down a dan buoy ahead and its fellow half a mile away. Steering carefully to round the buoy to leeward I noticed too late a small red dan buoy some fifty yards further out to which the net, rather unfairly, extended. We were properly caught, and before long made matters worse by drifting on to another net. We hauled away on the net and this time with some success, for we extracted a fine, big salmon and consigned it forthwith to the galley. A few other fish in sight in the net were unfortunately out of reach. There were several boats hanging about in the offing, none of which paid the least attention. A yacht sailing in those waters would surely attract some attention and if it suddenly lowered its sails and remained stationary by a dan buoy one would have expected the penny to drop.

A smoke canister had worked with the Greenlanders so we tried another. If anyone in those boats 2 miles away thought we were on fire they remained admirably calm. Then we got out our parachute flares and soon had the technique worked out. Sticks had to be fashioned for the rocket and the vertical exhaust-pipe by the doghouse made a fine launching pad. Each of us in turn had the privilege of touching off a rocket, with some jealous competition as to whose would fly highest and burn longest. Nearly two hours elapsed and five rockets had been fired before one of the distant boats started steaming towards us. One felt that had we been sinking or on fire it would have been a close run thing. The Norwegian who arrived got his net free fairly easily and told us that the net we were really wrapped up in belonged to his mate who had gone back to Holsteinborg but whom he would call up by radio telephone. Both boats came from Alesund. While waiting we watched the first boat haul his net. It came in over a roller with a man standing by extracting the fish. I reckoned that for every two yards of net they had a salmon, so that a half-mile of net catches a lot of fish. In view of the number of boats at work that came within our limited vision it is not surprising that our salmon rivers are feeling the effect.

When the other boat at last arrived they passed us a line and tried towing from various angles without success. Finally, with their consent if not approval, we began hacking away at the nylon net and its numerous ropes. We could not reach far down and when at length free we still had a long streamer of net and rope attached to the keelband. Some of this was round the propeller and the rest we lashed to the bulwarks to keep out of harm's way. Under way again and steering north we then found that the first Norwegian boat was busy re-laying his net right across our course. True he was flashing a lamp to warn us but in my aggrieved eyes he seemed to be acting with malice aforethought. We went about just in time to avoid a third incident. The salmon steaks that we ate that night more than made up for the loss of a few hours and five parachute flares. I thought the crew might have proposed a vote of thanks.

In the early part of the voyage I may have overpainted the charms of Greenland, laying some stress on the weather we should enjoy, cloudless skies, twenty-four hours of unbroken sunshine, the calm blue water dotted with picturesque icebergs glinting in the sun; whereas up to Godthaab the reality had been roughish seas, rain, a minimum of sun, and fog in which the vague shape of icebergs loomed menacingly. As we had found years before, one must go north, north at least of the Arctic Circle, to enjoy halcyon weather. This magic circle (Lat. 66° 30′) was not crossed until 5 August, until when we had been beating against fresh northerly winds and not doing very well. Igdlorssuit by 13 August, unaided by the engine, was by no means in the bag. To celebrate crossing the Arctic Circle we ate and drank rather more than usual. It offered an excuse for an additional drink beyond that of the customary Saturday night tot, we opened a Christmas pudding, while John produced a magnum of Spanish wine bought in Godthaab for this occasion. No certificates were issued to the crew, as I believe is done for the passengers on cruise ships, nor were all hands piped to bathe and skylark.

On the 6th, taking advantage of the first calm, windless day, we began clearing the propeller, and by patiently poking and probing with a boathook John at last succeeded. Our chances of reaching Igdlorssuit in time were thus

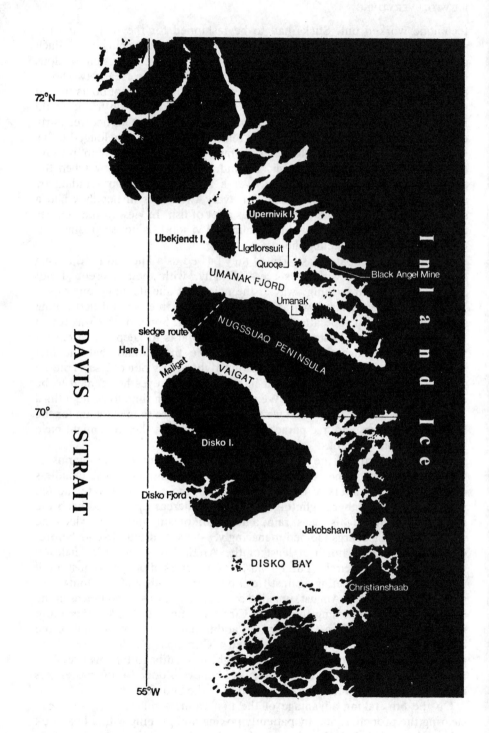

72°N

Upernivik I.

Ubekjendt I.

Igdlorssuit

Quoqe

UMANAK FJORD

Black Angel Mine

Umanak

sledge route

NUGSSUAQ PENINSULA

DAVIS

Hare I.

Maligat

VAIGAT

70°

STRAIT

Disko I.

Disko Fjord

Jakobshavn

DISKO BAY

Christianshaab

55°W

Inland Ice

improved. But clearing the net from the keelband defied all our efforts. We tried with a knife lashed to a boathook, and we tried attaching a 56 lb. weight, a piece of ballast, to give a vertical downwards pull. John, with no wet suit or any under-water gear, even offered to jump in. With the sea temperature at 3° C. I discouraged this, although, as I reflected, it might have silenced him for a bit if not for ever. While all this was going on we were drifting vaguely in fog towards the Qagsit Islands, two islands 10 miles out from the coast extensively surrounded by foul ground. In fact we were further inshore than we imagined.

Fog plays some queer tricks. At 2 am Brian who had just relieved me drew my attention to a dark object apparently not more than a couple of hundred yards away. Staring at it for a long time through binoculars neither of us could decide whether it was a rock, a great bunch of kelp, or some sea monster. Brian suggested rowing across to see, a matter of minutes. When the fog had thinned a little we recognised it as an island a good 2 miles away, certainly a long row. Later that morning, still in fog, only the lucky glimpsing of two islands to the west showed that we were inside the Qagsit. We took steps accordingly and went out to sea.

Another flat calm on 7 August allowed us to have another go at ridding the boat of its incubus the net, when we merely succeeded in breaking a boathook. By now it had become a race against time. By the 10th we had got up to Lat. 68° N. leaving five days to reach Lat. 71°, or rather more than 200 miles since we had to go round north of Disko Island. With time in hand I would have taken the longer way inside Disko through the strait called Vaigat where there is the largest concentration of freshly calved icebergs anywhere. Icebergs of all shapes and sizes, some like fortresses with sheer sides, others with pinnacled towers like glistening cathedrals, all floating serenely on the stillest of blue seas. As the *Pilot* records:

in June, after the break-up of the winter ice, thousands of icebergs some from 200ft. to 300ft. high, drift, backwards and forwards with the tidal streams, or in other directions according to the wind; these bergs render navigation dangerous and anchorage impossible.

Later on, as in August, when many of the bergs have gone out to sea, the Vaigat is not as bad as it is painted. When returning through it in August 1961 we managed well enough. These bergs are calved from the numerous glaciers that descend into the Vaigat from the ice-cap, two very large glaciers near Jakobshavn being principal offenders. For a visit to Jakobshavn one might need a more compelling reason than curiosity. As the *Pilot* says:

A peculiarity of Jakobshavn is the so-called *kanel* produced by the calving of large icebergs or by a discharge of ice from Jakobshavn Isfjord. Without warning a large or small wave comes rolling into the inner harbour; the water is violently disturbed and covered with white foam, while seaweed and vegetation on the bottom are torn up by the roots. The *kanel* appears in September and may be violent enough to tear vessels from their moorings.

Having seen the glaciers where they originate, with bergs a daily sight and, when becalmed, recognising old friends, marking their progress or lack of progress, seeing and hearing one split, or even capsize, one naturally becomes interested in their ultimate fate. Nearly all Arctic bergs originate from the glaciers of East and West Greenland and it is reckoned that 70 per cent come from the regions of Disko and of Umanak to the north. The twelve biggest glaciers of this area are estimated to discharge 5,400 bergs annually. The flow of the current carries the bergs northwards up the Greenland coast, round the head of Baffin Bay, and then southward down the Labrador coast to the region of Newfoundland. The time taken by a berg to reach Newfoundland, and, of course, only a few of the bigger ones survive that long, varies greatly. Shape, strandings, variations in local current, and other factors, all play a part. It is possible for two bergs calved from the same glacier on the same day to be separated by one or even two years in the time of their arrival at the Tail of the Grand Bank.

Slowly we worked our way up the west coast of Disko Island, frequently in fog, and using the engine more and more as time began to run out. On the 11th we ran it all night, thus ensuring for some of us a sleepless night. For the amateur, navigation is never an exact science and if fog has added to his uncertainties he must be prepared for some unexpected sights. North of Disko Island is Hare Island and between them is a 5-mile-wide channel called Maligat. Thinking that the channel might be infested with bergs I had decided to go north of Hare Island and on the 12th, until the fog lifted a little, that is what I thought we were doing. Land then showed up on either side and that to the north might or might not be Hare Island. There was another puzzle. What looked like another island lay to the north-east, whereas if we were in the Maligat strait looking to the east we should have seen an unbroken line of coast on the far side of the Vaigat. According to the chart the only place that might conceivably agree with what we saw was Disko fjord, 30 miles to the south, and that was too discouraging to believe. He who knows not where to go is in no hurry to move. Further prolonged study of chart and *Pilot* revealed that across the land to the east that we were looking at, the Nugssuaq peninsula, ran a wide valley, a well-known Greenlander sledging route. I guessed then that what looked like an island to the north-east was actually the tip of the peninsula and that fog lying in the wide valley had given it the appearance of an island. On that assumption we pressed on and although fog still hung over the valley we soon satisfied ourselves that we were at the northern end of the Vaigat and not in Disko fjord. Having rounded the tip of Nugssuaq peninsula our next mark was Ubekendt Island, 20 miles away, with Igdlorssuit another 15 miles up its eastern side. We had to motor all that night and a good part of the following day, hoisting our sails as we approached the settlement, not on account of any wind, but by way of a gesture and to astonish the natives. There is no harbour, hardly even a bay, and as we anchored off the beach of black sand at 3 pm on the 13th we were boarded by another and quite unexpected friend. This was Frank George of the Royal Institute of Navigation and for the life of me I could not think what had brought him to Igdlorssuit. In the role of surveyor he had come to measure glacier movement on the neighbouring island of Upernivik, not that glacier movement has any bearing on navigation, even in Greenland waters. I lost no time in going ashore to be greeted by the man I had expected to see, my friend Dr Drever, wearing a deerstalker hat and in spite of that looking every inch a benign and comparatively learned professor.

CHAPTER FOURTEEN

To the Mountains

IN RECENT years St Andrews University, with which I have a loose, un-academic connection, have built a hut at Igdlorssuit, as has, more recently, Manchester University. The two are side by side well clear of the settlement. In the matter of the hut Dr Drever, who had made several visits and who for many years has made a study of the rocks of Ubekendt Island, was the moving spirit. The layman who thinks that a few hours or even days devoted to the studying of a piece of rock would be more than enough is seriously mistaken. Geologists, as even the layman should know, have their own vast time-scale, and work accordingly. I believe that some of the Ubekendt rock is similar to that which has been brought back from the moon, but, as Tallulah Bankhead would say, there may be less in this than meets the eye. In the course of his visits Dr Drever has conceived a great liking and respect for the people of the settlement with whom he has had close relations, and is rightly concerned for the future of this self-contained, self-sufficient happy community. In fact his interest in them now threatens to outdo his interest in igneous rocks. On this occasion, largely through him, what was called the Scottish West Greenland Project had been active on the island since July, its main objective, besides several others, being 'the reconnaissance of possible sites on Ubekendt for a field centre designed to promote cross-cultural communication between people with an Eskimo cultural inheritance and people with other cultures'. Besides Dr Drever, the party included two high-powered professors (an American and a Dane) of Eskimology and Sociology. On a slightly more frivolous plane one cross-cultural feature, introduced some years ago by Dr Drever, had been a sort of local Derby Day, a day of jollification, the big event a race for kayaks from Umanak to Igdlorssuit, a distance of 50 miles. We missed this by arriving too late. I was told that entries for this formidable endurance test are falling off. Possibly the Greenlanders are becoming soft, like ourselves, or are learning from us that sporting events deserve more tangible rewards than honour and glory.

The settlement seemed to me to be much the same as when we had last seen it in 1961. Very little 'growth' here one was thankful to note. Like all other Greenlanders the people of Igdlorssuit are far from being of pure Eskimo descent, of whom nowadays there are few if any left. In the course of the last two centuries seamen and whalers of various nationalities and Danish officials and traders have seen to that. Yet they and their way of life appeared to us to have some resemblance to the real thing; the huskies, of which each family has a sledge team or more, the sledges lying about, the kayaks stored high up out of the reach of dogs, the racks of shark meat and cod drying in the sun, women sewing skins on to the frame of a newly-built kayak; all of which, in spite of the presence of a petrol pump, led us to think we were seeing primitive life in the Arctic.

From the huts a half-mile walk along the beach, the sea one side and a gravel fan sparsely covered with grass on the other, brought one to the heart of Igdlorssuit – the store, the post-office, and the petrol pump, the latter an innovation since 1961. The store, run by the Royal Greenland Trading Co., buys sealskins or any other skins and sells all that the community needs; and since the community is by now what we call civilised its needs are many – food, clothing, household goods, beer, tobacco, tools, fishing gear, boats, rifles, shotguns, ammunition, fuel for lighting, cooking, and heating, as well as for outboard engines. Thus although their main occupation has not changed in that they still live, though indirectly, by hunting and fishing, yet their way of life is very far from the self-sufficiency of their forebears when the seal or the walrus provided everything – clothing, boots, tents, kayaks, food for men and dogs, fuel for cooking and oil for lighting.

The few motor boats they have are used for fishing or for reaching places where seals may be found, with a kayak in tow or on board to be used in the final stages of the hunt. Even with modern firearms, hunting a seal calls for skill and patience; with only the harpoon of former times Nimrod himself would have been severely taxed; but in those days, of course, there were many more seals. The few seals we saw were mere fleeting glimpses of a head poked above water. A seal shot in the water in summer will probably sink anyway; hauled out on a floe they offer the hunter more chance, but even there they must be killed with one shot or they will roll into the water. In winter they are harpooned at breathing holes or stalked on the ice, both methods calling for the patience of Job and, considering the cold, a Job's fortitude. Though they are not fur seals, the skins of these ring and harp seals are valuable to the fur trade. At Igdlorssuit in 1961 I bought a dozen skins from which were made two short women's coats. The remnants provided me with only a waistcoat whereas I really wanted a pair of trousers like those worn by the oldest inhabitant of Igdlorssuit, a delightful character, shaped like a barrel, almost as broad as long, who walked about aided by a stick, a benign smile on his leathery, wrinkled face and a short cutty pipe stuck firmly in his toothless mouth.

There are some thirty brightly painted wooden houses, their immediate vicinity usually pretty squalid on account of the huskies and the absence of anti-litter laws or societies for the preservation of rural Greenland. The communal refuse dump is a long way off and everyone is expected to do their own thing. Unfortunately, what is everybody's business is nobody's business; which, by the way, was the explanation given to an enquiring visitor after the Irish 'troubles' of the twenties for the fact that while a number of harmless people had been shot or had their houses burnt, the most unpopular character, against whom everybody bore a grudge, had remained unharmed. Igdlorssuit has also a church and a school and thanks to the sensible arrangement of closing the school in summer, leaving the dark, winter months for study, the place swarmed with children who had little to do beyond pestering visitors. Rather like the dogs who led a carefree, idle, well-fed life all summer only to make up for it in winter by hauling sledges on long journeys over the ice. The Igdlorssuit dogs were lucky to be fed. At Holsteinborg, a place alive with dogs and where there are no sharks to be caught to provide dog-meat, we learnt when we were there in 1962 that the dogs had to fend for themselves in summer. They managed this by scouring the harbour and the fish factory where offal, scraps of whale or reindeer meat might be picked up and oil barrels licked. They even waded about off the beach looking for small fish. There are no dogs in Godthaab where keeping them is forbidden.

The children were not always a nuisance. Simon and I, for instance, employed a volunteer crew to tow an oil-drum from the settlement to *Baroque*, getting thoroughly wet on the way when jealous rivals had to be fought off. From infancy they play about in boats and kayaks, becoming good watermen. Naturally they liked to clamber over *Baroque* if given the chance and on shore they attended our movements closely. Taking a solitary walk one afternoon, congratulating myself on having escaped detection, I was half-way up a steep, stony gully when I heard shouts from below. Half a dozen urchins were in hot pursuit. But I managed to shake them off, the gully being not much to their liking. Although the island rises to over 4,000ft. it is not mountainous in the true sense of the word; for real mountains one must look across the 6-mile-wide channel to Upernivik Island where peaks of true Alpine character stab the sky and broad glaciers flow down to the sea. At Igdlorssuit, shut in by the hill behind, one's gaze rests constantly and inevitably upon these mountains, yet those who live there show no interest. The Greenlander seems to be immune from the love of 'high places and the golden mountain tops where dwell the Spirits of the Dawn'. And this is strange because they struck me as being very like Sherpas both in appearance and behaviour, the same short, sturdy figures and Mongolian features, their brown cheeks suffused with red, gay, cheerful, happy go-lucky, born gamblers, easily amused, and always ready to laugh either at us or themselves.

In the early thirties Igdlorssuit had an unusual visitor when Rockwell Kent, an American artist, built himself a house and lived there for a year in intimate contact with the natives. The house is now a ruin. *Salamina*, the interesting and entertaining book illustrated by himself, gives a true picture of life at Igdlorssuit, though even in the short span of forty years there have been changes; the houses, for instance, that then were mostly built of stones and turfs are now all of imported material. In writing about our first visit to Igdlorssuit in 1961 I felt constrained to comment upon Rockwell Kent, his book *Salamina*, and Ubekendt Island:

His descriptive powers are to be envied. He saw things through the eyes of an artist, a man with a soul, as opposed to a man personifying, as a French writer puts it, '*le mépris de vulgarisation, du clubalpinisme, et des yahous*'. For on the first sighting of Ubekendt by this yahoo it appeared to be an uncommonly dull and barren lump whereas Rockwell Kent saw it thus: 'Both by the suggestion of its name (unknown) and by its position and character – its seagirt location, the simple grandeur of its stark, snow-covered table-land and higher peaks, the dark cliff barrier that forms its eastern shore –

there is the glamour of imponderable mystery about the island which dignifies it even at the gateway of a region of stupendous grandeur. Its cliffs, proclaiming inaccessibility, preclude the thought of human settlements. When, therefore, on approaching its more mountainous north-eastern end, where, just ahead, steep mountain walls rise sheer from the water's edge, the barrier ends, the shore sweeps inward in a mile-wide crescent of smooth strand and, cupped by mountains, there appears a low and gently sloping verdant foreland, jewelled with painted buildings, one's spirit, in sudden awakening to a need, exults in grateful consciousness of its fulfilment.'

The crew together with odd bodies from the Manchester hut and a few Greenlanders who thrust their way in, filled the St Andrews hut to capacity. I was disappointed to learn that both my friends were leaving that evening by boat for Umanak and thence by helicopter to the airfield at Sondre Stromfjord. The hut was well stocked with provisions of which we were invited to take what we wanted. We were also told of a climber, David Meldrum, who in a day or two would be available to accompany us to Upernivik Island. At this open roadstead we kept an anchor watch, mainly to keep an eye on drifting floes of which there were in fact few, all the bergs being well out in mid-channel. During my watch next night I took the dinghy ashore to empty it of water and met David Meldrum who was taking the air on the beach. On shore, even at midnight, there were mosquitoes about though, like the seals, they seem to have diminished in numbers over the years. David, who had climbed on Upernivik with a St Andrews party in 1967, agreed to start on the 16th, bringing with him a Zodiac inflatable so that he could get back to Igdlorssuit on his own. At this time he was working for the Danish Geodetic Survey.

Pending our departure we put in some work on the boat and attended coffee parties in various houses. Such parties are the main social activity – Rockwell Kent has much to say about them in his book.

The clew of the mainsail needed a new cringle, a job I found difficult to do well with a strand of nylon rope; it does not hold its lay when unstranded as does tarred Italian hemp which is the proper stuff to use. We managed at last to cut away a lot more of the net still attached to the keel by swinging out the boom with enough weights suspended from it to heel the boat well over. Before we left Ilan collected the promised stores – fried onion, milk powder, honey, marmalade, Ryvita, all most welcome – and for one meal showed us how to live off the country in the manner of Stefansson's *The Friendly Arctic*. One of the local boats had brought in a small whale and in the course of my walk over the hills I had found a gigantic mushroom or some kind of fungus. Hence for supper we had mushroom soup and whale steaks.

Unless circumstances demand of them a very early start, as may happen in the Alps, mountaineers are not unduly quick off the mark. We hung about until midday before David had himself fettled up and ready to move. Towing the Zodiac we motored across to the south-west corner of Upernivik and along its south coast before turning into Pakavsa, a 2-mile-wide fjord separating Upernivik from the Qioqe peninsula. In 1961 I had had my eye on a peak on Qioqe of 7,500ft., the highest in the region. In mountaineering, if not in life, we needs must love the highest when we see it. Before sailing, however, I learnt that the peak had been climbed by the Italian Piero Ghiglioni, aged seventy-seven, and an Italian guide, climbed, too, from sea-level in the day without any bivouac. The friend who sent me the account added: 'There is hope for you yet.' Piero Ghiglioni was an exceptional man who would no doubt still be climbing had he not been killed in a car accident the next year. In any case had we tried that peak Charles Marriot (on whom be peace) and I would not have succeeded. From sea-level we attempted a peak of 6,500ft. and after eight hours, having reached about 5,500ft., Charles had a bad attack of what I call Mountaineer's Foot, the inability to put one in front of the other. Stung by that failure we had gone to Upernivik where we had spent most of our time looking for a peak within our grasp. Had we gone there first, where there were glaciers on which one could move freely and many unclimbed peaks of great character, we might have bagged several instead of only one. As I wrote afterwards: 'Instead of buzzing like elderly bees from flower to flower gathering very little honey, had we but established a high camp on Upernivik we might have drunk our fill.'

Having climbed there with a very active St Andrews party David knew well the mountains of Upernivik. He had with him, too, a map of the island and full accounts of two St Andrews expeditions. As we motored up the fjord between towering walls of red granite, many high, slender, and apparently inapproachable spires would make their startling appearance. Whereupon I would say to David: 'Well, I suppose that one has not yet been climbed', for in the eyes of a superannuated mountaineer some of the peaks looked not only as if they could not be climbed but that they were best left alone. Nothing of the sort. All had been climbed as well as several equally or even more difficult peaks on Qioqe. I doubt if there are any first ascents to be made now in that region – not that that matters, for the mountain is the same and will afford the same satisfaction when it is climbed for the five-hundredth time.

Since the war and particularly in the last fifteen years climbing standards have risen enormously, partly to the ever-increasing number of climbers, not only in England but throughout the world (the Japanese for instance), and partly owing to new equipment and new techniques. There is in some instances, too, an attitude new to mountaineering, that of death or glory, which sometimes succeeds and sometimes fails, and which in any case is foolish, because the glory is so transient. A man ought to rate his achievements only by the satisfaction they give him, for they will soon be outdone, outshone, and speedily forgotten by everyone but himself. Such climbers push their luck to the limit. In the Himalaya, for example, routes that are threatened by ice-falls to which a party may be exposed for days while it lays its fixed ropes, are cheerfully undertaken; whereas in the thirties no sober mountaineer, taught to eschew objective dangers, would have looked twice at such a route.

We hoped to anchor off the mouth of a small river, the place where the St Andrews party had established their first base camp, and since the river, though small, is fed by melting snow and melting glaciers and must carry down a lot of silt I expected to find off its mouth water shallow enough for an anchorage. In these steep-sided fjords an anchorage is hard to find, only

where glaciers and rivers debouch is there much chance. I see from the chart
that the depths in Pakavsa are 500 metres, or in more seamanlike terms 270-
odd fathoms. Within thirty yards or less of the rocks where the river came
tumbling down we got no bottom at 10 fathoms. I gave Simon another length
of line to bend on. We all make mistakes. Simon's bend was not what it
should have been and at the next cast we lost our 7 lb. lead. After that I gave
up and we made for the Qioqe side of the fjord where steep walls gave way to
a wide valley, a glacier coming down it half-way, and a sandy beach below.
Obviously a good anchorage although on the wrong side of the fjord. But we
had the Zodiac.

While we were crossing the fjord Simon hastily contrived another lead out
of two pieces of iron wired together. We anchored in 8 fathoms a hundred
yards from the beach, a beach unsullied but for a solitary tin and the inevitable,
indestructible plastic bag. As the sun sank in a cloudless sky a slender, knife-
edged ridge some 5,000ft. above cast its shadow across the glacier. The ridge
led to an even more slender peak which David assured me had been climbed
by a Scottish party in a climb lasting thirty-six hours, while an equally
fearsome peak to the north had been climbed by an Italian party. Air transport,
too, has been another contributory factor to the revolution in climbing without
which mighty few peaks in Greenland would as yet have been climbed.

On 17 August, yet another flawless day, the climbing party embarked in the
Zodiac and by 10 am had landed at the river mouth, crossing the fjord three
times as fast as we had in *Baroque*. Having moored the Zodiac, anchoring it
with stones to prevent it drifting back against the rocks, we shouldered our
rucksacks and set off up the left bank of the river. At the last moment Ilan
had decided to come with us for a walk. In case I had to wait half the night for
Simon and David I had brought a sleeping bag which I dumped there. David
should have warned me about the river. At that comparatively early hour
there was not much water coming down and at the mouth it was easily
fordable, but as we moved up the volume of water seemed to increase rapidly.
David and Simon soon forged ahead out of sight, I followed, while Ilan who
had on his feet only rubbers, remained at a respectful distance behind. My
chosen peak of some 4,500ft. lay across the river a couple of miles to the south
and so long as I followed the left bank it was not getting any nearer. The river,
now running with intimidating force, had to be crossed and at last I found a
place where although I should get wet I was not likely to be drowned. Happily
the rucksack containing food and camera got across dry. A freshwater bath
might have done the camera good, for after three months at sea in *Baroque* it
was pretty salty. I had no ice-axe and in crossing rivers an ice-axe for taking
soundings and for support, like a third leg, is invaluable. My last axe had gone
down with *Sea Breeze* and had not been replaced. In the original Ellesmere
Island plan I had assumed that Simon and John Harradine would do the
climbing and that in those comparatively unknown waters my lot would be to
look after the boat.

The broad, easy slopes of the stony glacis leading to the foot of the peak
provided a long, hot trudge. One could not plod along automatically with
some sort of rhythm, one's mind on something else; there were too many

boulders, large and small, so that every step had to be chosen. I sat down for a bite in the welcome shadow of a great rock in a thirsty land. The day was hot, the peak distant, and it did not really matter tuppence if I climbed it or not. Thus Belial, once more, with words clothed in reason's garb counselled ignoble ease. Having shed a few garments and wrung out wet trousers and socks I felt better and pressed on. A wide snow couloir led invitingly towards the summit but I found that in spite of the sun the snow remained extremely hard. Scraping a few tentative steps with my boots I soon realised that without an axe I would probably come unstuck and without an axe a slide in hard snow is difficult to stop. The first stop would probably be a violent one against some boulder where the snow ran out. But at the side of the couloir where snow met rock, progress was easy either on the rock, or on the snow, or in the gap between them.

Even the 20ft. summit boulder which from below I had already decided to forgo – such is the caution imposed by age – offered no resistance and was soon overcome. Judging from afar whether a thing can be climbed or not is as uncertain as judging from afar the navigability or otherwise of pack-ice. The only way is to go and see. In a cairn on the summit was a cigarette tin with the four names of the St Andrews party who had made the first ascent. From the time they had taken one gathered they were not very fit, and it was in fact their first climb undertaken merely to gain a view-point. The solo climber, too, is at an advantage; 'he travels the fastest who travels alone' with no one arguing the toss about the best route to take. This inoffensive summit, by the way, has been named 'Groyling' by the St Andrews party. So far as I know there is as yet no co-ordinating body to approve or disapprove of the names given to Greenland peaks, names now bestowed in haphazard fashion according to the whims and the nationality of the party that makes the first ascent.

From the top I could see the first obstacle, a steep snow couloir, that David and Simon would have to climb but, of course, no sign of the climbers. Even at this height yellow Icelandic poppies grew and flowered in modest profusion. Starting down the rocks of the south-east ridge I was soon tempted by a more direct route down another wide snow couloir. After a few more hours of sunshine the snow here had just the right consistency for a fast descent by making long strides with each heel dug down into the snow. With an ice-axe one could have made a fast glissade. The river had been much on my mind, for by the evening of so warm a day would be a boiling torrent. So I decided to try at the mouth where it flattened out after a steep drop and there I got across with unexpected ease. The Zodiac had drifted against the rocks in spite of our care but it had come to no harm. There was no sign of Ilan so I made a bed of heath and got into my sleeping bag, both to ward off mosquitoes and to keep warm, the sun having dropped behind the ridge. By eight o'clock I was getting worried. Unused to rough going, and ill-shod, Ilan, I felt sure, had sprained an ankle or fallen into the river, nor had I any idea which way he had gone. Half-an-hour later he turned up, unperturbed and seemingly untired in spite of having been wandering about since ten that morning, having much enjoyed his solitary stroll. The thought of food and drink easily persuaded us not to wait any longer and by 9 pm we were back on board enjoying coffee and scrambled eggs.

I sent John and Brian off to pick up the climbers. At 2 am they returned complaining with some reason that they were cold and clamouring for coffee. Again I began to worry and this time with some reason. Their peak was further away than mine and altogether in a different class, but it was only a thousand feet higher and should not have taken such a young and active pair all that time. On the other hand David had climbed it before and was experienced. At 3 am just as the Zodiac was about to start back again Brian saw a flare. So John went over alone and half-an-hour later, much to my relief, everyone was back on board. Simon was a rock climber, unused to snow and ice, and the descent of the snow couloir which by then was in bad condition had consumed a lot of time. The climb had been an eye-opener for Simon who found that mountaineering, as opposed to rock-climbing, involved toil and sweat.

David had now to get back to Igdlorssuit so having seen him off in the Zodiac we got under way down the fjord. The absence of wind gave us a chance to try out the great sweeps that Colin Putt had made, our immediate reaction to the loss of *Sea Breeze*. When near the land if there is no wind, whether there is ice about or not, a boat without an engine is liable to get into trouble. If there is any wind the boat can claw off the shore, but if there is a lot of ice about as well the boat cannot sail for fear of hitting a floe. With a pair of sweeps we might have succeeded in getting *Sea Breeze* close enough inshore to anchor before the gale broke and before the ice came down. The sweeps with their rowlocks fitted snugly into holes in the capping rail forward of the mast, and with two men on each we found we could move the boat at the rate of nearly a knot and turn her about easily.

CHAPTER FIFTEEN

Umanak and Homewards

UMANAK, WHERE we intended stocking up for the voyage home, is the administrative centre for this region. On the way there I had thought of visiting a new zinc-lead mine which had just become operational, but on second thoughts it seemed likely they would be too busy to welcome casual visitors. This Blank Angel mine, as it is called, is an exciting project, the ore having to be brought down 3,000ft. by aerial cableway from the top of Black Angel mountain. This will be the only mine now active in Greenland. The cryolite mine at Arsuk which has been worked for more than half a century has been worked out; a zinc-lead mine on the east coast north of Scoresby

Sound had closed down, likewise the coal mine on Disko Island. Future possibilities are a molybdenum deposit in East Greenland, an iron deposit at the bottom of Godthaab fjord, and uranium in South Greenland. No one yet knows whether there is gas or oil under the Greenland continental shelf, although the geological features are said to be favourable. The Danish Government is still pondering the implications of granting concessions which, if ever granted, would be under stringent safeguards against pollution.

From almost anywhere in the large bay called Nordost Bugt, in which Ubekendt and Upernivik islands lie, the small island of Umanak catches the eye. Only 4 miles long and less than 2 miles wide, it comprises an uncommonly sheer rock peak that rises to 3,856ft. Its obvious challenge, visible from 40 to 50 miles away, was first taken up by two German climbers, and it was climbed for only the second time much more recently by a St Andrews party. As we approached it Simon and I naturally looked long and hard at this great monolith trying to discover the line of weakness in its formidable defences. The settlement crouches on the only flat bit left at the eastern end of the island. The small harbour, its entrance less than a cable wide, is sheltered from all but easterly winds. When we anchored there, putting a stern line ashore, there were only one or two small floes inside the harbour. We enjoyed the luxury of having all-night in, setting no anchor watch.

Church, school, hospital and store cluster round the harbour, leaving the private houses to perch as they can on any flat bit of rock between the harbour and the base of the mountain. On the Monday we completed our shopping, took on more diesel oil by floating a drum across the harbour, and watered from the nearest tap, rowing it off in jerrycans. That afternoon it began to blow hard from the east and small bergs began making their way into the harbour. After the Vaigat this Nordost Bugt is the most prolific source of supply for icebergs. Many large glaciers descend from the inland ice to debouch into it and many such glaciers lie not far east of Umanak; they are constantly calving and an easterly wind accelerates the drift of the bergs down the fjord to Umanak Island; and while the depth of water across the entrance does not permit the entrance of any monsters it encourages them to take the ground and pile up just outside. Many small floes were worming their way in so we moved our berth out of the direct line of entrance and set an anchor watch to fend off intruders.

Next morning, 21 August, dawned bright and sunny, the east wind still at full blast not far from gale force, and the accumulation of ice outside warned us that it was high time to go. We got our anchor and motored to the entrance where there was still room enough to pass provided one could steer the necessary devious course. *Baroque*'s whimsical ways when under power have been noticed. She sheers relentlessly to starboard, a tendency that is barely counteracted by keeping the tiller hard over. To turn to port the engine must be put in neutral. At the critical moment in the pass, as we put her in neutral to turn to port, the wind took charge and blew her off to starboard. By going full astern we narrowly missed hitting the rocks on that side. Going astern with ice floes around is particularly hazardous because there is no telling which direction she will take. The wind soon obliged her to make up her mind and as soon as she pointed towards the harbour we went back, thankful to have escaped any damage.

Once more at anchor, warding off floes and wondering what next to do, we were presently boarded by a Greenlander who had his skiff moored close by. He began talking vehemently in a frightful mixture of Eskimo, Danish and English. The words 'ice' and 'come' frequently repeated were alone distinguishable but he was evidently voicing my own fears, namely that if we did not get out that day we might be there for some time, even for the winter. Accompanied by the Greenlander we rowed across to the harbour office to find someone who spoke English. A tow from the harbour tug, we learnt, would cost 100 kr. an hour for a minimum of six hours. While digesting this we saw that the tug in question, having just conducted an incoming vessel through the ice, had gone alongside *Baroque*. We took the hint, bundled the Harbour-master into the dinghy, and rowed back to talk to the man who mattered.

The skipper of the tug understood English far better than the Harbour-master. He and his crew had been inspecting *Baroque* above and below with interest and he grasped what we wanted almost at once. He looked like an American gangster and spoke like one. Completely ignoring the Harbour-master, who was still muttering about kroners, he merely drawled out 'Sure'. So in with the dinghy, up anchor, and away. While still inside the harbour, ignoring or forgetting our 7ft. 5in. draught, he towed us right over the projecting tongue of a floe on which we ought to have grounded but just managed to slide over. With this narrow shave averted we weaved an intricate course through the clutter of ice outside and soon reached more or less open water. Casting off, waiting neither for kroners nor even cigarettes, the friendly tug sped back to Umanak. Hoisting sail, the wind as fresh as ever and right astern, we in turn sped off down the fjord, thankful to be on our way. My intention had been to return through the Vaigat, visiting either Christianshaab or Jakobshavn on the way. Both harbours are small and liable to be encumbered with bergs of which, mindful of *Baroque*'s vagaries and our recent experience, I had for the present had enough. The open waters of Davis Strait, salmon nets notwithstanding, seemed the safer course.

In Davis Strait the winds follow roughly the lie of the coast and are either from south-east or north-west, the latter predominating. We enjoyed a fine spell of northerly wind which gradually increased until on 25 August it blew hard enough for us to log nearly a hundred miles.

She should have done better than that but by now we had a good growth of grass and weed on the hull. The seeds of this growth must have been sown, as it were, during our stay in Irish waters and the cold water in which we had been for the last two months had not prevented its grow-ing. Steering south, while the coast trended away to the south-east, we were a long way from land and near the middle of Davis Strait when we encountered the remnants of what is called the 'Middle Pack', the pear-shaped field of ice that extends south-wards from Baffin Bay down the middle and western half of Davis Strait. We had passed several ice-bergs and I had assumed that the scattered floes we now found ourselves among were merely debris from those that were breaking or disinteg-rating. The drop in sea temperature from 4° C. at noon to 1.5° C. at 6 pm should have warned me. Later that night we were still among floes which by then had become difficult to see and to avoid.

At first we hove-to but as she still forged slowly ahead we dropped the sails and lay a-hull, keeping double watches, with the engine ready to start should a floe bear down on the boat. At midnight the sea temperature fell to 0° C. and at 6 am to – 0.5° C.; the lowest we recorded. Sea water of average salinity freezes at –1.6° C. Strangely enough, just as we hove-to that night, a great bunch of salmon net rose to the surface to be dragged on board by Brian. This must have been all that remained after our last attempt to clear it at Igdlorssuit. Even lying a-hull did not ensure a quiet night. More than once the engine had to be started and more than once a nasty thud showed that it had not been started quickly enough.

We began sailing again at dawn and by breakfast-time had got clear of the ice, the last we were to see. In bleak, dismal weather we held on southwards, making nothing to the east, as we wanted to keep well outside the north-going current that sets up the coast. So far we had done well and might have made a fast passage but for various troubles, some of them serious, that now began to plague us. The increasing play in the tiller caused some alarm. The bolts holding the iron shoe which held the tiller to the rudder stock were worn and could not be tightened. As a temporary measure we lashed it with chain.

Then on 2 September, when we were some 200 miles west of C. Farewell, we met a gale at south-east, a direction that was worse than useless. The barometer fell to 989 mbs. and we remained hove-to for the next two days. Pumping became continuous, for the more violent squalls heeled her right over in spite of being close-reefed. Later we preferred to lie a-hull, thus keeping her more upright and lessening the drift to leeward. The snag is that instead of meeting the seas more or less bow on a boat lying a-hull is broadside on, presenting a more vulnerable target to breaking seas. There are exceptions, of course, but generally speaking a summer gale in the North Atlantic seldom lasts long enough to raise a dangerously high sea such as might be met with in the Roaring Forties.

All ills are good when attended by food – down below, digesting risotto and a pudding fit for a glass case, the whole washed down with mulled wine, one could ignore the seas outside and our inexorable drift in the wrong direction. Another bright feature was the state of the bonded store locker where we had far more than we would be allowed to take ashore. This we set about systematically to reduce. During this blow, besides a lot of pumping to do, we had some minor troubles. The hook of the topping-lift block broke allowing the boom to drop on to the doghouse with surprisingly little damage to that flimsy structure. The port side pinrail to which the peak and staysail halyards were secured came adrift and the wire life-line on that side parted. At sea one expects wear and chafe, especially if there is much bad weather, but in *Baroque*, arrange things as one might, some piece of gear always seemed to be rubbing against another.

On the evening of 5 September, the wind blowing harder as it often does when the barometer starts to rise, a small hand-mirror I used for shaving fell to the floor and broke. Sailors are traditionally superstitious. One writer whom I have consulted goes so far as to say 'they are puerile in their apprehensions of omens', and then lists a few of the things that no sailor cared to meet on land much less to have on board – bare footed women with flat feet, a red-headed man with flat feet, priests, hares, pigs, lawyers and cats. The playing of cards, or worse still losing overboard a mop or bucket, presaged evil of some kind, while the ringing of a glass certainly foretold the death of a shipmate and had to be stopped instantly. Similarly whistling, umbrellas, pins, and pieces of cut hair or finger nails were taboo. Sailing on a Friday or changing a ship's name are both inadvisable. Of mirrors there is no mention. Such things would seldom be found in the fo'c'sle of a sailing ship, so it is probably only landsmen who feel concern when they break. Be that as it may, no sooner had our mirror broken than Simon came down to report the boom sprung about four feet from the after end. With something of a struggle we got the sail down and lay a-hull.

Early next morning in his watch Simon, anxious to be doing, not only got the sail off the boom but in a fit of absent-minded enthusiasm unrove the peak halyards. The boom could be repaired without doing this and meantime we could not set the mainsail, as we might have done, loose-footed without the boom. Instead we set an old canvas jib abaft the mast and with that and the staysail made some progress, the wind having at last gone north-west. Contrary winds, and the time we had lost spent hove-to roused some concern for our water supply, for we were still west of C. Farewell and a long way from home. As one small economy we cut out the midday cocoa. We had on board a big coil of ⅜in. wire that Colin Putt had provided, with a view to it being needed for the mast. There was a long scarf in the mast and some observers might have described it in the words of Mr Chucks, the bos'un, as precarious and not very permanent. In fact it stood up manfully and gave us no concern. By revolving the boom with the reefing gear and keeping the wire under tension we put on some three feet of neat wire serving. Over this we put two of the old chain plates as splints with more wire serving over them, and on top of all a canvas coat to protect the sail when reefing.

In quieter weather Simon went aloft to hang a new block for the topping-lift and to reeve the peak halyards again. As a rock-climber, accustomed to modern methods, he had with him his climbing harness. In any seaway the ratlines would shake a man off, so he was hauled up by the stays'l halyards and sitting secure in his harness, which could be clipped on anywhere, he had both hands free to work. With the peak halyards rove we set the main-sail loose-footed, the wind being fair and the work on the boom not quite finished. Sailing thus imposes a heavy strain on the clew of the sail and by the end of the day the mainsail had to come down for repair. Next day with the boom ready we were back in business. Not for long, though. By nightfall, the wind blowing hard from south-east, we were once more hove-to.

Torn sails and sprung booms, which can be repaired, caused less concern than leaks which could not be traced, much less stopped. Drips through the deck and weeps through the topside planking did not account for the pumping we had to do and on 8 September this suddenly increased from 800 strokes a watch to over 2,000. We gave up counting. Having my young crew to get safely home I suggested making for Iceland, the only real advantage being that on a course for Iceland we could make good use of the persistent south-east winds. The distance to Reykjavik was 700 miles, only some 300 miles less than to Ireland, and since the boat would still have to be got home from there we decided to press on. Despite the double watches that the pumping necessitated and the numerous mishaps the crew remained in good heart. We kept her going that day steering north of east – the best we could do – until at midnight when the wind again increased and during my spell at the pump I found myself doing nearly a hundred strokes a minute. We took the sails down and lay a-hull.

Breaking mirrors or not, misfortune still dogged us. The wind at last packed up to leave us rolling about in thick fog, and when the sea subsided a little we started the engine in order to charge the batteries as well as to make good a few miles. The gear box began making strange noises and upon opening it up Simon found that a nut had come adrift and caused serious damage. Simon thought we might still go astern but otherwise the engine was now useless. This, of course, would be no handicap until we reached Lymington. Calms seldom last long and in mid-ocean one does better to wait for a wind. A sight that I got that evening put us just east of C. Farewell. Our latitude remained doubtful, since for six days we had had no meridian sight. A dirty night of wind and almost continuous heavy rain once more obliged us to heave-to, tearing the jib badly as we took it down. With the jib down in the cabin we had a prolonged sewing bee, three of us at work on it until well into the night and again next morning until it was finished.

By 15 September we began to think the long spell of southerly and south-easterly winds with almost incessant rain and drizzle had come to an end. The wind went round to north-west, and although it blew with some violence, we could lay the desired course. We ran on either close-reefed or sometimes under bare poles and under this rig, or lack of rig, she would make a good 3 knots, the helmsman having to work hard to keep her running straight. We were running like this when a Russian stern trawler, homeward bound, altered course to close and speak to us. 'Can we do anything for you?' they hailed in very good English. 'Please report us to Lloyds, London,' we replied. It was expecting a lot, I suppose, for them to be on speaking terms with London. A long embarrassed silence ensued, then, 'We wish you a happy voyage,' and with a parting blast on the siren and much waving they resumed their course. This looked like a genuine working trawler. Two other Russian trawlers we met in the Channel off Portland, loitering with intent as the police say, looked like equally genuine spy-ships.

On the 18th, the wind for once moderate, we made a notable discovery. In quiet conditions, with no water sloshing about below, Ilan heard water coming in under the galley floor. On lifting the boards we found a regular gusher of nearly an inch bore and rising about a foot. This discovery, while alarming, was none the less welcome. By heeling her over on the other tack we reduced the fountain sufficiently for Simon to clap over it a tingle of canvas and copper sheeting held down by many screws. With one main source of leakage thus reduced we were able to revert to single watches. The play in the tiller having become much worse we shipped the iron emergency tiller. This tiller was on the short side. Short though it was the force exerted by the rudder when hove-to during a gale was sufficient to bend it into almost a half-moon. Straightening it by clobbering took some time and while this was going on we reverted to the wood tiller until it finally came away, as it were, in the helmsman's hands.

This year we had some wild weather around the time of the equinox, thus fulfilling the expectations of those who believed in equinoctial gales. Lecky, the author of *Lecky's Wrinkles*, whom I accept as an oracle in most seafaring matters, holds that there are no such things as 'equinoctial gales'. 'Equinoctial gales,' he writes, 'constitute one of those prejudices of which it is well-nigh hopeless to disabuse the popular mind. Most careful observations prove conclusively that storms have no special connection with the equinoxes; yet how often does one hear a gale, occurring even three weeks one side or other of this event, referred to as an equinoctial gale.' In this Lecky has the support of the Meteorological Office who should know:

The use of this expression implies that gales are more frequent (and possibly more severe) within a few days of each equinox. At any particular location in the temperate North Atlantic, the normal pattern of gale frequency runs from a minimum in summer to a maximum in winter; from the available data there do not appear to be secondary maxima around the equinoxes. There is no reason to suggest that sudden changes of weather accompany the sun's transit of the equator. As in any other season, within the temperate belt some places will enjoy settled weather at the equinox while others will suffer boisterous weather according to the positions of anticyclones and depressions at that time.

Nevertheless, in spite of Lecky and the Meteorological Office this popular myth is probably inextinguishable. It would be an interesting piece of research to discover when and why it was ever started.

After a wild night on 20 September a seam in the mainsail began to go so that had to come down, the boom coming down of its own accord with some violence when the topping-lift parted. John, who went aloft sitting in Simon's harness, found the other lift badly stranded and both were sent down for splicing. These repairs were completed by next day, a day so warm and sunny that I had a bucket bath, the first and last of the voyage. On earlier voyages this had been a daily, before-breakfast ritual, observed faithfully until fairly high latitudes had been reached. On one voyage I remember one of the crew followed my example and this soon developed into an unspoken but well understood challenge as to who would give up first. In bucket baths as in more serious matters it is hard to live up to the precept of the Old English poet:

> Harder should be the spirit, the heart all the bolder,
> Courage the greater, as the strength grows less.

Yet another 'equinoctial gale' on the 23rd obliged us to lie a-hull. By now we were approaching the area defined as 'Shannon' in the Shipping forecasts, close enough to home for us to pick them up. The gale had abated by next day when we celebrated Simon's twenty-first birthday with a three-course meal – onion soup, *moussala* (a Greek speciality of Ilan's), and peaches in rum. Replete and lethargic, with the feeling that 'fate cannot touch me, I have dined today', we nevertheless had to turn out at midnight to reef.

September went out with a roar, gale succeeding gale, all from the right direction and giving us a great lift homewards, usually running with only the staysail and what we called our 'comic' sail set. The much-needed trysail was lying at the sailmakers and we felt the mainsail should be nursed, not wishing to have twenty or thirty feet of seam-stitching on our hands. We passed south of the Scillies on the night of the 30th, too far off to raise the Bishop light, but on the following night we saw the loom of the Lizard, our first English light. Whereupon, by way of welcome, the wind promptly went round to the east where it remained for the following four days blowing pretty fresh. Beating against it proved unprofitable. We fetched up on the French coast east of Ile de Batz and our next board took us back to England in the vicinity of the Eddystone. For some unseamanlike reason this light escaped the notice of the man on watch and when I came on at 2 am we seemed to be on the point of entering what looked like Fowey. Gybing with difficulty, for *Baroque* gybes with reluctance except accidentally, we stood out to sea and soon picked up the Eddystone light.

The east wind continued, as did our run of mishaps. In fact it blew so hard that we hove-to and let her drift rather than go on beating to small purpose. On our resuming sailing and sighting the Eddystone for the third time, the hook on the jib block broke. Once more and for the last time Simon went up to hang another block. More leaks too, under the galley floor where water was spurting up between two planks as she rolled. But by now the malice of the east wind was spent. Off Anvil Point on 6 October, the tide foul and the wind but light, Ilan and I played our last game of chess, a prolonged struggle, and by evening we were up with the Needles, carrying the last of the flood to Yarmouth where we anchored.

By sailing at dawn we expected to catch the tide and with the aid of our sweeps make our way up Lymington river. But the westerly wind died away by dawn and by the time we had crossed the Solent had come in fresh from the north. Our sweeps would be no good against that so we anchored off Lymington Spit. It was a Sunday and there were many yachts out even in October. The first yacht we hailed said he was bound for Poole and he seemed a little shaken when in reply to his query 'Where from?' we answered

'Greenland'. Presently, however, I got a lift into Lymington where I arranged for a tow that afternoon.

So in this undignified fashion *Baroque* ended her first voyage with me, a voyage that in some respects had been troublesome. Still we had all enjoyed ourselves – which is why one goes to sea – and in spite of her troubles *Baroque* had been what is called a happy ship. Once more I could appreciate the wisdom of Conrad's old shellback Singleton. 'Ships are all right, it's the men in them'; for whatever the faults of a ship, and *Baroque* had one or two, with a good crew these faults can generally be overcome. Conversely, however good the ship, with a poor crew one cannot get very far.

In climbing mountains or sailing the seas one often has to settle for less than one hoped. Instead of Ellesmere Island we had to settle for Greenland, and considering the short time we had to prepare her for a hard voyage she did well to get us there and the crew did well to get her back. In theory the skipper of a small boat should be able to do rather better than his crew anything that is required either on deck or aloft. With the handicap of age more had to be left to the crew and I was thankful to have Simon, active and competent, backed up by the others who were equally active if less competent. More important, however, is for them to have the right outlook. Activity can be instilled and competence can be acquired, but the right attitude must be ingrained – the cheerful acceptance and endurance of small privations and wearisome duties and the unquestioned belief that the success of the voyage and the care of the ship is what matters most. 'This ship, the ship we serve, is the moral symbol of our life.'

TRIUMPH AND TRIBULATION

Triumph and
Tribulation

First published by Nautical Publishing Company, 1977

Contents

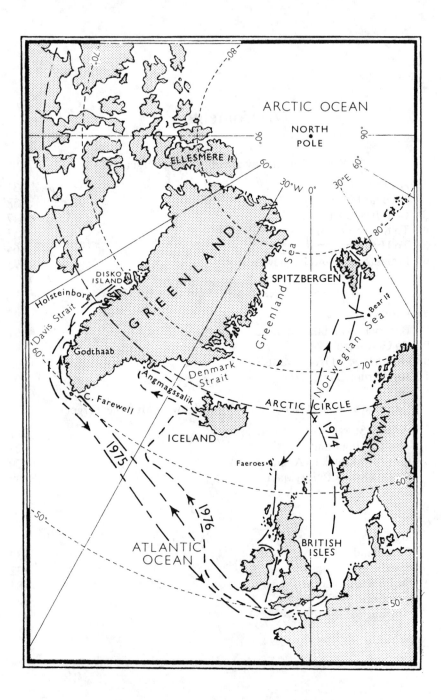

Part 1

Spitzbergen

CHAPTER ONE

A Fresh Start

COLONEL WILLIAM F. CODY, alias Buffalo Bill, earned his sobriquet by his association with buffaloes, an entirely successful association from the colonel's point of view. Years ago some American climbing friends took it into their heads to label me Himal Bill, a title that no doubt owed more to length of association with the Himalaya than to entire success. Having long since forsaken the Himalaya and instead made ten or more Greenland voyages I might now qualify for the title of Greenland Bill, or perhaps Eskimo Bill, not to be confused with Eskimo Nell, the heroine of a long sexual saga. To make so many voyages to the same region seems to imply a lack of imagination. From my point of view, however, Greenland is the ideal objective, combining remoteness, difficulty of access, the grandest scenery, an inexhaustible number of mountainous fjords each with its own character, and on the whole a region still sufficiently unfrequented for a man in a small boat to feel very remotely akin to the early seamen-explorers and to their successors the old whaling men from Hull, Leith, Dundee; and should he chance to find himself in difficulties among ice, to share in a much milder way their harsh experiences. All this being so, why go elsewhere? As the man from Texas advised: 'When you strike ile stop boring.'

Greenland had for me become a habit and habits are difficult to break. In 1974, however, we at last got out of the rut by going to Spitzbergen. Some might think this a change for the worse since it involved sailing much further north, so far north in fact that at one point we were within 600 miles of the North Pole. Though this proximity is illusory, since the 600 miles comprise mainly rough ice broken by leads of open water, it accounts for Spitzbergen having been chosen in the past as the jumping-off place for several attempts to reach the Pole, attempts that were remarkable for the variety of means employed. In 1827, from a base on the north coast, Perry and his naval party

made their effort by man-hauling the specially-fitted ship's boats. In 1897 Andrée began his fatal balloon flight from Danes Island at the north-west corner of Spitzbergen. Amundsen, in 1925, used two Dornier flying-boats; and in 1928, starting from Ny Alesund on the west coast, Nobile crashed the airship Italia on the return flight and in the subsequent search for the missing airship Amundsen lost his life. Finally, in 1931, Sir Hubert Wilkins, ahead of his time, used a submarine. In two of these ventures several lives were lost, and all except Parry's seemed designed to prove the capabilities of a particular form of transport.

Besides its proximity to the Pole Spitzbergen enjoys another feature that recommended it as a base for these sorties. In spite of the high latitude (up to 80°N.) the whole of the west coast is free from ice throughout the summer, and from July onwards the greater part of the north coast as well. Nowhere else in the world can a small, unstrengthened vessel safely reach so high a latitude, so that for anyone with the urge to penetrate remote regions, preferably mountainous, Spitzbergen is a powerful magnet and an obvious objective. For ten years it had figured high on my list but for one reason or another a visit had been deferred. For one thing, except on the east coast where access is less simple, it is all well known and, as Belloc says, when the unknown becomes known 'it loses that mysterious power of attraction which the unknown always possesses'. From early in the 17th century all the fjords, bays, and coves along the west coast were known and used by the whalers, mostly Dutch and British. When the whales and the whalers disappeared early in the 18th century Russian and Norwegian trappers appeared on the scene, nor did they confine themselves, like the whalers, to the coastal regions. In the present century expeditions to Spitzbergen have been numerous, particularly in the 'twenties and 'thirties when parties from Oxford and Cambridge worked there, crossing and recrossing it and no doubt climbing most of the mountains. And if all this were not enough there are the visiting cruise ships, starting with the *Lusitania* as far back as 1894 – a predecessor of the famous Cunarder of that name, built in 1903 and sunk by a German submarine in 1915.

Unlike Greenland, Spitzbergen has never had any indigenous population. Excluding those employed in the five or six coal-mines, which are worked all the year round, it is uninhabited. Yet Greenland, for most Europeans, is less well known, owing presumably to the absence there of any cruise ships; at least there have been none until this year (1974) when, I believe, a trial run was made to the west coast. The presence of ice on both the Greenland coasts is a discouraging factor for this kind of activity. On the other hand far fewer climbing parties go to Spitzbergen than to Greenland which, so much vaster, is enormously rich in mountains; nor do the comparatively few Spitzbergen peaks rank with those of Greenland for either stature, beauty, or climbing interest. The highest are in the interior where they are more like nunataks projecting from a miniature ice-cap – Mt Newton 5,445ft. is the highest – while those bordering the fjords within striking distance of a boat party, while steep and Alpine in character, are from only 2,000ft. to 3,000ft. high. Here, perhaps, was another reason for deferring my visit. No mountains are to be despised – what a world it would be were there none – yet ten years ago I may have felt that mountains of such modest height were below my standard, whereas by 1974, my altitude ceiling falling fast, there were just about my mark or even a little above it. Merit may be acquired merely by reaching some remote region, yet a voyage with an objective beyond that of getting there and back safely has more flavour, and for a mountaineer the objective is obviously mountains. In recent voyages therefore, since my own ardour and ability have diminished, I have always tried to include in the crew two climbers to undertake the serious climbing, leaving me free to potter on easier ground. Since nearly all the fjords on the west coast of Spitzbergen are littered with mountains we had a wide choice and would happily take whatever offered. In fact on this voyage climbing was a secondary objective. What I really wanted to do was to circumnavigate the island, a task harder to achieve probably than any of the mountains.

Unless we have been to a place our ideas of its geography are probably a little scattered. Spitzbergen, for instance, we all know of though strictly speaking there is no such place. The island I wanted to sail round is called Vestspitzbergen while the whole group or archipelago is known as Svalbard. The following quotation from the *Arctic Pilot* explains matters:

This ancient name (Svalbard) was first given nearly nine hundred years ago to a land discovered by the 'Northmen' some four days sail northward of Iceland, and from time to time there has been considerable controversy as to its exact location.

It is claimed that in all probability the archipelago was discovered by the Norwegians in 1194, and re-discovered by the Dutch navigator Barents in 1596. The English explorer Henry Hudson visited Svalbard in 1607.

In the Middle Ages all polar lands were held to be part of, or at least belong to Greenland, and the separateness of the two was not really determined until 1707, while the real circumnavigation of Vestspitzbergen was first performed by the Norwegian Elling Carlsen in 1863. The present Svalbard originates with the Treaty of Paris, 1920, by which measure the sovereignty of all lands embraced within the area between the parallels of Lat. 74 N. and 81 N. and the meridians of Long. 10 E. and 35 E. was vested in Norway. In August 1925 the Norwegian Government formally inaugurated their administration by sending an official, who hoisted their flag over the group, renaming it Svalbard.

Svalbard thus includes, Vestspitzbergen, Nordaustlandet, Barentsoya, Edgeoya, Prins Karls Forland, and the islets lying close to them, together with the smaller islands of Bjornoya, Hopen, Kong Karlsland, and Kvitoya.

Besides Elling Carlsen mentioned above as having circumnavigated Vestspitzbergen, another circumnavigator under sail was Frank Stuart Worsley, a professional seaman, who had been Shackleton's navigator on the famous voyage in the ship's lifeboat *James Caird* from Elephant Is. in the South Shetlands to South Georgia. But Worsley's track lay along the north coast of Vestspitzbergen, thence south to a point about half-way through Hinlopen Strait, and then counter-clockwise round Nordaustlandet, a far more difficult feat as there is usually a lot of ice east and north of Nordaustlandet. Worsley's vessel was the 100 ton trading barque *Island*, sheathed with steel plates forward for ice protection. He had with him an amateur crew of twelve. In the process they lost the propeller and so damaged the rudder that having got back to their starting point in Isfjord they finally accepted a tow to Norway.

It is time to introduce *Baroque*, the Bristol Channel pilot cutter that I had acquired in 1973 in place of *Sea Breeze*. The same year we sailed her to West Greenland. Before that voyage she had needed some attention, and after it she needed a lot more. She had been built in 1902 when the pilots based on Bristol Channel ports owned and sailed their own boats. After the First War, with the advent of steam, the pilotage service was put on a different footing, and the cutters, some sixty of them, were sold, many of them for conversion into yachts. It is now lost, but I once had a list of them and the prices they fetched – *Mischief*, for example, which I owned from 1954 until 1968, went for £350 and the top price was about £500. This sounds little enough but for today's money the figures would have to be multiplied by at least ten. One would like to know something about the pilot who gave his boat the curious name of *Baroque*, and why. According to the dictionary the word means whimsical, grotesque, irregular in shape. Grotesque might describe the doghouse which some misguided owner has stuck on her, but that is an addition of recent date. Pilot cutters had either a flush deck or perhaps a low cabin skylight. As for irregularity, detractors with keen eyes, viewing her sideways on, might point to her irregular sheer-line which sags a little amidships as if she were feeling tired. Which is not to be wondered at, though personally, I think the wavy sheerline gives her a rakish look. Nevertheless she is of a different shape to that of my two earlier boats, *Mischief* and *Sea Breeze*. She has less beam for a greater length, the bows are finer and more cutaway, and she is harder in the bilge. These finer lines do not seem to make her sail any faster than her predecessors while they markedly reduce the space on deck, particularly the foredeck, as well as the amount of stowage space below. However, in 1973 I had to take what I could get and with boats, as with women and horses, one must be 'to their faults a little blind, and to their virtues ever kind'. Always speak well of the bridge that has carried one over. There are not many boats built in 1902 that are still going strong or even going at all, and none that has sailed, as *Baroque* has, to Lat. 80° N.

On her first Greenland voyage she had proved a little wet; in fact a leak amidships under the galley floor might have been described by an oil-man as a gusher. On her return the leaks had to be stopped and some of the frames in way of the mast needed replacing or doubling. The chainplates on the starboard side had to be lengthened and a new keelband fitted. A jagged break in the keelband had contributed to our having become firmly enmeshed in a salmon net in Davis Strait. All this took time and March had arrived before the hull was being stopped preparatory to a coat of anti-fouling and her return into the water. Either from curiosity or too much zeal one of the men so employed stuck his knife clean through the hull between two planks. Mindful of their unhappy experience with *Sea Breeze* under similar circumstances the Yard hastened to give me the news by telephone and suggested a survey. In the winter of 1968–9 *Sea Breeze*, the Pilot Cutter I had just acquired in place of *Mischief*, had been hauled out for several months for a major overhaul during which no one had thought of examining the caulking. Sailing in May as usual for Greenland, while we were held up in the Solent for two days by strong westerlies, the caulking fell out piecemeal, and she had finally to be slipped again and recaulked throughout. So this time I asked my friend John Tew,* a surveyor, to have a look at the boat and I arranged to meet him in the yard. He had been concerned – in both senses of the word – over *Mischief* and *Sea Breeze* and naturally did not expect to find *Baroque* any more free from the ravages of time than they had been. When we met on the slipway where the boat was hauled out John Tew had finished his inspection. I could divine, without waiting to be told, that his news was bad:

> Yea, this man's brow, like to a title-leaf,
> Foretells the nature of a tragic volume.

The recaulking of the hull, a breast-hook to hold the bows together, and extra fastenings to make sure the coach-roof remained in place, were his minimum requirements. There were others but with the time and money available only these could be accepted, and even with these done John Tew, an exacting man, could not think of any class at Lloyds for which *Baroque* would qualify. The fact that we were bound for Arctic waters had to be considered. No waters are fool-proof and northern waters are less so than most. In the matter of weather, however, I should doubt if up there in *summer* the weather is any more inclement than around the British Isles.

This additional, unexpected expense was profoundly discouraging. It gave me a shock and like the shock treatment that leaves alcoholics with a disgust for alcohol, it almost extinguished my liking for old wooden boats or even for the sea. Why not retire to the middle of some continent, preferably mountainous, where the call of the sea would be inaudible. But hope springs eternal in even my breast and the gloom cast by this costly business was lightened by a satisfactory settlement of the crew problem, that annually recurring headache which often is not settled until the last moment and then not without misgivings.

Given a good crew the boat's shortcomings are of less moment while with a poor crew the ablest of boats seldom goes far. Simon Richardson, who had been a tower of strength on the previous voyage, wanted to come again, and in two volunteers from Yorkshire, Paul Reinsch and Alan Stockdale, who had sailed and climbed together, I felt I had two capable and reliable hands. We met on board one week-end during the winter and while this did not allow me to assess their respective characters and their likely behaviour at sea, at least it allowed them to assess the boat. Although a psychologist may think he can, in my experience a witch or a wizard is no more likely to divine a man's character and his suitability for a given task from a brief meeting. Such a meeting merely assures one that the man is blessed with the usual number of eyes and limbs, how he may react after a month or two's subjection to the strains and stresses imposed by the confined life in a small boat is but guesswork; unless, of course, having had ocean-going experience, he knows what to expect and what will be expected of him. Paul was a craftsman and knowledgeable about engines. He himself maintained a small boat at Whitehaven in which he and Alan had made a most enterprising voyage to St Kilda and thence to the small island of Rhona north of Cape Wrath. Both were keen climbers, well versed in modern technique and ironmongery, accustomed to camping and roughing it.

* John Tew died in October 1975.

For the first time for many years I had not even had to advertise for a cook, a post that is not easy to fill and not often filled to the satisfaction of everyone. Apart from standing no watches and having all night in, the cook, if he is up to his job, will find he has more work to do than anyone. A Cambridge undergraduate in his last year, Andrew Craig-Bennett, wrote to ask if I had a vacant berth. With the three I already had the only vacancy left was that of cook and when I had explained this to Andrew he gladly agreed to come in that capacity. He sounded to me the right sort so we omitted the formality of meeting, a formality, as I have said, of questionable value. He kept a boat of his own on the east coast where intricate shoals, short seas, and a harsh climate combine to form a rigorous training ground for amateur sailors. My only regret was that his experience would be more useful on deck than in the galley.

Thus a month before sailing day the boat was back in the water and I had what looked like a capable and experienced crew, so much so that I could promise myself an easy time, lying below reading mind-broadening literature, dodging the drips, digesting the duffs that Andrew would no doubt provide, and appearing on deck at infrequent intervals to take a sight. Such a complacent feeling of well-being – hubris, I think, is the word – is often the prelude to a change of fortune. Simon wrote to say that owing to the sudden death of his father he would have to withdraw. Thus, having no reserves in hand or even in sight, I went down to Lymington in mid-May in a thoughtful or even subdued mood. None of the feelers hastily put out had so far touched anything and it was late in the day to start advertising. Something might be hoped for from time and chance, factors upon which I have come to rely heavily, but time was short.

The two clear days I had before the crew started to arrive were spent replacing the wooden ratlines with rope. Although at Mylor the previous year the projecting ends had been sawn off they still stuck out far enough beyond the shrouds for the halyards to catch on them in a maddening way. I regretted having to do this because wooden ratlines always look neat whereas rope stretches and sags, and if much time has to be spent aloft, when navigating among ice, for example, wood is easier on the feet. The crew arrived on 20 May and we soon had the spars shipped and the rigging rove, leaving ample time for the innumerable, unforeseen jobs that keep cropping up when a boat is being got ready for sea.

Paul and Alan drove from Yorkshire in a car that Paul in a fit of extravagance unusual in Yorkshiremen had bought for £15. If he could keep that going, I reflected, he should have no difficulty with our engine. During the winter my friend Colin Putt, an engineering maestro from Australia, had put in a lot of work, among other things installing two new fuel tanks. The old ones were merely two 40 gal. oil drums which had rusted abominably. Colin replaced these with two of heavier gauge treated inside and out against rust. While fitting out we had a visitor, a tolerably ancient mariner, who told us that he had once owned *Baroque*, having come by her cheaply, in fact for nothing. Unwanted, neglected, she had been allowed to sink at her moorings in Cowes harbour. After some time under water she had been raised by our friend who for his trouble had been told to keep her. One could not help wondering whether the engine now installed had undergone this water cure.

Work progressed and sailing day approached without our coming any nearer to finding a fourth hand. The other three, who had not tried it, talked nonchalantly of sailing short-handed. The few likely converts that I knew had been drawn blank and to advertise at this late stage, even if successful, involved inevitable delay. The uninstructed might think that at a place like Lymington which more or less revolves round yachts – a thousand or so berthed there would be a conservative estimate – there would be a queue of eager applicants for a free holiday of four months at sea. I knew better. 'I have no great hopes of Birmingham,' Mrs Elton remarked, 'there's something dire about the sound of it.' Similarly I had no great hopes of Lymington. There may be nothing dire about the sound of it but I suspected that its yachting fraternity, wedded to modern boats, might think there was something dire about the sound of *Baroque*.

On this occasion those fickle allies time and chance did not fail us. About four days before we were due to sail a young Irishman, David White, turned up, having heard of our pressing need either through Simon Richardson or a friend of Simon's whom he had met in a bar. Bar acquaintances are not necessarily suspect, much depends on the bar. In *Mischief's* time, when two surveyors had condemned her, I had greatly benefited from the advice of one such chance-met acquaintance. David looked about 18 but was in fact 25 and had some unspecified job in Harrods. He knew nothing of the sea or of boats, had no special skills, and indeed nothing to recommend him except a cheerful smile, our sore need, and the fact that he could quit his job and be ready in time. With the three responsible men I already had I could well afford to include one greenhorn and on past occasions have had to be content with a far less favourable ratio. So I took him on and needless to say, later that same day I had an offer from a much more promising candidate whom I had to refuse. It had been touch and go, nor was I confident that David would join as promised. He seemed a volatile character, as bar acquaintances are apt to be.

CHAPTER TWO

To Bear Island

DAVID KEPT his word and we sailed on 1 June according to plan. As the great Von Moltke observed, few plans withstand contact with the enemy. If they do, and the enemy in this case was time, it is all the more satisfying. Casting off at the start of a long voyage is a pregnant moment, for me pregnant with doubts; doubts even about the wisdom of the voyage, of the crew, of the skipper himself, or whether some vital item has not been forgotten. Above all I was worried by horrid remembrances of *Baroque*'s behaviour on several occasions on her first voyage under power; particularly when we had attempted to leave Umanak, a small harbour with a narrow entrance, the entrance encumbered with grounded bergs, and a stiff breeze blowing directly in. After just missing hitting first a berg and then a rock we returned to our moorings and finally had to be towed out. The large propeller seemed to be so far offset on the port side that even with full contrary helm she edged constantly to starboard. To turn to port the engine had to be in neutral and with any sort of head wind, as at Umanak, she became unmanageable. To counteract this awkward tendency Colin Putt had made a drogue, a small sea-anchor with a heavy iron frame, to be streamed from midships on the port side to about level with the propeller. In theory the drag of this would turn her head to port. There had been no opportunity for a rehearsal and Lymington river, thick with yachts and the occasional ferry, seemed no place for an unrehearsed performance. Instead we took a tow through the narrowest part between the ferry stage and the Marina where the fairway is about 20 yards wide, and then, with prayers to the river gods and encouraging noises to *Baroque*, we cast off the tow-line. Men and women sometimes behave in unexpected ways, so do boats. Feeling, perhaps, that the eyes of England, or at least Lymington, were upon her *Baroque* played no tricks and answered the helm well enough. I had no difficulty in sticking to the strait and narrow path. At the river mouth we hoisted sail and turned east, bound for the North Sea, first stop Bear Island.

Frank Bullen, in the *Cruise of the Cachalot*, records that the old sperm-whaling ships, mostly American (one of them, by the way, is preserved in the Marine Museum at Mystic, Connecticut), in the course of voyages that might last two or three years, seldom called at any port. They avoided ports like the plague. All that they needed to replenish was water and the captain took care to do this at some remote, uninhabited island – Aldabra, for example, where the crew had neither the temptation nor the opportunity to desert. It is an example that I have found it advisable to follow in so far as to avoid if possible, a call at any port on the way out. Bound for East Greenland, for instance, it would be wiser not to call at Iceland. Bear Is. is only some 200 miles short of Spitzbergen, and while its name and its remoteness alike demanded a visit on our part, I reckoned it far enough from home to be, as it were, a point of no return should any of the crew by then be having second thoughts.

We made a brisk start, passing Dungeness at noon next day. The same evening, with Calais in sight, we went about to begin the long haul to the north, from Lat. 50° N. to Lat. 75° N., some fifteen hundred miles as the crow flies and no doubt many more as *Baroque* would sail. Even at that early stage it seemed likely that David would never be of much use on deck, whereas Andrew, who between spells in the galley lent us an able hand, would obviously be in his element. I therefore arranged for them to change places, a step that required some self-denial. The few days of Andrew's reign in the galley had been so brilliant that it seemed the act of a madman or of a sour ascetic to cut it short, while if David were to show as little aptitude in the galley as he had on deck we faced lean times. At the moment Paul and Alan were indifferent to food having not yet found their sea-legs. They would not notice any difference between the master's dishes and those that would now be served up by the apprentice. But besides cooking food Andrew had an amazing ability to eat it, while I, too, liked my victuals and am not over fond of resisting temptation where food is concerned. At sea, at any rate, where priorities are easily determined, one can agree with Epicurus that the beginning and root of all good is the pleasure of the stomach; even wisdom and culture must be referred to this.

Those twin topics food and seasickness must, I'm afraid, loom large in the early stages of any voyage. Paul was our chief sufferer. For many days even a moderately rough sea laid him out, so many that I became concerned, fearful that he might prove to be another chronic case for whom use and wont is no cure. For more than a fortnight he ate little enough and looked accordingly wan and spectre-like. However once the corner had been turned he reacted strongly, almost startlingly, making up for past omissions and speedily over-hauling or out-eating Andrew who until then had been our chief cormorant. The contest between these two was stubborn. Andrew did not surrender the crown easily but the writing was on the wall when Paul assumed what hitherto had been Andrew's prerogative, taking care of anything left over and scraping the bottoms of the pans. Neither of them went as far as Sherpas do, holding the plate up to the face and licking it, or if mugs were being used, as for pemmican soup or tea and tsumpa, then polishing out the mug with the forefinger and licking that. We had with us some copies of *The Times* which had accumulated at Lymington where I had not had the leisure for battling with the Crossword puzzles. Doing them now, seeking inspiration from the adjacent Personal Column, my eye lit on a curious notice. I showed it to Paul and Andrew and stuck it in the log-book in case they wanted to follow it up when they got back: 'Anorexia Nervosa, Compulsive fasting, stuffing. Box No. ...'

On the 3rd, the wind fresh and free, we passed the Galloper light vessel. When the wind died we ran the engine in order to learn what effect Colin Putt's patent steering drogue would have. She certainly required a little less help to keep her straight but as we had found when coming down Lymington river the fault had largely corrected itself. Her improved steering when under power as compared with the previous voyage is another unsolved sea mystery. Becalmed once more on the following day, not far from the Dogger Bank, we caught two nice cod on the bottom in 20 fms., and later two mackerel also from deep down. Fish and chips for supper followed by a duff of Andrew's making, for David was still feeling his way, and frequently stumbling, among the foothills of cookery, far from the gastronomic heights.

If the navigator is asked by one of the crew where the ship is, he feels obliged to commit himself or at least hazard a guess. On the other hand, if he is not asked and he thinks he knows where he is, he should not let pride tempt him into announcing to a suitably awe-struck crew what sea-mark or cape they will presently sight and where, or, as in this instance, what they will not sight. But every ass loves to hear himself bray. I thought we were too far east to sight Smith's Knoll light vessel and rashly imparted this unimportant piece of knowledge to the crew. No one unkindly reminded me of this. It was humiliation enough to read later the log-book entry to the effect that we had left that particular light vessel close to port at 4 am. Soon after breakfast we sighted a Shell–Esso gas platform and were in fact carried rather too close to it by a strong tide. A helicopter landed on it as we passed. For the Dogger area where we now were a gale warning had been put out. About Force 6 was all the wind we had and enough, too, for Paul and Alan to succumb and for David to experience some mishaps in the galley. Scalded cats are a common and reliable standard for judging leaping powers, and since David's back where the kettle landed had not been scalded, nor even marked, the leap he gave, and the accompanying yell, were the more remarkable. After this, and in the prevailing conditions, he did well to produce sausage and mash for supper, even if the sausages had to be scraped off the floor. Like onions, no ship should be without Tabasco Sauce. It gives a relish to the plainest fare and is probably a powerful germicide.

On the whole by the end of our first week at sea, in spite of Paul's persistent sickness and frequent bad news from the galley, I felt reasonably satisfied. We were well up the North Sea, about 150 miles east of Dundee and a like distance from the southern coast of Norway. The boat was drier as, of course, she should have been after recaulking and with a newly painted deck; but in any seaway she made quite a bit of water and there were still enough drips from the deckhead to be annoying. Plastic sheeting and drawing pins were again in demand. One reason for contentment lay in the crew who were cheerful, hard-working, and apparently enjoying themselves. In this last respect I was mistaken. A week had been enough for young David who now asked to be put ashore, life at sea falling short of his expectations and the prospect of months more of it quite insupportable. Request not granted. Quite apart from the replacement problem, probably insoluble, we could not afford to waste days beating to some port in Scotland, still less did I want to visit the complicated Norwegian coast of which I had charts only for the most northerly part. In a small crew the presence of one unhappy, unwilling member may well cause trouble. Happily I had no need to worry about that. The other three had the success of the voyage at heart as much as I had, that and the safety of the ship were all that mattered to them.

In Lat. 57° N., Long. 03° E., about ninety miles off the Norwegian coast, we sighted an enormous concrete island, a miniature town crowned by a chimney that almost rivalled that of Fawley, belching a flame of natural gas. Whatever one may think of the consequences of North Sea oil, some good, some possible dire, or of the curious conviction of the Scots or their loud-mouthed spokesmen, that they not only put the stuff there in the first place, but rediscovered it, provided the money and the know-how to sink the wells and bring it ashore, the sight of these man-made islands are astonishing testimonies to the enterprise and technical skill of twentieth-century man, led, to be honest, by Americans. The North Sea is no tranquil lake and the skill and seamanship needed to site precisely and then build these structures is almost beyond belief.

A man describing a passage such as this through well-known waters, unless he can paint in words the ever-changing scene of sea and sky in faint imitation of a Conrad, is reduced to recording trivial events such as the making up of a Norwegian courtesy flag which we had forgotten to bring. Sufficient red, white, and blue bunting were obtained by cutting up signal flags (which we were never likely to use) and we had made careful note of the right way to combine these colours from the occasional Norwegian vessel that passed with its ensign flying. After doing the rough groundwork I handed it over to Paul who was a much better hand with a needle. Then there was the curious encounter with the German tanker from Hamburg which having passed ahead of us westbound, when two miles away turned round and steamed straight back towards us. As he passed for the second time I hailed him with the loudspeaker – 'Are you all right?' – a question usually asked by the steamer of the yacht. We got no answer.

We read in Shakespeare of 'the poet's eye, in a fine frenzy rolling', similarly though more coarsely, when writing of these voyages I am occasionally able to make my own mouth water (and perhaps the mouths of a few equally uncouth readers) by recollecting some of the more memorable meals we enjoyed. In fact had I but a less defective memory and more descriptive powers it would be a grateful task in the long winter evenings of old age to compile a book of memorable meals – Gleanings of a Glutton, or some such title. A similar thing, more wholesome and less enervating, might be done for one's memorable bathes. But on this outward voyage, I'm afraid, meals were memorable only for the wrong reason – things improved immensely on the way home – and had it not been for Andrew hovering and helping in the background we had fared but ill. At sea the punctuality of meal-times is important, so that the man going on watch can have his meal beforehand, and the man coming off can have his before it gets cold. This calls for careful timing on the part of the cook and as yet David's timing was erratic. His first attempt to down us with a duff, a praiseworthy ambition, led to the stew appearing an hour-and-a-half late at 9 pm. Having coated himself and the galley floor with flour and squeezed the remnants into the largest available saucepan, he found he had no room on the stove for that and the stew. We could, of course, have had the pudding first like they do in Iceland, there is no need to be hide-bound in these matters. On another occasion a delay of two hours was explained by the belated discovery that he had filled the stove with methylated spirit instead of paraffin, a sort of Irish bull. Flour, I admit, is intractable stuff and in the hands of the amateur liable to spread itself. In the Himalaya after the day's march, I used to turn to and make bread, inside a tent if it happened to be raining. Emerging from the tent on one occasion, my boots white with flour, the inference was obvious, and henceforward my loaves were known as 'Foot-bread'. But as I have said, when David's vagaries became too much for Andrew, threatening to thwart his over-keen appetite, he took charge of the supper to our great benefit as well as his. Bully beef pie followed by syrup tart and baked custard is a random example that obviously bears his signature. He also tried to impress upon David the necessity of keeping things in their proper place, the galley shelves rapidly becoming a hurrah's nest, everything on top and nothing to hand; and having taken a degree in English he painted on the galley shelf in large letters, misquoting Shakespeare, 'Every item has a local habitation and a name.'

By the end of the second week we had not done so well. Head winds and short, steep seas, followed by a bout of hot, windless, anti-cyclonic weather slowed us down and pushed us close to the Norwegian coast. We logged only 280 miles in the week and by no means all of that was in the right direction. By then we had finished the fresh bread and had started on what I call the 'hard-bake' – bread that after slicing is rebaked. This lot had been cut too thick, baked too long, and was abominably hard. Instead of a bread-knife we used a fret-saw. By the 13th we had drifted to within ten miles of the coast south of Bergen, the barometer as high as ever at 1,030 mbs., no wind and no signs of any. We enjoyed sun and sea bathing but at the end of the third windless day it occurred to me to check our water supply. The main tank proved to be nearly dry, implying that we had used some 4 gallons a day instead of the normal allowance of 2½ gallons. More probably the header tank which supplies the main tank, owing to an air-lock, had not been full when we started. The tank that lurks beneath the cabin table, thus keeping cool those who sit round the table, was untouched so that we had twenty days supply in hand. Bear Is. was still some 700 miles away. Assuming the worst, that our daily average did not improve, it would be a close-run thing; but we were getting a good lift from the Norwegian current which sets north up the coast, and the spell of calm weather, unequalled in these latitudes in my experience, must soon end. The 'hard-bake', too, needed to be conserved. We cut out bread for breakfast and David tried his hand successfully at soda-bread, his native product. Is it possible that the daily intake of bicarbonate of soda in his bread accounts for an Irishman's effervescent behaviour?

In N. Lat. 65° the fine weather packed up and we were to enjoy no more until close to Spitzbergen. Bear Is. and the seas for a long way south are noted for overcast skies and fog. After carrying a fresh south-westerly wind all night, by midday of the 21st we had logged 84 miles and I reckoned that by tea-time we should be north of the Arctic Circle. Accordingly we began our celebrations in time by having a slug of whisky in our tea. Shortly after a hail from on deck gave us the welcome news that Father Neptune, or his Arctic representative, had come on board, apparently over the bows. By coincidence I had just made some baggy wrinkle for the topping lifts to save the mainsail from chafe and except for this round the waist he was naked, but the flippers on his feet, goggles, crown and trident, and a red beard, together made up a striking ensemble. He concluded a short, seamanlike speech of welcome by presenting me with a scroll, the necessary passport giving us the freedom of his domain. In return I gave him what the French call *un grand coup de whisky*, for in spite of being native to those parts he was obviously feeling cold. Andrew took charge of the subsequent banquet which comprised risotto Bolognese, alleviated by prunes and baked custard.

Even in the vicinity of N. Lat. 70° it was less cold than might be expected, less cold than it would have been in that latitude off Greenland, owing no doubt to the Norwegian current still running from the south. The sea temperature did not drop appreciably until we met what is called the

Spitzbergen current which runs west out of the cold Barents Sea. As usual on these voyages we were keeping a weather log for the Meteorological Office. Obviously we cannot transmit our observations at the time as does the great fleet of Voluntary Observing Ships – some 500 Selected ships and 50 Supplementary ships – but in the absence of any observations at all from waters little frequented by British ships our observations are of use for the records and are always welcome at Bracknell. Every six hours we recorded wind, cloud, visibility, pressure, air and sea temperatures. At the Arctic Circle the sea temperature was 55° F. and had fallen to 39° F. by the time we reached Bear Is. In a war-time debate about maritime affairs in which the subject of shark repellent had been mentioned, Winston Churchill took the opportunity to remark that 'His Majesty's Government was totally opposed to sharks'. As might be expected from a modern edition of Col Blimp I am totally opposed to the metric system and since the thermometers provided by Bracknell are graduated in Centigrade I have taken the trouble to translate back into Fahrenheit. Most of us had already donned our winter woollies and when the wind permitted we had the cabin heater lit. With much wind or the mainsail sheeted in, the down draught off the sail proved too much for the cabin heater and we had to do without. Besides colder water, the Spitzbergen current brings with it a lot of driftwood, massive logs brought down by rivers from the forests of Siberia. The east coast of Jan Mayen Is. is thickly strewn with such logs and hardly any of the Svalbard beaches that we visited were without their quota. On dark nights in a rough sea these great logs might be a hazard to a small vessel of light construction, but in these high latitudes it is late in the autumn before the nights get dark when no such vessels are likely to be about.

Before reaching Bear Is. we had some roughish weather. On three occasions in the last week of June we were either hove-to or lying-a-try, that is to say lying broadside on with no sails set. All this wind came from an easterly quarter so that by the 29th we had been set down nearly a hundred miles west of the island, so far that I was tempted to give it up and carry on for Spitzbergen in spite of water problems. Happily the easterlies subsided, the sea fell calm, and as we began making up lost ground the problem of finding Bear Is. began to loom large. Nowadays the navigator has to know only his own position, his objective's position being definitely fixed; but before the days of chronometers and Admiralty charts the navigator must have had as much or more doubt about the position of the island or cape he hoped to make as he had about the position of his ship, a consideration that makes the voyages of those days even more a cause for astonishment and admiration. Owing to the prevailing overcast our last noon sight for latitude had been two days before, and on the evening of the 30th a single snap sight from a fleeting glimpse of sun had put us 20 miles west of our dead reckoning position. With no certainty about our latitude this sight might well be far out.

Early on the morning of 1 July we handed the sails, there being no wind to speak of, and after breakfast started the engine and kept it going ruthlessly in the spirit of 'Pike's Peak or bust'. Assuming that our latitude was correct I determined to get into what I hoped would be the same longitude as Bear Is.

and then steer north, trusting largely to Providence and to a lesser extent to birds. As the *Pilot* observes:

At this time of year (summer) the island swarms with guillemots, and the flocks of these birds and the direction of their flight are of great use to vessels attempting to make Bjornoya in thick weather.

Which was exactly our position, for throughout the day we were pestered by drifting banks of fog. I spent hours on deck on the slight chance of the sun appearing and the still slighter chance that when it did the horizon immediately below would be clear. It did appear once for about ten seconds, long enough to take a sight, had not the horizon been indistinguishable, leaden-hued sky merging into leaden-hued sea, with no telling where one began or the other ended.

The guillemots had certainly increased in numbers – we felt we were getting warm – but were flying in all directions searching for food rather than Bear Is. Indeed in the prevailing calm conditions and no hours of darkness why should they bother to go home to roost. We would watch a flock set out purposefully as if it had to get there before closing time only to see it alight about half a mile away, merely changing its feeding ground. In one of Neville Shute's best stories, *The Trustee in the Tool-room*, there is a character who successfully navigates his small boat from San Francisco to Hawaii by watching aeroplanes and birds. The vapour trails of planes are, I should think better guides than birds; one could certainly sail from New York, say, and arrive at Shannon by following them.

In order to have supper in peace we stopped the engine. We had finished our sausage and mash and were contemplating a noble duff, David by now having mastered the art, when from on deck came the cry of 'Land'. Sure enough, its top just showing over a bank of fog, there could be seen the hard, black outline of a high rock. It was Stappen, the 610ft. high stack lying off the south end of Bear Island, some five miles away and broad on the port bow. Whether attributable to luck rather than skill, a landfall such as this gives the small boat sailor unbounded pleasure. The doubt, the long suspense, and then the satisfaction and thrill of seeing this slender black, pinnacle floating above the fog, the island itself still completely hidden. For me it compensated for some hideous mistakes of the past and even took some of the sting out of the Smith's Knoll episode. Among some memorable landfalls it reminded me of our first sighting of Heard Is. in the Southern Ocean when from 40 miles away the snow-capped summit of Big Ben (9,005ft.) appeared framed in a patch of blue in the middle of a great cumulus cloud high above the sea.

Against a strong west-going current we made slow progress towards Stappen so we altered course to north in order to round the north-west corner of the island. The Norwegian weather station Nordhamm, for which we were making, lies about half-way along the north coast. Closer in to the shore there were several trawlers about, for the island lies at the southern end of the Spitzbergen Bank which is a rich fishing ground. The *Arctic Pilot* has this description:

Bjornoya, the southernmost island of Svalbard, lies about 140 miles SSE of the southern point of Vestspitzbergen and about 225 miles NNW of the northern coast of

Norway. It is triangular in shape with the apex pointing southwards and it is about 9 miles long and 8 miles wide. The northern part is a plateau 110ft. to 150ft. high cut up by numerous shallow lakes, the coast being bounded by vertical cliffs. The south-eastern and southern parts are mountainous, the east coast being dominated by Miseryfjellet, a table mountain 1,758ft. high. The southern part of the island is also bounded by almost vertical cliffs, which in places reach an elevation of 1,300ft. In many places there are beaches at the foot of the cliffs on which landing can be affected but only in exceptionally favourable weather. Owing, however, to the very steep cliffs, it is only in a few places that access to the interior can be gained from the beaches. There are no sheltered harbours in Bjornoya and vessels surprised by the weather are forced to find shelter on the lee side of the island and to anchor close in under the cliffs. In fine weather anchorage may be obtained anywhere round the island. Within a distance of about 2 miles offshore there are depths of from 8 fms. to 20 fms., the bottom in most places sand.

The island was discovered by the Dutch navigator William Barents in 1596 on a voyage in search of the North-east passage. He called it, in Dutch, Bear Island. Stephen Bennet, who visited it seven years later, called it Cherrie Is. after his patron Sir Francis Cherrie, and the erroneously spelt Cherry Is. still appears on some charts. Whalers and walrus hunters were busy there throughout the 17th century and in the 18th century they were mainly Russians who hunted and wintered on the island. They were succeeded by Norwegians who finally finished off any bear or walrus that were left. There are coal seams on the northern part of the island and during the First War coal was mined, work being finally abandoned in 1925. Tunheim, the mining town, had at its best a population of 250.

An island situated so far north and yet not far enough north nor quite high enough to maintain glaciers and snow fields, has the worst of both worlds and appears truly desolate. 'A wilderness of barren stones' is the *Pilot*'s description, though in favoured spots there is some scant vegetation, saxifrages and a few grasses. The piles of whale and walrus bones littering the shores, and the graves of long-dead hunters, only emphasise the dreariness of the landscape. But teeming life still exists in the form of birds and during the breeding season the cliffs are almost covered with guillemots, little auks, kittiwakes, fulmar, and the burgomaster gull.

Turning eastwards along the north coast we soon spotted the radio masts and buildings of the weather station. An 'open bay' is the official description of Nordhamm and when we closed it at midnight, so little shelter did it seem to offer that I thought the word 'bay' might as well have been omitted. We anchored in 4 fms. with an ugly looking rock reef some fifty yards astern. A weather station is on duty all round the clock. As we came in they were busy launching a boat and presently six guests crammed into the cabin to be entertained with cocoa and rum.

CHAPTER THREE

Bear Island and Isfjord

ONLY ONE of our guests, who proved to be the Base leader, spoke fluent English. Since so many of the Danes and Norwegians I have met over the years spoke English, this surprised me, and it is a tribute to the efficiency of their schools that few of those who did speak English had ever visited England. So strong is the assumption I now have that any Dane or Norwegian will immediately understand what is said to him in English, that those who do not are at once written off as ignorant foreigners. And this by a man who speaks only his own language and very little of that.

Having seen our guests safely away in the small hours we met them again at breakfast in their spacious and comfortable mess-room. In fact the main building with everything under the one roof, its big double-glazed windows overlooking the sea, might be described by an estate agent as a desirable sea-side residence for a man of means with a large family – lounge, dining room, 14 bedrooms, the usual offices, own lighting and power plant, central heating throughout, shower baths and sauna, small private landing ground, own moorings, water frontage. In summer a ship calls once a week and in winter mail is dropped by air. Except, perhaps, in early spring the island is usually ice-free, while trawlers fish all the year round in the neighbouring waters. This accessibility is in striking contrast to that of another Norwegian weather station on the island of Hopen in the Barents Sea only some two hundred miles north-east of Bear Is.

We were told that there they had been troubled with Polar Bears and that the Svalbard Governor's own vessel, a vessel strengthened against ice, had within the last fortnight been stopped by ice when trying to reach Hopen. Later in the summer, on our way home, I had hoped to call at Hopen but by then things were not going as planned.

In relays we made use of the showers and sauna, for in view of the open anchorage two of us had always to be on board. Had not the wind been well north of east the high cliffs immediately to the east would have afforded shelter; throughout our short stay this wind gradually increased and without Norwegian assistance we should have had a wet time ferrying off water in our small pram dinghy. As it was they organised our water supply and brought it off in their motor launch. Their cook baked ten loaves specially for us and they also gave us a quantity of eggs and paraffin. In my experience these far-flung weather stations are exceedingly generous to visitors like ourselves; no doubt partly on the account of their rarity, just as in those countries where travellers are few there is most hospitality.

Many of the numerous lakes and tarns on the island hold Arctic char, and the Base leader showed us with pride an aquarium he had built in which he was breeding them. He had also successfully incubated a guillemot egg and was having problems in feeding the voracious chick with the right food. Back on board we spent an uneasy night, a stiff breeze blowing directly on shore. Instead of hauling the dinghy on board we stupidly left it lying astern and none of us on anchor watch noticed when the painter parted. In the morning we spotted it lying on the beach beyond the rock reef not far from our stern. In this reef there was one narrow gap through which the dinghy had found its way, ending up unharmed on the shingle beach instead of breaking up on the rocks, a piece of luck that our carelessness hardly merited. After breakfast we broke out our inflatable dinghy in which Andrew and I went ashore paying out a long warp, for with the wind then blowing the row back would be strenuous. Having made our farewells at the base we carried the wooden dinghy to a corner of the beach where the breakers were most moderate and then rowed back tied in tandem, one man in each dinghy, helped by the line from *Baroque* and another line held by a shore party to keep us from being blown on to some rocks. We got under way with difficulty owing to *Baroque*'s reluctance to pay off on the seaward tack in contrast to her suicidal desire to rush towards the land. With little enough room for manoeuvre in that direction we swallowed our pride, downed the mains'l, and got clear by using the engine. A fine breeze just forward of the beam made up for the usual overcast sky and the absent sun, and at the pace we were going Bear Is. soon disappeared in the murk. At 6 pm the air temperature was 36° F. and the sea 34° F. I added another sweater and a thicker pair of trousers.

All that night the continuing wind gave us a splendid sail, and for the first time on the voyage we scored a century, registering on the log 117 miles from noon to noon. We ran clear of the overcast, too. By 8 am we had the snows of Vestspitzbergen in sight glistening in the sun, while far to the north there was not a cloud in the sky. When Sorkapp, the southernmost point, came abeam to starboard we were in the lee of the land and quieter water. Some pack-ice had accumulated round the cape and we sailed through a line of small floes that had drifted to leeward. By this time we, too, had run into sunshine, a cloudless sky overhead and a sparkling, blue sea flecked with bits of ice. This is the sort of weather I have come to expect north of the Arctic Circle and do not always get, but for the next two months similar flawless days far outnumbered those with cloud and rain. For the past fortnight we had seen precious little sun and we now began to feel reasonably warm. That evening we had the wide Hornsund fjord abeam and greatly admired its fine peak Hornsundtind (4,691ft.), the most impressive mountain, I think, that we were to see. That night, thanks to the clear sky, we were allowed for the first time to see the sun at midnight; for us he would not be below the horizon again until the first week of August.

In the lee of the land *Baroque*'s immoderate burst of speed could not be sustained. Except for two short-lived blasts that obliged us to reef we had little enough wind in the next two days to Longyearbyen. These squally winds struck off the mouths of fjords and were no doubt caused by the funnelling effect of their mountainous shores. We met several ships, for what with colliers and cruise ships the west coast as far up as Isfjord is well frequented. One vessel closed us to speak and I regretted that the helmsman had stood on without calling me up, for we learnt later that she was the *Nordsyssel* with the Governor on board returning from a second and successful trip to Hopen. Our second day in Spitzbergen waters proved equally brilliant and the night not less so. As the Psalmist wrote: 'The night shineth as the day; the darkness and the light are both alike.' For the sake of 'One-upmanship' I took a meridian sight at midnight instead of noon. In contrast to the usual procedure of deducting the sun's altitude – in this case 10.38 – one adds it to 90° and then deducts the sun's declination; so that 100.38 less the declination of 22.32 gave our latitude as 78.06, provided this excursion into higher mathematics is not at fault and has been understood. With the land close aboard and most of it identifiable this hard-won piece of knowledge was not essential, but I felt that the midnight sun was there for use as well as an ornament to be admired and wondered at.

Longyearbyen, the administrative capital of Svalbard, lies some thirty miles up Isfjord, the largest fjord of those parts, 55 miles in length and 10 to 15 miles wide. Hudson (1603) called it the Great Indraught and it was Poole (1610) who named it Ice Sound. In spite of the name it is usually ice-free from June to November and is not completely frozen over until the end of December. The flat-topped hills of the southern side, with not a glacier to be seen, are in sharp contrast with the high, serrated rock ridges to the north, ridges that are separated by large glaciers which reach right down to the waters of the fjord. Longyearbyen itself lies in Adventfjord, a short arm of the main fjord on the southern side. On 7 July, after beating into Adventfjord, when we started the engine it chose that critical moment to go hay-wire, emitting clouds of white smoke. The small jetty was already overcrowded by the two vessels lying there, *Nordsyssel* and a Russian tug. So we shaped to anchor close off the jetty and had time for only one cast of the lead before coming gently to rest on the bottom. As we discovered the engine had no power in reverse, indeed by now it had no power at all. It was about low water so we adjourned for lunch, declining the kind offer of the Russian tug to pull us off.

We were boarded by an electrician from the coalmine, a man who had plenty to say and no complaints about life in Longyearbyen – good pay, no taxes, and no temptations to riotous living. In these querulous days it is encouraging to meet anyone without a grouse or a grudge. Among other interesting things he pointed out to us a small boat used by two enterprising Norwegians for collecting driftwood logs which they cut up into saleable timber. When we were afloat again, his dinghy with its outboard together with our long sweeps, were enough to move *Baroque* to the other side of the jetty where we anchored in 2 fms. It is all shallow and not good holding ground; during our stay we seemed to be either sitting on the bottom or dragging. The halcyon weather of the last few days had momentarily ended and under a lowering sky the beach of black sand where we used to land, strewn with lumps of coal, old rope, and other rubbish, wore a forlorn look. Overhead a cable-way carried coal in great buckets to the coal wharf a mile to the west.

On a wet day even the Garden of Eden may have looked sad and Long-yearbyen, whose very name suggests length and dreariness, is no garden. The drizzle that set in next day merely deepened its gloom. Near the jetty are a store, the power station, and engineering shops; on the hill above are the Governor's house and the church; from there one walks nearly a mile up a bleak, barren valley flanked by abandoned mine workings to reach the township proper, comprising the Post Office, a shop, the Coal Company's offices, and the houses of its employees. A small glacier at the valley head is a cheering sight. Attached to the Post Office is a sort of lounge and coffee bar where one may relax, if that is the word, and let the busy tide of Longyearbyen roll by. I noticed outside almost every house one or more skidoos, a Canadian contraption for motoring on ice. In winter, I believe, they have skidoo races.

Nobody in Longyearbyen walked and none of the vehicles that sped along the road between the harbour and the township ever offered us a lift. We probably rated as tourists. On this wet day it must have been the coal dust from the overhead cable-way that turned the mud at the roadside black, and the black footmarks that we left on the immaculate floor of the bakery earned us a severe rebuke from the baker. Buying bread involved paper-work and a lot of walking. The baker's bill had to be taken to the Company's office and paid, and then armed with the receipt one walked back to the bakery to collect the bread. I had a talk with the friendly Governor who put in a word on our behalf to the manager of the Coal Company which in effect runs Longyearbyen. We were allowed to buy what we needed at the Company store and they put at our disposal a diesel engine mechanic.

Paul had been wrestling with the engine ever since we arrived and had to confess himself baffled. Hence the calling in of the mechanic who after spending eight hours on the job could only suggest that we might need a new injector pump. Since the part would have to be ordered from Norway and brought out this did not help very much. Nevertheless, for his eight hours work the Company, having their shareholders to consider, billed me for £52. This exorbitant sum shook me and outraged Paul's frugal Yorkshire instincts so much that he immediately set to work again on the engine, discovered at last that the timing was at fault, and soon had it running perfectly. Although we had got nothing for our money the bill had to be paid in full, the Company insisting on the cash and not caring who got the credit. Meantime, at the end of our second day here David was missing. He had gone ashore for what was to be two hours and had not returned.

On the whole it had been a trying day but I see from my diary that Andrew and I sat up till midnight playing chess. Before leaving we had been unable to find a sea-going chess set – one in which the pieces will stay on a moving board – so Andrew set to work with his penknife and by this time had finished a set of hand-carved pieces complete with pegs at the base to fit into the handsome board that Alan made. The chessmen finished, Andrew had tried his hand at ships in bottles, while Paul, not to be outdone, started carving seals and polar bears.

At midnight we all turned in and for the first and last time set no anchor watch in the belief that we were securely anchored. It was a disturbed night.

At 1 am David announced his arrival on the beach and having been brought off fell into the water while climbing on board. Alan, roused by the commotion, went to help Paul who was having trouble fishing out David, for it is no easy matter hauling up a more or less inanimate body. I was on deck myself at 3 am when all seemed well, but half an hour later there was a bump and we found ourselves alongside a small vessel anchored much further out. Veering all the cable we had we dropped clear astern of her and then found that our cable was foul of her anchor. The two men on board whose sleep we had disturbed proved to be remarkably good-natured. Instead of venting a torrent of Norwegian Billingsgate they calmly made their appreciation, as the military say, got their anchor up, freed our cable, and anchored themselves again further away from the enemy.

David's long search for an escape from *Baroque* or an alternative means of getting home had failed, as inevitably it must in a place like Longyearbyen, especially if the searcher is without money. Consequently he was in a morose, unhappy mood, and most unwilling to face the inevitable. He had not yet attained to Lord Curzon's lofty philosophy: 'It is inevitable, therefore it can be approved'. But once we had left Longyearbyen, when with a little wishful thinking one could say that we were homeward-bound, he pulled himself together, cast care aside, and worked in the galley with zest and great success, running it more or less like clockwork with fewer and fewer calls upon Andrew to do some winding. Meantime he had something to occupy his mind in the matter of getting his clothes dried which he managed by having them steamed at the power station.

Paul, with the engine now going to his satisfaction, took a day off to go fossicking among the old mine workings. Industrial archaeology, he called it, and together with Alan triumphantly brought back some old miner's lamps which they lovingly cleaned and polished. All was grist to their mill. Besides lamps they had a pair of boots – miner's boots presumably – reindeer horns, and the skull of an Arctic fox, or maybe a domestic dog. As mementoes of Svalbard, for they had started collecting them at Bear Island, bones were highly prized by all the crew, bones of whales, seals, bears, and, of course, reindeer horns. Later on, at more than one anchorage, where there were the graves of old-time whaling men and trappers, I admired their restraint in not digging up a skeleton or two for their collection. These relics were not really welcome in the cabin, so we had a large box for them on deck.

We waited until 12 July in order to collect some expected mail and early that morning the cruise ship *Regina Magna* came in. Hundreds of tourists, Europeans, or at any rate middle-Europeans, disembarked to proceed by bus and taxi to the Post Office and the shop. A few of the hardier types preferred to walk and these became the prey of some enterprising Norwegian boys who had set up a stall by the roadside for the sale of fossils. Vestspitzbergen is rich in fossils.

Among the stores that we had bought were 24 loaves of white bread and it was the nature of this bread that really determined our next port of call. According to Sir Fopling Flutter, 'Beyond Hyde Park all is desert'; beyond Longyearbyen, too, all is, so to speak, desert, it is the last place where anything can be bought. If we failed in our circumnavigation we should, of course, have to return by the west coast, but if we succeeded I intended going directly home (after a call at Hopen) and this implied starting from Longyearbyen with stores, including bread, for two months. The only kind of bread that would keep that long without going mouldy is black bread, readily obtainable in Greenland, for instance, under the name of 'rugbrod'. It has the additional advantage of becoming harder with age so that as time goes on the crew eat less and less. None of this could be had at Longyearbyen but I readily assumed that Russians would eat nothing else, despising anything so cissy as white bread. The Russian mining town of Barentsburg was therefore to be our next stop.

The Russians lease two mines at Isfjord, one at Pyramiden at the head of the fjord and another at Barentsburg in Greenfjord on the same side of Isfjord as Longyearbyen and close to the entrance. Compared with most coal mines those in Vestspitzbergen are easy to work. The seams lie high up on the hillside so that instead of deep shafts having to be sunk they can be reached by adits driven in at the same level; moreover the mines are close to the sea and the coal goes direct from the mine to the ship's hold – in the case of Longyearbyen by a cable conveyor $2\frac{1}{2}$ miles in length. Finally owing to the frozen soil there are no water problems and little need for pit props.

Thanks to a fresh northerly breeze, by supper time we were off the Greenfjord entrance where we gybed and sailed in. Inside the wind died away, thus frustrating our hope of astonishing the natives by approaching the town under sail. Why the fjord was named Green Harbour by Poole in 1610 is not immediately obvious, unless it was because there are no glaciers in sight. Three ships lay at anchor waiting to load and one lay alongside a small jetty having coal poured into her in rather slow time. Unlike Longyearbyen the town is compact, all the buildings, badly in need of paint, huddled together a few hundred feet above the jetty. Three helicopters were parked nearby. Having cruised up and down and found no obvious anchorage for small craft we decided to anchor off a little bit of beach just ahead of the vessel coaling. By then (10 pm) a crowd of curious sightseers had gathered on the beach, many of them armed with cameras. Close in the water shoaled abruptly to 3 fms. Going hard astern had no effect – we should have remembered – so that we slid gently to rest on the mud almost eyeball to eyeball with the nearest Russian.

One could almost have waded, but I rowed ashore and presently got into conversation with one of the reception party. Conversation, implying two-way traffic, is hardly the word. While my new-found friend volleyed away in fluent German, the only words in that language that I could summon up were 'schwarzbrod' and 'funfzehn'. Apparently he got the message. It was too late then, but early next morning we should have our fifteen loaves of black bread. Meantime a kindly bystander, catching at least part of the message, rushed off and returned with four white loaves for which he firmly refused the proffered cigarettes.

Back on board we had a visitor, a young Norwegian working for a Norwegian company who were laying a pipe-line across Greenfjord to augment Barentsburg's water supply. He messed with the Russians and found it distressing – beans for the most part and liberal quantities of poor quality margarine with everything. Instead of beer, which was not to be had, they got a ration of two bottles of Vodka a month, and should we happen to have on board a copy of *Playboy* we could swop it for three bottles of Vodka. He confirmed what one would suspect, namely that Russia is not so destitute of coal deposits that they have to be eked out with Spitzbergen coal, and that the leasing of the mines there is more for the sake of maintaining a foothold.

Early next morning before anyone was about I went ashore again for a quick look round. The only way of getting from sea level to the town above, apart from the coal chute, seemed to be by way of a long flight of wooden steps. This possibly accounted for the mass of material piled anyhow on the beach almost down to tidemark – iron pipes by the mile, steel joists, cement, timber, drums of cable, coils of wire. Except for the absence of warlike stores it might have been a badly organised war-time beach-head. Half-way up the steps was a mammoth greenhouse crammed with plants which I could not identify from outside. The door was locked. In this they were one-up on Longyearbyen though the produce from a single greenhouse would not go far among the thousand or more inhabitants of Barentsburg.

When the whistle blew and work started our beach remained singularly empty. No one came near it. Copies of *Playboy* would have found no takers, trade and barter had ceased, the Iron Curtain lowered and the Cold War resumed. Word must have gone around that fraternising with yacht-owning, capitalist lackeys must cease. All cameras had been put away or confiscated. Hours passed and no one came near the beach or so much as looked at us. We had already kedged ourselves off the mud, so when noon came and found us still, as it were, in quarantine, we got our anchor and sailed for the north. So much for Russian black bread.

CHAPTER FOUR

To the Mountains

A NOTED feature on the west coast is Prins Karls Forland, a long, narrow island lying parallel to the coast and separated from it by a channel known as Forlandsundet. The island, nearly fifty miles in length, is well furnished with mountains and glaciers, the highest mountain rising to 3,500ft. The southern entrance to Forlandsundet is just off Isfjord and its northern exit is off Kongsfjord whither we were then bound. Conveniently enough, therefore, we could make the whole passage in the quiet waters of Forlandsundet. A bar runs right across the sound over which the greatest depth is 13ft. Ships of any size are therefore obliged to pass outside.

In discussing the naming of Prins Karls Forland the *Arctic Pilot* reveals in its laconic way something that would surprise or even startle a student of mountaineering history;

It was named Prince Charles Island by Fotherby (1616) after the son of James 1st, who afterwards reigned as Charles 1st, while at the same time it was known to Dutch whalers as Kijn Island, after a supercargo who *broke his neck while climbing a mountain on the island.*

Where in a matter such as this one's curiosity is never likely to be satisfied, it is maddening to have it aroused by the throw-away remark 'broke his neck while climbing' as if climbing in Spitzbergen early in the 17th century was a normal activity, and that Dutch whaling men, of all people, took part in it. De Saussure's ascent of Mt Blanc in 1787 is generally accepted as marking the beginning of mountaineering as a sport, although his motives were not altogether pure as they were a little tainted by science. Thus to learn that De Saussure's historic initiative had been anticipated by a hundred and fifty years or more is like discovering that cricket matches were played every Saturday afternoon in, say, Paris, long before they thought of it at Hambledon. Much depends upon what poor Kijn's motives for climbing were and that we shall never know. It is more than likely that he was not climbing for fun but on business, looking for whales or surveying ice conditions from some lofty look-out, and since we know neither this nor what mountain he was climbing, any claim to regard him as the father of mountaineering instead of De Saussure would be difficult to establish. To have one's name recorded in the *Arctic Pilot* is surely a kind of immortality and with that Kijn, Dutch supercargo and embryo mountaineer, will have to be content.

Before we had quite cleared the Isfjord entrance we were struck by another of those furious, short-lived blasts of wind blowing out of the fjord. For the two hours it lasted we dropped the stays'l and reefed down. Once inside Forlandsundet we had little enough wind while a steady drizzle so reduced visibility that the mountains on the Forland remained hidden. Thus when approaching the bar we were not as confident as we should have been to our whereabouts or of hitting off the channel. This channel, with a least depth of 2 fms. is half a mile long and only a cable and a bit wide. It is indicated by a pecked line on the chart and the point of departure for it on the Forland side is marked by a beacon which we failed to see. The least depth we got with the lead was 4 fms. but I suspect that by then the bar had long been crossed.

The ten-mile wide entrance to Kongsfjord is marked on the north side by a prominent peak called The Mitre, an apt name for once since it is cleft down the middle and when viewed from the south does resemble a bishop's mitre. It was so named by William Scoresby of Scoresby Sound fame, whaling captain, explorer, scientist, and finally Church of England parson, an all-rounder, man of action and man of intellect, the sort that is not bred nowadays. He not only named the Mitre but climbed both it and a neighbouring summit, finding the ridge between the two so sharp that he traversed it *à cheval*, a leg on either side. Scoresby's *Account of the Arctic Regions,* first published in 1820, is in two volumes, one dealing very thoroughly with whaling while the other, besides scientific matter, includes a general account of the west coast of

Vestspitzbergen in which his ascent of Mitre peak, a modest 1,233ft., is graphically described. Scoresby spent twenty-five years voyaging in Arctic waters, going to sea first at the age of fourteen in his father's whaling ship *Resolution*, and when writing of ships and the sea, the element whereon he was supreme, his style is severe, sober, seamanlike; but the rarified atmosphere of Mitre peak goes to his head and he becomes exuberant, almost intoxicated:

The prospect was most extensive and grand, mountain rising above mountain until by distance they dwindled into insignificancy; the whole contrasted by a canopy of deepest azure, and enlightened by the rays of a blazing sun, and the effect marked by a feeling of danger, seated as we were on a pinnacle of rock almost surrounded by tremendous precipices, all united to constitute a picture singularly sublime. Here we seemed elevated to the very heavens, and though in an hazardous situation, I was sensible only of pleasing emotions, heightened by the persuasion that, from experience in these adventures I was superior to the dangers with which I was surrounded. . . . The effect of the elevation and the brightness of the picture were such that the sea, which was at least a league from us, appeared within reach of a musket shot, mountains a dozen miles off, seemed scarcely a league from us, and our vessel, which we knew to be a league from the shore, appeared in danger of the rocks.

The ascent had been difficult enough, for as well as the *mauvais pas*, already mentioned, which they overcame by sitting astride, the looseness of the terrain had reduced them to more unorthodox methods, methods which no mountaineer would think of copying even when climbing a sandhill, and which the Alpine Club, had it then existed, would have certainly sneered at: . . . 'the ground gave way at every step and no progress was made; hence the only method of succeeding was by the effort of leaping and running, which under the circumstances could not be accomplished without excessive fatigue'. The descent, naturally, was worse: 'We found it really a very hazardous and in some instances a painful undertaking. The way now seemed precipitous. Every movement was a work of deliberation.' But Scoresby had in him the makings of a mountaineer, recognising at once the dangers implicit in descending loose rock and as readily hitting on a way of obviating the danger; 'We were careful to advance abreast of each other, for any individual being below us would have been in danger of being overwhelmed with the stones which we unintentionally dislodged in showers.' On this perilous Mitre peak adventure Scoresby does not seem to have taken the precaution which Martens, an earlier Spitzbergen explorer to whom he refers, deemed essential: 'The necessity,' writes Martens, 'of marking every step with chalk, as the adventurer climbs the rugged mountain, otherwise he will not know how to get down.' Frederick Martens' book, *A Voyage to Spitzbergen*, describes a voyage undertaken in 1671.

From Mitre Peak which started this long digression, it is time to return to Kongsfjord where we, too, hoped to do some climbing. I might add that in spite of Scoresby the Mitre did not seem worth a second ascent – devoid of snow or ice and probably what Baedeker would have written off as 'fatiguing and not repaying'. We also wanted to visit Ny Alesund, a place that formerly had been of some importance. The coal mines there had been abandoned but in 1937 the Norwegian Government converted most of the buildings into the North Pole Hotel and Ny Alesund blossomed as a short-lived tourist centre. Nowadays hotels are built in even more unlikely places. In 1950, the first party from the outside world ever to visit Thyangboche on the Nepal side of Mt Everest (Dr Charles Houston and his father, Mrs Betsy Cowles, Anderson Bakewell S.J., and the present writer) little imagined that in less than twenty-five years so remote a spot, sanctified by a Bhuddist monastery, would become a tourist centre complete with hotel.

Kongsfjord trends south-east and Ny Alesund lies on the south side some ten miles in. There are no hazards in the approach and on 16 July, a lovely, warm day, we anchored close to the small jetty. On a little peninsula opposite Ny Alesund there is a place with a familiar name, London; it is the site of a disused marble quarry and unlike its greater rival has now only one house. On this sunny day, if one ignored an overpowering concrete structure as high as a sky-scraper and as windowless as a pill-box, Ny Alesund with its mountain background wore a far more cheering aspect than either Longyearbyen or Barentsburg. The North Pole Hotel is, of course, no more so there were no brightly garbed Americans sunning themselves on the jetty, but I did have one pleasing encounter when I first went ashore. In the shadow of the giant pill-box a Land Rover passed, stopped, and the Norwegian driver hailed me by name. To my shame I failed to recognise him, for he proved to be the man who had been Commandant of the Norwegian station at Jan Mayen in '68 when we had to beach *Mischief* there and subsequently lost her. He was now in charge at Ny Alesund and had the ungrateful task of closing the station or at least running it down. Besides an air-strip and a weather station there was a European satellite tracking station with the familiar monster plastic dome housing the sensitive antennae. Of these only the weather station and the power plant necessary for lighting and heating were to remain. Ny Alesund has had nothing but setbacks. The hotel did not survive the war and long before that the coalmine had been closed down as the result of an explosion that killed a number of miners. We visited the old workings where even now the evidence of violent destruction, pieces of building and machinery strewn far and wide, is sufficiently striking.

My Jan Mayen friend drove me into the town where, in what might be called the High Street, he introduced me to Professor Harland, an old Spitzbergen hand, who was then in charge of a geological party of twenty from the Sedgewick Museum, Cambridge. Even in Lat. 79° N. such a fine, wide street as this deserved to be lined with something. Plane trees, of course, were out, lamp-posts were superfluous because of the absence of night, so instead they had lined it with Huskie's kennels, a dozen each side; ingenious kennels made from those great wooden drums on which cable is wound, the hub part with a door cut in it forming a commodious dog's home. Outside each, on a chain, sat the proud owner.

The Cambridge party were widely scattered while the Professor himself and several others were about to leave for the north coast in their two small cabin cruisers. By chance we met them there later. There are many empty houses in Ny Alesund and the building they were occupying may well have been part of the old hotel. No doubt they were drier but compared with us they seemed to be having a hard time, living entirely on pre-packed 12-man-day ration boxes. Consequently ever since their arrival in Spitzbergen they had not eaten bread or even any of the simpler flour products such as soda bread or chapatties. When the Professor, together with the Naval officer who was in charge of their boats, and a geological student, later visited us at tea-time they regarded our bread and butter as a rare treat. There is something to be said for pre-packed ration boxes in that they save the men in the field a lot of trouble, the trouble of having to think, to improvise, or to cook, and at the same time they must convince those same men that they are indeed on an expedition. To eke out our bread and flour we needed some biscuit so we did a swop with the Cambridge party – ten boxes of Lifeboat biscuit and a ration box in exchange for some flour, dried egg, and potatoes. Lifeboat biscuits are part of the emergency food carried in ship's lifeboats. On the longer voyages in *Mischief* I used to carry a lot of them and even in those days they were not cheap, 12/– (old shillings) for a box of 48 small biscuits. The small size is a point in their favour, for on them it is not possible to convey to the mouth unduly large quantities of butter and jam. A Norwegian whose own plans had come unstuck also had a number of ration boxes for disposal. I felt sorry for him but not quite sorry enough to pay the price he wanted for ration boxes.

The day of our arrival Andrew succumbed to a violent attack of migraine, as he did on more than one occasion later. In the matter of illness or accidents on the part of the crew all these voyages have been lucky; only twice have men had to be landed, one with a threatened appendicitis and the other with a tooth abscess, and each time we were reasonably close to a port. Paul, Alan, and I went to look at the old mine workings and, of greater interest, the *Italia* mooring mast and the Amundsen memorial. On 23 May 1928 airship *Italia*, designed and commanded by Gen Nobile, set out from Ny Alesund to fly to the North Pole. Three years earlier in the airship *Norge*, accompanied by Amundsen and Ellsworth, he had flown over the Pole to Nome in Alaska. In 1928 the *Italia* reached the Pole but on the return flight bad weather and other troubles forced Nobile to make a crash-landing off the coast of Northeastland. Only the cabin and its ten occupants, Nobile with a broken leg, survived the landing, the body of the airship together with the gondola and six men in it being blown away by the wind never to be seen again. The cabin party had ample food and the wireless set still worked. Every hour they sent out an SOS signal but their support ship at Barentsburg in Greenfjord was not listening. By chance a Russian amateur picked up the signal and a rescue on an international scale was speedily mounted. Amundsen, in spite of having quarrelled bitterly with Nobile over the conduct of the *Norge* expedition, was one of the first to respond and in so doing lost his life, his plane with two French pilots disappearing on the way to Spitzbergen. A Swedish airman finally located the wrecked cabin and brought back Nobile. On his second attempt, however, his plane overturned alongside the cabin and the task of rescuing the whole party, including two men who had walked ashore to Northeastland to seek help, was finally accomplished by a Russian ice-breaker. The stone memorial, suitably inscribed in Italian, commemorates

Amundsen's heroic end, in keeping with the life of that most illustrious explorer. On one of *Mischief*'s voyages I saw on South Georgia the memorial to another great explorer, Shackleton, who died at sea off South Georgia in 1922. Perhaps men of such achievements need no memorials but at Ny Alesund and even more in the grimmer surroundings of Grytviken I found them moving. Contemplating the ruins of Iona Dr Johnson wrote:

To abstract the mind from all local emotion would be impossible if it were endeavoured, and would be foolish if it were possible. Whatever withdraws us from the power of our senses; whatever makes the past, the distant, or the future predominate over the present, advances us in the dignity of thinking beings.

The gloriously fine weather continuing, Paul and Alan set off for a long ridge climb taking with them an assortment of ironmongery. This remained unused, for the rock, both here and elsewhere, proved to be almost uniformly soft and rotten, nowhere to be trusted, and on the whole unsuitable either for free or artificial climbing. A small peak much closer at hand attracted me. It was mainly snow and I had no axe, so I picked up a stake at the old mine workings and fashioned it into a shortened form of alpenstock. Two hours up and one down sufficed which meant that it cannot have been more than 2,000ft. The only hazards of this expedition were encountered on the approach march through what might be called the suburbs of Ny Alesund where Arctic terns, nesting by the roadside, made it their business to attack anyone on foot. They did not often press their attack home, usually pulling out of their dive before actually striking, but twice I received taps on the head. My alpenstock, flourished continuously like a bandmaster's staff, helped to keep them at bay.

Having seen all the sights, climbed two peaks, and put in some industrial archaeology at the old mine, we were ready to go. The *Nordsyssel* came in and occupied the jetty and after she had left we went alongside to fill up with oil and water. When we sailed on 18 July we had not far to go. Krossfjord, where we intended spending a few days, is merely a northern extension of Kongsfjord. It is well provided with mountains and at the head of its main branch is a popular tourist ship attraction, what the Pilot calls the 'immense glacier of Lilliehook'. If compared with some Himalayan or Greenland glaciers its immensity shrinks considerably. As the Red Queen said: 'I have seen hills compared with which these are valleys'. Icebergs, of course, are calved from glaciers, yet all the numerous glaciers of Vestspitzbergen between them produce nothing really worthy of the name. Anyone accustomed to Greenland waters where vast and slightly less vast icebergs are nearly always in sight, their diversity of shape, size, and colour a constant source of delight, will regret the absence of anything comparable around Vestspitzbergen. The glaciers are on a much smaller scale than those from which the Greenland bergs are calved, for these are fed by and descend from the great ice-sheet thousands of feet thick that covers most of the interior. With reference to the Lilliehook glacier the *Pilot* has this to say of bergs:

From this glacier large bergs are frequently calved, many with a height of 40 to 50ft. and a length and breadth of over half a mile. These are the only real icebergs calved on the west coast, for the masses of ice that break off from the considerable glaciers in the fjords are very much smaller. The reason for the larger size of the Lilliehook calvings appears to be the greater depth of water at the front of the glacier. None of the Lilliehook bergs, however, appear to reach the open sea, as having too great a draught, they ground either on the banks fringing the fjord or on the shoals near the entrance. Small vessels should keep well clear of the front of the Lilliehook glacier as it calves frequently, and the waves then raised are sufficiently high to be dangerous for a considerable distance.

It is not only the west coast that is devoid of sizeable icebergs, for neither on the north coast nor the east did we encounter any. Towards the head of Krossfjord there were a few floes and one miniature berg drifting about and I concluded that if we anchored there these were likely to prove a nuisance. There is another branch fjord that trends away to the north-east and since from the chart we could see that the glacier at its head did not reach the water there would be no floes there to bother us. The anchorage, too, was said to be good, so thither we went.

While proceeding up Krossfjord on the way to this other branch which is called Mollerfjord, we made out the cruise ship *Regina Maris* right up near the front of the Lilliehook glacier, the captain evidently doing his best to give his passengers their money's worth. Near the head of Mollerfjord on the east shore, a conspicuous boulder some 20ft. high makes a useful leading mark for the anchorage. On inspection its face proved to be fairly smooth and I mentioned this to the crew, as well as the fact that Darius, the great king, liked to have his victories and progressions commemorated upon any convenient rock face – at Bisitun near Kermanshah, for example. Paul and Andrew between them could no doubt have carved an elaborate inscription had we had time to spare. On the other hand we had plenty of paint.

In the morning I had myself rowed across to the west shore, a longish row, where a good looking peak of about my low standard challenged attention. Having ascended the south side by way of a convenient snow gully I descended the north side by a much steeper gully, steep enough in its upper part to oblige me to face inwards to kick steps, using the hands for support. The dinghy had been taken back so I walked round the head of the fjord, an estuary of mud flats and innumerable small streams left behind by the retreating glacier. Back by the conspicuous boulder I found Paul already hard at work with a paint brush and making a good job of it with the name *Baroque* and the date extending right across the face. Unfortunately this will not endure as long as the rock-carvings at Bisitun and whether in the future there will be the opportunity to touch it up is more than doubtful; in 1973 we were able to touch up the *Mischief* we had painted on the rock wall overlooking Godthaab harbour in 1963. Commemorative vandalism, as this might be called, recording one's name and date of visit, preferably in indelible pencil, is a weakness that tourists and trippers suffer from, particularly the British variety. But recording the name and date of a ship's visit to a remote place is, perhaps, more excusable and personally I enjoyed scanning the names painted on the wall at Godthaab, guessing at the various nationalities and even recognising the names of ships that one had met or passed.

Along the shores of Vestspitzbergen fjords huts or the remains of huts are a fairly common sight, the relics of Norwegian and Russian hunters of bygone days or of past expeditions. A hut half a mile from the big boulder seemed to be an objective for cruise ships and to be maintained by them in good order – shovels and brushes for clearing out snow, a stove and fuel, a stock of tinned food, a visitor's book, and a home-made chess set – the last item, in my opinion, not nearly so good as Andrew's. The visitor's book, which we took the liberty of signing, contained the names of hundreds of tourists, most of them German off the cruise ship *Europa*.

The most challenging peak within reach lay to the south on the far side of an arm of Mollerfjord at the head of which was a terribly broken glacier. The easiest approach was by water, thus avoiding the crossing of the glacier, so Paul and Allen got Andrew to row them across, a journey that took a good hour. The fog that had prevailed had lifted but above the 500ft. level thick clouds writhed around all the peaks, at times concealing and again revealing unexpected features in a way that baffled the beholder:

> The hills are shadows and they flow
> From form to form and nothing stands,
> They melt like mists; the solid lands
> Like clouds they shape themselves and go.

As might be expected the climbers could make nothing of it. They spent the day groping, knowing neither where they were nor where their peak lay. They did not get back until 9 pm by when the clouds had dispersed and all lay revealed. Even so they could not point out with any certainty on which of several buttresses they had spent an unrewarding day.

On the 21st, fine but windless, we waited for the tide to drift us down to Krossfjord where we expected to find some wind. In the fjord we passed yet another cruise ship, the French line *Renaissance*, and by evening were approaching the entrance with C. Mitre abeam. Both the chart and the *Pilot* warn the mariner of foul ground near the cape and although we were a good two miles off we saw close ahead white water breaking over a sunken rock. Without either our modern charts or pilotage directions, in unhandy ships, the Dutch and English whaling men of the 17th century who made so free with this coast must have been superbly skilful and daring seamen. No doubt the knowledge gained bit by bit was soon pieced together and became widely diffused throughout the fleets, and the fact that they sailed in company was an advantage, for it is a comfort to know that there are other ships in the vicinity. It may be regrettable but it is certainly true that these hazards and hardships were incurred for the sake of profit and that should not lessen one's admiration for such redoubtable characters.

We were bound for Magdalena fjord about 25 miles further north and in the course of an almost windless night managed to drift a good part of the way. At breakfast time the *Renaissance* passed again bound north. She turned up again late that evening in Magdalena fjord so she may well have spent the day steaming as far north as she could, possibly as far as N. Lat. 81° where she would probably be able to astonish her passengers by having the Polar pack in sight. Magdalena fjord runs east-north-eastwards and has at its head the 300ft. high ice front of the Waggonway glacier, at least a mile in width, rivalling as a tourist attraction the great Lilliehook glacier. This fjord, reputedly the most beautiful of Vestspitzbergen fjords, was visited first by Barents in 1596 who named it Tusk Bay from the finding of two walrus tusks. Fotherby in 1616 called it Maudlen Sound and the anchorage at its head Trinitie Harbour, which is now the Trinityhamna where we anchored that evening. Sailors are said to be conservative folk and accordingly the editor of the 1961 edition of the *Arctic Pilot* has based much of the description of Magdalena fjord upon a report by Lieut Beechey who visited the fjord in HMS *Trent* in 1818. Since 1818 there have, of course, been other visitors to Magdalena – there were several hundred there that evening – some of whom could have made a concise and up-to-date report for the *Pilot*; but despite the inevitable inaccuracies, I for one applaud the preference given to Lieut Beechey, for he must be the same Lieut Beechey who was on Parry's expedition in search of the North-west passage in 1829, still a lieutenant eleven years later, promotion no doubt being damnably slow in the piping days of peace subsequent to the Napoleonic war. A figure from the heroic days of Arctic exploration deserves to be thus remembered in the *Arctic Pilot* even if his observations no longer hold good.

A glaring example of this is the description of a glacier called Hangebreen not far from Trinityhamna:

Hangebreen, or Hanging Glacier, though the smallest in size, is the most remarkable of the glaciers visible. It is situated at an elevation of about 200ft. on the slopes of a mountain, in such an apparently precarious position that it looks as if a slight shock would precipitate it into the sea. Large portions do occasionally break away and fall down the mountain side, making this part of the fjord hazardous to approach in a small boat.

Since 1818 this little glacier has retreated so far from the water, diminished so much in size, and lies at such a gentle angle that it is hard to imagine any ice breaking off let alone reaching the water.

Still relying upon Lieut Beechey, attention is drawn to a striking contrast between the north and south sides of the fjord, the latter, on account of the steep mountains, seldom if ever being visited by the sun. Accordingly we read:

While on the southern side perpetual frost is converting into ice the streams of water occasioned by the thawing snow on those upper parts of the mountains which are exposed to the sun's rays, the northern shore is relieving itself of its superficial winter crust and refreshing a vigorous vegetation with its moisture.

On my reading this, averse as ever to avoidable hardship, I seriously thought of foregoing the well-known, secure anchorage of Trinityhamna and instead seeking an anchorage on the verdant, sun-bathed north shore. Yet, in July, both sides of the fjord appeared to be equally barren, the sun occasionally lit on Trinityhamna, and there was never any question of freezing, the numerous small streams running merrily night and day. Finally, for good measure, the *Pilot* adds: 'Landing is difficult anywhere in Magdalena fjord', whereas at

Trinityhamna nothing could be easier, the *Renaissance*, as we shall see, landing several hundred people that night.

With reason, mariners regard the Admiralty Pilots much as one would Holy Writ. Nevertheless, although attempts to bring the Bible up-to-date are to be deplored this should not apply to them. As there are some seventy volumes the mere keeping of them up-to-date is a sufficiently formidable task, and since the three volumes of the *Arctic Pilot* cannot be in great demand they probably have a low priority. On the whole, in the matter of Magdalena fjord and Lieut Beechey, it is better to be harmlessly misinformed than that his name should be forgotten.

As mentioned above the *Renaissance* came in that evening and we were able to witness a cruise ship in action, as it were. She anchored just outside Trinityhamna and although it had begun to rain smartly preparations began for giving her passengers a run ashore. A pontoon was positioned near the sandy beach of Trinityhamna and a gangway rigged from the pontoon to the shore, after which two or three big launches, each holding about fifty people, maintained a shuttle service from ship to shore. This went on until midnight. Pontoon and gangway were then dismantled, launches and accommodation ladders hoisted on board, and at 5 am she sailed. The whole business went smoothly like a familiar drill, as no doubt it was.

The sandspit where all this coming and going took place is called Graveneset. As the name implies it has on it a number of graves and a stone memorial inscribed 'Svalbardfrareri 1600–1750'. The sandspit forms a protecting arm round Trinityhamna which is a safe and pleasant anchorage, almost free from drifting floes, and with a number of peaks within striking distance. As far as I remember only one floe drifted in and that had on it a fat seal fast asleep, probably a harp seal, easy meat had we had on board a rifle and felt sufficiently brutal. 'God Almighty, what things a man sees when he is without a gun,' is a remark attributed to a Boer farmer. We had no weapons of any kind and the crew's respect for life would have profoundly shocked men like Lamont and Leigh Smith, wealthy Victorian yachtsmen whose passion for slaughter, particularly the slaughtering of walrus, Polar bears, and seals, led them to sailing in Arctic waters.

The next day, fine but dull, the climbers followed their vocation. Paul and Alan took on the two nearest peaks while I went for one more distant. The approach march involved a mile of boulder-hopping along the shore, a disagreeable pastime most often associated with Himalayan glaciers and their moraines. A long glacier walk and a gradual ascent on hard *névé* left only a few hundred feet of steeper snow to climb. Like most of the peaks we climbed one side fell away almost sheer and there almost every ledge and cranny of the crumbling cliff were the homes of countless little auks.

The next target chosen by Paul and Alan lay half-way up the Waggonway glacier, thus providing them with a long row, a long glacier walk, and a fine, long ridge to traverse. We had noticed two tents at the foot of the glacier and our climbers found them occupied by a party of Norwegians and Swiss. They were at the end of their stay, due to be picked up the following day, and already beginning to pack up. I went for a peak on the far side of a glacier known as Gully Glacier which descended to the water in a steep and broken ice-fall. Well above this, where I crossed, the mile-wide glacier consisted of smooth 'dry' ice, that is without any snow cover. The ice itself was by no means dry in the ordinary sense, the melt-water pouring off in deep runnels. Normally one avoids traversing a glacier alone but where there is no snow cover, as here, the crevasses are wide open and easy to avoid or to jump. As I began a long, slow plug up snow of variable quality I had leisure to ponder upon the immortal lines of one Joseph Cottle, a very minor poet:

> How steep, how painful the ascent;
> It needs the evidence of close deduction
> To know that I shall ever gain the top.

My peak was crowned with a rock tower that when viewed from afar might have been described as beyond the bounds of human possibility. From below I had certainly written it off as beyond my bounds and was content to forego it. As often happens, closer inspection diminished its terror and in fact it presented hardly any difficulty even to my faltering footsteps.

Rain and thick mist on the 26th gave us an excuse for staying at Trinity-hamna instead of sailing as intended. We spent the time writing letters with a view to handing them to the ship that was due to collect the Norwegian–Swiss party. She came in late at night and anchored near the Waggonway glacier a long way from us. As I had the anchor watch I set off in the dinghy to intercept her but she got her anchor and steamed away long before I had got within hailing distance. Having thus, as we thought, missed the post, Alan made up a mail-bag and fastened it to a pole near the Graveneset memorial, hoping that among the next shipload of tourists there would be someone curious enough to open it. No sooner had he done this than our old acquaintance *Regina Magna* came in, anchored off Gully glacier, and began landing her passengers on the far side of Graveneset. So we motored round towards her and then sent off Alan in the dinghy to hand over our mail to one of her launches. Thick fog having by now come down we went back to Trinityhamna for lunch and sailed late in the afternoon when the fog had lifted.

Readers will probably agree with me that all this tourist activity in Magdalena fjord and elsewhere, while convenient for posting letters, detracts not a little from the romance that even in these days should still cling to so distant and so desolate an island, an island where almost every name recalls the bold seamen and explorers of the past. From now on, however, we should be on our own. In a small boat on the north and east coasts of Vestspitzbergen one feels almost as far out on a limb as one could wish.

CHAPTER FIVE

To Hinlopen Strait

THE BEST TIME for tackling a place like Hinlopen Strait where ice is likely to be met would probably be late in August. Rather than hang about until then – though there were still places of interest to visit – I felt an impatient urge to try our luck as soon as possible and so to have done. I had on my mind the possibility of being stopped by ice at the southern end of the strait and faced with the long haul back round the north and west coasts, no doubt feeling sour and depressed by defeat. Not that that would have been the first time by any means, or the last, that we have had to sail home empty-handed, mission unaccomplished. In Magdalena fjord, therefore, we had climbed our last mountain. Those few we had climbed were modest enough in height and the rudimentary cairns that adorned most of them proclaimed that ours were not the first ascents. But there are no guidebooks for Spitzbergen mountains and for us they were as good as virgin peaks up and down which we had to find our own way. On that account alone they had given us a lot of pleasure and had been well worth a visit.

After so many days in sheltered waters we had now to put to sea and on quitting the fjord were soon reminded of such things as waves. A fresh head wind obliged us to reef down and raised such a short, steep sea that both Paul and David were temporarily overcome. Once more they had to find their sea-legs. The direction of the wind, too, discouraged us from trying a slightly shorter way to the north coast through Smeerenburg fjord inside Danes Is. and Amsterdam Is. These names remind one that this north-west corner of Vestspitzbergen which we were now rounding was more frequented by the whaling ships of the 17th century than any other part. At the height of the whaling industry of those days so much quarrelling and even fighting arose among the ships of the several nations engaged that finally an agreement was made to apportion the various harbours. Hence English Bay on Prins Karls Forland, for example, while Danes Is. and Amsterdam Is. were Danish and Dutch preserves. The expressive name of Smeerenburg, or Blubber town, the harbour on Amsterdam Is., speaks for itself. In its palmiest days between 1633 and 1643 Smeerenburg had 1,200 inhabitants, besides the crews of a hundred or more whalers lying in the bay. The Spaniards, French, and Hamburgers, as they were the weaker parties, had to be content with such harbours that the bully-boys of those days – the English and the Dutch – did not want. All of them, however, English and Dutch included, were indebted to or relied upon Biscayners, who from long experience of whaling off their own coast were employed throughout the fleets in the essential roles of harpooners and coopers.

Danes Is. is noteworthy on another account. It was from here that on 11 July 1897 Andrée embarked on his ill-fated balloon flight towards the North Pole. Nothing more was seen or heard of Andrée and his party for the next thirty years and only by the merest chance did the tragic ending to the flight become known. In 1930 a Norwegian sealer happened to anchor off White Is., a small island to the east of Northeastland. On going ashore they found the remains of a camp and the bodies of Andrée and his companions Strindberg and Fraenkel, and in the pocket of Andrée's coat, his diary. The flight had lasted for 65 hours before the balloon came down on the ice having made good some 350 miles to the north-east. In the colder air over the pack-ice the gas had contracted and although they threw out ballast and everything they could spare they could not keep the balloon aloft.

When the party fetched White Is. on 5 October they had with them enough bear and seal meat to last them through the winter. There Andrée's diary ends but Strindberg wrote some notes until on 17 October he died and was buried by the two survivors. How long after that they survived is not known. Various conjectures have been made as to why, with apparently ample food, they should all have succumbed – poisoned by eating bear liver or suffocated with fumes from their stove? Nansen and Johansen, when they left the *Fram* on her Polar drift, had been travelling over the ice for five months before they reached Franz Josef islands where they wintered successfully in similar hard or harder conditions, living on bear meat. Nansen, however, was an experienced Polar traveller and when reading the Andrée diaries some time ago I had the impression that he and his men started out poorly clad to withstand an Arctic winter, lacked the know-how to improvise, and may have died from cold and exhaustion. Hakluyt's Headland, a bold, 1,000ft. high granite cliff on Amsterdam Is. marks the north-western extremity of Vestspitzbergen. After passing this we continued north and for another thirty miles to reach 80° 04′ N. our furthest north, on 28 July. The sun slowly burnt up the sullen fog that lay in patches all round the horizon and by noon it shone from a cloudless sky upon a calm, unblemished sea. In the distant south the land lay glistening white and to the north open water, no ice anywhere in sight. The sight reminded me of words used by the great Elizabethan seaman-explorer John Davis when in 1587 he reached his furthest north off the cape he named, 'Sanderson his Hope of a North-west passage', now known as Sanderson's Hope off the west coast of Greenland; words that betray the jubilation he felt as seeing before him, as he mistakenly thought, the elusive North-west passage: 'No ice towards the north, but a great sea, free, large, very salt and blue, and of an unsearchable depth.' We would probably have reached 81° N. before encountering the Polar pack but we were not trying to establish a furthest north record for yachts and since there were no impediments in sight there was little merit to be acquired by going any further in that direction. We were bound round Vestspitzbergen and accordingly headed east.

Verlegenhuken at the entrance to Hinlopen Strait was 60 miles away almost due east. This is Fotherby's Point Desire which he named in 1614 and in normal years it marks the limit of open water along the north coast in the months from July to November. As long ago as 1924, in a book 'With Seaplane and Sledge in the Arctic', George Binney wrote: 'Of recent years the amelioration of ice conditions had been very marked; thirty years ago you could never be sure of rounding the northwest corner of Spitzbergen. Now you take for granted (after 1 July) open water as far as Verlegenhuken. It seems that the Atlantic current has become warmer and that its influence has extended north and east.'

The wind, which had been at north, now veered, forcing us off well south of east so that we fetched the coast at Mosselbukta, a bay ten miles south of Verlegenhuken. Either by being too far south or failing to keep a sharper look-out we missed sighting the curious island of Moffen which I much wanted to see. One would need good eyes anyway to spot it from a distance for it is only 6ft. high, sand and gravel, no vegetation at all. In the centre is a lagoon which, according to the *Pilot*, can be reached at high tide by small vessels. When Nordenskjold, the Swedish explorer who was the first to make the North-east passage, visited Moffen in 1861 he found the skeletons of thousands of walrus, killed by hunters. Mosselbukta, into which we penetrated before going about, is a spacious bay, originally known as Half-moon bay and much favoured by whalers. Frederick Martens, mentioned before, reported that in mid-July (1671) there were many ships in the bay beset by ice. Nordenskjold, too, had to winter there in 1872 when ice prevented him from passing east of Verlegenhuken. Besides being the first to traverse the North-east passage, a feat he accomplished in two seasons 1878–9 in the 300 ton steam-sailing vessel *Vega*, Baron Nordenskjold, the eminent Swedish explorer, broke new ground in Vestspitzbergen and Northeastland and also in Greenland where he attempted the crossing of the ice-cap at its narrow southern end.

In the case of Spitzbergen there is good reason, I think, for what may appear to be over-much harping on early voyages and the names bestowed upon capes, bays, and islands by the hardy, enterprising whalers, the men who in fact did most of the exploring, as well as those given by their successors, the professional explorers. On nearly all coasts nowadays, even on some of the remotest, alterations have been made by man in the shape of bases or weather stations or there are enough hints of man's recent presence effectively to curtain off the distant past from the imagination of the present-day visitor. Not so on the north and east coasts of Vestspitzbergen. The odd cairn seen upon headland or island that alone betokens man's presence might have been built by the whalers themselves, just as the graves that one comes upon are occupied by those same men; and apart from these the coast looked as unknown, forlorn, and inhospitable as it had to them. Hence one could the more easily ignore the lapse of time, to regard Fotherby, Martens, and their like, as almost contemporaries, for one was seeing no more than they had seen; here, if anywhere, one of the aims and one of the rewards of the amateur sailor might be achieved, that which appealed to Belloc when he wrote:

In venturing in sail upon strange coasts we are seeking those first experiences, and trying to feel as felt the earlier man in a happier time, to see the world as they saw it.

Making long boards we were up near the head of Musselbukta before we could point north up the coast towards Verlegenhuken. Late on the afternoon of the 29th we weathered this noted cape and at once began meeting some scattered floes. They were nothing to worry about except that further down the Strait they looked a good deal less widely scattered than one might wish. By turning the cape we now had the bitterly cold north-east wind in our favour and we made haste to reach the shelter of Sorgfjord and the secure anchorage at Hecla Cove. Sorgfjord lies on the west side of the entrance to Hinlopen Strait and extends about five miles southwards. As we turned into Hecla Cove late that evening the two small motor cruisers of our Cambridge friends were on the point of leaving, bound westwards. Shouts, a farewell wave, and the dipping of flags, and they were gone.

The bitter blast, which they would soon be facing, did not penetrate to Hecla Cove. We could almost have dined on deck. Sparta, however, emphatically begins outside, so we went below for supper, a three-course banquet to celebrate our arrival at the entrance to Hinlopen Strait. And as we turned to go below I at any rate spared a thought for the Cambridge party, cold no doubt, and dining – if they had not already dined – upon Lifeboat biscuits and whatever the compiler of their 12-man-day ration boxes might have ordained. The crowning mercy of our meal was the pudding, a pudding fit for a glass case, even though it were only a mock plum-pudding, its chief ingredient prunes, looking and tasting remarkably like the real thing, lubricated with rum butter, crowned with Hecla holly (a species unknown to Linnaeus), and carried in all alight and flaming by a triumphant Andrew.

The cove had evidently been the base of several bygone expeditions. Just above the little sandy beach were the remains of four huts, one of which, by sweeping out the snow, could easily have been made habitable. Another, circular in shape, had an 8ft. high brick pillar in the middle, no doubt a base for some scientific instrument. Except for what had accumulated inside the hut and some drifts by the water's edge, the vicinity was entirely free from snow; and since the drifts, though exposed to the sun, showed no signs of melting it looks as if the winter snowfall must be removed by evaporation, or perhaps by wind as on the north side of Everest. There were four distinct beaches and most of the driftwood lay on the highest and therefore the oldest of them. On some islands south of Northeastland driftwood has been found at a height of 130ft. above sea level, striking evidence according to the experts, not only of the land rising but of the slow rate of decomposition in these high latitudes, for several thousand years must have elapsed since the logs drifted ashore and the land began its slow rise.

On 30 July the wind had gone round to the south and blew so fresh that even in the cove we had difficulty in rowing against it. For Hinlopen Strait we needed a north wind or no wind at all, we therefore lay at earth. In Parry's day, if weather-bound in Hecla Cove, one would have found abundant wild life to observe or more likely to shoot. Seventy reindeer and three bears were shot by his party, while of birds they noted ivory and glaucus gulls, terns, eider duck, grouse, and geese. Parry apparently intended using reindeer – presumably the tame variety – to haul his sledges on the North pole attempts, as Nordenskjold did successfully in 1872 when he crossed the Northeastland ice-cap. In the end Parry relied upon man-power for hauling two, large, flat-bottomed boats that could be fitted with either wheels or steel runners as the surface required. Travelling by night to take advantage of slightly colder conditions, and with the most severe labour, the party of twenty-two officers and bluejackets hauled these two heavy boats, *Enterprise* and *Endeavour*, for 200 miles as far as 82° 45′ N. or 435 miles short of the Pole. Many days elapsed before Parry discovered the heartbreaking truth that besides the terribly broken nature of the ice, they were also contending with a strong southerly drift, a drift so strong that if they rested for a day they lost almost as much as they had gained on the march of the previous day. So on 27 July 1827, when thirty-six days out, they turned back for Hecla Cove and their ship HMS *Hecla*, Parry admitting: 'I could not but consider it useless fatigue to officers and men and unnecessary wear and tear for the boats, to persevere any longer in the attempt.' Their record of furthest north stood for the next 48 years.

From the mouth of Sorgfjord the coast runs east for some three miles to C. Foster before turning south and opening up Hinlopen Strait. Thus the force of a wind blowing up the full fetch of the Strait is not felt until one is well clear of C. Foster. We learnt this next day when, deceived by the moderate wind inside C. Foster, we decided to make a start. Clear of the cape, and by then reefed down, we made a long board to the east across the strait, and having gone about found that on the return leg we could point no better than at the cape we had just left. In other words we were making no southing at all. So we started back for the cove. Within a mile of it, by the wind again falling light, we were led to think we had given up too easily and were merely chicken-hearted, but once more beyond Cape Foster we soon realised that conditions were no better. Prolonged beating in confined waters, where neither tack can be held for long and little ground is gained, is a wearing exercise; moreover the increasingly numerous floes driven up the Strait by the southerly wind meant that others besides the helmsman would have to be on deck for long spells. After a third futile attempt that evening the message sank home and we retired to Sorgfjord to await better times.

Even the ruins of four huts and raised beaches are not an inexhaustible sight. Besides Hecla Cove there is an anchorage on the west side of the fjord off Graves Point, a name that aroused the morbid interest of the crew, their collection of bones far from complete. Thither we went and in the course of a peaceful night each of us in turn took a walk ashore, finding more raised beaches each with its load of driftwood, more derelict huts, and the graves. There were thirty of these, laid out in a line on the highest point, the heavy stones piled on each the only mark and memorial of some unnamed, forgotten man. The whalers penetrated as far east as this and the graves are most probably those of whaling men.

Early next morning a ship, the *Pole Star*, anchored half a mile south of us and after breakfast I rowed across for a gam with her captain. She might conceivably have come from south in which case they would know all about ice conditions in Hinlopen Strait. She was a vessel chartered by the Norwegian Polar Institute, a sealer type built for working among ice, carrying two helicopters and a bevy of bearded scientists. Having come by the north coast, as we had, they could tell us nothing about Hinlopen Strait, but unlike us they had sighted Moffen Is., landed on it by helicopter, and found there some forty walrus. So we had missed something worth seeing, the sea-horse in his native haunt. It is pleasant to think that they are returning to one of their old stamping grounds after having been persecuted almost to extinction.

A noted amateur in the walrus-killing line of business was Leigh Smith, the Victorian yachtsman already mentioned, whose yacht, by the way, like many others in those spacious days, was a vessel of 300 tons manned by a paid crew. Leigh Smith's two hobbies of shooting walrus and exploring were happily combined in several hazardous voyages to Spitzbergen, Northeastland, and as far east as Franz Josef Land, where in 1881 he lost his yacht *Eira* in the ice. A cape on Northeastland bears his name, a tribute to the man and to the sketch he made of that then almost unknown coast on a voyage in 1871. After the loss of *Eira*, crushed between pack-ice and shore-fast ice at C. Flora in Franz Josef Land, Leigh Smith's proceedings showed that he had the qualities needed in a successful seaman-explorer – leadership, resourcefulness, foresight, and the requisite know-how. The party of 25 officers and men wintered in an improvised hut and remained in good health in spite of having neither bedding nor fur clothing. Besides stores retrieved from *Eira* before she sank they killed and ate 24 walrus and 34 bears. The four ship's boats had been saved and during the winter they were made ready for the summer's voyage to Nova Zembla some 500 miles to the south. Sails were made and a quantity of fresh meat was boiled and tinned by the blacksmith. When they sailed on 21 June each boat had a compass, chronometer, sextant, charts. They were able to make a hot meal daily and brewed tea twice a day. On 1 August they landed at the western end of Matochkin Shar, the channel dividing Nova Zembla into two, and on the 3rd were picked up by Sir Allen Young in the relief ship *Hope*.

Another Victorian yachtsman with similar tastes though of less calibre as an explorer, was James Lamont. He made two voyages to Spitzbergen in 1858 and 1859, mainly in order to shoot as many seals and walrus as he possibly could, but he was also an enthusiastic amateur geologist. In spite of his ownership of a large yacht, yachting cannot be included among his hobbies; for in a book, *Seasons with the Seahorses*, published in 1861, he wrote: 'I sent the yacht round to Leith, while I travelled north by land, as I am not the least shamed to confess that I have a strong preference for land travelling, when it is practicable.'

But despite this professed dislike of the sea he knew what he was about and his remarks concerning ice navigation are worth quoting at length:

I am perceived on this occasion (1858) that nothing could be more impracticable for ice navigation than a long fore-and-aft rigged schooner yacht, as in threading the intricate mazes of the ice there was no possibility of stopping her 'way' to avoid collisions, as is done by backing the topsails of a square-rigged vessel, and her frail planking and thin copper were exposed to constant destruction from the ice. Her dandified painted gigs were also totally unsuited for the rough work of pushing in amongst the ice in pursuit of seal and walrus; indeed it was very fortunate that we did not succeed in harpooning one of the latter mighty amphibiae from the yacht's boats, for my subsequent experience of the strength and ferocity of these animals leads me to believe that he would infallibly have pulled us all to the bottom of the sea.

Accordingly at Hammerfest Lamont chartered a boat such as the Norwegian sealers used, a 30-ton sloop with a small square topsail, in which he cruised off the south coast of Edge Is. and in Storfjord, while his schooner yacht *Ginevra* spent the time out of harm's way in Isfjord. Incidentally he explored the head of Storfjord which is now called Ginevrabotnen, in which there is also a Lamont Is. On this second voyage he and his friend Lord Kennedy accounted for 46 walrus, 88 seal, 8 polar bear, 1 white whale, and 61 reindeer, while another 20 walrus and 40 seal were shot but sank. Not a bad bag. If the Victorians had an horror of slaughter they confined it to the slaughter of men, at least of white men, whereas now that animals are becoming scarce and men are proliferating we reserve most of our horror for the slaughter of the former. So much for our rude forefathers, but I confess that the sight of large quantities of game filled me with a similar blood-lust when I went in 1919 to what was then British East Africa, now Kenya. But it soon wore off and the time came when one would not so to speak cross the road for the sake of shooting an inoffensive buck however fine his head. The so-called dangerous game – elephant, rhino, buffalo, lion – were perhaps on a different footing, for the pursuit of these is less one-sided and a slight mistake may lead to the demise of the hunter, or at least to his becoming the hunted instead of the hunter.

The skipper of *Pole Star* had no advice to offer concerning Hinlopen Strait, nor did he rate highly our chances of getting through. At this stage I rather agreed, especially after our experience of the previous day. Strong southerly winds might well be a local phenomenon like the northerlies that blow down the Portuguese coast in late summer. In 1954, inexperienced and ignorant of these northerlies, I was bringing *Mischief* home from the Mediterranean, and after beating against them for eighteen days, when somewhere off Oporto, our progress or lack of progress was brought to an end by a mutiny on the part of the crew. Hinlopen Strait itself is a good eighty miles in length, and beyond there is another hundred miles to get round Edge Is. In the southern half of the Strait there are many islands around which ice might accumulate; ice and islands together with head winds would pose some problems. However, as we were to learn later, the woes we fear do not come; worse ones do.

The following summary of attempts to pass through Hinlopen Strait, taken from the *Arctic Pilot*, might well omit some successful passages by small sealing vessels of which nothing would be heard:

In 1827, during Parry's absence on his Polar journey, Lt Foster surveyed the Strait as far south as the islets named after him, about forty miles within the northern entrance. He was able to identify almost every feature laid down on the old Dutch charts, thus showing it to have been delineated from observations made on the spot.

In 1855 the map of Svalbard embodying the exploration of Duner and Nordenskjod (1861 and 1864) was published, carrying the survey to the southern end of the Strait. It was in 1864 that Nordenskjold rescued the crews of six boats that had been obliged to abandon their three walrus-hunting vessels beset in the ice south of Cape Leigh Smith and had succeeded in passing through the Strait from south to north.

In 1871 and twice in 1873 Leigh Smith attempted to pass through from north to south, but was stopped each time by ice; on the first and last occasion at the southern end of the Strait, and on the second attempt at the Foster Is.

In 1896 Sir Martin Conway succeeded in passing through from north to south but was held up by ice at its southern end and forced to return by the way he had come.

In 1900 De Geer, of the Swedish Arc of Meridian expedition, resurveyed the greater part of the Strait.

In August 1924 the Oxford University Expedition in the *Polarbjorn* and *Oiland* penetrated the Strait from north to south and ranged the southern coast of Northeastland, the return journey being made through the Strait.

In July 1925 Worsley in the *Island* passed through the Strait from north to south and succeeded in the circumnavigation of Northeastland.

In July 1930 the Norwegian vessel *Ringsael* passed through the Strait from north to south and proceeded along the southern coast of Northeastland without sighting any pack-ice.

Our fears about constant southerly winds were soon set at rest; we motored out that morning in fog and went on motoring throughout a completely windless day. As Dr Johnson robustly remarks of those who indulge too much in hopes and fears: 'Let us cease to consider what may never happen, and what when it shall happen will laugh at human speculation.' Thanks to a timely lifting of the fog we were soon able to see where we were going and to choose the best line through the increasing floes. At its northern end the Strait is at its narrowest only some five miles wide and this tended to concentrate the floes. Twice we were brought to a stand and to some intricate manoeuvring in order to find a way through. In a vessel like *Baroque* with a large turning circle and at that time with no power in reverse, we needed to avoid getting into a cul-de-sac where the only remedy would have been to warp her out backwards. The question of darkness did not arise but I intended anchoring for the night in order to give the engine, or rather ourselves, some rest. As might be supposed of such unfrequented waters there are no recognised or recommended anchorages. We had to find our own and I thought that off the Foster Is. (a group of three small islets) would be the most likely bet. Solely owing to drifting ice, in most of the anchorages occupied in the course of the next few days I had reason to remember a remark made in one of the *Mediterranean Pilot* volumes about anchoring in some bight off the North African coast: 'Anchoring anywhere in this bight must be prompted by necessity and not by any hope of tranquillity.'

As we had hoped we found a place to anchor that evening off the easternmost of the Foster group. Foster, it will be remembered, was Parry's second-in-command. We were in 7 fms. which was as close in as we dared go. There was a fine, big cairn on the summit of this 276ft. high islet to which after supper Alan and I made a pilgrimage in order to leave in it a message for mankind. On our return I rashly agreed to Paul and Andrew taking a run ashore, for the wind had begun to pipe up from the north and they might have problems getting back. We missed their help, too, in a prolonged tussle with a large floe that had got athwart our cable. At midnight, when Paul and Andrew were on their way back in the dinghy, I turned in. But not for long. Stirred up by the ever-freshening northerly wind the ice was now on the move southwards and several large floes were already menacingly close. If we were not to be pushed on to the rocks it was high time to move. On the south side of the group the westernmost islet boasted the merest suspicion of a cove and we sounded our way in until we were within almost spitting distance of the shore without finding any bottom. Not far off I noticed a floe that was obviously aground so we crept close to that and let go the anchor in 6 fms. Andrew swung the lead like a professional. Admiration mingled with alarm as he swung that lethal weight in a complete circle, or several circles before letting it go. Some of my less efficient leadsmen of past voyages have contrived to land the lead on the foredeck instead of in the sea; fortunately they swung it only a modest half circle, for after a full-blooded swing such as Andrew used a misdirected lead might have gone through the deck. With the sea temperature 33° F. the taking of soundings, hauling in the wet line and coiling it for another cast, was not for boys. Sometimes it needed two, one to take over while the other got some feeling back into his hands. Why not an echo-sounder? I have thought about it but as Dr Johnson remarked: 'Conveniences are never missed where they were never enjoyed.'

We sailed after breakfast on a cold, dull morning, the air temperature 34° F. The wind remained fresh at north-west and when out of the lee of the Foster Is. we set all plain sail and bowled along at 3 or 4 knots, the ice-floes sparse and widely scattered. On the previous day we had made good nearly forty miles and our objective this day, Wilhelm Is., lay about the same distance further south and closer to the western side of the Strait which thereabouts is a good thirty miles wide. South of the Foster group there is a long string of islets, the Vaigat Is., which encumber the middle of the Strait for a distance of 15 miles. Most of them are named after members of Nordenskjold's and other Swedish expeditions. Between the Vaigat islands and the coast of Northeastland there is a five-mile wide channel and even there the floes were far enough apart for us to sail unhindered. With a leading wind such as we now enjoyed one can weave a way through moderately close floes, whereas with a head wind one would be either running the boat off or getting her in irons. This north wind was a blessing, too, in that it stopped any more ice coming up from the south where it appeared to be pretty thick. At midday *Pole Star* passed bound south and in the afternoon we could still see her mast sticking up above the ice far to the south-east. Judging by her frequent changes of direction she seemed to be working through heavy ice.

By evening we were east of the Von Otter Is., the southernmost of the Vaigat group, with Wilhelm Is. still ten miles away and a lot of ice in between. Forgetting Wilhelm Is. for the moment we turned west and at 8 pm anchored off the south-west corner of Von Otter Is. where low, gently shelving gravel slopes enclosed a bay of moderate depths, free from floes. To our eyes, attuned to a harsh landscape of rock and ice, with only logs of driftwood to remind us of the existence of trees, Von Otter Is. looked friendly, almost benign. Having had our pasta sciuta, followed by a prime duff of noble proportions, we were relaxing on deck, taking the air, admiring the placid but austere scene, when a Polar bear strolled down to the beach. One had the impression that he felt satisfied, that he felt as we did: 'Fate cannot harm me,

I have dined today.' Taking no notice of *Baroque* he launched himself off and swam in leisurely fashion past the boat barely thirty yards away. Bears, I believe, are now protected in Svalbard, and none too soon for there cannot be many left. In many voyages north I had never seen a Polar bear and this alone made our Spitzbergen voyage worth while. During his anchor watch later that night Alan saw a female with two cubs.

I set great store on our making Wilhelm Is. It is a big island and its southern shore, where I wanted to be, still lay twenty miles away. As well as big, it is 1,820ft. high and from somewhere on its southern slopes I counted on seeing far to the south, far enough, I hoped, to be able to weigh up our chances of getting through. *Pole Star* had evidently met a lot of ice, and though she was well to the east of our course, possibly bound round Nordaustland, I did not feel over sanguine about our own prospects. When we sailed on 3 August the wind was still fresh at north, so fresh that we rolled in a reef. It was not until we drew near Thumb Point, the easternmost point of Wilhelm Is., that we met much ice. There we dropped the mains'l and proceeded under stays'l alone. From a couple of miles south of the island another string of islets stretches southwards for ten miles and in the gap between Wilhelm Is. and the northernmost of this string the ice at first sight looked impenetrable. I had begun to fear that this would beat us when Paul from the crosstrees reported open water beyond this barrier and also a possible lead through it. Once more one learnt not to judge ice conditions without a close inspection or without the use of the highest possible view point. We got through with little trouble, reset the mains'l, and ran on towards the island. We were still a good mile off shore when, not liking the colour of the water, I thought it time to take some soundings. None too soon either, for we were in 2 fms. of water and sailing fast towards the shore. Turning away we downed the mains'l and anchor in 3 fms., still a mighty long way from the beach.

For the last two days of overcast skies and northerly winds the air temperature had seldom risen above 35° F. Considering the amount of ice about that was reasonable enough and we had nothing to complain about. At sea between 79° and 80° N., even in August, one could hardly expect to feel warm. 'Comfort must not be expected by folks that go a pleasuring,' as Byron says. That evening, with a rising glass, the sky cleared, the sun came out, and the brown, barren slopes of Wilhelm Is. assumed a warm, welcoming glow. After tea I rowed ashore alone, for in view of the long row the less weight in the dinghy the better. Some snow drifts some 500ft. above the sea were the chosen vantage point towards which I plodded slowly up a boulder-strewn gully, resolved not to turn round for a glance southwards until I had reached them. I was well rewarded. On that clear, calm, sunny evening I reckoned I could see forty miles or more, at least as far as Edge Is., and all the way was a broad lead of open water bounded on the west by the coast of Barents Is., and on the east by a field of unbroken ice. Aware of how quickly ice conditions can change I had an uneasy feeling that we ought to push on that night; but there are never any lack of reasons for doing nothing – if you practise inaction, as the Taoist doctrine preaches, nothing is left undone – and mindful of how little rest we had had in the last few days I decided to stay. Back at the boat they told me another bear had been seen and were surprised, perhaps disappointed, that we had not met.

For all the rest we got that night we might as well have gone on. Twice we had to shift our berth on account of ice drifting athwart the cable, threatening to uproot the anchor or to damage the bowsprit. Before breakfast I went up the hill again, satisfied myself that conditions were unchanged, and after breakfast we started off in a flat calm – ideal conditions for motoring. For most of the morning we had on our port hand the long chain of islets, some almost hidden by the floes that had banked up around them. Messrs Lamont and Leigh Smith would have had a field day, for on the floes there were many seals. By noon we had C. Payer abeam, or rather the place where the cape had been. A glacier has overflowed the cape and now projects into the sea well beyond it. This cape marks the easternmost point of Vestspitzbergen and the entrance on that side to Hinlopen Strait, while on the Northeastland side the entrance point is an indeterminate glacier tongue. We were therefore through the Strait but still had to pass the east coasts of Barents Is. and Edge Is., a distance of about sixty miles.

A few miles south of the ice-engulfed C. Payer is Heley Sound, a narrow channel between Vestspitzbergen and Barents Is., leading into Ginevrabotnen, the head of Storfjord explored by Lamont. It was named after William Heley, an English supercargo in the whaling fleet in 1617, but it was not until 1858 that Johannes Nielsen of Tromso sailed through it and proved it to be a strait. Before then all charts showed it as a creek running northwards from Ginevrabotnen. Heley Sound was therefore a possible escape route for us had we felt desperate enough to take it. The *Pilot* has this to say:

In 1869 Heleysundet was explored by Lamont who called it Hell Sound and recorded as follows: 'The sound itself appeared like a winding river, being not more than four or five hundred yards across and two miles long. High precipices bounded the north side. ... Between these contracted shores a tremendous tide was running out at some 8 knots, carrying with it quantities of ice. On the opposite side an enormous glacier projected from Barents Is. far out into the East sea,' Two days after making these observations Lamont passed through in a boat at the top of flood tide, which sets north-eastward, and returned with the ebb. In August 1897 Arnold Pike, finding large floes in Freemansundet, steamed through Heleysundet in *Victoria*. He reported the navigation was most difficult on account of the violent currents, the rate of which he estimated at 10 knots.

For the last few days I had been pondering the question of whether to complete our circumnavigation of Vestspitzbergen by way of Freemansund between Barents Is. and Edge Is. or to go outside Edge Is. direct into the Barents Sea. The latter course would make a more complete and satisfying job of it and if we should meet a lot of ice off Edge Is. there would still be Freemansund to fall back on. In view of the mass of ice close to the eastward I thought we might well be stopped on the way round Edge Is.; on the other hand I was not all that keen on Freemansund which likewise has strong currents though nothing like so fierce as those of Heley Sound. Besides that there might be a concentration of ice in this comparatively narrow channel which averages three to four miles in width. That evening when we were some

ten miles east of the Freemansund entrance we did in fact meet a concentration of floes, and having got through them I decided to stand on to the south
in order to go round Edge Is. When a nice breeze set in from the east we
stopped the engine and set all plain sail, and at 10 pm on a lovely, sunny
evening, with the way ahead still clear as far as one could see, I turned in
feeling almost confident that we should get through.

At midnight Andrew reported ice ahead and on climbing to the cross-trees
I saw what looked like a solid wall of ice stretching out from the coast of Edge
Is. to merge with the field of ice that all day had lain along our port hand. We
were still two or three miles short of this seeming barrier and in any other
circumstances I should have closed with it for a proper look, to see how close
the floes really lay and whether there was open water in sight beyond them.
But the probably easier and certainly shorter alternative of Freemansund was
too tempting and unluckily I decided to take it, thus setting the scene for
another regrettable incident. Putting about we ran off to the north-west and
were soon back off C. Heuglin, the northernmost point of Edge Is. and ten
miles from the entrance to Freemansund.

CHAPTER SIX

Freemansund and Homewards

*There is nothing so distressing as running ashore – unless there is also a doubt as to which continent the shore
belongs.*

Lecky's Wrinkles.

Freemansund is thus described in the *Pilot*:

Freemansundet, a strait about 22 miles in length, with a least width of about 2½ miles,
separates Edgeoya from Barentsoya, and was named after Alderman Freeman, a
director of the Muscovy Company, who visited Svalbard in 1619. The strait is
reported to be too shallow and rocky to admit the passage of any but small craft, and
Nordenskjold, when looking down on it from an elevation of 1,066ft. at the summit of
Kapp Lee, the southern entrance point at the western end of the strait, observed that it
appeared to be much encumbered with sandbanks. However, Captain E. Lund of
Hammerfest sailed through the strait in August 1847 and in August 1870 Von Heuglin
passed through along the southern side of the strait. Freemansundet is entered from
eastwards between Kapp Heuglin (78° 15′ N. 22° 56′ E.) and Kapp Waldburg, the
south-eastern extremity of Barentsoya, about 9 miles westward. Foul ground extends
about 15 miles northward and north-westward of Kapp Heuglin and it is reported that
Kapp Waldburg is foul also. Zeiloyane are two islets lying in the middle of the eastern
entrance, about 4 miles west-north-westward of Kapp Heuglin.

The remark about the strait being too shallow and rocky for the passage of
any but small craft is out of date; both the Admiralty chart and the Norwegian

chart show a line of soundings which give a least depth of 6 fms. near the eastern entrance increasing to 24 fms. at the western end. However, these two charts did not agree about the Zeiloyane islets, either as to their position or number.

The breeze having died we were again under engine when at 4 am I took over the watch from Alan. What followed is not easy to explain and still less easy to excuse. Perhaps, having spent the last three days mostly on deck and enjoyed only disturbed nights, I was not as bright as I should have been. Zeiloyane, the two islets mentioned above, were in sight ahead and with the west-going ebb under us we were rapidly approaching them. We had already discovered that west of C. Heuglin along the north coast of Edge Is. the water was shoal and we intended passing north of the Zeiloyane islets. I had my eyes fixed on one but the northernmost looked to me like a spit of land projecting from the coast of Barents Is. What with the engine and the tide which, as we neared the islets seemed to gather speed for its rush through the channel, we must have been making 7 or 8 knots over the ground. Before I had really hoisted in what was happening we were heading between the two islets which are a mile or so apart. To attempt to pass between unknown islets however wide apart they may be is always a hazardous proceeding. A shoal extended the whole way between the two and the rate we were going ensured our being carried right up on the back of it before we ground to a stop.

If the crew thought the old man had taken leave of his senses, as they must have done, they studiously refrained from comment. As soon as the tide slackened a bit we ran out a kedge astern bringing the warp forward to the winch. The engine, as we knew, had no power in reverse and the winch alone failed to budge her. Circumstances had combined to make things as difficult as they could be. Although the ebb had been running for an hour or more we must have gone on at or near the highest level of water; it was three days after full moon so that the tides were taking off. The differences between high and low water proved to be only around 2ft. which in one way was a good thing because the boat remained more or less upright. What happens, I think, is that when the ebb starts running west the water piles up in the narrow, twenty-two mile long strait and thus continues to rise or at any rate maintains its level at the eastern end when it should be falling. Something similar occurs at the eastern end of the Magellan Straits where the water is pent up in the First and Second Narrows with the result that the west-going and east-going streams continue running in the channel for three hours after high and low water by the shore. There, too, as we found in Freemansund, the duration of slack water is barely noticeable.

Our next move was to take out half the ballast and jettison it over the side. We had no choice. The nearest islet was half a mile away and in the absence of any appreciable slack water there was no question of rowing a heavily-laden dinghy that far. In spite of a strong westerly wind blowing out of the strait – a wind that blew incessantly for the next few days – the sea remained calm and the boat motionless. There was thus no fear of the boat damaging herself by pounding, but we had something else to worry about. When the west-going stream started again it brought with it numerous ice-floes, large and small. The big ones grounded on the edge of the shoal about fifty yards away where they furnished a kind of protective barrier. There were, however, gaps in the barrier through which any piece of ice that drew less than 6ft. or 7ft. of water found its way, and by driving past the boat at a rate of several knots threatened disaster to either our rudder or our propeller. Bits of ice moving at that rate, even if they weighed only half a ton or so, could neither be stopped nor diverted with boat-hooks. Watching a small floe apparently on a collision course we could only hold our breath and hope. Twice the rudder sustained a savage blow. Nor were we much better off when the tide turned, when those that had already passed came back with the flood.

No one doubted that we should get her off in time – at least no doubts were expressed – but I felt that we had only to stay there long enough for the worst to happen. Damage to the rudder would be bad enough but if the propeller were damaged the chances of getting off would be much reduced; for by now it was clear that we must get her facing the way she had come so that the engine could be used to advantage. We were a sitting target for these floes, dependent entirely upon luck. We could not afford to be aground three days as *Mischief* had been on her first voyage in '54 when she stuck on a reef in a Patagonia fjord. In the course of three days 3 tons of ballast were ferried ashore and she floated off. In the meantime drifting ice of far smaller dimensions than the Freemansund floes stripped the propeller blades and bent the shaft. Happily on that occasion, by being away on the ice-cap at the time, I was not only free from blame but also escaped the strains and stresses resulting from the stranding of a vessel, especially for the owner.

In the afternoon, near high water, we made several attempts to pull her head round, for until we could get her pointing the way she had come and so make full use of the engine we should never get off. Having got us into this mess I at least should have had skilly for supper, instead we finished up with one of David's increasingly majestic duffs. Care weighing heavy upon me, I could only toy with this, notwithstanding the advice of that strong-minded gastronome Dr Oppimian – 'Whatever happens in this world, never let it spoil your dinner.' No doubt the reverend doctor had never assisted at a stranding, a stranding that might well become a shipwreck if a piece of ice with *Baroque*'s name on it hit her in a vital spot. The crew having disposed of the duff we turned with renewed vigour to taking out the remainder of the ballast and emptying all the water tanks but for a few gallons for immediate use. The crew worked like heroes, Paul groping away in the bilge prizing out the slimy chunks of pig-iron – some weighing 80 to 90 lbs. – from the filthy bed where for years they had lain undisturbed. In no time all were once more coated from head to foot in black, oily sludge. Besides all the ballast and most of the water, we threw overboard an old flax mainsail that we had been carrying as a spare. It dated from the days of *Mischief* and when wet, as the sails stowed on a rack in the peak always were, it must have weighed about four hundred-weight. Normally I get a lot of harmless pleasure from throwing overboard superfluous gear. The mainsail might be included in that category, but certainly not the ballast.

We had already lost a kedge and now Andrew went off in the dinghy with the big Fisherman type anchor hanging over the stern ready to drop in the selected spot. This anchor weighed about 1 cwt. and we were reconciled to losing that, too, for if she came off we were not going to risk going aground again while making an effort to retrieve it. The boat was now a lot lighter and in the course of the night by heaving away on the firmly embedded big anchor, little by little we brought her head round until at last she pointed in the right direction. The westerly wind still blew vigorously out of the strait. It seemed to be an almost permanent local feature and later when we were trying to make headway through the strait we had good reason to curse it. As they say in Africa, cross the river before you start reviling the crocodile's mother, and at this juncture, twenty-four hours after the first stranding, we wanted a west wind, the more the better. So with the whole mainsail and staysail set and drawing, the flood tide making, the engine flat out, the kedge warp quivering under the strain of the winch, and a subdued cheer from the crew, she began to move.

The big anchor had played its part, and having got in all the warp we could before it grew wide on the beam we cut it, and a moment later came to a shuddering stop alongside a large floe grounded on the edge of the shoal. We lost no time in playing our last card, another small kedge anchor of only about 25 lbs. weight. Surprisingly enough this diminutive anchor took good hold, and as we winched in on it – the sails, the engine, and the tide all working hard to assist – the boat reluctantly bumped her way off. We were too anxious to be clear of this baleful shoal to bother with the little anchor. This, too, became a sacrifice together with two other anchors, all the ballast, and the old mainsail. Our only remaining anchor was the 60 lbs. CQR which we normally used.

Giving the northernmost Zeiloyane islet the widest possible berth we headed for Freemansund, the ebb tide by then having begun to run. But even with the tide under us we made little progress against the westerly wind, so we sheered off to the north to anchor off the south-east corner of Barents Is. where we obtained a bit of a lee. In this short sail, while the absence of any ballast did not seem to make the boat unduly tender, the complaints that came from the rudder could hardly be ignored. After the two blows it had sustained from the ice, the fact that is was still there and still steering the ship was more surprising than the play one felt in the tiller and the occasional groans from under the counter.

When we sailed out next morning and were clear of the shelter of Barents Is. we faced the same west wind. Nevertheless we managed to make good some five miles inside the strait before the turn of the tide obliged us to make for the north shore where behind a little cape we found less wind and less current. Half a mile to the east the high ice front of the Freeman glacier projected well into the water. From this floes frequently broke off though few of them found their way into our shallow bay. Before beginning the long haul homewards we needed ballast and water and I had intended to look for these at some anchorage in Storfjord where one might expect to be free from the strong winds and currents of Freemansund. On going ashore that evening, however, I found a small trickle of water that if dammed up we could collect, as well as an assortment of reasonably sized stones. Like the plums in a poor man's duff they were not that plentiful and would need gathering, but we might go further and fare worse so I decided to stock up here. The plain that extended inland looked as barren as the beach, yet on it I counted eighteen reindeer busily grazing. Like yaks, they seem to subsist or even thrive on a diet of gravel slightly flavoured with moss.

The evil day had at last come when, our bread finished, we had to go on to biscuit, and since the supply of that was not abundant we agreed on a remarkably small daily ration. After a large dose of stiff porridge most of us went without the breakfast allotment, saving it for lunch when it could be used to convey to the mouth cheese, sardine or peanut butter, all more interesting than marmalade. We were lying a good 400 yards out and when deciding to fill up here with ballast and water I had assumed we could bring the boat much closer to the beach. Andrew went off in the dinghy to take soundings and when he found the water started to shoal almost under the bows I regretted my decision and had half a mind to push on. However, we blew up the inflatable dinghy and set to work with that and the pram dinghy, our working hours being limited by the duration of the ebb tide. The west wind, we found, almost sufficed to offset the effect of the west-going stream. When the flood ran, with the wind behind it, work had to stop.

Since the amount of stone that could be got into the space occupied by the jettisoned pig-iron, which we estimated to be nearly 3 tons, would not weigh nearly so much, we made additional space for ballast by emptying the food lockers under the bunks on either side of the cabin, stowing more in the main food locker forward which by now was half empty. Even when stones had been shoved into every available hole and corner the pessimists reckoned that we should not be carrying more than 2 tons. Others put it as high as $2\frac{1}{2}$ tons, while Andrew, despising guesswork, invoked the aid of Archimedes and his well-known Principles. Weighing on our spring balance a piece of iron and a piece of stone, he then measured the volume of water that each displaced and in due course, all calculations made and checked, announced smugly that our stone ballast would weigh exactly a quarter of the original pig-iron, or rather less than a ton. So much for what Goethe called the charnel house of science. Nothing has an uglier look than reason when it is not on our side and we hastened to tell Andrew what he could do with Archimedes and his bath-water.

For most of next day the wind proved too strong for the tide and it was not until after supper that ferrying began again. By midnight, when only one load of stones and two of water were needed to complete the job, a brief puff of wind discouraged the crew. I was set on getting away on the morning tide and the crew, seeing my disappointment, fell to again. By 2 am we were getting the dinghies on board for the last time. Ever since the stranding they had cheerfully given all they had in back-breaking, wet, and grimy toil to retrieve a bad situation. Accordingly, on the morning of 10 August, the west wind much less than usual, we completed the passage of Freemansund, home-ward bound at last. As we had suspected, the west wind prevailed only in Freemansund. For the rest of the day we drifted and sailed fitfully across a windless Storfjord. All that night we were puzzled and disquieted by a distant sound, a sort of 'melancholy, long, withdrawing roar', that might have been the growl of pack-ice or waves breaking on a shingle beach, except that we had seen no ice in Storfjord, nor in our tour round Spitzbergen had we come across any beaches of shingle. In thick weather and light airs we made our way slowly down the west coast of Storfjord, seeing little except for an occasional glimpse of a glacier whose brightness even the fog could not hide. Of these there are no less than ten on this seventy-mile stretch of coast.

The coast runs almost due south to Sorkapp which we passed when north-bound on 4 July in brilliant sunshine. It would have been a useful point from which to take our departure but this time fog hid everything. On a long voyage taking one's departure is a navigational luxury rather than a necessity and, according to Scoresby, whalers homeward bound from the Greenland Sea had only the vaguest notion of where they were starting from. As he writes:

When a ship has on board an ample cargo course is directed immediately homeward. It is not unusual for a ship to bear away without the navigators having first obtained any certain knowledge as to their longitude, not having perhaps seen any land for some weeks or even months; having neither a chronometer on board, nor the means of taking a lunar observation; they set out ignorant of the meridian on which they sail and sensible to their being liable to an error of five or six degrees of longitude. In such cases they steer a south-westerly course by the compass. If they steer too far to the eastward they make the coast of Norway, and if too far to the westward they probably make the Faeroes.

In other words, you can't go wrong. It all sounds like the rough and ready sailing directions for a Nova Scotiaman bound for Barbados: 'Steer south until the butter melts and then turn east.' Although we started off on a rather better footing than the homeward bound whalers we, too, were not fussy about our next landfall; except that Norway had to be avoided, indeed the whole of the North Sea, for we wished to return west-about. We would therefore take the wind as it served and if we got pushed too far to the west would call at the Faeroes for bread and water, otherwise we would make for Lerwick in the Shetlands. Having been there before I had a slight preference for the Faeroes, but as it happened we made neither.

For the first few days in the open sea the state of the rudder gave us more concern than any possible shortage of ballast which, if Andrew and Archimedes were right, might result in a capsize. The boat appeared to be no more tender than before and we never thought of reducing sail on that account, but the groans emanating from the rudder and the increasing play that could be felt were constant and unpleasant reminders of the possibility of losing it. To avoid imposing on it any additional strain we determined not to heave-to; instead, if the occasion arose, we lay-a-try with the helm unlashed. Meantime, during one's spell at the tiller, when the horrid spectre really took shape, one could pass the time devising ways of coping if the rudder did at last come adrift. What would Hornblower have done, I asked myself, and curiously enough we found the answer to that in a copy of *The Commodore* which happened to be on board. From either quarter stream a half-filled

barrel (or presumably any suitable weight) and by heaving in the port warp
and letting out the starboard, or vice versa, steer accordingly, learning as you
go by trial and error. Nothing could be simpler.

Until we reached home waters we made slow work of it, seldom having a
favourable slant of wind. The further south we got the more contrary the
weather, and in consequence the more occupation we had in the way of
pumping as well as the stitching of sails. The mainsail, a good, strong terylene
sail, had been put together on the wrong principle. The cloths, instead of
running up and down, ran fore and aft, so that if a seam opened near the leach
it might, and often did, open half-way across the sail towards the luff.
Moreover the seams had been machine stitched with thread that one would
hardly trust for a trouser-button. If the jib or stays'l needed repair they could
be taken below whereas the mains'l had to be attended to on deck as and
when the weather permitted. Nearly a fortnight after leaving Spitzbergen,
and two months since we had first crossed it, we recrossed the Arctic Circle,
an occasion that had to be suitably marked. It's a poor heart that never
rejoices and at sea the galley, or what comes out of it, is probably the most
likely cause of rejoicing. In preparation for this banquet more or less all hands
mustered in the galley, each bent on showing what he could do; nor was there
any fear of too many cooks spoiling the broth because each was too intent on
his own masterpiece to meddle with that of anyone else. Alan, sole architect
and creator, led off with the hors d'oeuvre – sardines submerged in a pungent
mixture of tomato puree and curry powder, tastefully draped with melted
cheese; Paul, possibly with left-wing tendencies, gave birth to Bortsch, thick
as glue and withal luscious; after these lofty flights David brought us back to
earth with homely Cottage Pie, while Andrew, a dab hand at pastry, clinched
matters with an outsize apple tart. Cocoa laced with rum followed as a
corrective.

Three southerly gales in a row drove us so far to the west that Thorshavn, in
the Faeroes, became the likeliest target. We had no charts for the Faeroes
and on 1 September when we were only a few miles off the weather was so
thick that I preferred not to try to find the place. Instead of waiting for the fog
to clear, the wind still fair for Scotland, we decided to carry on for Stornoway.
At this time the weather round the British Isles was extremely unsettled with
gale warnings in force for most areas. A low in the Irish Sea was said to be
moving north bringing with it a Force 10 gale. On the night of 3 September we
sighted the C. Wrath light, our first landfall, and although the night was dirty
enough the wind was nothing like Force 10. Being too far east we failed to
weather C. Wrath and in consequence spent a day bucketing about in a
confused sea and not enough wind with the islands of Rona and Sula Sgeir in
sight to the north. At least Paul and Alan had the pleasure of seeing again the
islands that had been their objective on their first cruise. By the evening we
were inside Lewis in calm waters, the wind so slight that we turned on the
engine. Whereupon a gush of oil and water mixed obliged Paul quickly to turn
it off, for obviously a liner had cracked or had a hole in it. The engine had
evidently been living on borrowed time and we had reason to be thankful that
this had not happened when we were aground or coming through Freemansund.

On the night of 6 September we sailed cautiously into Stornoway to anchor until morning when we went alongside to take on water and bread. As usual David disappeared for the day. So far as I know he had not a penny but he was no doubt rich in tall Spitzbergen yarns, rich enough to induce someone to pay for his drinks. I came across him on the quay some time after midnight pretending he was a Polar bear. Persistent head winds made for a slow passage through the Minches and then a hard south-easterly gale drove us well to the west of Tory Island off the north-west corner of Ireland. The prospect of having to sail down the west coast and of having no doubt to make frequent tacks to keep clear of the land was far from pleasing; but before we were quite reconciled to it the wind veered to south-west and soon rose to gale force. Whereupon we ran off to the east to enjoy a wonderful day's sailing with the rugged north coast of Ireland close aboard. Later in the day, in order to have a fair tide in Rathlin Sound, we slowed her down by dropping the mains'l and even so she continued to run at close on four knots. We surged through Inishtrahull Sound just as the lighthouse lit up and by day-break we were through the North Channel and off the Maidens by breakfast time. This was the first really fair wind we had had since leaving Spitzbergen and two days later another favourable gale gave us a final shove home. Having rounded Lands End at midnight of the 19th we anchored off Lymington river at midnight of the 21st. In the course of this fast run up Channel we were twice nearly run down by small coasters, having on both occasions to gybe hurriedly to avoid a collision. On a rough night in a lively sea a yacht's oil lamps might not easily be seen, and in the intoxication of *Baroque*'s wild rush for home we had forgotten to hoist the radar reflector. But close quarter situations with steamers, either large or small, should be avoided however many lights or radar reflectors one may be showing.

Since the engine had evidently had it we could hardly make bad worse by using it, so on the next day, a Sunday, we motored up the river. Through impatience and the desire to have done we started too soon on the young flood and owing to lack of water and the week-end traffic we twice took the mud. The first time must have been in sight of the Royal Lymington Clubhouse, yet notwithstanding this unseamanlike approach, as we passed, they gave us their customary finishing gun. For me it was not a happy return: a friend boarded us in the river to tell me that my sister with whom I lived, and with whom I had spoken by telephone from Stornoway, had died sud-denly on the day we left there. But it had been a happy voyage as well as a notable voyage in that we had accomplished our aim. On recent voyages this has not often happened; but, as I have said before somewhere, there is little point in setting out for a place that one is almost certain to reach. Of course, if failures become too frequent there may be something wrong with the objective, too ambitious perhaps, or even something wrong with oneself, too faint-hearted; yet if the blame for failure can be placed fairly and squarely upon natural causes, such as ice, it need not be taken too much to heart. I have in mind Scoresby Sound which we made three attempts to reach. Two of them were certainly frustrated by ice, while on the third the crew were unwilling to press on. Big mountains are seldom climbed at the first attempt which is more often a pioneering effort, breaking the trail for those who follow. Whether successful or not, on these voyages of mine there is a little of the pioneer's reward as well as four months sailing to look back on with pleasure, four months of endeavour to mull over, and that much more experience to store away. Experience is said to be the name men give to their mistakes and of the experience I gained in Spitzbergen that may well be true. Much, if not all, depends on the crew. I had with me a good crew and if a man chooses to put his ship aground in Freemansund that is what he needs.

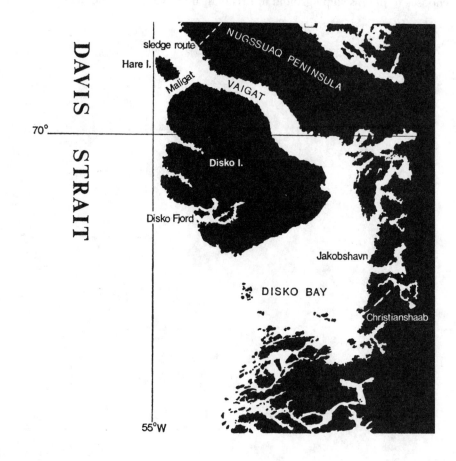

Part 2

West Greenland

CHAPTER SEVEN

Finding a Crew

BY THE AUTUMN of 1974 circumstances had changed for the worse. I had now to face living entirely alone like a Himalayan ascetic in his mountain cave – a spacious cave, I admit, far too spacious for one man. Instead of making it easier, this made it harder to get away either for long or short periods, what with the dogs who shared master's cave and other considerations. Increasing feebleness would oblige me to swallow the anchor some day and that day was not far off. Dwindling resources, too, along with inflated bills plus 25% VAT. Like Tallulah Bankhead, in similar hard times, one began to wonder where the next magnum was coming from. In this weak frame of mind I even questioned the making of another voyage, to regard *Baroque*'s circumnavigation of Spitzbergen as a fitting occasion, a memorable last act, upon which to ring down the curtain. Wisdom certainly pointed that way but whenever there has been a choice between wisdom and what many might regard as folly I have usually chosen the latter. Strenuousness, we are told, is the immortal path, sloth is the way of death. Well aware of this truth I left the question for the moment, with a slight bias in favour of action.

My real hope was that in the course of the winter, as has usually happened in the past, someone who had a mind to take part would write to ask if I had any plans for the coming year. This would act as a spur and be also a commitment, for to assure oneself that a voyage will be undertaken is not as binding as a promise to take someone else. Meantime I made infrequent journeys to Lymington to commune with *Baroque* and bit by bit to bring back for overhaul all the running rigging – the wire for renewal where needed, ropes to be turned end for end, and all the blocks, some twenty-five or so, to be taken apart, greased, and varnished. Wooden blocks ought to be cherished for even now they are not easily found. Soon the only place to buy them – at antique prices – will be those antique shops with a marine flavour, along with ship's wheels, copper navigation lamps, and gimballed brass cabin lamps. Several years ago a Southampton ship's chandler confessed to me that he had sold his entire stock of beautiful wooden blocks with bronze sheaves and pins to a scrap merchant who had promptly burnt the lot to retrieve the metal.

Without any ballast at all *Baroque* rode high in the water. The Spitzbergen rock she had brought home had been taken out and dumped on the quay and I had not yet acquired the necessary 3 tons of pig-iron. The pile of stones on the quay had steadily diminished; rock gardeners, amateur geologists, and souvenir hunters had been chiselling away at it until little remained. The Lymington Town Sailing Club took the biggest bit they could find and having affixed a suitable inscribed brass plate presented it to me at one of their meetings. Weighing some 30 lbs. it is on the heavy side for a paper weight but it makes an admirable door-stop.

The rudder which had sustained severe blows from passing floes when she was aground had been repaired. A new heel fitting was required and that the rudder had remained in place until we got home was a source of wonder. The engine had been taken out, a feat of some ingenuity if the amount of wrecking done was to be kept within bounds. By means of two small holes bored in the roof of the doghouse a chain lift could be inserted to raise the monster from its bed and then with not more than an inch to spare manoeuvred through the door opening on to the cockpit.

Either out of friendly curiosity or puzzled, perhaps, by some of the oddities that from time to time figure amongst my crews, many people ask how they are obtained. Do I resort to crimps or press-gangs? The method or lack of method employed in 1975 is a sample, though since this proved to be one of the more difficult years it is not quite a fair one. Contrary to my hopes the gloom of the winter months was not relieved by enquiries from anyone interested in making a northern voyage. Such enquiries are valuable because they show that the enquirer is keen, and it is better to be approached than to have to approach someone, someone who may get it into his head, perhaps rightly, that he is doing you a favour by coming. And, as I have said, that winter I particularly needed some encouragement, better still a commitment, to making a voyage. But no would-be voyagers, either youthful or elderly, showed any interest in *Baroque* or any plans I might have for using her in the summer. So when March came I was a worried man, for instead of taking this lack of interest as the required signal to stay quietly at home it made me the more obstinately determined to find a crew and go somewhere. The aforesaid crimps, had they been still in business would have been of no use. The ships they catered for were on the point of sailing and the essence of the contract was that the crew they provided should not wake up or recover from a drunken stupor until the ship was safely at sea, whereas I needed my crew at least a fortnight before sailing to help in fitting-out. Numerous feelers were put out to the proliferating Sailing Schools, Adventure Centres, and such like, but none of them touched anything. My first victim, a young man whose home was not far from Barmouth, came by chance, some friends having put me in touch with him. Nicholas was a rolling stone who so far had gathered no moss, nor any polish either. Among the many other jobs that he had held for a time was that of an instructor at an Adventure Centre in Scotland so that he had sailed a boat. He was currently driving a van in Swansea. First impressions were favourable and delight at having at last made a start inclined one to take a good deal for granted. Looking a bit like a bird himself, red-headed at that, bird-watching proved to be his real forte. Meantime the fact that he was employed driving a van ear-marked him for looking after *Baroque*'s engine.

In spite of our long partnership in Africa and the Himalayas in the 'thirties Eric Shipton and I seldom correspond and in fact seldom know at any given moment where the other is. A letter from him therefore came as a surprise, a welcome surprise because it asked me to consider taking with me his youngest boy John. When they bring you a heifer be ready with the rope, and anyway, for old time's sake this was a request that could hardly be refused. Assuming he would be a likely lad I took him on unseen. We talked by telephone but did not meet until later on at Lymington. Young John had spent the last three years bumming his way round the world and in the course of this had crewed on passage-making yachts. He therefore had ocean-going experience though some of the questions he asked and things he did during our first days at sea gave me some concern for those same yachts. However, he soon became a competent hand, uncomplaining, indefatigably cheerful, and ready to turn his hand to anything. I say uncomplainingly because although he had the wettest berth, forward of the galley and too near the foward hatchway, so that its occupant has to live under a permanent polythene canopy, John took this in his stride. Like father, he loved talking and arguments, but had such volubility, such a rush of words to the mouth, that when I was concerned I had to have everything repeated in slow time before I got the message.

The manager of the yard where *Baroque* lives put me in touch with Andrew Horsfield, a student at London University who had had some ocean-going experience. From what I was told I felt he would be my key-man, less volatile than the other two, and indeed he proved a tower of strength, reliable and responsible, always first on deck and last to leave, and a glutton for work. His coming with us, which I felt to be essential, meant a later start than I had bargained for since, owing to exams, he would not be available until 10 June. This would certainly lessen our chances of reaching Ellesmere Is. Its south coast, which was the only part we could hope to reach, lies as far north as 76° N. It is a big island, extending north to 83° N., a fact which made it a favoured jumping-off place for attempts on the North Pole, in particular Peary's successful attempt in 1909. Parts of the island attain to 5,000ft. though there are no mountains of a character that would attract a climber; for me the lure lay in its remoteness and comparative inaccessibility for a small boat. It had been our objective in 1972 when as a result of *Sea Breeze* breaking her boom when still 300 miles east of C. Farewell our plans had to be changed with ultimately disastrous consequences. It is some 800 miles north of Godthaab and since the winds up there in summer are usually light and more often than not from north-east, and since moreover ice would begin to form early in September, a start in mid-May would be desirable.

I now had three hands and needed only a fourth who would undertake the job of cooking. To have one man responsible for this all the time instead of the crew taking it in turns seems to me preferable if not essential on a long voyage. With everyone having a go, each man trusting to his successor to reduce chaos to order, the galley soon becomes a hurrah's nest, everything on top and nothing to hand, while what stores have been used and what remains is nobody's business. On several occasions in the past an advertisement in the Personal Column of *The Times*, the column that is used and perused by screwballs and other *lusus naturae*, has proved fruitful. On resorting to it again I found some new rules had been made as to what kind of advertisement qualified for insertion in so distinguished a place. Mine read 'Amateur cook (male) wanted for 4 months voyage' and they told me that this could only appear either in the 'Situations Vacant' column or under 'Holidays and Villas'. The first implied the paying of wages; as for the other, although *Baroque* might be regarded as a sea-going villa I wondered how many would regard cooking in her galley off Greenland as a holiday. Finally, as a concession, not to be regarded as a precedent, my advertisement did at length appear in the Personal Column and after all this bother produced precisely four replies. After they had learnt what was in store for them none of the four showed any further interest.

Similar advertisements in the not so distant past have produced at least a couple of dozen replies including several from women – hence, on this occasion, the stipulation 'male'. A woman in the galley would, I am sure, bring with her a little much-needed sweetness and light but old-fashioned prejudices have not allowed me to move with the times. Besides, there is the uneasy feeling that the Chinese sage may well have been right when he decided that discord is not sent down from Heaven but is brought about by women. Moreover few women have any understanding of duffs, especially if these have to be cooked in a bucket. They don't eat them and can hardly be expected to cook them. For a sea-cook one wants an all-rounder, a comprehensive genius like Alexis Soyer whose book *Gastronomic Regenerator* I have just been reading, a man who could dish up a banquet for the assembled crowned heads of Europe, make soup for fifty men at a time in the rigours of a Crimean winter, and find time to invent a stove, the Soyer Stove still used by the army in 1914–18.

About this time Solent Radio asked for an interview, holding out as an inducement that it would surely evoke an overwhelming response from would-be crew. So I reluctantly agreed to undergo this brief, distasteful ordeal and there is no doubt that Solent Radio had at least one listener for soon after I had a letter from a Captain Joslin. He was an ex-Master Mariner, *aetat* 70, evidently heartily sick of life ashore and withal conveying a hint that he could cook. To ask a Master Mariner to ship as cook in *Baroque* seemed to me verging on impudence, but we arranged to meet at Lymington where by now it was time for me to go to start fitting-out. Like master, except that they did not know what they were in for, my dogs had now to face up to four months hard in kennels, and having disposed of them and hopefully locked the front door I went down to Lymington on 21 May. Next day Captain Joslin came over from Winchester to have a look at the boat. It may have been the galley that shook him, for it had not been properly cleaned since the previous voyage, and he finally departed with a slightly reluctant 'No'. But within an hour he was back, having in the interim spoken by telephone with a forceful daughter who had apparently urged him to go. Next day he started work on the galley. His age naturally gave me pause, for although I could give him several years he had not been accustomed to small boat voyages in rude climates.

He looked a little frail but I assumed that if he did not thrive he would at any rate survive and I liked the idea of having on board a professional seaman to show how things should be done. Before we parted that evening he mentioned that he was due for a medical check. I feared the worst. Sure enough, two days later he rang to say he would have to cry off. Far from recommending a long sea voyage his doctor had firmly told him to stay at home.

Andrew, whom I kept informed of the state of play, posted a notice in some of the London colleges. This produced quite a few enquiries, mostly from those who would not be available until mid-June. Two who would be free in time I invited down to Lymington that first week-end when there were 3 tons of pig-iron ballast waiting to be tarred. On this test one of them scored only low marks but the other I rather took to, a 27-year-old Dane who had spent a short time in Greenland running the air-port hotel at Sondre Stromfjord. He had a care-free attitude, smoking cigars while he wielded the tar-brush. Unluckily he had first to go to Denmark to settle some private affairs and the affairs seem to have settled him. He wrote to say he would be unable to come.

Meantime, the cook problem still unsolved, we got on with the fitting out. Something could still be hoped for from those fickle allies time and chance, but with sailing day provisionally fixed for 5 June time was running out. Having set up the ratlines I could go aloft to hang the blocks for the throat and peak halyards and the strops and blocks for the jib and stays'l halyards. An elderly bystander reproved me for not leaving this to the young crew. John happened to be one of those unfortunates with no head for heights and never succeeded in reaching the crosstrees, while had it been left to Nicholas I should have had to listen to a steady, unstoppable flow of questions, suggestions, and doubts about the possibility of whatever was in hand. While I was busy aloft the boys were stowing the ballast. Simon Richardson, who had been mate on *Baroque*'s first voyage, had got this for me from a Portsmouth scrap yard, all in handy sizes, nothing heavier than 40 lbs. A few pieces were in the shape of the weight on a lead-line with an eye at one end, and when we lost our 7 lbs. lead, the line parting, we used one of these cut in half as a replacement. It did not take long to stow the ballast. Owing to her harder bilge, finer garboards, and a liberal use of concrete there seemed to be much less room for ballast than in either *Mischief* or *Sea Breeze*.

This done we could ship the spars – bowsprit, boom, gaff – and bend on the mains'l, and still had plenty of time for panting and varnishing. With praise-worthy zeal John and Nicholas scraped the whole of the capping rail down to bare wood – a long job – before varnishing it. Having sacrificed our big fisherman type anchor the previous voyage we acquired an equally heavy one which was lying rusty and forlorn under my store. According to the yard's oldest inhabitants it had once belonged to *Mischief*. Although it was rusted almost solid we managed to free the stock and when chipped and painted it looked as good as new. The cable, too, had to be laid out, cleaned up, and the appropriate links painted white at 5 fms. intervals. The three of us had therefore plenty to do. Dana, in *Two Years before the Mast*, quotes what he calls the Philadelphia Catechism:

> Six days shalt thou labour and do all that thou art able,
> And on the seventh, holystone the decks and scrape the
> cable.

Baroque's deck had been painted the previous year and it now had another coat in the hope of making it water-tight, so that we had no use for the holystone that we had used on the deck of *Sea Breeze* which still lay in the store. Holystones come in two sizes. A big one, the Sailor's Bible, which is applied standing up, and a smaller one, the Prayer Book, which is used kneeling.

By 30 May we were still without a cook. A telegram, 'Regret impossible', from the last of my always doubtful reserves had blasted that hope. Thus things looked desperate enough when young John bethought him of a London friend, Alec Ramsay, whom he rang. Alec professed interest and when I spoke to him later he decided to come down next day to look us over. In the end he agreed to come and promised to join on 4 June, giving himself three days to organise his affairs. He was a professional photographer and an amateur cook with no sea experience whatsoever but once he had got his sea-legs he never looked back. Keeping a close watch on stores and water, he fed us admirably and economically, and even in the most boisterous weather refused to lower his standards. Life's lottery includes a great many blanks but there are yet a few prizes and I regarded Alec's quite fortuitous presence on board as one of them. In his early days I could fault him on only one count, a strange reluctance or shyness in the matter of duffs. We were 36 days out and west of C. Farewell before, as it were, we struck pay-dirt. One of the spotted dog or dead-man's-leg variety, boiled in a cloth and bent at both ends to fit the pan, at last made its appearance. After that, as if a spell had been broken or a curse lifted, we had two a week, cooked in a more refined way in a basin instead of a dishcloth, and each better than the last.

On 1 June the stores came and were stowed, anything that was not in tins or jars – sugar, flour, dried fruit, etc. – being put first in heavy-duty plastic bags. As most of these had originally contained insecticide or fertiliser one had to be a little careful. For the first time we had to go without dried egg, none being obtainable. This is a useful ingredient for cakes, duffs, pancakes and such like, and in the form of omelettes or scrambled eggs, provided it is well laced with Tabasco sauce, makes a welcome breakfast change from porridge. We also took on the usual twice-baked bread, twenty-four loaves of it, and by an oversight a little of it remained when we returned to Lymington in September, on the hard side but still in prime condition and free from mould. Fresh bread will last only ten days or so at the outside before going mouldy so this twice-baked bread sees us through to Greenland where one can get black bread with its superior keeping qualities. In a vegetable locker on deck we had 1 cwt. of potatoes and $\frac{1}{2}$ cwt. of onions. Alec used onions almost daily for cooking as we ate them raw for lunch, yet this ½ cwt. lasted and kept so well that at the end of the voyage there were quite a few left for me to take home.

With Alec's joining on the evening of 4 June the crew, against all the odds, was complete except for the absent Andrew then undergoing the torture of examinations. We had arranged to pick him up at Castletown in Bantry Bay where we would already have put a few hundred miles of westing behind us. Giving Alec a day's grace to accustom himself to the boat I put sailing day back to 6 June. Having regard to the haphazard way in which they had been gathered together the crew proved to be a great deal better than I deserved. They accepted with equanimity the occasional peevishness of their ageing skipper and the far from occasional dampness of their quarters, doing all that was required of them with unfailing cheerfulness and willingness. Above all they got on well together and when not occupied with work or sail changing contrived to keep themselves amused – chess, Scrabble, even Monopoly for which John contrived a board. They spent much time, too, in argument and debate in which John and Nicholas were eminently vociferous, Alec quieter but equally fluent, and Andrew, who like Moses was very meek, putting in occasional soothing words. Inarticulate and hearing little, I took no part in these debates, but I gathered that in some respects John was almost as much of a Col. Blimp as I was and that Nicholas was against the Establishment or indeed any establishment. Besides his strident debating powers, Nicholas, our bird-man, had a habit of whistling or breaking into loud song, apparently involuntarily, whether on deck or below. Like the poet Gray who could stand only the hissing of the tea-kettle, I am averse to noise. It was like living in the monkey-house or an aviary, an aviary devoted mainly to the keeping of whooping cranes, whistling ducks, and macaws. However, we are all as God made us, some of us much worse, and he who will have eggs must bear with cackling.

CHAPTER EIGHT

Bantry Bay and the Atlantic

HAVING FILLED up with water and fuel and, as one hoped, in all respects ready for sea, on the morning of Friday 6 June we cast off and motored down the river. *Baroque*'s curious behaviour under power on her first voyage still haunted me. With the engine going she had always refused to turn to port and the only way of overcoming the effect of the offset propeller was to put the engine in neutral. On the second voyage she behaved better and we had no occasion to use the drogue which a friend had gone to the trouble of making in order to counteract this awkward tendency. On this third occasion going down the river my fears were soon forgotten, for she steered almost normally. Perhaps the rough treatment of those two voyages had ironed some kinks out of her hull. We went down to the Needles under mains'l and stays'l and set the jib when outside. I cannot remember ever making a kindlier start in more benign weather, yet with the Needles still in sight astern Alec and Nicholas were communing with the sea over the rail, the latter not sufficiently overcome to forget to tell us in his querulous voice what he wanted for supper.

John, who was happily immune, provided supper for two, letting his imagination run riot to the extent of opening a tin of bully and boiling some spuds. Alec, refusing to give in, cooked breakfast for us next morning but his frequent, forced visits to the deck while doing so resulted in abominably hard eggs. This quite spoilt my day for I am like the valetudinarian Mr Woodhouse who held that only an egg boiled very soft is not unwholesome. Having caught a few small mackerel we did better for supper; there were just enough for John and I who were the only ones interested. Happily the placid weather still prevailed. I shuddered to think of the resulting shambles had it been otherwise, with only John and a seasick Nicholas to work the boat, neither of them knowing where gear or tools had been stowed or even what some of the gear was properly called.

By the Sunday evening we were off the Lizard. A slight haze as well as a desire for a quiet night decided me to go south of the Scillies instead of north-about round the Seven Stones light vessel. The night proved quiet enough but did not pass without mishap. Coming on deck at midnight to relieve John I noticed a gaping seam in the mains'l. No one could fail to notice so large a hole but John had not allowed it to worry him and he now suggested that we should roll down a few reefs to hide it, sweeping the mess, as it were, under the carpet. By the time we had the sail down some twelve feet of seam had opened and it took me most of next day to close it. To sew in comfort we had to unreeve the clew earing and unlace the after part of the sail. On a warm and sunny evening, the sewing completed, John and I were hauling out the clew again and having something of a struggle as it needs to be bar taut. Francis Bacon, philosopher and essayist, remarked on the pleasure of watching a battle from a distant hill, and Nicholas, watching our struggles as he reclined on a mattress spread on the counter did not forget to ask if he was in the way.

The thickening fine-weather haze prevented our seeing anything of the Scillies or the Bishop Rock, but we were well to the south and could afford to start steering north-west for Bantry Bay where we were obviously going to be late for our rendezvous with Andrew. By the 11th, the appointed day, we were still 70 miles away with the wind blowing directly from where we wanted to go. Tacking, as we now had to do, emphasised once again another curious feature of *Baroque*. Most boats when on the wind under all plain sail will carry some weather helm, that is to say they tend to come up into the wind so that the tiller has to be kept up (towards the wind) to hold the boat straight. On the port tack, the wind blowing from the port side, *Baroque* conformed to this rule, while on the starboard tack she needed a lot of lee helm to keep her up to the wind. In her old age she is evidently beginning to stoop or droop to one side, for what little I have gathered of her past life does not account for her vagaries, it only makes it the more surprising that she is still afloat.

Recently a friend sent me a long article on Bristol Channel Pilot Cutters by B. R. Waite which had appeared in the *Yachting Monthly* in 1927. *Baroque* figures prominently in this with two pictures of her. At the end of the article is a list of eighteen Pilot Cutters which had been converted into yachts. Neither *Mischief* nor *Sea Breeze* are listed and many others must have been omitted because the whole fleet, some sixty in all, was sold after the First War when the pilotage went over to steam. According to this article, when the pilots owned and sailed them, the mast was supported only by the shrouds, no backstays at all; nor did they have a bobstay or any bowsprit shrouds; and it was the considered belief of the pilots that since their conversion to yachts, the vessels had lost a great deal of their speed owing to additions to the standing rigging and the fitting of rigging screws in place of deadeyes and hemp lanyards. The picture of *Baroque* confirms the absence of backstay, bobstay, and bowsprit shrouds. The paragraphs referring to *Baroque* are worth quoting in full; the *Saladin* mentioned, her rival, was one of the full-bodied type like *Sea Breeze* and *Mischief*, and had a displacement of 35 tons against *Baroque*'s 32 tons:

The difference of the under-water sections of *Saladin* and *Baroque*, as shown in the accompanying photographs, so interested the owners of the two craft that they arranged a friendly race. *Saladin* with her full forward sections proved to be appreciably the faster off the wind. On the wind there seemed to be little difference, and as *Baroque* was handicapped by the drag of a propeller, was the smaller of the two, and had a suit of well-worn winter sails bent, honours to windward might be considered equal. It is interesting to note that *Baroque* is not fitted with runners, where *Saladin* had all the runners and backstays usually carried by yachts. Whether *Baroque* proved her rival's equal to windward by virtue of the play allowed her gear or to her hard bilge and finer garboards forward is difficult to say, but *Saladin*'s superior speed off the wind seems undoubtedly due to her clean run.

Baroque is a particularly interesting example of these craft. Built for the pilot service by Hambley in 1902 she was sold when the service was disbanded and eventually found her way to Scarborough where owing to bad times she was left in the harbour to be sold for what she would fetch. Her present owner found her with a large hole in her planking through which the tide ebbed and flowed at will. Except for the hole in her side she was found to be sound so she was put ashore, thoroughly overhauled, one of her engines removed (her previous owner had installed two) and now has her headquarters at Hamble, from where she cruises winter and summer. She is an extremely comfortable and able craft, and has been fitted up internally by her owner who has made an excellent job of her accommodation.

The mention of *Baroque*'s propeller implies that this race took place when she was no longer a working boat and had been converted to a yacht. Poor *Baroque*! I have already recorded how she was fished up out of Cowes harbour and here she is again full of sea water at Scarborough. Not to mention the two engines inside her and the structural upheaval that these must have occasioned. Where I willingly agree with the writer of this article that she is an able boat, his remarks about her comfort and the excellent accommodation are questionable. Much depends on what you want to accommodate and, of course, since the writing of that article in 1927 she must have suffered many chops and changes at the hands of various whimsical owners. The Registry that I now have goes back only to 1951 and since then she has changed hands no less than eight times. And what a mixed lot these various owners have been – a consulting surgeon, a seaman, a banker, a blacksmith's striker, a plumber, a spinster, a horticulturist – any or all of whom may have wrought drastic changes in her either on deck or below, particularly the blacksmith's striker.

In anticyclonic weather, pleasant enough but inimical to progress, the wind light at north-west with patches of fog, two more days passed until at last late on Friday 13 June we secured alongside at Castletown. Fishing boats, mostly engaged in salmon-netting, left us little room, and my inexperienced crew, trying to pass warps ashore in bundles, did not show up very well. Andrew, who for two days had been playing Sister Anne with the harbour-master, came down at 10 pm with his gear and I was mightily relieved at this reinforcement. The crew went ashore, as they said, for a 'short walk', and announced their return at 2 am by jumping on to the deck from what sounded like a great height. Our sensitive poet Gray would not have liked this, nor did the skipper.

In the morning we had to move to make room for a Spanish trawler and we lay at close quarters stern to stern. Between us a small boat with an outboard engine came in to fill up with petrol from a drum on the quay, and at the same time the Spaniard decided to give his propeller a whirl. Pandemonium! The small boat shot out seawards in a cloud of petrol and our stern did its best to follow, the stern warp having parted. In the afternoon the Spaniard repeated the performance, fortissimo and more prolonged. One by one all our warps parted except the bow line. With Andrew busy on the quay retrieving broken warps I was alone on board wondering what Hornblower would have done if the quivering bow-line parted. The rest of the crew were amusing themselves ashore. Like some of my past crews they tended to regard a boat as a car, a necessary evil for getting from one place to another which, on arrival, one parked and forgot about. This time the Spanish bos'n, recognising our plight, brought some of his men to our assistance and with a running commentary of what must have been seamanlike Spanish oaths soon had things under control. We made ourselves fast once more as far as possible from Spain.

Having filled up with water we sailed that evening and met some roughish weather outside. Squalls of Force 6 continued throughout the night and most of the following day. None of the crew felt at all happy except John who in an excess of zeal fell into the drink. By sailing too close to the wind he had let the boat go about Chinese fashion and while I was gybing her back and he was getting in the main sheet he fell over the side. He had a hold on the life-rail, thank Heaven, and was able to drag himself back, for the rest of the crew were in no condition to respond smartly to any 'Man Overboard' drill. On one of the voyages south in *Mischief* one of the crew fell overboard while skylarking and it took a good twenty minutes to recover him. We were south of the Cape Verde Is. running under twin staysails so that these had to come down before anything could be done. The man had got into the lifebuoy we had thrown after him but we had gone so far before we were able to start back towards him that we had great difficulty in keeping him in sight. The answer is to keep on throwing things overboard until the boat has been turned round, like laying a trail. On the only other man overboard incident, also on a voyage south in *Mischief* the victim never had a chance, and why or how he came to go overboard is still a mystery. David Shaw, an officer on leave from the Royal Mail line, had the 6 am to 8 am watch, and when I came on deck before breakfast at about 7.30 am I found the boat on course, the helm lashed, and no helmsman. From the reading on the patent-log it seemed that it had stopped rotating soon after 6 am and on hauling in the log-line we found that it had broken well short of the rotator. Assuming that it had been broken by David grabbing hold of it, he had been in the water well over an hour and must have been a good four miles back. The weather was by no means bad but there were enough white horses to make it difficult to spot anything small. For two hours we sailed back on a reciprocal course, the crew up the shrouds on the look-out. After that we motored back along the course in zig-zag fashion and in fact went on searching until almost sundown. The water was warm and even without a lifebuoy a man might keep afloat for a long time and although the chances of our spotting him were remote it was not pleasant to think that he might well have seen *Mischief*. David Shaw was my key-man, while the rest of the crew, as events soon showed, were one and all what my New Zealand friends call pikers.

Crossing the North Atlantic from west to east is generally uphill work, a fight to make westing. The desired course for C. Farewell is about WNW. With a south-west wind we could just about lay the course while winds with a more westerly component, which were also more frequent, pushed us off course to the north. The perfect summer of 1975 enjoyed at home will long be remembered and it might be thought that the same warm, calm conditions would prevail well out into the Atlantic if not right across it; whereas once west of Ireland we ran into typical Western Ocean weather, no better and no worse than on many previous voyages. June is one of the quietest months and on five days the wind reached Force 7, there were five days of rain or drizzle, and an equal number of foggy days. Midsummer day was a bright exception, warm, cloudless, windless, with all hands except the skipper bathing over the side. The weather we experience is seldom so widespread as we tend to think, a fact that should worry (though it never does) those who believe in and talk of 'Equinoctial' gales. Within a day or so of the Equinox one observer to his great satisfaction experiences a gale just as he had foretold, while another 200 miles away and an equally convinced believer, has his hopes or expectations dashed by a flat calm.

All these minor prophets who tell us what things will be like fifty years hence, or even next year, should try their hands at the weather which happily enough still remains fairly unpredictable except perhaps for the next twenty-four hours. Two hundred miles or so west of Ireland one is out of the region covered by the Shipping Forecast and by that time anyway our small receiving set could no longer pick up the BBC. The Atlantic Weather Bulletin which covers as far as 40° W. is broadcast by W/T and even if we could have picked it up we had no one on board good enough at Morse. With the aid of the barometer and the appearance of the sky, particularly at dawn and sunset,

a man does his own forecasting and unless the presages of good or evil are glar-
ingly obvious he seldom gets it right. Some dispense even with a barometer
and certainly Joshua Slocum, the first single-handed circum-navigator, had no
such thing on board *Spray*. A man like Slocum, though, would be eminently
weatherwise, having spent many years as a master in sail where the vessel's
safety or at least the safety of her sails and spars depended on the master's
ability to read the signs aright. When Nicholas succeeded in wrecking our
barometer so that it fell 30 mbs. and refused to move, I felt deprived of help
as well as annoyed. No doubt in time I should have got used to its absence but
in fact it staged a slow recovery by itself without any tinkering on our part.

CHAPTER 9

To Godthaab

As a SEA-GOING CROW would fly it is only about a thousand miles from
Bantry Bay to C. Farewell. *Baroque* logged 1,300 miles and took 24 days over
it, during which we suffered the usual minor mishaps. Another seam opened
in the mains'l, outdoing the first one in length, and since the sail had to be
opened out to get at the seam, sewing could only be done in calm spells when
the sail lay quiet. There may be some reason for the cloths of a mains'l to be
sewn together horizontally rather than vertically (*Mischief*'s mainsails were all
made up this way by a very well known sailmaker) but if they are I should like
to see them sewn with sinews, preferably those of an elephant, instead of with
seaming twine. A tear in the jib was more serious. While handing the sail the
crew made a nonsense and got it wrapped round the bobstay. When finally
recovered it looked as if it had been caught up in some machine, the clew and
part of the sail in ribbons. At first sight I thought it beyond repair but down in
the cabin we pieced it together and with two or three of us stitching away for
two days it began to look like a sail; by the time we had reinforced it with
crude strips of canvas it was nearly as strong as ever, and for the rest of the
voyage, though we had to nurse it a little, we had no more trouble. Then we
had sanitary problems. The outlet pump on the lavatory broke down and, as
we soon discovered, *Baroque* is not well adapted for business over the side.
The guard rails finish well short of the counter so that there is nothing there to
hang on to and forward of that the double guard rails made things difficult
except for a contortionist. Working up till midnight Nicholas and Andrew
repaired the pump. At Godthaab I bought a galvanised bucket in case it
happened again.

Although another coat of deck paint had been lavished on her the boat
appeared to me to be no drier than the previous year, in other words she was
just as wet, the drips from the beams persisting insidiously, difficult to trace to

their source. As the Tibetans say, one can live comfortably even in hell if one knows how to go about it, and we all devised our own irrigation or anti-irrigation systems based on plastic sheeting and drawing pins. There were other sources probably besides the deck, for in rough weather she needed a lot of pumping. On 28 June when it blew hard out of a clear sky we had to double the watch at night with one man attending to the pump. Otherwise the man coming off watch, whose normal duty it was to clear the bilge, would have spent a lot of time doing this before he could get his head down. Next morning, the wind as fresh as ever, a wave pushed in one of the windows on the port side of the dog-house. In accordance with Sod's Law I had just come off watch and having taken off my oilskins was writing up the log on the chart table inside the dog-house. The log book as well as the chap writing in it got soaked. We boarded over the windows and I removed everything of moment like the navigational books to the bookshelf in the cabin which remained. uniquely dry. The following morning, the same wind still blowing, a wave broke the after window on the same side. As the door of the 'heads' was not really needed we used that to put over both the broken windows where it fitted snugly. Shortly afterwards we hove-to and a sight that I got later put us 40 miles north of our dead-reckoning position, the effect of leeway after three days of strong WSW winds. Although still 400 miles east of C. Farewell we were in 59° 30′ N. or almost on the latitude of the cape.

The wind continued unfavourable. By going on the starboard tack to gain southing we should also lose ground to the east and that went against the grain. The *Pilot* recommends keeping 70 miles south of C. Farewell, mainly to avoid meeting icebergs, and on all five previous voyages there had been little difficulty in so doing. On only one voyage had we sighted any ice and that when we were closing the land a little west of the cape. Several days of either fog or rain were a hindrance to precise navigation but on 8 July I reckoned we were fifty miles west of the cape and only a few miles south, and that afternoon we sighted a line of what looked like heavy pack-ice about two miles to the north. With the wind light we could just point WSW and on that course we soon found ourselves among scattered floes. So we started the engine and steered due south expecting to be very soon clear of the ice. Not a bit of it. Twenty-four hours elapsed before we won clear and that at the cost of two sprung planks.

By supper time (fried rice and apple crumble) when we stopped the engine, we were still surrounded by floes, no wind to speak of and foggy. After supper we resumed motoring. We must have done nearly twenty miles under the engine and had we but stuck firmly to a southerly course we might have got clear. Instead we tended inevitably to take the line of least resistance, steering towards where the floes appeared most widely scattered, and this was generally to the west. The crew enjoyed the novelty of steering through ice and they were getting plenty of practice. However, towards midnight Andrew cut things too fine, misjudged the distance between two floes, and gave poor *Baroque* a terrible wallop forward of the shrouds on the port side. With the cabin sole almost immediately awash it was clear we had suffered some damage and it did not take long to find that a plank had been sprung about a foot below the water-line forward of the galley. With canvas, a board, and a great many nails Nicholas and Andrew soon reduced the flow to a trickle and we restarted the engine.

By 4 àm the floes were far enough apart for us to cut the engine and set all plain sail, and when I took over from John at 6 am of a wonderfully clear, cloudless morning we were cruising along nicely over a perfectly calm sea. Unfortunately we were cruising westwards for all along our port hand, not more than fifty yards away, lay a wall of closely packed ice. Fine on the port bow and about forty miles away the mountains near C. Farewell showed blue in the early morning light, and to the north as far as one could see there were neither floes nor bergs to break the wide expanse of free and open sea. We had met no icebergs among the floes and now the absence of any in sight to the north was very curious, for one expects to see bergs rather than floes anywhere within seventy miles of C. Farewell. Pleasant sailing though it was on this fresh morning I had not been long at the tiller, enjoying the distant mountain prospect, before it occurred to me that we were wasting our time. Seen from the crosstrees the horizon is distant only some six miles; in the absence of a helicopter or a man-lifting kite one could not be sure, but it was highly probable that the ice on our port hand would not diminish to the west and that there would be ice close to C. Farewell and all along the coast to the west. The temptation of proceeding direct to the cape through apparently open water had to be resisted and I soon decided that the safest plan would be to sail east. We therefore went about and began to retrace our steps of the previous day.

Since our return the Meteorological Office have sent me a plot of the ice limits at this time, between 7 and 10 July, which shows the ice extending to some 60 miles east of C. Farewell and nearly 100 miles to the south. The following long extract from the *Arctic Pilot* explains the ice conditions off the cape:

Ice is brought down the east coast of Greenland to C. Farewell in the East Greenland current, and subsequently carried west of that cape by the West Greenland current. This ice was called the East Ice by the nineteenth century whalers to distinguish it from the West Ice of Baffin Bay. The Arctic pack forming the East Ice is called *Storis* literally 'large ice', by the Danes. It consists of very old floes, the last remnants of much larger ones originally formed in the Arctic Ocean and there increased to great thicknesses by rafting, up to 100ft. or more. On the long passage down the East coast the process of weathering and erosion by the sea continues, and by the time the storis reaches C. Farewell the original great floes have been broken up into small irregular ones which are frequently high. Sea erosion has hollowed them out at the water-line, often leaving long rams projecting below the surface. Many of the floes are of fantastic shapes. The majority have a total thickness of up to 20ft.; these float with from 3 to 4ft. above the surface. Some, however, stand higher out of the water, from 8 to 10ft. and occasionally 12ft. The total thickness of these is estimated to be from 30 to 40ft.

The amount of storis which rounds C. Farewell varies in different years and there are irregularities in its rate of movement and in the times of the beginning and ending of its passage past that cape. The rate of the East Greenland current seldom exceeds one knot and wind influence in opposition to the current may be strong enough to check the flow of ice or even for a time reverse it to a northerly direction. The main mass of the storis, consisting of large, thick floes, usually passes C. Farewell in April, but may be delayed until May. Off the south-west coast of Greenland the ice normally reaches furthest north in May, the northern limit being in the vicinity of Fiskernaes. Occasionally, in a heavy storis year, scattered floes drift as far north as Godthaab in May to August, and rarely, as in 1898 and 1940, even further north. In a light ice year the storis may not reach further north than C. Desolation, 140 miles north-west of C. Farewell.

The amount of ice passing C. Farewell is usually less in June and decreases rapidly towards the end of July. The flow usually ceases in the early part of August. From September to the beginning of next season's flow of storis, no appreciable amount of pack-ice passes C. Farewell in average years, though occasional scattered floes may be met. Every storis floe that passes C. Farewell ends by melting in the relatively warm water of the southern approaches to Davis Strait. As it rounds the C. Farewell region the storis spreads out to the southward to an average distance of 60 to 70 miles in April and May. It has been known to extend from 100 to 150 miles south of the cape. In general, the further the distance from the coast, the greater is the degree of scattering of the ice, but at any given distance the amount of scattering will depend on the total quantity of ice rounding the region of the cape at the time.

The main flow of bergs from the glaciers on the east coast of Greenland round C. Farewell occurs from April to August inclusive, the maximum number being usually in April with a gradual decrease from May to August. Off the cape several hundred large bergs have been reported in sight from a ship at one time. In autumn the number of bergs in this region decreases rapidly, and in winter the vicinity is more or less free from bergs, though occasional ones may be met in any month. The bergs are carried northward and north-westward by the West Greenland current. They end by melting in the central part of Davis Strait, the waters of which are relatively warm, so that no berg from East Greenland ever reaches the Great Bank of Newfoundland and the main transatlantic shipping tracks. The region in which bergs may be met off southern Greenland is much more extensive than that occupied by the storis, and no definite southerly limit can be given. The greatest distance at which bergs are met south of C. Farewell usually occurs in April and May; this is generally up to about 130 miles, but in 1922 bergs extended to 150 miles south of the cape. In April bergs may be found as far to the eastward as 60° N., 32° W.

All that morning we steered east or south-east among floes so thinly distributed that we sailed more or less unhindered. We expected soon to be in the clear and were disconcerted when the floes began to increase rather than diminish in numbers. By noon we had to hand the sails and revert to the engine and an hour later, patience now wearing thin, we still had to pick our way through narrow leads with no signs of any easier conditions ahead. But then from up the mast came the report of open water to the south and when I went up to have a look I saw an abrupt edge to the ice barely half a mile away and beyond it open water with never a floe in sight. A tenuous lead promised to take us a good part of the way but closer to the edge even the eye of faith could discern no opening at all. Had there been any pronounced ice edge the day before we would have shyed away from it, but we had been drawn among floes almost imperceptibly and I expected to emerge from it in the same way. Given the patience to carry on eastwards for a few more hours we might have done so but the sight of open water so close at hand was too tempting. At least we could have a look.

From up the mast it had been clear that we should not escape without a struggle and when we were within two to three hundred yards of the clean-cut ice-edge the struggle began. The narrow lead had petered out. More than that, it had closed in astern of us, providing us thus with at least an excuse for pushing on and for the vigorous tactics that this entailed. Where two floes were far enough apart to accept *Baroque*'s stem we nosed her in, and then with boathooks pushed one or both floes away until she could be squeezed through the gap. The pool beyond would be too small for manoeuvring, and the boat had no steerage way, so her stem would come to rest against the next floe. The crew would then jump on to the ice, push her bows into the nearest gap, and clamber back on board for more business with boathooks. It was all by no means so straightforward and there were times when progress in any direction seemed unlikely. Some floes were on the move, in which case we might get nipped, as we did once at the cost of another sprung plank. Some floes had projecting underwater tongues on which the keel stuck, and since the engine had no power in reverse the crew had to warp her off by hauling from the ice. An observer of the scene would have wondered what we were playing at and if he were at all apprehensive would have thought, like Brer Rabbit, 'that every minit wuz gwineter be de nex'. The shortest follies are the best but it took us more than two hours to conclude this folly. Fortunately the day was calm and clear. Only at the edge itself were the floes moving up and down in response to a gentle swell, while the several banks of fog that lowered in the distance remained stationary. Having at length got clear and put some water between us and the ice we hove-to for a belated lunch. The crew had done well in this trial of strength and nerve and if they had any doubts about the outcome, as once or twice I myself had, they did not let them appear. I made our position that evening 58° 30' N., 42° 30' W. or about 80 miles south-west of C. Farewell. The reader may think it strange that there are no pictures of this episode, of *Baroque*'s hand-to-hand fight with large chunks of ice. Pictures often tell the story better than the account, especially if the account is written by one with a limited vocabulary, a constrained mode of expression, and little or no imagination. In fact we were all too busy, including Alec, whose photographic talent and equipment outdid that of the rest of us put together; too concerned to get clear before wind or ice movement made things worse than they already were.

11 July proved to be a day on which a church might have appointed a General Thanksgiving to be read; a church, I mean, such as that adorned by the Rev Dr Oppimian who figures in Peacock's novels, not so much as a clergyman but as a high priest of good living, one of whose dictums – 'Whatever happens in this world never let it spoil your dinner' – as we have seen, is not always easily obeyed. The continuing fine, calm weather retarded progress as well as giving us a chance to straighten the port side capping rail, pushed inwards by a floe the previous day; also to attend to the new leak which was near the water-line and that much easier to get at. But the real cause for rejoicing was that after 36 days at sea a duff at last made its appearance, admittedly a trial shot and, unlike some of Alec's subsequent efforts, not a dish to be eaten on one's knees, but undoubtedly a duff, one of

the old-fashioned spotted-dog or dead-man's-leg variety, boiled in a cloth. Its shape lent it added interest. Because the ends had had to be bent to fit the saucepan it looked like a sickle moon rather than the conventional rolling-pin. On most voyages our duffs had been steamed in a basin, or on special occasions in a bucket, so this spotted-dick type presented me with the opportunity to regale the crew with the appropriate story, an unwonted exercise on my part and received by them with respectful laughter. The dramatis personae are the skipper, the mate, and the cabin boy of a small trading vessel, all apparently messing together. Such a duff as we had just eaten, though probably straighter, is brought in by the cabin boy, and the skipper, before dividing it up, politely asks him which he prefers, 'Middle or ends, boy'? As every schoolboy knows, or did know, the fag-ends of these spotted-dick duffs are invariably stodgy and devoid of currants, mere con-gealed suet, so the cabin boy naturally replies, 'Middle, if you please, sir'. Whereupon the skipper, with the explanatory remark, 'Well, me and the mate like ends,' proceeds to cut the thing in half.

For the next few days a lot of fog and little enough wind were our portion, more fog than I have known before in Davis Strait, though it is not to be denied that in summer in these northern latitudes fog is all too frequent. Like the sound of breakers, we kept hearing the growl of pack-ice to the north-west and owing to the presence of this ice the sea temperature was still only 2° C. On 14 July, when according to my hopes we should have been in Godthaab, we relished for the first time what I call a 'Greenland day', a pale blue cloudless sky and a vivid blue sea flecked here and there with dazzling white floes and bergy bits. We were only some thirty miles off the coast and so getting a useful lift from the current which follows the trend of the coast to the north-west. We saw our first icebergs, met an occasional trawler, and could obtain a rough check on our progress by the ice-blink reflected from the Frederikshaabs glacier with its ten-mile wide front. The glacier extends 35 miles inland and rises to a height of 6,000ft. The trawlers were engaged in salmon netting rather than trawling. According to a skipper we met at Holsteinborg the cod and halibut, owing to a fall in sea temperature, have deserted the banks which extend far up the west coast and which up to a few years ago were rich fishing grounds. On earlier Greenland voyages we used to see not only dozens of trawlers fishing these banks but also the three-masted Portuguese schooners anchored on one or other of the banks with their dories (sixty to each schooner) spread far and wide busy hand-lining for cod. Nowadays, as we learnt to our cost on *Baroque*'s first voyage, almost any fishing vessel one meets is either laying or standing by to haul in a half-mile long salmon net. Two days before reaching Godthaab we narrowly escaped an entanglement with a net such as had happened on the first voyage. I had the 6 am to 8 am watch on a perishing cold morning, thick fog and a biting north-east wind, the air temperature 2° C. When an iceberg loomed up I had to alter course smartly and passed within feet of a dan buoy at the windward end of a salmon net. Even in fog one can generally spot a berg in time to sheer away but a dan buoy, which is merely a pole with a small flag supported by a float, is another matter. Shortly after we met an Italian vessel *Ave Maria* at anchor, with one of her boats out busy laying buoys all over the place. Whether these were for nets or for some more obscure purpose we could not decide.

My flawless 'Greenland' days were notably scarce at this time when, if it were not foggy, it would be either raining or blowing. Early on the 19th it blew so hard that we had three rolls in the mains'l. Had the whole sail been up things might have been worse, for bird-man Nicholas chose that moment to execute an imperial Chinese gybe, his second. On this occasion the boom crashed over with enough violence to break the block and spread the hook of the backstay tackle. Normally when gybing the main sheet is hauled in until the boom is almost amidships before it is allowed to go over, whereas in an accidental gybe it slams over of its own accord and the violence with which it fetches up against the first obstruction, either the backstay or the main shrouds, depends upon how much of the main sheet is out and the strength of the wind. Chinese gybe, I suppose, referred originally to the way a Chinese junk would gybe, that is to say all standing, for with no heavy boom and the weight of the sail spread evenly by the battens with which it was fitted, this could be done with impunity. Among yachtsmen now it has a derisory meaning, an unseamanlike or lubberly performance by the helmsman, for which there is sometimes an excuse and sometimes not. For instance, an excessively heavy roll may make a gybe almost unavoidable especially with a gaff mainsail. To Englishmen there is, or at any rate used to be, nothing funnier than a foreigner, so that 'Chinese gybe', like other similar expressions, may be just a sailor's way of ascribing to foreigners anything ludicrous or lubberly. For something that has been forgotten we have 'left behind, like the Dutchman's anchor', or 'Dutchman's cape' for non-existent land, 'Irish pendants' for unwhipped rope's ends, and 'Paddy's hurricane' for a flat calm with the wind blowing vertically upwards. The Chinese crop up again in the expression '12 knots and a Chinaman'. Before the patent log came into use a log-line, log-ship (the piece of wood swimming upright at the end of the line), and a sand-glass were the means of ascertaining the vessel's speed. The line was divided by knots, usually twelve, each knot about 47ft. apart for a 28 second sand-glass. One man held the reel from which the line ran out, another tended the line, and an officer watched the sand-glass, and as soon as this ran out the line was checked and the number of knots that had been reeled off gave the speed of the ship. When doing more than 12 knots the man holding the reel was in peril. Apparently in one of the famous flyers of the last century her speed was such that when the line ran out the man holding the reel – a Chinaman, of course – was jerked overboard and lost. So that a vessel doing more than her normal speed – *Baroque*, for instance, doing 7 knots and trembling with excitement at that – might be reported as doing '12 knots and a Chinaman'.

After this damaging gybe we lay-a-try for most of a day of continuous rain with wind gusting to Force 8. By evening it had moderated and we started closing the land towards Godthaab fjord which I reckoned lay 30 miles to the south-east. At 10 pm we sighted the lighthouse on one of the numerous outlying islands. Lighthouses in Greenland are few and far between, existing only at the entrances of the busier ports. They are modest structures with equally modest lights – the Godthaab light, for instance is in a 23ft. high cement tower. In summer, when the nights are never properly dark, the structure will be made out long before the light shows. We lay off for the night, drifting north, and owing to a combination of baffling winds and batteries that were almost flat we did not make the harbour until late next afternoon.

CHAPTER TEN

Godthaab and Northwards

THE HARBOUR that lies some 12 miles up the fjord is now far more commodious than on our first visit in *Mischief* in 1961; indeed there have been further improvements since *Baroque*'s first visit in 1973. We had no difficulty in finding a berth at a long, wooden jetty of recent construction for the accommodation of small fishing boats. This now extends almost the whole length of the high rock wall on which the names of numerous visiting ships have been painted. *Mischief* still figures prominently and this time we added *Baroque*. Presumably because they are such rare birds, the Danes take the kindliest possible view of visiting yachts, which is to say that they completely ignore them. Our Q flag could be hauled down forthwith and without waiting for Customs or Immigration officials we were free to stretch our legs on shore. For the 35 days from Ireland we had averaged a pitiful 44 miles a day and were down to our last gallon of water.

At the main wharf across the harbour they had a large charging plant for keeping the batteries of the fork-lift trucks up to scratch, and the harbour master readily undertook to have our almost flat batteries put on charge. With a borrowed wheelbarrow we took them over. A wet and windy morning turned into an afternoon fine and warm enough to bring out the mosquitoes in some force, but with Godthaab rapidly becoming a concrete jungle they are less numerous then they were. On our first visit the Danish workmen making roads or erecting buildings all wore face veils. We made fruitless attempts to get at the leak on the port side, first by swinging out the boom with the heavy anchor and one of the crew on the end. Then we attached a long warp to the throat halyards and some friendly Danes in a motor boat took the warp and made it fast to a trawler on the far side of the harbour. But our mooring warps – which we could not let go – always prevented our heeling the boat over far enough to bring the sprung plank above water and in the end we gave up and instead put a cement box over the leak inside. What with boulders on the bottom and the absence of any wall to lean against I felt that we might do more harm than good by trying to beach her. Next day, 23 July, the Danish Royal Yacht came in, on her way to the airport up Sondre Stromfjord where the royal party were to be picked up. Her beautiful appearance was marred by the sloppiness of the crew, most of them with long hair streaming out from under their sailor's caps. The Danish navy, I think, is manned by National Service men serving for only a short time which must embitter the hair question. A man finishing his time with short hair would have to face several months of civilian ignominy before it grew again. The old *Mallemuken,* a small gunboat which I remembered from our 1961 visit, was also in harbour. We had had shower baths on board her – the only place one could get a shower at that time – and even then fourteen years ago, she had looked far from modern. Now there is a fine Sailor's Home down by the harbour where one can get a shower.

The fish factory, the only productive unit, did not appear to be working full time, yet Godthaab continues to grow and even to thrive though it is not easy to see why. New buildings were still going up while the amount of traffic that dashes about is astonishing when one remembers that there are no roads anywhere outside the township; all the cars and lorries were merely going from the harbour to the town or from one street to the next, and there are not that many streets. There is an oasis of peace and quiet round the old harbour which is still used by small fishing boats, their catch going to an adjacent open-air market where, I noticed, you could also buy wild rhubarb and odd bits of meat that might have been whale, seal, reindeer, or even dog. Here, too, are the church, the Hans Egede statue, and his original house built of stone, the only such house in Godthaab. Hans Egede was a Norwegian missionary who came to Godthaab in 1721, half expecting, or at least hoping, to find the Norsemen still there. He started missionary work among the Eskimo, established a commerce with Denmark, and was thus the founder of Godthaab. His son Paul continued the Greenland mission and completed the translation of the New Testament into Eskimo, a task left unfinished by his father who died in 1758.

The Norsemen or Vikings, referred to above, the toughest and most adventurous colonists of all time, are closely associated with Godthaab as well as with south-west Greenland. Eric the Red founded the so-called Eastern Settlement or Osterbygd around Julianehab in 986AD and in time it comprised 300 farms, a cathedral, churches, a monastery and a nunnery. The Vesterbygd or West Settlement around Godthaab was smaller, consisting of some ninety farms and four churches, seventy of the farms have been located. Whether the settlers died out because worsening ice conditions cut off essential supplies from Europe or whether the Eskimo exterminated them is conjectural. The annual Greenland carrier (Knarren) made its last voyage in 1369 and in 1406 the last vessel known to have reached Greenland arrived there by mistake and did not get away for four years. The rest is silence. John Davis, the great Elizabethan seaman-explorer who made three voyages in search of the North-west Passage, was the first European to rediscover Greenland. He visited Godthaab in 1585, had moderately friendly relations with the Eskimo who were then there, and made no mention of any Norsemen. Cape Desolation, north of Julienehaab, was so named by him, also Sanderson's Hope near Upernavik, which was his furthest north:

attained on his third Greenland voyage in 1587. On this voyage his eagerness
to push north on what might be a fruitless quest had to be reconciled with
regard for the pocket of his faithful backer William Sanderson, a London
merchant. So he sent his two larger vessels, *Sunshine* and *Elizabeth*, to fish on
the Grand Banks while he himself pushed north in *Helen*, a barely seaworthy
clinker-built pinnace of only 20 tons. In 72° 12' N. they sighted and named the
great cliff Sanderson's Hope, seeing, as Davis wrote, 'no ice towards the
north, but a great sea, free, large, very salt and blue, and of an unsearchable
depth'. But then a north wind drove them west until they encountered the
'Middle Pack' and were forced south.

It was time for us to push on northwards and sight Sanderson's Hope. We
sailed on the evening of 24 July and our departure was, as the phrase goes,
fraught with anxiety. To get water we went to the main quay whence, as the
harbour master said, we must leave by 5.30 pm to make room for an incoming
freighter. Though we needed only 20 gals. of fuel the harbour master had also
arranged for a bowser to come down to the quay to deliver it. At five o'clock,
with no sign of the bowser, the light airs of anxiety that were already playing
upon the brow of expectation rose to a stiff breeze when a large Danish
frigate suddenly appeared at the harbour entrance. I was about to abandon
our fuel and give the order to cast off when the frigate, instead of making for
the quay, let go her anchor in the middle of the harbour. The harbour is small
so that she lay not far from the quay. The bowser then arrived and we filled up
and paid our bill with about five minutes in hand. We were just moving away
from the quay, the engine going, when the bird-man reported no oil pressure
and stopped the engine. A slight breeze blowing down the harbour sufficed to
fill the stays'l and we managed to swing past the frigate without pranging her
with our bowsprit, and without saluting her either, as I suppose we should
have done, my *sangfroid* at that moment in abeyance. Hurriedly setting the
jib and mains'l we reached the harbour entrance almost at the same time as
the expected freighter. Heading as we were for one side of the narrow
entrance we had urgent need to go about, but it seemed better to run aground
than to be impaled as we crossed the bows of the freighter. We stood on in
hope as the distance to the rocks rapidly shortened and put about the moment
we had room.

The tide was making and in spite of a fair wind we had gained less than a
mile when the wind petered out and a dense fog came down. By this time the
engine was in action, the lack of oil pressure having proved a false alarm, and
we decided to carry on for the fjord entrance, the course being straightforward. The south side of the fjord is a string of islets and islands which we
needed to keep close on our port hand, so that the navigator was considerably
perturbed when one of these loomed up to starboard. Navigational errors, if
they do not end in disaster, can be laughed off and attributed to unknown
currents or acts of God. In this case we were probably set south by the tide.
Of such errors, errors on a more sublime though not impossible scale, the
Editor of *Lecky's Wrinkles* has a classic remark: 'There is nothing so distressing as running ashore, unless it be a doubt as to which continent the shore
belongs.'

Having regained the fairway we groped our way from island to island as each in turn came up out of the fog seldom more than a hundred yards away, ticking them off on the chart as one might the buoys marking a channel. Though many people do not mind or even prefer eating to the sound of what passes for music, few would enjoy eating to the thump of *Baroque*'s engine at close quarters. We usually stopped the engine if motoring and meal-time happened to coincide, but now in fog, close to islands, and a tide running, we had to keep going. This was particularly unfortunate because Alec had chosen to dish up something akin to a banquet – salmon (bought by Andrew) and sauce Hollandaise followed by treacle duff, an invitation to feats of higher gluttony. 'Never let it spoil your dinner', and no doubt that care-free gastronome Dr Oppimian would not have let a trifle of engine noise spoil his. I am more weak-minded. Noise, fog, and navigational worries altogether spoiled mine, and how glad I was when a little later we picked up the dim light on the outermost island, which in fact showed up rather better in the prevailing gloom of fog and twilight.

Two days of fog and northerly winds were an unusual combination, for it is southerly winds that usually bring fog. This kept us on the starboard tack steering almost due west and in such thick weather we were not sorry to be well away from land. Raw days they were, too, the fog bringing the air temperature down to 4° C. The perfect 'Greenland' day that followed allowed sights to be obtained and these showed that we were a good seventy miles from the coast and thus beyond the influence of the north-going current. Spanish omelette and yet another duff for supper, Alec by now having found them as easy to make as we did to eat. Lay on McDuff, was the word, and even at the rate of two or three a week no one felt like crying, 'Hold, enough'. After another cloudless day we had thirty-six hours of north-easterly wind of nearly gale force. We could make no progress on either tack in such a wind and when a seam went in the mains'l we lay-a-hull, rolling heavily in a short, steep sea. There were a few large bergs about, majestically contemptible of the seas that broke angrily against them. To avoid drifting on to a berg I found that with patience and the tiller hard over *Baroque* could be brought stern on to wind and sea, upon which she soon gathered steerage way and went with increasing speed at a fair lick down wind under bare poles.

Overnight the wind dropped and we enjoyed a warm, windless morning on which to do 8ft. of stitching in the mains'l. I also made up some baggywrinkle against an expected visit from Father Neptune, for we were now nearing the Arctic Circle. Still making westing, we were nearly a hundred miles from the coast, rather nearer to Baffin Is. than to Greenland, for hereabouts Davis Strait is only 180 miles wide. C. Dyer and Mt Raleigh, which we visited and climbed in 1962 were only 80 miles to the west. John Davis had led me to seek out Mt Raleigh. Nearly four hundred years ago, lying at anchor in Exeter Sound, he recorded: 'We lay under a brave mount the cliffs whereof were orient as gold. This mount we named Mt Raleigh.'

A cold foggy night succeeded this pleasant day, both air and sea temperatures falling to 2° C. To account for the drop in sea temperature from 5° to 2° C. I thought that there must be ice about and sure enough at noon we sighted a line of floes to the west. This was probably remnants of what the whalers used to call the Middle Pack, the great, pear-shaped field of ice that in spring and early summer extends from Baffin Bay down the middle and western half of Davis Strait. Having altered course to ENE we later passed close to more outlying floes and the presence of these together with some fitful sunshine decided me to invite Father Neptune on board forthwith although we were a few miles short of the Arctic Circle. The ice would make a suitable setting for the ceremony.

John came in over the bows stark naked except for the length of baggy-wrinkle round his waist. The deck broom had been converted into a passable trident, his crown glistened with silver foil, while his beard, also of baggy-wrinkle, should have lent him a venerable air. In fact it reminded me more of Leech's picture of Facey Romford than of Majesty. I welcomed him on the foredeck with a swig of rum, accepted humbly the scroll he presented (our *laissez-passer*), and turned to address the crew, most of them on their knees busy with cameras. 'Men, As we are now entering His Majesty's arctic domains he himself has graciously come on board to hand us in person the needed documents. Three cheers for His Majesty.' And when the cheers had subsided: 'He orders me to pipe all hands to dance and skylark and to splice the mainbrace.' As John and I had finished our rum we took advantage of this last order to have our glasses recharged. Sausage and mash were, perhaps, an ignoble conclusion to an auspicious day but no such criticism could apply to what followed – a weightily majestic chocolate duff accompanied by a smooth sauce, both, of course, the colour of royal purple.

A sight next day confirmed that we had crossed the Arctic Circle and the air temperature of 1° C. that had been recorded at 6 am was in accordance. A trawler, *Orion Arctic*, had passed in the night. We met her subsequently at Holsteinborg and learnt that she was on charter engaged in seismic survey, not in trawling. The Danish Government had recently allotted blocks off the west coast for oil exploration and *Orion Arctic* and two other vessels were already so engaged. We were now closing the land north of Holsteinborg, the coast littered with islets of barren rock and backed by snow mountains. On any day but this, a typical 'Greenland' day of brilliant sunshine, such a coast would have looked grim and forbidding but for us it had a warm and friendly appearance. Off this coast is the Great Hellefiske Bank that recently was rich in cod and halibut, the name alone suggesting to anyone as ignorant as myself 'hellish good fishing'. Hereabouts on *Baroque*'s first voyage we were pestered by salmon nets. This year we saw only one net and only two trawlers fishing for those few cod and halibut that had not left for new pastures. When becalmed, we put a line down near the bottom and succeeded in catching a worm, foul-hooked at that.

I had a mind to go through the Vaigat, the sixty-mile long channel between Disko Is. and the mainland. The slight extra distance would be worth incurring for Alec to get some professional studies of icebergs, for there is no other place where such majestic monsters can be seen in such great variety and great profusion. As the *Pilot* remarks: 'In June, after the break-up of the winter ice, thousands of bergs, some of them from 200ft. to 300ft. high, drift backwards and forwards with the tidal stream; these bergs render navigation dangerous and safe anchorage almost impossible.' The Jacobshavn Isfjord where two large glaciers descend from the inland ice is the main source of these bergs. In late summer of 1961 in *Mischief* we had passed through the Vaigat southbound, and apart from running aground in fog had encountered no great difficulty. To enter the Vaigat proper we had first to get into Disko Bugt at its southern end and the thirty-mile wide entrance is encumbered by a number of islands. With a fair wind taking us right up to the small island of Rotten it looked like a piece of cake until the wind headed us and began to blow with some strength directly out of the Vaigat. Moreover we were still on the wrong side of the Kronprinsens Islands, a large group that until recently were known as Whale Fish Islands, a name that stirs the imagination and conjures up visions of the old whaling fleets. Godhavn on Disko Is., ten miles north of the Whale Fish group, was the principal port of call for the whaling fleet on its way north. Anyhow, whatever the name of these islands, the north-east wind stopped us from getting past them. Having tacked several times without gaining much ground we finally bore away to the north-west to go outside Disko Is., foregoing the Vaigat but at least turning a foul wind into a fair wind.

CHAPTER ELEVEN

An Abrupt Conclusion

There is a world of difference between being outward
bound by choice and homeward bound by necessity.
R. T. McMullen, 'Down Channel'

BY THE TIME we reached the south-west corner of Disko Is., the wind was all over the place and fast dying. A little more patience and we might have been sailing or at any rate motoring through the Vaigat, but whether that would have prevented what was about to happen, or merely deferred it, is conjecture. We handed the sails, the mains'l with two rolls still in, and motored up the west coast of Disko Is. for a couple of hours before stopping for supper. For this kind of yachting, where comfort and the care of the stomach have priority over progress, some wag has recently coined the word 'gastro-navigation'. For supper we had potato pie and duff, a little heavy perhaps on the carbohydrates and a meal from which anyone with a keen sense of foreboding might have expected an uneasy night. And so it proved. With no wind we lay becalmed and drifting about two miles offshore, a shore fringed with grounded bergs, until very suddenly at about 1 am the wind came in with considerable violence from south-west. The crew responded smartly. Not only was it a fair wind for making northing but it also put us on a lee shore. Having regard to the strength of the wind the two rolls in the mainsail would be needed. We left them in and swigged up the sail. As the last inches were got out of the throat and peak halyards I began easing out the main sheet whereupon, with no warning, the boom broke clean in two. Had it not been for the sail wrapped round them the two separate pieces might have led us a proper dance. As it was, with a struggle, we soon had the whole lot inboard and secured, and the sail down. Setting the trysail we steered north-west to gain some much needed offing, for a thick drizzle now obscured the coast. To balance the trysail the jib had to come down. In the process it went overboard and was recovered badly torn with four feet of the luff wire sticking out. On the whole, a night to be remembered.

By morning I had decided against going any further north. This was 7 August and if we were to be back by the end of September we should have to start for home not much later than mid-August. True we were in only a semi-crippled state. In light winds we could use the mainsail without any boom and we had the trysail, but with that we should make no progress at all against head winds. We were just north of 69° N. Ellesmere Is. was still 450 miles away and Upernavik, which I had rather expected might be our furthest north this voyage, was 250 miles off. Water and food for the passage home could be had at Holsteinborg where there was also a slight possibility of having a boom made; though if that meant a long delay, as it well might, we could manage without. It might be slow work in Davis Strait but once south of C. Farewell the brave westerlies should hustle us along. So, to the disappointment of us all, we put about and headed south-east. Headed is the word, for we were not moving. The wind had gone almost as suddenly as it had come leaving behind a terrible lop in which we lurched and sidled closer to Fortune Bay – a misnomer, I thought – near the southern edge of Disko Island. Lop or no we had to get clear, besides the land, there were icebergs all round and we could see the white water over the sunk rock called Parry's Skaer. Labouring heavily in the confused sea, the propeller at times thrown clear of the water, we motored for two hours.

In recent years I have had no luck at all with spars. *Sea Breeze* broke her topmast, her bowsprit, the gaff twice, and finally the boom. *Baroque* sprung her boom the first voyage, and now the replacement, a hollow spar, had survived only two voyages. Chinese gybes, I suppose, are not conducive to long life in spars, but a boom should be man enough to withstand some occasional ill-treatment. Coming back across the Atlantic on her first voyage in 1956 *Mischief* had sprung her boom, but the replacement which, so far as I remember, was a solid spar and an inch thicker than the original, was still there in 1968 when we lost *Mischief*. It was a spar, I might add, whose size and weight struck terror into all beholders, particularly the crew; but if a man is going to be struck by a boom a little extra weight is neither here nor there, the effect will be equally lethal. Whether there is any real evidence for it – beyond that of my own ill-luck – it has been suggested that Pilot Cutters were liable to break their booms on account of the size of the sail, the length of the boom, and above all their roller-reefing gear. With the sheet made fast to a revolving iron collar at the extreme end of the boom the strain comes on only one point, and the more the sail is rolled the greater becomes the buckling effect as the leech comes further and further inboard. One would have thought that hand-reefing would produce the same effect, the leech, with two or three reefs pulled down, coming equally far inboard. Metal spars break, and anyhow such a spar would be an anachronism in a Pilot Cutter, so the only answer seems to be a solid and thick enough boom. One is reminded of the complaint of James Pigg, Jorrock's North-country huntsman, who when riding half-drunk through a gateway nearly had his leg torn off by one of the gate-posts: 'Sink. They dinna make their gates half wide enough.'

Mainly owing to lack of wind the 150 miles to Holsteinborg took us five days. Having unwrapped the mainsail from the boom we lashed the two pieces on deck and used the sail without the boom; but since this imposed a severe strain on the clew of the sail it could be done only in light winds. Nor, without a boom, did the sail prove very effective if the wind was ahead. On the 11th, by dint of much motoring we were near the Qagssit Islands, a group lying just off Holsteinborg. Despite the wonderfully clear, calm evening I decided not to try to find our way in that night, a lucky decision because we were soon enveloped in thick fog. Meantime, with a light Fisherman anchor and two long warps bent together we had anchored in 30 fms., and until the fog came down, from bearings taken to the islands and mountains beyond, we seemed to be holding well in spite of a strong north-going current. Ignorance now indeed proved to be bliss. We spent a quiet, untroubled night and only when the fog lifted, which it did not do until noon next day, did we find that we had drifted three miles north and closer inshore. With nothing to see and nothing to hear the man on anchor watch had no means of telling whether or not we were dragging. Perhaps if we had used the chain, its grumbling as it dragged along the bottom might have warned us. Anchoring with warps in fog, I felt, must be unseamanlike.

We did not get in until late that evening. The marks were not easy to pick up, though the leading lights for the final dog-leg approach to the harbour were very clear. We anchored short of the inner harbour used by small boats and while we were squaring up a young Greenlander who was alongside handed us a freshly caught cod. Andrew, taking the hint, put a line over the side and soon had two more fat cod. Fried cod for breakfast and fish chowder for supper. Going ashore that night for a quick look round I could recognise only the shipyard and the church with the whalebone arch over the gate, so much had the place altered since 1962. The main harbour where we had found barely room or even enough water to anchor has been enlarged and enclosed with wharves, and the beach off which we had lain, where starving huskies waded in search of fish, has disappeared under a road. The shopping centre – for there are now a few shops – is a short half-mile uphill from the harbour, far enough apparently to justify the presence of numerous taxis. In 1962 a taxi might well have been taken to avoid being mauled by the packs of huskies which then roamed everywhere like wolves, licking oil drums and even fishing, for it was the custom then to feed them only in winter when they worked pulling sledges. The Town Council or the local RSPCA have applied the screw. The only huskies to be seen were in wire cages outside the Greenlander houses where, one hopes, they are occasionally fed.

Next day, by swinging out the gaff with a weight on the end and bringing some ballast up on deck we canted the boat over far enough to put a tingle over the sprung plank. With no mooring warps to stop her she heeled over readily. An Englishman, a meteorologist from *Orion Arctic* which was now in harbour, paid us a visit. She was a Canadian vessel with a crew of at least half a dozen different nationalities. In contrast to this was the trawler *Greenland*, the crew all Faeroese and the skipper and mate, father and son. The skipper, who spoke excellent English, looked a proper seaman, quite distinct from the son with his spectacles, long hair, and beard. It was this skipper who told us that colder water had driven most of the fish away from the Greenland banks.

We all had showers at the well-run Seaman's Home and I paid a visit to the shipyard. In 1962, and it may be so still, this was the only place in Greenland where a vessel of moderate size could be hauled out. A helpful Dane was running it then and we had had *Mischief* hauled out to see if she had sustained any damage from some ice she had hit. Since then it has been enlarged and seemed to be busy enough with two small trawlers hauled out undergoing repair; moreover from some of the timber lying about I thought a boom could have been made. But even the enquiry stage was never reached. In the

Greenlander manager I met a blank wall. We had not a word in common and he showed no interest in the reason for my visit. The same afternoon, having done our shopping (mainly black bread), we went alongside for water, or rather alongside *Greenland*, the nearest we could get to the quay. Before we cast off they gave us two buckets of prawns, not as fresh as one might wish of prawns but fresh enough to eat.

Outside we had a fair northerly wind and a lively following sea. With her nose turned for home *Baroque* thought fit to kick up her heels while the compass behaved even more wildly, trying hard apparently to describe circles. On settling down, as later it did, the direction in which it pointed was obviously suspect. At noon next day with the sun due south the compass also pointed south, whereas with the local magnetic variation of 48° W. the compass should have pointed nearly south-east. We searched carefully to see if there was anything near the compass to account for its behaviour and found nothing. Thereafter, every day we compared the compass with the sun's bearing either at noon or whenever I took a sight and got an azimuth. As one goes south down Davis Strait and then eastwards across the Atlantic the westerly magnetic variation decreases by something like 5 deg. every 200 miles. Our compass ignored this and continued to point more or less true all the way home. It might well have been a gyro compass. Here was another unsolved mystery of the sea and on our return I consulted a compass adjuster in Southampton who reported:

I have today tested this compass for friction and period. The compass is not frictional which means the sapphire and pivot are satisfactory. The period was 13 seconds which was exactly the same as the period of a brand new Medina compass from stock. The error which you experienced is indeed very strange and as I understand it, the deviation was always approximately the same amount as the variation with opposite name so as to give a nil compass error throughout the return voyage. What caused the deviation to decrease with the variation is mysterious for a wooden boat. Are you sure there is not iron or steel near the compass position to give an induced effect, or any electric motor for steering gear, window wipers, clear view screens or auto-pilots nearby?

This is not the place to enter into the difference between variation and deviation, but in wooden boats the latter is usually small and in all the boats I have had we have ignored it, possibly not justifiably but at any rate without detriment. As regards the enquiries at the end of this report I could answer with my hand on my heart that there were no such things in *Baroque* nor ever likely to be.

Despite a lot of fog we made good progress. By the 17th the log had clocked up 3,000 miles for the voyage, and on the night of the 18th with fog all round and a clear sky overhead we lay becalmed off Godthaab. Meantime we had been living on the country, or rather the sea, eating a great many prawns mostly in curries, and now Andrew contributed to this rich living by catching two nice cod. We were over the Fyllas Bank and had anchored accordingly to fish. There were evidently still some of the hardier characters around, like the Serpentine Christmas Day bathers, who did not object to colder water. The fog did not clear until the following evening, a lovely tranquil evening with the slowly dispersing fog reluctantly revealing a glorious panorama of distant mountains. We were still motionless when a local trawler with a friendly Danish skipper on his way into Godthaab came skilfully alongside and passed us a line. We had a gam while his Greenlanders passed over a lot of red fish with big eyes and serrated spine, together with a huge box of prawns. I gave the skipper a bottle of whisky and, besides the sea-food, he gave us the latest weather report from Godthaab. It proved, I'm afraid, to be as far out as some of our own. All hands were busy next morning cleaning prawns and we had our first go at them for lunch, finding them sweet and tender, far better than those given to us at Holsteinborg. When we began moving again it was with the help of a slight breeze from north sent specially by Aeolus not so much for our benefit but to spite the Godthaab weather boys who thought it should be southerly Force 5 to 6.

For the next few days we continued to make good progress south, pestered though we were by bergs and bergy bits. The weather, too, was generally thick and by now, from 10 pm onwards, the nights were dark. Off this part of the coast, midway between Godthaab and C. Farewell, the cold current fans out to the west carrying with it numerous bergs and bergy bits. On the 22nd and 23rd, when we sometimes sighted up to ten bergs in a watch, the sea temperature varied between 5° C. and 2° C. For the next two days with the temperature at 7° C. we saw no bergs and then by steering east, when we got within fifty miles of C. Farewell, the temperature fell again to 2° C. and more bergs were sighted. The last berg was sighted on 27 August and thereafter the sea temperature rose steadily all the way across the Atlantic. This premature steering eastwards towards C. Farewell was the result of my stupidly toying with the idea of going through Prins Christians Sund, the fifty-mile long channel between the east and west coasts just north of C. Farewell. We had been through it from west to east in 1970, but then we were already inshore, knew more or less where we were and where the entrance was. At the eastern end there is a weather station where we had had a royal welcome and been given vast quantities of stores. This, rather than the spectacular scenery of the channel may have been what drew me towards it on this occasion. But the continuing thick weather, the dark nights, the number of bergs about, the strong current inshore, and the difficulty of identifying, among many others, the right fjord, together aroused enough apprehension to overcome my greed. Accordingly we resumed our southerly course. It would have been a difficult undertaking and not altogether prudent.

Even when well away from the coast we had some pretty severe frights during those few days, impressing upon us the difference that the dark nights made, particularly when combined with fog. On the afternoon of the 22nd, in the absence of wind, we had been motoring. By evening a fine north-westerly breeze enabled us to start sailing but brought with it thick fog. Andrew's startled cry brought me on deck at the jump and the brief glimpse I got of the berg that he had just missed hitting by a yard or two nearly spoilt my supper of pasta and apple dumpling. We set a double watch – one man forward on look-out – until 2 am when the fog cleared as the wind increased. There was far too much wind for the boomless mainsail which before breakfast, after a prolonged struggle, we got down. With so much belly in the sail we had to bring her into the wind before the throat halyards would render. Under the trys'l she still went at 4 knots, rolling with great abandon, so much so that Nicholas poured a jug of milk over me at breakfast.

Although we covered a lot of miles that day before this fresh quartering wind we did not outrun the bergs of which there were still far too many about. Curry and duff, for supper, by way of a change, encouraged me to dispense with a double watch for the oncoming night. There was a full moon and in the absence of fog I reckoned that bergs would show up from a mile or more away. However, coming on watch at 10 pm I soon realised that the moon was a hindrance rather than a help. Low in the sky and dead ahead, it turned the whole sea a silvery white, almost exactly the colour of ice. As a change from peering anxiously ahead I happened to glance aside where to my horror, barely three yards away, there was a piece of ice the size of a van with a long under-water tongue projecting towards us. We must have just skidded over it. As well as the moonlight, the breaking waves and the rise of the foredeck when the boat pitched, made it difficult to pick up anything directly ahead. The rest of my watch was spent literally and figuratively on tiptoe. On account of the over-high dog-house a short man always feels he is not seeing properly over it, and after this near-miss, having started breathing again, I felt in need of a hundred eyes and a powerful searchlight. A trawler that had passed us two nights before had kept his searchlight going all the time.

Further north in almost perpetual daylight icebergs are more a welcome break in a monotonous seascape than source of worry, but in the long nights of late summer further south, unless one is prepared to heave-to, they become something of a menace, for besides the berg itself there are the bergy bits and growlers to which they give birth and which are so much harder to spot. We were thankful when we saw what was to be our last, and two days later on 29 August we were well east of C. Farewell and a hundred miles to the south. For several days we had on board what bird-man Nicholas pronounced to be a dunlin. It soon got so used to us as to take food from our hands, any kind of food, not excluding curry and duff. For days on end the same gallant breeze blew steadily on our quarter, seldom more than Force 6 and never less than Force 5, so that even without benefit of mainsail we made a fast passage. In thirty days from Holsteinborg to the Bishop light, sighted on 14 September, she averaged 70 miles a day, logging over a hundred miles on at least seven days. No homeward run can be too fast, especially when one has had, as it were, to retire hurt, and when there is a broken boom lying on deck to remind one of it.

We reached Lymington 18 September with twelve days in hand. Had we been assured of making so fast a passage home we might have gone on for another week, reaching possibly Upernavik (72° N.) but no further. That one can never be quite confident of reaching any of the places I aim at may be part of their charm, and failure is at least an excuse for making another voyage. Nevertheless, success is sweet and to achieve it in the case of Ellesmere Is. we ought to have started earlier, say mid-May, though even that would barely allow for unforeseen things like breaking booms. Travelling hopefully is

within the reach of almost anyone while to arrive needs a little more judgement, determination, skill, and perhaps some luck. There are many ways to
the top of a mountain but the view is always the same; and there are many
ways of going to sea yet the views of those who do are various. Many go to
compete, some for the excitement of speed, or for the thrills of passage-
making, or merely to get away from it all. Some of us, by extending our
horizons, are trying in an amateurish way to recapture or at least get a faint
idea of days when, as Conrad wrote, 'the sea was great and mysterious and
ready to surrender the prize of fame to audacious men.' Days most often of
hardship and peril and never any lack of men to face them. To re-live their
experiences may be impossible and to try to do so may be foolish but it was
evidently the motive that inspired Hilaire Belloc's modest cruising, expressed
in the words that I have already quoted: 'In venturing in sail upon strange
coasts we are seeking those first experiences, and trying to feel as felt the
earlier man in a happier time, to see the world as they saw it.'

Part 3

East Greenland

CHAPTER TWELVE

A False Start

Lor, Brer Rabbit, you don't know what trouble
is. I'm de man what kin show you trouble.
Uncle Remus

AS I BEGIN to describe this voyage, the discrepancy between the target and the fall of shot provokes a wry smile. Wry smiles, I suppose, are better than no smiles but there will be few more of any kind. Only a Mark Tapley, who would take no credit for being jolly except in the most adverse conditions, only such a man could look with cheerful pleasure upon a voyage that thanks mainly to a half-hearted, dissident crew, missed its objective by a thousand miles and then failed with ignominy to bring the boat home.

Unlike the previous year, with winter merging into spring before I had had any offer, bite, or nibble from prospective crew, by Christmas I had gathered a promising nucleus. Owing to hard times the sail-training ship *Captain Scott*, based on the west coast of Scotland, had been laid up, and two of her former instructors, Brian Williamson and Hamish Brown, wrote to say they would like a voyage in *Baroque*. As well as their sea experience both were mountaineers. Then a man from Bristol offered to come. He had no sea experience so I suggested his coming as cook, to which he agreed with only moderate rapture. At the same time a David Burrows wrote to me about Spitzbergen. He was a retired business man (and a grandfather), owned a boat himself, and had had varied sailing experience including yacht deliveries. Living in Wells and keeping his boat in Wales he thus reversed my extraordinary habit of living in Wales and keeping a boat in Lymington. He wanted to sail his boat to Spitzbergen where she was to act as transport for a small shore-based expedition and having regard to the man and the boat this seemed to me a feasible plan. Later he wrote to say that nobody would insure the boat for

917

Spitzbergen waters and instead offered to come with me to which I readily agreed. Since he had only a part share in the boat he could not afford to ignore the insurance aspect as I have had to do ever since I started sailing in 1954.

So there I was, long before sailing day, with a full crew, a crew that on paper, except for the Bristolian, abounded with promise. My state of euphoria can be imagined. Thus deeply committed there was no room for the faint-hearted doubts of the previous winter. Ellesmere Is. – for that must certainly be our aim – seemed almost in the bag. My monthly visits to *Baroque* at Lymington may have moderated this ardour but did not dispel it. There are few more depressing sights than the inside of a boat like *Baroque* on a wet, winter's day. In winter she has a great canvas tent rigged over the deck from stem to stern, and since this is tied down in about thirty places and the day is probably windy, I untie only enough to crawl under to go below. Naturally it is dark below though not too dark to discover that it is also damp. However, with the stove alight, a dry sleeping bag, and no watch on deck to keep, if it is not ecstasy it is comfort. All the same the cheerless surroundings became no brighter as I pondered over the defects that were being put right and the bills that would accrue. Primarily, of course, a new boom, solid this time. The doghouse windows had to be renewed and strengthened (a waste of time and money as it turned out); 10ft. of underwater planking needed replacing; a samson post and the boom crutch were loose, as well as the engine seating. A soft spot in the mast needed an engraving piece which luckily could be done while the mast remained stepped. She had to be slipped for anti-fouling and for the repair of the planking, and finally a new lavatory had to be fitted, the old one having seized up solid. Altogether a thoroughly daunting amount of work to be done at present-day prices.

Of the crew so far I had met only David who called at Bodowen on the way to look at his boat lying in a small harbour a few miles north of Barmouth. The two Scots I took for granted, for surely with a background of climbing and sail training they would be of the right stuff; later Hamish looked me up on his way to the Atlas Mts. where he remained until a few days before we sailed. My Bristol man proved elusive. Twice I had advised him of my Lymington visits expecting that he would join me there to have a look at the boat, so that after his second failure to turn up I was not surprised to hear that he had taken another job and would not be available. I learnt this about a month before sailing day which I had fixed for 12 May, thus giving us three weeks start over that of 1975. On top of that came a letter from Brian Williamson to say that he had damaged a leg in a fall on Ben Nevis and would be out of action until the autumn. Thus at a stroke, as the politicians say, my crew had dwindled to two, one of whom, Hamish, would not be available for fitting out. Although this sort of thing had by now become usual I found it no less worrying.

But Brian Williamson was a responsible chap who appreciated my position and within a week had come up with the names of two Scottish climbers with whom I got in touch and who in the upshot made up the crew. Richard and Jim were bosom friends, both in their late twenties, married, and, I think, fathers, though that did not deter them from taking four months unpaid holiday. Nothing could be more outdated than two lines of Charles Kingsley:

> For men must work and women must weep,
> For there's little to earn and many to keep.

However, at that moment I was selfishly glad to have them and refrained from asking whether their wives had been consulted and what they thought. As Sancho remarked: 'A wife's council is bad, but he who will not take it is mad,' I did not see them until they joined though I learnt that Richard had had various jobs farming both in England and Norway, inshore fishing, and a spell as instructor at the Moray Firth Sea School. Two who joined us subsequently had also been there as instructors, so that even if this Sea School failed to furnish me with reliable hands it at least furnished a common topic of conversation and reminiscence. Jim, too, had had an unsettled career including a voyage as a refrigerator engineer. This distant connection with food impelled me to ask him to undertake the galley to which he willingly consented.

Thus thanks mainly to Brian Williamson we were again complete and I could proceed to Lymington in a fairly confident mood. David with his long experience would be a great asset; Hamish with his *Captain Scott* background should be more than useful; while Richard and Jim should at least be tough, for Scottish climbers, who do a lot of their climbing in winter, are reputedly hard men. During my absence Bodowen would be occupied at intervals by friends, or at least friends of a niece, for I myself for several obvious reasons have few friends left. It remained only to house in kennels my two dogs who can hardly have suspected a second act of treachery on master's part. That done I went down to Lymington on 1 May, the crew being due a day or two later. My first job was to set up the ratlines so that we could go aloft to start re-rigging the boat. Next day David arrived with a mountain of gear, a lot of it for the benefit of the ship – a bag of tools, an Aldis lamp, and a big quartz clock which kept remarkably accurate time, varying only a few seconds throughout the voyage. Richard and Jim came the following day, both burdened with more climbing equipment and gadgets than they were ever likely to use, especially on Ellesmere Is. where so far as I knew there were no peaks of Alpine character. Like yachting, climbing has been commercialised and those who participate are seemingly a 'soft sell' for the enterprising firms which provide superfluous but fashionable equipment. Richard appeared to be strong, well-built, fairly free from hair, while Jim, who was small, had hair down to his shoulders, reddish at that, not to mention a matted beard. He took pride in his hair, parting it in the middle and combing it admiringly in front of the small mirror in the galley. The beard's treatment was more offhand (the *mot juste*) merely being teasled out or scuffled with the fingers after meals to remove the bulkier debris. He had a powerful Scotch accent and later on, when his mouth became masked with hair, very few words that I could understand ever filtered through.

With Hamish still to come the four of us had enough to do to be ready in time. David at once showed his quality by taking on the manifold jobs that required some technical knowledge and skill with tools. Enthusiasm was rife as it always is either when fitting out for a long voyage, at the start of a mountaineering expedition, or even at the start of a war. A mountain expedition is usually short enough for enthusiasm to be sustained right up to the end. Wars may last for years but even for voyages that are reckoned in months enthusiasm at the start is not enough. More solid and less effervescent qualities are needed such as determination, endurance, forbearance, a sense of duty, and an obligation towards the ship we serve. Sir Francis Drake, that sovereign leader of men, may have had in mind this all too likely fading of early enthusiasm: 'It is not the beginning,' as he said, 'but the continuing of the same until it be thoroughly finished that yieldeth the true glory.'

On 10 May we embarked the stores. The lack of dried egg, apparently unobtainable, was a nuisance. Although duffs can be and were made by Jim without they are all the better when eggs are included; and in the form of scrambled egg or omelette, provided it is well laced with Tabasco sauce, dried egg makes a welcome change from porridge for breakfast. Everything that was not in tins had to be packed in plastic bags. On land one curses the plastic in which everything from wood screws to kippers is nowadays impenetrably wrapped, yet what a blessing it is to the man in a small boat, especially to one whose boat is inclined to be wet, either for protecting his bunk, his clothes, or his food. In the Himalaya before the plastic age had dawned one had to have bags made specially from canvas or some rubberised material for carrying the loads of sugar, atta, or satu, if they were to survive the monsoon rains or the mishaps that occur when fording rivers.

Hamish arrived that day and from the lack of interest he bestowed on our activities one had the impression that he rather regretted having left the Atlas Mts. Enthusiasm, whether to be sustained or not, was noticeably lacking. Certainly he had been travelling hard since leaving the Atlas, including a journey to Scotland, and possibly the contrast between *Captain Scott* and *Baroque* took some digesting. From April onwards the weather had been good with a lot of easterly winds, perfect conditions for a swift and painless passage down Channel, allowing the crew time to find their sea-legs. It broke just before we sailed – rain, westerlies, and gale warnings all round the coast. We had other worries, too, in the form of an intrusion by Southern Television who threatened to come again to see us off in spite of all the discouragement I could give them. Television camera men think they are conferring a favour by allowing you to appear in some obscure programme along with other unfortunates as obscure as oneself; whereas for thus making you look and feel a fool some compensation is surely due from them, preferably in kind – a coil of rope or a bottle of whisky.

Still having some mistrust of *Baroque*'s steering when under power I arranged for a tow through the narrowest part of the channel – expensive yachts lying on either hand – to as far as the fuelling berth where we had to fill up with diesel oil. The fact that it was raining and blowing hard did not prevent the camera men from carrying out their threat at a time when we had much to do besides mouthing vocables into a microphone while striking seamanlike attitudes. One of our fuel tanks had moved, as we belatedly discovered, making it extremely awkward to fill; and the twice-baked bread delivered the previous evening needed supplementing. There had to be enough of this to see us to Greenland and instead of twenty-four large loaves they had sent small loaves. An old and tried friend who was on board dashed off to the town, the shops not yet open, where by some undisclosed means he obtained a quantity of biscuit – the more or less edible cardboard variety. At nine o'clock we cast off and started down the river under our own steam, the Royal Lymington Yacht Club honouring us with a two-gun salute as we passed their clubhouse. *Baroque* played no tricks and although I am just wise enough to insure against third-party risks while in home waters, upon our reaching the river mouth clear of the lines of moored yachts I heave a sigh of relief. We were by no means there yet, but even more profound is the relief felt when clear of the British Isles. As Conrad wrote: 'The true peace of God begins a thousand miles from the nearest land.'

Arrived in the Solent, in view of the strong westerly wind, we decided to anchor to await better times as we have had to do on several previous occasions. There is something to be said for starting on the appointed day even if it does mean anchoring outside. The last minute shopping for forgotten items which threatens to go on and on is finally halted, those few who have come to see one off are not disappointed, while the crew, most of them with scant resources, can buy no more beer. By morning the wind had veered north-west and the barometer had risen so that in spite of the early shipping forecast which still muttered gale warnings we got under way with all plain sail, able to lay the course for the Needles channel. For the benefit of my friend Mr Lee, who had got us our biscuit and who, as I expected, was now lurking there in wait with his camera, we went as close as we could to Hurst Point. Outside the Needles where the wind had free play we put a roll in the mains'l and dropped the stays'l'. The evening forecast spoke of south-west winds of Force 7 to 8 whereas the wind fell light with none at all at times. Hamish seemed seedy but the rest shaped well.

No favouring slant of wind came our way. Contrary winds pushed us into Lyme Bay and early on the 16th, the same WSW wind blowing and a gale warning for the Plymouth area, I decided to anchor inside Start Point. The poor progress we were making hardly justified the effort and a calm spell might give Hamish, who now looked the worse for wear, a better chance of recovery. He had eaten nothing beyond some dates from the Atlas Mts. and except for standing his watch had remained prone ever since the start. He had unwisely told us that *Captain Scott* had been accustomed to leaving harbour when other vessels were seeking shelter and we could not help wondering how he had managed on those occasions. All next day we remained at anchor. To give our table a much needed new look David planed and holystoned it, while Richard and Jim went ashore for bread and a jerrycan of water. Having got doused in the surf they brought back some mouldy rolls wrapped in plastic, so this foray was not a success and one hoped that no eagle-eyed coast watcher had noted it and reported back to the Lymington Customs.

Out at sea again we raised the Eddystone light that night and by the 20th, a rough, windy day, when we were a week out from Lymington, we were still the wrong side of the Lizard. The crew were not cheerful and the presence of the melancholy Hamish holding his head in his hands did nothing to raise their spirits. The next day, as for some time I had expected and feared, he expressed a wish to be put ashore and in spite of the delay and doubt about finding a replacement I thought it best to comply. Luckily we were not too far off and the wind was fair for Falmouth. This was where I had bought *Baroque* in 1972 and mindful of the trouble I have had with her and was yet to have I sometimes wonder why. Was she a replica of Milton's 'fatal and perfidious bark, built in th' eclipse and rigged with curses dark'? Or was her skipper at fault, trying too high a faithful old servant, subjecting her to Chinese gybes, strandings, and the shunting of ice? As we made fast to a convenient buoy that evening the Customs launch came alongside. They sealed up our bonded stores and in reply to enquiries told us that our convenient buoy might cost us £1.50 a day. Though on pleasure bent, like Mrs Gilpin, I have a frugal mind so we moved forthwith to an anchorage. That done I went ashore to the Royal Cornwall YC to make my number and to ask for the use of their telephone. That was all I expected and in fact all I got, for I knew it would be no use enquiring there for crew. Later Richard and Jim put in calls to Manchester and Fort William thus making our shortage known in their respective circles. Hamish, now restored to health, left next day. Having contributed nothing to the gaiety of nations while at sea he now made amends by capsizing the dinghy alongside and falling into the drink. For the first and last time on the voyage the crew enjoyed a whole-hearted laugh. Hamish then got away in a motor boat (owned by yet another Moray Sea School Old Boy) wringing out his clothes as he went. This was on a Saturday and Jim had already hoisted in what that implied – curry and duff for supper.

On the Sunday, with an easterly wind blowing powerfully enough to have set us on our way a hundred miles or more, I landed on the Flushing shore and walked across to Mylor where *Baroque* had been fitted out for her first voyage. At the boatyard there I met the manager and a shipwright I knew who, as I had hoped, had someone for me in mind and strongly recommended him. After some search we learnt that he was away on a delivery job. At Flushing on the way back a young chap accosted me and having had a look at *Baroque* professed interest in the voyage. He had a job with a local tin-mining company and after dithering over the week-end finally decided in favour of tin. On the Monday I had another nibble from a curious chap who had neither house, flat, nor caravan but dwelt snail-like in his Volkswagen. He, too, was a yacht delivery man working for an agent in Plymouth. He would consult his agent, he said, and telephone me Yes or No at 10.30 am the next day. No call came and I suppose it was idle to expect promises to be kept by a man whose home was in a motor car. Having waited until 11 am I was about to push off in the dinghy when the club steward ran out to say there was a call for me. The steward of the Royal Cornwall, by the way, proved more helpful than the members. Evidently the jungle drums had been rumbling to some purpose, from the Scottish highlands to the south of England. A Mike Holland, speaking from Chichester, knew all about us and our need, seemed bent on joining, but thought it might take him a week to get ready. I suggested he should come down and have a look at me and the boat. He arrived that evening all kitted up and wanting only a morning in Falmouth for a final round-up. He slept on board while mother, who had driven him down, parked herself in a hotel. Mike, too, had been an instructor at the Moray Sea School, and although not a dedicated worker was a good hand and a likeable chap. Unluckily he proved to be ill adapted for a long voyage.

CHAPTER THIRTEEN

The Turning Point

WE SAILED on the 26th, a fortnight having already elapsed since we left Lymington, the crew change costing us nearly a week. It could have been much longer. Anchored in the roads were two smart French brigantines, sail training ships presumably, with two yards on the foremast, fore and aft rig on the main. Richard the fishing expert got to work and late that evening off the Lizard had a good haul of mackerel which we had for breakfast fried in oatmeal. And *à propos* of fishing, we witnessed an amusing scene near the Wolf rock the next afternoon – two French fishing boats speeding southwards, bursting their boilers, so to speak, the reason for their haste becoming clear when a naval vessel hove in sight well astern of them. At the time, and it was a rare event, we had our genoa set, a huge sail hanked to the topmast forestay imposing a severe strain on the mast. That would have been acceptable had there been any topmast backstays but after the first voyage I had abolished these in order to simplify the gear and cut out chafe, the genoa being so rarely set. One had to watch the topmast and guess how much it would bend before worse happened. When we had this sail up again next day we soon had to take it down on account of a heavy swell which made the mast whip. Unlike *Mischief* and *Sea Breeze*, both fitted with fidded topmasts that could be sent down, *Baroque* has a pole mast. To have the mast cut short, though it would suit my purposes, would certainly spoil her graceful appearance. She had no tops'l when I bought her and I have not had one made. Such a sail might be of value in Greenland waters where in summer light winds are the rule rather than the exception, and the reeving of the extra gear could be delayed until one had got there.

To come to a more homely subject, after this nautical digression. Originally in the 'heads' compartment there had been a shower as well as the lavatory. If you were shower-minded you stood in a deep well, the feet no doubt in bilge water; but we had always used the well for stowing bonded stores. The bulkheads surrounding this insanitary affair were lined with bits of black imitation stone, like sequins, the whole effect one of sombre gloom. David took this in hand. Abolished the taps and pipes (from which, rather surprisingly, water spurted), stripped the bulkheads and painted them white, boarded over the bottomless well, fitted shelves above, provided a footstool for the lavatory seat, and for good measure a handhold for use in rough weather. To commemorate this welcome transformation Richard affixed a plaque:

This loo designed and built
By David Burrows
Shipwright 1976

923

An obvious mistake in the spelling of 'shipwright' had to be put right. Spurred on by this the crew had one of their infrequent attacks of spontaneous effort. The brass lamps were polished and the panelling in the cabin – mahogany, I believe – given a shine. Of the gimballed brass lamps that look so well few survive the voyage; the brass fittings corrode and the globes break. As a general routine David worked most of the day, either on the engine, or tracking down leaks and stopping them, or many small jobs that were of benefit to the ship; Richard and Jim read voraciously or held long private conferences, while Mike mostly slept.

Meantime we had rounded the Seven Stones and were making some progress. Richard caught five unusually large mackerel and, as often happens, several racing pigeons alighted on board. The one to which we entrusted our message to mankind refused to push off until it had Ireland in sight. South of the Fastnet we had some roughish weather which laid Jim out and we had to forego our Saturday night curry and duff. The winds were mostly from the wrong direction and in the first week out from Falmouth we had made good a pitiful 240 miles. In the second week we did better, logging just under 400 miles, for by then we were beyond the influence of the anti-cyclonic weather that prevailed over the British Isles for most of a memorable summer. Iceland, on the other hand, had a very poor summer, while in the North Atlantic the month of June which is usually fairly quiet proved to be pretty boisterous. Besides a frightening bang like that from a 15-inch gun as Concorde passed overhead there were other disconcerting incidents. Because I had the mains'l down for stitching, we were motoring when Jim discovered that the port side fuel tank had again shifted and was dripping oil on to the hot exhaust pipe. The tank had to be emptied before we could get it upright and secured for a full due. A moderate gale on 8 June broke a pane in the galley skylight and an immoderate gale the following night made her leak so much that we handed the sails and lay-a-hull. The drips from the deckhead over my bunk obliged me to rig plastic gutters under two of the beams; but strangely enough Richard's bunk, almost directly under the fore-hatch, remained driest of all.

A flat calm on the 10th induced us to make use of the engine when we discovered the batteries were flat. Jim attributed this to salt water though in the doghouse where the batteries live there had so far been nothing more serious than drips. David immediately set about converting the anchor winch handle into a starting handle and at that time there may have been just enough left in the batteries for this plan to succeed. Meantime with no engine and no compass light we were still a lot better off than earlier Greenland-bound voyagers. 'Hellish dark and smells of cheese,' was James Pigg's report on the night's weather, having when drunk looked into a cupboard instead of out of a window. So it was that night except for the smell and the darkness was accentuated by a featureless layer of cloud that blended sea and sky together indistinguishably. Without a compass steering was difficult and within five minutes of taking over from me David executed a Chinese gybe, so I went back and stayed on until it began to get light. In such conditions one needs to discard hoods, hats, and towels round the neck in order to steer by feeling the wind.

Saturday 12 June might be called Black Saturday in that it put paid to any hope of our reaching Ellesmere Is. After heavy squalls of wind and rain the previous evening the sky had cleared but the wind remained fresh. With three rolls in the mains'l we were heading north, the best we could do, and at the awkward hour of 5 am a seam in the mains'l started to go. By the time enough hands had mustered to get the sail down some twenty feet of seam had gone as well as some bad tears crosswise. This was a serious blow for I could see little chance of repairing the sail at sea. It is far too big to have below for stitching and this could be done on deck only in more or less windless weather. These horizontal seams were a nuisance. A tear of an inch or so soon became an ell, and after the last voyage I had made a mental note to have narrow strips sewn every few feet vertically from head to foot. For me mental notes are not enough with the result that nothing had been done. On this occasion, after the sail had been repaired in rather amateurish fashion by a Reykjavik sailmaker, I added some cross strips myself. On land, bolting the stable door after the horse's departure is a well-known exercise; at sea it takes the form of handing a sail after it is ripped. With the wind backing and the glass falling, as they were, prudence should have suggested setting the trys'l instead of reefing the mains'l. The trouble is that roller reefing is too easy so that instead of changing sails one is inclined merely to put in more rolls.

This was only the start of Black Saturday. We set the trys'l, and after breakfast it began to blow in earnest, the barometer having fallen to 992 mbs. At two o'clock when we were doing 5 knots and making a lot of water, not to mention the odd spout through the skylight, we handed the trys'l and pressed on under the jib. Two hours later this had to come down for the sea had built up and waves were beginning to break with the usual menacing roars. Lying-a-hull with no sails set the vessel lies broadside on to wind and sea. Whether this is better or worse than heaving-to, when with a minimum of sail set she takes wind and sea on the weather bow, is a moot point. In either case the drift to leeward is the same, from 20 to 30 miles a day in a full gale. If lying-a-hull, there are no sails to blow out and there may be less strain on the rudder, on the other hand, if broadside on, a boat is more vulnerable than when lying bow on, especially if like *Baroque* she has a lofty and fragile doghouse. We had not been lying-a-hull long before a wave broke alongside and bashed in the starboard side of this erection, flooding the chartroom (for that is what is inside) with all the charts, navigational books, log books, sextant, chrono-meter watch, not to mention the batteries which on this occasion really did have a salt water bath. David got to work boarding up the hole and for good measure put boards over the port side as well. Meantime I got her before the wind and we ran under bare poles, a strategem that did not escape the notice of Poseidon, ruler of the waves, for one of these promptly broke over the counter, cracking a bit more of the doghouse, filling the cockpit, and in its retreat nearly dragging the skipper through the life-rails.

To keep her before the wind with no sail set was not easy and when darkness fell we once more lay-a-hull. It blew hard until morning when the wind veered north-west and dropped to a steady Force 6 at which it remained all day. Richard retired from his watch at 2 am to remain all day in his bunk suffering as he said from 'exposure'. Except for David, the crew seemed to be a little shaken by this gale. As I surveyed the scene on deck Mike took me aback by remarking that he assumed we should now be returning home, and no doubt he was equally astonished by my reply. He then said he would quit at the first opportunity and all three were decided we should go to Reykjavik for repairs, then about 500 miles to the north. Cape Farewell, for which the wind might be less favourable, was about 600 and from there to Godthaab another 400 miles. The lack of mains'l and engine, and the impossibility of finding at Godthaab a replacement for Mike, inclined me at first to agree; though over-riding these arguments should have been the fact that going to Reykjavik implied giving up Ellesmere Is. My own private thoughts about Mike were that if we got to Godthaab, the fact that we were still afloat and the high cost of getting away from there as compared with Reykjavik, might induce him to change his mind.

For the next three days the weather continued boisterous, though with winds mainly from west we were able to lay the course for Iceland. The serving of the eye-splice of the forestay round the mast had come off and to my annoyance chafed through the jib halyard, an almost new terylene rope. With no jib our speed fell off dismally and several days elapsed before we could get Jim aloft in his climbing harness with a top rope to reeve a new halyard. David made and discarded several versions of a starting handle for the engine and when his Mark V version, from which he expected success, failed like the others, he gave it up as a bad job.

The wind then began blowing from the direction of Iceland right in our teeth and when this had gone on for two days I altered course for C. Farewell hoping that by now the others would have recovered their nerve and see reason. We were then on the same latitude about 500 miles away and the wind was fair. Jim, who had become spokesman for the malcontents at once protested, calling it an 'undemocratic' decision, and at the sailor's Soviet he presently convened David and I found ourselves in a minority. Had I had any eloquence now was the time for an appeal to their better natures or even to their self-respect, but I felt mere disgust and no doubt allowed it to show. For me the voyage had now no aim and I could not feel much regard for those who had so tamely abandoned its objective. They were not the ill-conditioned lot that I had suffered from in '68 on *Mischief*'s last southern voyage – I felt no likelihood of being pushed overboard or knocked on the head – they merely lacked the requisite zeal. Giving up Ellesmere Is. also meant my failing to keep a promise of calling at Igdlorssuit, where we had been on *Baroque*'s first voyage, in order to bring back a Zodiac left there by a friend of mine, Professor Drever, who had recently died. To press on with an unwilling crew, who apparently expected the next gale to sink us, would be an ill task for which I had neither will nor strength. It is easy to criticise. When reviling it is not necessary to prepare a preliminary draft, but it occurs to me that for the state of affairs we had then reached I should have reviled myself. In the army one learnt that there were no bad regiments, battalions, batteries, there were only bad officers, and in the present case the skipper who had recruited his crew in the first place and who then failed to jolly them along and to infect them with some notion of high endeavour, was himself to blame. That said there is the truism about silk purses and sow's ears, and the fact that you can't hang soft cheese on iron hooks.

So once more we headed north, or rather well west of north which was the best we could point. And since the north-easterly wind continued to blow, in four days time we were in the latitude of Reykjavik and 120 miles west of it. Had we stood on for C. Farewell we should have rounded it by then. Angmagssalik on the east coast of Greenland was almost as near as Reykjavik. David suggested our going there, ignoring or ignorant of the fact that at this time of year, late June, ice conditions would almost certainly prevent it. Waiting in vain for a shift of wind we stayed too long on the starboard tack and by the time we went about to steer south-east we were nearly 150 miles north-west of our destination. At midnight of the 24th the wind, still at north-east, increased to gale force and although this gale had less vice than the earlier one the damage it did was more serious.

Under trys'l and jib she was going fast and working too much. In order to heave-to we had to drop the jib and set the reefed stays'l, and no sooner had the jib been dropped and the support given by its tight luff wire withdrawn, than the forestay parted. This 3in. circumference wire, in apparently good shape, passes inside the stemhead for almost a foot before emerging at deck level. The unseen bit inside the stemhead had rusted and there it parted. This in turn endangered the mast. In the lower part of the mast there is a long scarph which then began opening and shutting in ominous fashion as the mast swayed. Having downed the trys'l we managed to set up the forestay temporarily by means of a wire strop round the bowsprit and a tackle; and in daylight I managed to get the stay really tight with a length of chain rove through the stemhead and back to the anchor winch. It was too rough to deal with the mast. We did this next day when David and I put three wide bands of fencing wire round it. That done we set both jib and trys'l and crossed our fingers.

A fortnight had now passed since we turned north for Iceland. After copious priming with boiling water and a blow lamp heating the air-intake David made one more attempt to start the engine. By now, of course, not a flicker of life remained in the batteries. No joy, therefore, except that David lost his cool with the crew who were being less than helpful. The 28th, gloomy and cold, saw the last of our twice-baked bread and we turned to our edible cardboard. That night when the wind rose to nearly gale force we handed all sails, having in mind the state of the mast, a state that Mr Chucks the bos'n might have described as precarious and not very permanent. As we rolled and tossed, with no sails to steady her, a trawler passed, the first vessel we had seen for several weeks. Richard wished he was on board. On the contrary, I thought, they had reason to envy us who had nothing to do but lie and read in our lamp-lit bunks, in cool and airy surroundings instead of hot and stuffy, with no engine thumping away, and no racing propeller as she pitched.

Our mishaps were by no means over. We were aiming for Garhskali, a low, rocky point on the southern side of the wide Faxafloi bight at the back of which lies Reykjavik. On 30 June, when we had run our distance eastwards, confirmed by a snap sight which I got between rain squalls, Mike spotted an isolated rock of a peculiar shape. There was no such rock anywhere near Garhskali and by a process of elimination and comparison with views in the *Arctic Pilot* we decided it must be Eldey nearly twenty miles south of Garhskali. Eldey is a sheer-sided rock about 220ft. high lying off the coast about eight miles south-west of Reyjaknes at the south-west corner of the mainland. Until recently it was one of the largest gannetries in the world. Now the gannets seem to have been ousted by fulmars. It is unlit and from it a dangerous reef extends for thirty miles to the south-west. Had we not sighted Eldey we should have missed Iceland altogether and gone bumming on to the south-east. On this occasion the navigator was not entirely at fault, though he

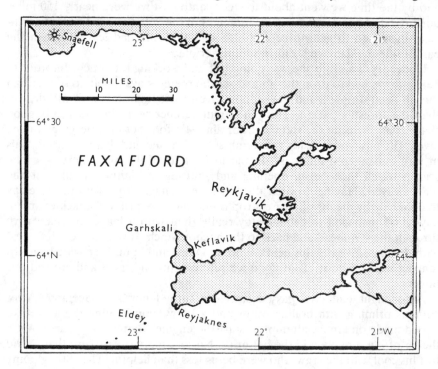

might have discovered earlier that the compass had resumed its behaviour of the previous voyage. Instead of the four points westerly variation that in this region it should have shown it had less than one point; so that when we were steering south-east by compass on the assumption that that would be east true, we were in fact steering nearly south-east true.

We closed the rock and having sighted Reyjaknes and its lighthouse, thus confirming that the rock was Eldey, we rounded it and made north up the coast. The wind had at last gone round to west putting us on a lee shore, a shore that remained obstinately hidden under low cloud throughout the day. Intent on keeping a good offing we steered west of north with the result that when we had run our distance to Garhskali we were a long way from the coast. We raised the Garhskali light that night and in the morning (1 July) a light breeze took us into Reykjavik roadstead where we anchored close to the harbour entrance. At the worst we could take a battery ashore for charging in order to use the engine for entering the harbour. However, when I went ashore to see the Customs and the harbour master the latter at once agreed to tow us in. A pilot came off that afternoon and as he watched patiently while we laboriously wound in the anchor cable with a Stilson wrench I wondered what he thought of us. The winch handle with which David had hoped to start the engine had not yet been restored to its original condition. We secured alongside a big floating crane, a convenient berth just abaft of five Icelandic gunboats, the whole fleet. They were dressed over-all in honour of the fiftieth anniversary of the Coastguard service and most of them were still undergoing repairs to hull damage sustained in the recent cod-war. Any ideas we may have had that the Red Ensign would not be welcome in Reykjavik were soon to be dismissed. We needed help of various kinds and willing helpers were easily found. The Icelanders no doubt felt they had been victorious and perhaps were all the more ready to be generous to the defeated.

CHAPTER FOURTEEN

From Reykjavik to Angmagssalik

WHEN WE put in here in 1972 to have a new boom made for *Sea Breeze* the local Odin Yacht Club had found for us the right man for the job. Through the Customs I tried to get in touch with them again. Nothing happened and no one from the Yacht Club ever came near us; instead the man himself, Jon Jonason, who had made the boom, turned up next morning accompanied by one Stefan Bjarnason as interpreter. Stefan deserves a word to himself for he became our main standby, sparing neither time nor trouble on our behalf. He was a naval architect by profession having studied at Newcastle University. After a spell in Nyasaland working for UNO designing fishing boats for use on Lake Nyasa, he had returned to Reykjavik where he now had the job of Harbour Pollution Inspector. Like many others in Reykjavik, where inflation is probably worse than in England, he had to have two jobs to make ends meet; after office hours, which were not unduly prolonged, he worked in his own profession.

Jon Jonason, widely known in Reykjavik as Jon Eleven (he had in his time been a noted footballer), has a small boat-building yard where he employs himself, his son, and one other hand. He has a liking for old boats and loves working in wood; in his shed was the hull of a 60ft. fishing boat which he expected to finish by the end of the year. In Iceland fishing boats have to be built to a very high standard and this one looked enormously strong. In his spare time Jon had built himself a small yacht – sails, fittings, and engine bought from England, the latter, I regret to say, proving highly unsatisfactory. Later on he sailed her round from his yard five miles away to bring up alongside us at our floating crane. To Jon I entrusted the job of repairing and strengthening the doghouse and of making up three iron bands for the mast. Having taken our batteries away for recharging he started work the same afternoon. Stefan took me to a wholesale fishmonger where I bought 1 kg. of halibut for £1.50. There are no fishmonger shops in Reykjavik (nor any butchers); presumably most of the 70,000 people living there get their fish from relatives or friends employed in fishing or in fish factories. Later when we moved to that side of the harbour where the fishing boats lie we were given all the fish we needed. Stefan presented me with some dried cod, stockfish, which is eaten raw like chewing gum, only worse. It is very expensive.

Before he left home Mike and the two other climbers were to spend a week in the mountains a long bus journey north of Reykjavik. Richard and Jim, by now practically penniless, had no qualms about allowing Mike to foot the bill, for nowadays the young expect and accept hand-outs from the Government milch-cow or from individuals as of right. Thus David and I had some time alone on board, a pleasant respite. On Sundays we used to walk out to the Meteorological Office, now housed in a new building some way beyond the airport. They had copies of the most recent ice charts from the Met. Office at Bracknell and now that our dwindling ambitions comprised only a brief visit to Angmagssalik we were interested in the ice conditions off the east coast. These appeared to be bad, or at least worse than normal, and were not likely to improve before the end of July or early August. We had a look, too, at the North Atlantic weather chart for 12th and 13th June which showed a large depression covering our position at that time with a low at the centre of 975 mbs. Those on duty there on Sundays welcomed our intrusion and gave us all the information they could, usually in perfect English. To get inside I found embarrassing, for the main door was kept locked and one had to press a button and speak into a hole in the wall to explain who one was. Usually a girl's voice replied in dulcet but distorted tone. I felt like Pyramus conversing with Thisbe: 'O sweet, O lovely wall, thanks courteous wall.'

One day a French yacht with a cheerful and capable crew of three came alongside, two months out via the Hebrides and the Faeroes. They knew all about *Mischief*'s voyages and were the first yachtsmen I have met who had similar aims, indeed even larger aims. On a voyage of indefinite extent they intended visiting the west coast of Greenland, Baffin Is., Labrador, California, Alaska, and thence down to the Patagonia channels, in fact most of the cold, mountainous regions that could be reached by sea. They had not quite done their homework, for they were not aware that they would probably meet ice off south-west Greenland, their first objective. I advised them to make for Godthaab and the mountains to the north and gave them my West Greenland charts of which they had very few. It would have done my three faint-hearted voyagers a world of good to have met these French lads and to have caught some of their bold, infectious spirit.

Meantime *Baroque* needed attention, primarily the forestay both below and aloft where the eye-splice had to be parcelled and served. The jib halyard rove by Jim had also been stranded. I only discovered this when sitting aloft in the bos'n's chair serving the splice suspended on that same halyard, or rather by the one frayed strand that remained. To replace the chain at deck level I got from a kindly stevedore a discarded 2½in. wire sling, cut off the damaged bit, and put a hard eye in one end. An equally kind engineering shop made up a long threaded 'U' bolt which served for tightening up instead of an expensive bottle screw. The other end of the sling was secured to the broken forestay with bulldog grips and to disguise this I covered the whole with overhand grafting painted black, decorated with Turk's heads painted white. Besides the forestay both wire topping lifts needed attention, one having to be replaced with rope. Of necessity the mast bands that Jon Eleven fitted had large outstanding lugs to take the bolts. As these hindered sail hoisting David made wood fairings to fit above and below the lugs so that the sail lacing would render over them. This worked pretty well although both the mains'l and trys'l lacing sometimes needed assisting over them by hand.

On 13 July the climbing party returned refreshed by the change of scene; Richard, for a time, slightly less bloody-minded. Mike left next day with assurances that he would send out a substitute. We had had one or two nibbles from Icelanders and from the Youth Hostel where we had made our want known. There was probably no connection but on the return of the climbing party I suffered a sleepless night. Consequently in the afternoon, having finished *The Times* crossword, I was dozing off when one of the pilots came on board to move us in order to make room for *Brendan*. This was the boat made from thirty-two cow-hides on a voyage from Ireland to America. Better off in one respect than St Brendan she had made her whereabouts known by radio telephone and she had also been sighted some eighty miles away. Rather than secure outside us, as she could have done, she was to have VIP treatment, and in view of the numbers of sight-seers who would want to go on board her we did well to be out of it. Owing to adverse winds three more days elapsed before *Brendan* arrived to receive a great welcome. To give her a fresh coating of some special grease they later slipped the boat at a yard near Jon's place where David and I had a look at her. They told us she was an excellent sea-boat and could do wonders with a following wind having on occasions logged over 100 miles a day on passage from the Faeroes. There was some talk of crew changes but I had no fear of any of my crew volunteering for the next leg of this bold and remarkably uncomfortable adventure. But on our return to Reykjavik later we learnt that she never sailed, a long spell of westerly winds having decided the crew to leave her there for the winter. Would St Brendan have concurred?

Our move across the harbour did not go smoothly. Besides cutting with its propeller the moorings of a small boat, the pilot boat that had us in tow rammed the quay wall with our bowsprit. On reaching the other side we were put in a berth alongside a wooden quay that at high tide would be submerged. A fishing boat owner suggested our lying against a nearby trawler that was undergoing repair and offered to tow us there. He did this with so much *élan* that our counter hit the steel hull of the trawler a terrible crack, starting a plank and displacing the counter itself a good three inches. More work for Jon

Eleven's shipwright who next day made good the plank and restored and strengthened the counter.

When the mains'l came back repaired we bent it on, Richard assisting, after which he announced his forthcoming departure, his passage home already arranged for with the British Consul. I made some suitable remark upon which he went below in dudgeon to confer with Jim who by now seemed to be the senior in this strange partnership. A few minutes later he was back on deck with the news that he had now decided to stay to which I foolishly consented. From the Consul, whom I knew of old, I learnt that he had merely outlined to Richard the necessary procedure when applying for assistance as a distressed British subject; among other things he would have had to produce a note from me saying that I refused to take him. A surprising number of people had been assisted back from Iceland in the past year and, less surprisingly, many of them had failed to refund the money. The same day I had a too laconic cable from Mike – 'Crew arriving 23rd' – which aroused speculation as to who this crew might be. In order of dread I feared it might be either a friend of Richard's, the girl with whom Mike had sailed home from the West Indies, an instructor from the Moray Sea School, or even Mike himself, by this time possibly regretting that he had not kept his hand to the plough. Richard now did his best to behave normally, even doing some work, instead of remaining aloof surrounded by an aura of morose gloom, or what may have been merely the mystic melancholy of a Scot too far from home; an attitude that in the army as I first knew it would have quickly had him booked by the sergeant-major on a charge of dumb insolence.

Varying our route, David and I walked one Sunday to the Met. Office by way of the beach were we came across a stream of hot water gushing out of a large drainpipe. This was a popular picnic spot where numerous families in bathing dresses larked about in the hot stream. All the houses and buildings in Reykjavik are heated by this constant supply of hot water from underground. Stefan showed us his modest bills for so many tons of hot water; at his house there were two inlets, one for the radiators and one for the hot taps. His water when used went down the drain but in newer houses the supply is re-cycled. Thus there is some compensation for living on an unstable island with the ever-present threat of eruptions.

The latest ice chart showed little change for the better and there were reports of a vessel having been stuck in the ice for two weeks. On the other hand, a pilot who had just flown back from Kulusuk, the air-strip 16 miles ENE of Angmagssalik, told me that the ice looked navigable; but what might look navigable from a thousand feet up might not look so good from *Baroque*'s cross-trees. Hoping for some real information from a man on the spot I went to the Danish consul and got the telephone number of Niels Underborg, skipper of a boat based at Angmagssalik, who had been of assistance to me in the past. No reply could be got from this Angmagssalik number (which saved me a costly telephone call) and later I found that Niels had retired to Denmark. For some odd reason the use of a telephone to obtain information about ice conditions seemed to me a little underhand. The early seamen–explorers, whose experience it has always been my aim in a faint and feeble way to recapture, had to go and find out; and in spite of ice reports, which are out of date by the time one is on the spot, this is what the man in a small boat had nowadays still to do. Anyway, our new crew having arrived as promised on the 23rd. I decided to sail on the 29th, hoping that by the time we were off the coast in early August the ice would be navigable. The new crew, another Hamish, a big chap and a climber, who was from the Moray Sea School, proved also, like Mike, to lack staying power. With a crew that in words of studious moderation might be called mercurial it is a mistake to visit such unremote places as Reykjavik or Angmagssalik from which escape is comparatively easy.

At considerable cost we stocked up with bread, rice, fish-loaf, potatoes, and onions, taking only enough for a month as I reckoned food would be cheaper in Angmagssalik assuming we got there. Shortly before we sailed a small vessel belonging to the Danish Geodetic Survey came in with eight geologists on board bound for East Greenland. She was named *Tycho Brahe* after the Danish astronomer and later she was to do me what I considered an ill turn. On the day we sailed, a day of incessant rain, Jon Eleven came to say farewell with a gift of two boxes of frozen haddock fillets earmarked for the American market, in other words the best. We cast off after lunch, but before we had cleared Engey Island not far from the harbour entrance, finding the wind dead ahead and the weather thick, we turned back and anchored in the roadstead. We beat out next day in better weather and when off Gardhskagi we hove-to in the hope of catching some cod. Richard had provided himself with lures recommended by the professionals but we had no luck; what with the tide and the boat fore-reaching, as she does when hove-to, we were probably moving too much.

In crossing Denmark Strait we had a lot of rain and winds of such variable strength that we spent most of the time reefing and unreefing. It is about 400 miles across and on 14 August, when we were less than a hundred miles from the Greenland coast the sea temperature dropped from 9° C. at 6 am to 3° C. at noon, indicating that we were then in the East Greenland current. At 3 am next morning when we were bowling along before a nice easterly breeze, the weather was so thick that I decided to double the watch with one man on look-out. So on being relieved at the helm I went forward and, as I had expected, soon began to sight the odd ice floe. By breakfast time we were surrounded by scattered floes and having retreated to open water we steered north-west along the edge of what I thought must be a detached field of ice – at least one hoped it was for we were still a long way from the coast. The previous evening Jim had reported hearing a distant rumble, a noise that no doubt came from this field of ice. A noon sight put us about 550 miles ESE of C. Dan and by evening we were some 30 miles from the land with ice visible ahead as well as to north and south. The glass was falling so we retreated a few miles to the west and hove-to.

This prudent decision failed to save us from a night of anxiety. When I took over at midnight from David he stayed up, for what with squalls of wind and rain, low visibility, and ice in the vicinity, some support was welcome. Even in such conditions a field of ice can be seen or heard in good time, it is the odd floe that drifts away on its own that is a menace to a small boat. Presently we had to let draw to sail clear of a floe and soon after that started the engine to avoid another. Even this did not rouse any curiosity on the part of the crew, but at 4 am when a line of ice appeared ahead we called them up to put the boat about. By breakfast time the wind had steadied to a good Force 6, the sea rough enough to conceal the odd floe lurking in the wave troughs. Quite suddenly we were confronted at close quarters by a cluster of floes and small bergs and in the rough water she missed stays. With little room to spare I had to gybe all standing and split the stays'l. After first making a nonsense of it the crew got the storm jib set and to my relief, after some heart-stopping moments, we were again under control. As the wind took off snow began to fall, the air temperature down to 1° C. This short-lived vicious northerly blow put me in mind of Lecky's warning that a falling barometer with a northerly wind is a signal that cannot be disregarded with impunity.

On 7 August we enjoyed for the first time what I call a 'Greenland' day, calm, cloudless, serene. For twenty miles we motored towards the land through widely scattered floes, skirting many majestic icebergs, while I sat on deck in the warm sun repairing the torn stays'l. With fog hanging low over the land, we had little idea how close we were or how far south of Angmagssalik, so when the ice became thicker we retreated to more open water and lay-to for the night. A night of wind and rain gave way to a day of drizzle and the same cold, northerly wind. I felt unwell, added a third sweater, and spent the day in my bunk, the crew standing my watches. 9 August was drier but otherwise no better; the same cold, northerly blast, drifting south, rolling damnably, knowing neither our own position nor that of the ice. However, we had the stays'l below and finished it, and if my stitches looked a bit erratic, those of Jim and Richard, plying their prentice hands, were frightful. We were not in a strong or even a satisfactory position. From what we had seen the ice near the coast seemed pretty thick, our bread was already finished and we had little biscuit left. We could wait for a few days but if we then failed to reach Angmagssalik we were in for a lean time. That evening the wind fell light leaving behind a nasty lop. To steady her we set all sail, pointing north-east but barely moving, with the hard, white line of the pack showing up to the north and to the west.

This waiting game would have been less trying could we but have stayed still. Unless we could keep on the move northwards we lost ground fast to the south, set down by the current. That we had lost a lot became clear next day when we motored for 30 miles in a north-westerly direction before meeting any ice. Early in the afternoon of this bright, windless day, motoring over the calmest of seas with no ice yet in sight, I had felt so confident of reaching the coast that I had the anchor got ready and hoisted our Danish courtesy flag. By 5 pm we were in contact with fairly close pack stretching in a wide arc from C. Dan to Sermilik fjord, close enough pack to discourage any attempt at bashing a way through. Sermilik fjord looked open and although we now had an engine that worked I felt that to enter would be courting a repetition of the 1972 disaster when we lost *Sea Breeze*. Much to the chagrin of the crew we turned about and sailed north-east, for by then a light breeze had come in.

The wind died at night, we drifted south, and at the start of yet another frustrating day we were once more south of Sermilik fjord. The ice seemed to have spread out from the coast and unlike the previous day it proved bitterly cold. To avoid the constant set to the south I thought of anchoring under Cape Tycho Brahe at the southern entrance to Sermilik fjord which at that moment looked reachable. By late afternoon I regretted we had not tried this. In thick, drizzly weather we were dodging in fairly thick ice on the north side of Sermilik, quite cut off from C. Tycho Brahe by a line of unnavigable ice. Once more we beat a retreat.

12 August, a dull, windless day, happened to be David's birthday and we nearly made it a really happy one. Having motored for three hours we entered the ice and found the going easy, so easy that I became confident of success and imparted this to David. He was at the engine controls while I

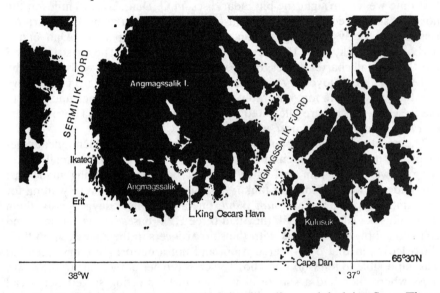

stood on deck – to see better – holding the tiller line and dodging floes. There were seals about, in the sea and on the ice, and when we were within a couple of miles of Ortumuviak we spotted some seal-hunters. Ortumuviak is a bold headland only some two miles south of King Oscar's Havn, the entrance to Angmagssalik, and had we found an inshore lead we were home and dry. As it was we were stuck, the ice ahead being too thick for us to penetrate and beyond it no hint of open water. One of the seal-hunters came on board – no kayak, but a fibreglass dory astern of which he towed a big harp seal he had just shot. Richard, who had spent some time in Norway, tried to converse in halting Danish of which our visitor understood little. He said there was open water ahead but having climbed to the crosstrees and spent some time there he seemed less confident. I took the hint and by seven o'clock we were back in ice-free water. Two more Greenlanders in a motor boat came out for a gam, one of a rather superior type, the other fulfilling one's idea of a real Eskimo, squalid, uncouth, with a perpetual amiable grin. They assured us we could not get in and would not get in next day either. This attempt, our third, had nearly succeeded. At moderate speed the engine used only ½ gal. an hour so that we had fuel enough for several more attempts. Bread was another matter and by now Jim had started to make soda-bread. I see from my diary that I was 'becoming a little browned off with all this fruitless manoeuvring in ice and shall be heartily glad to have done'.

On the 13th we enjoyed another flawless 'Greenland' day, the icebergs mirrored in the still water and beyond them a background of wild, jagged peaks. The ice in our vicinity had thickened and spread eastwards, so we used the engine to round the easternmost corner and then set sail for a light southerly breeze. On the way we met a Norwegian whaler busy seeking along the ice edge. We hoisted our ensign, waved, and made what noise we could, hoping to get some bread off him, but he ignored us and stood on. For the first time we had in sight the big radar discs on C. Dan about 15 miles to the north-west and reckoned we were just holding our own against the current. Besides an Early Warning station there is an air-strip at C. Dan and a harbour, Kulusuk, some 16 miles ENE of Angmagssalik. The air-strip is used mostly by small charter planes from Reykjavik. That night, as well as the lights at Kulusuk, we enjoyed a moderate display of aurora. In sharp contrast we spent the next day in fog, miserably damp and chill, tacking back and forth to the ice edge. All ills are alleviated by food and since this was a Saturday the curry and duff were the more welcome.

The onset of a south-westerly breeze, the first we had had, lent encouragement, for it might well open up the ice inshore. Having noted a small tanker lying-to we closed him and after a lot of backing and filling made fast alongside. It was a Canadian tanker, *Jos Simard*, and they were waiting for the American ice-breaker *South Wind*, due at 4 am next day, to assist them into Kulusuk. After Kulusuk they had three EWS bases on the Baffin Island coast to supply. I had a talk with the ship's officers in their mess, all in their shirt-sleeves in that over-heated room and not a uniform amongst them. It was impossible to tell who was who. The crew did better by going to the men's mess where they had a square meal. This lucky meeting solved our bread problem, for they gave us fifteen loaves, baked, I noticed, in Montreal, not by their cook. After this pleasant interlude we pushed on for our fourth attempt and were finally stopped off Ortumuviak in much the same place as before. In the evening on the way back, after getting stuck in a cul-de-sac where we took half-an-hour to turn round, we moored to a convenient floe, large, flat, and fitted with rudimentary bollards, with *Jos Simard* in sight a few miles away. This floe served the purpose though it was nothing like so substantial as the one we were moored to for five days in *Sea Breeze*. With ice-axes the bollards were soon improved and we were now able to stretch our legs, as it were, on shore. An ivory gull, the most beautiful of all the gulls, with pure white plumage, alighted on the floe for a short time. Jim, a keen and knowledgeable bird-watcher, identified it. I wanted to see what *Jos Simard* did. We did not want to follow in her wake – I had tried that lark in *Mischief* in '64 – nor did we want to go to Kulusuk, but from it there might be a shore-lead to Angmagssalik so by watching *Jos Simard* and the ice-breaker we might discover the most likely approach. My plan miscarried. When *South Wind* arrived on time they moved off and were soon out of sight, and instead of calling me at 4 am for my watch David, meaning kindly, let me lie and we remained moored to our floe.

At ten o'clock we got under way, high time, too, as the ice was on the move and thickening. Having reached open water we hoisted sail for a light breeze, steering for C. Dan off which there seemed to be little or no ice. Inside the cape the ice receded in a great bight towards Angmagssalik fjord and had it not been late evening we might have had a closer look; instead we hove-to for the night and proceeded to lose our hard-won northing. Indeed we seemed to lose more than ever. Next morning, after motoring for two hours through scattered floes, it was disheartening to find ourselves opposite C. Tycho Brahe on the south side of Sermilik fjord. However, the ice had apparently moved south. Towards Angmagssalik conditions looked much better and when we were eventually stopped I reckoned we were within a mile of Ortumuviak. Still we could see no open water close inshore while Sermilik fjord was now chock full of ice. It was late evening by then and nine o'clock before we were back in open water with all sail set for a nice south-westerly breeze. When a motor boat appeared in chase we hove-to and were presently boarded by the same Greenlander that we had met before. He had no seal in tow this time, instead he had a nice, new pair of sealskin boots. He was now confident we could get in and offered to show us the way, an offer which I accepted with some reluctance, for it would soon be dark. He headed towards the north side of Sermilik fjord at a brisk pace and only once or twice did he have to wait while we manoeuvred ourselves through some narrow passage. By midnight he had brought us into a moderately wide inshore lead a mile or two south of Ortumuviak. There he disappeared into the night leaving us to our own devices. We never saw the man again and since he would surely have looked us up in Angmagssalik, even if only to claim a reward, I think he must have come from the small settlement in Sermilik fjord.

By then it was dark, loose bits of ice hard to see, so I handed over to Richard who had keener sight. A half-moon shining directly down our course helped and if one could refrain from anxiously scanning our surroundings, a rocky shore on one side and ice on the other, immediately overhead the aurora was staging a remarkably brilliant display, bands of light, whorls, shimmering curtains, and transient flickering shafts. We passed close under Ortumuviak, the goal we had twice narrowly failed to reach, and beyond it we presently made out the faintly flashing light marking the entrance to King Oscar's Havn. On opening up the entrance we met a powerful wind blowing straight out of the fjord, and when we turned towards the entrance we had to keep the engine going hard to make headway against it. Watching the little light to starboard creep past fearfully slowly I could not forget the jostling floes and bergs to seaward of our narrow shore-lead, nor ignore the possibility of the engine failing or faltering and of our drifting back helplessly among them.

Having taken over the tiller I soon found that we could steer but in one direction, dead into the wind. The moment the bow fell off, however slightly, there was no recovering; one had to let her go right round in full circle and with gathering speed head once more into the wind. This being so we had no chance of reaching the harbour whose lights we could see away on the port hand; so we stood on for the head of the fjord hoping to find a lee under the mountains together with some sort of anchorage. As we groped our way in the dark towards the head of a small inlet, the wind already appreciably less, for a long time the leadsman reported 'no bottom'. Then suddenly 5 fms., and by the time the bunglers got the anchor over, only 2 fms. The occasional willie-waw that swept down from the mountains made her drag. We had to anchor afresh and by the time we had finished it was 6 am and time for breakfast – a welcome end to yet another night to remember. As I was turning in Hamish, who had the anchor watch, asked: 'Should you fall asleep do you want waking so that we can get to Angmagssalik?'

CHAPTER FIFTEEN

Angmagssalik to Reykjavik

THE GALE accompanied by rain went on throughout the following day. By then we had two anchors down and twice had to relay them on account of dragging. The next evening we thought the wind had moderated and discovered our mistake only when we emerged from the inlet into the main fjord. In half a mind to go back I foolishly ran on before the gale to find when we reached the harbour that it was almost blocked by ice. As we tried to creep through a small gap between a grounded floe and a Norwegian vessel lying at the quay the Norwegian chose that moment to cast off. In avoiding him we pranged the floe with our bowsprit, luckily without damage, and having backed out of the ensuing *melée* we anchored off a rocky shore some two cables from the harbour entrance. Our anchorage of former years, outside of and near the root of the quay, was merely a mass of ice. After more dragging, by 10 pm with two anchors down, we seemed at last to be fairly static. The wind had taken off and our only troubles were from drifting floes. On the whole it had been an unwise move, leaving a doubtful anchorage on a weather shore for a precarious anchorage on a lee shore with the addition of menacing floes.

The warning in the *Pilot* that has already been mentioned – 'Anchoring in this bight should be prompted by necessity and not in any hope of tranquillity' – certainly applied to our anchorage off that rocky shore, dictated by necessity and affording no tranquillity. David and I stayed on deck until 5 am busy at first fending off floes and then, when the tide ebbed, relaying the anchors in order to get clear of the boulders on which she began to bump. After inspecting the ice-strewn harbour I thought we should be better off inside, and having moved inside we secured to a small local boat which we were assured would not be moving for three days. When she moved that evening we went alongside the small quay where we learnt that a small tanker would shortly arrive. Finally we found some peace at the anchorage of former years whence by then most of the ice had drifted out. The harbour is small, the inner shallower half is a clutter of small boat moorings, at the one big mooring buoy there are usually two or three local boats, and at the quay itself there is room for only one vessel of any size.

After two days of wind and rain we were now enjoying the brilliant weather that I associate with Greenland, especially the east coast. The three younger crew went up what I call 'Spy-glass hill', the hill of nearly 2,000ft. that lies close behind the town, from which in 1964, when the ice had imprisoned us for three weeks, we used to scan the sea outside for possible routes of escape. In those days I used to climb it before breakfast in three quarters of an hour or less; next day when David and I thought to go up I was foundered 500ft. below the top. David, too, failed to make it, hastening down, as he said, in response to what he took to be cries for help, possibly from the skipper! This poor performance indicated to me that the wear and tear of a disheartening voyage had begun to tell on a frame no longer resilient – and worse was yet to come. Nevertheless, now that sufficient time has elapsed for the 1976 crew to become merely a distasteful memory, I am thankful to report that the Welsh equivalent of Spy-glass Hill is again well within compass. Thanks to rest, coupled with a diet of home-brewed beer, home-made bread, cheese, honey, and apple dumplings, spurred on, too, by my four-footed friends: – at 2,000ft. I no longer succumb to mountaineer's foot, the inability to put one in front of the other.

We devoted one morning to taking photographs of *Baroque* under sail in the fjord, dropping Jim, our expert photographer, in the dinghy and then making several runs past him. Next day the three young climbers set off for the peak that we had climbed in 1964. It is about 3,500ft. and they had a row of about a mile across the fjord, and a walk of three or four miles to the foot of the climb. Even so they took an unconscionable time. At four o'clock we spotted them through binoculars about half-way up but they did not get back until three o'clock next morning. Apparently they had tried a new route which failed to 'go' and in the end had to resort to the gully by which we had made the ascent. By this time I had made the rounds of Angmagssalik, meeting only one friend of 1964, Martin Petersen, the shipwright carpenter who had repaired *Mischief*'s damaged planks. He had now a fine, new workshop with power-driven saws and lathe. Martin has a little English, unlike the few more ancient Greenlanders who recognised me with whom I could exchange only grins. Another old acquaintance, one that I regarded as slightly ominous, was the Norwegian vessel with which we had nearly collided on our first approach. She was *Brandal*, the same vessel that had tried to tow the by then much battered *Mischief* from Jan Mayen to Norway in 1968, now on charter at Angmagssalik as a sort of maid-of all work, hard worked at that. None of her present crew had been on board in 1968.

On 25 August, another wet day, we went alongside the quay to fill up with water and fuel for the homeward passage which was to begin the next day. I intended going north of Iceland in order to call at the Island of Grimsey, thus just crossing the Arctic Circle. This crossing had become a ritual for *Baroque* which I felt could not be omitted even on this irresolute voyage. By noon a wind of almost gale force was blowing straight into the harbour and we were content to remain where we were. Had we wanted to move it had become almost impossible and at that moment my old friend *Brandal* hove in sight, back from one of her all too frequent local passages, evidently in a hurry to come alongside. A local boat moored round the corner of the quay had her stern sticking out far enough to prevent us dropping back and just off the quay was the large floe aground that had been there when we arrived and was still there when we left. And to confuse things further more floes were now drifting into the entrance. The harbour master (a Greenlander) soon sized up our predicament and *Brandal*'s. Summoning his gang he took charge very efficiently. Casting off the local boat they let her go down the harbour on a long warp and then paid out our warps until we could secure alongside her, whereupon *Brandal*, patiently lying-to outside, moved in to the quay.

There had been more than one black day on this voyage and the next day, 26 August, proved blackest of all. By morning there were three of us lying together on long warps from the quay, *Baroque* in the middle, and having disentangled ourselves we motored slowly towards the entrance keeping to the side opposite to the quay to avoid ice floes. We got too near the side. In Greenland fjords it is usually safe to go within spitting distance of a rock shore but not on this occasion. We should have gone astern, instead we came firmly to rest on a rock on a falling tide. As she floated easily enough at high water that evening I might have laughed the incident off as a minor mistake; what followed this mistake was disastrous and no laughing matter at all. Having wasted some time trying vainly to kedge off I picked up the first handy coil of rope, shackled it to the throat halyard block and sent Richard ashore to anchor it. We were close to the oil installation where some concrete posts came in useful as strong points. I had thought of using this coil of rope for the mainsheet and when I tried putting in an eye-splice had found the strands so tightly laid up that I gave it best. It proved to be nylon with apparently unlimited stretch. By the time I had grasped this and begun to unreeve the peak halyards for use as a masthead line *Baroque* had listed to 45° and was beyond recovery. The nylon line went on stretching until she finished up on her beam ends, the deck vertical. Meantime David had been trying to lighten her, sending ashore the heavy anchor and cable, draining the water tanks, and even lifting the floor-boards with a view to getting out the ballast – all to no purpose.

By afternoon we had four lines from mast to shore, a tackle on each, together with a very capable Greenlander who came along to encourage and assist. With David and I tailing behind he did most of the work as we gained a few inches on each line in turn in an effort to get the boat upright before the rising tide flooded her. I never saw the rest of the crew who must have gone shopping. At the extreme angle the boat lay over, the lines had little lifting power and needless to say the tide won, rising inexorably inch by inch, until long before we had her even half upright she was completely full of water.

Little enough that was of use or value had been got out – all the food, except that in tins, was destroyed, clocks, barometer, binoculars, camera, film, radio, clothes, sleeping bags, and worst of all the engine and batteries, all soaked in a mixture of diesel oil and sea water. A number of Danes and Greenlanders had gathered on the rocks to watch. One of the Greenlanders took the opportunity to pocket a thousand or so of David's cigarettes lying among the small pile of stuff that had been salvaged. When detected by David and forced to disgorge the bystanders merely laughed, evidently more in sympathy with the culprit than with his victim. Among the Danes was the man in charge of the oil installation who offered at a price, a high one, to pump out the boat. They ran a power line down, put a pump on board, and within an hour had all the water out. By then she had floated off so I got them to tow her to the buoy. We then began ferrying the salvaged stuff on board in the dinghy. I stood by until the last load had gone and it was about 10 pm before I got back on board.

What a homecoming! Anything floatable had floated so that debris lay about everywhere, a film of oil covered everything, the floorboards were up, and both pumps were at work. While lying on her beam ends a plank had been started. David slightly lessened the copious flow by cutting up a rag and stuffing bits in, but the pumps had to be kept going all night. A hut at the oil installation had kindly been put at our disposal and we took it in turns to row over and doss down for a couple of hours in a warm, dry room. Early in the morning I got hold of Martin who came off and speedily stopped the leak with his sawdust trick. A bucketful of sawdust with a long pole attached to the handle is capsized alongside bottom up, thrust smartly down to the vicinity of the leak where, by joggling the pole, the sawdust escapes and is sucked into the leak. A refinement is to have a box with a sliding lid, actuated by a line, fixed to the pole. When the box is in position the lid is drawn and the sawdust released. I arranged with Martin that after the week-end we would beach *Baroque* so that he could put tingles over the leak.

David and Jim had drained the engine and cleaned it out but the electrical parts needed professional attention. Through the hospital doctor, whom I knew, I got in touch with a Dane who ran a taxi and plant-hire business who sent two of his mechanics on board that evening. They soon had the cylinder off and took the batteries, dynamo, and starter motor to their workshop. From the doctor, by the way, we received other kindnesses including gifts of whale meat and arctic char and the use of his house to dry out our gear. Our beaching arrangements looked like being in jeopardy when the local hospital ship limped in with propeller trouble. The beach, which is reasonably smooth, is very small, and the hospital ship obviously had first claim; in the end, however, Martin, who is in charge of all repair work, got us in together. The acting skipper of the hospital ship paid me a visit along with his cook, also acting, who turned out to be an Englishman, a very dark one. The skipper's real motive was to buy spirits and I had to tell him I would rather he drank them on board, which he did with a will. Greenlanders can buy alcohol only in the form of beer (Carlsberg or Tuborg lager) and the sale of that is stopped on Fridays in the hope that the wives will be able to grab enough of their man's wages for housekeeping. The skipper looked forward to retiring early in order to devote all his time to the business or pastime of seal-hunting to which he was addicted. His English was nearly as good as that of the cook and both became increasingly voluble. Not surprisingly, from this rum session only one item of seal lore remains clear, namely that the blue-back skin is the best, followed by that of the ring seal.

Except for David the crew had now taken to sleeping ashore. The boat seemed the more wholesome for it though I realised that it would be difficult to sail without them. They turned up on the Monday and at high water we rowed the boat with our sweeps on to the beach in the wake of the hospital ship. The rise and fall of the tide is from 8 to 10ft. and in the absence of any wall to lean against we rigged lines to keep her upright. By late evening Martin had finished his tingles of felt covered with aluminium sheet and we kedged off as soon as she floated. Instead of the calm conditions of the morning there were violent gusts of wind and what with this and the numerous small craft yawing wildly at their moorings we had to anchor before we were in deep enough water. By midnight, with another three hours of ebb to go she was on the bottom. With the sweeps and a big baulk of timber David and I rigged legs and also took a long line from the mast ashore. Half of this long line turned out to be the same damned line that had literally let us down before, but the boat was still upright and every ten minutes or so we took in the slack by hauling on the throat halyards. The legs appeared to be taking most of the weight so when the mast line became block on block we let it go in order to shorten it, whereupon the lashing of the midships leg parted and over she went with a bang. She was nothing like right over and by pumping we kept the water down until she began to lift when, having rigged another masthead line, by heaving in on both we presently got her upright. David and I spent the night on deck, the crew's contribution being pumping and saving their gear from the threatened inundation.

My relations with them were becoming strained and these came to a head the next afternoon. After our all-night performance I wanted some sleep and with Richard prowling about on deck in his climbing boots I found it difficult. My suggestion that he should either come below or jump over the side was not well received. All three hastened below to announce that they were quitting, that they were unhappy, and that the boat was not safe. What, I think, they really wanted was to oblige me to leave the boat at Angmagssalik and so make me responsible for getting them home. Rather than this I reckoned that David and I could take her to Reykjavik and hope to get some more crew there. Richard took his gear ashore, Hamish packed his but continued using the boat as a restaurant, while Jim, who had some sense of duty, declared that 'he was ready to stick his neck out' but only as far as Reykjavik, and always provided the engine worked.

Owing to the exertions of the last few days I felt extremely weak and could only crawl around. We had once more to arrange for taking on water and fuel and before that could be done the fuel tanks needed draining off and a water pipe had to be repaired. When she was full of water the cabin water tank had come adrift and broken the outlet pipe. At this time *Tycho Brahe* came in.

She had landed her geologists at Kulusuk, whence they would fly home, and she was now homeward bound empty. Her skipper, whom I did not meet, apparently advised or even invited *Baroque*'s crew to take passage with him. Richard was on board like a shot and that night, or rather at three in the morning, a voice by my bunk was heard intoning: 'This is Hamish. I've come to tell you that I'm leaving.'

In the morning (4 September) we warped up to the quay astern of *Tycho Brahe* who was supposed to be leaving. Her skipper must have been of a cautious disposition for though she was a vessel built to shunt ice, and by then there was little enough left to shunt, he was waiting for a helicopter report on ice conditions. She finally got away, spurred on by *Brandal* which was again waiting to come in, with Richard and Hamish safely on board, Richard on deck busy with warps, Hamish out of sight below. On reflection I believe that *Tycho Brahe* did me a good rather than an ill turn. Without her Richard and Hamish looked like being marooned and the Danish authorities in Greenland dislike having on their hands penniless foreigners. I should have had to tell the local Governor that I was leaving behind two of my crew and he would no doubt have taken the line that since I had brought them there I should have to get them away, or in other words have them flown to Reykjavik. Some moderately kind words are no doubt owing to Jim, who all along had been apprehensive, for resisting the terrible temptation offered by *Tycho Brahe*, especially as the engine had not yet been started and might well never start. That was settled the same evening when the two mechanics came and in a short time had it running as well as ever. As there would no doubt still be some ice outside to negotiate this was a great relief.

After the severe strains we had recently put upon the mast the shrouds needed setting up again and also the forestay. David stripped down the water-logged barometer and finally got it to work. The ship's clock, the chronometer watch, and the wireless set were all too badly corroded, as well as my camera. Except for the clock which looks well when polished even if it does not go, I dropped them all overboard. David's quartz clock still functioned. I had intended sailing on 6 September but by the time the bill for the engine repairs – a hefty one – had been settled we had not enough time left to get clear of the ice before dark. When we left early the next morning, the water in the harbour and in King Oscar's Havn was covered with cat-ice. A field of fairly close pack extended from the entrance to C. Dan but south of this there were only a few scattered floes and a great many bergs. By 6 pm, after motoring all day, we were in ice-free water. Feeling greatly in need of a quiet sea voyage after the harrowing experiences of the past fortnight I had reason to be thankful. Storms, ice, and the damage they can do are acceptable as part of the game, but damage inflicted by one's own mistakes is more painful, less easily borne, and not readily forgotten.

The first three days of this short passage were calm, cloudless, and without a breath of wind. We motored more or less non-stop and when I insisted on stopping the engine for the sake of having four hours of quiet in the middle of the night, the other two regarded me as no better than a 'cissy'. On the fourth day we had all the wind we wanted and eventually hove-to with six rolls in the mains'l. She was leaking rather more than usual, a circumstance that might put a severe strain on Jim's fragile loyalty. In the morning, however, I discovered the source of this additional leak close to the head of my bunk and just above the water line. Every roll of the boat produced a miniature water-spout. Putting her about so that she heeled the right way, we hove-to while David tacked on a tingle of canvas, putty, and aluminium sheet. With Jim holding on to his feet he could just reach down far enough.

With no latitude sight the previous day, on the sixth day out we found we were heading for Snaefell (4,759ft.), the snow-capped mountain on the northern side of the wide Faxafloi bight. Mindful of the liberal error of our first landfall I had allowed too much for the vagaries of the compass, and besides that a strong north-going current sets up the west coast of Iceland. As we closed the land a fog-bank drifted in from seawards reducing visibility to barely a cable's length. An hour later it cleared with remarkable suddenness revealing, close on our port hand, the snowy dome of Snaefell glistening in the setting sun. We made Reykjavik next day, a week out from Angmagssalik, again securing to the floating crane. On this passage we did a lot more motoring than sailing, for since David and Jim had to do all the hoisting and changing of sails I was loth to call them up too often.

In the course of their long, fruitful collaboration over the recent engine problems they had become pretty matey and David now confided to me that the apprehensive Jim, if treated gently, would probably remain with us all the way home. This he finally agreed to do provided I would land him at his home-town Fort William or at worst Oban. Looking back it occurs to me that from quite early on democrat Jim had more or less dictated the course of this troubled voyage; he was by no means indispensable but apart from his steady if unflamboyant work in the galley he knew more about the engine than David, and being of slight build had less difficulty in reaching its more inaccessible parts. We needed now only one or two more hands in order to complete the last leg of the voyage. The weather seemed set fair and a fine, warm spell, unusual for Iceland, continued until we were just about to sail.

As the Bulgars say, you can go nowhere, not even to church, without cash. Not surprisingly I was now short of it and accordingly called on my friend Mr Holt at the Embassy. Aware of my crew problem he gave me the name of a friend of his who might help, a Mr Stefanson, a keen dinghy sailor and president of some local sailing association. After much telephoning Mr Stefanson found a man who although about to leave on holiday for Majorca professed a liking for sailing to England instead. He promised to visit *Baroque* that evening and needless to say failed to turn up. Without wishing to asperse them I must say I did find some Icelanders more prompt in their promises than in their performance, though it may well be that this applied only in such matters as shipping in *Baroque*. We had already made our wants known at the Youth Hostel and the next day Nicholas appeared, an American in his early thirties, looking and behaving, I thought, not unlike the stoical Red Indian. He did not enlarge on his past, we gathered only that he had some knowledge of computers and being anxious to forget it had taken to travel. He had a flight to Luxembourg next day, thence to Munich for some festival, and later to Nepal. He had no sea experience whatever but confessed to cooking and since he seemed keener on sailing to England than flying to Luxembourg I took him on. He brought his traps on board next day, having cancelled his flight, and also brought a Norwegian friend, John, who wanted to come. He had no sea experience either and a more unlikely looking sailor would be hard to find – lanky, bespectacled, flaxen hair down to his shoulders, and a beard. Nevertheless, in the very short time these two were with us one could see that John had in him the makings of a useful hand while Nicholas seemed to have no aptitude. John spoke a little English and both were inveterate smokers, rolling their own cigarettes. With these two and the two remaining original hands – if Nicholas took on the galley – I felt we could manage all right and fixed sailing day for 18 September. On the 16th the weather broke, raining and blowing hard from south-east, the direction from which Iceland gets most of its wind and rain since most depressions pass to the south. Short-handed though we were then, had we but sailed from Angmagssalik direct for the UK, by the time the fine spell broke we should have been on the south side of the depressions and enjoying westerly winds.

On the 18th it was still blowing hard from the same hostile quarter and that afternoon I walked out to the Meteorological Office to learn what the prospects were. A big low to the south was almost stationary, nor would the weather men promise anything better than south-easterlies Force 6 to 7 for the next day or two. After three days of wet weather with nothing to do we were all restive and anxious to be off, weather forecasts have been known to be wrong, and although I had a graveyard cough and a sore throat I decided to sail the next day, a Sunday. As a reward for this impatience it may be said that I deserved all that followed but those who say so should try lying alongside a crane in Reykjavik harbour for four wet and windy days.

Sheltered by the land we sailed down the coast in relatively calm conditions until we began to open up the strait between Reyjaknes and Eldey rock where we met the full force of the south-easterly. We were under stays'l and trys'l and even with the mains'l set, to beat through the strait in the teeth of a near gale would have been a thankless task. We kept her pointing west of south, thankful to have Eldey rock and its thirty mile-long reef to windward. With the rock still in sight and darkness falling we were about to have supper when the head of the stays'l blew out. Supper had to wait until we had both sails down and were lying a-hull, losing ground steadily to the west. The most astonishing thing about this rough start was how the landsmen Nicholas and John reacted. They failed to react at all. Neither showed any qualms of sea-sickness or uneasiness and carried on unconcernedly rolling endless cigarettes and eating their meals. Wind and rain continued all night and although the man on watch could shelter in the lee of the doghouse or inside I was thankful when David offered to take my watch. We lay-to all next day in the same disagreeable weather while I had the stays'l sent below and put in the morning stitching. Apart from that I lay at earth, missing meals, and thus remained ignorant of the consultations that were no doubt going on and unprepared for the impending 'bombshell', the name that journalists have for the unexpected.

Though still in the same quarter, by morning the wind had moderated and I was feeling more like myself. It was time to start sailing. Whereupon Jim piped up with a demand that we return to Reykjavik and to my astonishment and dismay David, who hitherto had been a tower of strength, doing his utmost for the success of the voyage, backed him up. 'Et tu Brute,' was my inevitable thought as he gave his reasons – the boat leaking, a new suit of sails needed, the skipper on the point of collapse, and another depression imminent. Naturally our two landsmen took no part in the heated dispute that followed, and considering their indifference to the weather of the last two days they must have wondered what all the fuss was about, that the two whom they took to be hardened sailors, accustomed to gales, should want to turn back. With David's support we could have taken the unhappy Jim home willy-nilly, but with the two of them bent on going back there was nothing to be done.

Besides the folly of ever spending a day or half a day in one's bunk, this episode brought home to me another disadvantage that this particular bunk had in addition to its proximity to the galley and the heads, its poor light, and a certain amount of dampness, namely that of being apart from and out of touch with the crew; so that even if one, as it were, smelt a rat, one could not, to continue the metaphor, nip it in the bud. This forced return to Reykjavik had enough implications, I think, to preclude its being received with good grace. A winter in Iceland, hauled out for something like seven months, would not improve *Baroque*, and it put paid to any lingering hopes I may have had of a voyage the following year. While Reykjavik is well placed geographically for a northern voyage, fitting out and the buying of stores there would be prohibitively expensive, and to that would be added the cost of flying out a crew.

David's imminent depression turned into an anti-cyclone that for the next week embraced Iceland and the surrounding waters. We sailed back in benign weather, sweetness and light everywhere except in *Baroque*, and by the time we made fast alongside our too familiar crane I had the stays'l repaired. Next morning Stefan, surprised by our return, took me out to Jon Eleven's yard where I made arrangements for the boat's wintering. She could not be hauled out at once as Jon had to get his slipway ready and a cradle built. He had a respect for old wooden boats, felt as much concern for *Baroque* as I did, and I was confident she would be in good hands. On returning I found David alone, Jim having already taken his gear ashore. For some reason he had undergone a change of mind and heart. I had misunderstood him and jumped to conclusions; his sole concern had been for my health and he was quite willing to finish the voyage.

Anxious as ever to get the boat home I took this revised version at its face value. As the Arabs say, the camel driver has his thoughts and the camel he has his, so I set about the unpromising task of finding a replacement for Jim. He had to be a man with some sailing experience, for we could not cope with three landsmen, and he had to be quickly available, for the season was well advanced. Having warned Jon Eleven that we might yet get away I gave myself until the next Sunday, 26 September, to find him. My friend Mr Stefanson seemed hopeful. He had two men in view and they promised to see me that evening. The one who turned up said he could not get away but he had strong hopes that Specky, as he was known, who had failed to come, would be a likely starter. On my reporting progress or the lack of it to Mr Stefanson he gave poor Specky a telephone lecture on the need for keeping appointments and got from him a firm promise to turn up next day at 4 pm. Even so I was not much surprised when at the appointed hour Mr Stefanson himself came on board to say that Specky had cried off. Our last hope was now the Fishermen's Union many of whose members apparently took a holiday at this time of year, generally in Majorca. *Baroque* could not compete with Majorca, for although for many Icelanders the sea is their livelihood we never found one who wanted to make it his playground.

On the Monday, therefore, we unbent the sails, unshipped the bowsprit, and unrove the running rigging, stripping her to a gantline as the saying goes. In the absence of anyone else able or willing the skipper, despite his recently alleged failing health, spent an hour or so aloft unshackling and sending down all the wire ropes, blocks, and strops. When the gear had been labelled Jon took it to his store. Nicholas and John were still on board to give us a hand, and apart from my own feelings over this mournful affair I felt that they had been badly let down. In due course, I hope *Baroque* will sail back to England and that will probably be my last voyage in her. As my birthday is in February it would be difficult to celebrate my eightieth north of the Arctic Circle, though I should have liked to have made a voyage in her in 1978 if only as a gesture of defiance. However, steeply rising costs and waning strength had already inclined me to call a halt, and now with the boat lying at Reykjavik, together with the frightening possibility that one might again be stuck with a similar crew, the decision is no longer in doubt. As Conrad's old seaman Singleton remarked: 'Ships are all right, it's the men in them.'

The verses below by Humber Wolfe are by way of farewell to the few who have followed my varied fortunes. They appeal especially to me now because three great beech trees below the window where I write are still stripping themselves. In the last verse perhaps poetic licence will allow the use of 'running close-hauled' though it grates on a seaman's ear. Just as it is proverbially impossible to blow and swallow at the same time, so is it to run and sail close-hauled.

> Listen! The wind is rising
> and the air is wild with leaves;
> we have had our summer evenings;
> now for October eves.
>
> The great beech trees lean forward,
> and strip like a diver, we
> had better turn to the fire
> and shut our mind to the sea
>
> where the ships of youth are running
> close-hauled on the edge of the wind,
> with all adventure before them
> and only the old behind.
>
> Bodowen, November 1976

APPENDIX 1

John Davis

JOHN DAVIS was born at Sandridge between Totnes and Dartmouth in about 1550. In the same neighbourhood was the home of John and Humphrey Gilbert, some years older than Davis, and of their younger brother Adrian who was about the same age. The half-brothers Carew and Walter Raleigh also lived there and were younger than Davis. All these must have been known to each other as boys and Adrian Gilbert and Walter Raleigh were life-long friends of Davis. Davis must have gone to sea early for he is not heard of again until 1579 when he was already a sea captain of known conduct and sufficiently properous to marry a Faith Fulford in 1582.

In 1576 Sir Humphrey Gilbert published his famous *Discourse* concerning the North-west Passage, adducing arguments in its favour which seem fantastic to us now but were no doubt convincing enough at the time. Davis had certainly studied this *Discourse*, and the loss of the little *Squirrel* with Humphrey Gilbert and his company must have made a deep impression coming so soon after the penning of the famous words with which the *Discourse* ends. These words have been quoted in a previous chapter. No doubt they inspired Davis to do and to dare, as they inspired lesser men.

Adrian Gilbert and Davis were already deep in plans for a northern voyage and in 1584 Sir Walter Raleigh (now knighted) persuaded the Queen to grant a charter in the names of himself, Adrian Gilbert, and John Davis for the search and discovery of a North-west Passage to China. Raleigh, too, induced William Sanderson, a wealthy London merchant married to a niece of Raleigh's, to back the venture. On this first voyage in 1585 Davis, as we have seen, after making his landfall at Cape Desolation, thus re-discovering Greenland, anchored in Godthaab fjord which he called Gilbert's Sound. There he had friendly meetings with the Eskimos. He then crossed his Strait to anchor in Exeter Sound, discovering and naming Capes Dyer and Walsingham, and finally explored Cumberland Sound in the belief that this might be the much sought North-west Passage.

In 1586 he sailed again with *Sunneshine* and *Mooneshine* as before, and *Mermaid*, a larger vessel of 120 tons. He landed first at old Sukkertoppen. Having crossed the Strait he again explored Cumberland Sound, satisfying himself that it was not a strait. Sailing south he passed the mouth of Hudson Strait and explored the Labrador coast whence he returned home bringing with him some salt cod and 500 sealskins.

On his third voyage in 1587, still backed whole-heartedly by Sanderson, he had the old *Sunneshine*, another vessel *Elizabeth*, and a clinker-built pinnace

Helen of only twenty tons. Having reached once more Gilbert Sound, Davis made a decision which shows us his inflexible determination. He owed it to his backers to make this voyage pay, so he dispatched his two bigger ships to fish the Grand Banks while he pushed north in the barely seaworthy *Helen*. He went as far as 72° 12′ north, to the great cliff he named 'Sanderson his Hope', seeing 'no ice towards the north, but a great sea, free, large, very salt and blue, and of an unsearchable depth'. A north wind drove them westwards until they encountered the 'middle pack' and were once more forced south to Cumberland Sound. Continuing south down the coast, off Hudson Strait they met with 'a mighty race, where an island of ice was carried by the force of the current as fast as our bark could sail'. On this voyage Davis had charted long stretches of coast on both sides of his Strait and much of the Labrador coast. Summing up these three voyages his biographer, Sir Clements Markham, wrote: 'Davis converted the Arctic regions from a confused myth into a defined area. He not only described and mapped the extensive tract explored by himself, but he clearly pointed out the work cut out for his successors. He lighted Hudson into his strait. He lighted Baffin into his Bay. He lighted Hans Egede to the scene of his Greenland labours.'

During the three following years Davis like all other seamen was engaged in the war against Spain. His command against the Armada seems disproportionate to his ability and experience, a vessel of twenty tons called *Black Dog* which acted as tender to the Lord Admiral in *Ark Royal*. She had a crew of ten men and an armament of three sakers. In those days, as in more recent times, interest and high connexions probably weighed more heavily than merit. With the Armada defeated, Davis himself fitted out a ship called *Drake* and joined the Earl of Cumberland's squadron, then cruising off the Azores for prizes and plunder. The squadron captured thirteen prizes. Davis continued this cruising until 1591, harassing the Queen's enemy, destroying his commerce, and profiting to a modest extent on his own account.

In fact as a result of these activities he was in a position to fit out an expedition more to his liking, nothing less than the passage of the Magellan Straits with a view to discovering the North-west Passage from the Pacific side. Unfortunately he was persuaded to join forces with Cavendish, the man who had completed in 1588 the third navigation of the globe. They sailed in 1591, the squadron comprising *Leicester, Roebuck, Desire* (in which Cavendish had sailed round the world), and *Dainty* owned jointly by Adrian Gilbert and Davis. Davis also contributed a large sum of money and at the pressing request of Cavendish took command of *Desire* instead of his own ship *Dainty*. The venture ended in disaster for all concerned.

Having reached the Straits in April 1592 Cavendish, discouraged by the cold and by continuous gales, proposed continuing the voyage by way of the Cape of Good Hope. When no one would agree to this he decided to return to Brazil to refresh before making a second attempt. After leaving the Straits the fleet got separated. Davis supposing they had gone to Port Desire, the usual rendezvous, went there to wait for them. Cavendish, in fact, with *Leicester* and *Roebuck*, had gone straight to Brazil and thence to England, he himself dying on the way. By August, when he had refitted as best he could, Davis, concluding that Cavendish had already returned to the Straits without calling at Port Desire, set out a second time to join him there. On the way he discovered what are now the Falkland Islands. After many buffetings, and having already been twice driven back, the *Desire* on October 9th passed into the Pacific. But a furious gale broke, sank their consort the little *Black Pinnace*, and drove them back again. By consummate seamanship *Desire* just managed to weather Cape Pillar and by the end of October they once more reached Port Desire. After refitting, they revictualled the ship for the voyage home with 14,000 dried and salted penguins, and sailed on December 22nd. The meat had been imperfectly dried, and soon a loathsome worm infested the whole ship – 'there was nothing they did not devour, only iron excepted'. Scurvy broke out and when the noisome, worm-ridden *Desire* struggled into Berehaven in June 1593 only sixteen of the crew remained alive and of these only five could stand.

Davis had lost £1,100 in this venture and returned a ruined and disappointed man to find that his wife, by whom he had had four children, had deserted him. He returned to his patrimony at Sandridge where he lived with his children and where he spent the next two years writing his *Seaman's Secrets*, dedicated to Lord Howard of Effingham and published in 1594: 'A brief account of such practices, as in my several voyages, I have from experience collected; those things that are needfully required in a sufficient seaman; because by certain questions demanded and answered I have not omitted anything that appertaineth to the secrets of navigation, whereby if there may grow any increase of knowledge or ease in practice it is the thing which I chiefly desire.' He also perfected at about this time the 'backstaff' or 'Davis Quadrant', an instrument that was a great improvement on the cross-staff and came into general use. And in 1595, harking back to his earlier voyages, he published an appeal to the Privy Council to show that 'there is from England a short and speedy passage to India by northerly navigation'.

In 1598 he sailed as chief pilot in a Dutch expedition to the East Indies. At Sumatra the two ships *Lion* and *Lioness* were nearly seized by treachery on the part of the Sultan, treachery largely averted by Davis who after a desperate fight on the poop of *Lion* finally drove the Malays out of the ship. Some sixty-four Dutch sailors were killed including one of the captains. The ships returned in July 1600.

In 1601 he sailed again as chief pilot on the first voyage made by the newly formed East India Company with a fleet of five ships commanded by James Lancaster in *Red Dragon*. Davis sailed in this ship and for his services he was to receive £500 if the voyage yielded two for one, £1,000 if three for one, and £2,000 if five for one. After a hazardous and adventurous voyage the ships returned home in 1603 laden with pepper and spices.

Davis remained a year at home before sailing on his last voyage. It had been a sad home-coming. The great Queen was dead. Adrian Gilbert, his half-brother and life-long friend, had died, and Sir Walter Raleigh, another constant friend, was already in confinement. He prepared a second edition of his *Seaman's Secrets* and before sailing became engaged to a Judith Havard, the marriage to be deferred until his return. He made a will by which his estate was to be divided between his children and his betrothed.

He went as chief pilot in a private venture to the East Indies undertaken by Sir Edward Michelborne with the ships *Tiger* of 240 tons and *Tiger's Whelp*, a pinnace. For Davis the voyage ended on the east coast of Malaya where the *Tiger* fell in with a Japanese junk, or rather a captured junk in the hands of ninety Japanese pirates. They lay alongside each other apparently on friendly terms. Michelborne hoping to obtain information regarding trade with China and the pirates resolving to seize the *Tiger* or die in the attempt, for their junk was unseaworthy. At sunset the storm broke. All the Englishmen who were in the junk at the time were killed and in the course of a fierce fight on the *Tiger* Davis met his death on 27 December 1605. Michelborne and his men finally overcame the pirates and Davis was buried at sea near the island of Bintang.

In his life John Davis had shown himself to be a thorough seaman, a scientific observer, an admirable organizer, loyal and faithful to his men, his friends, and his employers, and above all a man of daring enterprise. He fought in war against the Spaniards and in peace against treachery and pirates. His character is thus summed up by Sir Clements Markham: 'No part of his fame rests on his war services. He was essentially a man of peace. It was by the calm and collected way in which he faced, and encouraged others to face, the most terrible hardships and sufferings; by his ever-ready presence of mind and consummate seamanship in moments of danger, that he showed the stuff he was made of. The enemies against which he made war were the ice of the frigid zone, the storms of the far south, the pestilence of the tropics, and the evil designs of false companions. It was the mission of his life to study the forces of nature, and to mould and direct them for the good of his Queen and countrymen. If, as regards worldly success and his own fortunes, the life of Davis was, in some sort, a failure, in all that is worth living for, in valuable public services well performed, and in the acquisition of immortal fame, it was a success. With all his faults, John Davis, the great discoverer and scientific seaman, the consummate pilot, takes rank among the foremost seaworthies of the glorious reign of Queen Elizabeth.'

APPENDIX II

Tilman's Sailing/Mountaineering Record 1954–1977

Relevant pages and books are noted at the end of each item

1954
Purchased *Mischief* in Mallorca. Bristol Channel pilot cutter built in 1906 by Thos. Baker, Cardiff. Length: 45ft; Beam: 13ft; Draught: 7ft 6in; Thames Tonnage 29. Sailed (end of July) to Lymington via Gibraltar, with previous owner and his wife (to Gibraltar) and then David Drummond, three soldiers and 'a Scottish youth from the dockyard' for the voyage home. Two of the soldiers mutinied and were replaced at Oporto by Humphrey Barton and 'friend'. They arrived at Lymington on 5 November. pages 19–25

1955/56

Patagonia: Traverse of the Ice-cap (Lymington – Las Palmas – Montevideo – Magellan Straits – Punta Arenas – Puerto Bueno – Valparaiso – Callao – Panama – Bermuda – Lymington. 20,000 miles) in *Mischief* with Bill Procter, John Van Tromp, Michael Grove (to Panama), Charles Marriott (to Valparaiso), Gird Brewer (Montevideo to Punta Arenas), Jorge Quinteros (Punta Arenas to Valparaiso) and George di Giorgio (from Valparaiso). They reached Montevideo on 1 October and Punta Arenas in early November. They continued on 26 November and after a brief stop at Puerto Bueno reached Calvo Fjord on 15 December. Between 18 December and 27 January Marriott, Quinteros and Tilman traversed the ice-cap via the Calvo Glacier, Calvo Pass (7,500ft) and the Bismark Glacier to Lago Argentino. They placed 11 camps and returned by the same route. Meanwhile *Mischief* had struck a rock and sustained damage to her propeller. They reached Valparaiso on 24 February, where the engine was repaired, and sailed on 23 March making Callao by 5 April and Panama on 25 April. After passing through the canal they left on 1 May for the remaining voyage – across the Caribbean via Yukatan Channel to Bermuda and thence to Lymington by 9 July.   pages 19–132

1957/58

Circumnavigation of Africa after an attempt to reach Crozet Islands (Lymington – Las Palmas – Bahia Blanca – Cape Town – Durban – Beira – Comoro Islands – Aldabra – Aden – Port Said – Malta – Gibraltar – Lymington. 21,000 miles) in *Mischief* with Mike Clay (to Durban), Jim Lovegrove (to Gibraltar), Gerry Levick, Pat Green (to Cape Town), Howard Davies (to Durban), Allen Jolly (Cape Town to Durban) and David Smith, Douglas Moore and Ian Sibbald (all of whom joined at Durban). They sailed on 30 June and arrived at Cape Town on 16 October. They continued on 21 November but shortly afterwards the dinghy was lost in a gale making a Crozet landing impossible. This and other factors made Tilman abort the trip and return to South Africa. After crew changes *Mischief* left Durban on 23 December and returned to England via the Suez Canal and Gibraltar arriving back in Lymington in July 1958.   pages 595–623

1959/60

Crozet Islands (Lymington – Las Palmas – Cape Town – Crozet Islands – Kerguelen – Cape Town – St Helena – Lymington. 20,000 miles) in *Mischief* with Bill Procter, Jan Garnier, John Lyons (to Cape Town on the return), Jim Osborne and Roger Tufft. Left Lymington on 30 July, and arrived at Cape Town on 1 November and Crozet Islands in mid December. Tufft and Tilman set up a camp in America Bay, Possession Island on 29 December and ringed birds for the Californian Wild Life Society. Three peaks of about 3000ft were climbed and they returned to *Mischief* on 8 January. They then moved on to Port d'Hiver, Kerguelen, where Tufft and Tilman climbed two small peaks. Sailed for Baie du Morbihan (Port aux Francais) and left for Cape Town 2 February, reaching Cape Town in mid March and Lymington on 6 June.   pages 133–255

1961

West Greenland: Upernivik Island (Lymington – Belfast – Godthaab – Umanak Fjord – Godthaab – Lymington. 7,500 miles) in *Mischief* with David Hodge, Terry Ward (to Godthaab on the return), Charles Marriott, Michael Taylor-Jones, John Wayman and Dr J.B. Joyce (who left at Belfast). Left Lymington 14 May and after a stop at Belfast arrived at Godthaab on 4 July. Thence to Igdlorssuit and the Qioqe peninsula where Marriott and Tilman attempted a 6,500ft peak (coming within 200ft of success) before moving to Upernivik Island. Here Marriott and Tilman climbed a 6,370ft peak. During the return Terry Ward was taken off at Godthaab with appendicitis. Left Godthaab 28 August, arrived Lymington 26 September.   pages 263–323

1962

West Greenland and Baffin Island: Mt Raleigh (Lymington – Godthaab – Evighedsfjord – Holsteinborg – Baffin Island/Cumberland Peninsula – Lymington. 6,500 miles) in *Mischief* with Hans Hoff, Michael Rhodes, Roger Tufft, Shaun White and Roger Brown. Left Lymington 23 May, reached Godthaab 22 June and Evighedsfjord (Kangiussaq) on 30 June. Tufft and Tilman climbed Agssaussat (6,995ft) and later (anchorage at Tasiussaq) Amausuaq (4,620ft) and another peak. They were off Baffin Island on 31 July but found the coastal ice too thick and returned across the Davis Strait to Holsteinborg and Isortok to await more favourable conditions. They eventually returned to Baffin Island on 20 August anchoring at Exeter Sound where Tilman and Tufft climbed Mt Raleigh (5,700ft) and 'False' Mt Raleigh (Mt Mischief). They left on 26 August and arrived at Lymington 28 September.   pages 325–374

1963
The Crossing of Bylot Island (Lymington – Godthaab – Godhavn – Upernivik – Bylot Island – Godthaab – Lymington. 7,000 miles) in *Mischief* with Ed Mikeska, Mike Taylor, Bruce Reid, Stephen Pitt, Bob Sargent. Left Lymington 23 May and arrived Upernivik on 11 July. They crossed the Davis Strait and landed at Cape Liverpool on the northern coast of Bylot Island on 24 July (see jacket photograph). Reid and Tilman then made the fifty-three mile crossing of the island to the Sermilik Glacier above Pond Inlet – an arduous trip hampered by poor snow conditions and involving 15 camps and crossing a col of 5,700ft. They reached Pond Inlet on 8 August and were transported by Eskimos (in motor-driven kayaks) to rejoin *Mischief*. They left Pond Inlet on 15 August reaching Godthaab on 28 August and Lymington on 26 September.

pages 381–425

1964
East Greenland – attempt to reach Skjoldungen (Lymington – Faeroe Islands – Surtsey – Reykjavik – Angmagssalik – Holyhead – Barmouth – Lymington. 3,700 miles) in *Mischief* with Roger Coward, Charles Sewell, Martin Wareham, Bob Cook and Charles Marriott. They left Lymington on 30 May and reached Reykjavik on 27 June by way of Midvaag and Surtsey (the newly-formed volcanic island). Left on 7 July for Angmagssalik. *Mischief* was damaged while trying to follow the *Ejnar Mikkelsen* through the coastal ice to Angmagssalik (mid July) necessitating beaching and repairs. Prevented from leaving by dense coastal ice, Cook, Sewell and Tilman climbed Poljemsfjeld (3,380ft) and Cook and Tilman climbed Sofiasfjeld. They sailed on 9 August reaching Lymington on 10 September.

pages 426–456

1964/65
The Heard Island Expedition to climb Big Ben (Sydney – Albany – Kerguelen – Heard Island – Kerguelen – Heard Island – Albany – Sydney. 10,000 miles) in the schooner *Patanela* with Warwick Deacock (leader), Ed Reid, John Crick, Tony Hill, Philip Temple and Dr Russell Pardoe also Alec Theakston, Jim McCormick and Albert Rogers crewed to Albany where they handed over to Colin Putt, Dr Malcolm Hay and Grahame Budd. They left Albany on 27 November, reached Kerguelen on 1 January and Heard Island on 8 January where Putt, Deacock, Budd, Temple and Crick made a dangerous landing in heavy surf and established a camp. *Patanela* returned to a safer anchorage at Kerguelen. All members of the shore party made the first ascent of Big Ben (9,004ft) on 25 January. *Patanela* returned on 9 February, picked up the shore party, and arrived back at Sydney on 11 March.

pages 457–486

also *The Sea and the Snow* by Philip Temple (Cassell, Sydney 1966);
Spirit of the Storm by Warwick Deacock (*The Alpine Journal*, November 1965).

1965
East Greenland – second trip to Skjoldungen (Lymington – Heimaey – Reykjavik – Angmagssalik – Skjoldungenfjord – Lymington. 4,000 miles) in *Mischief* with Martin Wareham, Robert Bradley, Brian Hill, Brian Thomas, Brian Holloway. They left Lymington 25 June and after inspecting a new active volcano near Surstey, visited Heimaey and Reykjavik and arrived at Angmagssalik on 3 August and Skjoldungen on 10 August. Holloway and Tilman attempted a 5,000ft peak and climbed a smaller one. On 23 August they moved south to Sehesteds Fjord where Tilman and Holloway climbed another peak. Finally they moved further south to visit the weather station at Tingmiariut Fjord. After a fast passage they returned to Lymington on 19 September.

pages 487–505

1966/67
South Shetlands/Smith Island project (Lymington – Las Palmas – Montevideo/Puerto Buceo – Punta Arenas – South Shetland Islands – South Georgia – Montevideo – Azores – Lymington. 20,400 miles) in *Mischief* with Tom O'Shaughnessy, Mike Edwards, David Shaw (lost overboard), Roger Robinson and John Ireland (both of whom quit at Montevideo) and, variously, Carreo Javiel, Herbert Bittner, 'Louis', 'Robin', 'Roberto' and 'Sergio'. Left Lymington on 14 July. On 27 August just after leaving Cape Verde David Shaw was lost overboard whilst on watch. At Montevideo Ireland and Robinson left and were replaced by Javiel and Bittner. They reached Punta Arenas on 28 November and were joined by 'Louis'. Reached Smith Island on December 25 but were unable to land. *Mischief* continued to Port Foster, Deception Island with a demoralised crew who rapidly outstayed their welcome with the inhabitants.

They left Deception Island on 6 January and reached Montevideo via South Georgia on 16

February where all the crew, except Edwards, left and were eventually replaced by 'Roberto' 'Robin' and 'Sergio'. *Mischief* finally sailed for home on 21 March, and after a stop in the Azores arrived at Lymington on 15 July. A thoroughly unpleasant trip.   pages 543–593
see *The Book of Modern Mountaineering* by Malcolm Milne
(Arthur Barker, London 1968) for a good photograph of Smith Island (p. 167).

1968
Trip to Scoresby Sound (Sund) and Jan Mayen (Lymington – Faeroe Islands – Akureyri – Jan Mayen. 2,500 miles) in *Mischief* with Charles Marriott, Simon Beckett, Kenneth Winterschladen and Ian Duckworth. Sailed from Lymington on 31 May and after stops at the Faeroes and Iceland sighted Jan Mayen on July 15. After viewing Beerenberg and the north-west coast, *Mischief* rounded the South Cape to reach the south-east coast but during the night, with Duckworth on watch, hit a rock and was holed. Efforts to repair the hull at Batiska were unsuccessful and *Mischief* was further damaged by pack-ice. The boat was towed by a Norwegian ship for a short distance but then abandoned to sink a few miles east of Jan Mayen.   pages 631–658

1968
Purchased *Sea Breeze* from Sir Atholl Oakeley. Bristol Channel Pilot Cutter built in 1899 by J. Bowden, Porthleven. Length: 49ft; Beam: 14ft 4in; Draught: 7ft 6in; Thames Tonnage 33.
pages 659–665
see *Sea Breeze* by H.W. Tilman (*The Journal of Navigation*, January 1973).

1969
East Greenland – the second Scoresby Sound attempt (Lymington – Seydisfjord/Iceland – East Greenland coast – Lymington. 3,400 miles) in *Sea Breeze* with John Murray and Brian Potter. Also Mike Brocklebank, Ralph Furness (both of whom quit at Appledore) who were replaced by Dai 'Ken' Morgan and Colin Kavenan. They sailed from Lymington on 30 June but had to put in to Appledore to replace a broken bowsprit and for the crew change. They left on 15 July and made a fast passage to Iceland arriving at Seydisfjord on 29 July. Here Tilman and Potter climbed Strandertinder (3,310ft). After a passage beset by mist and pack-ice they arrived just south of Scoresby Sound on 8 August with broken pack-ice barring entry. At this point all the crew except Potter refused to continue and the attempt was curtailed. They returned to Lymington by early September. Another disappointing trip.   pages 659–689

1970
West Greenland – Cape Farewell area (Lymington – Faeringehavn – Ivigtut – Julienehaab – Prins Christian Sund – Lymington. 5000 miles) in *Sea Breeze* with Colin Putt, Ian Dillon, Bob Comlay and Andrew Harwich. They left on 5 June were off the west coast of Greenland by early July where they became marooned in pack-ice which took them well to the north of their target area. *Sea Breeze* finally made Faeringehavn on 14 July after five days in the ice.
After working back south well out to sea, they re-entered the pack-ice and reached Arsuk Fjord and Ivigtut. They then moved on to Torsukatak Fjord and thence Bredefjord (1 August) and Julianehaab. With increasing problems with the ice they worked down the coastline to Tasermuit Fjord where Putt and Dillon had 3 days climbing. They then moved further south to the Cape Farewell area and entered Torssukatak Fjord where they anchored at Stordalens Havn (photo 27). Here they made another short climb before ice forced them to move on to Augpilag-toq. Eventually a safe anchorage was found in Kangikitsoq Fjord from where Putt and Dillon made a four-day climbing trip into the interior. They then motored down Prins Christian Sund, stopping briefly at a Danish weather station, and set sail for home on 31 August arriving at Lymington on 27 September. A happy and eventful trip.   pages 691–728

1971
East Greenland – The third attempt to reach Scoresby Sound (Lymington – Faeroes – Rejkjavik – Isafjord – off Scoresby Sound – Angmagssalik – Sehestedsfjord – Lymington. 5,000 miles) in *Sea Breeze* with Bob Comlay, Max Smart, Marius Dakin and Peter Marsh (to Reykjavik) and Jim Collins (from Reykjavik). They sailed on 12 June taking a route by the North Sea to the Pentland Firth and thence by the Faeroes to Reykjavik. When leaving on 21 July they lost the propeller and had to put in to Isafjord for repairs. They continued on 31 July and were 60 miles off Scoresby Sound on 11 August when they met the pack-ice. After several probes, they gave up and

headed south making Angmagssalik on 25 August and thence to Sehestedsfjord on 2 September where an attempted climb was spoilt by bad weather. They set sail for home on 4 September and arrived back at Lymington on 27 September.   pages 735–757

1972
East Greenland – fourth attempt to reach Scoresby Sound (Lymington – Reykjavik – Isafjord – off Scoresby Sound – Sermilik Fjord. 3000 miles) in *Sea Breeze* with Brian Potter, Brian McClanagan, Mike Clare, Richard Capstick (to Reykjavik), John Lapin (Reykjavik to Isafjord) and Dougal Forsyth (from Isafjord). They sailed on 31 May intending to reach Ellesmere Island via Godthaab. On 19 June, when 300 miles south of Iceland, the boom broke necessitating a diversion to Reykjavik which they reached on 2 July. After repairs, they left on 10 July but put into Isafjord for a crew change. They continued on 18 July with Jan Mayen and Scoresby Sound as the new objectives. Jan Mayen was reached on 25 July and after a short stop they continued to Greenland and got within a few miles of Scoresby Sound (Cape Tobin) on 4 August when weather and ice conditions deteriorated. After various probes the engine broke down on 8 August. They sailed for Angmagssalik but in poor weather conditions sought refuge in Sermilik Fjord where, dodging ice floes without an engine, *Sea Breeze* hit a rock and sank. All the crew escaped and were eventually picked up by a coastal vessel and taken to Angmagssalik from where they flew to Reykjavik and thence back to Britain.   pages 757–778

1973
Purchased *Baroque* at Falmouth. British Channel Pilot Cutter built in 1902 by J. Hambly, Cardiff. Length: 50ft; Beam: 13ft 6in; Draught: 7ft 6in; Thames Tonnage 32.   pages 778–781

1973
West Greenland (Falmouth – Cork/Crosshaven – Bantry Bay – Godthaab – Umanak Fjord – Lymington. 5000 miles) in *Baroque* with Brian McClanaghan, John Harradine (to Cork), John Barrett (from Cork), Simon Richardson and Ilan Rosengarten. They left Falmouth on 29 May but put in to Cork for the crew change. Defects in the boat necessitated repairs at Crosshaven and Bantry Bay and they finally resumed the voyage on 26 June reaching Godthaab one month later. They proceeded north past Jacobshavn and Disko Island and reached Igdlorssuit on 13 August. Here they were joined by David Meldrum (St Andrews University) for a trip to Qalagtoq valley of Upernivik Island where Tilman made a solo ascent of Groyling and Meldrum and Richardson climbed Mount Change. After a brief visit to Umanak they started for home on 21 August and after a troublesome voyage got back to Lymington on 6 October. A happy trip.   pages 778–824

1974
Spitzbergen (Lymington – Bear Island – Isfjord – Mollerfjord – Magdalena Fjord – Stornoway – Lymington) in *Baroque* with David White, Paul Reinsch, Alan Stockdale and Andrew Craig-Bennett. They sailed on 1 June and by the North Sea route reached Bear Island on 2 July and Spitzbergen (Isfjord) on 7 July. They headed north to Ny-Alesund (16 July) where they did some modest climbing, Mollerfjord (more climbing), and thence to Magdalena Fjord where Reinsch, Stockdale and Tilman climbed peaks.

They then moved on to the dangerous Hinlopen Strait passing through on 31 July. With dense pack-ice threatening from the east they made haste along the coast but ran aground while trying to pass through Freemansund. Desperate measures were employed to refloat and after further difficulties they eventually made open water by 10 August thus completing a circumnavigation of Vestspitzbergen. On a difficult homeward passage (with a damaged engine) they reached Stornaway on 6 September and Lymington on 21 September. A fine adventure.   pages 831–883

1975
West Greenland – attempt to reach Ellesmere Island (Lymington – Bantry Bay – Godthaab – Holsteinborg – Lymington – 5000 miles) in *Baroque* with Nicholas Parker, John Shipton, Andrew Horsfield (from Bantry Bay) and Alec Ramsey. They left Lymington on 6 June making Bantry Bay by 13 June. Off Cape Farewell they encountered abnormally extensive pack-ice and reached Godthaab on 22 July after a slow passage. On 7 August, off Disko Island, the boom snapped and the trip was prematurely curtailed. They were unable to obtain a new boom at Holsteinborg and sailed home (boomless) arriving back on 18 September.   pages 885–915

1976
East Greenland: Angmagssalik – the original intention being Ellesmere Island (Lymington – Falmouth – Reykjavik – Angmagssalik – Reykjavik) in *Baroque* with David Burrows, 'Richard' (to Angmagssalik), Jim Gaitens, Hamish Brown (to Falmouth), Mike Holland (Falmouth to Reykjavik) and another 'Hamish' (Reykjavik to Angmagssalik). They left on 13 May but were delayed at Falmouth until 26 May by the crew change. At sea it was found that the engine could not be started because of flat batteries. On 12 June, during worsening weather, first the mainsail split, then a wave broke in and flooded the chartroom and finally another filled the cockpit. This sequence of events caused a breakdown of morale with all the crew except Burrows demanding a course change to Reykjavik where, after further mishaps, they arrived on 1 July. After repairs and the crew change they left on 29 July eventually arriving at Angmagssalik on about 20 August after adventures in fog in the Denmark Strait, dense coastal ice, and difficult inshore conditions. They sailed on 26 August but immediately grounded on a rock. As the tide receded they were unable to keep the ship upright and it was swamped in the next tide. Though *Baroque* was pumped out quickly this mishap left much damage and disarray. Richard and Hamish left. Tilman, Gaitens and Burrows sailed on 7 September and made Reykjavik by 14 September. With two new hands, an American 'Nicholas' and a Norwegian 'John', they sailed for home on 21 September but after two days with some heavy weather, Gaitens and Burrows forced a return to Reykjavik, where *Baroque* was stripped and laid up for the winter. A thoroughly unsatisfactory trip fraught with mishap and discontent.   pages 917–947

1977
Baroque comes home (Reykjavik – Holyhead – Lymington) with Frank George, Mike Phillips, Nigel Stacey and Robert Adams. Reykjavik 26 May – Lymington 12 June.   pages 948–950
Roving Commissions 18 (RCC Press, London 1978).

1977
South Shetlands (Southampton – Las Palmas – Rio de Janiero) in *En Avant* with Simon Richardson (skipper), Mark Johnson, Charles Williams, Roderick Coatman, Joe Dittamore and Robert Toombs. They left Southampton in early August and after a stop at Las Palmas reach Rio on 25 October and left for Port Stanley on 1 November. Nothing more was heard of her. Various possibilities exist about her demise, the most likely being (in the absence of any clues) that she foundered and sank.   see *High Mountains and Cold Seas* by J.R.L. Anderson (Gollancz, 1980) and *The Quest of Simon Richardson* by Dorothy Richardson (Gollancz, 1986).

other useful sources:

Ocean Voyaging Under Sail by H.W. Tilman (*The Journal of Navigation*, July 1972). A general account of the voyages in Mischief.

Adventures Under Sail Edited by Libby Purves (Gollancz, 1982). An anthology of items drawn from Tilman's sailing books.

H.W. Tilman – The Seven Mountain-Travel Books (Diadem/The Mountaineers, 1983) An omnibus edition of the author's books dealing with his mountaineering exploits before 1954.

Eric Shipton – The Six Mountain-Travel Books (Diadem/The Mountaineers 1985) An omnibus edition in which the author describes many expeditions and climbs that involved Tilman.

Crossing the Patagonian Ice-cap by H.W. Tilman (*The Alpine Journal*, November 1956).

Voyage to the Iles Crozet and Iles Kerguelen by H.W. Tilman (*The Geographical Journal*, September 1961).